# University Textbook Series

**February, 1980**

## Especially Designed for Collateral Reading

**HARRY W. JONES**
**Directing Editor**
Professor of Law, Columbia University

---

**ADMIRALTY, Second Edition (1975)**
Grant Gilmore, Professor of Law, Yale University.
Charles L. Black, Jr., Professor of Law, Yale University.

**ADMIRALTY AND FEDERALISM (1970)**
David W. Robertson, Professor of Law, University of Texas.

**AGENCY (1975)**
W. Edward Sell, Dean of the School of Law, University of Pittsburgh.

**BUSINESS ORGANIZATION AND FINANCE (1980)**
William A. Klein, Professor of Law, University of California, Los Angeles.

**CIVIL PROCEDURE, BASIC, Second Edition (1979)**
Milton D. Green, Professor of Law Emeritus, University of California, Hastings College of the Law.

**COMMERCIAL TRANSACTIONS, INTRODUCTION TO (1977)**
Hon. Robert Braucher, Associate Justice, Supreme Judicial Court of Massachusetts.
Robert A. Riegert, Professor of Law, Cumberland School of Law.

**CONFLICT OF LAWS, COMMENTARY ON THE, Second Edition (1980)**
Russell J. Weintraub, Professor of Law, University of Texas.

**CONSTITUTIONAL LAW, AMERICAN (A TREATISE ON) (1978) with 1979 Supplement**
Laurence H. Tribe, Professor of Law, Harvard University.

**CONTRACT LAW, THE CAPABILITY PROBLEM IN (1978)**
Richard Danzig.

**CORPORATIONS, Second Edition (1971)**
Norman D. Lattin, Professor of Law, University of California, Hastings College of the Law.

**CORPORATIONS IN PERSPECTIVE (1976)**
Alfred F. Conard, Professor of Law, University of Michigan.

**CRIMINAL LAW, Second Edition (1969)**
Rollin M. Perkins, Professor of Law, University of California, Hastings College of the Law.

**ESTATES IN LAND & FUTURE INTERESTS, PREFACE TO (1966)**
Thomas F. Bergin, Professor of Law, University of Virginia.
Paul G. Haskell, Professor of Law, Case Western Reserve University.

## UNIVERSITY TEXTBOOKS SERIES—Continued

**EVIDENCE: COMMON SENSE AND COMMON LAW (1947)**
John M. Maguire, Professor of Law, Harvard University.

**EVIDENCE, STUDENTS' TEXT ON THE LAW OF (1935)**
John Henry Wigmore.

**JURISPRUDENCE: MEN AND IDEAS OF THE LAW (1953)**
The late Edwin W. Patterson, Cardozo Professor of Jurisprudence, Columbia University.

**LEGAL CAPITAL, Second Edition (1980)**
Bayless Manning, Former Dean, Stanford Law School.

**LEGAL RESEARCH ILLUSTRATED (1977)**
J. Myron Jacobstein, Professor of Law, Law Librarian, Stanford University.
Roy M. Mersky, Professor of Law, Director of Research, University of Texas.

**LEGAL RESEARCH, FUNDAMENTALS OF (1977), with 1980 Assignments Pamphlet**
J. Myron Jacobstein, Professor of Law, Law Librarian, Stanford University.
Roy M. Mersky, Professor of Law, Director of Research, University of Texas.

**PROCEDURE, THE STRUCTURE OF (1979)**
Robert M. Cover, Professor of Law, Yale University.
Owen M. Fiss, Professor of Law, Yale University.

**THE PROFESSION OF LAW (1971)**
L. Ray Patterson, Dean of the School of Law, Emory University.
Elliott E. Cheatham, Professor of Law, Vanderbilt University.

**PROPERTY, Second Edition (1975)**
John E. Cribbet, Dean of the Law School, University of Illinois.

**TAXATION, FEDERAL INCOME, Second Edition (1979)**
Marvin A. Chirelstein, Professor of Law, Yale University.

**TORTS, Second Edition (1980)**
Clarence Morris, Professor of Law, University of Pennsylvania.
C. Robert Morris, Professor of Law, University of Minnesota.

**TRUSTS, PREFACE TO THE LAW OF (1975)**
Paul G. Haskell, Professor of Law, Case Western Reserve University.

**WILLS AND TRUSTS, THE PLANNING AND DRAFTING OF, Second Edition (1979)**
Thomas L. Shaffer, Professor of Law, University of Notre Dame.

# THE LAW OF ADMIRALTY

SECOND EDITION


By

GRANT GILMORE
Sterling Professor of Law, Yale Law School

and

CHARLES L. BLACK, Jr.
Henry R. Luce Professor of Jurisprudence
Yale Law School



Mineola, New York
THE FOUNDATION PRESS, INC.
1975

*Library of Congress Catalog Card Number:* 74-22911

Gilmore & Black, Admiralty Law 2nd Ed. UTB
4th Reprint—1980

To HELEN and BARBARA

*

# PREFACE TO THE SECOND EDITION

A few words of explanation about the differences between the original and this second edition may be helpful.

The general arrangement of topics has seemingly proven useful to the bench and bar, and no major changes have been made as to these. Rather, the text has been reworked to reflect caselaw and statutory developments of the years since first publication. Account has also been taken of new technological developments in ocean shipping and navigation. The bibliographic leads into the periodical and other literature have been updated. The aim throughout has been not to introduce change for change's sake—though the entire original text has been fully reconsidered—but rather to introduce the new material harmoniously into the book.

We have found it necessary, however, to scrap a good many sections of the original text and to do the discussion over completely. In some instances this was required by intervening statutory change. For example, the enactment of the Uniform Commercial Code in all jurisdictions (except Louisiana), the 1971 amendments to the Federal Maritime Lien Act and the 1972 amendments to the Longshoremen's and Harbor Workers' Compensation Act required a complete rewrite of Part I of Chapter III and of substantial portions of Chapters IX and VI. In other instances fundamental changes in the maritime law have been accomplished by judicial fiat—for example, the introduction by the Supreme Court in the Moragne case (1971) of a remedy for wrongful death under the general maritime law (Chapter VI). As to Chapter I, the major strategic change has to do with the new (1966) Rules of Procedure, which formally merge admiralty causes with the "civil action", reserving some special proceedings. The attempt is made to handle this change in such a way as to make it comprehensible, without totally discarding treatment of the older forms, since knowledge of these is indispensable to understanding innumerable key precedents. In Chapter VII, the section on Radar has been entirely rewritten, and the rest of the material updated and keyed to the 1965 Rules. In Chapter XI, the most important recent development has been the passage of the Merchant Marine Act of 1970.

We have found it necessary to add some new sections, to deal with problems which had not surfaced when the original edition was prepared. Thus the enactment of anti-pollution legislation, state and federal, whose relationship to the Limitation of Liability Act remains (at the date of writing) a total mystery, required the addition of extensive new material in Chapter X. The vast increase in the use of preferred mortgages during the 1960's required the addition of comparably extensive new material in Chapter IX, including discussions of the federal guaranty program and of novel methods of ship financing which had hardly been heard of until well after World War II. The introduction of containers has revolutionized both the technology and the law relating to the carriage of goods by sea (Chapter III, Part II).

We have, on occasion, been forced to the unhappy conclusion that our original discussion of one or another point was inadequate, unsound, or flatly wrong. Our policy has been to confess, and attempt to rectify, our own errors.

We have not attempted to indicate what changes in text and footnotes have been made from the original edition. The sequence of chapters remains the same and so, in general, does the sequence of sections within each chapter. So far as possible, we have retained from the original edition the numeration of section-numbers and footnotes; that was done in order to avoid the necessity of reworking the elaborate system of cross-references with which the original edition was provided. We have therefore been forced to adopt the somewhat inelegant solution of identifying new sections and new footnotes by adding letters in alphabetical sequence to the immediately preceding number. In almost all cases the lettered sections and footnotes constitute new material. Unlettered sections and footnotes may also be new when a discussion has been rewritten for one of the reasons suggested above.

The problem of acknowledgment is truly staggering—indeed unmanageable. For nearly two decades, members of bench and bar, people in the shipping industry, and above all, students at Yale and the University of Chicago Law Schools, have contributed innumerable suggestions. Adequate records of these do not exist. By this time, a work of this kind owes a great deal to the entire profession and even to the entire industry. We can only express regret that most of this indebtedness cannot now specifically be given a name. Where record or exact recollection does exist, we have owned the debt in footnotes.

Even so, some names can be and therefore should be mentioned here: Professor Preble Stolz; Congressman Bob Eckhardt; James Howard Smith of the London insurance world; Professor Avrom Udovitch of Princeton; Dr. Hans Ulrich Haensel of the Verband Deutscher Reeder; all the members of the Advisory Committee on Admiralty Rules, 1960–1970, and most especially its Reporter, the late Professor Brainerd Currie; George T. Nickell, Esq., of the Seattle Admiralty Bar; Professor Nicholas Healy; Abraham E. Freedman, Esq.; Sam Levinson, Esq.; most especially William Warner, Esq., who has been unfailingly helpful. Many, many students have helped, including James Petersen, Jay Powell, Richard Grande, Tom Richardson, John Kuhns, and especially Charles Palmer.

Arthur Charpentier and the entire staff at the Yale Law Library have been unflaggingly supportive; perhaps it will not be invidious to mention especially that daily yea-sayer, Jim Golden. Thanks are due to Dorothy Egan and the secretarial staff at Yale Law School, but it must be mentioned especially that Eileen M. Quinn's help was far more than secretarial, including much helpful checking, consultation, and constant and understanding management of the successive drafts.

There is one final regret we have to express, for a now largely irremediable omission in the preface to the first edition, an omission that occurred through sheer haste. We refer to the omission of express acknowledgment of our obvious great debt to the late Professor Gustavus H. Robinson, whose 1939 treatise first organized this subject for modern times.

Year after year, Harold Eriv has been all that could be desired in a publication chief—invisible as a taskmaster, unfailingly visible as a helper and friend.

G. G.
C. L. B., JR.

New Haven, Connecticut
December, 1974

*

# PREFACE TO THE FIRST EDITION

A preface is superfluous in respect of a work with such obvious purposes as this; but some acknowledgments are in order.

To Messrs. Kirlin, Campbell & Keating, to Wilbur E. Dow, Jr., Esq., and to William G. Symmers, Esq., for professional courtesies extended; to Commander Lane C. Kendall of the United States Merchant Marine Academy, for his helpful suggestions with respect to references on industrial background; to Mr. Austin Tobin of the New York Port Authority, for his furnishing of source-material concerning that body; to Robert Aronstein, Esq., of the New York Bar, for many helpful suggestions made in informal conversations; most especially, to William Warner, Esq., of Symmers, Fish, Warner & Nicol, for his attentive reading in manuscript of about half the chapters, and for the many valuable suggestions he made; to Barbara A. Black, for checking and preparing for publication the manuscript of about half of the book; to Terence Benbow, Esq., of the New York Bar and to Ronald Orloff, Class of 1957 Yale Law School, for assistance in research. William F. Drake, Class of 1957 Yale Law School, performed the tedious task of preparing the index and made many helpful suggestions en route. Many students, in their term papers or in class discussion, have contributed both ideas and documentation; their names are too many to list but a collective acknowledgment of indebtedness is gratefully made.

It goes without saying that none of those named bears any responsibility for any of the contents of the book.

Special thanks are due for a difficult and painstaking transcribing job to Mrs. Edna Rothenberger and her staff at the Columbia Law School Mimeograph Office and to Miss Theresa Brennan and her associates in the Yale Law School Secretarial Office; to Miles O. Price, Librarian of the Columbia Law Library, to the staffs of the Columbia and Yale Law Libraries, and especially to Mrs. Charlotte Sherr, for unflagging and most efficacious assistance in assembling the many volumes, legal and non-legal, that had to be consulted.

The Baker Memorial Library of Dartmouth College, Hanover, N. H., graciously made its facilities available during the summers of 1955 and 1956, as did the Library of the University of Texas Law School during the summer of 1955.

GRANT GILMORE
CHARLES L. BLACK, JR.

New Haven, Connecticut
March, 1957

*

# SUMMARY OF CONTENTS


Page

PREFACE TO THE SECOND EDITION ........ VII

PREFACE TO THE FIRST EDITION ........ XI

Chapter

I. Introduction: History and Jurisdiction ........ 1

II. Marine Insurance ........ 53

III. Carriage of Goods Under Bills of Lading ........ 93

Part I. The Relationship of the Bill of Lading to the Contract of Sale and Its Use in Financing Transactions ........ 93

Part II. Who Bears the Loss When Goods are Damaged or Lost? ........ 139

IV. Charter Parties ........ 193

A. The Voyage Charter ........ 197

B. Time Charters ........ 229

C. Demise or Bare-Boat Charters ........ 239

V. General Average ........ 244

VI. Rights of Seamen and Maritime Workers: Recovery for Death and Injury ........ 272

VII. Collision ........ 485

VIII. Salvage ........ 532

IX. Maritime Liens and Ship Mortgages ........ 586

X. Limitation of Liability ........ 818

XI. Governmental Activity in Shipping ........ 958


## APPENDICES


App.

A. The Documentary Council of the Baltic and White Sea Conference ........ 997

B. Time Charter ........ 1003

**Table of Cases** ........ 1011

**Index** ........ 1045


*

# TABLE OF CONTENTS


Page

PREFACE TO THE SECOND EDITION .......... VII

PREFACE TO THE FIRST EDITION .......... XI

CHAPTER I. INTRODUCTION: HISTORY AND JURISDICTION .......... 1

The Past—Or, The Rhodian Law and All That .......... 3
World Shipping and Its Law .......... 11
Admiralty Jurisdiction in the United States .......... 18
The Jurisdiction and Procedure of Courts .......... 18
"Waters" and "Vessels" .......... 31
Consequences of Admiralty Jurisdiction .......... 34
The "Saving Clause" .......... 37
Remedies; Admiralty and Equity .......... 40
Prize and Criminal Jurisdiction .......... 44
Substantive Law in Admiralty Cases .......... 45
Federal-State Conflict .......... 47
Note on Conflicts of Laws .......... 51

CHAPTER II. MARINE INSURANCE .......... 53

History .......... 54
General Principles .......... 56
What is Insured? .......... 58
Insurable Interest .......... 59
Certain Ways in Which the Policy May be Voided .......... 62
Express Warranties .......... 67
The Wilburn Boat Case .......... 68
The Risks Insured Against .......... 71
"Proximate Cause" .......... 76
Losses: "Memorandum" and F. P. A. .......... 79
Total Loss .......... 83
The Valued Policy .......... 86
Subrogation .......... 91

CHAPTER III. CARRIAGE OF GOODS UNDER BILLS OF LADING .......... 93

PART I. THE RELATIONSHIP OF THE BILL OF LADING TO THE CONTRACT OF SALE AND ITS USE IN FINANCING TRANSACTIONS .......... 93

The Negotiability of Bills of Lading .......... 94
Sale of Goods: The Passage of Property and the Risk of Loss: Mercantile Terms of Shipment: F.O.B.—C.I.F.—F.A.S. .......... 100
The Documentary Sale .......... 110
The Bank Letter of Credit .......... 114
A Note on Conflict of Laws Problems .......... 130

## CHAPTER III. CARRIAGE OF GOODS UNDER BILLS OF LADING—Continued

Page

PART II. WHO BEARS THE LOSS WHEN GOODS ARE DAMAGED OR LOST? 139
- Respective Coverages of Cogsa and Harter 145
- The Heart of Cogsa 149
- The Duty to Furnish a Proper Ship 150
- Care of the Cargo 155
- Navigation and Management of the Ship 155
- "Navigation and Management" as Against "Seaworthiness" 159
- Fires 161
- Perils of the Sea 162
- Act of God 163
- The Exceptions of Overwhelming Human Force 164
- Exceptions Having to Do with Fault of the Shipper or Defect in the Cargo 166
- Other Exceptions 167
- The Catch-All Exception 167
- The Substantive Effect of Negligence in Cogsa 169
- The "Both-to-Blame" Clause 173
- Deviation 176
- Burden of Proof 183
- The Requirement That a Bill of Lading Be Issued—The "Clause Paramount" 185
- Carriage Liens—Jurisdiction 186
- Valuation and Claims 187
- Cargo Insurance—"Benefit of Insurance" Clauses 189
- A Final Word on Goods Carriage and Cogsa 191

CHAPTER IV. CHARTER PARTIES 193
- Taxonomy and Nature 193
- A. The Voyage Charter 197
  - The Setting: Tramp Shipping 197
  - Clause 1: The Basic Terms 200
  - Clause 1 (cont'd): Safe Ports and Berths—"Always Afloat" 202
  - Clause 2: Liability for Goods Damage 207
  - Clause 3: Deviation 209
  - Clause 4: Payment of Freight 210
  - Clauses 5, 6 and 7: Loading, Unloading, and Demurrage 210
  - Clause 8: Liens (Herein of the Cesser Clause) 215
  - Clause 9: Bills of Lading in Voyage Charter Carriage 217
  - Further of the Cesser Clause 221
  - Clause 10: Strikes, War and Ice. "Frustration" and Connected Problems 223
  - Clauses 11–15 229

**CHAPTER IV. CHARTER PARTIES**—Continued Page
B. Time Charters 229
The Basic Arrangement 229
The Position as to Dispatch 231
Overlap and Underlap 231
Bills of Lading Under Time Charters 232
The "Breakdown" and "Exceptions" Clauses (15 and 16) 233
Frustration 236
C. Demise or Bare-Boat Charters 239
General Nature 239
How to Recognize a Demise 240
Legal Consequences of the Demise 241
The Charterer as Owner: Third Persons 242
Liens on Vessels Under Demise 242

**CHAPTER V. GENERAL AVERAGE** 244
Basic Ideas 244
The General Average Adjuster 248
The York-Antwerp Rules—Applicable Law 252
The Peril—The "Voluntary" Sacrifice—The "Common Venture" 254
Some Typical General Average Sacrifices and Expenditures 260
Time and Place as of Which Values are Calculated 263
The Effect of Fault 266
Jurisdiction and Liens 270
Evaluation of General Average 270

**CHAPTER VI. RIGHTS OF SEAMEN AND MARITIME WORKERS: RECOVERY FOR DEATH AND INJURY** 272
Introduction with Caveat 272
Maintenance and Cure: The Nature of the Remedy 281
Same: Amount of Recovery—Duration and Extent of Shipowner's Liability 297
Same: Shipowner's Right to Indemnity from Third Party for Maintenance and Cure Expenses 314
Same: Shipowners' Liability Convention 323
The Jones Act: Background 325
The Jones Act: Plaintiff (Herein of "Seamen" and "Vessels") 328
The Jones Act: Defendant 335
Jones Act: "An Action for Damages at Law, with the Right of Trial by Jury 340
Jones Act: "At His Election" 342
Jones Act: The Federal Employers' Liability Act 351
Assumption of Risk vs. Contributory Negligence 354
Same: Recovery for Wrongful Death Under FELA, the Death on the High Seas Act and the General Maritime Law 359

CHAPTER VI. RIGHTS OF SEAMEN AND MARITIME WORKERS: RECOVERY FOR DEATH AND INJURY—Continued

Page
Statutory Recovery Formulae ---- 360
A Place for Each Statute and Each Statute in Its Place ---- 362
From Moragne to Gaudet ---- 369
Same: What is "Negligence"? ---- 374
Unseaworthiness: The Scope and Nature of the Remedy ---- 383
Rights and Disabilities of Harbor Workers: Herein of the Constitutional Requirement of National Uniformity ---- 404
The Longshoremen's and Harbor Workers' Compensation Act of 1927; Scope and Purpose of the 1972 Amendments ---- 408
Constitutionality of LHCA; Judicial Review of Compensation Orders ---- 412
Coverage of LHCA—I: Its Territorial Application and Relationship with State Compensation Acts ---- 417
The 1927 Act (Herein of "Maritime but Local" and "the Twilight Zone") ---- 418
The 1972 Amendments ---- 423
Coverage of LHCA—II: Types of Employment ---- 427
The Problem of Successive Awards Under LHCA and State Compensation Statutes; the Effect of the Payment of Compensation Benefits on Damage Actions ---- 431
The Harbor Worker's Recovery of Damages Outside the Compensation System—I: The Sieracki-Ryan Period (1946–1972) ---- 436
Harbor Workers as Seamen ---- 438
The Shipowner's Indemnity Action ---- 442
The Nullification of § 905 ---- 446
The Harbor Worker's Recovery of Damages Outside the Compensation System—II: The 1972 LHCA Amendments ---- 449
Applicability of Maritime Law in Non-admiralty Courts ---- 456
Federal Jurisdiction in Death and Injury Cases Brought Outside the Admiralty Under the Saving to Suitors Clause ---- 468
Choice of Law in Actions Brought in the United States by Seamen Injured on Foreign-Flag Ships ---- 471

CHAPTER VII. COLLISION ---- 485
The Importance of Collision ---- 485
The Elements of Collision Liability ---- 486
The Standards of Proper Action ---- 488
The Effect of Fault ---- 492
Causation ---- 494
Collision Litigation ---- 498
The Navigation Rules: Application and Definitions ---- 500
"Lights and Shapes" ---- 501

CHAPTER VII. COLLISION—Continued Page
The Steering and Sailing Rules 503
The Fog Rules 504
The "Special Circumstance" and "General Prudential" Rules —"Negligence" 508
Radar 511
Custom 514
Towage in Collision Cases 515
Negligence Clauses in Towage Contracts 516
Pilotage in Collision Cases 520
"Ship-to-Shore" Collisions 522
Further on Damages 524
Critique of the Divided Damages Rule 528

CHAPTER VIII. SALVAGE 532
The Nature of Salvage—What Property May be Salved 532
Who May Become Salvors 541
The Salvage Award: How Computed—How Distributed 559
Liability for Salvage Award 574
Salvage Under Contract 578

CHAPTER IX. MARITIME LIENS AND SHIP MORTGAGES 586
Introduction: Land Liens and Maritime Liens 586
Theories About Maritime Liens: The "Personification" of the Ship 589
Enforceability of Liens When Owner is not Personally Liable. (1) Good Faith Purchasers without Notice 594
Same: (2) Liens Arising from Acts of Compulsory Pilots 597
Same: (3) Liens Arising When Ship is in Control of Charterers and the Like 600
Same: (4) Liens Arising While Ship is in Custodia Legis 602
Same: (5) Liens Arising While Ship is in Control of Sovereign 606
The Libel in Rem, the Libel in Personam and the Problem of Res Judicata 613
The "Personification" of the Ship: Conclusion 615
Claims Which Give Rise to Liens 622
Advances 633
The Executory Contract Doctrine 635
Liens Under the "General Maritime Law", State Statutes and the Federal Maritime Lien Act 642
The "Home Port" Doctrine and the State-Created Lien 643
The Federal Maritime Lien Act 652
Scope of the Lien Act: Its Relationship with State Statutes and the General Maritime Law 654
"Any Person Furnishing . . . to Any Vessel" 661

**CHAPTER IX. MARITIME LIENS AND SHIP MORTGAGES —Continued** Page

"It Shall Not be Necessary to Allege or Prove That Credit was Given to the Vessel" 664
Authority to Subject Chartered Vessels to Contract Liens: Introductory Note 668
Authority to Subject Chartered Vessels to Contract Liens: The General Maritime Law 670
Authority to Subject Chartered Vessels to Contract Liens: The Lien Act (1910–1971) 672
Authority to Subject Chartered Vessels to Contract Liens: Effect of the 1971 Deletion of the Duty of Inquiry Provision of § 973 685
The Ship Mortgage Act of 1920: Background and Constitutionality 688
Scope of the Mortgage Act 695
A Note on Patterns of Ship Financing 702
"Preferred Mortgages": Formal Requisites 706
"Preferred Mortgages": Recordation and Indorsement on Ship's Papers 712
The Ship Mortgage Act: Applicability of State or Federal Law 718
Equipment and the Title Retention Problem 727
Priorities Among Maritime Liens: Introduction 733
Priority as Determined by Class of Lien 737
Priority as Determined by Time of Accrual 742
Lien Priority as Affected by the Ship Mortgage Act 751
Priority of Government Claims 757
Loss of Lien: Laches, Limitation and Waiver 764
Same: Execution of Liens by In Rem Decree. (Herein of Distribution of Proceeds and Effect of Stipulation for Value) 786
Bankruptcy and Reorganization 806

**CHAPTER X. LIMITATION OF LIABILITY** 818

Background and Generalities 818
The Torrey Canyon and the Pollution Problem 824
The Structure of the Act 834
"The Appropriate Proceedings in Any Court" 847
Control by the Admiralty Court of Proceedings in Other Courts 862
The Conditions of Limitation: "Privity or Knowledge" 877
The "Personal Contract" Doctrine 898
The Limitation Fund 906
Claims for Loss of Life and Bodily Injury 919
The Nature of the Limitation Proceeding 927
The Voyage as the Limitation Period (Herein of the Treatment of Prior and Subsequent Claims) 946

Page

**CHAPTER XI. GOVERNMENTAL ACTIVITY IN SHIPPING** 958
The Past 959
The American Experience 963
U. S. Shipping Policy Under the 1936 Act 969
Problems After World War II 973
The Merchant Marine Act of 1970 974
Government as Promoter 978
Government as Participant 980
Government as Litigant 982
Regulatory Activity 986
Regulation of Rates and Trade Practices—The "Conferences" 990
Conclusion 996

## APPENDICES

App.
A. The Documentary Council of the Baltic and White Sea Conference 997
B. Time Charter 1003

**Table of Cases** 1011

**Index** 1045

†

# THE LAW OF ADMIRALTY

## Chapter I

## INTRODUCTION: HISTORY AND JURISDICTION

**§ 1–1.** The law of admiralty, or maritime law, may tentatively be defined as a corpus of rules, concepts, and legal practices governing certain centrally important concerns of the business of carrying goods and passengers by water. Insofar as the reference is to substantive law, the terms "admiralty" and "maritime law" are virtually synonymous in this country today, though the first derives from the connection of our modern law with the system administered in a single English court, while the second makes a wider and more descriptive reference.[1] The subject comprises the most important part of the private law that deals with the shipping industry, although, for historical and to some extent practical reasons, its coverage is by no means coextensive with the whole reach of that industry's legal concerns; [2] in some modern cases it has even been held to cover some mat-

1. The historical discussion in the first part of this chapter will make this point clear. See also De Lovio v. Boit, 7 Fed.Cas.No. 3776 at 441–3 (C.C.D.Mass.1815). "Maritime" is a fairly self-explanatory word. "Admiralty" is of course formed from "admiral"; that word, in turn, derives from an incomplete Arabic expression, *amīr-al* . . ., meaning "ruler of the . . ." Apparently common in the nomenclature of Arab officialdom in the Middle Ages, this phrase often (though not exclusively) occurred in expressions denoting maritime officers, such as *amīr-al-mā*, "ruler of the water," and *amīr-al-bahr*, "ruler of the sea." European Christians, taking the bound form, *amīr-al*, for an independent word, adopted it (in many disguises: "amiralis," etc.) to designate any high official, but ultimately borrowed the specialized use just mentioned, *without* taking over the final element *-bahr* or *-mā*. The word was meanwhile reshaped, both as to spelling and pronunciation, on false analogy with words in the etymological family of the Latin verb *admirare*: "admire," "admiration," etc. The whole history is set out in A New English Dictionary on Historical Principles (Murray ed. 1888) *s. v.* "Admiral"; the passage is worth reading, for it gives a glimpse of the interconnections of the Mediterranean world in which modern maritime law took form. (See also the Oxford Dictionary where the same story is told.)

2. "Maritime" matters connect and blend with shore transactions; thus the concept of "maritime concern" must shade off at the edges. This fact is reflected in the fuzziness of the borders of admiralty jurisdiction in the United States today; see *infra* at note 96. Then, too, the shipping industry is subject, as a matter of course, to law in general as well as to the special rules of the *lex maritima*; see *infra* at note 97.

ters quite unconnected with shipping [2a] (though the Supreme Court has recently cut back sharply on this development [2b]). Its tie with a single industry, and its separate, long-continued, and international traditions and history mark it off quite distinctly from the relatively interpermeating branches of shoregoing law—with which, nonetheless, it has numerous relations. Substantively, in the United States, it is federal law, and jurisdiction to administer it is vested in the federal courts, though not to the entire exclusion of the courts of the states.[3] Because of its special history, and its special-industry linkage, one cannot move about in it with any sureness without some knowledge both of its past and of the nature of the business it polices and serves. This chapter, therefore, (a) will sketch, *pari passu*, the history of the shipping industry and of its law, and (b) will try to convey an idea of some of the activities in shipping which today tender problems to law for solution. On all these matters vast libraries could be assembled; a schematic diagram is all that can be attempted here. Finally, we will turn (c) to consider the jurisdictional scheme which in the United States marks off admiralty as a separate subject.

In the latter connection, it is indispensable to note at the outset a recent change as regards the formal separateness of the "admiralty jurisdiction". Until 1966, each federal district court had an admiralty "side", with a separate docket, and rules of procedure peculiar to admiralty cases. In 1966 the separate "sides" were merged, the admiralty "suit" became a regular "civil action", and the Federal Rules of Civil Procedure were made generally applicable, with some special rules for certain cases heard under the "admiralty" jurisdictional grant.[3a] Despite this "unification", the admiralty power remains a separate and independent *ground of jurisdiction*, both constitutional and statutory. We will have more to say later about the new position.[3b]

**2a.** See *infra* § 1–10, at notes 98–98g.

**2b.** See *infra* § 1–10, at notes 98d & 98g.

**3.** The consequence of the famous "saving clause" in the basic Congressional grant of admiralty jurisdiction to the lower federal courts, in the Judiciary Act of 1789, 1 Stat. 76. For the subsequent history of this statutory provision, and a discussion of the whole "saving clause" question, see the text *infra* at note 116 *et seq.*

**3a.** See Rules of Civil Procedure for the U. S. District Courts, esp. Rules 1 and 9h, and the Supplemental Rules. For a discussion of recently emergent problems arising from unification, see Note, Powell, Admiralty Practice After Unification: Barnacles On the Procedural Hull, 81 Yale L.J. 1154 (1972); also L. Colby, Admiralty Unification, 54 Georgetown L.J. 1258 (1966); Wiswall, Admiralty: Procedural Unification in Retrospect and Prospect, 35 Brooklyn L.Rev. 36 (1968); Crutcher, Imaginary Chair Removed From the U. S. Courthouse, 5 Willamette L.J. 367 (1969). For background see B. Currie, Unification, etc., 17 Maine L. Rev. 1 (1965). The late Prof. Currie, Reporter of the Supreme Court's Advisory Committee on Admiralty Rules, was the chief architect and builder of unification.

**3b.** It may be helpful to mention at this point that current casebooks on Admiralty are Lucas (1969 with supplements from time to time) and Healy & Sharpe (1974).

## The Past—Or, The Rhodian Law and All That

§ 1–2. The ship (as Chesterton remarked of civilization as a whole) is a "relic of barbarism". The Sumerians had a word for it; we find it in miniature replica in Egyptian tombs; archaeology carries it still further back.[3c] The superior ease and even safety of water carriage made it the chief means, in late prehistory and in antiquity, of the carriage of goods and people over great distances.[4] We can be sure that from the earliest times "legal" problems, whether so-called or not, arose out of this carriage—that "trouble-cases" occurred and that customs took shape to channel conduct with a view to the avoidance of trouble. Of the functionally or formally "legal" dispositions that arose to do this work in ancient times we know very little. Nothing like a formal sea-code has survived even from Greek or Roman antiquity;[5] the few glimpses we get of the workings of what might today be called maritime law could at the most serve as bases for reconstructions of doubtful validity. A strong tradition says that a maritime code was promulgated by the Island of Rhodes, in the Eastern Mediterranean, at the height of its power; the ridiculously early date of 900 B.C. has even been assigned to this suppositious code—a date accepted uncritically by some legal scholars. But even the existence of such a code has been pretty well cast in doubt, and we know next to nothing of its contents, if it existed.[6] It is in-

3c. Apparently the sea and other great waters were made accessible, by the invention of the boat, very late in human evolution, a short time (in the relevant scale) before the introduction of agriculture. Washburn & Lancaster, The Evolution of Hunting, in Washburn & Jay, eds., 1 Perspectives on Human Evolution 214–216 (1968).

4. "Once started, seafaring quickly spread and by 3000 B.C. many ports had been established to handle the ever growing trade between the peoples of the ancient world." Armstrong, The Early Mariners 22 (1967). "This transport [i. e., in world commerce in general], from the earliest times until comparatively modern ones, was almost invariably by water; at first, because the ancient world was situated around the shores of a great ocean, and, later, because of the hazards and continual vexations to which all medieval traffic on land was subject." Sanborn, Origins of the Early English Maritime and Commercial Law 3 (1930). This may slightly overstate the case; see Genesis 37, 25, quoted in this connection in Day, A History of Commerce 10 (1938). The Rig-Veda "speaks in many places of ships and merchants sailing out into the open main . . ." Mookerji, Indian Shipping 85 (1912). There is a fascinating brief account of Akkadian, Sumerian, and Egyptian material in Hourani, Arab Seafaring in the Indian Ocean, 6 *et seq.* (1951).

5. The Digest provisions from the late Empire may be thought to constitute a partial exception; see *infra* at note 7. Story, however, remarks on the paucity of these: "Yet, how narrow is the compass, within which the whole maritime law of Rome is compressed! . . . But the very circumstance, that so little is here to be found . . . seems a decisive proof, that neither she, nor any more ancient nation, on the shores of the Mediterranean, had ever digested at any period a general system of maritime law." Story, Literature of the Maritime Law, in Miscellaneous Writings 97–8 (1852).

6. Two passages in Justinian's Digest seem to form the principal support of the "Rhodian Law" legend. One is cited in the note next after this. The other recounts that, when applied to for relief by a man plundered after shipwreck, Antoninus replied: "I am indeed lord of the world, but the Law is lord of the sea. This matter must be decided by the maritime law of the

teresting to note, however, that the root-principle of the highly distinctive maritime-law system of general average (under which, where something is sacrificed to save from a peril a ship and her cargo, the saved property contributes to make good the loss to the owner of the sacrificed property) is clearly stated in Justinian's Digest, and that the Rhodian Law is invoked as authority.[7] Glimpses such as this remind us that, though we do not know much about its early manifestations, maritime law is very old, and they bring to attention the fact that both commercial shipping and its law, in the forms in which they exist today, began in the Mediterranean.

Sea commerce never totally died out after the liquidation of the Roman power, but it became during the Dark Ages not so much a regular occupation as an extra-hazardous gamble of life and property.[8] It remained marginal until the rise of the great Italian trading city-states, in full swing by around 1000 A.D.[9] From this time until the era of the global Voyages of Discovery, shipping in the Mediterranean—stimulated perhaps principally by the Crusades—never flagged for long; by 1400, Venice, the greatest of the maritime pow-

Rhodians, provided that no law of ours is opposed to it." Digest 14.2.9; 2 The Digest of Justinian 389 (Monro transl. 1909). On this slender foundation has been reared an imposing edifice indeed; the quality of the masonry may be sampled in this comment, by an enthusiastic "Rhodian," on the Digest passage just quoted: "Retenons que ce fait date de 138–161 avant J. C., temps de l'empire d'Antonin." Passias, Essai Sur Le Droit Maritime Des Anciens Hellenes 33 (1932). The whole intricate matter is discussed by Benedict, The Historical Position of the Rhodian Law, 18 Yale L.J. 223 (1909). There is in existence a compilation, in Greek, of sea laws, some manuscripts of which refer to it as the "Rhodian Sea Law," but Ashburner, who edited the work, dates it between 600 and 800 A.D. (The Rhodian Sea Law cxii (Ashburner ed. 1909)). He thinks that a compiler of sea laws in that period, familiar with the remark attributed to Antoninus (see *supra*) "would be strongly inclined to call his book the Rhodian law, in order to add to its authority." *Id.* at lxviii.

7. Digest 14.2.1; 2 The Digest of Justinian 385 (Monro transl. 1909). The Digest itself contained a number of fairly detailed provisions regarding maritime matters. These are usefully summarized in Sanborn, *op. cit. supra* note 4, at 10–18. But *cf.* Story's remarks, quoted *supra* note 5.

8. Oakeshott, Commerce and Society 40–42 (1936); this author speaks (p. 42) of "the virtual breakdown of commercial intercourse," owing both to piracy and to systematic societal disintegration. *Cf.* Day, *op. cit. supra* note 4, at 33–35.

9. See Pirenne, Medieval Cities 77–92 (Halsey transl. 1948) for a spirited account. Lopez & Raymond, Medieval Trade in the Mediterranean World (1955) reproduces and annotates many commercial documents from this period; see especially Chapter XIV, Transportation by Sea, pp. 239–247. See also Clough & Cole, Economic History of Europe 58–60 (3d ed. 1952). Ganshof, The Middle Ages (1971) describes the relative position of the Italian city-states as maritime trading centers in this period (pp. 70–71) and follows their relative development through the end of the 12th Century (p. 104), laying stress on implications for international diplomacy. Genicot, Contours of the Middle Ages 136–139 (1967) credits the Christian triumph over Islam and subsequent Christian control of the Mediterranean with providing the impetus for the development of the Italian city-states as maritime trading centers. Brooke and Zarnecki, The Flowering of the Middle Ages 276–278 (1966), describes several of the men who were major figures in the period of developing trade. See also Tierney and Painter, Western Europe in the Middle Ages 213–215 (1970).

ers of the day, is said to have had 3000 ships afloat, with well-protected lanes established to Syria and elsewhere.[10] This period gave rise to what came to be called the law merchant, and saw the hesitant but unmistakable beginnings of the law of intellectual and industrial property. And it is to these times that we may trace in recognizable form the patterns of modern shipping and its associated law.[11]

§ 1–3. Special courts or tribunals sat in Mediterranean port towns to judge disputes arising among seafaring people, and the natural desire of judges and disputants for settled guidance led to the recording of judgments in individual cases and to the codification of the customary rules by which mariners and their courts considered themselves bound.[12] This dispute-settling activity, and the resultant code-making, must be looked on as part and parcel of the development of the law merchant, or *lex mercatoria;* trade and shipping were merely different phases of the same process, and the administering of maritime customary law by maritime tribunals was at the most a special aspect of that concession from local territorial jurisdiction which allowed to trading people the competency to iron out their own troubles among themselves.[13]

Two of the Mediterranean sea-codes may be mentioned: The Tablets of Amalfi,[14] near Naples, and the *Llibre del Consolat de mar*

10. Clough & Cole, *op. cit. supra* note 9, 61; McDowell & Gibbs, Ocean Transportation 9 (1954). On the influence of the Crusades, see Cunningham, Western Civilization in its Economic Aspects (Medieval and Modern Times) 125–129 (1910). On the expansion of maritime trade into the Atlantic and accompanying diplomatic activity see Ganshof, *op. cit. supra* note 9, 226–228.

11. Although, of course, it is certain that the customs of the earlier "Dark Ages" affected the more formal compilations of this later period.

12. There is a difference of opinion among specialists, apparently, as to which of these processes—recording of judgments or setting down of customs—came first. See Sanborn, *op. cit. supra* note 4, at 52. Whatever the answer, it seems clear that it was the need for guidance, in dispute-settling and probably also in dispute avoidance, that must have led to the writing down both of "precedent" and "rule."

13. "And even as the roundnesse of the Globe of the world is composed of the Earth and Waters; so the body of *Lex Mercatoria* made and framed of the *Merchants Customes*, and the *Sea-Lawes*, which are involved together as the seas and earth." So says Gerard Malynes, in his address "To the courteous Reader" of his Consuetudo, Vel, Lex Mercatoria (1636 ed.). Senior, Doctors' Commons and the Old Court of Admiralty 21 (1922) quotes this passage and remarks that the same "kinship" between the law maritime and the law-merchant "was a reality even when in the fourteenth century the bailiffs of Scarborough and Bristol dealt with them." But the relation was actually not one of "kinship" but of *inclusion.* Sanborn, *op. cit. supra* note 4, at 125, makes the point explicitly: "Such a division [i. e., into "maritime" and "commercial" law] . . . is a purely artificial one, and one that at no time has had any basis in fact."

14. The Amalfitan code can be seen in a facsimile edition, Tabula De Amalpha (with appended critical remarks by L. A. Senigallia, Naples 1934). The extant manuscript dates from the sixteenth century, but Senigallia says that the weight of authority would trace that part of it which is in Italian back to the fourteenth century, and the Latin part to a time prior to 1131. An English translation is available in 4 Black Book of the Admiralty 3 (Twiss ed. 1876).

of Barcelona.[15] Each of these in its day enjoyed prestige and even authority far beyond the port in which it was promulgated;[16] until the rise of modern states it would have been inconceivable to look on maritime law as deriving its force from a territorial sovereign, and these, like other sea-codes of the time, purported not so much to enact law for any territory as to state what was conceived already to be law by the custom of the sea.[17]

From the time of the Phoenician voyages to Britain, there had always been some maritime activity westward and northward of the Mediterranean basin, on the Atlantic littoral of the European mainland, to the British ports, and, in later times, to Scandinavia and the Baltic.[18] As this commerce grew in importance,[19] maritime courts naturally arose in Atlantic and Baltic port towns and new codes took their names from the localities where they were promulgated. The Laws of Wisby[20] and of the Hansa Towns[21] may be mentioned, but

15. A handsome facsimile of the first printed edition of this classic has been published (in 1953) in Barcelona, with a preface (in Spanish, French, and English) by Pedro Bohigas, who dates the first printing at c. 1484. The compilation itself probably took on definite shape some two centuries earlier. "A work conceived, elaborated, and completed in the Middle Ages, it served as a code of maritime law in important European countries up until the end of the eighteenth century." Preface, p. 35. For an English translation, see 3 Black Book of the Admiralty 50 (Twiss ed. 1874); the title is here given as The Good Customs of the Sea; a Catalan text faces the English.

16. Senigallia, the commentator on the facsimile Amalfitan Table, speaks (*op. cit. supra* note 14, at 31) of its "fame and authority in a broad zone of the southern Tyrhenian littoral." The Consolat de Mar was widely translated in the Mediterranean area, and as far north as Leyden. Llibre Del Consolat De Mar, *supra* note 15, at 45–46.

17. Ashburner, reviewing the authorities, concludes that they point "to the existence, if not of a general sea custom for the whole Mediterranean, at least of a custom extending beyond the jurisdiction of the individual state." The Rhodian Sea Law (Ashburner ed. 1909) cxxiii.

18. The Roman trade with Gaul and Britain is described in Charlesworth, Trade Routes and Commerce of the Roman Empire (2d ed. 1926) 179–221. All the British trade was of course by sea, and a good deal of the trade into and out of Gaul was over water.

19. In Pirenne, *op. cit. supra* note 9, at 92–105, there is an interesting account of the movement of trade to the North and into the Baltic, during the reawakening of commerce in the Middle Ages. "The two great centres of commercial activity in later medieval times were Lombardy and Flanders. The second of these regions steadily increased its commercial power." Oakeshott, *op. cit. supra* note 8, at 90. O. Tonning, Commerce and Trade on the North Atlantic, 850 A.D. to 1350 A.D. (1936) tells of the patterns of trade (involving the British Isles, Norway, Iceland, and Greenland) that grew up on the northern seas. See also Clough & Cole, *op. cit. supra* note 9, 61–62; Fayle, A Short History of the World's Shipping Industry 88 *et seq.* (1933). Ganshof, *op. cit. supra* note 9 at 218–231 contains an interesting discussion of the development of trade to the North, relating it to industrial and political developments. See also Tierney and Painter, *op. cit. supra* 215–218.

20. Wisby is a port on the island of Gotland in the Baltic, just off the coast of Sweden. The Laws of Wisby exist in many versions; sometimes the title "Gotland Sea Laws," or its equivalent, is used. Apparently they did not all originate in Wisby or in any one place. The whole subject is discussed by Sir Travers Twiss, in 4 Black Book of the Admiralty xxii *et seq.* English translations are given in

21. See note 21 on page 7.

the most interesting of all these medieval maritime codifications, to the English or American student, is the one that goes by the name of the Rules of Oleron.[22] It is said that this code was promulgated, on the small island off the French west coast from which it takes its name, by Eleanor of Aquitaine, on her return from her spectacular course of misconduct in the Holy Land, and that it was introduced into England by her son Richard the Lionhearted.[23] However that may be, it has always been regarded as having an especial importance for the maritime law of England, and hence for that of the United States.

The student will want to know how important it is that he be familiar with this or others of the medieval sea-codes. Probably a recognition of their names is all that is really needed even for ornamental purposes by the compleat admiralty proctor (if, under the unified Rules,[23a] one may still use that title). They could hardly state much living law for the concerns of modern shipping. Yet, once in a while, when more recent authority fails, a court may look back to them, and especially to the Rules of Oleron, for what analogical help may be vouchsafed.[24]

the same volume, at pp. 55 (Gotland Sea Laws) and 265 (Laws of Wisby). A translation of the latter collection is found in Peters, Admiralty Decisions in the District Court of the United States for the Pennsylvania District (1807). Appendix to Vol. I, lxvii–xc (reprinted in 30 Fed.Cas. 1189).

21. These are available in English translation, with a brief account of their origin, in Peters, *op. cit. supra* note 20, Appendix to Vol. I, xciii–cxi (reprinted in 30 Fed.Cas. 1197).

22. A number of printings of this code are available in English. Perhaps the most generally accessible is in 30 Fed.Cas. 1171, reprinting the version in Peters, *op. cit. supra* note 20, Appendix to Vol. I, iii–lxiii. A different version is found in 1 Black Book of the Admiralty 88–131, with French and English texts facing. In 2 Black Book of the Admiralty 212 ff., a version resembling the one given by Peters is printed under the title The Customs of Oleron. Actually, the expression "Rules of Oleron" must be treated as generic, designating a number of more or less similar collections of sea laws going by this name. (The same observation might be made of any of the more widely known medieval codes.) Straightening out the filiation of the various manuscripts would be a life's work; some idea of the complexity of the matter can be gained by the perusal of Twiss's remarks in the Introductions to the two volumes of the Black Book in which are printed the "Rules" and the "Customs." A concise account of textual and other questions is found in Burwash, English Merchant Shipping, 1460–1540. App. I, 171 *et seq.* (1947). Dr. H. L. Zeller has edited a number of the manuscripts of the "Rules" in his series, Sammlung Älterer Seerechtsquellen. The individual volumes in this series have facsimile pages of the manuscripts edited.

23. Cleirac gives credit to Eleanor: Us Et Coutumes De La Mer 2 (1661 ed.), and seems to imply, in the same passage, that Richard introduced the Rules into England. A less romantic view is stated by Sir Travers Twiss, in 1 Black Book of the Admiralty (Twiss ed. 1871) lxii; he thinks the "Rules," which have the sound of judgments in individual cases rather than of general precepts, are a compilation of decisions made at Oleron. (The discussion following seems to establish that these "Rules" entered England later than the time of Richard I; certainly there is no evidence they were around that early.)

23a. See *supra*, § 1–1, second paragraph.

24. "The law of Oleron, and other maritime codes, may still be usefully cited

As maritime commerce grew in importance, its law attracted the attention of those Continental legal scholars and commentators who were reworking and adapting to their times the Roman or "civil" law. Treatises and commentaries appearing during and after the Renaissance acquired status as classic systematizations of the subject.[25] Maritime law thus grew up and came of age under the tutelage of the civil law, and it still bears the imprint thus acquired, even when administered in the courts of common law countries.[26] As the great national states arose in Europe, the international law of the sea came to be assimilated into national law, or at least to be restated in authoritative codifications; the classic one is the Ordonnance de la Marine of Louis XIV.[27]

**§ 1–4.** Turning to England, it ought to be noted first that that country, though late in so doing, participated fully in the medieval development sketched above. Maritime courts sat in the English port towns, and adjudicated the causes before them by customary sea

in English courts." 1 Holdsworth, A History of English Law 559 (3d ed. 1922).

25. E. g., Étienne Cleirac, Us Et Coutumes De La Mer, first published in 1647 in Bordeaux. For a full account of Cleirac's work in maritime law, see Gros., L'Oeuvre De Cleirac En Droit Maritime (1924). Of the classic names, mention should be made of Roccus, Bynkershoek, Casaregis, Valin, Pothier, and Emerigon. Assessments of these and many more are to be found in Story, Literature of the Maritime Law, in Miscellaneous Writings (1852). This essay gives what is perhaps the most useful view, from the standpoint of the American lawyer, of the "maritime classics," for (whatever it may want of the critical spirit of later scholarship) it shows us how these writers impressed the man through whose work, largely, they influenced our maritime law. (For Story's place in American maritime law, see Dunne, Justice Joseph Story, 99–102, 109, 129 *et seq.* (1970)) The most imposing collection of old sea laws, with commentary, is Pardessus, Lois Maritimes Antérieures Au XVIIIe Siècle (1828–1845).

26. The story of the civilians in England is interestingly told in Senior, *op. cit. supra*, note 13.

27. Promulgated in 1681, it far outclassed its predecessor compilations, in comprehensiveness and structure. It was carried over nearly intact into the French Commercial Code of 1807. Chadelat, L'Elaboration de l'Ordonnance de la Marine d'Août 1681, Revue Historique De Droit Français Et Étranger, 4e Série, 32e Année, 74, 228 (1954), is a careful study of the circumstances of its construction, under the guiding genius of Colbert. Chadelat calls this Ordinance "the most celebrated of the laws of the Ancien Régime." *Id.* at 74. Its renown was world-wide; in Morgan v. Insurance Co. of North America, 4 Dall. 455, 458 (Pa.1806), Chief Justice Tilghman of the Supreme Court of Pennsylvania, confronted with a maritime law question on which no precedents were available, said: "But, although there is no adjudged case, the subject has not escaped the notice of writers on the marine law. In one of the ordinances of *Lewis* XIV. (A. D.1681) it is declared, that a charter party to carry goods *out* and *in*, if, during the voyage, the commerce is prohibited and the vessel returns, the outward freight only is earned; and *Valin*, in his commentary on this article, says, the law is the same, if the vessel is freighted *outward* only. These ordinances, and the commentaries on them, have been received with great respect, in the Courts both of *England* and the *United States*; not as containing any authority in themselves, but as evidence of the general marine law. Where they are contradicted by judicial decisions in our own country, they are not to be respected. But on points which have not been decided, they are worthy of great consideration."

law.[28] But the later English evolution had a special character. To the office of the Lord High Admiral (originally a naval official concerned with the command of the fleet and the suppression of piracy and wrecking) there was annexed a court which acquired a jurisdiction over civil cases of a maritime nature. Just how and when this happened is too cloudy and controversial for simple or even accurate summary,[29] but by the time of Richard II (1377–1400) the admiral and vice-admiral were transacting enough judicial business to move Parliament to limit their jurisdiction by statute to "a thing done upon the sea," [30] and in Tudor times the court was well established as a court of record, doing a large civil business.[31] It slowly but surely took away most of their business from the local maritime courts in the port towns, and attracted the easily aroused jealousy of the common law courts, as well as the dislike of those who feared it as a prerogative court and as one that conducted its trials (following the civil law with which the maritime law is closely related, and setting the practice still followed in this country in civil cases where the admiralty jurisdiction is invoked) without a jury.

These factors resulted in the rather anticlimactic eclipse of the court for almost two centuries. The common law judges, relying on controversial constructions of the statutes of Richard II mentioned above, began issuing writs of prohibition against proceedings in ad-

28. 1 Holdsworth *op. cit. supra* note 24, at 530–535.

29. The following summaries of the early history of the Admiralty court are useful: Mears, The History of the Admiralty Jurisdiction in 2 Select Essays in Anglo-American Legal History 312 (1908); Marsden's Introduction to 1 Select Pleas in the Court of Admiralty (being Vol. VI, Publications of the Selden Society, 1892); 1 Holdsworth, *op. cit. supra* note 24, at 544 ff.; Laing, Historic Origins of Admiralty Jurisdiction in England, 45 Mich.L.Rev. 163 (1946). A detailed description of the early Admiralty court which focuses primarily on the role of the Admiralty Registrar is found in Thompson, Admiralty Registrars—Some Historical Notes (1958). The upshot is that the available data permit only doubtful approximation; probably, an admiral's court was beginning to form, and to deal with piracy, wrecking, and the like, toward the beginning of the fourteenth century, and probably this court had begun to acquire some sort of civil jurisdiction toward the end of that century. Around this time there began to take shape the celebrated "Black Book of the Admiralty"—a compilation of sea laws and miscellaneous directions and other matter having to do with the admiral's office. For a general account of this collection see 1 Black Book of the Admiralty (Twiss ed. 1871), Introduction.

30. The quotation is from 13 Rich. II, c. 5 (1389). Another and more explicitly worded statute was passed two years later, 15 Rich. II, c. 3 (1391). Little is known of the grievances giving rise to the passage of these statutes; see Mears, *supra* note 29, at 329–30. Laing, *supra* note 29, at 169–170, says that "the prime objection to the new court was its connection with the civil law," because, principally, of the lack of a jury.

"The statutes of Ric. II do not appear to have prevented the evils which they were intended to meet, and in 1400 another Act [2 Hen. 4, c. 11] was passed by which a penalty was imposed upon those who sued in the Admiral's Court contrary to the statutes of Richard II." Marsden, *op. cit. supra* note 29, li.

31. 1 Holdsworth, *op. cit. supra* note 24, at 552; Laing, *supra* note 29, at 174–5. Some account of the intellectual atmosphere surrounding the study of maritime law in Britain in these early times is found in Senior, Early Writers on Maritime Law, 37 L.Q.Rev. 323 (1921).

miralty except within absurdly narrow limits. In a nutshell, the construction of the words of the statutes that limited the Admiral's court to things "done upon the sea" was extremely literal, so that, e. g., contracts having a maritime subject-matter but made on land (as most were) were held outside the jurisdiction of the Admiralty.[32] By the end of the seventeenth century, the court was of comparatively little importance; Pepys tells of a visit to one of its sittings: "I perceive that this court is yet but in its infancy (as to its rising again); and their design and consultation was, I could overhear them, how to proceed with the most solemnity, and spend time, there being only two businesses to do, which of themselves could not spend much time." [33] (It is puzzlingly interesting, however, that Pepys, whose main professional concern was maritime and naval business, speaks of a "rising again" as a thing to be looked for.)

Still, the court continued in being, and thus, on however narrow ground, there was firmly established in England a tribunal constituted at least in theory to deal with shipping matters; the common law courts did not manage to prevent this, as they did in the case of commercial law and commercial courts in general. And by statute, in the nineteenth century, the jurisdiction of the court over maritime matters was vastly enlarged.[34] It is now a part of the High Court of Justice, being united in a single Division with Probate and Divorce [35] —a linkage that underlines its civil law connections.

Meanwhile, the Voyages of Discovery had changed the pattern of shipping. The Mediterranean commerce yielded in importance to trade on the ocean routes, and thus the European maritime law system spread to farflung colonies. Of principal interest to us is the establishment of colonial courts of Vice-Admiralty in British North America. These were granted an ample general maritime jurisdiction in their commissions, for the Crown was not blind to the advantages of a prerogative court that sat without a jury. It has long been part of received lore that this jurisdiction was not sliced away by writs of prohibition, the statutes under which these had issued not applying to the colonies. The truth seems to be much more complicated than this, and is only partly recoverable. The formerly preva-

32. The story of this conflict has often been told. 1 Holdsworth, *op. cit. supra* note 24, at 553 ff.; Mears, *supra* note 29, at 354ff.; Laing, *supra* note 29, at 179 ff. Lord Coke led the attack, as he did that on the court of Chancery. This time his views won out, though he did not live to enjoy the full victory, which was not complete until after the Restoration.

33. Pepys, Diary, March 17, 1662–3; quoted in 1 Holdsworth, *op. cit. supra* note 24, 557.

34. 3 & 4 Vict. c. 65 (1840); 13 & 14 Vict. c. 26 (1850); 24 Vict. c. 10 (1861). Broadly speaking, the jurisdiction of the British admiralty now corresponds to our own; there subsist, however, minor technical differences. A valuable work on the last two centuries is Wiswall, The Development of Admiralty Jurisdiction and Practice Since 1800 (1970). For a survey of the admiralty jurisdiction throughout the Commonwealth see Fitzgerald, Admiralty and Prize Jurisdiction in the British Commonwealth of Nations, 60 Jurid.Rev. 106 (1948).

35. 1 Holdsworth, *op. cit. supra* note 24, at 639–40.

lent view had a definite influence on the development of admiralty jurisdiction under the Constitution. It seems to be the case that the colonial admiralty courts had a wider scope of business than the one at home, and that the earliest American experience was with an admiralty court exercising this fuller maritime jurisdiction.[36]

So matters stood at the time of the American Revolution. Except for certain brief hesitations of the Confederation, of interest mainly to the specialist in legal history,[37] the next step was the adoption of the Constitutional provision placing admiralty jurisdiction within the federal judicial power,[38] and the implementing of this grant by the relevant provisions of the Judiciary Act of 1789.[39] But since the constitutional provision still states the living law of this country, its interest is more than historical, and its consideration will be deferred to a later section.[40]

## World Shipping and Its Law

**§ 1–5.** Maritime law was secreted in the interstices of business practice. It arose and exists to deal with problems that call for legal solution, arising out of the conduct of the sea transport industry.

36. See De Lovio v. Boit, 7 Fed.Cas.No. 3776, at 442 (C.C.D.Mass., 1815); Crump, Colonial Admiralty Jurisdiction in the Seventeenth Century (1931). Reports of Cases in the Vice Admiralty of the Province of New York (Hough ed. 1925) contains an introduction by the editor, a distinguished admiralty judge, on the work of the court that was lineal predecessor to the present federal court for the Southern District of New York. For more recent and exact accounts, see Robertson, Admiralty and Federalism, 65–94 (1970); Ubbelohde, The Vice-Admiralty Courts and the American Revolution (1960); see also Setaro, The Formative Era of American Admiralty Law, 5 New York Law Forum 9 (1959); Wroth, The Massachusetts Vice-Admiralty Court, in Billias, *ed.*, Law and Authority in America 32 (1965). The last-named author says ". . . The court exercised jurisdiction in almost every type of case that has ever been claimed by admiralty." (p. 45). The use of prohibition seems to have been erratic; the records are exceedingly fragmentary. It is quite impossible to substantiate Story's view as expressed in DeLovio v. Boit, *supra*, and rather clear that his expressions there were at least hyperbolical.

37. The national government under the Articles of Confederation had no general admiralty powers; there were, of course, no national courts by which maritime law could have been administered, and such admiralty courts as existed were maintained by the states. But the Articles did provide that the Congress should have the exclusive power to lay down rules for prize cases (see *infra* at note 149) and empowered Congress to establish "courts for receiving and determining finally appeals in all cases of captures" (which included prize cases). A "Court of Appeals in Cases of Capture" was established, and disposed of more than a hundred cases. Its work is discussed, and citations given to authorities evaluating its place in constitutional history, in Hart & Wechsler, The Federal Courts and the Federal System 11, n. 18 (1953). The same Article gave Congress power to appoint courts "for the trial of piracies and felonies committed on the high seas," but this empowerment to exercise a criminal jurisdiction in admiralty (see *infra* at note 147) was never used. Hart & Wechsler, *loc. cit. supra*.

A review of admiralty jurisdiction in the States under the Articles of Confederation is found in 4 Benedict, Admiralty (6th ed. 1940) 438–449. See also Robertson, *op. cit. supra*, note 36, 95–103; Setaro, *op. cit. supra*, note 36.

38. U.S.Const. Art. III, § 2.

39. 1 Stat. 76 (1789).

40. See *infra* at note 52 *et seq.*

The student of the subject will do well to familiarize himself, as widely and deeply as he can, with the structure and doings of that industry; only thus can he handle his subject, either practically or academically.[41] Here we can only sketch a few of the principal characteristics of the industry as it exists today; it will be the aim of this section to show how the principal 'topics' dealt with in this book arise naturally out of the conduct of the business. In later chapters, we will go somewhat more deeply into the industrial background relevant to each chapter-topic.

Though individual and joint ownership still exist in some small trades, the bulk of economically significant shipping is now conducted by corporations possessing the financial resources required by the heavy initial and operating costs that mark the industry. These corporations vary in size from insubstantial entities operating one or a few marginal tramps to the great lines that conduct fleet operations on tight schedule. Corporate organization is of a complexity that reflects the great and growing complication of shipping and its multitudinous service industries.[42] Carriers in a given "trade" (operating, that is to say, within some defined geographic limits) are usually organized in a "conference", the main purpose of which is the setting of rates; such arrangements enjoy a conditional exemption from the anti-trust laws of the United States.[43]

41. The following works will be found useful for this purpose: Kendall, The Business of Shipping (1973); McDowell & Gibbs, Ocean Transportation (1954); Dover, The Shipping Industry, Its Constitution and Practice (1952); Bross, Ocean Shipping (1956); Thornton, British Shipping (1939) (this, like Dover, is a British treatment, but it must be remembered that the relations between British and American shipping are close, and that much of the American admiralty lawyer's work has to do with British shipping); Stevens, Shipping Practice (7th ed. 1952), containing considerable concrete know-how; Bes, Chartering and Shipping Terms (7th ed. 1970), a helpful glossary, with much trade information; Knight, Modern Seamanship (14th ed. 1966), Turpin & MacEwen, Merchant Marine Officers Handbook (4th ed. 1965)—both on technical aspects of ship operation; Woollam, Shipping Terms and Abbreviations (1963), (for common abbreviations).

Perhaps the most immediately useful book for the beginner starting to clear his way through the terminological jungle in the "statements of facts" in admiralty cases is Norman Ford, Ship Lore (1953), a simple account of the special language of seafaring people, with respect to parts of the ship, position of objects sighted etc. Periodicals are Fairplay Shipping Journal; Shipping World & Shipbuilder (London); New York Journal of Commerce; Marine News. Following the marine news in the New York Times is a good way to keep up with recent developments in the world of shipping.

42. See McDowell & Gibbs, *op. cit. supra* note 41, Chapter 12, Organization and Management, at p. 221. On the development from simple to complex organization, see Clough & Cole, *op. cit. supra* note 9, 465.

43. Shipping Act, 1916, § 15, 39 Stat. 733, 46 U.S.C.A. § 814. But see Federal Maritime Comm. v. Aktiebolaget Svenska Am.L., 390 U.S. 238, 88 S.Ct. 1005 (1968) which held that the Federal Maritime Commission could require proof of sufficient justification for antitrust violations before approving a restraint and giving it antitrust immunity. Carnation Co. v. Pacific Westbound Conference, 383 U.S. 213, 86 S.Ct. 781 (1965) held all shipping agreements not approved by the Federal Maritime Commission subject to the antitrust laws. In Marine Space Enclosures v. Federal Maritime Commission, 137 U.S.App.D.C. 9, 420 F.2d 577 (1969), the court required the Federal Maritime Commission to hold

The most significant function of shipping is the transport of goods. Passenger carriage is of far less importance to the world economy and to the industry, and is every year lessening in importance as air transport replaces it.

Two types of cargo operation may be distinguished. First, there are the "liners", sailing along fixed routes on preannounced schedules, and carrying "general cargoes"—that is, whatever is offered and accepted for shipment. Then there are the "tramps", which offer their capacity for the carriage of bulk cargoes as desired by the shipper, who ordinarily engages the whole of the ship; each voyage is thus a matter of special arrangement between shipowner and shipper. It would be a great mistake to carry over to this sort of operation the derogatory feel of the word "tramp"; the packaged and containerized shipments loaded on by liners are indeed important in international trade, but the world economy would wither away were it not for the work of the tramps that carry their bulk cargoes of fuel, food, ore, and other raw materials when and where needed in shipload lots.

It will be handy, however, to start our description of particular courses of dealing with the simplest transaction; the carriage by sea of a less-than-shipload shipment of goods, taken on board by a "general" ship (one holding herself out for the receipt of mixed cargoes as offered) and carried under a bill of lading. The shipment may actually originate in the port of lading or somewhere else; if the latter, then the shipper must get his goods to the port and shipside by whatever land transportation is available and of choice. Meanwhile, he will have reserved ("booked") space on the vessel, and will have been instructed by the carrier, at the time of booking, as to the day or days on which the goods are to be delivered at the dock. When they are so delivered, he will receive a "dock receipt"; at this point, the carrier takes over, loading the goods aboard (often using the services of a stevedoring company operating in the port) and issuing, in place of the dock receipt, a bill of lading. This highly important document serves as a written embodiment of the terms of the contract of carriage, as a receipt for the goods, and as a negotiable document of title. In this third capacity it is a vital part of the financing of the sale of the goods; it is usually forwarded through a bank to the buyer, together with a draft for the price of the shipped goods, an insurance policy, a seller's invoice, and whatever other documents are required by law, custom, or special agreement; on paying or accepting the draft, the buyer gets the other papers. (If the shipper is at an inland point, or if his overseas business is too light to justify the maintenance of a special department to handle the necessary documentary and physical work, he may engage the services of a

hearings before granting approval of shipping agreements where there was objection by a potential competitor on antitrust grounds. The operation of the conference system is briefly described in Rosenthal, *op. cit. supra* note 41, 33–51; a full account and evaluation is found in Marx, International Shipping Cartels (1953).

professional "freight forwarder",[43a] who will book space, take charge of the shipment on its arrival at port, go through the steps requisite to seeing it aboard, and turn the bill of lading over to the shipper.) Meanwhile, the goods are on their way, and, after whatever calls the ship must make, are set down at the port of destination and delivered to the holder of the bill of lading.[44]

This picture is now complicated by the "container revolution"; goods now often move from inland points in "containers" up to some 40 feet in length by 8 feet high, and 8 feet wide, which can be moved by truck and rail to shipside, be loaded intact there, and be finally delivered by truck or rail to inland destination. This containerized multimodal transport tenders new problems to law, but solutions so far connect with and branch out from the law governing traditionally packaged shipments. Beyond doubt, general revision, perhaps by international agreement, will soon have to take place, but meanwhile the older law must be understood.[44a]

Out of the simple fact that things can go wrong in such a set of transactions—that men may disagree as to the meaning of documents, that ships may be delayed with fault therefor in doubt, that goods may be spoiled or damaged through debatable carelessness—arise the legal problems dealt with in Chapter III, *infra, The Carriage of Goods under Bills of Lading.*

**§ 1–6.** The heavy shipper (especially of bulk commodities) may find it more economical to engage the carrying capacity of an entire ship—one of the "tramps" mentioned above, and often one specially designed to carry one particular sort of bulk cargo. The ancient document which will state the terms to which he and the shipowner agree is known as the charter party. There are several main kinds of charter parties, or charters, under which a whole ship is engaged—some adapted to other sorts of transactions than the one described—and many varieties of each kind, but all are contracts, and hence capable of generating in their special way all the disputes that contracts can produce—as to construction, performance, discharge, frustration, and so on; and most contemplate the carriage of goods by sea, with all the consequent chances of spoilage, delay, and the like, arising when goods are shipped. Out of these possibilities and actualities of trouble arise the questions dealt with in Chapter IV, *infra, Charter Parties.*

**43a.** On the freight forwarder and his functions, see Brooks, "Freight Forwarder Liability for Cargo Damage," 2 Journal of Maritime Law and Commerce 888 (1971); Aquascutum of London v. S.S. American Champion, 426 F.2d 205, 1970 A.M.C. 679 (1970); Chicago, M., Etc. R. Co. v. Acme Freight 336 U.S. 465, 484, 69 S.Ct. 692 (1949). For a modern set of problems, see Ullman, The Role of the American Ocean Freight Forwarder in Intermodal Containerized Transportation, 2 Journal of Maritime Law and Commerce 625 (1971).

**44.** For a more detailed discussion of the use of bills of lading in financing sales transactions, see Chapter III, Part I.

**44a.** For a thorough practical treatment of containerized shipment, see Tabak, Cargo Containers (1970).

Two highly significant observations may now be made. First, it is a logical possibility (and very often happens) that, when a ship is chartered for the carriage of goods, bills of lading for the goods are taken when they are loaded. Thus the two principal legal forms under which water carriage takes place are by no means mutually exclusive; quite commonly *both* are used with respect to a single shipment. This generates certain complex questions, with which we will deal in the chapter on charter parties. For now, it is important that we note for the first time how interconnected are the "topics" into which maritime law has arbitrarily to be separated for purposes of sequential analysis. Keeping this in mind will make it much easier to get into the subject; this book will be cross-referenced to bring the point often to mind.

Then, secondly, we ought to observe that bills of lading and charter parties are "contracts" of a very special kind. They are what have been called "type-contracts",[45] which is to say that most of their terms, other than time, price, and a few other variables, are worked out by industry consensus or invariant practice long before —in some cases centuries before—the parties "bargain". The formation of the contractual relationship requires no more than the filling in of blanks in printed forms. There is, of course, no general legal mandate that this be so; so long as certain special statutory requirements were met, shippers and carriers who found time heavy on their hands might dicker about every word in each shipping document. But goods are loaded in a hurry, and charter parties are arranged by wireless—and business men who do a heavy volume of one sort of transaction want to settle and routinize both practice and expectation. So in the main the terms under which goods are shipped are not renegotiated with each shipment, but are fixed by institutional practice and locked firm in printed forms. And the important point now is that this is not a feature peculiar to bills of

45. The "type-contract," or standardized (usually printed) commercial contract, is of immense importance in modern economic life. See Prausnitz, The Standardization of Commercial Contracts 15–16 (1937). This author adds a note of caution:

"So far our survey has shown how far contracts had already been stereotyped through the defects of the general law, the needs of the trade and the reservoir of legal experience, the notaries. It only needed one more factor to turn this mass of experience into a weapon. This new factor was the economic power of individual undertakings."

Even today, constant vigilance has to be exercised to prevent the overreaching facilitated by situations such as the one mentioned; in Chapter III, *infra*, we will see that drastic legislative action has been found needful, to offset the tendency of ocean carriers to use the standardized bill of lading as a weapon for avoiding liability for goods damage. For an interesting discussion of the extent to which the contracts govern the law today and their implications for democratic theory, see Slawson, Standard Form Contracts and Democratic Control of Lawmaking Power, 84 Harv.L.Rev. 529 (1971). See, generally, Kessler, Contracts of Adhesion, 43 Colum.L. Rev. 629 (1943); Eiber, The Significance of Standardized Mass Contracts in Insurance, 6 Journal of the American Society of Chartered Life Underwriters 84 (1951); Bolgan, The Contract of Adhesion, 20 Amer.J.C.L. 53 (1972). See Judge Frank's interesting dissent in Siegelman v. Cunard White Star Limited, 221 F.2d 189, 1955 A.M. C. 1691 (2d Cir. 1955), esp. 221 F.2d at 204 *et seq.*

lading and charter parties, but is generally characteristic of maritime law today. Much of the working law with which the admiralty practitioner has to deal consists not in law-at-large but in the interpretative glosses that have clustered around constantly used clauses in the type-contracts that are the structural steel of the industry. And the fact that judicial interpretations have accreted around these set clauses and phrases tends in turn to make doubly sure their continued use, for the maritime world grows to rely on continuance in settled interpretations, and to stabilize its documentary practice on that reliance. This, and not a mere love of verbal old lace, is the reason for the continued use in marine insurance policies, for example, of language so archaic as hardly to be comprehensible to the normal literate person today.[46]

**§ 1–7.** Up to now we have discussed shipping as a going concern, but ships must be built and kept in operation. Perversely, contracts for their building have been held "not within the admiralty jurisdiction",[47] which may be noted as the first of the vagaries that mark our subject as of human devising. But their sale must be financed, and this often involves the creation of security interests enforced in admiralty. The more important of these will be dealt with in Chapter IX, *infra.*

Ships require a vast and bewilderingly various amount of supply and repair. An outgoing ship will normally have taken on some stores and fuel for her voyage at the port of lading. She will have run up a wharfage bill, and incurred various port fees. She will have been loaded by stevedores. She will probably be taken out by a pilot, and assisted at the start of her voyage by tugs. From time to time she will have to be repainted and repaired. A host of special callings and industries has arisen to furnish these and a hundred other supplies and services, and maritime liens are granted to secure payment. These transactions create legal problems, also treated in Chapter IX.[48]

The personnel requirements of the industry are heavy and exacting. Chief importance, economically and in volume of litigation, goes to the subject of seamen's injuries, and the remedies that have been devised for these will form the subject-matter of Chapter VI.

46. See Calmar S. S. Corp. v. Scott, 345 U.S. 427, 430–433, 73 S.Ct. 739, 741, 742, 1953 A.M.C. 952 (1953); Chapter II, *infra,* at note 21. Some of the incomprehensibility of marine, as of other commercial documents, arises not from archaism but from a tendency toward standardized abbreviation; see Chapter IV, *infra,* at note 8, *et seq.*

47. People's Ferry Co. v. Beers, 61 U.S. (20 How.) 393 (1858), is conventionally cited to this point, though it may be read as holding no more than that a *lien* is not given by the maritime law to the shipbuilder; see *infra* at note 107. But later cases have treated it as having held that the shipbuilding contract itself is outside the jurisdiction. Morewood v. Enequist, 64 U.S. (23 How.) 491, 494 (1860); Thames Towboat Co. v. The Francis McDonald, 254 U.S. 242, 243, 41 S.Ct. 65, 66 (1920). Ultimately—perhaps soon—this rule may have to respond to the critical ideas expressed in the last two paragraphs of § 1–10, *infra.*

48. See Chapter IX, *infra.*

In going their rounds, ships sometimes run into serious mishap. They collide with one another, for example, more often than seems plausible to the landlubber—often enough, at least, to give rise to a volume of important litigation and to justify a special chapter (*infra*, Chapter VII, *Collision*) largely devoted to the ascertainment and adjustment of consequent liabilities.

Whether through collision or otherwise, a ship or its cargo may be in such a spot as to require emergency assistance; the peculiar maritime rules compensating the furnisher of such assistance with a sort of bounty, paid out of the value of the saved property, form the subject-matter of the topic called *Salvage*, and are taken up in Chapter VIII, *infra*. The ship, on the other hand, may seek to extricate herself from peril by taking some action that damages or destroys a part of herself or her cargo, in order to save the rest (e. g., throwing goods overboard to lighten the ship in a storm). The system of subsequent *pro rata* contribution, by which the loss is equalized among saved and sacrificed interests, is one of the most ancient peculiarities of the maritime law—still very much alive today, and dealt with in Chapter V, *infra*, *General Average*.

In case of collision or other marine disaster, claims subsequently asserted against a ship and her owner may be very large in number and in aggregate amount. In the United States, as in most maritime countries, a statutory plan is provided for the limitation of total liability, under designated circumstances, to the value of the vessel or to an amount calculated on her tonnage.[49] The federal courts exercising of admiralty jurisdiction administer this system; we will examine it in Chapter X, *infra*, *Limitation of Liability*.

**§ 1–8.** We come now to a subject that blankets the whole ground already covered. Insurance may or may not have originated in maritime commerce, but it was certainly first used in volume there, and (more to the point) there is no other industry quite so thoroughly committed to the insurance idea. Almost every important possibility of loss in the conduct of ocean shipping is normally insured against. If you glance over the matters already taken up in this section, you will see that this means there is an insurance angle to every one of them. If goods are damaged en route, the shipper is usually insured against the damage and the carrier is almost always insured against the liability that may be brought home to him. When a seaman (usually uninsured) is injured, it is his employer's insurance company that normally pays the claim. If goods have to pay general average, their underwriter does it for them; collision damage is usually made well by insurance, with liability to be settled later.

Now where it is normal that insurance carriers pay off incurred liabilities, and that they also pay for physical damage, being thereby subrogated to the claims of their policyholders, it is easy to see that a very large proportion of maritime litigation must involve at least one

49. R.S. §§ 4283–4289 (1875), 46 U.S.C.A. §§ 183–189.

insurance company as the factual if not the technical "party in interest". To the admiralty lawyer, therefore, the subject of *Marine Insurance* (Chapter II, *infra*) is of immense importance. The prevalence of insurance also has important bearings on the evaluation, from the standpoint of policy, of statutory and decisional rules everywhere in the maritime law.

*Governmental Activity in Shipping* (Chapter XI, *infra*) is another all-pervasive theme. The earliest and most constant form this has taken is in the establishment of regulatory and administrative machinery to police many important concerns of the industry. More recently, the federal government has entered the picture as subsidizer and promoter of ship construction and operation.[50] And especially during World War I, and during and since World War II, government has figured as owner, charterer, or operator of vessels performing functions which would previously have been classed as private. None of these governmental entrances into the picture has radically altered the underlying industrial pattern or the traditional legal system. But the active presence of government is of great importance both to the student of the working of the shipping industry and its law, and to the admiralty practitioner—and it brings home the great public interest, economic and strategic, that inheres in the merchant marine.[51]

Thus, ships are financed and built, mortgaged, bought and sold; men almost of a world apart take them over the seas; goods are loaded aboard them and carried from here to yonder. Armies of supply- and repairmen keep them seaworthy and well-bunkered; pilots wait at Sandy Hook; tugs churn out on call. In spite of all precautions, collisions occur; help is rendered; sacrifices are made as the price of safety. And over the whole stretches the worldwide network of marine insurance, and everywhere is felt the active hand of government, in regulation or aid or participation. And out of this confusing but well-ordered complex of vital work come the cases of trouble and the problems in counseling with which the admiralty lawyer has to deal.

## Admiralty Jurisdiction in the United States

### The Jurisdiction and Procedure of Courts

**§ 1–9.** The empowerment of the courts of the United States to draw upon and administer the maritime law derives from constitutional language extending the "judicial power of the United States" to "all cases of admiralty and maritime jurisdiction." [52] In Section

50. Merchant Marine Act, 1936, §§ 501–511, 601–612, 49 Stat. 1995–2007, 46 U.S.C.A. §§ 1151–1182. In 1970 the Act was amended to establish a Commission on American Shipbuilding and to provide increased subsidy to shipbuilding. 46 U.S.C.A. §§ 1151–1183a. On the whole subject, see infra, Chapter XI, §§ 11–7 and 11–8.

51. A review of the importance of merchant shipping through history, with a brief assessment of the present position and abundant references, is found in McDowell & Gibbs, *op. cit. supra* note 41, Chapter 1, Sea Power and National Power, pp. 7–33 (bibliography at 32–33).

52. U.S.Const. Art. III, § 2. The almost total lack of light on the genesis of this clause in the deliberations of the convention is brought out in Putnam, How the Federal Courts Were

9 of the Judiciary Act of 1789, Congress implemented the constitutional grant:

> ". . . the district courts . . . shall also have exclusive original cognizance of all civil causes of admiralty and maritime jurisdiction . . . saving to suitors, in all cases, the right of a common law remedy, where the common law is competent to give it; . . ." [53]

The above-mentioned (§ 1–1) modern "unification" of the admiralty suit and the civil action, under a single set of procedural Rules, makes necessary a rather complicated approach to the problem of "jurisdiction in admiralty". As briefly noted above, for some 175 years the admiralty jurisdiction of the district courts was kept separate from other branches of jurisdiction; the "admiralty docket" was a thing apart, and the admiralty suit was handled under an entirely separate set of procedural rules. Since 1966, the litigant invoking the constitutional and statutory admiralty jurisdiction does so by means of a "complaint", indistinguishable formally from the ordinary civil complaint. The consolidated rules, however, still make some provision for differential treatment when the admiralty jurisdiction is invoked, as well as for the special handling of some matters previously existing only "in admiralty". It may sometimes happen that some independent ground of jurisdiction, in addition to the admiralty ground, may exist—as, e. g., diversity of citizenship—and the new "complaint", without some special provision, might not reveal which ground was being invoked—and therefore, whether the special rules for treating admiralty matters were to be applied. It is provided in the new federal Civil Rules, therefore, that the complaint may declare on its face that it is the admiralty jurisdiction that is being appealed to; [53a] if this declaration is not inserted, and if an independent non-admiralty ground of jurisdiction appears, the action will go forward under general civil procedure, not subject to the special provisions made for cases in which the admiralty jurisdiction is invoked.

In this attenuated sense, it may be said that there are still "admiralty" cases—those cases, namely, in which the only constitutional and statutory ground of jurisdiction is the admiralty ground, or in which, there being more than one ground, the admiralty ground is opted for in the complaint.

The major complication lies in the fact that all the cases from 1787 to 1966 (comprising, of course, a very large portion of the precedents with which the student and practitioner must deal) are set in the frame of the older terminology and practice. Such cases are

Given Admiralty Jurisdiction, 10 Cornell Law Q. 460 (1925). For a later critique of Judge Putnam's views, see Robertson, *op. cit. supra* note 36, 10–17.

53. 1 Stat. 76–77. The provision has been carried over, in somewhat altered language, into 28 U.S.C.A. § 1333; see *infra* at note 125.

53a. Rule 9(h), Rules of Civil Procedure for the United States District Courts.

spoken of as being "in admiralty", the complaint is the "libel", and so on. It seems, therefore, too early to discard the older frame of reference. But the reader should remember that today's equivalent to a case's being "in admiralty" is its being either a case in which the admiralty ground is the only ground of federal jurisdiction, or a case in which, out of more than one possible ground of such jurisdiction, the plaintiff in his complaint designates the admiralty ground. This equivalency, which is very nearly complete, makes the older material easy to restate in modern terms.

In this book, since the cited cases mostly antedate the unification, we will often use the older terminology, in which the older leading opinions are all written. It must steadily be borne in mind, however, that no case is any longer "in admiralty", in the older sense; the admiralty clause in Article III of the Constitution, and the successive statutory implementations, are *grounds for jurisdiction* in ordinary civil actions, with some modification in procedural treatment when these grounds are with warrant invoked.

The constitutional language, and the statutory grant of "cognizance" quoted above,[53b] have, by interpretation and inference, been made the basis of a wide federal power, not only as to jurisdiction of courts but also as to substantive law,[54] over matters maritime.

Consideration of the effect of the so-called "saving clause" in the language quoted above must be deferred until a little later along, after enough has been said about certain distinctive features of admiralty procedure (and correlative substantive conceptions) to make intelligible a delineation of just what is "exclusive" and just what is "saved". Right now we are interested in the affirmative effect of the language just preceding the "saving clause". This is that, from the organization of the federal judiciary down to the present, the federal courts have taken jurisdiction (without reference to amount in controversy, diversity of citizenship, or the presence of any other "federal question") of all causes of action arising under the maritime law.[55]

Just what cases are these? The answer to this will always be a little vague at the borderline, no matter how long the process of judicial inclusion and exclusion goes on, and there were large doubts indeed, in the early days of the Republic, as to the extent of the power conferred. In the leading early case, De Lovio v. Boit,[56] an opinion

53b. Supra at note 53.

54. See *infra* § 1–16.

55. Glass v. The Sloop Betsey, 3 U.S. (3 Dall.) 6 (1794); Ex parte Easton, 95 U.S. 68 (1877). For general discussions of the jurisdiction, see Beeks and Moss The Exclusive Admiralty Jurisdiction, 27 Wash.L.Rev. 176 (1952); Black, Admiralty Jurisdiction: Critique and Suggestions, 50 Colum.L. Rev. 259 (1950). A superb note, From Judicial Grant to Legislative Power: The Admiralty Clause in the Nineteenth Century, 67 Harv.L.Rev. 1214 (1954), should be read as to several of the matters under discussion here.

56. 7 Fed.Cas. 418, No. 3776 (C.C.D. Mass.1815), followed in the landmark case of Insurance Co. v. Dunham, 78 U.S. (11 Wall.) 1 (1871), see *infra* note 71.

by Story suggests several possible ways for defining the category. The words might have been intended to refer to the practice of the British Court of Admiralty during early colonial times or at the American Revolution, but Story believed (and the belief gained nearly uncontradicted generality) that the restrictions that hampered that court were enforced by writs of prohibition based on statutes not applicable to the colonies; it would thus have seemed gratuitous as well as crippling to accept its limits as those of the newly constituted American admiralty tribunals. This test was accordingly rejected, in De Lovio v. Boit and generally in our early precedents,[57] though it cannot be said to have left no trace at all.[58] Another possible reference might be to the jurisdiction of the colonial courts of vice-admiralty;[59] still another might (especially in view of the use of the word "maritime") be to the jurisdiction of maritime courts throughout the shipping world. Story suggested in De Lovio that these two tests came down to much the same thing, since he believed that the colonial admiralty courts, like the seacourts of other nations, enjoyed a wide jurisdiction over maritime affairs, uncircumscribed by the narrowly literal "locality test" that had confined the English Court of Admiralty.[60] De Lovio v. Boit concludes with a formulation that is imprecise, as was unavoidable, but that has, in the end, set the style for later courts: the jurisdiction, says Story, "comprehends all maritime contracts, torts, and injuries. The latter branch is necessarily[61] bounded by locality; the former extends over all contracts (wheresoever they may be made or executed, or whatsoever may be the form of the stipulations) which relate to the navigation, business or commerce of the sea. . . . "[62]

57. Waring v. Clarke, 46 U.S. (5 How.) 441, 454–458 (1847); Morewood v. Enequist, 64 U.S. (23 How.) 491 (1860); Insurance Co. v. Dunham, 78 U.S. (11 Wall.) 1, 24 (1871); Ex parte Easton, 95 U.S. 68, 70 (1877); see also The Lottawanna, 88 U.S. (21 Wall.) 558, 574–577 (1875).

The emancipation of the jurisdiction from dependence on the English model, and its broadening to its present scope, were not performed without some conflict; see the account in The Gilbert Knapp, 37 F. 209 (E.D.Wis. 1889).

58. One such trace may be in the rule that shipbuilding contracts are not within the jurisdiction. People's Ferry Co. v. Beers, 61 U.S. (20 How.) 393 (1858), the case that is taken to have established this rule (see *supra* note 47), seems to rest in part on the fact that the shipbuilding contract is "made on land, to be performed on land." *Id.* at 402. See also the general doubts, as to the propriety of our extending the jurisdiction beyond the English precedents, expressed by Mr. Justice Woodbury in New Jersey Steam Navigation Co. v. Merchants' Bank, 47 U.S. (6 How.) 344, 420–22 (1848).

The rule of The Plymouth, 70 U.S. (3 Wall.) 20 (1866), that no tort is maritime unless the substance and consummation are on water, may be another trace of the English "locality" influence. This rule has now been drastically modified by statute: see *infra*, note 75. For what may be a modern revival of the "locality test", see *infra*, n. 98f.

59. See *supra* at note 36.

60. 7 Fed.Cas. at 442. But see *supra* at n. 36.

61. For the fate of this "necessity," see *infra* Chapter VII, at note 151.

62. 7 Fed.Cas. at 444. Generally, see Deutsch, Development of the Theory of Admiralty Jurisdiction in the U.S., 35 Tulane L.Rev. 117 (1960); Stolz, Pleasure Boating and Admiralty:

**§ 1–10.** The resultant conception of our admiralty jurisdiction has been one of fairly complete coverage of the primary operational and service concerns of the shipping industry, with a few anomalous exceptions. To the modern student, the history of the growth of the jurisdiction, and the high-level concepts that have been suggested as keys to its definition, may be of interest, but he ought also to be aware that certain fields, without arguing the matter, may now be taken as settled within the jurisdiction, and others as equally certainly excluded from it. The contours of the jurisdiction appear from a list of most of the principal included causes:

> Suits on contracts for the carriage of goods [63] and passengers; [64] for the chartering of ships (charter parties); [65] for repairs, supplies, etc., furnished to vessels,[66] and for services such as towage,[67] pilotage,[68] wharfage; [69] for the services of seamen and officers; [70] for recovery of indemnity [71] or premiums [72] on marine insurance policies.

Erie at Sea, 51 Calif.L.Rev. 661 (1963). (This article, despite its deceptively narrow title, is a mine of information and thought on admiralty jurisdiction.)

63. New Jersey Steam Navigation Co. v. Merchants' Bank, 47 U.S. (6 How.) 344 (1848) (Daniel, J., dissented, and two of the concurring justices felt it necessary to resort to the theory that the action, which was for the loss of cargo, was on a "marine tort" rather than on the contract of carriage.); Brittan v. Barnaby, 62 U.S. (21 How.) 527 (1859). (The Court did not notice the jurisdictional point at all in deciding the case, which involved the carriage of goods under a bill of lading, but Daniel J., dissented, on the ground that the courts of admiralty are without jurisdiction "of charter parties or bills of lading," *id.* at 538.) Suits of this kind are now regarded as unquestionably within the jurisdiction, and constitute a large part of the business of the admiralty court; see Chapters III and IV, *infra*.

64. The Moses Taylor, 71 U.S. (4 Wall.) 411 (1867).

65. Morewood v. Enequist, 64 U.S. (23 How.) 491 (1860). Counsel in this case tried yet again to persuade the court to backtrack and accept the theory that the American admiralty jurisdiction was to be defined in terms of the English view. By this time, the court is getting a bit testy, and speaks of the issue before it as "The question now (it is hoped for the last time) mooted before us." *Id.* at 495.

66. The General Smith, 17 U.S. (4 Wheat.) 438 (1819); North Pac. S. S. Co. v. Hall Bros. Marine Ry. & Shipbuilding Co., 249 U.S. 119, 39 S.Ct. 221 (1919).

67. See The Knapp, Stout & Co. Company v. McCaffrey, 177 U.S. 638, 20 S.Ct. 824 (1900).

68. Ex parte McNiel, 80 U.S. (13 Wall.) 236, 242–43 (1871).

69. Ex parte Easton, 95 U.S. 68 (1877).

70. Sheppard v. Taylor, 30 U.S. (5 Pet.) 675 (1831).

71. Insurance Co. v. Dunham, 78 U.S. (11 Wall.) 1 (1871). But a contract to procure insurance on a vessel is not "maritime in character". Warner v. The Bear, 126 F.Supp. 529, 1955 A.M.C. 1123 (D.Alaska 1955). But see Isbrandtsen Co. v. United States, 233 F. 2d 184, 1956 A.M.C. 1028 (2d Cir. 1956), where it was held that a carrier's failure to procure insurance for cargo placed on shore was a breach of a maritime obligation implied by the contract of carriage.

72. The Guiding Star, 18 F. 263 (C.C.S. D.Ohio 1883).

Suits in tort for collision damage,[73] or for any physical damage to ships or cargoes on navigable waters; [74] (by special statute [75]) for any damage caused by a vessel, whether or not consummated on land; for personal injuries to seamen,[76] passengers,[77] and probably to all others while aboard

73. Waring v. Clarke, 46 U.S. (5 How.) 441 (1847).

74. Philadelphia, W. & B. R. R. v. Philadelphia & Havre de Grace Steam Towboat Co., 64 U.S. (23 How.) 209, (1860); Fireman's Fund Ins. Co. v. City of Monterey, 6 F.2d 893, 1925 A.M.C. 989 (N.D.Cal.1925). In United States v. Standard Oil Co. of California, 156 F.2d 312, 1946 A.M.C. 1160 (9th Cir. 1946) it was held that damage done on shore by the breach of a maritime contract is compensable in admiralty; this case antedates the statute cited in the next note.

75. 62 Stat. 496 (1948), 46 U.S.C.A. § 740. For amendment to 1948 Act see 1965 A.M.C. 974. This statute will be discussed in the chapter on Collision (VII). It has been held to apply not only to damage physically caused by a vessel, but also to a tort committed by a shipowner "while or before the vessel is being unloaded, . . . The impact of which is felt ashore at a time and place not remote from the wrongful act." Gutierrez v. Waterman S. S. Corp., 373 U.S. 206, 210, 83 S.Ct. 1185, 1188, 1963 A.M.C. 1649, 1653, rehearing denied 374 U.S. 858, 83 S.Ct. 1863 (1963). A suit for oil pollution has been held within the statute, State of California By and Through Dept. of Fish and Game v. S. S. Bournemouth, 307 F.Supp. 922, 1970 A.M.C. 642 (1969), *noted* 2 Journal of Maritime Law and Commerce 200 (1970); Perth Amboy No. 1, 168 F.Supp. 925, 1959 A.M.C. 2532 (S.D.N.Y.1958).

76. London Guarantee & Accident Co. v. Industrial Accident Commission of California, 279 U.S. 109, 49 S.Ct. 296, 1929 A.M.C. 495 (1929); *cf.* The Osceola, 189 U.S. 158, 23 S.Ct. 483 (1903); Atlantic Transport Co. v. Imbrovek, 234 U.S. 52, 34 S.Ct. 733 (1914). In Dunn v. Wheeler Shipbuilding Corp., 86 F.Supp. 659, 1949 A.M.C. 1953 (E.D.N.Y.1949) a wrongful death action based on allegation that errors in design of a ship had ultimately resulted in death of libellant's decedent on navigable waters, was held to involve a "maritime" tort.

77. The Admiral Peoples, 295 U.S. 649, 55 S.Ct. 885, 1935 A.M.C. 875 (1935). This case involved a "borderline" situation—the injured woman fell from the gangplank while disembarking. The Court held the tort within the jurisdiction, on the ground that the gangplank was "part of the vessel."

The subject of liability to passengers for injury may be summarily handled here, as the principles involved differ little from those in use ashore. The liability basis is negligence; there is no "insurer" relation and no "warranty" (on both points cf. the law as to Carriage of Goods, *infra* Chapter III, Part II). (The only apparent exception is the unconditional responsibility of the carrier for misconduct of his people toward the passengers. See New Jersey Steamboat Co. v. Brockett, 121 U.S. 637, 7 S.Ct. 1039 (1887)). The "negligence" may consist of course, in failure to handle the ship skillfully, with the result that disaster ensues, in the form of collision or otherwise, with consequent injury to the passenger.

Most passengers' injury suits are brought under the "saving clause" (see *infra* § 1–13) in order to get a jury, but many such suits are brought into the admiralty forum when the carrier files a limitation petition (see *infra* Chapter X) and thus forces all persons asserting claims into concourse. Passengers, like others, may benefit posthumously from the Death on The High Seas Act, (see *infra* note 133), and presumably from the newly-created general maritime cause of action for wrongful death, *infra* note 79b.

A 1936 statute forbids stipulations in the contract of passage (1) for immunity from or limitation of amount of liability for negligence, and (2) for periods for filing notice of claim or filing of suit less than six months and one year respectively. 49 Stat. 960, 1480, 46 U.S.C.A. §§ 183(b) and (c).

Siegelman v. Cunard White Star Limited, 221 F.2d 189, 1955 A.M.C. 1691 (2d Cir. 1955) decided that, where a ticket stipulated for English law and for a one-year statute of limitations English

a vessel on navigable waters.[78] (The jurisdiction in personal injury cases is partly statutory.[79])

Suits for wrongful death. Where these occur outside territorial waters, the federal Death On The High Seas Act applies.[79a] Where the death occurs within the territorial jurisdiction of the United States, the Supreme Court has recently held that the general maritime law creates a cause of action.[79b] Earlier, such a cause of action had been referred to the law of the State within whose bounds the death occurred.[79c]

Suits on claims for salvage,[80] general average,[81] and maintenance and cure (the seaman's ancient right to be

law has to apply to the questions of effectiveness of waiver by an agent in New York of the one-year provision, and of the interruption of the one-year period by the necessity of the plaintiff's obtaining letters of administration. The opinion of the court, and perhaps even more the dissent of Judge Frank, interestingly illustrate some phases of the carrier-passenger relation.

**78.** It was long unsettled whether any tort whatever, occurring on navigable waters, is within the jurisdiction. Certainly, the courts have used language broad enough to support this conclusion. "Every species of tort, however occurring, and whether on board a vessel or not, if upon the high seas or navigable waters, is of admiralty cognizance." The Plymouth, 70 U.S. (3 Wall.) 20, 36 (1866). But in the Imbrovek case, *supra* note 76, it was left open whether the maritime employment of the libellant was a needful element of his right to access to admiralty. See Admiralty Jurisdiction in Tort Actions, 23 Wash. & Lee L.Rev. 345 (1966). See esp. note 98d *infra*.

**79.** Merchant Marine Act of 1920, § 33, 41 Stat. 1007, 46 U.S.C.A. 688—popularly known as the Jones Act; Death on the High Seas Act, 1920, 41 Stat. 537, 46 U.S.C.A. 761. The admiralty jurisdiction has been held exclusive as to cases under the latter act, see *infra* note 133, but the seaman suing under the Jones Act may sue either at law or in admiralty, and he usually picks the former, for he wants to present his case to a jury.

**79a.** *Supra* n. 79.

**79b.** Moragne v. States Marine Lines, Inc., 398 U.S. 375, 90 S.Ct. 1772, 1970 A.M.C. 967 (1970) noted 44 Temple L. Q. 292, 293 (1971). On this exceedingly important case, see Chapter VI, *infra*, §§ 6–32 *et seq.*

**79c.** The immediately prior (and highly confused) state of the law on this is sketched in Moragne, *supra* n. 79b. See also Levinson, Recovery for Wrongful Death on Offshore and Inland Waters, 5 Willamette L.J. 379 (1969).

**80.** Mason v. The Blaireau, 6 U.S. (2 Cranch) 240 (1804) (admiralty jurisdiction assumed); see also Houseman v. Cargo of the Schooner North Carolina, 40 U.S. (15 Pet.) 40, 48 (1841). For discussion of salvage as a substantive topic, see *infra* Chapter VIII.

**81.** Strangely, there was difficulty in establishing admiralty jurisdiction over this most maritime of subjects (see *supra* at note 7, and *infra* Chapter V). The English court of admiralty did not take jurisdiction in general average cases. Lowndes and Rudolph, General Average 311–12 (7th ed. 1948). In Cutler v. Rae, 48 U.S. (7 How.) 729 (1849), the Supreme Court held that admiralty had no jurisdiction over a libel in personam (see *infra* at note 106) to enforce payment of general average after release of the cargo; expressions in the case would support the view that admiralty had no jurisdiction over general average at all. Du Pont de Nemours & Co. v. Vance, 60 U.S. (19 How.) 162 (1857) held that a cargo claim for general average could be enforced in admiralty by in rem process against the vessel; this clearly established that admiralty had jurisdiction in general average cases and Cutler v. Rae was

supported and cared for by his ship when injured in her service, irrespective of fault.) [82]

Petitions for limitation of shipowners' liability [83] (statutory).

Proceedings to foreclose preferred ship-mortgages [84] (statutory), or to enforce bottomry [85] or respondentia bonds.[86]

Suits to recover ships wrongfully taken or withheld.[87]

(Detailed discussion of all of these is reserved for the appropriate chapters.)

confined to holding that the ship's lien on cargo for general average was lost by delivery, and that no in personam suit in admiralty could be brought on the promise implied on receipt of the goods. The force of Cutler v. Rae, even as so narrowed, was regarded, by judges in the later years of the century, as weakened or destroyed by the leading case of Insurance Co. v. Dunham, 78 U.S. (11 Wall.) 1 (1870); that case, though holding only that suits on marine insurance policies were within the jurisdiction, used language so broad as to make it seem clear that such a distinctively maritime obligation as general average must be included. To this effect, see Coast Wrecking Co. v. Phoenix Ins. Co., 7 F. 236, 242 (E.D. N.Y.1881) ("Cutter [*sic*] v. Rae must be considered to have been overruled by the subsequent case of Insurance Co. v. Dunham. . . ."); Bark San Fernando v. Jackson & Manson, 12 F. 341 (E.D.La.1882) (the court held squarely *contra* Cutler v. Rae, relying on Insurance Co. v. Dunham); National Board of Marine Underwriters v. Melchers, 45 F. 643, 645 (E.D.Pa. 1891) ("That case [Cutler v. Rae] . . . cannot be regarded as authority."); Pacific Surety Co. v. Leatham & Smith Towing & Wrecking Co., 151 F. 440, 442 (7th Cir. 1907). In Compagnie Française de Navigation a Vapeur v. Bonnasse, 19 F.2d 777, 1927 A.M.C. 1325 (2d Cir. 1927), certiorari denied 275 U.S. 551, 48 S.Ct. 114 (1927), it was held that the liability on a bond given to cover ship's liability in general average was maritime and within the jurisdiction; *cf.* The Emilia S. De Perez, 22 F.2d 585, 1927 A.M.C. 1839 (D.Md.1927). These cases have firmly established general average within the jurisdiction.

82. Harden v. Gordon, 11 Fed.Cas. 480, No. 6,047 (C.C.D.Me.1823) (full discussion by Mr. Justice Story); The Osceola, 189 U.S. 158, 23 S.Ct. 483 (1903); see *infra*, Chapter VI.

83. Norwich & N. Y. Transp. Co. v. Wright, 80 U.S. (13 Wall.) 104, 122–24 (1872); see *infra* Chapter X.

84. The Thomas Barlum, 293 U.S. 21, 55 S.Ct. 31, 1934 A.M.C. 1417 (1934).

85. The Grapeshot, 76 U.S. (9 Wall.) 129 (1870). At p. 135 *et seq.*, the Court discusses the nature of the bottomry bond, which is a sort of mortgage on a ship, entered into for the purpose of raising money in case of necessity in a foreign port. The advance of communications has caused bottomry and respondentia (see *infra* note 86) bonds to pass virtually out of use.

86. Franklin Ins. Co. v. Lord, 9 Fed. Cas. 712, No. 5,057 (C.C.D.Mass.1826). The court here discusses the respondentia bond, which resembles bottomry except that the cargo rather than the ship is pledged.

87. The so-called "possessory" and "petitory" actions. The Schooner Tilton, 23 Fed.Cas. 1277, No. 14,054 (C.C. D.Mass.1830). It has been held that possessory libels may be used to break up a sit-down strike aboard; Korthinos v. S. S. Niarchos, 175 F.2d 730, 1949 A.M.C. 1135 (4th Cir. 1949), certiorari denied 338 U.S. 894, 70 S.Ct. 241 (1949).

See also Atamanchuck v. Atamanchuck, 61 F.Supp. 459, 1945 A.M.C. 1244 (D. N.J.1945).

The following is a sampling[88] of causes that might be thought to be included, but actually are not:

Suits on contracts for the building[89] and sale[90] of vessels; for the payment of a fee for procuring a charter;[91] for services to a vessel laid up and out of navigation.[92]

88. This is all that is feasible or at least desirable at this point. "Close cases" could of course be multiplied, as is always true when a high-level abstraction such as "maritime" has to be used to draw a line between concrete cases. The test of maritime subject matter has proved itself "not always easy of application." Cory Bros. & Co. v. United States, 51 F.2d 1010, 1011, 1931 A.M.C. 1442 (2d Cir. 1931). In that case, the court had to deal with the claim of an agent, employed to handle ship's business in Pernambuco, for reimbursement of expenses incurred in defending a suit for cargo damage. Doubting that the suit (despite its seeming connection with maritime concerns) could be entertained in admiralty, the court found another ground of jurisdiction. Contrast the more hard-shelled view of the Supreme Court in Minturn v. Maynard, 58 U.S. (17 How.) 477 (1855); the shore agent sued for balance of money due him for disbursements on ship's business, but the court said, "There is nothing in the nature of a maritime contract in the case." . . . "The case is too plain for argument." Cases like these, and the ones cited in the notes immediately following, will warn the student that the concept of "maritime concern" is not to be given a straightforward lay meaning—that it is not only vague but highly artificial—and inconsistent even in its artificiality. It should be stressed that the important cases in admiralty are *not* the borderline cases on jurisdiction; these may exercise a perverse fascination in the occasion they afford for elaborate casuistry, but the main business of the court involves claims for cargo damage, collision, seamen's injuries and the like—all well and comfortably within the circle, and far from the penumbra. (The last sentence was quoted with approval in Executive Jet Aviation, Inc. v. City of Cleveland, 409 U.S. 249, 93 S.Ct. 493, 1973 A.M.C. 1 (1972).

The reading of a few cases denying admiralty jurisdiction will give the student some feel for the line as drawn. *E. g.*: Mulvaney v. Dalzell Towing Co., 90 F.Supp. 259, 1950 A.M.C. 1053 (S.D.N.Y.1950)—breach of contract to compromise and settle claim for death of seaman; Goumas v. K. Karras & Son, 140 F.2d 157, 1944 A.M.C. 60 (2d Cir. 1944), affirming 51 F.Supp. 145 (S.D.N.Y.1943), certiorari denied 322 U.S. 734, 64 S.Ct. 1047 (1944)—false representations that working conditions aboard ship were good, resulting in picketing, etc., of libellant, who procured the crew, by its disappointed members; The Richard Winslow, 71 F. 426 (7th Cir. 1896)—storage of grain in vessel during off-navigation season on Great Lakes, after carriage (but *cf.* Richardson v. Conners Marine Co., 141 F.2d 226, 1944 A.M.C. 444 (2d Cir. 1944), where a contract for day-to-day storage on New York harbor barges was held maritime); Kamara v. The Atlantic Emperor, 97 F.Supp. 722, 1951 A.M.C. 1304 (E.D.Pa.1951)—"blacklisting" seamen.

89. See *supra* note 66. The "borderline" problem is the distinguishing of "repair" from "rebuilding." See New Bedford Dry Dock Co. v. Purdy, 258 U.S. 96, 42 S.Ct. 243 (1922).

90. The Ada, 250 F. 194 (2d Cir. 1918); Grand Banks Fishing Co. v. Styron, 114 F.Supp. 1, 1953 A.M.C. 2172 (D. Me.1953). But *cf.* MacDonald v. United States, 79 F.Supp. 953 (E.D.N.Y. 1948) (contract to convert a vessel from a cargo ship to a mule carrier held maritime. *Cf. supra* note 89, on the "repair" vs. "rebuilding" question.) A comment on the Grand Banks case attacks the rule excluding ship sale contracts; see Admiralty Jurisdiction and Ship-Sale Contracts, 6 Stanford L.Rev. 540 (1954). The Supreme Court has never squarely decided the point. See Flota Maritima v. Motor Vessel Ciudad de la Habana, 181 F.Supp. 301, 1960 A.M.C. 496 (D. Md.1960), affirmed 335 F.2d 619, 1966 A.M.C. 1999 (4th Cir. 1966); Richard Bertram & Co. v. Yacht Wanda, 447 F.2d 966, 1971 A.M.C. 1841 (5th Cir. 1971).

91. Rhederei Actien Gesellschaft Oceana v. Clutha Shipping Co., 226 F.

92. See note 92 on page 27.

Proceedings to foreclose ship-mortgages other than those designated as "preferred" in the Ship Mortgage Act.[93]

Suit on breach of an agreement to procure insurance on a cargo.[93a]

Suits for injuries occurring on "artificial island" drilling rigs.[93b]

The following are doubtful areas, where generalization is dangerous:

Quasi-contractual claims arising out of maritime transactions.[94]

339 (D.Md.1915); The Thames, 10 F. 848 (S.D.N.Y.1881). Such services are looked on as "preliminary to," rather than part of, the maritime activity. This is one of the vague ideas that has to be reckoned with in the twilight zone of jurisdiction. (As to contracts to procure insurance, see Warner v. The Bear, 126 F.Supp. 529, 1955 A.M.C. 1123 (D.Alaska 1955), *supra*, note 71.)

92. The Andrew J. Smith, 263 F. 1004 (E.D.N.Y.1920); Murray v. Schwartz, 175 F.2d 72, 1949 A.M.C. 1081 (2d Cir. 1949). On the often troublesome question of when a ship actually is "dead," see Hercules Co. v. The Brigadier General Absolom Baird, 214 F.2d 66, 1954 A.M.C. 1201 (3d Cir. 1954).

93. Bogart v. The John Jay, 58 U.S. (17 How.) 399 (1854); *cf. supra* at note 84.

93a. See Koch-Ellis Marine Contractors, Inc. v. Phillips Petroleum Co., 219 F.2d 520, 1955 A.M.C. 558 (5th Cir. 1955), and case cited.

93b. Rodrigue v. Aetna Casualty and Surety Co., 395 U.S. 352, 89 S.Ct. 1835, 1969 A.M.C. 1082 (1969).

94. Archawski v. Hanioti, 350 U.S. 532, 76 S.Ct. 617, 1956 A.M.C. 742 (1956) has changed the picture on the jurisdiction in quasi-contract. Respondent received money for passage, kept the money, and did not furnish the passage. The Court upheld admiralty jurisdiction over the suit for restitution, saying, "We conclude that, so long as the claim asserted arises out of a maritime contract, the admiralty court has jurisdiction over it." 350 U.S. at 535, 76 S.Ct. at 620. In Sword Line, Inc. v. United States, 228 F.2d 344, 1956 A.M.C. 47 (2d Cir. 1955), on rehearing, 230 F.2d 75, at page 77, 1956 A.M.C. 1277 (2d Cir. 1956), the court found admiralty jurisdiction over a libel to recover overpayments of charter hire, setting up a broad test of "inherent maritime character of the underlying transaction . . . ." Judgment affirmed 351 U.S. 976, 76 S.Ct. 1047. These cases seemingly go a long way to establishing the jurisdiction over quasi-contractual claims. For background, see Chandler, Quasi Contractual Relief in Admiralty, 27 Mich.L.Rev. 23 (1928); Comment, Present Status of Quasi-Contractual Relief in Admiralty, 23 Calif.L.Rev. 343 (1935).

In Krauss Bros. Lumber Co. v. Dimon S. S. Corp., 290 U.S. 117, 54 S.Ct. 105, 1933 A.M.C. 1578 (1933) the Court granted relief, in rem against the ship, for a freight charge exceeding the contract rate and paid by mistake. The Court did not discuss with any fullness the jurisdictional point, but the opinion suggests (290 U.S. at 122, 54 S.Ct. at 106) a distinction between excessive payments exacted in breach of contract and other sorts of payment of money under circumstances where good conscience demands repayment.

The Krauss case might be read to have established quasi-contractual jurisdiction in admiralty. But no such use of it was made for a long time. In Silva v. Bankers Commercial Corp., 163 F.2d 602, 1947 A.M.C. 1266 (2d Cir. 1947) suit for restitution of advance freight was brought on the civil side on a diversity basis; the court not only indicated that it still entertained the view that admiralty jurisdiction did not exist, but even went on to hold that state law applied to the unjust enrichment question presented. The procedure in this case perhaps gives the clue to an explanation of the failure of the Krauss case to germinate; as a practical matter counsel cannot afford to take a chance that

"General agency" and "management of the vessel" agreements. A "general agency" agreement has been held outside the jurisdiction[94a] but an agreement for managing the vessel within it.[94b]

Torts occurring on navigable waters, but having no other maritime connection.

"Mixed" contracts i. e., those of which part would be, if standing alone, within the jurisdiction, and part without.[95]

admiralty jurisdiction will be sustained in quasi-contractual suits, and voluntarily use the ordinary civil procedure. But see Pontin Lighterage Co. v. American Export Lines, 126 F. Supp. 824, 1955 A.M.C. 50 (E.D.N.Y. 1954), where an action by a lighter company to recover from a steamship company amounts which the lighter company had paid its employees in connection with work done for the steamship company was held within the admiralty jurisdiction. The court cited the Krauss case for the proposition that the test to be applied "is not the form of the action but the subject matter and questions involved." *Id.* at 826.

See also Home Ins. Co. of New York v. Merchants Transp. Co., 16 F.2d 372, 1927 A.M.C. 57 (9th Cir. 1926), affirming 12 F.2d 931 (W.D.Wash.1926) (restitution denied to a marine insurance company that had paid a loss on allegedly false proofs); S/A Industrias Reunidas F. Matarazzo v. Compania De Vapores San Antonio, S. A., 126 F.Supp. 558, 1955 A.M.C. 306 (S.D.N. Y.1954) (no jurisdiction of suit to recover overpayment of freight).

As the article and comment cited in this note *supra* make clear, there is no warrant in history, venerable precedent, principle, or common sense for denying to the admiralty courts jurisdiction over the quasi-contractual claims. If the court is set up as the special industrial court of the shipping business, then obviously its expertness is just as much needed when the theory of action happens to be *quasi ex contractu* as at any other time.

**94a.** P. D. Marchessini & Co. (N.Y.) v. Pacific Marine Corp., 227 F.Supp. 17, 1964 A.M.C. 1538 (S.D.N.Y.1964). This case is distinguished, and a rather different approach taken to the "general agency" problem, in Hinkins, S. S. Agency v. Freighters Inc., 351 F.Supp. 373, 1973 A.M.C. 348 (N.D.Calif.1972), citing this text. See Note, 4 Journal of Maritime Law and Commerce 480 (1973).

**94b.** Hadjipateras v. Pacifica, S. A., 290 F.2d 697, 1961 A.M.C. 1417 (5th Cir. 1961). In this case, citing the present section, Judge John Brown upheld the jurisdiction, saying of the contract, "It concerns a ship . . . Its very purpose is to effectuate the physical economic operation and employment of a vessel." 290 F.2d at 703. With respect, the same thing is true of the "general agency" agreement; the case cited in the last preceding note is of dubious defensibility. *Cf.*, also, Economu v. Bates, 222 F.Supp. 988, 1965 A.M.C. 1289 (S.D.N.Y.1963) with Hadjipateras v. Pacifica S. A., *supra.* It is predicted that the Supreme Court, when the issue reaches it, will hold "general agency" and other vessel-management agreements within the jurisdiction—along with actions for accountings on them. (See also Interocean S. S. Corp. v. Amelco Engineering Co., 341 F.Supp. 995, 1971 A.M.C. 1661 (N.D. Calif.1971)).

**95.** Obviously, agreements to perform maritime services (*e. g.*, to carry goods) may be part of contracts involving other types of agreements as well (*e. g.*, to assemble and deliver the same goods). When suit is brought in admiralty for the breach of an obligation in such a contract, a number of problems can arise, of which the chief is: Where the breached obligation is in itself maritime, does its association with non-maritime elements take it out of the jurisdiction? Berwind-White Coal Mining Co. v. City of New York, 135 F.2d 443, 1943 A.M.C. 682 (2d Cir. 1943) is a good illustration. The contract involved imposed a duty to remove a railroad trestle—clearly a non-maritime obligation—and to restore the bottom of a slip to its former condition—a maritime service. The actual damage was alleged to have resulted from faulty perform-

Torts having to do indirectly with the business of shipping, such as the tort of inducing breach of a maritime contract.[95a]

Causes of action "pendent" to admiralty claims.[95b]

"Products liability." [95c]

(None of these lists is anywhere near exhaustive.)

In the main, the outlines of the jurisdiction seem to have been pretty well drawn. Its evaluation requires the balancing of two factors pulling in opposite directions. First, if there is any sense at all in having a separate basis for admiralty jurisdiction in the federal courts, it must be because there is a federal interest that can best be implemented by thus dealing with the major concerns of the shipping industry—with all of them, and not just with a few of them selected on antiquarian criteria. On the other hand, the actual concerns of the shipping industry may reach as far as the last ranch that sends cattle to port, and, even without stretching the matter at all, maritime transactions are inseparably connected with and shade into the non-maritime.[96] Also, there are aspects of the shipping industry

ance of the latter duty. The court, following a long line of cases, saw the problem as one of "separability." If the maritime duties were capable of "being divided from the rest," so that they might be separately adjudicated, then admiralty could deal with them. On the facts, the court found this amputation feasible, and took jurisdiction. Obviously, this formula cannot produce hairline clarity; cases stand on their own facts. *Cf.* Compagnie Française de Navigation v. Bonnasse, 19 F.2d 777, 1927 A.M.C. 1325 (2d Cir. 1927), certiorari denied 275 U.S. 551, 48 S.Ct. 114 (1927).

"Separability" may defeat the effort to bring the breach of the non-maritime component before the admiralty court. In Armstrong Cork Co. v. Farrell Line, 81 F.Supp. 848, 1948 A.M.C. 1708 (E.D.Pa.1948) suit was brought in admiralty for damage suffered by goods on land, merely because they were held under a "dock receipt," a maritime contract. The court held that the obligations owed the cargo while on the dock were separable from the maritime obligations evidenced by the "dock receipt," and declined jurisdiction.

Sometimes "separability" is not insisted on, where the maritime component clearly dominates the contract. United Fruit Co. v. United States Shipping Board Merchant Fleet Corp., 42 F.2d 222, 1930 A.M.C. 1404 (D.Mass.1930). Many courts, like the one just cited, say that the rule is that the contract must be "wholly" maritime, and then add that this "wholeness" is to be found not in literal exclusion of all non-maritime matters but in their being "carried with" the dominantly maritime parts (Gronvold v. Suryan, 12 F.Supp. 429, 1936 A.M.C. 105 (W.D.Wash.1935)). Neither this brand of "wholeness" nor the concept of separability can do more than suggest factors to be considered by a court faced with a "mixed contract" problem. See also Armour & Co. v. Ft. Morgan S. S. Co., 270 U.S. 253, 46 S.Ct. 212, 1926 A.M.C. 327 (1926); American Stevedores, Inc. v. Porello, 330 U.S. 446, 67 S.Ct. 847, 1947 A.M.C. 349 (1947); D. C. Andrews & Co. v. United States, 124 F.Supp. 362, 1954 A.M.C. 2221 (Ct.Cl.1954).

**95a.** See Orient Mid-East Lines v. Bowen, 255 F.Supp. 627, 1966 A.M.C. 623 (S.D.N.Y.1966).

**95b.** Romero v. International Terminal Operating Co., 358 U.S. 354, 79 S.Ct. 468, 1959 A.M.C. 832 (1959); See Notes, Pendent Jurisdiction in Admiralty, 18 Wayne L.Rev. 1211 (1972); 1973 Wisc.L.Rev. 594. No more in admiralty than elsewhere has "pendency" developed its general logic.

**95c.** See Dudley v. Bayou Fabricators, 330 F.Supp. 788, 1971 A.M.C. 2492 (S.D.Ala.1971).

**96.** See *supra* at note 2. See also Schoening v. 102 Jute Bags of Stand-

which naturally fall within some area of general governmental concern that is defined on other than single-industry lines; an example is the problem in anti-trust created by its organization into "conferences".[97] The line drawing the admiralty jurisdiction must compromise the claims of these sets of factors. The reasons that have been given for the decisions that have pricked out the line have not always been satisfactory; some of them have had an archaic flavor that leaves one in doubt whether the writing judge realized that he was driving in one fence-post around the industry-law of modern shipping, and not composing an epilogue to *The Ancient Mariner*. Some lines of decision are pretty clearly wrong; there seems no good reason, for example, for excluding from the jurisdiction a contract to build a ship, while the exclusion of some quasi-contractual claims arising in the same fields in which the court would have jurisdiction in cases of express contract bars the court arbitrarily from doing full justice in areas where the separate jurisdiction is admittedly appropriate and needful. But in the main, it had seemed until recent years that the courts were moving toward putting themselves in a better and better position to do their job. Of late, certain disturbing tendencies have appeared.

Whether a given inclusion within or exclusion from the jurisdiction is warranted must depend on the general sense and policy of having the jurisdiction at all. It is hard to think of any better reason for having this jurisdiction than its aptness for providing a special-industry court for the maritime industry.[98] If this is right, then some modern decisions wander far off the mark. One thinks of the cases bringing airplane accidents within the jurisdiction, just because the plane happens to crash on navigable waters,[98a] and the inclusion of such mishaps as surfboard accidents [98b] or motorboat accidents on lakes substantially landlocked.[98c] Happily, these cases have (to some

ard Canadian 3R Asbestos Spinning Fibre, 132 F.Supp. 561, 1955 A.M.C. 760 (E.D.Pa.1955), where it was held that admiralty jurisdiction was not conferred by the mere fact that converted goods had been transported over navigable waters.

**97.** See *supra* at note 43.

**98.** See Black, Admiralty Jurisdiction: Critique and Suggestions, 50 Colum.L. Rev. 259 (1950) at 260, 276 *et seq.*, 280, *et passim.* See also Stolz, *op. cit. supra*, at 665 *et seq.*

**98a.** Weinstein v. Eastern Airlines, 316 F.2d 758, 1965 A.M.C. 2258 (3rd Cir. 1963) *certiorari denied* 375 U.S. 940, 84 S.Ct. 343 (1963). See White, The Admiralty Jurisdiction Adrift, 28 U. Pitt.L.Rev. 635 (1967). See Comment, Admiralty Jurisdiction: Airplanes and Wrongful Death In Territorial Waters, 64 Columbia L.Rev. 1084 (1964); Crenshaw, Airplanes in the Admiralty Jurisdiction: A Short History, 18 S. Car.L.Q. 572 (1966); F. A. Moore, Federal Practice, 330 (1971)

**98b.** Davis v. City of Jacksonville Beach, 251 F.Supp. 327 (M.D.Fla.1965). *Cf.* King v. Testerman, 214 F.Supp. 335, 1963 A.M.C. 2054 (E.D.Tenn.1963). (Water skiing accident) More recently, the Fourth Circuit has applied the Executive Jet case, *infra*, n. 98d, to dismiss as outside the jurisdiction, a case of injury to a waterskier by the towing boat. Crosson v. Vance, 484 F.2d 840, 1973 A.M.C. 1895 (4th Cir. 1973).

**98c.** Madole v. Johnson, 241 F.Supp. 379, 1966 A.M.C. 2610 (W.D.La.1965). But *cf.* Chapman v. City of Grosse Point Farms, 385 F.2d 962, 1968 A.M. C. 386 (6th Cir. 1967); McGuire v.

not yet certain extent) been overruled, at the highest level.[98d] It may be hoped that this overruling is thoroughly general. On the other hand, some transactions closely connected with maritime transportation have been excluded, on the ground they were "merely preparatory" to such transportation.[98e] Ideally, the jurisdiction out to include those and only those things *principally connected* with maritime transportation. Summarily, the lower courts have been over-inclusive as to torts, and under-inclusive as to contracts.[98f] On some of these issues, the Supreme Court has not yet committed itself; perhaps a more rational general directive may be forming now.[98g]

### "Waters" and "Vessels"

§ **1–11.** Up to now we have said nothing of the so-called "test by waters". The jurisdiction is defined by reference to maritime matters, but these in turn are defined with regard to the character of the waters where or with reference to which the given transaction or occurrence takes place. Obviously, the high seas are included, as well as ports and harbors communicating with them; it should be said at once that the "three-mile limit" has nothing to do with admiralty jurisdiction, which subsists as well within it as without it. It was not so obvious, in the early nineteenth century, that the Great Lakes and the navigable rivers were included, and it is tempting to go into the history of the gradual extension of the jurisdiction to include them, but the law is now too well settled to make this worthwhile.[99] Briefly, the admiralty jurisdiction of the United States ex-

City of New York, 192 F.Supp. 866, 1962 A.M.C. 516 (S.D.N.Y.1961).

**98d.** Executive Jet Aviation, Inc. v. City of Cleveland, 409 U.S. 249, 93 S. Ct. 493, 1973 A.M.C. 1 (1972). The holding was that claims arising out of an airplane crash were not within the admiralty jurisdiction, but the discussion seemed to establish that some definite maritime flavor was henceforward to be a prerequisite for all admiralty tort jurisdiction. See Notes, 4 Journal of Maritime Law and Commerce 637 (1973); 34 Ohio State Law Journal 355 (1973); 14 Boston College Industrial and Commercial L.Rev. 1071 (1973); 26 Ark.L.Rev. 390 (1973); 47 Tulane L.Rev. 1143 (1973). See also the discussion in Swaim, Admiralty: The Fifth Circuit "Returned to Navigation", 19 Loyola L.Rev. 617, at 617–624 and 634–639 (1973).

**98e.** See, e. g., *supra* at n. 91.

**98f.** The conjecture is hazarded that we have here to do with the "locality test" *redivivus*. Contracts clearly concerned with maritime matters are commonly executed (and are often to be performed) on land; torts totally unconnected with maritime matters often occur on navigable waters. It is the disappointing fact that many recent lower court cases, aberrant on any functional point of view, can be explained by these simple—and, one had hoped, irrelevant—facts.

**98g.** Actually, one half of such a directive, excising the non-maritime tort that chances to "occur" on navigable water, seems to be contained in Executive Jet, *supra* note 98d. The other half would be an equally general affirmative holding drawing into the jurisdiction all torts and contracts having principally to do with maritime commerce. Two such holdings could frame a new rationality in the law of admiralty jurisdiction.

**99.** Briefly: In 1825, the Supreme Court held the jurisdiction limited to tidal waters. The Thomas Jefferson, 23 U.S. (10 Wheat.) 428 (1825). In 1847, the Court sustained jurisdiction

tends to all waters, salt or fresh, with or without tides, natural or artificial, which are in fact navigable in interstate or foreign water commerce, whether or not the particular body of water is wholly within a state, and whether or not the occurrence or transaction that is the subject-matter of the suit is confined to one state.[100] Thus, the Erie Canal is within the jurisdiction, though wholly within the State of New York, for it is navigated in interstate water commerce.[101] The status of the Great Lakes and the Mississippi and its tributaries is clear; they are within the jurisdiction.[102] What decisions there are point to the commonsense conclusion that small bodies

*infra corpus comitatus* (within the body of a county, and hence within the jurisdiction of common law courts), but still spoke as though it assumed the jurisdiction was limited to tidal waters. (The actual spot involved was in the Mississippi, far inland but still tidal.) Waring v. Clarke, 46 U.S. (5 How.) 441 (1847). In 1845, Congress passed a statute extending the jurisdiction to the Great Lakes, which are non-tidal, and "navigable waters connecting said lakes." 5 Stat. 726 (1845). In 1851, the Court upheld this act against constitutional objection, and on unnecessarily broad grounds—saying not merely that Congress might extend the admiralty jurisdiction of the District Courts to the Great Lakes, but that the jurisdiction subsisted there and on other navigable waters throughout the nation (Genesee Chief v. Fitzhugh, 53 U.S. (12 How.) 443 (1851)). For the view (almost certainly correct) that the Court selected the "admiralty" ground rather than the Article I, § 8 "commerce" ground, for sustaining this Act, because of fears that an amply recognized interstate commerce power might be used to regulate or prohibit the slave trade, see Stolz, *op. cit. supra* note 62, at 681 *et seq.* The earlier "tidal" cases were overruled. The case next succeeding in the same volume of the reports, Fretz v. J. C. Bull & Co., 53 U.S. (12 How.) 466 (1851), was not covered by the statute, for it involved a collision on the Mississippi; the court disposed of the jurisdictional point in a single perfunctory sentence, citing the Genesee Chief. Though it took some time and reiteration to bring it home to the bar (see The Magnolia, 61 U.S. (20 How.) 296 (1858); The Hine v. Trevor, 71 U.S. (4 Wall.) 555 (1867); The Eagle, 75 U.S. (8 Wall.) 15 (1869)), the extension of the jurisdiction to all the significant interior waters was complete. For a recent reaffirmation, see Dow Chemical Co. v. Dixie Carriers, Inc., 330 F. Supp. 1304, 1972 A.M.C. 145 (S.D. Texas 1971), affirmed 463 F.2d 120, certiorari denied 409 U.S. 1040 (1974). See Sprague, The Extension of Admiralty Jurisdiction, etc. in Law, A Century of Progress 294 (1937).

100. See cases cited in the preceding note. Also: The Daniel Ball, 77 U.S. (10 Wall.) 557 (1871); The Robert W. Parsons, 191 U.S. 17, 24 S.Ct. 8 (1903). The last case held that the jurisdiction extended to a case involving a horse-drawn barge on the Erie Canal, engaged in purely intrastate commerce. The opinion and dissent fully canvass the earlier cases. In Wilburn Boat Co. v. Fireman's Fund Ins. Co., 348 U.S. 310, 75 S.Ct. 368, 1955 A.M.C. 467 (1955), the Court called an insurance policy on a small houseboat on Lake Texoma, an artificial inland lake between Texas and Oklahoma, a "maritime contract . . . within federal jurisdiction." In Davis v. United States, 185 F.2d 938, 1951 A.M.C. 93 (9th Cir. 1950), certiorari denied 340 U.S. 932, 71 S.Ct. 495 (1951), Lake Tahoe, on the California-Nevada border, was held "navigable waters" for purposes of the Motorboat Act of 1940.

It is well to keep in mind that, despite its extension to inland waters, the admiralty jurisdiction has its greatest significance, by far, in relation to ocean commerce, and to activities ancillary thereto.

101. The Robert W. Parsons, *supra* note 100.

102. Genesee Chief v. Fitzhugh, 53 U.S. (12 How.) 443 (1851); The Hine v. Trevor, 71 U.S. (4 Wall.) 555 (1867).

of water, wholly in one state and not navigable in interstate or foreign water commerce, are not included.[103]

(The leading peculiarity of admiralty practice on the Great Lakes is that, by statute, jury trial is provided.[104] In this book, we are going to discuss our subject principally in terms of ocean commerce; the student will realize that practically all of the concepts, rules, and so on, can be transplanted to the tideless shores of the inner waters.)

Occurrences on foreign navigable waters may also ground admiralty jurisdiction.[104a]

Another definitory limitation on the jurisdiction needs to be mentioned. For some purposes, admiralty courts deal only with vessels and their cargoes and personnel. Once in a while, the question arises whether some marginal structure (a floating drydock, a moored showboat, a pumpboat, or something of the sort) is properly to be called a "vessel". The student will not find this set of questions to be of great importance; practically all of the business that comes before the admiralty court directly or indirectly concerns what are indubitably "vessels". In the dealings of the courts with the structures and objects that have raised the question actively, a single clear test is hard to discern; perhaps the best approximation would be to say that the term "vessel" is applied to floating structures capable of transporting something over the water.[105]

103. Shogry v. Lewis, 225 F.Supp. 741, 1965 A.M.C. 2745 (W.D.Pa.1964); In re Madsen's Petition, 187 F.Supp. 411, 1963 A.M.C. 488 (N.D.N.Y.1960); Stapp v. The Steamboat Clyde, 43 Minn. 192, 45 N.W. 430 (1890); Commonwealth v. King, 150 Mass. 221, 22 N.E. 905 (1889). It has, however, been recently held that a lake not now navigable in interstate commerce is within the jurisdiction, on the ground, to put the matter baldly, that it used to be so navigable. Madole v. Johnson, 241 F.Supp. 379, 1966 A.M.C. 2610 (W. D.La.1965). The case involved a motorboat accident. It is to be hoped that either Congress or the appellate courts will utter requirements more conformant to reality. See, generally, McCaughan, Federal Maritime Jurisdiction Over Inland Intrastate Lakes, 26 Wash. & Lee L.Rev. 1 (1969).

104. 5 Stat. 726 (1845), 28 U.S.C.A. § 1873. See Connors v. Brown S. S. Co., 117 F.Supp. 179, 1954 A.M.C. 518 (W.D.N.Y.1954); Miller v. Standard Oil Co., 199 F.2d 457, 1953 A.M.C. 589 (7th Cir. 1952), certiorari denied 345 U.S. 945, 73 S.Ct. 836 (1953), noted 21 Geo.Wash.L.Rev. 483 (1953). See Barrett, Verdict of Great Lakes Jury, 2 Journal of Maritime Law and Commerce 672 (1971).

104a. Wall Street Traders v. Sociedad Espanola de Construcion N., 236 F. Supp. 358, 1965 A.M.C. 290 (S.D.N.Y. 1964).

105. Pleason v. Gulfport Shipbuilding Corp., 221 F.2d 621, 1955 A.M.C. 794 (5th Cir. 1955). See also the following cases: Cope v. Vallette Dry-Dock Co., 119 U.S. 625, 7 S.Ct. 336 (1887)—floating drydock not a vessel; Evansville & Bowling Green Packet Co. v. Chero Cola Bottling Co., 271 U.S. 19, 46 S. Ct. 379, 1926 A.M.C. 684 (1926)—unpowered wharfboat not a vessel; Kenny v. City of New York, 108 F.2d 958, 1940 A.M.C. 186 (2d Cir. 1940)—deck scow towed to location and used for fireworks display a vessel. The question whether a given structure is a vessel may get mixed up with the question whether something which clearly will be or once was a vessel is yet far enough advanced in construction to qualify (see Thames Towboat Co. v. The Schooner Francis McDonald, 254 U.S. 242, 41 S.Ct. 65 (1920)—and note that this problem may be restated, under some circumstances, in terms of the rule that

## Consequences of Admiralty Jurisdiction

**§ 1–12.** So far we have dealt with the question "What cases are within the admiralty jurisdiction?" Though in the given instance the answer may be so obvious as to be almost automatic, each case, to stay in court and to be dealt with as a case heard under the admiralty grant of jurisdiction, must pass this test. If the answer as to the given case is "No", the court cannot proceed with the case as an "admiralty" case; if no other ground of federal jurisdiction appears, the case must be dismissed. If the answer is "Yes", what are the consequences?

Reference must here be made back to the explanation of the modern position, § 1–9 *supra*. Briefly, if the admiralty jurisdiction is invoked in a civil complaint, and if a court holds this invocation well-founded, the case will in appropriate instances receive the special procedural treatment provided by the Rules, but will in general proceed as an ordinary civil action. As was said above, however, the older cases, understanding of which is indispensable, were decided at a time when the admiralty docket was separate. Not, then, for antiquarian reasons, but so as to be able to understand cases still of authority, the student must be taken through a brief account of the position as it stood before 1966.

Admiralty cases were formerly docketed and heard on a separate "side" of the federal district court, where a special terminology and

shipbuilding contracts are not maritime; see *supra* at note 89) or, on the other hand, has so deteriorated or been so altered in form or function as no longer to be a vessel (see Hercules Co. v. The Brigadier General Absolom Baird, 214 F.2d 66, 1954 A.M.C. 1201 (3d Cir. 1954)—and note that *this* problem may often be restated, as in the case cited, in "dead ship" terms; see *supra* at note 92).

The Fifth Circuit has recently emphasized *capability* of use in navigation as the criterion. M/V Marifax v. McCrory, 391 F.2d 909, 1968 A.M.C. 965 (5th Cir. 1968) ("Even fifteen years of resting inertia does not destroy navigability", 391 F.2d at 910); Miami River Boat Yard, Inc. v. 60 Foot Houseboat, 390 F.2d 596, 1968 A.M.C. 336 (5th Cir. 1968) (powerless houseboat held a "vessel"). On the other hand, the same court has held that a floating drydock, moored by chains and cables to a dock, is not a "vessel". Keller v. Dravo Corp., 441 F.2d 1239, 1971 A.M.C. 1797 (5th Cir. 1971), certiorari denied 404 U.S. 1017, 92 S. Ct. 679 (1972). See also Cook v. Belden Concrete Products, Inc., 472 F.2d 999, 1973 A.M.C. 285 (5th Cir. 1973), rehearing denied 472 F.2d 1405 (5th Cir. 1973).

An airplane is generally held not to be a vessel. Noakes v. Imperial Airways, 29 F.Supp. 412, 1939 A.M.C. 1048 (S.D.N.Y.1939); United States v. Cordova, 89 F.Supp. 298, 1950 A.M.C. 483 (E.D.N.Y.1950). The Air Commerce Act of 1926, § 7(a), 44 Stat. 572, 49 U.S.C.A. § 177(a) makes this rule explicit, in so far as navigation and shipping laws are concerned. But seaplanes while on the water are subject to the International Rules of Navigation; see *infra* Chapter VII. In Lambros Seaplane Base v. The Batory, 215 F.2d 228, 1954 A.M.C. 1789 (2d Cir. 1954) the court regarded a seaplane fished out of water as a "vessel" for salvage purposes (see *infra* Chapter VIII, § 8–3), but, since the salvage libel was dismissed on other grounds, the case cannot be regarded as a square holding on the "vessel" point. In any case, a decision that an airplane may be subject of salvage need not imply that it is a "vessel." (As to airplane accidents as "maritime torts", when the crash is on "navigable waters", see *supra* at notes 98a and 98d.)

procedure were used; these were in part traditional and in part prescribed by the Admiralty Rules promulgated by the Supreme Court and by the rules of the lower courts for admiralty cases. Some of the terminology may be gotten at by simple equivalences with code-procedure terms: the "complaint" was called the "libel"; the "plaintiff" was called the "libellant"; the "defendant" was the "respondent". Admiralty lawyers were "proctors".

Trial, following the civil-law tradition with which the maritime law is closely connected, was to the judge rather than to a jury, and procedure was rather non-technical and simple, though perhaps no more so than under any modern code. Depositions were frequently taken and used, for witnesses were likely to be long gone before a suit could be reached on the docket. Thus far, the differences from shore-going procedure are easily comprehensible and (except for the absence of the jury) rather minor.

There was one peculiarity, however, which is of great intrinsic importance, and which must be taken up at this time because some understanding of it is still prerequisite to comprehension of the jurisdictional allocation between state and federal courts. To it we now turn.

Admiralty libels were of two sorts: *in personam* and *in rem.* The *in personam* suit is unproblematical to the shore lawyer; it is a suit against a named natural or corporate person, asserting a personal liability. The *in rem* suit is virtually unknown outside the admiralty court,[106] and understanding of its nature is not to be approximated without some conception of the substantive concept that underlies it: the "maritime lien". In American admiralty law, the maritime lien is a necessary condition for success in the suit *in rem.*[107]

Upon the occurrence of certain mishaps or the non-fulfillment of certain obligations arising out of contract or status, the maritime law gives to the party aggrieved a right conceived of as a property interest in the tangible thing involved (usually but not always a ship) in the (often as yet unascertained) amount of the accrued liability. This right is called a maritime lien. Thus, the unpaid furnisher of supplies to a vessel has such a right; [108] the seaman's wages

106. The procedure has sometimes been borrowed. *E. g.*, The Federal Food, Drug and Cosmetic Act of 1938, § 304, 52 Stat. 1044, 21 U.S.C.A. § 334, provides that forfeiture cases under the Act "shall conform, as nearly as may be, to the procedure in admiralty." Hence such case styles as "U. S. v. 29 Bottles, More or Less, of Ocean-Lax."

107. The Propeller Commerce, 66 U.S. (1 Black) 574, 580 (1862); The Rock Island Bridge, 73 U.S. (6 Wall.) 213 (1867); The Resolute, 168 U.S. 437, 18 S.Ct. 112 (1897). As the last case shows, the objection that, on the merits, no lien exists in the given case, is not "jurisdictional"; a court with power over the *res* has jurisdiction to proceed and determine on the merits whether a lien exists. Recent cases with useful discussions on the "nature" of the lien, and the correlative in rem proceeding, are Todd Shipyards Corp. v. City of Athens, 83 F. Supp. 67, 1949 A.M.C. 572 (D.Md.1949) and State, to Use of Maines v. A/S Nye Kristianborg, 84 F.Supp. 775, 1949 A.M.C. 1329 (D.Md.1949).

108. The Nestor, 18 Fed.Cas. 9, No. 10,126 (C.C.D.Me.1831). Under the older law, there was no lien in the "home port," unless the state law

are secured by such a right in his ship;[109] the ship's claim for freight creates a lien in the cargo carried.[110] These are only a few of the cases in which the lien arises; throughout the book, when dealing with transactions giving rise to the lien, we will specify in more detail. The "unification" of procedures has in no way touched the substance of the maritime lien.

For now, we will consider only the maritime lien on the ship or vessel; cargo liens, and those on freight, have special peculiarities which can be best considered in the chapter on *Carriage of Goods* (III).

The maritime lien differs from others in that it is (at least as far as ships are concerned) entirely independent of possession,[111] is non-consensual, and is commonly said not to be extinguished by transfer to a bona fide purchaser without notice of its existence.[112] It may arise even though the owner of the vessel in which it subsists is not personally liable;[113] on the other hand, a personal maritime liability may exist without the lien;[114] many transactions and occurrences give rise to both a personal liability and a maritime lien.

The lien is enforced by a direct proceeding against the vessel or other property in which it subsists. The style of such a proceeding (*"The Minnie A"*; *"2000 Barrels of Linseed Oil"*) gives the clue to its theoretical nature. Such a proceeding was (until the 1966 "unification") called a *suit* (commenced by a *libel*) *in rem*—"against the thing".

The assertor of the lien was under the old procedure called the *libellant in rem.* His first step was the filing of a libel stating his case; the vessel in which he claimed a lien was then taken into the custody of the court. The owner of the vessel appeared as "claimant" and conducted the defense. He might and usually did "bond" the claim, thus procuring the release of the vessel, but if he did not do

gave one. The General Smith, 17 U.S. (4 Wheat.) 438 (1819); Peyroux v. Howard, 32 U.S. (7 Pet.) 324. The whole subject is now blanketed by statutes; see *infra,* Chapter IX, and *cf.* Dampskibsselskabet Dannebrog v. Signal Oil and Gas Co., 310 U.S. 268, 60 S.Ct. 937, 1940 A.M.C. 123 (1940).

109. This has been called a "sacred lien," inhering as long as a plank of the ship remains; The John G. Stevens, 170 U.S. 113, 119, 18 S.Ct. 544, 546 (1898).

110. In re One Hundred and Fifty-One Tons of Coal, 18 Fed.Cas. 702, No. 10,520 (C.C.S.D.N.Y.1859) See *infra* Chapter III, Part II, at note 143.

111. The Rock Island Bridge, 73 U.S. (6 Wall.) 213, 215 (1867).

112. The Bold Buccleugh, 7 Moo.P.C. 267 (1850–51); The Rock Island Bridge, *supra* note 111; Plamals v. Pinar Del Rio, 277 U.S. 151, 156, 48 S.Ct. 457, 458, 1928 A.M.C. 932 (1928). For important practical qualifications of this formulation, based on operation of the doctrine of laches, see *infra,* Chapter IX, § 9–77 *et seq.*

113. United States v. Brig Malek Adhel, 43 U.S. (2 How.) 210, 233–4 (1844); The China, 74 U.S. (7 Wall.) 53 (1869), as interpreted in The Barnstable, 181 U.S. 464, 468, 21 S.Ct. 684, (1901). See *infra,* Chapter IX, § 9–5 *et seq.*

114. The General Smith, 17 U.S. (4 Wheat.) 438 (1819).

so, and if the lien was established on the merits, the vessel would be sold publicly by an officer of the court, and the proceeds used to pay the lienor, any balance, of course, going to the claimant. *This sale differed from the ordinary judicial sale of a chattel in that the title transferred was not merely that of the claimant but a title "good against the world".*[115]

(This procedure, with the substantive concepts underlying it, was of course not as simple as all that. Additional lienors might turn up and intervene, in which case priority among the liens might be the really important question, where the value of the vessel on sale was insufficient to pay all. There was, too, the substantive question, in every case, of the existence or non-existence of the lien; not by any means all maritime claims gave rise to liens, and there were difficult borderline cases. These complications and others will be taken up later along in the book.)

*The important thing under the unified Rules is that, saving matters of mere terminology, the in rem proceeding, as the remedial correlate of the maritime lien, is especially preserved, and the old in rem cases are, in effect, as good law as ever.*[115a] Despite unification, one therefore not only may, but (for clarity) must distinguish *in personam* and *in rem* actions "in admiralty" (i.e., under the admiralty jurisdiction), just as before. The next Section should be read with this understanding. Hereinafter, the present tense will be used in referring to maritime liens and to proceedings *in rem.*

## The "Saving Clause"

**§ 1–13.** The Judiciary Act of 1789, it will be recalled, while bestowing "exclusive" admiralty jurisdiction on the District Courts, saved "to suitors, in all cases, the right of a common law remedy where the common law is competent to give it." [116] Obviously, the "exclusivity" and the "saving" are pretty much correlatives. What is "exclusive" and what is "saved"?

Summarily, the result of the cases is that a suitor who holds an *in personam* claim, which might be enforced by suit *in personam* in admiralty, may also bring suit, at his election, in the "common law" court—that is, by ordinary civil action in state court, or in federal court without reference to "admiralty", given diversity of citizenship and the requisite jurisdictional amount.[117]

115. The Trenton, 4 F. 657 (E.D.Mich. 1880). See *infra* Ch. IX, §§ 9–85 *et seq.*

115a. The "action in rem," to give it its modern name, is specifically provided for in Rule C, Supplemental Rules for Certain Admiralty, and Maritime Claims, in Rules of Civil Procedure for the United States District Courts.

116. *Supra* at note 53.

117. Leon v. Galceran, 78 U.S. (11 Wall.) 185 (1871); Rounds v. Cloverport Foundry & Machine Co., 237 U.S. 303, 35 S.Ct. 596 (1915); The Knapp, Stout & Co. Company v. McCaffrey, 177 U.S. 638, 20 S.Ct. 824 (1900).

It has been decided by the Supreme Court that he may *not* sue in federal court, *absent* diversity, on the theory that a maritime claim "arises under" the laws of the United States.[118]

Where, on the other hand, the claim asserted is in the nature of a maritime lien, enforceable "in admiralty" by *in rem* process, *only* the federal court as a court of admiralty may take jurisdiction. Thus, in the leading case of The Moses Taylor,[119] a California statute, conferring on the state courts power to administer *in rem* proceedings against vessels, was struck down, and in The Hine v. Trevor,[120] decided later in the same term of court, it is made explicit that the right to proceed *in rem* in any other court than the "court of admiralty" cannot be saved to suitors by the saving clause, for such a proceeding is not a "common law remedy" at all. Where, on the other hand, a state court merely enforces or secures enforcement of its judgment by levy on or attachment of a vessel as part of the defendant's goods, with a view to compelling appearance or to subjecting *the defendant's interest* therein to sale to satisfy the judgment, this proceeding lacks the distinctive character of the proceeding *in rem*, is one known to the common law and is hence saved to suitors under the saving clause.[121]

The exclusion of the state courts from the *in rem* proceeding is pretty definitely based, in the cases, on the belief that such a proceeding is not a "common law remedy".[122] It may be puzzling, therefore, to find that state courts have not been excluded from exercising jurisdiction in proceedings of an *equitable* nature, dealing with maritime subject-matters.[123] Such proceedings are certainly not "common law remedies" *stricto sensu*. Perhaps such cases can be harmonized with the above-discussed construction of the saving clause by reference to the fact that the admiralty court itself has been thought not to possess the powers of the courts of equity (a point discussed further along in this chapter), so that cases of this sort are not within the

118. Romero v. International Terminal Operating Co., 358 U.S. 354, 79 S.Ct. 468, 1959 A.M.C. 832 (1959).

119. 71 U.S. (4 Wall.) 411 (1867). (But see C. J. Hendry Co. v. Moore, 318 U. S. 133, 63 S.Ct. 499, 1943 A.M.C. 156 (1943)—forfeiture of a net after in rem proceeding in state court, based on infraction of game laws, upheld on ground that common law courts, in England, the Colonies, and the States, had historically exercised such a jurisdiction. The reasoning of this case reinforces the point that the exclusion of state courts from in rem proceedings rested squarely on the phrase "common law remedy"; see *infra*, at note 122.) For a discussion of the background of The Moses Taylor and The Hine v. Trevor, see Chapter IX, § 9–27.

120. 71 U.S. (4 Wall.) 555 (1867).

121. Rounds v. Cloverport Foundry & Machine Co., 237 U.S. 303, 35 S.Ct. 596 (1915); see Three Jacks, (Jackson v. Inland Oil and Transport), 318 F.2d 802, 1963 A.M.C. 1355 (5th Cir. 1963).

122. The Hine v. Trevor, 71 U.S. (4 Wall.) 555, 571 (1867).

123. The Knapp, Stout & Co. Company v. McCaffrey, 177 U.S. 638, 20 S.Ct. 824 (1900)—equitable enforcement of a lien arising out of a maritime transaction; Red Cross Line v. Atlantic Fruit Co., 264 U.S. 109, 44 S.Ct. 274, 1924 A.M.C. 418 (1924)—specific enforcement of an arbitration agreement.

admiralty jurisdiction at all, and hence, *a fortiori*, not within the exclusive jurisdiction. Or the term "common law" may be taken in its widest intendment, to include all legal, equitable and statutory rights and remedies, other than the distinctive admiralty *in rem* proceeding.[124]

In any event, perhaps attempting to codify these cases, the Revisers of the Judiciary Code in 1948 (with a slight further amendment in 1949) changed the wording of the saving clause, which now reads:

> "The district courts shall have original jurisdiction, exclusive of the courts of the States, of:
>
> "(1) Any civil case of admiralty or maritime jurisdiction, saving to suitors in all cases all other remedies to which they are otherwise entitled." [125]

Obviously, this quite unnecessary [126] change in phraseology, apparently motivated in part by a stylistic preference, might imperil those decisions which, like The Moses Taylor [127] and The Hine v. Trevor,[128] exclude state courts from entertaining *in rem* proceedings, though empowered by state statute to do so, on the square and sole ground that such proceedings are not "common law remedies". They certainly are "any other remedies"; whether one is "otherwise entitled" to them (taking "otherwise" as the mere automatic-writing surplusage it appears to be and thus sidestepping the vortex "otherwise than what?" [129]) is the very question that has to be decided all over again without the aid of the wording on the sole basis of which it was decided under the saving clause, old style. A subsequent Supreme Court case intimates that, by main force, the new language will be taken to mean the same thing as the old.[130]

124. The latter view seems to be the one taken in the Red Cross case, *supra* note 123.

125. 28 U.S.C.A. § 1333.

126. In the Reviser's Note to the new Title 28, the explanation offered of the change is that it is "simpler and more expressive of the original intent of Congress and is in conformity with Rule 2 of the Federal Rules of Civil Procedure abolishing the distinction between law and equity." 28 U.S.C.A. § 1333, Reviser's Note.

In the view of the problem broached in the text, as to the construction of this language, it seems unnecessary to comment on the claim of "simplicity." As far as the "intent of Congress" goes, it seems it would have been best to let the courts be the judges of that, and, if we must tamper with the language used (and so thoroughly glossed) at least to codify quite clearly the main effect of the judicial decisions, which was to exclude the state courts from in rem suits.

127. *Supra* note 119.

128. *Supra* note 120.

129. See Black, *supra* note 98, at 271–2.

130. "We take it that this change in no way narrowed the jurisdiction of the state courts under the original 1789 Act." Madruga v. Superior Court of California, 346 U.S. 556, 560, n. 12, 74 S.Ct. 298, 300, 1954 A.M.C. 405 (1954). Whether it *expanded* it is the point under discussion here, of course, but the fact that the court relegates the actual statute in force to a footnote, and discusses the case as though the 1789 language still had the force of law, may be a hint of what will happen if it ever has to be decided wheth-

On the assumption, nowhere contradicted, that this is the right view, we can summarize as follows: Where the suit is *in personam*, it may be brought *either* in federal court under the admiralty jurisdiction (which must in that case either be specially invoked by the plaintiff or visibly be the only ground of federal jurisdiction) *or*, under the saving clause, in an appropriate non-maritime court, by ordinary civil action. Where the suit is *in rem*, only the federal court, acting under its admiralty power, has jurisdiction.[130a] The distinction is not always easy. In the case of Madruga v. The Superior Court of California,[131] the Supreme Court was asked to decide whether the partition suit of a part owner of a vessel could be brought in state court under the saving clause. Such a suit certainly deals primarily with the thing, but the majority of the Court considered it as not possessing the characteristics of the admiralty suit *in rem*, and allowed it to proceed. The decisive distinction seems to have been that the California court was acting only on the interest of the defendant —that its judicial sale, if the case went that far, would not convey a title good against the world, or extinguish interests of those not parties to the suit.[132]

One very important caution must be added at this point. The allocation of jurisdiction just sketched is the one that has been derived from construction of the section of the Judiciary Act dealing *generally* with admiralty cases; it is a correct picture only for cases not otherwise provided for by statute. A proceeding to foreclose a preferred ship mortgage, for example, cannot be brought in state court under the saving clause, for the federal statute creating such mortgages prescribes that the federal court shall be the exclusive forum in which they can be foreclosed.[133]

## Remedies; Admiralty and Equity

**§ 1–14.** A word ought now to be said about the remedial machinery of which the federal district court disposes, when its ad-

er in rem proceedings are now open to state courts, by virtue of the 1948 language. Further, the lower court in Madruga had actually held that the 1948 revision at least made it clearer that the state jurisdiction extended to the case. 40 Cal.2d 65, 251 P.2d 1, 1953 A.M.C. 1059 (1952). The Supreme Court refuses to place any reliance on this ground or even to discuss it seriously (see discussion in the text immediately following). See also the Reviser's Note, *supra* note 126; whatever the demerits of that utterance, it would seem to refute the view that substantial change was intended.

130a. For translation into modern terms, see § 1–9 *supra*.

131. *Supra* note 130. See Notes: Jurisdiction of State Courts over Actions for the Sale of a Vessel, 42 Geo. L.J. 534 (1954); Admiralty: Partition of Ships: Concurrent Jurisdiction of State and Admiralty Courts, 42 Calif. L.Rev. 331 (1954).

132. 346 U.S. at 561, 74 S.Ct. at 301.

133. Ship Mortgage Act, 1920, subsec. K. 41 Stat. 1003, 46 U.S.C.A. § 951. It has been held that a suit under the Death on the High Seas Act, 41 Stat. 537 (1920), 46 U.S.C.A. § 761, must be brought on the admiralty side, and may not be brought at law under the "saving clause". Higa v. Transocean Airlines, 230 F.2d 780, 1956 A.M.C. 122 (9th Cir. 1955). See Comment, 55 Colum.L.Rev. 907 (1955).

miralty jurisdiction is invoked. The successful *in personam* suit based on the general maritime law usually terminates in a money judgment. Statutes have conferred special remedial powers on the court; thus, ship mortgages of a specified kind can be foreclosed,[134] and orders are issued enjoining the prosecution of claims against which limitation is being sought in a proceeding in admiralty brought under the limitation statute.[135] But in the general run of non-statutory maritime cases, the admiralty court has been thought not to possess the distinctive remedial powers of the court of equity.[136] It cannot issue injunctions,[137] decree specific performance of contracts,[138] or (ordinarily) order the reformation of instruments.[139] And, as we have seen, it has been to a great extent barred from granting any relief at all on claims sounding in quasi-contract—for these, though often "legal" in form, are "equitable" in origin and flavor.[140]

This whole set of limitations has been attacked,[141] and it does indeed seem irrational and crippling. If a separate court of admiralty is needed to entertain suits for damages for maritime torts or for the breach of maritime contracts, it seems absurd for that court to deny itself the power to enjoin the same torts, or to decree specific performance of the same contracts. Cases concerning the reformation of instruments call more urgently than most for that special-industry expertise which is one of the assumed bases for the existence of a separate admiralty court. Any court that is to deal with a factual subject-matter ought to have the remedial powers necessary to do complete justice with respect to the cases arising out of that subject-matter.

Though the court is said to lack the "jurisdiction" of equity, it may apply equitable principles to the subjects within its jurisdiction—or thus the polarized saying runs.[142] Obviously, the exception could conceivably widen until little of the rule was left. It may

134. See *supra* note 133.

135. Old Supreme Court Admiralty Rule 51; now Rule F(3), Federal Rules of Civil Procedure. See *infra* Chapter X.

136. See The Eclipse, 135 U.S. 599, 608, 10 S.Ct. 873, 876 (1890).

137. Sound Marine & Machine Corp. v. Westchester County, 100 F.2d 360, 1939 A.M.C. 210 (1938), certiorari denied 306 U.S. 642, 59 S.Ct. 582 (1939).

138. Paterson v. Dakin, 31 F. 682 (S.D. Ala.1887); see Hirsch v. The San Pablo, 81 F.Supp. 292, 1948 A.M.C. 1992 (S.D.Fla.1948).

139. Andrews v. Essex Fire & Marine Ins. Co., 1 Fed.Cas. 885, No. 374 (C.C. D.Mass.1822); Koninklijke Nederlandsche Stoomboot Maatschappij v. Yglesias & Co., 37 F.2d 103, 1930 A.M.C. 867 (S.D.N.Y.1930). But see Rice v. Charles Dreifus Co., 96 F.2d 80, 1938 A.M.C. 476 (2d Cir. 1938).

140. See *supra* note 94.

141. Morrison, The Remedial Powers of the Admiralty, 43 Yale L.J. 1 (1933).

142. "The reasoning of the District Court was based on the view that a claim of fraud in the transfer of a vessel was a matter for determination by a court of equity and therefore outside the bounds of admiralty jurisdiction. There is a good deal of loose talk to this effect in the reports, concurrent with talk that courts of admiralty exercise their jurisdiction upon equitable principles." Swift & Co. Packers v. Compania Colombiana Del Caribe, S.A., 339 U.S. 684, 689–690, 70 S.Ct. 861, 865, 1950 A.M.C. 1089 (1950).

be that some widening is in process. In Swift & Co. Packers v. Compania Colombiana Del Caribe, S.A.,[143] the libellants sued *in personam* for nondelivery of cargo, and placed a foreign attachment on a vessel (*not* the one involved in the original transaction) that had belonged to the respondent until a time shortly before the libel was filed, when the vessel had been transferred to a Colombian subsidiary hastily organized by the respondent. The respondent attacked the attachment on the ground that the vessel was no longer its property, while the libellant asked the court to disregard and set aside a transfer made under such circumstances to a mere corporate *alter ego.* Looking into an allegedly fraudulent transfer is of course a distinctively "equitable" function; the lower court had declined to do so, and had dissolved the attachment.[144] The Supreme Court held, however, that a court of admiralty, having jurisdiction of the claim for cargo loss, could, in the exercise of the jurisdiction, look into and in a proper case disregard or set aside a fraudulent transfer of the sort alleged. The language of Mr. Justice Frankfurter is worth quoting:

> ". . . The issue of fraud arises in connection with the attachment as a means of effectuating a claim incontestably in admiralty. To deny an admiralty court jurisdiction over this subsidiary or derivative issue in a litigation clearly maritime would require an absolute rule that admiralty is rigorously excluded from all contact with nonmaritime transactions *and from all equitable relief, even though such nonmaritime transactions come into play, and such equitable relief is sought, in the course of admiralty's exercise of its jurisdiction over a matter exclusively maritime.* It would be strange indeed thus to hobble a legal system that has been so responsive to the practicalities of maritime commerce and so inventive in adapting its jurisdiction to the needs of that commerce. Controversies between admiralty and common law are familiar legal history. See Mr. Justice Story's classic opinion in De Lovio v. Boit, 7 Fed.Cas. 418, No. 3,776, 2 Gall. 398; 4 Benedict on Admiralty cc. 61–63 (Knauth ed. 1940). We find no restriction upon admiralty by chancery so unrelenting as to bar the grant of any equitable relief even when that relief is subsidiary to issues wholly within admiralty jurisdiction. Certainly there is no ground for believing that this restriction was accepted as a matter of course by the framers of the Constitution so that such sterilization of admiralty jurisdiction can be said to have been presupposed by Article III of the Constitution." [145] [Emphasis supplied]

143. 339 U.S. 684, 70 S.Ct. 861 (1950); see Comment, Admiralty Courts and Equity Doctrines, 29 Tex.Law Rev. 244 (1950).

144. 83 F.Supp. 273, 1949 AMC 126 (D.C.Z.1948) affirmed 175 F.2d 513 (5th Cir. 1949).

145. 339 U.S. 684, 691–692, 70 S.Ct. 861, 866 (1950).

The italicized words have given ground for hope that a "doctrinal trend" is in the making that would render the ordinary equitable remedies of specific performance and injunction available to the admiralty court, in case of maritime contract or tort. Certainly, in such cases, these remedies would *ex hypothesi* be "sought in the course of admiralty's exercise of a jurisdiction over a matter exclusively maritime." Indeed, the fraudulent transfer alleged in the Swift case is a good deal more remote from the actual occurrence—cargo loss—that was the ground of admiralty jurisdiction, than could be true as to the factors calling for specific relief in a given case against a maritime tort or the breach of a maritime contract. On familiar principles, these are usually intrinsic to the transaction.

In a fairly recent case,[145a] the Supreme Court has said "Equity is no stranger to admiralty; admiralty courts are indeed authorized to grant equitable relief." [145b] (The very issue tendered, however, was the awarding of counsel fees.)

The modern procedural unification of admiralty with the ordinary civil action may at least sharpen the issues herein. It is hard to think, for example, that the federal courts will be content permanently to decline to enjoin the commission of maritime torts—given all the normal grounds for injunction—just because one jurisdictional ground rather than another has been invoked, when the litigation is on the same docket, and under the same Rules, as those pertaining to civil actions wherein injunctions are freely awarded. Indeed, it is the view of one of the ablest commentators on the "unification" that that unification has, as a matter of law, made equitable remedies freely available in admiralty.[145c] It is to be observed, moreover, that few if any of the rules banning equitable relief "in admiralty" have the sanction of a square Supreme Court holding.[145d] It is to be hoped that the Supreme Court, taking its lead from the spirit if not the letter of unification, will finally sweep away this entirely irrational limitation on remedies.[145e]

**145a.** Vaughan v. Atkinson, 369 U.S. 527, 82 S.Ct. 997, 1962 A.M.C. 1131 (1962) rehearing denied 370 U.S. 965, on remand 206 F.Supp. 575 (1962).

**145b.** 369 U.S. at 530, 82 S.Ct. at 999.

**145c.** Colby, Admiralty Unification, 54 Georgetown L.J. 1258, 1268–9 (1966).

**145d.** In The Eclipse, *supra* n. 136, the denial of specific performance of the contract of sale might have been rested on admiralty's not having jurisdiction over such contracts—itself also an irrational rule. The rest of what is said in The Eclipse is dictum.

**145e.** On these matters, see Payne v. S.S. Tropic Breeze, 423 F.2d 236, 1970 A.M.C. 1850 (1st Cir. 1970); Stern, Hays & Lang, Inc. v. M/V Nili, 407 F.2d 549, 1969 A.M.C. 13 (5th Cir. 1969) (broad general statement of affirmative effect of Rules, 407 F.2d at 551); Cummins Diesel Michigan, Inc. v. The Falcon, 305 F.2d 721, 1963 A.M.C. 214 (7th Cir. 1962); Hadjipateras v. Pacifica S.A., 290 F.2d 697, 1961 A.M.C. 1417 (5th Cir. 1961). See also the discussion in Powell, *op. cit. supra* n. 3a, 81 Yale L.J. 1154, and Note in 39 U.Cinn.L.Rev. 819 (1970). In lower court decisions, the power of the admiralty court remains severely circumscribed. See New York State Waterways Ass'n v. Diamond, 469 F.2d 419, 1973 A.M.C. 1232 (2d Cir. 1972).

### Prize and Criminal Jurisdiction

**§ 1–15.** We are now through with the main business of this jurisdictional outline; what follows may be regarded as somewhat parenthetical. We have dealt, so far, with the jurisdiction over ordinary civil cases, and such cases will be our exclusive concern in the rest of the book. Traditionally, the admiralty court possesses a jurisdiction in criminal law and in prize; a word about these is in order.

The British court was much concerned, in its early days, with criminal matters—piracy, wrecking, and the like. Since the criminal jurisdiction of the common law courts was territorial, the jurisdiction of the admiralty over crimes committed at sea constituted an essential supplement. The practice was early instituted, however, of trying those criminal cases that fell within the admiralty jurisdiction "according to the course of the common law"—that is, of using the procedure of the common law courts, including trial to a jury.[146] Essentially, the theory and practice of the American criminal jurisdiction under the admiralty power are quite similar to the early English model. Some federal statutes define and prescribe punishment for crimes committed "within the admiralty and maritime jurisdiction." The constitutional warrant for these statutes rests on the fact that the judicial power over admiralty cases includes a criminal as well as a civil jurisdiction. But cases brought under these statutes go forward as ordinary criminal cases, are tried to a jury, and are not usually thought of as "admiralty" cases at all.[147]

The prize proceeding, long in substantial disuse with us, consists in the subjection to condemnation and sale of vessels and cargoes having some "enemy" taint in wartime. It was early held that the district courts sitting in admiralty had a "prize" as well as an "instance" jurisdiction.[148] Machinery was readied for prize activity at the end of World War II, and several German vessels were condemned.[148a] The whole subject of prize is of little practical interest to the modern American admiralty lawyer.[149]

146. 28 Henry VIII c. 15 (1536); for an account of this statute, see 1 Holdsworth, History of English Law 550–552 (3d ed. 1922).

147. For full illustration of the points here made, see United States v. Flores, 289 U.S. 137, 53 S.Ct. 580 (1933); United States v. Ross, 439 F. 2d 1355, 1971 A.M.C. 2351 (9th Cir. 1971), certiorari denied 404 U.S. 1015, 92 S.Ct. 686 (1972).

148. Glass v. The Sloop Betsey, 3 U.S. (3 Dall.) 6 (1794). The "instance" jurisdiction comprises the civil (which is what we are going to be concerned with in the rest of the book), the criminal, and (in England) the jurisdiction for enforcing certain "droits" or "rights" of the Crown in property found on or by the sea. See 1 Holdsworth, *op. cit. supra* note 24, at 549.

148a. Department of Justice files Nos. 61–012–12, 1–14 inclusive; mimeographed Letter, Department of Justice, "Prize Court Cases During World War II" WEB: TFMcG, 61–012–12–1, 44–4–8–0, May 12, 1954 (probably still available on request). Apparently no Japanese vessels were condemned. (The authors are indebted for this information to George T. Nickell, Esq.)

149. The subject is well covered in Knauth, Prize Law Reconsidered, 46 Colum.L.Rev. 69 (1946).

### Substantive Law in Admiralty Cases

**§ 1–16.** The Constitution extends the *judicial* power to admiralty cases, but is silent as to the substantive law to be applied to such cases. Federal statutes have set forth law that partially covers some important fields, but a vast amount of the maritime law applied today has no statutory or obvious constitutional warrant. At the time of the adoption of the Constitution, it probably seemed "self-evident" that there already was in existence a corpus of maritime law which might, indeed, have been rejected in the courts of any nation strong enough to make that decision stick, but which certainly needed no express or implied legislative action on the part of any one nation to make it valid; clearly that would have been the received view in the days when maritime law was actually forming.[150] To the positivist legal philosophy prevalent in the late nineteenth and early twentieth centuries, it seemed equally "self-evident" that if, say, the courts of the United States enforced as valid law certain provisions relating to compensation for salvage, then these provisions must have been "uttered" by the "sovereign" in question—the United States—and must derive their validity from this fact, regardless of the source upon which the "utterance" was modelled.[151] Probably, the choice between these views involves little more than aesthetic preference, for any decision can logically be explained with careful enough qualification on the basis of either one of them. The Constitutional language lends itself as well to one as to the other; from a grant of judicial power, it may equally well be inferred either that the maritime law has been "incorporated by reference" into the law of the United States or that the United States has taken note of the existence and validity of the general maritime law and empowered its courts to try cases to which it applies. Insofar as these views have any non-logical tendency to push decision or attitude one way or another, it might be preferable to look on maritime law as a system not depending for its validation on any inferred national legislation, for this view gives accent to the desirability of international uniformity.[151a]

150. ". . . A case in admiralty does not, in fact, arise under the Constitution or laws of the United States. These cases are as old as navigation itself; and the law, admiralty and maritime, as it has existed for ages, is applied by our Courts to the cases as they arise." So Chief Justice Marshall in American Ins. Co. v. Canter, 26 U.S. (1 Pet.) 511, 545–6 (1828). And see *supra* at note 17; *but cf. supra* at note 118.

Cf.: "Maritime law, the common law of seafaring men, provides an established network of rules and decisions suited to the necessities of the sea." United States v. Webb, Inc., 397 U.S. 179, 191, 90 S.Ct. 850, 856, 1970 A.M.C. 265, (1969).

151. ". . . There is no mystic over-law to which even the United States must bow. When a case is said to be governed by foreign law or by general maritime law that is only a short way of saying that for this purpose the sovereign power takes up a rule suggested from without and makes it part of its own rules." The Western Maid, 257 U.S. 419, 432, 42 S.Ct. 159, 160 (1922). This classic aphorism seems not to take into account that the "sovereign" is just as much a fiction as is the "mystic overlaw."

**151a.** On the modern movement to effect international unification by diplomatic means, see Yiannopoulos, The

As was inevitable when the "maritime law" was placed in the hands of judges trained in the Anglo-American common law tradition, maritime law amongst us has been heavily influenced, substantively and methodologically, by shoreside law. Concepts sometimes visibly move from one to the other without remark. In Petition of Kinsman Transit Co.,[151b] for example, the celebrated "Palsgraf" [151c] doctrine is treated as fully applicable in admiralty. In Watz v. Zapata Offshore,[151d] land-developed doctrines of liability of the remote vendor are applied in admiralty. And in the celebrated Moragne case,[151e] the general maritime law wrongful death action is firmly bottomed on analogy with shoreside statutes.[151f]

Even more important is the methodological assimilation; federal judges as "admiralty" judges reason much as they do in other cases. There is really nothing forbiddingly esoteric about admiralty law. It is just law, in a special factual setting.

Whatever the theory, it is the fact that it was assumed at first, and later expressly stated, that those courts to which judicial jurisdiction over maritime cases was granted were thereby empowered and obligated to apply to such cases, in the absence of statute, the rules of the general maritime law. Certainly the early opinions (especially those of Story) prove that the courts looked on the maritime system they were administering as international in scope, for they are replete with citations to the continental European authorities, not for persuasive analogy but "as evidence of the general marine law." [152] As the nineteenth century wore on, the bases of the substantive maritime law became settled in this country, and the emergent problems came to be more and more those arising out of special national conditions. For both these reasons, overt reliance on foreign authorities diminished; only the rare case now requires recourse to the Rules of Oleron or Cleirac or Bynkershoek.[153] Still, it is a striking experience to open a French treatise on General Average. In place of the radical incomprehensibility, to the common-law man, of the whole frame of ref-

Unification of Private Maritime Law by International Conventions, 30 Law & Cont.Prob. 370 (1965).

151b. 338 F.2d 708, 1964 A.M.C. 2503 (2 Cir. 1964), certiorari denied Continental Grain Co. v. City of Buffalo, 380 U.S. 944, 85 S.Ct. 1026 (1965).

151c. Palsgraf v. Long Island R. R., 248 N.Y. 339, 162 N.E. 99 (1928), reargument denied 249 N.Y. 511, 164 N.E. 564 (1929).

151d. Watz v. Zapata Off-Shore Co. 431 F.2d 100, 1970 A.M.C. 2307 (5th Cir. 1970).

151e. *Supra* n. 79b. On the interesting methodological aspect of Moragne, see Note (M. J. Bean) The Legitimacy of Civil Law Reasoning in the Common Law, 82 Yale L.J. 258 (1972).

151f. There is a good statement of the general selective adoption of the common law by the maritime law, in Igneri v. Cie. de Transports Oceaniques, 323 F.2d 257, 259–260, 1963 A.M.C. 2318, 2321 (2d Cir. 1963), certiorari denied 376 U.S. 949, 84 S.Ct. 965 (1964).

152. See *supra* note 27 (remarks of Justice Tilghman) and *cf.* Marshall, quoted *supra* note 150.

153. By the time of The John G. Stevens, 170 U.S. 113, 18 S.Ct. 544 (1898), the Supreme Court is refusing even to discuss foreign codes and like materials.

erence of a French treatise on, say, Property, one finds oneself in a familiar world of one-to-one correspondence with the well-known.

The "general" maritime law in the United States, insofar as it remains unmodified by statute, contains, then, two parts. First, is the corpus of traditional rules and concepts found by our courts in the European authorities, and applied here with no more variation than is normal when purportedly identical bodies of law are applied in decision by courts in different cultural ambients without common appellate review (cf. the "common law" in England and Kansas). Second are rules and concepts improvised to fit the needs of this country, including, of course, modifications of the first component.

A second inference (rather forced perhaps, but practically very necessary) from the conferring of the judicial power in admiralty cases was to the effect that Congress thereby was empowered to alter and supplement the general maritime law.[154] Many statutes—some of great importance—have been passed in the exercise of this power. None, apparently, has ever been declared unconstitutional.[155] Some have added to the judicial jurisdiction; some have changed or filled out substantive rules of maritime law; a few have added whole new chapters of law to the corpus. There is, of course, a constitutional puzzle here. If the general maritime law is given effect in this country as a result of a constitutional provision, how can Congress change it by statute? This doubt troubled very little the onrushing nationalism of the nineteenth century. We need not worry about it at all, partly because over a century of precedent sets it pretty much at rest, and partly because the conception of the commerce power that now prevails would probably suffice, without reference to any inference from the admiralty judicial power, to validate every statutory enactment in question. And of course Congress may legislate for maritime matters under any of the powers given it.

### Federal-State Conflict

**§ 1–17.** These, then, are the components of federal law in maritime cases: the general maritime law as above described, and applicable Acts of Congress. Just as there has been conflict between the state and federal courts over judicial jurisdiction in certain maritime cases, so there has been a good deal of trouble in the relations between this federal maritime law and the common law and statutory enactments of the states. The state-federal conflict in admiralty is one of the sub-problems of federalism. The nation as a whole has a vital interest in the shipping industry as a whole, but states such as New York and Washington are also deeply concerned with the local problems created by the shipping that touches their ports, and they have

154. Panama R. R. v. Johnson, 264 U.S. 375, 44 S.Ct. 391, 1924 A.M.C. 551 (1924).

155. See American Bridge Co. v. The Gloria O., 98 F.Supp. 71, 73, 1951 A.M.C. 1388 (E.D.N.Y.1951).

articulated this interest in a mass of legislation dealing with shipping matters.[155a]

One constitutional truism may be got out of the way at once: Such state legislation is clearly invalid where it actually conflicts with the established general maritime law or federal statutes. Other problems are not so simple. Thus, the maritime law was long held to deny recovery for wrongful death, yet state statutes granting such recovery where injuries indubitably took place within admiralty jurisdiction were upheld, as merely supplementing the maritime law.[156] But when the states sought to provide workmen's compensation for injuries suffered by longshoremen within the admiralty jurisdiction, the Supreme Court, in a series of hard-fought cases, (leading off with the celebrated decision in Southern Pacific Co. v. Jensen) and in the face of vigorous dissent of the highest prestige, held that such enactments infringed the Constitution, in that they invaded the federally reserved field of maritime law and interfered with its uniform and harmonious operation.[157]

These latter cases are now in a sense drowned law, since Congress has enacted a Federal Longshoremen's compensation statute.[158] (Their meaning and fate will be more fully explained in the chapter (VI, *infra*) on Seamen's Rights.) But, however one may react emotionally to the bringing to bear of their high-flown vaguenesses to the barring of the tiny and doubtless pathetically needed recoveries that were at stake, it is difficult not to think that the *major* premise they state is a sound one. If there is any sense at all in making maritime law a federal subject, then there must be some limit set to the power of the states to interfere in the field of its working.

Nevertheless, the cases on this point cannot be wholly harmonized. A fairly recent utterance of the Supreme Court on the matter of substantive law jurisdiction as between the States and the national government is Wilburn Boat Co. v. Fireman's Fund Ins. Co.[159] In this case, the Court decided that there is no rule of federal origin or application defining the effect of warranties in marine insurance policies,[160] and that, in the absence of such a rule, the Court would not fashion one, but would allow a state statute to have effect. The insured vessel plied the waves of Lake Texoma, a small artificial lake

**155a.** See D. Currie, Federalism and the Admiralty: "The Devil's Own Mess" 1960 S.Ct.Rev. 158, (1960); also D. Currie, Federal Courts, Cases and Materials 693 *et seq.* (1968).

**156.** The Hamilton, 207 U.S. 398, 28 S. Ct. 133 (1907). For the present and radically different position, see *supra* at n. 79b.

**157.** Southern Pac. Co. v. Jensen, 244 U.S. 205, 37 S.Ct. 524 (1917); Knickerbocker Ice Co. v. Stewart, 253 U.S. 149, 40 S.Ct. 438 (1920); State of Washington v. W. C. Dawson & Co., 264 U.S. 219, 44 S.Ct. 302, 1924 A.M.C. 403 (1924). See *infra*, Chapter VI, §§ 6–43 to 6–44.

**158.** Longshoremen's and Harbour Workers' Compensation Act, 1927, 44 Stat. 1424, 33 U.S.C.A. §§ 901–950.

**159.** 348 U.S. 310, 75 S.Ct. 368, 1955 A.M.C. 457 (1955).

**160.** See *infra* Chapter II, at note 69 *et seq.*

between the two States suggested by its name, but, as Mr. Justice Frankfurter pointed out in his concurrence, the reasoning employed by the majority would subject a marine policy on the Queen Mary to such state laws as might be brought into play by her touching at New York, New Orleans, and Galveston. Viewed in this light, the decision seems to make serious inroads on the uniformity of the maritime law. Marine insurance is the world-wide maritime subject *par excellence*; subjection of the jural relations arising out of the policy to control by all the seaboard states of the Union is the antithesis not only of the Jensen thesis but also of the common sense underlying that thesis and somewhat obscured by the emotional appeal of the plaintiffs in cases of the Jensen type. The Wilburn case clashes with the whole theory that makes maritime law a federal subject, for if the general substantive law that has hitherto been thought to be implicitly accepted or adopted, *on a national basis,* by the implications of Art. 3, § 2 of the Constitution, does not include a corpus of law governing the chief incidents of the marine insurance policy, then it is hard to say what it does cover. This is not to say, of course, that States might not be left with some regulatory power over marine insurance in the *interstices* of the federal law; they have that as to all maritime matters. But the question of the effect of an express warranty in a marine policy is not interstitial but is a prime issue of insurance law; it might be thought that the "sovereignty" that controls that matter must be taken to control everything else in the field. It is to be hoped that future decisions will confine this case within narrower bounds than this; Mr. Justice Frankfurter's concurrence, on the ground that the facts of the very case made it of predominantly local concern, points the way.

The later case of Kossick v. United Fruit Co.[160a] points in a direction just opposite to that of the Wilburn Boat case. In Kossick, the Court held the general maritime law to govern the validity (as against a State statute-of-frauds objection) of an agreement between seaman and employer regarding liability for defective medical treatment. Strangely, no effort has been made by the Court to harmonize the cases.[160b]

Despite its possible implications, the majority opinion in the Wilburn case does not purport to abolish altogether the federal substantive maritime law, or the requirement that state legislation not impair its working. Nor does Kossick purport to overrule Wilburn Boat. Hence, the line will still have to be drawn from case to case. The concepts that have been fashioned for drawing it are too vague, as we have seen, to ensure either predictability or wisdom in the line's actual drawing. All that can be said in general is that the states may not

**160a.** 365 U.S. 731, 81 S.Ct. 886, 1961 A.M.C. 833 (2d Cir. 1961), rehearing denied 366 U.S. 941, 81 S.Ct. 1657 (1961). See also Taylor v. Crain, 224 F.2d 237, 1955 A.M.C. 1499 (3d Cir. 1955) state "dead man's statute" not applicable in admiralty.

**160b.** Irwin v. Eagle Star Ins. Co., 455 F.2d 827, 1973 A.M.C. 1184 (5th Cir. 1972), certiorari denied 409 U.S. 852, 93 S.Ct. 118 (1972), rejected limitation of Wilburn by Kossick. Kossick is further discussed in Chapter VI *infra*, § 6–11, text following note 58a.

flatly contradict established maritime law, but may "supplement" it, to the extent of allowing recoveries in some cases where the maritime law denies them [160c]; that states may legislate freely on shipping matters that are of predominantly local concern, but that they may not so act as to interfere with the uniform working of the federal maritime legal system.[161] These generalities have worked out differently in different fields, and, as the two cases just mentioned demonstrate, the law has not reached a firm resting-place.[161a] In subsequent chapters in the book, where the subject-matter is one as to which the state-federal problem has arisen, we will examine that problem in the particular context.

The latest utterance of the Supreme Court on this subject has upheld the Florida Oil Pollution Act against the objection that that Act intruded impermissibly on the federal admiralty power.[161b]

One striking peculiarity may, however, be mentioned before we finish with this topic. In certain cases, states have been upheld in creating maritime liens on the basis of transactions and occurrences that do not, under the general maritime law, give rise to such liens. But so jealously guarded is the exclusive federal jurisdiction over the suit *in rem* that these liens, though substantively the creatures of state law, can be enforced only in the federal district courts, acting under the admiralty jurisdictional grant.[162]

**§ 1–18.** Brief mention should be made of a question closely connected or even identical with the above. What law is to be applied to cases of a maritime nature brought in state court under the saving clause? The general answer might seem clear: The same substantive law ought to be applied as would have been applied had the suit been brought in admiralty. Specifically, the general maritime law, where applicable, ought to rule, even though suit is brought in state

**160c.** On the other hand, the rule that state law giving contribution in tort cases may not "supplement" maritime law has recently been reaffirmed; see Atlantic Coast Line R.R. Co. v. Erie Lackawanna R.R. Co., 406 U.S. 340, 92 S.Ct. 1550, 1972 A.M.C. 1121 (1972) and cases cited.

**161.** In Maryland Casualty Co. v. Cushing, 347 U.S. 409, 74 S.Ct. 608, 1954 A.M.C. 837 (1954), the Court had to decide on the validity and application of a Louisiana "direct action" statute (providing that suit might be brought directly against the insurance carrier of an alleged tort-feasor) in a case where a petition for limitation of liability had been filed by the party alleged to be primarily liable. It is infeasible to discuss the case at this point, for its intelligent evaluation requires an understanding of the peculiarities of the limitation proceeding (see *infra* Chapter X). It should be read after that chapter has been worked through, for the illustration it offers of the problems that may arise when state statutes are thrust into a worked-out federal statutory scheme in the maritime field. Annotations are found in 40 Va.L.Rev. 621 (1954) and 103 U.Pa.L.Rev. 263 (1954).

**161a.** See Note, The Aftermath of Wilburn, 5 Willamette L.J. 529 (1969).

**161b.** Askew v. American Waterways Operators, Inc., 335 F.Supp. 1241, rehearing denied 411 U.S. 325, 93 S.Ct. 1590, 1973 A.M.C. 811 (1973). See Chapter X, *infra*, § 10–4(b).

**162.** The Glide, 167 U.S. 606, 17 S.Ct. 930 (1897); Vancouver S. S. Co. v. Rice, 288 U.S. 445, 53 S.Ct. 420, 1933 A.M.C. 487 (1933). For a discussion of the state lien statutes see *infra* Chapter IX.

court.[163] It seems generally undesirable that the choice of a forum should at the same time be a choice of applicable substantive law. Yet some cases cast doubt on this general principle. In Caldarola v. Eckert,[164] Mr. Justice Frankfurter writing, the Supreme Court seemed to hold that, where a longshoreman brought suit for personal injuries sustained on board ship, the state court that tried the case correctly applied the state substantive rule as to the duty of care owed to one in his position, instead of the maritime law rule that would unquestionably have been applied had the suit been brought in admiralty. This is exactly the sort of thing which an entire branch of the body of doctrines known as Conflict of Laws is designed to prevent; it is submitted that the language in the case that seems to be saying that a different substantive law applies simply because a different court was sued in must be the result of inadvertence.[165] We will come back to the problem of applicable law in cases brought under the saving clause as it arises with respect to specific subject-matters in the chapters following.

On the other hand, in the Kossick case just discussed,[165a] the action was in federal court on *diversity* grounds. In consonance with Erie R. R. v. Tompkins,[165b] it would seem that holding a state statute of frauds to be without effect, as contravening the controlling maritime rule, would have to be tantamount to a holding that it would have been without effect in the state court as well. Indeed, the whole Kossick opinion breathes a spirit of federal maritime law supremacy over state law very hard to reconcile with the Calderola opinion and holding.

### Note on Conflicts of Laws

**§ 1–19.** Up to now, we have avoided discussion of the problem of international conflicts of laws. The courts of the United States take jurisdiction, subject to some reservations imposed by their own application of the doctrine of *forum non conveniens*,[166] of suits on

163. Chelentis v. Luchenbach S. S. Co., 247 U.S. 372, 38 S.Ct. 501 (1918); Pope & Talbot v. Hawn, 346 U.S. 406, 74 S.Ct. 202, 1954 A.M.C. 1 (1953). The matter is extensively discussed *infra* Chapter VI. See the effective article by Stevens, Erie R. R. v. Tompkins and the Uniform General Maritime Law, 64 Harv.L.Rev. 246 (1950); also Comment, Do Admiralty Rules Still Govern Maritime Cases in Common-Law Courts? 26 Tex.L.Rev. 312 (1948). In diversity cases on the civil side of federal court, maritime law is applied to those issues governed by it. Troupe v. Chicago, Duluth & Georgian Bay Transit Co., 234 F.2d 253, 1956 A.M.C. 1367 (2d Cir. 1956).

164. 332 U.S. 155, 67 S.Ct. 1569, 1947 A.M.C. 847 (1947). See Comment, 26 Tex.L.Rev. 312 (1948).

165. Mr. Justice Frankfurter, who wrote for the Court in Caldarola, clearly repudiates any such doctrine in his concurrence in Pope & Talbot v. Hawn, *supra* note 163. For further light on this perplexing matter, see § 6–61 *et seq.*, *infra*, and the discussion of state and federal law as to preferred ship mortgages in Chapter X.

165a. *Supra* at n. 160a.

165b. 304 U.S. 64, 58 S.Ct. 817 (1938).

166. See Charter Shipping Co. v. Bowring, Jones, & Tidy, 281 U.S. 511, 50 S.

maritime claims arising out of transactions and occurrences anywhere in the world.[166a] Obviously, modern conceptions as to choice of law would make it unthinkable to apply to all such cases the substantive rules of our own maritime law; even in non-statutory areas, though in theory the general maritime law throughout the world may be one, the court must face the fact that interpretations and applications vary, and that it would be highly unjust to apply our own views to maritime occurrences having no connection with the United States beyond the circumstance that suit is brought here. The choice of applicable substantive law is thus a problem of fairly frequent incidence in admiralty cases.[167] Throughout the book, we will notice the conflicts problems where these arise.

Ct. 400, 1930 A.M.C. 1121 (1930). An article by Bickel, The Doctrine of Forum Non Conveniens as Applied in The Federal Courts in Matters of Admiralty, 35 Corn.L.Q. 12 (1949), discusses the whole problem; see also the excellent comment, Admiralty Suits Involving Foreigners, 31 Tex.L. Rev. 889 (1953).

On the problem of forum non conveniens as among the districts, and transfer under 28 U.S.C.A. § 1404(a), see Note, 28 N.Y.U.L.Rev. 430 (1953).

166a. See *supra* at n. 104a.

167. The complexity of the problems, and of the factors going into solution, can be seen in Lauritzen v. Larsen, 345 U.S. 571, 73 S.Ct. 921, 1953 A.M.C. 1210 (1953), and in the Romero case (supra n. 118). Both these cases are discussed *infra*, Chapter VI.

# Chapter II

# MARINE INSURANCE

**§ 2–1.** Treatment of marine insurance at this point in a textbook on admiralty may surprise those who are familiar with its relegation, in some modern casebooks and treatises, to a minor position, or to no position at all. The feeling seems to have prevailed in academic circles that it is at the most an inaccessibly esoteric subject somehow connected with the main body of maritime law, but hardly so clearly of the essence as are such matters as Seaman's Injuries or Collision.

Yet the marine insurance contract is as unquestionably an integral part of the admiralty and maritime jurisdiction as is any other subject-matter. It was in deciding this very point, in fact, that Story wrote the opinion in De Lovio v. Boit,[1] already referred to,[2] which laid the new foundations of admiralty jurisdiction in the United States. Because all important possibilities of marine loss or liability are normally insured against, insurance is tied in *de facto* with a very high proportion of marine litigation; insurance companies are actively connected in intimate working relation with the admiralty practitioner.[3] To consider the rules and concepts of maritime law without reference to the all-pervading "insurance angle" is a stultifying process indeed.

For these reasons, we have felt that the subject ought to receive some general treatment near the beginning of this book. Special aspects may better be taken up in connection with topics covered later. Thus, some problems in the insurance of cargo can be dealt with best in association with the treatment of cargo damage, in the chapter on *The Carriage of Goods Under Bills of Lading*.[4] For now, our aim will be to give such treatment of the general characteristics of the marine insurance contract as will render obvious or intelligible such particular connections.

Finally, it may not be impertinent to add a word of advice, one which, it may be hoped, will send the student on a wider voyage of discovery than the confines of this chapter: There is no better way to a four-square understanding of the whole pattern of the maritime law and the maritime industry than the study of the subject of marine insurance.[5]

1. 7 Fed.Cas. 418, No. 3,776 (C.C.D. Mass.1815).

2. *Supra*, Chapter I, at note 56 *et seq.*

3. "Dans la plupart des procès maritimes les parties ne plaident qu'en nom; derrière ces figurants ce sont les assureurs qui mènent la lutte." Smet, Les Assurances Maritimes: Traité Théorique Et Pratique De Droit Comparé, Preface (1934).

4. *Infra*, Chapter III, Part II, at § 3–47 et passim.

5. In this conservative field, there is still value, as to business background,

## History [5a]

§ 2–2. Of the working of any kind of marine insurance in antiquity, we have only glimpses and guesses.[6] As a body of practice recognizably ancestral to the modern marine insurance system, it seems to have developed right along with the corpus of maritime law, in the late Middle Ages and into the Renaissance.[7] Undoubtedly, as in the case of maritime law in general, its customs became somewhat standardized before they were articulated in extant codes. In 1435, an ordinance issued by the magistrates of Barcelona (the city in which the Consolat de Mar was promulgated [8]) sought to regulate the business,[9] and similar codes appeared throughout the maritime world. By about 1600, the business was quite well established, as is shown by the elaborate dispensations of the *Guidon de la Mer,* a set of rules for its conduct said to have been published in Rouen around this time.[10]

Marine insurance was in full use in England in the time of Queen Elizabeth, A Chamber of Assurances being established in 1575.[10a] In 1601, Parliament actually passed a statute setting up a special court for the trial of insurance cases,[11] but this court was little used.[12] From 1613 dates the celebrated *Tiger* policy (so-called because it insured a ship of that name) now in the Bodleian Library; [13] it is striking in-

in Winter, Marine Insurance (3d ed. 1952) (hereafter cited as Winter). Rodda, Marine Insurance: Ocean and Inland (3d ed. 1970) hereinafter cited as Rodda, should also be consulted, as should Buglass, Marine Insurance and General Average in the United States (1973). Dover, A Handbook to Marine Insurance (6th ed. 1962) (hereafter cited as Dover) is of great value. Shorter, and useful, though British-oriented, is Keate, Guide to Marine Insurance (12th ed. 1958). See also Huebner and Black, Property Insurance, Part II, pp. 265 *et seq.* (1957). Many of the general works on shipping, listed *supra,* Ch. I, note 41, treat phases of marine insurance. The standard law treatise is Arnould, Marine Insurance (15th ed. 1961), now constituting Volumes 9 and 10 of the collection, British Shipping Laws (*cf. infra* at note 24) (hereafter cited as Arnould); see also Ivamy, Marine Insurance (6th ed. 1969). Vance, Handbook on the Law of Insurance (3d ed. 1951) has a useful chapter on marine insurance, at p. 908 *et seq.*

5a. Probably the best general historical account now in print is in Dover, *supra* note 5, Chapter I.

6. Trenerry, The Origin and Early History of Insurance (1926), esp. pp. 107–131.

7. *Cf. supra* Chapter I, at note 11 *et seq.*; See Vance, The Early History of Insurance Law, in 3 Select Essays in Anglo-American Legal History 98 (1909).

8. See *supra,* Chapter I, at note 15.

9. 5 Pardessus, Lois Maritimes 493 *et seq.* For an account of this ordinance, see Martin, The History of Lloyd's and of Marine Insurance in Great Britain 23 *et seq.* (1876).

10. Martin, *op. cit. supra* note 9, at 41 *et seq.*

10a. Dover, *op. cit. supra* n. 5, 15–16.

11. 43 Eliz. c. 12 (1601). This statute was reenacted, in amended form, in 1662, 13 & 14 Car. 2, c. 23.

12. 1 Holdsworth, A History of English Law 571 (3d ed. 1922). For discussion of the lack of a satisfactory tribunal for the decision of insurance cases, prior to the time of Lord Mansfield, see Vance, *supra* note 7, at 111–116; 8 Holdsworth, *op. cit.,* 283–293 (1926).

13. Martin, *op. cit. supra* note 9, at 46 *et seq.* Apparently the "Tiger" policy was not an original but a copy; the "Three Brothers" policy, 1656, seems to be the earliest original now

deed to note how similar some of the language in this policy is to that in common use today.

In the seventeenth century, the London marine underwriters formed the habit of gathering at the then much frequented coffee houses to transact business and discuss matters of common concern. Of these establishments, Edward Lloyd's became the most important. By the middle of the next century, this house had become the recognized center of the business, and the underwriters who came there formed an association which retained the now famous name even through subsequent changes in location. "Lloyd's" thus was and is an association of individual underwriters; in addition some corporate underwriters have done and do a considerable volume of business in England.[14]

In the United States, marine insurance was slow in starting;[15] the British underwriters tended to dominate the field. Almost from the beginning, this country showed a preference for the corporate form; stock and "mutual"[16] companies arose, and some prospered, but there was little individual underwriting on the Lloyd's pattern, after the eighteenth century.[17] At the present, the American marine insurance market is substantial, but the operations of British concerns are still of high importance in this country.[18]

The modern Anglo-American law of marine insurance, though of course rooted in custom,[19] developed in the cases.[20] To a very high degree, the working law consists in judicial interpretation of fixed clauses, often of a high antiquity, in the marine insurance policy.[21] The English Marine Insurance Act of 1906[22] is an important codification; in this country, the law of the subject is not codified, but forms a part of the "general" maritime law.[23] The courts of the Unit-

extant in English. See 30 Law Notes 239 (1927). A facsimile of the "Tiger" policy is found as a frontispiece to Gillingham, Marine Insurance in Philadelphia, 1721–1800 (1933).

14. On Lloyd's, past and present: Dover, *op. cit. supra* n. 5, 34 *et seq.*; Martin, *op. cit. supra* note 9; Straus, Lloyd's: A Historical Sketch (1937); Grey, Lloyd's: Yesterday and Today (1922). A most readable recent work on Lloyd's is Brown, Hazard Unlimited (1973).

15. For interesting material on early days, see Gillingham, *op. cit. supra* note 13.

16. Winter 24–26.

17. Winter 20 *et seq.*

18. See Note, 64 Harv.L.Rev. 446 (1951).

19. See Universo Ins. Co. of Milan v. Merchants Marine Ins. Co., [1897] 1 Q.B. 205, 2 Q.B. 93.

20. The development was slow and unsatisfactory until relatively recent times, probably because of the (not well explained) lack of any satisfactory court for insurance cases; see *supra*, note 12, and authorities there cited; also Review of Phillips on Insurance, attributed to Joseph Story, 20 North American Review 47 (1825).

21. *Cf. supra* Chapter I, at notes 45–46. On the archaic quality of the policy, see Calmar S. S. Corp. v. Scott, 345 U.S. 427, 73 S.Ct. 739, 1953 A.M.C. 952 (1953) and Ferrante v. Detroit Fire & Marine Ins. Co., 125 F.Supp. 621, 1954 A.M.C. 2026 (S.D.Cal.1954).

22. 6 Edw. 7, c. 41.

23. Insurance Co. v. Dunham, 78 U.S. (11 Wall.) 1, 31 (1870). Extreme cau-

ed States, notably the Supreme Court, have expressly announced and followed a policy of deference to the English decisions in the field,[24] recognizing not only the longer experience of those courts but also the great desirability of uniformity, given the close connections of the American and British insurance markets. While there is a substantial amount of marine insurance litigation, there is perhaps not as much as might be expected, given the ubiquitousness of marine insurance.[24a] There is a strong tendency to settle. Insurance companies do not make a practice of litigating fine points to avoid liability. But the subject is of great out-of-court importance.

## General Principles

**§ 2–3.** Marine insurance is at first a field bewilderingly strange to the shoreside lawyer, but this strangeness may soon be made to vanish. The first step toward simplification is to note that the policy, which is the documentary heart of the matter, expresses a *contract*, and is thus a member at least of a familiar phylum in legal taxonomy. There are two parties: the "assured" ("insured", "policyholder") and the "assurer" ("insurer", "carrier", "underwriter"). In the United States, the assurer is nearly always a corporation. The essence of the contractual position in which these parties stand is simple: the assured agrees to pay a premium, and the assurer agrees that, if certain losses or damage occur to certain interests of the assured, at risk in a marine venture, the assurer will indemnify the assured.[25] The complications of marine insurance are complications of this simple scheme: they arise out of the complexities of the policy which is the written embodiment of the contract, or out of the discernment by the courts of unexpressed terms and conditions.

By far the greater part of marine insurance in this country and in England is effected through the services of brokers, who, though technically agents of the assured,[26] are compensated by a commission

tion is now necessary in this regard, in the light of the surprising decision in Wilburn Boat Co. v. Fireman's Fund Ins. Co., 348 U.S. 310, 75 S.Ct. 368, 1955 A.M.C. 457 (1955), discussed in the text *infra* at note 69 *et seq.*

24. Queen Ins. Co. of America v. Globe & Rutgers Fire Ins. Co., 263 U.S. 487, 493, 44 S.Ct. 175, 176, 1924 A.M.C. 107 (1924); Calmar S. S. Corp. v. Scott, 345 U.S. 427, 442–443, 73 S.Ct. 739, 747, 1953 A.M.C. 952 (1953); Note, 64 Harv.L.Rev. 446, 449 (1951). The statement in the text may be weakened, to a now unknowable degree, by the Wilburn Boat case, *supra* note 23. Smet, *op. cit. supra* note 3, reviews the laws of the principal maritime nations; see also, for comparative material, Inter American High Commission, Marine Insurance and General Average, Comparative American Legislation and the York-Antwerp Rules (U. S. Govt. Printing Office 1927).

24a. Nicholas J. Healy explains the recent upswing in volume of marine insurance litigation by reference to the growing number of "sizable losses". Healy, The Hull Policy: Warranties Representations, Disclosures and Conditions, 41 Tulane L.Rev. 245 (1967).

25. Williams v. New England Ins. Co., 29 Fed.Cas.No.17,731 at 1384 (C.C.D. Mass.1869).

26. Eagle Star & British Dominions v. Tadlock, 22 F.Supp. 545, 548, 1938 A.M.C. 499 (S.D.Cal.1938), affirmed sub nom. Walsh v. Tadlock, 104 F.2d 131 (9th Cir. 1939); Connecticut Fire Ins. Co. v. Davison Chemical Corp., 54 F.

deducted from the premium paid through them to the underwriter, and who act as intermediaries both in the placing of the risk and in handling subsequent claims for losses. The first step is the application for insurance, on vessel, cargo, or some other marine subject matter, filled out from the specifications of the prospective insured and presented to the underwriter by the broker. The underwriter may decline the risk entirely; in the usual case, he names the rate of premium and the special conditions, if any, upon which he will accept it. If these are satisfactory, the broker and the underwriter indicate their assent by signing or initialling the appropriately annotated application, which then becomes a "binder". The contract of insurance is now perfected except for formality; the agreement that has been made is sufficiently detailed to enable a clerk familiar with the business to select the appropriate printed form, fill in a few blanks, and affix or stamp on the special clauses, if any, which have been agreed on. The policy is then signed by the underwriter or his agent and delivered to the assured, usually through the broker.[27] (This account is highly schematised, and is merely an abstraction from the complicated course of dealing at, say, Lloyd's.[27a])

The fixing of rates and special conditions requires a vast knowledge of the nature of vessels and cargos, and of the conditions of commerce and navigation.[28] "Classification" societies furnish up-to-date reports on vessel condition, and surveyors employed by underwriters supplement these with *ad hoc* inspection where desired and possible. Works of reference, informally communicated information, and the loss records kept in the office are the bases for calculation, by the cargo underwriter, of the probable susceptibility of various commodities to decay, rust, sweating, damage from salt air, and the like. A tendency to specialization is inevitable.[29]

The policy that issues may cover the risks of a single designated voyage, or may insure for a period of time.[30] Cargo is almost invari-

Supp. 2, 6, 1944 A.M.C. 384 (D.Conn. 1944); Winter 110 *et seq.*; Dover, 61 *et seq.*

27. On the course of trade, see Winter 128 *et seq.*

27a. See Dover, Chapter II, pp. 61–129.

28. For an example of the complexity of the problems facing the underwriter, see Sachs, The Insurance of Commercial Fishing Vessels, 1955 Ins.L.J. 28.

29. Winter, Ch. 14, Cargo Insurance as an Underwriting Problem, p. 227 *et seq.*

30. See Bradlie v. Maryland Ins. Co., 37 U.S. (12 Pet.) 378 (1838). For an interesting problem in coverage of a policy, with respect to losses accruing after its expiration due to causes operating while it is in force, see Export S. S. Corp. v. American Ins. Co., 106 F.2d 9, 1939 A.M.C. 1095 (2d Cir. 1939), certiorari denied 309 U.S. 686, 60 S.Ct. 809 (1940), and notes, 24 Minn.L.Rev. 428 (1940); 20 B.U.L.Rev. 151 (1940); 17 N.Y.U.L.Q.Rev. 293 (1940); 18 N.C.L.Rev. 157 (1940); 49 Yale L.J. 114 (1939). For the "continuation clause," which provides for optional extension of time policies where the vessel is "at sea, or in distress, or at a port of refuge or call" on expiration day, see Connecticut Fire Ins. Co. v. Davison Chemical Corp., 54 F.Supp. 2, 1944 A.M.C. 384 (D.Md.1944); Vogel, The Hull Policy: The Perils and Held Covered Clauses, 41 Tulane L.Rev. 259, 273 *et seq.* (1967).

ably insured by voyage, for that is the natural duration of its status as cargo. Vessels are usually insured for a given period of time, most commonly year by year. Cargo policies may be on a single lot, or may be "open" to cover cargo as shipped by the insured; in the latter case, though a full-form policy is not usually issued for each shipment, the net effect is that each lot of cargo is insured for the particular voyage involved just as though a separate contract and policy existed.[31] Insurance on vessels, called "hull insurance", may cover one ship or a whole fleet.[32]

Containerization,[32a] which has raised so many new questions, has raised the question whether containers are "vessel" or "cargo". The new American Institute Clauses expressly exclude containers from insurance on hull.[32b]

### What is Insured?

**§ 2–4.** Most easily comprehensible as subjects of marine insurance are vessels (with all their appurtenances) and cargo. There are, however, a number of intangible possibilities of loss that arise when a vessel puts to sea, though almost always these intangible subject-matters of insurance are tied in some way to the physical vessel and cargo, so that loss or damage of one is loss or damage of the other. Thus, expected "freight", including charter hire, may be lost to the vessel owner if his ship is sunk or damaged beyond proceeding.[33] Anticipated profits or commissions to be derived from the sale of goods at sea are sometimes insured.[34] A peculiar form of policy that has come into use in relatively modern times is written on "disbursements"—i. e., money already expended on a ship.[35] Insurance on

31. Orient Mutual Ins. Co. v. Wright, 64 U.S. (23 How.) 401 (1860); Forster v. Insurance Co. of North America, 139 F.2d 875, 1944 A.M.C. 131 (2d Cir. 1944). See Slavenburg Corp. v. Boston Ins. Co., 332 F.2d 990, 1964 A.M.C. 1120 (2d Cir. 1964) and City Stores Co. v. Sun Ins. Co., 357 F.Supp. 1113, 1973 A.M.C. 44 (S.D.N.Y.1972). On the "certificates" issued under such "open" or "floating" policies, see Thayer, Marine Insurance Certificates, 49 Harv.L.Rev. 239 (1935); New York & Oriental S. S. Co. v. Automobile Ins. Co. of Hartford, 37 F.2d 461, 1930 A.M.C. 328 (2d Cir. 1930), noted 30 Colum.L.Rev. 890 (1930). See also Winter 58–59.

32. Winter 262–3.

32a. See *supra*, Chapter I, § 1–5.

32b. Hicks, The American Hull Institute Clauses, 2 Journal of Maritime Law and Commerce 787, 789 (1971). See also, for general problems on insurance in container shipments, McDowell, Containerization: Comments on Insurance and Liability, 3 Journal of Maritime Law and Commerce 503 (1972).

33. Insurance Co. of the Valley of Va. v. Mordecai, 63 U.S. (22 How.) 111 (1860); Hugg v. Augusta Ins. & Banking Co., 48 U.S. (7 How.) 595 (1849); Simmes v. Marine Ins. Co., 22 Fed. Cas. 150, No. 12,862 (C.C.D.C.1825). For a freight insurance case involving questions of "frustration" (see *infra* Chapter IV, at note 135 *et seq.*) see Kulukundis v. Norwich Union Fire Ins. Society [1936] 41 Com.Cas. 239, noted 52 L.Q.Rev. 465 (1936).

34. Patapsco Ins. Co. v. Coulter, 28 U. S. (3 Pet.) 222 (1830). See Unson, Insurance on Expected Profits, 19 Phil. L.J. 390 (1940).

35. International Navigation Co. v. Atlantic Mutual Ins. Co., 100 F. 304 (S. D.N.Y.1900), affirmed 108 F. 987 (2d Cir. 1901), certiorari denied 181 U.S.

some of these intangible values may seem (and has seemed to some commentators) essentially the same as insurance on the connected goods or vessels, but a different treatment is accorded policies on profits, disbursements, commissions, and the like, and they must therefore be treated as something different from those on tangible maritime property.[35a] "Protection and indemnity" insurance is written to protect shipowners against certain liabilities.[36]

Most striking is the use of the words "lost or not lost" following the description of the insured subject matter. In former times (as to some extent today) it was often impossible to be certain, when insurance was taken out, whether the insured ship or cargo was already at the bottom of the sea. These words import a promise by the insurer to pay off even though the loss had already occurred at the time of his subscription.[37] Naturally, not only this provision but the whole policy would be voided if the insured had actually known of the loss.[38]

The generalities that follow may be taken to refer principally to insurance on the oldest and still the most important subjects: vessel [38a] and cargo.[38b]

## Insurable Interest

**§ 2–5.** It has been feared that if it were possible to take out "insurance" on goods or vessels through the destruction of which the insured stood to lose nothing, the marine policy, instead of serving the indemnification function for which it was devised, might become the means of gambling on the misfortunes of others, and would even give the "insured" an interest in the loss of marine property. The public policy against "insurance" of this kind has been embodied in the rule that no contract of marine insurance is valid unless the insured has an "insurable interest" in the subject matter at the time of loss.[39]

623, 21 S.Ct. 926 (1901). Winter 278–9, explains that in modern times "disbursements" insurance is in effect additional insurance of a limited type on hull.

**35a.** For discussion of all these intangible interests, see Haehl, The Hull Policy: Additional Insurance Permitted, 41 Tulane L.Rev. 315 (1967).

**36.** See *infra* at note 94, *et seq.*

**37.** General Interest Ins. Co. v. Ruggles, 25 U.S. (12 Wheat.) 408, 413 (1827).

**38.** Insurance Co. v. Lyman, 82 U.S. (15 Wall.) 664 (1873). For a close case, see Pendergast v. Globe & Rutgers Fire Ins. Co., 246 N.Y. 396, 159 N.E. 183 (1927), noted 37 Yale L.J. 1159 (1928).

**38a.** See the valuable Symposium on Hull Insurance in 41 Tulane L.Rev. at 231 *et seq.* (1967).

**38b.** See Cabaud, Cargo Insurance, 45 Tulane L.Rev. 988 (1971), for a thorough treatment of all principal problems.

**39.** Hart v. Delaware Ins. Co., 11 Fed. Cas. 683, No. 6,150 (C.C.D.Pa.1809); Chase v. Hammond Lumber Co., 79 F. 2d 716, 1935 A.M.C. 1502 (9th Cir. 1935). The concept of "insurable interest," in relation to all forms of insurance, has been studied exhaustively by Harnett & Thornton, Insurable Interest in Property: A Socio-Economic Reevaluation of a Legal Concept, 48 Colum.L.Rev. 1162 (1948). These authors are skeptical of the value both of the technical distinctions drawn in this field and of the utility of the

No exhaustive definition of the term "insurable interest" has ever given satisfaction. Though it has no direct force as law in this country, the definition in the English Marine Insurance Act, 1906, is probably as good a summary as any of the English and American cases on the point:

> "(1) Subject to the provisions of this Act, every person has an insurable interest who is interested in a marine adventure.
>
> "(2) In particular a person is interested in a marine adventure where he stands in any legal or equitable relation to the adventure or to any insurable property at risk therein, in consequence of which he may benefit by the safety or due arrival of insurable property, or may be prejudiced by its loss, or by damage thereto, or by the detention thereof, or may incur liability in respect thereof." [40]

Two concurrent tests are set up: a technical relation to the insured subject matter that can be qualified as "legal" or "equitable", and a consequent practical interest in safety and arrival. It is to be noted that this definition does not purport to be exhaustive.

The leading American case of Hooper v. Robinson [41] thus treats the subject:

> "A right of property in a thing is not always indispensable to an insurable interest. Injury from its loss or benefit from its preservation to accrue to the assured may be sufficient, and a contingent interest thus arising may be made the subject of a policy. Lucena v. Craufurd et al., 3 Bos. & Pul. 75; s. c. 5 id. 269; Buck & Hedrick v. Chesapeake Insurance Co., 1 Pet. 151; Hancock v. Fishing Insurance Company, 3 Sumn. 132.
>
> "In the law of marine insurance, insurable interests are multiform and very numerous.
>
> "The agent, factor, bailee, carrier, trustee, consignee, mortgagee, and every other lien-holder, may insure to the extent of his own interest in that to which such interest relates; and by the clause, 'on account of whom it may concern,' for all others to the extent of their respective interests, where there is previous authority or subsequent ratification.

"anti-wagering" concept. Their views seem borne out by experience in the marine insurance field where the "valued" policy (see *infra* at note 133) and the "honor" policy (see text *infra*, at note 44 *et seq.*) pretty well get around the technical requirements, without there being any evidence of "wagering" or any other evil consequences. See Arnould § 11.

40. 6 Edw. 7, c. 41, § 5 (1906).

41. 98 U.S. 528 (1879).

> "Numerous as are the parties of the classes named, they are but a small portion of those who have the right to insure." [42]

Obviously, all who hold any sort of general or security title to maritime property have insurable interests in it. Equally obviously, persons without any such interest or any factual expectation of benefit from the preservation of the property have none. In between there are doubtful cases, and the solutions have been piecemeal rather than based on any clear general test. Probably the furthest the concept of "insurable interest" has been pushed is in the discernment of such an interest in the shareholder of a company owning a ship, sufficient to support his insurance on the ship to the value of his derivative "interest" in her.[43] Persons who merely expect some general benefit from the successful conclusion of a marine venture, in the absence of any definite connection on their part with the subject matter at risk, have no insurable interest in the venture, however well-founded may be their expectations.

Some interests are insured "P.P.I., F.I.A."—"Policy Proof of Interest, Full Interest Admitted".[44] This means that the underwriter agrees not to raise the defence of lack of insurable interest. These policies are called "honor policies." This device is used where it is questionable whether the interest insured would technically qualify as "insurable", but where commercial practice is to insure it. The commonest cases are policies on "disbursements". In effect, such policies insure additional amounts on hull, but, since previous policies on hull have insured up to the full stipulated value, it would be difficult to establish an insurable interest. In theory, they seem to be intended to insure amounts "disbursed" on the ship—but money already spent can hardly be said to be at risk. It is, actually, hard to say just what the theory of disbursements insurance is, for the point obviously cannot be litigated so long as the insurer respects the "honor" term—which he always does.[45]

42. 98 U.S. at 538. Semble, that the seller's right of stoppage *in transitu* gives him an insurable interest. Kalimian v. Liberty Mutual Fire Ins. Co., 300 F.2d 547, 1963 A.M.C. 1730 (2d Cir. 1962). But cf. York-Shipley, Inc. v. Atlantic Mutual Ins. Co., 474 F.2d 8, 1973 A.M.C. 584 (5th Cir. 1973), holding shipper on c. i. f. terms retains no insurable interest.

43. Seaman v. Enterprise Fire & Marine Ins. Co., 18 F. 250 (C.C.E.D.Mo. 1883). See Note, Insurable Interest of Shareholder and Creditor in Corporate Property, 15 Geo.L.J. 73 (1926).

44. Hall & Co. v. Jefferson Ins. Co., 279 F. 892 (S.D.N.Y.1921); Roddick v. Indemnity Mutual Marine Ins. Co., [1895] 1 Q.B. 836; see In re London County Commercial Reinsurance Office, Ltd., [1922] 2 Ch. 67; Winter 279, 285, 320–321.

45. "Honor policies" thus come under judicial scrutiny only when the control of the policy has passed away from the underwriter, when he is contesting some other point, or when their existence is material in a suit between other parties. See Mackay, "Honour" Obligations in Marine Insurance, 97 Cent.L.J. 209 (1924). For the British position, see cases cited *supra*, note 44; also Abrahams, Honour Policies, 81 L.J. 452 (1936), and Arnould §§ 11, 363. "Honor" policies are apparently not *prima facie* void in the United States, but the insurer may escape by affirmatively establishing the absence of insurable in-

It is not always clear when the policy is issued just what (or whose) interest is to be insured. Policies are sometimes written "for the account of whom it may concern"; if it was the intent of the person taking out the insurance that the interest of the party seeking indemnity be covered, and if that party actually had an insurable interest, then the indemnity is payable by the insurer to that person.[46]

### Certain Ways in Which the Policy May Be Voided

**§ 2–6.** Even though a policy is in proper form, on an insurable subject matter and running in favor of one having an insurable interest, certain circumstances may make it void *ab initio* or void it after the risk has attached.

Of considerable importance is the special application to this field of general doctrines on misrepresentation and concealment. The marine insurance contract is *uberrimae fidei*—the highest degree of good faith is exacted of those entering it, for the underwriter often has no practicable means of checking on either the accuracy or the sufficiency of the facts furnished him by the assured before the risk is accepted and the premium and conditions set.[47] The first and most obvious consequence is that the underwriter may avoid the policy if a wilful misrepresentation, or an innocent one of a material fact, made by the assured in connection with the formation of the contract, has been one of the inducements to the underwriter's entering it.[48] So much is familiar law applicable to contracts in general; the only peculiarity is that the nature of the transaction gives new definition to the concept of materiality, for a fact is material if, to a prudent underwriter, its existence affects the risk he is assuming.[49] The high good faith exacted, moreover, is inconsistent even with nondisclosure of information pertinent to the risk, and the assurer may avoid a policy if it appears that the assured has concealed any material fact.[50]

terest; see Hall v. Jefferson Ins. Co., 279 F. 892 (S.D.N.Y.1921); Rep. of China v. National Union F. I. Co., 163 F.Supp. 812, 1958 A.M.C. 1529 (D.Md. 1958).

46. Hooper v. Robinson, 98 U.S. 528 (1879); Hagan v. Scottish Union & Nat. Ins. Co., 186 U.S. 423, 22 S.Ct. 862 (1902). See Winter 147, and Welded Tube Co. v. Hartford Fire Ins. Co., 1973 A.M.C. 555 (E.D.Pa. 1973), citing this text.

47. McLanahan v. Universal Ins. Co., 26 U.S. (1 Pet.) 170, 185 (1828); Sun Mutual Ins. Co. v. Ocean Ins. Co., 107 U.S. 485, 510, 1 S.Ct. 582, 599 (1883); Arnould § 550.

48. Wathen v. Public Fire Ins. Co., 61 F.2d 962 (2d Cir. 1932); see Hazard's Adm'r v. New England Marine Ins. Co., 33 U.S. (8 Pet.) 557 (1834); Arnould § 550 *et seq.*

49. Btesh v. Royal Ins. Co. of Liverpool, 49 F.2d 720, 1931 A.M.C. 1044 (2d Cir. 1931); Ruggles v. General Interest Ins. Co., 20 Fed.Cas.No.12,119, at 1324 (C.C.D.Mass.1825), affirmed General Interest Ins. Co. v. Ruggles, 25 U.S. (12 Wheat.) 408 (1827); Arnould § 557.

50. Gulfstream Cargo Ltd. v. Reliance Ins. Co., 409 F.2d 974, 1969 A.M.C. 781 (5th Cir. 1969); King v. Aetna Ins. Co., 54 F.2d 253, 1931 A.M.C. 1940 (2d Cir. 1931); Moses v. Delaware Ins. Co., 17 Fed.Cas. 891, No. 9,872 (C.C.D.Pa. 1806); Arnould § 590 *et seq.*; Note, Proposal For Marine Insurance, 168 L.T. 535 (1929).

Similar in effect is the breach of any of the "warranties" implied by law or expressed in the policy.[51] Of these one of the most striking (and distinctively maritime) is the implied warranty of seaworthiness of the insured vessel or of the vessel on which insured goods are carried. The word "warranty" is multivocal throughout the law; here it has its most drastic meaning.[51a] Where the implied warranty is held to exist, and where it is breached—i. e., where the vessel is not in fact seaworthy at the beginning of the voyage or at the inception of the risk—then no recovery can be had on the policy.[52] This result does not depend on the knowledge [53] or fault [54] of the assured. This warranty is implied in all voyage policies, unless clear language to the contrary is used; in England, the courts have held that it is not to be read into time policies,[54a] but some American courts seem to have thought otherwise, at least where the insured vessel is in port at the time the risk takes hold, though the authority for this proposition is quite slender.[55]

The Fifth Circuit in 1957 stated one view of the American position as follows:

> "The English Rule is clear that in a Time Hull policy such as this one, there is no '* * * warranty that the vessel at any particular time shall have been seaworthy * * *' but 'If, however, through the personal misconduct of the owner, the ship be sent to sea in an unseaworthy state, he cannot recover for a loss brought about by such

51. The difference between "representation" and "warranty" is discussed in Hearn v. Equitable Safety Ins. Co., 11 Fed.Cas.No.6,300, at 968 (C.C.D.Mass. 1872), affirmed 87 U.S. (20 Wall.) 494 (1874); see also, Arnould § 555. A warranty is either implied by law or written in the policy, while a representation is "collateral"; a warranty must be "strictly" complied with while a representation need only be substantially true. On all these matters, see Healy, The Hull Policy: Warranties Representations, Disclosures and Conditions, 41 Tulane L. Rev. 245 (1967).

51a. But note the shift in effect of "breach", in the language quoted below, at n. 55a.

52. Stetson v. Insurance Co. of North America, 215 F. 186 (E.D.Pa.1914); New Orleans, T. & M. R. Co. v. Union Marine Ins. Co., 286 F. 32, 1923 A.M.C. 183 (5th Cir. 1923); Arnould § 695 *et seq.* The warranty can be negated by the terms of the policy; Eagle Star & British Dominions Ins. Co. v. George Moore & Co., 9 F.2d 296, 1926 A.M.C. 126 (9th Cir. 1925). On the question of applicability of the warranty to liability policies, see Sorenson v. Boston Ins. Co., 20 F.2d 640, 1927 A.M.C. 1288 (4th Cir. 1927), certiorari denied 275 U.S. 555, 48 S.Ct. 116 (1927) and Note, 41 Harv.L.Rev. 537 (1928). The burden of proof as to unseaworthiness lies on the assurer. Hanover Fire Ins. Co. v. Holcombe, 223 F.2d 844, 1955 A.M.C. 1531 (5th Cir. 1955).

53. Richelieu & Ontario Nav. Co. v. Boston Marine Ins. Co., 136 U.S. 408, 429, 10 S.Ct. 934, 940 (1890).

54. Bullard v. Roger Williams Ins. Co., 4 Fed.Cas.No.2,122 at 646 (C.C.D.R.I. 1852).

54a. Arnould § 706.

55. Union Ins. Co. of Philadelphia v. Smith, 124 U.S. 405, 8 S.Ct. 534 (1888); Henjes v. Aetna Ins. Co., 132 F.2d 715, 719, 1943 A.M.C. 27 (2d Cir. 1943), certiorari denied 319 U.S. 760 (1943); see Compañia Transatlantica Centroamericana, S. A. v. Alliance Assur. Co., 50 F.Supp. 986, 1943 A.M.C. 976 (S.D.N.Y.1943); Note, 41 Harv.L. Rev. 537 (1928).

wilful act or default.' 2 Arnould, Marine Insurance (13th Ed. 1950), § 697, pp. 637–638.

"But the American Rule, in a rare departure from a determined course of parallel uniformity, Queen Ins. Co. of America v. Globe & Rutgers Fire Ins. Co., 263 U.S. 487, 44 S.Ct. 175, 68 L.Ed. 402, implies for a time policy, as does the English Rule as of the commencement of the voyage for voyage policies. 2 Arnould, op. cit. supra, §§ 691, 695, a warranty of seaworthiness as of the very moment of attachment of the insurance. And, unlike the English Rule which limits the warranty to the commencement of the voyage, the American Rule takes it somewhat further to extend, in point of time, a sort of negative, modified warranty. It is not that the vessel shall continue absolutely to be kept in a seaworthy condition, or even that she be so at the inception of each voyage, or before departure from each port during the policy term. It is, rather, stated in the negative that the Owner, from bad faith or neglect, will not knowingly permit the vessel to break ground in an unseaworthy condition. And, unlike a breach of a warranty of continuing seaworthiness, express or implied, which voids the policy altogether, the consequence of a violation of this 'negative' burden is merely a denial of liability for loss or damage caused proximately by such unseaworthiness.

"How this came to be the rule of general acceptance for all Time policies is obscure, for traced as it apparently is to expressions in Union Insurance Co. of Philadelphia v. Smith, 124 U.S. 405, 8 S.Ct. 534, 31 L.Ed. 497, there seems to have been slight critical awareness that the policy in Union contained not alone an express warranty of seaworthiness, but an express exclusion of losses caused by unseaworthiness or by incompetence of Master and Mariners, which might imply a contractual undertaking for a continuing obligation by Master and crew members acting generally as agents for the owners to take all prudent requisite steps to keep the ship seaworthy." [55a]

In the same year, The Second Circuit said: "Appellees correctly disclaimed defense of an implied warranty of seaworthiness, since these are time policies". A footnote expands the idea:

"There are statements in the following cases that the rule may be somewhat different in this country, i. e., that, although there may be no implied warranty of seaworthiness in a time policy, yet if the vessel is in port where repairs may be made, the insured cannot recover for any loss subsequently occurring when the vessel is at sea which is caused by the want of diligence in making the repairs; *Union Ins. Co.* vs.

55a. Saskatchewan Govt. Ins. Office v. Spot Pack, Inc., 242 F.2d 385, 388–9, 1957 A.M.C. 655, 661–2 (5th Cir. 1957). [Footnote by the court omitted.]

*Smith,* 124 U.S. 405; *New York & P. R. S. S. Co.* vs. *Aetna Ins. Co.,* 204 Fed. 255, 258 (2CA); *Henjes* vs. *Aetna Ins. Co.,* 1943 A.M.C. 27, 132 F.(2d) 715, 719 (2CA). However, as pointed out *supra,* the statement in the *Union Ins. Co. case* was *obiter,* for the case involved an express warranty against unseaworthiness. That this was *obiter* is noted in the *New York & P. R. S. S. Co. case,* 204 Fed. 255, 258, and had been noted by Judge LEARNED HAND in the district court, 192 Fed. 212, 214–215. The statement of the so-called American rule in 204 Fed. at 258 was also *obiter,* since the court found no want of diligence. So too was the statement in the *Henjes case, supra,* where there was a breach of an express promisory warranty." [55b]

No case has been found squarely basing decision on the so-called "American Rule", and the guess is ventured that the Supreme Court, if the issue is even tendered it, will not uphold this warranty.[55c]

Seaworthiness is a comprehensive term, and a relative one. The requirement is that the vessel not only be staunch and strong, but also that she be fitted out with all proper equipment in good order, and with a sufficient and competent crew and complement of officers.[56] But these requirements are relative to the voyage or service proposed.[57] A ship that is in one or another of these respects unseaworthy for an Atlantic crossing in December may nevertheless be seaworthy for a coasting run to the South in the same season. In cargo policies, the warranty of seaworthiness of the vessel comprises fitness to carry the particular cargo; thus, a ship lacking refrigeration is unseaworthy for the carriage of a cargo that will spoil unless refrigerated.

The burden cast on vessel owners is a heavy one. One sees few cases in the recent reports in which this defense is raised by underwriters [57a]; perhaps it is not insisted upon in practice when due diligence has in fact been exercised to make the vessel seaworthy, and when the actual loss bears no relation to the unseaworthiness. The stern requirement in the background, with its drastic penalty, doubtless had a wholesome effect on the discipline of the shipping industry in early, less well-policed days; it may not be too farfetched to see in it a principal cause of the connotation of the word "shipshape." It is questionable, however, whether present conditions fully justify the continuance of the stringent warranty. It is clear that an insured

**55b.** N.Y., N.H. & H. R. R. Co. v. Gray, 240 F.2d 460, 466, 1957 A.M.C. 616, 621 (2d Cir. 1957) certiorari denied 353 U.S. 966, 77 S.Ct. 1050 (1957).

**55c.** See, generally, Chamlee, The Absolute Warranty of Seaworthiness: A History and Comparative Study, 24 Mercer L.Rev. 519 (1973).

**56.** See The Southwark, 191 U.S. 1, 8–9, 24 S.Ct. 1, 3 (1903); Aguirre v. Citizens Casualty Co., 441 F.2d 141, 1971 A.M.C. 1134 (5th Cir. 1971); Arnould § 695.

**57.** Compañia de Navegacion Interior, S. A. v. Fireman's Fund Ins. Co., 277 U.S. 66, 74–78, 48 S.Ct. 459, 461, 1928 A.M.C. 923 (1928); American Merchant Marine Ins. Co. v. Margaret M. Ford Corp., 269 F. 768 (2d Cir. 1920).

**57a.** But see *supra* at n. 55a.

should not recover for losses caused by lack of care to make his vessel seaworthy. But once he has exercised this care (and the modes of its exercise have become more and more standardized), it seems somewhat contradictory of the general idea behind insurance to penalize him so drastically for a condition for the existence of which he is blameless; this impression is strongest as to the case of the insured who has used due diligence and then suffered a loss not even connected causally with the seaworthiness defect.

Cargo policies usually expressly waive the seaworthiness warranty, in recognition of the realistic fact that the cargo owner cannot control the vessel's state.[57b]

Similar in operation to the seaworthiness warranty, though taking effect later in the course of the voyage, is the doctrine of "deviation". In voyage policies, the assurer is deemed to have intended to accept only that risk that inheres in the expeditious prosecution of the voyage by the usual commercial route. Where the vessel without excuse[58] departs from this route, or delays unreasonably in pursuing the voyage, the policy is ousted.[59] The contract of insurance, once ousted by a deviation, is gone forever; return to the proper course does not restore it.[60]

Whether a ship has deviated is a question that must always be settled by reference both to the policy and to the usages of the particular trade concerned.[61] Where the policy is silent, specifying only *termini*, usage governs; a call at an intermediate port that is customarily touched by ships engaged on the voyage insured is not a deviation.[62] Special terms in the policy may vary the matter either way; liberties to touch and call, or to do anything else that would otherwise be a deviation, may be granted, or there may be laid down a more circumscribed route than usage would require.[63] "Held covered" clauses, moreover, often blunt the effect of the deviation warranty, by providing that, in the event of deviation, the insurance shall continue to cover, at a premium to be arranged.[63a] Since most voyage policies are, in modern times, actually on cargo (see *supra* § 2–3) it is very

**57b.** Cabaud, *op. cit. supra* n. 386, 45 Tulane L.Rev. at 995–6 (1971).

**58.** See Arnould § 428 *et seq.*; Note, 11 Cornell L.Q. 385 (1926).

**59.** Hearne v. Marine Ins. Co., 87 U.S. (20 Wall.) 488 (1874); Oliver v. Maryland Ins. Co., 11 U.S. (7 Cranch) 487 (1813); Glidden v. Manufacturers' Ins. Co., 10 Fed.Cas. 476, No. 5,482 (C.C.D. Mass.1832); Arnould § 431.

**60.** Burgess v. Equitable Marine Ins. Co., 126 Mass. 70 (1878).

**61.** Columbian Ins. Co. v. Catlett, 25 U.S. (12 Wheat.) 383 (1827); Arnould §§ 444–447.

**62.** Bentaloe v. Pratt, 3 Fed.Cas. 241, No. 1,330 (C.C.E.D.Pa.1801); see Bulkley v. Protection Ins. Co., 4 Fed.Cas. 614, No. 2,118 (C.C.D.Conn.1835); Martin v. Delaware Ins. Co., 16 Fed. Cas. 894, No. 9,161 (C.C.D.Pa.1808); Arnould § 445.

**63.** Hughes v. Union Ins. Co., 16 U.S. (3 Wheat.) 159 (1818); Winthrop v. Union Ins. Co., 30 Fed.Cas. 376, No. 17,901 (C.C.D.Pa.1807); Arnould § 447.

**63a.** See Vogel, The Hull Policy: The Perils and Held Covered Clauses 41 Tulane L.Rev. 259, 276 (1967).

important that current practice is in effect to waive the deviation warranty in cargo policies.[63b]

### Express Warranties

§ 2–7. Any fact whatever may be made the subject of an "express warranty"—that is, the initial or continued validity of the policy may be made conditional on the existence of any state of facts.[64] Such a warranty, to be effective, must somehow be expressed in the actual policy,[65] but the words "warrant" or "warranty" need not be used. Whether a given sentence or phrase in a policy is to be given the effect of a warranty must therefore be referred to the "intention of the parties".[66] Generally, any assertion of fact in the policy, whether in the main body or on the margins, is likely to be treated as a warranty of the fact asserted. Once a warranty is spelled out, the fact must be and remain exactly in conformity with the warranty, or the policy is voided.[67] The assurer may, however, be estopped from asserting the breach of warranty, by (for example) taking an active part in salvage operations.[67a]

(Clarity is not furthered by the additional circumstance that sometimes when the word "warrant" or some derivative is actually

**63b.** See Cabaud, *op. cit. supra* n. 38b, 45 Tulane L.Rev. at 990 (1971).

**64.** Fidelity-Phenix Ins. Co. v. Chicago Title & Trust Co., 12 F.2d 573, 1926 A.M.C. 787 (7th Cir. 1926)—vessel warranted a "passenger steamer" was not; no recovery allowed on policy, regardless of causal connection between breach of warranty and loss; Levine v. Aetna Ins. Co., 139 F.2d 217, 1944 A.M.C. 62 (2d Cir. 1943)—vessel warranted equipped with searchlights, but was not; same result as in preceding case. In Insurance Co. v. Thwing, 80 U.S. (13 Wall.) 672 (1872), there was a warranty against "loading" more than a specified tonnage. The insured took on coal beyond the warranted amount. The Court reversed a judgment for the insured, on the ground that the jury should have been instructed that, if the coal was carried for hire, it was "cargo" and the warranty was breached. No causal connection appeared between the "overloading" and the loss sued on. See also Ciconett v. Home Ins. Co., 179 F.2d 892 (6th Cir. 1950). For trenchant criticism of the "warranty" doctrine, with much interesting historical material, see Vance, The History of the Development of the Warranty in Insurance Law, 20 Yale L.J. 523 (1911). On express warranties generally, see Arnould, Chapter 19.

**65.** Arnould § 639.

**66.** See Henjes v. Aetna Ins. Co., 132 F.2d 715, 1943 A.M.C. 27 (2d Cir. 1943), certiorari denied, 319 U.S. 760, 63 S.Ct. 1316 (1943), for a close question of "intent." The "warranty" was against a certain kind of towing; the loss occurred just after the insured vessel cut loose from the forbidden tow. The court found that the "intention of the parties," while not supporting a full "warranty" which would have ousted the policy forever, did not contemplate such an abrupt reinstatement. Note, Insurance: Warranty or Description of Risk, 173 L.T. 296 (1932).

**67.** See cases cited *supra* note 64; but *cf.* Wilburn Boat Co. v. Fireman's Fund Ins. Co., *infra* at note 69 *et seq.* Where the "warranty" would work great hardship, courts are prone to construe the policy language quite strictly in the insured's favor. See Saskatchewan Govt. Ins. Office v. Ciaramitaro, 234 F.2d 491, 1956 A.M.C. 1400 (1st Cir. 1956).

**67a.** Reliance Ins. Co. v. The Escapade, 280 F.2d 482, 1961 A.M.C. 2410 (5th Cir. 1960).

used in the policy, its effect is not to create a "warranty" in the above sense at all, but merely to define the policy's coverage and to exclude from the potential liabilities of the underwriter certain losses. Thus the words "warranted free of particular average" do not mean (as would be absurd) that the policy is void if a "particular average", or partial loss, occurs, but rather that the underwriter does not pay on such losses.[68] These vagaries of terminology are to be deplored, but the modernizer of language usage would be well advised to seek scope for his talents in another field than marine insurance.)

### The Wilburn Boat Case

§ 2–8. The persistently problematic case of Wilburn Boat Co. v. Fireman's Fund Ins. Co.[69] must be treated at this point. The policy was on a small houseboat used for carriage of passengers on Lake Texoma. The following warranties were in the policy:

> "It is Also Agreed that this insurance shall be void in case this Policy or the interest insured thereby shall be sold, assigned, transferred or pledged, without previous consent in writing of the assurer."
>
> "Warranted by the assured that the within named vessel shall be used solely for private pleasure purposes during the currency of this policy and shall not be hired or chartered unless permission is granted by endorsement hereon." [70]

The boat burned, and the insurance company defended the suit under the policy on breach of warranty grounds. The Court of Appeals for the Fifth Circuit, following what it took to be orthodox views as to marine insurance law and the supremacy of federal maritime law in this field, upheld this defense, regarding as inapplicable certain Texas statutes which would have voided the agreement against pledging and made the breach of the passenger carriage warranty available only if the breach contributed causally to the loss.[71] The Supreme Court reversed, holding that no "federal" rule had been fashioned to deal with the consequences of the breach of warranties in marine policies,[71a] and that it would be impolitic for the court to fashion one. The decision was therefore to leave the matter to the States, and the case was remanded with directions to give effect to the Texas statutes.

68. See *infra* at § 2–12.

69. 348 U.S. 310, 75 S.Ct. 368, 1955 A.M.C. 457 (1955). See MacChesney, Marine Insurance and the Substantive Admiralty Law, 57 Mich.L.Rev. 555 (1959).

70. 348 U.S. at 311, 75 S.Ct. at 369.

71. Wilburn Boat Co. v. Fireman's Fund Ins. Co., 201 F.2d 833, 1953 A.M.C. 284 (5th Cir. 1953).

71a. At this point in the Wilburn reasoning, one is totally puzzled, for Insurance Co. v. Thwing, *supra* note 64, seems squarely to have decided this very point, or at least inevitably to have rested on the assumption of the correctness of the strict rule. How many Supreme Court cases does it take to "fashion" a federal rule?

The reader will by this time have an accurate enough picture of the place of marine insurance in the whole body of maritime law and ocean commerce to see the point in the statement, made in discussing this case in Chapter I, that it is hard to say what is to be governed by a federal maritime law, if the question of the effect of a breach of warranty in a marine policy is not so governed.[72] The decision in Wilburn is hard indeed to reconcile with the postulate of there being a federal maritime law at all; it is even harder to square with the assumption that the law of marine insurance is a part of that law. The opinion of the Court poses as its first question "Is there a judicially established federal admiralty rule governing these warranties?" [73] This seems to suggest the possibility that those questions of law concerning which litigation in the federal courts has been active enough to satisfy the Court's criteria of "establishment" are to be considered as ruled by maritime admiralty law, while those which for any reason (in this relatively non-litigious field) happen not to have reached the federal courts in volume are to be relegated to the legislative competency of the States. This is, with deference, a nightmarish solution; yet, if it is not the one envisaged, why pose the question in that way?

There is, for example, a well-established "federal" rule (at least in the sense that the federal courts have enunciated it) to the effect that, for the purpose of calculating whether a "constructive total loss" on a policy has taken place, the actual repaired value (rather than the insured value) of the ship is to be taken as the basis for deciding whether the cost of salvage, repair, etc., exceed half the ship's "value" —the criterion of the existence of the constructive total loss.[74] There is respectable (though old) state authority holding the reverse.[75] Are the federal courts to continue following their own rule, and bring the states into line, if necessary, by use of the certiorari jurisdiction of the Supreme Court? If so, in the light of Wilburn, then it must be for one of two reasons:

> (1) *States are to be allowed to deal with marine insurance substantive law only when it happens that such cases have not presented themselves to the federal courts in such number or with the issues so posed as to result in decision of the point involved.* This criterion would make a sheer crazy quilt of the subject. Some of the most important and obvious propositions in marine insurance law are rarely litigated.[75a]

72. See *supra*, Chapter I, at note 159 *et seq.*

73. 348 U.S. at 314, 75 S.Ct. at 370.

74. See *infra*, at note 125.

75. See Phillips, *loc. cit. infra* note 125.

75a. Yet this seems the view taken, *e. g.*, in Liman v. Amer. Steamship Owners Mutual Protection and Indemnity Ass'n, 299 F.Supp. 106, 108, 1969 A.M.C. 1669, 1672 (S.D.N.Y.1969) and in Navegacion Goya, S.A. v. Mutual Boiler and Machinery Ins. Co., 1972 A.M.C. 650 (S.D.N.Y.1972). For a general

(2) *States may interfere by statute, but not by decisional law.* Perhaps it is enough to point out the collision between this point of view and the philosophy of Erie R. R. v. Tompkins.[76]

Yet there is no reasonable general criterion, based on anything that has ever been put forward as a justification for federal substantive competence in the admiralty field, which could distinguish between (1) the question whether breach of an express warranty voids the policy and (2) the question whether the repaired or insured value of the ship should be used for the purpose mentioned. If anything, the first question is closer to the center of marine insurance law than is the second.

Unless, therefore, one of the unsatisfactory criteria listed above is to be applied, and the field carved up on such an irrelevant basis into bits and pieces, the implication of Wilburn would appear to be that marine insurance law as a whole is to be excised from the general maritime law inferentially adopted by the Constitution. Yet that would not only be entirely arbitrary; it would deeply disturb the whole philosophy of Insurance Co. v. Dunham,[77] and therefore of the federal admiralty jurisdiction. Dunham settled the foundations of the judicial jurisdiction in contract by holding the marine insurance contract within it, but it did so in great part, and quite explicitly, on the ground that marine insurance law was a part of the general maritime law. It is a true *tour de force* to hold that the federal maritime law is supreme in regard to seamen's suits for maintenance and cure and for indemnity for injuries suffered through unseaworthiness,[78] and at the same time to hold that marine insurance is not governed by federal law.

It is utterly impossible to be at all sure, even yet, how the Supreme Court will at last resolve these perplexities and contradictions. Wilburn may mean merely that the States are to have a limited competency to regulate certain terms of marine policies. It could as a matter of cold logic be read to mean that there is no federal maritime law at all.[78a] It may very well turn out to mean anything between

survey, see Note, The Aftermath of Wilburn, 5 Willamette L.J. 529, 534 *et seq.* (1969). The author of the Note concludes that the first of the alternatives in the text has been generally followed, and collects cases.

**76.** 304 U.S. 64, 58 S.Ct. 817 (1938).

**77.** 78 U.S. (11 Wall.) 1 (1871); see *supra*, Chapter I, note 56.

**78.** *Cf.* Pope & Talbot v. Hawn, 346 U.S. 406, 74 S.Ct. 202, 1954 A.M.C. 1 (1953).

**78a.** But this, as pointed out in Chapter I, is an impossible reading, in the light of the subsequent Kossick case. See *supra*, Chapter I, at n. 159a. Actually, Wilburn Boat seems not to have travelled outside the insurance field; see Note, 5 Willamette L.J. 529 at 541–2 (1969). In Crosson v. N. V. Stoomvaart Mij "Nederland", 409 F.2d 865, 1969 A.M.C. 1363 (2d Cir. 1969), the court rejected application of Wilburn to the choice of law governing recoverability of shipowner's counsel fees in indemnity action against a stevedore.

The multiple confusion ensuing upon Wilburn Boat can be illustrated by the opinion in Continental Sea Foods, Inc. v. New Hampshire Fire Ins. Co.

these extremes. Even eighteen years after the decision, it still seems unwise to cast this chapter in the form of a series of guesses, based on the set of possibilities as to the effect of Wilburn. The reader is sufficiently warned, however, of the incertitudes that case has introduced. The lower federal courts cannot authoritatively resolve those uncertainties; we will not know what Wilburn Boat means unless and until the Supreme Court clarifies the position further.[78b] In the long meanwhile, it has seemed best to try to sketch what would, before Wilburn, have been taken to be the law—since the effect of Wilburn is far from fully known.

### The Risks Insured Against

§ 2–9. The marine insurance policy, though it gives a wide shelter, does not protect against every sort of loss that may happen to vessel or cargo. The principal risks actually insured against are set out in the "perils" clause which is supplemented by "specially to cover" clauses, or restricted by clauses in effect eliminating one or more of the insured risks. The following clause sets out the common "perils":

> "Touching the adventures and perils which we the assurers are contented to bear and do take upon us in this voyage: they are of the seas, men-of-war, fire, enemies, pirates, rovers, thieves, jettisons, letters of mart and countermart, surprisals, takings at sea, arrests, restraints, and detainments of all kings, princes, and people, of what nation, condition or quality soever, barratry of the master and mariners, and of all other perils, losses, and misfortunes, that have or shall come to the hurt, detriment, or damage of the said goods and merchandises, and ship, &c., or any part thereof." [79]

*et al.*, 1964 A.M.C. 196 (S.D.N.Y.1963). The district judge denies the "revolutionary" character of Wilburn, saying that two prior Second Circuit decisions Levine v. Aetna Ins. Co., 139 F.2d 217, 1944 A.M.C. 62 (2d Cir. 1943) and Shamrock Towing Co. v. American Ins. Co., 9 F.2d 57, 1926 A.M.C. 433 (2d Cir. 1925) "in considering the effect of non-compliance with warranties in a marine insurance policy, discussed and relied upon New York cases." 1964 A.M.C. at 198. But the Levine case concerned events on Lake Owasco, one of the smaller finger lakes, almost certainly not considered by the court to be within the admiralty jurisdiction at all, and perusal of the Shamrock Towing opinion clearly shows that case to have been decided primarily on the authority of Arnould on Marine Insurance, a British text, and of federal cases; the "accord" with New York cases is pointed out as an afterthought, and certainly without any "discussion" of them.

**78b.** See Healy, *op. cit. supra* n. 51, 41 Tulane L.Rev. at pp. 254 *et seq.*

**79.** From the Lloyd's policy in the First Schedule of the British Marine Insurance Act, 1906, 6 Edw. 7, c. 41. This form is standard for British policies; American policies are much the same, with minor verbal changes (e. g., "perils of the lakes" may be substituted where geographically appropriate).

The burden of proof is on the insured to bring his loss within one of the perils, if the issue is raised by evidence for stringent modern application, see Northwestern Mutual Life Ins. Co. v. Linard, 498 F.2d 556, 1974 A.M.C. 877 (2d Cir. 1974).

This clause, it will be seen, includes many risks of warlike operation. For a long time, the ordinary marine policy has contained the "free of capture and seizure" (F. C. & S.) clause, eliminating such risks from the policy. The perils clause in a policy containing the F. C. & S. clause is to be read, therefore, as though the war risks were not enumerated in it. War risk insurance is written separately, with a perils clause of its own, covering the risks that are eliminated from the ordinary marine policy by the F. C. & S. clause.[80]

The perils clause which would appear in the war risk policy (an entirely separate policy, issued perhaps by another underwriter), though changed slightly from time to time, will read substantially as follows:

> "This insurance is only against the risks of capture, seizure, destruction or damage by men-of-war, piracy, takings at sea, arrests, restraints, detainments and other warlike operations and acts of kings, princes and peoples in prosecution of hostilities or in the application of sanctions under international agreements, whether before or after declaration of war and whether by a belligerent or otherwise, including factions engaged in civil war, revolution, rebellion or insurrection, or civil strife arising therefrom, and including the risks of aerial bombardment, floating or stationary mines and stray or derelict torpedoes and weapons of war employing atomic fission or radioactive force; but excluding claims for delay, deterioration and/or loss of market, and warranted not to abandon (on any ground other than physical damage to ship or cargo) until after condemnation of the property insured."

The net effect is that there are two sorts of insurance in use today: ordinary marine and war risk. The perils clause in the ordinary marine policy does not mean what it says, but covers only those risks which are not knocked out by the F. C. & S. clause. (As would be expected, there is some difficulty in distinguishing "war risks" from "marine risks", and the line may change with slight changes in the wording of the clauses in standard policies.[80a])

Of the marine perils, by far the most important are those "of the seas". What is covered is not any loss that may happen *on* the sea, but fortuitous losses occurring through extraordinary action of the elements at sea, or any accident or mishap in navigation.[81] By

80. Calmar S. S. Corp. v. Scott, 345 U. S. 427, 430 *et seq.*, 73 S.Ct. 739, 741, 1953 A.M.C. 952 (1953); Winter 325 *et seq.*; Note, 10 Modern L.Rev. 211 (1947). *Cf. infra*, Ch. XI, at note 130.

80a. For full treatment, see Haehl, The Hull Policy: Coverages and Exclusions Frequently Employed, 41 Tulane L.Rev. 277 (1967).

81. Western Assur. Co. of Toronto v. Shaw, 11 F.2d 495, 1926 A.M.C. 578 (3d Cir. 1926), certiorari denied 273 U.S. 698, 47 S.Ct. 93 (1926); Compañia Transatlantica Centroamercana S. A. v. Alliance Assur. Co., 50 F.Supp. 986, 1943 A.M.C. 976 (S.D. N.Y.1943); Read v. Agricultural Ins. Co., 219 Wis. 580, 263 N.W. 632, 1936 A.M.C. 25 (1935); Arnould § 800

far the greatest number of claims for marine loss, and of the insurance problems connected with other topics treated in this book, arise under this clause. Extraordinary action of the wind and waves is a sea peril.[82] Collision, foundering, stranding, striking on rocks and icebergs, are all covered under these words.[83] Even a swell from a passing ship may be a "peril of the sea".[83a] On the other hand, ordinary wear and tear are not included under the coverage of this or any other phrase in the clause, nor are losses which are anticipatable as regular incidents of sea carriage in general or of navigation in a particular part of the world.[84]

**§ 2–10.** The rest of the marine perils are of less importance, and may be mentioned briefly. "Fire" is pretty much self-explanatory.[85] "Barratry" refers to serious misconduct of the master or mariners.[86] The "thieves" insured against, in English law, are only those whose theft is accompanied by violence;[87] the weight of American authority seems to establish that secret theft and pilferage are to be included[88]—certainly a more satisfactory view from the standpoint

*et seq.*; Notes, 60 Scot.L.Rev. 56 (1944) 192 L.T. 158 (1941) 14 Austr.L.J. 399 (1941); 23 Cornell L.Q. 610 (1938).

**82.** Arbib & Houlberg v. Second Russian Ins. Co., 294 F. 811, 1924 A.M.C. 16 (2d Cir. 1923); Aetna Ins. Co. v. Sacramento-Stockton S. S. Co., 273 F. 55 (9th Cir. 1921).

**83.** Peters v. Warren Ins. Co., 39 U.S. (14 Pet.) 99, 108 (1940); American-Hawaiian S. S. Co. v. Bennett & Goodall, 207 F. 510 (9th Cir. 1913); Lanasa Fruit S. S. & Importing Co. v. Universal Ins. Co., 302 U.S. 556, 58 S. Ct. 371, 1938 A.M.C. 1 (1938); Quinlivan v. Northwestern Fire & Marine Ins. Co., 31 F.2d 149, 1929 A.M.C. 372 (W.D.N.Y.1929) reversed on other grounds 37 F.2d 29 (2d Cir. 1930); Arnould Chapter 23.

**83a.** Spooner & Sons v. Connecticut Fire Ins. Co., 314 F.2d 753, 1963 A.M.C. 859 (2d Cir. 1963).

**84.** Hazard's Adm'r v. New England Marine Ins. Co., 33 U.S. (8 Pet.) 557 (1834); Coles v. Marine Ins. Co., 6 Fed.Cas. 65, No. 2,988 (C.C.D.Pa.1812); Arnould § 825. An unusually high tide was held not a "peril of the sea" in Glover v. Philadelphia Ins. Co., 1956 A.M.C. 1210 (City Court, Baltimore, Md.1956). The mere fact that a vessel developes a leak, in ordinary weather and seas, does not establish causation by a "peril of the seas". Tropical Marine Products Co. v. Birmingham Fire Ins. Co., 1956 A.M.C. 567 (S.D.Fla.1955). But see N. Y. N. H. & H. R. R. v. Gray, 240 F.2d 460, 1957 A.M.C. 621 (2d Cir. 1957), certiorari denied 353 U.S. 966, 77 S.Ct. 1050 (1957). On "perils" in general, and particularly sea perils, see Vogel, The Hull Policy: The Perils and Held Covered Clauses, 41 Tulane L.Rev. 259 (1967).

**85.** See Waters v. Merchants' Louisville Ins. Co., 36 U.S. (11 Pet.) 213 (1837); Kuljis v. Union Marine & General Ins. Co., 4 F.Supp. 424, 1933 A.M.C. 1232 (W.D.Wash.1933), reversed on other grounds 70 F.2d 231 (9th Cir. 1934); Arnould § 818. Fire has been held to be both a "peril of the sea" and an independently named peril. Belle of Portugal, 421 F.2d 390, 1970 A.M.C. 30 (9th Cir. 1970).

**86.** For a modern discussion, see National Union Fire Ins. Co. v. Republic of China, 254 F.2d 177, 1958 A.M.C. 721 (4th Cir. 1958); see also Marcardier v. Chesapeake Ins. Co., 12 U.S. (8 Cranch) 39, 49 (1814); Patapsco Ins. Co. v. Coulter, 28 U.S. (3 Pet.) 222, 230 (1830); Intermondale Trading Co. v. North River Ins. Co., 100 F.Supp. 128, 1951 A.M.C. 936 (S.D.N.Y.1951); Arnould § 836 *et seq.*

**87.** Arnould § 834.

**88.** Atlantic Ins. Co. v. Storrow, 5 Paige 285 (N.Y.Chanc.1835); American Ins. Co. v. Bryan & Maitland, 1 Hill 25 (N.Y.1841); see 3 Kent, Commentaries *303 (14th ed. 1896); Arnould § 834.

of the insured. Many American policies, however, use the phrase "assailing thieves," which brings them back in line with the English view.[89] (It has been held that the term "assailing thieves" does not protect against theft of the whole vessel.[89a]) The general words at the end of the perils clause have been construed *ejusdem generis* with the preceding enumerated perils; they have not had much effect, for the "perils of the sea" are already so broad in scope that there is little left for a general phrase to cover, within *ejusdem generis* limits.[90] Sometimes, however, the general words have effect; the moving and damaging of a yacht, for the purpose of stealing property on board has been held to be "if not a theft . . . so very much like a theft . . ." as to fall under the "all other like perils" clause.[90a]

The constructions placed on the perils clause have in some cases resulted in restrictions of coverage which have become undesirable under modern conditions. Sometimes, moreover, a specific coverage may be desired, and it may be uncertain whether the traditional perils would include it. Hence many modern policies contain one or more "specially to cover" clauses of the following type:

> "This insurance also specially to cover (subject to the Average Warranty) loss of or damage to the subject matter insured directly caused by the following:
>
> "Accidents in loading, discharging or handling cargo, or in bunkering;
>
> "Accidents in going on or off, or while on drydocks, graving docks, ways, gridirons or pontoons;
>
> "Explosions on shipboard or elsewhere;
>
> "Breakdown of motor generators or other electrical machinery and electrical connections thereto, bursting of

89. Arnould § 834; Winter 184–5.

89a. Felicione & Sons Fish Co. v. Citizens Casualty Co. of N. Y., 430 F.2d 136 (5th Cir. 1970) certiorari denied 401 U.S. 939, 91 S.Ct. 936, 1971 A.M.C. 819 (1971); *noted* 2 Journal of Maritime Law and Commerce 688 (1970); 2 St. Mary's L.J. 274 (1970).

90. Union Marine Ins. Co. v. Charles D. Stone, & Co., 15 F.2d 937, 1927 A.M.C. 7 (7th Cir. 1926); Watson v. Providence Washington Ins. Co., 106 F.Supp. 244, 1952 A.M.C. 1812 (E.D.N.C.1952), appeal dismissed 201 F.2d 736 (4th Cir. 1953). See Arnould § 852. The most celebrated decision of recent times under the "general" clause was doubtless Thames & Mersey Marine Ins. Co. v. Hamilton, Fraser & Co., 12 App.Cas. 484 (1887). A pump, insured as part of the machinery of a vessel, clogged through valve failure and was damaged. The House of Lords held this accident arose neither through a "peril of the sea" nor through a cause ejusdem generis with the enumerated perils. (The judgments review the older authorities.) This was a disquieting decision, for it more than suggested that many costly accidents that might be suffered by the expensive machinery on steam vessels were not covered by the standard marine policy. The result was the inclusion of the celebrated "Inchmaree" clause in hull policies, extending special coverage not only to machinery breakage but to many other classes of loss not covered by the standard perils clause as restrictively construed. The clause discussed in the next paragraph in the text is a modern form of the "Inchmaree" clause.

90a. Feinberg v. Insurance Co. of North America, 260 F.2d 523, 1959 A.M.C. 11 (1st Cir. 1958).

boilers, breakage of shafts, or any latent defect in the machinery or hull, (excluding the cost and expense of replacing or repairing the defective part);

"Contact with Aircraft or with any land conveyance;

"Negligence of Master, Charterers other than an Assured, Mariners, Engineers or Pilots;

Provided such loss or damage has not resulted from want of due diligence by the Assured, the Owners or Managers of the Vessel, or any of them. Masters, Mates, Engineers, Pilots or Crew not to be considered as part owners within the meaning of this clause should they hold shares in the Vessel." [91]

Some insurance today is written against "all risks"—against all losses, that is, attributable to external causes.[92]

Besides the perils clause, modified and expanded as indicated, recovery under the policy can be had on the entirely separate "sue and labor" clause. This is not a new addition, but is an ancient component of the policy, as may be judged from the phraseology of a typical specimen:

"And in case of any loss or misfortune, it shall be lawful and necessary to and for the assured, . . . factors, servants and assigns, to sue, labor and travel for, in and about the defense, safeguard and recovery of the said goods and merchandises, or any part thereof, without prejudice to this insurance; nor shall the acts of the insured or insurers, in recovering, saving and preserving the property insured, in case of disaster, be considered a waiver or an acceptance of an abandonment; to the charges whereof, the said Insurance Company will contribute according to the rate and quantity of the sum herein insured. . . ."

Under this clause, the underwriter may become liable for certain charges incurred by the assured in caring for the insured property, whether or not there is any actual loss or damage. Where sue-and-labor charges are incurred and loss also occurs, the underwriter may become liable for more than the policy amount, which limits only a claim for loss of or damage to the goods or vessel.[93]

91. On the history and modern functioning of this "Inchmaree" clause, see Ferrante v. Detroit Fire & Marine Ins. Co., 125 F.Supp. 621, 1954 A.M.C. 2026 (S.D.Cal.1954), and Tetreault, The Hull Policy: The "Inchmaree" Clause, 41 Tulane L.Rev. 325 (1967).

92. Winter 193; Arnould § 856; on the practice in insurance generally, see Landis, All Risks Insurance, 1951 Ins.L.J. 709; Cunningham, Is "Inherent Vice" Covered By All-Risk Clauses? 1951 Ins.L.J. 261. See also Redna Marine Corp. v. Poland, 46 F.R.D. 81, 1969 A.M.C. 1809 (S.D.N.Y.1969).

93. Ciconett v. Home Ins. Co., 179 F.2d 892 (6th Cir. 1950). The underwriters contribute under this clause only where the charges are incurred to avert a loss for which they would be answerable. Biays v. Chesapeake Ins. Co., 11 U.S. (7 Cranch) 415 (1813). It has been held that, where the clause contains no specific promise by the in-

Hull policies (i. e., those insuring vessels) frequently contain a "collision and running down" clause covering liability incurred for damage to another vessel and cargo or to any other object or structure, through collision or striking, and sometimes personal injury liabilities similarly incurred. This clause in its older forms covered some but not all of the important liabilities that might be incurred by the shipowner through the operation of his ship; this sparseness of coverage was deliberate, for it was felt desirable to leave the owner with a substantial interest in the careful operation of his vessel. Owners, however, protected themselves by "club" insurance, and the supposed spur to diligence was thus removed. Policies today are written protecting owners against all important forms of liability.[94] The standard hull policy contains a "collision and running down" clause, somewhat limited still in its application. The Protection and Indemnity policy covers against collision liability not covered by the "collision and running down" clause, as well as against all other important possibilities of liability: loss of life and bodily injury, damage to cargo, repatriation expenses, etc. The "clubs," however, are still active. These are associations of shipowners banded together to spread and absorb liabilities falling on their members; they are called, for short, P. and I. Clubs, for Protection and Indemnity.

Containerization (see *supra* § 1–5) has created and will continue to create novel problems for the P. & I. clubs and insurers. How, for example, shall these policies handle liability to cargo incurred during one of the land legs of a multimodal through shipment? [95]

## "Proximate Cause"

**§ 2–11.** It is a prerequisite to the liability of the underwriter, under any of the clauses, that the loss be "proximately caused" by the peril insured against and claimed under.[96] Causes of marine loss are frequently concurrent; to decide which of concurrent causes is "proximate" has evoked that refinement of reasoning to which one is accustomed when "proximate cause" is mentioned. The most important modern questions that have arisen in this regard came up because of

surer to reimburse, he is not bound to do so. American Merchant Marine Ins. Co. v. Liberty Sand & Gravel Co., 282 F. 514 (3d Cir. 122), certiorari denied 260 U.S. 737, 43 S.Ct. 96 (1922). This seems unnecessarily narrow; money expended under the clause might arguably be recovered under either implied-in-fact contract or quasi-contractual theories. The opinion reviews many cases on the clause. See Winter 195 *et seq.*, and Bruns, The Hull Policy: Sue and Labor, etc., 41 Tulane L.Rev. 359 (1967).

94. There is a far-ranging Symposium on the P. & I. Policy in 43 Tulane L. Rev. 457 *et seq.* (1969). See Winter 272–273, 306, 402–403. Bernard, Protection and Indemnity Insurance (1945, 2d printing 1950) gives information on practical aspects of P. & I. insurance; see also, Libby, Some Aspects of Protection and Indemnity Insurance, 1952 Ins.L.J. 684.

95. See Reynardson, The Reaction of Protection and Indemnity Associations to Through Transit Risks, 2 Journal of Maritime Law and Commerce 837 (1971).

96. Lanasa Fruit S. S. & Importing Co. v. Universal Ins. Co., 302 U.S. 556, 58 S.Ct. 371, 1938 A.M.C. 1 (1938); Note, 23 Cornell L.Q. 610 (1938); Arnould § 811.

the division, described above,[97] between war risk and ordinary marine insurance. In Muller v. Globe & Rutgers Fire Ins. Co.,[98] for example, the vessel carrying the insured cargo was taken in charge by an English cruiser as she neared the British coast during World War I. The officer in command of the boarding party insisted on a night passage through waters that were dangerous because, for military reasons, the lights that ordinarily assisted navigation were extinguished. The vessel was lost, and with it the cargo. The assured sued his *war risk* underwriters, who defended on grounds that appear in the following extract:

> "The second contention herein raises ultimately the question of proximate cause, of which, after centuries of litigation, the Squib Case still remains the best and classic example. That the Canadia and her cargo was seized, arrested, and detained within the meaning of the policy we think too plain to require more than mention; the sole query is whether her loss proximately resulted therefrom.
>
> "Counsel have, we think, collated all the reported cases whose facts are suggestive; but it should be remembered that, however desirable is the exercise of ordered thought and arrival at a logical result, proximate cause is a question for the jury, unless there is but one inference possible from the settled facts. Therefore decisions of judges are rarely precedents in the same way as are legal rulings. Donegan v. Baltimore, etc., R.R., 165 Fed. 869, 91 C.C.A. 555; Erie R.R. v. Russell, 183 Fed. 722, 106 C.C.A. 160. Of the cases noted below, the Ionides decision best serves as text or starting point. From that ruling it is argued that, if (as was there held) going ashore at a notoriously dangerous point (Hatteras), whose lighthouse had been extinguished as a war measure, was not a 'consequence of hostilities,' but a sea peril, neither was a stranding on the unlighted Fair Isle proximately caused by any action of 'kings, princes, and people,' and more especially the British cruiser Hilary.
>
> "The contention is not unattractive, and we fully recognize it as a rule of law, supported by reason and the authorities quoted, that a mere increase of sea peril, by removal for belligerent purposes of all or any aids to navigation, does not per se afford ground for recovery under such 'war risk' as this, in respect of a loss due to the absence of accustomed assistance. Such act, indeed, no more than restores the dangers of the seas to their normal.
>
> "But the problem still remains whether the Canadia's loss was proximately due to sea peril, and solution primarily depends on the meaning of 'proximate,' as construed by judicial commentators. That cause is proximate which sets the other causes in motion; only when causes are independent is

97. *Supra* at note 80.

98. 246 F. 759 (2d Cir. 1917).

the nearest in time looked to. Insurance Co. v. Boon, 95 U.S. 117, 24 L.Ed. 395, a case whose facts are instructive and interesting. If there is an unbroken connection between act and injury, the act causes the injury; an intervening act is not the proximate cause of injury, unless it is efficient to break the causal connection (Milwaukee, etc., R.R. v. Kellogg, 94 U.S. 469, 24 L.Ed. 256).

"These rules are guides to ascertaining whether, as matter of fact, the Hilary's seizure of the Canadia caused the loss of the latter, and here both the facts and reasoning of British, etc., Co. v. The King, 33 Times L.R. 520, are illuminating. There a merchant vessel, chartered by the crown as a transport and insured substantially against war risks, was compelled to navigate without lights in the Mediterranean, and while so doing was rammed and sunk by a French man of war. Rowlett, J., held in substance that the obligation, imposed by military necessity, of doing so dangerous a thing as to run at night without lights, made such obligation the proximate cause of collision.

"We entertain a similar view in this cause. The Hilary did not say to the Canadia, 'Go to Kirkwall, as you intended; the lights are out, and you must pick your own way,' but compelled her to pursue an imposed and dangerous route, and especially to go by night in charge of a naval officer whose local knowledge was perhaps deficient, and certainly not useful. Not only did a belligerent's necessity create the peril of unlighted seas, but by 'acts of kings, authorized in prosecution of hostilities,' the Canadia was forced to run risks that even in time of war she could and would have escaped under the uncontradicted evidence. Furthermore, the very purpose of compelling such navigation was to prevent aid and comfort reaching enemies of Great Britain; therefore the insured cotton was lost in the continuing process of detaining the ship that carried it, for purposes of search, and seizure, too, if the facts found had warranted it.

"Thus we find no intervening cause, breaking the causal connection between the control assumed by the Hilary's boarding party, and the loss of the ship. There was no time when the shipmaster was left to navigate his own ship in his own way; she was lost while he was doing what he had to do. A workman compelled to handle familiar tools with one eye blindfolded, and injured by his own blundering use of them, is in truth injured by the person who put compulsion upon him." [99]

99. 246 F. at 762, 763; see Arnould §§ 904 *et seq.*; Derby, What Are Warlike Operations Under F. C. & S. Clause in Marine Policies, 33 Calif.L.Rev. 128 (1945); Merchant Ships and Warlike Operations, 195 L.T. 223 (1943); Note, 51 Yale L.J. 674 (1942); Note, 59 L.Q.Rev. 6 (1943); Standard Oil Co. of N. J. v. United States, 340 U.S. 54, 71 S.Ct. 135 (1950), and Notes, 31

During World War II, the problem of selection between the war peril and the marine peril, in cases where both concurred in producing the loss, became so acute that in 1945 the United States War Shipping Administration, then the principal war risk underwriter,[100] entered into an Overall War-Marine Risk Settlement Agreement [101] with the marine underwriters, clearing up a number of doubtful classes of cases and even providing for some compromise settlements where the vagueness of "proximate cause" doctrine left the law and the justice of the matter in doubt.[102] Where possible, the sound plan is for the assured to place his marine and war risks with the same underwriter, so that the question which sort of risk has caused a loss can have no practical importance.

### Losses: "Memorandum" and F. P. A.

**§ 2–12.** Some losses, though caused by insured perils, are not payable at all. The traditional policy contained a clause of the following sort, known (rather non-committally) as the "memorandum":

> "Memorandum. It is also agreed, that bar, bundle, rod, hoop and sheet iron, wire of all kinds, tin plates, steel, madder, sumac, wickerware and willow, (manufactured or otherwise), salt, grain of all kinds, tobacco, Indian meal, fruits, (whether preserved or otherwise), cheese, dry fish, hay, vegetables and roots, rags, hempen yarn, bags, cotton bagging and other articles used for bags or bagging, pleasure carriages, household furniture, skins and hides, musical instruments, looking-glasses, and all other articles that are perishable in their own nature, are warranted by the assured free from average, unless general; hemp, tobacco stems, matting, and cassia, except in boxes, free from average under *twenty per cent.* unless general; and sugar, flax, flax seed, and bread are warranted by the assured free from average under *seven per cent.* unless general; and coffee in bags or bulk, pepper in bags or bulk, and rice, free from average under *ten per cent.* unless general." [103]

Clearly, this clause applies only to cargo, or perhaps in rare cases, to ship's appurtenances.

B.U.L.Rev. 258 (1951); 37 Cornell L.Q. 99 (1951); 63 Harv.L.Rev. 1455 (1950); 26 N.Y.U.L.Rev. 362 (1951); also Libby, McNeil & Libby v. United States, 340 U.S. 71, 71 S.Ct. 144, 1951 A.M.C. 14 (1950). See Esso Standard Oil Co. v. United States, 221 F.2d 805, 1955 A.M.C. 1191 (2d Cir. 1955), affirming *per curiam*, on the District Court opinion, 122 F.Supp. 109, 1954 A.M.C. 1292 (S.D.N.Y.1954).

100. See *infra*, Chapter XI, at note 130.

101. Printed in 1945 A.M.C. 1014.

102. Thus, cases of damage incurred by "bumping or surging" against other vessels or structures in harbors in advanced-operations areas, where overcrowding due to war conditions prevailed, were to fall 50–50 on the war and marine risk underwriters respectively; see 1945 A.M.C. 1021.

103. See Washburn & Moen Mfg. Co. v. Reliance Marine Ins. Co., 179 U.S. 1, 2, 21 S.Ct. 1 (1900).

Several new terms are introduced in the "memorandum", and must be defined before the subject of losses can be tackled. An *average* is a partial, as opposed to a *total* loss. A *general average* is that sort of partial loss which is incurred when some of the values at risk in the marine venture are sacrificed to save the remainder from peril; thus the general average loss might consist in either (1) the incurring of a liability, on the part of insured goods that are saved by such a sacrifice, to contribute to the owners of the sacrificed goods, or (2) that portion of the loss of the sacrificed goods which, in the "levelling out" of loss under general average doctrines, remains uncompensated by the contributions of others.[104] An average which is not "general" —a partial loss, that is to say, which falls on the owner of the goods alone and is not partly compensated by general average contribution— is a "particular average".[105] (These terms are all equally applicable to losses to vessel or other interests, though the "memorandum" in which we first encounter them deals principally or entirely with goods.)

Now we can translate. "Looking glasses . . . warranted by the assured free from average unless general" means, "If looking glasses suffer a partial loss, other than the liability to make a general average contribution, or the sacrifice of the looking glasses themselves in a general average situation, then the underwriter will not pay such loss; he will, on the other hand, (since total loss is not "average"; see above) pay for a total loss." Similarly, "rice, free from average under ten percent, unless general," means "The underwriter will not compensate the owner of the rice for any partial loss or damage (except a general average loss as defined) unless the loss amounts to ten percent or more of the value of the rice." [106]

The rationale of the "memorandum" is easy to see. Where certain commodities are subject in the ordinary course of events to spoilage or breakage, or to other forms of deterioration normally expectable from the nature of the goods, underwriters were loath to assume the risk of loss from these causes.[107] Especially in early days, when merchants travelled with their goods, it was far more reasonable that they should take precautions against such loss than that underwriters should insure against them; even today, careful packaging and other precautions can protect against many such losses. On the other hand, the underwriter's function was to indemnify against loss through for-

104. See *infra* Chapter V, esp. the general explanation at the beginning of the chapter; Sharpe, Contribution to General Average, 21 L.Q.Rev. 155 (1905).

105. *Cf. infra*, Chapter V, at note 7.

106. This language means what it says. If the loss exceeds ten percent, the underwriter pays the whole loss; the percentage is not a "deductible." The reason for this is clear when one considers the rationale of the memorandum; if a loss rises above the memorandum percentage, then that is presumptive evidence that the cause was not one of the "inherent susceptibility" causes against the operation of which the memorandum is designed to protect the underwriter. *Cf.* the similar treatment of the F.P.A. clause, discussed in the text *infra*.

107. Winter 211–212.

tuitous and more or less catastrophic causes.[108] Where very heavy partial loss was expectable through inherent susceptibility and similar causes, the commodity in question was placed in the first part of the memorandum, and "warranted free of average unless general"—that is, insured against total loss and general average losses only. The reason the general average loss is included is that such a loss never comes about through the inherent characteristics of particular goods; the venture *as a whole* has to be in peril before a "general average situation" can be said to exist.[109] Where partial losses to be anticipated from the nature of the goods, and from the casualties that might normally be expected to happen to them in the course of a voyage, do not exceed, at an estimate, some percentage, then the underwriters, as in the later clauses of the memorandum, are willing to assume responsibility for such losses when above the calculated percentage.

Though no single policy would ever insure all the "memorandum articles", they were lumped together in this way, with a general term in the bargain, for two reasons. One was the desire to achieve a uniform rate of premium on goods insurance; the risk assumed was thus equalized and standardized by this clause.[110] The other was that, in many early cargo policies, the underwriter might not even know what goods he was insuring; the policy might describe the subject matter simply as "goods aboard the good ship Helen G."

The growing diversity of shipped commodities has, however, outrun the memorandum, and the prevalent custom now is to employ, where the result achieved by the memorandum is desired, a "free of particular average" (F.P.A.) clause of the following sort:

"Free of particular average unless seven percent".

Using the definitions above, the reader will see that this means the same as "free of average under seven percent unless general", for any "average" which is not "general" is "particular" by definition. Such a clause therefore achieves the same result for a single commodity as is effected by the memorandum, and suitable "particular average" terms can thus be selected for each commodity.[111]

**§ 2–13.** These clauses, it will be remembered, were intended to exempt the underwriter only from losses normally expectable because of the character of the goods. A given partial loss may, however, take place demonstrably because of some fortuitous maritime casualty, even though the characteristics of the insured goods might lead one to expect a heavy incidence of partial loss from causes of the "inherent susceptibility" type. It was a bit hard on owners of looking glasses, say, to refuse to insure against breakage caused by ship collision,

108. See the discussion of "perils of the sea," *supra* at note 81 *et seq.*

109. See *infra*, Chapter V, at note 35.

110. Winter 211.

111. This is one of the points at which extreme expertness is called for on the part of the cargo underwriter; see *supra* at note 29. For examples of FPA clauses in modern use, see Larsen v. Insurance Co. of North America, 252 F.Supp. 458, 1965 A.M.C. 2576 (W.D.Wash., 1965).

merely because looking glasses are frequently broken in the ordinary course of events. To take care of this, two slightly variant clauses have been used. The first is the "Free of Particular Average, English Conditions", or F.P.A., E.C. Clause:

> "Free of particular average unless the vessel be stranded, sunk, or burnt, or in collision".

The Free of Particular Average, American Conditions (F.P.A., A.C.) Clause, reads:

> "Free of particular average unless caused by stranding, sinking, burning, or collision with another vessel".

The difference between the clauses is patent when they are read literally, and courts have read them literally. Thus, the underwriter, by the operation of the English Conditions clause, is deprived of his F.P.A. protection if the vessel is stranded in course of the voyage, even though the actual particular average suffered has no causal connection with the stranding.[112] Doubtless this is a narrow and overliteral construction having little to do with the purpose of the clause, but it is an expression of what is on the whole a good tendency —that of construing strictly language inserted by the underwriter to cut down his own liability.

Where an F. P. A. clause states a percentage under which particular averages will not be paid, this does not operate as a "deductible". If the average exceeds the named percentage, then it is payable in full. Thus, under a clause reading "free of particular average unless five percent", when a particular average of six percent is suffered, the underwriter pays six percent, and not just one percent. This is in line with the purpose of the clause, which is included to disembarrass the underwriter of claims in a percentage considered normally expectable, given the character of the commodity; when the percentage selected to mark the limit of normal expectability is exceeded, then the inference is that the whole loss is of a fortuitous and unusual sort, and ought to be paid in full.[113]

Hull policies usually contain "minimum franchise" clauses similar in effect to the F. P. A. clauses in cargo insurance; these are included to immunize the underwriter from being bothered with losses so small and so normally expectable as to shade off into mere operating expenses. Sometimes, hull policies are written with "deductible average" clauses; under these, no matter how large the loss, the assured pays the amount of the "deductible" before the underwriter pays anything.[114]

112. London Assur. v. Companhia de Moagens do Barreiro, 167 U.S. 149, 17 S.Ct. 785 (1897); Arnould § 895.

113. *Cf. supra* note 106. F.P.A. clauses exhibit a wide variety of phraseology; see Jones Const. Co. v. Niagara Fire Ins. Co., 170 F.2d 667, 1951 A.M.C. 1401 (4th Cir. 1948).

114. Winter 201, 284.

### Total Loss

**§ 2–14.** So far we have considered only partial as opposed to total losses. Of the latter there are two sorts: actual and constructive.

In often-quoted language, Lord Abinger thus defines the actual total loss:

> "The underwriter engages that the object of the assurance shall arrive in safety at its destined termination. If, in the progress of the voyage, it becomes totally destroyed or annihilated, or if it be placed, by reason of the perils against which he insures, in such a position, that it is wholly out of the power of the assured or of the underwriter to procure its arrival, he is bound by the very letter of his contract to pay the sum insured." [115]

Where it is no longer possible that the goods or the ship can arrive at their destination *in specie,* then an actual total loss has occurred.[116] This result may be brought about by the physical destruction or deep-sea sinking of the insured property,[117] by capture or theft,[118] or by the breaking up or alteration of the goods or vessel to such an extent that they can no longer be looked on as existing *in specie.*[119] Actual total loss has also been held to have occurred when goods are so damaged in the course of the voyage that, while they still exist *in specie* at that time and can be sold where they are, there is no reasonable possibility that they can be transported to their destination without complete destruction or loss of identity.[120]

The concept of constructive total loss is a little more difficult.[121] In English law, when, by the operation of a peril insured against, insured property has been damaged to the extent that, though it continues to exist *in specie,* and might reach its destination *in specie,* the cost of bringing the latter result about would exceed the value of the goods or ship, then the assured may treat the loss as total, on condition that he notify the underwriter of his election and "abandon" to him all his own rights in the insured subject matter.[122] One of the

115. Roux v. Salvador, 3 Bing.N.C. 266, 285–6 (1836).

116. Morean v. U. S. Ins. Co., 14 U.S. (1 Wheat.) 219 (1816); Monroe v. British & Foreign Marine Ins. Co., 52 F. 777 (1st Cir. 1892); Arnould § 1048 *et seq.*

117. See Burt v. Brewers' & Malsters' Ins. Co., 9 Hun 383 (N.Y.Sup.Ct.1876), affirmed per curiam 78 N.Y. 400 (1879); Carr v. Security Ins. Co., 109 N.Y. 504, 17 N.E. 369 (1888), affirming 38 Hun 86 (N.Y.Sup.Ct.1885); Arnould § 1049 *et seq.*

118. See Arnould § 1052.

119. Great Western Ins. Co. v. Fogarty, 86 U.S. (19 Wall.) 640 (1874); Arnould § 1050.

120. Hugg v. Augusta Ins. & Banking Co., 48 U.S. (7 How.) 595, 604–8 (1849); for authoritative interpretation of this case, see Great Western Ins. Co. v. Fogarty, 86 U.S. (19 Wall.) 640, 644 (1874).

121. See Lord, The Hull Policy: Actual and Constructive Total Loss and Abandonment, 41 Tulane L.Rev. 347 (1967); Note, Constructive Total Loss Doctrine In Marine Insurance, 51 Colum.L.Rev. 526 (1951).

122. Marine Insurance Act, 1906, 6 Edw. 7, c. 41, § 60; Arnould § 1082.

few clearcut and important differences between English and American marine insurance law is that, in the United States, the insured may claim for a constructive total loss where the cost of repair, reconditioning, refloating, or the like would exceed *half* the value.[123] This discrepancy between the usually concordant systems of law has led to readjustment by the inclusion of special clauses in the standard policies; many hull policies in both countries incorporate a clause adopting the British rule, in something like the following terms:

> "No recovery for a constructive total loss shall be had hereunder unless the expense of recovering and repairing the vessel shall exceed the insured value." [124]

This clause effects another change in the law. In this country and in England, it had been held that the value, for purposes of calculating whether an actual total loss could be claimed on, was to be taken as the actual repaired value, which might be more or less than the insured value.[125] Standard practice in drafting hull policies now stipulates that the insured value shall be the guide. Thus, even in the United States, under such a policy, a constructive total loss of a vessel does not take place unless the cost of repairs, etc., would exceed the insured value.

In a close case, of course, few things are harder to ascertain with assurance than whether certain measures for saving or reconditioning property will in the end cost more than the value, or half the value, of the property. No nice mode of calculation is available to the master or the insurance company surveyor who, perhaps with Hurricane Carol reported on an uncertain and menacing course, stands off from a vessel driven on the rocks by Hurricane Barbara and tries to decide how badly she is damaged under water and how much trouble it will be to raise her. Abandonment must be made promptly, but the right to abandon often rests on facts that are impossible to ascertain promptly—or, rather, on a prediction. The American law fixes the right to abandon on the basis of facts as they are when abandonment is tendered.[126] Thus, if the reasonable probability, at the time the assured tenders abandonment and elects to claim for a constructive total loss, is that the cost of repair and like expenses will exceed the amount (either the insured value or half thereof, depending on the policy stipulation) required for the exist-

123. Marcardier v. Chesapeake Ins. Co., 12 U.S. (8 Cranch) 39 (1814); Jeffcott v. Aetna Ins. Co., 129 F.2d 582, 1942 A.M.C. 1021 (2d Cir. 1942), certiorari denied 317 U.S. 663, 63 S.Ct. 64 (1942); see Rock Transport Properties Corp. v. Hartford Fire Ins. Co., 312 F.Supp. 341, 1970 A.M.C. 590 (S.D.N.Y.1970).

124. See Winter 394. Such a clause is valid; Delta Supply v. Liberty Mutual Ins., 211 F.Supp. 429, 1963 A.M.C. 1540 (S.D.Tex.1962).

125. Bradlie v. Maryland Ins. Co., 37 U.S. (12 Pet.) 378, 398 (1838); 2 Phillips, Insurance § 1539 (5th ed. 1867); Arnould § 1085.

126. Rhinelander v. Insurance Co. of Pa., 8 U.S. (4 Cranch) 29 (1807); Calmar S. S. Corp. v. Scott, 209 F.2d 852, 1954 A.M.C. 558 (2d Cir. 1954); 2 Phillips, *op. cit. supra* note 125, at 348.

ence of the right to abandon, the abandonment is good and binds the underwriter, who must pay for a constructive total loss even though later events may show that the repair costs are less than the required amount.[127] English law, on the other hand, provides for a second guess; the state of things at the time of the attempted abandonment must support the right to abandon, but, even where this state of facts has existed, the abandonment is defeated if at the time of action brought it appears that the conditions necessary to establish a constructive total loss no longer exist.[128]

These questions can only arise, of course, where the underwriter has refused to accept an abandonment; where the tendered abandonment is accepted, the rights of the parties are fixed irrespective of whether the facts at any time actually justified the tender.[129] Sometimes, however, it is difficult to say whether an abandonment has been accepted. The "sue and labor" clause, it will be remembered, protects the underwriter against the inference that, by taking steps to preserve the goods, he has by implication accepted abandonment,[130] while, on the other hand, acceptance (or for that matter, tender) need not be by the use of any set verbal formula, but may be picked up from the circumstances.[131] Each case must be decided on its own facts; it is fortunate that these matters, like most others involving insurance claims, are usually settled by out-of-court agreement.

Constructive total loss, it will be seen, is distinguished on one side from actual total loss, and on the other from partial loss. The principal effect of the first distinction is that no formal abandonment need be made in respect of the actual total loss, while the tender of abandonment, either accepted by the underwriter or binding upon him because of the existent facts, is a prerequisite to a claim under a constructive total loss. The principal importance of the constructive total loss doctrine on the other side (apart from the convenience to any assured of receiving payment of the policy value without proof of particular damages and charges and without bothering any further with a badly damaged ship or cargo) is to the assured whose policy protection is against total loss only.[132]

127. Later events, such as actual cost of repairs, will of course be evidence of what the facts were, but are not in themselves decisive. Bradlie v. Maryland Ins. Co., 37 U.S. (12 Pet.) 378, 397–8 (1838).

128. Arnould § 1090.

129. Copelin v. Phoenix Ins. Co., 76 U. S. (9 Wall.) 461 (1870); Arnould § 1192.

130. Indemnity Marine Assur. Co. v. Cadiente, 188 F.2d 741, 1951 A.M.C. 878 (9th Cir. 1951).

131. Copelin v. Phoenix Ins. Co., 76 U. S. (9 Wall.) 461 (1870); Canada Sugar-Refining Co. v. Insurance Co. of North America, 175 U.S. 609, 20 S.Ct. 239 (1900); but see Indemnity Marine Assur. Co. v. Cadiente, 188 F.2d 741, 1951 A.M.C. 878 (9th Cir. 1951); Arnould § 1193 *et seq.*

132. Under the "memorandum" or F.P. A. clauses; see *supra*. See Barry, Casual Comments Upon Particular Average and Constructive Total Loss, 9 Va.L.Rev. 344 (1923). See also Calmar S. S. Corp. v. Scott, 209 F.2d 852, 1954 A.M.C. 558 (2d Cir. 1954).

§ 2–15. Aside from total losses and particular or general averages, the insurer often has to pay charges incurred under the "sue-and-labor" [132a] clause, and, where clauses are included in the policy protecting the assured against liability, these also may be invoked. Thus, in a marine disaster of any dimensions, it is perfectly possible for the assurer to be out a great deal more than the value of the principal subject matter of the insurance.

To summarize on losses, the following are the principal sorts, with a brief characterization of the treatment given:

I. Under the "perils" clause, as supplemented or restricted:

A. *Particular average, or partial loss other than general average.* These are payable in full in all cases unless some other treatment is stipulated for in the policy, but it usually is; see the treatment above of the "memorandum", F.P.A. clauses, and the less frequently encountered "deductible" clause.

B. *General Average,* of two kinds: the liability to contribute in general average, and the loss falling on the goods sacrificed. General average losses are paid as a matter of law, and no policy in common use ever stipulates to the contrary.

C. *Actual Total Loss.* This largely self-explanatory term is defined above. The carrier pays the full insured value.

D. *Constructive Total Loss.* This liability arises at the election of the assured where the circumstances are such (see above) as to give him the right of election. His election must be accompanied by an abandonment of his interest to the underwriter. Payment is as for actual total loss.

II. *Under the sue-and-labor clause.* Charges incurred by the assured in fulfilling his duties under this clause are reimbursable.

III. *Under any other head of liability provided for in the policy.* The most common one, which can serve as an example, is the "collision and running down" clause, under which a claim for indemnification from collision liability is paid.

### The Valued Policy

§ 2–16. Most marine insurance policies are "valued". This means that the assurer and the assured have agreed in advance on the total value of the insured subject matter. In the absence of fraud, concealment or an intent to wager, this stipulation is binding on both

132a. See Seaboard Shipping v. Jocharanne Tugboat Co., 461 F.2d 500, 1972 A.M.C. 2151 (2d Cir. 1972), citing text; Teneria El Popo v. Home Ins. Co., 207 Misc. 84, 136 N.Y.S.2d 574, 1955 A.M.C. 328 (Sup.Ct.1954).

of them, whatever the true worth of the insured property may be.[133] The "valuation" is to be distinguished carefully from the "sum insured"; it is entirely possible that a policy may be written valuing a ship at $1,000,000, but insuring only $500,000 of that amount.

The bindingness of the valuation has many consequences. The most obvious is that, where the valuation and the insured sum are the same, that amount is the amount payable in the event of a total loss, regardless of "actual value" at the time of loss or at any other time. Where the insured sum is, say, only one-half of the stipulated value, the underwriter pays only the insured sum; the assured may have to make up the difference out of his own pocket, or there may be other policies in force.

The practice of "valuation" may, of course, turn out in the event to be advantageous to one party or the other, depending upon whether an over- or an under-valuation is stipulated for, and on the trend of the market between the issuance of the policy and the loss. But the courts have firmly refused to allow the chance hardship or windfall to produce an exception to the binding effect given to the valuation.[134] The practice of valuation, supported by this firm judicial attitude, is of high utility; it obviates the necessity of wrangling, in or out of court, over matters that are notoriously difficult of ascertainment.

The adjustment of partial losses on valued policies is a matter that can become intricate. Where the insured sum is less than the valued sum, the underwriters liability is to pay that proportion of a particular or general average that the insured sum bears to the valued sum.[135] For the rest, exactly as in the case of the total loss, the assured has to rely on other insurance if he has any, or on his own resources. The calculation of the *amount* of the partial loss payment is a little difficult, in the case of goods at least. A discussion of the problem is a good way to introduce the reader to the outskirts of the intricacies of marine insurance practice.

Let's say that goods insured under an F.P.A., A.C. clause [136] are valued at a fixed sum, and are damaged by contact with sea water, caused by a collision. For purposes of simplicity, we will assume that the damage is uniform throughout the entire shipment covered, at

133. Leo v. Ins. Co. of North America, 275 F.2d 766, 1960 A.M.C. 832 (2d Cir. 1960); Rosenthal v. Poland, 337 F. Supp. 1161, 1972 A.M.C. 627 (S.D.N.Y. 1972); New York & Cuba Mail S. S. Co. v. Royal Exchange Assur. 154 F. 315 (2d Cir. 1907); Standard Marine Ins. Co. v. Nome Beach Lighterage & Transp. Co., 133 F. 636 (9th Cir. 1904) certiorari denied 200 U.S. 616, 26 S.Ct. 753 (1906); see Aetna Ins. Co. v. United Fruit Co., 304 U.S. 430, 58 S. Ct. 959, 1938 A.M.C. 707 (1938); Arnould § 394 *et seq.*

134. See authorities cited *supra* note 133, esp. The Cuba Mail case. But the valuation clause does not work an estoppel for all purposes; a general average contribution by cargo is reimbursible by the insurer only in the proportion the policy valuation bears to the "sound value" on the basis of which the average adjustment is made. Gulf Refining Co. v. Atlantic Mutual Ins. Co., 279 U.S. 708, 49 S.Ct. 439 (1929).

135. Western Assur. Co. v. Southwestern Transp. Co., 68 F. 923 (5th Cir. 1895).

136. See *supra* at note 112.

least to the extent that apportionment is impracticable, and that the goods arrive in saleable though damaged state at the port of destination. What procedure shall be followed to arrive at the amount payable by the underwriter?

Step 1: What is wanted first is a *proportion* of damage for application to the policy value, so as to determine what the loss is to be taken to be. This is arrived at by ascertaining (1) the *actual sound worth* (*not* the policy value) of the goods, if they had arrived in an undamaged state (estimated by reference to the market), and (2) the amount the goods are actually worth (ascertained, usually, by public sale) in their damaged condition. The proportion of damage they have suffered may be expressed by a fraction, the numerator of which is the actual sound worth minus the actual damaged worth, and the denominator of which is the actual sound worth. Letting P = proportion of damage, *sw* actual sound worth, *dw* actual damaged worth, and *ad* the amount of actual damage,

$$ad = sw - dw$$

and

$$P = \frac{ad}{sw}$$

It is to be noted that the policy value plays no part in the calculations so far. This is because what is sought at this stage is not an amount of money payable, but a *fraction*, expressing the proportion of damage to the goods. It would be senseless to try to arrive at this proportion by comparing, say, the price actually brought by the damaged goods to the policy value, or by using, in place of *ad* as above defined, a figure arrived at by subtracting the actual damaged worth from the stipulated policy value, for that obviously tells us nothing about the *proportion* of damage sustained, unless it just happens that the policy value is the same as the actual sound worth. The anomalies that would be introduced by such a proceeding, where market fluctuations had made the actual sound worth differ from the policy value, may be readily seen. If, say, goods had been damaged to the extent of twenty percent, as defined in the equation above, but if the market had meanwhile risen so that the sound worth was thirty percent above the valuation in the policy, it is apparent that the goods would actually bring more in their damaged state than the policy valuation, so that, unless some method of arriving at a fraction or proportion of damage, without recourse to the policy valuation, were worked out as in the equations above, the assured would receive nothing on account of the loss sustained. On the other hand, if the market had broken so that the sound worth of the goods was now only fifty percent of the policy valuation, goods damaged to twenty percent would bring only forty percent of the policy valuation and the underwriter would have to pay sixty percent on an actual loss amounting to twenty percent. The purpose of a stipulation for value in the policy is to settle, as between the parties, the sum the goods *are to be taken to be worth;* the only way to give effect to this stipulation, in case of partial loss, is to arrive at a fraction or proportion of damage, without recourse to the policy value, and *then* to apply that fraction to the policy value to determine what the loss *is to be taken to be,* regardless of errors in valuation or fluctuations in the market.

Step 2: With the fraction $\frac{ad}{sw}$ or P ascertained, the loss (L) that, pursuant to the binding valuation (V), *is to be taken to have been suffered,* is easily arrived at: $L = P \times V$.

Step 3: If there is only one underwriter, and the sum he has insured (insured sum $= i$) is the same as the policy value, then the final step is automatic; the underwriter simply pays L as arrived at in the last step. Sometimes, however, the insured sum may not be as great as the policy valuation, either because the insured has spread the insurance among several underwriters or because he prefers to stand as his own insurer for a part of the value. In such a case, each underwriter will, for obvious reasons, pay only that proportion of L which the insured sum in the policy he has subscribed bears to the valued sum. Letting A = amount payable in such a case,

$$A = \frac{i}{V} \times L.$$

Thus, putting all the equations together:

$$A = \frac{i}{V} \times V \times \frac{sw-dw}{sw} = i \times \frac{sw-dw}{sw}$$ [137]

The above calculations, while interesting, have no more intrinsic importance than many that might have been selected from the field of marine insurance. They are a valuable example, however, of the close interworkings of law and simple mathematics in the commercial parts of the maritime law, and they happen to raise an interesting point as to the dangers of rule-sloganization when lawyers balk the arithmetic. Bedazzled by the above simple equations, some authorities have concocted the maxim "A partial loss on goods opens the policy" [138] (i. e., ousts the valuation in the policy). This slogan, which the reader who has followed the above development will realize is a rather surprising outcome of a process that gives the most carefully appropriate effect to the policy valuation, seems to be an infelicitous attempt to crystalize one or both of these aspects of the process of calculation:

1. *The fact that, in arriving at the proportion of damage to goods, the policy valuation is not taken into account.*

137. For an authoritative explanation of this process, see London Assur. v. Companhia de Moagens do Barreiro, 167 U.S. 149, 171–72, 17 S.Ct. 785, 793 (1897); also the long discussion in International Navigation Co. v. Atlantic Mutual Ins. Co., 100 F. 304 (S.D.N.Y. 1900) affirmed 108 F. 987 (2d Cir. 1901), certiorari denied 181 U.S. 623, 21 S.Ct. 926 (1901).

138. See International Navigation Co. v. Atlantic Mutual Ins. Co., *supra* note 137, 100 F. at 325; Arnould § 395.

This is, of course, not to disregard the valuation, but to refrain from using it for a purpose for which it is wholly inapt. If a claim were made under a policy for the loss overboard of a part of a shipment of steel girders, it would be impossible to establish what proportion was lost overboard by looking at the policy valuation. Similarly, if one needs to know how badly goods have been damaged by wetting, the policy valuation cannot help; if what is needed is a proportion of damage, no better method has been suggested than actual damage as against sound market worth. To apply the fraction thus derived to the policy value, for the purpose of evaluating the loss, is to give, as we have seen, the fullest effect to the valuation, by protecting it against market fluctuation.

2. *The fact that, when the equations are all put together, V, or the policy value, appears once in the numerator and once in the denominator, so that algebraic simplification cancels it out.* If this is the source of the slogan, then it is equally true that a total loss opens the policy. In such a loss, P as arrived at in Step 1 above is, *ex hypothesi,* 1, but the rest of the calculations could be set up exactly as in Steps 2 and 3: that is to say, in a total as well as in a partial loss, the insurer pays that proportion of the loss (which in the total loss case is taken to equal the value) as the insured sum bears to the value. Thus, if one wanted to go to the trouble, one could say that (since, in total loss, L = V)

$$A = V \times \frac{i}{V} = i$$ [139]

The truth is that the valuation term is given its full proper application in case of partial loss on cargo, and that giving it this application happens, as a matter of algebra, to result in its falling out of the final simplified formula for calculating the amount payable.

The mode of calculation we have gone through is not applied to hull insurance, for ships are not ordinarily sent on voyages merely to be sold at the end, and the sound market value would be much more difficult to establish than in the case of goods.[140] The cost of repairs is the usual measure of payment on claims for particular average to hull,[141] with such deductions as may be provided for in the policy or by law to make up for the replacement of old parts and materials with new.[142]

139. Values as in the calculations *supra.*

140. See Gulf Refining Co. v. Atlantic Mutual Ins. Co., 279 U.S. 708, 713, 49 S.Ct. 439, 440, 1929 A.M.C. 825 (1929).

141. Arnould § 1024; International Navigation Co. v. Atlantic Mutual Ins. Co., *supra* note 137, 100 F. at 318 *et seq.* But see Compañia Maritima Astra, S. A. v. Archdale, 134 N.Y.S.2d 20, 1954 A.M.C. 1674 (Sup.Ct.1954).

142. See Arnould § 1026; Winter 270.

## Subrogation

**§ 2–17.** Underwriters often pay losses which have occurred in such a way as to create liability in a third party to the assured. Thus, the assurer may pay for damage to goods caused by improper stowage, though the carrier of the goods is at the same time liable to the consignee for such damage. Obviously, it would be equally inequitable to allow the cargo owner to recover twice, or to allow the shipowner to escape liability merely because an insurance policy, with which he has no concern, has resulted in the indemnification of the cargo owner. Similarly, underwriters often pay for collision damage to an insured vessel though the owner-insured has a good claim against the other vessel for the damage, and the same equities appear to exist here.

The doctrine of subrogation is the device the law has adopted to solve this problem. When the assurer has paid a claim with respect to which the assured has rights against a third party, the assurer becomes, in effect, the beneficial owner of those rights, entitled to sue (either in his own name or in the name of the assured) to assert the right against the third party.[143]

The practice of abandonment works a similar result, for, in addition to his rights directly in the thing abandoned, the assured also abandons rights of action connected with the loss. Thus, the abandonment of a vessel that has become a constructive total loss in collision gives to the underwriter the assured's right of action against the other colliding vessel.[144] The subrogated underwriter may also recover for such expenses in taking care of the insured property as would have been incurred by a prudent insured owner.[145]

We cannot here go into the intricacies of subrogation.[146] But its operation in general is of interest to the student of admiralty law, because it is this doctrine perhaps more than any other that explains the great practical importance of marine insurance in the maritime law world. Particularly with the inclusive coverage afforded by many modern policies (and given the speed with which underwriters pay

143. Liverpool & Great Western Steam Co. v. Phenix Ins. Co., 129 U.S. 397, 462, 9 S.Ct. 469, 479 (1889); Mobile & Montgomery Ry. v. Jurey, 111 U.S. 584, 593–595, 4 S.Ct. 566, 571 (1884); Arnould §§ 1225 *et seq.* On the topic in insurance law generally, see King, Subrogation under Contracts Insuring Property, 30 Texas L.Rev. 62 (1951). The insurer is subrogated to the insured's rights of action only up to the amount paid on the policy; see Aetna Ins. Co. v. United Fruit Co., 304 U.S. 430, 436, 58 S.Ct. 959, 961, 1938 A.M.C. 707 (1938).

144. Comegys v. Vasse, 26 U.S. (1 Pet.) 193, 213–217 (1828).

145. Brown and Root, Inc. v. American Home Assurance Co., 353 F.2d 113, 1965 A.M.C. 2689 (5th Cir. 1965).

146. The general policy of "subrogation" has lately been searchingly questioned, see 2 Gilmore Security Interests in Personal Property § 42.7 *et seq.* (1965), but the maritime field seems at least so far to have been unaffected. Change in this field would have radical effects; see *supra*, note 3. As to subrogation of the cargo underwriter, public policy in form of this seems clearly implied in the voiding of the "benefit of insurance" clause by the Carriage of Goods by Sea Act, see *infra*, Chapter III, Part II, § 3–47.

off as contrasted with the slowness and resistance of private parties, including carriers, in dealing with claims), it is easy to see that most suits asserting commercial liabilities in admiralty are likely to be in the hands of the underwriters, who have paid off the loss long ago and who are now seeking to recoup from the party allegedly liable. This fact alone would serve to tie this chapter to virtually all of the rest of the book.

# Chapter III

# CARRIAGE OF GOODS UNDER BILLS OF LADING

## PART I. THE RELATIONSHIP OF THE BILL OF LADING TO THE CONTRACT OF SALE AND ITS USE IN FINANCING TRANSACTIONS

**§ 3–1.** A bill of lading is, in the first instance and most simply, an acknowledgement by a carrier that it has received goods for shipment. Secondly, the bill is a contract of carriage. Thirdly, if the bill is negotiable (as, for practical purposes, all ocean bills are) [1] it controls possession of the goods and is one of the indispensable documents in financing the movement of commodities and merchandise throughout the world. In Part II of this Chapter, we shall discuss principally the contractual aspect of the bill, as set forth in a hitherto little explored jungle of fine print clauses, and the limitations on freedom of contract expressed in the governing American statutes which are the Harter Act of 1893 [1a] and the Carriage of Goods by Sea Act of 1936 (hereafter referred to as Cogsa).[2] The liability of the ocean carrier for breach of its contract of carriage is only one aspect of the complex of legal rules and commercial practice relating to bills of lading. Because it is the aspect that most directly concerns the shipping industry and because the contractual liability of the ocean carrier has come to be significantly different from the contractual liability of carriers by rail, road and air, we shall in Part II explore the jungle of clause and statute in detail. Here, we shall more briefly consider the bill as a control device and as a financing document.

In the following discussion we shall take up aspects of the law of negotiable instruments, of documents of title, of sales, of letters of credit and of security transactions. Except for letters of credit, these areas of commercial law have long been governed by codifying statutes, the earliest of which were the Uniform Negotiable Instruments Law (1896) and the Uniform Sales Act (1906).[2a] These Uniform Acts have now, throughout the country, been repealed and superseded by the Uniform Commercial Code (hereafter U.C.C. or Code)

1. However, David Crystal, Inc. v. Cunard Steam-Ship Co., Ltd., 339 F.2d 295 (2d Cir. 1964), certiorari denied sub nom. John T. Clark & Son v. Cunard Steam-ship Co. Ltd., 380 U.S. 976, 85 S.Ct. 1339 (1965), apparently involved a non-negotiable bill. The goods were delivered against a delivery order which had been forged in the office of the owner-consignee's customs broker. Cunard was held liable to the owner for misdelivery but, over a dissent by Friendly, J., was allowed to recover over from its stevedore which had actually made the delivery.

1a. 27 Stat. 445 (1893) 46 U.S.C.A. §§ 190–196.

2. 49 Stat. 1207 (1936), 46 U.S.C.A. §§ 1300–1315.

2a. On the codifying statutes relating to bills of lading, see § 3–3 *infra*.

which has been enacted in all American jurisdictions except Louisiana.[2b] The Code also, for the first time, codifies the law of letters of credit (see § 3–12 *infra*). In point of fact, with respect to most of the issues we shall be concerned with, the Code makes little or no change in the pre-Code law and much of the pre-Code case law retains a continuing vitality.

### The Negotiability of Bills of Lading

**§ 3–2.** The term "negotiability", most familiar in the context of short term instruments for the payment of money, means not one but many things.[3] Its most commonly understood and most dramatic aspect is the privileged status conferred upon the good faith purchaser, known as the holder in due course. An even more important aspect of negotiability may well be the degree to which the piece of paper on which the note, bill or check is written has come to represent the debt for which the instrument is given. The debt is said to be "merged" in the instrument. Merger leads to a variety of conclusions which are commercially of the highest importance. One is that, in most circumstances, if the instrument is discharged, so is the underlying debt. A second is that the only payment which will discharge an instrument is payment to a holder—*i. e.* to one who is physically in possession of the piece of paper.[4] A third is that the instrument (and the debt) will be discharged by such a payment even though the payment is made to one who has no right to the instrument—that is, to a thief. Thus while the holder is protected by his possession of the instrument, the obligor is also protected by the rule which allows him to pay any holder.[5] And finally, creditors of a holder, who wish to reach an instrument as part of their debtor's assets, may do so only by attaching the paper itself, as if it were a chattel, and not by serving garnishment process on the obligor.

**§ 3–3.** Ocean bills of lading have been treated as negotiable for well over a hundred years.[6] Railroad bills, originally thought of as non-negotiable, gradually achieved during the nineteenth century

2b. Ezer, Uniform Commercial Code Bibliography (1972), published by the Joint Committee on Continuing Legal Education of the American Law Institute and the American Bar Association, is an invaluable reference tool on the Code.

3. For a discussion of the principal attributes of negotiability, see Gilmore, The Commercial Doctrine of Good Faith Purchase, 63 Yale L.J. 1057, 1062 *et seq.* (1954).

4. There are acts other than payment which will discharge a negotiable instrument—*e. g.*, cancellation by the holder. See generally Britton, Handbook of the Law of Bills and Notes, (2d ed. 1961) Ch. 6; U.C.C. § 3–605.

5. Under U.C.C. § 3–603 payment to a thief will not discharge the instrument if the payment is made "in bad faith." With that exception the paying party is protected (*i. e.* granted a discharge) even if he pays "with knowledge of a claim of another person to the instrument." If an adverse claimant wants to block a payment, he must either put up satisfactory indemnity or procure a restraining order.

6. Llewellyn, Cases and Materials on the Law of Sales (1930) 78. Professor Llewellyn's volume, now unfortunately out of print, contains not only a rich collection of case material but much perceptive comment on historical development and commercial practice.

what was referred to as quasi-negotiable status.[7] In the United States the Uniform Bills of Lading Act (1909)[8] gave full negotiability to bills issued in intra-state commerce; the Federal Bills of Lading Act (1916),[9] often referred to as the Pomerene Act, which largely reproduced the provisions of the earlier Uniform Act, did the same for all bills issued in the United States in interstate and foreign commerce.[10] Cogsa (1936) did not repeal or amend the Pomerene Act, which continues to apply to ocean bills.[11] Since the Pomerene Act does not apply to bills of lading issued in foreign countries for shipment to the United States, the negotiability of such bills would depend on the law of the country of issue.[12] The law of negotiability is, however, a sort of *ius gentium*—in broad outline although not in each detail everywhere the same.

A negotiable instrument calls for the payment of money and represents a debt. A bill of lading calls for the delivery of goods and represents or covers goods. The law of money instruments has developed over a three hundred year period and has been spelled out in almost infinite detail by case law as well as in the detailed provisions of the Negotiable Instruments Law of 1896 and Article 3 of the U.C.C.[12a] By contrast the law of negotiable bills of lading and similar documents of title has been a species of improvisation over the past fifty or seventy-five years. The successive codifications of the law of documents of title have been fragmentary affairs and the case law harvest has not been large. Gaps exist in the law of documents which have long since been filled in the law of instruments. As new problems arise in the documentary field the natural analogy to which the courts turn is the more fully developed law of money instruments. The law of documents of title is therefore in a sense open-ended: to a necessarily indefinable extent it is supplemented as need arises by the law of the companion field.

Article 7 of the U.C.C. on Documents of Title covers both bills of lading and warehouse receipts (which were formerly covered by the Uniform Warehouse Receipts Act (1906)). Article 7 continues the

7. See Gilmore, *op. cit. supra* note 3, at 1076–1081.

8. The text of the Act (hereafter referred to as UBLA) is set out in 4 Uniform Laws Annotated (1922).

9. 39 Stat. 538–545 (1916); 49 U.S.C.A. § 81–124.

10. The Pomerene Act, with respect to foreign commerce, covers "[b]ills of lading . . . for the transportation of goods . . . from a place in a State to a place in a foreign country. . . ." 49 U.S.C.A. § 81.

11. Section 3(4) of Cogsa (46 U.S.C.A. § 1303(4)) provides that "nothing in this Act shall be construed as repealing or limiting the application of any part of the [Pomerene] Act. . . ."

12. See § 3–19 *infra* for a discussion of conflict of laws problems.

12a. A handy compendium of NIL case law is Brannan, Negotiable Instruments Law (7th ed. by Beutel, 1948). The best general treatment of negotiable instruments law is Britton, *op. cit. supra* note 4, which has not been revised to deal with Article 3 of the U.C.C. No satisfactory general treatise on Article 3 has yet appeared although there is a considerable law review literature.

full negotiability provisions of U.B.L.A., extending them to warehouse receipts as well as to bills of lading, and in general makes little or no substantive change in the pre-Code law. The language and terminology of Article 7, however, differ notably from the language and terminology of the pre-Code Uniform Acts. The Federal (Pomerene) Act has not as yet been conformed to Article 7 and there is no reason to believe that it ever will be.

Bills issued in the United States or its territories in connection with transactions involving interstate or foreign commerce continue to be governed by the Pomerene Act, so that Article 7 is technically irrelevant. However the possibility that courts will look to Article 7 when, strictly speaking, they should look to the Pomerene Act should not be ignored and Article 7 can in any case be appealed to as an authoritative source for the resolution of ambiguities and inconsistencies in the older statute. Fortunately there has been no litigation involving the negotiability or the proper negotiation of bills of lading for a long time and there is no reason to believe that there will be any in the future. Thus the possibility of statutory confusion is a theoretical rather than a real problem.[13]

**§ 3–4.** In the adaptation of the law of money instruments to documents of title, the proposition of greatest commercial importance has been the documentary analogue to the rule that the only payment which will discharge an instrument is payment to the holder.

A carrier which has issued a non-negotiable bill of lading normally discharges its duty by delivering the goods to the named consignee; [14] the consignee need not produce the bill or even be in possession of it; the piece of paper on which the contract of carriage is written is of no importance in itself. A carrier which has issued a negotiable or order bill thereby places itself in a radically different situation. Just as the maker of a note effects his discharge only by payment to the holder, so the carrier will be discharged only by delivery to the holder of the bill.[15] The piece of paper on which the bill is written now becomes indispensable; the goods are locked up in the bill, in the same way that the debt is merged in the instrument. A seller who ships on an order bill can, by insisting on payment before the bill is delivered to his buyer, protect himself against an insolvent's obtaining possession of the goods much more effectually than by his common-law remedy of stoppage in transit.[16] A bank which advances

13. Since the Pomerene Act continues to apply to ocean bills, the following discussion will be documented with citations to that Act as well as to the sections of UBLA from which the sections of the Pomerene Act were copied. References to the analogous sections of U.C.C. Article 7 have also been included.

14. UBLA § 12; Pomerene Act § 9 (49 U.S.C.A. § 89); U.C.C. § 7–403.

15. UBLA §§ 12, 13; Pomerene Act §§ 9, 10 (49 U.S.C.A. §§ 89, 90); U.C.C. § 7–403.

16. The remedy, now codified in U.C.C. § 2–705, allows a seller to order a carrier to stop delivery to a consignee and redeliver the goods to the seller if the buyer has become insolvent. However, "If a negotiable document of title has been issued for goods the bailee [i. e. the carrier] is not obliged

money against goods covered by a negotiable bill of lading has the goods as security so long as it or a correspondent retains possession of the bill. The carrier which delivers goods without taking up and canceling its order bill remains liable to anyone who has purchased the bill for value and in good faith, before or after the improper delivery, and even though the delivery was made to a person legally entitled to possession of the goods.[17]

To the rule just discussed there is one exception whose theoretical interest is greater than its commercial importance. A bill may be issued to a shipper who has no title to the goods. The thief, who has procured the bill to be issued, will seek to obtain advances against it, so there are good chances that the bill will end up in the hands of a good faith purchaser. On this state of facts the law protects the true owner of the goods and, incidentally, the carrier which has innocently issued its bill to the thief. The true owner may replevy the goods from the carrier or from anyone into whose hands they have passed after delivery.[18] The carrier is doubly protected: if, without knowledge of the true owner's claim, it delivers the goods to the holder of the bill, the carrier is discharged.[19] If, on the other hand, it delivers the goods to the true owner without taking up the outstanding bill, it is equally protected against any good faith purchaser of the bill. The section of the Pomerene Act which makes the carrier liable to the holder of an order bill for delivery of the goods without cancellation of the bill provides that the carrier is to be so liable only with respect to bills "the negotiation of which would transfer the right to the pos-

to obey a notification to stop until surrender of the document" (§ 2–705(3)(c)). The stoppage in transit remedy, much used by sellers in the nineteenth century, has now almost dropped from sight, no doubt because goods are shipped under negotiable bills whenever the seller mistrusts his buyer's ability to pay. Furthermore modern case law has developed the doctrine that receipt of goods on credit by an insolvent buyer is a species of fraud which entitles a seller who moves promptly to reclaim the goods from the insolvent buyer or, possibly, his trustee in bankruptcy. A leading case on this branch of sales law is California Conserving Co. v. D'Avanzo, 60 F.2d 528 (2d Cir. 1933). The "fraud by insolvency" rule, is codified in U.C.C. § 2–702. In re Kravitz, 278 F.2d 820 (3d Cir. 1960) made it doubtful whether the seller's right to reclaim under § 2–702 as originally drafted was effective against the buyer's trustee in bankruptcy. In many states (e. g. New York) § 2–702 has been amended in an attempt to deal with the threat of Kravitz.

17. UBLA § 14; Pomerene Act § 11 (49 U.S.C.A. § 91); U.C.C. § 7–403. In addition to the exception discussed in the following paragraph of the text, the carrier is also privileged to sell goods, without canceling the bill, to satisfy its lien or because goods are unclaimed, perishable or hazardous.

18. Against the carrier, see Salant v. Pennsylvania R. Co., 188 App.Div. 851, 177 N.Y.S. 475 (1919), affirmed 231 N. Y. 607, 132 N.E. 907 (1921); Lux, Jr., Mercantile Co. v. Jones, 177 Ark. 342, 6 S.W.2d 302 (1928). Abbe v. Erie R. Co., 97 N.J.L. 212, 116 A. 778, (1922) is not to the contrary, despite its citation in 4 Uniform Laws Anno. (Supp. 1955) s. v. § 24. Against a good faith purchaser, see Kendall Produce Co., Inc. v. Terminal Warehouse & Transfer Co., 295 Pa. 450, 145 A. 511 (1929) ("true owner" vs. bank which had discounted draft on security of attached bill of lading); Albers Bros. Milling Co. v. Drumheller, 280 F. 217 (W.D. Wash.1922).

19. UBLA §§ 12, 13; Pomerene Act §§ 9, 10 (49 U.S.C.A. §§ 89, 90); U.C.C. §§ 7–403, 7–404.

session of the goods," [20] and a bill issued to one without title is not such a bill. The issuance of a bill to one who has voidable title—that is, one who has acquired the goods by fraud rather than by theft—does carry the title to the goods with it, and in disputes between defrauded owner of the goods and good faith purchaser of the bill, the title derived from the bill will prevail.[21] The determination of who owns the goods is not, and ought not to be, any business of the carrier; in all such cases it will be well advised to require the claimants to interplead, and in most cases it does just that.[22]

**§ 3–5.** Other aspects of negotiability do not require extended discussion here. A person to whom a bill has been "duly negotiated" acquires title to the goods, as well as title to the document itself, except in the single case of the bill issued to one without title to the goods; the taker by due negotiation also, and subject to the same exception, acquires "the direct obligation of the carrier" under its bill.[23] An order bill properly indorsed may be negotiated "by any person in possession of the same, however such possession may have been acquired" [24] and the validity of the negotiation is not impaired by its being a breach of duty on the part of the transferor or "by the fact that the owner of the bill was deprived of the possession of the same by fraud, accident, mistake, duress, loss, theft, or conversion".[25] The purchaser who is protected is, of course, the purchaser for value, in good faith and without notice of claims.[26] By analogy to the negoti-

20. UBLA § 14; Pomerene Act § 11 (49 U.S.C.A. § 91); U.C.C. §§ 7–403, 7–503. The U.C.C. formulation (§ 7–403) is that "the bailee must deliver the goods to a person entitled under the document . . . unless . . . the bailee establishes . . . (a) delivery of the goods to a person whose receipt was rightful as against the claimant. . . ." Under § 7–503 a bill issued to a person without title "confers no right in goods" against a true owner.

21. A person who has voidable title to goods has the power to transfer perfect title to a purchaser in good faith, without notice and for value. This was the rule of Uniform Sales Act § 24, which is carried forward in U.C.C. § 2–403. A purchaser who takes a bill of lading by due negotiation acquires "such title to the goods as the consignee and consignor had or had power to convey to a purchaser in good faith and for value." UBLA § 32; Pomerene Act § 31 (49 U.S.C.A. § 111). U.C.C. § 7–503 is to the same effect. Since a consignor with voidable title has power to transfer perfect title to a purchaser of the goods, a purchaser of a bill issued to such a consignor likewise gets perfect title.

22. Section 20 of UBLA (§ 17 of the Pomerene Act, 49 U.S.C.A. § 97) provides that "If more than one person claims the title or possession of goods, the carrier may require all known claimants to interplead . . . ." The Article 7 interpleader section is § 7–603.

23. UBLA § 32(b); Pomerene Act § 31(b) (49 U.S.C.A. § 111(b); U.C.C. § 7–502.

24. UBLA § 31; Pomerene Act § 30 (49 U.S.C.A. § 110); U.C.C. § 7–501.

25. UBLA § 38; Pomerene Act § 37 (49 U.S.C.A. § 117); U.C.C. § 7–502. The terms "loss" and "theft" appear in the Pomerene Act but not in UBLA. The U.C.C. provision follows the Pomerene Act.

26. *Ibid.* U.C.C. § 7–501(4) adds the idea that a negotiation which is "not in the regular course of business or financing or involves receiving the document in settlement or payment of a money obligation" is not a "due negotiation."

able instrument law rule that a holder in due course must take the instrument before maturity, the documentary case law, in the absence of specific statutory language, has developed an analogous concept of "staleness" with reference to bills of lading: one who purchases a bill outstanding more than a reasonable time after its issue does not take by "due negotiation" and receives only the title of his transferor.[27] The cases have been few and it is far from clear how old a bill must be to be stale. Under the N. I. L. every instrument was presumed to have been issued for a valuable consideration [28] and every holder was presumed to be a holder in due course; [29] thus the burden of proof normally borne by plaintiff in a contract action was cast on the defendant.[29a] No doubt the same presumptions run in favor of purchasers of order bills; the statutes, however, are blank and the issue has not been litigated.[29b] Negotiation of order bills is made by indorsement of the order party plus delivery: the indorsement may be blank or special, and, as under negotiable instrument law a blank indorsement converts the bill to "bearer paper" so that subsequent negotiation may be by delivery alone.[30] Unlike the general indorser of a negotiable instrument, who engages that if the bill is not paid on due presentment he will pay it, the indorser of a bill does not engage to take back the bill if the carrier fails to make delivery. The indorser warrants only the genuiness of the bill and, in substance, his own good faith and authority to transfer both bill and goods; [31] if the indorser is a seller of goods, but not if he is a bank to which the bill has been pledged, he also makes the standard sales warranties with respect to the quality and condition of the goods.[32] The warranty as to

27. See discussion in Saugerties Bank v. Delaware & Hudson Co., 236 N.Y. 425, 141 N.E. 904 (1923). U.C.C. Article 7 contains no express provision on "staleness." However the Official Comment to § 7–501 remarks that under the "regular course of business or financing" provision of § 7–501(4) (see note 26 *supra*) "unexplained staleness of a bill of lading may appropriately be recognized as negating a negotiation in 'regular' course."

28. NIL § 24.

29. NIL § 59.

29a. Article 3 of the U.C.C. reaches the same result by providing (§ 3–307) that, except in cases where forgery is put in issue, "production of the instrument entitles a holder to recover on it unless the defendant establishes a defense."

29b. Official Comment 4 to U.C.C. § 7–501 is to the effect that the presumptions are to be implied even though they are not explicitly stated in Article 7.

30. UBLA §§ 28, 29; Pomerene Act §§ 27, 28 (49 U.S.C.A. §§ 107, 108); U.C.C. § 7–501.

31. UBLA § 35; Pomerene Act § 34 (49 U.S.C.A. § 114); U.C.C. §§ 7–505; 7–507.

32. *Ibid.* That banks do not, by their indorsements of bills of lading, make "sales warranties" results from UBLA § 37, Pomerene Act § 36 (49 U.S.C.A. § 116). See Bank of Italy v. Colla, 118 Ohio St. 459, 161 N.E. 330 (1928); Stacey-Vorwerk Co. v. Buck, 42 Wyo. 136, 291 P. 809 (1930); *cf.* Bishop & Co., Inc. v. Midland Bank, 84 F.2d 585 (9th Cir. 1936). A few early cases to the contrary have been either overruled or discredited. See Note 26 Colum.L.Rev. 63 (1926) and a communication on the same subject from Professor Williston (the draftsman of UBLA) in 26 Colum.L.Rev. 330 (1926). However, under § 7–508 collecting banks do not warrant the genuineness of a bill and under § 7–507 sellers who negotiate or transfer bills do not make any warranties with respect to the goods (although such warranties,

the goods obviously does not cover damage to the goods in transit unless, by the terms of the contract of sale, the risk of loss remains on the seller during the transit period. Where a purchaser of a bill fails to secure his transferor's indorsement and such an indorsement is necessary for negotiation, the statutes provide that the missing indorsement may be compelled; as under negotiable instrument law the indorsement (for purposes of the "dueness" of the negotiation) takes effect when made and not at the time when the bill was transferred.[33] Finally, when an order bill has been issued, the goods may no longer be attached or levied upon; a creditor seeking to reach the goods must by appropriate process first obtain possession of the document.[34] To the rule just stated there is the recurrent exception in favor of the true owner whose goods have been stolen; he may disregard the outstanding bill and replevy the goods directly from the carrier.[35]

### Sale of Goods: The Passage of Property and the Risk of Loss: Mercantile Terms of Shipment: F.O.B.—C.I.F.—F.A.S.

**§ 3–6.** It has been said that the law of sales of goods, both in its case law formulation during the 19th century and in its codification in the Uniform Sales Act, was barely adequate to deal with the transfer in a local market, for cash, between a seller and a buyer who dealt face to face, of such uncomplicated objects as horses and haystacks. During the 1920's and 1930's a favorite theme of academic writers in the law reviews was that sales law, as exemplified in the Uniform Sales Act, had become hopelessly out of touch with the commercial realities of the 20th century. The point was made that the number of sales cases, as reported in the digests, had sharply declined since the beginning of the century. The explanation for that decline, or so the argument ran, was that the mercantile community, disenchanted with the law, had somehow organized a mass flight from the courts and had elected to settle its disputes extra-legally, principally through the medium of commercial arbitration.[36] Revision of the Uniform Sales Act became an urgent goal of law reform.

We need not concern ourselves with the merits of the case against the Sales Act—although in this quarter there is some disposition to believe that the Act was a good deal better than its detractors made out and that the American mercantile community could have gone on living under its provisions quite as easily as the mercantile communi-

unless effectively disclaimed, would arise under the contract of sale and U.C.C. Article 2 on Sales).

33. UBLA § 34; Pomerene Act § 33 (49 U.S.C.A. § 113); U.C.C. § 7–506.

34. UBLA § 25; Pomerene Act § 24 (49 U.S.C.A. § 104) provides that a creditor in attaching a bill "shall be entitled to such aid from courts of appropriate jurisdiction by injunction and otherwise . . . as is allowed at law or in equity in regard to property which cannot readily be attached or levied upon by ordinary legal process." U.C.C. § 7–602 is to the same effect.

35. See cases cited note 18 *supra*.

36. For a different explanation of why the number of cases reported in the digests under the rubric "Sales" may have declined, see Gilmore, On Statutory Obsolescence, 39 U. of Colo.L. Rev. 461 (1967).

ties in England and the former British dominions have gone on living under the provisions of the Sale of Goods Act of 1887. Through a series of accidents the campaign to revise the Sales Act ultimately flowered in the grandiose project of recodifying the entire commercial law in the Uniform Commercial Code. Professor Karl Llewellyn, who had been the leading academic critic of the original Sales Act, became the principal draftsman of the new one—eventually known as U.C.C. Article 2 on Sales—as well as the Chief Reporter for the Code as a whole.

From early drafts of Article 2—then known as the Uniform Revised Sales Act—it is clear that Professor Llewellyn had initially contemplated a radical restructuring of sales law. However, the conservative memberships of the sponsoring organizations [37] did not take kindly to radical law reform. In the lengthy course of drafting, the Chief Reporter's bright vision of a brave, new mercantile world suffered the fate of either being rejected outright or of being watered down into a kind of mush. Article 2 in its final form differed from the Uniform Sales Act principally in details of style and in the adoption of a novel terminology.

Even though the revolution did not quite take place, the shift from the Uniform Sales Act to Article 2 will unsettle sales law for a generation or more. An Article 2 provision may have been intended to restate, without change of meaning, the analogous Sales Act section from which it was drawn. However, the restatement comes out in quite different language. No practitioner can afford to assume that the two formulations mean the same thing until he has heard directly from the relevant court of last resort. It is also true that commercial sales litigation—as distinguished from consumer sales litigation—comes up only sporadically, mostly in periods of depression, so that the message may be a long time coming. Another unsettling factor is that courts, during the Sales Act period, took the statute lightly. Nothing is less common in the Sales Act case law than a careful analysis of the actual statutory text. Now-a-days courts, weaned on the Internal Revenue Code, treat statutes like Holy Writ and brood anxiously over commas. Article 2, although to a lesser degree than the rest of the Code, is drafted in the currently fashionable style which aims at an unearthly precision and tightness. Case-law adaptation of the statutory rules to the new problems which will arise in litigation will be difficult to the point of impossibility if current methods of statutory interpretation are applied to a statute which is itself drafted in the current style. There is, finally, a peculiar time-gap problem. The bulk of the Article 2 drafting was done in the early 1940's along lines laid down in the 1930's. In most states Article 2, along with the rest of the Code, came into force during the middle and late 1960's. The courts thus face the problem of dealing with the issues which will be litigated during the 1970's and 1980's in the light of guide-lines laid

37. The American Law Institute and the National Conference of Commissioners on Uniform State Laws.

down before World War II. No doubt the detached professorial observer in his study will enjoy the spectacle of things to come in sales law a good deal more than the harried practitioners and judges on the firing line.

§ 3–7. In this section, before taking up the mercantile terms of shipment (such as F.O.B. and C.I.F.) which are incorporated in most commercial contracts, we shall briefly explore the sales law background out of which the mercantile terms grew.[38]

During its formative period—that is, the first half of the 19th century—sales law seems to have been thought of as being essentially a branch of property law. The courts developed rules for determining the exact point in time at which the ownership of the goods or, in the term which came into use, the property in the goods [39] passed from seller to buyer. Under the rules, which will be described presently, the property typically passed while the goods were still in the seller's possession and control—that is, before tender or delivery to the buyer. From that point on the goods were held at the buyer's risk—if they were accidentally damaged or destroyed, he still had to pay for them at the agreed contract price.[40] Furthermore the property-passing point determined the remedies available on breach or repudiation. On breach or repudiation before the property passed, the non-breaching party was limited to a contract action for damages—which were typically measured by the differential between contract price and market price on the date when and at the place where the goods ought to have been delivered.[41] On breach or repudiation after the property passed, what can be described as property remedies became available. The seller could sue the defaulting buyer for the full price of the goods (holding or storing them at buyer's expense until the conclusion of the litigation) [42] or, alternatively, could sell (or "resell") the goods and collect the contract price plus the expenses of resale less the proceeds of resale.[43] The buyer, at least theoretically, could re-

38. The standard treatise on pre-Code sales law is Williston, Sales (3rd ed. 1948, in 4 vols.). Professor Williston was the draftsman of the Uniform Sales Act, (hereafter referred to as U.S.A.). The Williston treatise has not been, and presumably will not be, revised to take account of U.C.C. Article 2. On Article 2 see Duesenberg & King, Sales and Bulk Transfers under the Uniform Commercial Code (1966).

39. The terms "property" and "title" were used interchangeably. In the Uniform Sales Act Professor Williston adopted the practice of using the term "property" with respect to rights between seller and buyer and the term "title" with respect to rights of third parties. That refined distinction did not, however, come into most legal or judicial discussion.

40. USA § 22.

41. USA § 64. Western Hat & Mfg. Co. v. Berkner Bros., Inc., 172 Minn. 4, 214 N.W. 475 (1927) was a leading case on the proposition that an action for the price did not lie unless property had passed. On the computation of damages (contract less market) under the Sales Act, Frankel v. Foreman & Clark, Inc., 33 F.2d 83 (2d Cir. 1929) is instructive, and see further note 43 *infra*.

42. USA § 63. An interesting case, with a brilliantly obscure opinion by Cardozo, J., is Glass & Co. v. Misroch, 239 N.Y. 475, 147 N.E. 71 (1925).

43. USA § 60. If seller, by a turn in the market, should resell the goods for more than the contract price he

cover the goods in an action of replevin or their value in an action for conversion. However, in the real world, the buyer's property remedies withered on the vine; for reasons which we need not explore here he rarely, if ever, got either the goods or a money judgment for their value.[44]

It is clear enough that the common-law property rules worked to the distinct disadvantage of the buyer. He became responsible for goods which he could not control and in which, at the time the rules were formulated, he probably did not have an insurable interest even if insurance had been available. He could not get the goods without paying for them, unless the seller had agreed to extend credit, and indeed stood to lose the goods both to competing purchasers from the seller and to the seller's creditors (as well as, in later times, the seller's trustee in bankruptcy). The reasons for the adoption or invention of the rules by the early 19th century courts, both English and American, are obscure. Conceivably they may have been a remote echo of fraudulent conveyance law which, from the 17th century on, had stigmatized as fraudulent the retention of possession of goods by a seller after they had been sold.[45] From this point of view it was the buyer's duty to get the goods from the seller with the least possible delay—so that the seller's creditors would not be misled by his continuing possession and apparent ownership. Certainly a pre-insurance rule of law which cast the risk of loss on the buyer at the earliest possible point and well before delivery encouraged him to do just that.

When sales law was codified both in England and in this country, no thought seems to have been given to the possibility or desirability of making any changes in the well-established and familiar property rules. In their pure common-law state they were incorpo-

could keep the profit without accounting to the buyer. Resale could be made even after seller had commenced an action for the price. An excellent discussion of seller's right to resell under USA § 60 is found in D'Aprille v. Turner-Looker Co., 239 N.Y. 427, 147 N.E. 15, 38 A.L.R. 1426 (1925) (opinion by Cardozo, J., with Lehman, J. dissenting). Technically, damages measured by the difference between contract and resale were not the same as damages measured by contract and market, since the relevant market price was that obtaining on the scheduled date of delivery and in a damage action under USA § 64 evidence of resale at a later date should not be admissible in evidence. See Frankel v. Foreman & Clark, Inc., 33 F.2d 83 (2d Cir. 1929). The distinction, however, tended to break down during the latter part of the Sales Act period and many courts admitted evidence of later resale without question in cases where title had clearly not passed at the time of breach. Cases illustrative of this trend were Riverside Coal Co. v. Elman Coal Co., 114 Conn. 492, 150 A. 280 (1932), Obrecht v. Crawford, 175 Md. 385, 2 A.2d 1 (1938). See generally Comment, Lost Profits as Contract Damages: Problems of Proof and Limitations on Recovery 65 Yale L.J. 992 (1956). Article 2 (which does not make the availability of remedies depend on the location of title) apparently allows the seller a free choice in all cases between the contract less market and the contract less resale measures of damages; see §§ 2–703, 2–706 and 2–708.

44. See the cases cited in note 47 *infra*.

45. This venerable rule seems first to have been announced in Twyne's Case, 3 Co.Rep. 806, 76 Eng.Rep. 809 (Star Chamber, 1601).

rated lock, stock and barrel in the codifying statutes and used to determine both the risk-shifting point and the shift from contract to property remedies.

We may briefly summarize the rules as they appeared in the Uniform Sales Act, stated as a series of presumptions. In the case of specific goods in a deliverable state property was presumed to pass at the time when the contract was executed, even though the time of delivery or of payment or both was postponed. In the case of a sale of specific goods where some action like packaging, sorting, weighing or counting the goods remained to be done at the time the contract was executed, property passed automatically when the required action was performed. When the subject matter of a contract of sale was goods which at the time the contract was executed were either unascertained or not yet in existence, the property concept became more complicated: property did not pass automatically when the seller ascertained, acquired, or manufactured the goods but passed only when, following ascertainment, acquisition or manufacture, there occurred what was called an unconditional appropriation of the goods to the contract.[46] "Appropriation" was a mystical term of uncertain contours and shifting content. Its distinguishing feature was that it required a "bilateral consent" on the part of both buyer and seller; nothing that the seller could do unilaterally by setting the goods aside, marking or tagging them as property of the buyer, or by giving notice would pass the property if the buyer's consent was found to be lacking. On the other hand, the buyer's consent could be "expressed or implied, and may be given before or after the appropriation is made."[47]

The future or forward contract of sale of goods to be manufactured or otherwise acquired by the seller had become commercially predominant by the end of the 19th century. Such contracts were, of course, governed by the "appropriation" rules, whose open-ended fuzziness may have been their greatest strength. Armed with such a weapon, it would be a poor court which could not arrive at what seemed to it a just solution in any case, at whatever cost to predictability in the law. In all probability a careful study of the turn of the century case law would disclose that the old common-law property

46. The property rules were stated in USA § 19.

47. *Ibid.* Illustrative cases on appropriation are Western Hat & Mfg. Co. v. Berkner Bros., Inc., 172 Minn. 4, 214 N.W. 475 (1927); Bundy v. Meyer, 148 Minn. 252, 181 N.W. 345 (1921); Mitchell v. Weiner, 94 Conn. 446, 109 A. 164 (1920). In Proctor & Gamble Co. v. Peters, White & Co., 233 N.Y. 97, 134 N.E. 849 (1922) the buyer attempted unsuccessfully to support a conversion action on the theory that appropriation had taken place before the goods were resold to a third party. From the buyer's point of view, he could lose out against seller's creditors even though appropriation was conceded since in many states retention of goods by a seller after sale (*i. e.* passage of property) was either presumptively or conclusively fraudulent against creditors. See USA § 26 and Ely & Walker Dry Goods Co. v. Adams Mfg. Co., Inc., 105 F.2d 906 (2d Cir. 1939).

rules, even before their incorporation in the codifying statutes, had entered into a period of breakdown.

At all times and in all places the mercantile community hates with a passionate hatred any trace of uncertainty or confusion in the applicable law. The ambiguities of property law were, clearly enough, poor materials with which to build a stable structure of commercial law. The merchants, therefore, proceeded to manufacture their own bricks by developing a series of shipping terms—F.O.B., F.A.S., C.I.F. and the like—which began to appear in the case reports round about 1900. These terms were designed to regulate by contract the rights of the parties to sales transactions in which seller and buyer were at a distance from each other and, of necessity, seller had to arrange for the shipment of goods to buyer. Naturally enough the codifying statutes had nothing to say about these new-fangled mercantile inventions. The Uniform Sales Act remarked, in terms so vague as to be meaningless, that if a seller "in pursuance of a contract to sell" delivered conforming goods to a carrier, he was presumed to have "unconditionally appropriated" them unless the contract required seller to pay the freight or to deliver the goods "to the buyer or at a particular place." [48]

The true meaning of the mercantile shipment terms was thus left to be worked out by the courts. These shorthand descriptions of contractual arrangements have come, after a half century of use and of judicial construction, to have well-understood and reasonably precise meanings.[49] No doubt some of the inferences which the courts drew from these mercantile symbols came initially as a surprise to the business men who had invented them, and some of the early cases show the courts wrestling with a jargon which might better have been Greek from the sense which the unhappy judges were able to make of it. In time, however, the legal meaning and the business understanding of the shipment terms came together, each having borrowed from the other. This field of law, in which there has been almost no litigation for a generation, is one of the happiest examples of what sometimes appears to be the merely theoretical possibility of a harmonious adjustment between business practice and the law which purports to govern it.

The shipment terms serve several functions. 1) They determine the point at which the risk of loss passes from seller to buyer. 2)

**48.** USA § 19 (rule 4(2)).

**49.** American mercantile understanding of the meaning of the shipment terms is set out in the Revised American Foreign Trade Definitions (1941), which were adopted by a committee representing the United States Chamber of Commerce, the National Council of American Importers, Inc., and the National Foreign Trade Council, Inc. The Uniform Sales Act contained no specific reference to the shipment terms. Article 2 reformulates the Foreign Trade Definitions (hereafter FTD) in §§ 2–319, 2–320, and 2–321. The Article 2 reformulation is discussed in § 3–8 *infra*. The International Chamber of Commerce has also issued a set of International Rules for the Interpretation of Trade Terms ("Incoterms 1953") which differ in some respects from the American formulation.

They determine what performance by the seller amounts to a tender which will put the buyer, if he thereafter refuses to accept delivery, in breach. 3) They are a widely used means of quoting price.

In a shipment F.O.B. (Free on Board), the risk passes to buyer at the F.O.B. point. If the contract term is "F.O.B. cars at seller's factory", the buyer bears the risk of loss during transit. The seller completes his performance when he delivers conforming goods to the carrier. The price quoted does not include freight. Contrariwise if the term is "F.O.B. point of destination", seller bears the risk during transit, completes his performance only by tender at that point, and the price quoted normally includes freight.[50]

The term F.A.S. (Free Alongside) is a variant of F.O.B., used exclusively in connection with water carriage. The usual phrasing is "F.A.S. vessel" at some named port. The seller completes his performance and the risk passes to buyer on delivery of the goods alongside the vessel in whatever manner may be customary in the port; the buyer furnishes instructions covering the name, sailing date and loading berth of the vessel.[51] There is an important distinction between the term "F.A.S. vessel" and the term "F.O.B. vessel." In the former case seller delivers at the wharf but is under no duty to see to the loading: a "received for shipment" bill of lading would be an appropriate document for him to tender. "F.O.B. vessel", however, requires seller to bear the risk until the loading has been completed; only an "on board" bill of lading would evidence the completion of his duties.[52]

The principal shipment term used in overseas transactions has long been C.I.F. (Cost, Insurance, Freight). The C.I.F. term is followed by the name of the port of destination: when goods are shipped from Liverpool to New York, the term reads "C.I.F. New York." A C.I.F. price quotation includes the invoice price of the goods plus insurance and freight to the named port of destination.[53] The seller

50. See FTD II–IIF; U.C.C. § 2–319; 2 Williston *op. cit. supra* note 38 at §§ 280–280b.

51. See FTD III; U.C.C. § 2–319.

52. See FTD II–E and III; U.C.C. § 2–319 (in particular Comment 4).

53. Since the freight is included in the CIF price, seller normally prepays the freight. Not infrequently, however, the freight is deducted from the invoice and the goods shipped "freight collect". FTD III provides that seller must "provide and pay for transportation to named point of destination" and Comment 6, after referring to the practice of shipping "freight collect", cautions "*the Seller should always prepay the ocean freight* unless he has a specific agreement with the Buyer, in advance, that goods can be shipped freight collect" (italics in original). U.C.C. § 2–320(2)(b) provides that Seller must "load the goods and obtain a receipt from the carrier . . . showing that the freight has been paid or provided for" and Comment 5 adds that the Seller "has no option to ship 'freight collect' unless the agreement so provides". Under a contract which requires the buyer to pay on presentation of documents it is hard to see how he can be prejudiced by a "freight collect" shipment; indeed he will be benefited since in most cases the goods will not arrive until after the documents have been presented. On the other hand, under a contract which stipulates for credit, the buyer is prejudiced by a "freight collect" shipment if he is made to pay the freight before the ex-

completes his performance by procuring the necessary documents (bill of lading, insurance policy or certificate and invoice plus any others that may be called for by the particular contract) and forwarding them to the buyer. Unless the contract calls for an "on board" bill of lading, a "received for shipment" bill is appropriate. Under a C.I.F. term the buyer (for whose benefit the insurance is carried) bears the risk of loss in transit.[54] Where buyer prefers to take out his own insurance (as he will when he carries a blanket or floating policy), the term used is "C. & F." (Cost and Freight). The "C. & F." term has the same meaning, so far as seller's performance and the passage of risk are concerned, as C.I.F. except that the seller does not see to the insurance coverage.[55]

Confusion was generated in the early days of the development of the law of C.I.F. contracts by the propensity of merchants unfamiliar with the meaning of the term to annex inconsistent contractual conditions. Thus a contract which provides "C.I.F. New York—No arrival, no sale" is hopelessly self-contradictory. The C.I.F. term means that buyer bears the risk of loss in transit (but has the insurance to reimburse him). "No arrival, no sale" means exactly the opposite.[56] The two terms cannot stand together; if litigation ensues, the court must disregard one or the other. At one time there was much case-law discussion of the nature of a "true C.I.F. contract" and a few unfortunate holdings by courts which seemed to feel that any reference in the contract to the situation as it might exist at the port of destination was necessarily inconsistent with the C.I.F. term.[57] The education of both mercantile and judicial communities seems to have made great strides. There have been no recent cases involving such impossible combinations as "C.I.F.—No arrival no sale"; on the other hand the courts have learned to construe terms like "Net landed weights to govern" as calling for incidental adjust-

piration of the credit period. Nevertheless, in Dixon, Irmaos & Cia. Ltda. v. Chase Nat. Bank, 144 F.2d 759 (2d Cir. 1944), certiorari denied 324 U.S. 850, 65 S.Ct. 687 (1945), where seller shipped "freight collect" under a contract extending a 90 day credit, the Second Circuit affirmed a finding of the trial court that "the tender of documents showing a deduction of freight from the invoices was not a deviation from the requirement of defendant's credits [*i. e.* letters of credit issued by the Chase Bank] calling for C.I.F. shipment" (144 F.2d 759, 763). As the provisions of FTD and U.C.C. quoted above indicate, the Dixon, Irmaos holding on this point, was out of line with mercantile and banking practice. The Dixon, Irmaos case is further discussed § 3–17 *infra*.

54. See FTD V; U.C.C. § 2-320; 2 Williston *op. cit. supra* note 38, §§ 280c–280e.

55. See FTD IV; U.C.C. § 2–320(4), Comments 16 and 17.

56. FTD has no provision on the meaning of the "no arrival, no sale" term. U.C.C. § 2–324 provides (in part) that such a term means that "the seller must properly ship conforming goods and if they arrive by any means he must tender them on arrival but he assumes no obligation that the goods will arrive unless he has caused the non-arrival". Comment 4 to § 2–324 discusses the meaning to be attributed to a "no arrival, no sale" term in a C.I.F. contract.

57. See discussion and cases cited in 2 Williston *op. cit. supra* note 38 at § 280f.

ments when the goods arrive safely, but not as being destructive of the normal C.I.F. arrangement.[58]

It will be noted that a common feature of all the shipment terms was to make the time of delivery to the carrier the earliest possible point at which the risk of loss could shift to buyer. Thus the mercantile community had in effect contracted out of the property rules of sales law under which the buyer bore the risk of goods still in the seller's possession and control.

§ 3–8. The most widely publicized innovation in the Code's recodification of sales law is that Article 2 abandons the touchstone of "property" as a criterion for determining the rights of the parties to the sales transaction. Obviously the "property" or "title" still has to be somewhere and its location will continue to determine such things as the incidence of property taxes. Thus, of necessity, Article 2 provides (in § 2–401) rules for determining where the "title" is, while sternly warning that the "rights, obligations and remedies" of seller and buyer are to be determined "irrespective of title to the goods." Under Article 2 these "rights, obligations and remedies" are determined, not by metaphysical inquiries into who has the "property," but—as the Code supporters put it—functionally with reference to performance under the sales contract. It might therefore be assumed that the pre-Code law on such matters as the point at which the risk of loss shifts from seller to buyer would become irrelevant on the date of the Code's going into force in any jurisdiction. The assumption would be hazardous. Except for its adoption of a radically new terminology, Article 2 carries the pre-Code law forward without substantial change.

Article 2 (§§ 2–319, 2–320 and 2–321) "codifies" the true meaning of the mercantile shipment terms which are typically incorporated in the commercial contracts with which we are concerned. The Article 2 formulations were designed to reproduce without change of meaning the American mercantile understanding of the terms as stated in the Revised American Foreign Trade Definition (1941). Necessarily the Foreign Trade Definitions were restated in Code terminology—so that there is at least a theoretical possibility of confusion. And it is obvious that a statutory formulation is a different animal from a formulation agreed to by private mercantile associations, however prestigious they may be. The freezing of the meaning of the shipment terms in a statute vintage 1940's will pose obvious problems if changing business practices make it necessary or de-

58. 2 Williston, *loc. cit.* note 57 *supra*, concluded his discussion with the remark that "if possible, apparently inconsistent terms should be harmonized, and if this cannot be done a special provision should be held to modify the ordinary inferences from a c. i. f. contract only so far as is necessarily required, unless the inconsistency goes to the very essence of the characteristic features of c. i. f. bargains." To the same effect is U.C.C. § 2–320, Comment 14: "the dominant outlines of the C.I.F. term are so well understood commercially that any variation should, whenever reasonably possible, be read as falling within those dominant outlines rather than as destroying the whole meaning of [the C.I.F.] term . . ."

sirable to reformulate the mercantile understanding.[58a] Those problems have not, however, yet arisen: the summary of what the terms mean which was set out in the preceding section still holds, regardless of whether reference is had to the Foreign Trade Definitions or to Article 2.

The Sales Act term "appropriation" is not used in Article 2. Section 2–501 goes into detail about what is called "identification" of goods to a contract and at first glance "identification" appears to be the Article 2 analogue to "appropriation." Indeed the rules for determining when goods are identified to the contract closely follow the property rules of the Sales Act with the exception that, in the case of "future goods," there is no requirement that the buyer consent to the seller's "identification" of the goods. However, the only consequences of "identification" under § 2–501 are that the buyer receives an "insurable interest" and what is mysteriously referred to as a "special property" in the goods identified. It is easier to say what the § 2–501 "special property" is not than what it is. It is not "title," which is handled quite differently under § 2–401 and it has nothing to do with the shifting of the risk of loss.

The Article 2 rules on risk-shifting are set out in § 2–509. If the contract "requires or authorizes the seller to ship the goods by carrier," subsection (1) provides that the risk shifts at the delivery point. In the case of commercial contracts which incorporate one of the mercantile shipment terms that point would be determined by the Article 2 (or FTD) formulation of the true meaning of the term. Since almost all commercial shipments are made F.O.B., F.A.S., C.I.F. or what not and since the Article 2 formulation is designed merely to restate the pre-Code mercantile and judicial consensus, there is in effect no change from pre-Code law (even if the FTD are not incorporated by reference). Subsection (2) of § 2–509 covers the case of goods "held by a bailee to be delivered without being moved." Subsection (3) states a rule for all cases not within subsections (1) or (2)—that is, for cases where the seller does not ship the goods and where the goods are not held by a bailee. The rule is that the risk passes to the buyer on receipt of the goods if the seller is a merchant and on tender if the seller is not a merchant. The residual rule of subsection (3), which is of scant commercial importance, thus rejects the old property rules under which the buyer could bear the risk of goods still in the seller's possession and control. The Article 2 risk of loss treatment is rounded out in § 2–510 which provides in substance that, if one party is in breach, he continues to bear the risk even though, apart from the breach, the § 2–509 rules would allocate the risk to the other party. However, the non-breaching party under §

**58a.** It should be noted that the Article 2 definitions of the terms all carry the tag "unless otherwise agreed." Thus it remains possible for the parties to contract for the Foreign Trade Definitions (as they now exist or as they may be subsequently modified). Despite that flexibility the possibilities of confusion are obvious if it ever comes to pass that the official public statute says one thing and the private mercantile "statute" says a different thing.

2–510 can recover only "to the extent of any deficiency in his effective insurance coverage"—which seems to mean that the party in breach gets the benefit of the non-breaching party's insurance.[58b]

## The Documentary Sale

**§ 3–9.** In a documentary contract of sale the buyer is required to pay (or accept) drafts on presentation of documents, without the right to inspect the goods beforehand. To state the case from the seller's point of view: in a documentary contract tender is made by presentation of documents and not by delivery of goods. By selling "against documents" the seller insures that an insolvent or fraudulent buyer will not get the goods without paying for them. The goods move under a negotiable bill of lading; the buyer cannot get the goods from the carrier until he has the bill; he will receive the bill only after payment or acceptance. In sales within the continental United States, a documentary term is unusual: most shipments are made on open credit under non-negotiable bills of lading. Only a seller who doubts the solvency or the honesty of a buyer will insist on payment against documents. In overseas transactions, on the other hand, a documentary arrangement is almost always used. The reasons are obvious: credit information about the distant buyer is hard to come by; litigation in a foreign country is risky and expensive. Overseas documentary contracts today usually involve the issuance of a letter of credit by the buyer's bank. Before taking up the letter of credit,[59] however, we shall describe the simple documentary sale in which no bank financing is involved beyond the occasional discount of a draft by seller's bank.

The seller first procures from the carrier a bill of lading to his own order. He then draws a bill of exchange or draft on the buyer in the amount of the contract price. The draft may be drawn payable on demand (or at sight) or payable at some stated period (30, 60 or 90 days) after acceptance. The draft is sometimes made payable to the order of a bank with which the seller has made arrangements to handle the paper for collection; more frequently it is made payable to the seller's own order (the seller thus appearing as both drawer and payee) and is also indorsed by the seller. To the draft the seller attaches the bill of lading which he indorses, a commercial invoice and whatever other documents may be required by the contract (*e. g.* an insurance policy or certificate [60] in a C.I.F. shipment, consular certifi-

**58b.** For a discussion of the insurance provision and of a comparable provision in U.C.C. Article 9, see 2 Gilmore, Security Interests in Personal Property § 42.7 (1965).

**59.** See § 3–12 *infra* for a discussion of letters of credit.

**60.** Insurance certificates are issued under blanket insurance policies and entitle the holder of the certificate to rights under the policy. Under English case law such certificates have been held not to be a proper tender under a C.I.F. contract. Under American case law and practice the certificates are a good tender. See Kunglig Jarnvagsstyrelsen v. Dexter & Carpenter, Inc., 299 F. 991 (S.D.N.Y.1924), affirmed 20 F.2d 307 (2d Cir. 1927), certiorari denied 275 U.S. 497, 48 S.Ct. 121 (1927). FTD V provides that among the documents which seller

cates of quality or of origin etc. etc.). The seller hands the set of documents to a bank for collection; if the seller's credit standing is satisfactory the bank may, in addition to acting as a collecting agent, discount the draft—*i. e.* make available to seller for immediate withdrawal the face amount of the draft less the bank discount charge, which is calculated with reference to the number of days it will presumably take to make the collection. The status of a discounting bank with respect to the documents in its possession is as follows: 1) if the buyer (rightfully or wrongfully) dishonors the draft, the bank may have recourse on the draft against the seller as drawer or indorser but does not have any action on the draft against the buyer as drawee;[61] 2) the bank holds the bill of lading in pledge and may sell the bill (or the goods) to satisfy its loan. The bank, whether it has discounted the draft or merely taken it for collection, forwards the documents to a bank at the buyer's place of business. That bank presents the draft and documents to the buyer. If buyer refuses to pay or accept, the presenting bank may return the documents or request from seller's bank instructions on how to proceed. If the buyer honors a demand draft, the presenting bank delivers the bill of lading and other documents to the buyer on payment. If the draft calls for payment at some period after acceptance, the question arises whether the bill of lading is to be delivered to the buyer against his acceptance or whether the bank should retain the bill until payment of the draft at maturity. The Uniform Bills of Lading Act provided that where a draft was drawn payable at more than three days after sight, it should be presumed that the buyer was entitled to the bill of lading on his mere acceptance; the UBLA provision is carried forward in U.C.C. Article 2.[62] For no discernible reason, that provision was omitted from the Federal Bills of Lading (Pomerene) Act. The omission is not thought to be of any significance, and the rule of UBLA and Article 2, which is in accord with commercial reality, should apply: a time draft implies an extension of credit, and unless buyer is entitled to the goods during the credit period he might as well buy for cash. Acceptance of a time draft with the bill of lading held back until payment makes no kind of sense. On the other hand, once the bill goes over to the buyer, the seller (or discounting bank) has lost any security in the goods; the buyer is now directly liable on his acceptance, but

must procure are an "insurance policy or negotiable insurance certificate". U.C.C. § 2–320(2)(c) requires seller to "obtain a policy or certificate of insurance" and discusses the point in Comment 9.

61. The standard negotiable instruments rule is that a draft (or bill of exchange) "of itself" does not operate as an assignment of the funds in the hands of the drawee available for its payment and the drawee is not liable on the bill unless and until he accepts it. This rule which developed at common law was codified in the N.I.L. and is carried forward without change in U.C.C. § 3–409. The buyer can—*e. g.* by accepting the goods if they are shipped under a straight bill of lading or delivered to him by mistake of the carrier under an order bill—render himself liable on the draft on what is sometimes called a theory of "virtual acceptance". See such cases as George F. Hinrichs, Inc. v. Standard Trust & Sav. Bank, 279 F. 382 (2d Cir. 1922); First Nat. Bank of McClusky v. Rogers-Amundson-Flynn Co., 151 Minn. 243, 186 N.W. 575 (1922).

62. UBLA § 41; U.C.C. § 2–514.

that liability is worth whatever the buyer is worth. Since most domestic documentary arrangements are inspired by seller's distrust of buyer, the acceptance is an unsatisfactory substitute for security in the goods. The seller who is willing to extend credit is about as well off under an open account shipment as he is under the more cumbersome arrangement of delivery of the bill of lading against buyer's acceptance. Perhaps for that reason the use of time drafts in domestic documentary sales is a rarity.

**§ 3–10.** Under a documentary contract the seller makes a proper tender only by a due presentment of the specified documents. If the contract calls for presentment in New York on September 15 of a bill of lading covering a carload of grapes of specified grade and quality by rail from California, the buyer is under no duty to accept anything but a tender of the bill of lading itself.[63] The seller may not put the buyer in breach by tendering the grapes in New York on September 15 or on any other date. The buyer may properly refuse a tender of the goods for any reason or for no reason. A seller who insists on payment against documents puts himself at the mercy of his buyer unless he is able to present a full set of documents in perfect order.[64]

The law of the sale of goods has traditionally been marked by a rule of tender much stricter than the analogous rules in real property transactions. The seller's tender must conform exactly as to time, place, manner, quantity and quality—or the technically minded buyer is privileged to reject, without regard to whether he is damaged by the non-conformity.[65] In practice the harsh edges of the perfect ten-

63. The importance of exact documentary tender is well illustrated by Mitsubishi Goshi Kaisha v. J. Aron & Co., 16 F.2d 185 (2d Cir. 1926). The contract called for shipment "f. o. b. sellers' tank car, Pacific Coast", payment "net cash against shipping documents". Seller tendered a bill of lading covering a car which had in fact left from the Pacific Coast at a proper time. The car had, however, been either diverted or reconsigned at Dallas and the bill of lading read from Dallas to East Rochester instead of from a Pacific Coast point. No question was raised by the buyer as to the conformity of the goods or the time of their arrival. *Held:* the tender was bad. "There is no room in commercial contracts," wrote Judge Learned Hand, "for the doctrine of substantial performance." *Cf.*, however, Lamborn v. National Bank of Commerce, 276 U.S. 469, 48 S.Ct. 378 (1928) applying a somewhat less strict approach, with four justices dissenting. See Bank of Nova Scotia v. San Miguel, 196 F.2d 950 (1st Cir. 1952), an interesting case where buyer rejected conforming goods because of an imperfect documentary tender.

64. National Importing & Trading Co. v. E. A. Bear & Co., 324 Ill. 346, 155 N.E. 343 (1927), although holding for the seller, indicates the difficulty that courts find in dealing with the slightest discrepancy in a documentary context. The contract called for "shipment from the Orient . . . in April . . . terms of payment: Net cash sight draft against bill of lading." Seller tendered a bill of lading showing the goods on board March 31 although it was conceded that the ship sailed on April 1. The majority of the Court concluded that "[W]e cannot hold, as a matter of law that time of shipment was of the essence of this contract, and that the vendee had a right to rescind the same . . . [because] the albumen was placed upon the steamer on March 31 instead of April 1." Two judges dissented, remarking that "[a] shipment on March 31 was no more a shipment in April than a shipment on January 31 or May 31."

65. See 2 Williston *op. cit. supra* note 38 §§ 453a, 458 *et seq.* USA § 44 stated a strict rule of tender with respect to quantity. Article 2, which relaxes

der rule have been smoothed down in cases where the goods themselves are tendered: either a clause in the contract or trade custom or the past practice of the parties will be construed to permit minor discrepancies and an innocent delay of a day or two will not necessarily be fatal. The softening of tender requirements has been particularly noticeable in long-term or instalment contracts where a rule of "materiality" has developed under which the buyer is not privileged to denounce the entire contract because of a merely technical breach in one instalment.[66] In the documentary field, however, the rule of perfect tender—or of "strict compliance"—continues to maintain itself to an extraordinary degree.

**§ 3–11.** The documentary buyer must pay "blind"; unless the contract expressly provides otherwise, he has no right to inspect the goods beforehand. He is not, of course, stripped of his contractual remedies if, on inspection after payment, the goods prove to be non-conforming. However, since the price will already have been paid, the buyer's action for damages or recovery of the price will have to be brought where jurisdiction over the seller can be procured. The buyer's remedy is against the seller alone: discounting or collecting banks which have indorsed the bill of lading make no warranties as to the condition of the goods [67] and attempts by buyers to attach or garnish the money paid over on seller's drafts have regularly met with failure.[68] The documentary sales contract does not however insulate the seller from buyer's claims asserted in advance of payment to nearly the degree that a bank letter of credit does. If the buyer believes that the goods are defective—as may be the case when previous shipments by the same seller have not met specifications or when the carrier has permitted an unauthorized inspection—he may refuse payment of the draft. If the seller thereafter sues for the price, all the

tender rules in instalment contracts, see note 66 *infra*, restates the strict tender rule with respect to all other contracts in § 2–601: "if the goods or the tender of delivery fail in any respect to conform to the contract, the buyer may . . . reject the whole . . ." On the strict tender rule in sales law see the materials collected in Kessler & Gilmore, Contracts—Cases and Materials, 823–845 (1970).

66. Under USA § 45, relating to instalment contracts, "it depends in each case on the terms of the contract and the circumstances of the case, whether the breach of contract is so material as to justify the injured party in refusing to proceed further and suing for damages for breach . . .". Helgar Corp. v. Warner's Features, Inc., 222 N.Y. 449, 119 N.E. 113 (1918) contains an excellent discussion by Cardozo, J. of the common-law background. U.C.C. § 2–612 goes even further toward a "substantial performance" rule in providing that a buyer must accept a non-conforming instalment if seller gives adequate assurance of cure unless "the non-conformity or default with respect to one or more instalments substantially impairs the value of the whole contract". Even under the Code, however, the substantial performance rule of § 2–612 does not apply "if the non-conformity is a defect in the required documents".

67. See note 32 *supra* and parallel text.

68. See Vickers v. Machinery Warehouse & Sales Co., 111 Wash. 576, 191 P. 869 (1920); Blatz Brewing Co. v. Richardson & Richardson, 245 Wis. 567, 15 N.W.2d 819 (1944). Occasionally the attachment has been allowed, as in National Bank of Commerce v. Morgan, 207 Ala. 65, 92 So. 10 (1921). There do not appear to be any recent cases of this type.

buyer's defenses and set-offs will be available to him as in any action on a contract.

The taking out by a seller of a bill of lading to his own order reserves not only effective control of the goods but a security interest in the goods as well. However the reservation of the security interest has no effect on the normal rules for the allocation of risk of loss.[69] That is to say, the terms C.I.F., F.O.B., F.A.S. and the like continue to have their normal operation although used in conjunction with a seller's order bill of lading.

Any contract of sale is documentary which expressly provides for "payment (or acceptance) against documents." Since the documentary term is uncommon in transactions within the continental United States, it will not be read into a contract by implication. In overseas transactions the reverse is true and consequently the shipment terms which are most closely associated with such transactions have come to be looked on as carrying the documentary term by necessary implication. Thus the C.I.F. term has long been thought to require the buyer to pay against documents without the right of inspection whether or not the "payment against documents" language appears in the contract.[70] Article 2 also applies the C.I.F. rule to shipments F.A.S. and F.O.B. vessel.[71]

## The Bank Letter of Credit

**§ 3–12.** A bank letter of credit (or, more simply, a bank credit) may be described as an engagement, undertaking or promise by a bank to pay money to or on behalf of the customer for whom it has issued the credit. Definitional purists have been made unhappy by the fact that banks enter into many engagements to pay money to or for their customers which are not, in commercial understanding, letters of credit. In practice, however, no one has ever had any trouble distinguishing a letter of credit from a loan agreement or a guaranty although it is true that there are such things as authorities to pay or purchase which ambiguously straddle the line. The best, or at all events the easiest, solution to the riddle is to say that any document issued by a bank which says it is a letter of credit is a letter of credit.[72]

69. See U.C.C. § 2–505. The Article 2 rules on risk of loss (§§ 2–509, 2–510) have been discussed § 3–8 *supra*.

70. FTD V, Comment 7: "*The Buyer* should recognize that *he does not have the right to insist on inspection of goods prior to accepting the documents*" (italics in original). U.C.C. § 2–320, Comment 12. The proposition was first established in a celebrated English case, Clemens Horst & Co. v. Biddell Bros., [1912] A.C. 18 (House of Lords, 1911), the most notable opinion in the case having been that delivered by Kennedy, L. J. in the Court of Appeal ([1911] 1 K.B. 934, 952).

71. U.C.C. § 2–319(4).

72. The leading American text on letters of credit is Ward and Harfield, Bank Credits and Acceptance (4th ed. 1958). U.C.C. Article 5, which will be presently discussed in the text, codifies, to some extent, the law relating to letters of credit. Mr. Henry Harfield, the co-author of Ward and Harfield, has contributed a "Practice Commentary" to Article 5 as it appears in McKinney's Consolidated Laws of New York Annotated.

Wichita Eagle & Beacon Publishing Co. v. Pacific National Bank of San Fran-

Credits may be "clean" or "documentary." Under a clean credit the bank agrees to pay drafts drawn under the letter (and invites other banks to negotiate such drafts) on production of the letter by the beneficiary. The traveler's letter of credit is the most familiar example of the clean credit. Under a documentary letter of credit the bank agrees to pay drafts only if the drafts are accompanied by documents which are specified in the letter. In the following discussion we shall be concerned only with documentary credits.

Documentary credits are most commonly used in financing international sales transactions. They could equally well be used in financing domestic sales transactions but in fact rarely are: an attempt to promote their use in domestic transactions after World War II met with scant success.[72a] Documentary credits are also used in a wide range of non-sales transactions.[72b] We shall, however, limit our dis-

cisco, 343 F.Supp. 332 (N.D.Cal.1971) is instructive on the definitional issue. The Bank contended that its "Letter of Credit" was really a performance bond or surety agreement. Judge Levin, giving judgment against the Bank, held in effect that anything the Bank chose to describe as a Letter of Credit was a letter of credit. The events in the case had taken place before U.C.C. Article 5 had become effective in California, but Judge Levin remarked that he "drew guidance" from § 5–102 which, in more elegant language, takes the position stated in the text. On the Wichita Eagle case, see further note 72b *infra*.

See further on the definitional issue the Barclay's Bank case digested in note 72b *infra* at end.

**72a.** Mentschikoff, Letters of Credit: The Need for Uniform Legislation, 23 U. of Chi.L.Rev. 571, 615 *et seq.* (1956) took an optimistic view of the prospects for increasing domestic use of letters of credit financing. Domestication of the letter of credit was, in Professor Mentschikoff's view, one reason why nationally uniform legislation was urgently needed. Professor Mentschikoff was Associate Chief Reporter for the Uniform Commercial Code. She devoted the bulk of her article to an attack on the position taken by a few New York banking counsel who had urged the deletion of Article 5 from the Code. What eventually happened in New York will be explained *infra* this section.

**72b.** For example, in Fair Pavillions, Inc. v. First Nat. City Bank, 19 N.Y. 2d 512, 227 N.E.2d 839 (1967) the beneficiary of the credit was a building contractor who had contracted to construct a building at the New York City World's Fair for Exhibitions de France, Inc. This turned out to have been a prudent arrangement. Both Exhibitions de France and its American representative collapsed into insolvency and the contractor, after litigation, recovered from the bank.

In Wichita Eagle & Beacon Publishing Co. v. Pacific National Bank of San Francisco, 343 F.Supp. 332 (N.D.Cal. 1971) the beneficiaries of the credit were the lessors under a 99 year lease. As in the New York Fair Pavillions case, this turned out to have been a prudent arrangement on the part of the lessors. The Bank's defense in the Wichita Eagle case was that the Letter of Credit was not really a letter of credit (see Note 72 *supra* at end). It is to be expected that banks will make this contention when credits are used in unusual situations in order to benefit from the generous rules on discharge of sureties.

In Barclay's Bank D.C.O. v. Mercantile Nat. Bank, 339 F.Supp. 457 (N.D.Ga. 1972) an Atlanta bank which had either issued or confirmed a credit sought to escape liability on the ground that the "credit" was really a "guaranty" and therefore ultra vires and void. This sort of thing is also to be expected as banks which have not previously engaged in the letter of credit business get their feet wet. The "credit" was held to be a credit under U.C.C. § 5–103 and the bank was held liable.

For a novel use of a letter of credit in a maritime setting, see Brock v. S/S Southampton, 1964 A.M.C. 800A (D. Or.1964), 231 F.Supp. 283, 1964 A.M.C.

cussion to credits issued in connection with international sales transactions which involve overseas shipment. In such a transaction the buyer under the sales contract is the bank's "customer" for whose account the letter of credit is issued. The bank is the "issuer." The seller is the "beneficiary." [72c] In the letter the bank undertakes to pay the seller's drafts up to the amount of the credit if the drafts are presented before the expiration date of the credit and are accompanied by the required documents. The letter of credit, by substituting the bank's promise to pay for the buyer's promise under the sales contract, protects the seller against the substantial risks which he incurs by shipping goods to a distant point even against documents: as beneficiary of the credit the seller need no longer worry about the buyer's becoming insolvent while the goods are in transit or about the buyer's unjustified refusal to pay the price when documents are presented. The typical American bank credit of this type involves the importation of goods into this country from abroad—thus an American buyer and a foreign seller. However, American banks also issue credits (or "confirm" credits originally issued by banks in other countries) in connection with shipments which have no points of contact in this country. And American sellers whose foreign buyers have established credits abroad may insist on the credits being "confirmed" in this country.

The seller who requires his buyer to provide a letter of credit naturally insists on a credit from an internationally known bank. Thus letter of credit financing has always been, and presumably always will be, the quasi-monopoly of the largest banks in the major financial centers of the world. In this country the New York City banks, which got into the letter of credit business shortly after World War I when New York challenged London as the world's money center, have played the predominant role.

The law relating to letters of credit was developed in this country by the courts during the 1920's and 1930's. The bulk of the litigation was localized in New York, with the result that only in New York did there come into existence anything even resembling a reasonably comprehensive body of case law. Elsewhere the case law harvest was scanty or non-existent. In time, and particularly after World War II, banks throughout the country, who were eager to capture what they regarded as their rightful share of a lucrative financing business, found the absence of precedents disturbing. Perhaps, the case arising, the local court would follow the New York precedents which were generally regarded (by bankers) as satisfactory. But

1905 (D.Or.1964): at the request of a shipowner and his agent banks issued their letters of credit to a maritime union to be used in paying crew's wages. The proceeds having been so used, the banks were held entitled to maritime liens against the ship (see Chapter IX, § 9–20, Note 89). In the Venizelos case, text following Note 72j *infra*, the letter ran to the shipowner as beneficiary and covered payments of freight and demurrage under a charter-party.

72c. This is the Article 5 terminology (see § 5–103) which has come into general use.

perhaps not. One could only wait and see—a situation which bank counsel find revolting.

The sponsors and draftsmen of the Uniform Commercial Code decided to include in their project a codification of the law of letters of credit. During the early stages of the drafting of the letter of credit statute—which became Article 5 of the Code—the group of New York City letter of credit specialists had little or nothing to do with it. There does not seem to have been any intent to exclude the New York group on the part of the Code authorities, who were on the whole not ill-disposed toward banks in New York or anywhere else. But the fact was that the original version of Article 5 was put together without the advice or consent of the New York lawyers who regarded themselves as pre-eminently qualified in this esoteric branch of law.

When the Code was first seriously proposed for enactment in the early 1950's, the large New York City banks and their counsel arrayed themselves in hard-line opposition.[72d] Their hostility, initially aroused by Article 5, was generalized to include the entire Code and indeed the bankers' campaign against the Code succeeded in holding up its enactment in New York for the better part of ten years.[72e] Meanwhile, in the rest of the country the banking community, after some initial hesitation, came out in favor of the Code, including Article 5, and in many states worked actively to secure the Code's enactment.

The Code sponsors, who were understandably eager to add New York to the list of Code states, agreed to rewrite Article 5 to meet the criticisms directed against it in New York.[72f] In the course of the rewrite many detailed provisions were deleted from the original version and the final draft became almost skeletonic—which may not have been altogether a bad thing. The sponsors even consented to the inclusion of the following extraordinary provision (§ 5–102(3)):

> "This Article deals with some but not all of the rules and concepts of letters of credit as such rules or concepts have developed prior to this act or may hereafter develop. The fact that this Article states a rule does not by itself require, imply or negate application of the same or a converse rule to a situation not provided for or to a person not specified by this Article."

In that skeletonized form and with § 5–102(3) directing the courts not to take the Article seriously in any case Article 5 was accepted in all the states which enacted the Code—except New York.

The New York opposition succeeded in obtaining from the New York legislature what might be described as the functional equivalent

**72d.** See generally the article by Mentschikoff cited note 72a *supra*.

**72e.** The Code was enacted in New York in 1962 and became effective in 1964.

**72f.** See the 1963 Report of the New York Law Revision Commission. Many of the Commission's criticisms are referred to in the Practice Commentary and in the New York Annotations attached to Article 5 in McKinney's Consolidated Laws of New York Annotated.

of a declaration that Article 5, as enacted, should not apply to credits issued by New York banks. In language that would have appealed to that great draftsman, Humpty-Dumpty, § 5–102(4) of the New York version provides:

> "Unless otherwise agreed, this Article 5 does not apply to a letter of credit or a credit if by its terms or by agreement, course of dealing or usage of trade such letter of credit is subject in whole or in part to the Uniform Customs and Practice for Commercial Documentary Credits fixed by the Thirteenth or by any subsequent Congress of the International Chamber of Commerce."

The provision just quoted does not say in so many words that the International Chamber of Commerce may rewrite the New York law of letters of credit whenever it sees fit but its failure to say exactly that may be put down to inadvertence on the part of the draftsman. The Uniform Customs and Practice for Commercial Documentary Credits (hereafter UCP) was first promulgated by the International Chamber of Commerce before World War II, was revised in 1951 and revised again in 1962.[72g] The banks in most trading countries throughout the world have, through their banking associations, adhered to the 1962 revision of UCP, which became effective July 1, 1963. (The Code itself became effective in New York on September 27, 1964.)

UCP is not in any sense a comprehensive "codification" of letter of credit law or even practice. Apart from a few general guiding provisions, UCP is a sort of manual for bank clerks. It goes into immense detail about the kinds of documents that banks will (or will not) accept and explains the meaning to be attributed to such phrases as "circa," "about," "middle of the month" and so on. On this level UCP serves an extremely useful function: it insures, so far as language can, that banks throughout the world will give a uniform meaning to terms frequently used in credits. When UCP goes beyond the bank clerk level, the reader will do well to bear in mind that the UCP rules, in their successive revisions, were drafted by international bankers and their counsel in a distinctly non-adversary setting. It is true that only professionals engage in letter of credit financing. It is also true that the banks which issue credits and the merchants who use the credits do not at all points share the same interest. And it is, finally, true that the banks wrote the rules.

Let us assume, arguendo, that no one will be ungentlemanly enough to suggest that New York § 5–102(4) represents an unconstitutional delegation of legislative power to the International Chamber of Commerce in Congress assembled. Under § 5–102(4) the effect of "subjecting" a credit to UCP is to make Article 5 inapplicable. The credit then becomes the creature of New York case law, old and

72g. UCP, in the 1962 revision, is reprinted in West's McKinney's Forms, Uniform Commercial Code under § 5–102. Brochure # 222 of the International Chamber of Commerce sets forth both the French and English texts of UCP.

new. It is also not unreasonable to take the statutory reference to UCP as a legislative endorsement of whatever UCP, in its present version or in any future version, may contain. That is, at all events, the understanding of the situation in New York banking circles.[72h] The credit "by its terms" may incorporate UCP by reference. The New York "Practice Commentary" to § 5–102(4) suggests that banks may unilaterally thus incorporate UCP without notice to or authorization from its customer. A credit may also become "subject" to UCP by "agreement, course of dealing and usage of trade." The Practice Commentary goes on to suggest that this means that a credit which makes no reference to UCP may nevertheless be subject to it (and not to Article 5) even though the beneficiary may never have heard of UCP and may have assumed that he was getting an Article 5 credit. "It is normally distasteful," says the Practice Commentary, "to subject one party to a contract to a body of rules as to whose applicability he has neither acquiesced nor been notified. Nevertheless, this appears to be the result required and intended by [§ 5–102(4)]. . . ." It should finally be noted that § 5–102(4) is oddly prefaced by the phrase "unless otherwise agreed"—a bit of semantic nonsense which seems to mean (if it means anything) that Article 5 (or parts of it) could be made relevant by "agreement" (whose agreement?) even though the credit was "subject" to UCP.

It is too early to tell what the courts will make of this act of "abdication" by the New York legislature.[72i] Venizelos, S. A. v. Chase Manhattan Bank [72j] may be a straw in the wind. Chase had confirmed a credit originally issued by a bank in Mexico. In determining the liability of a "confirming bank," Judge Smith, for the Second Circuit, cited the relevant sections of Article 5 (§§ 5–103(1)(f), 5–107(2)) without referring to the slightly different treatment of the question in UCP Article 3 and without inquiring whether Chase's confirmation had in some way become "subject" to UCP. Fair Pavillions, Inc. v. First Nat. City Bank [72k] may be another straw. In the Appellate Division [72l] Stevens, J. (giving judgment for the bank) seems to have assumed that Article 5 was relevant and made no reference to UCP. The Court of Appeals reversed and ordered judgment entered for the plaintiff-beneficiary. Van Voorhis, J., for the Court of Appeals, made no reference in his opinion either to Article 5 or to UCP but remarked that the cancellation clause in the credit, if construed as the bank contended that it should be construed, would be "a drastic provision which . . . would place one party at the mercy of another. That is against the general policy of the law [case citation omitted]." It may be that "the general policy of the law" and even

72h. See the Practice Commentary (note 72 *supra*) to § 5–102(4).

72i. The word "abdication" is taken from Mr. Henry Harfield's Practice Commentary to § 5–102(4) (see note 72 *supra*).

72j. 425 F.2d 461, 1970 A.M.C. 1421 (2d Cir. 1970).

72k. 19 N.Y.2d 512, 227 N.E.2d 839 (1967).

72*l*. 24 A.D.2d 109, 264 N.Y.S.2d 255 (1965).

Article 5 itself have more of a future in New York than was envisioned by the draftsman of § 5–102(4).[72m]

We have discussed the New York situation at length because New York has been, and will continue to be, predominant in the development of letter of credit law. New York lawyers now have their own peculiar problems. In other states Article 5 will be the primary source of law even with respect to credits which incorporate UCP—although it must be remembered that Article 5, as enacted, had already been rewritten to meet, so far as it was possible to do so, the wishes of the New York bar. Article 5 in its present "skeletonized" form, will frequently have to be supplemented by case law precedents. In using the current New York letter of credit cases, non-New Yorkers will be well advised to give thought to the altogether extraordinary situation in which the New York courts now find themselves.

**§ 3–13.** Involved in a letter of credit arrangement are three separate contracts. There is, first, the contract of sale between seller and buyer. Secondly, there is the contract between the issuing bank and its customer, the buyer, which provides for reimbursement of any advances made by the bank for its customer's account. Thirdly, there is the letter of credit itself, which is in substance a promise by the bank to pay drafts drawn by the beneficiary, the seller, up to a stated amount if presented at the bank before the expiration date of the credit with specified documents attached.

Few things are more clearly settled in the law than that the three contracts which make up the letter of credit arrangement are to be maintained in a state of perpetual separation. The bank's obligation under its letter is absolute, provided only that the terms of the letter have been complied with. The bank will not be excused from honoring drafts because, by reason of its customer's insolvency, it can no longer expect reimbursement. Nor will known non-conformity of the goods excuse the bank, even when the drafts are in the hands of the seller himself.[73] And when drafts have come into the hands of a hold-

**72m.** It seems in the highest degree unlikely that either the confirmation in Venizelos or the credit in Fair Pavillions was not made "subject" to UCP (which, as indicated in the text, had a relevant provision on the liability of a confirming bank). There is no suggestion in any of the opinions delivered in the two cases that counsel for the banks had objected to the introduction of the Article 5 material. In Marine Midland Grace Co. of N. Y. v. Banco del Pais, 261 F.Supp. 884 (S.D.N.Y. 1966) the credits involved expressly incorporated UCP. The court noted that, because of the incorporation, Article 5 did not apply to the case.

73. Maurice O'Meara Co. v. National Park Bank, 239 N.Y. 386, 146 N.E. 636, 39 A.L.R. 747 (1925). In Sztejn v. J. Henry Schroder Banking Corp., 177 Misc. 719, 31 N.Y.S.2d 631 (Sup.Ct. 1941) Justice Shientag held (in denying a motion to dismiss the complaint) that a bank which had issued a letter of credit would be restrained from honoring drafts presented by one not a holder in due course where the allegations as to the nonconformity of the goods evidenced fraud and not a "mere" breach of warranty. U.C.C. § 5–114 codifies both the O'Meara case and the Sztejn limitation on (or interpretation of) it. See further the second appeal in the Banco Espanol case discussed in note 77 *infra*.

er in due course, the issuing bank must pay even when the accompanying documents are known to have been forged.[74] As UCP puts it:

> "Credits, by their nature, are separate transactions from the sales or other contracts on which they may be based and banks are in no way concerned with or bound by such contracts. . . . In documentary credit operations, all parties concerned deal in documents and not in goods." [75]

The bank is entitled to reimbursement from its customer only if it pays against a proper set of documents. Its primary (indeed its only) duty toward its customer is to examine the documents with "reasonable care to ascertain that they appear on their face to be in accordance with the terms and conditions of the credit." [76] Beyond the documents the bank is not obliged or even allowed to go. The rule of strict compliance or of perfect tender here applies with special force. At least in theory the bank must reject a tender which deviates in the slightest degree from the ideal. In practice the rule is modified from necessity: it would be a rare set of documents that could meet the impossible standards of purity which the theory demands, and credits are, after all, designed to facilitate payments, not to serve as escape hatches for buyers who have repented of their bargains.[77] Nevertheless, at a time of sharp market breaks, a bank officer who cannot, at his customer's request, discover some plausible reason for dishonoring drafts is hardly worthy of the name.

It is of obvious importance that the description of the goods in the documents should correspond with their description in the letter of credit. Nevertheless, each of the documents will contain a description, and it will be a careful and a lucky seller who can insure that the several descriptions match exactly. Too many documents are filled out by too many different hands—steamship employees, insur-

74. See U.C.C. § 5–114.

75. UCP General Provision C; Article 8. On UCP, see § 3–12 *supra*. Quotations from UCP in the text are, unless otherwise indicated, from the 1962 Revision.

76. UCP Article 7. U.C.C. § 5–109 says that "An issuer must examine documents with care so as to ascertain that on their face they appear to comply with the terms of the credit" and further provides that "An issuer's obligation to its customer includes good faith and observance of any general banking usage . . ."

77. Ward & Harfield, *op. cit. supra* note 72, after stating the rule of strict compliance, remark (at p. 77): "Like most theories, however, this is one which has been altered in practice by pragmatic considerations. The fact is that banks frequently pay, notwithstanding deviations from the terms of the letter of credit . . ."

Banco Espanol de Credito v. State Street Bank and Trust Co., 385 F.2d 230 (1st Cir. 1967), certiorari denied 390 U.S. 1013, 88 S.Ct. 1263 (1968) is an excellent illustration of the need to temper the theoretical rule of strict documentary compliance to commercial realities. In a remarkable opinion, Judge Coffin collected many authorities, old and new. On a second appeal following further proceedings, 409 F.2d 711 (1st Cir. 1969), the State Street Bank argued that it was excused from honoring drafts drawn under its credits under the rule of the Sztejn case as codified in U.C.C. § 5–114(2). (See note 73 *supra*.) *Held* that Banco Espanol had become a holder in due course of the drafts, so that the excuse was not available.

ance company clerks, government functionaries—for verbal identity to be a likely issue. The one document which is always under the seller's control is the commercial invoice. Therefore, as UCP provides:

> "The description of the goods in the commercial invoice must correspond with the description in the credit. In the remaining documents the goods may be described in general terms." [78]

Despite which helpful statement, it is clear that the description in general terms in the bill of lading or insurance certificate must be close enough to the particular description in the commercial invoice and the credit so that no reasonable man—or no reasonable bank—could doubt that the two descriptions refer to the same lot of goods.[79] So the decision goes back to the bank, which is after all paying out its own money.

In theory the bill of lading called for by a credit must be "clean": that is, it must bear no notations which indicate that the goods or the containers in which they are packed were, when received by the carrier, in any manner defective. A bill bearing such a notation is "foul" and not a document which "on its face appears to be in order". At this point the interests of shipper and carrier are opposed: the shipper wants a clean bill, with which he can compel the bank to honor his drafts; the carrier, to protect itself from claims, insists on noting on the bill all possible reservations as to the "apparent good order and condition" of the goods received. Since the carrier controls the form in which its bills are issued, a technically clean bill is as common as a white blackbird, a blue moon, or a pink elephant.[80]

78. Article 30.

79. In Laudisi v. American Exchange Nat. Bank, 239 N.Y. 234, 146 N.E. 347 (1924) the credit covered a shipment of Alicante Bouchez grapes. The invoice described the grapes in the terms used in the credit, but the bill of lading read simply "grapes". *Held*: the tender was good. Cf. however Bank of Italy v. Merchants' Nat. Bank, 236 N.Y. 106, 140 N.E. 211 (1923) in which the credit called for "dried grapes" and the bill of lading covered "raisins". *Held*: an improper tender. In Rayner & Co., Ltd. v. Hambro's Bank, Ltd. [1943] 1 K.B. 37, it was held that a credit covering "Coromandel groundnuts" was not satisfied by presentation of a bill of lading for "machine-shelled groundnut kernels" (the accompanying invoice being in proper terms) and that evidence of a trade usage under which Coromandel groundnuts and machine-shelled groundnut kernels were the same thing was not admissible. The Rayner case is criticized and the Laudisi case approved in Ward and Harfield *op. cit. supra* note 72 at 50 *et seq.* On its facts, however, Rayner may well be thought to be closer to the Bank of Italy case than to Laudisi. A leading English text, Gutteridge and Megrah, The Law of Bankers' Commercial Credits (3d ed. 1962) says that there is "a marked difference between English and American law" represented by the Rayner and Laudisi cases but goes on to suggest, citing Midland Bank Ltd. v. Seymour, [1955] 2 Lloyds List Rep. 147 (per Devlin, J.), that judicial ingenuity can save the day by taking the decision in Rayner as "permissive and not peremptory" and distinguishing it out of existence (at p. 86 *et seq.*).

80. A curious and doubtful practice has grown up under which carriers sometimes issue a clean bill for goods damaged at the time of receipt against a letter of indemnity from the shipper who agrees to save the carrier harm-

Banks, which find their letter of credit business profitable, have bowed to the carrier's strategic position in deciding what notations are to go on the face of bills of lading. The credits continue to call for "full set clean bills of lading." UCP, incorporated in the credits by reference, provides:

> "A clean shipping document is one which bears no superimposed clause or notation which expressly declares a defective condition of the goods and/or the packaging.
>
> "Banks will refuse shipping documents bearing such clauses or notations unless the credit expressly states clauses or notations which may be accepted." [81]

The 1962 Revision of UCP deleted the following paragraph which had appeared in the 1951 version (Article 18):

> "The following should not be considered such reservations: a) clauses which do not expressly state that the goods or packaging are unsatisfactory, e. g., 'secondhand cases', 'used drums', etc.; b) clauses which emphasize carriers' non-liability for risks arising through the nature of the goods or the packaging; c) clauses which disclaim on the part of the carrier knowledge of contents, weight, measurement, quality or technical specification of the goods."

less with respect to any claims which may be brought against it as a result of the misrepresentations in the bill of lading. In one of the few cases to discuss this practice, Continex, Inc. v. S. S. Flying Independent & Isbrandtsen Co., Inc., 106 F.Supp. 319, 1952 A.M.C. 1499 (S.D.N.Y.1952) Judge McGohey remarked: "When a carrier issues a clean bill of lading for goods manifestly damaged he is estopped to deny the assertion against a purchaser of the bill of lading who has been misled to his damage by reliance on the representation." The letter of indemnity practice is briefly discussed in Knauth, The American Law of Ocean Bills of Lading (4th ed. 1953) at 183 and 411.

In Empresa Central Mercantil de Representacoes, Ltda. v. Republic of the United States of Brazil, 257 F.2d 747, 1958 A.M.C. 1809, (2d Cir. 1958) the carrier, "through the connivance of the shipper," issued a clean bill for damaged goods and was held liable for damages to the consignee.

Freedman v. The Concordia Star, 250 F.2d 867, 1958 A.M.C. 1308 (2d Cir. 1958) was another clean bill for damaged goods case but the libel against the carrier was dismissed because it did not appear that the purchaser of the goods had relied on the clean bill of lading.

In Groban v. S. S. Pegu, 331 F.Supp. 883, 1972 A.M.C. 460 (S.D.N.Y.1971) the goods had been damaged by exposure before being loaded. *Held* that the notation on the bill of lading that the goods had been received "in second hand condition" was sufficient to protect the carrier.

81. Article 16.

In Dorsid Trading Co. v. S. S. Rose, 343 F.Supp. 617, 1973 A.M.C. 457 (S.D. Tex.1972) the bill of lading provided: "The term 'apparent good order and condition' when used . . . with reference to iron, steel or metal products does not mean that the goods, when received, were free of visible rust or moisture." The bill further provided that, if the shipper so requested, a "substitute" bill would be issued setting forth the actual condition of the goods, with respect to rust or moisture, on their receipt. Two Texas bankers testified that they would regard such a bill as "clean". The District Judge was apparently shocked by their testimony but the point was not involved in the decision of the case.

By the deletion the banks appear to have increased their own freedom to manoeuvre. Presumably banks could reject bills which noted that the goods were packed in "second hand cases" or "used drums" unless the bank's customer had instructed the bank to provide in the credit that such notations were acceptable. On the other hand the bill of lading "clauses" referred to in (b) and (c) of the deleted paragraph would not seem in any case to tarnish the bill's "cleanness."

**§ 3–14.** In the nineteenth century a bill of lading was a bill of lading: when issued by an ocean carrier it recited, over the master's signature, that goods had been loaded on board the good ship "Barbara B". In our own century the tightness of shipping space consequent upon war and threat of war, together with developments in the organization of the shipping industry, has brought into use of a variety of forms all known as bills of lading. Most common of these relatively new types of bills is the "Received for Shipment" bill, which acknowledges receipt of goods by the carrier at wharf or dock for subsequent loading and shipment. In exports of cotton from the United States variants of the "Received for Shipment" bill have grown up known as "Port" and "Custody" bills.[82] Except for such Port or Custody bills, UCP requires that, unless otherwise specified in the credit, bills "must show that the goods are loaded on board".[83] The ocean carriage of goods may be preceded or followed by carriage by rail or truck. Efforts have been made to popularize "through" bills of lading. Such bills have not come into widespread use and will be accepted by banks only when issued by steamship companies or their agents.[84] Furthermore, all bills of lading issued by forwarding agents will be refused by banks, as well as, UCP continues, with a splendid foreshortening of past and present, "bills of lading covering shipment by sailing vessels".[85]

82. The Port bill is issued only against cotton which has arrived in the port of shipment and provides for shipment on a named vessel which must likewise be in port. In the Custody bill the cotton must have arrived at the port of shipment and have been delivered to the signatory of the bill, but the vessel named need not have arrived in port; the cotton must, however, be loaded on board within three weeks from the date of the bill on the named vessel or a substituted vessel, substitution being permitted only when, by reason of loss, accident or *force majeure*, the named vessel is unavailable. Article 17 UCP provides that Port or Custody bills for shipment of cotton from the United States will be accepted by banks. Knauth *op. cit. supra* note 80 reproduces at 365 *et seq.* the Liverpool Agreements which led to the Port and Custody bills as well as a fascinating account of the fraud and confusion in the cotton industry which led to their adoption (at 394 et seq.)

83. Article 18. In the 1951 version of UCP Article 19 provided that "Received for Shipment" bills were acceptable. U.C.C. § 2–323(1) provides that a "Received for Shipment" bill is proper under a C.I.F. or C. & F. contract of sale. Banking practice and mercantile practice appear to be diverging at this point.

84. UCP Article 17. See Knauth *op. cit. supra* note 80 at 141. On the liability of the issuer of a "through" bill, see U.C.C. § 7–302.

85. Article 17.

§ 3–15. Bills of lading are often issued under a charter party.[86] A time charterer who operates a vessel as a "general ship" will issue (through the master) bills of lading to the shippers who engage his services. A voyage charterer will frequently (for the purpose of making documentary presentment to banks or buyers) take a bill or bills of lading from the owner. Now we have two contractual documents covering the contract of carriage: charter party and bill of lading. The charter party will be the more detailed and, since it is not subject to the mandatory provisions of Cogsa, will often contain provisions more favorable to the carrier than those in the bill of lading. In order to preserve the terms of the charter party for his benefit, the owner will require that the bill of lading contain some such legend as "subject to terms of charter party." The incorporation of the charter party terms is of particular importance to the owner in order to preserve his charter party lien against subfreights where a time-charterer issues bills to shippers.

A bill of lading which states that it is "subject to" a charter has obvious drawbacks from the point of view of a purchaser, who will typically not have access to the other document and thus no way of knowing what terms are incorporated by the reference. In a documentary exchange between merchants it may be doubted that a "subject to" bill would be a good tender. Where a bank letter of credit is involved, UCP has a specific provision: "Bills of lading which are issued under and are subject to the conditions of a Charter Party [will be rejected unless specifically authorized in the credit]."[87] It may be noted that the unacceptable bill is one which is both "issued under" and "subject to" the charter party. Presumably this means "subject to" the charter party even in the hands of a good-faith purchaser of the bill. Since purchasers of bills will take free of the charter party unless they have notice of its terms,[88] a bill would be acceptable, even though issued under a charter party, if it did not bear some sort of "incorporation by reference" legend.

§ 3–16. Letters of credit call for "a full set" of ocean bills of lading. From time immemorial ocean carriers have issued their bills in "sets of parts"—that is to say, two (or occasionally three) duplicate originals, one of which being accomplished, the others, in the traditional phrase, to stand void.[89] Ocean bills were originally

86. For discussion of the issuance of bills of lading under charter parties, see Chapter IV, §§ 4—10, 4—17.

87. Article 17.

88. See Chapter IV, § 4—10, especially text at note 91 *et seq.*, for discussion of the incorporation of the charter terms in the bill.

89. The issuance of bills in sets is discussed in 2 Williston *op. cit. supra* note 38 § 441. Neither Cogsa nor the Uniform or Federal (Pomerene) Bills of Lading Act contains any provision covering the peculiar problems of bills in sets (except the prohibitory clause referred to in note 91 *infra*). U.C.C. § 7–304 codifies the issuance of bills in sets and may be taken as a brief statement of current understanding of their effect. The Comment to § 7–304 incorrectly states that this branch of law is codified in "the Hague and Warsaw Conventions and in the Carriage of Goods by Sea Act . . .".

issued in this form as a means of insuring against the perils of the sea: parts were forwarded to destination by different vessels, so that the chances of one of the parts arriving were doubled or tripled. They continue to be so issued today for substantially the same reason, although the perils of our own century are as apt to proceed from acts of men as from what our ancestors chose to call acts of God. With a world in which peace and war have become indistinguishable, it remains as wise as it was a hundred years ago to provide for the safe arrival of documents by sending duplicates forward by alternative routes. The usual practice today is to send one part by air while the others follow by water.

Each of the parts is an original, negotiable document. The carrier is under a duty to deliver against whichever part is first presented, and, by so doing, discharges its liability on the other parts.[90] The parts are of course meant to be separated physically, since they arrive at destination by different routes. A holder in possession of two or more parts may, if he is fraudulently inclined, separate them in quite another sense by negotiating each part to a different purchaser. To prevent that type of fraud U.C.C. Article 7, like the earlier Bills of Lading Acts, forbids the issuance of domestic bills of lading in sets of parts.[91] In ocean commerce, however, the needs of safe communication have continued to outweigh the possibility of fraudulent misuse. From the dearth of litigation, it may be concluded that such fraudulent negotiation is more a theoretical than a real danger. If the separate parts do come into the hands of two or more good faith purchasers, the purchaser to whom the first due negotiation was made prevails: if the other parts are outstanding, he may recover them from their holders; if the carrier has delivered against one of the other parts, the holder with prevailing title may recover the goods from whoever has received them [92]—although it is doubtful whether he could recover the goods if after delivery they had been resold to a good faith purchaser.[93]

**§ 3–17.** The documents required by a letter of credit are usually presented to the issuing bank by another bank in the same city to which they have been forwarded by the seller or his bank. On the

90. This is of course the condition under which the carrier issues the bill, see text at note 89 *supra*. See U.C.C. § 7–304(5).

91. UBLA § 6; Pomerene Act § 4 (49 U.S.C.A. § 84). A proviso to § 4 of the Pomerene Act permits bills to be issued in sets of parts "for transportation of goods to Alaska, Panama, Puerto Rico, the Philippines, Hawaii, or foreign countries . . .". Under U.C.C. § 7–304: "Except where customary in overseas transportation, a bill of lading must not be issued in a set of parts."

92. See 2 Williston *op. cit. supra* note 38 at § 441. U.C.C. § 7–304(3).

93. There appear to be no cases on the point. The conclusion in the text is based on the thought that a subsequent indorsee receiving goods from a carrier in good faith would have at least voidable title and until his title had been avoided could transfer good title to a good faith purchaser. U.C.C. § 2–403. However, § 7–403 makes no exception for such good faith purchasers. On good faith purchasers and voidable title see note 21 *supra*.

expiration date of the credit the presenting bank may be in possession of only one part of the bill of lading (usually the one that has been forwarded by air), while the credit calls for the full set. In that situation, the presenting bank tenders the available part with an indemnity agreement against any loss which might arise from a fraudulent negotiation of the missing part or parts. Such an indemnity agreement, when tendered by a leading bank, is regularly accepted.[94]

Despite banking practice in tendering and accepting such indemity agreements, it has been banking opinion that the issuing bank has the right to stand on the terms of the letter of credit, to refuse the indemnity and to dishonor the drafts. In Dixon, Irmaos & Cia. Ltda. v. Chase National Bank,[95] the Chase Bank had refused a tender by the Guaranty Trust Company of one part of a bill of lading plus an indemnity agreement in customary form. The Chase Bank's credit was a confirmation[96] of a credit originally issued by the Banque de Bruxelles on behalf of a Belgian importer. The expiration date of the Chase credit, and the day on which the Guaranty Trust Company made presentment, was May 15, 1940—and since at that time Belgium was being overrun by the German army the Chase Bank might well have thought that its chances of being reimbursed were remote. It dishonored, assigning as the principal reason the failure of the Guaranty Trust Company to present the full set of bills of lading. The Second Circuit held that the dishonor was unjustified. The Chase Bank had not objected either to the form of the indemnity or to the standing of the Guaranty Trust Company. In such circumstances, the court found, the existence of a custom among New York banks to accept the indemnity agreement in lieu of the missing part was "established beyond dispute". Therefore, the term in the credit requiring "full set bills of lading" had to be construed in the light of the custom, and the tender had been sufficient. The Dixon Irmaos decision, praised by some commentators,[97] was severely attacked by spokesmen representing the banking point of view for its holding that custom can prevail over the unambiguously expressed terms of a contract, particularly a banking contract.[98] Nevertheless, the decision stands as governing law. Neither UCP nor Article 5 of the Code covers the issue.[99]

94. See the opinion of Swan, J., in Dixon Irmaos & Cia. Ltda. v. Chase Nat. Bank, 144 F.2d 759 (2d Cir. 1944), certiorari denied 324 U.S. 850, 65 S.Ct. 687 (1945).

95. See note 94 *supra*.

96. A "confirming" bank adds its own liability to that of the issuing bank and itself undertakes to honor drafts. See U.C.C. § 5–107(2); UCP Article 3; Ward & Harfield *op. cit. supra* note 72 at 25.

97. See Honnold, Letters of Credit, Custom, Missing Documents and the Dixon Case: A Reply to Backus and Harfield, 53 Colum.L.Rev. 504 (1953); Honnold, Footnote to the Controversy over the Dixon Case, 53 Colum.L.Rev. 973 (1953).

98. See Backus and Harfield, Custom and Letters of Credit: The Dixon Irmaos Case, 52 Colum.L.Rev. 589 (1952).

99. Drafts of Article 5 up to 1951 contained a provision codifying the Dixon, Irmaos result whenever documents were to be sent from overseas. See U.C.C. (Spring, 1950, Spring, 1951 drafts) § 5–118. The provision was

The contemporary critics of the Dixon Irmaos holding appear to have been motivated principally by a metaphysical rage at the introduction of parol evidence as to banking custom in any situation. The holding could not conceivably be described as "anti-bank" since any bank which regularly engages in the letter of credit business finds itself quite as often in the position of the Guaranty Trust (the presenting bank in Dixon Irmaos) as it does in that of the Chase Bank (the issuer). In this century it has gradually become clear, even to the legal mind, that there are few contract terms, if indeed there are any, which are so "unambiguously clear" on their face that they cannot, in case of need, be supplemented or explained by evidence relating to custom or usage.[99a] From this point of view Dixon Irmaos was in the mainstream of twentieth century legal development while its critics were nostalgically looking back to a vanished Utopia. Good sense eventually prevailed, even within the New York banking establishment, since no attempt was made to do anything about Dixon Irmaos, either generally or specifically, in the 1951 and 1962 revisions of UCP or in Article 5 of the Code as enacted in New York. Indeed, one of the general provisions of Article 1 of the Code (§ 1–205) takes what might be described as a liberal position on the introduction of evidence on "Course of Dealing and Usage of Trade" and it should be kept in mind that a New York credit to which Article 5 does not apply (because the credit is "subject" to UCP) is still governed generally by New York law which now includes § 1–205.[99b]

**§ 3–18.** When a bank has honored drafts drawn under its letter of credit, the bill of lading and the other documents which accompany the drafts are delivered to it. The bank now no longer has any

deleted from the November, 1951, draft and from all subsequent drafts. Under § 5–113 indemnities to induce honor, unless otherwise explicitly agreed, apply only to defects in the documents and not to defects in the goods and expire at the end of ten business days following their receipt. The Official Comment to § 5–113 goes out of its way to make clear that the issue litigated in Dixon, Irmaos "is beyond the scope of this section."

**99a.** The classical exposition was by Wigmore, who has been followed by all subsequent commentators. See 9 Wigmore on Evidence §§ 2400–2478 (3d ed. 1940).

**99b.** Pre-Code New York law seems on the whole to have been consistent with § 1–205. See B. M. Heed, Inc. v. Roberts, 303 N.Y. 385, 103 N.E.2d 419 (1952) and cases cited in the New York annotations to § 1–205 in McKinney's Consolidated Laws of New York Annotated.

In Marine Midland Grace Trust Co. of New York v. Banco del Pais, S.A., 261 F.Supp. 884 (S.D.N.Y.1966) the issue was whether Marine Midland had properly dishonored drafts drawn under its credits within a "reasonable time" after presentment, as required by UCP which had been incorporated in the credits by reference. The two banks submitted conflicting affidavits on the issue of what was a "reasonable time" in the light of New York banking custom. The District Court sensibly held that the conflicting affidavits raised a triable issue of fact so that motions for summary judgment were denied. No further proceedings in the case were reported. If Article 5 had applied to the case, the issuer, under § 5–112, would have had three days in which to honor or dishonor. Marine Midland argued that under New York banking custom it had ten days.

On the non-applicability of Article 5 to New York credits which are "subject" to UCP, see § 3–12 *supra*.

right of recourse against the seller;[100] it must look for reimbursement exclusively to its customer, the buyer, and, failing such reimbursement, to its security interest in the goods. If the customer has become insolvent during the period between the issuance of the letter and its performance, the bank holds the bill of lading as pledgee and may sell it or the goods to satisfy its advance.

The customer's arrangement with the bank may require him to put the bank in funds before the bank pays the draft. If his credit standing is satisfactory, an alternative arrangement widely used is for the bank to release the shipping documents against a trust receipt under which the bank retains a security interest in the goods (and the bill of lading) until its loan has been paid. The trust receipt practice grew up at common law in the early part of the century and was codified in the Uniform Trust Receipts Act (UTRA) which was widely enacted during the 1930's.[101] UTRA has been superseded by U.C.C. Article 9 on Secured Transactions which, however, carries forward the pre-Code trust receipt practice without substantial change. As a matter of nomenclature the pre-Code trust receipt is now an Article 9 security interest but the trust receipt terminology continues in use. The bank may perfect its security interest by filing a financing statement; if it does not file, the interest is nevertheless perfected, automatically and without any filing requirement, for 21 days after the delivery of the bill of lading to the bank's customer.[102] At the end of the 21 days the bank's interest becomes unperfected unless by that time it has either filed or regained possession of the bill of lading (or the goods).[103] Article 9

100. Usually drafts are drawn by the seller on the issuing (or confirming) bank; payment extinguishes the draft and discharges the seller's liability as drawer. However even where the seller draws not on the bank but on his own buyer, so that the issuing bank takes the draft by negotiation, the bank has been denied recovery back against the seller: Bank of East Asia v. Pang, 140 Wash. 603, 249 P. 1060 (1926). Under U.C.C. § 5–111 the beneficiary and banks which handle his drafts make certain warranties on transfer or presentment and the issuer could have a recovery for breach of warranty. The Practice Commentary and the New York annotations to § 5–111 in McKinney's Consolidated Laws of New York Annotated suggest that the § 5–111 warranties go well beyond the existing New York case law. Conceivably § 5–111 is a section which might find favor with New York issuers who are otherwise wholeheartedly devoted to UCP.

101. On the common law development of the trust receipt and its codification in UTRA, see 1 Gilmore, Security Interests in Personal Property, Ch. 4 (1965).

102. The purpose of the automatic 21-day perfection provision (§ 9–304(5)) is to avoid cluttering the files with notices of short-term, self-liquidating transactions. UTRA §§ 7, 8 gave a 30-day period of protection without filing. The UTRA 30-day period was cut back to 21 days in § 9–304(5) to avoid a possible conflict with § 60 of the Federal Bankruptcy Act on Voidable Preferences.

103. If the bill was surrendered for the goods on the 21st day, it is possible that the bank would get another 10 days of perfection without filing under § 9–306 on proceeds. However, the statute is hopelessly unclear on the point and, if it were construed to give the extra 10 days of perfection without filing, might be found to be in conflict with § 60 of the Federal Bankruptcy Act. On the 21-day automatic perfection provision (§ 9–304(5)), see 1 Gilmore, *op. cit. supra* note 101, § 14.6.2. On § 9–309, 2 *id.* § 25.4.

(like UTRA before it) recognizes the special character of negotiable documents of title. Unless the bank takes the bill of lading in pledge, perfection, even by filing, protects the bank only against lien creditors or trustees in bankruptcy. Absent a pledge and despite perfection, the bank loses to a purchaser who has taken a bill of lading (or a warehouse receipt substituted for the bill) by "due negotiation" even though the bank's customer had no authority to sell the bill or the goods or to procure a warehouse receipt in place of the bill.

Section 9–309 provides:

> "Nothing in this Article limits the rights of . . . a holder to whom a negotiable document of title has been duly negotiated (section 7–501) . . . and such [a holder] take[s] priority over an earlier security interest even though perfected. Filing under this Article does not constitute notice of his security interest to such [a holder]."

## A Note on Conflict of Laws Problems

**§ 3–19.** Disputes involving bills of lading may arise between a holder of a bill and the carrier; between successive holders of a bill; or between a holder of a bill and a person claiming rights of property in the goods apart from the bill. The dual nature of the bill, which is in one aspect merely a contract of carriage and in another aspect the symbolic representative of the goods, has led to odd results in the choice of law governing the several types of disputes.

In actions against the carrier for negligent stowage or care of the goods during transit, conflict of laws principles would lead to the law of the jurisdiction in which the bill was issued. However, in litigation in the United States under ocean bills of lading which cover shipments to or from ports of the United States, that solution has been superseded by statute. Under Cogsa bills the liability of the carrier, American or foreign, with respect to shipments to or from ports of the United States whether the bill was issued in the United States or abroad, will be determined by the United States Cogsa.[104]

104. Thus, for example, in Schroeder Bros., Inc. v. The Saturina, 226 F.2d 147, 1955 A.M.C. 1935 (2d Cir. 1955) the United States Cogsa was applied to a shipment from Italian ports to New York in an Italian owned and operated ship. See also J. Gerber & Co. v. S. S. Sabine Howaldt, 310 F. Supp. 343, 1970 A.M.C. 441; (S.D.N.Y. 1969); Trans-Amazonica Iquitos, S. A. v. Georgia Steamship Co., 335 F.Supp. 935, (S.D.Georgia 1971). The reverse situation—what law will the courts of foreign countries (Cogsa or non Cogsa) apply to disputes arising under bills issued in the United States or by American ships—is far from clear. Knauth, the American Law of Ocean Bills of Lading (4th ed. 1953) 154 *et seq.* has a brief discussion. In Petition of Isbrandtsen Co. (The Edmund Fanning) 201 F.2d 281, 1953 A.M.C. 86 (2d Cir. 1953), the court seems to have approved the incorporation of the United States Cogsa in a bill of lading covering a shipment in an American ship from German ports to Korea. The lower court had held to the contrary (105 F.Supp. 353, 1952 A.M.C. 1147 (S.D.N.Y.1952).

A lively focus of litigation in recent years has been the validity of stipulations in bills of lading for the application of foreign law or for the localiza-

§ 3–20. Different considerations apply to disputes between successive holders where the issue is whether there has been a "due negotiation" of the bill. Neither the Harter Act nor Cogsa covers the question of what rights are acquired by negotiation. The Federal Bills of Lading (Pomerene) Act, which applies to ocean bills issued in the United States for shipment to a foreign country but not to bills issued abroad for shipment to the United States, does contain provisions on rights acquired by negotiation.[105] It does not follow, however, that United States courts will apply the Pomerene Act to determine the due negotiation of bills issued in the United States and foreign law to bills issued in other countries. In this situation the courts will apply to negotiable bills of lading the negotiable instruments rule that rights acquired by negotiation will be determined by the law of the jurisdiction where the negotiation took place.[106] Thus if

tion of litigation in the courts of a foreign country when the bills were issued in connection with shipments to or from ports of the United States and thus subject to the United States Cogsa. On this point, see § 3–25 *infra*, note 23.

105. See § 3–3 *supra*.

106. Ehrenzweig, Private International Law (1967) comments (at p. 226) that "No cases seem to have arisen determining the law applicable to the rights of successive holders of bills of lading." In the absence of case authority, Ehrenzweig cites the rule suggested in the text.

United States v. Guaranty Trust Co., 293 U.S. 340, 55 S.Ct. 221 (1934) is a, or perhaps the, leading case on this seldom litigated issue. The United States Veterans Bureau drew a check on the United States Treasury and mailed it to the payee in Yugoslavia where it was negotiated under a forged endorsement of the payee's name. The negotiation was effective under Yugoslavian law but ineffective under American law. *Held*, that Yugoslavian law applied.

The First Restatement of the Conflict of Laws (1934) "codified" the rule of the Guaranty Trust Co. case in § 349, using the facts of that case as an "illustration." The Comment to § 349 suggested that the rule was applicable "to any instrument made negotiable by common law or by statute, whether a bond, note, bill of exchange, share certificate or warehouse receipt." The Restatement also provided in § 261(3) that: "The validity of a conveyance of a document in which title to a chattel is embodied . . . is determined by the law of the jurisdiction where the document is at the time of the conveyance." It is unclear why the Restaters dealt separately with "documents" in § 261 if § 349 was meant to cover such things as "warehouse receipts." However, no harm was done since both sections stated the same rule.

The Restatement of Conflicts (Second) (1971) seems to have introduced a certain amount of confusion. Restatement (Second) § 216 (like § 349 in the First Restatement) "codifies" the Guaranty Trust Co. case which it uses as an "Illustration" and cites (in the Reporter's Note) as the leading authority. The caption of § 216 is "Transfer of Interests in Negotiable Instrument." Conveyances of chattels are dealt with in §§ 244–250. In that sequence both § 248(2) and § 249(2) provide that "As between persons who are not both parties to the conveyance" the effect of a conveyance of an interest in a document in which "title to a chattel is embodied" (§ 248) or in which "a right is embodied" (§ 249) will "usually" be determined by the law of the state "where the document was at the time of the conveyance." In the commentary to both §§ 248 and 249 the statement is made that "as between the parties" the validity of the conveyance is to be determined by the rule stated in § 244. The rule of § 244 is that the validity and effect of a conveyance of a chattel is to be determined by the law of the state which "has the most significant relationship to the parties, the chattel and the conveyance" (subsection (1)) which will "usually" be the state where the chattel was located at the time of the conveyance (subsection (2)).

a bill issued in the United States and subject to the Pomerene Act was negotiated in England, both American and English courts would look to the law of England to determine the rights of the purchaser. In the same way, if an English bill not subject to the Pomerene Act was negotiated in New York, both American and English courts would apply American law. Fortunately state law (represented by the UCC Article 7) and federal law (the Pomerene Act) are identical in substance as to rights acquired by negotiation, so the problem of choosing between state and federal law is of only theoretical interest.[106a]

It should be borne in mind that the rule stated in the preceding paragraph applies only to rights acquired by negotiation. The question of what law is applicable to determine the validity and negotiability of a bill of lading will be taken up in the following section.

**§ 3–21.** Disputes involving the right to possession of the goods between a person who claims under the bill and a person whose claim is based on some other ground bring in still other considerations. Under American law, for example, a bill issued to a person who has no title to the goods does not cut off the true owner's interest: he may replevy the bill or the goods from the carrier or any one into whose possession they may have come, good faith purchaser or not.[107] Here the question is the validity of the bill: is it mere waste paper or is it, in truth or at any rate in law, the document of title which it purports to be? In this situation by analogy to the prevailing rule on the determination of negotiability courts will presumably look to the law of the jurisdiction where the bill was issued;[108] if valid (and

The opinion will be hazarded that the true meaning of Restatement (Second) is that the rule of the Guaranty Trust Co. case applies (or "usually" applies) to negotiations of bills of lading as well as to negotiations of negotiable instruments. (The commentary to § 248 does not mention Guaranty Trust but the Reporter's Note to § 249 cites it as the leading authority.)

**106a.** On the relationship between U.C.C. Article 7 and the Pomerene Act, see § 3–3 *supra*.

**107.** See § 3–4 *supra*.

**108.** There is relatively little authority on the point and what authority there is is divided. See Goodrich, Handbook of the Conflict of Laws (4th ed. by Scoles 1964) 322; Stumberg, Principles of Conflict of Laws (3d ed. 1963) 250. Restatement of the Conflict of Laws (First) (1934) § 336 provided that: "The law of the place of contracting determines whether a mercantile instrument is negotiable. . . ." However Restatement (Second) (1971) § 214 provides that the obligation of the maker of a note and of the acceptor of a draft is determined by the local law of the state designated as the place of payment or, if no place of payment is designated, by the local law of the state in which he delivered the instrument. The following § 215 provides that the obligations of indorsers and drawers are determined by the local law of the state in which the indorser or the drawer delivered the instrument. The Comments and Notes to §§ 214 and 215 do not comment on the rule of § 336 of the First Restatement or on why it seems to have been abandoned in the Second Restatement.

Neither Restatement refers expressly to the negotiability of bills of lading (or documents of title). However, Restatement (Second) § 248(1) (which is identical in substance with Restatement (First) § 261(1)) provides that: "Whether the title to a chattel is embodied in a document is determined by the local law of the state where the chattel was at the time the document was issued."

negotiable) there, it will be valid (and negotiable) everywhere and vice versa.[108a]

Carrier's liability, then, will be determined (at least in most Cogsa countries) by the law of the forum; rights acquired by negotiation by the law of the jurisdiction where the negotiation took place; and the validity and negotiability of the bill by the jurisdiction in which the bill was issued. Still a fourth situation is illustrated by a case, decided in the 1950's, whose commercial importance, as well as the continuing dearth of authority on the point, make it worth separate discussion.

In Barrett v. Bank of the Manhattan Co.[109] the bank had issued its letter of credit (on behalf of a New York customer) covering a shipment of 500 bales of Hessian bags from Calcutta, India, to Manila, Philippine Islands. The bill of lading (which had evidently been issued in India) was delivered to the bank in New York and there released by it to its customer who executed a trust receipt in favor of the bank. Subsequently the bill of lading was surrendered in Manila, where the goods were warehoused and a warehouse receipt was substituted for the original document. Several months later on default in the loan the warehouse receipt was turned over to the bank by its customer and the bank sold the bags to satisfy its loan. Insolvency proceedings were instituted against the customer and it appeared that the turning over of the warehouse receipt to the bank could be set aside as preferential under State law unless the bank's prior security interest was valid under the applicable law.[110] The bank had filed in New York which had enacted the Uniform Trust Receipts Act. As to the law of the Philippines, which had not enacted UTRA, the court found that a

See note 106 *supra* on the treatment in the two Restatements of the law applicable to the negotiation of negotiable instruments and negotiable documents of title. Once again the opinion will be hazarded that, at least with respect to documents of title, Restatement (Second) means the same thing as Restatement (First) and that both Restatements are consistent with the statement in the text.

U.C.C. § 1–105 provides that, with some exceptions which are not relevant here, "[W]hen a transaction bears a reasonable relation to this state and also to another state or nation the parties may agree that the law either of this state or of such other state or nation shall govern their rights and duties." The Comments to §§ 214 and 215 of Restatement (Second) assume that U.C.C. § 1–105 applies to choice of law provisions in negotiable instruments—and, if that is so, the Code section would seem to apply equally to negotiable documents of title. Furthermore Restatement (Second) § 244(2) (on the conveyance of chattels) expressly assumes the effectiveness of choice of law provisions. On the applicability of § 244 to conveyances of documents of title, see note 106 *supra*. It should be noted, however, that the U.C.C. § 1–105 choice of law rule does not apply to security transactions under Article 9 which states its own choice of law rules in §§ 9–102 and 9–103. See text following note 120 *infra*.

See further the Cogsa litigation discussed in § 3–25 *infra*, note 23.

108a. Ehrenzweig, *loc. cit. supra* note 106, seems to accept the position taken in the text.

109. 218 F.2d 763 (2d Cir. 1954).

110. The transaction was not voidable under Section 60 of the Federal Bankruptcy Act because the petition in bankruptcy had not been filed until more than four months after the turning over of the warehouse receipts. 218 F.2d 763, 765.

trust receipt was there recognized as valid at common law—*i. e.* valid against creditors (including a trustee in bankruptcy) without filing.

The Barrett case raised for the first time the problem of the law applicable to the perfection of a non-possessory security interest in negotiable documents of title where the goods covered by the documents are in one jurisdiction and the documents themselves are in another jurisdiction. (The opinion in Barrett does not state where the bank's customer kept the documents during the loan period but the warehouse receipt was eventually turned over to the bank in New York. The substitution of the warehouse receipt for the original bill of lading was evidently made with the bank's knowledge or at least its consent.) The traditional method of creating security interests in negotiable instruments and negotiable documents has been by pledge—that is by transfer of possession of the instrument or document to the pledgee (or, to use U.C.C. Article 9 terminology, the secured party). The idea that there could be such a thing as a non-possessory (i. e., without possession taken or retained by the secured party) security interest in a negotiable document first came in with the common law trust receipt and received its first statutory recognition in UTRA.[111] Thus the problem litigated in Barrett could never have come up before the invention of the trust receipt and was unlikely to have come up before the enactment of UTRA.[112] The problem, briefly stated, is where the secured party is supposed to perfect his interest (by filing or otherwise). In Barrett the two possible choices were the Philippines (where the bill of lading was surrendered and the goods were warehoused) and New York (where the trust receipt was executed and the warehouse receipt was turned over to the bank). New York was also the state where the bank's customer, which was engaged in "importing, exporting and dealing in commodities," seems to have been domiciled.

The actual decision on the Barrett facts was almost absurdly simple. The bank won whether Philippine law (said to recognize trust receipts without a filing requirement) or New York law (the bank having properly filed in New York under UTRA) was applied. But suppose either that Philippines law had not recognized trust receipts or that the Philippines, like New York, had enacted UTRA or a comparable filing statute (and that the bank had filed only in New York). At that point decision, far from being absurdly simple, would have become almost impossibly complex. It may be noted that the first assumption (the security interest in question is recognized in one jurisdiction but not in the other) could come up any day in an international context and that the second assumption (the security interest is recognized in both jurisdictions, both of which have filing

111. On trust receipt financing, UTRA and the currently applicable provisions of U.C.C. Article 9, see § 3–18 *supra*. Article 9 follows UTRA in recognizing non-possessory security interests in negotiable documents.

112. Theoretically the problem could have come up at common law if one of the jurisdictions recognized the trust receipt and the other jurisdiction did not.

statutes) could come up any day in two states both of which have enacted U.C.C. Article 9. New York banks which do "trust receipt" financing for customers in Connecticut or for New York customers who warehouse the goods in Connecticut must decide whether they are supposed to file in New York or in Connecticut or maybe in both states. Unfortunately Article 9 itself is hopelessly obscure on the point and Judge Learned Hand's opinion in Barrett, which is also hopelessly obscure, is the only relevant judicial discussion.

Judge Hand concluded his Barrett opinion with the observation:

> "We base our decision strictly upon the Philippine law, without indicating how we might decide the issue, had there been no evidence as to, and, a fortiori, had there been evidence against, the validity of 'trust receipts' in the Philippines." [113]

However, he devoted the greater part of a fairly lengthy opinion to the proposition that New York law applied so that the bank was protected by its UTRA filing. Thus the opinion can be read either way. Indeed it can be read to mean that the bank would lose unless it held a perfected interest both in the Philippines (where the goods were kept) and in New York (where the bill of lading was turned over, the trust receipt was executed and the warehouse receipt was kept at least part of the time). It will be suggested that the proper result in Barrett was to apply New York law, but for reasons different from those suggested by Judge Hand.[114]

In the course of his analysis Judge Hand quoted from a 19th Century Supreme Court case:

> "The old rule, expressed in the maxim mobilia sequuntur personam, by which personal property was regarded as subject to the law of the owner's domicile, grew up in the Middle Ages. . . . In modern times . . . that rule has yielded more and more to the lex situs, the law of the place where the property is kept and used." [115]

Thus the creation and perfection of security interests in personal property should be determined by the law of the state where the property was when the security interest was created (or, in Article 9 terminology, "attached"). (We may disregard for present purposes the problems created by subsequent interstate movement of the property.) Judge Hand next referred to the doctrine that when "title to a chattel is embodied in a document," the relevant situs becomes that

113. 218 F.2d 763, 768.

114. The present writer may not be an altogether trustworthy guide through the conflicts jungle. In his discussion of Barrett in the first edition of the treatise he argued at length that the law of the Philippines should determine perfection of the bank's security interest. In another discussion of Barrett written some years later he reversed his position and argued for the applicability of New York law. 1 Gilmore, Security Interests in Personal Property (1965) § 24.3. We must not let consistency become the hobgoblin of our little minds.

115. Pullman's Palace-Car Co. v. Commonwealth of Pennsylvania, 141 U.S. 18, 22, 11 S.Ct. 876, 878 (1891).

of the document and not that of the goods covered or represented by the document. Judge Hand assumed that, under the law of India where the Barrett bill of lading had been issued, title to the Hessian bags had indeed become "embodied" in the bill of lading.[116] Since New York was the situs of the bill of lading when the trust receipt was executed, it followed that the bank had a good New York trust receipt, perfected by its New York filing. (Judge Hand did not discuss the substitution of the warehouse receipt for the bill of lading in Manila.) Judge Hand then left open the question "whether the doctrine of the 'embodiment' of the chattel in the document should be applied, even though the chattel be in a jurisdiction which refuses to recognize 'trust receipts.' "[117] That question did not have to be answered since the law of the Philippines did, or so the court found, recognize trust receipts. Wherefore, judgment went for the bank against its customer's trustee in bankruptcy.

It is submitted that the true reason why perfection of the bank's security interest should have been determined by New York law was that the bank's customer was doing business and apparently domiciled in New York. In determining such questions there is a great deal more to be said, on grounds of policy and commercial convenience, for the maxim "mobilia sequuntur personam" than Judge Hand or Professor Beale (the Reporter for the First Restatement of the Conflict of Laws) may have assumed.[118] Judge Hand was, of course, dealing with a statute (UTRA) which, he assumed, required filing in the state where the goods (or the documents) were when the security interest attached. However, an ingenious student note on Barrett pointed out that the filing provisions of UTRA § 13 said nothing about the location or situs of goods or documents within the state but referred instead to the "trustee" under the trust receipt transaction (the bank's customer in Barrett) having a "place of business" within the state.[119] Thus UTRA § 13 could be construed as providing (in all UTRA states) that the proper place to make a trust receipt filing on a business enterprise engaged in interstate operations but domiciled (or having its "principal place of business") in New York was not here, there and elsewhere wherever goods (or documents) might be kept but only in the domiciliary state.[120]

116. On "embodiment" Judge Hand cited the Restatement of the Conflict of Laws (1934). On the treatment of these problems in the successive Conflicts Restatements, see notes 106 and 108 *supra*. The Reporter's Note to Restatement (Second) § 248(1), quoted in note 108 *supra*, cites Barrett as authority for the proposition that the law of the state where a document is issued determines whether it "embodies" the title to the chattel.

117. 218 F.2d 763, 767.

118. For an argument in favor of the domiciliary rule (mobilia sequuntur personam) see 1 Gilmore, *op. cit. supra* note 114, § 22.3.

119. 66 Yale L.J. 565 (1957).

120. It may be doubted whether the draftsman and sponsors of UTRA consciously intended to adopt such a domiciliary filing rule. However, many of the accounts receivable statutes enacted during the 1940's did expressly adopt such a rule. See 1 Gilmore, *op. cit. supra* note 114, § 17.5.

However, the possible meanings of UTRA § 13 have become irrelevant with the enactment of U.C.C. Article 9. Article 9 does adopt a domiciliary filing rule for "mobile equipment" (§ 9–103(2)) and provides in § 9–103(1) that filing with respect to security interests in "accounts" and "contract rights" is to be made in the state where the debtor "keeps his records concerning them" (which would normally be his domicile or "chief place of business"). As to all other collateral § 9–102 provides that "this Article applies so far as concerns any personal property and fixtures within the jurisdiction of this state." The § 9–102 rule, which would apply to security interests in documents, appears to be a straight situs rule; "within the jurisdiction of this state" means "physically located within this state." [121] The application of situs theory to non-possessory interests in documents of title makes little sense theoretically. It may be assumed (or hoped), however, that the debtor, as in Barrett, will normally "keep" the documents where he is domiciled or doing business. In such cases the § 9–102 situs rule will lead to the same result as a domiciliary rule —thus achieving, as Judge Hand did in Barrett, the right result for the wrong reasons.

The Article 9 place of perfection rules have been drastically rewritten in a revision of the Article promulgated in 1972. The § 9–102 situs rule has been deleted and § 9–103, which covered both the "validity" and "perfection" of security interests, has been rewritten in terms of "perfection" only.[122] In the revision of § 9–103 the domiciliary rule (the debtor's "chief executive office" in the United States) is applied to the perfection of security interests in intangibles and mobile equipment as well as to the perfection of non-possessory interests in "chattel paper." Unfortunately that desirable rule was not extended to cover non-possessory interests in documents of title. The general rule for collateral not covered by the domiciliary rule is stated in § 9–103(1)(b) of the 1972 revision:

> "[P]erfection and the effect of perfection or non-perfection of a security interest . . . are governed by the law of the jurisdiction where the collateral is when the last event

121. The time reference in § 9–102 is presumably to the time when the security interest attaches. Section 9–103(3) provides that if a security interest attaches to collateral and is perfected in State A but the collateral is thereafter removed to State B the secured party must reperfect his interest in State B within four months after the removal. That section also provides that if collateral is to be kept in State B the interest must be perfected in State B even though it may have initially attached in State A. Thus, if the bank's customer in Barrett had, with the bank's consent, kept the documents in Connecticut the bank would have had to perfect (file) in Connecticut even though the bill of lading had been turned over and the security agreement executed in New York.

122. According to the revised commentary (Reasons for 1972 change) these changes "make . . . clear that Article 9 does not govern problems of choice of law between the original parties and that this question is governed by the general choice of law provision in Section 1–105." The § 1–105 provision is quoted in note 108 *supra*.

occurs on which is based the assertion that the security interest is perfected or unperfected." [123]

This evidently states a situs rule and attempts to pin-point a moment in time in the concluding "last event" clause. What the "last event" would be on the facts of a case like Barrett may not be entirely clear. However the mysteriousness of the "last event" clause may be, on the whole, a good thing since mysterious statutory language must be construed (or manipulated) by courts. If the Barrett situation arises in litigation which involves two Article 9 states, we may hope that the "last event" will be found to have taken place in the state of the debtor's domicile. Of course, until the mystery has been resolved, secured parties who allow their debtors to remain in possession of documents of title will (if the 1972 revision is enacted) be well advised to perfect by filing in all states which could conceivably be "last event" candidates.

Our discussion so far has assumed that the Barrett situation arises in litigation which involves two (or more) Article 9 states. The situation can, of course, as in Barrett itself, come up in litigation which involves a state in the United States and a foreign country. If the case was litigated in a court in the United States the court would have to decide whether the interest had to be "perfected" in the United States or in the foreign country or conceivably (as Judge Hand's Barrett opinion can be read to suggest) in both. Presumably the Second Conflicts Restatement is the most authoritative source for current general conflicts theory in this country. Fortunately the Second Restatement is not as irrevocably wedded to situs theory as was the First Restatement. According to Restatement (Second) § 222 the "General Principle" is that "interests . . . in a thing" are to be determined by the law of "the state which, with respect to the particular issue, has the most significant relationship to the thing and the parties. . . ." The "most significant relationship" principle is reiterated in § 244 (Validity and Effect of Conveyance of Interest in Chattel) and § 251 (Validity and Effect of Security Interest in Chattel) along with the additional statement (in both sections) that "[i]n the absence of an effective choice of law by the parties" greater weight will be given to "location" (or situs) than to any other "contact." Banks in this country which engage in financing international transactions like that in Barrett will do well to ponder the advisability of including choice of law provisions in their loan agreements or security instruments. In the absence of such a provision, Restatement (Second) points vaguely toward a situs rule but the commentary suggests that domicile may also be weighed in the balance.[124] It is

123. The "general rule" is made subject to the provisions on wandering collateral summarized in note 121 *supra* which have been carried forward without substantial change from the original § 9–103.

124. The following statement appears in the commentary to § 251: "In determining the state of most significant relationships and thus of the applicable law, the forum will consider other contacts in addition to the loca-

true that Restatement (Second) § 251 refers expressly to "Validity" and "Effect" and does not refer to "Perfection." Even so, the next time the Barrett situation surfaces, at least in an international context, the state of conflicts theory which the court will have to deal with will presumably be perceived as considerably more open-ended, fluid or fuzzy than the flat situs rule which, in Judge Hand's opinion, had carried the day.

## PART II. WHO BEARS THE LOSS WHEN GOODS ARE DAMAGED OR LOST?

**§ 3–22.** The main problem to which the remainder of this chapter is addressed is a simple one. When goods are loaded aboard and a bill of lading is given, it normally follows (however pessimistic might be the impression gained from studying the subject only through reading the cases in which it did not follow) that the goods are carried with reasonable dispatch to their destination and delivered in good order to the consignee. Sometimes, however, the goods or some of them are damaged on the way, and sometimes they fail to arrive at all. We are concerned here with a simple question: When one of these things happens, in what cases does the carrier have to pay, and in what cases does the loss remain where it falls, on the shipper or his successor (the holder of the bill of lading) or on the underwriter on the cargo policy? [1]

By far the most important body of law for dealing with this question, when it arises in regard to the ocean commerce which is our principal concern in this book, is contained in the Carriage of Goods By Sea Act of 1936 [1a] (herein referred to as Cogsa). This section will therefore be organized mainly as an analysis of and commentary on the more important sections of that Act. Some background is, however, necessary.

The general law of maritime carriage made the public [1b] carrier of goods by sea absolutely responsible for their safe arrival, unless loss or damage was caused by the Act of God or of the public enemy, or by the inherent vice of the goods or the fault of the shipper—*and*

tion of the chattel, or group of chattels, at the time the security interest attached. So the forum will consider the domicil, nationality, place of incorporation and place of business of the parties." The commentary to § 244 contains a statement which is identical in substance. On the applicability of the "chattel" rules to conveyances of (and presumably security interests in) documents of title under Restatement (Second), see note 106 *supra*.

1. There is a wealth of modern material in the Admiralty Law Institute Symposium on Carriage of Goods by Water, 45 Tulane L.Rev. 697–1013 (1971), and a valuable historical discussion in Bradley, Maritime Contracts on the Western Rivers, 38 Ins. Couns.J. 372 (1971). For business and technical background, see Kendall The Business of Shipping (1973).

1a. 49 Stat. 1207 (1936), 46 U.S.C.A. §§ 1300–1315.

1b. See Chiang, The Characterization of a Vessel as a Common or Private Carrier, 48 Tulane L.Rev. 299 (1974).

(even where the loss was caused by one of these) the carrier was not negligent or otherwise at fault.[2] Except for the qualification indicated this liability did not rest on fault. All the shipper had to do to make his case was to prove receipt for carriage in good order, and non-delivery or delivery in bad order. If the carrier could not show that one of the "exceptions" just listed was the cause of the loss or damage, he had to pay.

When the bill of lading came into general use as a receipt for goods and as a document of title, shipowners, naturally desirous of diminishing this stringent liability, began to set out on the face or back of the bill various "exceptions"—clauses, that is to say, stipulating that they should not be liable to the holders of the bill of lading for damage or loss of the goods suffered in certain ways or from certain causes. These may be looked on as contractual additions to the common-law "exceptions" (Act of God and the public enemy, inherent vice) listed in the last paragraph. During the nineteenth century, the aggregate of such clauses to be found in the usual bill of lading was large, and bills were more or less standardized in this respect, so that one could speak, *e. g.*, of *the* "exception of rust" in reference to the customarily included clause stipulating that the carrier was not to be liable for damage to the goods caused by rust.[3]

Before these clauses came into use, it had not been of much importance (unless the carrier invoked one of the "common law" exceptions listed above) whether or not the carrier had been at fault in any respect, for his liability, outside the common-law exceptions, was that of a warrantor of safe arrival, and fault was immaterial. When the exceptive clauses came into extensive use, the courts held that the exemption conferred by such clauses was to be subjected to two "overriding obligations": the obligation to use due care with respect to the cargo, and the obligation to furnish a "seaworthy" ship at the beginning of the voyage.[4] Proof that one of these obligations had been breached, and that the breach had contributed to cause the damage, might be brought forward by the shipper, to take his case out of an "exception" under which the carrier had brought it. This seems always to have been the rule as to the common-law "exceptions," carried over to the new and numerous "exception" clauses.[5]

2. See Propeller Niagara v. Cordes, 62 U.S. (21 How.) 7, 23 (1859); The Willdomino, 300 F. 5, 9, 1924 A.M.C. 889 (3d Cir. 1924), affirmed 272 U.S. 718, 47 S.Ct. 261 (1927); Knauth, Ocean Bills of Lading 116 (4th ed. 1953). Probably the best extended discussion is in Carver, Carriage of Goods by Sea 1–20 (12th ed. 1971). These common law "exceptions" are stated by different authorities in slightly variant forms. See also Note, 32 Neb.L. Rev. 600, 601–602 (1953).

3. For a listing of the more common "exceptions," see Note, 23 Va.L.Rev. 590, 595, note 27 (1937).

4. See Propeller Niagara v. Cordes, 62 U.S. (21 How.) 7, 23 (1859); The Xantho, [1887] 12 A.C. 503, 515; Lockett Co. v. Cunard S. S. Co., 21 F. 2d 191, 1927 A.M.C. 1057 (E.D.N.Y. 1927); Carver, *op. cit. supra* note 2, § 100. See also, generally, Chamlee, The Absolute Warranty of Seaworthiness: A History and Comparative Study, 24 Mercer L.Rev. 519 (1974).

5. See Carver, *op. cit. supra* note 2, § 19; Clark v. Barnwell, 53 U.S. (12 How.) 272, 280 (1851).

§ 3–23. Since carriers commonly inserted in the bill of lading a clause exempting them from liability for damage flowing from breach of the *warranty* of seaworthiness, the "overriding obligations," breach of which, if a "promoting cause" of loss, would take a case out of a common-law or bill of lading exception under which the carrier had brought it, came in practice to be: (1) the duty to use due care with respect to the cargo, and (2) the duty to use due diligence to furnish a seaworthy vessel. These obligations, now imposed by statute,[6] are of immense importance in the law of carriage of goods by sea. As a matter of construction of the bill of lading contract, in the days before statutory regulation supervened, they remained unless *clearly and expressly* excepted;[7] we will presently consider the position when "negligence," by that name, was excepted.

Thus, when goods were carried under a bill of lading with "exceptions," the shipper still could make a *prima facie* case by proving delivery to the carrier in good order and receipt from him in bad, or entire failure to deliver; but if the carrier could go forward and establish that the damage fell within one of the "exceptions"—and there were many to choose from, and more could readily be added at need—then he was exonerated, unless the shipper, taking up the burden of proof, could establish that, though the damage was within an excepted cause, a concurrent or "promoting" cause was some default of the carrier in one of the respects set out in the last paragraph.[8]

Substantively, one could state this as a rule that the carrier who had issued a bill "excepting," say, rust was liable for the damage caused by rust, if his negligence had caused the rusting, but we have put it in burden-of-proof form because of the immense difference it makes, in regard to cargo damage claims, who has to prove what. All the consignee usually has the means of knowing is that the goods have been lost or have turned up damaged. Clearly, the carrier and not the shipper is the one in a position to know and to be able to prove most facts concerning events on the voyage. The allocation of burden of proof may make more difference than the nature of the substantive rules in the actual outcome of litigation and in the negotiating position in regard to claims settlement.[9]

6. See *infra* at note 33 *et seq.*

7. Phillips v. Clark, [1857] 2 C.B., N.S., 156; Carver, *op. cit. supra* note 2, 103 and cases cited; see The Xantho, [1887] 12 A.C. 503, 515. Since, as we shall see, "negligence" clauses were held invalid in our federal courts, the question whether, as a matter of *construction,* a carrier was immunized from liability for negligence, was of importance mainly in the British courts. But see New Jersey Steam Navigation Co. v. Merchants' Bank, 47 U.S. (6 How.) 344, 383–4 (1848); Compania de Navigacion La Flecha v. Brauer, 168 U.S. 104, 119–120, 18 S.Ct. 12, 15–16 (1897); Kenney v. New York Central & H. R. R. Co., 125 N.Y. 422, 425, 26 N.E. 626, 627 (1891).

8. Clark v. Barnwell *supra* note 5. This burden of proof rule was carried forward under the Harter Act (*infra* at note 14); see The Monte Iciar, 167 F.2d 334, 1948 A.M.C. 615 (3d Cir. 1948). For the burden of proof position under Cogsa, see *infra* at note 129 *et seq.*

9. See Note, 27 Texas L.Rev. 525, 530 (1949).

The draftsmen of ocean bills of lading in the last century did not rest content with exceptions of physically described perils and causes. Bills came to include stipulations that the carrier was not to be liable even for the results of his own negligence or that of the ship's people. Thus, where these clauses were upheld, the position of the carrier became, roughly speaking, the reverse of the one he had occupied under the general maritime law. Instead of being absolutely liable, irrespective of negligence, he enjoyed an exemption from liability, regardless of negligence, as wide as his bargaining position enabled him to contract for.[9a]

The British courts generally upheld the validity of these "negligence" exceptions,[10] while the Federal courts in this country held it against public policy for the carrier to contract out of liability for his own negligence or that of his people, and declined to give effect to the "negligence" clauses.[11] Thus, when goods were carried under such a bill, the accidents of accessibility of courts or amenability to service made a crucial difference in the outcome of litigation. And the difference in judicial doctrine at least ran parallel to differences in national interest. With the decline of the clipper ships and the triumph of steam, the British merchant marine came to be dominant in the Atlantic,[12] and most of the bills of lading containing these extreme stipulations against liability for negligence were issued by British ships. The United States, on the other hand, was vitally interested in both export and import of cargo, and great dissatisfaction was felt, on the part of American cargo interests, with bills of lading that agreed, in effect, that the goods would be carried when, where, and in what manner was pleasing to the carrier.[13]

§ 3–24. This was the problem to which Congress sought to provide an answer in the Harter Act of 1893.[14] That act was a compro-

9a. Caterpillar Overseas, S. A. v. S. S. Expeditor, 318 F.2d 720, 722, 1963 A.M.C. 1662, 1665 (2d Cir. 1963), certiorari denied 375 U.S. 942, 84 S.Ct. 347 (1964), citing text.

10. Carver, *op. cit. supra* note 2, §§ 134 *et seq.* See *In re* Missouri S. S. Co., 42 Ch.D. 321 (1889), where the British court upheld a "negligence" clause in a bill of lading issued by a British line to an American in Massachusetts. Conceding *arguendo* that the clause would be invalid in the place of issuance, the court, in determining as a conflicts matter that its validity was to be referred to British law, used the argument that the parties must have "intended" the application of the law that would make it valid. Practically, such decisions meant that Americans exporting in British bottoms were, notwithstanding United States law, subjected to the impact of the negligence clauses when they had to sue in England.

11. Liverpool & Great Western Steam Co. v. Phenix Ins. Co., 129 U.S. 397, 438–463, 9 S.Ct. 469, 470–480 (1889). There were state decisions following the British rule, a fact which, in the days before any clear delineation of federal supremacy in substantive maritime law, further muddled the picture. See Rubens v. Ludgate Hill S. S. Co., 65 Hun 625, 20 N.Y.S. 481 (Sup.Ct.Gen.Term, 1st Dep't 1892), affirmed without opinion 143 N.Y. 629, 37 N.E. 825 (1894).

12. See *infra,* Chapter XI at note 46.

13. See Knauth, *op. cit. supra* note 2, 116 (and, generally, 115–131, for a detailed account of the commercial, judicial and legislative history behind the modern statutes regulating ocean carriage).

14. 27 Stat. 445 (1893), 46 U.S.C.A. §§ 190–196.

mise between the interests that sought (by the inclusion of exculpatory clauses in bills) full exoneration for the carrier from all claims based on his negligence, and those who (relying on the view of the federal courts) sought to hold carriers responsible for the consequences of every sort of negligence. By Sections 1 and 2 of the Act, it was made unlawful for any bill of lading covering a shipment "from or between ports of the United States and foreign ports" to contain clauses relieving the vessel or her owners from liability "for loss or damage arising from negligence, fault or failure in proper loading, stowage, custody, care, or proper delivery" of the cargo, or weakening or lessening the obligation to use diligence to "properly equip, man, provision and outfit said vessel, and to make said vessel seaworthy . . . ."[15] Thus, the cargo interests got some protection against the "negligence" clauses. On the other hand, the carrying interests got something too. Section 3 of the Act provided:

> "*Limitation of liability for errors of navigation, dangers of the sea and acts of God.* If the owner of any vessel transporting merchandise or property to or from any port in the United States of America shall exercise due diligence to make the said vessel in all respects seaworthy and properly manned, equipped, and supplied, neither the vessel, her owner or owners, agent, or charterers, shall become or be held responsible for damage or loss resulting from faults or errors in navigation or in the management of said vessel . . . ."[16]

The net position came down to this: The shipowner could not contract out of the duty to use care to put his vessel in good shape for the voyage, or the duty to care properly for the goods while they were in his hands or aboard. On the other hand, if he did use due care to send a seaworthy vessel on the voyage, he could not be held for the defaults of those he put in charge, in regard to running her. The rationale of the last provision is fairly easy to see. The safety of his own vessel was taken to be sufficient spur to the owner to lead him to do what he could to bring it about that the people to whom he entrusted her would use care in her navigation and management.

This compromise was so well thought of that when, between 1921 and 1924, representatives of the shipping world and of the maritime nations sought by conference to arrive at terms suitable for uniform worldwide treatment of the shipper-carrier relation under ocean bills of lading,[17] the "Hague Rules" which they adopted, first as a set of clauses for voluntary inclusion in bills of lading and then as a Convention to which the adherence of maritime nations was invited, embodied the Harter Act compromise in its main outline. In 1936, the

15. 27 Stat. 445 (1893), 46 U.S.C.A. §§ 190–191.

16. 27 Stat. 445 (1893), 46 U.S.C.A. § 192.

17. See Knauth, *op. cit. supra* note 2, 125–127.

United States adhered to the Convention, and Congress passed in implementation the Carriage of Goods By Sea Act,[18] which with minor differences follows verbatim the Hague Rules.[19]

So much for background. The Harter Act was supplanted in important part by Cogsa, but is still law for some sorts of carriage and at some points in other sorts. Because of the overwhelming importance of Cogsa, however, we will treat the Harter Act comparatively along with the analysis of the newer statute.

Reference ought at this point to be made to the "container revolution" described in Chapter I.[19a] In the last fifteen years or so, a very great deal of international transport has come to be carried in "containers", of such size as to be movable as units behind trucks, or piggyback on flatcars, from any inland point to the ship, and from the ship to any inland point, without being opened. This combined transport raises new legal questions; the courts are struggling with these, under statutes enacted quite without prevision of or provision for this revolution, and attempts at rationalization through international negotiation are in progress.[19b] Given the intense conservatism of maritime law,[19c] it is pretty certain that knowledge of the older law, relating to conventionally packaged goods, will be essential or at least helpful in dealing with the problems arising out of containerization.

18. *Supra* note 1a. See Scarburgh v. Compania Sud-Americana De Vapores, 174 F.2d 423, 424 (2d Cir. 1949). There is a discussion of the background and theory of Cogsa, citing this text, in Nichimen Co. v. M/V Farland, 462 F.2d 319, 326 et seq., 1972 A.M.C. 1573 (2d Cir. 1972); see also Encyclopedia Britannica, Inc. v, S. S. Hong Kong Producer, 422 F.2d 7, 1969 A.M.C. 1741 (2d Cir. 1969).

An international Protocol, modifying the Hague Rules which are the basis of Cogsa, was adopted in Brussels in 1968. This Protocol is colloquially known as the Visby Amendment. Ratification is slow; for now, it is best to proceed on the assumption that Cogsa will continue to be the law. See De Gurse, The "Container Clause" in Article 4(5) of the 1968 Protocol to the Hague Rules, 2 Journal of Maritime Law and Commerce 131 (1970) and *cf.* § 3–48 *infra.*

19. For variations which may make a difference, see *infra* at notes 81 *et seq.*, 97 *et seq.*, 136 *et seq.* For the original French text of the Rules, and the official American translation, see Knauth, *op. cit. supra* note 2, 40 *et seq.* Private international law questions in ocean transport are surveyed in Knauth, Renvoi and Other Conflicts Problems in Transportation Law, 49 Colum.L.Rev. 1 (1949).

19a. See *supra* § 1–5.

19b. See Simon, Latest Developments in the Law of Shipping Containers, 4 Journal of Maritime Law and Commerce 441 (1973); Massey, Prospects for a New Intermodal Legal Regime, 3 Journal of Maritime Law and Commerce 725 (1972); also Schmeltzer & Peavy, Prospects and Problems of the Container Revolution, 1 Journal of Maritime Law and Commerce 203 (1970); Hickey, Legal Problems Relating to Combined Transport and Barge Carrying Vessels, 45 Tulane L.Rev. 863, esp. pp. 885–900 (1971); Bissell, The Operational Realties of Containerization . . . ., 45 Tulane L. Rev. 902 (1971); Spitz, Cargo Risk Problems—Container Operator's Dilemma, 45 Tulane L.Rev. 925 (1971). The International Chamber of Commerce has recently promulgated new Rules for Combined Transport; these do not of course have the force of law. See Maritime Law Association Doc. No. 584, p. 6265 (1974).

19c. See, *e. g.*, Crutcher, The Ocean Bill of Lading—A Study in Fossilization, 45 Tulane L.Rev. 697 (1971).

## Respective Coverages of Cogsa and Harter

**§ 3–25.** Cogsa, like Harter, regulates the terms of ocean carriage by the indirect but highly efficacious device of dealing with the terms of the ocean bill of lading. The enacting clause gives the theory:

> "*Be it enacted by the Senate and House of Representatives of the United States of America in Congress assembled,* That every bill of lading or similar document of title which is evidence of a contract for the carriage of goods by sea to or from ports of the United States, in foreign trade, shall have effect subject to the provisions of this Act." [20]

Thus, a bill of lading covered by Cogsa is to be read as though Cogsa were incorporated by reference.[21]

An inspection of Cogsa, particularly of sections 3 and 4, shows that the Act is a limited code of rules governing the most important of the rights and responsibilities, liabilities and immunities arising out of the relation of issuer to holder of the bill of lading, with respect to goods damage or loss. (This loss or damage may occur through delay, without physical damage to cargo.[21a]) Harter is less comprehensive, and in part at least proceeds on a different theory. Its sections 1 and 2 lay down no positive rules of law, but simply forbid certain stipulations in the bill of lading contract. Section 3 of Harter does, indeed, grant certain immunities from liability as a matter of law.[22]

Cogsa allows a freedom of contracting out of its terms, but only in the direction of *increasing* the shipowner's liabilities, and never in the direction of diminishing them.[23] This apparent onesidedness is a

20. 49 Stat. 1207 (1936), 46 U.S.C.A. § 1300. The frequency with which this Act will be cited in this chapter makes it unwieldy to repeat formal citations. Generally, section numbers of the Act will be employed. Where clarity requires it, fuller citations will be given.

21. See Shackman v. Cunard White Star, Ltd., 31 F.Supp. 948, 1940 A.M.C. 971 (S.D.N.Y.1940). This principle may be subject to the reservation that, where a carrier wilfully omits the "clause paramount" expressly provided for by the Act, he may be estopped to claim its benefits; see *infra* at note 137 *et seq.*

21a. See Commercio Transito Internazionale, Ltd. v. Lykes Bros. Steamship Co., 243 F.2d 683, 1957 A.M.C. 1188 (2d Cir. 1957).

22. See *supra* at notes 15–16.

23. §§ 3(8), 5. This passage was cited with approval in Encyclopedia Britannica, Inc. v. S. S. Hong Kong Producer, 422 F.2d 7, 12, 1969 A.M.C. 1741 (2d Cir. 1969). There was danger to this principle in Wm. H. Muller & Co. v. Swedish-American Line, Ltd., 224 F.2d 806, 1955 A.M.C. 1687 (2d Cir. 1955) certiorari denied 350 U.S. 903, 76 S.Ct. 182 (1955). (See *supra* Chapter III, Part I, note 104). The bill of lading, on a shipment from Sweden to Philadelphia, was beyond all question subject to Cogsa. Yet the court gave effect to a clause stipulating for Swedish law and suit only in Sweden. Such a clause seems to fly in the face, as clearly as may be, of the precisely-stated rule of Cogsa that every bill of lading in foreign commerce into or out of the United States shall "have effect" subject to Cogsa. Under the Muller decision, the bill "had effect" subject not to Cogsa but to Swedish law. True, Sweden has adopted the Hague Rules, but no country has a statute exactly like the U. S. Cogsa, which latter statute Congress has said, with all possible clarity, is to apply. If the foreign law is

less favorable to the shipper than Cogsa, then his rights are "lessened" in violation of section 3(8) of Cogsa; it is manifestly unreasonable to put on him the burden of proving this to be so in the given case, if for no other reason than that either the shipper's rights are "lessened" or the stipulation for foreign law is valueless to the carrier, and the latter has no interest in asserting it.

The stipulation for suit abroad seems also to offend Cogsa, most obviously because it destroys the shipper's certainty that Cogsa will be applied. Further, it is entirely unrealistic to look on an obligation to sue overseas as not "lessening" the liability of the carrier. It puts a high hurdle in the way of enforcing that liability. And section 5 of Cogsa makes it plain that no provisions directly or indirectly disadvantaging the shipper were to be permitted.

Finally, the case seemed impossible to reconcile with the holding in Knott v. Botany Worsted Mills, 179 U.S. 69, 21 S.Ct. 30 (1898) that section 1 of The Harter Act "overrides and nullifies" (179 U.S. at 77, 21 S.Ct. at 33) a stipulation for ship's-flag law. The Supreme Court said: "The power of Congress to include such cases . . . cannot be denied in a court of the United States." 179 U.S. at 74, 21 S.Ct. at 31, 32. Congress seems to have done so in Cogsa, just as clearly as or more clearly than in Harter. (Cerro De Pasco Copper Corp. v. Knut Knutsen, 187 F.2d 990, 1951 A.M.C. 630 (2d Cir. 1951), which the court purports to follow in Muller, is summarily and clearly distinguishable since the carriage there was not "to or from" the U. S., and Cogsa did not apply.)

In Sociedade Brasileira De Intercambio Comercial E. Industrial, Ltda. v. S. S. Punta Del Este, 135 F.Supp. 394, 1955 A.M.C. 2288 (D.C.N.J.1955) the court refuses to give effect to a stipulation for Uruguayan law and courts, partly on the ground that the bill of lading in suit contained a "clause paramount"—*i. e.*, one stating that Cogsa was to be applicable. But surely that can make no difference in an American court, for Congress has already said it is to be applicable.

With respect, it seems the Muller court ought to have left the question of "reasonableness" of such a stipulation with Congress, for Congress has settled the question in language which is none the less clear for being general —or, more to the point, sweeping.

Fortunately, in Indussa Corp. v. S. S. Ranborg, 377 F.2d 200, 1967 A.M.C. 589 (2d Cir. 1967), The Second Circuit *en banc* (citing text) overruled the Muller case, invalidating a stipulation for foreign law and a foreign forum. For a vigorous defense of the Indussa holding, see Mendelsohn, Liberalism, Choice of Forum Clauses, and the Hague Rules, 2 Journal of Maritime Law and Commerce 661 (1971). It has, however, been held that Cogsa does not invalidate a three-month limit on arbitration. Kurt Orban Co. v. S. S. Clymenia, 318 F.Supp. 1387, 1971 A.M.C. 778 (S.D.N.Y.1970), noted, 2 Journal of Maritime Law and Commerce 897 (1971). This holding seems clearly out of line with Indussa. The Supreme Court has shown a reluctance to speak on these issues; see The Monrosa v. Carbon Black Export Co., 359 U.S. 180, 79 S.Ct. 710, 1959 A.M.C. 1327 (1959) rehearing denied 359 U.S. 999, 79 S.Ct. 1115 (1959).

The recent case of M/S Bremen v. Zapata Off-Shore Co., 407 U.S. 1, 92 S.Ct. 1907, 1972 A.M.C. 1407 (1972) upheld a "choice of forum" clause in a towage contract, but it was explicitly noted that Cogsa was inapplicable, 407 U.S. at 10, n. 11, 92 S.Ct. at 1913. Thus the Bremen case need not be held to disturb the Indussa. See Black, The Bremen, Cogsa, and the Problem of Conflicting Interpretation, 6 Vanderbilt Journal of Transnational Law 363 (1973). The *Bremen* is also noted in Juenger, Supreme Court Validation of Forum Selection Clauses, 19 Wayne L. Rev. 49 (1972), and the choice-of-forum problem is discussed in historic depth in Nadelman, Choice-of-Court Clauses in the United States, 21 Am.J. of Comp.Law 124 (1973). See also Notes, 58 Cornell L.Rev. 416 (1973); 33 La.L.Rev. 481 (1973). (The Bremen is further discussed in Chapter X, *infra.*)

A recent District Court case has upheld a "choice of forum" clause in a bill of lading, but in the very peculiar circumstances the clause operated to benefit the *shipper*, and hence inverted the situation contemplated and covered by § 3(8). Roach v. Hapag-Lloyd, 358 F.Supp. 481, 1973 A.M.C. 1968 (N. D.Calif.1973).

commonsense recognition of the inequality in bargaining power which both Harter and Cogsa were designed to redress, and of the fact that one of the great objectives of both Acts is to prevent the impairment of the value and negotiability of the ocean bill of lading. Obviously, the latter result can never ensue from the increase of the carrier's duties. So far as is known, no carrier has availed itself of the latitude afforded by this provision.

(In Holden v. S. S. Kendal Fish,[23a] the carrier had contracted to pay invoice value plus freight and insurance as measure of damages; the court held market price at destination to be the proper measure, and invalidated the contractual term, which would have benefitted the cargo owner. This result is questionable; Cogsa's policy against freedom of contract probably ought to be held to be for the benefit of cargo only.)

Cogsa, as the enacting clause tells us, applies only in *foreign* commerce. The exact period during which the Act defines rights and duties on which liability can be predicated is "from the time when the goods are loaded on to the time when they are discharged from the ship." [24] Undoubtedly, therefore, during this period in foreign carriage the substantive sections (1–3) of Harter are superseded by Cogsa, for the matters previously covered by these sections during this period are explicitly provided for in the later Act.

Harter, on the other hand, applied to both foreign and domestic water carriage under bills of lading. Unlike Cogsa, Harter contains no limitation of its effect to any period of time; the period of its application has to be inferred. Sections 1 and 2 of Harter speak of duties as to loading, stowage, custody, care and delivery.[25] A duty as to "delivery" manifestly applies not only until goods are discharged but until they are delivered; "custody and care" would seem to reach from receipt by the carrier until delivery. Cogsa expressly saves Harter from repeal in so far as it applies to the periods prior to loading and after discharge from the ship.[26] Thus, in the absence of stipulation, Harter still applies:

(1) To all "coastwise" trade—that is, to bills of lading covering shipments by water from one port of the United States to another.[27]

23a. 395 F.2d 910, 1968 A.M.C. 2080 (5th Cir. 1968).

24. § 1(e).

25. See *supra* at note 15.

26. Cogsa § 12, 46 U.S.C.A. § 1311.

27. Even a towage contract may be covered by the Harter Act, where the contract is actually one of "affreightment" rather than "towage"—*i. e.*, where the shipper simply places his cargo in the custody of the barge-owner, who proceeds to tow it to destination. Sacramento Navigation Co. v. Salz, 273 U.S. 326, 47 S.Ct. 368, 1927 A.M.C. 397 (1927). For the position as to "negligence" stipulations of the tug owner in the contract of "mere" towage, see Bisso v. Inland Waterways Corp., 349 U.S. 85, 75 S.Ct. 629, 1955 A.M.C. 899 (1955). The Court, over vigorous dissent, declined to give effect to a clause exempting the tug from liability for negligent towage. See also Boston Metals Co. v. The Winding Gulf, 349 U.S. 122, 75 S.Ct. 649, 1955 A.M.C. 927 (1955).

(2) To the period, even in foreign trade, during which the carrier has custody of the goods, before they are loaded on the ship and after they are unloaded from the ship.[28]

By express provision of Cogsa, the bill of lading may validly stipulate for coverage by Cogsa rather than Harter in domestic voyages.[29] This is the so-called "coastwise option." There is no provision for contracting out of Harter and into Cogsa as to the period prior to loading and between loading and delivery. Such a stipulation is, however, often included in Cogsa bills. Usually there is no difference between the two Acts. Cogsa imposes a duty to use care in respect of the cargo.[30] Harter, in its presently relevant provisions,[31] forbids stipulations which eliminate the duty to use care in respect of the cargo. Thus, except for unimportant differences in phraseology, the two Acts come down to much the same thing, as to liabilities which might be incurred before loading or after unloading.

(Some limitation of value clauses, invalid under Cogsa, might be valid under Harter. It has been held in the Second Circuit, however, that the validity of such a clause cannot be revived when goods, having been carried under Cogsa, are unloaded but still in custody of the carrier.[31a])

As the discussion develops, it will be seen that Cogsa and Harter are at many points so much alike that the differences may be looked on as merely verbal or stylistic. For this reason, it is universal practice, followed here, to cite Harter Act cases to Cogsa points, where applicable. Thus (for example) there is no reason to suppose that the

28. Caterpillar Overseas, S. A. v. S. S. Expeditor, 318 F.2d 720, 1963 A.M.C. 1662 (2d Cir. 1963), certiorari denied 375 U.S. 942, 84 S.Ct. 347 (1964), citing text. The case held that a contractual attempt to equate "discharge" with "delivery" was invalid, as tantamount to an attempt to contract out of the Harter Act. See also Isthmian S. S. Co. v. California Spray-Chemical Corp., 300 F.2d 41, 1962 A.M.C. 1474 (9th Cir. 1962). The reservation must be noted that the Harter Act § 3 immunity with regard to negligent navigation and managemet (see *supra* at note 16) is conditioned on the exercise of due diligence to make the ship seaworthy, and that this condition is satisfied or not as of the moment of "breaking ground" or commencing the voyage. See Gilchrist Transp. Co. v. Boston Ins. Co., 223 F. 716, 718–19 (6th Cir. 1915); The Newport, 7 F.2d 452, 454, 1925 A.M.C. 1193 (9th Cir. 1925). In this sense, it can be said that the benefits of § 3 are not available to the carrier except as to events taking place subsequent to the start of the voyage. But this does not mean that the other provisions of the Harter Act do not apply, as on their face they appear to, after receipt of the goods but before sailing. The points seem to be clinched by the provision in Harter, § 1, as to "loading"; obviously, this must apply before the voyage begins.

Proper "delivery" denotes placement in a fit place. Levatino Co. v. S. S. Hellenic Hero, 1969 A.M.C. 695 (S.D.N.Y. 1969).

29. Cogsa § 13, 46 U.S.C.A. § 1312. There appears to be a growing tendency for Harter Act bills to stipulate for Cogsa.

30. § 3(2).

31. See *supra* at note 15.

31a. David Crystal, Inc. v. Cunard S. S. Co., 339 F.2d 295, 1965 A.M.C. 39 (2d Cir. 1964), certiorari denied 380 U.S. 976, 85 S.Ct. 1339 (1965); Leather's Best, Inc. v. S. S. Mormaclynx, 451 F.2d 800, 1971 A.M.C. 2383 (2d Cir. 1971), on remand 346 F.Supp. 962 (E. D.N.Y.1972).

term "seaworthiness" means anything different under Cogsa from what it did and does under Harter, and the older cases are freely used to establish its construction under the new Act.[32]

It is now settled that only the carrier, and not the stevedore handling goods, gets the benefit of Cogsa's limitations of liability.[32a] Presumably the same would be true of the Harter Act. But the result may be different if the bill of lading expressly covers the stevedore by providing for his enjoying the Cogsa benefits.[32b]

### The Heart of Cogsa

**§ 3–26.** Before we discuss particular sections and clauses, it will be advisable to look over the ground-plan of that part of Cogsa which defines the "responsibilities and liabilities" of the carrier, on which claims for cargo damage may be predicated, and the "rights and immunities" under which the carrier can avoid liability. Sections 3(1) [33] and 3(2) state the broad affirmative grounds on which cargo may recover; Sections 4(1) and 4(2) set out the "exceptions" from liability which are now enjoyed as a matter of statute rather than of contract. 3(1) and 4(1) must be read together, as they both deal with the subject of the carrier's duty with respect to seaworthiness of the vessel. Section 3(2) states a general duty of using due care with respect to the cargo, and Section 4(2) is a rather miscellaneous list of causes and circumstances for effects of which the carrier is not to be held liable. The reader will recognize, in Section 3(1) and (2), though in somewhat altered form, the two "overriding obligations" of the carrier discussed in the first section of this chapter, and in Section 4(2) the "exceptions" formerly incorporated in bills of lading.

It is rather rare that any one subsection or clause comes up for construction by itself. The foregoing account of the rough structure of these crucial sections will make it clear that the fight will normally be about whether a given sequence of events is to be classified under one section *or* another. The case-law is multifarious and disorganized, but what clarity in organization it can be given must come from grouping it around lines drawn between one subsection or clause and another. Thus, the question "What is 'negligence in the navigation and management of the ship'?" is never asked in isolation, but in a question of the form: "Is the set of facts under examination to be classed

**32.** For a survey of the similarities between the two Acts, see Note, 27 Va. L.Rev. 1078 (1941).

**32a.** Herd & Co. v. Krawill Machinery Co., 359 U.S. 297, 79 S.Ct. 766, 1959 A.M.C. 879 (1959).

**32b.** Carle & Montanari, Inc. v. American Export Isbrandtsen Lines, Inc., 275 F.Supp. 76, 1967 A.M.C. 1637 (S. D.N.Y.1967), affirmed 386 F.2d 839, 1967 A.M.C. 2529 (2d Cir. 1967), certiorari denied 390 U.S. 1013, 88 S.Ct. 1263 (1968). See Doak, Liabilities of Stevedores, Terminal Operators, and Other Handlers in Relation to Cargo, 45 Tulane L.Rev. 752, 760 (1971). This coverage of the stevedore, it has been held, must be specific and clear, for the contract is one of adhesion. Cabot Corp. v. S. S. Mormacscan, 441 F.2d 476, 1971 A.M.C. 1130 (2d Cir. 1971), certiorari denied 404 U.S. 855, 92 S.Ct. 104 (1971). See also Rupp v. International Terminal Operating Co., 479 F.2d 674, 1973 A.M.C. 1093 (2d Cir. 1973).

**33.** See *supra* note 20.

as an instance of negligent management of the ship, or of negligence in the care of the cargo?"

When the sections are read together, one interesting generality emerges. So far as these crucially important provisions go, the carrier's "insurer's" liability is a thing of the past. His liability for cargo damage must now be predicated on fault only. A quick skimming of the four subsections we are now examining will show that this is so: Sections 3(1) and 3(2) impose liability only in case of negligence; section 4(1) limits a certain sort of liability to a negligence basis; 4(2)(a) to (p) confer specific immunities, and 4(2)(q) nails the point down by providing that the carrier shall not be responsible for loss or damage resulting from "any other cause arising without the actual fault and privity of the carrier and without the fault or neglect of the agents or servants of the carrier . . . ." This general immunity from liability without fault is, of course, enjoyed by the carrier without the necessity for stipulation in the bill of lading.

It should be said at once (though it will clearly appear shortly) that, though the carrier cannot be held for losses occurring without fault, it neither follows nor is true that he can be held for every act of negligence of himself or his agents. One of the specific "exceptions," 4(2)(a), grants an immunity in case of negligence of a certain sort; another, 4(2)(b), drastically cuts down the normal operation of *respondeat superior* doctrines as to negligence resulting in loss by fire, though leaving the carrier responsible for "personal" negligence in this regard. The question whether the 4(2)(c) to (p) exceptions excuse the carrier from liability even for negligence in the cases they cover, may not have a general solution, since these exceptions differ widely in type among themselves; we will return to this question after the clause-by-clause discussion of these provisions has furnished the basis for a more concrete treatment.

### The Duty to Furnish a Proper Ship

§ 3–27. The carrier's first duty is defined in Section 3(1):

"The carrier shall be bound, before and at the beginning of the voyage, to exercise due diligence to—

"(a) Make the ship seaworthy;

"(b) Properly man, equip, and supply the ship;

"(c) Make the holds, refrigerating and cooling chambers, and all other parts of the ship in which goods are carried, fit and safe for their reception, carriage and preservation."

The reader will recognize the term "seaworthy" as one already encountered in marine insurance. Just as, in the marine policy, the assured warrants that the ship is seaworthy, so, under the general maritime law, the carrier warranted to the shipper that the carrying ship was seaworthy.[34] The concept of unseaworthiness alone, without the expansion in Cogsa Section 3(1)(b, c) above, would, in Anglo-American maritime law, include proper manning, equipping, and supplying, and fitness to receive and care for the cargo,[35] but the additional clauses make clear the comprehensiveness of the duty, and may have been necessary in rules, such as those of which Cogsa is a near copy, designed to be applied in countries where a different concept of seaworthiness may prevail.

Section 3(1) cuts down the warranty of seaworthiness to an obligation to use due diligence to make the vessel seaworthy. The abolition of the warranty need not be left to inference from the limited language of this section, however, for Section 4(1) says explicitly:

> "Neither the carrier nor the ship shall be liable for loss or damage arising or resulting from unseaworthiness unless caused by want of due diligence on the part of the carrier to make the ship seaworthy, and to secure that the ship is properly manned, equipped, and supplied, and to make the holds, refrigerating and cool chambers, and all other parts of the ship in which goods are carried fit and safe for their reception, carriage, and preservation in accordance with the provision of paragraph (1) of section 3. Whenever loss or damage has resulted from unseaworthiness, the burden of proving the exercise of due diligence shall be on the carrier or other persons claiming exemption under this section." [36]

Thus, where unseaworthiness causes a loss, and where the defect that caused the loss is itself attributable to a want of due diligence on the part of the carrier, cargo can recover. The Harter Act, as it actually operated, attained the same result in a different way. Section 2 of that Act,[37] as we have seen, prohibits contracting out

34. The Caledonia, 157 U.S. 124, 15 S. Ct. 537 (1895). But it seems never to have been even suggested, in the goods carriage cases, that breach of this warranty "ousted" the bill of lading contract, as the breach of the insurance seaworthiness warranty ousts the policy; the carrier is liable only for damages *causally connected* with unseaworthiness.

35. The Southwark, 191 U.S. 1, 24 S.Ct. 1 (1903); R. T. Jones Lumber Co. v. Roen S. S. Co., 270 F.2d 456, 1960 A.M.C. 46 (2d Cir. 1959); The Benjamin Noble, 244 F. 95, 97 (6th Cir. 1917) affirmed *sub nom.* Capitol Transp. Co. v. Cambria Steel Co., 249 U.S. 334, 39 S.Ct. 292 (1919). See Note, 19 Va.L. Rev. 526 (1933).

36. See The Toledo, 122 F.2d 255, 1941 A.M.C. 1219 (2d Cir. 1941), certiorari denied 314 U.S. 689, 62 S.Ct. 302 (1941). On the scope of the remaining "due diligence" obligation, see Villareal, The Concept of Due Diligence in Maritime Law, 2 Journal of Maritime Law and Commerce 763 (1971).

37. 27 Stat. 445 (1893), 46 U.S.C.A. § 191. As to what constitutes due diligence, see Erie & St. Lawrence Corp. v. Barnes-Ames Co., 52 F.2d 217, 218–19, 1931 A.M.C. 1994 (W.D.N.Y.1931); Gold Dust Corp. v. Munson S. S. Line, 55 F.2d 900, 1932 A.M.C. 240 (2d Cir. 1932). The duty to use due diligence cannot, of course, be cut down by any clause in the bill of lading or any other contractual arrangement (Cogsa § 3(8)), and is non-delegable. See The Point Brava, 1 F.Supp. 366, 1933 A.M.C. 146 (N.D.Cal.1932).

of the obligation to use due diligence to make the vessel seaworthy. It was early held that this provison did not of its own force eliminate the warranty of seaworthiness, though it did impliedly permit contracting out of the warranty.[38] Naturally, carriers commonly inserted clauses in bills of lading reducing the warranty to the point permitted by the Harter Act—to an obligation to use due diligence in this respect. Thus, in a case ruled by a normally drawn bill of lading under Harter, the carrier could be held only for damage ensuing from his failure to use due diligence to make his vessel fit for the service—the same result as under Cogsa.

The House of Lords has held, in an important decision, that this obligation is non-delegable; and is not discharged by turning the vessel over to impeccably reputable repairmen.[38a] In practice though not in theory, this restores much of the seaworthiness warranty.

The obligation to use due diligence to make the vessel seaworthy, like the warranty it has replaced, is either fulfilled or not fulfilled when the vessel "breaks ground" on the voyage.[39] There may be close cases here; in Mississippi Shipping Co. v. Zander & Co., Inc.[39a] for example, the Fifth Circuit held that the voyage had begun when undocking maneuvers started, so that failure to stop and repair an injury then occurring was not a failure in the "seaworthiness" obligation, but one in "management", for the consequences of which the carrier was exempt. (see *infra* § 3–29).

(The reader will compare this timing of the warranty with the similar rule as to the warranty of seaworthiness in marine insurance.[40])

The specific content of the term "seaworthiness" seems much the same in carriage law as it is in marine insurance. In the chapter on that subject, we called it both "a comprehensive and a relative term."[41] Both these points are made, in the present context, by the

38. The Carib Prince, 170 U.S. 655, 18 S.Ct. 753 (1898).

38a. Riverstone Meat Co. v. Lancashire Shipping Co. [1961] A.C. 807, 1961 A.M.C. 1357.

39. Horn v. Cia de Navegacion Fruco, S. A., 404 F.2d 422, 1968 A.M.C. 2548, 2558 (5th Cir. 1968), certiorari denied 394 U.S. 943, 89 S.Ct. 1272 (1969). Erie & St. Lawrence Corp. v. Barnes-Ames Co., 52 F.2d 217, 1931 A.M.C. 1994 (W.D.N.Y.1931); The Steel Navigator, 23 F.2d 590, 591, 1928 A.M.C. 388 (2d Cir. 1928). The obligation may, however, revive if the vessel puts into a port of refuge, and be breached by sailing thence in an unseaworthy state caused by lack of due diligence, at least of the managing personnel of the owner. The Isis, 290 U.S. 333, 344–345, 54 S.Ct. 162, 164, 1933 A.M.C. 1565 (1933). It is not always easy to tell when the voyage has begun; see Greenwood, Problems of Negligence in Loading, etc., 45 Tulane L.Rev. 790, 802–805 (1971); Tetley and Cleven, Prosecuting the Voyage, 45 Tulane L. Rev. 807 (1971).

39a. 270 F.2d 345, 1959 A.M.C. 2143 (5th Cir. 1959), vacated 361 U.S. 115, conformed to and recalled in part 273 F.2d 618 (2d Cir. 1960).

40. Union Ins. Co. v. Smith, 124 U.S. 405, 427, 8 S.Ct. 534, 546 (1888). See *supra*, Chapter II, at note 51 *et seq.*

41. See *supra* Chapter II, at note 56. For detailed review of judicial opinions on seaworthiness, see Longley, Common Carriage of Cargo, 41–60 (1967).

opinion, written by Judge Learned Hand, in Edmond Weil, Inc. v. American West African Line, Inc.[42] In that case, the ship sailed with a deck cargo of ammonia cylinders and mahogany "curls" (roots), as well as a cargo under deck. From the deck on which cargo was stowed (and which also, of course, constituted the protective covering of the under-deck cargo), protruded certain tubes, formerly used to carry electric wiring, but now empty and capped. During rough weather on the voyage, some of the ammonia cylinders broke loose, rolled about the deck, and broke off some of the tubes, opening holes in the deck, through which seawater entered and damaged the cargo below. On the issue of seaworthiness as tendered by these facts, Judge Hand says:

> "The first question is whether the ship was unseaworthy. Arguendo, we will assume that the 'kick-tubes' did not make her so if she had carried no deck cargo; and, perhaps also, even when she carried certain kinds of deck cargo. Indeed, we might go still further, and assume that she was seaworthy, just as she rode, for a summer voyage, for example in the Mediterranean. But she was to cross the Atlantic in January, ending in latitudes over 40°; and the question is whether, with the deck cargo she actually did carry and the 'kick-tubes' in her deck, she was reasonably fitted for such a voyage. The Silvia, 171 U.S. 462, 464, 19 S.Ct. 7, 43 L.Ed. 241; The Southwark, 191 U.S. 1, 9, 24 S.Ct. 1, 48 L.Ed. 65; Societa Anonima, etc. v. Federal Insurance Co., 2 Cir., 62 F.2d 769, 771; The Smyrna, 4 Cir., 62 F.2d 1048, 1050; The J. L. Luckenbach, 2 Cir., 65 F.2d 570, 572; The Galileo, 2 Cir., 54 F.2d 913, 914. The fact that the 'kick-tubes' had caused no trouble in the past was relevant, but far from conclusive; it took only a minimum of foresight to perceive that they would stand up against very little violence. True, as they were placed on the deck, they were out of the way; set either close to the bulkhead, alongside the hatch coamings, or around the mast. It would take a direct hit to break them off; but it would not take a heavy hit, and each one, if broken, would open a hole over an inch in diameter directly into the 'tween-deck. An ammonia cylinder, weighing 200 pounds, free to plunge about on an open deck in a heavy seaway, was an engine before which such a fragile obstacle was no better than an eggshell. The safety of the cargo stowed below deck was therefore absolutely dependent upon the continued solidity of the pack; and, in the way the cylinders were made fast, that solidity depended upon each one's keeping its position in the pyramidal stack. As soon as one slipped out from between its fellows, the hold of the rest upon each other was lost, and all would inevitably

42. 147 F.2d 363, 1945 A.M.C. 191 (2d Cir. 1945).

escape. There were the nets, to be sure, but these did not go clear to the deck, and could not be expected to hold if they had, once the pack broke up.

"The consequences of any such break being so great, the least care that could be demanded was that the cylinders should be made fast against all but the most unexpected and 'catastrophic' storms; and such care the ship did not in fact bestow as the event proved. During the watch between 4 a. m. and 8 a. m. on January 11, the 'West Kebar's' log records a wind force of 8 on the Beaufort Scale—39 to 46 miles—and for the watch from 8 a. m. to 12 M., '9–10.' Nine is a 'strong gale'—47 to 54 miles—; 10 is a 'whole gale' 55 to 63 miles. Kimball, the expert of the Weather Bureau upon such matters, computed that, at noon on the 11th, the 'West Kebar' was 300 miles from the storm centre. (The master put her further away.) The storm itself Kimball thought was 'about 125 miles across, and the area of gales extending out from the center was about 700 miles'; so that at noon on the 11th, the ship was, so far as we can tell, only 50 miles inside the perimeter of the surrounding gales."[43]

Additional illustrations of the comprehensiveness of the term seaworthiness are found in such modern cases as Hydaburg Cooperative Ass'n v. Alaska S. S. Co.[43a] where inadequate markings on pipe outlets were held to make the ship unseaworthy, and Horn v. Cia de Navegacion Fruco,[43b] where insufficiency of crew had the same effect. It has even been held that a vessel likely to be delayed by litigation is "unseaworthy" for cargo carriage.[43c]

Since the law of marine insurance implies a warranty of seaworthiness in every voyage policy, including one on cargo,[44] the scaling down of the carrier's warranty of seaworthiness to an obligation to use due diligence might be thought to put the cargo owner in an unfortunate position, since, if the vessel is actually unseaworthy, the marine insurance doctrine voids his insurance, though he may have no claim against the carrier, since the latter may have exercised due diligence. For this reason, and because the application of the marine insurance seaworthiness warranty doctrine as a whole is unsuitable to the modern position of the cargo owner,[45] marine policies on cargo now commonly contain a clause stipulating that "the sea-

43. 147 F.2d at 365–366.

43a. 404 F.2d 151, 1969 A.M.C. 363 (9th Cir. 1968).

43b. 404 F.2d 422, 1968 A.M.C. 2548 (5th Cir. 1968).

43c. Morrisey v. S. S. A. & J. Faith, 238 F.Supp. 877, 1966 A.M.C. 71 (N.D. Ohio 1964).

44. See *supra* Chapter II, at note 52 *et seq.;* 2 Arnould, Marine Insurance § 689 (14th ed. 1954).

45. In the days when the owners of ships carried goods on their own account, and when, in any case, the shipper had opportunity to make investigation before selecting a vessel, the rule may not have worked great hardship.

worthiness of the vessel as between the assured and the underwriters is hereby admitted."

## Care of the Cargo

**§ 3–28.** Section 3(2) of Cosga provides:

> "The carrier shall properly and carefully load, handle, stow, carry, keep, care for, and discharge the goods carried."

Thus, after having provided a vessel seaworthy in the broadest sense, the carrier may still be held liable for fault in any of the respects enumerated, if the goods are consequently damaged. The main problem posed by this subsection is that of how it is to be read with Section 4. That section, as we have seen, confers on the carrier certain immunities from liability for damage arising from designated causes. Such immunity may be logically inconsistent with an obligation properly to "carry," etc.; at the least, the sections must be read together.[46]

## Navigation and Management of the Ship

**§ 3–29.** Section 4(2) sets forth a list of causes for which the carrier shall not be liable. Of these the most striking and perhaps the most important is 4(2)(a):

> "Act, neglect, or default of the master, mariner, pilot, or the servants of the carrier in the navigation or in the management of the ship";

It will be recalled that a similar immunity is granted by the Harter Act, "*if*" due diligence shall have been exercised to make the ship "*in all respects*" seaworthy.[47] In the famous case of The Isis,[48] the Supreme Court read Section 3 of Harter literally, and held that the condition had to be met before the immunity could be availed of, whether or not the actual loss or damage was causally connected in any way with the unseaworthiness defect left uncorrected through a failure to use due diligence. Thus, under the Isis rule, a ship, on a voyage subject to the Harter Act, may sail with inadequate or antiquated charts, thereby increasing the risk of her coming to grief in dangerous waters through which she is to pass in the course of the voyage. Before reaching these waters, or even after successfully negotiating them, she may negligently collide with another vessel, damaging herself and her cargo. If the defect with regard to the charts is considered (as it might well be[49]) sufficiently serious to

46. The student can get an idea of some of the problems involved in care of cargo from Leeming, Modern Ship Stowage (1942), a publication of the Department of Commerce. This work has been cited by the courts that have to find a standard of care under Cogsa; see General Foods Corp. v. The Troubador, 98 F.Supp. 207, 210, 1951 A.M.C. 662 (S.D.N.Y.1951).

47. See *supra* at note 16.

48. 290 U.S. 333, 54 S.Ct. 162, 1933 A.M.C. 1565 (1933). Noted 34 Colum.L. Rev. 357 (1934); 47 Harv.L.Rev. 715 (1934).

49. See The Maria, 91 F.2d 819, 1937 A.M.C. 934 (4th Cir. 1937).

render the vessel not "in all respects seaworthy," and if, as would normally be true as to patent defects of this kind, the deficiency is held to be attributable to a want of due diligence, then, under Harter, the vessel would be liable for the cargo damage, though the latter was not even remotely caused by the seaworthiness defect. This looks like a harsh rule, and has been much criticized. But there is a great deal to be said in favor of the Isis decision. The actual wording of Section 3 of the Harter Act will certainly bear the construction put upon it, and that construction is, quite properly, a restrictive one against the immunization of carriers from liability for their own negligence, and against those whose overreaching, in bills of lading "exceptions," was sought to be curbed by the other sections of Harter.[49a]

In any event, the rule of the Isis is now abolished by Cogsa where that Act applies. The 4(2)(a) immunity is not stated in conditional form; seaworthiness is dealt with elsewhere, as we have seen. Thus, under Cogsa, the Isis problem cannot even arise.

The cases which have defined the scope of the exemption from liability for negligence in the navigation and management of the ship have mostly been concerned with deciding whether a given fault is to be classified as of this sort or is to be regarded as one having to do with the custody, care, etc., of the cargo, for which the carrier is liable. Since the line that has to be drawn in the case governed by Cogsa is the same as that under Harter, the Harter Act cases are important not only for the construction of that Act itself but also for the direct help they give in pinning down the distinction, in Cogsa, between a Section 3(2) liability and a Section 4(2)(a) immunity. The somewhat different phraseology has never been thought to carry any material difference in meaning.[50]

The difficulty in drawing the line arises from the fact that, read naturally, the two clauses overlap, for many actions which might be spoken of as faults or errors in management or even in navigation might equally well be viewed as failures in the duty to use due care with respect to the cargo.[50a] Few clearcut concepts have appeared for dealing with the problem; the feel of it can only be acquired by reading cases.

**49a.** The rule still applies in Harter Act cases; Blanchard Lumber Co. v. S. S. Anthony II, 259 F.Supp. 857, 1967 A.M.C. 103 (S.D.N.Y.1966).

**50.** From quite early, the trend has been to construe the carrier's immunities under the Harter Act strictly, and not to extend them to doubtful and uncertain cases. The Jeanie, 236 F. 463, 471 (9th Cir. 1916). This tendency continues under Cogsa. As to this topic and others where the two Acts differ only in minor stylistic respects, Harter and Cogsa cases are here cited without distinction; this practice is also followed in recent opinions, where the Harter Act jurisprudence is taken as applicable to Cogsa except where the Acts obviously differ in substance.

**50a.** See Note, Error in Navigation or Management of a Vessel—a Definitional Dilemma, 13 Wm. & Mary Law Rev. 638 (1972).

A leading case is Knott v. Botany Worsted Mills.[51] Wool belonging to the libellants was stowed in a hold forward of a wooden bulkhead, which was not water-tight. At a subsequent port of call, the ship took on a shipment of wet sugar, from which drainage is to be expected, and stowed it aft of the wool, on the other side of the bulkhead. The vessel was "trimmed by the stern" at this time—that is, the stern was lower than the bow, so that the drainage from the sugar ran back, and was carried off by scuppers. On the discharge of cargo at a second port of call, the trim of the ship changed, and she was "down by the head," so that the drainage from the sugar ran the other way; there being no provision for carrying it off at the forward end of the hold, some of it penetrated the bulkhead and damaged the wool. The Supreme Court, holding that these facts added up to a failure to use due diligence in respect of the cargo, quoted with approval the language of the opinion in the District Court below:

> " 'The primary cause of the damage was negligence and inattention in the loading or stowage of the cargo, either regarded as a whole, or as respects the juxtaposition of wet sugar and wool bales placed far forward. The wool should not have been stowed forward of the wet sugar, unless care was taken in the other loading, and in all subsequent changes in the loading, to see that the ship should not get down by the head. There was no fault or defect in the vessel herself. She was constructed in the usual way, and was sufficient. But on sailing from Para she was a little down by the head, through inattention, during the changes in the loading, to the effect these changes made in the trim of the ship and in the flow of the sugar drainage. She was not down by the head more than frequently happens. It in no way affected her seagoing qualities; nor did the vessel herself cause any damage to the wool. The damage was caused by the drainage of the wet sugar alone. So that no question of the unseaworthiness of the ship arises. The ship herself was as seaworthy when she left Para as when she sailed from Pernambuco. The negligence consisted in stowing the wool far forward, without taking care subsequently that changes of loading should not bring the ship down by the head. I must therefore regard the question as solely a question of negligence in the stowage and disposition of cargo, and of damage consequent thereon, though brought about by the effect of these negligent changes in loading on the trim of the ship. . . . The change of trim was merely incidental, the mere negligent result of the changes in the loading, no attention being given to the effect on the ship's trim, or on the sugar drainage. . . . Since this damage arose through negligence in the particular mode of stowing and

51. 179 U.S. 69, 21 S.Ct. 30 (1900).

changing the loading of cargo, as the primary cause, though that cause became operative through its effect on the trim of the ship, this negligence in loading falls within the 1st section. The ship and her owner must therefore answer for this damage, and the third section is inapplicable.' "[52]

Perhaps the nearest thing to a general rule for drawing this line is to be found in The Germanic.[53] The steamer in that case was heavily iced on reaching port, and, since she was late, unloading and coaling proceeded with greater speed than was conducive to the exercise of care. Due to unbalanced loads, she listed heavily and shipped water through her ports, finally sinking at her pier. Negligence was found; the question was whether it concerned the "management" of the vessel or the care of the cargo. The court, finding it to be the latter, laid down a rule:

> ". . . If the primary purpose is to affect the ballast of the ship, the change is management of the vessel, but if, as in view of the findings we must take to have been the case here, the primary purpose is to get the cargo ashore, the fact that it also affects the trim of the vessel does not make it the less a fault of the class which the first section removes from the operation of the third. We think it plain that a case may occur which, in different aspects, falls within both sections; and if this be true, the question which section is to govern must be determined by the primary nature and object of the acts which cause the loss.
>
> "A distinction was hinted at in argument, based on the fact that the damage was not to the cargo removed, but to that left behind in the ship. If the damage was attributable to negligence in unloading, it does not matter what part of the cargo is injured. The fact referred to does bring out, however, that the negligence in removing the cargo was negligence only because of its probable effect on the ship, and was negligence towards the remaining cargo only through its effect on the ship. But, although this may be conceded, the criterion which we have given is undisturbed. That 'in' which, as the statute puts it, the fault was shown, was not management of the vessel, but unloading cargo; and, although it was fault only by reason of its secondary bearing, the primary object determines the class to which it belongs."[54]

52. 179 U.S. at 73–74, 21 S.Ct. at 31.

53. 196 U.S. 589, 25 S.Ct. 317 (1905).

54. 196 U.S. at 597–8, 25 S.Ct. at 318.

The following have been held errors in "navigation" or "management": Ballasting into deep tank where cargo was stored, instead of into empty tank, Firestone Synthetic Fibers v. M/S Black Heron, 324 F.2d 835, 1964 A.M.C. 42 (2d Cir. 1963); failure to remove water from bilges, resulting in moistening and spoilage of hides, The Merida, 107 F. 146 (2d Cir. 1901); change of course and failure to put in for repairs, Corsair v. J. D. Spreckels & Bros. Co., 141 F. 260 (9th Cir. 1905); leaving port in disregard of

It seems clear that the bill of lading may not validly provide that a given sort of negligence shall fall on one side or the other of this line, for that is exactly equivalent, logically and practically, to a stipulation for exoneration. In a modern Fifth Circuit case,[54a] for example, the bill of lading provided that any fault in the operation of the refrigerating equipment should be considered a fault in the management of the ship; the court held this clause to be without effect.

One final word: If an entirely new start could be made, it might well be that the most rational way to draw the line we are talking about would be to classify as "navigation and management" any fault which endangers the *ship* or a part thereof, and as "custody and care of the cargo" any fault which endangers the *cargo* alone, without substantial danger to the ship. This would hold the carrier in just those cases where he is not himself motivated, by self-interest, to be careful. It is possible that this was the rationale of the Harter Act distinction. It would be very difficult to introduce such a rule now, after hundreds of decisions; perhaps this thought could play a part in future legislation or conventions—though complete discard of the "fault" concept may be more likely—and perhaps preferable.

### "Navigation and Management" as Against "Seaworthiness"

**§ 3–30.** Since, under Cogsa, the cargo owner can collect from the carrier if damage to his goods is attributable to a lack of due diligence in providing a seaworthy vessel, but must bear his own

weather warning, Hanson v. Haywood Bros. & Wakefield Co., 152 F. 401 (7th Cir. 1907); tipping ship to examine propeller, The Indrani, 177 F. 914 (2d Cir. 1910); washing down of leaking sulfuric acid drums with water, increasing corrosive power of acid and damaging flour in hold below, The Milwaukee Bridge, 26 F.2d 327, 1928 A.M.C. 1063 (2d Cir. 1928), certiorari denied 278 U.S. 632, 49 S.Ct. 31 (1928); selecting an unsafe anchorage and failing to give signals of distress, Luria Bros. & Co. v. Eastern Transp. Co., 89 F.2d 900, 1937 A.M.C. 778 (2d Cir. 1937); failure to make frequent inspection of brass caps on sounding pipes, with result that water entered, The Newport News, 199 F. 968 (S.D. N.Y.1912). (Often, these are holdings in the alternative, the other possibility being that there is no negligence of any kind.)

The following have been held errors in the duties owed to cargo: Use of an improper refrigerant, Barr v. International Mercantile Marine Co., 29 F.2d 26, 1929 A.M.C. 53 (2d Cir. 1928); so directing discharge from after hold as to bring about depression of bow and wetting of cargo there, The Joseph J. Hock, 70 F.2d 259, 1934 A.M.C. 507 (2d Cir. 1934); stowage of leaky acetic acid drums near iron plates, Armco International Corp. v. Rederi A/B Disa, 151 F.2d 5, 1945 A.M.C. 1064 (2d Cir. 1945); failure to observe condition of thermometers in refrigerating compartments, The Samland, 7 F.2d 155, 1925 A.M.C. 1198 (S.D.N.Y.1925); failure to close lid of ventilator before running hose over it, Lockett Co. v. Cunard S. S. Co., 21 F.2d 191, 1927 A.M.C. 1057 (E.D.N.Y.1927); improper ventilation of hold, The Rita Sister, 69 F.Supp. 480, 1946 A.M.C. 910 (E.D. Pa.1946). For an example of the technical problems of stowage, see The Norte, 69 F.Supp. 881, 1947 A.M.C. 381 (E.D.Pa.1947).

Thoughtful reading of the cases in this note will result in some accurate feeling for the problem under discussion.

**54a.** Horn v. Cia de Navegacion Fruco, 404 F.2d 422, 1968 A.M.C. 2548 (5th Cir. 1968).

loss if it is caused by negligence in the navigation and management of the ship,[55] some cases turn on the question whether a given negligent act of the carrier or his agents is to be looked on as one or the other of these.

These cases always concern some condition or state of manning or equipment in which the ship actually began the voyage, for the question whether the shipowner has done all that is required as to seaworthiness is answered, as we have seen, as of the moment of sailing,[56] so that the question can never arise whether an act or omission after sailing is to be placed on one side or the other of the line. (Thus the cases dealing with the distinction between "seaworthiness" and "navigation and management" arise in a more constricted temporal frame of reference than do those which prick out the line between "navigation and management" and "care of the cargo." One may be negligent as to the cargo at any stage of the voyage.)

The most common case in which this line has to be drawn is that of the vessel that sails in a state which, if not corrected, would imperil the cargo, but which may be corrected with greater or less ease and as a matter more or less of routine after the vessel is at sea. Two close cases in the Supreme Court draw the line with niceness, if not (as would have been impossible) with very great resolving power for other cases. In International Nav. Co. v. Farr & Bailey Mfg. Co.,[57] the ship sailed with ports open near cargo; the hold where the ports were located was used exclusively for cargo; the hatches were battened down over the hold, and no one had any plans for inspecting or otherwise dealing with these ports. When the vessel reached its destination, the cargo was found wet with sea water, which had obviously come in through the ports. This damage was held to be attributable to the unseaworthiness of the vessel. In The Silvia,[58] on the other hand, the ship sailed with ports left open on purpose to light the hold, in a position where they were entirely accessible and could have been closed at any time without trouble. A ship sailing in such a state was held not unseaworthy; the failure to close the ports when weather arose making this advisable was an error in the management of the ship. In Farr, however, the court stresses the point that each case must be decided on all of its facts, and it is impossible to elaborate an entirely satisfactory rule in this matter.[59]

55. §§ 3(1) and 4(2)(a).

56. See *supra* notes 28, 39.

57. 181 U.S. 218, 21 S.Ct. 591 (1901).

58. 171 U.S. 462, 19 S.Ct. 7 (1898).

59. See also: The Steel Navigator, 23 F.2d 590, 1928 A.M.C. 388 (2d Cir. 1928); The Aakre, 122 F.2d 469, 1941 A.M.C. 1263 (2d Cir. 1941) certiorari denied 314 U.S. 690, 62 S.Ct. 360 (1941); The President Polk, 43 F.2d 695, 1930 A.M.C. 1358 (2d Cir. 1930); The Oritani, 40 F.2d 522, 1930 A.M.C. 230 (E.D.Pa.1929); The Yungay, 58 F.2d 352, 1932 A.M.C. 123 (S.D.N.Y. 1931).

## Fire

**§ 3–31.** Sections 4(2)(b) to (p) of Cogsa enumerate certain causes of damage to cargo which are "excepted." It is handy to treat the exception of fire separately, for it has a separate history in American law, and the wording and theory of 4(2)(b), the clause in which it occurs, raises a special problem.

In 1851, Congress passed the Fire Statute,[60] which provided that the vessel owner was not to be liable to the shipper for losses caused by fire on board, "unless such fire is caused by the design or neglect of such owner." It has been held that the "design or neglect" through which the owner loses this exemption must be personal to him; negligence on the part of the master, mariners, or other agents is not brought home to him, for this purpose, by *respondeat superior* doctrines.[61] The concept of "personal" fault is hard to apply to a corporate owner, but the courts have found it in the fault of the managing agents to whom the corporation delegates the tasks of inspection, decision on precautions, and the like.[62]

Cogsa, in Section 4(2)(b), excepts "Fire, unless caused by the actual fault or privity of the carrier." Section 8 then proceeds to save the Fire Statute from repeal. It has been assumed that "actual fault or privity" have the same meaning as "design or neglect," and no case proceeds on any other theory. A leading difference (which could never actually eventuate in conflict) may be that the Cogsa exception covers any "carrier" (such as a time-charterer liable on bills of lading) whether or not he is an "owner".[62a]

The authoritative Second Circuit Court of Appeals has recently held that "unseaworthiness" of firefighting equipment means liability for the owner, notwithstanding the fire exemption.[62b]

60. Rev.Stat. § 4282 (1875), 46 U.S.C.A. § 182. *Cf.* Chapter X, §§ 10–6, 10–20 to 10–25.

61. Walker v. The Western Transp. Co., 70 U.S. (3 Wall.) 150 (1866).

62. Williams S. S. Co. v. Wilbur, 9 F. 2d 622, 1926 A.M.C. 32 (9th Cir. 1925), certiorari denied 271 U.S. 666, 46 S.Ct. 482 (1926); Arkell & Douglas, Inc. v. United States, 13 F.2d 555, 1926 A.M. C. 1123 (2d Cir. 1926), certiorari denied 273 U.S. 735, 47 S.Ct. 243 (1926); United States v. Charbonnier, 45 F.2d 174, 1930 A.M.C. 1875 (4th Cir. 1930); The Edmund Fanning, 105 F.Supp. 353, 369, 1952 A.M.C. 1147 (S.D.N.Y. 1952), modified 201 F.2d 281 (2d Cir. 1953). Negligence in providing means to combat fire defeats the fire exception as much as does fault in connection with the ignition of the fire. Asbestos Corp. Ltd. v. Compagnie de Navigation Fraissinet, 480 F.2d 669, 1973 A.M.C. 1683 (2d Cir. 1973).

62a. Automobile Ins. Co. v. United Fruit Co., 224 F.2d 72, 1955 A.M.C. 1429 (2d Cir. 1955), certiorari denied 350 U.S. 885, 76 S.Ct. 138 (1955). See Thede, Statutory Limitations (Other Than Harter and Cogsa) of Carrier's Liability to Cargo—Limitation of Liability and the Fire Statute, 45 Tulane L.Rev. 959, 980 (1971).

62b. Asbestos Corp. v. Compagnie de Navigation Fraissinet, 480 F.2d 669, 1973 A.M.C. 1683 (2d Cir. 1973), noted, 5 Journal of Maritime Law and Commerce 129 (1973).

## Perils of the Sea

§ 3–32. Cogsa, in § 4(2)(c) provides that the carrier shall not be responsible for damage occurring through perils of the sea. Generally speaking, this phrase has the same meaning in a bill of lading or in Cogsa as it has in the "perils clause" of the marine insurance policy.[63] The important difference is that, as a bill of lading exception, the term does not include losses caused by the carrier's negligence, or that of his agents.[64] In the law of carriage, it is defined as a fortuitous action of the elements at sea, of such force as to overcome the strength of the well-found ship or the usual precautions of good seamanship.[65] Thus, in a sense, the absence of negligence as a concurring cause may be said to enter into the very definition of a sea peril, so that, in order to establish an exception under this clause, the ship would have to establish freedom from negligence. This seems to be about the effect of Wessels v. The Asturias,[66] where the court said:

> "Without meaning to set up a hierarchy of presumptions or of rules relating to burden of proof, we think that the taint of sweat damage is sufficiently answered if the carrier shows that the cargo has an unavoidable tendency to cause sweat, or that the weather conditions made it impossible to ventilate the cargo properly. In our view, the carrier remains liable if it fails to provide, without excuse, sufficient ventilation, or if its improper stowage contributes to the sweat, or if it is otherwise negligent in handling the cargo. Sweat, then, can be regarded as a peril of the sea only when all available and reasonable precautions are taken to avoid it. This is, of course, not new doctrine: '* * * although the loss occurs by a peril of the sea, yet if it might have been avoided by skill and diligence at the time, the carrier is liable.' Clark v. Barnwell & Ravenal, supra, 12 How. at page 280, 13 L.Ed. 985." [67]

This case concerned the relation of the "perils of the seas" exception to the duty to care properly for the cargo. Where the "skill and diligence" which might have overcome an alleged sea peril concern the

63. See *supra* Chapter II, at note 81.

64. Liverpool & Great Western Steam Co. v. Phenix Ins. Co., 129 U.S. 397, 438, 9 S.Ct. 469, 470 (1889); Arbib & Houlberg v. Second Russian Ins. Co., 294 F. 811, 816, 24 A.M.C. 16 (2d Cir. 1923); The Xantho, [1887] 12 A.C. 503, 510.

65. Chiswick Products, Ltd. v. S. S. Stolt Avance, 387 F.2d 645, 1968 A.M.C. 324 (5th Cir. 1968). The Frey, 106 F. 319 (2d Cir. 1901); The Giulia, 218 F. 744, 746 (2d Cir. 1914); R. T. Jones Lumber Co. v. Roen S. S. Co., 213 F. 2d 370, 1955 A.M.C. 1990 (7th Cir. 1954); see Poor, Charter Parties and Ocean Bills of Lading 200–202 (4th ed. 1954).

66. 126 F.2d 999, 1942 A.M.C. 360 (2d Cir. 1942).

67. 126 F.2d at 1000. Accord: Compagnie de Navigation Fraissinet and Cyprien Fabre, S. A. v. Mondial United Corp., 316 F.2d 163, 169, 1963 A.M.C. 946, 950 (5th Cir. 1963).

navigation and management of the ship, it could make no difference in result, under Cogsa, whether the loss was caused by the sea peril or by negligence in navigation and management, for the carrier has a good exception under either head.[68]

There seems to be a similar relation between the "perils of the sea" exception and the liability for failure to use due diligence to furnish a seaworthy ship. In a sense, "seaworthiness" and "peril of the sea" are related by definition, for the seaworthiness of a vessel consists in part of her ability to stand up under reasonably expectable conditions, while the peril of the sea, on the other hand, is the sort of action of the marine elements that is not reasonably expectable and that consequently can overcome the strength of the seaworthy ship.[69] Thus, where sea water unexplainedly enters the hold, there is a presumption of unseaworthiness, for the well-found vessel does not ship sea water in the hold under normal conditions; the carrier's hope of rebutting this presumption lies in establishing that the entry of sea water was caused by a "peril of the sea"—an occurrence so violent and unusual as to overcome the defenses of even a seaworthy ship.[70] Of course, even if the sea water entered because of unseaworthiness, the carrier, under Section 4(1) of Cogsa, is not liable unless he failed to use due diligence to make her seaworthy.

### Act of God

**§ 3–33.** This common-law term, found in Section 4(2)(d) of Cogsa, has been called

> " . . . a mere short way of expressing this proposition. A common carrier is not liable for any accident as to which he can shew that it is due to natural causes directly and exclusively, without human intervention, and that it could not have been prevented by any amount of foresight and pains and care reasonably to be expected from him." [71]

Some cases point to the conclusion that, to qualify as an "Act of God," an occurrence must be brought about wholly without human intervention, negligent or not.[72] It is certain that human negligence as

**68.** §§ 4(2)(a) and 4(2)(c).

**69.** See Virgin Islands Corp. v. Merwin Lighterage Co., 251 F.2d 872, 1958 A.M.C. 294 (3d Cir. 1958), certiorari denied 357 U.S. 929, 78 S.Ct. 1369, on remand 177 F.Supp. 810, 1959 A.M.C. 2133 (D.Virgin Islands 1959). Duche v. Thomas & John Brockelbank, 40 F.2d 418, 1930 A.M.C. 114 (2d Cir. 1930); The Naples Maru, 106 F.2d 32, 1939 A.M.C. 1087 (2d Cir. 1939); The Cypria, 137 F.2d 326, 1943 A.M.C. 947 (2d Cir. 1943).

**70.** Herman v. Compagnie Générale Transatlantique, 242 F. 859, 861 (2d Cir. 1917); The Plow City, 122 F.2d 816, 818, 1941 A.M.C. 1564 (3d Cir. 1941), certiorari denied 315 U.S. 798, 62 S.Ct. 579 (1942); see The Folmina, 212 U.S. 354, 29 S.Ct. 363 (1909).

**71.** Nugent v. Smith, [1876] 1 C.P.D. 423, 444.

**72.** Forward v. Pittard, [1785] 1 T.R. 27, 33–34; Compania De Vapores Insco, S. A. v. Missouri Pac. R. Co., 232 F.2d 657, 1956 A.M.C. 764 (5th Cir. 1956). See Gans S. S. Line v. Wilhelmsen, 275 F. 254 (2d Cir. 1921), certiorari denied 257 U.S. 655, 42 S.Ct. 97 (1921).

a contributing cause defeats any claim to the "Act of God" immunity, or, rather, that the absence of human negligence or fault as a concurring cause is a part of the definition of the "Act of God." [72a] For a reason which will appear when we take up Section 4(2)(q), it is now of less practical interest, so far as Cogsa is concerned, to draw with precision the line of definition around the "Act of God," a line, incidentally, that has proven quite difficult to draw.

### The Exceptions of Overwhelming Human Force

**§ 3–34.** These are 4(2)(e) Act of War, (f) Act of public enemies, (g) Arrest or restraint of princes, rulers, or people, or seizure under legal process, (h) Quarantine restrictions, and (k) Riots and civil commotions.[73] With these may be grouped (j), which reads:

> "Strikes or lockouts or stoppage or restraint of labor from whatever cause, whether partial or general: *Provided,* that nothing herein contained shall be construed to relieve a carrier from responsibility for the carrier's own acts; " [74]

Exceptions (e), (f) and (g), saving one minor point, are the principal perils which are eliminated from the marine insurance policy by the F. C. & S. clause, and which are covered by war risk insurance.[75] Doubtless the three clauses overlap to some extent; an act performed in the prosecution of war might be the act of an enemy of the carrier's country, though the term might equally well be applied to the actions of military or naval forces of a nation at war with some country unconnected with either the carrier or the goods.[76] A "restraint of princes" may be an act performed for purposes connected with the prosecution of war, or some other sort of act, such as the prohibition, for sanitary reasons, of the entry of the ship into the port of discharge, or the refusal of permission to land the cargo.[77] Quarantine, (h), probably would be covered by the general clause excepting "restraint of princes," for quarantine has been so treated in the decisions.[78] "Seizure under legal process" (g) refers to the arrest or seizure in civil courts (of the cargo at least) under judicial process issuing in the normal course of the administration of private justice, and these words are added to clause (g) because such a seizure is not comprised within the coverage of the general "restraint of princes" concept, which has to do with executive or administrative action, and not with ordinary

**72a.** This passage was cited with approval in Mamiye Bros. v. Barber Steamship Lines, Inc., 241 F.Supp. 99, 108, 1966 A.M.C. 1175, 1186 (S.D.N.Y. 1965); *affirmed* 360 F.2d 774, 1966 A.M.C. 1165 (2d Cir. 1966), certiorari denied 385 U.S. 835, 87 S.Ct. 80 (1966).

**73.** § 4(2)(e), (f), (g), (h), (k).

**74.** Cogsa § 4(2)(j).

**75.** See *supra* Chapter II, at Note 80.

**76.** See Carver, *op. cit. supra* note 2, § 173.

**77.** See Carver, *loc. cit. supra* note 76; Poor, Charter Parties & Ocean Bills of Lading § 72 (5th ed. 1968)

**78.** The Progress, 50 F. 835 (3d Cir. 1892). But where the quarantine is imposed through the fault of the carrier, no immunity is conferred. Hearty v. Ragunda, 114 F.Supp. 869, 1954 A.M.C. 716 (S.D.N.Y.1953).

civil administration of justice.[79] It is not settled, apparently, whether the "seizure" that is excepted is that of the goods only or whether the shipowner gets a good exemption under this head if damage is caused by the arrest of the vessel under *in rem* process or by way of attachment,[80] but this doubt would not, it seems, extend to the "restraint of princes" subclause, which excepts "restraints" of any kind.

Clause (j), "strikes and lockouts," presents a special problem, because of the words which follow the statement of the exception.[81] These words were not in the Hague Rules or the Convention, but were added by Congress when Cogsa was enacted. It has been pointed out that while "a strike is almost always a matter of money, and can be ended by a money payment," courts, in charterparty cases, have taken the view that the carrier is not bound to make an offer of increased wages in order to retain the benefit of the strike exception.[82] These cases, however, are not particularly helpful in the construction of the troublesome words in Cogsa, because they were decided under charterparties which did not contain these words. We have little aid, actually, in deciding what can have been meant by the proviso, but only as a last resort would it be appropriate to say that it has *no* meaning, which is what is being said, in effect, when cases construing the strike exception *simpliciter* are cited for the construction of the Cogsa strike exception with this proviso. A possible construction might include one or more of the following propositions:

1. *If the strike causing the damage or loss is precipitated or prolonged by unlawful action on the carrier's part, he loses the exception.* In most industrial countries today, there is a considerable body of fairly definite law, and authoritative judicial and administrative decisional material, defining "unfair labor practices," and it is even conceivable that a strike might be provoked or prolonged by some act or acts wrongful under general legal provisions outside the scope of the specialized law of "labor relations." It would seem that a carrier should not be allowed to plead exoneration on the basis of a strike that he himself contributed to causing, in a manner defined as wrongful by the applicable law. This proposition would seem closely analogous to, if not identical with, the operation of the "over-riding obligations", discussed in § 3–22 *supra*.

79. Clarke S. S. Co. v. Munson S. S. Line, 59 F.2d 423, 427, 1932 A.M.C. 900 (E.D.N.Y.1932) affirmed per curiam 64 F.2d 1011 (2d Cir. 1933); see Carver, *op. cit. supra* note 2, § 175.

80. With The Brunswick, 263 F. 907 (E.D.La.1920), and The Estrada Palma, 8 F.2d 103, 1923 A.M.C. 1040 (E. D.La.1923), compare The Penobscot, 1940 A.M.C. 1217, 1232–4. It seems clear in any case that if the seizure of the vessel comes about through the fault of the carrier he cannot have the exception. This seems to be assumed even in The Estrada Palma, *supra*, 8 F.2d at 104.

81. See *supra* at note 74.

82. Knauth, *op. cit. supra* note 2, 223, citing Hawkhurst S. S. Co. v. Keyser, 84 F. 693 (N.D.Fla.1897) affirmed 87 F. 1005 (5th Cir. 1898); The Toronto, 174 F. 632 (2d Cir. 1909); The Themis, 244 F. 545 (S.D.N.Y.1917), affirmed, sub. nom. Gans S. S. Line v. Wilhelmsen, 275 F. 254 (2d Cir. 1921), certiorari denied 257 U.S. 655, 42 S.Ct. 97 (1921).

2. *If the carrier incites a strike or intentionally refrains from settling it, with the motive of putting himself in a position to plead the strike exception, then he loses the exception.* The fear of this seems to have been one motive for the inclusion of the proviso.[83] There is considerable overlap, probably, with 1, but the overlap is not necessarily complete, for it might be possible, within the large leeways of conduct afforded by the law of labor relations, for a carrier to bring about or prolong a work stoppage without using means forbidden in themselves, but with the motive of being able to plead the exception. Such a motive would be hard to prove, but there would seem to be no reason, if any shipper happens to be able to prove it, why a carrier should not lose the strike exception on such a showing. (This case is probably almost entirely imaginary, but it cannot be so treated in the face of the proviso's inclusion.)

3. *The carrier loses the exception if he fails to make reasonable efforts (including reasonable offers to the strikers) to avert or end the strike.* In so far as this construction of the proviso does not overlap with 1 and 2, it would impose a very heavy burden indeed on the carrier, for, even where his conduct with respect to the strike was both lawful and properly motivated, he would be required to go further and act affirmatively to bring the strike to an end, and his bargaining position vis-a-vis labor would be arbitrarily altered in the interest of cargo. In view of the two other quite reasonable constructions which have been proposed, it would seem unwarranted to see in the proviso anything so drastic. At the most, an inexplicably unreasonable attitude toward ending the strike by settlement might be evidentiary of the sort of motivation required to bring 2 into operation.

It should be emphasized that all this is mere conjecture on the possible meaning of a proviso very deliberately included, and hence, presumably, to be given some effect. It is to be noted that this conjecture concerns the effect of fault of the carrier in *causing* the inception or continuance of the strike. It is not conjectural that, if a strike has damaged goods or threatens damage, the carrier owes a duty to minimize or avert the damage by the exercise of due care.[84]

## Exceptions Having to Do with Fault of the Shipper or Defect in the Cargo

§ 3–35. These are (i) Act or omission of the shipper or owner of the goods, his agent or representative, (m) Wastage in bulk or

83. See Knauth, *loc. cit. supra* note 82.

84. Schroeder Bros., Inc. v. Saturnia, 226 F.2d 147, 1955 A.M.C. 1935 (2d Cir. 1955). See General Foods Corp. v. U. S., 104 F.Supp. 629, 1952 A.M.C. 310 (S.D.N.Y.1952). But it has been held that a ship may under appropriate circumstances discharge cargo at an alternate port, when the port of destination is strike-bound. Hirsch Lumber Co. v. Weyerhaeuser S. S. Co., 233 F.2d 791, 1956 A.M.C. 1294 (2d Cir. 1956). See also *infra*, at note 95. The mere threat of a future strike has been held not to bring the strike exception into play. British West Indies Produce v. Atlantic Clipper, 353 F.Supp. 548, 1973 A.M.C. 163 (S.D.N.Y. 1973).

weight or any other loss or damage arising from inherent defect, quality, or vice of the goods, (n) Insufficiency of packing, (*o*) Insufficiency or inadequacy of marks.[85] These exceptions arise out of considerations of simple justice and existed at common law.[86] "Marks" may require some explanation. When goods are delivered to a general ship, each separate shipment, consisting of one or more packages, is marked on each package with a set of initials, or a geometrical design, or both, in aid of ready identification. The name and address of the consignee are rarely put on the package. Instead, the "mark" is copied on the bill of lading, a copy of which is of course taken on the voyage, and when it is time to unload the packages are "cut out of the herd" by their "brands". Where the marks are insufficient, or where they are obliterated, it is very difficult or impossible to identify the goods belonging in any one shipment.[87]

### Other Exceptions

**§ 3–36.** Clause (p)—"latent defects not discoverable by due diligence"[88]—obviously overlaps with Section 4(1), for the "latent defects" which usually result (absent contractual or statutory provision) in carrier liability are those which make the ship unseaworthy, and Section 4(1) has already immunized the carrier from liability for unseaworthiness where due diligence has been exercised. This exception may help out when a latent defect in shore apparatus, or in other cargo, causes a loss.

The exception of "saving or attempting to save life or property at sea" (*l*) should be considered in connection with deviation, which will shortly be taken up.

### The Catch-All Exception

**§ 3–37.** Section 4(2)(q) provides:

> "Neither the carrier nor the ship shall be responsible for loss or damage arising or resulting from . . . any other cause arising without the actual fault and privity of the carrier and without the fault or neglect of the agents or servants of the carrier, but the burden of proof shall be on the person claiming the benefit of this exception to show that neither the actual fault or privity of the carrier nor the fault or neglect of the agents or servants of the carrier contributed to the loss or damage."

This section may be looked on as the lineal descendant of the multitudinous bill of lading "exceptions"—rust, sweat, bursting of pipes, breakdown of machinery, and so on. The Cogsa bill of lading need not and usually does not contain any of these, for all exceptions

85. § 4(2)(i), (m), (n), (*o*).

86. See *supra* at note 2.

87. See Horn, International Trade, Principles & Practices 622–624 (3d ed. 1951). On insufficiency of package, see The Rita Sister, 69 F.Supp. 480, 1946 A.M.C. 910 (E.D.Pa.1946).

88. Cogsa § 4(2)(p).

that could be devised by human wit are contained in 4(2)(q). But they are all conditioned, substantively, on their arising "without the fault" of the carrier or his people. Thus, even in England, where stipulations for exoneration from negligence liability were formerly upheld,[89] Cogsa has changed the rule in this regard. Of greater importance in this country is the shift in burden of proof brought about by this section; the carrier must now, to enjoy any of the immunities conferred by this catch-all section, shoulder the burden of proving his own freedom from contributing fault.[90] And this is no mere burden of going forward with the evidence, but a real burden of persuasion, with the attendant risk of nonpersuasion.[91]

The presence of this section ought to have some tendency to make it unnecessary to define some of the other exceptions with precision. All we now need to know, e. g., as to the defining characteristics of the "Act of God" is that freedom from fault is one of them, for, once a carrier has established freedom from fault, it does not make any difference whether the cause of the damage is an "Act of God" or "any other cause." Similarly, as to "perils of the seas," it is instructive to look over, in the present connection, the passage from Wessels v. The Asturias, quoted above.[92] If "sweat is a peril of the sea when reasonable precautions are taken to avoid it," then to establish it as a peril of the sea one must show that reasonable precautions were taken. But once this is shown, it makes no difference whether it is a peril of the sea or not, for if it is not, it falls under 4(2)(q), the catch-all section.[93] Of course, as to some of the 4(2) exceptions, the burden of proof advantage gained for the carrier by avoiding recourse to 4(2)(q) may be of value.

89. See *supra* at note 10.

90. See The Vizcaya, 63 F.Supp. 898, 902, 1946 A.M.C. 469 (E.D.Pa.1945), affirmed sub. nom. Beck v. The Vizcaya, 182 F.2d 942 (3d Cir. 1950), certiorari denied 340 U.S. 877, 71 S.Ct. 124 (1950). *Cf. supra* at notes 8, 9.

91. The West Kyska, 155 F.2d 687, 1946 A.M.C. 997 (5th Cir. 1946), certiorari denied 329 U.S. 761, 67 S.Ct. 115 (1946). In Copco Steel & Engineering Co. v. The Prins Frederik Hendrik, 129 F.Supp. 469, 1955 A.M.C. 2052 (E. D.Mich.1955), the carrier argued that the burden of proof should be on the cargo as to a loss falling within a *bill of lading* exception also covered by § 4(2)(q), on the theory that the inclusion of the exception (apparently "rust") in the bill of lading shifted the burden. The court disposed of this contention summarily under the plain language of Cogsa § 3(8).

92. *Supra* at note 67.

93. Thus a question such as that raised in The G. R. Booth, 171 U.S. 450, 19 S.Ct. 9 (1898), could not have any substantive importance under Cogsa. In that case, an explosion of detonators carried as cargo had made a hole in the side, admitting sea water which damaged other cargo. There was a bill of lading exception of "perils of the sea"; the Court held that sea water entering under such circumstances could not be denominated a sea peril, and that the ship was liable. Under Cogsa, such a course of events, though excluded from the "peril of the sea" coverage, would fall under § 4(2)(q), if (as it appears could have been done) the carrier establishes his freedom from negligence.

### The Substantive Effect of Negligence in Cogsa § 4(2)(a) to (p)

§ 3–38. As we have seen, the liability of the carrier for cargo loss or damage can never be established, under the sections we have been examining, unless he has been negligent. The substantive question remaining is whether the exceptions in 4(2)(a) to (p) exempt him from liability for damage caused by the excepted perils, even though he has been negligent and his negligence may have contributed to or been somehow causally connected with the result.

Some of the clauses speak for themselves on this issue. 4(2)(a) explicitly excepts a certain kind of negligence. 4(2)(b) by clear implication leaves the carrier liable for fire damage incurred through his actual fault or privity, but insulates him from the effect of the negligence of his ordinary agents.

4(2)(c) and (d) ("perils of the sea" and "Act of God") are in a special position, for, as we have seen, absence from negligence is in a sense a part of the definition of each of these perils, so that it would seem inevitable that the carrier remain liable if his negligence concurred in causing the loss. It is probably misleading to say that negligence takes the carrier out of these exceptions; it would be more accurate to say that he never was within them if he was negligent. The same is true, on its face, of 4(2)(p): "Latent defects not discoverable by due diligence."

4(2)(j) must be eliminated before any general solution in regard to the rest of the clauses can be attempted. We have already looked at the cryptic language that limits this exception: "Provided, that nothing herein contained shall be construed to relieve a carrier from responsibility for the carrier's own acts." Whether the carrier would remain liable for the consequences, to cargo, of a strike, where his own negligence precipitated the strike or aggravated the result, is a question that would have to be settled by the construction of this special provision, and not on the basis of general considerations.[94]

As to the exceptions we have considered so far, the question as to the effect of negligence is answered by the nature of the exception itself; we may thus eliminate them from further consideration. The remainder, save one, fall into two classes: 1. *Actions of third parties* —(e) Act of War, (f) Act of public enemies, (g) "Restraint of princes" and seizure under legal process, (h) Quarantine, (k) Riots. 2. *Acts of the shipper or inherent vice of the goods*—including (i) and (m), which name (in somewhat more extended language) these causes, and (n) Insufficiency of packing and (*o*) Insufficiency or inadequacy of marks. The odd clause, not normally falling in either class, is (*l*), Saving or attempting to save life or property at sea. The classification of the causes as to which this negligence problem actually subsists serves a purpose which will shortly appear, and also shows how narrow and special a question is really posed.

94. See *supra* at note 81 *et seq.*

But it is even narrower than we have so far seen. For even if the carrier sometimes remains responsible for damage within the exceptions listed, when his negligence is a concurring cause, that result obviously cannot follow when the only concurring negligence is in the "navigation and management" of the ship—for 4(2)(a) exempts the carrier in such a case, and two concurring excepted causes cannot add up to a liability. Thus, before we even try to answer it, the question "Do the exceptions in 4(2)(a) to (p) immunize the carrier from the results of his own negligence?" boils down to "Does the fact that a loss is brought within one of the ten perils enumerated in the last paragraph immunize the carrier regardless of his negligence in some other respect than that of navigation and management of the ship?"

As a matter of fact, the crucial question may be narrower than that. For "negligence" in this context is a mixed bag. The reference may be (1) to a failure to use due care to "prevent the spread of the mischief"—to minimize and not to aggravate the damage that has been caused by an excepted peril; or (2) to the carrier's negligence as a cause of the incidence of the excepted peril. It seems that the first of these does not pose a very serious question. If the mere happening of damage through an excepted peril releases the carrier from responsibility to take due measures to care properly for the cargo, then that must be because the happening of the damage has somehow brought an end to the obligation imposed by Section 3(2), and, once that inconsequent proposition is stated, it will find few supporters.[95] At the least, the carrier who was negligent in failing to minimize damage occurring though one of the ten perils we are considering would be liable for that portion of the damage caused by such negligence, and the often well-nigh uncarryable burden of apportionment, to avoid paying all, seems his to shoulder.[96] Thus we probably have to do only with the problem posed where the actual incidence of the excepted cause is itself wholly or partly caused by the negligence of the carrier.[96a]

Thus far, the narrowings of our question have been purely theoretical. Practically, we are now in a position to observe a further narrowing result, if the three preceding paragraphs are considered together. As to the first of the classes into which the perils we are now considering were divided (*Actions of third parties*) it is easy to see that by far the greater part of the negligence which can operate as a concurring cause with the incidence of the peril will have to do

**95.** The exemption for "fire" (§ 4(2)(b)) has been held not to protect a carrier who failed to use due diligence to extinguish a fire for which he would not have been primarily responsible. American Mail Line, Ltd. v. Tokyo Marine & Fire Ins. Co., Ltd., 270 F.2d 499, 1959 A.M.C. 2220 (9th Cir. 1959). See also *supra* at n. 62b.

**96.** See Schnell v. The Vallescura, 293 U.S. 296, 55 S.Ct. 194, 1934 A.M.C. 1573 (1934); Armco International Corp. v. Rederi A/B Disa, 151 F.2d 5, 1945 A.M.C. 1064 (2d Cir. 1945).

**96a.** This passage is cited with approval in Lekas & Drivas, Inc. v. Goulandris, 306 F.2d 426, 431, 1962 A.M.C. 2366, 2373 (2d Cir. 1962). The case holds, however, that the mere raising of an issue of concurring carrier's fault does not put the burden of disproving such fault on the carrier.

with the navigation or management of the ship. Failures in due care which produce a special vulnerability to capture, torpedoing, civil commotions, etc., are likely to be such as ought to be avoided for the sake of the ship and the whole venture, and not specifically for the sake of the cargo, alone or principally. As to these acts of negligence, of course 4(2)(a) immunizes in any case. It is only in regard to those cases—hard to imagine with plausibility—in which negligence with respect specifically to the cargo brings about the incidence of one of these "third-party perils" that the question we are now examining can become important.

On the other hand, probably a great majority of the acts of negligence concurring with the causes in the second class above—those having to do with acts of the shipper or characteristics, etc., of the goods—consist in failure to prevent the "spread of mischief"—to minimize damage. If we are right in the view that negligence of this type must be answered for, regardless of the connection of the loss with one of the excepted perils here under discussion, then in this second group we are left, so far as the really doubtful branch of our question is concerned, only with those rare cases where the negligence of the carrier contributed to cause the actual original incidence of the excepted cause. As to some of the causes in this group—e. g., insufficiency of packing—it is hard to see how this can ever be.

We may note in passing that it is well-nigh incredible—and should give pause to those who place a high faith in the magically clarificatory powers of "uniform legislation"—that a statute which embodies the fruit of years of discussion by attested experts should leave thus in the dark, for solution by elaborate inference, a simple and fairly important question—and one, moreover, to which attention ought to have been urgently directed by over a half-century of debate about the negligence exceptions. The statute as a whole gives us little help. 4(2)(a) suffices to establish, for what it is worth, that the rules are not intended to hold the carrier in every case of negligence—but it also suggests that, where an immunity from liability for negligence is to be conferred, the draftsmen of the Rules know how to say so. This last point might be impressive were it not for 4(2)(p), which suggests that, where it is *not* intended that, by any misconstruction, a negligent carrier be exempted, they know how to say that too. 4(2)(q) again suggests that, where freedom from concurrent negligence is to be a substantive condition to the enjoyment of an exemption, the Act will say so—but this is not a conclusive point, for the special burden-of-proof provision in 4(2)(q) might have made it advisable, or natural, to be explicit there as to the effect of negligence, while leaving the matter implicit elsewhere.

The American Cogsa, in contrast to the Rules adopted in the Convention, and therefore to the versions in force in some other countries, *dropped* from Section 3(2) the opening phrase italicized in the following extract: "*Subject to the provisions of Article IV* [i. e., Section 4 in the American statute] the carrier shall properly and carefully load, handle, stow, keep, care for, and discharge the goods carried." A leading authority on the Act in this country, regards this omission as of no significance, mainly, it seems, because the only significance he could attribute to it would be the absurd one of the nullification of all of Section 4.[97] It may be, however, that a more sensible meaning can be given to it in the present context—that Congress, by effecting an omission of a phrase that subjected the cargo-care duty to the Section 4 immunities, intended to make it plain that, notwithstanding the setting up of those immunities, the duty to use care persisted, which could only mean that the immunities were lost or somehow qualified when negligence was a concurring cause of damage, except where, as in 4(2)(a), negligence is expressly excepted. This is a telling point, but, in the absence of relevant legislative history it cannot be concluded for sure that this is the effect to be given to a simple omission of certain words, perhaps merely thought unnecessary.

Perhaps the solution is to be found in the fact that Cogsa is not intended to be a whole code of law with respect to the carriage of goods by sea, but only, so far as material here at least, a set of compulsory terms to be read into bills of lading. This concept at least furnishes a base for solving our present problem, for there is no question whatever that if, prior to the enactment of Harter and Cogsa, these very same exceptions had appeared verbatim in a bill of lading, the carrier who had established that a loss fell under one of them could still be held liable if the shipper could establish negligence as a concurring cause.[98] In the United States, this result would follow even if there were a stipulation to the contrary in the bill, for such a stipulation, as we have seen, would have been against public policy.[99] But even in Britain, where "negligence" exceptions were upheld, they had to be clearly spelled out, and mere exceptions of general "causes" such as the ones we are now examining did not work an exemption at all where concurrent negligence could be proved.[100] It is not self-evident that the effect of the Cogsa language must be the same as the effect of the same language in a bill of lading printed by the carrier and forced, so far as the exceptive clauses go, on the shipper, for the judicial attitude as to negligence in respect to such bill of lading clauses was based in part on their "ambiguity"—which was resolved against the party drawing the contract—and in part, doubtless, on an inequality in bargaining power which is not of any relevance as to a statute. But the "ambiguity" remains, as we have abundantly seen, and must be resolved somehow. It seems fairly good sense to resolve it as it was resolved in the decided cases that actually construed the very terms of art that were copied into the Act; or, to put it with a slightly different point, to proceed on the assumption that the framers of an act that prescribes terms for bills of lading meant them to be construed just as they would be construed if they appeared in a bill of lading. It seems good sense, too, in independence of the foregoing points, to construe a genuinely dubious phrase so as

97. Knauth, *op. cit. supra* note 2, 147–8.

98. See *supra* at note 8.

99. See *supra* at note 11.

100. See *supra* at note 7.

not to immunize a carrier from the consequences of his negligence. Thus, on the whole, the better supported and sounder view would seem to be that, where a carrier brings himself under one of these excepted causes, he may nevertheless be held liable if his negligence concurred as a cause in producing the damage or was itself a cause of the incidence of the peril. The carrier, as we have shown, does not lose by this nearly as much as might be thought from its general statement.

### The "Both-to-Blame" Clause

§ 3–39. An interesting and intricate question in regard to the substantive effect of § 4(2), and more particularly of § 4(2)(a) (the clause immunizing the shipowner from liability for errors of the master and crew in navigating and managing the ship) arose in United States v. Atlantic Mutual Ins. Co.,[101] the case in which the Supreme Court finally passed adversely on the validity of the celebrated "Both-to-Blame" clause, a standard feature, since the 'thirties, of bills of lading in the North Atlantic and elsewhere.

The situation which gave rise to the use of the clause is easy to understand, if taken step by step. The basic problem is that of adjustment of liability for damage to cargo where two ships collide and where both are negligent and hence liable. It is convenient to focus attention on the cargo of only one of the ships, and to designate the vessels, with respect to it, as "carrying" and "non-carrying."

First, from our discussion of Cogsa § 4(2)(a), it should be obvious that the carrying ship is not directly liable to its cargo for damage sustained by the latter, for § 4(2)(a) immunizes the ship from liability to its own cargo for negligence in the navigation of the ship. Negligence causing collision is clearly of this type.

Secondly, however, the non-carrying ship *is* liable to the cargo on the carrying ship for damages sustained. Cogsa, like the Harter Act, regulates only the relations between cargo and carrying vessel.[102] And the negligence of the carrying vessel is not "imputed" to its cargo; so far as that cargo is concerned, the two vessels are simply joint tort-feasors, each liable *in solido* for the full amount of damage were it not that § 4(2)(a) of Cogsa relieves the carrying ship. The non-carrying ship, not being so shielded, is fully liable.[103]

101. 343 U.S. 236, 72 S.Ct. 666, 1952 A.M.C. 659 (1952); noted 52 Colum.L. Rev. 1056 (1952); 51 Mich.L.Rev. 430 (1953). For the lower court opinions, see United States v. Farr Sugar Corp., 191 F.2d 370, 1951 A.M.C. 1435 (2d Cir. 1951); United States v. The Esso Belgium, 90 F.Supp. 836, 1950 A.M.C. 719 (S.D.N.Y.1950). The opinions in the three courts are replete with references to authorities.

102. See The Delaware, 161 U.S. 459, 471, 16 S.Ct. 516, 522 (1896).

103. See the review of authorities in the Court of Appeals opinion in the case under discussion, United States v. Farr Sugar Corp., 191 F.2d 370, 376, 1951 A.M.C. 1435 (2d Cir. 1951). For a modern example see O/Y Finlayson-Forssa A/B v. Pan Atlantic S. S. Corp., 259 F.2d 11, 1958 A.M.C. 2070 (5th Cir. 1958), certiorari denied 361 U.S. 882, 80 S.Ct. 153 (1959).

Thirdly, it must be here noted (though the subject will be more fully discussed in Chapter VII) that, where collision occurs owing to mutual fault, damages are divided equally between the two vessels—such decree being entered as will bring it about that each will have suffered equally. Thus, in such a mutual-fault collision, if Vessel A is damaged $250,000 worth, and Vessel B is damaged $500,000 worth (with no cargo damage in the picture on either side), Vessel A will have to pay Vessel B $125,000, so that each will have suffered a net damage of $375,000.

But (and here's the rub) where cargo damage *is* involved, a part of the damages of the *non-carrying* ship will consist in the liability it has incurred to cargo on the other ship, and that item will be thrown into the adjustment.[104] So, in the example just given, if (in addition to the physical hull damage) cargo on Vessel B had been damaged $500,000 worth, that cargo could sue Vessel A and recover that amount. Vessel A's damages suffered from the collision would now be $250,000 plus $500,000, or $750,000. Since Vessel B (which, on the assumption that no cargo on Vessel A had been damaged, would not be under any additional liability) has been damaged only $500,000, she must now pay $125,000 to Vessel A, to equalize the damage at the figure of $625,000 apiece. Thus instead of receiving $125,000, Vessel B pays out that amount. The net difference, $250,000 is just half of the $500,000 damages recovered by Vessel B's cargo in its suit against Vessel A. It is easy to see that, where this liability of the non-carrying ship to cargo is entered as an item in the collision adjustment under the half-damages rule mentioned above, the carrying ship will always pay half of it, whether by way of increase in the amount it owes or of decrease in the amount owed it.

Thus the "anomaly" arises that the carrying ship—immunized by § 4(2)(a) against claims of its cargo for damages attributable to negligent navigation—actually ends up paying half the damages so suffered by its cargo. And the anomaly is sharpened by the fact that, if it *alone* had been negligent, it would have paid nothing on account of its own cargo, for that cargo would have had nobody to sue.

The Both-to-Blame clause sought to remedy this "anomaly" by providing, in the bill of lading contract, that the cargo would indemnify the carrying ship against this loss. A common version provided:

> "If the ship comes into collision with another ship as a result of the negligence of the other ship and any act, neglect or default of the master, mariner, pilot or the servants of the Carrier in the navigation or in the management of the ship, the owners of the goods carried hereunder will indemnify the Carrier against all loss or liability to the other or non-carrying ship or her owners insofar as such loss or

104. *Ibid.*

liability represents loss of or damage to, or any claim whatsoever of the owners of said goods, paid or payable by the other or non-carrying ship or her owners to the owners of said goods and set off, recouped or recovered by the other or non-carrying ship or her owners as part of their claim against the carrying ship or Carrier. The foregoing provisions shall also apply where the owners, operators or those in charge of any ship or ships or objects other than, or in addition to, the colliding ships or objects are at fault in respect of a collision or contact."

Had this clause been upheld, the following cumbersome machinery would have finally settled the cargo damage matter.

1. The cargo would sue the non-carrying ship and collect full damages.

2. The non-carrying ship, in the collision cause, would throw this liability into the damages account, so that the carrying ship would pay half.

3. The carrying ship would sue the cargo interest for that half under the contractual provision of the Both-to-Blame clause.

Of course, consolidation of suits could reduce the complexity of this litigation. It is spelled out in full merely to show schematically the functioning of the clause.

The operation of the clause, of course, produced another "anomaly"—this one shocking to cargo. Where only the non-carrying ship was negligent, cargo could recover in full and keep the money, for there would then be no half-damage decree in the collision suit. But where the carrying ship had been negligent as well, cargo, through no fault of its own, had to pay one-half of its recovery to its own ship.

The Supreme Court declared the clause invalid in an opinion which showed how much vitality remained in the traditional American notions on "negligence" clauses of all sorts in contracts of carriage.[105] Pointing out that the public policy of this country had, prior to the Harter Act, been resolute in denying to carriers the right to escape by "contract" the consequences of their negligence, the Court further noted that the Harter Act and Cogsa, being compromises, carved out definite exceptions to this principle. But it declined to extend these exceptions by inference to include a matter not expressly covered. Unquestionably, the Both-to-Blame clause, absent Harter and Cogsa, would be invalid. Both those acts grant *immunities* from certain liabilities, but they do not purport to validate a contractual provision such as this.

The Both-to-Blame clause now belongs to the ages, or at least sleeps in an enchanted cave awaiting the magic touch of Congress, and

105. See *supra* at note 11.

we would not have dwelt so long on it were it not that the philosophy of the opinion in the case is of interest.[105a] It shows the Supreme Court firmly opposed to the view that the carrier's rights under Harter and Cogsa are to be extended by analogy inference, or appeals to symmetry and "reasonableness." The exculpatory sections of these acts, it may now be said on authority, represented limited concessions to the carrier interests. Over vigorous dissent on this very point, by Mr. Justice Frankfurter, the Court refused to see in these enactments any general repudiation of antecedent policy, long hardened into rules of law.

This seems, on the whole, a sound view. It is idle to expect entire symmetry and freedom from anomaly in a compromise of interest such as is embodied in these statutes. The idea of carrier's exemption from liability for the negligence of his people is not itself wholly free from anomaly, if viewed in the wider context of shore law. To allow a start to be made toward the "contractual" extension of this change in settled law is simply to put a wide power in the hands of carriers, because the "contracts," of course, are dictated by them, and are in fact adopted simultaneously by wide segments of the trade.[106] It seems best to read Cogsa and Harter narrowly and literally in this respect.

## Deviation

**§ 3–40.** "Deviation" is a notion which came into the law of carriage from marine insurance; we have already dealt with it in that context.[107] The accepted view before Cogsa was that deviation ousts

**105a.** The clause still appears in many bills of lading, perhaps in the hope that it may be given effect in a foreign forum. See Waesche, Cargo's Rights in Collision Cases, 45 Tulane L.Rev. 781, 787 (1971).

**106.** The Supreme Court was realistically aware of the fact that the Both-to-Blame clause was instituted by concert among carriers; see 343 U.S. at 240, 241, 72 S.Ct. at 237. The Court of Appeals opinion is more explicit:

". . . The shipowners stress the consensual nature of the clause, arguing that a bill of lading is but a contract. But that is so at most in name only; the clause, as we are told, is now in practically all bills of lading issued by steamship companies doing business to and from the United States. Obviously the individual shipper has no opportunity to repudiate the document agreed upon by the trade, even if he has actually examined it and all of its twenty-eight lengthy paragraphs, of which this clause is No. 9. This lack of equality of bargaining power has long been recognized in our law; and stipulations for unreasonable exemption of the carrier have not been allowed to stand. Liverpool & G. W. Steam Co. v. Phenix Ins. Co., 129 U.S. 397, 441, 9 S.Ct. 469, 32 L.Ed. 788; Inman v. South Carolina R. Co., 129 U.S. 128, 139, 9 S.Ct. 249, 32 L.Ed. 612; Sante Fé, P. & P. R. Co. v. Grant Bros. Const. Co., 228 U.S. 177, 184, 185, 33 S.Ct. 474, 57 L.Ed. 787. Hence so definite a relinquishment of what the law gives the cargo as is found here can hardly be found reasonable without direct authorization of law. Actually the shippers, through official bodies, appear to have registered their opposition where they could and successfully at that, *viz.*, in the halls of legislation." 191 F.2d at 374.

(The passage in the text at this point was quoted, and its content reaffirmed, in Encyclopaedia Britannica v. S. S. Hong Kong Producer, 422 F.2d 7, 13, 1969 A.M.C. 1741 (2d Cir. 1969).)

**107.** See *supra* Chapter II, at note 58 *et seq.* For a general and up-to-date

the contract of carriage embodied in the bill of lading clauses, deprives the carrier of "exceptions" in so far as they apply to damage sustained during or after the deviation, and thus substitutes an "insurer's" liability for the narrower liability stipulated for in the bill of lading contract.[108] Doubtless this line of decision was influenced by the fact that, before the liberal use of "held covered" [109] clauses and other devices for avoiding the harsh effects of deviation in marine insurance, the cargo lost its insurance coverage when the ship deviated, and it was felt just that the carrier, through whose fault this had come about, should bear the consequences. It is questionable whether the stringent application of the doctrine in carriage law is appropriate anymore, unless insurance coverage is actually lost by cargo, and it is arguable that Cogsa has done away with this harsher aspect of deviation law and substituted a liability for damage actually caused by the deviation.[110]

Deviation, in the geographical sense, is a departure from the voyage; the first job, therefore, in any deviation case is to decide what the contract voyage is to be taken to be. In the absence of stipulation in the bill of lading, the voyage may be taken to be the normal route of sailing between the port of loading and the port of discharge, as defined by geography and by trade customs which the parties are taken to have incorporated by reference.[111] Most standard-form bills of lading today contain, however, a clause of the following type:

> The scope of voyage herein contracted for shall include usual or customary or advertised ports of call whether named in this contract or not, also ports in or out of the advertised, geographical, usual or ordinary route or order, even though in proceeding thereto the ship may sail beyond the port of discharge or in a direction contrary thereto, or depart from the direct or customary route. The ship may call at any port for the purposes of the current voyage or of a prior or subsequent voyage. The ship may omit calling at any port or ports whether scheduled or not, and may call at the same port more than once; may, either with or without the goods on board, and before or after proceeding toward the port of discharge, adjust compasses, dry dock, go on ways or to repair yards, shift berths, take fuel or stores, remain in port, sail without pilots, tow and be towed, and save

discussion, see Lee, The Law of Maritime Deviation, 47 Tulane L.Rev. 155 (1972).

108. The Willdomino v. Citro Chemical Co., 272 U.S. 718, 725, 47 S.Ct. 261, 262 (1927); Niles-Bement-Pond Co. v. Dampkiesaktieselskabet Balto, 282 F. 235 (2d Cir. 1922).

109. Such clauses provide that, in the event of departure from the described voyage covered by the policy, the risk is to be "held covered" at an additional premium to be arranged. See Winter, Marine Insurance 169 (3d ed. 1952); Dover, Handbook to Marine Insurance 263 (6th ed. 1962).

110. See *infra*, § 3–41, for a fuller discussion of this point.

111. Hostetter v. Park, 137 U.S. 30, 11 S.Ct. 1 (1890).

or attempt to save life or property, and all of the foregoing are included in the contract voyage.

It would seem hard to "deviate" from such a voyage. But the courts have indicated that such a clause must be construed or limited only to authorize reasonable departure from the normal route.[112] A construction which would give the ship all the liberties which seem literally to be granted by the clause would run afoul of the public policy and statutory provisions forbidding the carrier to contract out of liability for his own wrongdoing, and would, specifically, contradict Section 3(2) of Cogsa, which imposes a duty to ". . . properly . . . carry the goods."[113] Unreasonable departure from the normal course of sailing has always been considered highly improper carriage of goods. To allow the carrier to define the permissible scope of his conduct, without reference to the requirements set by the statute, would be to allow him to set his own standard of proper carriage. Thus, it would appear that, even under such a voyage clause as the one quoted, a deviation occurs when the liberties conferred by the clause are pushed beyond reasonableness, in the light of the carrier's duties to cargo.

In Section 4(4), Cogsa provides:

> "Any deviation in saving or attempting to save life or property at sea, or any reasonable deviation shall not be deemed to be an infringement or breach of this Act or of the

112. P & E Shipping Corp. v. Empresa Cubana Exportadora E Importadora De Alimentos, 335 F.2d 678, 1964 A.M.C. 2006 (1st Cir. 1964). A good general discussion, holding for the ship but making clear, on full review of authority, that these "liberties" clauses must be reasonably construed, is found in Grace & Co. v. Toyo Kisen Kabushiki Kaisha, 7 F.2d 889, 1925 A.M.C. 1420 (N.D.Cal.1925), affirmed 12 F.2d 519 (9th Cir. 1926), certiorari denied 273 U.S. 717, 47 S.Ct. 109 (1926). The clause covers only "delays fairly ancillary to the prescribed voyage." Dietrich v. U. S. Shipping Board, 9 F.2d 733, 742, 1925 A.M.C. 1173 (2d Cir. 1925). See also General Hide & Skin Corp. v. United States, 24 F.2d 736, 1928 A.M.C. 357 (E.D.N.Y.1928); Romano v. West India Fruit & S. S. Co., 151 F.2d 727, 1946 A.M.C. 90 (5th Cir. 1945); Poor, Charter Parties and Ocean Bills of Lading 194 *et seq.* (4th ed. 1954); Scrutton, Charterparties 291 (15th ed. 1948).

113. As Judge Knox said, in a slightly different context: "According to my view of the verity of things, a liberty or deviation clause which relieves a shipowner from the performance of the obligations of a contract to carry goods directly and without unnecessary delay from the point of shipment to the port of destination, and which obligation, in the absence of the liberty clause, would strictly be binding upon him, may well be nothing more or less than an exemption in favor of the shipowner from his liability to carry and deliver goods safely. In so far as the liberty relieves the shipowner from such deterioration and damage as come to the goods as a result of the exercise of the privileges of the liberty, it is an exemption of that precise character. I see no reason, therefore, why such a clause should not fairly be regarded as an 'exception.'" Centrosoyus-America, Inc. v. United States, 31 F.2d 610, 611, 1929 A.M.C. 289 (S.D.N.Y.1929). In the Grace case, *supra* note 112, the court makes it clear that "reasonable" construction is required to save the "liberties" clause from invalidity under Harter. The case is even stronger under Cogsa, since the provisions of § 4(4) dealing with "reasonable" deviation would make no sense if carriers could so define the voyage as to make it impossible for deviation to be found.

contract of carriage, and the carrier shall not be liable for any loss or damage resulting therefrom: *Provided, however, That if the deviation is for the purpose of loading or unloading cargo or passengers it shall, prima facie, be regarded as unreasonable.*" [Emphasis supplied]

Theoretically, this section seems to be defining (in part) "reasonable" deviation, and setting out, expressly and by implication, what the consequences of "reasonableness" or "unreasonableness" are to be, once a deviation is ascertained. Thus, the section might not be thought to help out much in regard to the "scope of the voyage" clause question touched on in the last paragraph, for the question of "reasonableness" cannot arise until the question of "deviation" is settled, and that can be done only after the scope of the voyage is defined. But this is probably too close and technical a reading. The draftsmen of the Rules on which Cogsa is based must have been aware of the standard use of voyage clauses very wide on their face, and of the judicial practice of construing such clauses down to reasonable limits. It is submitted, therefore, that the concept of "reasonable deviation," in this section, may be taken as equivalent to "reasonable departure from the normal course of sailing, or the contract course as defined by a *reasonable construction* of the voyage clause." Such a reading is in line with the whole theory of the Act, which is to subject the bill of lading contract to overriding statutory requirements.[114]

The proviso italicized in the quotation of Section 4(4) above did not appear in the Convention text of the Rules, but was added by the American Congress when Cogsa was enacted. The rationale of the rule it states seems to be that the carrier ought not to be allowed to deviate with no other motive than the increase of his own revenues; thus, the proof required to overcome the *prima facie* unreasonableness of such a deviation would have to show something more than mere reasonableness from the point of view of the *carrier*; most deviations of this sort are reasonable from his point of view, for they are performed, usually, in his interest, and the deliberate addition of these words cannot be taken merely to have set up a straw man for the carrier to knock down. Of course, this proviso does not imply that any deviation, other than for the two purposes mentioned, is "reasonable"; it simply makes it easier to establish unreasonableness in the named cases.[115] The carrier, throughout the performance of the voyage, is always subject to the Section 3(2) duty to care for and carry the goods properly, and his decision on a route would seem to be improper and unreasonable whenever it is made in disregard of that duty.

114. For a valuable discussion of this clause, see Deutsch, Deviation Under the Carriage of Goods By Sea Act, 21 Ore.L.Rev. 365 (1942). For "unreasonable deviation", see P & E Shipping Corp. v. Empresa Exportadora E Importadora De Alimentos, 335 F.2d 678, 1964 A.M.C. 2006 (1st Cir. 1964).

115. For a case illustrating the effect of this proviso, and showing the sort of evidence needed to establish "reasonableness", see Haroco Co. v. The Tai Shan, 111 F.Supp. 638, 1953 A.M.C. 887 (S.D.N.Y.1953), affirmed on opinion of district court, sub nom. Frederick H. Cone & Co. v. The Tai Shan, 218 F.2d 822 (2d Cir. 1955).

**§ 3–41.** Cogsa must clearly be taken to have abolished all legal effect of any deviation other than "unreasonable." What is the effect of "unreasonable" deviation?

A case can be made out, on the face of the Act, for the proposition that Cogsa has abolished the harsh doctrine which put the carrier in an "insurer's" position after deviation, and substituted a liability for that damage with which the deviation has some causal connection. Section 4(2) might be thought to have that effect, since, read as a whole, it immunizes the carrier from liability for loss arising from *any cause*, except where his fault is a concurring cause of the loss, and from some losses even where this is the case. Clearly, a loss actually *caused by* unreasonable deviation is not excepted by anything in Section 4(2), for only 4(2)(q) could apply, and it cannot operate because a loss caused by deviation is *ex hypothesi* "contributed to" by the fault of the carrier or his servants—their fault, namely, in deviating. Obviously, a carrier whose deviation has contributed to the causing of the loss ought not to be given the benefit of any of the other exemptions. But to go further than this and hold the carrier liable strictly as an insurer for any loss, however caused, occurring during or even after a deviation, may be thought directly contradictory of the terms of 4(2). This construction is shored up by the wording of Section 4(4), quoted above. The carrier is not to be "liable for any loss or damage *resulting*" from reasonable deviation. It is maintainable that the draftsmen of such a passage must have had in mind that the carrier should not be liable, even in the case of unreasonable deviation, for loss or damage other than that *resulting from* the deviation. In the past, the drastic effect of deviation has been rested on the notion of an "ouster" of the contract of carriage, and a consequent reinstatement of the underlying strict liability of the public carrier without contractual protection.[116] But it is questionable whether a statute can be "ousted" in this way.

The opposite view would seem to rest on the idea that Cogsa simply defines what the terms of the bill of lading contract are to be, as long as it is in effect, and that there is no clear intention discernible in the statute to alter the effect of deviation on the actual remaining in effect of the bill of lading contract. This broad theory as to the operation of Cogsa is too indispensable a tool in understanding its working elsewhere for it to be rejected out of hand in any context. But, as applied to the present question, it may be thought not to sit comfortably with the fact that Section 4(4), already quoted, does deal with the question of permissible deviation, defining, however vaguely, what deviations are to have legal effect, and doing so, as we have seen, in terms which seem to imply that the only effect deviation is ever to have is to subject the carrier to liability for loss caused by it.

116. See *supra* at note 108.

In Jones v. The Flying Clipper,[117] the court, in holding that a deviation displaced the $500-per-package limitation of Cogsa,[118] used language indicating a conviction that Cogsa had in no way changed the substantive law concerning the result of deviation, and cited an English case [119] to this effect. But the Jones case did not speak with entire clarity on the issue now under discussion, for the court finds it necessary to point out that the "causal relation between the deviation and the sea water damage is not in dispute." [120] Other early cases after Cogsa are even less decisive.[121]

More recently deviation has been held by the Second Circuit not to deprive the carrier of the benefit of the Fire Statute (see *supra* § 3–31) unless causally related to the loss by fire.[121a] But the whole of § 4(2) of Cogsa is just as "statutory" as the Fire Statute, and ought no more to be subject to "ouster" by a causally unconnected deviation than is the older statute. The Seventh Circuit has held that an unreasonable deviation did not oust the $500 per package limitation in Cogsa § 4(5).[121b] This result was rested on the special wording of § 4(5), but § 4(2) is as definite, if not as emphatic, as § 4(5). No rational ground appears for "ousting" § 4(2) upon the occurrence of deviation, while not "ousting" the Fire Statute or § 4(5) of Cogsa. But if § 4(2) is not "ousted", the carrier is not liable for damage not *caused by* his fault—including his fault in deviating.[121c]

Certainly, a construction is appealing which would abolish the drastic effect of deviation, leaving the carrier liable for damages caused by the undoubted breach of duty involved. "Deviation" is no more serious a matter to cargo than other gross faults of the carrier; yet no other breach of duty has such drastic consequences. The reason for the old rule seems to have been that the cargo lost its insurance when the vessel deviated, so that it was felt appropriate and just

**117.** 116 F.Supp. 386, 1954 A.M.C. 259 (S.D.N.Y.1953), noted 40 Va.L.Rev. 356 (1954); 102 U.Pa.L.Rev. 797 (1954); 1 Bus.L.Rev. 106 (1954).

**118.** See *infra* at note 150.

**119.** Stag Line v. Foscolo, Mango & Co., [1932] A.C. 328.

**120.** 116 F.Supp. at 387.

**121.** For various faint sidelights, see The Lafcomo, 64 F.Supp. 529, 1946 A.M.C. 903 (S.D.N.Y.1946), modified 159 F.2d 654 (2d Cir. 1947), certiorari denied 331 U.S. 821, 67 S.Ct. 1310 (1947); Haroco Co. v. The Tai Shan, 111 F.Supp. 638, 1953 A.M.C. 887 (S.D.N.Y.1953); affirmed on opinion of district court sub nom. Frederick H. Cone & Co. v. The Tai Shan, 218 F.2d 822 (2d Cir. 1955); The Tregenna, 35 F.Supp. 118, 1940 A.M.C. 1415 (S.D.N.Y.1940), reversed 121 F.2d 940 (2d Cir. 1941); Romano v. West India Fruit & S. S. Co., 151 F.2d 727, 1946 A.M.C. 90 (5th Cir. 1945); The Rio Verde, 69 F.Supp. 880, 1946 A.M.C. 1576 (S.D.N.Y. 1946).

**121a.** Frederick H. Cone & Co., Inc. v. The Tai Shan, 218 F.2d 822, 1955 A.M.C. 420 (2d Cir. 1955).

**121b.** Atlantic Mutual Ins. Co. v. Poseidon Schiffahrt, 313 F.2d 872, 1963 A.M.C. 665 (7th Cir. 1963), certiorari denied 375 U.S. 819, 84 S.Ct. 56 (1963).

**121c.** In World Wide S. S. Co. v. India Supply Mission, 316 F.Supp. 190, 1971 A.M.C. 498 (S.D.N.Y.1970), the court appears to have assumed that the deviation must be causally connected with the loss sought to be averaged, if a deviation is to oust a carrier's claim to general average.

to put the vessel in the insurer's position.[122] But at present cargo policies usually contain clauses which provide that, in the event of deviation, the risk shall be "held covered," notwithstanding. If and when the cargo owner learns of a deviation, it becomes his duty to notify the insurance company, and to pay an additional premium to be arranged. Often, the cargo interest will not learn of deviation until after loss, but is protected by this clause in the interim.[123] When insurance is actually lost by deviation, and when the cargo interest suffers thereby, it would seem not too great a strain upon notions of causation to charge the carrier with the loss, which is foreseeable as a possible result of his fault, thus preserving the good sense which was the starting point of the application of deviation law to the shipper-carrier relation.[124]

Any possible relaxation of the drastic penalty attached to deviation ought, however, to be kept in strictest isolation from the entirely different attempt to relax, by insistence on literal construction of absurdly wide voyage clauses, the duty, imposed by Section 3(1), properly and carefully to carry and care for the cargo. That duty, by the terms of the Act, overrides every contractual stipulation, whether in the form of a voyage clause or otherwise, and permeates every phase of the performance of the contract of carriage. For losses *causally connected* with the breach of that duty the carrier is liable, regardless of any clause of any name or type, and, indeed, without even any reference to the notion of deviation.

**§ 3–42.** Of late years there has been a tendency to import the notion of "deviation" into situations where no change of route is involved, on the theory that various forms of misconduct of the carrier are so serious as to amount to a departure from the whole course of the contract, with the consequence that the bill of lading protection is ousted, as in the case of deviation properly so called, and the insurer's liability reimposed. The stowage of cargo on deck, when stowage underdeck is called for by contract or custom, has been held to have this effect.[125] Delay has been brought under this concept.[126]

122. See *supra* at note 109; Knauth, *op. cit. supra* note 2, 249.

123. See *supra* note 109.

124. It would seem, too, that the necessity for paying an additional insurance premium is a damage proximately caused by the deviation, and should be recoverable as such.

There may be a trend in recent cases toward the views expressed in this section. See, *e. g.*, International Drilling Co. v. M/V Doriefs, 291 F. Supp. 479, 486–487, 1969 A.M.C. 119, 127 (S.D.Tex.1968). Hays, J. (in a dissent from a judgment not directly in point) speaks of the views expressed in this text as "generally accepted"—citing the discussion herein; Encyclopedia Britannica v. S.S. Hong Kong Producer, 422 F.2d 7, at 20 (2d Cir. 1969). Puzzling is Searoad Shipping Co. v. E. I. duPont de Nemours & Co., 361 F.2d 833, 835–6, 1966 A.M.C. 1405 (5th Cir. 1966), certiorari denied 385 U.S. 973, 87 S.Ct. 511 (1966), for the court speaks of an "insurer" liability but also heavily stresses the *causal relation* between the "deviation" and the damage, and indeed, states the rule in *causal* terms.

125. Searoad Shipping Co. v. E. I. duPont de Nemours & Co., 361 F.2d 833, 1966 A.M.C. 1405 (5th Cir. 1966), certiorari denied 385 U.S. 973, 87 S.Ct.

126. See note 126 on page 183.

In many such cases, the concept of deviation did not need to be introduced, for the loss was causally connected with obvious negligence or other fault. It would seem unwise to extend analogically and by way of metaphor a doctrine of doubtful justice under modern conditions, of questionable status under Cogsa, and of highly penal effect.

This problem is becoming acute with the advent of containerization (see *supra* §§ 1–5, 3–24). Most containers are designed to be carried safely on deck, and, for technical reasons of ship's balance, and loading and unloading, it cannot be foretold which of a ship's load of containers it will be necessary to carry on deck.[126a] It is therefore often (if not normally) impossible to issue a "below deck" bill of lading at the time of receipt of the container. On the other hand, the issuance of an "on deck" bill takes the goods out of the protection of Cogsa,[126b] and so impairs or destroys the commercial acceptability of the bill—and may turn out to have been quite unnecessary, since in fact the container may be carried below deck.

The provision of Section 4(4) permitting deviation to save life or property at sea reproduces a similar provision in the Harter Act.[127] It is largely self-explanatory, except for the caution that the deviation must go no further than necessary, or the immunity is lost. Thus a vessel which took another vessel off the rocks, and towed her to a place of safety where tugs were available, was within the permitted limits up to that point, but deviated unjustifiably when she towed the disabled vessel further along into a safer harbor, instead of leaving her to the tugs.[128]

## Burden of Proof

**§ 3–43.** We have seen that, under the general prestatutory law, the shipper made out his *prima facie* case by proving loss of or damage to the goods while they were in the hands of the public carrier.[129] The Harter Act effected no change. If the carrier wanted to establish an exemption, he had to take up the burden and bring the loss within an "exception" established by law or by contract.[130]

511 (1966); St. Johns N. F. Shipping Corp. v. S. A. Companhia Geral, etc., 263 U.S. 119, 44 S.Ct. 30, 1923 A.M.C. 1131 (1923); Jones v. The Flying Clipper, 116 F.Supp. 386, 1954 A.M.C. 259 (S.D.N.Y.1953), see *supra* note 117. But see DuPont de Nemours v. S.S. Mormacvega, 493 F.2d 97, 1974 A.M.C. 67 (2d Cir. 1974), where deck stowage was held not to have the effect of deviation when it was "reasonable," citing § 3–41 of this text.

**126.** See The Citta Di Messina, 169 F. 472 (S.D.N.Y.1909); Knauth, *op. cit. supra* note 2, 261–265; Carver, *op. cit. supra* note 2, 511.

**126a.** See Bissell, The Operational Realities of Containerization, etc., 45 Tulane L.Rev. 902, 917–920 (1971).

**126b.** Encyclopaedia Britannica v. S.S. Hong Kong Producer, 422 F.2d 7, 1969 A.M.C. 1741 (2d Cir. 1969).

**127.** Harter Act § 3, 27 Stat. 445 (1893), 46 U.S.C.A. § 192.

**128.** In re Meyer, 74 F. 881, 894 (N.D. Cal.1896).

**129.** *Supra* at note 2.

**130.** The Frey, 106 F. 319, 320–21 (2d Cir. 1901); The Rosalia, 264 F. 285, 288 (2d Cir. 1920).

Cogsa might, on its face, seem to have changed this rule, for Section 3(1) and 3(2), which are the affirmative basis on which a shipper must rely for recovery, are cast in terms of negligence, and it might seem that a libellant relying on one or both of these sections would have to establish, as his own *prima facie* case, breach of one of the duties imposed and consequent damage. But Cogsa is, as we have seen, not a complete code of the law of carriage, but a codification of some of the terms according to which bills of lading are to take effect. Section 3(1) and 3(2) merely restate, in modified form, the overriding obligations previously implied by law in the bill of lading contract,[131] and there is no indication that they were meant to effect so drastic a change as the imposition of the requirement that the shipper affirmatively establish negligence in order to make out a *prima facie* case. That they were not intended to have any such effect is conclusively established by the fact that such a construction would make nonsense of the allocations of burden of proof as to negligence in Section 4(2). Section 4(2)(q) provides that the carrier shall be exonerated from loss arising from any cause other than those listed in 4(2)(a) to (p), only if he sustains the burden of proving freedom from fault. Such a provision would have nothing to operate on if the shipper had the initial burden of proving negligence or other fault in every case.[132]

Once the damage is established, the carrier, it would seem, has two main lines of possible escape. He may take up the burden of establishing that the loss falls within 4(2)(a) to (p). If he does this successfully, then either (as in 4(2)(a)) he is exonerated regardless of his negligence; or (as in 4(2)(c)) he will, in effect, already have established his own freedom from negligence as a part of the process of bringing himself under the exception; or, if the exception he has brought himself under is one to which his own contributing fault would disentitle him, the burden will shift to the shipper to prove the carrier's negligence or other fault.[132a]

If on the other hand, the nature of the carrier's explanatory evidence is such that it appears either that the loss was due to the un-

131. See *supra* at notes 6, 33.

132. This passage is quoted with approval in Mamiye Bros. v. Barber S.S. Lines, 241 F.Supp. 99, 109–110, 1966 A.M.C. 1175, 1188 (S.D.N.Y.1965), affirmed 360 F.2d 774, 1966 A.M.C. 1165 (2d Cir. 1966), certiorari denied 385 U.S. 835, 87 S.Ct. 80 (1966). The shipper makes his prima facie cases by proving delivery to the carrier in good order and receipt in bad or non-receipt; the burden of explanation is on the carrier. Spencer Kellogg & Sons v. Great Lakes Transit Corp., 32 F.Supp. 520, 529, 1940 A.M.C. 670 (E.D.Mich.1940); American Tobacco Co. v. The Katingo Hadjipatera, 81 F. Supp. 438, 445, 1949 A.M.C. 49 (S.D. N.Y.1948), affirmed 194 F.2d 449 (2d Cir. 1951), certiorari denied 343 U.S. 978, 72 S.Ct. 1076 (1952); General Foods Corp. v. The Troubador, 98 F. Supp. 207, 1951 A.M.C. 662 (S.D.N.Y. 1951). Proof of good condition on loading is not always easy; see *e. g.*, American Tobacco Co. v. Goulandris, 281 F. 2d 179, 1962 A.M.C. 2655 (2d Cir. 1960). But a clean bill of lading will suffice, when the goods are of a nature permitting easy inspection; Kupfermann v. U. S., 227 F.2d 348, 1955 A.M.C. 2171 (2d Cir. 1955).

132a. Lekas & Drivas, Inc. v. Goulandris, 306 F.2d 426, 1962 A.M.C. 2366 (2d Cir. 1962).

seaworthiness of the ship or to some cause covered only by the omnibus exception 4(2)(q), the burden of establishing his freedom from fault remains with him, by express provision of 4(1) and (4)(2)(q).[132b]

As we have seen when dealing with the substantive effect of negligence or other fault in 4(2)(a) to (p), what this comes down to is that the carrier (with the special exceptions of 4(2)(a) and (b)) has sooner or later the burden of establishing his own freedom from fault except where he has shown that the loss was caused by overwhelming force of third persons, some fault in the shipper or the goods, or the attempt to save life or property. This leaves with him the burden of explaining a loss and exonerating himself from the imputation of fault in almost all cases in which it has not been demonstrated that at least a part of the fault lies with somebody else. This scheme of allocation of burden of proof seems well-constructed.[133]

### The Requirement That a Bill of Lading Be Issued—The "Clause Paramount"

§ 3–44. We have covered the crucial sections of Cogsa; it remains to deal with a few miscellaneous provisions.

Section 3(3) requires that the carrier or his agent actually issue a bill of lading, showing the "marks," the quantity, and the apparent condition of the goods. No penalty is provided in Cogsa for the failure to issue such a bill, but it may be that Sections 4 and 5 of the Harter Act,[134] which require the issuance of a bill and impose a fine for failure to issue it on demand, are to be regarded as still in force as to this provision, even where Cogsa otherwise applies.[135]

Cogsa goes further and requires that an outbound bill of lading contain a "clause paramount," reciting that the bill is to be governed by the provisions of the Act.[136] This was an addition by Congress to the Rules. No provision is to be found for enforcing this requirement. It has been suggested that the carrier who issued a bill without the

132b. This burden is not insuperable; see *e. g.*, Manhattan Fruit Exp. Corp. v. Royal Netherlands S.S. Co., 271 F. 2d 607, 1960 A.M.C. 180 (2d Cir. 1959), certiorari denied 363 U.S. 812, 80 S.Ct. 1249 (1960).

133. For an excellent discussion of the burden of proof problem, see Note, 27 Texas L.Rev. 525 (1949). It would seem plain that attempted contractual alteration of this burden of proof scheme must fail, as being a lessening, in practical effect, of the ship's Cogsa liability; see *supra* § 3–25, and Encyclopaedia Britannica v. S.S. Hong Kong Producer, 422 F.2d 7, 13, 1969 A.M.C. 1741, 1747 (2d Cir. 1969).

134. 27 Stat. 445–6 (1893), 46 U.S.C.A. §§ 193–4.

135. A fine point of statutory construction is involved. Cogsa § 12 expressly saves Harter from repeal only in so far as it relates to duties, etc., of the carrier before loading and after discharge. § 4 of Harter seems to impose a duty to issue a bill of lading for merchandise "received by the owner, master, or agent of the vessel for transportation . . . ," but a shipped bill could not of course be required until the goods were loaded. It might be argued that this provision in Harter, though not expressly saved by Cogsa, is not repealed by implication, since it is not inconsistent with Cogsa, but only adds a penalty to a duty Cogsa imposes.

136. § 13, 46 U.S.C.A. § 1312.

clause paramount might be deprived of the protection of the Act and of his bill of lading contract, rendered "illegal" by this omission, and be held to perform the contract of carriage on the "insured" basis of the common law.[137] This may look drastic, but it seems on the other hand a lame conclusion to be forced to the position that a positive requirement such as this has been laid down with no penalty whatever for its infraction.

It should be borne in mind, moreover, that mere inadvertent omission of a required clause of this sort is an impossibility in the standardized bills of lading issued in ocean carriage. When a bill of lading is issued in the United States for an outward foreign shipment, with the clause paramount omitted, the probability is that the carrier is hoping to evade the requirements of Cogsa; this is a feasible enterprise if the shipment is to a non-Cogsa country which will apply its own law if Cogsa is not mentioned in the bill of lading.[138] The fact that the "clause paramount" is required only in *outbound* bills of lading suggests that it was this hope which Congress meant to thwart. The "reading in" of Cogsa, notwithstanding the absence of the clause paramount, will of course be done if the carrier, thwarted in the evasive scheme, is successfully subjected to suit in the United States, but that hardly meets the need for a sanction; all it means is that the scheme didn't work this time. Under these circumstances, it may not seem too drastic to hold the carrier estopped from claiming the benefit of the statute, or of the exceptions in his illegal bill, while permitting the cargo to claim whatever benefit the statute gives. An "equality" in this matter is fictitious; bills of lading are drawn up by carriers.

The bill of lading, though its function as the embodiment of the contract of carriage is now largely absorbed by the provisions of Cogsa, still functions as a receipt for the goods; in this capacity it is of value as evidence, being *prima facie* proof of the receipt of the goods as described in it.[139]

## Carriage Liens—Jurisdiction

§ 3–45. Every valid claim for cargo loss or damage creates a maritime lien against the ship.[140] Thus, where we have spoken of a liability of the "carrier" the reader may supply "and of the ship." Such a lien is of course enforced by the action *in rem* within the ad-

137. See Knauth, *op. cit. supra* note 2, 158–161. Mr. Knauth seems to disapprove of this suggestion.

138. See Knauth, *op. cit. supra* note 2, 161. As Mr. Knauth says, this scheme cannot work if the carrier can be sued in the United States, but very often this is not possible. To attribute no legal consequence whatever to the omission of the clause paramount is to conclude that Congress, in this deliberately added proviso, meant merely to express an aesthetic preference.

139. Cogsa § 3(4).

140. Bulkley v. Naumkeag Steam Cotton Co., 65 U.S. (24 How.) 386 (1860); Demsey and Associates v. S.S. Sea Star, 461 F.2d 1009, 1972 A.M.C. 1440 (2d Cir. 1972), citing text.

miralty jurisdiction, as described in Chapter I.[141] Cogsa and Harter contain prohibitions against the carrier or the vessel's contracting out of these liens.[142]

Similarly, the ship has a lien on the cargo for freight, and other charges arising out of the ship-cargo relation and the bill of lading contract.[143] Such a lien can certainly be enforced by the action *in rem*, but is is questionable how far it ought to be regarded as a genuine maritime lien in the strict sense, for it does not survive unqualified delivery of the goods, and hence seems more like the possessory lien of the carrier at common law.[144] Even where delivery is qualified by a reservation of the lien, this cannot survive transfer of the goods to a bona fide purchaser for value without notice of the lien, though survival under these circumstances is often said to be one of the most striking characteristics of the maritime lien on the ship.[145]

The reciprocal susceptibility to liens arising out of the carriage relationship comes into being, it seems, only when the goods are loaded aboard. At that time, the ship and the cargo are regarded as pledged to one another for the performance of the obligations of the venture. Cleirac's phrase, invariably quoted in this connection, is the classic epitomization: "Le batel est obligé à la marchandise, et la marchandise au batel." [146] Thus, a ship may not be proceeded against *in rem* for refusal to receive cargo, though the refusal may be in breach of the maritime contract of carriage.[147]

All suits based on cargo loss or damage, or any other breach of the contract of carriage, are within the admiralty jurisdiction.[148] *In personam* actions may, of course, be brought either in federal court under the admiralty jurisdiction or in the state courts (or, in a proper case, on the civil side of the federal courts), under the saving clause; a good many suits for small claims are actually brought in state courts. The maritime liens arising out of the shipper-carrier relation may be enforced only in federal court under admiralty jurisdiction.[149]

## Valuation and Claims

**§ 3–46.** Cogsa sets a maximum of $500 which may be recovered on any package or "customary freight unit." [150] These words have created a wilderness of problems.

141. See *supra* Chapter I, § 1–12.

142. Harter Act § 1, 27 Stat. 445 (1893), 46 U.S.C.A. § 190; Cogsa § 3(8).

143. The Bird of Paradise, 72 U.S. (5 Wall.) 545, 555 (1867).

144. See 4885 Bags of Linseed, 66 U.S. (1 Black) 108 (1861).

145. Harmer v. Bell (The Bold Buccleugh) 7 Moo.P.C.C. 267 (1850–51).

146. Quoted by the Court in Osaka Shosen Kaisha v. Pacific Export Lumber Co., 260 U.S. 490, 497, 43 S.Ct. 172, 173, 1923 A.M.C. 55 (1923).

147. Osaka Shosen Kaisha v. Pacific Export Lumber Co., 260 U.S. 490, 43 S.Ct. 172, 1923 A.M.C. 55 (1923). The matters referred to in the preceding paragraphs are further discussed *infra*, Chapter IX.

148. *Supra* Chapter I, at note 63.

149. See *supra* Chapter I, at note 117 *et seq.*

150. § 4(5).

The West Kyska [151] involved the loss overboard of thirteen pieces of steel, unpackaged but billed for freight by the hundredweight. The carrier sought to limit liability to $6500, being thirteen times $500; but the court held that the "customary freight unit," one hundred pounds, was the applicable unit for valuation, and allowed a larger recovery. Billing freight at a high unit—say, in an appropriate case, a thousand pounds or a ton—would be an obvious means of attempting to cut down recoveries, but it is to be assumed that courts would give full force to the word "customary" in the statute. "What is a package?" is sometimes a hard question. A giant machine shipped in 126 pieces, was treated as so many packages or package-like units; [152] a tractor machine, unpackaged, was divided (in contemplation of law) into units of 40 cu. ft., valued at $500 each.[153] On the other hand, in a decision which practically converted Cogsa into an exoneration statute, the Second Circuit held that a whole locomotive was, if not a "package", then a "freight unit",[153a] limiting liability for its destruction to $500.

Containers (see *supra* §§ 1–5, 3–24) pose special problems here, and the law cannot be said to have come to rest. In a case decided with evident hesitation and very much on its own facts, the Second Circuit has held that a container is not a "package", where the separate packages in the container are described.[153b] As the court says, "The problem demands a solution better than the courts can afford, preferably on an international scale. . ." [153c]

The basis for fixing damages for loss of cargo under the general law is the market price at the port of destination on the day of arrival or when the vessel should have arrived.[154] Before Cogsa was enacted,

151. 155 F.2d 687, 1946 A.M.C. 997 (5th Cir. 1946), certiorari denied 329 U.S. 761, 67 S.Ct. 115 (1946).

152. Stirnimann v. The San Diego, 148 F.2d 141, 1945 A.M.C. 436 (2d Cir. 1945). See also Brazil Oiticica v. The Bill, 55 F.Supp. 780, 1944 A.M.C. 883 (D.Md.1944), affirmed per curiam 145 F.2d 470 (4th Cir. 1944).

153. Middle East Agency v. The John B. Waterman, 86 F.Supp. 487, 1949 A.M.C. 1403 (S.D.N.Y.1949).

153a. Isbrandtsen Co. v. United States, 201 F.2d 281, 1953 A.M.C. 86 (2d Cir. 1953). See also Island Yachts, Inc. v. Federal Pacific Lakes Line, 345 F.Supp. 889, 1971 A.M.C. 1633 (N.D.Ill., 1971).

153b. Leather's Best, Inc. v. S.S. Mormaclynx, 451 F.2d 800, 1971 A.M.C. 2383 (2d Cir. 1971) on remand 346 F.Supp. 962 (1972). The lower court holding is discussed in Simon, Note, 2 Journal of Maritime Law & Commerce 190 (1970); but *cf.* Standard Electrica S.A. v. Hamburg Sudamerikanische, etc., 375 F.2d 943, 1967 A.M.C. 881 (2d Cir. 1967), certiorari denied 389 U.S. 831, 88 S.Ct. 97 (1967) noted by Reed, 43 Notre Dame Lawyer 259 (1967), where a pallet, upon which six cartons were shipped, was held to be a "package". The majority and dissenting opinions contain discussions of the "package" problem. And see also Royal Typewriter Co. v. Hamburg-Amerika Linie, 483 F.2d 645, 1973 A.M.C. 1784 (2d Cir. 1973). On the whole problem, see DeOrchis, The Container and the Package Limitation, 5 Journal of Maritime Law and Commerce 251 (1974).

153c. 451 F.2d at 814 (2d Cir. 1971).

154. St. Johns N. F. Shipping Corp. v. S. A. Companhia Geral, etc., 263 U.S. 119, 125, 44 S.Ct. 30, 31, 1923 A.M.C. 1131 (1923); The Ansaldo San Giorgio I v. Rheinstrom Bros. Co., 294 U.S. 494, 55 S.Ct. 483, 1935 A.M.C. 419 (1935); The Lafcomo, 64 F.Supp. 529,

it seems to have been a common practice for the bill of lading to stipulate for "invoice plus disbursements (freight and insurance)" as the measure of loss, and these stipulations were upheld.[155] Under Cogsa, it has been held that such a clause, when it "lessens" the carrier's liability, offends Section 3(8).[156]

Suit for cargo damage under Cogsa must be brought within one year from the date when the goods were delivered or should have been delivered.[157] Under Cogsa, no notice of damage or presentation of a claim is, or can be made by contract, a prerequisite to the filing of a suit;[158] it is to the advantage of cargo, however, to give notice of damage on delivery if the damage is patent, or within three days if it is concealed, for if this is not done cargo will have to bear the burden of proving that the goods were not delivered "as described in the bill of lading."[159]

### Cargo Insurance—"Benefit of Insurance" Clauses

**§ 3–47.** In this chapter, we have touched at several points the connection of the rules governing the shipper-carrier relation with the doctrines and practices of marine insurance. Some general view of this connection may be in order.

Standard cargo insurance protects against most of the risks for which the ship is not responsible. In the rough these are fire, negligence in the navigation and management of the ship which, in an insurance policy on cargo, is a "peril of the sea" and (without regard to burden of proof) any other insured cause arising without the carrier's fault. If war risk insurance is carried, the cargo is protected against most of the "acts of third persons" exceptions in Cogsa, 4(2). "Inherent vice" losses are almost never protected against by cargo insurance.

532, 1946 A.M.C. 903 (S.D.N.Y.1946), modified on other grounds, sub nom. Pioneer Import Corp. v. The Lafcomo, 159 F.2d 654 (2d Cir. 1947), certiorari denied 331 U.S. 821, 67 S.Ct. 1310 (1947). For some problems in the application of this rule, see Wood, Damages In Cargo Cases, 45 Tulane L. Rev. 932 (1971).

155. Smith v. The Ferncliff, 306 U.S. 444, 59 S.Ct. 615, 1939 A.M.C. 403 (1939).

156. Sanib Corp. v. United Fruit Co., 74 F.Supp. 64, 67 (S.D.N.Y.1947). For a decision invalidating the "pro rata" clause, limiting recovery to such fraction of the valuation as the damage suffered bears to the actual value, see Pan-Am Trade & Credit Corp. v. The Campfire, 156 F.2d 603, 1946 A.M.C. 644 (2d Cir. 1946), certiorari denied 329 U.S. 774, 67 S.Ct. 194 (1946). These decisions seem clearly correct; § 3(8) is in a sense the key to the Act, for it assures that the cargo interest will receive the broad benefits granted to it without gradual erosion by carefully contrived clauses in the bills of lading drawn up by carriers in concert. The only way it can fulfil this function is by being construed to mean what it says, without too great attention to arguments based on a "convenience" which usually turns out to be carrier's convenience.

157. § 3(6).

158. § 3(6); Balfour, Guthrie & Co. v. American-West African Line, 136 F.2d 320, 1943 A.M.C. 954 (2d Cir. 1943), certiorari denied 320 U.S. 804, 64 S.Ct. 437 (1944). *Cf.* Newport Rolling Mill Co. v. Mississippi Valley Barge Co., 50 F.Supp. 623, 1943 A.M.C. 793 (E.D.La. 1943) (Harter Act).

159. § 3(6).

The most important gap in the cargo owner's coverage may be created by the "particular average" conditions of his policy.[160] If his coverage is "free of particular average," he must himself bear any partial loss for which the ship is not responsible. Often, as we have seen, the F.P.A. clause is so drawn as not to apply when the vessel is stranded, sunk, burnt, or in collision, and one type of F.P.A. clause on cargo goes further:

> "Warranted free from Particular Average unless the vessel or craft be stranded, sunk, or burnt, but notwithstanding this warranty the Underwriters are to pay the insured value of any package or packages which may be totally lost in loading, transhipment or discharge, also for any loss of or damage to the interest insured which may reasonably be attributed to fire, explosion, collision or contact of the vessel and/or craft and/or conveyance with any external substance (ice included) other than water, or to discharge of cargo at port of distress, also to pay landing, warehousing, forwarding and special charges if incurred for which Underwriters would be liable under a policy covering Particular Average. This clause shall operate during the whole period covered by the policy."

This clause extends even particular average coverage to losses often not claimable against the ship (fire, and, to a great degree, negligence in navigation). Still, the cargo owner insured against total loss and general average only can find himself, in the event of loss, without a claim against either the ship or the insurance company.

As a matter of business judgment, he may elect to pay a larger premium and insure with a low particular average franchise. He may, also, procure an "all risk" policy, at a correspondingly higher premium than that charged for insurance against the limited perils in the "perils clause," and thus assure that no loss can happen through the incidence of a cause neither insured against nor creating liability in the ship.

Cargo insurance, of course, insures against some losses for which the ship is responsible, for the cargo underwriter pays on many claims even though negligence of the ship has been a concurrent cause of the loss. Wherever this happens, it is the practice for the insurance company to pay the cargo at once, and put in a claim against the ship as subrogee.[161] It is greatly to the advantage of cargo to be able to look to the underwriter instead of the carrier for payment, even where the latter is clearly liable, for ocean carriers are not noted for the ease and dispatch of their claims settlement procedures.

Thus, the operation of the doctrine of subrogation is such that a carrier often finds itself sued, in the name of the shipper, by the insurance company that has already reimbursed the shipper for the loss The reader who has followed this chapter closely will be aware that

160. See *supra* Chapter II, at note 111. 161. See *supra* Chapter II, at note 143.

ocean carriers are not the sort of people to take that kind of thing lying down, as long as a bill of lading clause can prevent it. The clause was forthcoming; it provided that the carrier was to have "the benefit of the shipper's insurance," which meant that the carrier was not to be liable for any damage reimbursed by cargo insurance; under such a clause, there was nothing for the underwriter to be subrogated to since the clause by its own terms extinguished liability in those circumstances where subrogation would have occurred. The "benefit of insurance" clause was upheld by the courts,[162] but the insurance companies devised a system for circumventing it; they merely "loaned" the amount of the insurance liability to the cargo owner, while he (in a suit financed and managed by them) sued the carrier for the damage. The "loan" was repaid out of the proceeds of the suit. This device, known as the "loan receipt," was generally successful in defeating the "benefit of insurance" clause.[163]

These maneuvers are unnecessary under Cogsa, for that Act expressly outlaws the benefit of insurance clause, in Section 3(8).

### A Final Word on Goods Carriage and Cogsa

§ 3–48. Because of the containerized multimodal revolution, already sufficiently described, this whole subject must be regarded as very much in flux. International conventions for dealing with it on a new basis rather clearly impend; it may even be that a no-fault system will gain favor, and that carrier liability, without fault, will be extended to the full value of the goods, on the quite plausible economic theory that this requirement would motivate just that degree of care costing as much as would the loss of goods thereby averted, thus ending up, so far as the whole economic society is concerned, in a desirable equilibrium. In a work such as the present, it has seemed unsuitable to try to present a static picture of the process of total international reconsideration now in progress.[163a] But the profession should be aware that major change probably impends.

One problem that will have to be solved, if actual uniformity is to be attained, is *international uniformity of interpretation* of texts agreed to internationally.[164] The best solution here might be an international specialized tribunal exercising a discretionary jurisdiction (similar to the certiorari jurisdiction of the American Supreme

162. Phoenix Ins. Co. v. Erie & Western Transp. Co., 117 U.S. 312, 6 S.Ct. 750 (1886).

163. Luckenbach v. W. J. McCahan Sugar Co., 248 U.S. 139, 39 S.Ct. 53 (1918).

163a. See the discussion in Lucchese v. Malabe Shipping, 351 F.Supp. 588, 1973 A.M.C. 979 (D.Puerto Rico 1972); Maritime Law Association Document No. 578, Oct. 1973, at p. 6153. Documents giving account of work in progress are issued from time to time by the United Nations Commission On International Trade Law.

164. In General Motors Overseas Operation v. S.S. Goettingen, etc., 225 F. Supp. 902, 1964 A.M.C. 940 (S.D.N.Y. 1964), *e. g.*, it was shown by affidavit that "peril of the sea" has different meanings to German and American courts. See also Selvig, The Paramount Clause, 10 Amer. J. of Comparative Law 205 (1961); Mendelsohn, *op. cit. supra* n. 23, 2 Journal of Maritime Law and Commerce at 666.

Court) over cases involving the interpretation of international agreements (Cogsa, or its probable successors) governing goods carriage. The jurisdiction of such a court should be discretionary, for some latitude of interpretation is tolerable (as it is among the American judicial circuits). The establishment of such a tribunal would raise constitutional questions, here and in every country, but it is believed these are not insuperable.[165]

Meanwhile, the accessible publication of reports of decisions, translated into several languages of wide currency, might promote uniformity by comity.

165. See Black, The Bremen, Cogsa, and the Problem of Conflicting Interpretation 6 Vanderbilt Journal of Transnational Law 363 (1973).

# Chapter IV

# CHARTER PARTIES

## Taxonomy and Nature

**§ 4–1.** The term "charter party," often shortened to "charter," designates the document in which are set forth the arrangements and contractual engagements entered into when one person (the "charterer") takes over the use of the whole of a ship belonging to another (the "owner"). Actually, a charter of less than the entire ship is possible, but occurs quite infrequently. It is not unknown, however, even in modern times.[1] We will be concerned here only with charters engaging the whole capacity of a vessel.

In general, suits brought on the breach of an obligation incurred in a charter party are within the admiralty jurisdiction.[1a] For most defaults in performance, so long as the agreement is executory, the remedy is *in personam,* with the corollary that suit may also be brought in the ordinary civil courts under the saving clause.[2] Some breaches of charter obligations, however, create maritime liens;[3] in such a case, of course, proceeding may be *in rem,* under the admiralty jurisdiction only,[4] and in procedural compliance with the supplemental Federal Rules applicable.[4a]

Charter parties are highly standardized.[5] There are three main types[5a]:

> A. *The Voyage Charter.* In this form, the ship is engaged to carry a full cargo on a single voyage. The vessel is manned and navigated by the owner. Manifestly, such a charter is merely a special kind of contract of carriage. This form is adaptable to any commercial situation in which the thing wanted is the moving of a shipload of cargo from one point to another. It is the form most frequently encountered.

1. See Pacific Veg. Oil Corp. v. M/S Norse Commander Corp., 264 F.Supp. 625, 1967 A.M.C. 1895 (S.D.Tex.1966).

1a. *Supra* Chapter I, at note 65.

2. See *infra* at note 78 and *supra* Chapter I, at note 117.

3. See *infra* at note 73 *et seq.*

4. See *supra* Chapter I, at note 119.

4a. Rules of Civil Procedure for the United States District Courts, Supplemental Rules for Certain Admiralty and Maritime Claims, esp. Rules C and E. See *supra,* Chapter I, §§ 1–1 and 1–9.

5. For a discussion of early charter forms, see Prausnitz, Standardization of Commercial Contracts 13–14 (1937); for modern forms, see the authorities cited in note 9, *infra.*

5a. The differences among the three kinds of charters are discussed in Randolph v. Waterman S.S. Corp., 166 F.Supp. 732, 1960 A.M.C. 2382 (E.D. Pa.1958). See § 9–51(a) *infra* for discussion of the current financing arrangement under which the "true owner" of a vessel sets up a dummy corporation to hold title and then "charters" the vessel from the dummy. For the right of such a "charterer" to institute proceeding under the Limitation of Liability Act, see § 10–10 *infra.*

B. *The Time Charter.* In this form, as in the voyage charter, the owner's people continue to navigate and manage the vessel, but her carrying capacity is taken by the charterer for a fixed time for the carriage of goods anywhere in the world (or anywhere within stipulated geographic limits) on as many voyages as approximately fit into the charter period. She is therefore under the charterer's orders as to ports touched, cargo loaded, and other business matters. The time charter is used where the charterer's affairs make it desirable for him to have tonnage under his control for a period of time, without undertaking the responsibilities of ship navigation and management or the long-term financial commitments of vessel ownership. The company operating regular liner service may, for example, find itself temporarily short of tonnage and wish to place another vessel in the service; it can do this with relatively slight trouble and without indefinitely long commitment if it can find a suitable vessel to take on time charter.

C. *The Demise or Bareboat Charter.* In this form, the charterer takes over the ship, lock, stock and barrel, and mans her with his own people. He becomes, in effect, the owner *pro hac vice,* just as does the lessee of a house and lot, to whom the demise charterer is analogous. Obviously, such an arrangement is suitable to the needs of anyone who wants, for a time, to be in the position of the owner of a vessel, but who does not want to go to the expense and trouble of buying one or having one built. The demise, as well as the time charter, may answer the need of the shipping line temporarily short on tonnage; whether a company in this position wants to take a ship on time or on demise will depend on whether the advantages of the complete control enjoyed by the demise charterer seem, in the actual situation, to outweigh the rather heavy responsibilities that he assumes, as owner, in effect, for the time being.[6] In recent years, the main use of the demise charter has been as a device for putting the government into the shipping picture; the government may, e. g., demise a vessel owned by it to a private company, for operation by that company, or conversely, the government may (in wartime or other emergency) get the tonnage it needs by taking vessels from private companies on demise. (The government has also frequently employed the time charter in both these ways.)[7]

Theoretically, a ship might be demised for a voyage, but in practice virtually all demise charters are for a period of time. It needs

6. In 1952, a typical American line had 22 ships in operation, of which 17 were owned and 5 chartered. McDowell & Gibbs, Ocean Transportation 221 (1954).

7. *Id.* at 187. See *infra* Chapter XI, at notes 128 & 129.

to be noted, therefore, that the phrase "time charter" (B, above) is a term of art; it is not used, as one might assume, to denote all charters running for a fixed period, but refers only to non-demise charters so time-limited.

Although a voyage charter is simply a contract for the carriage of definite goods between definite points and a time charter might be looked on as a sort of contract for the carriage of such goods as may from time to time be specified, on such voyages as may be ordered, and though both these forms of charter thus operate on the same subject matter as do bills of lading, the charter party is in no sense an *alternative* to the other embodiment of the carriage contract—the bill of lading—in the documentation of goods carriage. Bills of lading are, on the contrary, issued in the great majority of cases of carriage under charter. Voyage and time charters usually stipulate expressly for the issuance (by the master, who is under the owner's control) of bills of lading for the goods carried; in the demise situation, the charterer himself controls the master, and bills of lading are issued just as they would be if the ship were under the hand of her general owner; the personal liability, however, is that of the demise charterer. Time or demise charterers often operate the vessel they control as a "general ship," taking package cargo from all comers and giving bills of lading. Thus bills of lading and charter parties may be and commonly are involved in the same situation.

Nor need a vessel be under only one charter at a time. The demise charterer of a ship, for example, may desire to charter her to someone else (called the "subcharterer") for a voyage, and he may do so unless prohibited by the terms of the charter under which he himself entered the picture.

From what has been said, it will be seen that the charter party is merely a contract, subject in general to all the rules and requirements of contract law. As is the case with that even more highly standardized contract, the marine insurance policy, the special law of charter parties consists almost entirely in the accumulated gloss of judicial decision surrounding certain more or less stereotyped terms and clauses.[8] Standardization has not resulted in simplicity or lucidity, from the layman's point of view. The phrasing of charters is laconic, and a single short (and often, to the uninitiate, obscure) expression may refer to a whole set of complicated practices perfectly familiar to those who deal regularly in such matters. A good handbook on shipping practice, or a trade dictionary of shipping, can sometimes do more to render a charter party case comprehensible than all the legal acumen in the world.[9] Standardization has resulted in the

8. *Cf. supra* Chapter I, at note 45, and Chapter II, at note 21.

9. The following will be found useful: Stevens, Shipping Practice (9th ed. 1971); McDowell & Gibbs, Ocean Transportation 185–203 (1954); MacMurray and Cree, Shipping & Shipbroking 97–172 (3d ed. 1934); Dover, The Shipping Industry 42–68 (1952); Bes, Chartering and Shipping Terms (7th ed. 1970). For those who can even limp along in German, Capelle, Die Frachcharter in Rechtsvergleichender Darstellung (1940) may be of use; the book is a survey of char-

stereotyping not of one charter form alone but of a really bewildering variety of special forms, each regularly used for some one purpose or set of purposes, and each with a name of its own: *"Burma Rice Charter Party," "Baltimore Berth Grain Charter Party (Form C)"*, etc.

As the foregoing discussion will have implied, charters are not *in themselves* subject to Cogsa (see *supra* Chapter III, Part 2, *passim*), though bills of lading issued concurrently with or under a charter may be and often are subject to Cogsa. But immunity from Cogsa's requirements depends on the charter's being a real and not a sham charter, designated as such for the purpose of evading Cogsa.[9a] Nor need it be shown that the ship was a "common" carrier for Cogsa to apply; even specialized "private" carriage may be subject to Cogsa.[9b]

The law of charters is in any case federal law, as to which uniformity is required.[9c] However, since most points of charter law involve construction of the charter, the principles are much the same as those of ordinary contract law.

In such a field, it is not surprising that arbitration (often made compulsory by the charter itself [10]) has largely taken the place of litigation. It is only infrequently, today, that a court is called on to construe a charter. Some questions of a more general nature do, however, get into court. The infrequency of litigation does not, any more than in the marine insurance field, imply that the subject is unimportant to the admiralty lawyer.

terparty practice throughout the world, and most of the clauses discussed are in English. Rørdam, Treatises on the Baltcon Charterparty (1954) is an interesting monograph on a single form. For a recent general account, both supporting and citing this text, see Zock, Charter Parties in Relation to Cargo, 45 Tulane L.Rev. 733 (1971).

9a. See Jefferson Chemical Co. v. M/T Grena, 413 F.2d 864, 1969 A.M.C. 2443 (5th Cir. 1969). In that case, an agreement called a "charter", but actually involving the use from time to time of some 10–15% of the space on several vessels from time to time, was held common carriage, subject to Cogsa.

9b. Nichimen Co. v. M/V Farland, 462 F.2d 319, 1972 A.M.C. 1573 (2d Cir. 1972), extensively citing this text.

9c. Jack Nielson, Inc. v. Tug Peggy, 428 F.2d 54, 1970 A.M.C. 1490 (5th Cir. 1970). See *supra*, § 1–17.

10. In Red Cross Line v. Atlantic Fruit Co., 264 U.S. 109, 44 S.Ct. 274, 1924 A.M.C. 418 (1924), it was held that a state court might enforce an agreement to arbitrate contained in a charter; see *supra* Chapter I, at note 123. In 1925 Congress enacted a federal Arbitration Act, 43 Stat. 883, 9 U.S.C.A. §§ 1–15, providing for irrevocability and specific enforcement of agreements to arbitrate, in (*inter alia*) "maritime" transactions. The background and effect of this Act are exhaustively discussed in Kulukundis Shipping Co. v. Amtorg Trading Corp., 126 F.2d 978, 1942 A.M.C. 364 (2d Cir. 1942), noted 29 Va.L.Rev. 338 (1942). The federal courts may be called on to order an arbitration, Industrial Y Frutera Colombiana v. The Brisk, 195 F.2d 1015, 1952 A.M.C. 738 (5th Cir. 1952), or to enforce an award. Application of States Marine Corp. of Delaware, 127 F.Supp. 943 (S.D.N.Y.1954). See also *infra* at note 93 *et seq.*

The federal policy in favor of arbitration is sometimes invoked in charter cases to overcome technical objections; see *e. g.*, Carcich v. Rederi A/B Nordie, 389 F.2d 692, 1968 A.M.C. 299 (2d Cir. 1968); Eastern Marine Corp. v. Fukaya Trading Co., 364 F.2d 80, 1966 A.M.C. 1959 (5th Cir. 1966).

The "fixture" of a ship—the bringing to successful conclusion of the negotiations precedent to signing the charter—is complicated work, performed by a corps of brokers who maintain an elaborate network of intelligence that enables them to bring together the needed tonnage and the cargo waiting or in process of assembly.

Though they have much in common, the three basic charter party forms differ so widely among themselves, with respect to practical and legal considerations, that it is considered best to take them up separately. This method will necessitate some repetition and cross-reference, but it is believed to be more conducive to clarity than is the treating of all three of these dissimilar arrangements in a jumble. First, we will examine the voyage charter, the most important of the three. Secondly, we will turn to the time charter, emphasizing the points wherein it differs from the voyage charter. Finally, we will treat briefly the demise.

## A. THE VOYAGE CHARTER

### The Setting: Tramp Shipping

§ 4–2. The simplicity of the voyage charter makes it adaptable to many sorts of transactions, but its greatest importance is as the basic document in the carriage of bulk cargoes by the tramp fleet of the world. Tramp shipping is a topic of great fascination; Commander Lane C. Kendall of the United States Merchant Marine Academy some years ago devoted to the subject an article that does justice to both its practical and its romantic sides, and that is still of considerable interest and validity.[11] In large debt to his summation,[11a] we will take up those aspects essential to an understanding of the place of the voyage charter in this vital branch of the shipping industry.

The tramp is a vessel that seeks employment in carriage of goods at such times and between such places as opportunity may offer—in contrast to the "liner," which operates on schedule between prearranged termini. Liners are usually operated as "general ships," taking on a miscellaneous packaged or containerized cargo belonging to different shippers. The charter therefore plays a minor part in the operation of the scheduled line. By contrast, the tramp seeks and usually gets a full cargo loaded by a single shipper. Such cargoes are most often in bulk or in standard packages, and typically consist of the raw materials, fuels, and unprocessed foods so vital to the world economy—wheat, oil, lumber, iron ore, and the like.

11. Kendall, Tramp Shipping, Polaris, Summer 1952, p. 37. For an indispensable updating by the same author, see Kendall, The Business of Shipping, 15–47 (1973). For recent policy regarding tramp shipping, see *infra* Chapter XI, at note 101d *et seq.*

11a. Later works of interest are Cufley, Ocean Freights and Chartering (1962); Bes, Chartering and Shipping Terms, *supra* note 9.

The firm desiring to ship such a cargo—often because it has contracted for its sale and delivery at some foreign port, but sometimes merely in expectation of finding such a market—will normally turn over the problem of procuring the required tonnage to its cargo broker, whose greatest asset is his contact with the network of brokers and shipowners' representatives all over the world. In America, he may first survey the New York market to see if a suitable vessel is being offered, but if nothing turns up there he may, by cabled request to a British correspondent, institute inquiries on the great Baltic Exchange in London. All his telephoning and legwork, as well as that of any representatives or correspondents he may bring into the picture, is aimed at finding a tramp that will be completing a prior charter sometime shortly before the shipment he is interested in has to be made, at some port reasonably close to the port from which that shipment will leave. Sooner or later, he will probably find some shipbroker whose principal has a vessel that will be so circumstanced as to be able and willing to undertake the charter he is offering. There will follow some negotiation over terms, but if differences can be ironed out, the charter will be "fixed" and signed.[12]

This inquiry and negotiation are carried on by cable or wireless, except where all concerned are in a single city. In New York, brokers work by telephone; in London, they meet in the Baltic Exchange. Speed is essential. Brokers rather than principals do a good deal of the work. These factors are a partial explanation for the standardization of voyage charters; in this institutional context, it would be simply impossible to chaffer, in each case, over all the terms of the proposed contract. Consequently, each "trade" (*e. g.*, the Australian grain trade) has developed a standard charter form; each such form can be referred to by a short title, or even a code name. Such a form, in a given trade (*e. g.*, the *Chamber of Shipping Australian Grain Charter 1928*, code name "Austral") is the outcome of negotiations between the interests involved in that trade. Its terms take account of and attempt to cover by express stipulation those matters which have proven to be productive of misunderstanding. Thus, the Australian charter cited in the parenthesis allocates between the parties the responsibility and cost of bagging enough of a bulk shipment of wheat to prevent shifting and so to satisfy the applicable Australian regulations. Manifestly, a multitude of such matters cannot be negotiated *ad hoc*. And it seems to be the general opinion that the charter forms in use are not one-sided, but are reasonably fair as between shipping and cargo interests. There are no statutes in this country (or, generally, elsewhere) regulating the terms of charter parties, as the terms of bills of lading are regulated by the Carriage of Goods by Sea Act.[13] It has traditionally been felt, apparently, that

12. A vivid account of negotiations preceding the fixture of a voyage charter is found in Kulukundis Shipping Co. v. Amtorg Trading Corp., 1941 A.M.C. 1347 (S.D.N.Y.1941), reversed (on grounds not presently material), 126 F.2d 978 (2d Cir. 1942).

13. 49 Stat. 1207 (1936), 46 U.S.C.A. §§ 1300–1315. (The abbreviation "Cogsa"

the bargaining power of charterers and owners is near enough equal that they may be left to contract freely, a situation in sharp contrast to the great disparity between ship lines and the shippers of package cargo. Nonetheless, it has been the settled rule that "exceptions in a . . . charter party, inserted by the shipowner for his own benefit, are unquestionably to be construed most strongly against him." [14]

Of late, this freedom of contract may be changing. In Bisso v. Inland Waterways, Corp., cited and discussed *infra* § 7–15, the Supreme Court used language which might extend to charterparties, wherever disparity in bargaining power actually appeared. So far, the Court has not spoken on this issue; lower federal court decisions are not free from ambiguity.[14a] Obviously, only the Supreme Court can decide authoritatively whether and to what extent the Bisso rule is to prevail in charter-party cases. It seems that any really practical solution will have to come from an international convention, comparable to the one underlying Cogsa; the strong assertion of national "public policy", in this most international of fields, is highly problematic.

As a matter of practice, many charter party forms stipulate for the applicability of Cogsa or the Harter Act to the charterer-owner relations; such a stipulation is of course valid, and prevails even where no bill of lading is issued.[15]

In this subchapter, we are going to proceed by considering a single one of the many charter forms—the *Uniform General Charter 1922* (code name "Gencon")—a form selected because of its relative simplicity. This form is printed as an appendix; [16] the text that follows here will refer frequently to it. To follow the discussion in the text it will be necessary for the reader to turn frequently to the charter itself. We will discuss its provisions, and go into some of the problems of law that have arisen in regard to similar clauses and phrases.

will hereafter be used.) See The Monarch of Nassau, 155 F.2d 48, 1946 A.M.C. 853 (5th Cir. 1946); Horn v. Cia. de Navegacion Fruco, S.A., 404 F.2d 422, 429, 1968 A.M.C. 2548, 2553 (5th Cir. 1968), citing text. But see *supra* § 4–1, at notes 9a–9c.

14. Compania de Navigacion La Flecha v. Brauer, 168 U.S. 104, 118, 18 S.Ct. 12, 15 (1897); Mechling Barge Lines, Inc. v. Derby Co., Ltd., 399 F.2d 304, 1968 A.M.C. 1436 (5th Cir. 1968).

14a. Recent cases, either unclear in tendency or emanating from district courts, are cited in Zock, Charter Parties in Relation to Cargo 45 Tulane L.Rev. 733, 741, note 51 (1971).

15. J. B. Effenson Co. v. Three Bays Corp., Ltd., 238 F.2d 611, 1957 A.M.C. 16 (5th Cir. 1956). United States v. The South Star, 210 F.2d 44, 1954 A.M.C. 418 (2d Cir. 1954); see also United States v. Wessel, Duval & Co., 115 F.Supp. 678, 1953 A.M.C. 2056 (S.D.N.Y.1953).

16. *Infra*, Appendix A. This charter is apparently still in use (see Zock, *op. cit. supra* note 9, 45 Tulane L.Rev. at p. 736, note 21) but is selected in this text for its simplicity and lack of specialization, rather than for its being frequently encountered. Actually, charters vary so much that none can strictly be said to be "typical".

## Clause 1: The Basic Terms

§ 4–3. This clause expresses the gist of the contract, identifying the parties, designating and describing the vessel, naming the cargo, and setting the contract voyage and the freight.

Statements made about the vessel, whether descriptive of her characteristics or stating her position and situation, may, if such a construction appears reasonable, be treated as warranties, breach of which entitles the charterer either to avoid the contract entirely or to proceed with it and sue for such damages as he may have suffered from the breach.[17] A leading case on the problem of deciding which of these terms are to be treated as warranties is Watts v. J. B. Camors & Co.[18] In that case, the owner of the Highbury sued the charterer for the latter's refusal to take the vessel when tendered, pursuant to a charter that described her as "of the burden of 1,100 tons, or thereabout." Her actual tonnage was 1,203 tons, and the charterer's defense was that the representation in the charter party was to be treated as a warranty, entitling him to decline the vessel, as he had done. But the Court noted that the charter provided for the loading of 11,5000 quarters of wheat as the contemplated cargo, and that the Highbury was actually capable of carrying this amount. Applying what seems at this distance to be common sense, the Court regarded the capacity stipulation as "controlling" the tonnage representation, since it was carrying capacity rather than tonnage that was of interest to the charterer; the defense was rejected.

The blank following the word "now" in the first sentence of the clause under examination would normally be filled in with some statement as to the present position of the vessel, sometimes with the addition of the information that she is "about to sail." This sort of representation is frequently held to amount to a warranty.[19] But in Lovell v. Davis [20] the Supreme Court refused to find a warranty in the statement that the vessel was "now lying in the harbor of New Orleans," when she was actually at sea, it appearing that this statement was

17. Davison v. Von Lingen, 113 U.S. 40, 5 S.Ct. 346 (1885); Horn v. Cia de Navegacion Fruco, S.A. 404 F.2d 422, 429, 1968 A.M.C. 2548, 2554 (5th Cir. 1968); Romano v. West India Fruit & S. S. Co., 151 F.2d 727, 731, 1946 A.M. C. 90 (5th Cir. 1945); Simonetti v. Foster, 2 F. 415 (D.Mass.1880). On the question whether a given statement is to be taken to be a warranty, the statement of the court in the Romano case, *supra*, is interesting: "The owner, agreeing that the speed of a vessel may be warranted, insists that the inserted clause was not a warranty at all because not expressly declared to be. But this will not stand up under the authorities. As Denholm Shipping Co. v. W. E. Hedger Co., 2 Cir., 47 F.2d 213 points out, the failure to use the word 'warranty' in a statement of this kind is unimportant. What is important is whether the statement was positively and unequivocally made as a statement of fact and whether the natural tendency of its making was to induce the chartering of the ship." 151 F.2d at 731.

*Cf. supra* Chapter II, at note 51. And see Carver, Carriage of Goods by Sea 293–307 (12th ed. 1971).

18. 115 U.S. 353, 6 S.Ct. 91 (1885).

19. Davison v. Von Lingen, 113 U.S. 40, 5 S.Ct. 346 (1885); Olsen v. Hunter-Benn & Co., 54 F. 530 (S.D.Ala.1892).

20. 101 U.S. 541 (1880).

not material, and that the charterer knew of the actual position of the vessel.

Actually, as to statements of past or present fact, the courts seem to apply what amounts to a test of materiality to determine whether the statement is to be taken to be a warranty.[21] It is questionable, therefore, whether the "warranty" terminology adds much at this point, where the charterer is claiming the right to avoid, since it seems clear as a general matter that he would in any case be entitled to disaffirm the contract for material misrepresentation, where this is found.[22]

Some so-called "warranties" are, however, promissory in character. Though Gencon does not contain it, there is sometimes a statement that the vessel is to proceed to the port of loading with "all possible dispatch." Failure to proceed with all dispatch has been held a breach not merely of contract but also of warranty, entitling the charterer to back out.[23]

It will be handy here to take up, out of order, Clause 11, which also concerns the matter of delay. If the provision for declaration of option to cancel 48 hours before expected arrival were not included, the charterer could wait until the vessel actually arrived and was tendered, and then cancel because of failure of the vessel to make the cancellation date[24]—obviously a rather hard disposition. The 48-hour provision forces him, on demand, to make up his mind while the vessel is on her way to the loading port. It will be noted, on careful reading of the second sentence in Clause 11, that the sentence sets up, at least in so far as it provides for cancellation, an alternative to the fixed cancellation date of the first sentence. If the blank in the first sentence is not filled in by agreement then presumably the optional cancellation date would arrive ten days after the "expected ready" day in Clause 1.

The strictness with which carefully worded commercial documents are sometimes construed by the courts is nowhere better illustrated than in Sanday v. U. S. Shipping Board Emergency Fleet Corp.[25] In that case, the charterers repudiated a ship, under the

21. See the statement quoted from the Romano opinion, supra note 17, and the Watts and Davis decisions discussed in the text.

22. See Note, 23 Va.L.Rev. 211 (1936).

23. Lowber v. Bangs, 69 U.S. (2 Wall.) 728 (1865). But whether such a warranty exists is of course a question of intention and hence of construction, and circumstances or other terms in the charter may negate it. Massari v. Forest Lumber Co., 290 F. 470, 472, 1923 A.M.C. 1111 (S.D.Fla.1923).

Somewhat similar is the warranty that the vessel will be "ready to sail" from the loading port, or "expected ready to load," on or about a named date. Dexter & Carpenter Co. v. United States, 13 F.2d 498, 1926 A.M.C. 1415 (S.D.N.Y.1926). But whether a warranty or a mere statement of expectation is involved is, again, a matter of construction. Petroleum Export Corp. v. Kerr S. S. Co., 32 F.2d 969, 1929 A.M.C. 905 (9th Cir. 1929).

24. The Progreso, 50 F. 835 (3d Cir. 1892); Karran v. Peabody, 145 F. 166 (2d Cir. 1906); The Samuel W. Hall, 49 F. 281 (S.D.N.Y.1892).

25. 6 F.2d 384, 1925 A.M.C. 542 (2d Cir. 1925), certiorari denied 269 U.S. 556, 46 S.Ct. 19 (1925).

cancellation clause, some days before the cancellation day, but at a time when it was, from her position, clear that she could not arrive on time. There was no question but that they were, under these circumstances, relieved of their own obligation under the charter. But they sought to go further and to hold the owner in damages for breach of the charter, on the theory that the cancellation date was also to be taken to be the date when it was agreed that the vessel would be tendered. This theory the court declined to accept, insisting that the cancellation date was material *only to cancellation*, and not to defining an affirmative obligation on the owner's part. There is implied, as the court in Sanday recognized, an obligation to get the ship there in a "reasonable" time, but the libellant had failed to prove "unreasonableness," and the cancellation date did not *ipso facto* establish "a promise of the owner to tender the ship on or before the cancellation day or at any other definite time." [26]

### Clause 1 (contd): Safe Ports and Berths—"Always Afloat"

**§ 4–4.** Typically, a single port is named as the port of loading, filling in the first blank in the second paragraph of the clause, though this is not invariably true.[27] But it is very common for the charterer to be given the option of discharge at one or more ports within a given geographic range. The words "as ordered on signing Bills of Lading," following the port-of-discharge blank, mean that the option must be exercised at the time of loading and before the vessel sails. Sometimes the rate of freight will be variable, depending on the choice made.[28] The charterer is given this option for the sound commercial reason that he may not, at the time the charter is fixed, know where the best market for his goods will be found.

Two frequently-encountered provisions affect the charterer's freedom of choice as to ports and berths to which he may order the vessel. The first is the so-called "safe-ports" clause. Our Gencon form does not contain such a clause; where, however, the range of ports set out as available contained any ports that might be unsafe, the words filling in the blanks would probably stipulate for "safe ports" only. The following is a typical formula, found in a charter that got into litigation:

> "thence to Queenstown or Falmouth, (as directed by charterers or their agents), for orders to discharge, always

26. 6 F.2d at 385. For the position where no cancellation date is stated, see Schooner Mahukona Co. v. Charles Nelson Co., 142 F. 615 (N.D.Cal.1906).

27. Farr v. Hain S. S. Co., 121 F.2d 940, 1941 A.M.C. 1282 (2d Cir. 1941).

28. See the example given by Kendall, *supra* note 11, Polaris, Summer 1952 at p. 42. In Warren Corp. v. Picton S. S. Co., 100 F.2d 212, 1938 A.M.C. 1544 (1st Cir. 1938), it was held that the charterer's election of discharging ports, once made, binds him, and that extra expenses caused by his going back on it are recoverable by the ship. Interesting sets of facts, illustrating current practice, are found in two Arbitrations: Argonaut Navigation Co. v. French Supply Council, 1950 A.M.C. 1477 (1950); same parties, 1950 A.M.C. 1823 (1949).

> afloat, either at a safe port in the United Kingdom or on the continent of Europe between Havre and Hamburg (both included), Rouen excepted, or at option of charterers to order vessel from Barbadoes to proceed to Delaware breakwater for orders to discharge at New York or Boston or Philadelphia or Baltimore, or so near the port of discharge as she may safely get and deliver the same, always afloat, in a customary place and manner, in such dock as directed by charterers, agreeably to bills of lading." [29]

This extract well exhibits the use of the "safe ports" clause. It is to be noted that the phrase is not used with regard to Boston, New York, Philadelphia, or Baltimore; the safety of these named ports is already known; but the alternative range of discharge ports—anywhere in the United Kingdom or on the continent of Europe between Havre and Hamburg except Rouen—is so wide and indefinite that the owner feels it necessary to reserve the right to decline to risk his vessel in an unsafe port, without being in default under his contract.

The Gazelle [30] is a typical and well-known "safe ports" case. The charter provided for delivery "to a safe, direct, Norwegian or Danish port, as ordered on signing bills of lading . . . " The charterers tendered bills of lading naming Aalborg; these the master refused to sign, on the ground that this port was unsafe for his vessel, because of a bar across the fiord or inlet through which he had to pass to reach it. The Court sustained the master's contention, and awarded as damages the net freight the vessel would have earned under the charter, plus the expenses of taking the cargo out, and wharfage and towage charges incurred.

Closely connected with the "safe ports" stipulation is the provision, found in our charter and appearing in variant forms in most, that the vessel shall be obligated to go only "so near thereto [i. e., to the port of loading or discharge] as she may safely get and always lie afloat." This may be looked on as a stipulation for a "safe berth." [31] The dispute with regard to this clause sometimes concerns the question of who is to pay for lighterage or other expenses necessitated by alleged inability of the ship to tie up safely at the designated wharf. A classic case on this matter is Mencke v. A Cargo of Java Sugar.[32] The charterer had designated New York as the port of discharge. One of the relevant clauses of the charter has already been quoted; [33] another provided:

> "All goods to be brought to and taken from alongside of the ship, always afloat, at the said charterers' risk and expense,

29. Mencke v. A Cargo of Java Sugar, 187 U.S. 248, 251, 23 S.Ct. 86, 87 (1902).

30. 128 U.S. 474, 9 S.Ct. 139 (1888).

31. But a mere stipulation for a safe berth does not always imply an undertaking that the vessel will be afloat at low tide. Oil Transfer Corp. v. Spentonbush Fuel Transport Service, 1940 A.M.C. 820 (S.D.N.Y.1940).

32. 187 U.S. 248, 23 S.Ct. 86 (1902).

33. *Supra* at note 29.

who may direct the same at the most convenient anchorage; lighterage, if any, to reach the port of destination, or deliver the cargo at port of destination, remains for account of receivers, any custom of the port to the contrary notwithstanding." [34]

The designated point of discharge was above the Brooklyn Bridge; it was found that the vessel's masts were too high to permit her to pass under that structure. The court agreed with the vessel owner that the designated dock was not, under these circumstances, a place to which the ship might "safely get . . . in a customary place and manner."

Most "safe port" and "safe berth" cases have involved the question whether the shipowner or the master was at fault for not going into the designated port or berth—or the connected question (as in the case just discussed) of the proper allocation of extra expenses consequent on the owner's or the master's refusal to send the ship to the designated port or berth. It is clear on the face of it that, if the port or the berth is unsafe, the master is excused from taking his ship in, and the charterer must bear the extra expense, such as lighterage, entailed by the refusal. In fairly recent times, in some authorities, a quite different consequence has been suggested for the "safe port" and "safe berth" clauses: that the charterer, regardless of fault, be held liable for damages to the ship resulting from her having entered an unsafe port, or tied up at an unsafe berth.[34a] It is submitted that these authorities go too far. It will be convenient first to take this question upon the reason of the thing.

It is quite inconsonant with the positions of the parties, in the usual case, to charge the charterer with the consequence of the master's having entered an unsafe port or tied up at an unsafe berth. It is the master who ordinarily has the best means of judging the safety of a port or berth, first because he is an expert in navigation, furnished with aids thereto, secondly because he knows his vessel (including its draft and its present trim), and thirdly because he is on the spot. The charterer, on the other hand, need not be a nautical expert at all, knows nothing about the vessel except its capacity, and normally is far from the scene of decision as to safety; his designations of port and berth are made (and are known to be made) on commercial rather than on nautical grounds.

Further, the master, by the very words of the usual clauses, is *not* obligated to take his vessel to any unsafe port or berth. The very

34. 187 U.S. at 251, 23 S.Ct. at 87.

34a. Poor On Charter Parties and Ocean Bills of Lading (5th ed. 1968) seems to state the rule as imposing liability on the charterer for ship's damage attributable to entering an unsafe port, unless the shipowner has accepted the port "as safe with full knowledge of its dangers . . ." § 5. See also the extended discussion in Carver, Carriage of Goods by Sea, §§ 375–6, 976–987 (12th ed. 1971); Ivamy, Ordering a Vessel to an Unsafe Berth, 20 The Solicitor 215 (1953); and American cases cited *infra*, note 36. For a comparative treatment, see Ramberg, Unsafe Ports and Berths (1967).

purpose of the clauses is to free him of this obligation. Since these clauses can be and have been given this meaning, it is by no means necessary that they be given the quite different meaning of creating an affirmative liability of charterer to ship, in case of mishap. Indeed, as just suggested, they might easily be read to contradict this latter meaning, since they place it outside the charterer's power to force the master to imperil the ship. If the charterer, by the clauses, is disabled from forcing the ship into an unsafe place, then his designation of an unsafe berth can hardly be said to cause the ship's going there.

Finally (and this cannot be irrelevant to an evaluation of the suitability of the allocation of risk), the ship can and almost invariably does carry insurance covering damage to her; the realistic question, in nearly every case, is whether the ship's hull underwriters or the charterer shall pay.

In the usual case of entry into an unsafe port or berth, therefore, the entry is effected by decision of the master (whose business it is to know) although (by operation of the very clauses under examination) he might validly have refused, and the ensuing damage is of a sort normally insured by the policy on hull. Very clear language, or compelling special circumstances, ought to be required, before the liability is shifted to the charterer, who may know nothing of the safety of ports and berths, and who is much less certain to be insured against this sort of liability.

As already suggested, this clarity of language is missing in the clauses. They might easily be taken as no more than limits on the ship's obligation and the charterer's correlative power.

Special circumstances vary from case to case. It is possible, though most unlikely, that a charterer will be aware of factors making a *port* unsafe, while the master will not have such knowledge, nor have any reason to have it. It is possible, and fairly likely, that the charterer or consignee may have knowledge of the conditions at a given *berth* which make it unsafe, while the master will neither have, nor reasonably be charged with having, such knowledge. In such cases, it may well be that the charterer or consignee ought to be held liable, not because of the "safe port" and "safe berth" clauses, but because it ought to be held to be an actionable wrong for him to invite the ship without warning into a peril known to him, with or without the clauses. There may be cases, too, where the charterer or (more frequently) the consignee is so situated as reasonably to be charged with a duty of inquiry, particularly as to berth.

Absent such special factors, it is submitted that there is no reason, in policy or in interpretation, for holding the charterer liable for ship's damage, on the basis of the safe-port and safe-berth clauses. The Supreme Court seems so to have held, about a hundred years ago, in a case not since overruled or weakened in that Court. In Atkins v. Fiber Co., the district court (the illustrious Judge Benedict sitting), confronted with a claim for damages to a vessel owing to her having entered a port concededly unsafe, said:

> The master is the navigator, presumed to know best the channel of the ports within the natural range of the adventure, and the capacities of his vessel; and he is the proper person to determine whether his vessel can or cannot enter any particular port.
>
> In this case the second port was to be designated at Kingston, where the owners did not intend to be except in the person of the master; and they must have intended that the master should act for them in determining the question which would arise when the second port should be designated, and must be there decided.
>
> If, then, the port named was deemed an unsafe port for his vessel, and so not within the privilege given by the charter, it was the duty of the master, as the sole representative of the owners, to have made known his objections at the time. Not having done so he must be deemed to have waived the right to object, and, the condition having been waived, no action can now be maintained for the breach of it.[35]

In its subsequent opinion, in an appeal taken on another ground, the Supreme Court said of the opinion in which these words occur:

> In regard to the merits—after a careful examination of the record—we have found no reason to dissent from the views of the learned district judge by whom the case was heard. However full might be our discussion, we should announce the same conclusions. They are clearly expressed and ably vindicated in his opinion. To go again through the process by which they were reached would be a matter rather of form than substance. [Formal footnote omitted.] [35a]

Nevertheless, some subsequent cases have intimated that the charterer is to be liable for damage resulting from entry into an unsafe place, on orders of charterer or consignee.[36] Most, perhaps all,

35. Atkins v. Fibre Disintegrating Co., 2 Benedict 381, 2 Fed.Cas.No. 601, at p. 79. See also The Terne, 64 F.2d 502, 505–6, 1933 A.M.C. 662 (2d Cir. 1933), certiorari denied 290 U.S. 635, 54 S.Ct. 53 (1933).

35a. Atkins v. The Disintegrating Co., 85 U.S. (18 Wall.) 272, 299 (1873).

36. Besides the secondary sources in note 34a *supra* and cases therein cited, see Universal Tramp Shipping Co. v. Irish Salt Mining Co., 1970 A.M.C. 1783 (D.Mass.1970); Park S. S. Co. v. Cities Service Oil Co., 188 F.2d 804, 1951 A.M.C. 851 (2d Cir. 1951), *certiorari denied* 342 U.S. 862, 72 S.Ct. 87 (1951); Cities Service Transportation Co. v. Gulf Oil Refining Co., 79 F.2d 521, 1935 A.M.C. 1513 (2d Cir. 1935); Eastern Mass. St. Ry. Co. v. Transmarine Corp., 42 F.2d 58, 1930 A.M.C. 1454 (1st Cir. 1930), *certiorari denied* 282 U.S. 883, 51 S.Ct. 86 (1930). Though it is usually unclear in the "hard-shelled" safe-berth-warranty cases whether the charterer or consignee was actually at fault, some expressions certainly intimate that this is not a requirement; to that extent, for the reasons given in the text, the decisions ought to be disapproved and their rule reconsidered. In commercial cases such as these, it is realistically (as in all cases it is theoretical-

of these cases could be explained on "special circumstance" grounds.[36a] But some have used the language of "warranty", which, pushed to its extreme, would reach results quite inconsistent with the language approved by the Supreme Court in the Atkins case.

No reason supports this extension. It is to be hoped that the Supreme Court will one day take up a case raising this question, and reaffirm the principle of the Atkins decision, confining charterer's liability to the case wherein his special knowledge or actions make it reasonable to charge him.

## Clause 2: Liability for Goods Damage

**§ 4–5.** This clause addresses itself, in the charter-party context, to the problem that was the subject matter of Part II, Chapter III, above, on the carriage of goods by sea. The first thing to be noted is that Cogsa does not apply to charter parties.[37] Charter party carriage, moreover, is normally looked on as "private" carriage,[37a] and, as pointed out above, there are no statutory rules forbidding the adjustment of risk for goods damage in any manner provided by the charter.[38]

The general maritime law, however, read into every charter a warranty of seaworthiness of the vessel, equivalent to the warranty

ly) true that a denial of certiorari implies no view on the merits.

The ship may, it has been held, recover "dead freight" (see *infra* at note 75) where passage out of the loading port is impossible with a full cargo and where charterer's designation of a berth is responsible for this condition. Carbon Slate Co. v. Ennis, 114 F. 260 (3d Cir. 1902).

It is submitted that this, too, ought to depend on charterer's fault, but here the relevant fault would be a refusal, after notice, to designate a berth the ship can get out of laden; it ought to be the master's business to ascertain whether this condition exists—at least in the normal case.

Generally speaking, the voyage charterer is responsible for the consequence of his own misperformance of any of his duties under the charter. Where, e. g., it was his duty to load, and a workman was injured by an unsafe appliance furnished by the charterer, the latter had to indemnify the owner for the liability the latter incurred. Ace Tractor & Equipment Co. v. Olympic S. S. Co., 227 F.2d 274, 1956 A.M.C. 144 (9th Cir. 1955).

**36a.** Park S. S. Co. v. Cities Service Oil Co., *supra* note 36 illustrates this. The pilot who actually selected the berth was distinctly found to have been negligent (see the findings in the District Court, 93 F.Supp. 201, 207–8 (S.D.N.Y.1950)) and to be a "borrowed servant", for whose acts the charterer was responsible. (188 F.2d at 806). Thus the issue of liability as for warranty was not actually tendered. (Even so, the justice of the holding may be questioned, on the "agency" point.) Similar remarks might justly be made on Venore Transportation Co. v. Oswego Shipping Co., 363 F.Supp. 1366, 1973 A.M.C. 2150 (S.D.N.Y.1973).

**37.** Cogsa § 5, 49 Stat. 1211 (1936), 46 U.S.C.A. § 1305. But carefully compare the authorities cited *supra*, § 4–1, at note 14a. Though the statute does not cover charters, it may be that an emerging "public policy" does.

**37a.** See especially, however, the Nichimen case, *supra* note 9b, where Judge Henry Friendly, speaking for the Second Circuit, says (undoubtedly correctly) that there is no reason why the parties to a voyage charter may not, if they wish, make the bill of lading the document regulating their relations—which would make Cogsa the governing law. 462 F.2d at p. 328, 1972 A.M.C. at p. 1584.

**38.** *Supra* at note 13. See Texas Co. v. Lea River Lines, 206 F.2d 55, 1953 A.M.C. 1894 (3d Cir. 1953).

of seaworthiness read into the contract of carriage entered into by the "general" ship.[39] As we have seen, Cogsa abolished this warranty as to public carriers, issuing bills of lading, substituting an obligation to use due diligence to make the vessel seaworthy.[40] The clause we are now considering produces much the same result; the difference is that it is only the "personal" want of due diligence on the part of the owners or their managers that is to count. The intended effect of this clause seems to be to make the owner responsible for the negligence of a narrower class of persons than those for whom he would have to answer under the ordinary doctrines of *respondeat superior*.[41]

The concept of seaworthiness, in its inclusiveness and its relativity to the character of the voyage and of the cargo, is just the same as in the carriage of goods by the public carrier.[42] A kind of unseaworthiness that is of major importance in charter party cases is that which consists in unfitness to carry the particular cargo. An often-cited and interesting case is Church Cooperage Co. v. Pinkney.[43] The charter on which suit was brought was for the carriage of a cargo of whiskey-barrel shooks from Galveston to Buenos Aires. The vessel had been carrying creosote, which has a tendency to permeate a ship and to communicate its odor to goods subsequently carried; the fact that the vessel was carrying creosote was stated in the charter, which also contained the clause: "Vessel agrees to have holds as clean as possible." In the suit by the charterer for contamination of his shooks, rendering them unsuitable for use in the wine barrels for which they were destined, the court rejected the contention that, given the knowledge by the charterer of the creosote carriage and the express statement in the charter of what amounted to a due diligence obligation, the warranty of seaworthiness was contracted out of by implication.[44] Clearly, under the charter we are considering

39. See Work v. Leathers, 97 U.S. 379 (1878); Horn v. Cia de Navegacion Fruco, S. A., 404 F.2d 422, 1968 A.M.C. 2548 (5th Cir. 1968); Ionian S. S. Co. of Athens v. United Distillers of America, Inc. 236 F.2d 78, 1956 A.M.C. 1750 (5th Cir. 1956); The Caledonia, 157 U.S. 124 (1895); New England S. S. Co. v. Howard, 130 F.2d 354, 1942 A.M.C. 1057 (2d Cir. 1942).

40. Cogsa, §§ 3(1), 4(1), 49 Stat. 1208–1210 (1936), 46 U.S.C.A. §§ 1303(1), 1304(1).

41. The incorporation by reference of Cogsa in the charter party would of course cut the seaworthiness warranty down to Cogsa dimensions. *Cf.* Ore S. S. Corp. v. D/S A/S Hassel, 137 F. 2d 326, 1943 A.M.C. 947 (2d Cir. 1943).

42. See *supra* Chapter III, Part II, at note 34 *et seq.* In texts and cases, no distinction is observed so far as the citation of authorities is concerned. For the difference in burden of proof, however, see Commercial Molasses Corp. v. New York Tank Barge Corp., 314 U.S. 104, 62 S.Ct. 156, 1941 A.M.C. 1697 (1941); a full discussion of the problem is found in a thoughtful Comment, 41 Mich.L.Rev. 693 (1943); see also Notes, 42 Colum.L.Rev. 699 (1942); 30 Geo.L.J. 400 (1942); 16 Tulane L.Rev. 464 (1942); 27 Va.L.Rev. 1078 (1941).

43. 170 F. 266 (2d Cir. 1909), certiorari denied 214 U.S. 526, 29 S.Ct. 704 (1909).

44. *Cf.* The Carib Prince, 170 U.S. 655, 18 S.Ct. 753 (1898), cited *supra* Chapter III, Part II, note 38; and see The Toledo, 122 F.2d 255, 1941 A.M.C. 1219 (2d Cir. 1941), certiorari denied 314 U.S. 689, 62 S.Ct. 302 (1941). See Note, 84 L.J. 269 (1937).

a different result would be reached, for the seaworthiness warranty is expressly abolished. But the case, and others like it, is of interest in exhibiting the wide scope of the notion of seaworthiness itself. Modern tramps are often of specialized design, constructed and equipped to carry only certain kinds of cargo; as to such vessels, "seaworthiness" will comprise the technical efficiency of the special design and equipment—e. g., ventilators and refrigeration.[45] The tramp designed for carriage of many and variegated sorts of cargo has, on the other hand, the headache, suggested by the Church Cooperage case, of being sure that a previous cargo has not so affected the holds as to make the vessel an unsuitable receptacle for the goods currently shipped.

A modern case,[46] involving the charter of a Mississippi barge, reiterates the rule that the warranty of seaworthiness is implied in every charter, unless the contrary is stipulated for, and that the contrary stipulation, to be effective, must be unequivocal and clear. The charter contained a provision that "The Charterer has had the barge inspected and found same to be in first-class condition"; a cursory inspection had actually been made. The court held that all this was not enough to abolish the seaworthiness warranty, and held the owner for damages resulting from its breach.

In the absence of stipulation the owner, as bailee, is responsible for damage to goods caused by negligence in their custody and care. Gencon, in the clause we are considering, cuts this liability down to one for negligent *stowage*, immunizing the ship from liability for negligence in the care of the goods once the voyage is begun. And even the liability for negligent stowage is cut down by the excision of damage caused by proximity to or contact with other goods.

As we have noted, some charters today incorporate by reference either Cogsa or the Harter Act or both, as a measure of the liability of the owner to the charterer. There can of course be no public policy objection to this.[46a]

### Clause 3: Deviation

**§ 4–6.** Little need be said about this, since the topic of deviation has already been given full treatment in the Chapters on Marine Insurance and Carriage of Goods,[47] and the concept is much the same in the charter party situation.[48] Obviously, this clause has the same

45. See The Southwark, 191 U.S. 1, 24 S.Ct. 1 (1903), and *supra* Chapter III, Part II, at note 35.

46. Jordan, Inc. v. Mayronne Drilling Service, 214 F.2d 410, 1954 A.M.C. 1807 (5th Cir. 1954).

46a. J. B. Effenson Co. v. Three Bays Corp., 238 F.2d 611, 1957 A.M.C. 16 (5th Cir. 1956); American Oil Co. v. S.S. Ionian Challenger, 366 F.2d 509, 1966 A.M.C. 2244 (2d Cir. 1966).

47. See *supra* Chapter II, at note 58 *et seq.*, and Chapter III, Part II at note 107 *et seq.*

48. See Farr v. Hain S. S. Co., 121 F. 2d 940, 1941 A.M.C. 1282 (2d Cir. 1941). As with "seaworthiness," the deviation cases are freely cited across the border between bill of lading and charter party carriage. See Notes, 54 Harv.L.Rev. 707 (1941) and 21 Va.L. Rev. 227 (1934). But for a caution as to equivalence of effect, see the text at the end of this Section.

intendment as the wide "scope of the voyage" clauses in standard bills of lading, and, like them, ought to be given a reasonable construction.[49]

Charters, however, are not subject to Cogsa unless Cogsa has been incorporated by reference in the charter. Hence the argument from Cogsa with respect to that Act's abolition of the more drastic consequences of deviation (namely, the converting of the carrier into an insurer; see *supra* § 3–41) would not literally apply to deviation from the chartered voyage. It is submitted, however, that (if the thesis stated in § 3–41 is correct) Cogsa has not only changed the law of bills of lading but also has by fair analogic implication stated a new public policy on the deviation question—a policy reaching to voyage charters and to deviation under these.

### Clause 4: Payment of Freight

**§ 4–7.** This clause gives the clarity of express and detailed stipulation to the rule that freight is due and payable on delivery.[50] The tightness of the cash position in which some tramps may find themselves is reflected in the stipulation for advances to cover expenses at the port of loading.

As we have seen, it is common practice today for bills of lading to provide that freight is due and payable on loading, goods lost or not lost. This practice seems to be spreading to charter parties, and it is common to find provision for the payment of all or a substantial part of the freight on loading.[51]

### Clauses 5, 6 and 7: Loading, Unloading, and Demurrage

**§ 4–8.** These clauses are to be read in the light of the basic position of the parties to a voyage charter as to the value of time. The charterer is usually interested in reasonable promptness, and may in special circumstances be in a hurry. But time is always of direct and vital financial significance to the owner, since his income from the vessel depends on the dispatch with which she can complete each charter, and since, moreover, he needs to be able to predict with some accuracy when she will be free again, so as to be able to arrange another fixture. The rates of loading and unloading are, practically speaking, dependent on or at least limited by the rate at which cargo is brought alongside by the charterer, and taken away by the consignee.[51a] For

49. See *supra* Chapter III, Part II, § 3–40. Very little geographic deviation can be "reasonable" under a voyage charter engaging the whole capacity of a ship for a single run from one named port to another.

50. See The Harriman, 76 U.S. (9 Wall.) 161 (1870); Burn Line v. U. S. & A. S. S. Co., 162 F. 298 (2d Cir. 1908), certiorari denied 212 U.S. 580, 29 S.Ct. 689 (1909); Richardson & Sons v. Jenkins S. S. Co., 44 F.2d 759, 1931 A.M.C. 315 (6th Cir. 1930), certiorari denied 283 U.S. 821, 51 S.Ct. 345 (1931).

51. Bes, *op. cit. supra* note 9, 7. See Société Purfina Maritime v. 8598.09 Long Tons of Diesel Oil, 43 F.Supp. 807, 1942 A.M.C. 484 (S.D.Cal.1942), affirmed as modified 133 F.2d 552 (9th Cir. 1942), certiorari denied 318 U.S. 781, 63 S.Ct. 858 (1943).

51a. The theory and types of demurrage, and of certain Federal Maritime Commission rules relating thereto, are

this reason, these clauses embody an agreement as to what is to be taken as a reasonable rate of loading or unloading and a set of penalties for undue delay.[52]

The first step is the agreement as to the time which is to be allowed for each of these operations, without the charterers' or their successors' in interest incurring any liability. The allowed time is stated in days, called "lay days" in trade parlance. Sometimes the statement is in hours,[53] though the expression "lay hours" has made no headway. There are several different forms the lay day provision may take. If "running days" are called for, then every calendar day counts against the time allowed, without allowance for Sundays and holidays.[54] If "working days" are stipulated, then the number of days allowed is counted by skipping Sundays and those holidays on which work is not performed in the port of loading or of discharge, as the case may be.[55] The expression "weather working days" excludes from the count not only holidays but also days on which weather conditions prohibit work.[56] Of these three expressions, obviously, the first is the most favorable from the ship's point of view.[57]

The charter we are examining (Gencon) uses the expression "running working days". Since, as the set of definitions just given makes clear, this is a self-contradictory expression, it must be intended that one or the other of the words will be stricken out. In the blank immediately preceding (see the first sentences in Clauses 5 and 6) a number will be inserted. Gencon thus allocates lay days severally to loading and unloading; in some charters, an aggregate number of days is allowed for both operations, by the device of stipulating that lay days shall be "reversible." [58]

If the lay days are exceeded, then the charterer has to pay demurrage. Clause 7 stipulates for the allowance of ten days on demurrage altogether, at ports of loading and discharge. This simply means that the stipulated sum per day or part thereof must be paid to the vessel as a sort of liquidated compensation for holding her up. Such fixed demurrage is called "contract demurrage."

discussed in American Pres. Lines, Ltd. v. Federal Mar. Bd., 317 F.2d 887, 1963 A.M.C. 2380 (D.C.Cir.1962). While this discussion directly relates to demurrage incurred by bill of lading consignees, it has application to straight voyage-charter demurrage as well.

52. See Ivamy, The Efficient Loading and Discharge of Cargo Vessels, 21 The Solicitor 35 (1954). If the owner, through the fault of the charterer, incurs a liability to a third party during loading, he may be entitled to an indemnity from the charterer; see *supra* note 36.

53. See case treated *infra* at note 60 *et seq.*

54. Bes, *op. cit. supra* note 9, p. 77; Poor, Charter Parties & Ocean Bills of Lading § 40 (5th ed. 1968). (The word "days" alone has the same meaning. Pedersen v. Eugster, 14 F. 422, 423 (E.D.La.1882).

55. Sorensen v. Keyser, 52 F. 163 (5th Cir. 1892); Hughes v. J. S. Hoskins Lumber Co., 136 F. 435 (D.N.J.1905).

56. The India, 49 F. 76 (5th Cir. 1891).

57. Bes, *loc. cit. supra* note 54.

58. Warren Corp. v. Britain S. S. Co., 100 F.2d 283, 1938 A.M.C. 1548 (1st Cir. 1938).

After the ten days on contract demurrage have expired, the charterer of course still remains liable for further delay, but the liability now is one for non-contract demurrage, which will be fixed by the court just as would any other unliquidated claim for damages. Non-contract demurrage may also be referred to as "damages for detention."

Disputes about demurrage in modern times usually go to arbitration, but occasionally a novel question gets litigated. Such a case was Atwater Fuels v. Pocahontas Fuel Co.,[59] in which delay at the loading port was occasioned, as it often is, by failure of the charterer to provide a cargo on time. The case was problematical because the charter was oral and informal, specifying little more than the date on which the vessel was to report for loading. The court noted, however, that the same parties had concluded another charter "for a series of like voyages . . . by a sister ship" of the one involved in the case. This other charter contained a full basis for computation of demurrage, and the court imported these terms into the oral and informal charter in suit.

Another modern demurrage case[60] illustrates the difficulty of providing in advance for all misunderstandings that can arise out of the attempt to deal contractually with such a complicated subject. The voyage was a peculiar one: the cargo, corn, was carried in a single flotilla, consisting of one ship and one barge, until a canal impassable by that flotilla was reached. Then it was transferred into five smaller vessels, and carried to destination on them. Lay days of "72 hours after the arrival of the grain" were allowed for unloading, and demurrage was stipulated at $12.50 an hour. Four of the smaller vessels were delayed beyond 72 hours. The court had to decide whether the "$12.50 an hour" was payable on each vessel, or only on the last vessel. Obviously what had happened was that neither party had thought about the matter, or at least that they had had quite different understandings. The court reached the conclusion that demurrage was payable on each vessel, and held the charterer accordingly for a large demurrage bill.

Some charters contain a provision for "dispatch money," which is in the nature of a reward to the charterer for loading or unloading more rapidly than provided for—*i. e.*, in less time than the stipulated "lay days."[61] Dispatch, where payable, is usually stated, just as is demurrage, in terms of a rate per day and pro rata part thereof.

The expression of demurrage terms in charters is subject to wide variation. Sometimes "lay days" are not set out as such, but rather it is stipulated that cargo shall be loaded or unloaded at a fixed rate per day;[62] in such a case, the approximate figuring of lay days is a

59. 185 F.2d 337, 1951 A.M.C. 439 (1st Cir. 1950).

60. Sarnia Steamships, Ltd. v. Continental Grain Co., 125 F.2d 362, 1942 A.M.C. 117 (7th Cir. 1941).

61. See The West Nosska, 2 F.Supp. 547, 1928 A.M.C. 1631 (S.D.N.Y.1928); The Seaboard Pioneer (arbitration), 1950 A.M.C. 1408 (1950).

62. See The West Nosska, *supra* note 61.

matter of simple arithmetic, once the quantity of cargo is ascertained. Sometimes, it is simply provided that loading or unloading shall proceed "with all dispatch," or "with customary dispatch"; in case of dispute, the court has to take proof of custom.[63]

It has been said that there is a "wilderness of law upon the subject of demurrage." [64] Since the demurrage case almost invariably involves the question whether the stipulations of the charter have been transgressed, and since the bewildering variety of phraseology in the many charter forms now or formerly in use brings it about that two cases are rarely exactly alike, it is quite impossible to systematize the holdings. The most that we can do here is to indicate a few problem areas, giving a few representative cases.

First, there is the problem of when the lay days actually start to run. This will depend on the wording of the charter, on the custom of the port, and on the often quite unique facts of the individual case.[65]

Secondly, the delay in loading or unloading is often occasioned by circumstances beyond the control of the charterer; inability to get a berth to which to order the ship is an illustration. When such a case comes to court, it is necessary to decide whether, given the actual terms of the charter, the charterer is to be excused; these tend to be the most significant financially of the demurrage cases, for some delays imposed by outside circumstances may be of quite long duration. The general rule is that the charterer, having undertaken absolutely to see the ship loaded in a stated time, assumes the risk of all casualties preventing this, and the obligation of paying demurrage if anything goes wrong. There are, however, well-recognized exceptions; in United States v. Atlantic Refining Co.,[66] the District Court rehearses them:

> "It is well recognized that demurrage is extended freight and that the risk of vicissitudes which prevent the loading or discharge of cargo within the stipulated lay days lies unconditionally with the charterers. Yone Suzuki v. Central Argentine Ry., 2 Cir., 27 F.2d 795; The Marpesia, 2 Cir., 292 F. 957. But, this absolute liability to pay demurrage is subject to three exceptions: (1) specific exonerating clauses in the charter party; (2) the delay being attributed to the fault of the shipowner or those for whom he is responsible; and (3) a vis major amounting to 'a sudden or unforeseen interruption or prevention of the act itself of loading or discharging,

63. Steamship Rutherglen Co. v. Howard Houlder & Partners, 203 F. 848 (2d Cir. 1913); see Williams v. Theobald, 15 F. 465 (D.Cal.1883). For the position when the charter says nothing about the time of loading or unloading, see Empire Transp. Co. v. Philadelphia & R. Coal & Iron Co., 77 F. 919, 925–6 (8th Cir. 1896).

64. Steamship Rutherglen Co. v. Howard Houlder & Partners, 203 F. 848, 851 (2d Cir. 1913).

65. See Aktieselskabet Fido v. Lloyd Brasileiro, 283 F. 62, 69 (2d Cir. 1922), certiorari denied 260 U.S. 737, 43 S.Ct. 97 (1922); Poor, *op. cit. supra* note 54, §§ 35–39.

66. 112 F.Supp. 76 (D.N.J.1951).

not occurring through the connivance or fault of the charterers.' "[67]

On its facts, the case illustrates rather well the basic demurrage situation. It is worth noting to start with that the stipulated rate for time in excess of the lay days was $120 an hour, and that the bill for 124 hours and 55 minutes of demurrage came to $14,990. This rate, since the vessel was a War Shipping Administration ship, was fixed by regulation, but is not believed to be very far if at all out of line with general practice. Demurrage is important money and even minutes are mentioned without thought of the rule *de minimis*.

The charter was of a tanker, and the cargo crude oil. The port of loading was Atreco, Texas, in the Port Arthur area near the great refineries. Of the 72 hours allowed for loading and unloading, 21 hours and 10 minutes were consumed there, including an interruption of 8 hours and 10 minutes while a barge alongside, operating an open gasoline engine, created what was thought by the charterer's employees to be a fire hazard, with the result that loading stopped; responsibility for the presence of this barge was disputed.

But the main trouble arose at the discharging port, in the Philadelphia area. The designated point of discharge was the Port Mifflin terminal of the charterer. The vessel proceeded up the Delaware river in charge of a local pilot, and came to anchor, as was apparently customary, about a mile south of the designated point of discharge. There she waited for another pilot and tugs to take her to her berth. But these failed to show up, owing to a strike of tugboat employees, and about a week elapsed before Navy tugs arrived and towed the vessel to the Port Mifflin pier. The actual discharge was completed in 18 hours and 15 minutes.

On these facts, the charterer contended, first, that the strike excused it for the delay. The contention seems not to have been that the strike constituted *vis major*, for the court brushes this aside as not even arguable, since it could "hardly be claimed that the strike . . . was so unusual, extraordinary and unexpected a circumstance as to be equivalent to vis major."[68] The contention was rather that, assuming the strike caused the delay, there was a "specific exonerating clause"[69]—namely, the general "exceptions" clause, providing, inter alia:

> "And neither the Vessel, her Master or Owner, nor the Charterer, shall, unless otherwise in this Charter expressly provided, be responsible for any loss or damage or failure in performing hereunder, arising or resulting from:—Act of God, act of war, act of public enemies, pirates or assailing thieves, arrest or restraint of princes, rulers of people, or seizure under legal process provided bond is promptly furnished to

67. 112 F.Supp. at 80. See also, Pa. R. R. v. Moore-McCormack Lines, Inc., 370 F.2d 430, 1967 A.M.C. 5 (2d Cir. 1966), citing this text.

68. 112 F.Supp. at 80.

69. See *supra* at note 67.

release the Vessel or cargo; strike or lockout, or stoppage or restraint of labor from whatever cause, either partial or general; or riot or civil commotion."

This contention the court rejected, citing Continental Grain Co. v. Armour Fertilizer Works,[70] where it was said:

> "The general 'strike exception' clause in the charter party does not prevent the running of demurrage; some similar phrase is necessary in conjunction with the demurrage clause to free the charterer from the burden of paying demurrage when the delay is due to strikes, etc.
>
> "A review of the cases, wherein the courts have held that charterers were not liable for demurrage for delays due to strikes, reveals that, in addition to the general 'strike exception' clause, the charters also contained stipulations exonerating the charterers from liability for demurrage when the delay was due to strikes, riots, etc., said stipulations being incorporated in or appurtenant to the 'lay day' or 'demurrage' clauses of the charter parties." [71]

This rule, interpreting the "strike" exception clause as not referring to demurrage, is confirmed by the Second Circuit's affirmance of Compagnia de Navegazione Rome v. Kulukundis [71a].

But the charterer had another string to its bow, and this time the arrow went home. Turning the question of necessity for excuse around, the charterer urged that it had done its duty in designating a safe berth, and that it was up to the vessel, unless excused, to get there—undoubtedly a sound general proposition. Since the tugboat strike was the only available excuse, the question became one as to its adequacy, and this, in turn, raised the question whether the master might have brought the vessel into berth on her own power and without a pilot. This the court, after a careful review of the testimony, concluded he might have done this, and demurrage was accordingly denied.[72]

### Clause 8: Liens. (Herein of the Cesser Clause)

**§ 4–9.** This clause confirms the liens which would in any case have been enjoyed by the carrier-owner,[73] and stipulates for certain others. The lien for freight is of course basic; it does not differ in principle from the lien for freight on goods carried by a general ship.[74]

70. 22 F.Supp. 49, 1938 A.M.C. 414 (S.D.N.Y.1938).

71. 22 F.Supp. at 53.

71a. 182 F.Supp. 258, 1960 A.M.C. 1191 (E.D.N.Y.1959), affirmed 277 F.2d 161, 1960 A.M.C. 1190 (2d Cir. 1960).

72. See exception (2) in the passage quoted at note 67 *supra*.

73. The classic discussion of the liens arising out of the shipper-carrier relation is in the opinion of Judge Hough in The Saturnus, 250 F. 407 (2d Cir. 1918), certiorari denied 247 U.S. 521, 38 S.Ct. 583 (1918).

74. See *supra* Chapter III, Part II, at note 143 *et seq.*

"Dead freight" requires some explanation. The charterer, as we have seen in Clause 1, binds himself to ship a "full and complete cargo." Freight, as such, is payable only on the quantity actually shipped. If for any reason the charterer does not furnish a complete cargo, the freight payable will be less than anticipated. "Dead freight" is the amount paid to offset this difference; it is calculated by taking the freight which would have been due on the shortage, and subtracting the extra expenses, if any, to which the vessel would have been put in carrying the cargo not shipped.[75]

The lien of the ship on the cargo is possessory; the cargo may be held until charges are paid.[76] The charterer and his successors as owners of the cargo are given maritime liens, non-possessory and enforceable by *in rem* process, against the ship, for damage to or non-delivery of the goods, under circumstances where the vessel is liable for these, and for some other defaults in the performance of the contract of carriage evidenced by the charter.[77] In general, the maritime lien in favor of cargo arises only as a result of a default occurring *after* the cargo is loaded and the physical relation of ship and cargo is thus established;[78] the principle is the same as in the case of general ship carriage. Thus, a proceeding *in rem* does not lie for the vessel's breach of the charter by failure to arrive at the loading port in time.[79] The cargo interest has, however, been held to have a lien on the ship for damage occurring after cargo had been taken in charge by ship's officers, preparatory to its being loaded.[79a]

For a long time, charters have commonly contained the so-called "cesser" clause, reading in one form as follows:

> "The charterer's liability shall cease as soon as the cargo is shipped and the advance of freight, dead freight, and demurrage in loading (if any) are paid, the owner having a lien on the cargo for freight, demurrage, and average." [80]

It is said that this clause first came into use to protect charterers who were mere agents for other persons desiring to ship cargo, and who

75. New York & Cuba Mail S. S. Co. v. Guayaquil & Q. R. Co., 270 F. 200, 202 (2d Cir. 1920), certiorari dismissed, 257 U.S. 642, 42 S.Ct. 51 (1921); Steamship Co. of 1912 v. C. H. Pearson & Son Hardwood Co., 30 F.2d 770, 1929 A.M.C. 343 (2d Cir. 1929). See Rederi A/B Pulp v. Republic Chemical Co., 274 F.2d 428, 1960 A.M.C. 1415 (2d Cir. 1960).

76. The Eddy, 72 U.S. (5 Wall.) 481 (1867); see 4,885 Bags of Linseed, 66 U.S. (1 Black) 108 (1861).

77. The Maggie Hammond, 76 U.S. (9 Wall.) 435, 449–50 (1870); Cooper v. Pinedo, 212 F.2d 137, 1954 A.M.C. 899 (5th Cir. 1954).

78. Osaka Shosen Kaisha v. Pacific Export Lumber Co., 260 U.S. 490, 43 S.Ct. 172, 1923 A.M.C. 55 (1923); The Saturnus, 250 F. 407 (2d Cir. 1918), certiorari denied 247 U.S. 521, 38 S.Ct. 583 (1918). See California & Eastern S. S. Co. v. 138,000 Feet of Lumber, 23 F.2d 95, 1928 A.M.C. 73 (D.Md. 1927). See *infra*, Chapter IX, § 9–22 *et seq.*

79. Belvedere v. Compania Plomari De Vapores, S. A., 189 F.2d 148, 1951 A.M.C. 1217 (5th Cir. 1951).

79a. Bulkley v. Naumkeag Steam Cotton Co., 65 U.S. (24 How.) 386 (1860).

80. This common form is from Capelle, *op. cit. supra* note 9, p. 475.

wished to "get out from under" as soon as the ship was loaded.[81] Whatever its origin, its main intendment is fairly clear. The idea is that the ship, once the cargo is loaded, shall have to look to its lien on the cargo for payment of amounts due it under the charter, and that the personal liability of the charterer shall cease at that point. The charterer who has sold the cargo has no further control over the transaction after he has put the goods alongside or aboard, and it is commercially reasonable that he should desire to bow out of the picture, rather than to have hanging over his head contingent liabilities dependent on what may happen after he thinks the transaction is finished.

A leading American case on the construction of the cesser clause, Crossman v. Burrill,[82] laid down the principle that the clause "is to be construed, if possible, as inapplicable to a liability with which the lien is not commensurate." [83] This is in conformity to the simple idea behind the clause—the substitution of the security of the possessory lien in the goods for the personal liability of the charterer. Whether the lien on the goods exists and is enforceable as against the claim for delivery of the consignee will often depend on the wording of the bill of lading issued when the goods are shipped and transmitted to the consignee. Thus it will be handy at this point to take up the issuance of bills of lading for goods loaded pursuant to voyage charters and then to return to the cesser clause with a fuller understanding of the context in which it operates.

### Clause 9: Bills of Lading in Voyage Charter Carriage

**§ 4–10.** Often the charterer-shipper will be making the shipment in performance of one or more contracts for sale of the shipped goods, and will want bills of lading to present with his other documents in satisfaction of the contract, *c. i. f.* or other.[84] Sometimes the goods will not yet have been sold, but are being shipped on the expectation that they can be sold while in transit. In these and in other less typical cases, the charterer will want bills of lading for the cargo shipped; by far the greater part of voyage charter carriage entails their use.[85]

This regular and open association between charters and bills of lading is to be distinguished, of course, from the use of a charter as a sham for the purpose of evading Cogsa.[85a]

The first thing to notice about Clause 9 is the provision as to freight. The owner looks to his lien on the cargo for the payment of freight. But the holder of a bill of lading will have the right to de-

81. See Francesco v. Massey, L.R. 8 Exch. 101, 103 (1873); also The Eliza Lines, 61 F. 308, 326 (C.C.D.Mass. 1894), affirmed 114 F. 307 (1st Cir. 1904). (Reversed on other grounds, 199 U.S. 119, 26 S.Ct. 8 (1905).

82. 179 U.S. 100, 21 S.Ct. 38 (1900).

83. 179 U.S. at 108, 21 S.Ct. at 40.

84. See *supra* Chapter III, Part I, especially § 3–15.

85. See Thornton, British Shipping 132 (1939).

85a. See *supra* at note 9a.

livery at destination on tender of the freight named in the bill of lading.[86] If, therefore, the charterer wants for any commercial reason (as, e. g., the satisfaction of a stipulation in his contract of sale) to get a bill of lading for all or any part of the cargo quoting a freight rate lower than does the charter, he must make up the difference in cash.

A more complex problem is presented by the phrase "without prejudice to this charter party." Two sets of questions arise: (1) To what extent, under the law applicable to bills of lading, *can* the provisions of the charter party override the legal rights and duties subsisting between the carrier and the holder of the bill of lading? (2) What does it take, by way of clausing of the bill of lading, to incorporate by reference the terms of the charter party?

The first of these questions must be answered by reference to the Carriage of Goods By Sea Act, 1936, as to all carriage to which that Act applies. The material provision is in Section 5 of the Act:

> "The provisions of this Act shall not be applicable to charter parties, but if bills of lading are issued in the case of a ship under a charter party they shall comply with the terms of this Act." [87]

This language hardly calls for construction; it must mean that, however clearly they may be incorporated, by reference or *in extenso*, in the bill of lading, any and all charter party terms, in order to have effect as bill of lading terms, must conform to Cogsa; in so far as they go beyond the limits set by Cogsa, they are invalid. Whether "notice" is brought home to the bill of lading holder is quite immaterial to this question, for the bill of lading is expressly subject to Cogsa, and "notice" cannot make valid a bill of lading term that infringes Cogsa by altering, to the detriment of the holder of the bill of lading, the dispositions of Cogsa.

We have seen, *e. g.*, that Clause 2 in Gencon immunizes the shipowner from liability for goods damage in some cases (for example, negligent custody of the cargo other than its stowage) in which Cogsa imposes liability. Clearly, such a provision cannot, under the statutory language we have quoted, be valid against a holder of the bill of lading, no matter how clearly his attention may be directed to it. It would indisputably be invalid if it were included in a bill of lading *not* issued under a charter party, for it directly lessens the liability of the carrier, in violation of Section 3(8) of Cogsa, and the fact that it enters the bill of lading through incorporation by reference cannot save it, if Cogsa Section 5, quoted above, is to make any sense at all.

The only apparent exception occurs when the bill of lading has remained in the hands of the charterer. It had been held in a number

86. If the bill of lading is marked "freight prepaid," the vessel cannot collect freight from the consignee who took the bill for value and without notice, even though freight is actually owing. The Robin Gray, 65 F.2d 376, 1933 A.M.C. 770 (2d Cir. 1933), certiorari denied 290 U.S. 653, 54 S.Ct. 70 (1933).

87. 49 Stat. 1211 (1936), 46 U.S.C.A. § 1305.

of pre-Cogsa cases that, in such a case, the bill of lading is a mere receipt as between the parties to the charter, and that the charter controls.[88] This rule still has validity.[88a] Practically, this distinction may make sense, for, so long as the bill of lading remains in the possession of the charterer himself, we have to do with parties who can usually be assumed to be of something like equal bargaining power (at least that is the assumption which underlies the abstention of Congress from attempting to regulate charter terms) and the problem of clogs on negotiability is not present. It would be somewhat anomalous, in the light of the exemption of charter parties from the coverage of Cogsa, if the charterer could bring it about that Cogsa applied merely by taking a bill of lading and holding it throughout the period of carriage. Technically, this distinction (between the effect of the bill of lading in the hand of the charterer and in that of a subsequent holder) can be justified under the language of Cogsa by holding that, as between the parties to the charter, the bill of lading is not "evidence of a contract," or at least not of the one they have made, and so is not, *as between them*, subject to the Act. This technical device is supported, or at least made admissible, by the definitions section of Cogsa:

> "(b) The term 'contract of carriage' applies only to contracts of carriage covered by a bill of lading or any similar document of title, insofar as such document relates to the carriage of goods by sea, *including any bill of lading or any similar document as aforesaid issued under or pursuant to a charter party from the moment at which such bill of lading or similar document of title regulates the relations between a carrier and a holder of the same.*" [Emphasis supplied.] [89]

Certainly, this language leaves it open that, as between owner and charterer, the bill of lading may not "regulate the relations" and thus constitute a contract of carriage. This cannot be true of the transferees of the bill of lading, for the bill of lading (whatever it may "incorporate by reference" from the charter) is the only document which can regulate their relations with the owner, as they are not parties to the charter, and the bill must therefore conform strictly to Cogsa once it has been transferred.[90]

It should be obvious that the carrier, quite apart from Cogsa, cannot unilaterally alter the charter contract by issuing bills of lading with terms more favorable to him.[90a]

88. The Iona, 80 F. 933 (5th Cir. 1897); Carr v. Austin & N. W. R. Co., 14 F. 419 (C.C.E.D.Tex.1882); The Chadwicke, 29 F. 521 (S.D.N.Y.1887).

88a. North American Steel Products Corp. v. Andros Mentor, 1969 A.M.C. 1482 (S.D.N.Y.1967); Jefferson Chemical Co. v. M/T Grena, 292 F.Supp. 500, 1968 A.M.C. 1202 (S.D.Tex.1968); Zock, Charter Parties in Relation to Cargo, 45 Tulane L.Rev. 733, 742–744 (1971).

89. 49 Stat. 1208 (1936), 46 U.S.C.A. § 1301(b).

90. A view very similar to the one here expressed is found in Temperley, Carriage of Goods by Sea Act, 1924, 15–17 (1932). See also Zock, *loc. cit. supra* n. 88a.

90a. See Hellenic Lines, Ltd. v. Embassy of Pakistan, 467 F.2d 1150, 1972 A.M.C. 2216 (2d Cir. 1972).

Even within the limits set by Cogsa, however, there is some room for contracting, and as to these matters the question is not one of the *validity*, as a bill of lading provision, of the term sought to be read into the bill of lading from the charter, but rather one of the efficacy of the language used to bring about its incorporation.[91] Since the written or stamped endorsements on bills of lading, having the aim of incorporating by reference the provisions of the charter, are of great variety, and since decisions as to their effect necessarily turn on the construction of the particular form of words employed, little is to be gained by a parade of cases. Generally, the courts require a clear manifestation of intention to incorporate the entire charter, or the particular term sought to be enforced against the consignee. Where, for example, the bill of lading was endorsed "freight as per charter and all its conditions," provisions as to demurrage were not incorporated.[92] In Son Shipping Co. v. De Fosse & Tanghe,[93] the Second Circuit Court of Appeals had to do with an incorporation clause, in the bill of lading, reading as follows:

> "This shipment is carried under and pursuant to the terms of the charter dated Antwerp, June 29th, 1948 between Son Shipping Company and De Fosse & Tanghe, charterer, and all the terms whatsoever of the said charter except the rate and payment of freight specified therein apply to and govern the rights of the parties concerned in this shipment." [94]

The question presented was whether this language effectively incorporated a charter provision providing for compulsory arbitration of all differences, so as to bind the parties to the bill of lading. Reversing the District Court, the appellate court held that it did.[94a]

Liability for demurrage seems to be what is most frequently sought to be enforced by the ship against the consignee, under the bill of lading clauses incorporating the charter party. The ship's aim is to get a lien against the goods for all demurrage or other charges that

91. There is no automatic incorporation of the charter in the bill of lading, in the absence of notice. The Titania, 131 F. 229 (2d Cir. 1904).

92. Dayton v. Parke, 142 N.Y. 391, 399–402, 37 N.E. 642, 644–645 (1894).

93. 199 F.2d 687, 1952 A.M.C. 1931 (2d Cir. 1952). For fact-variations on incorporation of the arbitration clause by reference to the charter in a bill of lading, see Southwestern Sugar & Molasses Co. v. The Eliza Jane Nicholson, 126 F.Supp. 666, 1955 A.M.C. 746 (S.D.N.Y.1954); Chilean Nitrate Sales Corp. v. The Nortuna, 128 F.Supp. 938, 1955 A.M.C. 1576 (S.D.N.Y.1955); Instituto Cubano De Estabilizacion Del Azucar v. The Golden West, 128 F.Supp. 754, 1955 A.M.C. 2128 (S.D.N.Y.1955); Savannah Sugar Refining Corp. v. S. S. Hudson Deep 288 F. Supp. 181, 1968 A.M.C. 745 (S.D.N.Y. 1967), rehearing denied 288 F.Supp. 183, 1968 A.M.C. 748 (S.D.N.Y.1968); Production Steel Co. of Illinois v. S. S. Francois L. O., 294 F.Supp. 200, 1968 A.M.C. 2529 (S.D.N.Y.1968).

94. 199 F.2d at 688.

94a. See, Davies, Incorporation of Charter-party Terms Into a Bill of Lading, 1966 J.Bus.L. 326 (1966); McMahon, The Hague Rules and Incorporation of Charter Party Arbitration Clauses Into Bills of Lading, 2 Journal of Maritime Law & Commerce 1 (1970).

may accrue under the charter, and so to clause the bill of lading that this lien can be enforced at the port of discharge as against the consignee's claim for delivery.

### Further of the Cesser Clause

**§ 4–11.** We have now considered all the elements necessary to an understanding of the operation of the cesser clause in actual cases—the tenor of the clause itself, the liens which it substitutes for the charterer's personal liability, the position of the bill of lading holder, and the nature of the claims which are most often the subject of dispute under the clause. We can now take a brief look at a few of the questions that have arisen with respect to the construction and operation of the clause.

First arises the question, whom does it exonerate? In an opinion which is a classic on the whole subject of the cesser clause,[95] the court had to deal with the contention, by a consignee who held a bill of lading incorporating the charter party, that the cesser clause was incorporated in the bill of lading, and that the holder thereof was thereby released, just as was the charterer, from liability for demurrage. The court rejected this plea, and it has frequently been stated that any other decision would totally defeat the operation of the cesser clause scheme, which rests on the notion of the release of the charterer on condition that the goods be liable. It seems, however, that some of these comments—and perhaps the Yone Suzuki opinion itself—fail to distinguish adequately between release of the lien on the goods and release of the consignee from personal liability. To construe an "incorporation clause" in the bill of lading as importing the cesser clause, and so doing away with the vessel's lien on the goods for amounts due under the charter, would not only defeat the cesser clause scheme but would also be the sheerest nonsense, since the cesser clause itself (or a connected clause in the charter) usually provides for a continuance of the lien on the goods, and even if it were "incorporated" in the bill of lading that lien would not be abolished. The personal liability of the consignee is another matter. To read the documents as exempting him from personal liability (in consequence of the incorporation of the cesser clause in his bill of lading) would not be to defeat the cesser clause scheme at all; that scheme envisions the substitution of the *lien on the goods*, rather than anybody's personal credit, for the personal obligations of the charterer.

Nevertheless, the only person one can be sure is released from personal liability by this clause is the charterer himself. From what liabilities is he released? We have already mentioned one common formulation: from those, only, for the non-fulfilment of which the carrier gets a lien on the goods.[96] Other formulae of limitation have,

95. Yone Suzuki v. Central Argentine Ry., 27 F.2d 795, 1928 A.M.C. 1521 (2d Cir. 1928), certiorari denied 278 U.S. 652, 49 S.Ct. 178 (1929).

96. *Supra* at note 83.

however, been drawn: In Steamship Rutherglen Co. v. Howard Houlder & Partners,[97] the court said:

> "The charterers contend that they were relieved of liability for anything occurring at Dalny by virtue of the cesser clause, which reads:
>
> 'Charterers' liability to cease on cargo being shipped and freight paid.'
>
> "The freight was paid at New York on the shipment of the cargo, and the owners make no claim for demurrage or anything else occurring there. The clause would protect the charterers from liability for anything done at the discharging port by others, but not for anything which they had themselves agreed to do. The charter contemplates that the charterers will receive the cargo at Dalny. It provides that in certain circumstances they will be obliged to provide lighters, and that for delay in discharging, due to certain excepted causes, they are not to be liable, and that the vessel is to be consigned to their agents. Accordingly the cesser clause does not protect them from liability for delay incurred in discharging at Dalny not within the exceptions."

Spelled out, this seems to mean that, even as between the charterer and the owner, the cesser clause merely immunizes the former from liabilities other than those arising through his own breach of duty. Where he stays in the picture *de facto*, and is in default in respect to some remaining legal duty, he is not protected.

A more recent affirmation of this principle seems to be contained in American Tobacco Co. v. The Katingo Hadjipatera, where the charterer had actually performed stowage of the cargo, on which bills of lading were issued to third parties. The stowage was negligent, and damage ensued. The ship, of course was liable, and sought to hold the charterer as the guilty party. The court held that the cesser clause did not immunize the charterer from liability over to the shipowner.[98]

Another way of putting this might be to say that the charterer is protected *only as such*. If he continues to hold the bills of lading, then he may, as holder of these, be subjected to some liability from which he would have been immunized as charterer, by operation of the cesser clause.[99]

On the other hand, the cesser clause does not bring the charter obligations automatically and wholly to an end, substituting therefor the bill of lading obligations. Where, for example, a charter provision as to arbitration had been carefully negotiated, while the bill of

97. 203 F. 848, 850–51 (2d Cir. 1913).

98. 81 F.Supp. 438, 448, 1949 A.M.C. 49 (S.D.N.Y.1948), modified on other grounds, 194 F.2d 449 (2d Cir. 1951), certiorari denied 343 U.S. 978, 72 S.Ct. 1076 (1952).

99. The Eliza Lines, 61 F. 308, 326 (C. C.D.Mass.1894), affirmed 114 F. 307 (1st Cir. 1904), reversed on other grounds 199 U.S. 119, 26 S.Ct. 8 (1905); *cf.* The Chadwicke, 29 F. 521, 524–5 (S.D.N.Y.1887). See Note, 54 Jurid.Rev. 55 (1942).

lading arbitration clause was boilerplate, the charter provision was enforced.[99a]

We have noted that the charter we are examining has no cesser clause. One might, of course, be stamped or affixed. Even where it is not, it will be seen that Clause 8 can be read as a sort of limited cesser clause, as to port-of-discharge demurrage liability, since it exonerates the charterer from such liability where the ship can get satisfaction out of its lien on the goods.

### Clause 10: Strikes, War and Ice. "Frustration" and Connected Problems

**§ 4–12.** These clauses are alike in that they contain detailed provisions for dealing with the arising of contingencies seriously threatening the whole venture embodied in the charter. Their actual provisions are fairly clear, and we will not go through them one by one. Their major interest consists in their suggesting of the set of problems that arise when proceeding with the charter voyage as planned becomes either impossible or so difficult or risky that it cannot reasonably be required.

When the supervening block to smooth performance as planned produces only minor trouble, then the resulting disputes are dealt with by deciding whether some express or implied excuse exonerates the defaulting party from liability. The charter as a whole stands. We have briefly touched on implied excuses in connection with the subject of demurrage; in form, the charterer contracts absolutely either to load and unload in the lay days or to pay for not doing so, but we have seen that the courts read into the contract certain "exceptions" to this absolute duty.[100] Expressed "exceptions" that excuse from the performance of some undertaking in the charter may be simple and absolute; or they may, like the clauses here, set up some agreed handling of the new situation, by way of substituted or altered performance.

But trouble may be too serious to be dealt with in any of these ways. Performance of the contract as a whole may be rendered substantially impossible, or conditions may have so altered that a perfunctory going through with those parts of it which still can be performed would be a mockery of the original intent. In such a case, a court is likely to find that the charter as a whole is "frustrated," and has come to an end, freeing both parties from their obligations. It is a melancholy reflection, but not a very surprising one, that the necessity for the elaboration of intricate legal doctrines dealing with the problem of what to do when plans are totally upset has been felt chiefly in the present century, and in connection with the outbreak of war.

**99a.** Ministry of Commerce, etc., Greece v. Marine Tankers Corp., 194 F.Supp. 161, 1961 A.M.C. 320 (S.D.N.Y.1960).

**100.** *Supra* at note 67.

The so-called "doctrine" of frustration is not susceptible of very precise statement. Contracts in general are not made subject to a clause *rebus sic stantibus,* and within wide limits the courts take the view that parties remain bound to go through with their agreements regardless of supervening events making performance more onerous. But where some radical alteration of conditions has swept away all the assumptions on which the contract was made, making impossible the fruition of its commercial object, then the courts have spoken of frustration, and have declared (under a fiction of "constructive conditions" or otherwise) that the charter is no longer in existence. "Frustration of a charter party is a change of conditions so radical that accomplishment of the commercial object of the charter is made impossible." [101] Manifestly, no amount of verbal nicety or spatial metaphor can conceal the fact that such a formula raises questions of *degree,* and that the "line" is or ought to be drawn on the basis of commercial reasonableness and substantial fairness.

It has been emphasized that the doctrines of impossibility and frustration are not in any sense peculiar to charter parties or to maritime law in general; [102] it is the fact, however, that charter parties, since they embody arrangements for the transport of goods throughout the world in ships that are prime strategic assets, are especially vulnerable to frustration by political and military happenings. The solutions worked out by the courts have three components: the general doctrines of contract law as applied in this field, the special rights and obligations created by the clauses of the particular charter, and the specific facts of each case.

World War I was prolific of cases involving the frustration problem. In Texas Co. v. Hogarth Shipping Co.,[103] the charter was for a voyage from Texas to South Africa. The agreed time for tender was between April 15 and May 15, 1915. On April 10, the British government requisitioned the ship, which was then in British waters. Tender, of course, became impossible, but the charterer sued for its damages, on the theory that the owner was *absolutely* bound either to tender or to pay for his failure to do so. This was high ground indeed; the Supreme Court found the air too rarified, saying:

> "It long has been settled in the English courts and in those of this country, federal and state, that where parties

101. United States v. M/V Marilena P, 433 F.2d 164, 167, 1969 A.M.C. 1155, 1159 (4th Cir. 1969), citing this text. See The Claveresk, 264 F. 276, 281 (2d Cir. 1920).

102. Scrutton, Charterparties 95 (17th ed. 1964); see Restatement, Contracts § 288 (1932); 6 Corbin, Contracts §§ 1353–1361 (1962); Gow, Some Observations on Frustration, 3 Int'l & Comp.L.Q. 291 (1954); McNair, Frustration of Contract by War, 56 L.Q. Rev. 173 (1940); Webber, Frustration of Contract, in 4 Current Legal Problems 283 (Keeton & Schwarzenberger ed. 1951); Schroeder, The Impact of the War on Private Contracts, 42 Mich.L.Rev. 603 (1944). For a skeptical view as to the actual acceptance of the doctrine in this country, see Anderson, Frustration of Contract—A Rejected Doctrine, 3 De Paul L.Rev. 1 (1953).

A very full comparative discussion is Ramberg, Cancellation of Contracts of Affreightment on Account of War and Similar Circumstances (Göteborg 1969).

103. 256 U.S. 619, 41 S.Ct. 612 (1921).

enter into a contract on the assumption that some particular thing essential to its performance will continue to exist and be available for the purpose and neither agrees to be responsible for its continued existence and availability, the contract must be regarded as subject to an implied condition that, if before the time for performance and without the default of either party the particular thing ceases to exist or be available for the purpose, the contract shall be dissolved and the parties excused from performing it. . . . Another application widely recognized is where a ship chartered for a voyage, after the date of the charterparty and before the time for the voyage, is accidentally destroyed by fire, lost at sea, or injured in such degree as not to be available for the service. The Tornado, *supra*, was a suit on a contract of affreightment where the ship, before beginning the voyage, was accidentally burned and thereby prevented from undertaking it. This court held that the contract was dissolved, saying, p. 349:

" 'We are of opinion that by the disaster which occurred before the ship had broken ground or commenced to earn freight, the circumstances with reference to which the contract of affreightment was entered into were so altered by the supervening of occurrences which it cannot be intended were within the contemplation of the parties in entering into the contract, that the shipper and the underwriters were absolved from all liability under the contract of affreightment. The contract had reference to a particular ship, to be in existence as a seaworthy vessel and capable of carrying cargo and earning freight and of entering on the voyage. All the fundamental conditions forming part of the contract of the ship-owner were wanting at the time when the earning of freight could commence.'

"Here the ship, although still in existence and entirely seaworthy, was rendered unavailable for the performance of the charterparty by the requisition. By that supervening act she was impressed into the war service of the British Government for a period likely to extend—and which as it turned out did extend—long beyond the time for the charter voyage. In other words, compliance with the charterparty was made impossible by an act of state, the charterer was prevented from having the service of the ship and the owner from earning the stipulated freight. The event apparently was not anticipated and there was no provision casting the risk on either party. Both assumed that the ship would remain available and that was the basis of their mutual engagements. These, we think, must be regarded as entered into on an implied condition that, if before the time for the voyage the ship was rendered unavailable by such a supervening act as the requisition, the contract should be at an end and the parties absolved from liability under it." [104]

In this case "frustration" is merged with "impossibility" in a rather literal sense: illegality and extreme risk were involved in Essex S. S. Co. v. Langbehn.[105] The charter was executed July 9, 1914, and the vessel reached Galveston, the port of loading, on August 12. The charter party provided:

> "Vessel to load and being so loaded shall proceed to Rotterdam; one port only, as ordered on signing bills of lading. Charterers have the privilege of ordering the vessel to Antwerp to discharge. Charterers have the privilege of ordering the vessel to Hamburg to discharge." [106]

The charterer had advertised Hamburg as the ship's destination, and proposed to order her there; to the master, on the other hand, such a voyage would have been unthinkable, for war had broken out between Germany and England on August 4, and the vessel was British. The charterer, on the master's refusal to go to Hamburg, declared the charter cancelled; his defense to the shipowners' suit was, in effect, frustration of the contract. It seems to have been the owners' theory that the charter was not ended by the practical impossibility of the ship's going to Hamburg, but that the range of ports open to the charterer was simply thereby diminished. But the court held that the charter was brought to an end as a whole, and affirmed a judgment for the respondent.

Calmar S. S. Corp. v. Scott,[107] a more recent pronouncement of the Supreme Court in this field, shows some parsimony in the application of the "frustration" doctrine. The suit was against war risk underwriters on hull; they were presumptively liable unless the voyage had been "frustrated" before the loss occurred, for the policy was for the "voyage." [108] The Portmar had sailed from San Francisco for Manila, under charter, on November 28, 1941. The attack on Pearl Harbor occurred while she was at sea, and on December 11 she received routing orders from the Navy; from that time on her movements were under government control. She deflected her course to Sydney, where she touched briefly, and then proceeded to Brisbane, where she was unloaded; her cargo was sorted and part put back on board, after which she went to Port Darwin. Here she took on troops and equipment, and joined a military expedition to Koepang, on Timor. Forced to turn back by air attacks, she returned to Darwin, where she was bombed and strafed by the Japanese. Her master was forced to beach her, and she was abandoned. On these facts the court held that the voyage was not frustrated at the time of the loss, and that the underwriters were liable.

104. 256 U.S. at 629–631, 41 S.Ct. at 614.

105. 250 F. 98 (5th Cir. 1918).

106. 250 F. at 100.

107. 345 U.S. 427, 73 S.Ct. 739, 1953 A.M.C. 952 (1953).

108. See *supra* Chapter II, at note 30.

There was a dissent, and it does seem as though the case backtracks a good deal on the frustration doctrines of the World War I decisions. But there is a complicating factor which makes it questionable how far the case can be taken to go into the frustration problem in general. The insurance, the court held, covered war risks incurred while under "Seizure . . . by . . . Great Britain or any of its . . . allies." Thus the court could have rested (and perhaps did rest) its holding not on the ground that the *insured voyage* was still in existence at the time of loss, but rather that the *risk* was extended, by this provision, beyond the voyage. The following language hints at this:

> "The Koepang expedition was undoubtedly a venture inconsistent with the voyage specified in the Portmar's insurance. We are prepared to assume, though of course we do not decide, that the Koepang trip would have terminated, on grounds of abandonment of voyage, the coverage of a policy warranted free of war risks or of one warranted completely free of British capture, and that, under such a policy, had the Portmar subsequently sustained damage not attributable to war causes, cf. *e. g.*, Standard Oil Co. v. United States, 340 U.S. 54, 71 S.Ct. 135 there would have been no recovery. We assume that in those circumstances the Court of Appeals could have inferred as it did, on the basis of the Koepang venture and of the military situation, that the Portmar was to be retained indefinitely under requisition, and that her voyage was therefore over. But the point of this policy is that here the underwriters, by virtue of the saving clause, did insure against risks of British requisition. They insured, in other words, against consequence of a forced interruption of the voyage, which must necessarily throw into doubt the chances of completing the voyage as planned. Circumstances which may make out a change of voyage and cause termination of coverage under a policy warranted free of risks arising from seizure need not do so under one of insurance against such risks. In one as in the other, if they are both written for a voyage, there is an implied warranty that no different voyage will be undertaken. But it is a warranty which must be construed in light of the express provisions of the policy, and which may mean different things in different policies." [109]

The great variety of circumstances which may present themselves in frustration cases is illustrated in The Innerton,[110] another World War II case. The charter was from Houston to "one or two safe ports in the United Kingdom or one or two ports out of Antwerp, Rotterdam, Amsterdam, or Queenstown," as designated on signing bills of

109. 345 U.S. at 439–440, 73 S.Ct. at 745–746.

110. 141 F.2d 931, 1944 A.M.C. 570 (5th Cir. 1944).

lading. The ship was ready to load September 19, 1939, approximately two weeks after war broke out.

On September 6, the British Board of Trade issued an order, forbidding British ships in the Innerton's position from putting to sea, except under license from the Board's Licensing Committee. Applications for licenses were twice refused, for the voyage as described in the charter, but it was intimated that a license would be granted for shipment under a charter providing for discharge in United Kingdom ports only. The charterers nevertheless required that the vessel be tendered for loading; the owner refused, on the ground that the charter had been frustrated by operation of law. The suit was by the charterer, for damages.

Regarding it as "reasonably certain" that the Board of Trade would have issued a license for carriage to the United Kingdom, the court declined to look on the contract as frustrated, since the charterer might have designated a United Kingdom port. As long as this possibility was open, the charter could not be said to be either impossible of performance or commercially frustrated.[111]

Closure of the Suez Canal in 1956 produced a large crop of "frustration" cases. In Transatlantic Financing Corp. v. United States,[111a] the Court of Appeals for the District of Columbia Circuit helpfully reviews the then (1966) recent decisions and authorities. The holding, a reasonable one, was that a charter naming no route was not "frustrated" or rendered impossible of performance merely because closure of the Suez Canal forced the vessel to go around the Cape of Good Hope, rather than by the shorter "usual and customary route." The opinion is valuable for its supporting the proposition that "frustration" law is not basically different in the charter situation from what it is as to contracts in general.

It should be strongly emphasised that the incidence and effect of general doctrines on frustration may be deflected by specific clauses

111. General doctrines of "frustration" and the like cannot, of course, come into play where the actual documents (charter or bills of lading) make explicit provision for the contingency that arises, or generally impose the risk of change of circumstance on one of the parties. Thus, where freight is agreed to be earned on loading, regardless of future events, it is not returnable merely because government action frustrates the voyage. Allanwilde Transport Corp. v. Vacuum Oil Co., 248 U.S. 377, 39 S.Ct. 147 (1919); International Paper Co. v. The Gracie D. Chambers, 248 U.S. 387, 39 S.Ct. 149 (1919); Standard Varnish Works v. The Bris, 248 U.S. 392, 39 S.Ct. 150 (1919); Société Purfina Maritime v. 8598.09 Long Tons of Diesel Oil, 43 F.Supp. 807, 1942 A.M.C. 484 (S.D. Cal.1942), affirmed as modified 133 F. 2d 552 (9th Cir. 1942), certiorari denied 318 U.S. 781, 63 S.Ct. 858 (1943). See also: Borup v. Western Operating Corp., 130 F.2d 381, 1942 A.M.C. 1111 (2d Cir. 1942); The Wildwood, 133 F. 2d 765, 1943 A.M.C. 320 (9th Cir. 1943); Pope & Talbot v. Blanchard Lumber Co., 159 F.2d 134, 1947 A.M.C. 325 (9th Cir. 1947).

111a. 363 F.2d 312, 1966 A.M.C. 1717 (D.C.Cir.1966). To the same effect (though each case in this field turns on its own commercial and documentary facts): Glidden Co. v. Hellenic Lines Ltd., 275 F.2d 253, 1960 A.M.C. 810 (62d Cir. 1960).

in the charter, providing for the treatment of war emergency, requisition, or other contingency.[111b]

### Clauses 11–15

§ 4–13. Clause 11 has already been dealt with. Clause 12 reminds us that general average [112] is payable in the case of carriage under charter just as in the case of general ship carriage; for the purpose and effect of the stipulation for payment even where the general average is "necessitated through the neglect or default of the owner's servants," see the discussion, in the chapter on General Average, of the Jason clause.[113]

The remaining clauses call for no particular comment in this place.

## B. TIME CHARTERS

§ 4–14. A standard time charter, that approved by the New York Produce Exchange, revised 1946, will be found printed as an Appendix.[114] Many of its clauses are self-explanatory. Our method here will be to proceed by pointing out differences from the voyage charter already discussed, and by mentioning a few of the other peculiarities of the time charter which are not adequately exhibited by this method but which are suggested by the form we are considering.

### The Basic Arrangement

The part of our form that precedes the numbered clauses states the basic terms of the charter, except for the matter of payment of hire, which is taken care of in Clause 4.

The time charter is, compared with the voyage charter, an arrangement of some permanency, and it is clear from these clauses that the charterer is being assured of a good deal more about the character of the ship he is getting than is the case in the voyage charter. As in the latter form, these statements may be treated as warranties.[115]

Most important, it is to be noted that the warranty of seaworthiness, implied by law in every charter,[116] is not only not abolished but is

111b. *E. g.*, Navios Corp. v. The Ulysses II, 161 F.Supp. 932, 1958 A.M.C. 1925 (D.Md.1958), affirmed, 260 F.2d 959, 1959 A.M.C. 18 (4th Cir. 1958).

112. See *infra* Chapter V.

113. *Infra* Chapter V, at note 82.

114. *Infra* Appendix B. This old stalwart was in active use at least as late as 1965 (see Eastern Marine Corp. v. Fukaya Trading Co., 364 F.2d 80, 1966 A.M.C. 1959 (5th Cir. 1966)), and remains an excellent basis for discussion of time-charter problems.

115. Denholm Shipping Co. v. W. E. Hedger Co., 47 F.2d 213, 1931 A.M.C. 297 (2d Cir. 1931); The Atlanta, 82 F.Supp. 218, 1948 A.M.C. 1769 (S.D. Ga.1948); Poor, *op. cit. supra* note 54, §§ 1, 3.

116. See *supra* at note 39. An insubstantial breach of this warranty, resulting in a few days' delay at the inception of a twelve-month time charter, was held insufficient to justify repudiation of the vessel, in Aaby v. States Marine Corp., 181 F.2d 383, 1950 A.M.C. 947 (2d Cir. 1950), certiorari denied 340 U.S. 829, 71 S.Ct. 66

reinforced by the word "good" in the description of the vessel, and by the provision that she is to be "tight, staunch, strong, and in every way fitted for the service." [117] It is further agreed, in Clause 1, that the owners will keep the vessel fit throughout the charter term.

The filling in of blanks and the crossing out of words will make specific just what goods are to be carried, and what the trading limits are to be. The actual limits of trading may be left as wide as indicated in the form or may be cut down either by cancelling some of the named areas or by making note of limitations in the appropriate blank. In any event, the "safe port" and "safe berth" questions are at least as important in time charters as in voyage charters, for in the former the charterer has almost invariably a wider range of ports to which the vessel may be ordered. The decision whether a port is safe has to be made by the master, who is the owner's man, and of course there is much room for difference of opinion as to the correctness or reasonableness of this judgment.[118]

The designation of the "trading limits" may have an indirect effect on other terms of the charter. It will be noted that, by the terms of Clause 1, the owners pay for the insurance of the vessel. In Seas Shipping Co. v. U. S. War Shipping Administration,[119] the charterer ordered the ship on a voyage of such a nature that the owner had to pay an extra premium on his hull policy, and the owner sought to hold the charterer for this amount. But the court noted that the voyage in question lay within the limits set by the charter, and held that the premium must be paid by the owner.

Clauses 1 and 2 interestingly reflect the basic time charter arrangement. The owner runs and mans the ship; accordingly, Clause 1 places on him the responsibility of procuring and paying for those things which are connected with that duty.[120] The charterer says where she is to go and with what she is to be loaded; he bears the expenses that vary with the manner in which he exercises these options. The provision as to fumigation (Clause 2) marks the exact line. Where illness of the crew necessitates fumigation, the expense is for the own-

(1950), noted 29 Texas L.Rev. 113 (1950). The case discusses the nature of the warranty in time charters. See also Note, 12 Modern L.Rev. 372 (1949).

117. See Luckenbach v. W. J. McCahan Sugar Refining Co., 248 U.S. 139, 150, 39 S.Ct. 53, 55 (1918); The Fort Gaines, 21 F.2d 865, 1927 A.M.C. 1778 (D.Md.1927).

118. See Christophersen v. Donald S. S. Co., 187 F. 975 (2d Cir. 1911), affirming 175 F. 1002 (S.D.N.Y.1910); Tweedie Trading Co. v. Clan Line, 207 F. 70 (2d Cir. 1913). On owner's claim against charterer for designating an unsafe berth, see Park S. S. Co. v. Cities Service Oil Co., 188 F.2d 804, 1951 A.M.C. 851 (2d Cir. 1951), certiorari denied 342 U.S. 862, 72 S.Ct. 87 (1951). See discussion of this case in note 36a, *supra*, and see § 4–4 for full discussion of the "safe port" and "safe berth" question.

119. 97 F.Supp. 129, 1951 A.M.C. 503 (S.D.N.Y.1951).

120. Materialmen can acquire liens on the vessel for supplies ordered by them. Dampskibsselskabet Dannebrog v. Signal Oil & Gas Co., 310 U.S. 268, 60 S.Ct. 937, 1940 A.M.C. 123 (1940). It is to prevent this that the second sentence of Clause 18 is inserted in the Time Charter in our Appendix. The subject is more fully discussed in Chapter IX *infra*.

er's account, for they are his men.[120a] Where fumigation is necessary because of ports visited or cargo carried, the charterer pays, for it is his exercise of his options that has caused the trouble.[121]

### The Position as to Dispatch

**§ 4–15.** In the voyage charter, we saw that the owner's interest strongly impels him to the rapidest possible completion of the voyage, so that his vessel can take another engagement. In consequence, the demurrage device is provided to operate as a spur on the cargo interest to save as much time as possible, and to compensate the owner for undue delay. In the time charter, the position is reversed. The owner is being paid by calendar and clock time (see Clause 4), and will receive just the same hire regardless of the efficiency of employment of the vessel. If the charterer delays loading or unloading, that is of no concern to the owner. The charterer, on the other hand, is paying for time, and it is to *his* economic interest to see that this time is efficiently employed. The charter contains provisions designed to assure that he gets his money's worth. In the general unnumbered clause at the head of the charter, it is provided that the vessel is to report for the service with sufficient power to "run all the winches at one and the same time"—so that the cargo may be loaded at maximum speed. During loading and unloading, it is expressly provided (Clause 23) that the vessel shall work day and night, if required.[122] Besides the provision, already noted, that the owner is to keep the vessel in efficient state, it is explicitly made the duty of the Captain to "prosecute his voyages with the utmost dispatch." (Clause 8) And Clause 15 provides that the vessel shall go off hire when time is lost through any cause involving the matters of vessel repair and management for which the owner has assumed responsibility.

It is to be noted, moreover, that the description of the vessel contains a rather detailed statement as to her speed fully laden, and her fuel consumption. This statement expresses a warranty.[123]

### Overlap and Underlap

**§ 4–16.** It will be noted that the first blank in the first sentence in the second paragraph of the charter is preceded by the word "about"; the period of the charter is thus given some elasticity. It is recognized that redelivery on a scheduled day is not usually practicable, in view of the nature of ocean shipping. There is a lot of law behind this word "about"; the words "overlap" and "underlap" are the relevant terms of art. As a matter of fact, though the word "about" usually appears in time charters, the doctrines of overlap and under-

**120a.** See Peterson v. S.S. Wahcondah, 235 F.Supp. 698, 1965 A.M.C. 2433 (E.D.La.1964).

**121.** *Cf.* the holdings as to quarantine cited *infra* notes 132–133.

**122.** See Poor, *op. cit. supra* note 54, § 54.

**123.** The Ceres, 72 F. 936 (2d Cir. 1896), certiorari denied 163 U.S. 706, 16 S.Ct. 1199 (1896); The Astraea, 124 F. 83 (E.D.N.Y.1903).

lap would apply even if it were omitted, for courts recognize the impracticability of redelivery on a set day.

The simplest operation of the doctrine of overlap is, of course, the excuse furnished the charterer for failure to redeliver at the end of the fixed period. An early leading case is Straits of Dover S. S. Co. v. Munson.[124] In that case, redelivery was nearly three months late on a three months charter. The vessel had been greatly delayed by accidents beyond the charterer's control. The owner, charter rates having risen, wanted payment for the overlap at the new higher rates. But the court held that the three-months period was fixed with the implied understanding of its subjection to the contingencies of navigation, and that the charter, and hence the charter rate of hire, continued in force down to redelivery.

The courts have gone even further than this, however, and (at least where the word "about" is used) have read the doctrines of overlap and underlap into the terms of the charter not merely for the purpose of excusing delay in redelivery but even of establishing an affirmative right to a charter period differing from the "flat" period specified. Most interesting is the often cited case of The Rygja.[125] The charter was for a term of "about" six months, with option in the charterer to renew for another six months. The charterer exercised this option, and, because of a dispute as to when and where the ship was to be redelivered, it became necessary for the court to decide when the *second* term had ended. Since it was to run six months from the end of the first term, the question then became, "When did the first term end?" The facts were that the voyage on which the ship was engaged toward the end of the first flat period had not been completed until some seven weeks after the six months' term; under the doctrine of overlap, the charter (absent the question of renewal) would not have come to an end until that voyage was completed. Under these circumstances, the court held that the second term of six months began not at the expiration of the six months' flat period of the first term, but at the later date on which the overlapping voyage was completed—with the result that the second term did not expire one year from the beginning of the charter, but at a later time.

### Bills of Lading Under Time Charters

**§ 4–17.** Clause 8 provides that the master is to sign bills of lading as presented. Clause 18 reserves to the owners a lien on all cargoes and sub-freights (i. e., freight due from shippers of goods) for amounts due under the charter, which means, mainly, the charter hire.

The owner naturally desires to be immunized as far as possible from liability to the holders of bills of lading signed by the master. He cannot prevent, of course, the arising of the usual liens against his

124. 95 F. 690 (S.D.N.Y.1899), affirmed on opinion of District Court, 100 F. 1005 (2d Cir. 1900). See also Western Canada S. S. Co. v. United States, 1955 A.M.C. 2057 (W.D.Wash.1955).

125. 161 F. 106 (2d Cir. 1908).

vessel, where these accrue because of cargo damage or non-delivery, even when he cannot be held personally liable.[125a] Cogsa, as we have seen, applies to all bills of lading issued by vessels under charter.[126] This means not only that no charter-party term can validly be "incorporated" in a bill of lading where its effect would be to weaken the liability of the carrier—whether the carrier be the charterer or the owner—but that the liability of the ship *in rem* cannot be diminished.[127] But the further provision of Clause 8 (that the master shall be under the direction of the charterers as regards "employment and agency"), may be an attempt to isolate the owner from *in personam* liability to the cargo interest.[128]

The provision for liens on cargo and subfreight can apply only when there is freight actually owing on a shipment of goods; payment in the ordinary course to the charterer by the third-party shipper discharges the latter's obligation and with it the lien.[129] And of course the lien on cargo cannot be enforced beyond the amount of freight actually due on that cargo; as to the third-party shipper, this means, usually, the freight stipulated in the bill of lading.[130]

### The "Breakdown" and "Exceptions" Clauses (15 and 16)

**§ 4–18.** Many things can happen to prevent the performance by one party or another of one or more obligations under the charter. Where the other party suffers some damage from such a default, the question always arises "Who is to pay?", or what other adjustment is to be made. Charter parties go into great detail in arranging in advance for the taking care of these derailments of the adventure. We have already touched on the general subject in the section on voyage charters, in connection with demurrage and in our discussion of the strike, war and ice clauses and the topic of frustration. But a voyage charter envisions, in comparison with a time charter, a relatively simple and brief arrangement; the owner and his time charterer are bound up in a long-continued, complicated arrangement, and the chances of something going wrong are correspondingly greater. The two clauses under examination attempt to deal with the problem of adjustment of claims when this happens.

**125a.** Demsey & Associates, Inc. v. S. S. Sea Star 321 F.Supp. 663, 1970 A. M.C. 1088 (S.D.N.Y.1970). See the court's note 5.

**126.** *Supra* at note 87.

**127.** Cogsa, § 3(8), speaks of the liability of the ship as well as that of the carrier. 49 Stat. 1209 (1936), 46 U.S. C.A. § 1303(8).

**128.** Where the charterer procures the master's signature to bills of lading containing terms less favorable to the ship than those comprised in the charter party, and where the ship consequently incurs a liability, it has been held that the owner has a right of indemnity against the charterer. Field Line v. South Atlantic S. S. Line, 201 F. 301 (5th Cir. 1912). See, generally, Poor, *op. cit. supra* note 54, §§ 9–11.

**129.** Larsen v. 150 Bales of Sisal Grass, 147 F. 783 (S.D.Ala.1906); Actieselskabet Dampsk. v. Harrison & Co., 260 F. 287 (S.D.N.Y.1918).

**130.** American Steel Barge Co. v. Chesapeake & O. Coal Agency Co., 115 F. 669, 672 (1st Cir. 1902). The owners lien on cargo and subfreight depend on the clause. Oceanic Trading Corp. v. Vessel Diane, 423 F.2d 1, 1970 A.M. C. 351 (2d Cir. 1970).

The charterer, as we have seen, is paying for time. The "breakdown," or, as it is sometimes called, the "cesser of hire" clause relieves him, under some circumstances, from paying for time he doesn't get. The list of causes, delay in consequence of which stops the hire, will be seen to be those which prevent the full working of the vessel. There is no fault component in this clause; the owner simply agrees that, regardless of fault, he will cease to receive hire if time is lost through any of the specified causes.

The "exceptions" clause (16) may work to the benefit of either party, though it is usually the owner who can bring himself under it. In plain language, it means that neither party shall be liable to the other for the consequences of any of the enumerated causes.

Borderline cases arise under each of these two clauses, but the most interesting problem is their interrelation. The first and most obvious consequence of their being read carefully together is the perception that the "exceptions" clause cannot prevent the stoppage of hire under the "breakdown" clause, even though the ship is put out of service by one of the "excepted" causes. If this were not so, the breakdown clause would largely be nullified, for most of the causes which stop hire are also "excepted." The "exceptions" clause thus must be a shield against liability rather than a limitation on the stoppage of hire.

It is perhaps not so obvious, but nevertheless undoubtedly correct on careful reading, that the stoppage of hire clause cannot be filled out by the "exceptions" clause. What this means is brought out in Clyde Commercial S. S. Co. v. West India S. S. Co.,[131] where the exceptions clause, so far as now material, was as in the charter we are examining, and where the breakdown clause read:

> "(15) That in the event of the loss of time from deficiency of men or stores, breakdown of machinery, stranding, fire or damage preventing the working of the vessel for more than twenty-four running hours the payment of hire shall cease until she be again in an efficient state to resume her service. * * *"

The vessel left Colon after a short delay owing to the illness of two of her officers; this was a "deficiency of men," and the court held she went off hire for that time. When she arrived at Sabine, Texas, she was placed in quarantine for nearly eleven days, not because of any condition existing on the ship or among the crew but solely because she came from Colon, a port considered "infected" at that time under Texas law. The charterer deducted from the hire for this time too, and the owner sued. Quarantine, the court noted, is a "restraint of princes," and is hence excused under the exceptions clause.[132] But all this means is that the *owner* is not liable for the delay. Neither quarantine specifically nor "restraint of princes" generally was one

131. 169 F. 275 (2d Cir. 1909), certiorari denied 214 U.S. 523, 29 S.Ct. 702 (1909).

132. *Cf. supra* Chapter III, Part II, at note 78.

of the causes specified in the clause as justifying the cesser of hire. A quarantine restraint did not make it impossible for the charterer to pay hire; hence such payment is not excused under the "exceptions" clause. The precise line is neatly shown by other quarantine cases, in which the quarantine is imposed or prolonged for reasons having to do with the state of health of the crew, rather than because of the provenance of the vessel. Quarantine, in such a case, is still a "restraint of princes," but it arises from a "deficiency of men," and, while the owner could not be held liable for its consequences, at least unless his fault contributed to the result, the payment of hire is excused.[133] Thus, the two clauses are to be read together, but they are not to be fused.

On the same facts as Clyde, the actual breakdown clause in our charter (Clause 15) would raise a further question, for it provides for cesser of hire in the event of loss of time "by any . . . cause preventing the full working of the vessel . . . " Though this appears to be comprehensive, a court might still reach the same result as in the Clyde case, on the theory that "full working" refers to the capacity of the vessel herself and not to externally imposed compulsion.

The question has arisen whether the owner can be held liable, over and above the cesser of hire, for delays covered by the breakdown clause, or whether that clause states the sole remedy for such delay.[134] It seems clear that the clause should not be read to imply something radically different from what it says. It provides for the stopping of hire in certain contingencies, but the charter party contains other undertakings of the owner, and there is nothing in a provision for the ceasing of hire which implies that the owner shall not be liable for the breach of these, in accordance with ordinary rules of law. This conclusion seems commercially reasonable; the charterer, in the case of breakdown, always loses the use of the vessel, and a stipulation that he not pay for that use is not at all in the nature of "damages", liquidated or not, but simply an assurance that he will not pay for something he does not get. Damages for delay are on quite a different footing; they are not a mere device for adjusting price to the quantum of the thing received, but compensate the party for the consequences of the other's fault. The practical question is, of course, to be evaluated in the light of the "exceptions" clause. The owner cannot be held for damages ensuing from any of the causes named there, unless his own fault contributed. But reading the two clauses together makes it even clearer that the "breakdown" clause is not to be taken as a provision, in effect, for liquidated damages, for, as we have seen, the owner is immunized entirely, by the "exceptions" clause, from liability arising from most of the causes named in the "breakdown" clause. The latter clause, it seems clear, ought to be read to

133. Gow v. Gans S. S. Line, 174 F. 215 (2d Cir. 1909); Noyes v. Munson S. S. Line, 173 F. 814 (S.D.N.Y.1909). *Cf.* Northern S. S. Co. v. Earn Line S. S. Co., 175 F. 529 (2d Cir. 1910).

134. See The Bjornefjord, 271 F. 682 (2d Cir. 1921).

mean just what it appears to say, and not to contain wide implications beyond its apparent tenor.

## Frustration

**§ 4–19.** The topic of frustration, which we have already dealt with in the Voyage Charter section, connects directly with those of exceptions and cesser of hire. Those topics have to do with the treatment of minor hitches in performance; when performance becomes impossible, or when conditions have so changed that the purpose and object of the contract may be said to be gone, then the courts speak of frustration, and the charter is held to have come to an end.[135]

Time charter frustration problems do not differ in principle from those in the voyage charter situations, but the fact-situations are different. A good illustration is Atlantic Fruit Co. v. Solari.[136] The libellant held two Dutch steamers under time charter, and subchartered them, also on time, to the respondents. The respondents started using the vessels to carry foodstuffs from North and South America to the Italian military authorities; the year was 1915.

The Dutch government, worried about its neutrality and anxious to protect vessels and crew from the hazards such a trade entailed, ordered its consul at Genoa not to permit the crews to sign on for any more voyages, so long as the vessel was under charter to either of the parties to the case. After diplomatic negotiation, the Dutch government rescinded this order, on condition that the vessel not trade to the ports of any belligerent; the libellant, the Atlantic Fruit Company, signed an agreement to that effect, whereupon the vessel was released, and the subcharterer notified to furnish sailing orders. The latter took the position that these developments had ended the charter, and paid no more hire. Of the principal question raised, Judge Augustus Hand said:

> "It is urged that this action by the government, which deprived the subcharterers of the use of the ships for a substantial portion of the charter period, constituted a 'frustration,' and relieved the respondents from the payment of charter hire, and I agree with this contention. I am well aware of the English decisions which express doubt as to whether any 'restraint of princes' can amount to a 'frustration' in a time charter. Here, however, was a case where the Dutch government did not, according to the allegations of the libel, simply at one time restrain the sailing of the vessel, but decreed that it would not permit the crew to be signed *'for any voyage while the said vessel was under charter to the respondents or libelant.'* This, I think, was a decision to annul completely the rights of the charterers. If the restraint had been a temporary matter pending negotiation, it might very likely be regarded as not sufficient to amount to a 'frustra-

135. See the discussion, *supra*, of Clause 10 of the Voyage Charter.

136. 238 F. 217 (S.D.N.Y.1916).

> tion'; but when, under the allegations of the libel, it was coupled with a declaration that the charterers could never use the ship, and continued for about two months, I think the respondents had a right to treat the decree as amounting to a 'frustration,' which ended relations between them and the libelant. As was said in the case of Embiricos v. Sydney Reid & Co., [1914] L.R. 3 K.B. 45, quoting the remarks of Lord Gorell in The Savona, [1900] L.R. 3 K.B. 252: 'I do not think this case can be decided by what happened afterwards.'" [137]

The time charter is often frustrated by a requisition of the ship by the government, on a new time charter. In such a case, the charterer has appealed for the court to give him, and not the owner, the benefit of the (usually higher) rate paid by the government. There seems much equity in his claim; in the Isle of Mull,[138] the court puts it strongly:

> ". . . The strong reasons in favor of the charterer's claim may be thus stated: The charter confers upon it the right to the use of the vessel for the specified period. This right, although not a demise, is a property right. There is the strongest presumption against the intention of the British government to appropriate this property of the charterer without compensation. Yet the government, in the stress of a war involving its highest interest, if not its existence, cannot take time to adjust the rights of the charterer and the owner. The government needs the vessel, and takes it from the owner, because the owner is in actual possession by its master and crew, and pays the owner with whom it deals a lump sum, leaving it to meet other claimants. But it pays the owner for the use, not for the vessel itself. Therefore, since the charterer had legal right to the use of the vessel, the owner, after paying itself the amount due under the contract and compensation for any losses sustained, holds the remainder for the charterer. To allow the owner to retain the excess paid by the government, would be to allow it to avail itself of the act of the government, a third party, to enrich itself at the expense of the charterer by the practical appropriation of the charterer's property right." [139]

But the same opinion gives the other side of the thing:

> "The argument in favor of the owner's rights to the entire compensation for the use of the vessel paid by the British government is this: The requisition of the ship by the government for an indefinite period completely frustrated the

137. 238 F. at 224.

138. 278 F. 131 (4th Cir. 1921), certiorari denied 257 U.S. 662, 42 S.Ct. 270 (1922).

139. 278 F. at 133.

contract and put an end to all rights of both parties under it. This is true, first, because under the general law the contract ceases to operate when the particular thing contracted for ceases to be available for the purpose contemplated; and, second, because under the restraint of princes clause the requisition of the ship relieved the owner of all obligation to the charterer for the service of the ship, and as a consequence from all obligation to account for the hire of it." [140]

In the actual case, the decision was for the owner.[141]

It will be seen that the frustration principle, as applied to government requisition of vessels under time charter, has to be accommodated to the operation of "the cesser of hire" and "restraint of princes" clause. The logic of the Clyde Commercial Steamship case,[142] treated in the section on the breakdown clause, above, is that the "restraint of princes" (which a governmental requisition certainly is), far from bringing the charter to an end, does not even suspend the payment of hire; on the other hand, it does excuse the owner from not having the vessel at the full disposition of the charterer. An extrapolation of this logic would lead unquestionably to the conclusion that governmental requisition does not end the time charter, but that, on the contrary, the obligation to pay hire continues through the charter term, even though the vessel is in the hands of government; obviously, on equitable principles, the corollary would be that the hire paid by the government would belong to the charterer. But the courts have declined to take this logic to its conclusion; the distinction made is one of degree:

> "Ordinarily that governmental pressure, which is restraint, is but temporary; and the usual restraint clause, such as we have before us, is drawn on that assumption. Thus in Clyde, etc., Co. v. West India, etc., Co., 169 Fed. 279, 94 C.C.A. 551, we found a quarantine detention to be within the restraint clause, and held that such temporary delay did not even stop the daily hire due by charter, not only because the words of the clause did not provide for such stoppage, but because the charterer 'had the use of the vessel for which it was to pay, notwithstanding the interruption.'
>
> "Whether a given act suspends or dissolves a relation is, like most matters, a question of degree. It was well put arguendo by Lord Haldane, when he pointed to the restraint clause as an instance of providing for the 'partial or temporary suspension of certain obligations' of a charter, yet said:

140. 278 F. at 134–5.

141. See also Permanente S. S. Co. v. Hawaiian Dredging Co., 65 F.Supp. 321, 1945 A.M.C. 1447 (N.D.Cal.1945); Henjes Marine, Inc. v. White Const. Co., 58 N.Y.S.2d 384, 1945 A.M.C. 1240 (Sup.Ct.1945). In these two cases, involving demise charters, governmental requisition was held to have frustrated the charter and put an end to the obligation to pay charter hire. See Note, 40 Harv.L.Rev. 305 (1926).

142. *Supra* note 131.

" 'To the extent to which the perils mentioned interfere with the fulfillment of [charter] obligations, the parties are exempted from liability for nonperformance.' Tamplin, etc., Co. v. Anglo-Mexican, etc., Co., [1916] 2 A.C. 397, at pages 406–409.

"Evidently the interference may be total; it may amount to prevention.

"The same kind of restraint, the same act of power, may at one time or in one instance produce but a temporary delay, changing the contractual obligations of no one, and at another time, or when operating on other attending circumstances, may so change the relation of parties as to destroy the contract itself." [143]

## C. DEMISE OR BARE-BOAT CHARTERS

### General Nature

**§ 4–20.** The fact that the demise charter bears the same generic name as the time and voyage charters we have been considering is likely to lead one into thinking of the demise as quite similar in practical use and legal import to the other two. Nothing could be farther from the truth; a better first approximation would be to say that the demise is linked to the time and voyage charters only by an accident of nomenclature arising out of a past in which the types were not as standardized and isolated from one another as they are today. The charters we have studied so far are one and all contracts for the carriage of the goods designated by one person in the ship of another person, who himself remains in control of the navigation of the vessel. The demise, in practical effect and in important legal consequence, shifts the possession and control of the vessel from one person to another, just as the shoreside lease of real property shifts many of the incidents of ownership from lessor to lessee. The owner of a demised ship still has interests in her, just as the lessor has interests in the house and lot he has leased to somebody else. But the principal interests the shipowner has are in receiving the agreed hire and getting the vessel back at the end of the term; there are none of the problems that arise out of the intimate cooperative association created when one firm's ship, under its control, is carrying goods for another firm.[144]

The demise charter is thus not a documentary device for the *conduct* of the business of shipping; it is rather an instrument for vesting in one person most of the incidents of ownership in a capital asset of that business—the ship—while another retains the general ownership and the right of reversion. Its use among private firms has

143. The Claveresk, 264 F. 276, 281–2 (2d Cir. 1920).

144. There are, however, atypical arrangements of great complexity. See Polar S. S. Corp. v. Inland Overseas S. S. Corp., 136 F.2d 835, 1943 A.M.C. 857 (4th Cir. 1943), certiorari denied 320 U.S. 774, 64 S.Ct. 83 (1943). The text above refers to the typical demise pattern.

for a long time been far less frequent than that of the other forms of charters.[144a] Of recent years, it has been used very considerably by the government, as a device for implementing the various public activities in shipping which have been forced by the lack of tonnage in times of war and emergency, and by the necessity of maintaining control over what tonnage there was. During World War II, the government took over and operated, directly and through "general agency" agreements, a good many privately owned ships. Rather than condemn and pay for a ship itself, the device frequently used was the taking of the ship on demise from the private owner. Then after the war, when the government found itself the owner (in consequence of the heavy shipbuilding program) of a great many vessels for which it had no use, it proved handy, in many cases, to demise these ships to private firms.[145]

Most demise charters today and in the recent past thus have or had the government as one of the parties [145a]; the forms of the charters are in such cases the result of governmental regulatory activity, and are promulgated and regularly used by the public agencies involved. To such transactions the old cases have little application, and in a work such as this it seems useless to study in any detail the current governmental practice, for in a new situation this is subject to change with a rapidity practically impossible to the maritime law in general.

For all these reasons, our treatment of the demise will be quite brief. Enough has already been said to give some idea of its place and use.

## How to Recognize a Demise

**§ 4–21.** The first problem is of course that of distinguishing the demise from the regular time and voyage charters. The test is one of "control"; if the owner retains control over the vessel, merely carrying the goods furnished or designated by the charter, the charter is not a demise; if the control of the vessel itself is surrendered to the charterer, so that the master is his man and the ship's people are his people, then we have to do with a demise. As the Supreme Court has said, "To create a demise the owner of the vessel must completely and exclusively relinquish 'possession, command, and navigation' thereof to the demisee".[146]

144a. "Demise charters are infrequently used in commercial practice . . ." Zock, Charter Parties in Relation to Cargo, 45 Tulane L.Rev. 733, 735 (1971).

145. See *infra* Chapter XI, at note 129.

145a. The reference here is to formal demises, rather than to the informal, oral, short-term demise of small craft encountered in local situations, sometimes fixed by telephone.

146. Guzman v. Pichirilo, 369 U.S. 698, 699, 82 S.Ct. 1095, 1962 A.M.C. 1142, 1143–4 (1st Cir. 1962), citing this text. See also United States v. Shea, 152 U.S. 178, 14 S.Ct. 519 (1894); Davison Chemical Corp. v. The Henry W. Card, 144 F.2d 705, 1944 A.M.C. 1058 (2d Cir. 1944); Romano v. West India Fruit & S. S. Co., 151 F.2d 727, 729–30, 1946 A.M.C. 90 (5th Cir. 1945); Salmons Dredging Corp. v. The Herma, 180 F.2d 233, 1950 A.M.C. 839 (4th Cir. 1950).

In the forms actually used for chartering today, it is usually quite clear which of these arrangements is intended. It is common practice, as well, for the charter to contain an express stipulation in this regard; the time charter we have examined, in its Clause 26, expressly provides that it is not to be construed as a demise; it could not be in any case, for, as in most time charters, it is perfectly clear that the owner retains control over the navigation and management of the vessel.

A few cases occur in which a fictitious "demise" is used as a sham to take the real owner out of the danger zone of liability, particularly for personal injuries.[146a]

### Legal Consequences of the Demise

§ 4-22. The primary obligation of the owner is to furnish the vessel in seaworthy state at the beginning of the term.[147] The charterer's obligations are to redeliver the vessel in as good condition, ordinary wear and tear excepted, as that in which he received her,[148] and to pay hire. If the vessel, on return, is damaged, there arises a (rebuttable) presumption that the charterer was negligent.[148a]

Demise charters often provide for survey (that is, full inspection by attested experts) on delivery and redelivery, so that disputes as to the charterer's fulfilment of his duty of redelivery unimpaired may be minimized. These surveys are a nuisance, and their necessity may explain some of the decline in the use of demise charters among private firms. Common forms also provide for periodic joint inspections, and for reports by the charterer to the owner on the movements of the vessel; the owner, like the lessor of a house and lot, retains an interest in his property, and desires to keep in touch.

The responsibility for providing insurance is usually allocated by the charter. A typical arrangement is that the hull insurance is provided by the owner for his own account, while the protection and indemnity coverage is arranged by the charterer. The charterer may, if he wishes, also insure such interest as he has in the vessel; his loss, in the event of hull damage or loss of the ship, would be the damages he suffers through loss of the use of the vessel, or through incurring a liability for not returning her safely.[149]

**146a.** See, e. g., Stevens v. Seacoast Co., 414 F.2d 1032, 1969 A.M.C. 1911 (5th Cir. 1969).

**147.** Work v. Leathers, 97 U.S. 379 (1878); Maine Seaboard Paper Co. v. The Maurice R. Shaw, 46 F.Supp. 767, 1942 A.M.C. 1630 (D.Me.1942).

**148.** Kenny v. City of New York, 108 F.2d 958, 1940 A.M.C. 186 (2d Cir. 1940); Howard v. Dobbins-Trinity Coal Co., 111 F.2d 571, 1940 A.M.C. 800 (2d Cir. 1940), certiorari denied 311 U.S. 691, 61 S.Ct. 73 (1940).

**148a.** Sears Oil Co. v. Reinauer Transportation Co., 1966 A.M.C. 1729 (S.D. N.Y.1966). On demisee's offer of proof of freedom from negligence, it has been held the presumption drops out of the case. Hudson Valley Lightweight Aggregate Corp. v. Windsor Bldg. and Supply Co., 446 F.2d 750, 1971 A.M.C. 1608 (2d Cir. 1971).

**149.** See Arnould, Marine Insurance § 317 (15th ed. 1961).

## The Charterer as Owner: Third Persons

**§ 4–23.** The most important consequences of the distinction between the demise and the other forms of charters flow from the fact that the demise charterer is looked on as the owner of the vessel *pro hac vice.*[150]

In consequence, he qualifies as the "owner" for purposes of the statutes relating to limitation of liability; he can thus limit under those statutes where the voyage and time charterers clearly cannot.[151]

Far less palatable are some of the other consequences of standing in the owner's position. In general, all *in personam* liabilities arising out of the ship's operation are brought home to the demise charterer. It may be of immense economic importance to him that he, as owner, is the warrantor of seaworthiness of the vessel to seamen who work aboard her, and that he in consequence may be held liable for personal injuries suffered as a result of breach of the absolute duty to provide a safe place to work and safe implements to work with.[152] He is the "employer" for purposes of personal injury liabilities to seamen under the Jones Act, since the crew is hired by him.[153] The vessel, so far as third persons are concerned, is his vessel, and the men are his men; such of their defaults as are attributable to the owner and employer under *respondeat superior* doctrines are his to answer for.[154]

## Liens on Vessels Under Demise

**§ 4–24.** We have seen that the time charterer, as the party responsible for furnishing certain supplies, can create liens on the vessel, and that the time form makes provision to insure the minimization of this threat to the owner's interest.[155] In the demise, the general owner has a much more difficult problem, because the charterer's people are running the vessel for all purposes, and their activities cannot be closely supervised. Yet the plastering of a vessel with liens is just as definite a diminution in her value as is physical damage, and the owner wants to make the charterer pay as he goes, and not conduct operations on the credit of the vessel.

150. Leary v. United States, 81 U.S. (14 Wall.) 607, 610 (1872); see Reed v. United States, 78 U.S. (11 Wall.) 591, 601 (1871).

151. Rev.Stat. § 4286 (1875), 46 U.S.C.A. § 186. See The Atlas No. 7, 42 F.2d 480, 1930 A.M.C. 1029 (S.D.N.Y.1930). *Cf. infra* Chapter X, § 10–10.

152. Reed v. S.S. Yaka, 373 U.S. 410, 83 S.Ct. 1349, 1963 A.M.C. 1373 (1963). Cannella v. United States, 179 F.2d 491, 1950 A.M.C. 858 (2d Cir. 1950). See Vitozi v. Balboa Shipping Co., 163 F.2d 286, 1947 A.M.C. 1160 (1st Cir. 1947); Muscelli v. Frederick Starr Contracting Co., 296 N.Y. 330, 73 N.E. 2d 536, 1947 A.M.C. 1110 (1947), noted 34 Cornell L.Q. 92 (1948).

153. See Cromwell v. Slaney, 65 F.2d 940, 1933 A.M.C. 1514 (1st Cir. 1933). Close questions of fact can arise in such cases. See Loe v. Goldstein, 101 F.2d 967, 1939 A.M.C. 627 (9th Cir. 1939).

154. See, *e. g.*, The Barnstable, 181 U. S. 464, 21 S.Ct. 684 (1901), where the demise charterer was held primarily liable for collision damage.

155. *Supra* note 120.

Most demise charters therefore provide that neither the charterer nor the master shall have the power to create liens on the vessel. This provision is obviously without effect with respect to liens arising by operation of law; liens for crew's wages and salvage are often expressly allowed by the clause, but it is clear that tort liens and general average liens cannot be prevented from coming into being by any documentary manipulation or by "notice." [156] Nor can such a provision prevent the arising of liens in favor of shippers of goods under bills of lading, in case of liability for damage or loss, for Cogsa expressly forbids the lessening of the liability not only of the owner but of the ship.[157] The main purpose and effect of the provision is to prevent the arising of liens for repairs, supplies, and the like, and this purpose is achieved only where notice, actual or constructive, is brought home to persons dealing with the ship, of the fact that they are trading not on her credit but on that of the charterer. The question of the quantum of "putting on inquiry" necessary to defeat the would-be lienor can be dealt with only in the framework of the whole subject of maritime liens, statutory and non-statutory, and is taken up in the chapter devoted to that subject.[158]

156. It has been held that the seaman's lien for maintenance and cure (treated in Chapter VI *infra*) cannot be affected by the terms of the charter. Solet v. M/V Capt. H. V. Dufrene, 303 F. Supp. 980, 1970 A.M.C. 571 (E.D.La. 1969). The Edward Pierce, 28 F.Supp. 637, 1939 A.M.C. 1260 (S.D.N.Y.1939).

157. See *supra* at note 127; Karobi Lumber Co. v. S.S. Norco, 249 F.Supp. 324, 1966 A.M.C. 315 (S.D.Ala.1966), citing text.

158. *Infra* Chapter IX, § 9–42 *et seq.* See Note, 44 Yale L.J. 697 (1935).

# Chapter V

# GENERAL AVERAGE

### Basic Ideas

**§ 5–1.** The root notion of general average goes back at least to Roman times; in the Digest we read:

> "It is provided by the Rhodian Law that if merchandise is thrown overboard to lighten the ship, the loss occasioned for the benefit of all must be made good by the contribution of all." [1]

So in the Rules of Oleron:

> "ART. 8. A ship leaves Bordeaux or elsewhere, and it happens that a storm takes it at sea and the ship cannot escape without throwing out goods from within. The master is bound to say to the merchants: 'Signors, we cannot escape without throwing out the wines and the goods.' The merchants, if there are any, shall signify their good will who shall agree to this jettison, and that the master's reasons are most clear; and if they do not agree, the master ought, nevertheless, not to fear to throw out as much as shall seem to him good, swearing himself and the third of his crew on the Holy Gospels, when he shall have come safe ashore, that he did it of no malice, but to save their lives, the ship, the goods, and the wines. Those which have been thrown out ought to be appraised at the rate of those which shall come safe, and shall be divided pound by pound amongst the merchants; and the master out to share on account of the ship or his freight, at his choice, to restore the damage. The mariners ought to have each a ton (*tonnel*) free, and the rest shall contribute to the jettison according to what he has, if he defends himself on the sea like a man; and if he does not defend himself, he shall have nothing free: and the master shall be believed upon his oath. And this is the judgment in this case." [2]

The general principle underlying these dispositions has come down to modern times, and is a part of the sea law of all the principal

1. 2 The Digest of Justinian 385 Monro transl. 1909, Digest 14.2.1; See Lowndes & Rudolf, General Average §§ 1–4 (9th ed. 1964, now Vol. 7 in the collection, British Shipping Laws). (This book actually comprises Lowndes, General Average, and Rudolf, York-Antwerp Rules, revised and combined. It will be cited hereinafter as Lowndes & Rudolf.)
(James Thomas Richardson, Esq., Yale Law School 1972, was especially helpful in preparing this chapter for the second edition.)

2. Lowndes & Rudolf § 7. See Chapter I, *supra*, at note 22.

maritime nations.[3] It has recently been held that the right is not statutory, even where it is alluded to or time-limited by a foreign statute, but a creature of the "general" maritime law.[3a] The requisites of general average in the United States are thus set out by Mr. Justice Grier in Barnard v. Adams: [4]

> "In order to constitute a case for general average, three things must concur:—
>
> "1st. A common danger; a danger in which ship, cargo, and crew all participate; a danger imminent and apparently 'inevitable,' except by voluntarily incurring the loss of a portion of the whole to save the remainder.
>
> "2d. There must be a voluntary jettison, *jactus*, or casting away, of some portion of the joint concern for the purpose of avoiding this imminent peril, *periculi imminentis evitandi causa*, or, in other words, a transfer of the peril from the whole to a particular portion of the whole.
>
> "3d. This attempt to avoid the imminent common peril must be successful." [5]

When a ship is on her voyage carrying cargo, three things may be said to be "at risk": the ship, the cargo, and the freight. The first two are self-explanatory. "Freight," in maritime law and commercial parlance, never refers to the goods carried, but rather to the compensation which the shipowner is to receive for carrying the goods; the shipowner's interest in freight is "at risk" because under the general maritime law of carriage he cannot collect it unless the goods are delivered to their destination, so that loss of the goods entails loss of the freight as well.[6]

Actually, modern bills of lading very frequently provide that freight is to be considered as earned and payable when the goods are loaded on; in such a case, freight is obviously not "at risk," and should not enter into the general average statement. (In this connec-

3. For a valuable comparative review, see Felde, General Average and the York-Antwerp Rules, 27 Tul.L.Rev. 406 (1953). Barclay, The Definition of General Average, 7 L.Q.Rev. 22 (1891), assembles comparative material on this topic. Buglass, Marine Insurance and General Average in the United States (1973) contains much useful practical information. See also Inter American High Commission, Marine Insurance and General Average, Comparative American Legislation (U. S. Govt. Printing Office 1927). For problems consequent on containerization (see *supra* Chapter I, § 1–5) see Lyons, Some Thoughts on General Average in the Container Age, 2 Journal of Maritime Law and Commerce 165 (1970).

3a. Argyll Shipping Co. v. Hanover Ins. Co., 297 F.Supp. 125, 128, 1968 A.M.C. 2195, 2198–9 (S.D.N.Y.1968).

4. 51 U.S. (10 How.) 270 (1850).

5. 51 U.S. (10 How.) at 303. See Lowndes & Rudolf §§ 33 *et seq.*; Note, 15 Harv.L.Rev. 488 (1902). A very thorough and quite interesting "illustrative opinion" on general average, taking up some modern aspects, is in Cia. Atlantica Pacifica S.A. v. Humble Oil & Refining Co., 274 F.Supp. 884, 1967 A.M.C. 1474 (D.Md.1967).

6. *Cf. supra*, Chapter II, at note 33, and cases there cited, on freight as an insurable subject-matter at risk in the sea "venture".

tion a recent decision must be queried. Construing a charter provision of dubious meaning as providing that the 80% of freight prepaid was "earned" on sailing, the lower court held this "freight" was "at risk" for cargo's account, and was therefore a part of the contributory value.[6a] The appellate court reversed, holding the construction of the charter to have been wrong, and the 80% of freight not to have been "earned".[6b] It is submitted that the lower court decision was questionable in a more fundamental respect. Prepaid earned freight is for all practical purpose merged in sound value at the arrival port, and in any case nothing but that value is actually "at risk"; the concept of "risk", as to freight irretrievably prepaid, is highly problematic.) Mishaps at sea may result in the loss or diminution of the value of one or more of these interests. The ship may be damaged in a storm; the cargo may be pilfered, or spoiled by delay; the right to receive freight may be lost to the shipowner because, owing to frustration of the voyage, loss of the cargo, or some other cause, the cargo cannot be delivered and the freight earned.

Usually, the interest that sustains the loss has to bear it alone, and has no right of contribution from the other interests. The maritime adventure is not, in general, a common or joint one; the separate owners of the property at risk take their own chances. Any loss so treated, if less than a total loss, is called a "particular average," the word "particular" being the opposite of "general."[7] The owner who suffers such a loss may have a right of *indemnity* against some other party to the marine adventure; the most usual instance is the cargo-owner whose cargo is damaged, and who may have a right to recover his loss from the vessel or her owner, if the loss occurs under circumstances such that the law of the carriage of goods makes the vessel liable.[8] But there is no right, in the usual case of loss through marine mishap, of contribution from the other interests on the basis of general average.

Where, however, the property at risk in the venture actually comes into a position of peril, and where a voluntary sacrifice is made of one part, with the result that the rest is saved, the property saved must contribute, not a full indemnity to the owner of the sacrificed property, *but in such amount as to insure that all shall have suffered equally.* In Pacific Freighters Co. v. St. Paul Fire & Marine Ins. Co.,[9] the court sums up what it calls "the mechanics of apportionment": "The value of each of the contributing interests is multiplied by a fraction which has as its numerator the sum of the general average expense and has as its denominator the sum of the contributing

6a. Waterman S.S. Corp. v. United States, 258 F.Supp. 425, 1967 A.M.C. 905 (S.D.Ala.1966).

6b. United States v. Waterman S.S. Co., 397 F.2d 577 (5th Cir. 1968).

7. On the use of these terms in marine insurance, see *supra*, Chapter II, at note 105.

8. See, generally, Chapter III, Part II, *supra*.

9. 109 F.2d 310, 1940 A.M.C. 195 (9th Cir. 1940); see also Nicaraguan Long Leaf Pine Lumber Co. v. Moody, 211 F.2d 715, 719, 1954 A.M.C. 658 (5th Cir. 1954).

values." [10] Thus, in a highly simplified example given merely to make the principle clear, let us imagine that a vessel under charter is worth $1,000,000, her cargo (all belonging to one owner), worth $1,000,000, and the freight, to be earned on arrival, $100,000. Let's suppose that, in a storm, it became necessary, in the judgment of the master, to throw overboard, in order to lighten the ship, cargo worth $100,000, freight on which, if it had arrived, would have been $10,000, and that, in order to accomplish this jettison in a hurry, it was also necessary to cut a hole in the deck over the hold, damaging the ship to the extent of $5,000. The "vessel interest" (ship plus freight) was worth, as a whole, $1,100,000, and has incurred a total damage of $15,000 (injury to deck plus loss of freight). The cargo was worth $1,000,000, and has been damaged $100,000 worth. All three interests together were worth $2,100,000, and were damaged by the general average acts in the total amount of $115,000, or 115 parts in 2100. The end to be reached by calculation is that each interest shall suffer in just this proportion. The application of this proportion to the cargo interest at risk ($1,000,000) gives, to the nearest cent, $54,761.-90; and the same proportion of the vessel interest (ship and freight) totalling $1,100,000 comes to $60,238.10. Since the cargo, by the jettison, has suffered $100,000, a sum greater than its proper share of the loss, the ship must pay to the cargo owner the difference between that amount and the $54,761.90 the cargo should end up out of pocket, or $45,238.10. This payment, together with the $15,000 it has suffered by lost freight and damage to the deck, will put the ship out of pocket to a total of $60,238.10, which, as we have seen, is its proper proportion of the general average loss.

Those familiar with the intricacies of general average adjustment would smile at the simplicity of this example, and at the cumbersomeness of the calculations, but it is believed that the student who will go through the last paragraph with care, working out the arithmetic and understanding the ideas behind the process of calculation, will have a satisfactorily concrete notion of the practical consequences of general average doctrine.[11] It should be carefully noted that the general average adjustment does not make anybody whole; the owner of the sacrificed property continues to bear his proper share of the loss, but no more than that.

§ 5–2. The modern law of general average may be looked on as an extension by analogy and by generalization of the right to contribution in case of throwing overboard of cargo, of voluntary destruction of a part of the ship, and like literal "sacrifices." The extension has been wide, but the root-principle remains remotely recognizable. Thus, it is held in this country that the extra wages a ship has to pay her crew, while the vessel is in a "port of refuge," to which she has been taken because further prosecution of the voyage has become

10. 109 F.2d at 312.

11. For other examples, see Rosenthal, Techniques of International Trade 281 (1950); 2 Arnould, Marine Insurance § 990 (15th ed. 1961).

dangerous, is a "general average expense." [12] This seems a long way from the cutting off of a mast and throwing it into the sea, to lighten a ship in a storm, but the idea still is that a sacrifice (in this case the incurring of a liability for extra wages) has been voluntarily made for the purpose of taking the whole adventure, ship and cargo, out of danger, and that the interests thus extricated from peril ought to chip in all around. The payment of money, or the incurring of a liability to pay money, under circumstances giving rise to a right to contribution in general average, is called a "general average expenditure" or "expense," in contradistinction to the more physical "sacrifice." [13] Both may be lumped together as "general average acts."

It ought perhaps to be mentioned that, in modern times, most general average acts are *ship's acts,* giving rise to a right of contribution running in the ship's favor against cargo; whatever may have been the case in the medieval wine trade, general average now is mainly ship's doctrine.

The application of the basic principle of general average to the complex actualities of modern navigation has led in the cases to the arising, and partial settling, of a number of clusters of questions: What sort or degree of peril suffices to produce a "general average situation," and to what extent is the master's judgment to be respected after the event, even if he may have wrongly estimated the peril? When may a sacrifice be said to be "voluntary"? What effect does it have on the right to receive contribution that the peril may have resulted from the fault of one of the parties to the adventure? How, precisely, are the interests which are benefited by the sacrifice, and hence subject to contribution, to be defined and given a money value? These and similar questions are raised and answered in the case-law; we will shortly mention a few of the cases.

But first, in order to understand the workings of the modern general average system a little more clearly than can be accomplished through the reading of opinions which are in the main rather old, it is essential that we take a brief look at the work of a corps of specialists, the "general average adjusters," who actually perform the enormously intricate investigations and calculations behind the general average statement, and at the York-Antwerp Rules,[13a] which, despite their lack of formal legal status, function in fact as a sort of code governing the subject in modern times.

## The General Average Adjuster

§ 5–3. The actual work of preparing the adjustment in general average is performed by the "adjuster." [14] This specialist is, in this

12. The Star of Hope, 76 U.S. (9 Wall.) 203, 236 (1870).

13. The Star of Hope, *supra,* note 12, 76 U.S. (9 Wall.) at 228. See Lowndes & Rudolf § 242, where this dichotomy is criticized as somewhat inaccurate; it is useful, none the less, for a first approximation.

13a. See *infra,* § 5–5.

14. On the matters discussed here, see generally Winter, Marine Insurance 405–422 (3d ed. 1952); Dover, A Handbook to Marine Insurance 679 (1962). The procedure described is merely typical; as a matter of law, even the appointment of an adjuster

country, often associated with an insurance broker; the larger marine insurance brokerage houses all have one or more adjusters. In the normal course, when the master of a vessel considers that a "general average situation" has arisen, and that an adjustment will have to be stated, he notifies his owner, who in turn notifies the broker through whom insurance on the ship was placed. The broker's adjuster then takes over. It is interesting to note that, although an adjuster in this position is to some extent allied with the vessel interest, the members of this profession enjoy a very high reputation for fairness to ship and cargo alike.

The adjuster must, personally or through a representative, investigate the entire course of events on the basis of which general average contribution is to be claimed, with a view to determining whether, in the first place, a general average situation is to be taken to have occurred at all, and, if it has, which of the many losses and disbursements are to be classified as general average charges and which are to be borne by the interests on which they have fallen. Of prime interest to him will be the ship deck and engine logs, where actions taken should be fully recorded, and the radio log, where there will be a record of communications with salvors and others. Before the cargo is discharged at the port of destination, the adjuster makes a rough calculation of the contribution that is likely to be due from each shipment of cargo; he errs, if at all, on the side of overestimation, for one purpose of this calculation is the setting of the amount of the deposit [14a] to be exacted as a condition of delivering the cargo, and it is a great deal easier to make a refund later than it is to collect any excess from a large number of cargo owners. When this deposit has been paid by the cargo owner, and the cargo received, the cargo owner, if insured, can usually get a refund in full from his insurance carriers, who notify the adjuster that they have indemnified the cargo owner and now stand in his shoes so far as the adjustment is concerned. Perhaps more often, the insured cargo owner simply notifies his underwriter that a general average contribution may be due, and the underwriter gives, in lieu of a cash deposit, an "underwriter's guarantee"; the adjuster will usually accept this, and allow delivery of the cargo, looking to the insurance company for later payment. (The exaction of a cash deposit is not, however, unknown; in Hoskyn & Co. v. Silver Line,[15] the cargo interest alleged that a deposit of $125,000 had been required by the ship as a condition of delivery.)

is not essential to the accrual of the general average liability. Det Forenede Dampskibs Selskab v. Insurance Co. of North America, 31 F.2d 658, 1929 A.M.C. 581 (2d Cir. 1929), certiorari denied 280 U.S. 571, 50 S.Ct. 28 (1929). But it is the duty of the master, on the completion of a voyage on which a general average sacrifice of cargo has taken place, to procure an adjustment and to take security from other cargo before it is delivered; if he neglects this, the ship will be held for the whole amount. Heye v. North German Lloyd, 33 F. 60 (S.D.N.Y. 1887), affirmed 36 F. 705 (C.C.S.D.N.Y.1888).

14a. See Pineus, General Average Deposits, 4 Journal of Maritime Law and Commerce 619 (1973).

15. 63 F.Supp. 452, 467–8, 1943 A.M.C. 510 (S.D.N.Y.1943), affirmed 143 F.2d 462 (2d Cir. 1944), certiorari denied 323 U.S. 767, 65 S.Ct. 116 (1944).

Concurrently, the consignee is usually required to execute a "General Average Agreement", engaging to pay such sums as may be found due on adjustment.

(Parenthetically but importantly, it may be noted that virtually all marine insurance policies, however restricted their coverage in other regards, insure in full against general average losses,[16] so that a general average adjustment in the end is almost invariably in greatest part a distributing of loss among insurance companies. A few cargo owners still act as self-insurers.)

The adjuster must now enter on a very complicated set of calculations both of damage and of value, in order to determine balances due. We cannot go into the intricacies of all this, but the main aims are simple: to find a valuation for each *contributing interest*—vessel, freight at risk if any,[17] and each shipment of cargo—and to estimate as correctly as may be the value of each *general average sacrifice or expenditure*. The total contributory value and the total of the general average sacrifices and expenditures can be found by addition, and, just as in the simple example given above, the adjuster can then calculate the proportion or percentage which each interest should bear, and convert this to a dollar amount for each interest.

The final embodiment of his work is the "Statement of General Average." This commences with a "narrative" of the events giving rise to the claim for general average contribution. This may be followed by a copy of the "sea protest," filed by the master at the port of refuge and containing the master's account of the relevant happenings. Next may come extracts from ships' logs and more informal reports of master and chief engineer, reports of surveys of the vessel, documents establishing her valuation, and the like. Sacrifices and disbursements, described and valued, will then be set forth, and the contributing interests will be listed, with the contributory value of each, the amount it is to be assessed, and the balance owed by or to each interest.

§ 5–4. It will be seen that the adjuster must, in the course of his work, make determinations on all questions of law and fact, however difficult, that can possibly arise in a general average situation. It is rather rare that his determinations are questioned. When they are, the matter is usually settled informally. Sometimes a reference is arranged, advisory or binding, to some recognized authority. Negotiations usually proceed in a friendly spirit of give and take, for, as we have seen, the parties in interest are usually marine insurance companies.

It is a striking fact that litigation involving general average rarely reaches the courts any more. There have been perhaps thirty reported cases in the last twenty years, and these have been mostly concerned with the question whether general average was payable at all, and not with the details of adjustment. Using the Rules of

16. See *supra*, Chapter II, at note 103 *et seq.*

17. See *supra*, at note 6.

Practice of his Association,[18] and the insight and know-how derived from experience in a profession with a high *esprit de corps,* the adjuster performs a function which, in one sense, is judicial in character, settling claims on the facts and the law. If his profession did not exist, and his work came to the courts in great volume, they would undoubtedly find it a heavy burden to handle. But the adjusting profession does its job so well that the vast majority of the claims with which it deals are processed to the satisfaction of the community concerned, and the courts never hear of them. This phenomenon might be looked on—along with the growing practice of arbitration in all maritime cases—as part of a swing back to the medieval custom by which the members of the mercantile community adjusted their disputes among themselves, without recourse to the general judicial system.[19]

As a matter of law, in the absence of agreement, the "adjustment" has no binding effect, being advisory merely.[20] Any party could (though few do) go to court on the propriety of anything in the adjustment. Two cases, from different circuits, seem to diverge on the effect, as to the bindingness of the adjuster's determinations, of the cargo underwriter's having signed a standard agreement to pay "so much of the loss and expenses . . . as upon an adjustment of the same to be stated by . . . [the designated adjusters] . . . according to the provisions of the contract of affreightment and to the laws and usages applicable, may be shown by the statement to be a charge upon said cargo . . . " In Corrado Societa Anonima Di Navigazione v. L. Mundet & Son,[21] it was held that this was an agreement merely to pay such sum as might be due under the contract of affreightment, and law and usage; the adjustment was held to have no binding effect. The Second Circuit Court of Appeals, in Navigazione Generale Italiana v. Spencer Kellogg & Sons,[22] treated a similar clause in a somewhat less clear way; some language of the court might lend support to the view that the "agreement" was held to be an agreement to abide by all the determinations of the adjusters, but the opinion emphasizes that all the items allowed actually seemed

18. Reproduced in Lowndes & Rudolf § 991ff. These Rules of course change in minor particulars from time to time.

19. This passage is cited with approval and quoted in Cia. Atlantica Pacifica S.A. v. Humble Oil & Refining Co., 274 F.Supp. 884, 892, 1967 A.M.C. 1474, 1489 (D.Md.1967). See *supra,* Chapter I at note 13.

20. The Santa Anna Maria, 49 F. 878 (D.S.C.1892). See also United States v. Atlantic Mutual Ins. Co., 298 U.S. 483, 491, 56 S.Ct. 889, 891, 1936 A.M.C. 993 (1936), where the adjuster's statement is said to be nothing more "than a provisional estimate and calculation which his principal, the owner, was free to adopt or to put aside". This is doubtless true as a matter of law, but it suggests a less important position than the adjuster actually occupies.

21. 18 F.Supp. 37, 1936 A.M.C. 1740 (E.D.Pa.1936), affirmed 91 F.2d 726 (3d Cir. 1937), certiorari denied 302 U.S. 751, 58 S.Ct. 271 (1937).

22. 92 F.2d 41, 1937 A.M.C. 1506 (2d Cir. 1937), certiorari denied 302 U.S. 751, 58 S.Ct. 271 (1937), noted 16 Texas L.Rev. 257 (1938). But see Globe & Rutgers Fire Ins. Co. v. United States, 105 F.2d 160, 163, 1939 A.M.C. 912 (2d Cir. 1939).

proper, and that "no successful attack"[23] had been made on any of them. This opinion may merely mean, then, that an "agreement" of the sort quoted stipulates only that the adjustment shall be taken to be correct *prima facie*. If it means more than that, then it seems clear that at the least an ambiguous agreement is being pushed too far. On familiar principles, such an ambiguity, if it exists, ought to be resolved against the party who drew the agreement. Indeed, one might go further and say that the agreement is not ambiguous at all, but on its face only binds the signer to pay what is really due, ". . . according to the provisions of the contract of affreightment and to the laws and usages applicable . . . ."

In a recent case from the federal district court for Maryland, *prima facie* effectiveness, subject to rebuttal, has been given the statement of the adjuster, when such an agreement as the one in the foregoing paragraph has been entered into.[23a] This seems a thoroughly reasonable compromise, and has the effect of leaving open pure questions of law, since the "rebuttal" in such a case must consist not in the offering of testimony but in the tendering of legal argument.

### The York-Antwerp Rules—Applicable Law

**§ 5–5.** Law and practice on the adjustment of general average vary to some extent throughout the maritime world, and uniformity has long been desired. After some thirty years of discussion and experiment, a Conference of the Association for the Reform and Codification of the Law of Nations, held at Liverpool and attended by representatives of the shipping world, adopted the so-called York-Antwerp Rules of 1890.[24] These Rules never had the force of law, but were very widely adopted in bills of lading throughout the world, by the use of clauses incorporating them by reference, so that, in effect, a large proportion of the world's commerce came to be carried, as a matter of contract, under their terms.[25] These 1890 Rules, eighteen in number, did not embody a complete code of the subject, but dealt in the main with relatively narrow problems as to which dispute or variance existed at the time of their adoption.

In 1924, the 1890 Rules were supplemented and somewhat amended, and there were added a set of "lettered" rules, stating general principles.[26] In 1949, a third version was promulgated, known as

**23.** 92 F.2d at 45.

**23a.** Cia. Atlantica Pacifica S.A. v. Humble Oil & Refining Co., 274 F. Supp. 884, 896 *et seq.*, 1967 A.M.C. 1474, 1492 *et seq.* (D.Md.1967). See also Empire Stevedoring Co. v. Oceanic Adjusters Ltd., 315 F.Supp. 921, 1971 A.M.C. 795 (S.D.N.Y.1970).

**24.** Lowndes & Rudolf §§ 497–498; for text of all successive versions of the Rules, see *id.* at §§ 901 *et seq.* For accounts of the deliberations preceding promulgation of these and the later Rules, see Lowndes & Rudolf Chapter 10 §§ 481–529; Felde, *supra* note 3, 27 Tul.L.Rev. 427 *et seq.*

**25.** See Morrison S. S. Co. v. Greystoke Castle, [1947] A.C. 265, 296.

**26.** Lowndes & Rudolf §§ 509 *et seq.* For text of the 1924 Rules, see *ib.*, §§ 901 *et seq.*

the "York-Antwerp Rules, 1950." [27] These, like the 1924 Rules, consist of "lettered" rules dealing with general principles and "numbered rules" dealing with special problems. Very recently still another version has been adopted, the York-Antwerp Rules 1974.[27a]

It is important to keep in mind that none of the versions of these Rules is binding as law. Bills of lading may stipulate for any version, or for some of the Rules and not others, in one version, or even in more than one. Thus, a standard clause in American bills of lading in recent use read:

> "10. General average shall be adjusted, stated, and settled, according to Rules 1 to 15, inclusive, 17 to 22, inclusive, and Rule F of the York-Antwerp Rules 1924, at such port and place in the United States as may be selected by the Carrier, and as to matters not provided for by these Rules, according to the laws and usages at the port of New York." [28]

American commercial interests seem generally to have accepted the 1950 Rules in their entirety, and standard bills of lading issued in this country now stipulate for them without editing.[28a]

The tendency in courts and in the adjusters' profession is to defer to the Rules, and they are so nearly invariably found in bills of lading as to make an awareness of them necessary to the modern student of general average. In the pages that follow, we will include in the discussion not only the judicial treatment but also dispositions in the York-Antwerp Rules, where they contain anything relevant.

In the absence of contrary stipulation, the substantive law (including adjusters' customs) governing a general average adjustment is that of the port at which the voyage ends.[29] Bills of lading issued by American steamship lines usually contain a clause stipulating for adjustment according to the law and customs of the port of New York or of San Francisco.

27. For text, see Lowndes & Rudolf, *loc. cit. supra*, n. 26; Felde, *supra* note 3, 443 *et seq.;* 1949 A.M.C. 1683. In our text hereafter, the Rules will be referred to simply by number or letter.

27a. This version can be found in Healy & Sharpe, Admiralty: Cases & Materials, p. 830 (1974).

28. This in consequence of American dissatisfaction with some of the 1924 Rules; see Lowndes & Rudolf §§ 519 *et seq.*

28a. It is too early to say whether the 1974 Rules (*supra* at note 27a) will win a similar acceptance, though it is probable this will happen, given the smallness of the changes introduced.

29. National Board of Marine Underwriters v. Melchers, 45 F. 643 (E.D. Pa.1891); Lowndes & Rudolf, §§ 331 *et seq.* Normally, of course, this means the port of destination. (But see Lowndes & Rudolf, in the sections just cited, for variations). The Southern Prince, 47 F.Supp. 470, 1942 A.M.C. 1247 (S.D.N.Y.1942); see Charter Shipping Co. v. Bowring, Jones & Tidy, 281 U.S. 515, 50 S.Ct. 400, 1930 A.M.C. 1121 (1930); Note, 22 Harv.L. Rev. 611 (1909). For an additional complication, see Putnam, General Average Liability with Cargo for Successive Ports, 2 Colum.L.Rev. 275 (1902).

The connected cases of Charles Pfizer & Co. v. 912 Bags of Tartar and 58 Bags of Uva Ursi Leaves,[30] and Compania Trasatlantica v. Charles Pfizer & Co.,[31] are interesting in connection with several of the matters taken up in this and in the preceding section. General average was claimed against cargo, on the basis of sacrifices and expenses incurred by the ship in connection with a stranding. The ship sought to exact a bond, as condition of delivery of the cargo. The court, in the first case,[32] held that, since the bill of lading stipulated for adjustment in Barcelona, the ship could insist that the bond contain a similar stipulation. But the tendered bond went further and required the admission of matters of fact; it also failed to refer to certain of the York-Antwerp Rules, which were contracted for in the bill of lading. The court held that such a bond could not be required as a prerequisite to delivery of the cargo. Thus matters stood; no bond, seemingly, was given, but the carrier proceeded to an adjustment in Spain, and again sued for the contribution shown as due by the adjustment.[33] This time, however, the court dismissed the claim because the Spanish adjuster apparently used *all* the York-Antwerp rules, instead of Nos. 1–15 and 17–22, as stipulated in the bill of lading.[34] The burden of proof as to the payability of general average, said the court, is on the party claiming the contribution; the court therefore refused to presume that the variance in rules applied made no difference in the result.

### The Peril—The "Voluntary" Sacrifice—the "Common Venture"

**§ 5–6.** Sacrifices and expenditures incurred merely to help a ship along do not come under general average; extrication from *peril* must be the motive of what is done.[35] But the peril need not be already upon the ship in order to make actions taken to escape it compensable in general average;[36] timely action is to be encouraged, and a wide latitude is given the master in making up his mind as to the degree of peril existing and the necessity of the steps taken.[37] It has, however, been held that, where a peril does not exist at all, a reasonable belief that it does cannot convert the steps taken to avert it into general average acts; in the very case[38] the master had ordered

30. 40 F.Supp. 123, 1941 A.M.C. 1338 (E.D.N.Y.1941).

31. 96 F.Supp. 217, 1951 A.M.C. 699 (E.D.N.Y.1951).

32. *Supra*, note 30.

33. *Supra*, note 31.

34. See *supra* at note 28.

35. Columbian Ins. Co. v. Ashby & Stribling, 38 U.S. (13 Pet.) 331, 338 (1839); Lowndes & Rudolf §§ 48 *et seq.*

36. Aktieselskabet Fido v. Lloyd Brasileiro, 283 F. 62, 71 (2d Cir. 1922), certiorari denied 260 U.S. 737, 43 S.Ct. 9 (1922), (general average status accorded to loss caused by delay in unloading overheated coal, though fire had not yet broken out); Lowndes & Rudolf § 49.

37. The Star of Hope, 76 U.S. (9 Wall.) 203, 230 (1870); Willcox, Peck & Hughes v. American Smelting & Refining Co., 210 F. 89 (S.D.N.Y.1913).

38. Ravenscroft v. United States, 1936 A.M.C. 696 (E.D.N.Y.1936), affirmed 88 F.2d 418 (2d Cir. 1937), certiorari denied 301 U.S. 707, 57 S.Ct. 940 (1937). See also Lowndes & Rudolf § 48. But *cf.* The Wordsworth, 88 F. 313 (S.D.

water forced into a ship's hold under the mistaken belief that fire existed there, and cargo damaged by the water claimed a general average contribution, which was denied. The result of this case seems hard, for it is certainly arguable that the same equity which is said to underlie general average as a whole ought to require contribution from all interests to those whose property is injured by steps taken in good faith to avert a peril thought to exist. York-Antwerp Rule A (1974) might naturally be construed to include such a case within general average:

> "There is a general average act when, and only when, any extraordinary sacrifice or expenditure is intentionally and reasonably made or incurred for the common safety for the purpose of preserving from peril the property involved in a common maritime adventure."

A "purpose of preserving from peril" surely may exist, even though a mistake may be made as to the existence of the peril.

Sometimes it may be questioned whether the position of difficulty in which the ship finds herself is to be regarded as dangerous enough to justify its being qualified as "peril." In The Alcona,[39] a ship stranded on a river bottom lightened herself by transferring cargo to a barge, and was then floated with the help of tugs; in denying her claim that these expenses were of a general average nature, the court insisted on the presence of peril as a constituent of the general average situation, and did not find this ingredient in the vessel's unfortunate predicament. Yet, in Navigazione Generale Italiana v. Spencer Kellogg & Sons,[40] the court said ". . . when a vessel is stranded she and her cargo are practically always in a substantial peril."[41] This, if intended as a statement of fact, is much too broad, and there seems no reason for stating such a proposition as a conclusion or presumption, overriding the facts of each case.[42] The Spencer Kellogg opinion contains, however, some interesting summing-up on "peril":

> "There must be fair reason to regard a vessel in peril in order to require a contribution in general average. While the courts in some cases have used expressions indicating that both in general average and in salvage cases it is essential that the property at risk be subject to an immediately

N.Y.1898). In the latter case, cargo was damaged when the master (informed that the forepeak was flooded and erroneously believing this was due to a hole in the ship) opened sluices and drained the forepeak. The Ravenscroft court distinguished The Wordsworth on the ground that in that case a peril (the flooded forepeak) had actually existed, though the master made a mistake as to the exact origin of the peril and the best means of averting it.

39. 9 F. 172 (E.D.Ill.1881).

40. 92 F.2d 41, 1937 A.M.C. 1506 (2d Cir. 1937), certiorari denied 302 U.S. 751, 58 S.Ct. 271 (1937).

41. 92 F.2d at 44.

42. *Cf.* United States v. Wessel, Duval & Co., 123 F.Supp. 318, 1954 A.M.C. 2070 (S.D.N.Y.1954).

impending danger, we think the 'imminency' of the peril is not the critical test. If the danger be real and substantial, a sacrifice or expenditure made in good faith for the common interest is justified, even though the advent of any catastrophe may be distant or indeed unlikely. In pointing out the broad discretion which must be allowed in such cases to the master of the vessel, Judge Hough said in Willcox, Peck & Hughes v. American Smelting & Refining Co. (D.C.) 210 F. 89, 91: 'If he finds danger in a landlocked harbor, in shallows, at anchor, or moored to a wharf, it should be no answer to register a landsman's opinion as to the necessary absence of danger at such a place.'

"As Curtis, J., said in Lawrence v. Minturn, 17 How. 100, 109, 15 L.Ed. 58, where the necessity of a jettison of cargo was questioned: 'It is true, that when it was actually made, the sea was smooth, and the ship in no immediate danger. But it satisfactorily appears, that these boilers and chimneys could not be thrown overboard, without the greatest risk, when there was any considerable sea. To require delay until a storm, would be, in effect, to prohibit the sacrifice.' "[43]

§ 5–7. An objection of quite another tenor has been raised when the peril is so great that the whole adventure must necessarily be lost unless the sacrifice is made. It has been argued that such a sacrifice cannot be said to be "voluntary," or even a "sacrifice," in view of the fact that the loss of the "sacrificed" property, along with everything else, would have occurred in any case. This difficulty has been felt in cases of "voluntary" stranding, where a vessel that would have been lost, with her cargo, if she had not gone ashore, took timely action and deliberately ran aground, saving the cargo but being herself severely damaged, sometimes to the point of not being worth floating and repairing. The most puzzling case of this sort is the one in which the vessel would inevitably have gone ashore, and all the master did was select the most advantageous place for taking the ground. It does, indeed, seem a paradox to treat as a "sacrifice," made for the benefit of the whole venture, the mere making of such a choice. Yet the American cases go a long way in that direction. In Barnard v. Adams,[44] the vessel, with cargo aboard, had apparently been in desperate straits, almost certain to be driven on rocks and broken up. Her master ran her on shore at a less dangerous point; she was not worth refloating after the storm had passed, but some of the cargo was saved, and against this cargo the ship made a claim for general average. The Supreme Court, over a vigorous dissent, allowed the claim, saying:

"It is evident from these propositions, that the assertion so much relied on in the argument, namely, 'that if the peril be inevitable there can be no contribution,' is a mere truism,

43. 92 F.2d at 43.

44. 51 U.S. (10 How.) 270 (1850).

as the hypothesis of the case requires that the common peril, though imminent, shall be successfully avoided. Those who urge it must therefore mean something else. And it seems, when more carefully stated, to be this, 'that if the common peril was of such a nature that the "*jactus*," or thing cast away to save the rest, would have perished anyhow, or perished "inevitably," even if it had not been selected to suffer in place of the whole, there can be no contribution.' If this be the meaning of this proposition, and we can discover no other, it is a denial of the whole doctrine upon which the claim for general average has its foundation. For the master of the ship would not be justified in casting a part of the cargo into the sea, or slipping his anchor, or cutting away his masts, or stranding his vessel, unless compelled to it by the necessity of the case, in order to save both ship and cargo, or one of them, from an imminent peril, which threatened their common destruction. The necessity of the case must compel him to choose between the loss of the whole and part; but, however metaphysicians may stumble at the assertion, it is this forced choice which is necessary to justify the master in making a sacrifice (as it is called) of any part for the whole." [45]

If the stranding, however, is in substantially the same place as it would have been even if the master had not ordered it, the right to general average contribution has been denied.[46]

The York-Antwerp Rules (1950) made the following provision for voluntary stranding cases:

"RULE V. *Voluntary Stranding.*

"When a ship is intentionally run on shore, and the circumstances are such that if that course were not adopted she would inevitably drive on shore or on rocks, no loss or damage caused to the ship, cargo and freight or any of them by such intentional running on shore shall be made good as general average, but loss or damage incurred in refloating such a ship shall be allowed as general average.

"In all other cases where a ship is intentionally run on shore for the common safety, the consequent loss or damage shall be allowed as general average."

The 1974 Rules [46a] change this materially:

"Rule V. *Voluntary Standing.* When a ship is intentionally run on shore for the common safety, whether or not she might have been driven on shore, the consequent loss or damage shall be allowed in general average."

45. 51 U.S. (10 How.) at 303–304. See also Columbian Ins. Co. v. Ashby & Stribling, 38 U.S. (13 Pet.) 331 (1839); Lowndes & Rudolf §§ 209 *et seq.*

46. The Major William H. Tantum, 49 F. 252 (2d Cir. 1891).

46a. See *supra* at note 27a.

This would seem to reaffirm, for shipping conducted under the 1974 Rules, the doctrine of the American cases on voluntary stranding. The more general theoretical point, as to the possibility of "sacrifice" when loss is inevitable anyway, remains. Perhaps, the solution is to be sought in the fact that it is not easy, at the time or after, to make an accurate judgment as to whether loss was "inevitable" or merely highly probable, and that it would be undesirable to put a master in the position, at the time when his ship and cargo are in the greatest danger, of having to choose between chancing it a little longer or incurring a certain loss for which no general average contribution could be had. The unfettering of the master's judgment from considerations as to who will pay is one of the main merits alleged for general average,[47] and it may seem that this is most clearly needful when the peril is greatest. All this is, however, subject to the reservations, as to the actual motivating impact of general average doctrine, alluded to at the end of this Chapter.[47a]

**§ 5–8.** Another interesting problem raising a similar theoretical question arises when water is poured into the hold to put out a fire in the cargo. As to cargo not on fire nor threatened immediately by the fire, but damaged by the water, there is little problem; such damage is clearly of a general average nature.[48] But what of the cargo actually on fire, or so situated as to be certain to catch fire? Can it claim a general average contribution for damage done to it by the water? Under the York-Antwerp Rules (1974) the matter is provided for as follows:

> "RULE III. *Extinguishing Fire on Shipboard.*
>
> "Damage done to a ship and cargo, or either of them, by water or otherwise, including damage by beaching or scuttling a burning ship, in extinguishing a fire on board the ship, shall be made good as general average; except that no compensation shall be made for damage by smoke or heat however caused.[49]

Though "peril" is an essential ingredient of general average, and the peril must be a common one rather than one threatening a particular interest, it need not menace all interests equally. Thus where ore and nitrates were in the same cargo, it was held that, though the nitrates were in greater peril than the ore, the latter interest had to contribute.[50]

47. Lowndes & Rudolf § 11.

47a. See *infra*, § 5–16.

48. The Roanoke, 59 F. 161 (7th Cir. 1893), adopting, on this point, the opinion of the District Court, 46 F. 297 (E.D.Wis.1891); see also The Ronaoke, 53 F. 270 (E.D.Wis.1892).

49. See also The Rapid Transit, 52 F. 320 (D.Wash.1892); Lowndes & Rudolf § 130 *et seq.*

50. Willcox, Peck & Hughes v. American Smelting & Refining Co., 210 F. 89 (S.D.N.Y.1913).

Another fire case raised a further interesting question in regard to the voluntariness of the sacrifice. In Ralli v. Troop,[51] fire aboard was put out by drastic measures (pouring in large quantities of water, scuttling) ordered not by the master but by port authorities. The court held that the damage sustained as a result of these acts was not a general average, since neither the master nor anyone acting under his authority had ordered what was done. The reasoning was, in part, that the port authorities, unlike the master, could not be taken to have acted primarily for the purpose of saving the vessel and cargo (the essential animus of general average), but rather for the purpose of preventing the spread of fire in the port.[52] If the action of the fire department is taken for the benefit of the ship and cargo, and if the master or someone else in authority invokes this action, it has been held that Ralli does not apply, and that damage done is of a general average nature.[53] But the Ralli rule has been held to prevent the arising of a general average claim for the voluntary grounding of a burning vessel, when she had already been "seized", though only theoretically, by a federal court, and hence was not in the lawful possession of those who grounded her.[53a]

**§ 5–9.** Several cases have denied general average contribution because the sacrifice made did not have the purpose of saving a *common* venture from disaster. In Dabney v. New England Mutual Marine Ins. Co.,[54] the claim was against an insurer, presumably under a policy insuring only against general average loss, for the value of oranges thrown overboard so as to make room for persons taken aboard from another vessel that was in sinking condition. Admitting (in some rather fly-blown rhetoric) the moral duty the captain was under to take the people aboard, the majority of the court held, in effect, that the jettison was "proximately caused" by the fulfilment of this duty rather than by the taking of action to avert a sea peril threatening the common venture subsisting between the receiving ship and her cargo, and denied general average status to the sacrifice. There was a vigorous dissent.

Where one vessel is towing another under a towage contract, and the towing vessel sacrifices the towed vessel to save herself, the towed vessel cannot recover under general average, since the two are not bound up in a "common adventure." [55] Where, however, the vessel in tow is a mere barge, under the control, for all purposes, of the

51. 157 U.S. 386, 15 S.Ct. 657 (1895). The case is criticized in Lowell, General Average, 9 Harv.L.Rev. 185 (1895).

52. 157 U.S. at 419–420, 15 S.Ct. at 670.

53. The Northern No. 30, 24 F.2d 975, 1928 A.M.C. 606 (E.D.N.C.1928); The Beatrice, 36 F.2d 99, 1924 A.M.C. 914 (S.D.N.Y.1924). But see The Moran No. 16, 40 F.2d 466, 1930 A.M.C. 631 (2d Cir. 1930).

53a. Tampa Tugs and Towing, Inc. v. M/V Sandanger, 242 F.Supp. 576, 582, 1965 A.M.C. 1771, 1780 (S.D.Calif. 1965).

54. 96 Mass. (14 Allen) 300 (1867).

55. The J. P. Donaldson, 167 U.S. 599, 17 S.Ct. 951 (1897); see also The John Perkins, 13 Fed.Cas. 702, No. 7,360 (C. C.D.Mass.1857).

master of the towing vessel, it would seem that the venture is actually one, and that the same principles of general average should apply as in the case of cargo carried on a single ship. This is the holding in the 1962 case of S. C. Loveland Co. v. United States,[56] and seems eminently correct.

### Some Typical General Average Sacrifices and Expenditures

**§ 5–10.** It is believed that the student's feel for the subject of general average can be heightened by a review of a few of the more typical sorts of sacrifices and expenditures. These may affect either cargo or ship.

Jettison, or casting overboard, is the classic instance.[57] Jettison of cargo to lighten the vessel is the usual sort, but cargo may be thrown overboard for some other purpose—*e. g.*, to clear the way to a fire, so that it may be extinguished. On the ship's side, a mast or other structure may be cut away and jettisoned.[58]

The jettison of cargo carried on deck is not in general compensable, partly because it is hard to establish whether such action was really voluntary, and partly because it is so easy a step that there has been fear lest the master order it unnecessarily.[59] The well-recognized exception is as to cargo carried on deck in accordance with established custom in the particular trade.[60] The York-Antwerp Rules (1890) provided that no jettison of deck cargo should be made good, thus embodying the general rule without the exception.[61] But the 1924 revision, which has been carried over *verbatim* into the 1974 version, in effect restored the exception:

> "RULE I. *Jettison of Cargo.*
>
> "No jettison of cargo shall be made good as general average, unless such cargo is carried in accordance with the recognized custom of the trade."

56. 207 F.Supp. 450, 1963 A.M.C. 260 (E.D.Pa.1962). In Sacramento Navigation Co. v. Salz, 273 U.S. 326, 47 S.Ct. 368, 1927 A.M.C. 397 (1927) a carrier gave bills of lading for carriage of cargo on a barge both owned and towed by him. The Court held the contract one of "affreightment" rather than "towage", and applied the Harter Act (see *supra* Chapter III, Part II, n. 27.) The shipper and carrier, in such a case, seem bound up in just the sort of "common venture" required by general average concepts; the mere physical duality of the transporting means seems an irrelevant distinction. This suggestion seems first to have been made by Prof. Robinson. Robinson, Admiralty 778 (1939).

57. See *supra* at note 1. The case of the prophet Jonah is customarily mentioned in this connection; see Lange v. Emery Co., 18 F.2d 744, 746, 1927 A.M.C. 844 (2d Cir. 1927), certiorari denied 275 U.S. 540, 48 S.Ct. 36 (1927).

58. Patten v. Darling, 18 Fed.Cas. 1306, No. 10,812 (C.C.D.Mass.1859); The Margarethe Blanca, 14 F. 59 (E.D.Pa. 1882).

59. Lowndes & Rudolf §§ 106 *et seq.*; see Lawrence v. Minturn, 58 U.S. (17 How.) 100, 113 (1855). On the whole subject, see Deutsch, Deck Cargo, 27 Calif.L.Rev. 535 (1939).

60. The John H. Cannon, 51 F. 46 (D. Md.1892); Nicaraguan Long Leaf Pine Lumber Co. v. Moody, 211 F.2d 715, 1954 A.M.C. 658 (5th Cir. 1954); Lowndes & Rudolf §§ 113–122.

61. Rule I (1890).

This means that where, as in certain lumber trades, cargo is customarily carried on deck, such cargo, if thrown overboard in a general average situation, is entitled to contribution. The recent case of Nicaraguan Long Leaf Pine Lumber Co. v. Moody [62] illustrates the point. Although a custom to carry on deck was regarded by the court as having been satisfactorily proved, the bill of lading provided: "All lumber loaded on deck at shipper's risk." It was held that this stipulation (which would doubtless have immunized the carrier against successful suit if the lumber had been lost simply through his negligence) had no effect on the right to general average, so that the owner of jettisoned lumber was granted contribution.

Damage done to the ship in accomplishing a jettison of cargo is a general average sacrifice, as is damage done (to cargo or ship) by water entering the holds, when they are opened to get out the scapegoat cargo.[63] Generally, any damage caused by the performance of a general average act is itself compensable in general average. York-Antwerp Rule 2 (1974) provides:

> "RULE II. *Damage by Jettison and Sacrifice for the Common Safety.*
>
> "Damage done to a ship and cargo, or either of them, by or in consequence of a sacrifice made for the common safety, and by water which goes down a ship's hatches opened or other opening made for the purpose of making a jettison for the common safety, shall be made good as general average."

As we have seen, damage done to ship or cargo through measures taken to extinguish fire is of a general average nature.

Any damage done to a ship or her engines through using them in some extraordinary way for the purpose of extricating the ship and cargo from peril may be a general average sacrifice.[64] Payments made by the ship to salvors are also included, as expenditures.[65]

One interesting form of quasi-expenditure is the incurring of a liability to a third party. Where, *e. g.*, the ship can only avert disaster by running into a pier and damaging it, thus becoming liable

62. 211 F.2d 715, 1954 A.M.C. 658 (5th Cir. 1954).

63. Lange v. Emery Co., 18 F.2d 744, 1927 A.M.C. 844 (2d Cir. 1927), certiorari denied 275 U.S. 540, 48 S.Ct. 36 (1927); Lowndes & Rudolf § 129.

64. Willcox, Peck & Hughes v. American Smelting & Refining Co., 210 F. 89 (S.D.N.Y.1913); see International Navigation Co. v. Atlantic Mutual Ins. Co., 100 F. 304 (S.D.N.Y.1900), affirmed 108 F. 987 (2d Cir. 1901), certiorari denied 181 U.S. 623, 21 S.Ct. 926 (1901) Lowndes & Rudolf § 180. York-Antwerp Rule VII (1974) limits such claims to cases where the ship is actually ashore, and disallows other claims arising from working ships machinery.

65. McAndrews v. Thatcher, 70 U.S. (3 Wall.) 347, 365–6 (1866); the editors of Lowndes & Rudolf say (§ 244) that non-contract salvage is not, strictly speaking, a general average expense, but rather a charge secured by a lien imposed ratably on vessel, cargo, and freight. The net effect is about the same. *Cf. infra,* Chapter VIII.

to the pier owner for the damage, the resultant monetary loss is treated as a general average expenditure.[66]

An important and difficult set of problems arises as to the inclusion of expenses in the "port of refuge." Quite often the damage sustained at sea is such that it is unsafe to go on, and the vessel puts in at some intermediate port for repairs. In going in and leaving, she incurs certain expenses which are allowed as general average, under the York-Antwerp Rules and in the American cases, and while laid up she runs up bills for provisions, wages, and so on, which also go in the adjustment as ship's expenses.[67] Where purely temporary repairs are necessary to enable the vessel to go on, the cost of these is also allowable.[68]

**§ 5–11.** General average *expenditures*, comprising port of refuge expenses of this kind as well as payments to salvors, and the like, are perhaps the largest part today of those losses compensable by general average contribution. Almost always, the money is laid out by the ship. Sometimes, as in the case of crew's wages while the ship is safely moored in the port of refuge, the "peril" concept is stretched close to the breaking point. Sometimes, as in the hiring of tugs to help a vessel off a strand, the line is a thin one between relief from peril and mere helping through difficulty. The courts should be vigilant to see that the extension by analogy of the principle of general average does not encroach upon the equally valid and much more important principle that the shipowner is under a duty to employ whatever means are needful to fulfil his contract of carriage, even though difficulties of various sorts may result in its costing him a little more than he had hoped.

Damage to cargo through discharging or other handling in the port of refuge is allowed as general average, but decay owing to the delay has been disallowed on the highly dubious ground that "all men know that delay does not cause decay." [69]

66. Austin Friars S. S. Co. v. Spillers & Bakers, [1915], 3 K.B. 586; The Seapool, [1934] p. 53.

67. Hobson v. Lord, 92 U.S. 397 (1876); United States v. Los Angeles Soap Co., 83 F.2d 875, 1936 A.M.C. 850 (9th Cir. 1936); York-Antwerp Rules, (1974) Rule X; Lowndes & Rudolf §§ 280 *et seq.*; Carver, Expenses at a Port of Refuge, 8 L.Q.Rev. 229 (1892).

68. See The Queen, 28 F. 755 (S.D.N.Y. 1886); Shoe v. George F. Craig & Co., 189 F. 227 (E.D.Pa.1911), modified on other grounds, 194 F. 678 (3d Cir. 1912).

69. Hills Bros. Co. v. United States, 39 F.2d 136, 1930 A.M.C. 623 (S.D.N.Y. 1930). In Anglo-Argentine Agency v. Temperley Shipping Co., [1899] 2 Q.B. 403, cattle were shipped from Buenos Aires for the U.K.; the contract of carriage provided that the steamer was not to call *en route* at Brazilian or Continental ports, since to do so would make it impossible to land the cattle in the U.K., under then applicable disease control regulations. Owing to a leak, the master put into Bahia. Barred from the U.K., the cattle had to be sold at a loss in Antwerp. This decline in value was held to be general average.

York-Antwerp Rule C (1974) now governs most situations. It provides:

"Only such losses, damages or expenses which are the direct consequence of the general average act shall be allowed as general average.

It should be noted that such a ruling operates to bar from general average one of the most common cargo claims; see *supra,* § 5–2, for the dominant importance of ship's claims in modern general average.

Interest, commissions and other special fees are commonly allowed the ship for general average expenditures she makes.[69a]

Of relatively recent emergence is the notion of "substituted expenses." York-Antwerp Rule F provides:

> "Any extra expense incurred in place of another expense which would have been allowable as general average shall be deemed to be general average and so allowed without regard to the saving, if any, to other interests, but only up to the amount of the general average expense avoided."

Thus, where the cost of being towed to the port of destination—not normally a general average act—is less than the expenses of staying in the port of refuge to await repair—which are usually allowable in general average—the doctrine of "substituted expenses" would allow the towing cost as a "substitute" for the port of refuge costs, thus saving money all around.[70]

### Time and Place as of Which Values are Calculated

**§ 5–12.** The York-Antwerp Rules (1974) are clear on this point:

> "RULE G. General average shall be adjusted as regards both loss and contribution upon the basis of values at the time and place when and where the adventure ends.
>
> "This rule shall not affect the determination of the place at which the average statement is to be made up." [71]

Thus, the property liable to contribute in general average is valued for this purpose as of its arrival at the port of destination.

An interesting result ensues when property which would otherwise have to contribute is lost *en route,* subsequent to the general average act. Obviously, there is nothing left on which to contribute.

"Loss or damage sustained by the ship or cargo through delay, whether on the voyage or subsequently, such as demurrage, and any indirect loss whatsoever, such as loss of market, shall not be admitted as general average."

**69a.** Moore-McCormack Lines v. The Esso Camden, 244 F.2d 198, 202, 1957 A.M.C. 971, 975 (2d Cir. 1957); Oliver J. Olson & Co. v. American Steamship Marine Leopard, 356 F.2d 728, 1966 A.M.C. 1064 (9th Cir. 1966).

**70.** Lowndes & Rudolf §§ 311–312. The "substituted expenses" doctrine raises questions of too great intricacy for extended discussion here; see Hugg v. Baltimore & Cuba Smelting & Mining Co., 35 Md. 414 (1872); Earnmoor S. S. Co. v. New Zealand Ins. Co., 73 F. 867 (N.D.Cal.1896), affirmed 79 F. 368 (9th Cir. 1897); Shoe v. George F. Craig & Co., 194 F. 678 (3d Cir. 1912); Wilson v. Bank of Victoria [1867] 2 Q.B. 203. Summarily, the sparse case law leaves the doctrine of "substituted expenses" in a cloudy state. Consequently, an attempt is usually made to get agreement in advance on the substitution; see The Plow City, 23 F.Supp. 548, 1938 A.M.C. 1265 (E.D. Pa.1938).

**71.** See also Rule XVII.

Where an entire venture, ship and cargo, is so lost, after general average sacrifices have been made, no adjustment can be drawn up, for there are no contributory values. Where the sacrifices have been of physical property at risk—by jettison and the like—this result is self-evidently equitable; everybody has lost all he had, and all are therefore on a plane of equality. Some commentators have felt a difficulty when the general average acts have in part consisted in the spending of money by the shipowner.[72] A subsequent total loss of ship and cargo leaves him out of pocket with nobody to look to for contribution, unless he is given an *in personam* right against the cargo owner.

A fairly recent British case (as recency goes in this field) was decided in the Court of Appeal against the claim of the shipowner who sought personal general average contribution from cargo owners for port of refuge expenses followed by total loss of ship and cargo after the voyage was resumed. The Court of Appeal relied on Rule 17 of the York-Antwerp Rules, which was incorporated in the bill of lading.[73] The lower court [74] had rendered the same decision on the basis of common law; the judges in the Court of Appeal expressly declined to consider this ground.

A connected question would arise if an attempt were made to enforce against the owners of cargo a claim for contribution to make up the excess of general average expenditures over arrived value—to enforce, in other words, a general average contribution greater than one hundred percent. Such a claim, if ever made, would require a re-searching of the whole theory of general average. Its allowance, it seems, would have to rest on the theory that the master acts as an "agent" for all parties in making the expenditure—one of the bases on which general average has been sought to be rested. But this "agency" is a mere fiction, set up to explain the traditional rules of general average; [75] like all fictions, it is malleable, and one may still

72. E. g., Carver, Carriage of Goods by Sea §§ 949–954 (12th ed., 1971); Lowndes & Rudolf (§§ 343 *et seq.*). Summarily, there seems to be no significant case authority for recovery of general average on such facts. The British cases seem clearly to have rejected it. See authorities cited in Lowndes & Rudolf, § 954.

73. Chellew v. Royal Commission on Sugar Supply, [1922] 1 K.B. 12; followed and applied in Green Star Shipping Co. v. London Assur. [1933] 1 K. B. 378.

74. Chellew v. Royal Commission on Sugar Supply, [1921] 2 K.B. 627.

75. The process is well described in Lowndes & Rudolf § 40:

"Such considerations and even phrases as natural justice or general utility as the basis of rights between contracting parties, though no doubt secretly underlying the decisions of our judges, do not ordinarily appear on the surface so frequently as the familiar medieval notions of implied contracts or implied agency. Hence, in proportion as the subject of general average came to be more familiar, it seems to have been felt to be more consonant to the spirit of the English common law, that, in seeking to place this right of contribution on a secure basis, some implied contract or implied agency should, if possible, be found for it to rest on. Several such easily presented themselves. It might be supposed, for instance, that, at the time of shipping or entering into the contract for shipping the goods, all

ask: "To what does the fictitious 'agency' extend? To the creation of a personal liability on the part of the cargo owner, or merely to the creation of a charge on cargo, limited by its value?"[76] The operations of general average law up to now can be explained perfectly well on the basis of the latter, more limited sort of "agency."

Strongly counter to the claim would be the theory that general average doctrine is to be explained on the ground of unjust enrichment;[77] the unjust enrichment of the consignee can extend no further than the value of what he receives.

To the present writers, it seems that the subjection of the consignees of cargo to claims for contribution over and above the arrived value of cargo would create endless complications, not the least of which would be the effect on the acceptability of bills of lading if the transferee had to apprehend that he might be purchasing not an asset but a liability (and perhaps even quite a large liability, if expenditures had been heavy and little was saved). There is no "principle" favoring such a result, for the supposed "principles" are merely fictions, elaborated to explain a peculiar legal institution coming down from antiquity. What such a claim would involve would be an extrapolation, far beyond its traditional scope of operation, of a rule

shippers impliedly contract with the shipowner and with each other, that the master shall have authority in case of danger to make all needful sacrifices, to the expense of which they, the shippers, will contribute their share; or it may be supposed that a similar engagement is made between the parties, at the moment of danger, treating them as if on the spot, as they originally were; or, again, if an implied agency is preferred, the master may be supposed to have, in virtue of his office, an authority to do for each cargo-owner, as well as for the shipowner, whatever any one of those parties would have had the duty or the power to do had he been on the spot; so that the master's act should on each occasion be taken to be and treated as if it were, the act of his appropriate principal."

Obviously, concepts arrived at in this way cannot serve as a basis of inference!

76. *Cf.* Bark San Fernando v. Jackson, 12 F. 341 (E.D.La.1882), where the court said: "The obligation of the cargo to contribute, in a proper case of general average, is a maritime obligation for which the cargo is bound, but not the consignees. When the cargo is delivered there is an implied obligation, or, if a bond is taken, an express obligation, on the part of the consignees to contribute the share due by the cargo so received by them." This chimes completely with the holding, in Det Forenede Dampskibs Selskab v. Insurance Co. of North America, 31 F.2d 658, 1929 A.M.C. 581 (2d Cir. 1929), certiorari denied 280 U.S. 571, 50 S.Ct. 28 (1929), that the right to bring suit for general average arises "upon the implied obligation at the termination of the venture and acceptance of the goods . . . ."

77. See Felde, *supra* note 3, 413. The unjust enrichment theory is certainly adequate to explain the whole of general average law and practice, without recourse to fictitious "contracts" and "agencies." Strong analogical support for this theory is to be found in the recent case of Lambros Seaplane Base v. The Batory, 215 F.2d 228, 1954 A.M.C. 1789 (2d Cir. 1954), where the court held that no claim for salvage lay in the absence of the acceptance of the property by the owner, on the ground that "acceptance of the benefit" creates the personal liability. General average and salvage are closely connected; at the very least, the Batory case shows that there is nothing incomprehensible or anomalous in a liability to pay for action taken to save one's property, limited by the value of the property and based on the "benefit received."

which is, whatever its merits as applied up to now, something of an anomaly in law.[78]

### The Effect of Fault

§ 5–13. It has been said that there can be no general average contribution when the peril arises through the fault of some party to the adventure; it is probably more exact to say that the party at fault cannot claim contribution. Though the fault of the shipper of cargo may once in a while come into play, the usual case in which the issue arises is one in which the fault which has necessitated the general average sacrifice is that of the ship.

The American law, before the passage of the Harter Act, gave no general average right to the ship through whose fault the peril arose,[79] and, from the same public policy which struck down clauses exonerating the ship from liability to the cargo for negligence,[80] it followed that a bill of lading clause giving the ship such a right would have been invalid. When the Harter Act was passed, the contention was made that its third section, by exonerating the shipowner from liability (under certain conditions) for cargo damage due to negligence in the navigation and management of the ship, had at the same time automatically removed the bar against his being entitled to general average contribution where his negligence in these respects had created the peril. In The Irrawaddy,[81] the Supreme Court rejected this contention, holding that, of its own force, the Harter Act had made no change in the antecedent rule as to general average, and that, as a matter of law, the ship at fault had no right to general average contribution. The next step taken by the vessel interests was, as might have been predicted, the inclusion of a clause in bills of lading, providing that, where the general average situation arose through negligence of the ship, from the effects of which she would be exonerated by the Harter Act, her owners having exercised due diligence to make her seaworthy, general average was to be payable; this clause came to be known as the Jason clause, after the case which finally held it valid.[82] The reasoning of the Jason opinion was that, while

78. The specialness of general average, and the fallacy of supposing its doctrines to be derivative from "principles" of high abstractness, is decisively shown by the fact that no similar regimen prevails in any other branch of law, though there are undoubtedly many situations in which the sacrifice of a part (or the incurring of an extraordinary expenditure) is performed for the benefit of some whole. See Ralli v. Troop, 157 U.S. 386, 405, 15 S.Ct. 657, 664 (1895); note, The Applicability of General Average to Aircraft, 47 Colum.L.Rev. 1203 (1947). We have to do in this field with a special dispensation of sea-law, no more suitable than is the maritime lien for elaborate extension by inference and analogy.

79. See The Portsmouth, 76 U.S. (9 Wall.) 682 (1870).

80. Liverpool & Great Western Steam Co. v. Phenix Ins. Co., 129 U.S. 397, 9 S.Ct. 469 (1889).

81. 171 U.S. 187, 18 S.Ct. 831 (1898); see also The Mary F. Barrett, 279 F. 329 (3d Cir. 1922), noted 11 Calif.L. Rev. 24 (1922).

82. The Jason, 225 U.S. 32, 32 S.Ct. 560 (1912).

the third section of the Harter Act had not of its own force changed the law of general average, it had in effect abolished the public policy against contractual stipulations relieving the ship from the consequences of her negligence in navigation and management, thus removing any objection to a bill of lading provision stipulating for general average in this situation.

The Jason clause, in some form, is now standard in all bills of lading. The following is the new-style version in use in bills covering carriage under Cogsa: [83]

> "In the event of accident, danger, damage, or disaster, before or after commencement of the voyage resulting from any cause whatsoever, whether due to negligence or not, for which, or for the consequence of which, the Carrier is not responsible by statute, contract or otherwise, the goods, shippers, consignees, or owners of the goods shall contribute with the Carrier in general average to the payment of any sacrifices, losses, or expenses of a general average nature that may be made or incurred, and shall pay salvage and special charges incurred in respect of the goods."

This clause is, of course, so drafted as to take advantage of every immunity granted by Cogsa or by any other statute. In a general average case, the issue as to liability of the cargo to contribute may often, therefore, involve exactly the same questions as would have arisen had the case been one of cargo damage, for, under such a clause, the ship is entitled to recover general average expenses in just exactly the same cases as those in which it would have been immunized against cargo claims, had cargo been damaged.[83a]

Thus, in Hoskyn & Co. v. Silver Line, Ltd.,[84] general average expenses consequent upon a fire caused by negligence were conceded to be subject to contribution under a Jason clause similar to the one quoted, for, under the Fire Statute and Cogsa § 4(2)(b), the ship was not liable. On the other hand, in The Venice Maru,[85] the Second Circuit Court of Appeals—applying a Jason clause of the older style that, following the phraseology of the Harter Act, laid down "due diligence to make the vessel seaworthy" as a condition for enjoyment by the ship of the right to general average contribution—held that the shipowner who had failed to exercise due diligence could not recover in general average, even though immunized under the Fire Statute from liability to cargo.

83. *I. e.*, The Carriage of Goods By Sea Act, 1936, 49 Stat. 1207, 46 U.S.C.A. §§ 1300–1315. See *supra*, Chapter III, Part II, at note 1.

83a. This is the case, *e. g.* in Amer. Mail Line, Ltd. v. Tokyo Marine & Fire Ins. Co., 270 F.2d 499, 1959 A.M.C. 2220 (9th Cir. 1959).

84. 63 F.Supp. 452, 1943 A.M.C. 510 (S.D.N.Y.1943), affirmed 143 F.2d 462 (2d Cir. 1944), certiorari denied 323 U.S. 767, 65 S.Ct. 116 (1944).

85. 133 F.2d 781 (2d Cir. 1943), affirmed 320 U.S. 249, 64 S.Ct. 15 (1943).

Under the new-style Jason clause, quoted above, the court, in Isbrandtsen Co. v. Federal Ins. Co.,[86] held that, under Cogsa, it is immaterial whether due diligence to make the vessel seaworthy has been used or not, if there is no causal connection between unseaworthiness and the general average situation (in the actual case, a stranding.)[87]

There is only one reference in Cogsa to general average; in Section 5, it is provided that "Nothing in this Act shall be held to prevent the insertion in a bill of lading of any lawful provision regarding general average." [88] It is usually assumed that both the presently used Jason clause and the clause incorporating the York-Antwerp rules are within the latitude afforded by this Section. Since the word "lawful" undoubtedly has some force, it may be suggested that two types of clauses would still be invalid: (1) Clauses giving a right to general average to the ship even under circumstances where she would be liable for goods damage under Cogsa; obviously, the lawfulness of the Jason clause extends no further than the immunity coverage of Cogsa. (2) Any clause having the effect of extending the right of general average contribution entirely outside its traditional bounds—to a situation, e. g., where the requisite "peril" did not exist; such a clause would only in name concern "general average," and would, it seems, run indirectly afoul of Cogsa, § 3(8) or of the negative implication in the first sentence of § 5.[89]

**§ 5–14.** Another interesting relation of Cogsa to general average arises from Rule D of the York-Antwerp Rules (1974):

> "Rights to contribution in general average shall not be affected, though the event which gave rise to the sacrifice or expenditure may have been due to the fault of one of the

**86.** 113 F.Supp. 357, 1952 A.M.C. 1945 (S.D.N.Y.1952), affirmed on opinion of District Court, 205 F.2d 679 (2d Cir. 1953), certiorari denied 346 U.S. 866, 74 S.Ct. 106 (1953).

**87.** *Cf. supra*, Chapter III, Part II. Bill of lading clausing is extremely conservative, mostly because old boilerplate is thoughtlessly carried forward. The old Harter Act-style Jason clause was used for a 1953 voyage from Tampa to Ecuador, in Schade v. National Surety Corp., 288 F.2d 106, 1961 A.M.C. 1225 (2d Cir. 1961). The court duly required proof of due diligence, and affirmed a judgment that found this proof wanting. It may be suggested that this result is unduly hard on the carrier. Since the carriage was undoubtedly subject to Cogsa, a Cogsa Jason Clause would have been lawful, and the inclusion of the Harter Act Jason Clause was clearly an inadvertence; perhaps its conditional form, irrelevant under Cogsa, might have been treated as *pro non scripto*.

On the effect of fault and the Jason clause, the following cases are interesting: The West Arrow, 80 F.2d 853, 1936 A.M.C. 165 (2d Cir. 1936); United States v. Los Angeles Soap Co., 83 F.2d 875, 1936 A.M.C. 850 (9th Cir. 1936); Corrado Societa Anonima Di Navigazione v. L. Mundet & Son, 91 F.2d 726, 1937 A.M.C. 1257 (3d Cir. 1937), certiorari denied 302 U.S. 751, 58 S.Ct. 271 (1937)—applying the Irrawaddy rule where charter contained no Jason clause; Globe & Rutgers Fire Ins. Co. v. United States, 105 F. 2d 160, 1939 A.M.C. 912 (2d Cir. 1939), certiorari denied 308 U.S. 611, 60 S.Ct. 175 (1939); The Maria, 15 F.Supp. 745, 1936 A.M.C. 1314 (S.D.N.Y.1936).

**88.** 46 U.S.C.A. § 1305.

**89.** 46 U.S.C.A. §§ 1303(8), 1305.

> parties to the adventure; but that shall not prejudice any remedies or defenses which may be open against or to that party in respect of such fault."

Since, as we have seen,[90] American bills of lading did not customarily stipulate for the 1924 "lettered" Rules, it is only recently that this Rule (in a slightly different 1950 form) has come to be incorporated in such bills. Rule D, it would seem, when construed as it must be to meet the requirements of Cogsa, neither adds to nor subtracts from the Jason clause, quoted above. It seems quite clear that Rule D cannot be given such effect as to bring it about that general average is due from cargo even where Cogsa would impose a liability on the ship for cargo damage (as, e. g., where the mishap was caused by lack of due diligence to make the ship seaworthy) for such a construction, if not directly offending against Cogsa § 3(8),[91] would merely produce a circuity of actions, inasmuch as cargo could recover from the ship, as damages, the same sum that had been exacted as general average.[92] The Jason clause on the other hand, gives the ship everything she can have under Cogsa—namely, a right to general average contribution in every case in which the cause of the trouble is one for which the ship is not responsible. The Jason clause, it seems, is still needed to bring this result about, for Rule D does not affirmatively confer a right to general average contribution, and such a right does not exist under our law, absent a Jason clause, in any case where the ship's fault has produced the peril, regardless of her responsibility, under the Harter Act or Cogsa.[93] The York-Antwerp Rules, being neither statute nor treaty, could not, it would seem, in any way diminish the cargoes rights under Cogsa.

Deviation, which has been discussed in the chapters on Marine Insurance and Carriage of Goods,[94] is another ship's fault which may affect the right to general average contribution from cargo. In the past, deviation has been given its usual drastic effect: the deviating ship can never enforce a claim for general average.[95] If we are right in supposing that Cogsa has reduced the penalty for deviation to that of responsibility for loss or damage wholly or partly *caused* by departure from the contracted course,[96] then it seems to follow that the ousting of the ship's right to general average contribution should be limited to a similar scope—that, in other words, deviation ought now to bar the ship's general average claim when and only when the peril arises wholly or in part as a *result* of the deviation.[96a] Wheth-

90. *Supra*, at note 28.

91. 46 U.S.C.A. § 1303(8).

92. Liability to make general average contribution under such circumstances would seem obviously to be a damage suffered as a result of the operation of a cause for the consequences of which the ship is made liable by Cogsa.

93. The Irrawaddy, *supra* note 81.

94. See *supra*, Chapter II, at note 58 *et seq.*; Chapter III, Part II, at note 107 *et seq.*

95. See Note, 21 Va.L.Rev. 227 (1934).

96. *Supra* Chapter III, § 3–41.

96a. The assumption that this is now the correct rule seems to underlie the

er or not this is the position as a matter of law, the present form of the Jason clause, quoted above, creates a right to general average whenever the peril arises through causes for which the ship is not responsible; if, therefore, Cogsa is now to be read as making the deviating ship responsible only for losses caused by the deviation, clearly the Jason clause creates a general average right, even in favor of a deviating ship, where the general average peril is not caused by the deviation.

### Jurisdiction and Liens

**§ 5–15.** General average claims may be asserted in ordinary civil actions, where the process of the shoregoing courts is adequate to deal with them,[97] but today what little litigation there is on this subject is mostly carried on in the admiralty court.

Cargo has a maritime lien on the ship for general average contributions when due,[98] and the ship's claims against cargo create just the same sort of possessory lien as in the case of freight.[99]

In practice, as we have seen, the ship exacts a general average bond and some sort of security—a cash deposit, an insurance company's guarantee, or some less customary equivalent—before delivering the cargo.

### Evaluation of General Average

**§ 5–16.** Few features of maritime law can with any realism be questioned as to their fundamental right to exist. Changes may be proposed and may come, but there must (so long as modern commerce is recognizably the same) be a law of collision, of goods damage, of personal injuries, and so on.

General average, on the other hand, is by no means self-evidently a necessary or useful institution on the whole. Its abolition would be thinkable, whether or not desirable. If it were abolished, no gap would be left that must indispensably be filled. Accordingly, there has been recurrent talk of the possibility of doing away with general average altogether, with suitable adjustments in hull, cargo, and liability insurance carriage, and in related rules of carriers' liability.[100]

In this connection, a most interesting modern work is Knut S. Selmer's The Survival of General Average: A Necessity or an An-

reasoning in World-Wide S.S. Co. v. India Supply Mission, 316 F.Supp. 190, 1971 A.M.C. 498 (S.D.N.Y.1970).

97. Under the "saving clause"; see *supra*, Chapter I, at notes 53, 117. For a full canvass of remedies available in general average cases, see United States v. Atlantic Mutual Ins. Co., 298 U.S. 483, 489, 56 S.Ct. 889, 890, 1936 A.M.C. 993 (1936).

98. The Odysseus III, 77 F.Supp. 297, 1948 A.M.C. 608 (S.D.Fla.1948).

99. Wellman v. Morse, 76 F. 573 (1st Cir. 1896).

100. See Lowndes & Rudolf, §§ 11, 1101 *et seq.* The Maritime Law Association of the United States has recently begun study of possible "simplification" of general average; M.L.A. Document No. 559, pp. 5976 *et seq.* (1971).

achronism?[101] Selmer explores, by statistical sampling, the costs of the general average adjustment and distribution, and finds these costs considerable; most of them, he concludes, could be avoided by limiting contribution to salvage money actually expended, and by letting other losses fall where they hit, with some necessary changes in hull and cargo insurance, and in rules of ship's responsibility to cargo.

He then turns to "the traditional defense", as he calls it, of general average. General average, it is said, affects the behavior of the ship's master in a position of peril, since it assures that the cost of all measures taken, whether sacrificial of vessel's or of cargo's interest, will be shared equally, thus freeing the master from the temptation to prefer the vessel.

Selmer points out that general average, as actually administered, does not, even now, make it a matter of indifference whether ship or cargo be sacrificed. More fundamentally, however, he doubts whether shipmasters are actually influenced to any appreciable degree by their knowledge of the possibility of a general average adjustment. Of more importance are pride of craft, and the frequent lack of really viable alternatives to the action taken. He concedes, however, that little scientific support can now be given to either side of this question—that it must be resolved on the basis of common sense.

It is likely that debate as to the desirability of totally abolishing general average will recur for a long time. As a practical matter, it seems quite unlikely that so firmly entrenched an institution will actually be done away with in the foreseeable future. The recent revision of the York-Antwerp Rules [101a] seems to evidence a general expectation that general average is to be with us yet a long while.

101. Published in Norway by the Oslo University Press and in London by Sir Isaac Pitman & Sons (1958).

101a. See *supra* at note 27a.

# Chapter VI

# RIGHTS OF SEAMEN AND MARITIME WORKERS: RECOVERY FOR DEATH AND INJURY

## Introduction with Caveat

**§ 6–1.** Since 1940 the Supreme Court has been rewriting the law under which crew members and harbor workers may recover for death and injury. The rewrite job has gone far enough to make it clear that a revolution has taken place. If the Court adheres to its present position, the main outlines of the new law are reasonably clear, although the lower courts will be occupied for a generation in filling in the details. It is, however, less than a foregone conclusion that the Court will adhere to its position. At no time has that position commanded unanimity within the Court: single and multiple dissents have been common, and the Court has been narrowly divided on basic issues of law and policy. Changes in the Court's membership and shifts in the thinking of individual justices could convert a protesting minority into a comfortable majority. Another possibility is Congressional action—a solution which the Court itself has urged in several opinions.

Much of the present chapter is not much more than a progress report. So long as the volcano continues in eruption, no charts can be guaranteed reliable even until the next term of Court. Many of the old landmarks have disappeared for good. New ones have been tossed up, which may or may not be permanent additions to the map. There are unsuspected reefs whose existence will be determined by the usual method of hit or miss. The perils of the sea, which mariners suffer and shipowners insure against, have met their match in the perils of judicial review.

**§ 6–1(a).** The preceding section has been left in the form in which it appeared in the first edition of the treatise. In this section we turn to the course of events from the mid-1950's until the mid-1970's.

During the 1950's and 1960's the Supreme Court majority did indeed, despite occasional setbacks, remain faithful to the revolution which had been wrought from the 1940's on. The division within the Court appeared to grow progressively more bitter and, on more than one occasion, unseemly charges of unprincipled conduct were leveled by one faction against the other. In the late 1950's the Court devoted an inordinate amount of its time and energies to cases of this type, with results which one commentator characterized as "the devil's own mess."[1] After 1960 the number of such cases in which the

1. D. Currie, Federalism and The Admiralty: "The Devil's Own Mess," 1960 Sup.Ct.Rev. 158.

Court granted certiorari declined sharply, perhaps because the lower federal courts had accepted the fact that the Justices, at least those temporarily in the majority, really meant what they had been saying. There was one brief, happy moment when it appeared possible that the Justices had put aside their contentious quarrels and were prepared to work harmoniously together in fashioning a new synthesis.[1a] That optimistic view of the matter was not, for long, tenable. Since 1970 the reconstituted majority of the Court has made at least a beginning on the job of dismantling the structure which had been put together during the preceding thirty years.[1b] In the dismantling job, so far as it has progressed at the moment of writing, the new majority (if indeed there is a new majority), instead of overruling the earlier cases, has distinguished them away on grounds which, to the surviving Justices of the former majority, have seemed tenuous if not altogether outrageous.

In 1972 Congress enacted amendments to the Longshoremen's and Harbor Workers' Compensation Act which were designed to negate two of the propositions which the Court had established during the 1940's and 1950's.[1c] These propositions were that harbor workers (as well as traditional seamen) were entitled to recover from ships and shipowners for injuries caused by unseaworthiness of the ship and that shipowners held liable to harborworkers in such actions were entitled to be indemnified by the employers of the harborworkers if the employers had contributed to the condition which resulted in unseaworthiness. The amendments, which have not been given a retroactive effect, remain to be judicially construed. The Supreme Court will in due course determine the extent to which the amendments have displaced the Court's earlier formulations.

What the Supreme Court did during its thirty years war was greatly to expand the liability of shipowners and other employers of maritime labor for injuries suffered in the course of employment. The expansion of liability was accomplished by shifting the recovery from negligence to unseaworthiness and by converting the shipowner's liability for unseaworthiness into what the Court often described

**1a.** Moragne v. States Marine Lines, Inc., 398 U.S. 375, 90 S.Ct. 1772, 1970 A.M.C. 967 (1970), discussed § 6–32 *infra*. Moragne was one of the few cases involving personal injury and death claims decided since the 1940's in which the Court was unanimous. Justice Harlan, who wrote the Moragne opinion, had typically dissented in other cases.

**1b.** See Usner v. Luckenbach Overseas Corp., 400 U.S. 494, 91 S.Ct. 514, 1971 A.M.C. 277 (1971), discussed §§ 6–39, 6–44(a) *infra*; Victory Carriers, Inc. v. Law, 4€4 U.S. 202, 92 S.Ct. 418, 1972 A.M.C. 1 (1971), discussed § 6–44a *infra*, note 251f. The two cases cited have, rightly or wrongly, been taken by most commentators to signalize a basic shift in the Court's position. See, e. g., George, Ship's Liability to Longshoremen Based on Unseaworthiness—Sieracki through Usner, 32 Louisiana L.Rev. 19 (1971); Note, 47 Tulane L.Rev. 183 (1972). Justices Black, Douglas, Brennan and Harlan dissented in Usner; Justices Douglas and Brennan dissented in Victory Carriers, which was a 5–2 decision, Justices Black and Harlan having retired from the Court.

**1c.** The amendments, which do much more than merely negate the propositions referred to in the text, are discussed § 6–46 *et seq. infra*.

as a species of absolute liability which had nothing to do with fault. The beneficiaries of the Court's labors, and their lawyers, naturally approved of what was being done and indicated their approval by instituting thousands upon thousands of personal injury and death actions. The conservative legal establishment, a substantial part of the federal judiciary (including the minority justices on the Supreme Court itself) and most academic commentators disapproved, finding no warrant for the Court's developing jurisprudence in "history, reason [or] logic." [1d] The widespread criticism of the Court's work fanned the flames of controversy and no doubt led many defendants to litigate to the bitter end cases in which judgments for plaintiffs were a foregone conclusion (so long as the Court maintained its course).

In the 1970's we are in a better position than we were in the 1950's to set the Supreme Court's maritime law revolution in some kind of perspective. Since the 1940's there has been in our law of civil obligations, alike in contract and in tort, what can only be described as an explosion of liability.[1e] The most dramatic illustration of this process has been in the so-called products liability cases under which manufacturers have been held to strict or absolute liability (that is, liability without regard to fault or negligence) to those who suffer personal injury or property loss by reason of defectively manufactured goods. The strict liability idea, pioneered by the California Court during the 1950's, achieved widespread acceptance within ten years, including "codification" in § 402A of the Second Restatement of Torts.[1f] It is reasonable to assume that the Justices of the Supreme Court of the United States, insulated by the Court's docket from most private law issues, knew little or nothing about such developments. It is therefore of the highest jurisprudential interest that the majority of the Court, working in its chosen field of maritime personal injury litigation, achieved, during the 1950's and 1960's, results strikingly similar to those being achieved at the same time by the state courts with respect to manufacturer's liability for defective goods. We need not, of course, conclude that whatever is is right; the doctrine of the products liability cases has been attacked by respectable commentators quite as savagely as the Supreme Court's unseaworthiness doctrine has been. But we will do well to bear in mind that the "extraordinary expansion" [1g] of the unseaworthiness doctrine was not in any sense an isolated phenomenon or an aberration

**1d.** The quotation in the text is from Justice Stewart's majority opinion in Usner, Note 1b *supra*, 400 U.S. at p. 497, 91 S.Ct. at p. 516, 1971 A.M.C. at p. 280.

**1e.** For the detail of this development on the contract side, see Gilmore, The Death of Contract (1974).

**1f.** The volume of the law review literature on the products liability cases since the mid-1960's matches the volume of maritime personal injury litigation. For a Symposium which collects diverse views by various legal and economic hands, see Products Liability: Economic Analysis and the Law, 38 U. of Chi.L.Rev. 1 (1970).

**1g.** Stewart, J., in the Usner case, Note 1b *supra*, 400 U.S. at p. 497, 91 S.Ct. at p. 516, 1971 A.M.C. at p. 279.

attributable to half a dozen Justices; it was part and parcel of the judicial revolution which has reshaped our law of civil obligations during the post-World War II period.

It is a truism in law as it is in politics that periods of revolutionary ferment are succeeded by periods of repose and consolidation. Typically, what has been accomplished during the first period is not undone during the second period. As a literary theme it may become fashionable to deplore the excesses of the previous period, but in fact little is done about them. Let us assume for the sake of the argument that the current majority of the Supreme Court is out of sympathy with or even antipathetic to what the previous majority did in the field of maritime personal injury litigation. In all probability all that will happen is that there will be no further expansion of remedy; at most there will be a few insignificant cutbacks. The main outlines of the body of law which the Supreme Court fashioned from the 1940's through the 1960's will remain unchallenged. The fact that the new majority has so far chosen to proceed by distinguishing instead of by overruling may well be taken as indicative of our future course. There remains the possibility of drastic legislative intervention. It seems a fair guess, however, that Congress has shot its bolt for the next generation or so with the 1972 amendments to the Longshoremen's and Harborworkers' Compensation Act. Furthermore, it is by no means impossible that, when the amendments have run the gauntlet of judicial construction, it will turn out that there is much less there than meets the eye. Justice Black was the principal architect of the new law; his ghost will not necessarily be saddened at the events of the next ten or fifteen years.

**§ 6–2.** A preliminary survey will locate the principal features of the pre-1940 lawscape.

In 1903 Justice Brown wrote in The Osceola:

> ". . . the law may be considered as settled upon the following propositions:
>
> 1. That the vessel and her owners are liable, in case a seaman falls sick, or is wounded, in the service of the ship, to the extent of his maintenance and cure, and to his wages, at least so long as the voyage is continued.
>
> 2. That the vessel and her owner are, both by English and American law, liable to an indemnity for injuries received by a seaman in consequence of the unseaworthiness of the ship, or a failure to supply and keep in order the proper appliances appurtenant to the ship. Scarff v. Metcalf, 107 N.Y. 211.
>
> 3. That all the members of the crew, except, perhaps, the master, are, as between themselves, fellow servants, and hence seamen cannot recover for injuries sustained through the negligence of another member of the crew beyond the expense of his maintenance and cure.

> 4. That the seaman is not allowed to recover an indemnity for the negligence of the master, or any member of the crew, but is entitled to maintenance and cure, whether the injuries were received by negligence or accident."[2]

The four propositions of The Osceola have been reproduced in hundreds of cases as the classical statement of the liability of the ship and her owner to sick and injured seamen. Like holy writ they are ritually invoked, respectfully recited, rarely analyzed and never criticized. The facts of the case have been lost from sight: even the admiralty casebooks merely reprint the four propositions with no indication of the context in which Justice Brown delivered his celebrated statement.

In The Osceola a crew member had libeled the ship *in rem* to recover for injuries received in carrying out an order given by the master. As presented to the court, the case was one of the few which have ever raised a question of pure operating negligence: counsel for the injured seaman conceded that the ship was in all respects seaworthy and that the sole cause of the accident was an improvident order given by the master, which was properly carried out by the crew. The District Court gave judgment for the libellant. On appeal, the Circuit Court certified three questions to the Supreme Court: 1) whether the ship is liable to a crew member "by reason of an improvident and negligent order of the master in respect of the navigation and management of the vessel"; 2) whether the master and crew were fellow servants; 3) whether, as a matter of law, the vessel or its owners were liable to the libellant on the facts of the case. The Supreme Court unanimously denied recovery. Justice Brown first reviewed the continental sources and the American cases. In addition to the traditional remedy of maintenance and cure, the cases, as Justice Brown analyzed them, allowed recovery of an "indemnity" for unseaworthiness while they denied recovery for negligence in "navigation and management". The unseaworthiness indemnity was looked on as an American innovation, which had perhaps been stimulated by the English Merchants' Shipping Act of 1876 which allowed such a recovery; the Continental codes restricted the seaman to his maintenance and cure alone. Justice Brown then stated his four propositions, whose form and sequence are to some degree explained by the phraseology of the questions certified by the Circuit Court. The third and fourth propositions are repetitious and overlapping and the third (on the fellow servant rule) is made unnecessary by the fourth (no recovery for negligence of either master or crew without regard to the fellow servant rule).

Justice Brown's statement of shipowner's liability to crew members was couched in terms reminiscent of those used in the then recently passed Harter Act, which dealt with shipowner's liability to cargo. The Harter Act rule was that the shipowner should not be

2. 189 U.S. 158, 23 S.Ct. 483, 487 (1903).

liable to cargo for damage resulting from "faults or errors in navigation or the management of [the] vessel" provided that the owner had used "due diligence" to furnish a seaworthy vessel.[2a] In The Osceola the Circuit Court, using Harter Act terminology, had certified the question whether the vessel was liable for the master's negligence "in respect of the navigation and management of the vessel". The answer was: No. Since the seaworthiness of the Osceola had been conceded, there was no occasion for the Circuit Court to ask or for the Supreme Court to answer the question whether, in the context of seaman's injuries, the owner was under an absolute duty to furnish a seaworthy ship or merely under a Harter Act duty to use "due diligence" to do so. The holding in The Osceola is the fourth proposition (no recovery for injuries caused by master's negligence); the second proposition (recovery for injuries caused by unseaworthiness) was dictum and neither the facts of the case nor the questions certified required Justice Brown to analyze with care the extent of the owner's duty to provide a seaworthy ship.

§ **6–3.** In 1920 Congress undercut the fourth proposition of The Osceola by passing the Jones Act which in substance provided that a seaman injured in the course of his employment by the negligence of owner, master or fellow crew members could recover damages for his injuries.[3] The Jones Act was abominably drafted and the case law construing it soon became a trackless maze, bristling with danger points and honeycombed with pitfalls. Nevertheless, between 1920 and 1950 it was the principal vehicle for personal injury recoveries by seamen against shipowners. As the law then stood, "unseaworthiness" and "negligence" were discrete concepts. "Unseaworthiness" went to the structure of the ship and the adequacy of her equipment and furnishings; "negligence" went to the direction and control of operations aboard ship. The injured seaman (unless he was the master) had always been under someone's orders, so that the allegation of negligence was always available except for off-duty injuries. The Jones Act provided for jury trial; if plaintiff brought an unseaworthiness action he could in most situations have his jury by bringing suit in a non-admiralty court under the saving to suitors clause, but it was by no means clear how much of the maritime law followed him when he sued outside the admiralty. The Jones Act abolished contributory negligence as a defense; it was possible that contributory negligence might bar plaintiff in an unseaworthiness action brought in state court or on the civil side of the federal court. Nor was it settled whether the shipowner's duty to provide a seaworthy ship was absolute or was satisfied by proof of due diligence. Finally, it was believed that plaintiff had to elect between the Jones Act and the unseaworthiness doctrine and could not go to the jury on both counts. Thus for a variety of reasons, suits under the Jones Act were counted by the hundreds while the unseaworthiness actions fell off to a trickle.

**2a.** The Harter Act is discussed in Chapter III, Part 2.

3. The Jones Act is discussed *infra* §§ 6–20 to 6–37.

§ 6–4. In 1917 the Supreme Court, in Southern Pacific Co. v. Jensen,[4] held a state workman's compensation statute unconstitutional as applied to a longshoreman who had been injured under circumstances which constituted a maritime tort. In 1926 the Court held that a longshoreman was a "seaman" entitled to sue under the Jones Act.[5] In response to these decisions Congress passed the Longshoremen's and Harbor Workers' Compensation Act of 1927.[6] The Act made the compensation remedy exclusive against the injured worker's employer, but preserved the worker's right to bring tort actions against any third party. Under the customary employment pattern the harbor worker is hired by a master stevedore or other independent contractor and not by the shipowner. Following the passage of the Longshoremen's Act, the remedies available to such workers were as follows: against his employer, he was restricted to his statutory compensation award. Consequently he could not sue under the Jones Act, which was thought to cover only actions by employees against employers. If the circumstances of his injury constituted a maritime tort, the harbor worker, like any other person injured by or on board a ship, could bring an action *in personam* against the shipowner or *in rem* against the ship, or, under the saving to suitors clause, could proceed outside the admiralty. Doctrinally, the harbor worker's tort action was not thought of as being the same as the crew member's action to recover an indemnity for unseaworthiness, but the differences, if any, between the two were never explored in the cases. If the harbor worker sued the shipowner outside the admiralty in order to have his damages assessed by a jury, he was faced by the same legal obscurity as the crew member who invoked the unseaworthiness doctrine outside the admiralty: would the maritime law follow him into state court, and would his contributory negligence bar the action (under the state law rule) or merely serve to mitigate damages (under the admiralty rule)? Between 1927 and 1950 most harbor-worker litigation involved the question whether the injured worker should have sought compensation under the Federal Act (for a maritime tort) or under the applicable State Act (for a nonmaritime tort). There were relatively few actions brought by harbor workers against shipowners.

§ 6–5. The state of the law outlined in the preceding sections has been radically changed. In the first edition of the treatise we commented that the following propositions had (as of 1957) been established:

1. The shipowner's duty to furnish a seaworthy ship is absolute and is not satisfied by due diligence.[7]

4. 244 U.S. 205, 37 S.Ct. 524 (1917). The case is discussed § 6–45 *infra.*

5. International Stevedoring Co. v. Haverty, 272 U.S. 50, 47 S.Ct. 19, 1926 A.M.C. 1638 (1926) discussed § 6–21 *infra* text following note 107.

6. The Act is discussed §§ 6–45 to 6–52 *infra.*

7. See infra §§ 6–38 to 6–44.

2. The term "unseaworthiness" (at least in the context of suits to recover for personal injuries) is broad enough to include almost all (perhaps all) types of operating negligence in the navigation and management of the ship.[8]

3. A crew member may join an unseaworthiness count with a Jones Act count and is not required to elect between them: both counts may go to the jury.[9]

4. Most (perhaps all) types of harbor workers are "seamen" entitled to recover for unseaworthiness.[10] (The harbor worker still cannot sue under the Jones Act, since the Longshoremen's Act restricts him to his compensation remedy against his employer and Jones Act actions are though to lie only against employers. The unseaworthiness actions are against shipowners who are not the direct employers.)

5. In actions brought in non-admiralty courts under the saving to suitors clause, by harbor workers or by crew members, maritime law probably prevails over most (perhaps all) state law rules which are inconsistent with the maritime law.[11]

As of 1974 our 1957 propositions numbered 1, 3 and 5 need little or no change and what changes there have been are all further expansions of remedy. (1) The duty to furnish a seaworthy ship is still absolute and after 1957 the Court continued steadily to expand the concept of unseaworthiness. (3) In 1963 the Court concluded that where a count for maintenance and cure is joined to counts under the Jones Act and for unseaworthiness, all three counts must go to the jury.[11a] (5) Maritime law clearly prevails over inconsistent state law in actions brought under the saving to suitors clause, at least where the maritime law rule is more favorable to plaintiff's recovery than the state law rule; it is possible that plaintiff may have the best of both worlds and claim the benefit of a state law rule that is more favorable to him than the maritime rule would be.

Through 1970 it seemed that "unseaworthiness" had to all intents and purposes swallowed up "negligence" (Proposition 2). The 1971 Usner case [11b] reestablished the category of "operating negligence" as distinct from the category of unseaworthiness. In actions by crew members in which a Jones Act count is routinely joined with an unseaworthiness count and both counts go to the jury, the Usner holding seems to be of no importance whatever. Usner might have had significant results in harborworkers' actions to recover for unseaworthiness but those actions are no longer available for the reasons indicated in the following paragraph.

8. See *infra* § 6–39.

9. See *infra* §§ 6–23 to 6–25.

10. See *infra* §§ 6–53 to 6–55.

11. See *infra* §§ 6–58 to 6–61.

11a. Fitzgerald v. United States Lines Co., 374 U.S. 16, 83 S.Ct. 1646, 1963 A.M.C. 1093 (1963), discussed § 6–9 *infra*, text following note 45d.

11b. Usner v. Luckenbach Overseas Corp., 400 U.S. 494, 91 S.Ct. 514, 1971 A.M.C. 277 (1971), discussed §§ 6–39, 6–44(a) *infra*.

The 1972 amendments to the Longshoremen's and Harbor Workers' Compensation Act provided that such shore-based maritime workers may no longer recover under the unseaworthiness doctrine but may recover for negligence chargeable to the ship or shipowner. Proposition 4 has thus been abrogated by statute. It remains to be seen how much of what was characterized as "unseaworthiness" during the 1950–1970 period will hereafter be characterized as "negligence". The Usner case, which pre-dated the amendments, may have an unexpected significance if there is a revival of negligence litigation in this context.

There has never been a time when the courts did not have to deal with a substantial volume of personal injury cases. Following the passage of the Jones Act in 1920 the cases came in flood. By 1950 the Supreme Court had not only practically guaranteed recovery in the damage action but had added a new class of plaintiffs, harbor workers dubbed seamen *pro hac vice*. From 1950 until 1970 the flood reached unprecedented proportions. Since 1970 both Court and Congress have shown an interest in flood-control measures. The 1972 amendments to the Longshoremen's Act have been hailed as a much-needed reform which will substantially lighten the dockets of the overburdened federal courts.[11c] However, it is, notoriously, much easier to let the genie out of the bottle than to coax him back in. Neither ambiguously tentative shifts of direction by the Court nor half-way measures by Congress will effectively reduce the volume of litigation; indeed, both the Court's shift and the 1972 amendments may well be litigation breeders, at least in the short run. Congress could shift the burden from the courts to an administrative agency by subjecting all maritime workers (including traditional seamen) to a mandatory and exclusive compensation system. There appears to be absolutely no likelihood of such a move by Congress. All that being so, personal injury and death litigation will bulk as large in the digests over the next generation as during the past generation.[12]

11c. See Friendly, Federal Jurisdiction: A General View 131 *et seq.* (1973).

12. A Note on the footnotes to this Chapter:

The radical reconstruction of maritime personal injury law since 1940 has made much of the older case law of little more than antiquarian interest. The volume of personal injury litigation since 1945, and particularly since 1950, has been so great that exhaustive citation of recent lower court cases would be an almost impossible task. These cases were decided against a rapidly changing background and many of them were of merely transitory interest; since the Supreme Court has claimed the field of maritime personal injury litigation as its own, lower court decisions have suffered from rapid technological obsolescence. Thus exhaustive citation to them would be fruitless and unhelpful. The case law annotations to this chapter will therefore be in general restricted to citation of (1) the pre-1940 leading cases which have a bearing on the formulation of the "new law"; (2) Supreme Court cases from 1940 to date; (3) lower court cases since 1940 which are illustrative of developing trends or deal with issues still left unsettled by the Supreme Court.

2 Norris, The Law of Seamen (3d ed. 1970, with annual cumulative supplement) contains exhaustive collections of cases.

### Maintenance and Cure: The Nature of the Remedy

**§ 6–6.** The seaman's right to maintenance and cure for illness or injury occurring while he is in the service of the ship is often analogized to workmen's compensation. While the origins of the right are customarily traced back to the mediæval sea codes, it appears to have been first recognized in this country by Justice Story in two cases which he decided on circuit. The quotations from Harden v. Gordon [13] and Reed v. Canfield [14] which regularly adorn modern opinions explain the right partly on humanitarian and partly on economic grounds. The doctrine not only protected the childlike and improvident seaman (who is usually "poor and friendless" and apt to acquire "habits of gross indulgence, carelessness and improvidence"), but served "the great public policy of preserving this important class of citizens for the commercial service and maritime defence of the nation".[15] Even the shipowners derived an ultimate benefit from being made to assume these charges, since, as Story shrewdly pointed out, seamen were thereby encouraged "to engage in perilous voyages with more promptitude, and at lower wages".[16]

The analogy to workmen's compensation is on the whole misleading. The theory of compensation was to substitute for a tort action based on negligence the remedy of a compensatory award, determined by an administrative agency, without regard to the employer's fault or negligence. Since the compensation statutes made the award the workman's exclusive remedy against his employer, there was a mutual give and take: the workman gave up the chance of a large verdict from a sympathetic jury but received the certainty of some compensation; the employer gave up the chance of escaping liability altogether and agreed to pay something whenever any of his employees was injured in the course of his employment.[17]

The shipowner's liability for maintenance and cure resembles that of an employer subject to a Workmen's Compensation Act only in that it is a liability without fault which is based on the employment relationship. The shipowner's liability is not restricted to injury or illness "arising out of" or causally related to the seaman's shipboard duties; except for injury and illness caused by the seaman's gross and willful misconduct or existing at the time the seaman signed on and knowingly concealed by him, the shipowner is liable for any injury which occurs or any illness which manifests itself while the seaman is under articles. Not only is the shipowner's liability more extensive than liability under any Workmen's Compensation Act, but the right to maintenance and cure is not the seaman's exclusive remedy

13. 11 Fed.Cas. 480, Case No. 6,047 (C.C.D.Me.1823).

14. 20 Fed.Cas. 426, Case No. 11,641 (C.C.D.Mass.1842).

15. Harden v. Gordon, *supra* note 13 at 483.

16. *Ibid.*

17. See generally Larson, Workmen's Compensation (originally published 1952, revised and reissued 1970–1973).

against his employer: he may also recover damages for negligence under the Jones Act or for breach of the duty to provide a seaworthy ship.[18]

The "poor and friendless" seaman is thus the beneficiary of a system of accident and health insurance at shipowner's expense more comprehensive than anything yet achieved by shorebound workers. Naturally, the suggestion that Congress pass a workmen's compensation act for seamen is opposed by the seamen and their representatives, who have so far been successful in their opposition. Since 1927 there has been no serious effort to substitute a compensation system for the Jones Act—unseaworthiness—maintenance and cure combination.[19] Meanwhile the seaman has prospered both as to his damage recovery, which has steadily become more certain, and as to the maintenance and cure recovery which has correspondingly widened in scope.[19a]

**§ 6–7.** Maintenance and cure is available only to seamen in the primitive sense: the members of the crew (including the officers and master). Harbor workers, who have won the assimilated rank of "seamen" for some purposes, are not entitled to maintenance and cure.[20] A modern ship's company includes many specialists who perform duties far removed from those of the able-bodied seaman. No distinction is drawn on this ground, however: the bartender, the musicians, the maids and stewards have the same rights as the deckhands and the engine crew.[21] The traditional seaman lived on the

18. Pacific S. S. Co. v. Peterson, 278 U.S. 130, 49 S.Ct. 75, 1928 A.M.C. 1932 (1928). The case is discussed *infra* § 6–24.

19. See note 325 *infra.*

19a. On whether claims for maintenance and cure are subject to limitation of liability, see Chapter X, § 10–26, text following Note 113c. See further in Chapter X, § 10–40 and the reference to the maintenance and cure cases in note 161i. Several District Court cases have suggested that the claims are not subject to limitation but the issue has never been authoritatively decided and must be regarded as open.

20. At least no case has awarded maintenance and cure to a harbor worker. In Flanagan & Sons, Inc. v. Carken, 11 S.W.2d 392 (Tex.Civ.App.1928) it was held that even though at that time under the doctrine of the Haverty case (note 5 *supra*) harbor workers were considered "seamen" for purposes of bringing suit under the Jones Act, they were not entitled to recover maintenance and cure. In Weiss v. Central R. Co. of N. J., 235 F.2d 309, 1956 A.M.C. 1473 (2d Cir. 1956) it was assumed that plaintiff, unless he was a "seaman," was not entitled to maintenance and cure. The majority of the Court decided that a railroad worker, who had only occasional duties afloat on ferry boats crossing the Hudson River, was a seaman, entitled to sue under the Jones Act as well as to claim maintenance and cure. The opinions by Judge Clark and by Judge Lumbard (dissenting) contain an exhaustive collection of the authorities on the seaman-harbor work distinction.

21. See, e. g., Mahramas v. American Export Isbrandtsen Lines, Inc., 475 F.2d 165, 1973 A.M.C. 587 (2d Cir. 1973) (hairdresser in beauty shop). Both Judge Anderson's majority opinion and Judge Oakes' dissent collect other cases of this type. The plaintiff in Mahramas was denied maintenance and cure on the ground that she had not incurred any out-of-pocket expenses, see § 6–12 *infra.*

In Steuer v. N. V. Nederl-Amerik Stoomvaart Maatschappf (Holland-Amerik-lijn), 362 F.Supp. 600, 1973 A.M.C. 1634 (S.D.Fla.1963) the plaintiff was a

vessel which he left only for brief periods of shore leave. There are, however, many workers employed on harborcraft and the like who live at home and commute to work day by day. No one seems to have doubted that such workers, if they are injured or become ill while they are at work, are "seamen" entitled to maintenance and cure and the other maritime remedies;[21a] their off-duty injuries and illnesses raise problems in the light of the "shore-leave" cases which will be subsequently discussed.[21b]

Any seaman has the right to maintenance and cure no matter what type of ship he serves on, provided only that the fundamental test of admiralty jurisdiction is met: the structure must qualify as a vessel.[21c] Coastwise, river, harbor and Great Lakes vessels are liable for maintenance and cure[21d] equally with transatlantic liners; pleas-

Jewish rabbi who had received free passage on a Caribbean cruise ship on the understanding that he would conduct religious services on two occasions during the cruise. The rabbi and his wife (who paid for her passage) lived in passenger accommodations and were treated as passengers. The arrangement was not a continuing one but applied only to the particular voyage. The rabbi did not sign shipping articles. He suffered a heart attack while sightseeing in San Juan and sought to recover his hospital expenses (cure) in the amount of approximately $18,000. Judge Roettger, denying the claim, commented that a full-time ship's chaplain would unquestionably be entitled to maintenance and cure but that "to conclude that Rabbi Steuer was a seaman would be an impossible strain on the imagination and would defy not only the law but common sense."

**21a.** See, e. g., George v. Chesapeake and Ohio Railway Co., 348 F.Supp. 283 (E.D.Va.1972) (tug pilot who worked 12-hour shifts and lived at home); Richardson v. St. Charles-St. John the Baptist Bridge and Ferry Authority, 284 F.Supp. 709, 1968 A.M.C. 1485 (E.D.La.1968) (deckhand on ferry-boat); Hudspeth v. Atlantic and Gulf Stevedores, Inc., 266 F.Supp. 937, 1967 A.M.C. 2108 (E.D.La.1967) (deckhand on harbor tug). On whether such shore-based seamen are entitled to maintenance and cure for injuries suffered when they are on shore, see § 6–8 *infra*, text following Note 40b; on whether they are entitled to a living allowance (maintenance) in addition to their medical expenses, see § 6–12 *infra*.

**21b.** See § 6–8 *infra*.

**21c.** With the development of off-shore oil-drilling from stationary rigs, initially in the Gulf of Mexico, the question obviously arose whether workers employed on such rigs whose duties had little or nothing to do with traditional seaman's work were seamen entitled to maintenance and cure and to damages under the Jones Act. (In this context the Jones Act cases and the maintenance and cure cases are interchangeable.) Most of the action was in the Fifth Circuit which held in a series of cases beginning with Offshore Company v. Robison, 266 F.2d 769, 1950 A.M.C. 2049 (5th Cir. 1959) (Jones Act and unseaworthiness) that such workers were Jones Act seamen entitled to the general maritime law remedies including maintenance and cure. Judge Wisdom's Robison opinion included a careful review of the gradual expansion of the meaning of the terms "seaman" and "vessel" under the Jones Act and the general maritime law. See also Boatel, Inc. v. Delamare, 379 F.2d 850, 1968 A.M.C. (5th Cir. 1967) (Jones Act); Vincent v. Harvey Well Service, 441 F.2d 146, 1971 A.M.C. 2541 (5th Cir. 1971) (Jones Act; Judge Brown equated the Jones Act cases with maintenance and cure cases).

For a good review of what are vessels for this purpose, see Sims v. Marine Catering Service, 217 F.Supp. 511, 1964 A.M.C. 377 (E.D.La.1963).

See further the discussion of who are seamen under the Jones Act, § 6–21 *infra*.

**21d.** In Rowald v. Cargo Carriers, Inc., 243 F.Supp. 629, 1968 A.M.C. 1397 (E.D.Mo.1965) Judge Meredith rejected without discussion the contention that shipping on the inland waterways is

ure yachts equally with commercial vessels. A shore-based worker whose duties take him on navigable waters only occasionally may be a seaman with rights to maintenance and cure if he is injured while afloat.[22] On the other hand a night watchman on a dead ship tied up at a wharf and no longer a vessel for jurisdictional purposes would presumably not have the right. Seamen who are employed directly by the United States have been held deprived of their right to maintenance and cure (as well as of their right to sue under the Jones Act or to recover for unseaworthiness) on the ground that their exclusive remedy is under the Federal Employees' Compensation Act.[23] Foreign seamen on ships of foreign registry, not owned by American citizens, will be remitted in most instances to the law of the ship's flag.[24]

The right runs both against the ship and the shipowner.[24a] It creates a maritime lien, entitled to the highest priority,[24b] and may be

not liable for maintenance and cure. This appears to be the only case in which such a contention has ever been made.

22. See the Weiss case, note 20, *supra*.

23. According to a 5–4 decision in Johansen v. United States, 343 U.S. 427, 72 S.Ct. 849, 1952 A.M.C. 1043 (1952), civil service seamen serving in Army Transport vessels may not sue the United States for their personal injuries under general maritime law or pursuant to the Jones Act and the Public Vessels Act, 43 Stat. 1112 (1925), 46 U.S.C.A. §§ 781–790.

Their sole remedy is the Federal Employees' Compensation Act, 39 Stat. 742 (1916) which, as amended, currently appears in 5 U.S.C.A. § 7902, §§ 8101 *et seq.*; 18 U.S.C.A. § 292, §§ 1920 *et seq.*

Following Johansen it was suggested that the rule of that case applied only to seamen on "public vessels" of the United States and that seamen on government-owned "merchant vessels" were entitled to the usual maritime remedies. See Inland Waterways Corp. v. Doyle, 204 F.2d 874 (8th Cir. 1953). However, in Patterson v. United States, 359 U.S. 495, 79 S.Ct. 936, 1959 A.M.C. 1640 (1959), rehearing denied 360 U.S. 914, 79 S.Ct. 1293, (1959), the Court, in a brief per curiam opinion, held that Johansen, which the Court refused to overrule, applied both to merchant and to public vessels. In Amell v. United States, 384 U.S. 158, 86 S.Ct. 1384, 1966 A.M.C. 1391 (1966) and in United States v. Demko, 385 U.S. 149, 87 S.Ct. 382, 1967 A.M.C. 1666 (1966) (per Black, J., who had dissented without opinion in Patterson) the Johansen-Patterson sequence was reaffirmed. See also Johnson v. United States, 402 F.2d 778 (5th Cir. 1968), certiorari denied 394 U.S. 930, 89 S.Ct. 1195 (1969).

In the case of ships owned by the United States and operated for it during World War II by "general agents," the Supreme Court held, as a matter of construction of the wartime agency contract, that the proper defendant in actions for maintenance and cure (or for damages under the Jones Act) was the United States and not the general agent. See § 6–60 *infra*.

24. See *infra* § 6–63 *et seq.*

24a. Occasionally a seaman may have rights to maintenance and cure against successive employers, if, for example, he is originally injured on a ship owned by A and his condition is aggravated while subsequently serving on a ship owned by B. See, e. g., Gooden v. Sinclair Refining Co., 378 F.2d 576, 1968 A.M.C. 210 (3d Cir. 1967) (the opinion, by Judge Seitz, collects other cases of this sort). Gooden and a companion case, Gore v. Clearwater Shipping Corp., 378 F.2d 584, 1968 A.M.C. 396 (3d Cir. 1967), discuss the rights of the successive employers to contribution or exoneration among themselves, see § 6–18 *infra*, text following note 94i.

24b. On the priority of the lien for maintenance and cure, see Fredelos v. Merritt-Chapman & Scott Corp., 447 F.2d 438, 1971 A.M.C. 2192 (5th Cir. 1971), discussed Chapter IX, § 9–61, note 308a.

enforced by libel *in rem* against the ship or by libel *in personam* against the owner.[25]

In the normal course of events the shipowner and the seaman's employer are the same person. No doubt for this reason it has been customary to say, as we put it in the first edition of the treatise, that: "Since the right [to maintenance and cure] arises out of the employment relationship, the employer is the person liable." Cases have occasionally arisen in which the plaintiff, concededly a seaman, has been employed by someone other than the shipowner. For example, in Mahramas v. American Export Isbrandtsen Lines, Inc.[26] the plaintiff was a hairdresser in a cruise ship's beauty shop; although she signed the ship's articles she was employed by the owners of the beauty shop who operated it as independent contractors. Claiming to have been injured by reason of defective equipment on the ship she brought the customary three-count action for unseaworthiness, for damages under the Jones Act, and for maintenance and cure. The unseaworthiness action, in its modern guise, does not rest on the employment relationship;[27] thus there was no doubt that she could bring that count against the shipowner in personam (or the ship in rem). Actions under the Jones Act, however, like actions for maintenance and cure, have been thought to lie only against an employer. For that reason the majority of the Court, over a persuasive dissent by Judge Oakes, held that the Jones Act and maintenance and cure counts could be brought only against the owners of the beauty shop and dismissed those counts of the libel in personam against the shipowner (the plaintiff in Mahramas did not attempt to libel the ship in rem).[27a] We shall defer discussion of the merits of the question until a later point[27b] where, as a matter of policy, we shall adopt the position taken by Judge Oakes in his Mahramas dissent.

At this point, however, there should be pointed out a possible line of distinction between Jones Act actions and maintenance and cure actions which has, so far, not been much explored in the reported cases. Actions under the Jones Act can be brought only in personam;[27c] thus, if it is assumed (as the majority held in Mahramas) that only the employer can be sued under the Jones Act, that is the end of the matter. The maintenance and cure action, however, as we have pointed out, can be brought in rem as well as in personam. Even if it is assumed that, in a Mahramas situation, the shipowner is not liable in personam for maintenance and cure (because he is

25. The Osceola, 189 U.S. 158 (1903).

26. 475 F.2d 165, 1973 A.M.C. 587 (2d Cir. 1973). On the plaintiff's status as a "seaperson" see Note 21 *supra* and the accompanying text.

27. See § 6–38 *et seq. infra.*

27a. The same result had been reached in a maintenance and cure action in Sims v. Marine Catering Service, 217 F.Supp. 511, 1964 A.M.C. 377 (E.D.La. 1963) (messman employed by catering service on vessel owned by oil company engaged in off-shore development). As in the Mahramas case, the libels in Sims were in personam only.

27b. See § 6–21(a) *infra* (Jones Act).

27c. See § 6–22 *infra.*

not the employer), it does not necessarily follow that the ship is not liable in rem.[27d]

In Solet v. M/V Captain H. V. Dufrene [27e] the plaintiff was injured in the course of his work on a shrimp trawler owned by Dufrene. Dufrene had let or chartered the trawler to a Captain Parfait who had engaged Solet as a deckhand under an arrangement whereby Solet and another crew member were to share in the profits (if any). Judge Rubin concluded that Dufrene was not Solet's employer. Therefore Solet's Jones Act count against Dufrene was dismissed as well as his count for maintenance and cure against Dufrene in personam. Judge Rubin then went on to suggest that the maintenance and cure remedy depended, historically, not so much on the employment relationship as on "the seaman's special dependence on his vessel." Therefore:

> "While Solet's failure to prove a common law employer-employee relationship prevents him from recovering damages under the Jones Act and maintenance and cure from Dufrene personally, it does not prevent him from acquiring a lien, enforceable by an *in rem* proceeding against the trawler for this claim under the older standards applicable in determining liability for maintenance and cure." [27f]

Maintenance and cure plaintiffs will be well advised to proceed in rem whenever there is any doubt about the shipowner's being the employer and the vessel is amenable to in rem process.[27g]

In the first edition of the treatise we suggested that a maintenance and cure action brought by a plaintiff who had been employed by a bareboat or demise charterer would lie only against the charterer-employer and not against the shipowner. That statement appears to be correct with respect to the shipowner's in personam liability [27h] even if we adopt the position taken by the dissenting judge in Mahramas. In Mahramas the employer was in no sense responsible for the operation of the ship; here the charterer is, by hypothesis, responsible so that (except for injuries resulting from conditions of

**27d.** For a discussion of situations in which a ship may be libeled in rem although the shipowner is not liable in personam, see Chapter IX, § 9–5 *et seq.*, particularly § 9–18(a). A libel in rem by a Mahramas type plaintiff would concededly be a novel twist on some old doctrine but the idea does not seem to be unreasonably far-fetched.

**27e.** 303 F.Supp. 980, 1970 A.M.C. 571 (E.D.La.1969).

**27f.** 303 F.Supp. at p. 988, 1970 A.M.C. at p. 582.

**27g.** On venue requirements for in rem process, see Chapter IX, § 9–85.

**27h.** In Haskins v. Point Towing Co., Inc., 421 F.2d 532, 1970 A.M.C. 14 (3d Cir. 1970) it was held that a shipowner was not liable in personam for maintenance and cure to a seaman who had been employed by a bareboat charterer. Judge McLaughlin dissented on the ground that summary judgment for the defendant had been improper since there was evidence on which the jury could have found that the plaintiff had in fact been employed by the shipowner-defendant and not by the charterer. Welsh v. Utah Dredging Co., 403 F.2d 217 (3d Cir. 1968) appears to be to the same effect. See also the Solet case, text at Note 27e, *supra*.

unseaworthiness which existed before delivery of the ship under the charter) there appears to be no theory under which the owner could (or should) be held to personal liability. However, our earlier discussion of the shipowner's non-liability seems to have overlooked the possibility, suggested by the Solet case, that the maintenance and cure plaintiff could proceed in rem against the ship even if the owner's non-liability in personam is conceded. Indeed in rem liability for events which occur while the ship is in the possession and control of demise charterers traces back to the venerable authority of The Barnstable.[27i] If the maintenance and cure plaintiff was successful in his in rem action, there is no doubt that the shipowner would be entitled to indemnity from the charterer-employer, with the exception previously suggested of injuries resulting from pre-demise conditions of unseaworthiness.[27j] Indeed the principal holding in The Barnstable itself was that the owners, under the charter, were entitled to such an indemnity.

Whatever the theoretical possibilities may be of proceeding in rem against the ship or in personam against a shipowner who is not the employer, it is of course entirely clear that the maintenance and cure plaintiff can always proceed against his employer. A perfectly possible result in such situations is that the employer will be held liable for maintenance and cure with respect to injuries caused by unseaworthiness or operating negligence for which the shipowner is wholly responsible. We shall defer until a later section our discussion of whether the employer so situated would be entitled to indemnity from the shipowner.[27k]

The right to maintenance and cure arises when the seaman signs articles and continues until he has received his discharge.[28] It is the fact of employment or, more accurately, the fact that the seaman is engaged in the service of the ship which creates the right and not the form of contract: a term in a contract under which the seaman purported to waive the right would unquestionably be held void. Even fishermen who operate under the traditional lay system, in which the crew looks to a share of the profits from the voyage for its wages, are entitled to maintenance and cure, against the argument that they have become in a sense part owners.[29]

**§ 6–8.** The seaman may recover for any injury or illness suffered without his misconduct during the employment period. The

**27i.** 181 U.S. 464, 21 S.Ct. 684 (1901), discussed Chapter IX, § 9–10. On the current status of the rule in The Barnstable, see Chapter IX, § 9–18(a).

**27j.** The Solet case, text at note 27e *supra*, illustrates the exception.

**27k.** See § 6–18, *infra*.

**28.** Farrell v. United States, 336 U.S. 511, 69 S.Ct. 707, 1949 A.M.C. 613 (1949). The reference in the text to signing articles is not of course meant to suggest that only members of the ship's company who sign on in the traditional form are entitled to maintenance and cure.

**29.** Old Point Fish Co. v. Haywood, 109 F.2d 703, 1940 A.M.C. 145 (4th Cir. 1940). See also the Solet case, text at Note 27e *supra*.

injury or illness need not result from or be in any way causally related to his shipboard duties. The Supreme Court has made this proposition crystal clear in a series of cases beginning with Calmar S. S. Corp. v. Taylor.[30] In that case the seaman suffered from Buerger's disease, an incurable malady of the veins and arteries which tends to be progressive and may cause death. The seaman alleged that the disease had been caused by an injury to his foot which resulted from stubbing his toe against an object on the floor of the ship's boiler room where he was on duty; the Court, however, accepted the trial judge's finding that there was no connection between the foot injury and the disease. The Court, recognizing that in most prior cases "the efficient cause of the injury or illness was some proven act of the seaman in the service of the ship", held that all that was necessary was that the seaman become incapacitated "when subject to the call of duty". Chief Justice Stone commented that "the practical inconvenience and the attendant danger to seamen in the application of a rule which would encourage the attempt by master or owner to determine in advance of any maintenance and cure whether the illness was caused by the employment, are manifest." The owner may even be held liable for maintenance and cure with respect to an illness from which the seaman was suffering before he signed on, so long as the sailor did not knowingly conceal his condition at the time he applied for employment. In applying the "knowingly concealed" phase of the rule, the courts have been liberal toward the seaman, who is considered to be endowed with an invincible ignorance.[30a] The practice of having prospective employees examined by a physician may backfire against the shipowner on the ground that he has taken it upon himself to discover the true condition, thereby releasing the seaman from any duty beyond truthfully answering the questions put by the physician.[31]

30. 303 U.S. 525, 58 S.Ct. 651, 1938 A.M.C. 341 (1938).

30a. See Sammon v. Central Gulf S. S. Corp., 442 F.2d 1028, 1971 A.M.C. 1113 (2d Cir. 1971) (maintenance and cure awarded although seaman had failed to disclose a prior condition which recurred during his employment). Gore v. Clearwater Shipping Corp., 378 F.2d 584, 1968 A.M.C. 396 (3d Cir. 1967) is to the same effect. *Cf.*, however, McCorpen v. Central Gulf S. S. Corp., 396 F.2d 547, 1968 A.M.C. 1147 (5th Cir. 1968). Judge Thornberry's opinion in McCorpen collects cases on the distinction between mere failure to disclose and willful concealment. Siders v. The Ohio River Co., 351 F.Supp. 987 (W.D.Pa.1970, 1971), affirmed 469 F.2d 1093 (3d Cir. 1972) is another willful concealment case in which maintenance and cure was denied.

Occasionally defendants in maintenance and cure actions who have made voluntary maintenance and cure payments will counterclaim to recover the payments made on the ground that they were fraudulently procured through concealment or misrepresentation. See Bergeria v. Marine Carriers, Inc., 341 F.Supp. 1153, 1972 A.M.C. 1629 (E.D.Pa.1972), holding that such a counterclaim was within the admiralty jurisdiction. In Alvarez v. American Export Isbrandtsen Lines, Inc., 1971 A.M.C. 359 (S.D.N.Y.1970), judgment was awarded to the defendant-shipowner on such a counterclaim. See also the Fletcher case, note 40 at end.

31. Rosenquist v. Isthmian S. S. Co., 205 F.2d 486, 1953 A.M.C. 1249 (2d Cir. 1953); Ahmed v. United States, 177 F.2d 898, 1950 A.M.C. 53 (2d Cir. 1949); Saar v. Sun Oil Co., 124 F.Supp. 684, 1954 A.M.C. 2138 (E.D.Pa. 1954). See also Hazelton v. Luckenbach S. S. Co., Inc., 134 F.Supp. 525, 1955 A.M.C. 2096 (D.Mass.1955).

After Taylor, the Supreme Court explored the no-causal-relationship proposition further in several cases which involved injuries on shore leave. In Waterman S. S. Corp. v. Jones,[32] the seaman, who was leaving the ship on authorized shore leave, not connected with the ship's business, fell into an open ditch at a railroad siding which was apparently on an appropriate route to the street from the pier at which the ship was moored. In Aguilar v. Standard Oil Co.,[33] the seaman, who was returning from authorized shore leave which had been granted for his "personal business", was injured by a motor vehicle on premises through which he had to pass to reach his ship. The two cases were consolidated for argument and decided together in an opinion by Justice Rutledge which has since become almost as mandatory a source for quotation as Justice Story's opinion in Harden v. Gordon.[34] Noting that the question of the shipowner's liability for injuries incurred on shore leave not on ship's business was being decided by the Court for the first time, Justice Rutledge wrote:

> ". . . Unlike men employed in service on land, the seaman, when he finishes his day's work, is neither relieved of obligations to his employer nor wholly free to dispose of his leisure as he sees fit. Of necessity, during the voyage he must eat, drink, lodge and divert himself within the confines of the ship. In short, during the period of his tenure the vessel is not merely his place of employment; it is the framework of his existence. For that reason, among others, his employer's responsibility for maintenance and cure extends beyond injuries sustained because of, or while engaged in activities required by his employment. In this respect it is a broader liability than that imposed by modern workmen's compensation statutes. Appropriately it covers all injuries and ailments incurred without misconduct on the seaman's part amounting to ground for forfeiture, at least while he is on the ship, 'subject to the call of duty as a seaman, and earning wages as such.'
>
> "* * *
>
> "We think that the principles governing shipboard injuries apply to the facts presented by these cases. To relieve the shipowner of his obligation in the case of injuries incurred on shore leave would cast upon the seaman hazards encountered only by reason of the voyage. The assumption is hardly sound that the normal uses and purposes of shore leave are 'exclusively personal' and have no relation to the vessel's business. Men cannot live for long cooped up aboard ship, without substantial impairment of their efficiency, if not also serious danger to discipline. Relaxation beyond the confines of the ship is necessary if the work is to go on, more

32. 318 U.S. 724, 63 S.Ct. 930, 1943 A.M.C. 451 (1943). The Waterman case and the Aguilar case, note 33 *infra*, were decided in the same opinion.

33. Note 32, *supra*.

34. 11 Fed.Cas. 480, Case No. 6,047 (C.C.D.Me.1823).

so that it may move smoothly. No master would take a crew to sea if he could not grant shore leave, and no crew would be taken if it could never obtain it. Even more for the seaman than for the landsman, therefore, 'the superfluous is the necessary . . . to make life livable' and to get work done. In short, shore leave is an elemental necessity in the sailing of ships, a part of the business as old as the art, not merely a personal diversion." [35]

Farrell v. United States [36] went a step beyond the Jones and Aguilar cases. Farrell was a merchant seaman attached to a cargo and troop ship docked at Palermo in 1944. Like Aguilar he was injured while returning from shore leave, but the circumstances of Farrell's injury were not in his favor. In the first place, he had overstayed his leave by two hours. Returning late, on a dark and rainy night, he lost his way and entered the shorefront by the wrong gate a mile from where his ship was moored. Making his way to the ship, he fell over a guard chain into a drydock which was lighted sufficiently for night work then in progress. His fall, wrote Justice Jackson, "was due to no negligence but his own". Nevertheless, Farrell was held entitled to "the usual measure of maintenance and cure at the ship's expense". In that holding the Court was unanimous although the Justices were divided on the proper amount of Farrell's recovery.

Warren v. United States [37] raised the problem of injuries received on shore leave during the seaman's period of relaxation and amusement. Warren and some companions went ashore at Naples in 1944, did some sightseeing, drank a bottle of wine and went to a dance hall. Warren went out of the dance hall on an unprotected balcony which overlooked the ocean. Leaning over the edge of the balcony, he attempted to support himself by an iron rod which was apparently attached to the side of the building. The rod came loose and Warren fell, breaking a leg. Like Aguilar, Jones and Farrell, Warren was held entitled to maintenance and cure, this time over dissents by Justices Jackson, Clark and Frankfurter.

The opinions in the three Supreme Court shore leave cases all recognize that the seaman forfeits his right to maintenance and cure by his own willful misconduct. As Justice Rutledge put it in Aguilar, "the traditional instances are venereal disease and injuries received as a result of intoxication, though on occasion the latter has been qualified in recognition of a classic predisposition of sailors ashore". It may be that changing attitudes toward sexual activity and the

35. 318 U.S. 724, 731, 733, 63 S.Ct. 930, 934, 935, 1943 A.M.C. 451, 458, 459. While Justice Rutledge's language suggests that he had in mind shore leave in foreign ports, the lower courts have held that injuries which occur on shore leave in the home port are also covered: Smith v. United States, 167 F.2d 550, 1948 A.M.C. 761 (4th Cir. 1948); Lawler v. Matson Nav. Co., 108 F.Supp. 946, 1953 A.M.C. 154 (N.D.Cal.1952).

36. 336 U.S. 511, 69 S.Ct. 707, 1949 A.M.C. 613 (1949).

37. 340 U.S. 523, 71 S.Ct. 432, 1951 A.M.C. 416 (1951).

analogy of the Army's handling of the problem (it is not misconduct to contract venereal disease; it is misconduct to fail to report infection) will lead to a relaxation of the venereal disease rule. A colorful 1948 case decided by a New York state court may be indicative: maintenance and cure was awarded to a seaman who had suffered a broken leg in jumping from a window of a Yugoslavian brothel following a dispute over financial arrangements.[38] In line with Justice Rutledge's recognition of the "classic predisposition of sailors ashore", even a finding that a seaman's injuries resulted from his drunkenness has been held not to bar his recovery.[39] Misconduct on board ship as well as misconduct ashore will forfeit the right, but the courts have not been inclined to construe misconduct as including what the opinions refer to as "horseplay".[40] It is apparent from the Farrell case (plaintiff fell over a guard chain into a lighted dry-dock) that negligence or contributory negligence of even the grossest kind will not of itself qualify as misconduct and forfeit the right.[40a]

38. Koistinen v. American Export Lines, Inc., 83 N.Y.S.2d 297, 194 Misc. 942, 1948 A.M.C. 1464 (N.Y.City Ct. 1948).

39. Bentley v. Albatross S. S. Co., 203 F.2d 270, 1953 A.M.C. 645 (3d Cir. 1953). But see Victoria v. Luckenbach S. S. Co., Inc., 141 F.Supp. 149, 1956 A.M.C. 1626 (S.D.N.Y.1956).

In Blouin v. American Export Isbrandtsen Lines, Inc., 1970 A.M.C. 712 (S.D. N.Y.1970) the court concluded that chronic alcoholism which had aggravated a pre-existing condition of hypertension would bar a maintenance and cure award with respect to the hypertension on grounds of misconduct. An award was made, however, because of a heart condition which had first manifested itself during the plaintiff's employment.

In Whatley v. United States, 1970 A.M. C. 1556 (S.D.N.Y.1970) the plaintiff had been beaten up and robbed while he was on shore leave in Saigon. The court dismissed his action for damages on the ground that the plaintiff had been at fault and was responsible for his own misadventure, but nevertheless awarded him maintenance and cure.

40. See Murphy v. Light, 224 F.2d 944, 1955 A.M.C. 1986 (5th Cir. 1955) certiorari denied 350 U.S. 960, 76 S.Ct. 348 (1955); Meyer v. Dollar S. S. Line, 49 F.2d 1002, 1931 A.M.C. 1059 (9th Cir. 1931). A maintenance and cure award was held barred by misconduct in Watson v. Joshua Hendy Corp., 142 F.Supp. 335, 1956 A.M.C. 1630 (S.D.N.Y.1956).

In Gulledge v. United States, 337 F. Supp. 1108, 1972 A.M.C. 1187 (E.D.Pa. 1972) judgment went against the plaintiff in his action to recover damages for injuries suffered in a fight with a fellow member of the crew. He did, however, recover an award for maintenance and cure even though the evidence suggested that the plaintiff had been the aggressor. The court held that the burden of proof to show the plaintiff's gross misconduct with respect to the maintenance and cure count was on the defendant and had not been met.

In Fletcher v. Keystone Tankship Corp., 1970 A.M.C. 1812 (S.D.Tex.1969), the plaintiff had shot and killed a fellow crew-member. Subsequently the shipowner entered into a settlement with the heirs of the dead man. After criminal proceedings against him had been dismissed by reason of insanity, the plaintiff sought to recover both damages and maintenance and cure. The court not only dismissed both counts of his action but gave judgment for the defendant on a counterclaim for the amount of the settlement and attorneys' fees in connection with it.

40a. That the burden of proof is on the defendant to plead and prove such misconduct as will bar a maintenance and cure award, see the Gulledge case, note 40 *supra*; 2 Norris, note 12 *supra*, § 558 (without citation of authority). Norris collects the willful misconduct cases at § 602 *et seq.*

The Supreme Court opinions in the Taylor case and the shore leave cases seem to have left no further room for dispute about the circumstances under which maintenance and cure may be recovered. With the exception of borderline cases on misconduct, there is no reason to anticipate further litigation of this sort. The remedy has become absolute.

The Supreme Court's extension of the maintenance and cure remedy to shore leave injuries has led to some uncertainty in subsequent lower court decisions in cases which involve what have been called "commuter seamen" [40b]—that is seamen who live at home and commute to work daily or who spend fixed periods on the vessel and on shore. Such seamen are of course entitled to maintenance and cure with respect to shipboard injuries and diseases which manifest themselves during the employment period.[40c] Whether they are also entitled to maintenance and cure for injuries suffered during their periods on shore is a question as to which a certain amount of judicial disagreement appears to be developing. In several cases the situation has been that the seaman was injured in the course of his trip to or from work. The Ninth Circuit approved an award under such circumstances in Williamson v. Western Pacific Dredging Corp.;[40d] Judge Browning was at pains to point out that the Court "intimate[d] no opinion" as to what the decision would have been if the plaintiff's injury had occurred while he was at home. The Fifth Circuit seems to be in the course of working out a fairly complicated distinction based on whether the plaintiff was or was not "answerable to the call of duty" at the time of his injury.[40e] Presumably plaintiffs injured on shore but not in the course of their trips to and from work will have considerable difficulty in persuading courts and juries that their injuries occurred in the service of the ship.[40f]

**40b.** See Comment, Maintenance and Cure, the Jones Act and Land-Based Seamen, 46 Tulane L.Rev. 877 (1972).

**40c.** See text at note 21a *supra* and the cases cited in the note.

**40d.** 441 F.2d 65, 1971 A.M.C. 2356 (9th Cir. 1971), certiorari denied 404 U.S. 851 (1971).

**40e.** See Sellers v. Dixilyn Corp., 433 F.2d 446, 1971 A.M.C. 425 (5th Cir. 1970). Plaintiff, employed on an offshore oil rig, spent seven days on the rig and seven days on shore. He was paid only for the time he spent on the rig and was free to do whatever he wanted while he was on shore. Maintenance and cure was denied. *Cf.* Vincent v. Harvey Well Service, 441 F.2d 146, 1971 A.M.C. 2541 (5th Cir. 1971) (a Jones Act case) in which the automobile in which the plaintiff was injured was provided by the employer and driven by a fellow-employee who was paid to furnish transportation. Judge Brown, distinguishing the Sellers case, observed that the employer's interests were served by the arrangement and made out an occurrence in the "service of the ship".

**40f.** See Baker v. Ocean Systems, Inc., 454 F.2d 379, 1972 A.M.C. 287 (5th Cir. 1972) (maintenance and cure denied to a "diver-tender" who was injured in a cocktail lounge after his return from work). In O'Neill v. Perini Corp., 1972 A.M.C. 112 (D.Mass.1971) maintenance and cure was denied for an injury suffered while the plaintiff was off-duty and at home. In Haskell v. Socony Mobil Oil Co., 237 F.2d 707, 1956 A.M.C. 2277 (1st Cir. 1956) maintenance and cure was denied to a seaman who was injured in an automobile accident while he was living at home during a period of accumulated leave.

**§ 6–9.** Maintenance and cure may be sought either in a separate action or under one count in an action to recover damages for negligence or unseaworthiness.[41] The usual reason for bringing a separate maintenance and cure action is that some third party, and neither the ship nor the shipowner, is the only possible tortfeasor in sight: the shore leave cases, in which the seaman is injured while away from the ship, have made this a not infrequent situation. Occasionally counsel who regards himself as more than usually astute will separate the maintenance and cure action from the damage action in the hope of getting a double recovery from the shipowner. It is obvious on principle that a plaintiff who has recovered medical expenses, a living allowance and unearned wages under the name of maintenance and cure has no right to recover them a second time in a damage action. Thus any maintenance and cure expenses which have been recovered as damages ought to be subtracted from a maintenance and cure award and vice versa. When a jury has awarded damages on principles best known to itself, it may be easier to say that the deduction ought to be made than to make it. Nevertheless the trial judge, on appropriate motion, can, and often will, achieve rough justice.[42] The separation of the maintenance and cure items from the damage items of the recovery is probably harder to control judicially when they all go to a jury together in the same action, so that the more than usually astute counsel who brings the maintenance and cure action separately when there is no need to do so may well be outsmarting his own client.[42a]

Maintenance and cure, which is a right arising under maritime law, may of course be recovered in admiralty where the action may be *in rem* or *in personam*. The recovery may also be had outside the admiralty under the saving to suitors clause.[43]

41. Calmar S. S. Corp. v. Taylor, 303 U.S. 525, 58 S.Ct. 651, 1938 A.M.C. 341 (1938); Pacific S. S. Co. v. Peterson, 278 U.S. 130, 49 S.Ct. 75, 1928 A.M.C. 1932 (1928).

42. McCarthy v. American Eastern Corp., 175 F.2d 724, 1953 A.M.C. 1864 (3d Cir. 1949) certiorari denied 338 U.S. 911, 70 S.Ct. 349 (1950). See also Yates v. Dann, 124 F.Supp. 126, 1955 A.M.C. 1078 (D.Del.1954) reversed on other grounds 223 F.2d 64, 1955 A.M.C. 1214 (3d Cir. 1955); Gomes v. Eastern Gas & Fuel Associates, 132 F. Supp. 29, 1955 A.M.C. 1560 (D.Mass. 1955). In Moss v. Hendy Corp., 1955 A.M.C. 360 (N.D.Cal.1955), the District Judge ordered a maintenance and cure libel consolidated for trial with a civil action under the Jones Act. Stendze v. The Neptune, 135 F.Supp. 801, 1956 A.M.C. 583 (D.Mass.1955) indicates the difficulties of making an allocation.

42a. Astute counsel will do well to ponder Siders v. The Ohio River Co., 351 F.Supp. 987 (W.D.Pa.1970, 1971), affirmed 469 F.2d 1093 (3d Cir. 1972); further proceedings 351 F.Supp. 995 (W.D.Pa.1972). The action was in the usual three counts. At the request of plaintiff's counsel the maintenance and cure count was tried to the court first. The judge dismissed the maintenance and cure count and the dismissal was affirmed on appeal. When the Jones Act and unseaworthiness counts came on for trial, the same judge held that, on the ground of collateral estoppel, the earlier dismissal of the maintenance and cure count required dismissal of the other two counts.

43. Recovery for maintenance and cure in a state court action was approved in Garrett v. Moore-McCormack Co., 317 U.S. 239, 63 S.Ct. 246, 1942 A.M.C. 1645 (1942). The Garrett case also made clear that when the action is brought outside the admiralty, maritime and not state law will apply; see *infra* § 6–58 *et seq.*

In cases brought on the civil side of federal court and tried to a jury in which the plaintiff joined a count for maintenance and cure to counts for damages under the Jones Act and for unseaworthiness, a controversy developed during the 1950's as to the proper handling of the maintenance and cure count. There had come to be general agreement that both the unseaworthiness count under the general maritime law and the negligence count under the Jones Act were to go to the jury without any requirement that the plaintiff elect between them.[44] In some Circuits the maintenance and cure count was also allowed to go to the jury along with the other two counts;[45] in other Circuits the maintenance and cure count was kept from the jury and decided by the court on the theory that maintenance and cure was not a common law remedy within the saving clause.[45a]

The developing confusion was compounded by the Supreme Court's decision in Romero v. International Terminal Operating Co.[45b] Romero was the usual three-count action brought on the civil side of federal court. The majority of the Court held that, absent diversity, there was no "federal question" jurisdiction over the general maritime law counts for unseaworthiness and maintenance and cure under 28 U.S.C.A. § 1331. However, when the general maritime law counts were joined to a Jones Act count (as to which no jurisdictional question arose) then, on a theory of "pendent jurisdiction," there would be, even in the absence of diversity, federal jurisdiction over all three counts. Having got that far, Justice Frankfurter's majority opinion observed: "We are not called upon to decide whether the District Court may submit to the jury the 'pendent' claims under the general maritime law . . . "

The confusion engendered by that sibylline utterance was dramatically illustrated by the Second Circuit's extraordinary division in Fitzgerald v. United States Lines Company.[45c] The Court heard the case *in banc*. All the judges agreed, in an opinion by Judge Friendly, that, if diversity jurisdiction existed, all three counts should go to the jury. On what should be done in the absence of diversity jurisdiction the Court split three ways. Judge Friendly, supported by three other judges, concluded that Romero meant that the maintenance and cure count could not be sent to the jury and must be decided by the court. Three judges joined in an opinion by Judge Clark

44. See § 6–23 *infra*.

45. See, e. g., Rosenquist v. Isthmian, S. S. Co., 205 F.2d 486, 1953 A.M.C. 1249 (2d Cir. 1953). In Weiss v. Central R. Co. of New Jersey, 235 F.2d 309, 1956 A.M.C. 1473 (2d Cir. 1956) Judge Clark suggested that while the maintenance and cure count could properly go to the jury along with the other counts, the trial judge could also in his discretion pass on the maintenance and cure count himself.

45a. See, e. g., Jordine v. Walling, 185 F.2d 662, 1951 A.M.C. 43 (3d Cir. 1950).

45b. 358 U.S. 354, 79 S.Ct. 468, 1959 A.M.C. 832 (1959). The Romero case is discussed § 6–62, *infra*.

45c. 306 F.2d 461, 1962 A.M.C. 2251 (2d Cir. 1962).

which concluded that all three counts must be sent to the jury. Two judges joined in an opinion by Judge Smith which concluded that the trial judge had discretion either to send all three counts to the jury or to keep the maintenance and cure count from the jury and decide it himself.

The Supreme Court granted certiorari in Fitzgerald and gave a totally unexpected answer to the puzzle it had propounded in Romero.[45d] Justice Black noted approvingly that: "For years it has been a common, although not uniform, practice of District Courts to grant jury trials to plaintiffs who join in one complaint their Jones Act, unseaworthiness, and maintenance and cure claims when all the claims . . . grow out of a single transaction or accident." Indeed the opposite practice of keeping the maintenance and cure claims from the jury was "unfortunate, outdated and wasteful . . . cumbersome, confusing, and time consuming," raised "needless problems" and placed "completely unnecessary obstacles in the paths of litigants seeking justice in our courts . . . ." "Fortunately," Justice Black added, there was no "statutory or constitutional obstacle" to reaching a sensible solution, even without reconsidering Romero which the Court declined to do. While jury trials in admiralty cases are not constitutionally required, neither are they constitutionally forbidden. Congress has largely left to the Supreme Court "the responsibility for fashioning the controlling rules of admiralty law." Therefore, by way of fashioning a new rule, "we hold that a maintenance and cure claim joined with a Jones Act claim [45e] must be submitted to the jury when both arise out of one set of facts." Justice Harlan, who expressed himself to be "wholly in sympathy with the result reached by the Court," dissented on the ground that the proper way to fashion a new admiralty rule was under the Court's rule-making powers. Thus the Court was unanimous on the desirability of the result. The Court chose to decide Fitzgerald on the assumption that diversity jurisdiction was lacking; obviously the "rule" in Fitzgerald is equally applicable to diversity cases, as Justice Black suggested in a footnote and as all the judges of the Second Circuit had assumed when they heard the case *in banc.*

The remand in Fitzgerald is of particular interest. At trial there had been a jury verdict for the defendant on the unseaworthiness and Jones Act counts, following which the District Court had made a small maintenance and cure award. That disposition of the case was affirmed by the Second Circuit. The Supreme Court's grant of certiorari was limited to the maintenance and cure count, so that the judgment entered on the jury verdict on the other two counts still stood. Nevertheless the Court remanded the case so that the plaintiff could have the jury trial on the surviving maintenance and cure

**45d.** Fitzgerald v. United States Lines Co., 374 U.S. 16, 83 S.Ct. 1646, 1963 A.M.C. 1093 (1963).

**45e.** Although Justice Black did not expressly refer to the unseaworthiness claim in this passage of his opinion, he evidently meant that, if all three claims are joined, they must all go to the jury.

count that he would have had on all three counts the first time around if the trial judge had not fallen into "error".

The Supreme Court's uncharacteristically forthright resolution of the jury trial issue in Fitzgerald has effectively removed the problem from litigation. In Haskins v. Point Towing Company[45f] the Third Circuit concluded that under Fitzgerald the plaintiff could have the best of both worlds by designating his unseaworthiness and maintenance and cure counts as admiralty claims under Rule 9(h) F.R.C.P.[45g] (thus preserving the procedural advantages of admiralty practice such as the use of in rem process and the availability of interlocutory appeals) and his Jones Act count as being at law (thus entitling him to a jury trial on all three counts).[45h] All this did Haskins no good, however, since on a second appeal the Court approved the District Court's action in giving summary judgment for the defendant on all counts.[45i] The Second Circuit has taken the position that Fitzgerald has not limited the power of the trial judge to enter summary judgment on a Jones Act claim when he feels that there is no evidence to go to the jury and then decide the general maritime law claims himself.[45j] That may be a narrow reading of Fitzgerald but it is certainly not an implausible one; however, if attention is focused on the terms of the remand in Fitzgerald, the argument could be made, not implausibly, that the plaintiff is entitled to a jury trial on the general maritime law counts, no matter what happens to the Jones Act count (at least if it is assumed that the Jones Act count was not frivolous).

**45f.** 395 F.2d 737, 1968 A.M.C. 1193 (3d Cir. 1968).

**45g.** Judge Freedman noted in his Haskins opinion that in the 1966 procedural unification nothing was done one way or the other about the Fitzgerald case. That is, the Fitzgerald holding was not "codified" as a Rule; neither was it rejected. In all the cases of this sort which have been decided since 1966 the judges have assumed, as Judge Freedman did in Haskins, that Fitzgerald is still the governing law despite the failure of the 1966 draftsmen to embody it in a Rule.

**45h.** In Blake v. Farrell Lines, Inc., 417 F.2d 264 (3d Cir. 1970) a longshoreman brought unseaworthiness actions against shipowners who then impleaded the longshoreman's employer in an action for indemnity. The Court held that under Fitzgerald the indemnity action could be consolidated with the unseaworthiness actions and tried to the jury. In Bergeria v. Marine Carriers, Inc., 341 F.Supp. 1153, 1972 A.M.C. 1629 (E.D.Pa.1972) Judge Becker concluded that the Blake reading of Fitzgerald meant that a shipowner's counterclaim to recover maintenance and cure payments voluntarily made (see note 30a *supra*) should go to the jury along with the plaintiff's Jones Act and unseaworthiness counts. See also Jewell v. The Ohio River Co., 431 F.2d 691 (3d Cir. 1970), digested note 55c *infra*.

**45i.** 421 F.2d 532, 1970 A.M.C. 14 (3d Cir. 1970).

**45j.** Mahramas v. American Export Isbrandtsen Lines, Inc., 475 F.2d 165, 1973 A.M.C. 587 (2d Cir. 1973), Judge Anderson commented: "If the rule were otherwise, any plaintiff could receive a jury trial on his admiralty claims simply by alleging a Jones Act count, whether or not he had any evidence to support it, and, of course, the time has still not come when one is entitled to a jury trial in every admiralty suit." (475 F.2d at pp. 172–173; 1973 A.M.C. at p. 596.)

### Same: Amount of Recovery—Duration and Extent of Shipowner's Liability

**§ 6–10.** How much can be recovered for maintenance and cure and for how long a period after discharge the shipowner's liability continues are matters less clearly settled than the circumstances which create the right in the first place. Most current cases on maintenance and cure involve one or both of these questions.

Both the Taylor case (incurable disease not causally related to seaman's duties) [46] and the Farrell case (injury while on shore leave) [47] dealt with the amount of recovery and the duration of liability. In the Taylor case the trial court had found that the seaman was entitled to recover the cost of medical treatment so long as such treatment might be necessary. On the assumption that the plaintiff's disease was incurable, the judge felt that there should be a lump sum award based on life expectancy, and entered a judgment for $7,000. Accepting the medical findings, the Supreme Court disapproved the lump sum award, at least in cases where there was no causal relationship between the employment and the illness. Such an award, it seemed to Chief Justice Stone, was not only without support in prior case law but was not justifiable on policy, both because it was too speculative and because it was not well adapted as a safeguard during illness to the notoriously improvident beneficiary. Turning to the proper measure of recovery, the Chief Justice wrote:

> "The seaman's recovery must therefore be measured in each case by the reasonable cost of that maintenance and cure to which he is entitled at the time of trial, including, in the discretion of the court, such amounts as may be needful in the immediate future for the maintenance and cure of a kind and for a period which can be definitely ascertained." [48]

In the Farrell case, the seaman was totally and permanently disabled as a result of his injuries: he had been blinded and suffered post-traumatic convulsions which were expected to become more frequent and could not be cured. From time to time he would require medical care to ease attacks of headaches and epileptic convulsions. The District Court held that the shipowner's duty to furnish maintenance and cure did not extend beyond the time when the maximum cure possible had been effected; therefore, Farrell was found not entitled to maintenance or to medical expenses after the time when his condition had been diagnosed as hopeless. An award was made for a period of six months following his discharge from hospital.[49] The Supreme Court, in an opinion by Justice Jackson, affirmed, four justices dissenting on the ground that Farrell should receive his con-

46. See text at note 30 *supra*.

47. See text at note 36 *supra*.

48. 303 U.S. 525, 531, 58 S.Ct. 651, 655, 1938 A.M.C. 341, 346 (1938).

49. The District Court opinion in the Farrell case was not reported. The award made by the District Court is referred to in Justice Douglas' dissent, 336 U.S. 511, 523, 69 S.Ct. 707, 713, 1949 A.M.C. 613, 622 (1949).

tinuing medical and maintenance expenses, presumably for life. Justice Jackson took the occasion to disclaim any inference from the Taylor case that a distinction could be drawn between injury and illness caused by, and injury and illness not caused by, the employment: treating Farrell's case as one caused by the employment, an assumption hardly warranted by the facts, he concluded that both types of claims were on the same footing:

> ". . . For any purpose to introduce a graduation of rights and duties based on some relative proximity of the activity at time of injury to the 'employment' or the 'service of the ship,' would alter the basis and be out of harmony with the spirit and function of the doctrine and would open the door to the litigiousness which has made the landman's remedy so often a promise to the ear to be broken to the hope." [50]

In any case, he added, Farrell, whose injuries resulted from his own negligence, was not a claimant who could reasonably hope to benefit from the suggested distinction: "If we should concede that larger measure of maintenance is due those whose injury is caused by the nature of their employment, it would seem farfetched to hold it applicable here." With respect to the allowable measure of recovery, Justice Jackson wrote:

> "Maintenance and cure is not the only recourse of the injured seaman. In an appropriate case he may obtain indemnity or compensation for injury due to negligence or unseaworthiness and may recover, by trial before court and jury, damages for partial or total disability. But maintenance and cure is more certain if more limited in its benefits. It does not hold a ship to permanent liability for a pension, neither does it give a lump-sum payment to offset disability based on some conception of expectancy of life. Indeed the custom of providing maintenance and cure in kind and concurrently with its need has had the advantage of removing its benefits from danger of being wasted by the proverbial improvidence of its beneficiaries. The Government does not contend that if Farrell receives future treatment of a curative nature he may not recover in a new proceeding the amount expended for such treatment and for maintenance while receiving it." [51]

Since the Supreme Court has not returned to these questions, the Taylor and Farrell cases are still the basic sources of law. Under those cases the shipowner's liability continues only until the point of maximum cure, whatever that may be, is reached. There can be no lump sum recovery for partial or total disability, computed on the basis of life expectancy: the seaman must seek such recovery

50. 336 U.S. 511, 516, 69 S.Ct. 707, 710, 1949 A.M.C. 613, 617 (1949).

51. 336 U.S. 511, 519, 69 S.Ct. 707, 711, 1949 A.M.C. 613, 623 (1949).

in his actions for negligence or unseaworthiness, where they are available (as they were not in Farrell's case). It should be noted that Taylor expressly reserved the question of lifetime maintenance and cure for an incurable condition caused by the seaman's duties and that Farrell did not completely deny the possibility. But Justice Jackson's opinion suggested that the possibility would be considered only when the seaman had himself been entirely free from negligence, which would mean, apart from an Act of God, that the shipowner must have been negligent or the ship unseaworthy. In such cases, as the opinion pointed out, the recovery could be had in the damage action, so that it became merely theoretical speculation whether the same recovery could also be had under a maintenance and cure count.

The rule that the seaman will be abandoned to his own devices at the time his condition becomes hopeless may sound harsher than in fact it is. The rule is obviously a manipulable one: no two men (or judges) need agree on when the point of maximum cure or improvement has been reached. Furthermore, as will be pointed out in the following section, the seaman is not foreclosed by a present denial of future benefits; he can try again and recover further benefits if he can pursuade judge or jury that, because of changes in his own condition or advances in the medical art, there is now a possibility of further improvement. And finally, in all the cases in which the maintenance and cure count goes to the jury under the Fitzgerald rule,[52] the situation is beyond control. In Neff v. Dravo Corporation [52a] an award was approved for medical treatment which would do no more than maintain the plaintiff in his present state, but most courts, whatever they may do in fact, continue to recite the "maximum cure" limitation on recovery.[52b]

**§ 6–11.** Neither Taylor nor Farrell sets any time limit on the duration of the shipowner's liability, so long as there is a chance of improvement in the claimant's condition. The majority opinion in Farrell seems to take the position that "cure" means improvement, or the possibility of improvement, and that Farrell could not recover medical expenses necessary to maintain him in his present condition without further deterioration; this position was bitterly attacked by the four dissenting justices. On the other hand the majority opinion

52. See text following note 45c, *supra*.

52a. 407 F.2d 228 (3d Cir. 1969).

52b. See, e. g., Berke v. Lehigh Marine Disposal Corp., 435 F.2d 1073, 1971 A.M.C. 323 (2d Cir. 1970). Judge Waterman's opinion collects maximum cure cases and expressly criticizes the Third Circuit's decision in Neff, note 52a *supra*. 2 Norris, note 12 *supra*, collects cases on the maximum cure limitation in §§ 562, 563.

Among the older cases see Sims v. U. S. War Shipping Administration, 186 F.2d 972, 1951 A.M.C. 461 (3d Cir. 1951), certiorari denied 342 U.S. 816, 72 S.Ct. 31 (1951); Stanovich v. Jurlin, 227 F.2d 245, 1956 A.M.C. 402 (9th Cir. 1955). On the difficulty in determining the point of maximum cure sometimes in the future, see Gomes v. Eastern Gas & Fuel Associates, 132 F.Supp. 29, 1955 A.M.C. 1560 (D.Mass. 1955). "Cure" in the phrase "maintenance and cure" originally meant "care." One of the odd by-products of the Farrell case is that the meaning of "cure" has now shifted to that of recovery from disease or injury.

assumed (and with this the dissenting justices would have agreed) that if, at a future time, by reason of advances in medical knowledge, it should become possible to ameliorate Farrell's condition, he would then be entitled to an additional recovery. The shipowner's liability thus appears to be unlimited in time, and can be revived, with respect to an apparently hopeless case, by new discoveries which make a resumption of treatment advisable.[53]

The claimant can recover only for past medical expenses actually incurred, plus, as the Taylor opinion suggests, "such amounts as may be needful in the immediate future for the maintenance and cure of a kind and for a period which can be definitely ascertained".[54] It follows that the seaman may bring successive suits and that a prior recovery will not bar a subsequent action.[55] In Sobosle v. United States Steel Corporation[55a] the plaintiff had suffered injuries while employed on the defendant's ship in 1946. She was denied recovery under the Jones Act on the ground that no negligence on the defendant's part had been shown but a maintenance and cure award was made in a companion admiralty action, covering her expenses and maintenance down to the time of trial (March 14, 1951). Plaintiff subsequently filed a second maintenance and cure libel under which an award was made from the date of the first trial to the date of the second trial (May 2, 1957). At that time her physician had recom-

53. Sims v. United States War Shipping Administration, 186 F.2d 972, 973, 1951 A.M.C. 461, 462 (3d Cir. 1951) certiorari denied 342 U.S. 816, 72 S.Ct. 31 (1951); ". . . the libellant developed and manifested gastroduodenitis, which condition continued to evidence itself thereafter and during the remainder of the voyage and which, either in its original form or in subsequent phases has practically incapacitated him for work of the kind of which he is capable up to the present time [six years from the end of the voyage]." Koslusky v. United States, 208 F.2d 957, 959, 1954 A.M.C. 230, 233 (2d Cir. 1953): "The respondent argues that when the libellant was found fit for sea duty and signed on board the Grace Abbott in May, 1945, maximum improvement in his condition had been reached and therefore liability for maintenance and cure beyond that time is unjustified. But there is evidence showing that when the libellant left the service of the Grace Abbott he was suffering from the same injuries for which the respondent was under a duty to provide maintenance and cure. Moreover, the judge below discredited the fitness report made in May, 1945, and the record shows that the libellant's injuries were of a recurring nature. We cannot say that the award is unreasonable since it was not until his final discharge in 1951 from the Marine Hospital on Staten Island that it was clear that no further improvement in the libellant's condition would be possible." But see Desmond v. United States, 105 F.Supp. 9, 1953 A.M.C. 375 (S.D.N.Y.1952), reversed on other grounds 217 F.2d 948, 1955 A.M.C. 17 (2d Cir. 1954), certiorari denied 349 U.S. 911, 75 S.Ct. 600 (1955), holding that in an action under the Suits in Admiralty Act the two year statute of limitations applied to bar recovery except for the two years preceding the filing of the libel. To the same effect is Williams v. United States, 228 F.2d 129, 1956 A.M.C. 80 (4th Cir. 1955).

54. On the recovery of the plaintiff's living allowance (maintenance) as distinguished from his recovery of medical expenses (cure), see § 6–12 *infra*. The recovery of medical expenses is subject to the limitations discussed in the following paragraph of the text.

55. Calmar S. S. Corp. v. Taylor, 303 U.S. 525, 58 S.Ct. 651, 1938 A.M.C. 341 (1938); Robinson, Admiralty 299 (1939): "Thus the seaman is to keep biting at his cherry."

55a. 359 F.2d 7, 1966 A.M.C. 886 (3d Cir. 1966).

mended shock therapy which she refused to undergo; the District Court refused to make any further awards until she agreed to undergo the recommended treatment. Almost seven years later she applied for further relief; at this time her original physician had died and her present physician no longer recommended shock therapy. The Third Circuit, in a notable opinion by Judge Freedman, concluded that her refusal to undergo shock therapy in 1957 had been, under the circumstances, reasonable and held that she was entitled to file a third libel and proceed de novo subject to the defendant's right to show that it had been prejudiced by the delay under the admiralty doctrine of laches.[55b] The Sobosle case is no doubt exceptional on its facts but the underlying idea that the plaintiff is entitled to successive recoveries (at least so long as there is a possibility of improvement) seems never to have been doubted.[55c]

The seaman does not have a free hand in choosing his own physician and deciding on his own treatment. The United States Public Health Service maintains Marine Hospitals at which seamen may receive low cost or free care and treatment. An ill or injured seaman who has been given a "hospital ticket" by the master and provided with transportation to the nearest Marine Hospital will usually be held to have acted at his own risk and expense if he either refuses to enter the Marine Hospital and to follow the advice of the Public

**55b.** In most recent laches litigation a claim becomes time-barred only when unexcused delay by the plaintiff in bringing his action has resulted in prejudice to the defendant in making his defense and the burden of proof to show prejudice is on the defendant. See the discussion in Chapter IX, § 9–77 *et seq.* The older cases held that a "presumption of prejudice" resulted from mere unexcused delay, so that the burden of showing that the defendant had not been prejudiced was put on the plaintiff. The "presumption of prejudice" line was followed in Burke v. Gateway Clipper, Inc., 441 F.2d 946, 1971 A.M.C. 1623 (3d Cir. 1971) with respect to unseaworthiness and maintenance and cure claims which were filed more than ten years after they had accrued. West v. Marine Resources Commission, 330 F. Supp. 966, 1971 A.M.C. 418 (E.D.Va. 1970) which held that unseaworthiness and maintenance and cure courts joined to a Jones Act count were governed by the three-year Jones Act statute of limitations seems out of step with most current litigation. See § 6–25 *infra*, note 149 and the accompanying text.

**55c.** The doctrine of the Sobosle case was followed in Jewell v. The Ohio River Co., 1967 A.M.C. 1724 (W.D.Pa. 1966), affirmed per curiam 431 F.2d 691 (3d Cir. 1970). The plaintiff in Jewell had recovered both maintenance and cure and damages under the Jones Act in earlier actions. The maintenance and cure claim in the second action was joined with a Jones Act claim for damages for a negligent failure to furnish maintenance and cure (see § 6–13 *infra*, text following note 67). The Third Circuit's per curiam opinion suggested that under the Fitzgerald case (note 45d *supra* and the accompanying text) both claims should be tried to the jury.

In Hugney v. Consolidation Coal Co., 345 F.Supp. 1079 (W.D.Pa.1971) it was held that the fact that the plaintiff had received awards on his Jones Act and maintenance and cure claims in a limitation of liability proceeding did not bar him from bringing a subsequent action to recover further maintenance and cure as well as damages for failure to provide maintenance and cure. Judge Marsh assumed that claims for maintenance and cure are not subject to limitation of liability. On that unsettled issue, see Chapter X, § 10–26, text following note 113c; § 10–40, note 161i.

Health Service physicians or if he consults private physicians or enters another hospital.[56]

Nevertheless if the judge concludes that the facilities or treatment afforded the seaman are inadequate, he may allow recovery for expenses incurred outside the Public Health Service system or even order the seaman removed at the shipowner's expense to a place where adequate treatment is available. The latter possibility is dramatically illustrated by the 1955 case of Williams v. United States.[57] Williams, a Negro messboy, had shown signs of insanity while serving on a merchant vessel owned by the United States. He left the ship at Newport News, Virginia, and was later committed, not to a Marine Hospital, but to a state hospital in Virginia, which was the only public or private institution available to Negro mental patients in that state. His illness was diagnosed as schizophrenia. At the time of trial he had been confined in the state hospital for about three years, having received free care as a resident of the State. Judge Hoffman, after comparing the facilities of the state hospital with the minimum standards set by the American Psychiatric Association, concluded that the facilities were woefully inadequate and that Williams had not received proper treatment. The Judge conceded that no duty rested on the shipowner to investigate the facilities of a state-supported institution. The inadequacy of the facilities had, however, now been brought to the shipowner's notice. Therefore, he concluded,

> "The respondent, in the light of this opinion, will probably conclude to bring about the transfer of libellant from Central State Hospital to an institution providing proper and adequate care. The care and treatment there afforded the libellant should be the maximum reasonably possible under the circumstances. If the respondent does not elect to transfer libellant, the effect of such a decision may give rise to further litigation." [58]

56. Benton v. United Towing Co., 120 F.Supp. 638, 641, 1954 A.M.C. 995, 999 (N.D.Cal.1954) affirmed 224 F.2d 558, 1955 A.M.C. 1738 (9th Cir. 1955): ". . . since it appears that Benton could have obtained free hospitalization at the Marine Hospital, he is not entitled to his medical expenses." But see Luth v. Palmer Shipping Corp., 210 F.2d 224, 1954 A.M.C. 502 (3d Cir. 1954). In Oswalt v. Williamson Towing Co., 357 F.Supp. 304, 1973 A.M.C. 2306 (N.D.Miss.1973) a maintenance and cure award was denied on the ground that the plaintiff had unreasonably refused the defendant's offer of free medical care. Judge Keady's opinion collects a number of cases which have held that the seaman's refusal to accept medical care offered by his employer does not bar a maintenance and cure award if the refusal is found to have been, under the circumstances, reasonable. See particularly the Sobosle case discussed in the text following note 55a *supra*. In George v. Chesapeake and Ohio Railway Co., 348 F.Supp. 283 (E.D.Va.1972) the plaintiff's use of a private physician and a private hospital were held not to bar a maintenance and cure award because the treatment offered him by his employer was (or might reasonably have been thought to be) inadequate. Robinson v. Pocahontas, Inc., 477 F.2d 1048, 1973 A.M.C. 2268 (1st Cir. 1973) is to the same effect.

57. 133 F.Supp. 319, 1955 A.M.C. 1323 (E.D.Va.1955), affirmed 228 F.2d 129, 1956 A.M.C. 80 (4th Cir. 1955).

58. *Id.* at 327, 1955 A.M.C. at 1334. Judge Hoffman dismissed a claim for maintenance during the period while

Kossick v. United Fruit Co.[58a] contributed a certain amount of confusion to these issues, particularly since the case, when it finally arrived in the Supreme Court, seemed to bear little resemblance to the case which Judge Bicks had initially discussed in the District Court. From the District Court opinion it appeared that Kossick had brought an action in two counts against his employer, the United Fruit Company. One count was for maintenance and cure. The second count was for damages for breach of contract. The facts alleged with respect to the second count were that the Fruit Company had insisted that Kossick go to a United States Public Health Service Hospital for treatment and had promised Kossick that it would assume responsibility for the consequences of any incompetent or negligent treatment he might receive; that Kossick, relying on the promise, had gone to the Hospital and that his condition had been seriously aggravated by the incompetence or negligence of the Hospital personnel;[58b] he claimed damages in the amount of $250,000. Kossick's counsel drafted his second count as a simple breach of contract action and not as a general maritime law action or an action under the Jones Act.[58c] His reason for this complicated strategy seems to have been that the action, if pleaded under the general maritime law or under the Jones Act, might have been time barred;[58d] by pleading it as an action for breach of contract he hoped to plead himself into the longer New York statute of limitation for contract actions. The difficulty with his approach was that the alleged contract between Kossick and the Fruit Company, being oral, was clearly unenforceable under the New York statute of frauds. Oral contracts are, however, enforceable under the general maritime law.[58e] Thus, to win his case (as he eventually did) counsel had to plead himself into the state statute of limitations to avoid the maritime law time bar but at the same time to keep on the maritime law side to avoid the state statute of frauds. Anyone who can do that could (if he was a camel) pass through the needle's eye with room to spare.

Williams had been cared for in the hospital as well as a claim for damages based on the theory that his condition had been aggravated by improper care. He was affirmed on both points by the Fourth Circuit, see note 57 *supra*. Other cases involving maintenance and cure claims for mental disease are Rofer v. Head & Head, Inc., 226 F.2d 927, 1955 A.M.C. 2204 (5th Cir. 1955); Brahms v. Moore-McCormack Lines, Inc., 133 F.Supp. 283, 1955 A.M.C. 2240 (S.D.N.Y.1955). In Siders v. The Ohio River Co., 351 F.Supp. 987 (W.D.Pa.1970, 1971), affirmed 469 F.2d 1093 (3d Cir. 1972) maintenance and cure was denied where it appeared that the plaintiff suffered from a schizophrenic condition which long antedated his employment.

**58a.** 166 F.Supp. 571, 1958 A.M.C. 2548 (S.D.N.Y.1958), affirmed 275 F.2d 500, 1960 A.M.C. 837 (2d Cir. 1960), reversed 365 U.S. 731, 81 S.Ct. 886, 1961 A.M.C. 833 (1961), rehearing denied 366 U.S. 941, 81 S.Ct. 1657 (1961).

**58b.** According to Justice Harlan's opinion, 365 U.S. 731, 732 n. 1, 81 S. Ct. 889 n. 1, any action by Kossick against the United States had "apparently" become time-barred under 28 U.S.C.A. § 2401(b).

**58c.** See § 6–13 *infra* on actions for damages for failure to provide maintenance and cure.

**58d.** See 166 F.Supp. at p. 573.

**58e.** Union Fish Co. v. Erickson, 248 U.S. 308, 39 S.Ct. 112 (1919).

In the District Court the Fruit Company moved to strike the second count on the ground that the contract alleged was nonmaritime and therefore unenforceable under the statute of frauds. (The sufficiency of the first count on maintenance and cure was not questioned in the motion or involved in the District Court's opinion.[58f]) Judge Bicks granted the motion and was affirmed by the Second Circuit but reversed by a majority of the Supreme Court which held in an opinion by Justice Harlan that the alleged contract was maritime and thus not subject to the statute of frauds.[58g] All this is no doubt of the highest jurisprudential interest but has precious little to do with the law of maintenance and cure.[58h]

Meanwhile, what had happened to the maintenance and cure count? We are told by Judge Magruder in his opinion for the Second Circuit that that count had been discontinued "without prejudice and without costs to either party" and that Kossick had not appealed from the discontinuance.[58i] No reasons were given for this action on the maintenance and cure count, which was not reported. Presumably the trial judge felt that the Fruit Company had fulfilled its duty by arranging for Kossick to be treated at the Public Health Service Hospital and was not responsible for the incompetence or negligence of the Hospital's personnel. On this aspect of the case Justice Harlan cautioned that it is not necessarily true that the employer fulfills his duty by arranging for the seaman to enter a Public Health Service Hospital:

> "[T]he duty to afford maintenance and cure is not simply and as a matter of law an obligation to provide for entrance to a public hospital. The cases . . . hold no more than that a seaman who can receive adequate and proper care free of charge at a public hospital may not 'deliberately refuse the hospital privilege, and then assert a lien upon his vessel for the increased expense which his whim or taste has created' [quoting from The Bouker No. 2, 241 Fed. 831, 835 (2d Cir. 1917)]. Presumably if a seaman refuses to enter a public hospital, or, having entered, if he leaves to undergo treatment elsewhere, he may recover the cost of such other treatment upon proof that 'proper and adequate' care was not available at such hospital." [58j]

However, in Kossick's case, as Justice Harlan noted, the Court agreed with the courts below that no facts were alleged which would make the Fruit Company liable apart from the contract which Kossick was

**58f.** See 166 F.Supp. at p. 574.

**58g.** Justice Harlan's only reference to counsel's complicated pleading was that the Court would not change its conclusion "because of any suspicion that this complaint may have been contrived to serve ulterior purposes." 365 U.S. at p. 742, 81 S.Ct. at p. 894.

**58h.** The Kossick case is further discussed § 6–61, *infra*.

**58i.** 275 F.2d at p. 502.

**58j.** 365 U.S. at p. 737, 81 S.Ct. at p. 891. Following the passage quoted Justice Harlan cited Williams v. United States, discussed in the text following note 57 *supra*.

to get a chance to prove. No further proceedings in the case were reported.

What the nonjurisprudential aspects of the Kossick case come down to is that the employer initially fulfills his duty by arranging for the seaman to have free treatment at a Public Health Service Hospital; the seaman who refuses the treatment will normally have no right to recover his medical expenses; but if he can show that the treatment offered at the Hospital is not "proper and adequate," then it becomes the employer's duty to see that proper and adequate treatment is provided; if the employer fails to do so, the seaman can then recover whatever medical expenses he may reasonably incur. And of course it goes without saying that the employer can, by contract, assume greater responsibilities than those imposed on him by law.

**§ 6–12.** In addition to his medical expenses the incapacitated seaman is entitled to a living allowance (maintenance). The period of time for which he may have maintenance is presumably the same period for which he is entitled to medical expenses: until he has recovered or until the maximum cure has been achieved. Allowances for as much as a year or two are not uncommon and even longer ones are occasionally made: in 1953 the Second Circuit affirmed a maintenance award which ran from November 29, 1944, to January 18, 1951.[59]

In its origins the right to maintenance was no doubt based on the thought that the traditional blue-water seaman lived on the ship which furnished him with his meals and lodging. Therefore, when he was injured or became ill in the service of the ship and was forced to live ashore, he should get a living allowance in lieu of what he would normally have received from the ship. The conditions of life of many, if not most, maritime workers today bear little resemblance to the paradigm derived from the days of sailing ships. If the life of the law was logic and not experience, it might be assumed that maintenance awards would be denied to shore-based workers who live at home and provide their own sustenance. It might also seem to follow that, even in the case of the traditional seaman, maintenance awards would not be made except for expenses actually incurred; the seaman who lived free with his family, relatives or friends during his period of convalescence would get nothing except his necessary medical expenses. And it might even follow that any earnings which the seaman might have during that period should be deducted from any maintenance award to which he might be otherwise entitled. The traditional view may well have been that the right to maintenance was restricted to the seaman's out-of-pocket expenses during his enforced absence from the ship.[60] In recent litigation, however, the idea seems to have been

59. Koslusky v. United States, 208 F.2d 957, 1954 A.M.C. 230 (2d Cir. 1953). See the Sobosle case, text following note 55a *supra*.

60. For an expression of the "traditional view", see 2 Norris, note 12 *supra*, §§ 572, 573 (collecting cases). The Second Circuit followed the traditional view in Mahramas v. American Export Isbrandtsen Lines, Inc., 475 F.2d 165, 1973 A.M.C. 587 (2d Cir. 1973). Johnson v. United States, 333 U.S. 46, 68 S.Ct. 391, 1948 A.M.C. 218 (1948) is

making its way that the right to maintenance, whatever the origins of the right may have been, should not be restricted in any of the ways that have been suggested. As might be expected in a period during which a rule of law is, arguably, being transformed into its own opposite, the resulting pattern is by no means all of a piece.

Vaughan v. Atkinson [61] was the Supreme Court's principal contribution to maintenance and cure law during the 1960's. Vaughan had developed tuberculosis while he was employed on the defendants' vessel. After a period of hospitalization at a United States Public Service Hospital he was discharged as an out-patient and remained in that status for more than two years. During that period his employer failed or refused to make voluntary payments for Vaughan's maintenance and medical expenses. Vaughan, as Justice Douglas described his situation, was "on his own . . . and required to work in order to survive"; he supported himself by driving a taxi. At the trial the District Judge concluded that his earnings as a taxi-driver should be deducted from his maintenance award. A divided panel of the Fourth Circuit affirmed the deduction, over a dissent by Judge Sobeloff, on the theory that seamen (like discharged schoolteachers) are required to mitigate damages. The Supreme Court reversed in an opinion by Justice Douglas; Justice Stewart, joined by Justice Harlan, dissented; Justices White and Frankfurter did not participate in the decision. The outer reaches of the Vaughan holding are notably fuzzy. According to Justice Stewart's dissent, Vaughan's return to work, so far as the record indicated, had been "completely voluntary" and was not "brought on by economic necessity." If the holding is interpreted in the light of the dissent, Vaughan seems to hold that there is no duty to mitigate damages and no accountability for money received from other sources during the period when the plaintiff is entitled to maintenance. On the other hand Justice Douglas' majority opinion emphasized the facts that Vaughan had been "required to work in order to survive" [62] and that the employer's failure to make voluntary

usually cited as the leading case on the proposition that only out-of-pocket expenses can be recovered as maintenance. The principal issue in Johnson was the proper standard of negligence to be applied in Jones Act cases (that aspect of the case is discussed § 6–36 *infra*); the majority of the Court, in an opinion by Justice Douglas, reversed the Ninth Circuit which had denied plaintiff his Jones Act recovery. The Ninth Circuit had also denied plaintiff a maintenance and cure award on the ground that he had incurred no expenses. Justice Douglas devoted only a brief paragraph at the end of his opinion to the maintenance and cure point, as to which the Ninth Circuit was affirmed. Neither the offhand discussion of the no expenses-no maintenance proposition in Johnson nor its equally casual reaffirmance in Vaughan v. Atkinson, see note 62 *infra*, can be taken as foreclosing further discussion of the issue.

61. 369 U.S. 527, 82 S.Ct. 997, 1962 A.M.C. 1131 (1962). Another aspect of the Vaughan holding is discussed § 6–13 *infra* text following note 71c.

62. Judge Sobeloff in his dissenting opinion when the case was before the Fourth Circuit had referred to Vaughan's "being compelled under economic pressure to sustain himself by part-time taxi driving." 291 F.2d 813, 816, 1961 A.M.C. 2261, 2266 (4th Cir. 1961). Justice Douglas distinguished Vaughan from Johnson v. United States (note 60 *supra*) on the ground that in Johnson the plaintiff had lived on his

payments had been "callous . . . willful and persistent." Thus if the holding is interpreted in the light of the majority opinion, the case could be said to hold that the plaintiff's earnings are deductible from his maintenance award unless he was forced back to work by his own economic necessity reinforced by his employer's "callous . . . willful and persistent" behavior.

The lower courts seem to have steered a middle course between the broadest and narrowest possible readings of Vaughan. Maintenance seems never to have been awarded for periods during which the plaintiff was receiving free care and medical attention in hospital—a result which is consistent with the idea that, if there are no expenses, there is no right to maintenance. On the other hand the recent cases, almost without exception, award maintenance at a flat rate per day (usually $8.00 but occasionally $6.00 [62a]) without any further inquiry. The customary $8.00 rate seems to have become established by the late 1940's; awards in pre-World War II cases were at lower rates. Despite the continuing inflation since the 1940's the $8.00 rate (which is frequently specified in collective bargaining agreements between shipowners and maritime unions [62b]) has not been increased. The failure to adjust the rate to reflect inflation suggests that maintenance is no longer regarded as a living allowance sufficient to support even the proverbially impecunious unmarried male seaman in the modest circumstances to which he is thought to be entitled. If all he has to live on is his daily maintenance award, he will have to supplement it by finding work; if his earnings are deducted, he will starve. The disappearance from recent cases of the once not uncommon inquiry into the plaintiff's collateral earnings reflects these facts of life. It could of course be argued that a hypothetical seaman lucky enough to be endowed with a large private income would not be entitled to maintenance but the case is not likely to arise in real life. It is true that the Second Circuit in 1973 reiterated the proposition that a plaintiff who incurred no expenses is not entitled to maintenance but it is fair to add that the judges seemed to be skeptical of the plaintiff's entire story.[62c]

Haughton v. Blackships, Inc.[62d] is instructive on a problem of which we shall undoubtedly hear more in the future. Haughton, who had been injured while employed on the defendant's ship, recovered damages for his injury as well as an award for maintenance and cure. Haughton had received retirement benefits from a fund established under a collective bargaining agreement which was composed entirely of contributions made by the shipowners. The Fifth Circuit, revers-

parents' ranch "without cost to himself" and had received his maintenance "wholly from others."

**62a.** 2 Norris, note 12 *supra*, § 607, note 8, has an exhaustive list of awards, Circuit by Circuit.

**62b.** For a specimen clause, see Judge Sobeloff's dissent in Vaughan v. Atkinson, 291 F.2d 813, 819, n. 8, 1961 A.M.C. 2261, 2270, n. 8.

**62c.** See the Mahramas case, note 60 *supra*.

**62d.** 462 F.2d 788 (5th Cir. 1972).

ing the District Court, held, in an opinion by Judge Bue which relied principally on cases decided under the Federal Employer's Liability Act, that the benefits received by Haughton were not to be deducted from his recovery. While the Court's attention was principally directed to the damage recovery, Judge Bue's opinion seems equally applicable to the maintenance and cure award.[62e]

The case of the shore-based worker who lives at home and receives neither his meals nor his lodging from the ship presents obvious theoretical difficulties with respect to maintenance awards. The most ambitious discussion of this issue which the judicial literature so far provides was undertaken by Judge Rubin in Hudspeth v. Atlantic & Gulf Stevedores, Inc.[62f] Judge Rubin, after a careful review of the authorities, concluded that the shore-based seaman was entitled to exactly the same maintenance award as the traditional blue-water seaman.[62g] The other recent cases which have dealt with maintenance awards to shore-based workers have approved the awards, usually without discussion of the theoretical complications.[62h]

**62e.** With the Haughton case, *cf.* Thomas v. Humble Oil & Refining Co., 420 F.2d 793, 1970 A.M.C. 25 (4th Cir. 1970). In Thomas a collective bargaining agreement provided that payments (in excess of the customary rate for maintenance) should be made to disabled seamen from Humble's Disability Benefit Plan and provided further that "Maintenance shall not be paid concurrently with payments under the Disability Benefit Plan." *Held,* that Thomas was not entitled to a maintenance award in addition to the payments he had received under the Plan. Judge Bue's Haughton opinion carefully distinguished Thomas. See also Gypsum Carrier, Inc. v. Handelsman, 307 F.2d 525, 1963 A.M.C. 175 (9th Cir. 1962), holding that payments received under a Fund (to which employers made no contributions) created by the California Unemployment Disability Act were not deductible either from a Jones Act recovery or from a maintenance and cure award. See further Blake v. Delaware & Hudson Railway Co., 484 F.2d 204, 1973 A.M.C. 2177 (2d Cir. 1973) (an FELA case); Russo v. Matson Navigation Co., 486 F.2d 1018, 1973 A.M.C. 2334 (9th Cir. 1973) (following the Haughton case).

**62f.** 266 F.Supp. 937, 1967 A.M.C. 2108 (E.D.La.1967).

**62g.** Judge Rubin drew particular attention to Judge Clark's majority opinion in Weiss v. Central R. Co. of New Jersey, 235 F.2d 309, 1956 A.M.C. 1473 (2d Cir. 1956), digested note 20 *supra.* He concluded that the only case that was "in any part contrary" to his conclusion was Alexandervich v. Gallagher Bros., 298 F.2d 918, 1962 A.M.C. 317 (2d Cir. 1961) in which a maintenance award in favor of a cook who worked two weeks out of every three was ordered reduced by one-third because he spent only two-thirds of his time on the ship. Judge Rubin noted that Judge Kaufman's majority opinion in Alexandervich gave "no reason for the reduction during the usual shore period"; Judge Clark who had written the majority opinion in the Weiss case entered a forceful dissent in Alexandervich. With Alexandervich, *cf.* Crooks v. United States, note 62h *infra.*

**62h.** Crooks v. United States, 459 F.2d 631 (9th Cir. 1972) (no "double recovery" in awarding maintenance at $8.00 per day for entire relevant period although plaintiff worked two-thirds of his time on shore and only one-third of his time at sea; Judge Merrill's opinion collects cases on both sides of the issue, although he overlooked the Alexandervich case, note 62g *supra*); Williamson v. Western Pacific Dredging Corp., 441 F.2d 65, 1971 A.M.C. 2356 (9th Cir. 1971), certiorari denied 404 U.S. 851, 92 S.Ct. 90 (1971); George v. Chesapeake and Ohio Railway Co., 348 F.Supp. 283 (E.D.Va. 1972); Dardar v. State of Louisiana, 322 F.Supp. 1115, 1971 A.M.C. 1560 (E.D.La.1971); Richardson v. St. Charles-St. John the Baptist Bridge & Ferry Authority, 284 F.Supp. 709, 1968 A.M.C. 1485 (E.D.La.1968) (per

The long-term shift in the maintenance concept was admirably summed up by Judge Merrill in Crooks v. United States.[62i] After noting that maintenance had originally been looked on as a substitute for the board and lodging which the seaman was assumed to receive from the ship, and thus as a supplement to wages, he went on:

> "With the maintenance obligation recognized as persisting beyond the tenure of employment, it was in effect severed from the wage obligation and attached to the obligation for cure."

If the right to maintenance is divorced from the employment contract, the argument that a disabled seaman who is entitled to maintenance is subject to a common-law contractual duty to mitigate damages loses most of its theoretical underpinning. As the duty to mitigate damages disappears, so do the ideas that earnings and other income should be deducted from the maintenance award and that only out-of-pocket expenses (which, under conventional contract damage theory, would measure the plaintiff's economic loss) are recoverable. The cases seem to be heading in the direction suggested by Judge Merrill's analysis in the Crooks case but, in the absence of clarification of the issue by the Supreme Court, a judicial consensus may well be a long time emerging.

The third item of recovery in a maintenance and cure action is for unearned wages. The period for which wages may be recovered after the onset of illness or the injury depends on the type of service in which the ship was engaged. For ocean going ships, the rule is said to be that wages are recoverable for the balance of the voyage; in Farrell v. United States the Supreme Court held (four judges dissenting) that the voyage period was not extended when the seaman signed wartime articles of employment "for a term of time not exceeding 12 (Twelve) calendar months".[63] There is nothing in Justice Jackson's opinion in Farrell to suggest that the period for recovery of wages could not be extended by contract; the holding was merely that the contract in question, executed in wartime when for security reasons the ship's prospective voyage could not be spelled out, had not done so. In coastwise shipping it is customary to sign on crew members not for a voyage but for a period of time, and recovery of wages until the end of the term is regularly granted.[64] With re-

Rubin, J.); Rowald v. Cargo Carriers, 243 F.Supp. 629, 1968 A.M.C. 1397 (E. D.Mo.1965).

62i. Note 62h *supra*.

63. 336 U.S. 511, 520, 69 S.Ct. 707, 711, 1949 A.M.C. 613, 620 (1949).

64. See the dissenting opinion in Farrell v. United States, 336 U.S. 511, 521, 69 S.Ct. 707, 712, 1949 A.M.C. 613, 621 (1949); Jones v. Waterman S.S. Corp., 155 F.2d 992, 1946 A.M.C. 859 (3d Cir. 1946); Enochasson v. Freeport Sulphur Co., 7 F.2d 674, 1925 A.M.C. 1203 (S.D.Tex.1925). Presumably the same rule applies to inland and Great Lakes shipping. See the interpretation of the Farrell case in The Pioneer (Vitco v. Joncich), 130 F.Supp. 945, 949, 1955 A.M.C. 1366, 1372 (S.D. Cal.1955), affirmed 234 F.2d 161, 1956 A.M.C. 1639 (9th Cir. 1956) holding that a seaman was entitled to wages for the whole of the 12 month "tuna season" on the Pacific coast: ". . . the maritime law attaches

spect to land-based workers employed on harborcraft, ferry boats, oil rigs and the like, the terms of the contract of employment will presumably determine the length of time for which wages may be recovered.[64a] The recovery of unearned wages has become the least important part of the maintenance and cure award. Not only has the employer's liability for maintenance been largely expanded, but the disabled plaintiff's loss of future earnings becomes an element of damages in action for unseaworthiness and under the Jones Act.[64b] In Robinson v. Pocahontas, Inc.[64c] it was held that unearned wages could be included in a maintenance and cure award even though no specific demand for wages had been made in the maintenance and cure count of the complaint.

**§ 6–13.** The shipowner's duty is not only to pay for the seaman's maintenance and cure but to take all reasonable steps to make sure that the seaman, when he is injured or becomes sick, receives proper care and treatment.[65] If proper treatment is not available aboard ship, it is the master's duty to put into the nearest available port where the treatment can be had.[65a] If hospitalization is required, the master must see that money for transportation to the hospital is provided, and, if the seaman is unable to travel alone, must make arrangements for him to make the trip in safety.[66] If the seaman is forced to

to the seaman's contract of employment the right to receive his agreed wages throughout the period of employment . . . ; which historically has meant 'to the end of the voyage,' since 'the general custom in ships, other than the coastwise trade, is to sign on for a voyage rather than for a fixed period.' (Farrell v. U. S. . . . )

"Generally speaking then, whether the employment is for a voyage or for a definite time . . . , it is the shipowner's obligation to pay a seaman, who falls ill or is injured while in the service of the vessel, full wages throughout the period of employment." And see Harriman v. Midland S. S. Line, 208 F.2d 564, 1954 A.M.C. 67 (2d Cir. 1953), an action to recover damages for an unlawful discharge, which held that on the Great Lakes, a seaman employed for the season is still so employed although he signs monthly "Articles" as the season progresses. The Harriman case held the statutes relating to Articles for foreign-going ships inapplicable to Great Lakes shipping. See also Medina v. Erickson, 226 F.2d 475, 1955 A.M.C. 2211 (9th Cir. 1955), certiorari denied 351 U.S. 912, 76 S.Ct. 702 (1956). Rofer v. Head & Head, Inc., 226 F.2d 927, 1955 A.M.C. 2204 (5th Cir. 1955).

**64a.** In Dardar v. State of Louisiana, 322 F.Supp. 1115, 1971 A.M.C. 1560 (E.D.La.1971) the plaintiff, who was injured on February 25, 1968, was paid his full salary through September 3, 1968.

**64b.** See, e. g., the Dardar case, note 64a supra.

**64c.** 477 F.2d 1048, 1973 A.M.C. 2268 (1st Cir. 1973).

**65.** For the details of the duty to furnish proper care and treatment, see 2 Norris, note 12 *supra*, § 583 *et seq.*

**65a.** The Iroquois, 194 U.S. 240, 24 S. Ct. 640 (1903); Hendy Corp. v. Clavel, 189 F.2d 37, 1951 A.M.C. 1118 (9th Cir. 1951); Holliday v. Pacific Atlantic S. S. Co., 197 F.2d 610 (3d Cir. 1952) certiorari denied 345 U.S. 922, 73 S.Ct. 780 (1953). But see Medina v. Erickson, 226 F.2d 475, 1955 A.M.C. 2211 (9th Cir. 1955), certiorari denied 351 U.S. 912, 76 S.Ct. 702 (1956). Payne v. Tanker Co., Inc., 1955 A.M.C. 694 (E.D.Va.1954).

**66.** Spellman v. American Barge Line, 176 F.2d 716, 719, 1954 A.M.C. 724, 728 (3d Cir. 1949); "Merely furnishing means of transportation without making sure that they are employed by a mentally ill seaman may not amount

leave the ship in a foreign port, he must be provided with transportation back to the United States.[67]

If the master or owner fails to provide proper care and as a result the seaman's condition is aggravated, the shipowner is liable not only for the increased medical expenses and maintenance that may become necessary but also for resulting damages.[68] That is to say, following such a breach of duty the seaman may recover full tort damages, including compensation for total or partial disability which, the Taylor and Warren cases held, was not recoverable in an ordinary or unaggravated maintenance and cure action.

Such damages may be recovered either in an action for maintenance and cure or in an action for negligence under the Jones Act. In Cortes v. Baltimore Insular Line [69] a seaman had fallen ill of pneumonia aboard ship and died in a hospital where he had been taken following the ship's return to its home port. His administrator brought suit for damages, alleging that the death was the result of the master's failure to give proper care. Justice Cardozo held that maritime law gave the seaman a remedy in damages for breach of the duty to provide maintenance and cure. That remedy, however, abated on death: "Death is a composer of strife by the general law of the sea as it was for many centuries by the common law of the land." [69a] Justice Cardozo found nothing inconsistent, however, in the idea that the shipowner's breach of duty gave rise to liability not only under maritime law but also under the Jones Act: the seaman deprived of proper medical care suffers a "personal injury" quite as much as the sailor who falls from a defective rigging and breaks his leg. The Jones Act expressly provides that an action may be brought by a deceased seaman's personal representative. Thus, if the allegations of negligence were borne out in proof, the administrator could recover under the Jones Act.

In Sims v. United States War Shipping Administration [70] the Third Circuit applied the reasoning of the Cortes case to decree liability in damages when the failure to give proper care occurred not during the voyage but after its termination. Sims was discharged

to affording a method of transportation at all. Giving a bus ticket to a person who is mentally ill is hardly a method of affording safe transportation."

67. See Luth v. Palmer Shipping Corp., 210 F.2d 224, 1954 A.M.C. 502 (3d Cir. 1954) certiorari denied 347 U.S. 976, 74 S.Ct. 788 (1954); Ladjimi v. Pacific Far East Line, Inc., 97 F.Supp. 174, 1951 A.M.C. 979 (N.D.Cal.1951).

68. Cortes v. Baltimore Insular Line, 287 U.S. 367, 53 S.Ct. 173, 1933 A.M.C. 9 (1932); Sims v. United States War Shipping Administration discussed text following note 70 *infra*; Ladjimi v. Pacific Far East Line, note 67 *supra*; Medina v. Erickson, note 65 *supra*. See De Zon v. American President Lines, 318 U.S. 660, 63 S.Ct. 1025, 1943 A.M.C. 483 (1943).

69. 287 U.S. 367, 53 S.Ct. 173, 1933 A.M.C. 9 (1932).

69a. In Moragne v. States Marine Lines, Inc., 398 U.S. 375, 90 S.Ct. 1772, 1970 A.M.C. 967 (1970) it was held that a remedy for wrongful death is provided by the general maritime law. See § 6–32 *infra*.

70. 186 F.2d 972, 1951 A.M.C. 461 (3d Cir. 1951) certiorari denied 342 U.S. 816, 72 S.Ct. 31 (1951).

on January 18, 1945. During the voyage he had developed gastroduodenitis, from which he continued to suffer thereafter. Physicians prescribed a special diet and rest; Sims had no money to buy the items in the diet or to support himself without working. The War Shipping Administration, which denied any liability to Sims for maintenance and cure (apparently in the belief that he was not sick but malingering), refused to make funds available to him after request by Sims' attorneys. Sims was forced to go on working and to do without the diet; as a result his condition was aggravated and his illness prolonged. Judge Goodrich held that the United States was liable not only for the increased medical expenses for curing the aggravated condition but for damages with respect to all injuries suffered by Sims after he had, through his attorneys, given notice of his needs. In reaching this conclusion, Judge Goodrich accepted the trial court's finding that the War Shipping Administration had refused Sims' claim in the good faith but mistaken belief that the claim was fraudulent. The opinion does not indicate how the damages are to be assessed, except that Sims was to get more than his medical expenses and maintenance.[71]

Presumably it was the tangled factual and legal situation in the Cortes case which led the Supreme Court to hold that the action for damages for breach of the duty to furnish maintenance and cure could be brought under the Jones Act as well as under the general maritime law. No one, however, has ever sought to limit the Jones Act option under Cortes to situations in which, for some reason, the general maritime law action is barred; the plaintiff has a free option to claim damages (including punitive damages) under a general maritime law count or under a Jones Act count. By adding a Jones Act count for damages to his general maritime law count for maintenance and cure the plaintiff, under the Fitzgerald case,[71a] is entitled to have both claims tried to a jury.[71b]

In Vaughan v. Atkinson [71c] the Supreme Court added a new wrinkle to the damage recovery. The plaintiff's claim for damages in addition to his medical expenses and maintenance had been disallowed by the District Court on the ground that such damages were recoverable only when the defendant's failure to make the required payments voluntarily had caused or aggravated the plaintiff's disability (of which there was no evidence in Vaughan's case). The dismissal of the damage claim was affirmed by a divided panel of the Fourth Cir-

71. For a damage computation, see Ladjimi v. Pacific Far East Line, note 67 *supra*.

71a. Fitzgerald v. United States Lines Co., 374 U.S. 16, 83 S.Ct. 1646, 1963 A.M.C. 1093 (1963) rehearing denied 375 U.S. 870, 84 S.Ct. 26, discussed § 6–9 *supra*, text following note 45d.

71b. See Jewell v. The Ohio River Co., digested note 55c *supra*, which is of particular interest in that the plaintiff, who had already had one Jones Act recovery, was allowed to bring a second Jones Act action to recover his maintenance and cure damages.

71c. 369 U.S. 527, 82 S.Ct. 997, 1962 A.M.C. 1131 (1962). Another aspect of the Vaughan holding is discussed § 6–12 *supra*, text following note 61.

cuit but did not come before the Supreme Court, at least as the majority interpreted the grant of certiorari.[71d] However, the plaintiff had also sought unsuccessfully to recover an award for counsel fees and the Court considered that that aspect of the case was properly before it.[71e] On the ground that the defendant's attitude and behavior had been "callous . . . willful and persistent" and that his "recalcitrance" had forced plaintiff "to hire a lawyer and go to court to get what was plainly owed him", the majority of the Court, speaking through Justice Douglas, held that counsel fees should be awarded under the admiralty court's equity powers. Justice Stewart, joined by Justice Harlan, felt that, on this issue, the case should have been remanded to the District Court for further canvassing of the circumstances which motivated the respondents' failure to make maintenance payments. "If" [Justice Stewart observed] "the shipowner's refusal to pay maintenance stemmed from a wanton and intentional disregard of the legal rights of the seaman, the latter would be entitled to exemplary damages in accord with traditional concepts of the law of damages."

It will be noted that the Justices were, in effect, unanimous on the damage recovery. The dissenting Justices felt that the exemplary or punitive damages, if plaintiff was found entitled to them, should be awarded as such; the majority Justices, perhaps because of their narrow interpretation of the grant of certiorari and in order to avoid further proceedings, awarded what were essentially punitive damages under the name of counsel fees.[71f] It should be further noted that all the Justices were seemingly in agreement that the punitive damages were recoverable whether or not it was shown that the defendant's breach of duty had "caused" or "aggravated" the plaintiff's disability, provided that the defendant's behavior could be characterized as "callous", "willful", "wanton", "intentional", and so on. And although the case was a general maritime law action, there can be no doubt that the Vaughan holding is equally applicable in cases where the damages are sought under a Jones Act count and the case is tried to a jury.[71g]

Since Vaughan it has, of course, become routine for plaintiff's counsel to include a demand for counsel fees in all maintenance and cure actions. Typically the court will deny (or instruct the jury to deny) the award unless the defendant's behavior case be character-

**71d.** "Claims for damages for the illness and for wages, disallowed below, are not presented here." 369 U.S. at p. 528, n. 1, 82 S.Ct. at p. 998 n. 1, 1962 A.M.C. at p. 1132 n. 1 (per Douglas, J.).

**71e.** The case was being handled on a 50% contingency fee basis. Justice Douglas commented that the Court expressed no opinion on whether a 50% fee was reasonable.

**71f.** In Robinson v. Pocahontas, Inc., 477 F.2d 1048, 1973 A.M.C. 2268 (1st Cir. 1973), Judge McEntee noted that Justice Stewart's dissent in Vaughan was "seemingly in agreement with the majority's fundamental premise . . . ." The Robinson case approved a jury verdict for maintenance and cure in the amount of over $20,000 of which $10,000 was designated as punitive damages in addition to $45,000 under Jones Act and unseaworthiness counts.

**71g.** See the Robinson case, note 71f *supra*.

ized in one or more of the pejorative adjectives which are so plentifully sprinkled through the Vaughan opinions.[71h]

Another item in maintenance and cure awards which can only be classified as punitive is the award of pre-judgment interest on the amounts which the plaintiff recovers for medical expenses and maintenance. If the court feels that the defendant should have made the payments voluntarily and without delay, interest on these items will run from the dates when the payments ought to have been made. In the Vaughan case the District Court, which had refused to award the plaintiff any other maintenance and cure damages, did award pre-judgment interest and that award was not challenged on the appeals. Pre-judgment interest has also been awarded in addition to counsel fees or punitive damages.[71i]

### Same: Shipowner's Right to Indemnity from Third Party for Maintenance and Cure Expenses

**§ 6–14.** The shore leave cases have increased the number of situations in which the seaman has a right to maintenance and cure from a non-negligent employer and at the same time a damage action against a third party. As a result recent litigation has brought into prominence the question of the employer's right to indemnity from the third party. Case law conflicts have developed and the problem will not be resolved until the Supreme Court has passed upon it.

We need not discuss the situation in which both the employer and the third party are chargeable with negligence in connection with the plaintiff's injury: the Supreme Court has held that, in the absence of statute, the right of contribution among tortfeasors in maritime law

**71h.** See the discussion by Judge Rubin in Hudspeth v. Atlantic and Gulf Stevedores, 266 F.Supp. 937, 1967 A.M.C. 2108 (E.D.La.1967) (denying counsel fees) and in Solet v. M/V Captain H. V. Dufrene, 303 F.Supp. 980, 1970 A.M.C. 571 (E.D.La.1969) (awarding "a reasonable attorney's fee" and ordering a hearing to determine what the fee should be as well as whether damages in addition to the fee should be assessed). See further Judge McEntee's opinion in the Robinson case, note 71f *supra*.

In Reed v. People-to-People Health Foundation, 336 F.Supp. 18, 1972 A.M.C. 1200 (E.D.Pa.1972), which was the usual three-count action, it was held that the plaintiff was entitled to an award of counsel fees but would be awarded only one-third of his actual fee on the assumption that only one-third of counsel's time had been devoted to the maintenance and cure count. That pointless complication suggests that we would be better off calling punitive damages "punitive damages" instead of calling them "counsel fees".

In Gore v. Clearwater Shipping Corp., 378 F.2d 584, 1968 A.M.C. 396 (3d Cir. 1967), discussed text following note 94i *infra*, it was held that awards of counsel fees under Vaughan could not be recovered in an indemnity action against a previous employer of an injured seaman although the previous employer was held liable to indemnify subsequent employers for their ordinary (or non-punitive) maintenance and cure expenses.

**71i.** See the Robinson case, note 71f *supra*. The Court held that in a case which goes to the jury under Fitzgerald (text following note 45d *supra*) it is for the jury to decide whether or not to add pre-judgment interest. In Robinson the trial judge had added the interest himself, which was held to be error.

is limited to both-to-blame collision cases.[72] Nor is any difficulty presented by cases in which there is a pre-existing contractual relationship between the shipowner-employer and the third party assumed to be solely at fault. In Ryan Stevedoring Co., Inc. v. Pan-Atlantic Steamship Corp.[73] the Supreme Court held that a shipowner who had been held liable to a harbor-worker in an unseaworthiness action could recover indemnity from the harbor worker's employer when the latter, engaged to perform stevedoring services, was responsible for the condition of unseaworthiness. The lower courts were quick to construe the Ryan holding as allowing the shipowner-employer to recover his maintenance and cure expenses from any third party whose negligence caused the injury if the third party had been engaged in performance of a contract with the employer.[73a]

Our present discussion is concerned with cases where a shipowner who is in no way at fault seeks indemnity for maintenance and cure expenses from an independent tortfeasor responsible for the seaman's injury. The case can arise from shipboard injuries where the seaman is injured in a collision with another ship, the other ship being solely at fault. Now that the shipowner's liability for shore leave injuries has been established, a typical case will be the shipowner against the negligent owner or operator of the automobile, the tavern, the dance hall or whatever shoreside instrumentality was the occasion of the seaman's injury.

When the injured seaman joins the shipowner and the tortfeasor in the same action, the cases are in accord that the entire judgment, both for damages and for maintenance and cure, should run in the first instance against the tortfeasor, the shipowner being only secondarily liable for that part of the judgment allocable to maintenance and cure.[74] Thus the shipowner will not have to pay unless execution is

72. Halcyon Lines v. Haenn Ship Ceiling & Refitting Corp., 342 U.S. 282, 72 S.Ct. 277, 1952 A.M.C. 1 (1952), discussed § 6–55 *infra*, text following note 362.

73. 350 U.S. 124, 76 S.Ct. 232, 1956 A.M.C. 9 (1956), discussed § 6–55 *infra*.

73a. United States v. Tug Manzanillo, 310 F.2d 220 1963 A.M.C. 365 (9th Cir. 1962); Moore-McCormack Lines v. Boston Line and Service Co., 1968 A.M.C. 520 (D.Mass.1968). In United States v. Gallagher, 322 F.Supp. 426, 1971 A.M.C. 684 (W.D.Wash.1970) Judge Beeks described the result in the Manzanillo case as "a clear fallout from Ryan". On the Gallagher case, see note 94h *infra*.

74. Seely v. City of New York, 24 F.2d 412, 1928 A.M.C. 944 (2d Cir. 1928) (collision); The Jefferson Myers, 45 F.2d 162, 1930 A.M.C. 1911 (2d Cir. 1930) (libellant injured during unloading); Thibeault v. Boston Towboat Co., 28 F.Supp. 152, 1939 A.M.C. 1077 (D.Mass.1939) (roof boards of loading platform of freight car float gave way), affirmed Mystic Terminal Co. v. Thibeault, 108 F.2d 813, 1940 A.M.C. 183 (1st Cir. 1940). Cf. Gomes v. Eastern Gas & Fuel Associates, 127 F.Supp. 435, 1955 A.M.C. 97 (D.Mass. 1954), which held that a seaman who is struck by an automobile and settles with the automobile owner does not thereby release his claim against his employer for maintenance and cure. But the shipowner is entitled to setoff whatever recovery the seaman obtained applicable to the items which would be covered by maintenance and cure, and the burden is upon the seaman to separate those items for which the shipowner would not be entitled to credit. On the difficulty of performing the separation, contributing to a setting aside of a verdict for the seaman, see Gomes v. Eastern Gas & Fuel Associates, 132 F.Supp. 29, 1955 A.M.C. 1560 (D.Mass.1955).

returned unsatisfied against the "primary debtor".[74a] These holdings, despite the esoteric suretyship terminology, seem entirely sound. The ordinary plaintiff who recovers a tort judgment collects his medical expenses, lost wages and living costs while incapacitated as items in his damages. The seaman who sues a negligent third party may have the same recovery; he also has his peculiar maritime right to recover maintenance and cure from his employer without regard to fault; but he has no right to a double recovery. If the seaman recovers first from the tortfeasor and then proceeds against his employer for maintenance and cure, the employer should receive a credit for any maintenance and cure expenses recovered from the tortfeasor. It is reasonable that the result should be the same when the seaman joins the two defendants in the same action.

**§ 6–15.** The courts have found the case more difficult when the shipowner, having made maintenance and cure payments, brings his own action for indemnity, or when the shipowner, being sued for maintenance and cure, seeks to implead the tortfeasor. On the face of it, such situations do not seem to be notably different from those just discussed. Nevertheless the separate indemnity action as well as the impleader have been found to involve several obscure questions of law. The leading case *against* indemnity is The Federal No. 2,[75] decided by the Second Circuit in 1927. The leading case *for* is Jones v. Waterman Steamship Corp.,[76] one of the first shore leave cases, decided by the Third Circuit in 1946.

In The Federal No. 2,[77] a seaman employed on a barge was injured by a towing hawser which swept across the barge's deck. The injury was caused by the negligence of the tug's crew. The employer, having paid the seaman's expenses, libeled the tug *in rem* both for reimbursement of the expenses and for damage to the barge which had subsequently come into collision with the tug. The reimbursement claim was denied. The court felt that no question of subrogation was involved, since the barge-owner's liability to care for the injured seaman arose out of the contract of employment and was independent of the tug's negligence. Apart from cases allowing recovery for a tortious and deliberate attempt by a third party to interfere with the employer-employee relationship, the court professed itself unable to discover a case in which an employer had been allowed to recover from a third party loss or damage occasioned the employer by a tort against an employee. The closest analogy to such a recovery was said to be the parent's right to recover for loss of services or for expenses incurred in the care of a child, but that recovery was "based on the recognition of the natural parental obligation to care for and

**74a.** The text was quoted and approved by Judge Rubin in Richardson v. St. Charles-St. John the Baptist Bridge and Ferry Authority, 284 F.Supp. 709, 1968 A.M.C. 1485 (E.D.La.1968).

**75.** 21 F.2d 313, 1927 A.M.C. 1471 (2d Cir. 1927).

**76.** 155 F.2d 992, 1946 A.M.C. 859 (3d Cir. 1946).

**77.** See note 75, *supra*.

maintain the infant child" and similar considerations explained the husband's recovery for injury to his wife.

> "But this social condition does not exist in the relationship of a seaman and his employer. It is a contract obligation, which he must perform, that imposes this responsibility, even though it be a special damage he suffers from a tortious act. The cause of the responsibility is the contract; the tort is the remote occasion." [78]

§ **6–16.** Jones v. Waterman Steamship Corp.[79] presented not only the indemnity question but the effect of a release executed by the seaman and the question whether the employer, when sued by the seaman, could implead the tortfeasor. Jones had left his ship on shore leave and was crossing the pier on his way to the streets when the lights on the pier went out. In the darkness he fell into an open ditch along a railroad siding owned by the Reading Company. The Reading Company's failure to fill in or fence off the ditch was alleged as the negligent act which caused Jones' injury. Jones first brought a civil action for damages against the Reading Company. Subsequently Jones settled his claim against Reading for $750 and executed a general release in Reading's favor. Jones also brought a civil action (not in admiralty) against Waterman, his employer, for maintenance and cure. In that action Waterman impleaded Reading as a third-party defendant under Rule 14(a) of the Federal Rules of Civil Procedure.

With respect to the release, the Court held in the first instance that Jones' release of Reading did not bar his action against Waterman. That holding is clearly correct and has been followed without question in subsequent cases where releases or settlements have also appeared.[80] Jones' action against Waterman would not have been barred by a judgment against Reading in the tort action, and the settlement and release, if made in good faith, could have no greater effect. Secondly, the Court held that Jones' release of Reading did not operate as a release of any claim which Waterman might have against Reading. Conceptually, this holding was based on the thought that, while Jones' claim against Reading was in tort, his right to maintenance and cure from Waterman was contractual. Waterman's right (if he had one) to indemnity from Reading was in no sense derivative from Jones' tort claim and thus could not be affected by the release. Once again the holding seems sound: A and B cannot, by an agree-

78. 21 F.2d 313, 314, 1927 A.M.C. 1471, 1473. Given the contractual arrangement between the owner of the barge (the plaintiff's employer) and the owner of the tug, The Federal No. 2, on its own facts, would not be followed anywhere today. See text following note 73 and the cases cited in note 73a. Such vitality as the case may still have would be in cases where there is no contractual relationship between employer and tortfeasor. On the current attitude of the judges of the Second Circuit toward The Federal No. 2, see text following note 94d *infra*.

79. 155 F.2d 992, 1946 A.M.C. 859 (3d Cir. 1946).

80. Muise v. Abbott, 160 F.2d 590, 1947 A.M.C. 735 (1st Cir. 1947); Gomes v. Eastern Gas & Fuel Associates, 127 F.Supp. 435, 1955 A.M.C. 97 (D.Mass. 1954).

ment between themselves, destroy an independent right which C has against B.[80a]

Having held, further, that Reading was properly impleaded, the Court decided that Waterman's claim was based not on maritime but on common law. In support of this holding, the Court said merely: "Under the decisions of the American courts [citing none] there is no doubt that Waterman's cause of action does not lie within the purview of the maritime law." [81] Thus, regarding Waterman's third-party complaint against Reading (in a civil action) as based on diversity of citizenship, the Court concluded that the rule of Erie R. Co. v. Tompkins [82] applied and that the solution lay in Pennsylvania law. Finding no Pennsylvania cases, however, the Court embarked on a review of "general law" and persuaded itself to the conclusion that "the general law in the United States . . . seems settled" that an employer can recover for loss occasioned to him by injuries to his employees for which a third party is responsible. Thus the researches of the Third Circuit led it to a reading of prior law exactly opposite to that which the Second Circuit had reached in The Federal No. 2. Commenting on that case, Judge Biggs wrote:

> "We are of the opinion that the relationship of the shipowner to the seaman is more closely analogous to that of father and child than to that of an employer to a mere employee. We prefer to impose a higher degree of dignity upon the ship-seaman relationship, awarding to it a status or a 'social condition' in excess of that given under the ruling in The Federal No. 2." [83]

Waterman was therefore entitled to recover from Reading (if Reading's negligence was proved) any amounts it might have to pay Jones for maintenance and cure.

**§ 6–17.** One of the analogies which the Third Circuit looked to in the Waterman case was a lower court decision which held that the United States could recover the cost of hospitalization for an injured soldier from the tortfeasor responsible for his injuries.[84] The reversal of that holding by the Supreme Court in United States v. Standard Oil Co.[85] shook the Third Circuit's conceptual structure. Justice Rutledge's reasoning in his Standard Oil opinion was fugitive and difficult to seize; ultimately he seemed to ground the holding on the thought that the United States, as sovereign, could, through Congress, control the situation and that, since Congress had not acted, the Court would not, on more or less remote common-law analogies, invent a right of recovery. If the case is taken as resting on the

**80a.** See United States v. Tug Manzanillo, 310 F.2d 220, 1963 A.M.C. 365 (9th Cir. 1962).

**81.** 155 F.2d 992, 997, n. 3, 1946 A.M.C. 859, 865, n. 3.

**82.** 304 U.S. 64, 58 S.Ct. 817 (1938).

**83.** 155 F.2d 992, 1000–1, 1946 A.M.C. 859, 870–1.

**84.** United States v. Standard Oil Co., 60 F.Supp. 807 (S.D.Cal.1945).

**85.** 332 U.S. 301, 67 S.Ct. 1604, 1947 A.M.C. 1017 (1947).

special status of the United States, the holding should not be conclusive, or even persuasive, in litigation between private parties. It is, however, possible to take the case more broadly, and there was nothing in the opinion to give aid or comfort to the judges of the Third Circuit in their conclusion that the right of employers to recover for injuries to their employees has been generally recognized in American law. The Standard Oil opinion did not cite either Waterman or The Federal No. 2 or discuss the maintenance and cure cases.[85a] Nevertheless, the rationale of the Standard Oil case seemed clearly enough to favor the approach of the Second Circuit in the Federal No. 2 over the approach of the Third Circuit in Waterman.

**§ 6–18.** It is unfortunate that so relatively simple a situation has become enmeshed in technicalities and that the shipowner's right to indemnity cannot be decided without learned discussion of common law forms of action and the pleading *quod servitium amisit.* The equities are clearly with the shipowner. The tortfeasor, if he is required to indemnify the shipowner, is not being made to pay anything which (assuming his negligence) could not have been recovered from him directly in a tort action. The cases are in accord that if the seaman first recovers medical expenses from the tortfeasor, the shipowner gets a credit if he is subsequently sued for maintenance and cure.[86] If so much is recognized, it seems unduly technical to forbid the indemnity when the seaman proceeds in reverse chronological order and first collects his maintenance and cure from the shipowner. Furthermore, if the seaman joins both shipowner and tortfeasor as defendants, the cases hold without exception that the maintenance and cure items in any judgment are to be collected in the first instance from the tortfeasor.[87] Under those circumstances the shipowner ought not to be deprived of his right over by plaintiff's failure to make the joinder. So far the holdings in the Jones case are sound, even if the rationalizations in the opinion are occasionally weak. There is less reason to follow the Third Circuit in its assumption that the indemnity action is not a maritime law question and that state law applies. The maintenance and cure action is of course maritime and will be governed by maritime law no matter in what court it is pursued.[88] The indemnity action seems closely enough related to be equally considered as maritime: indeed only the Third Circuit in the Waterman opinion has ever suggested that it was not.[89] The trouble with the state law approach is not only the certainty of a hodge-podge of conflicting decisions but the fact that the shipowner might be deprived

**85a.** In the Standard Oil case, the Supreme Court affirmed the Ninth Circuit's reversal of the District Court's holding. Judge Bone's elaborate and learned opinion for the Ninth Circuit, 153 F.2d 958 (9th Cir. 1946), had indeed twice cited The Federal No. 2 with approval.

**86.** See cases cited *supra* note 74.

**87.** See cases cited *supra* note 74.

**88.** See *infra* §§ 6–53, 6–59.

**89.** In the Richardson case, text following note 93 *infra*, Judge Rubin, following Waterman, expressly rejected the state law approach. In all the other cases the judges have assumed without discussion that state law was irrelevant.

of his indemnity by state statutes of limitation which would not bar the maintenance and cure claim. The indemnity recovery should be allowed, as a question of maritime law, either by direct action against the tortfeasor or by impleader. The action should be for indemnity only; there should be no additional recovery, beyond maintenance and cure payments, for "loss of services".

In the indemnity cases decided since World War II the long-term trend seems to have been toward the position taken by the Third Circuit in Waterman. During the 1950's the Supreme Court's denial of indemnity in the Standard Oil case led several courts to conclude that the Waterman position was no longer tenable [90] and The Federal No. 2 was of course followed in the District Courts within the Second Circuit.[91] Even during that period, however, there were cases which followed Waterman. Judge Skelly Wright commented in Pure Oil Company v. Geotechnical Corporation [92] that The Federal No. 2 might still be the law in the Second Circuit and that the denial of recovery received "some support, although very meager" from the Supreme Court's Standard Oil opinion but concluded that Waterman stated the better rule.

The problem was comprehensively reexamined by Judge Rubin in Richardson v. St. Charles-St. John the Baptist Bridge and Ferry Authority.[93] Richardson, a deckhand on a car-ferry, was injured by a car which was being negligently driven off the ferry. He filed separate suits (which were consolidated for trial) against the tortfeasor and against his employer and the employer filed a cross-claim against the tortfeasor. Judge Rubin noted that if Richardson had joined both the tortfeasor and the defendant in a single action any resulting judgment (including the employer's maintenance and cure expenses) would run in the first instance against the tortfeasor.[93a] Since Richardson's two suits had been consolidated Judge Rubin might perhaps have stopped there but instead he elected to go on to a full-dress consideration of the indemnity problem. He clearly intended his analysis to apply not only to the procedural situation in the case before him but also to cases in which the seaman sues only his employer who then impleads the tortfeasor as well as to cases in which the employer has voluntarily made a settlement with the seaman and seeks recovery from the tortfeasor in an independent action. After remarking that, in his opinion, the Supreme Court's dis-

**90.** Gomes v. Eastern Gas & Fuel Associates, 127 F.Supp. 435, 1955 A.M.C. 97 (D.Mass.1954). See also Maryland Casualty Co. v. Paton, 194 F.2d 765, 769 (9th Cir. 1952); Frank C. Sparks Co. v. Huber Baking Co., 9 Terry 9, 96 A.2d 456, 459 (Sup.Ct.Del.1953).

**91.** See Irwin v. United States, 111 F. Supp. 912, 1953 A.M.C. 913 (E.D.N.Y. 1953), affirmed on other grounds 236 F.2d 774, 1957 A.M.C. 132 (2d Cir. 1956).

**92.** 129 F.Supp. 194, 1955 A.M.C. 566 (E.D.La.1955). See also Sillanpa v. Cornell Steamboat Co., 1954 A.M.C. 1189 (N.Y.Sup.Ct.1954).

**93.** 284 F.Supp. 709, 1968 A.M.C. 1485 (E.D.La.1968).

**93a.** See text at note 74a *supra*.

cussion of the problem in the Standard Oil case had not undermined the reasoning in Waterman, he reviewed both Waterman and The Federal No. 2, concluding that:

> "[T]he result reached in The Federal No. 2 is a poor one from the standpoint of policy. Determination of who should bear the cost of maintenance and cure ought not to turn on the sequence or the manner in which the seaman chooses to sue the parties. Yet, under the approach taken in Federal No. 2, this is exactly what occurs. . . .
>
> ". . . 'Equity is no stranger in admiralty' [93b] . . . and equity is done in such situations by placing primary liability for maintenance and cure on the tortfeasor who caused the seaman's injury." [93c]

In Mahramas v. American Export Isbrandtsen Lines, Inc.[93d] Judge Anderson suggested, in somewhat guarded language, that the time had come when the judges of the Second Circuit themselves might be willing to scrap The Federal No. 2 in favor of Waterman. Mahramas was an odd case in which the plaintiff had been employed not by Isbrandtsen but by the operators of a beauty shop on one of Isbrandtsen's cruise ships. The Court held that the plaintiff was not in any case entitled to recover maintenance and cure but that, if she had been so entitled, she could have recovered it only from her employer and not from Isbrandtsen.[93e] Piling hypothetical on hypothetical, Judge Anderson then observed:

> "[W]e see no reason why an employer, not the owner, could not seek indemnification against the owner for any maintenance and cure that he became liable for because of the ower's negligence. We question the continued validity of Federal No. 2 . . . to the extent that it would prohibit such an indemnification, see Jones v. Waterman S. S. Corp. . . ." [93f]

**93b.** Quoting Vaughan v. Atkinson, 369 U.S. at p. 530, 82 S.Ct. at 999, 1962 A.M.C. at p. 1133, see text following note 71e *supra*.

**93c.** 284 F.Supp. at p. 716, 1968 A.M.C. at pp. 1494–1495. In Savoie v. Apache Towing Co., 282 F.Supp. 876, 1968 A.M.C. 951 (E.D.La.1968) (seaman injured in collision with another ship found to be solely at fault) Judge Mitchell also elected to follow Waterman with respect to the employer's right to indemnity from the tortfeasor. The Fifth Circuit has not considered the issue directly but the opinions in both Richardson and Savoie cite Myles v. Quinn Menhaden Fisheries, Inc., 302 F.2d 146, 1962 A.M.C. 1626 (5th Cir. 1962) as impliedly adopting the Waterman approach. In Slade, Inc. v. Scurlock Oil Co., 418 F. 2d 847 (5th Cir. 1969) an attempt to recover maintenance and cure expenses from a third party failed because the employer (who had made voluntary payments to his employees) had not borne the burden of proof with respect to the third party's negligence. The Court did not express any opinion on whether the employer would have had a right to indemnity if the third party's negligence had been proved.

**93d.** 475 F.2d 165, 1973 A.M.C. 587 (2d Cir. 1973).

**93e.** See note 21 *supra* and text following note 26.

**93f.** 475 F.2d at p. 170, n. 7, 1973 A.M.C. at p. 593, n. 7.

Since the operators of the beauty shop were in a contractual relationship with Isbrandtsen, their right to indemnity, if they had been held liable for maintenance and cure, would seem in any case beyond dispute.[93g] However, Judge Anderson could have pointed out that the rule of The Federal No. 2 had been cut back by the contractual relationship cases without going to the length of citing Waterman as governing authority.

The Third Circuit, which had pioneered the indemnity approach in the Waterman case, extended it in a pair of companion cases which it decided in 1967.[93h] In the Gooden case it appeared that the plaintiff had injured his back while serving on a ship owned by Texaco. Subsequently, after having been pronounced fit for duty, his injury was "heightened" while serving on a ship owned by Sinclair. The Court held, in an opinion by Judge Seitz, that the plaintiff could recover his maintenance and cure expenses from either Sinclair or Texaco (subject to the usual prohibition of double recovery). As to whether Sinclair or Texaco should bear the ultimate liability the Court concluded that if Texaco had been at fault (because of negligence or unseaworthiness) in the plaintiff's original injury, then Sinclair could recover from Texaco whatever maintenance and cure expenses it might be required to pay; on the other hand, if neither Texaco nor Sinclair had been at fault, then Sinclair could recover only one-half its payments by way of contribution. The case was remanded for findings on the circumstances of the original injury. The Gore case presented the same situation with the exception that after the plaintiff's original injury on a ship owned by A he had suffered aggravation of the injury on ships owned by B, C, D, E, and F and that the original injury had been caused by A's negligence (or the unseaworthiness of his ship). The plaintiff brought actions for maintenance and cure against all six shipowners. *Held,* in a second opinion by Judge Seitz, that he could recover from any of them and that B, C, D, E, and F were entitled to indemnity from A. However, the right to indemnity, it was further held, did not include the right to recover awards of counsel fees which the District Court had made under Vaughan v. Atkinson.[93i] In the course of of his opinion in the Gooden case Judge Seitz naturally reexamined the present state of the Waterman case and concluded that the Supreme Court's Standard Oil opinion had not necessarily affected it ("a matter of opinion") and that the reaffirmation of the admiralty court's equity powers in Vaughan v. Atkinson had indeed given further support to the "equitable result" in Waterman.[93j]

**93g.** See text following note 73 *supra* and the cases cited in note 73a. See also note 78.

**93h.** Gooden v. Sinclair Refining Co., 378 F.2d 576, 1968 A.M.C. 210 (3d Cir. 1967); Gore v. Clearwater Shipping Corp., 378 F.2d 584, 1968 A.M.C. 396 (3d Cir. 1967).

**93i.** See text following note 71c *supra.*

**93j.** In current litigation only the Ninth Circuit has rejected Waterman and followed The Federal No. 2. In United States v. Gallagher, 467 F.2d 1103, 1972 A.M.C. 2521 (9th Cir. 1972) the facts were that Frey, a crew member on a vessel owned by the

### Same: Shipowners' Liability Convention

**§ 6–19.** In 1939, by presidential proclamation, the Shipowners' Liability (Sick and Injured Seamen) Convention became effective in the United States.[94] The Convention, which was prepared by the International Labor Organization, contains a detailed treatment of the liability of shipowners for maintenance and cure. It was accepted by the United States subject to the "understanding" that it was to apply to "navigation on the high seas only".[95] The "high seas" reservation is obscure: it might mean that the Convention should apply to all maintenance and cure claims brought by seamen employed on ocean-going ships, or it might mean that the Convention should apply only to claims based on injuries suffered while the ship was actually navigating the high seas. Evidently the Convention was not to apply to river, harbor and Great Lakes shipping, and, possibly, not to coastwise shipping. Thus it appeared that two bodies of maintenance and cure law were to develop, one based on the Convention, the other on general maritime law as interpreted by American courts. This unhappy development has not taken place. The Convention, which has almost never been referred to in the cases and has never been the basis of decision in any case, was judicially done to death in 1951 by a deft stroke in Justice Douglas' opinion in Warren v. United States.[96]

A recurrent phrase in the several articles of the Convention is that "national laws and regulations may make exceptions" to the rules stated. Article 2 provides that the shipowner shall be liable

United States, was injured while returning from authorized shore leave in a taxi operated by Gallagher whose negligence caused Frey's injuries. Frey brought a damage action against Gallagher which led to an out-of-court settlement; the amount of the settlement is not stated in the Gallagher opinions. In addition to whatever he received from Gallagher, Frey received payments from the United States for his medical expenses and maintenance. The United States then sought to recover indemnity from Gallagher. In the District Court (322 F.Supp. 426, 1971 A.M.C. 684 [W.D.Wash. 1970]), Judge Beeks remarked that he felt the equities were with the United States but that he was constrained to follow The Federal No. 2 because the Ninth Circuit had indicated its approval of that rule in its opinion in the Standard Oil case (see note 85a *supra*). On appeal Judge Hufstedler categorically restated the Ninth Circuit's position but without discussing the post-World-War II cases. She and her colleagues seemed to feel that the United States should have protected itself by intervening in Frey's action against Gallagher. Gallagher's settlement with Frey might have covered Frey's medical expenses; if it had and he was also required to reimburse the United States he would be made to pay twice for the same thing. It is true enough that Frey had no right to recover his medical expenses twice, and that Gallagher should not be made to pay them twice. But there must have been a better way of sorting out the tangled equities in the case than by resurrecting the doctrine of The Federal No. 2.

94. Proclaimed September 29, 1939, 54 Stat. 1693. The Convention is reprinted in 1938 A.M.C. 1297 and 6 Benedict, Admiralty 294 (6th ed. 1940).

95. This "understanding" was added to Article 20 of the Convention.

96. 340 U.S. 523, 71 S.Ct. 432, 1951 A.M.C. 416 (1951). For the facts of the Warren case, see text at note 37 *supra*.

in respect of "(a) sickness and injury occurring between the date specified in the articles of agreement for reporting for duty and the termination of the engagement", but that "national laws and regulations" may make exceptions as to "injury incurred otherwise than in the service of the ship" and "injury or sickness due to the wilful act, default or misbehaviour" of the seaman. In the Warren case (which involved shore leave injuries) counsel for the seaman argued that the Convention made the shipowner's liability absolute during the employment period and that only by legislation could "national laws and regulations" make an exception. Since Congress had passed no "excepting" legislation the Court could not consider either the fact that Warren's injuries were not incurred "in the service of the ship" or the fact that Warren might have been injured through his own negligence. Although the Court had decided to allow Warren's recovery, Justice Douglas paused for a moment to dispatch the Convention. The Court had held in Erie R. Co. v. Tompkins, he pointed out, that the phrase "the laws of the several states" as used in the Judiciary Act of 1789 included judicial decisions as well as statutes. "No reason is apparent why a more restricted meaning should be given the phrase 'national laws and regulations' " used in the Convention.[97] That *tour de force* finished the Convention, since any court in any case could now vary its provisions in any way it saw fit. There is more to be said for Justice Douglas' deed on grounds of judicial statesmanship than on ground of statutory construction. On the verbal level, the French text of the Convention uses the phrase "la législation nationale" as the equivalent of "national laws and regulations" in the English text.[98] There can be little doubt that the draftsmen of the Convention meant that its rules should govern unless displaced by statute, and Justice Douglas' citation of Erie sounds like a bit of deadpan judicial humor. On the other hand, the Convention had become a dead letter. Several of its articles called for implementing legislation which Congress had never bothered to pass. The argument made to the Court, if accepted, would have made the shipowner liable even for injuries incurred in wilful disobedience of orders, or for that matter while the seaman was taking part in a mutiny, until Congress enacted the appropriate exceptions. Furthermore, taking the Convention seriously would have led to the development of different sets of rules for "high seas" claims and non-high seas claims. At the time of the Warren case, the Convention had been in force for nearly 15 years but no one had ever paid any attention to it. Rightly or wrongly, Justice Douglas buried the Convention; it has not since been heard from.[99]

97. 340 U.S. 523, 526–527, 71 S.Ct. 432, 434, 1951 A.M.C. 416, 418 (1951).

98. Article 20 provides that both the French and English texts are authentic. Both the French and English texts are reprinted in 54 Stat. 1693 *et seq.* (1936).

99. In Desmond v. United States, 217 F.2d 948, 1955 A.M.C. 17 (2d Cir. 1954) there is a passing reference to the Convention in an opinion by Judge Frank, but the Convention was not the basis of decision.

### The Jones Act: Background

**§ 6–20.** In 1915 Congress passed an omnibus statute captioned "An Act to promote the welfare of American seamen in the merchant marine of the United States; to abolish arrest and imprisonment as a penalty for desertion . . .; and to promote safety at sea".[100] The Act, which takes up twenty-odd pages in the Statutes at Large, dealt with such matters as seamen's wages, working conditions on shipboard, desertion, and life-saving equipment. The twentieth and last section, which bore no relation to the preceding nineteen sections, read: "That in any suit to recover damages for any injury sustained on board vessel or in its service seamen having command shall not be held to be fellow-servants with those under their authority." By those few lines the Congress apparently intended to change the maritime law as stated in The Osceola under which an injured seaman could recover more than his maintenance and cure only in an action based on unseaworthiness and could not recover damages for negligence of master or crew in the navigation or management of the ship.[101] At least, if that was not the intention, no one has ever been able to suggest what the intention was. The draftsman of Section 20 had evidently read the third proposition in The Osceola to mean that the reason why seamen could not recover damages for negligence was that all the members of the crew were fellow-servants and consequently the negligence of each was attributed to all, thus barring the action; on that reading, the abolition of the fellow-servant relationship removed the only barrier to recovery and the action could be maintained under maritime law with no need for affirmative Congressional action.

The judges of the Second Circuit and the Supreme Court shortly combined to give Congress a lesson on "How to read a case" of a type familiar to any first term law student. In Chelentis v. Luckenbach S. S. Co.,[102] a seaman, who had been ordered to perform duties on deck, was injured when a wave swept across the deck, knocked him down and broke his leg. There was no allegation that the ship was unseaworthy. Thus Chelentis was a replica of The Osceola: the sole cause of the injury was an order improvidently given. Chelentis brought a common law action in state court, which was removed to Federal court because of diversity of citizenship. The theory of the case, according to the summary of argument in the Supreme Court report, was that Chelentis, in a common law action outside the admiralty, could recover damages on common law tort principles without regard to the maritime law. Alternatively, if maritime law was relevant, Section 20 of the Act of 1915 had removed the only barrier to recovery under that system of law. The case presented three important issues for decision: whether plaintiff had a right to sue

100. 38 Stat. 1164 (1915).

101. For a discussion of The Osceola, see § 6–2 *supra*.

102. 243 F. 536 (2d Cir. 1917), affirmed 247 U.S. 372, 38 S.Ct. 501 (1918).

outside the admiralty under the saving to suitors clause; whether, if he did, the case was governed by common law or by maritime law; whether, if the action was maintainable and maritime law applied, Section 20 of the Act of 1915 allowed recovery. The trial judge, the Second Circuit and five justices of the Supreme Court were in harmonious agreement. *One*: the action was maintainable outside the admiralty. *Two*: maritime and not common law applied. (This facet of the Chelentis case, resurrected a generation later after having been almost forgotten, has in recent years become of considerable importance.) [103] *Three*: under maritime law Chelentis could not recover and Section 20 of the Act of 1915 was, in Justice McReynolds' word, "irrelevant". The reason why it was irrelevant was that, on a proper reading of The Osceola, the fourth proposition (no recovery for negligence of master or crew) and not the third (fellow servant doctrine) controlled. Since the fellow servant doctrine had never been the bar to recovery, its abrogation by Congress was of no moment and left matters exactly as they had always been.

On the "how to read cases" level, there can be no quarrel with the Chelentis holding. It is another matter whether Congress should have been made to put on the dunce cap and stand in the corner. If Section 20 had been given its obvious (indeed its only) meaning, the Court would have spared much grief to itself, to the inferior federal judiciary, to the bar and to all parties litigant. The theory of Section 20 had been that, with the removal of the only maritime law bar to recovery, the seaman's action for negligence could proceed on ordinary maritime law principles and there would no longer have been any need to distinguish between unseaworthiness and operating negligence. It must be a matter of regret that the Court refused this simple solution and instead goaded Congress into doing it the hard way.

Congress did it the hard way in 1920. Section 33 of the Merchant Marine Act of 1920 "amended" Section 20 of the Act of 1915 to read as follows:

> "Any seaman who shall suffer personal injury in the course of his employment may, at his election, maintain an action for damages at law, with the right of trial by jury, and in such action all statutes of the United States modifying or extending the common-law right or remedy in cases of personal injury to railway employees shall apply; and in case of the death of any seaman as a result of any such personal injury the personal representative of such seaman may maintain an action for damages at law with the right of trial by jury, and in such action all statutes of the United States conferring or regulating the right of action for death in the case of railway employees shall be applicable. Jurisdiction in such actions shall be under the court of the district in

103. See § 6–58 *et seq. infra.*

which the defendant employer resides or in which his principal office is located." [104]

The Merchant Marine Act of 1920 established the Shipping Board, enacted the Ship Mortgage Act and made important amendments to the Maritime Lien Act of 1910. Like its predecessor Section 20 of the Act of 1915, Section 33, which came to be known as the Jones Act, was a little noticed provision, unrelated to the balance of the statute. As it made its way through committee to the floor of House and Senate, it can hardly have drawn much attention. In due course its constitutionality as a permissible modification or extension of maritime law was upheld [105] by a Supreme Court which might better have struck it down as offensive to the due process clause by reason of impossibly bad drafting.

Older editions of the United States Code Annotated prefaced the statute with a seventy-page essay entitled Commentary on Maritime Workers, supplemented by a diagrammatic "Chart to Illustrate the Jurisdiction of the Courts". The editors evidently felt that without such aids there was no hope for the traveler who ventured into the wilderness of Jones Act case law. The Commentary and Chart no longer appear in the current (1958) edition; perhaps the editors decided that there was no hope for the traveler, however well equipped he might be. The main volume in the 1958 edition collects 307 pages of case law annotations; the pocket part (1958–1973) collects another 241 pages. These impressive page counts do, however, distort the true situation. The great period for Jones Act litigation was from 1920 until approximately 1950: during that period the Act was the vehicle for almost all seamen's personal injury and death actions. During the 1940's the Supreme Court reformulated the traditional doctrine of unseaworthiness in a way which made the unseaworthiness action much more attractive to plaintiffs than a Jones Act action.[105a] The curious practice grew up (with results which will be described in the following sections) of joining a Jones Act count with an unseaworthiness count. One reason for continuing to use a Jones Act count was to make sure that plaintiff was entitled to a jury trial, which might not have been available in the general maritime law action for unseaworthiness even when that action was brought in a non-admiralty court under the saving to suitors clause. Another reason for continuing to use a Jones Act count in death cases (as distinguished from personal injury cases) was that until 1970 the accepted doctrine was that the general maritime law provided no remedy for wrongful death.[105b] Thus Jones Act counts have continued to swell the volume of the U.S.C.A. annotations but the truth is, at least in personal injury actions, that since 1950 the unseaworthiness count

104. 41 Stat. 1007 (1920); 46 U.S.C.A. § 688.

105. Panama R. Co. v. Johnson, 264 U. S. 375, 44 S.Ct. 391, 1924 A.M.C. 551 (1924), discussed § 6–22 *infra.*

105a. On this development see § 6–38 *et seq. infra.*

105b. The 1970 case was Moragne v. States Marine Lines, Inc., 398 U.S. 375, 90 S.Ct. 1772, 1970 A.M.C. 967, discussed § 6–32 *infra.*

has been the essential basis for recovery with the Jones Act count preserved merely as a jury-getting device. And since 1970 the only function of the Jones Act count in death cases is to preserve the right to jury trial. There has really been no substantive growth in the Jones Act case law since 1950; the action has been elsewhere. The resulting pattern is cumbersome and lacks elegance but practitioners have learned to live with the double-gaited pleading so that no real harm is done.

### The Jones Act Plaintiff (Herein of "Seamen" and "Vessels")

**§ 6–21.** The Jones Act plaintiff must be a "seaman" who is injured (or killed) "in the course of his employment".[106] The "course of . . . employment" requirement at least excluded passengers, guests, trespassers, pirates (unless of course the pirate was suing his own employer) and so on. Who else might be excluded (or included) was, as a matter of initial construction, impossible to say. After a half-century of litigation the answer to the riddle is not apparent. The Supreme Court has alternated between giving the term "seaman" an exceedingly broad construction and giving it a much narrower one. Consequently defendants have been encouraged to argue, in all but the most obvious cases, that plaintiff is not a Jones Act seaman and that the action must be dismissed. Thus there has always been, there continues to be, and presumably there will go on being a substantial volume of depressing litigation of this type.

Before going further, we should attempt to clarify what the consequences are of a holding that a particular plaintiff is not a Jones Act seaman. As a general proposition, anyone who is the victim of a maritime tort is entitled to bring an action in admiralty in rem or in personam or to pursue his remedy outside the admiralty under the saving to suitors clause. The fourth proposition of The Osceola had barred "seamen" from the exercise of this normal remedy with respect to injuries caused by "negligence of the master, or any member of the crew". The only purpose of the Jones Act was to remove

106. In the first edition of the treatise we commented that the phrase "in the course of his employment" had taken on, in the Jones Act context, a somewhat broader meaning than it had in the context of Workmen's Compensation Acts: "It may be read as equivalent to the 'in the service of the ship' formula used in the maintenance and cure cases." Justice Douglas adopted that formulation in Braen v. Pfeifer Oil Transportation Co., Inc., 361 U.S. 129, 80 S.Ct. 247, 1960 A.M.C. 2 (1959), commenting that "the scope of a seaman's employment or the activities which are related to the furtherance of the vessel are not measured by the standards applied to land-based employment relationships." (361 U.S. at p. 132, 80 S.Ct. at p. 250, 1960 A.M.C. at p. 5.) In Braen the plaintiff, who was employed as mate on a barge, had been ordered to perform some carpentry work on a raft. He was injured attempting to board the raft. "The fact that the raft was not presently being used to service [defendant's] barge is in our opinion immaterial. [Plaintiff] was acting "in the course of his employment" at the time of his injury, for at that moment he was doing the work of his employer pursuant to his employer's orders. No more is required by the Jones Act. . . ." (361 U.S. at p. 133, 80 S.Ct. at p. 250, 1960 A.M.C. at p. 6.) On the "service of the ship" formula used in the maintenance and cure cases, see § 6–8 *supra.*

the bar created by The Osceola, so that seamen would have the same rights to recover for negligence as other tort victims. It follows, therefore, that, if plaintiff is a seaman, he can recover under the Jones Act; if he is not a seaman, he can recover under the general maritime law. If that is so, what difference can it make (apart from technicalities of pleading and procedure) whether plaintiff is thought to get his remedy under the statute or under the general maritime law?[106a]

It must be remembered that the propositions of The Osceola did not merely put seamen under a special disability (no recovery for negligence); they also gave seamen special rights (to recover maintenance and cure as well as "indemnity" for unseaworthiness). With the enactment of the Jones Act the special disability was removed but, it was universally assumed, the seaman-plaintiff continued to be entitled to his special rights. That is, if he was a seaman he could recover under the Jones Act for negligence and under the general maritime law for unseaworthiness as well as maintenance and cure. If he was not a seaman he lost not only his right to sue under the Jones Act but also his special rights under the maritime law. Thus (to answer the question put at the end of the preceding paragraph) it made a great deal of difference whether plaintiff was entitled to sue as a seaman or merely as the victim of a maritime tort. And as the Supreme Court refashioned the unseaworthiness remedy into a species of absolute liability without fault, it came to make a great deal more difference than it had when the Jones Act was first enacted. From the earliest days of Jones Act litigation the courts assumed, without discussion, that the decision on whether plaintiff was a seaman determined not only his right to sue under the Jones Act but his right to recover maintenance and cure and the indemnity for unseaworthiness under the general maritime law.

During the 1920's and 1930's most seamen's personal injury actions were brought under the Jones Act without additional counts under the general maritime law. The courts therefore addressed themselves to the question of seamen's status in terms of the Jones Act. With the refashioning of the unseaworthiness remedy during the 1940's the practice became established of always joining an unseaworthiness count (and frequently a maintenance and cure count) to the Jones Act count. Through an understandable inertia the courts have in most cases continued to peg their discussions of seaman status to the Jones Act count; the decision on that count determines the fate of the other two counts. We may now return to our interrupted discussion of who is a Jones Act seaman.

106a. In addition to the answer to the question which will be suggested in the following paragraph of the text, one further point may be made. As the Jones Act case law developed, it gradually became clear that the standard of negligence applicable to Jones Act cases was considerably less onerous, from a plaintiff's viewpoint, than the standard of negligence which had been applied to ordinary maritime tort actions. See § 6–34 *et seq. infra.* Thus, even if we consider only the recovery for negligence, the plaintiff may be better off under the Jones Act than under the general maritime law.

First indications were that "seaman" was to receive the broadest possible construction. In International Stevedoring Company v. Haverty [107] the Court held that a longshoreman injured while stowing freight in the hold of a vessel was a Jones Act seaman and could bring a Jones Act action against his employer. As Justice Holmes put it: "[A]s the word is commonly used, stevedores are not 'seamen'. But words are flexible." The Haverty holding could have led, with the greatest of ease, to the conclusion that all maritime workers injured in the course of their employment were Jones Act seamen.

Haverty, however, shortly became a casualty of the war between the Supreme Court and Congress over the constitutionality of the application of state workmen's compensation statutes to shore-based maritime workers.[108] In 1927 Congress, bowing to the Court's constitutional strictures, enacted the Longshoremen's and Harbor Workers' Compensation Act, which made the compensation remedy exclusive against the worker's employer. The Longshoremen's Act clearly enough prohibited Haverty from suing the International Stevedoring Company (his employer) under the Jones Act.[108a] There remained the possibility that a Haverty-type plaintiff could bring a Jones Act action against the shipowner (who was not his employer). The Jones Act requires that the plaintiff's injury occur "in the course of his employment" but does not clearly say that the action can be brought only against his employer. Indeed the Supreme Court has never held that the Jones Act defendant must be the plaintiff's employer, although most judicial and academic discussions have assumed that that is what the Act means.[109] However, no Haverty-type plaintiff showed up to test the possibility of bringing a Jones Act action against a shipowner who had not employed him and the Haverty holding receded into the limbo of forgotten case law. Even when the Supreme Court held that stevedores were seamen for the purpose of bringing actions against shipowners (who were not their employers) under the unseaworthiness doctrine,[110] no one (including the Justices) suggested that stevedores had, ipso facto, become Jones Act seamen. The 1972 amendments to the Longshoremen's Act provided that stevedores and other shore-based workers can no longer bring unseaworthiness actions against shipowners but can bring negligence actions against them. It will no doubt occur to counsel for some Haverty-type plaintiff to argue that the Haverty holding has now been resurrected; we shall defer exploration of that possibility until we take up the 1972 amendments.[111]

107. 272 U.S. 50, 47 S.Ct. 19, 1926 A.M.C. 1638 (1926).

108. See § 6–45 *et seq. infra.*

108a. Swanson v. Marra Bros., Inc., 328 U.S. 1, 66 S.Ct. 869, 1946 A.M.C. 715 (1946).

109. See the following section, § 6–21(a), for further discussion of this point.

110. Seas Shipping Co. v. Sieracki, 328 U.S. 85, 66 S.Ct. 872, 1946 A.M.C. 698 (1946), discussed § 6–54 *infra.*

111. See § 6–57 *infra.*

Following the Haverty episode, the Supreme Court continued to express its approval of a broad construction of "seaman." [112] It seems never to have been questioned that any member of a ship's company who actually goes to sea, no matter what his (or her) duties may be, is a seaman.[113] But there are a great many maritime workers who do not go to sea but who are assigned duties on or about structures which float on navigable waters. If these workers are employed by the owners of the structures (as distinguished from longshoremen who are customarily employed by independent contractors) are they "seamen"?

In a trio of cases decided in the late 1950's the Supreme Court seemed to have concluded that all such workers are seamen or at least that they are entitled to have the seaman question decided by a jury.[114]

In Senko v. LaCrosse Dredging Corp.[115] the facts were, as Justice Reed stated them in his majority opinion, that Senko was employed as a handyman in connection with a dredging operation being conducted by the defendant. His duties included the carrying and storing of supplies and the general maintenance of a dredge which, throughout the period of his employment, was anchored to the shore. He was injured by the explosion of a coal stove while placing signal lanterns from the dredge in a shed on land.[116] He sued in State court under

112. There was, however, one class of traditional seamen who found themselves excluded both from the Jones Act and from the general maritime law remedies. These were seamen employed by the United States whose exclusive remedy, the Supreme Court held, was under the Federal Employees' Compensation Act. See note 23 *supra*. For the status of seamen employed on vessels owned by the United States but operated by "general agents", see § 6–60 *infra*. On whether United States courts will take jurisdiction of personal injury actions by foreign seamen employed on foreign-flag ships, see § 6–63 *et seq. infra*.

113. See, e. g., Mahramas v. American Export Isbrandtsen Lines, Inc., 475 F.2d 165, 1973 A.M.C. 587 (2d Cir. 1973) (female hairdresser in beauty shop). Both the majority and dissenting opinions collect other cases of this type. The Mahramas case is discussed in § 6–21(a) *infra*.

114. The Court had taken a more restrictive approach in a case decided only a few years earlier, Desper v. Starved Rock Ferry Co., 342 U.S. 187, 72 S.Ct. 216, 1952 A.M.C. 12 (1952). The Ferry Company operated a fleet of sightseeing boats which were used only during the summer months and were laid up during the winter months. Desper, who had operated one of the boats during the 1947 season, was rehired in March, 1948, to work on reconditioning the boats for the summer and to operate one of the boats when the season began. While engaged in such work on a "moored barge", he was killed by an explosion. His administratrix brought a death action under the Jones Act. In the District Court there was a jury verdict and judgment for plaintiff. The Seventh Circuit reversed and the reversal was affirmed in the Supreme Court (Justices Black and Douglas dissenting without opinion). In holding that, as a matter of law, Desper was not a Jones Act seaman, Justice Jackson wrote: "To be sure, he was a probable navigator in the near future, but the law does not cover probable or expectant seamen but only seamen in being . . . . [T]here was no vessel engaged in navigation at the time of the decedent's death." (342 U.S. at pp. 190–191, 72 S.Ct. at p. 218, 1952 A.M.C. at p. 14.)

115. 352 U.S. 370, 77 S.Ct. 415, 1957 A.M.C. 891 (1957).

116. It was assumed at one time that the Jones Act applied only to injuries which occurred on navigable waters. See Robinson, Admiralty 332 (1939).

the Jones Act and won a jury verdict and judgment, which was, however, reversed on appeal on the ground that there was insufficient evidence to support the finding that Senko was a member of a crew (or seaman). The Supreme Court, over a dissent by Justice Harlan joined by Justices Frankfurter and Burton, held that "there was sufficient evidence . . . to support the finding that [Senko] was a member of the dredge's crew."[117] "Sufficient" seemed to mean that he worked mostly on the dredge and that, if the dredge had been moved, he would have had "a significant navigational function."

Senko was followed by Grimes v. Raymond Concrete Pile Co.[118] Grimes was employed as a pile-driver in the construction of a "Texas Tower" (a structure permanently affixed to the floor of the ocean). He was injured while being transferred from a tug to the tower. Reversing the First Circuit, the Court held, in a brief per curiam opinion, that the "evidence presented an evidentiary basis for a jury's finding whether or not [Grimes] was a member of a crew of any vessel."[119] Justice Harlan, joined by Justice Whittaker, dissented. Justice Frankfurter at this time had adopted the practice of merely noting, in Jones Act cases of this type, that in his opinion certiorari should not have been granted.

The third case in the series was Butler v. Whiteman.[120] Once again the Court reversed per curiam a dismissal of a Jones Act action, citing Senko and Grimes, but without even indicating what the facts had been. According to Justice Harlan's by now customary dissent the facts were that the plaintiff had been employed as a laborer doing odd jobs on the defendant's wharf. A barge was moored, apparently permanently, to the wharf and a tug was lashed to the barge. The tug had, for several months, been withdrawn from navigation because it was inoperable; nor a year it had had neither a captain or a crew. Work was being done on the tug in an attempt to refit it for service and the plaintiff had been engaged in cleaning the tug's boiler. He was drowned, having last been seen going from the barge toward the tug. Justice Harlan commented: "[I]t taxes imagination to the breaking point to consider this unfortunate individual to have been a seaman . . .".

In O'Donnell v. Great Lakes Dredge & Dock Co., 318 U.S. 36, 63 S.Ct. 488, 1943 A.M.C. 149 (1943) it was held that plaintiff could recover under the Jones Act for injuries suffered while he was working on a wharf where he was hit by an object which fell from the ship. Thus Senko did not break new ground in holding that plaintiff could recover for injuries suffered on land.

117. The state appellate courts had not passed on the issues of whether the dredge was moored in navigable waters or whether the defendant was chargeable with negligence. The Supreme Court remanded the case with directions to review those issues; if they were decided in Senko's favor, the jury verdict was to be reinstated.

118. 356 U.S. 252, 78 S.Ct. 687, 1958 A.M.C. 1014 (1958).

119. In addition to Senko, the per curiam opinion cited Gianfala v. Texas Co., 350 U.S. 879, 76 S.Ct. 141 (1955) in which the Court had reversed, without opinion, a Fifth Circuit holding that workers employed on an oil-drilling rig in the Gulf of Mexico were not seamen.

120. 356 U.S. 271, 78 S.Ct. 734 (1956).

If the Supreme Court had stopped with Senko, Grimes and Butler, the situation would have been fairly clear: any worker whose duties had the slightest contact with a structure on navigable waters was entitled to a jury verdict on his seaman status and a jury finding that he was a seaman could not be set aside. And both Grimes (the Texas Tower) and Butler (the permanently moored barge and the inoperable tug) strongly suggested that it made not the slightest difference whether the "structure" was in any sense a vessel in, or even capable of, navigation.[121]

The Supreme Court did not let matters rest there. West v. United States [121a] involved a Liberty Ship owned by the United States which, after having spent several years in the "moth ball" fleet, was being reactivated for sea-duty during the Korean War. The United States had turned the ship over to a contractor for a complete overhaul. Roper v. United States [121b] involved another Liberty Ship in the mothball fleet which had been used as a warehouse to store grain. The grain having been sold, the ship was moved (not under its own power) to a wharf where the grain could be offloaded. The plaintiffs were an employee of the contractor (West) and a longshoreman employed by the stevedoring firm which was offloading the grain (Roper). These were not Jones Act cases but unseaworthiness cases, the plaintiffs claiming to be within the doctrine of the Sieracki case.[121c] *Held* in both West and Roper that, since the ships had been withdrawn from navigation ("dead ships"), the plaintiffs (whoever they might be) were not entitled to the warranty of seaworthiness. Given the close relationship between, indeed the identity of, the unseaworthiness action and the Jones Act action it follows (if the law has any logical content whatever) that Jones Act plaintiffs like unseaworthiness plaintiffs must be employed on vessels in navigation. If that is so, the apparent implications of Senko, Grimes and Butler were overruled sub silentio in West and Roper.[121d]

**121.** See also the Gianfala case, note 119 *supra*.

**121a.** 361 U.S. 118, 80 S.Ct. 189, 1960 A.M.C. 15 (1959).

**121b.** 368 U.S. 20, 82 S.Ct. 5, 1961 A.M.C. 2499 (1961).

**121c.** See note 110 *supra* and the accompanying text.

**121d.** The West opinion, by Justice Clark, did not refer to any of the three earlier cases. The Roper opinion, also by Justice Clark, cited Butler for the proposition that the determination of whether a ship is in navigation is "a question of fact", did not cite either Senko or Grimes and referred to the "limitation . . . applied in libels under the Jones Act, where it has long been held that recovery is precluded if the ship involved is not a vessel involved in navigation", citing the Desper case, digested note 114 *supra*. West was a unanimous decision; in Roper, Justice Douglas, joined by Chief Justice Warren and Justice Black, dissented on the ground that the ship was in navigation and not a dead ship.

In Mroz v. Dravo Corp., 429 F.2d 1156 (3d Cir. 1970) the vessel on which the plaintiff was injured (on May 26, 1965) had been tied up (both literally and figuratively) by a strike which had begun on March 31, 1965. Judge Maris, citing Senko but not citing either Roper or West, commented: "Whether or not on May 26, 1965, the plaintiff was a member of a crew of a vessel and whether that vessel was then in navigation were questions of fact which the jury in this case decided upon a full and fair charge by the

The Supreme Court has not further clarified these issues. The disarray into which the lower courts have fallen may be illustrated by two Fifth Circuit cases, Barrios v. Louisiana Construction Materials Company [121e] and Cook v. Belden Concrete Products, Inc.[121f] In both cases counts under the Jones Act were joined with counts for unseaworthiness. In Barrios the plaintiff was employed as an oiler on a dragline which was used in dredging operations mostly on land. He was injured while helping to load the dragline on a barge for transportation to a work site. A jury verdict and judgment for plaintiff were affirmed on appeal. Judge Morgan, citing Senko and Grimes, observed that, since those cases were decided, "it has been clear that it is a rare case in which a court may conclude as a matter of law that an injured individual is not a seaman within the meaning of the Jones Act . . . . [E]ven where the facts are largely undisputed, the determination of whether an individual is a seaman will ordinarily be left to the jury." In Cook the plaintiff was employed as a carpenter and when he was injured was working on a floating construction platform moored on navigable waters. The platform had no motive power of its own but was moved from one construction site to another by tugs or land-based cranes. The District Court gave summary judgment for the defendant which was affirmed on appeal. The question for decision, said Judge Clark, was whether the platform was a "vessel". He concluded that the platform was "legally indistinguishable from a floating drydock". In Cope v. Vallette Dry-Dock Co., 119 U.S. 625, 7 S.Ct. 336 (1887) the Supreme Court had held that a floating dry-dock was not a vessel and consequently could not be the subject of salvage. Since the construction platform was "legally indistinguishable" from a dry dock, it could not be a vessel for purposes of the Jones Act. Judge Clark did not cite Senko, Grimes, Butler, or any other recent Supreme Court decisions. With deference, we will suggest that Cook, on the facts of his case, sounds more like a "seaman" than Barrios did, on the facts of that case. Even in a Circuit as steeped in admiralty law as the Fifth, the plaintiff's fate, in cases of this sort, seems to depend on the luck of the judicial draw.[121g]

trial judge." (429 F.2d at p. 1165–1166.) A judgment for plaintiff entered on the jury's verdict was affirmed.

**121e.** 465 F.2d 1157, 1972 A.M.C. 2659 (5th Cir. 1972).

**121f.** 472 F.2d 999, 1973 A.M.C. 285 (5th Cir. 1973).

**121g.** The Cook case was followed in Powers v. Bethlehem Steel Corp., 477 F.2d 643, 1973 A.M.C. 2023 (1st Cir. 1973) (affirming the District Court which entered judgment for defendant notwithstanding a jury verdict for plaintiff in a Jones Act—unseaworthiness—maintenance and cure action). Despite the apparent mandate of Senko and Grimes, a good many current cases approve the practice of deciding seaman status cases for defendant by summary judgment, directed verdict or even (as in the Powers case) by judgment notwithstanding verdict.

Under the Outer Continental Shelf Lands Act, 67 Stat. 462, 43 U.S.C.A. § 1331 *et seq.*, permanently affixed offshore installations are removed from admiralty or maritime law and treated as "artificial islands". See Rodrigue v. Aetna Casualty & Surety Co., 395 U.S. 352, 89 S.Ct. 1835, 1969 A.M.C. 1082 (1969). In a series of cases beginning with Offshore Oil Co. v.

### The Jones Act Defendant

**§ 6–21(a).** The Jones Act plaintiff, as we saw in the preceding section, must be a "seaman" who suffers injury or death "in the course of his employment" on (or in connection with) a "vessel". In one of its early Jones Act cases the Supreme Court held that actions under the Jones Act could not be brought in rem against the ship.[121h] The Jones Act does not, however, specify against whom the in personam action is to be brought—being in this respect unlike the Federal Employers' Liability Act which clearly covers only actions by railroad employees against the railroads which employ them.[121i]

In the normal situation the Jones Act defendant is a) the plaintiff's employer, and b) the operator of the ship on which the plaintiff was injured. Suppose, however, that the employer has no control over the operation of the ship (the Jones Act being restricted to injuries caused by operating negligence). Can the operator be sued under the Jones Act although he is not the plaintiff's employer? Alternatively, can the employer be sued under the Jones Act although he does not operate the ship? And, if the non-operating employer can be sued under the Jones Act, is he liable only for his own negligence or is he liable for the operator's negligence as well? The Jones Act case law does not clearly answer any of these questions.

In Mahramas v. American Export Isbrandtsen Lines, Inc.[121j] a divided panel of the Second Circuit discussed all three of the questions put in the preceding paragraph. Mrs. Mahramas was a hairdresser employed in the beauty shop of one of Isbrandtsen's ships. The beauty shop was operated by House of Albert under a concession contract with Isbrandtsen. Mrs. Mahramas was required to have seaman's papers and to sign the ship's articles. Isbrandtsen furnished her subsistence and quarters. It was found, however, that "she was hired and paid solely by House of Albert . . . and took orders

Robison, 266 F.2d 769, 1959 A.M.C. 2049 (5th Cir. 1959) the Fifth Circuit has held that employees working on movable oil-drilling rigs and the like may qualify as Jones Act seamen. Judge Clark's opinion in the Cook case collects a number of cases of this type.

See further the discussion, § 6–7 *supra*, of who are seamen entitled to recover maintenance and cure.

**121h.** See § 6–22 *infra*, text following note 127.

**121i.** On the Federal Employers' Liability Act, which the Jones Act incorporates by reference, see § 6–26 *et seq. infra*.

It is true that the last sentence of the Jones Act (text at note 104 *supra*) obliquely refers to "the defendant employer." (On the construction which the Supreme Court gave to the "jurisdiction" provision of that sentence, see § 6–22 *infra*.) As a drafting matter, the obvious way of making clear that the action could be brought only against the seaman's employer would have been to say in the first sentence: "Any seaman . . . may . . . maintain an action *against his employer* . . ." Nothing in the first sentence suggests such a limitation. The fugitive reference to "the defendant employer" in the jurisdiction (or venue) sentence does not seem to be entitled to much, if any, weight.

**121j.** 475 F.2d 165, 1973 A.M.C. 587 (2d Cir. 1973).

only from House of Albert's supervisor on the ship." Mrs. Mahramas claimed to have been injured by reason of defective equipment in her quarters. She brought the usual three-count action (Jones Act, unseaworthiness, maintenance and cure), naming both Isbrandtsen and House of Albert as defendants. The District Court dismissed the Jones Act and maintenance and cure counts against both defendants—against Isbrandtsen because it was not the "employer" and against House of Albert because "it did not own or control the ship." The Court further held that the complaint stated a good cause of action against Isbrandtsen for unseaworthiness and for negligence under the general maritime law but that, following dismissal of the Jones Act counts and in the absence of diversity of citizenship, the plaintiff was not entitled to have a jury pass on her claims. The Court discharged the jury and denied any recovery against Isbrandtsen on the general maritime law claims.

The denial of recovery was affirmed on appeal, although Judge Anderson (speaking for himself and Judge Kaufman) concluded that the District Court had fallen into error on several points. The District Court had been correct in dismissing the Jones Act and maintenance and cure counts against Isbrandtsen and in taking the remaining counts against Isbrandtsen from the jury and deciding them on the merits against Mrs. Mahramas. It had been error to dismiss the two counts against House of Albert who was liable as "employer" even though it had no control over the operation of the ship. The error, however, had been harmless since, as to the Jones Act count, House of Albert would have been liable only for its own negligence and not for Isbrandtsen's and, as to the maintenance and cure count, Mrs. Mahramas was not entitled to recovery because it did not appear that she had incurred any out-of-pocket expenses.[121k]

Judge Oakes dissented with respect to the dismissal of the Jones Act count against Isbrandtsen which, he felt, should have been submitted to the jury along with the unseaworthiness count. He did not discuss the disposition of the maintenance and cure count or the proposition that House of Albert, as a Jones Act defendant, was not liable for Isbrandtsen's negligence in operating the ship. His argument that a Jones Act action should lie against Isbrandtsen was susceptible of two interpretations: 1) that, on the facts, Isbrandtsen could be considered the "employer" (Mrs. Mahramas signed the ship's articles and received subsistence and quarters from the ship); 2) that the Jones Act action should lie against the person in control of the ship and chargeable with negligence even if that person is not, technically, the plaintiff's employer.

In all probability there will never be a great many "concession" cases exactly like Mahramas.[121l] The issues decided by the Mahramas

121k. On the disposition of the maintenance and cure count, see § 6–12 *supra*, particularly note 60 and the accompanying text.

121*l*. The Second Circuit had decided one earlier case of this type, Schiemann v. Grace Line, Inc., 269 F.2d 596, 1960 A.M.C. 572 (2d Cir. 1959)

majority are not, however, by any means restricted to female hairdressers in beauty shops. There are a great many maritime workers who qualify as "seamen" and who may suffer work-related injuries on vessels operated by persons who may not be, technically, their employers. The issues warrant further analysis—in particular the basic holding in Mahramas that Jones Act actions (as well as maintenance and cure actions) can be brought only against an "employer" and that the plaintiff can have only one employer at a time.[121m]

According to Judge Anderson's Mahramas opinion: "There has never been any question that the Jones Act applies only between employees and their employers." That proposition has, indeed, been repeated hundreds, if not thousands, of times in judicial opinions and in the academic literature.[121n] On the other hand, nothing about the Jones Act is either true or false until the Supreme Court has held it to be so. Cosmopolitan Shipping Company v. McAllister [121o] is regularly cited as having so held.

McAllister was the last in a series of cases in which a shifting Supreme Court majority analyzed the legal relations created by the World War II "general agency" contract under which "general agents" were engaged to take care of certain aspects of the operation of ships owned by the United States.[121p] The Court eventually concluded that the United States, not the general agent, was the "employer" [121q] and held, in McAllister, that an injured seaman could not

(barber employed by a concessionnaire on a Grace Line ship). Schiemann brought actions, apparently under the Jones Act, both against his employer and Grace. Both actions were dismissed but only the dismissal of the action against Grace was appealed. A divided panel affirmed the dismissal. Judge Clark dissented on the ground that the jury should have been allowed to pass on "plaintiff's employment status" in the light of the facts that Grace in fact controlled his "work activities", that he had signed the ship's articles and was subject to the ship's rules, regulation and discipline. Sims v. Marine Catering Service, 217 F.Supp. 511, 1964 A.M.C. 377 (E.D.La.1963) was another concession case. As in Schiemann and Mahramas it was held that the Jones Act libel lay only against the concessionaire-employer (who was held liable for damages under the Jones Act as well as for maintenance and cure) and not against the operator of the ship. See also Solet v. M/V Captain H. V. Dufrene, 303 F.Supp. 980, 1970 A.M.C. 571 (E.D.La.1969), discussed § 6–7 *supra*, text following note 27e.

**121m.** On the importance of the employment relationship in the maintenance and cure cases, see § 6–7 *supra*, text following note 25.

**121n.** See, e. g., Gilmore & Black, The Law of Admiralty, § 6–21 (1st ed. 1957): "[T]he only action maintainable under the Jones Act is, and certainly ought to be, by the injured seaman against the shipowner who employs him."

**121*o*.** 337 U.S. 783, 69 S.Ct. 1317, 1949 A.M.C. 1031 (1949). Fink v. Shepard S. S. Co. and Gaynor v. Agwilines, Inc., 337 U.S. 810, 69 S.Ct. 1330, 1949 A.M.C. 1045 (1949), decided the same day as McAllister, presented the same issue and were "controlled" by the McAllister decision.

**121p.** The series of cases on the "general agency" contract is analyzed in § 6–60 *infra*.

**121q.** Seamen employed by the United States are usually restricted to their remedies under the Federal Employees' Compensation Act, see note 23 *supra*. Seamen employed on vessels operated by "general agents" during World War II were, by special legislation, excluded from FECA and given their customary remedies under the

sue the general agent under the Jones Act. Justice Reed's opinion assumed that the Jones Act defendant must necessarily be the plaintiff's employer and added the comment that: "We have no doubt that, under the Jones Act, only one person, firm, or corporation can be sued as employer." [121r] Since the Court had decided that the United States was the employer, the general agent was not. Having got so far, Justice Reed then devoted another half-dozen pages to a careful analysis of exactly what the general agent's functions were. His conclusion was that: "[A]n agent such as Cosmopolitan, who contracts to manage certain shoreside business of a vessel operated by the War Shipping Administration, is not liable to a seaman for injury caused by the negligence of the master or crew of such a vessel." [121s] What McAllister comes down to is that Cosmopolitan could not be sued under the Jones Act because a) it was not McAllister's employer and b) it was not the operator of the ship. McAllister (which was a 5–4 decision) tells us nothing about what the Supreme Court majority might have held if it had concluded that Cosmopolitan, although not the employer, was the operator. Thus, Justice Reed's remarks about the employment relationship rank as dictum and his lengthy demonstration of the fact that Cosmopolitan did not operate the ship (but merely "manage[d] certain shoreside business") suggests that even the McAllister majority regarded the question as open and unsettled. And if McAllister did not hold that the Jones Act defendant must be the plaintiff's one and only employer (which it did not), then no other Supreme Court case comes even close to establishing that proposition.[121t]

The Jones Act was designed to remove the bar created by the fourth proposition in The Osceola [121u] and to allow seamen to recover damages for work-related injuries caused by shipboard operating negligence. On policy grounds there seems to be no good reason for limiting the recovery to actions against "employers"; this is particularly true in the light of the fact that the action for unseaworthiness, which has become the identical twin of the Jones Act action, is not so limited. The long-standing assumption that the only possible Jones Act defendant is the plaintiff's one and only employer should be recon-

Jones Act and the general maritime law. The legislation is set out in Justice Reed's McAllister opinion, 337 U.S. at p. 788, n. 8, 69 S.Ct. at p. 1320, n. 8, 1949 A.M.C. at pp. 1034–1035, n. 8.

121r. 337 U.S. at p. 791, 69 S.Ct. at p. 1322, 1949 A.M.C. at p. 1036.

121s. 337 U.S. at p. 801, 69 S.Ct. at p. 1326, 1949 A.M.C. at p. 1044.

121t. In an early FELA case, which is cited both in McAllister and in Mahramas, the Supreme Court had held that a porter employed by the Pullman Company could not bring an FELA action against a railroad. Robinson v. Baltimore & Ohio Railroad, 237 U.S. 84, 35 S.Ct. 491 (1915). In his Mahramas dissent Judge Oakes commented 1) that "the definition of 'seaman' was never made dependent on the meaning of 'employee' as used in [FELA]" and 2) that he doubted whether the Supreme Court "facing the problem afresh" would decide the Robinson case in the 1970's the same way that it decided the case in 1915. In FELA litigation, Robinson was followed as recently as 1963 in Gloster v. Pennsylvania R. Co., 214 F.Supp. 207 (W.D.Pa.1963).

121u. See § 6–2 *supra*.

sidered. As Judge Oakes' Mahramas dissent suggests, there are two ways of going about this reconsideration. One is to conclude that, in Mahramas-type situations, the plaintiff has two employers: at least for purposes of the Jones Act there is no reason why a seaman cannot serve two masters.[121v] The other is to conclude that Jones Act liability rests essentially on control of the ship's operation and not on the employment relationship—an approach which the McAllister case certainly leaves open.

There is no reason to quarrel with the subordinate holding in Mahramas (that the "employer" can be sued under the Jones Act even when he does not have operational control of the ship) [121w] although that holding, on the Mahramas facts, sounds like a bad joke when linked to the further proposition that the non-operating employer is responsible only for his own, and not for the ship's, negligence. If A (employer) assigns his employee to work on a ship operated by B and the employee is injured by negligence chargeable to B, there seems to be no good reason why A should not be required to make his employee whole. Rights to indemnity or contribution between A and B could be settled by contract between them or worked out according to equitable principles. The injured plaintiff should not be required in factual situations which will frequently be obscure, to guess whether A or B should bear the ultimate liability on pain of losing his action if he guesses wrong.[121x]

In Barrios v. Louisiana Construction Materials Co.[121y] the Fifth Circuit also concluded that a non-operating employer could be held liable under the Jones Act. Judge Morgan concluded that the cases on this point were "in substantial conflict" but that "On the facts of this case, we think it is clear that [the employer] is a proper Jones Act defendant even though the jury determined that it did not have operational control over the vessel." In Barrios the employer, although he did not have "operational control", did supervise the operations which led to the plaintiff's injury and the employer's negligence was "a cause of the injury". Thus the employer was held liable in the Jones Act action and denied recovery of indemnity against the vessel's operator, whose concurring negligence was found to be "passive" rather than "active."

121v. See also Judge Clark's dissent in the Schiemann case, note 121 *supra*.

121w. In justifying this holding Judge Anderson relied principally on the Haverty case, § 6–21 *supra*, text following note 107.

121x. With respect to actions covered by § 905(b) of the Longshoremen's and Harbor Workers' Compensation Act (as amended in 1972), the statements in the text will require qualification. For a discussion of § 905(b), see § 6–57 *infra*.

121y. 465 F.2d 1157, 1972 A.M.C. 2659 (5th Cir. 1972).

## Jones Act: "An Action for Damages at Law, with the Right of Trial by Jury"

**§ 6–22.** The Jones Act did not bother to explain in what courts and under what form of pleading the seaman's action "at law with . . . trial by jury" was to be brought. In admiralty? If so, *in rem* or only *in personam* and with a jury or without? In state court under the saving to suitors clause? In federal district court on the civil side? Was jurisdiction exclusive or concurrent? Necessarily such bothersome questions were among the first which the courts had to settle.

The Supreme Court made a good start in its first Jones Act case, Panama R. Co. v. Johnson.[122] The action had been brought on the civil side of the federal court and tried to a jury. Before the Supreme Court counsel for the shipowner argued that the Act was unconstitutional because it sought to deprive the admiralty court of jurisdiction over maritime causes of action; the argument was based on reading the Act to mean that the action under it was to be only "at law", *i. e.* not in admiralty, and the reading was not unreasonable. "It must be conceded," wrote Justice Van Devanter, "that the construction thus sought to be put on the statute finds support in some of its words, and also that if it be so construed a grave question will arise respecting its constitutional validity".[123] To save the Act, its true meaning was declared to be that "the statute leaves the injured seaman free . . . to assert his right of action . . . on the admiralty side of the court. On that side the issues will be tried by the court, but if he sues on the common law side there will be a right of trial by jury." [124] All this was, as the Court hardly tried to conceal, the purest judicial invention. The proposition has, however, never since been questioned.

The next question was whether jurisdiction over the common law branch of the Jones Act action was exclusively in the federal district courts or concurrently in those courts and in the state courts. The second sentence of the Act ("jurisdiction . . . shall be under the court of the district in which the defendant employer resides or in which his principal office is located") supported the view that federal jurisdiction was exclusive. In the Johnson case suit had not been brought in either of the districts specified, but the defendant had nevertheless made a general appearance. Justice Van Devanter commented briefly that "jurisdiction" in the second sentence of the Jones Act meant not "jurisdiction" but "venue", so the defendant, by appearing, had waived his right to object. The discovery that "jurisdiction" meant "venue" settled the question whether Jones Act actions were maintainable in state courts: Engel v. Davenport [125] and Pana-

122. 264 U.S. 375, 44 S.Ct. 391, 1924 A.M.C. 551 (1924).

123. *Id.* at 390, 44 S.Ct. at 395, 1924 A.M.C. at 557.

124. *Id.* at 391, 44 S.Ct. at 395, 1924 A.M.C. at 558.

125. 271 U.S. 33, 46 S.Ct. 410, 1926 A.M.C. 679 (1926).

ma R. Co. v. Vasquez [126] held that state and federal courts had concurrent jurisdiction.

In Plamals v. The Pinar Del Rio [127] the Supreme Court took up the question whether the Jones Act action in admiralty could be brought *in rem* and decided that it could not. Proper venue for a libel *in rem* against a ship is wherever the ship is. The jurisdiction —*i. e.* venue—provision of the Jones Act, on the other hand, specified the district of the employer's residence or principal office. The Court concluded that the draftsman had chosen this subtle fashion of indicating that in admiralty only an action *in personam* could be brought.[128]

The Plamals holding has the effect of subordinating the seaman's personal injury claim under the Jones Act to all maritime lien claims, since, in American law, the lien and the libel *in rem* go hand in hand.[129] The seaman's Jones Act claim, being based on tort, would normally import a lien with a high order of priority. Under the Plamals case he has no lien and consequently in any proceeding where lien claimants have libeled the ship *in rem* the Jones Act claim will be paid only after all lien claims have been satisfied.

It has usually been assumed that actions under the Jones Act, as well as general maritime law actions for unseaworthiness and for maintenance and cure are subject to limitation of liability. In several recent maintenance and cure cases, however, District Courts have taken the position that maintenance and cure claims are not subject to limitation.[130] If that is so, then it would seem to follow that claims under the Jones Act and for unseaworthiness are not subject to limitation either. The issue must be regarded as open and unsettled until it has been passed on by the higher courts.

If seamen's death and injury actions are subject to limitation, then not only may plaintiffs find themselves removed to the admiralty court without benefit of jury but, against shipowners held entitled to limitation, the best they can hope for is to share pro rata in the limitation fund.[131] It is an obscure question whether maritime lien priorities are observed in the distribution of the limitation fund; [132] if they are, the seaman, who has no lien under the Jones Act, may

126. 271 U.S. 557, 46 S.Ct. 596, 1926 A.M.C. 984 (1926).

27. 277 U.S. 151, 48 S.Ct. 457, 1928 A.M.C. 932 (1928).

128. Granted that "jurisdiction" means "venue" the courts still found, and continue to find, many subsidiary ambiguities to wrestle with. For an able discussion of procedural problems under the Jones Act, see Comment, The Tangled Seine: A Survey of Maritime Personal Injury Remedies, 57 Yale L. J. 243, 263 *et seq.* (1947), in particular note 109. See also 2 Norris, note 12 *supra*, § 679.

129. See Chapter IX, § 9–19.

130. See Chapter X, § 10–26, text following note 113c.

131. On the limitation fund, see Chapter X, § 10–29 *et seq.* On whether seamen employed on non-passenger-carrying commercial vessels are entitled to the $60 per ton fund for personal injury and death claims established by amendments to the Limitation of Liability Act in 1935, see § 10–35.

132. See Chapter X, § 10–39.

come at the bottom of the list. Thus in any situation where multiple claims in excess of the value of the ship are brought against a shipowner, the Plamals holding puts the Jones Act claim in an unfavored position. These results follow, not from the nature of the seaman's action, but from the Court's reading of the peculiar language used in the statute. However, if a Jones Act count is joined with general maritime law counts for unseaworthiness and for maintenance and cure, there is no reason to believe that the plaintiff would not be entitled to his lien priority (if indeed such priorities are observed in distribution) despite the non-lien status of the Jones Act count taken by itself. These theoretical problems have not surfaced in litigation for reasons which will be suggested in our discussion of the rules which the courts have worked out for the equitable distribution of limitation funds.

### Jones Act: "At His Election"

§ 6–23. The Jones Act says that an injured seaman may "at his election" bring suit under the Act. As a matter of English grammar, "at his election" could be taken to mean "if he chooses" or "if he desires", with the way open to the conclusion that the Jones Act gave the seaman a remedy additional to his maritime remedies for maintenance and cure and for unseaworthiness. Under such an approach it could be argued that a seaman injured both because of unseaworthiness (*e. g.*, a defective appliance) and negligence (*e. g.* an order that the seaman use an appliance known to be defective) could have three separate recoveries: for maintenance and cure, for unseaworthiness and for negligence. It is unquestioned law that both the Jones Act and the unseaworthiness remedies are additional to maintenance and cure: the seaman may have maintenance and cure and also one of the other two.[133] It is equally unquestioned that the seaman may not have separate or cumulative damage recoveries for the same injury under unseaworthiness and under the Jones Act. "At his election" cannot be read "if he chooses" in order to support two recoveries (in addition to maintenance and cure) for the same injury. It follows that "election" in the Jones Act has its normal legal meaning of "a choice between" two inconsistent courses of action.

It was long thought that the election was between a Jones Act suit for negligence and a maritime law action for unseaworthiness. Robinson correctly stated the general understanding as of 1939 in blackletter text: "He [the seaman] must elect . . . between his right to indemnity under the prestatutory law and his right to indemnity under the provisions of the Seamen's [Jones] Act."[134] This meant at least that if plaintiff pleaded both an unseaworthiness count and a Jones Act count he could be required to elect between them before verdict and that both counts could not go to the jury.

133. Pacific S. S. Co. v. Peterson, 278 U.S. 130, 49 S.Ct. 75, 1928 A.M.C. 1932 (1928). See text following note 137 *infra*. Almost all Jones Act cases include an additional count for maintenance and cure.

134. Robinson, Admiralty 335 (1939).

Some courts thought that the rule went further and that a plaintiff who pleaded both counts could be required to elect between them before trial, one count or the other being subject to defendant's motion to strike.[135] The election between unseaworthiness and Jones Act was required whether the forum of litigation was the admiralty court, the civil side of federal court or a state court.

The present state of the law is that the only election required under the Jones Act is between a suit in admiralty (without a jury) and a civil action in state or federal court (with a jury). No election need be made between Jones Act and unseaworthiness; plaintiff may (and regularly does) plead both; he may go to trial on both; he may go to the jury on both (under separate instructions for the two counts); if a jury verdict for plaintiff is supportable on either count, the resulting judgment will stand.

Unlike most aspects of Jones Act case law, the proposition stated in the preceding paragraph was not, in the first instance, laid down by the Supreme Court. It developed, rather, on the Circuit Court level in an attempt to make sense out of two of the early Supreme Court Jones Act cases in the light of the Supreme Court's later development of the unseaworthiness remedy. Eventually, the Supreme Court accepted the resolution proposed by the Circuit Courts without itself ever having passed on the matter. This curious development will be traced in the following two sections.[136]

**§ 6–24.** The principal authority in support of the older rule (plaintiff must elect between his Jones Act remedy and his unseaworthiness remedy) was a passage from Justice Sanford's opinion in Pacific S. S. Co. v. Peterson:

> "What then were the 'alternatives' accorded to an injured seaman by the maritime law, as modified, between which the statute grants him an election? Plainly, we think, the right under the new rule to compensatory damages for injuries caused by negligence is not an alternative of the right under the old rule to maintenance, cure and wages—which arises, quite independently of negligence, when the seaman falls sick or is injured in the service of the ship, and grows out of that which was termed in The Montezuma (C.C.A.), 19 F.2d 355, 356, the 'personal indenture' created by the relation of the seaman to his vessel. . . .
>
> "The right to recover compensatory damages under the new rule for injuries caused by negligence is, however, an alternative of the right to recover indemnity under the old rules on the ground that the injuries were occasioned by un-

135. See, *e. g.* Skolar v. Lehigh Valley R. Co., 60 F.2d 893, 1933 A.M.C. 88 (2d Cir. 1932). The Skolar case is no longer good law in the Second Circuit (or anywhere else), see text at note 142 *infra.*

136. For the Supreme Court's acceptance of the no-election rule, see § 6–25, *infra,* text following note 144.

> seaworthiness; and it is between these two inconsistent remedies for an injury, both grounded on tort, that we think an election is to be made under the maritime law as modified by the statute. Unseaworthiness, as is well understood, embraces certain species of negligence; while the statute includes several additional species not embraced in that term. But, whether or not the seaman's injuries were occasioned by the unseaworthiness of the vessel or by the negligence of the master or members of the crew, or both combined, there is but a single wrongful invasion of his primary right of bodily safety and but a single legal wrong, Baltimore S. S. Co. v. Phillips, supra, 321, for which he is entitled to but one indemnity by way of compensatory damages." [137]

Justice Sanford's language seemed clearly enough to mean that the seaman must elect at some point between the two remedies, although there was no indication whether the election should be made before trial or only before going to the jury. Justice Sanford's remarks were, however, as other judges subsequently pointed out, merely dicta and thus persuasive but not binding. In the Peterson case the plaintiff had apparently accepted payments for wages to the end of the voyage and for medical expenses. He then brought suit under the Jones Act alone; there was no allegation of unseaworthiness. Defendant's counsel argued that plaintiff by accepting the payments had elected to recover under the maritime law and could not sue under the Jones Act. The holding in Peterson was that there was no requirement of election between maintenance and cure and the Jones Act; the two remedies were "consistent and cumulative". The remarks about election between Jones Act and unseaworthiness were merely speculation since there had been no unseaworthiness count in the pleading.

Nevertheless, even as dicta, Justice Sanford's remarks were taken to have settled the matter. To understand the full meaning of the doctrine of the Peterson case, however, we must turn to Baltimore S. S. Co. v. Phillips,[138] decided a year before Peterson.

In Phillips, plaintiff had brought an earlier action in admiralty [139] alleging that his injury was caused by negligence in failing to provide a safe place to work, and to use reasonable care to avoid striking him (the injury had been caused by the fall of a "strongback" used to support a portion of the hatch) and by the unseaworthiness and insufficiency of the ship's gear and tackle. By amendment to the pleadings it was further alleged that defendant had failed to provide a proper gear or socket to support the strongback, that the officers of the ship were incompetent and that there was a special duty owing to plaintiff (who was 18 at the time of the injury) because of his youth and inexperience. After trial the dis-

137. 278 U.S. 130, 137, 138, 49 S.Ct. 75, 77, 1928 A.M.C. 1932, 1936, 1937 (1928).

138. 274 U.S. 316, 47 S.Ct. 600, 1927 A.M.C. 946 (1927).

139. The West Cape (Phillips v. United States), 286 F. 631, 1923 A.M.C. 350 (D.Md.1923).

trict judge found that the cause of plaintiff's injury was none of the matters alleged but rather the grossly negligent way in which the dunnage had been taken out of the hold. For this negligence, he held, plaintiff could recover only maintenance and cure. Plaintiff did not appeal but instead instituted an action in New York state court which was removed to the federal court. In the second action the complaint alleged negligence in the control and operation of the ship and its appliances. It was argued that the second action was barred by the judgment in the first action as *res judicata.* The trial court concluded that the second action was not barred; the case was tried to a jury which gave plaintiff a verdict; judgment for plaintiff was affirmed by the Second Circuit on appeal.

From the statement of the pleadings in the two cases, as summarized in the Supreme Court's Phillips opinion, it is by no means clear under what theories the two actions were brought. The Supreme Court treated the case as if the first action (in admiralty) had been brought under maritime law for unseaworthiness and the second action (at law) under the Jones Act for negligence. Even so, the Court held, the plea of *res judicata* was good. The Court reasoned that the Jones Act had not created a new nonmaritime cause of action but had given seamen a new ground for recovery under maritime law. That being so, both grounds (unseaworthiness and Jones Act) could have been pleaded in the first action. If the trial judge had erroneously come to the contrary conclusion, his error should have been challenged on appeal and was not subject to collateral attack in the second action.

Thus, Phillips held that a judgment in an unseaworthiness action barred a subsequent action under the Jones Act (and obviously the proposition would also be true in reverse). The two grounds of recovery could both be pleaded in the same action and, since they could be, they had to be. But, added Peterson, citing and accepting Phillips, plaintiff, although required to plead both grounds, could also be required to elect between them (possibly before trial, certainly before going to the jury). The Phillips holding, plus the Peterson dictum, meant that plaintiff could never secure a judicial determination on both his possible grounds of recovery. Before he could persuade the oracle to speak, he must inform it which horn of the dilemma he chose to grasp and his choice, once made, was irrevocable; there was no way in which he could learn what the oracle might have said if he had grasped the other horn.

The result dictated by the combination of the Phillips and Peterson cases, illogical on any ground, could only work without severe injustice to plaintiffs so long as there was a reasonably well understood distinction between negligence and unseaworthiness. If under the case law the two concepts were allowed to overlap, plaintiff was being required to make a choice both meaningless and impossible. If he chose negligence and the Jones Act, he might learn on appeal that the evidence at trial had proved only unseaworthiness, or *vice versa,* and in either case he was forbidden to try again by the *res judicata* rule of Phillips. At the time of the Phillips case there probably was a fairly clear distinction between unseaworthiness and negligence, although the seeds of confusion had already been sown. By 1947, however, a commentator was able to write that "the Jones Act 'negligence' notion and the 'unseaworthiness' idea overlap and blend indistinguishably".[140] Seamen-plaintiffs in personal injury actions were thus put to a choice between two concepts which had become factually indistinguishable. Since the fiction that the two concepts were distinguishable persisted (and still to a degree persists) what he was really being called upon to do was to guess whether the court to which an appeal lay would consider that the facts provable or proved constituted unseaworthiness or negligence.

§ 6–25. The unhappy situation in which plaintiffs found themselves by reason of the Phillips-Peterson rules and the impossibility of predicting what any court on any given state of facts would hold to be unseaworthiness and what negligence, led the judges of the Third Circuit to reexamine the doctrine of election. Their conclusion was that the only election required by the Jones Act is "an election of remedies between a suit in admiralty and a civil action"; in whichever forum the plaintiff elects he may plead both negligence and unseaworthiness and have both counts submitted to the jury if he has elected the civil action. The reasons behind the Third Circuit doctrine were well expressed by Judge Maris in McCarthy v. American Eastern Corp.:

> "Moreover, it seems clear to us that the rationale of the decision in Baltimore S. S. Co. v. Phillips necessarily excludes the interpretation of the phrase 'at his election' for which the defendant contends. For the doctrine of res judicata, which the court applied in that case, is bottomed upon the proposition that a party should not be afforded a second chance to litigate a question as to which he has already had the opportunity of a day in court. If a seaman in asserting a cause of action derived both from the old rules of the maritime law and the new rules of the Jones Act must confine himself to only one of these grounds for recovery and forever lose the benefit of the other by the application of the doctrine of res judicata that doctrine applies in a very much harsher form to those who have always been regarded as wards of the admiralty in special need of protection than it does to all other litigants. For not only would an injured seaman have to decide at his peril, and in advance of judicial determination, which of two possible bases of his case was better grounded in law and fact, but he would also have to stake his whole possibility of recovery upon that choice, being barred from ever at any time asserting the other ground. He would thus be denied the right to any day in court upon

140. The Tangled Seine, *op. cit. supra* note 128 at 259 (n. 79).

what may turn out to have been his only valid ground for relief. And in some cases the choice might well be the nice one, often baffling to the most experienced lawyer, as to whether the injury was due to the failure of the owner to furnish suitable appliances or to the negligence of the crew in their use. We cannot believe that Congress when it passed the Jones Act as a measure for the relief of injured seamen intended that it should put them at their peril to any such choice as this." [141]

In Balado v. Lykes Bros. S. S. Co.[142] the Second Circuit announced its concurrence with the Third. In earlier cases the Second Circuit had indicated approval of the Peterson doctrine of election between negligence and unseaworthiness.[143] In the Balado case Judge Augustus Hand wrote:

> ". . . we find the analysis by Judge Maris [in the McCarthy case] . . . most persuasive. In accordance with the view there expressed we think there will be no necessity for such an election in the future. In our opinion election is required by the Jones Act only between a trial by jury and a suit in admiralty." [144]

141. 175 F.2d 724, 725, 1953 A.M.C. 1864, 1867 (3d Cir. 1949), certiorari denied 338 U.S. 868, 70 S.Ct. 144 (1949) rehearing denied 338 U.S. 939, 70 S.Ct. 343 (1950). Two earlier cases had foreshadowed the holding in the McCarthy case: Branic v. Wheeling Steel Corp., 152 F.2d 887, 1946 A.M.C. 66 (3d Cir. 1946), certiorari denied 327 U.S. 801, 66 S.Ct. 902 (1946); German v. Carnegie-Illinois Steel Corp., 156 F.2d 977, 1946 A.M.C. 1590 (3d Cir. 1946). In Yates v. Dann, 223 F.2d 64, 1955 A.M.C. 1214 (3d Cir. 1955), while reaffirming the doctrine of the McCarthy case, the Circuit reversed a district court which, after trial and a jury verdict which plaintiff claimed to be inadequate, had granted a new trial in admiralty (without a jury) in which the issue of damages was redetermined: "It is possible that a seaman who has already instituted an action at law may still begin an entirely new suit in admiralty on the same legal basis. [Citing cases.] It may also be true that the "spirit of modern pleading" will allow a claimant to transfer his whole case from the law side to admiralty at any time before trial. [Citing cases.] But if the election required by the Jones Act means anything at all, it must mean that a plaintiff suing under its provisions cannot in the same action have the issue of defendant's liability tried at law with a jury and the issue of damages resulting from the identical liability tried by the court in admiralty without a jury." (*Id.* at 66–67, 1217.)

142. 179 F.2d 943, 1950 A.M.C. 609 (2d Cir. 1950).

143. Skolar v. Lehigh Valley R. Co., 60 F.2d 893, 1933 A.M.C. 88 (2d Cir. 1932); McGhee v. United States, 165 F.2d 287, 1948 A.M.C. 139 (2d Cir. 1947).

144. 179 F.2d 943, 945, 1950 A.M.C. 609, 612.

In Williams v. Tide Water Associated Oil Co., 227 F.2d 791, 1956 A.M.C. 136 (9th Cir. 1955) the Ninth Circuit followed the Second and Third Circuits in adopting the McCarthy-Balado doctrine of no election. Justice Denman's opinion contained an exhaustive collection of the cases, state and federal, through 1955. The McCarthy-Balado line of reasoning was inferentially approved in Doucette v. Vincent, 194 F.2d 834, 1952 A.M.C. 458 (1st Cir. 1952) and was assumed by Judge Aldrich to be the law of the First Circuit in Warren v. Weber & Heidenthaler, Inc., 1955 A.M.C. 1054 (D.Mass.1955). In Nunes v. Farrell Lines, Inc., 227 F.2d 619, 1956 A.M.C. 40 (1st Cir. 1955), the Court approved without comment a jury trial on negligence, unseaworthiness and maintenance and cure. Pate v. Standard

The Supreme Court approached the Jones Act election problem with all deliberate speed. It never reversed a lower court on the ground that the general maritime law counts had been improperly submitted to the jury along with the Jones Act count. At times, in cases which did not involve the Jones Act, it seemed to approve the joinder of counts for negligence and for unseaworthiness, with both counts going to the jury.[145] If non-seamen could get to the jury on both counts, it might seem hard to articulate a theory under which Jones Act seamen could not.[145a] Nevertheless, in Romero v. International Terminal Operating Company[146] the *pro hac vice* majority, in an opinion by Justice Frankfurter, left open the question whether, in the absence of diversity jurisdiction, general maritime law counts for unseaworthiness and maintenance and cure should be submitted to the jury when joined with a Jones Act count. Four years after Romero the Court, which was for once unanimous on the substance of the ruling, held in Fitzgerald v. United States Lines Company[147] that, on grounds which came as a surprise to most observers, the general maritime law counts, when joined to a Jones Act count, must be sent to the jury even in the absence of diversity jurisdiction.[148]

The practice of pleading and going to trial on both the general maritime law counts and the Jones Act count created a number of potential procedural traps for plaintiff's counsel. Even though we have been living with this situation for twenty years or more, it

Dredging Corp., 193 F.2d 498, 1952 A.M.C. 287 (5th Cir. 1952) also suggested approval in a dictum. In Hill v. Atlantic Navigation Co., 1954 A.M.C. 2150 (E.D.Va.1954), Judge Bryan concluded that the Fourth Circuit had also adopted the no election rule, citing The Fletero v. Arias, 206 F.2d 267, 1953 A.M.C. 1390 (4th Cir. 1953).

145. See, e. g., Pope & Talbot, Inc. v. Hawn, 346 U.S. 406, 74 S.Ct. 202, 1954 A.M.C. 1 (1953), in which the majority of the Court approved the submission of negligence and unseaworthiness counts to the jury in a stevedore's action against a shipowner brought on the civil side of federal court. See also Boudoin v. Lykes Bros. S. S. Co., Inc., 348 U.S. 336, 75 S.Ct. 382, 1955 A.M.C. 488 (1955), in which Justice Douglas, writing for the court, remarked without further comment that plaintiff "based his claim for recovery both on negligence and on breach of the warranty of seaworthiness. The case was tried by the court upon waiver of jury. The District Court found for the plaintiff, holding that the shipowner breached its warranty of seaworthiness and that its officers were negligent."

145a. In McAllister v. Magnolia Petroleum Co., 357 U.S. 221, 78 S.Ct. 1201, 1958 A.M.C. 1754 (1958), Chief Justice Warren, citing the Hawn case, note 145 *supra*, the Second, Third, and Ninth Circuit cases previously mentioned and the discussion in the first edition of the treatise, commented that: "Recent authorities have effectively disposed of suggestions in earlier cases that an injured seaman can be required to exercise an election between his remedies for negligence under the Jones Act and for unseaworthiness." (357 U.S. at p. 223, n. 2, 78 S. Ct. 1203 n. 2). The McAllister case is discussed, text following note 150a *infra*.

146. 358 U.S. 354, 79 S.Ct. 468, 1959 A.M.C. 832 (1959).

147. 374 U.S. 16, 83 S.Ct. 1646, 1963 A.M.C. 1093 (1963).

148. See § 6–9 *supra* for discussion of the Romero-Fitzgerald sequence. Technically, Justice Black's Fitzgerald opinion dealt only with the maintenance and cure count but, for the reasons explained in our earlier discussion, Fitzgerald settled the question for the unseaworthiness count as well.

would be a gross overstatement to say that the available case law furnishes a reliable guide on how to avoid the danger spots.

By way of illustration, the Jones Act incorporates the three-year statute of limitations which was added to the Federal Employers' Liability Act by a 1939 amendment.[149] The general maritime law counts, in the absence of a limitation period established by federal statute, are governed by the doctrine of laches, which has come to mean inexcusable delay on the plaintiff's part coupled with resulting prejudice to the defendant. As a measuring point for determining when the delay bars the action the admiralty courts have traditionally looked to the state statutes which would be applicable if the action was not subject to federal maritime law.[150] When the general maritime law counts are joined with a Jones Act count, what is to be done if it appears that the general maritime law counts a) would be barred by laches in less than the three years applicable to the Jones Act count, or b) would not be barred by laches until after the three years had run?

The Supreme Court gave a partial answer to the problem in McAllister v. Magnolia Petroleum Co.[150a] McAllister brought the usual three count action more than two years but less than three years after his injury. All three counts were submitted to the jury and judgment was entered on the jury verdicts, making a maintenance and cure award but deciding the Jones Act and unseaworthiness counts for the defendant. The defendant appealed from the maintenance and cure award, which was affirmed. The plaintiff appealed only from the judgment on the unseaworthiness count, assigning errors in admitting evidence and in instructing the jury. The Texas appellate courts did not pass on the assignments of error, since the unseaworthiness action was held barred by a two-year Texas limitation statute on personal injuries. The majority of the Supreme Court, in an opinion by Chief Justice Warren, held that, in the light of the fact that the plaintiff had to put forward his Jones Act and unseaworthiness claim in a single action, both claims were entitled to the three-year Jones Act limitation period. Three dissenting Justices (Whittaker, Frankfurter, and Harlan) read the majority opinion as saying that a state statute could extend the limitation period for unseaworthiness actions to more than three years but could not cut it back to less than three years; that position, said the dissenters, was "quite inconsistent." Justice Brennan, concurring, said that he found no indication in the majority opinion that the unseaworthiness limitation period could be extended beyond the Jones Act period by a longer state statute.

149. 53 Stat. 1404, 45 U.S.C.A. § 56. The original FELA statute of limitations had been two years. On the problem of the applicability of FELA amendments to the Jones Act, see § 6–26 *et seq. infra.* That the 1939 amendment extending the limitation period does apply to Jones Act litigation, see Chief Justice Warren's opinion in the McAllister case, note 150a *infra*, 357 U.S. at p. 225, n. 6, 78 S.Ct. 1204, n. 6, 1958 A.M.C. at 1758, n. 6.

150. On laches, see the discussion in Chapter IX, § 9–77 *et seq.*

150a. 357 U.S. 221, 78 S.Ct. 1201, 1958 A.M.C. 1754 (1958).

McAllister established only that three years was to be the minimum limitation period for the general maritime law counts when they were joined with a Jones Act count. It left open whether the limitation period for the general maritime law counts could be extended beyond three years and, in such a case, whether the Jones Act limitation period would be comparably extended. Where the action is brought under the general maritime law without a Jones Act count the courts have, without exception, assumed that the doctrine of laches determines whether plaintiff's delay bars his action and the laches cases decided during the 1960's were, on the whole, extremely favorable to dilatory plaintiffs.[150b] There has been curiously little discussion of what happens when the Jones Act count is added to the general maritime law counts.

In Burke v. Gateway Clipper, Inc.[150c] plaintiff instituted the usual three-count action more than ten years after his injury. The trial court dismissed all three counts as time-barred. The Third Circuit, in a per curiam opinion, affirmed dismissal of the Jones Act count but remanded the case for further proceedings with respect to the general maritime law counts. As to the Jones Act count, the Court evidently felt that the action must be brought within the statutory limitation period unless for some reason the statute was tolled or the defendant estopped. The dearth of case law authority is illustrated by the fact that the Court placed principal reliance on Engel v. Davenport,[150d] a case which held that the Jones Act limitation period (which was then two years) could not be cut back by the application of a shorter state limitation statute even when the action had been brought in state court. As to the general maritime law counts, the Court held in the Burke case that the plaintiff must be given a chance to carry his burden of proving that his delay was excusable and that the defendant was not prejudiced.[150e]

The Burke case suggests that (subject to the rather limited holding in the McAllister case) when different procedural requirements apply on the one hand to the general maritime law counts and on the other hand to the Jones Act count, the case will be, so to say, split in two and the two parts left to go their separate ways. If the Jones Act action is time-barred or if the venue is improperly laid, that does not mean that the general maritime law action must also be dismissed. On the other hand, defects in the Jones Act count will not be cured by placing that action under the protective umbrella of the general maritime law action.

**150b.** See Chapter IX, § 9–80, text following note 402.

**150c.** 441 F.2d 946, 1971 A.M.C. 1623 (3d Cir. 1971).

**150d.** 271 U.S. 33, 46 S.Ct. 410, 1926 A.M.C. 679 (1926).

**150e.** Under the Third Circuit rule, illustrated by the Burke case, the plaintiff bears the burden of proof both on delay and on prejudice. In other Circuits the rule is that if plaintiff excuses his delay, the burden shifts to defendant to show prejudice. See Chapter IX, § 9–81, text at and following note 409a.

The position taken by the Third Circuit in Burke is certainly not unreasonable and might well commend itself to the present majority of the Supreme Court. On the other hand, it is possible to read the Supreme Court cases decided during the 1950's and 1960's (or some of them) as saying that the injured seaman as plaintiff may choose whichever of two inconsistent rules is the more favorable to his recovery.[150f] Under that approach it could be argued that if the general maritime law is procedurally more favorable to the plaintiff than the Jones Act, then the general maritime law should apply to the entire action (including the Jones Act count) just as McAllister may be said to have held that if the Jones Act is procedurally more favorable to plaintiff than the general maritime law, then the Jones Act applies to the entire action (including the general maritime law counts). Whether that argument would commend itself to the majority of the Supreme Court during the 1970's is, at the moment of writing, unknown.

### Jones Act: The Federal Employers' Liability Act

§ 6–26. Congress, when it passed the Jones Act, apparently did not want to waste any time on thinking about the special problems of maritime workers. As a thought-saving device, the draftsman hit on the odd expedient of incorporating another statute by reference. The Jones Act provides that in actions under it "all statutes of the United States modifying or extending the common-law right or remedy in cases of personal injury to railroad employees shall apply". The statutes thus adopted into the Jones Act are Sections 51 to 60 of Title 45 of the United States Code, commonly known as the Federal Employers' Liability Acts and hereinafter as FELA.[151]

Under FELA any employee of an interstate carrier by rail may recover damages from the carrier for injury or death "resulting in whole or in part from the negligence of any of the officers, agents, or employees of such carrier, or by reason of any defect or insufficiency, due to its negligence, in its cars, engines, appliances, machinery, track, roadbed, works, boats, wharves or other equipment." [152] Contributory negligence on the part of the injured employee "shall not bar a recovery, but the damages shall be diminished by the jury in proportion to the amount of negligence attributable to such employee".[153] As originally passed FELA abolished the defense of assumption of risk "in any case where the violation by such common carrier of any statute enacted for the safety of employees contributed to the injury or death of such employee". In 1939 the assumption of risk section was broadened to abolish the defense also "in any case

150f. See, e. g., Kossick v. United Fruit Co., 365 U.S. 731, 81 S.Ct. 886, 1961 A.M.C. 833 (1961), discussed § 6–11 *supra*, text following note 58a. See further the discussion in § 6–61 *infra*.

151. 35 Stat. 65 (1908), 36 Stat. 291 (1910), 36 Stat. 1167 (1911), 53 Stat. 1404 (1939), 62 Stat. 989 (1948), 45 U.S.C. §§ 51–60. The sections of FELA will be referred to by their U.S.C. section number.

152. § 51.

153. § 53.

where such injury or death resulted in whole or in part from the negligence of any of the officers, agents, or employees of such carrier".[154] Any attempt by a carrier to exempt itself from liability under FELA by any "contract, rule, regulation or device" is declared to be void.[155] Actions must be "commenced within three years from the day the cause of action accrued"; [156] federal and state courts are given concurrent jurisdiction,[157] with the proviso that no action "brought in any State court of competent jurisdiction shall be removed to any court of the United States".[158]

The Jones Act says merely that "all" statutes relating to personal injuries of railroad employees shall apply to seamen's actions under the Jones Act. The Supreme Court has construed this to mean that the provisions of FELA apply to Jones Act actions where their application appears reasonable and do not apply where their application appears unreasonable.[159] This proposition unavoidably shrouds the relationship between the two statutes in a sort of floating ambiguity, which becomes peculiarly intense whenever FELA is amended. There is no reason to believe that amendments to FELA do not carry over to the Jones Act (although the Supreme Court has never so held), but, even if there is a carry-over, it must be decided anew in each case whether the particular amendment can "reasonably" apply to the Jones Act.[159a]

154. § 54.

155. § 55.

156. § 56. As originally enacted, the limitation period was two years; the three year provision was introduced in 1939.

157. *Ibid.*

158. The no removal provision was originally included in § 56. In 1948 the provision was dropped from § 56 but a companion provision was retained in the Judicial Code (28 U.S.C. § 1445), see text at note 166 *infra.*

159. The Supreme Court has also made clear that in applying FELA in a Jones Act setting, an undue literalness is to be avoided. See Cox v. Roth, 348 U.S. 207, 75 S.Ct. 242, 1955 A.M.C. 942 (1955) in which it was held that a Jones Act action did not abate on the death of the defendant tortfeasor on the "analogy" that FELA provides (§ 57) for the prosecution of actions against receivers of insolvent railroads. (The admiralty rule was that actions do not survive, see § 6–29 *infra.*) Justice Clark wrote: "The Jones Act, in providing that a seaman should have the same right of action as would a railroad employee, does not mean that the very words of the FELA must be lifted bodily from their context and applied mechanically to the specific facts of maritime events. Rather, it means that those contingencies against which Congress has provided to ensure recovery to railroad employees should also be met in the admiralty setting. Applying such a rule here, we conclude that Congress, having provided that railroad employees could recover regardless of the "survival" of the tortfeasor railroad, intended that the death of the tortfeasor should not defeat recovery under the Jones Act." (*Id.* at 209, 944). See also the discussion of the Jones Act concept of "negligence", § 6–34 *infra.*

159a. "When the Jones Act was adopted in 1920 the period of limitations for the FELA was two years. Some authorities have suggested that the Act of Aug. 11, 1939, 53 Stat. 1404, which extended the FELA period to three years, did not effect a similar extension for the Jones Act. *E. g.*, 3 Benedict, Admiralty (6th ed., Knauth, 1940), § 469. The contrary must now be taken to have been established. [Citing cases.]" McAllister v. Magnolia Petroleum Co., 357 U.S. 221, 225 n. 6, 78 S.Ct. 1201, 1204 n. 6, 1958 A.M.C. 1754, 1758 n. 6 (1958) (per Warren, C. J.).

The Supreme Court's "rule of reason" in fitting FELA and the Jones Act together was foreshadowed by the doctrine announced in Panama R. Co. v. Johnson.[160] In that case, to save the Jones Act from "grave" constitutional objections, the Court decided that the Jones Act merely added a new remedy to the maritime law (over which admiralty courts had jurisdiction) and was not an attempt to create an exclusive common-law remedy for a maritime tort. Thus FELA put to sea. What that meant was neatly brought out in The Arizona v. Anelich [161] and Beadle v. Spencer,[162] companion cases which involved the availability in Jones Act cases of the defense of assumption of risk.

§ 6–27. At the time the two cases were decided, FELA abolished assumption of risk as a defense in cases where the carrier's violation of a safety statute contributed to the employee's death or injury.[163] In actions brought by railway workers under FELA it had been settled that assumption of risk was still a good defense when a safety statute had not been violated. In the two Jones Act cases it was argued that a seaman injured or killed by a defective appliance on the ship was subject to the assumption of risk defense so long as the ship was not in statutory violation with respect to the appliance. (Of course the detailed railroad safety statutes did not apply to ships. Thus the argument, if successful, would have made assumption of risk generally available to Jones Act defendants.) In reply, Justice Stone dusted off the "maritime law" theory of the Jones Act:

> "The Jones Act thus brings into the maritime law new rules of liability. The source from which these rules are drawn defines them but prescribes nothing as to their operation in the field to which they are transferred. 'In that field their strength and operation come altogether from their inclusion in the maritime law' by virtue of the Jones Act. The election for which it provides 'is between the alternative accorded by the maritime law as modified and not between that law and some non-maritime system.' Panama Railroad Co. v. Johnson, 264 U.S. 375, 388, 389, 44 S.Ct. 391, 394; and see Chelentis v. Luckenbach S.S. Co., 247 U.S. 372, 380, 381, 38 S.Ct. 501; Pacific S.S. Co. v. Peterson, 278 U.S. 130, 49 S.Ct. 75, 76." [164]

On a review of the cases, he concluded that assumption of risk had never been recognized as a defense under maritime law. Since the Jones Act was "remedial, for the benefit and protection of seamen who are peculiarly the wards of admiralty . . . to enlarge that protection, not to narrow it", it could not be supposed that a defense

**160.** 264 U.S. 375, 44 S.Ct. 391, 1924 A.M.C. 551 (1923).

**161.** 298 U.S. 110, 56 S.Ct. 707, 1936 A.M.C. 627 (1936).

**162.** 298 U.S. 124, 56 S.Ct. 712, 1936 A.M.C. 635 (1936).

**163.** See text at note 154 *supra*.

**164.** 298 U.S. 110, 119, 56 S.Ct. 707, 709, 1936 A.M.C. 627, 631.

not previously available under maritime law had now been made so. Consequently, not the limited abolition of the defense by FELA but its complete abolition by maritime law gave the solution.

The Arizona and Beadle v. Spencer lend themselves to two interpretations. One is that everything in FELA is incorporated in the Jones Act unless the incorporation would narrow rights granted seamen by the maritime law. The other interpretation of the two cases is that only those provisions of FELA which "reasonably" apply to the circumstances of maritime injury come over, without regard to the narrowing or broadening of rights. In most situations the two interpretations would supplement and not contradict each other, so that the cases may well be taken to stand on both grounds. Since Congress, when it amends FELA, rarely seems to remember that it is also (probably) amending the Jones Act, the second interpretation suggested is an obviously necessary part of the judicial armament.

### Assumption of Risk vs. Contributory Negligence

**§ 6–27a.** The Supreme Court continued its discussion of assumption of risk under the maritime law and the Jones Act in Socony-Vacuum Oil Co. v. Smith.[165] One of Smith's assigned duties was to check periodically to determine whether a bearing was overheating. The facts assumed were that there was a safe way to check the bearing (standing on the engine-room deck) as well as a dangerous way (standing on a step which, as Smith knew, was defective). Smith elected to do it the dangerous way (no doubt because it was easier to get at the bearing), fell, and was injured. The Court assumed, in an opinion by Justice Stone, that the case was not covered by its two previous assumption of risk cases [165a] since neither had presented the situation where the injured plaintiff was assumed to have had a choice between a safe way to do the job and a dangerous way. The majority of the Court, however, (McReynolds, J., dissenting) concluded that assumption of risk was not available as a defense even if the plaintiff had deliberately or for his own convenience chosen the dangerous way over the safe way. Consistently with the opinions delivered in the two earlier cases, Justice Stone developed this point as one of maritime, and not of FELA, law, relying principally on a relatively ancient case which had been decided by "the eminent admiralty judge, Addison Brown".[165b]

Smith's action, then, could not be barred under the assumption of risk doctrine. He had, however, as the Court viewed his case, been guilty of contributory negligence. Justice Stone observed that:

> "Any rule of assumption of risk in admiralty, whatever its scope, must be applied in conjunction with the established admiralty doctrine of comparative negligence and in har-

165. 305 U.S. 424, 59 S.Ct. 262, 1939 A.M.C. 1 (1939).

165a. See § 6–27 *supra*.

165b. The Julia Fowler, 49 F. 277 (S.D.N.Y.1892).

> mony with it. Under that doctrine contributory negligence, however gross, is not a bar to recovery but only mitigates damages." [165c]

Thus, on the contributory negligence issue as on the assumption of risk issue, the Court elected to go by way of the maritime law rather than by way of FELA.[165d] That simplified matters when, after the 1940's, unseaworthiness rather than the Jones Act became the principal basis for recovery: the points the Court had made in its Jones Act cases during the 1930's applied automatically (as maritime law) to the unseaworthiness cases of the 1950's, whether or not the unseaworthiness count was (or could have been) joined with a Jones Act count.[165e]

After the Smith case there was clearly no future in arguing assumption of risk in Jones Act and/or unseaworthiness cases. Counsel for defendants quickly grasped the point that what had once been called assumption of risk at common law could now plausibly be called contributory negligence under the maritime law (or FELA § 53), with the result (if the shift in terminology was successful) of reducing the damages even if they could not be barred completely. Thus the courts in the Jones Act and unseaworthiness cases (as in the FELA railroad cases [165f]) have been driven to construct fragile distinctions between situations in which the plaintiff's alleged contributory negligence really is contributory negligence (which the jury should be instructed to consider in reduction or mitigation of damages) and situations in which the contributory negligence allegation is an impermissible attempt to sneak the assumption of risk doctrine in by the back door.

The Second Circuit reviewed the contributory negligence vs. assumption of risk issue in Rivera v. Farrell Lines, Inc.[165g] Rivera was a messman whose duties required him to work in the crew pantry. The plumbing in the pantry was defective and the pantry floor was frequently wet. This condition had often been reported to the ship's officers but had not been corrected. Rivera, who knew of the dangerous condition, slipped and fell on the wet floor while performing his duties, injuring his back. In Rivera's Jones Act action the defense that Rivera had been contributorily negligent was submitted to the jury over objection by Rivera's counsel. The jury, finding that he was chargeable with contributory negligence, brought in a general verdict in his favor without indicating by how much the damages had been reduced. A unanimous panel of the Second Circuit reversed on the ground that the evidence went only to the now abolished defense of assumption of risk and did not support a

**165c.** 305 U.S. at p. 431, 59 S.Ct. at p. 266, 1939 A.M.C. at p. 7.

**165d.** For the FELA contributory negligence provision, see text at note 153 *supra*.

**165e.** See, e. g., Pope & Talbot, Inc. v. Hawn, 346 U.S. 406, 74 S.Ct. 202, 1954 A.M.C. 1 (1953) (unseaworthiness action brought by repairman).

**165f.** For collections of FELA cases see the annotations, 45 U.S.C.A. § 53, notes 33, 34.

**165g.** 474 F.2d 255, 1973 A.M.C. 602 (2d Cir. 1973).

finding of contributory negligence. Judge Oakes proposed this formula for making the distinction:

> "In common law days the knowledgeable acceptance by an employee of a dangerous condition when and if such acceptance was necessary for the performance of his duties was assumption of risk. 2 F. Harper and F. James, The Law of Torts, Section 21.4 (1956). Contributory negligence, on the other hand, connotes some careless act or omission on the part of the employee over and above that knowledgeable acceptance. Mumma v. Reading Co., 247 F.Supp. 252, 256–57 (E.D.Pa.1965) [a FELA case]." [165h]

Judge Oakes then reviewed and rejected the arguments which had been made in support of the contributory negligence allegation: that Rivera, knowing of the dangerous condition, should have exercised extra care; that he should have refused to work in the pantry, until the condition had been corrected; that he should have mopped up the floor before going into the pantry. (As to a fourth argument—that Rivera could have performed his duties without going into the pantry —Judge Oakes commented that the issue had not been presented at trial in such a way as to put Rivera's counsel on notice that he should offer rebutting evidence.) [165i]

The Ninth Circuit in DuBose v. Matson Navigation Company [165j] took a quite different course from that taken by the First and Second Circuits in their Rivera cases. DuBose was assigned to work in such cramped quarters that other crewmen passing behind him continually bumped his leg. Without complaining to the ship's officers, DuBose continued working and eventually, as a result of the bumping, suffered a cyst on his leg. DuBose brought a Jones Act action which was apparently tried to the court without a jury. The trial judge held that DuBose was chargeable with contributory negligence in having failed to report the dangerous condition to his superior and consequently reduced the damage award by 75 per cent. DuBose appealed on the ground that the finding "of contributory negligence . . . was improper and tantamount to a finding of assumption of risk . . ." Judge Barnes, writing for a unanimous panel, affirmed on the authority of Socony-Vacuum Oil Company v. Smith.[165k] The

165h. 474 F.2d at p. 257, 1973 A.M.C. at p. 604.

165i. In Rivera v. Rederi A/B Nordstjernan, 456 F.2d 970, 1973 A.M.C. 804 (1st Cir. 1972) (longshoremen's unseaworthiness action) the First Circuit took the same approach that the Second Circuit took in its Rivera case. Plaintiffs complained of the ventilation in the hold where they had been ordered to work; the foreman, after reporting the condition to the ship's officers, ordered them to go on working; they did so and were overcome by carbon monoxide fumes. Judge McEntee wrote: "To say that plaintiffs were contributorily negligent in these circumstances would be to state that in continuing work they assumed the risk of obeying orders. We will not allow assumption of risk to masquerade as contributory negligence."

165j. 403 F.2d 875, 1969 A.M.C. 290 (9th Cir. 1968).

165k. See text following note 165 *supra*.

Third Circuit also approved a contributory negligence finding in Mroz v. Dravo Corporation [165l] in which it appeared that the plaintiff's emphysema condition had been aggravated by a long exposure to diesel fumes and smoke.[165m]

When courts are required to sort cases into two heaps without being given a workable formula for distinguishing between the cases which are to go in the assumption of risk heap and those that are to go in the contributory negligence heap, results like those we have been reviewing are to be expected. The important point to bear in mind is that the courts have indeed been maintaining the two heap rule: not every allegation or finding that plaintiff is chargeable with contributory negligence will survive the countervailing argument that defendant is, essentially, attempting to reintroduce assumption of risk. The formula which Judge Oakes proposed in the Second Circuit Rivera case is as good as any but will hardly serve to bring the argument to an end.

**§ 6–28.** Another FELA provision whose applicability to Jones Act actions has long been conceded is the prohibition of removal of actions from state to federal courts. Originally the prohibition of removal clause was contained both in FELA and in a companion section of the Judicial Code. In 1948, in connection with the revision of the Judicial Code, the prohibition clause was dropped from FELA but retained as Section 1445(a) of the Code. On the basis of this statutory rearrangement, it was argued that the prohibition of removal no longer applied to actions brought under the Jones Act, but the courts rejected the argument.[166]

A more complicated question arises when a Jones Act count is joined with an unseaworthiness count, a maintenance and cure count, or both. Under the modern doctrine that no election is required between the Jones Act and the unseaworthiness counts, the issue becomes whether the Jones Act count communicates its own irremovability to the normally removable maritime counts. In Pate v. Stand-

165l. 429 F.2d 1156 (3d Cir. 1970). *Cf.* however, Benson v. American Export Isbrandtsen Lines, Inc., 478 F.2d 152, 1973 A.M.C. 1766 (3d Cir. 1973) in which the majority of the Court held that the trial court had erred in denying plaintiff's motion for a directed verdict on the issue of contributory negligence and in letting the issue go to the jury. The opinions in Benson do not discuss the relationship between contributory negligence and assumption of risk.

See further Urti v. Transport Commercial Corp., 479 F.2d 766, 1973 A.M.C. 1437 (5th Cir. 1973), holding that there was no evidence to support a jury verdict of contributory negligence and that the trial court had committed reversible error in denying plaintiff's motion for a new trial.

165m. Judge Oakes, in the Second Circuit Rivera case, note 165g supra, distinguished the DuBose and Mroz cases on the ground that they "involved conditions which almost imperceptibly and over a long period of time led to an illness suffered by a single seaman." A less ingenious but perhaps more candid statement might be that what is dismissed as assumption of risk in the First and Second Circuits can still qualify as contributory negligence in the Third and Ninth Circuits.

166. See Pate v. Standard Dredging Corp., 193 F.2d 498, 1952 A.M.C. 287 (5th Cir. 1952).

ard Dredging Corp.[167] the Fifth Circuit held that the Jones Act count made at least the unseaworthiness count irremovable. In reaching this conclusion the Court looked to § 1441(c) of the Judicial Code which provides that "Whenever a separate and independent claim or cause of action, which would be removable if sued upon alone, is joined with one or more otherwise nonremovable claims or causes of action, the entire case may be removed . . ." Inspiring itself from the Supreme Court's holding in Baltimore S.S. Co. v. Phillips[168] (judgment in seaworthiness suit *res judicata* as to subsequent suit under the Jones Act), the Fifth Circuit concluded that the unseaworthiness count was not "a separate and independent claim or cause of action" from the Jones Act count and hence, by negative implication from § 1441(c), neither was removable.[169] The pleadings in the Pate case also contained a maintenance and cure count and the Fifth Circuit found this one a harder nut to crack. By unquestionable authority a maintenance and cure claim is "separate and independent" from both a Jones Act claim or an unseaworthiness claim for purposes of *res judicata* or § 1441(c) or anything else.[170] Thus the elegant solution which the Court had found for the unseaworthiness count apparently left it in the situation of the amateur floor painter who inadvertently paints himself into the corner furthest removed from the door: the same reasoning which had proved the unseaworthiness count irremovable now proved that all three counts were removable (since under § 1441(c) the presence of one "separate and independent" claim makes the whole case removable). The Court got out of its corner in the Pate case by finding that the maintenance and cure count did not state the $3000 amount in controversy then requisite for federal diversity jurisdiction. If the maintenance and cure claim had been for $500 more, the Court would either have had to hold the case removable or get itself a new theory.

The cases to date have assumed that a Jones Act count makes the entire case irremovable, whether or not joined with unseaworthiness and maintenance and cure counts. The Pate opinion, however, suggests a lurking danger for plaintiff's counsel who feels that his chances are better in State court: to make sure that his case cannot be removed, he should be careful to state the maintenance and cure claim in less than the jurisdictional amount (or to abandon the maintenance and cure count, where there is no reasonable doubt of defendant's liability for negligence or unseaworthiness, and go for his entire recovery in the damage action).[170a]

167. Note 166 *supra*.

168. 274 U.S. 316, 47 S.Ct. 600, 1927 A.M.C. 946 (1927), see text at note 139 *supra*.

169. The Pate holding has been followed in several District Court cases. See Nickerson v. American Dredging Co., 129 F.Supp. 602, 1955 A.M.C. 1299 (D.N.J.1955), accepting the Fifth Circuit's reasoning in Pate and collecting other citations.

170. Pacific S. S. Co. v. Peterson, 278 U.S. 130, 49 S.Ct. 75, 1928 A.M.C. 1932 (1928), see text at note 137 *supra*.

170a. The issues discussed in this section seem to have disappeared from litigation in recent years—no doubt

### Same: Recovery for Wrongful Death Under FELA, the Death on the High Seas Act and the General Maritime Law

**§ 6–29.** In the Harrisburg [171] the Supreme Court held that no cause of action for wrongful death was provided by the general maritime law. In The Hamilton [171a], which involved a high seas collision between ships owned by Delaware corporations, the Court held that the gap in the maritime law created by The Harrisburg could be filled by allowing a recovery for wrongful death under a statute of the State of Delaware. Then or later statutes providing recovery for wrongful death were enacted in all states.[171b] On March 30, 1920, Congress enacted the Death on the High Seas Act (DOHSA) [171c] which provided a recovery for death "caused by wrongful act, neglect or default occurring on the high seas beyond a marine league from the shore of any State [Territory or dependency]." [171d] On June 5, 1920, Congress enacted the Jones Act [171e] which incorporated the wrongful death provisions of the Federal Employers' Liability Act [FELA].[171f] DOHSA and the Jones Act, enacted almost simultaneously, were hopelessly inconsistent with each other both as to the nature of the wrongful death recovery and as to the classes of beneficiaries entitled to recover. From 1920 until 1970 the lower federal courts, with occasional help from the Supreme Court, attempted to impose a degree of order on this statutory chaos. In 1970 the Supreme Court overruled The Harrisburg in Moragne v. States Marine Lines, Inc. [171g] and held, in a unanimous decision, that a remedy for wrongful death was provided by the general maritime law. The Supreme Court did not attempt in

because most plaintiffs now elect to bring their actions in federal court in the first instance. Rodriguez v. National Bulk Carriers, Inc., 1962 A.M.C. 2052 (D.Mass.1962) reproduced the situation in the Pate case (including the fact that the maintenance and cure count was stated in less than the jurisdictional amount) and was decided on the authority of Pate. In Preston v. Grant Advertising, Inc., 375 F.2d 430, 1967 A.M.C. 1274 (5th Cir. 1967), the trial court's refusal to remand to the state court a case allegedly "predicated on the Jones Act" was affirmed. The Court commented, per curiam: "We find that the complaint fails to allege sufficient facts to support a cause of action under the Jones Act."

171. 119 U.S. 199, 7 S.Ct. 140 (1886). The Harrisburg followed, and relied on, Mobile Life Insurance Co. v. Brame, 95 U.S. 754 (1878) in which the Court had held that, in this country as in England, no recovery for wrongful death was provided by the common law.

171a. 207 U.S. 398, 28 S.Ct. 133 (1907).

171b. On the various types of death and survival statutes, see 2 Harper and James, The Law of Torts §§ 24.2, 25.13 *et seq.* (1956). See also Justice Brennan's majority opinion in the Gaudet case, discussed § 6–33 *infra*.

171c. 41 Stat. 537, 46 U.S.C.A. §§ 761–768. The sections of DOHSA will be cited by their U.S.C.A. section numbers.

171d. § 761. Under § 767 DOHSA does not apply "to the Great Lakes, or to any waters within the territorial limits of any State, or to any navigable waters in the Panama Canal Zone."

171e. 41 Stat. 1007, 46 U.S.C.A. § 688.

171f. Note 151 *supra*.

171g. 398 U.S. 375, 90 S.Ct. 1772, 1970 A.M.C. 967 (1970).

Moragne to explain what the components of the new maritime wrongful death actions were to be or how recovery under the new action was to be related to the various and diverse recovery formulae provided by the two federal statutes and the fifty state statutes. The determination of such issues, said Justice Harlan in Moragne, "should await further sifting through the lower courts in future litigation." Since 1970 the lower courts have been diligently sifting the issues left undecided in Moragne. In Sea-Land Services, Inc. v. Gaudet [171h] a bitterly divided Supreme Court made its first post-Moragne contribution to the process of defining the new maritime law wrongful death action.

In the following sections we shall outline the pre-Moragne state of law (§§ 6–30, 6–31), analyse Moragne (§ 6–32), and indicate where (so far) we seem to be going (§ 6–33).[171i]

### Statutory Recovery Formulae

**§ 6–30.** It has become customary to distinguish between death statutes and survival statutes.[172] Under death statutes the interest protected is that of the decedent's family and other dependents; the amount of recovery is determined by what the members of the protected class would have received from the decedent during his life. "Received" originally meant (and in many, if not most, jurisdictions may still mean) "received in money"; there may be a growing tendency to allow recovery for such nonpecuniary values as loss of companionship, grief on the part of the surviving beneficiaries, and so on.[172a] Under survival statutes, the interest protected is that of the decedent himself; the decedent's representative recovers for pain and suffering before death, medical expenses, lost wages (and, sometimes, with a sort of humanitarian illogic, funeral expenses). Historically death statutes came first in most jurisdictions and were later supplemented by survival statutes. The end result of this secular legislative process will no doubt be that both interests will be protected in all jurisdictions; while the process continues each state must be looked on as a law to itself.

FELA, which the Jones Act incorporates, contains both a death provision (§ 51, which was part of the original 1908 statute) and a survival provision (§ 59, which was added by a 1910 amendment). Under § 51 the carrier, if negligent, is made liable for the death of an employee to his personal representative for the benefit of "the

**171h.** 414 U.S. 573, 94 S.Ct. 806, 1973 A.M.C. 2572 (1974), rehearing denied 415 U.S. 986 (1974).

**171i.** For obvious reasons the sequence of material presented in the following sections does not correspond to the sequence in the first edition of the treatise. In effect, §§ 6–30 and 6–31 condense the material presented in §§ 6–29—6–33 of the first edition; §§ 6–32 and 6–33 are new.

**172.** See Harper and James, *loc. cit. supra* note 171b; Malone, American Fatal Accident Statutes—Part I: The Legislative Birth Pains, [1965] Duke L.J. 673; Malone, The Genesis of Wrongful Death, 17 Stanford L.Rev. 1043 (1965).

**172a.** On this issue see the Gaudet case discussed § 6–33 *infra*.

surviving widow or husband and children of such employee; and, if none, then of such employee's parents; and, if none, then of the next of kin dependent upon such employee." Under § 59 "any right of action given by this chapter to a person suffering injury shall survive to his or her personal representative" for the benefit of the same classes of people listed in § 51. The two rights given by § 51 and § 59 are, according to an early Supreme Court FELA case, "quite distinct". "One [under § 59] is for the wrong to the injured person and is confined to his personal loss and suffering before he died, while the other is for the wrong to the beneficiaries and is confined to their pecuniary loss through his death." [173] If the employee is killed instantly, there can only be a claim under § 51; if he is injured and subsequently dies as a result of his injuries, there can be claims under both sections.

The exact wording of the Jones Act in the clause incorporating the FELA death provisions is: "in case of the death of any seaman as the result of any such personal injury". It might have been argued that only claims for death following injury and not claims for instantaneous death were meant to survive, and conceivably that only the FELA § 59 right was meant to be incorporated. The draftsman of the Jones Act was not noted for either the niceness or the clarity of his drafting; the courts have disregarded the obscure language of the incorporation clause and assumed that rights under both § 51 and § 59 are brought over from FELA to the Jones Act.

DOHSA contains a death provision (§ 761) but does not contain a survival provision. No plausible reason has ever been suggested to explain why Congress, which incorporated the FELA survival provision in the Jones Act, should not have included a survival provision in DOHSA. If DOHSA had been construed as statutes are supposed to be construed, there could have been no recovery for the decedent's pain and suffering before death or for the other pre-death items of damage normally recoverable under survival statutes. As we shall see, the courts hit upon a variety of devices under which the decedent's pre-death damages were included in the recovery awarded in DOHSA actions.

To make matters even worse, the § 761 list of DOHSA beneficiaries is not the same as the § 51 list of FELA beneficiaries. Under § 761 the decedent's personal representative recovers "for the exclusive benefit of the decedent's wife, husband, parent, child or dependent relative." Under that formula all those who are in fact dependent upon the decedent can share in the recovery in the amounts that the decedent would have contributed to their support. Under the FELA (Jones Act) formula, on the other hand, three successive classes of beneficiaries are listed (1: spouse and children; 2: parents; 3: dependent next of kin) and the existence of a prior class bars any recovery on behalf of members of a subsequent class.[174] If

173. St. Louis Iron Mountain & Southern R. Co. v. Craft, 237 U.S. 648, 658, 35 S.Ct. 704, 706 (1915).

174. It should be noted that the only express references to dependency are with respect to "next of kin" (FELA)

a decedent had, for example, contributed to the support not only of his wife but of his aged parents, all three could recover under DOHSA but only the widow could recover under the Jones Act.[175] Just as it made no sense to incorporate the FELA survival provision in the Jones Act without including a survival provision in DOHSA, so it made no sense to set up different classes of beneficiaries under the two statutes. In much the same way that the courts found ways of treating DOHSA as if it had included a survival provision, they also found ways of allowing most Jones Act plaintiffs in death actions to take advantage of the broader DOHSA schedule of beneficiaries.

### A Place for Each Statute and Each Statute in Its Place

**§ 6–31.** A description of the jigsaw pattern which the courts put together between 1920 and 1970 is essential to an understanding of why the Supreme Court decided in Moragne that the situation had become intolerable. It is necessary to distinguish between Jones Act plaintiffs and other plaintiffs as well as between on-shore deaths (that is, deaths occurring beyond the territorial reach of DOHSA [176]) and deaths on the high seas (covered by DOHSA).

1. *Jones Act plaintiffs—on-shore deaths*: In Lindgren v. United States [177] the decedent was instantly killed when he fell from a lifeboat which was slung from the davits of a vessel which was being reconditioned in a floating drydock in the port of Norfolk, Virginia. The decedent was the vessel's third mate; he was killed while performing his assigned duties; his administrator brought an action under the Jones Act.[178] The District Court found that the death was

and "relatives" (DOHSA). Neither Act expressly states a dependency requirement for parents, children or a surviving spouse. Nevertheless since pecuniary loss to the beneficiary is the basis for recovery the dependency idea cannot be lost sight of. The dependency of infant children may, perhaps, be conclusively presumed. On the other hand, it is hard to see how a recovery could be made out in favor of the surviving wealthy parents of a decedent who were in no way dependent upon him. In Civil v. Waterman S. S. Corp., 217 F.2d 94, 1955 A.M.C. 21 (2d Cir. 1954), the Second Circuit, over a vigorous dissent by Judge Learned Hand, approved an award to a widow who had been separated from the decedent and had not received any support from him for nearly twenty years before his death. The theory of the majority was apparently that the widow, by state law, could have required her husband to support her. The denial of an award, said Judge Clark, "seems unusually harsh: a husband may be killed with impunity civilly if he has been faithless. Here libellant had actually attempted to pursue her husband for support; the failure of that attempt does not suggest that she would have failed to assert her natural and legitimate rights had she been able to locate him and found him with a paying job."

175. For a discussion of the two formulae see The Four Sisters, 75 F. Supp. 399, 1947 A.M.C. 1623 (D.Mass. 1947) (father and sister). For the holding in The Four Sisters, see note 183 *infra*.

176. See note 171d *supra* and the accompanying text.

177. 281 U.S. 38, 50 S.Ct. 207, 1930 A.M.C. 399 (1930).

178. The vessel was a merchant vessel of the United States; the action against the United States, as the Jones Act employer, was under the Suits in Admiralty Act. Justice Sanford noted at the end of his opinion that the Court had not considered the effect of the Federal Employees Compensation Act. Subsequently, see note

caused by the negligent installation of the release gear of the lifeboat; that finding was not disturbed on appeal. The decedent's heirs were a nephew and a niece who had not been dependent on him; thus, they were not within the classes of beneficiaries stated in FELA §§ 51 and 59.[179] The administrator claimed that he should be entitled to recover damages for the wrongful death, for the decedent's estate and his heirs, under the Virginia Death Statute which did not contain a dependency requirement. Justice Sanford, for a unanimous Court, wrote an opinion inspired by the national uniformity principle of the Jensen case:[180] by enacting the Jones Act, Congress had preempted the field; recovery for a seaman's wrongful death within territorial waters could be had only under the FELA death provisions. Furthermore, Justice Sanford added, the Jones Act recovery "precludes the right of recovery for indemnity for his death by reason of unseaworthiness of the vessel, irrespective of negligence, which cannot be eked out by resort to the death statute of the State in which the injury was received."

The Lindgren case was decided at a time when the unseaworthiness remedy was little used and the election provision of the Jones Act was generally thought to require a choice between recovery under the Jones Act and recovery under the unseaworthiness doctrine.[181] Nevertheless, a quarter of a century later in Gillespie v. United States Steel Corporation[182] the majority of the Court in an opinion by Justice Black refused to reconsider Lindgren and reaffirmed the proposition that FELA death provisions could not be supplemented by state statutes either in a Jones Act action or in an unseaworthiness action. In an impressive dissent, which no other member of the Court joined, Justice Goldberg collected lower court cases in which the Lindgren holding, in the light of later developments, had been characterized as "deplorable", "anomalous", "archaic", "unnecessary", and "hard to understand". But the majority of the Court, at the time Gillespie was decided, was not moved.

2. *Jones Act plaintiffs—high-seas death:* The surviving beneficiaries of crew members killed on the high seas fared a good deal better than the beneficiaries of those killed in territorial waters. In Lindgren Justice Sanford expressly reserved the question whether the Jones Act superseded DOHSA in the same way that it superseded state death statutes. In the absence of further word from the Supreme Court, the lower federal courts concluded that the Lindgren rule had no application to high-seas deaths. When the first edition of the treatise was prepared in the mid-1950's, we commented that:

23 *supra*, the Court held that seamen employed on vessels owned by the United States were restricted to their rights under the Compensation Act and could not sue under the Jones Act or under the general maritime law.

179. See text preceding note 173 *supra*.

180. On the Jensen case, see § 6–45 *infra*.

181. On the election provision, see § 6–23 *supra*.

182. 379 U.S. 148, 85 S.Ct. 308, 1965 A.M.C. 1 (1964).

"[T]he lower federal courts are in agreement that the Jones Act is not exclusive [with respect to high-seas deaths] and that a seaman's personal representative can sue [either under the Jones Act or under DOHSA] and, occasionally, under both." [183] The Supreme Court never quarreled with the lower courts on this issue and in his Moragne opinion Justice Harlan suggested that the Supreme Court had indeed accepted the proposition that actions could be brought on behalf of a Jones Act seaman killed on the high seas not only under the Jones Act but for unseaworthiness, and that in the unseaworthiness action recovery could be had under DOHSA.[184]

3. *Other plaintiffs, high-seas deaths*: The enactment of DOHSA in 1920 apparently rendered obsolete the Supreme Court's suggestion in The Hamilton [185] that state wrongful death statutes could be applied to deaths on the high seas.

DOHSA covered the death of any "person" caused by "wrongful act, neglect, or default occurring on the high seas". In the case of a crew member killed on the high seas, "wrongful act, neglect or default" came, as we have seen, to include death caused by non-negligent unseaworthiness and the recovery in the action brought by his personal representative came to include both recovery for pecuniary loss suffered by his dependents under DOHSA § 761 as well as for the decedent's pain and suffering before death under the survival provision of FELA § 59.[186] In the case of a decedent who was not a crew member there was, in the typical case, no right to recover under the unseaworthiness doctrine (restricted to seamen and to certain types of harbor workers who would, in the normal course of events, be killed in territorial waters and not on the high seas). An action brought under DOHSA on behalf of a decedent who was neither a crew member nor a harbor worker was thought of as an action for a maritime tort with recovery based on negligence. Thus the DOHSA phrase "wrongful act, neglect or default" opened to include death caused by non-negligent unseaworthiness in the case of a seaman's death but was restricted to death caused by negligence in the case of the death of any other "person".

DOHSA, as we have noted, did not include a survival provision authorizing recovery for pain and suffering before death. In a case where the DOHSA action could be combined with a Jones Act action,

183. See, e. g., The Four Sisters, 75 F. Supp. 399, 1947 A.M.C. 1623 (D.Mass. 1947) (in which a recovery under DOHSA for the benefit of the decedent's brother and sister was allowed following a recovery under the Jones Act for the benefit of the plaintiff's father). See further Civil v. Waterman S. S. Corp., 217 F.2d 94, 1955 A.M.C. 21 (2d Cir. 1954).

184. 398 U.S. at p. 396 n. 12, 90 S.Ct. at p. 1785 n. 12, 1970 A.M.C. at pp. 983–984 n. 12. Justice Harlan in Moragne cited to Justice Brennan's opinion in Kernan v. American Dredging Co., 355 U.S. 426, 430 n. 4, 78 S.Ct. 394 n. 4, 1958 A.M.C. 251, 254, n. 4 as his source for the Supreme Court's acceptance of the proposition. He also cited with approval in the same context Doyle v. Albatross Tanker Corp., 367 F.2d 465, 1967 A.M.C. 201 (2d Cir. 1966).

185. Note 171a *supra* and accompanying text.

186. See § 6–30 *supra*.

the pain and suffering recovery could be had under the Jones Act count. Where that joinder could not be made, the apparent meaning of DOHSA was that there could be recovery only for pecuniary loss suffered by the decedent's dependents. However, after some initial hesitation, the courts concluded that DOHSA, in this situation, was not meant to be "exclusive" and that, under the rule of The Hamilton, the DOHSA recovery for the dependents' pecuniary loss could be supplemented by a recovery for the decedent's pain and suffering before death under the survival provision of some conceivably relevant state statute (e. g., a statute of the defendant's state of incorporation).[187]

Nothing in DOHSA limited recovery to "persons" killed by or on board ships. The courts concluded that a person killed in an airplane crash on the high seas is quite as much a DOHSA "person" as anyone killed on or by a more traditional vessel.[188]

4. *Other plaintiffs—on shore deaths*: The fact that DOHSA did not cover deaths in territorial or inland waters was evidently meant to mean, and was taken to mean, that recovery for such a death (other than the death of a Jones Act seaman) was to be had under the relevant statutes of the state in whose territorial waters the death occurred.[189] That rule presented no great problems until after the Supreme Court's decision in Seas Shipping Co. v. Sieracki [189a] had promoted certain types of harbor workers to the status of seamen *pro hac vice* entitled to recover under the reformulated doctrine of unseaworthiness. In the pre-Sieracki cases of this type recovery depended on proof that the defendant was guilty of a maritime tort (i. e., chargeable with negligence) with the state statutes being brought in to provide the remedy which, under The Harrisburg, was not available under the maritime law. After Sieracki negligence no longer had to be proved, provided the decedent had been within the protected class. *Quaere*: what was to happen if the remedial state statute provided recovery only for deaths caused by the defendant's negligent or tortious behavior? The Supreme Court's attempts to answer that question without overruling The Harrisburg can fairly be described as a jurisprudential disaster.

In The Tungus v. Skovgaard [189b] the decedent was a maintenance foreman who had been called on board a vessel unloading at a New Jersey port to repair a malfunctioning pump. He slipped on oil which

187. See Petition of Gulf Oil Corp., 172 F.Supp. 911, 1960 A.M.C. 341 (S.D. N.Y.1959) in which Judge Palmieri collected the authorities in an elaborate opinion.

188. See, e. g., Dugas v. National Aircraft Corp., 438 F.2d 1386, 1971 A.M.C. 1056 (3d Cir. 1971).

189. In addition to The Hamilton, text at note 171a *supra*, the Supreme Court held a state statute applicable to a death in territorial waters in Western Fuel Co. v. Garcia, 257 U.S. 233, 42 S.Ct. 89 (1921); the Garcia case, decided shortly after the enactment of DOHSA in 1920, involved a death which occurred in 1916.

189a. 328 U.S. 85, 66 S.Ct. 872, 1946 A.M.C. 698 (1946); see § 6–55 *infra* for a discussion of this aspect of the Sieracki case.

189b. 358 U.S. 588, 79 S.Ct. 503, 1959 A.M.C. 813 (1959).

had collected on the deck as a result of the pump's malfunction and was killed when he fell into a tank of hot oil. The Court was unanimous on the propositions that the decedent was a Sieracki-type seaman and that his death was caused by the vessel's unseaworthiness. Four members of the Court joined in an opinion by Justice Stewart which took the position that there could be recovery only if the New Jersey wrongful death statute "encompassed" death caused by non-negligent unseaworthiness; the Stewart group accepted a finding by the Third Circuit that the New Jersey statute was, as a matter of state law, to be so construed. Four other members of the Court ("the Tungus dissenters") joined in an opinion by Justice Brennan which took the position that there should be recovery no matter how the New Jersey courts construed the New Jersey statute; the only function of the state statute was to fill the gap in the maritime law created by The Harrisburg; the substantive right of recovery was provided by the federal maritime law. The ninth member of the Court, Justice Frankfurter, concurred with the Stewart group but felt that the case should have been remanded so that the New Jersey court could be asked to make an authoritative construction of its own statute. Thus five members of the Court (the Stewart group, which included Harlan, Clark and Whittaker, plus Frankfurter) favored a state law solution; four members (Brennan, Warren, Black and Douglas) favored a federal law solution.[189c]

The unhappy sequel to The Tungus came in two cases decided the following year, Hess v. United States [189d] and Goett v. Union Carbide Corporation.[189e] Hess involved a death which occurred within Oregon territorial waters. Oregon had enacted, in addition to a wrongful death statute, an Employers' Liability Act which (or so it was assumed) set a "higher" standard of liability than the wrongful death statute or the general maritime law. The lower courts refused to consider the possible applicability of the Liability Act on the ground that a state statute could not constitutionally impose higher standards than those set by the federal maritime law. That disposition of the case was reversed and the case was remanded so that the applicability of the Liability Act could be considered. The Hess majority consisted of Justices Stewart and Clark (from the Tungus majority) and the four Tungus dissenters who noted that they joined the opinion of the Court "solely under compulsion" of The Tungus in the belief that "as long as the view of the law represented by that ruling prevails in the Court, it should be applied even handedly, despite the con-

189c. United New York and New Jersey Sandy Hook Pilots Ass'n v. Halecki, 358 U.S. 613, 79 S.Ct. 517, 1959 A.M.C. 588 (1959), decided the same day as The Tungus, was a replica of the other case (including the fact that the death had occurred in New Jersey territorial waters) except that the Tungus majority (the Stewart group plus Frankfurter) concluded that the decedent had not been a Sieracki-type seaman; the case was remanded for determination whether recovery could be supported on a negligence theory. The Tungus dissenters also dissented in Halecki.

189d. 361 U.S. 314, 80 S.Ct. 341, 1960 A.M.C. 527 (1960).

189e. 361 U.S. 340, 80 S.Ct. 357, 1960 A.M.C. 550 (1960).

trary views of some of those originally joining it that state law is the measure of recovery when it helps the defendant, as in Tungus, and is not the measure of recovery when it militates against the defendant as it does here."[189f] Justices Harlan, Frankfurter and Whittaker, who had been in the Tungus majority, dissented in Hess. The Goett case, decided the same day as Hess, marked a descent into a still lower circle of the Court's private jurisprudential hell. In Goett the Fourth Circuit had held, reversing the District Court, that there was no basis for recovery either on negligence theory or unseaworthiness theory. The case was reversed and remanded so that the Circuit could explain whether it had determined the negligence issue under West Virginia law (as required by Tungus) or under maritime law. The Goett majority consisted of Justice Clark and the four Tungus dissenters, who filed the same memorandum they had filed in Hess. Justice Stewart joined Justices Harlan, Frankfurter and Whittaker in dissent. In effect eight of the Justices thought that the mandate in Goett was nonsense, a bad joke played by the Tungus dissenters on their now dissenting colleagues.

The only thing that can be said in favor of the series of cases initiated by The Tungus is that the Court had manoeuvered itself into such an untenable and absurd position that the only solution was to tear down the entire structure and make a fresh start. The opportunity to do that presented itself ten years after the debacle of the Hess and Goett cases.

**§ 6–32.** In Moragne v. States Marine Lines, Inc.[189g] the decedent, a longshoreman, was killed while working on a vessel within Florida territorial waters. His widow brought an action against the owner of the vessel to recover both for her own pecuniary loss and for her husband's pain and suffering before death. The action joined a count for negligence under maritime law with a count for unseaworthiness. In the District Court the defendant successfully moved for dismissal of the unseaworthiness count on the ground that the Florida wrongful death statute did not "encompass unseaworthiness as a basis of liability." An interlocutory appeal to the Fifth Circuit followed. The Circuit, under a procedure made available by Florida law, certified to the Florida Supreme Court the question whether the state's wrongful death statute "encompassed" unseaworthiness. The Florida Court answered that it did not. "Compelled" by The Tungus, the Fifth Circuit then affirmed the dismissal of the unseaworthiness count. (Thus Moragne presented the situation hypothesized in The Tungus from which the Court had escaped in that case by virtue of the Third Circuit's ingenious finding that the New Jersey wrongful death statute did encompass unseaworthiness.)

The Supreme Court granted certiorari and, in a unanimous opinion by Justice Harlan, not only overruled both The Harrisburg and The Tungus (along with its sequels) but in effect overruled the

**189f.** 361 U.S. at pp. 321–322, 80 S.Ct. at p. 347, 1960 A.M.C. at p. 535.

**189g.** 398 U.S. 375, 90 S.Ct. 1772, 1970 A.M.C. 967 (1970).

Lindgren and Gillespie cases as well and, in the course of its housecleaning operations, reduced both DOHSA and the FELA death provisions incorporated in the Jones Act to the level of nonstatutory Restatements.

We need not concern ourselves with the detail of Justice Harlan's meticulously reasoned demonstration of why the Supreme Court should never have adopted the rule of The Harrisburg in the first place, of why that rule should now be abandoned and of why the overruling of The Harrisburg necessarily disposed of The Tungus and its ilk. It is enough to say that the demonstration was carried out with the assured touch of a great master.

In Moragne the Court announced that it was creating (or restoring) a remedy for wrongful death (including death caused by unseaworthiness) on navigable waters under the non-statutory general maritime law. This reform, Justice Harlan suggested, would do away with at least three "anomalies". His first anomaly was that some victims of accidents in territorial waters could recover under the unseaworthiness doctrine if they were injured but not if they were killed; the reference was evidently to Jones Act seamen under the Lindgren and Gillespie cases. The second anomaly was that there could be recovery under DOHSA for deaths on the high seas caused by unseaworthiness but none for such deaths within the territorial waters of states whose wrongful death statutes did not encompass the unseaworthiness doctrine (the situation hypothesized in Tungus and made flesh in Moragne). The third anomaly was that Sieracki-type seamen could recover for deaths caused by unseaworthiness within territorial waters if the relevant state statute was construed to allow the recovery while true or Jones Act seamen (once again, under Lindgren and Gillespie) could not.

From Justice Harlan's discussion of the "anomalies" which the Moragne decision was designed to avoid, several conclusions clearly follow. The Moragne remedy covers deaths within territorial waters as well as deaths on the high seas. The remedy provides recovery for deaths caused by negligence as well as for deaths caused by unseaworthiness although in the latter case the decedent must have been a person (e. g., a Jones Act seaman) entitled to the warranty of seaworthiness. As to deaths within state territorial waters, the question whether a state wrongful death statute affords recovery for unseaworthiness is no longer relevant since the remedy is provided by maritime law.

Justice Harlan, in his remarkably far-ranging opinion, also addressed himself to several questions about the interrelationship of the Moragne remedy and the existing statutory remedies, state and federal. DOHSA, for example, contains a provision (§ 761) which has been taken to mean that jurisdiction in DOHSA suits is vested exclusively in the federal courts on the admiralty side; despite that provision, Justice Harlan suggested, actions for wrongful death on the high seas under Moragne could be brought under the saving to suitors clause in non-admiralty courts with a right to jury trial. For another example, the two-year DOHSA statute of limitations (§ 763) would give way to the admiralty doctrine of laches.[189h] From Justice Harlan's DOHSA examples, it seems to follow that the comparable FELA death provisions incorporated in the Jones Act would also be treated as guidelines for the development of the maritime death action rather than as statutory commands.

In conclusion Justice Harlan turned to the questions of what the measure of damages under Moragne should be and of what beneficiaries should be entitled to recover. The United States, which participated in the argument as amicus curiae, had suggested that the DOHSA death provisions should be followed on the theory that DOHSA is the most comprehensive of the federal statutes relating to wrongful death on navigable waters. Justice Harlan rejected the suggestion without committing the Court to any particular solution:

> "We do not determine this issue [of eligible beneficiaries] now, for we think its final resolution should await further sifting through the lower courts in future litigation. . . . If still other subsidiary issues should require resolution, such as particular questions of the measure of damages, the courts will not be without persuasive analogy for guidance. Both the Death on the High Seas Act and the numerous state wrongful-death acts have been implemented with success for decades. The experience thus built up counsels that a suit for wrongful death raises no problems unlike those that have long been grist for the judicial mill." [189i]

Justice Harlan's suggestion to the lower courts was evidently that, in working out the details of the maritime law remedy for wrongful death, they should feel free to make use of whatever sources, state or federal, might come to hand.

### From Moragne to Gaudet

§ 6–33. In Sea-Land Services, Inc. v. Gaudet [189j] a bare majority of the Supreme Court took an expansive view of the Moragne wrongful death remedy and seems to have held that the new remedy is not to be limited either by statutory provisions, state or federal, or by the case law, state or federal, construing such statutory provisions. Of course, until Moragne created the wrongful death remedy under the maritime law, all recoveries for wrongful death had been based on statutes. Thus Gaudet, if it is to be taken as representing the settled view of the majority of the Supreme Court, amply confirms our comment (written before Gaudet had been decided) that the Moragne case had

189h. On the treatment of laches in Jones Act—unseaworthiness actions in the light of the three-year FELA statute of limitation incorporated in the Jones Act, see § 6–25 *supra*, text following note 149. On laches generally, see Chapter IX, § 9–77 *et seq.*

189i. 398 U.S. at p. 408, 90 S.Ct. at p. 1792, 1970 A.M.C. at p. 993.

189j. 414 U.S. 573, 94 S.Ct. 806, 1973 A.M.C. 2572 (1974), rehearing denied 415 U.S. 986 (1974).

"reduced both DOHSA and the FELA death provisions incorporated in the Jones Act to the level of nonstatutory Restatements." Under Gaudet, indeed, all the state statutes seem to have joined the federal statutes on the scrap heap. The maritime law death remedy, as explicated in Gaudet, is now more comprehensive and provides for a greater recovery than had previously been available under the federal death statutes or under most state death statutes. From the point of view of the surviving beneficiaries, there are now obvious advantages if their decedent's fatal accident occurs on navigable waters (or at all events within the admiralty jurisdiction) rather than on an interstate highway.

The Gaudet majority consisted of Justices Blackmun, Brennan, Douglas, Marshall and White, with Justice Brennan writing the majority opinion. Chief Justice Burger and Justices Powell, Rehnquist, and Stewart dissented, with Justice Powell writing an opinion in which the other dissenters joined. The Gaudet majority may seem to have been somewhat precariously constituted. The reader will be in a better position than the writer is to have an opinion on whether Gaudet is a case for all seasons or merely a winter's tale.

Gaudet, a longshoreman, was seriously injured while working on a Sea-Land vessel in Louisiana territorial waters. He brought an unseaworthiness action as a Sieracki-seaman in which he recovered a judgment of $140,000 for his disability, pain, and suffering and loss of earnings. (The jury had reduced its verdict from $175,000 to $140,000 because Gaudet was found to have been 20% contributorily negligent.) Gaudet died, as the result of his injuries, while an appeal from the judgment was pending in the Fifth Circuit. The judgment was affirmed and was paid to Gaudet's estate. Thereafter Gaudet's widow instituted a wrongful death action under Moragne to recover for her own loss as the result of her husband's death. The District Court dismissed the wrongful death action as barred on grounds of res judicata by the recovery in the unseaworthiness action. The Fifth Circuit reversed the District Court and remanded the case for further proceedings without committing itself to what the damages in the wrongful death action were to be except that it cautioned the District Court to avoid any double recovery in the light of the fact that Gaudet's loss of future wages had already been recovered in the unseaworthiness action.[189k] The Supreme Court granted certiorari and not only affirmed the Circuit's reversal of the District Court's dismissal but went on to indicate how the damages in the wrongful death action were to be calculated. We shall discuss *first* the holding that the widow's wrongful death action was not barred by her husband's recovery in the unseaworthiness action and *second* the theory of recovery in the wrongful death action.

For the majority Justice Brennan conceded that: "To be sure, a majority of courts interpreting state and federal death statutes have

**189k.** 463 F.2d 1331, 1972 A.M.C. 2573 (5th Cir. 1972). Judge Clark wrote the opinion for a unanimous panel; a petition for rehearing was denied.

held that an action for wrongful death is barred by the decedent's recovery for injuries during his lifetime." So far as the federal statutes were concerned, the FELA death provisions incorporated in the Jones Act had been consistently so interpreted both in FELA and in Jones Act cases. The question had apparently not arisen in DOHSA litigation, a fact noted in both the majority opinion and the dissent. Justice Brennan disposed of the majority interpretation of the death statutes with the suggestion that "the bar [of the second action] does not appear to rest . . . so much upon principles of res judicata or public policy as upon statutory limitations on the wrongful death action." The Moragne wrongful death remedy is, however, "not a statutory creation but judge-made." Moragne "requires" that "the shape" of the new remedy "be guided by the principle of maritime law that 'certainly it better becomes the humane and liberal character of proceedings in admiralty to give than to withhold the remedy, when not required to withhold it by established and inflexible rules.' "[189l] "No statutory language or 'established and inflexible rules' of maritime law", Justice Brennan concluded, require that the death action brought by Gaudet's widow be "precluded merely because the decedent, during his lifetime, [was] able to obtain a judgment for his own personal injuries."

The personal injury and death actions in Gaudet were brought under the unseaworthiness doctrine under the theory that Gaudet, a harbor-worker, was a Sieracki-seaman. The 1972 amendments to the Longshoremen's and Harbor Workers' Compensation Act stripped harbor workers of their right to sue under the unseaworthiness doctrine; Gaudet's personal injury action and his widow's death action would be brought today for negligence under § 905(b) of the Compensation Act (added in 1972).[189m] Conceivably the Court, without overruling Gaudet, could hold that the Gaudet "no preclusion" rule does not apply to successive § 905(b) negligence actions. Conceivably also, the Court, without overruling Gaudet, could hold that the "no preclusion" rule does not apply to successive actions in which a Jones Act count is joined with an unseaworthiness count. That way, however, lies simple madness. If the Court does not overrule Gaudet, then it must follow, if the law is to have an ounce of sense, that the "no preclusion" rule applies not only to "pure" unseaworthiness actions but to "mixed" maritime law and statutory actions and indeed to "pure" statutory actions (say, under the Jones Act, the circumstances being such that operating negligence can be proved but unseaworthiness cannot). And if a Jones Act seaman's widow can bring her Gaudet death action under the FELA death provisions, why should a railroad worker's widow, bringing her death action under the same

189l. 414 U.S. at 583, 94 S.Ct. at 814. Justice Brennan's quotation was from the opinion of Chase, J., in The Sea Gull, 21 Fed.Cas. 909 (No. 12,578) (C.C.D.Md.1865), a pre-Harrisburg wrongful death case in admiralty which Justice Harlan had resurrected in his Moragne opinion. The Sea Gull did not, of course, involve the issue presented in Gaudet.

189m. See § 6–57 *infra*.

FELA provisions, be treated differently? [189n] The preceding comments are not meant to suggest that the Gaudet no preclusion rule is absurd, outrageous or wicked. According to a French proverb, whoever says A must go on to say B. The Gaudet Court has most of the alphabet ahead of it.

The Court's holding that the death action was not barred by the personal injury recovery led it into a discussion of the measure of damages which should be applied in the death action. Justice Brennan for the majority accepted the proposition that the damages already recovered in Gaudet's personal injury action (e. g., loss of future earnings) should not be recovered a second time in the death action (as, e. g., loss of support from the same future earnings). He concluded, however, that there were items of damage recoverable in the death action which had not been (or might not have been) recovered in the personal injury action. Such items included Gaudet's funeral expenses as well as the "monetary value" of whatever "services" Gaudet, if he had lived, might have been expected to provide for his family (including "the nurture, training, education and guidance that a child would have received had not the parent been wrongfully killed") to the extent that the "services" had not already been compensated in the judgment in the personal injury action.[189o] Justice Brennan then proceeded to consider whether in the death action the widow could recover for the loss of her husband's "society" (including, as Justice Brennan put it, "love, affection, care, attention, companionship, comfort and protection"). In what may well be the least convincing footnote (No. 17) in the history of our jurisprudence, Justice Brennan cautioned that: "Loss of society must not be confused with mental anguish or grief, which are not compensable under the maritime wrongful death remedy. The former entails the loss of positive benefits, while the latter represents an emotional response to the wrongful death." [189p] The reason for the curious distinction taken in the footnote may have been that several Circuit Courts of Appeal, in post-Moragne cases, had concluded that damages for what was most often called "survivor's grief" were not recoverable in Moragne death actions.[189q] "Insofar as" such cases "are inconsistent with our hold-

**189n.** 414 U.S. at 601, 94 S.Ct. at 823. Justice Powell's dissent makes the point, which it is hard to quarrel with, that the Gaudet holding "undoubtedly portends an express overruling of the [FELA cases holding that the decedent's own recovery bars the subsequent death action] that the Court bypasses today."

**189o.** Justice Powell in his dissent noted that: "I do not address the correctness of the Court's holding that Moragne allows the recovery of loss of services . . . or funeral expenses . . ." (Case citations omitted). 414 U.S. at 605 n. 14, 94 S.Ct. at 806 n. 14.

**189p.** In support of his footnote 17 proposition, Justice Brennan quoted at some length from Speiser, Recovery for Wrongful Death, § 3.45 (1966), an authority which is repeatedly cited in the course of his opinion.

**189q.** Petition of Canal Barge Co., Inc., 480 F.2d 11, 1973 A.M.C. 843 (5th Cir. 1973); Greene v. Vantage S. S. Corp., 466 F.2d 159, 1972 A.M.C. 2187 (4th Cir. 1972); Simpson v. Knutsen, 444 F.2d 523, 1972 A.M.C. 415 (9th Cir. 1971); In re United States Steel Corp., 436 F.2d 1256, 1971 A.M.C. 914 (6th Cir. 1970), certiorari denied sub nom. Lamp v. United States Steel Corp., 402 U.S. 987, 91 S.Ct. 1649 (1971).

ing, we disagree," Justice Brennan added in still another footnote.[189r] The conclusion was that, although recovery under many wrongful death statutes including DOHSA was limited to "pecuniary loss" suffered by the beneficiaries, the Moragne wrongful death remedy includes damages for "loss of society" (but not for "mental anguish or grief"). The dissenters attacked this aspect of the Gaudet holding as wrong in law, wrong in policy, and certain to lead to what Justice Powell referred to as "duplicative recoveries".

Presumably the Gaudet holding that the Moragne death remedy includes recovery for loss of services and society applies to all such death actions and not only to the death action which, as in Gaudet, is brought following a personal injury recovery by the decedent during his lifetime. In the usual case where there will not have been a pre-death personal injury recovery, the Moragne death action no doubt includes recovery both for the decedent's pain and suffering before death and for the survivors' loss of the decedent's services and society.[189s] Thus in Moragne death actions both the pain and suffering and the loss of services and society will have to be translated, by court or jury, into monetary equivalents. The recovery for pain and suffering before death (as well as for the other items recoverable in the right of the decedent) are subject to reduction for contributory negligence (in Gaudet's own action the recovery was reduced by 20%). There is nothing in Justice Brennan's opinion in Gaudet to suggest that the recovery for loss of services and society is subject to a comparable reduction.

If a majority of the Supreme Court continues to stand by the Gaudet holdings, the bountiful crop of post-Moragne lower court cases has been rendered obsolete. Among the Circuits the Fifth has been the most active. In Petition of Canal Barge Co., Inc.[189t] Judge Godbold had described the Fifth Circuit's approach to the Moragne problem in this way:

> "The methodology for the 'further sifting' contemplated by Moragne has thus been firmly established in this circuit. In shaping the new remedy we look first to existing maritime law to which Moragne has allowed access in a death action. We next examine the remedial policies indicated by Congress in the federal maritime statutes. Heed to these statutes will assist in ensuring that 'uniform vindication of federal policies' mandated by the Moragne Court.

**189r.** n. 23, citing, however, only the 9th and 6th Circuit cases, see note 189q *supra.* It may be that the Fifth and Fourth Circuit cases had not been available at the time Gaudet was argued and briefed.

**189s.** The FELA death provisions incorporated in the Jones Act cover both the decedent's own loss and the loss to his surviving beneficiaries; the courts have reached the same result under DOHSA which contains only a provision providing for recovery by the beneficiaries. See § 6–31 *supra.* It would be strange if the Moragne death remedy was to be construed more narrowly than the existing statutory death remedies.

**189t.** See note 189q *supra.*

> . . . Finally we look for 'persuasive analogies' in the state wrongful death acts. The importance of the role of these state acts is accented by their long and successful contribution to the growth of federal maritime law, and in their assistance in influencing the direction of admiralty law toward solution of contemporary maritime problems. [Citing the first edition of the treatise.] To the extent that policies developed under state death remedies are applicable in a maritime context, then, those policies should influence the content of the new maritime death remedy." [189u]

That "methodology" seems to have led Judge Godbold and his colleagues into error in the Canal Barge case, in which they held that "survivor's grief" damages were not recoverable in a Moragne death action.[189v] The key to the Moragne death remedy under Gaudet seems to be the "principle of maritime law" expressed by Judge Chase in The Sea Gull [189w] and quoted by Justice Brennan in Gaudet:

> "[I]t better becomes the humane and liberal character of proceedings in admiralty to give than to withhold the remedy, when not required to withhold it by established and inflexible rules."

And since the Moragne remedy is, per Gaudet, "not a statutory creation but judge-made," it appears that "established and inflexible rules" which require withholding rather than giving will be hard to come by.

A notable feature of the legal history of the twentieth century has been the progressive codification of the substantive law. For the past fifty years statutory reform has largely replaced judicial reform. The Moragne-Gaudet sequence is a fascinating example of the reverse process. The existing statutes, state and federal, have been reduced to at most "persuasive analogies" which the courts may, if they see fit, disregard as they go about fashioning the remedy for wrongful death under the general maritime law. The results of codification have been, on the whole, disappointing. It may be that we are coming to see, on an almost instinctive level, that the slower and more reflective process of judicial reform is preferable to the abrupt statutory cure. If that is true, the symbolic importance of Moragne may some day overshadow its topical importance in the A.M.C. Digests *sub nom*: Death.

### Same: What is "Negligence"?

§ 6–34. It is entirely clear that Congress did not intend the Jones Act to be an all-inclusive statute, stating the only ground of personal injury recovery for seaman against ship-owner-employer.

**189u.** 480 F.2d at p. 31, 1973 A.M.C. at pp. 869–870.

**189v.** See notes 189q, 189r *supra* and the accompanying text.

**189*w*.** See note 1891 *supra*.

The Supreme Court was undoubtedly correct in concluding that by the Jones Act Congress had meant to leave the pre-statutory unseaworthiness remedy intact and merely to add a remedy, previously not available, for injuries resulting from operating negligence.[190]

There is no reason to believe that anyone, in the process of drafting the Jones Act and enacting it, ever gave thought to the question whether the new remedy for negligence and the old remedy for unseaworthiness should be separate or overlapping concepts. For example, was the Jones Act meant to cover only cases where the sole cause of the injury was an order improvidently given or negligence on the part of a fellow crew member in executing an order? Or was it meant in addition to cover cases where the shipowner had been negligent in failing to use due diligence to furnish a seaworthy ship, even though recovery for that type of negligence was already available under maritime law? If the Jones Act was to be narrowly read as affording a remedy only in cases where no remedy had been available before, the courts had their work cut out for them: arguments about whether the proximate cause of the injury was a defective piece of machinery (thus unseaworthiness) or negligence in the use of machinery itself in good order would necessarily go on forever.

Congress gave some support, perhaps inadvertent, to a broad construction. The Jones Act itself says nothing about negligence but incorporates by reference the FELA provision that the carrier shall be liable for

> "injury or death resulting in whole or in part from the negligence of any of the officers, agents, or employees of such carrier, or by reason of any defect or insufficiency, due to its negligence, in its cars, engines, appliances, machinery, track, roadbed, works, boats, wharves or other equipment." [191]

The first branch of the FELA provision obviously covered, when translated into maritime terms, negligence on the part of the master and crew. The second branch ("defect or insufficiency . . . in its cars, engines, appliances . . . or other equipment") with equal obviousness covered what the maritime law had always called unseaworthiness. It should be noted that both branches of the FELA provision are expressly conditioned on negligence; thus under the Jones Act it could hardly be argued that a shipowner could be liable without fault even on the unseaworthiness side.[191a]

Perhaps because of the clear language of FELA, the contention that the Jones Act gave a remedy only where the maritime law had given none seems never to have been seriously put forward. In the earliest Jones Act cases the Supreme Court approved, at least by im-

**190.** Panama R. Co. v. Johnson, 264 U.S. 375, 44 S.Ct. 391, 1924 A.M.C. 551 (1923).

**191.** § 51.

**191a.** See, however, the discussion of Kernan v. American Dredging Co., 355 U.S. 426, 78 S.Ct. 394, 1958 A.M.C. 251 (1958), § 6–37 *infra*, text following note 202.

plication and without discussion, pleadings whose allegations of negligence clearly crossed over to the unseaworthiness side. The idea that the new remedy could properly overlap the old was eventually stated as doctrine by Justice Cardozo in Cortes v. Baltimore Insular Line:

> "While the seaman was still alive, his cause of action for personal injury created by the statute may have overlapped his cause of action for breach of the maritime duty of maintenance and cure, just as it may have overlapped his cause of action for injury caused through an unseaworthy ship. Pacific Co. v. Peterson, supra, p. 138; Baltimore S. S. Co. v. Phillips, 274 U.S. 316, 321, 324, 47 S.Ct. 600. In such circumstances it was his privilege, in so far as the causes of action covered the same ground, to sue indifferently on any one of them. The overlapping is no reason for denying to the words of the statute the breadth of meaning and operation that would normally belong to them, . . ..[192]

**§ 6–35.** A second general proposition, which the Supreme Court did not establish by direct holding but, rather, allowed to creep quietly into the literature, is that common law standards of negligence, even as those standards are applied in railroad cases decided under FELA, do not necessarily apply to the conditions of maritime employment: the shipowner's duty may be higher than that of the shore employer and the quantum of negligence needed to establish his liability less. Once again Justice Cardozo in the Cortes case expressed this necessarily vague concept on the broad level of doctrine:

> "We do not read the act for the relief of seamen [i. e. the Jones Act] as expressing the will of Congress that only the same defaults imposing liability upon carriers by rail shall impose liability upon carriers by water. The conditions at sea differ widely from those on land, and the diversity of conditions breeds diversity of duties. This court has said that 'the ancient characterization of seamen as "wards of admiralty" is even more accurate now than it was formerly.' . . . Out of this relation of dependence and submission there emerges for the stronger party a corresponding standard or obligation of fostering protection . . .
>
> "The act for the protection of railroad employees does not define negligence. It leaves that definition to be filled in by the general rules of law applicable to the conditions in which a casualty occurs. [Citing cases.] Congress did not mean that the standards of legal duty must be the same by land and at sea. Congress meant no more than this, that the duty must be legal, i. e. imposed by law; that it shall have been imposed for the benefit of the seaman, and for the pro-

192. 287 U.S. 367, 374–375, 53 S.Ct. 173, 175, 1933 A.M.C. 9, 12–13 (1932).

motion of his health and safety; and that the negligent omission to fulfill it shall have resulted in damage to his person. When this concurrence of duty, of negligence and of personal injury is made out, the seaman's remedy is to be the same as if a like duty had been imposed by law upon carriers by rail."[193]

A proposition so broadly phrased has no direct point of contact with the real world. It is the expression of an attitude, none the less important because it cannot be seized by its four corners and brought down to earth. Furthermore, the idea that the shipowner owes a higher duty, an "obligation of fostering protection," must be considered in connection with the modern theory which has converted the shipowner's duty to furnish a seaworthy ship into an absolute obligation. Even without the long established practice of pleading and going to the jury both on the Jones Act and on unseaworthiness,[194] it would be a rare court in an unusual case which would take the negligence issue away from the jury and an even rarer appellate court which would reverse a jury verdict for plaintiff as opposed to the weight of the evidence.

**§ 6–36.** The Jones Act plaintiff bears the burden of going forward with evidence on the essential elements of a negligence action: the existence of a duty; the negligent violation of the duty by defendant; and the causal relationship of violation to injury. On the first two issues his burden is lightened by the doctrine of the shipowner's "higher duty" announced in the Cortes case. On the proximate cause issue his burden is likewise reduced to featherweight by the Supreme Court's development of its own special brand of *res ipsa loquitur*, which it has described as a rule of "permissible inferences from unexplained events." In Johnson v. United States[195] plaintiff and another crew member were working together rounding in two blocks. Plaintiff was on the main deck; his co-worker above him on a meccano deck, a structure of beams erected on the main deck. Plaintiff bent over to coil the line on the deck and was hit by one of the blocks which fell on him from above. The co-worker was not called to testify and no evidence was introduced to explain what caused the block to fall. Nor was there any indication that plaintiff himself had been guilty of contributory negligence. The action was in admiralty, without a jury. The trial court gave a judgment to plaintiff and was reversed by the Ninth Circuit which felt that plaintiff was required to show something more than that the accident had taken place. Six justices of the Supreme Court agreed with the trial judge and reversed the Circuit. Justice Douglas said:

> "The rule of *res ipsa loquitur* . . . means that the facts of the occurrence warrant the inference of negligence, not that they compel such an inference. . . .

193. *Id.* at 377–378, 53 S.Ct. at 176, 1933 A.M.C. at 14–15.

194. See § 6–25 *supra.*

195. 333 U.S. 46, 68 S.Ct. 391, 1948 A.M.C. 218 (1948).

"[Under the Jones Act] the shipowner becomes liable for injuries to a seaman resulting in whole or in part from the negligence of another employee. . . . And there is no reason in logic or experience why *res ipsa loquitur* is not applicable to acts of a fellow servant. . . . True, the doctrine finds most frequent application in cases of injuries arising from instruments or properties under the employer's exclusive control. . . . Inherent, however, in the negligence inferred in that type of case is an act or a failure to act by an individual. . . .

"No act need be explicable only in terms of negligence in order for the rule of *res ipsa loquitur* to be invoked. The rule deals only with permissible inferences from unexplained events." [196]

It does not seem to be overstating the Johnson case much, if at all, to conclude that plaintiff makes his prima facie case by showing that he was injured and that the injury could have been caused by the negligence of the shipowner (in furnishing defective equipment) or of a fellow crew-member. In a case tried to the court (like Johnson) that is enough to justify the trial judge in giving plaintiff a verdict; in a case tried to a jury, the jury would be allowed to draw whatever "permissible inferences" occurred to it. Apparently the only way in which defendant can win a directed verdict is to establish by indisputable and uncontroverted evidence both the cause of the accident and its own freedom from negligence.[197]

196. *Id.* at 48, 49; 68 S.Ct. at 393, 1948 A.M.C. at 220, 221.

197. In Schulz v. The Pennsylvania R. Co., 350 U.S. 523, 76 S.Ct. 608, 1956 A.M.C. 737 (1956), the Johnson case was reaffirmed in a five to four decision. The trial judge had directed a verdict for defendant, stating: "There is some evidence of negligence, and there is an accidental death. But there is not a shred of evidence to connect the two." The Circuit Court affirmed the direction of the verdict. The Supreme Court reversed. Justice Black's majority opinion emphasized the constitutional right to trial by jury and commented: ". . . negligence cannot be established by direct, precise evidence such as can be used to show that a piece of ground is or is not an acre. . . . Fact finding does not require mathematical certainty." The following lower court cases from the early 1950's are instructive on Jones Act negligence theory as it had then developed: Gold v. Groves, 182 F.2d 767, 1950 A.M.C. 984 (3d Cir. 1950); Hill v. Atlantic Nav. Co., 218 F.2d 654, 1955 A.M.C. 542 (4th Cir. 1955); Nunes v. Farrell Lines, Inc., 227 F.2d 619, 1956 A.M.C. 40 (1st Cir. 1955). In the Gold and Nunes cases, which were at law, the trial judge directed a verdict for defendant on the ground that there was no evidence either of negligence or unseaworthiness: in both cases the direction of a verdict was reversed. The Hill case was in admiralty; the trial judge dismissed the case after trial on the ground that the libellant had not shown that his injuries were caused by anything under the control of the owners or operators of the ship; the Circuit reversed on *res ipsa loquitur* theory. In all three cases there was the customary joinder of counts under the Jones Act and for unseaworthiness, so that there is the usual impossibility of deciding whether they would have been handled the same way if there had been only the Jones Act negligence count. In Hawley v. Alaska S. S. Co., 236 F.2d 307, 1956 A.M.C. 1877 (9th Cir. 1956) the action was under the Jones Act alone without any allegation of unseaworthiness. A directed verdict for defendant on the ground that there had been

**§ 6–37.** In the context of a seaman's action to recover damages for personal injuries (as distinguished from the action to recover damages for the seaman's death) the question of what constitutes negligence for purposes of the Jones Act became, for all practical purposes, irrelevant during the 1950's. The Supreme Court accepted the proposition, initially put forward by the lower federal courts, that the injured seaman could join a Jones Act court with an unseaworthiness count, that he was not required to elect between the two counts and that both counts (if the plaintiff had elected to sue at law) went to the jury.[198] By the time this cross-breeding had been accomplished the unseaworthiness action (or count) had itself become what the Supreme Court described as "a species of liability without fault." [199] The damages recoverable under the unseaworthiness count were the same as the damages recoverable under the Jones Act count. It appeared that anything that could be described as "negligence" under the Jones Act count could be described as "unseaworthiness" under the companion count.[200] Plaintiff did not have to make a showing that the defendant had been in any way negligent in order to recover under the unseaworthiness count. Thus it became irrelevant whether he had carried even his attenuated burden of showing negligence under the Jones Act count.

The one situation in which the two counts could not be combined was in an action to recover for a seaman's death. Under The Harrisburg there was no right to recover for wrongful death under the general maritime law (unseaworthiness). Under Lindgren v. United States the Jones Act provided the exclusive remedy in the case of a seaman's death in territorial waters and could not be supplemented by state wrongful death acts.[201] Thus negligence of some sort still had to be shown in such a Jones Act death action. It was in such a case, Kernan v. American Dredging Company,[202] that the Supreme Court made one of its most significant contributions to Jones Act negligence theory. In Moragne v. States Marine Lines, Inc.[203] the Supreme Court overruled The Harrisburg and, in effect, also overruled Lindgren. Thus since Moragne (1970) all seamen's death actions can be brought under the general maritime law and the unseaworthiness doctrine without a showing of negligence. It might seem therefore

no evidence of negligence, was affirmed on appeal with one judge dissenting. Although the Hawley case was decided several months after the Supreme Court's decision in the Schulz case, Schulz was not cited in the Circuit Court's opinion. See also Stankiewicz v. United Fruit S. S. Corp., 229 F.2d 580, 1956 A.M.C. 559 (2d Cir. 1956).

198. See § 6–23 *et seq., supra.*

199. On the Supreme Court's reformulation of the unseaworthiness action, beginning in the 1940's, see § 6–38 *et seq., infra.*

200. At least that was the general understanding until the Supreme Court decided Usner v. Luckenbach Overseas Corp., 400 U.S. 494, 91 S.Ct. 514, 1971 A.M.C. 277 (1971), discussed § 6–39 *infra,* text following note 221d.

201. See §§ 6–29, 6–31 *supra.*

202. 355 U.S. 426, 78 S.Ct. 394, 1958 A.M.C. 251 (1958).

203. See § 6–32 *supra.*

that the Kernan case became irrelevant on the day Moragne was decided and should, in any up-to-the-minute discussion, get no more than the briefest foot-note mention. However, for reasons which will be subsequently developed,[204] the Jones Act negligence cases in general and the Kernan case in particular may take on a considerable importance in negligence action brought against shipowners by harbor workers who are not Jones Act seamen and who, since the 1972 amendments to the Longshoremen's and Harborworkers' Compensation Act, are no longer entitled to sue under the unseaworthiness doctrine. We shall, therefore, examine the Kernan case with care, even though its irrelevance for purposes of the Jones Act must be, since Moragne, conceded.

In Kernan the decedent lost his life in a fire on board a tug which was operating on the Schuylkill River in Philadelphia. An open-flame kerosene lamp which was being carried on the deck of the tug's tow and not more than three feet above the water had ignited inflammable vapors which resulted from an accumulation of oil and gasoline on the river (caused by spillage or leakage from shore-side refineries and storage tanks). A Coast Guard navigation rule required a lamp to be carried and displayed at a height not less than eight feet from the water; the tow did not carry such a lamp. The conceded purpose of the navigation rule was to prevent collisions; it had nothing to do with preventing fires. If the deck-lamp had been carried at the prescribed height, the vapors would not have been ignited and the fatal fire on the tug would not have resulted. Although the deck-lamp in fact caused the fire and the death, no negligence was chargeable to the master of the tug or its owners in allowing such a lamp to be so carried; in those happy days the presence of the oil and gasoline on the river was not reasonably foreseeable. Carrying the lamp three feet above the water was, however, a violation of the Coast Guard navigation rule.[205]

All nine Justices agreed on the statement of the case which has just been set forth: the fatal fire was caused by the violation of a navigation rule which (the rule) had nothing to do with the prevention of fires and which (the violation) was non-negligent so far as the resulting fire was concerned. Five Justices (Warren, Black, Douglas, Clark, Brennan) concluded that there should be a recovery in the Jones Act death action. Four Justices (Frankfurter, Burton, Harlan, Whittaker) dissented.

Both Justice Brennan for the majority and Justice Harlan for the dissenters dealt at length with a long series of Supreme Court

204. See § 6–57 *infra*, text following note 378t.

205. Justice Harlan in his dissent suggested that the violation of the navigation rule consisted in the absence of a lamp at the eight-foot level rather than in the presence of the lamp at the three-foot level. If that line had been pursued, there would have been no causal relationship between the violation and the fires. However, for the purpose of his dissent, Justice Harlan accepted the finding that the presence of the deck-lamp which had in fact caused the fire was in itself a violation of the rule.

FELA railroad accident cases in each of which (1) the proximate cause of the accident was a defective appliance; (2) the defective appliance constituted a violation of either the Safety Appliance Act or the Boiler Inspection Act; (3) the accident which in fact resulted was not the type of accident which the statutory requirement had been designed to prevent. Both Justice Brennan and Justice Harlan agreed that the Supreme Court FELA cases had in effect imposed absolute liability on the railroads in this situation: the railroads, once being found in statutory violation, are liable for all resulting accidents without regard to the statutory purpose. Both Justices also agreed that the FELA "absolute liability" rule had no counterpart in the general or common law of torts.

Only after recording all these points of agreement did the Justices come to the basic issue on which the Court divided. For Justice Harlan and his colleagues the FELA cases depended on the "special relationship" (as Justice Brennan put it) between the original FELA and the railroad safety statutes or (as Justice Harlan put it) on the Court's interpretation of the Congressional intent in enacting the safety statutes. According to Justice Harlan there was no basis in FELA (taken by itself) for the imposition of absolute liability. Nor had there been in the field of maritime legislation any expression of Congressional intent comparable to the railroad safety statutes.

> "[The majority of the Court, he concluded] reads out of the FELA and the Jones Act the common-law concepts of foreseeability and risk of harm which which lie at the very core of negligence liability and treats these statutes as making employers in this area virtual insurers of the safety of their employees. . . .
>
> "I cannot agree that Congress intended the federal courts to roam at large in devising new bases of liability for negligence which these Acts imposed on employers." [206]

Justice Brennan for the majority naturally took a much broader view of the FELA railroad cases. For one thing he rejected Justice Harlan's contention that the FELA cases depended on the safety statutes: "the basis of liability is the FELA." Even more significantly, he related the railroad developments to community acceptance of the idea that "the industrial employer had a special responsibility toward his workers, who were daily exposed to the risks of the business and who were largely helpless to provide adequately for their own safety." After reviewing the FELA cases he concluded:

> "The courts, in developing the FELA with a view to adjusting equitably between the worker and his corporate employer the risks inherent in the railroad industry, have plainly rejected many of the refined distinctions necessary

206. 355 U.S. at pp. 451, 452, 78 S.Ct. at pp. 406, 407, 1958 A.M.C. at pp. 269, 270.

in common-law tort doctrine for the purpose of allocating risks between persons who are more nearly on an equal footing as to financial capacity and ability to avoid the hazards involved . . . .

"We find no difficulty in applying these principles, developed under the FELA, to the present action under the Jones Act, for the latter Act expressly provides for seamen the cause of action—and consequently the entire judicially developed doctrine of liability—granted to railroad workers by the FELA." [206a]

At the time Kernan was decided the Court had, as we have suggested, made Jones Act negligence irrelevant in seamen's personal injury actions by its development of the unseaworthiness doctrine. No doubt all the Justices were disturbed at what Justice Harlan in Moragne later referred to as the "anomaly" that, under The Harrisburg and Lindgren, negligence still had to be proved in the death action. In 1958, however, the Court was still a dozen years away from the forthright solution which it unanimously adopted in Moragne: overrule The Harrisburg and Lindgren and let the death action like the personal injury action be brought under the general maritime law. The Kernan majority may have sought to correct the anomaly, at least in any case where a violation of a rule or a statute could be found, by making the shipowner's "negligence" liability under the Jones Act quite as absolute as his liability under the unseaworthiness doctrine. In that view of the case Kernan was a half-way house on the way to Moragne. Justice Harlan's Kernan dissent may have had somewhat the better of the legal argumentation but there is quite a lot to be said for the proposition that the only good anomaly is a dead anomaly.

It would be a waste of time to collect the cases on the almost infinite range of acts and omissions which have been held to constitute Jones Act negligence. The Second Circuit recently remarked, per curiam: "Absent a situation involving res ipsa loquitur [citing the first edition of the treatise] mere proof that an accident occurred is not evidence of anyone's negligence [or, for that matter of the ship's unseaworthiness]." [206b] But, even without the helpful presence of res ipsa loquitur, it has been a long time since a great deal more than that has been required in Jones Act (or FELA) cases. It is error to charge a Jones Act jury that the employer's negligence must have been a "substantial factor" in causing the injury (or death); the correct charge is that the jury may give a verdict for plaintiff if it finds that the employer's negligence "played any part, even the slightest." [206c]

**206a.** 355 U.S. at pp. 438, 439, 78 S.Ct. at pp. 401, 402, 1958 A.M.C. at pp. 261, 262.

**206b.** Traupman v. American Dredging Co., 470 F.2d 736, 1973 A.M.C. 28 (2d Cir. 1972).

**206c.** See Farnarjian v. American Export Isbrandtsen Lines, Inc., 474 F.2d 361, 1973 A.M.C. 917 (2d Cir. 1973) (under the circumstances the error was harmless); Caddy v. Texaco, Inc., 292 N.E.2d 348, 1973 A.M.C. 954 (Mass.1973). The source of the "even

The true measure of the Jones Act's success is that it became the prime cause of its own obsolescence. By an entirely logical albeit somewhat involved development, which will be next discussed, its addition of a "new" remedy to the maritime law had the unanticipated effect of broadening the old remedies, so that the new remedy, hedged about as it was with the technical restrictions we have discussed, itself became unnecessary.

### Unseaworthiness: The Scope and Nature of the Remedy

**§ 6–38.** Until the mid 1940's the seaman's right to recover damages for injuries caused by unseaworthiness of the ship was an obscure and relatively little used remedy. Robinson, writing in 1939, devoted 35 pages to the Jones Act, 10 to maintenance and cure and 6 to "Indemnity, under General Admiralty, for Ship's Defects".[207] The division of space accurately reflected the relative importance of the three remedies as of that time. Today the unseaworthiness doctrine has become the principal vehicle for personal injury recoveries.[208] Until the 1940's it had been assumed that plaintiff was required to elect between an unseaworthiness count and a Jones Act count.[208a] During the 1950's the election requirement disappeared and the common practice came to be to join the Jones Act count with an unseaworthiness count (as well as, frequently, with a maintenance and cure count). The Jones Act count and the unseaworthiness count overlap completely: they derive from the same accident and look toward the same recovery. As a matter of jurisprudential elegance or even of common sense it would have been desirable (and would still be desirable) to abandon the cumbersome fiction that two causes of action are involved and to restate the seaman's cause of action for death or injury as being what it is. That has not been done and, in all probability, will never be done. After ten or fifteen years of confusion the admiralty lawyers and the admiralty judges came to understand that the Jones Act count and the unseaworthiness count are Siamese twins. The only danger here is the possibility that a non-admiralty lawyer will be retained to handle such a case or that a non-admiralty judge will be called on to decide one.

the slightest" charge is Rogers v. Missouri Pacific R.R., 352 U.S. 500, 77 S. Ct. 443, 1957 A.M.C. 652 (1957) (an FELA case).

**207.** Robinson, Admiralty 291–344 (1939).

**208.** A large law review literature developed in connection with the Supreme Court's extension of the unseaworthiness doctrine. Among the earlier reviews of the new action Tetreault, Seamen, Seaworthiness and the Rights of Harbor Workers, 39 Cornell L.Q. 381 (1954) was notable both for its scholarly reconstruction of the historical development and for its analysis. The present writers acknowledge a considerable debt to Mr. Tetreault. Byrne, Liability for Personal Injury and Death, Including Third Party Liability and the *Ryan* Doctrine, 43 Tulane L.Rev. 509 (1969) is a comprehensive review of the historical background and the case law through the 1960's. Chamlee, The Absolute Warranty of Seaworthiness: A History and Comparative Study 24 Mercer L.Rev. 519 (1973) traces the 19th century development of the warranty in the cargo and insurance cases as contrasted with its later development in the seamen's death and injury cases.

**208a.** See § 6–23 *et seq. supra.*

The first American case to have recognized a duty of shipowner to seaman to furnish a seaworthy ship appears to have been The Cyrus.[209] However in that and other early cases there was no suggestion that for a breach of the duty a seaman could recover damages for personal injuries: unseaworthiness merely gave the seaman a privilege to leave the service of the ship without coming under the penalties for desertion and without forfeiting his wages. Until late in the 19th century the shipowner's obligation to provide maintenance and cure marked the limit of his liability to seamen injured as a result of either the ship's unseaworthiness or negligence on the part of the master and fellow crew members.

The first authoritative statement which recognized the right to recover damages for injuries caused by unseaworthiness was made in The Osceola.[210] Justice Brown's second proposition, that both ship and shipowner are "liable to an indemnity for injuries received by seamen in consequence of the unseaworthiness of the ship, or a failure to supply and keep in order the proper appliances appurtenant to the ship" represented a long step forward in the history of seamen's rights. The proposition was dictum since the holding in The Osceola was that no recovery could be had for injuries caused by operating negligence. Nevertheless it proved to be an influential dictum and during the twenty-year period between the handing down of The Osceola and the passage of the Jones Act there came to be a substantial volume of litigation over the "indemnity for . . . unseaworthiness."

With the passage of the Jones Act the unseaworthiness action quickly fell out of favor. It was generally assumed to be the law that plaintiff was required to elect between the Jones Act and the unseaworthiness doctrine; as of 1930 or thereabouts, when the Jones Act case law had performed the minor miracle of making sense out of the statute, election of the Jones Act had distinct advantages.[211]

**§ 6–39.** The revolution in the law began with Mahnich v. Southern S. S. Co.,[212] in which the Supreme Court held in effect that "unseaworthiness" included "operating negligence". After Mahnich plaintiff no longer had to prove that his case fell on the right side of the line; the Supreme Court had erased the line.

Mahnich was injured when a staging collapsed, throwing him to the deck. The cause of the accident was the parting of a piece of defective rope which had been used to rig the staging. The version of the facts which the Supreme Court adopted was that the staging had been properly rigged and that there was sound rope on board available for the job. The mate, however, selected defective rope and Mahnich's injury was "attributable to the negligence of the boatswain

209. 7 Fed.Cas. 755, Case No. 3,930 (D. Pa.1789).

210. 189 U.S. 158, 23 S.Ct. 483 (1903), The Osceola is discussed in § 6–2 *supra.*

211. See § 6–3 *supra.*

212. 321 U.S. 96, 64 S.Ct. 455, 1944 A.M.C. 1 (1944).

and the mate in failing to observe the defect." The lower court opinions throw considerable doubt on whether the defect in the rope could have been observed, but that issue became irrelevant in view of the Supreme Court's handling of the case.

Mahnich was injured on August 17, 1934. His action was not instituted until 1940—the reason for the six year delay having been, apparently, that he wished to keep on good terms with his former employer who had, he thought, promised him a job if ever he needed one. When the promise was not kept, he brought suit to recover maintenance and cure for medical expenses between 1938 and 1940 and to recover damages.

Looking at the case from counsel's point of view, we might conclude that the maintenance and cure claim had a fair chance of success (it was in fact successful) but that the damage claim was hopeless. There could be no possibility of using the Jones Act, since the three year statute of limitations had long since run. As for unseaworthiness, the Supreme Court had considered the following set of facts in 1928 in Plamals v. The Pinar Del Rio: [213] a seaman was injured by a fall from a staging which had collapsed when a defective piece of rope supporting it had parted, the mate having selected the defective rope when sound rope was available. "The record," wrote Justice McReynolds in Plamals, "does not support the suggestion that the 'Pinar del Rio' was unseaworthy. The mate selected a bad rope when good ones were available." In a lifetime of litigation no lawyer could hope to find a precedent more nearly in point and more disastrous to his case. Presumably counsel decided to litigate on the strength of the maintenance and cure claim and, having got that far, thought he might as well take a whirl at the nearly hopeless unseaworthiness claim. The strategy at trial was to present the facts so as to get out from under the incubus of Plamals. If that proved not successful, counsel's best effort "on the law", and a most ingenious best, was an argument drawn from Socony-Vacuum Oil Co. v. Smith,[214] which the Supreme Court had recently decided. The facts of the Smith case were these: a seaman had been injured as a result of performing an operation in a dangerous way when there was a safe way, known to him, in which the operation could have been performed. Suit was under the Jones Act; the defense was assumption of risk. The Supreme Court affirmed a judgment for plaintiff: defendant's negligence lay in failing to provide a safe place to work and assumption of risk was no defense under the Jones Act.[215] Both Plamals and Smith, the argument ran, involved doing something dangerously when it could have been done safely; Plamals denied recovery; Smith

213. 277 U.S. 151, 48 S.Ct. 457, 1928 A.M.C. 932 (1928).

214. 305 U.S. 424, 59 S.Ct. 262, 1939 A.M.C. 1 (1939), discussed § 6–27a *supra*.

215. On the assumption of risk point the Smith case merely reiterated the conclusion which the Court had reached in The Arizona v. Anelich, 298 U.S. 110, 56 S.Ct. 707, 1936 A.M.C. 627 (1936) and Beadle v. Spencer, 298 U.S. 124, 56 S.Ct. 712, 1936 A.M.C. 635 (1936), both discussed *supra*, § 6–27, text following note 161.

allowed it; therefore Smith must have overruled Plamals sub silentio. All this had, of course, nothing in the world to do with whether unseaworthiness included "operating negligence," which was the crucial issue in Mahnich's case. However, on that feeble reed, counsel, his trial strategy on the facts having failed, rode through to victory.

The district court awarded maintenance and cure but, on the unseaworthiness issue, found Plamals controlling both on the facts and the law; no recovery.[216] The Third Circuit first affirmed per curiam without opinion,[217] then, on reargument, affirmed again by a divided court.[218] Plamals, said Judge Goodrich for the majority, was squarely in point and, as for the argument drawn from the Smith case, "we do not, as we read the opinion, find even a dictum to support the position of the libellant here." Judge Biggs, dissenting, felt both that Mahnich's case was distinguishable from Plamals on the facts and that there was something to the Smith case argument (Smith, as Judge Biggs put it, had "mitigated" the effect of Plamals). On certiorari the Supreme Court reversed, two justices dissenting.

Chief Justice Stone's opinion, which was written in uncharacteristically broad and general language, disdained the easy way out and accepted the factual identity of Plamals and Mahnich. Beyond that point the line of argument became difficult to follow. The first point was that the shipowner's duty to a seaman to furnish a seaworthy ship was absolute, not predicated on negligence and not satisfied by the exercise of due diligence: this point, at best only remotely involved on the facts of Mahnich, had not figured in the opinions below; the flat statement that the duty was absolute was in itself a revolutionary departure. "If the owner is liable for furnishing an unseaworthy appliance, even when he is not negligent," the Chief Justice continued, "*a fortiori* his obligation is unaffected by the fact that the negligence of the officers of the vessel contributed to its unseaworthiness." The ship was unseaworthy in that the staging from which Mahnich fell was supported by a defective rope, and "[a]ny negligence of the mate in selecting the rope and ordering its use as a part of the staging, or of the boatswain in using it for that purpose, could not relieve respondent of the duty to furnish a seaworthy staging." Furthermore, the fact that there was sound rope on board was no excuse to the owner:

> "We have often had occasion to emphasize the conditions of the seaman's employment, see Socony-Vacuum Co. v. Smith, *supra,* 430–431 and cases cited, which have been deemed to make him a ward of the admiralty and to place large responsibility for his safety on the owner. He is subject to the rigorous discipline of the sea, and all the conditions of his service constrain him to accept, without critical examination

216. 45 F.Supp. 839, 1941 A.M.C. 1627 (E.D.Pa.1941).

217. 129 F.2d 857 (3d Cir. 1942).

218. 135 F.2d 602, 1943 A.M.C. 668 (3d Cir. 1943).

> and without protest, working conditions and appliances as commanded by his superior officers. These conditions, which have generated the exacting requirement that the vessel or the owner must provide the seaman with seaworthy appliances with which to do his work, likewise require that safe appliances be furnished when and where the work is to be done. For, as was said in The Osceola, *supra*, 175, the owner's obligation is 'to supply and *keep in order* the proper appliances appurtenant to the ship.' (Italics supplied.) It is not enough that the 'Wichita Falls' had on board sound rope which could have been used to make the staging seaworthy, if in fact the staging was unsafe because sound rope was not used." [219]

Wherefore (?) the doctrine of the Plamals case (that unseaworthiness did not include operating negligence) was overruled, partly because of the hazardous conditions of maritime employment, partly because of the shipowner's absolute duty to furnish a seaworthy ship.

Before Mahnich the great danger in any unseaworthiness action was that the case would be dismissed if the proximate cause of the injury was found to be operating negligence rather than the defective nature of the equipment or appliance. After Mahnich no amount of negligence on the part of the master, the officer in charge or fellow crew members was fatal, if plaintiff could find some handhold of unseaworthiness to cling to.

Indeed, as the Supreme Court continued to develop the unseaworthiness idea during the 1950's and 1960's, it appeared that not even the slightest handhold of unseaworthiness was any longer required: pure and simple operating negligence had itself become a species (or subcategory) of unseaworthiness.

Thus, in Crumady v. The J. H. Fisser [220] a longshoreman was injured when a boom, which was part of the vessel's unloading gear, fell on him. The unloading gear, which was in perfect condition, was designed to carry a three-ton load and had a cut-off device or circuit-breaker to shut off the current whenever the safe load was exceeded. "Employees of the ship", before turning the vessel over to the stevedores for unloading, had set the circuit-breaker to operate only when a six-ton load was carried. The boom fell on Crumady when it was carrying a load of more than three tons. The majority of the Court (Justices Harlan, Frankfurter and Whittaker dissenting) held that the careless or deliberate missetting of the circuit-breaker constituted unseaworthiness. In Mascuilli v. United States [221] the Court seemed to take a long step beyond even the Crumady case. In Mas-

219. 321 U.S. 96, 103–104, 64 S.Ct. 455, 459, 1944 A.M.C. 1, 7–8.

220. 358 U.S. 423, 79 S.Ct. 445, 1959 A.M.C. 580 (1959), on remand 176 F.Supp. 595 (D.N.J.1959), affirmed 272 F.2d 396 (3d Cir. 1959).

221. 387 U.S. 237, 87 S.Ct. 1705, 1967 A.M.C. 1702 (1967), appeal after remand 411 F.2d 867 (3d Cir. 1969).

cuilli the District Court's essential finding was that: "the vessel and all of its equipment was in a seaworthy condition at all times and remained so throughout the entire loading operation. The accident was caused solely by the negligent operation of the stevedoring crew using seaworthy equipment in such a manner as to cause the accident to occur so instantaneously that the Third Officer was unable to warn anyone or prevent its happening." [221a] On that finding the Third Circuit affirmed the denial of liability for unseaworthiness.[221b] The Supreme Court granted certiorari (over the objection of Justices Harlan, Stewart and White) and reversed per curiam, merely citing Mahnich and Crumady.

In Waldron v. Moore-McCormack Lines, Inc.,[221c] the "humanitarian" majority of the Court may have inadvertently cast doubt on the proposition that operating negligence and unseaworthiness were equivalents. Plaintiff, a seaman, was injured carrying out a mate's order to uncoil a heavy rope. He brought an action which combined a Jones Act negligence count with an unseaworthiness count. The mate had ordered the plaintiff and one other seaman to uncoil the rope. There was testimony at the trial that three or four men should have been assigned to the job. Plaintiff's case was that the mate's improvident order was "negligence" which rendered the ship "unseaworthy". The trial judge dismissed the unseaworthiness count but sent the negligence count to the jury, which, on that count, found for the defendant. The Second Circuit affirmed the judgment for defendant but the Supreme Court reversed, with Justice Black writing the majority opinion and Justice White, joined by Justices Harlan, Brennan and Stewart, dissenting. The ground of reversal was that it had been error to dismiss the unseaworthiness count. Justice White, in his dissent, reasonably pointed out that the only possible ground for finding the ship unseaworthy was that the mate's order had been improvident or negligent; the jury's finding that there had been no negligence would necessarily, on these facts, have required a finding that there was no unseaworthiness either; thus the dismissal of the unseaworthiness count was at most harmless error. The Waldron majority would have been on firmer ground if it had reversed on the ground that there should have been a directed verdict for the plaintiff. However, the members of the Waldron majority were committed to the slogan: All power to the jury. It may be that their reluctance to reverse a jury verdict led them to solve the case by (impliedly) holding that, even on such facts, operating negligence and unseaworthiness were, in some unexplained fashion, discrete concepts. Whatever the proper explanation of the holding may be, Justice Stewart, who had joined the dissent, cited Waldron repeatedly in his majority opinion in the Usner case, which will be next discussed.

221a. 241 F.Supp. 354, 362 (E.D.Pa. 1965) (Finding No. 35).

221b. 358 F.2d 133, 1966 A.M.C. 2503 (3d Cir. 1966).

221c. 386 U.S. 724, 87 S.Ct. 1410, 1967 A.M.C. 579 (1967).

In Usner v. Luckenbach Overseas Corporation [221d] the reconstituted majority of the Supreme Court held that the Mahnich—Crumady—Mascuilli sequence did not mean that operating negligence, without more, constituted unseaworthiness. Usner, a longshoreman, was injured when a winch-operator (a fellow-employee) lowered a sling from a boom in such a manner as to strike him and knock him to the deck. The cause of the injury was, thus, the negligent operation of seaworthy equipment. Usner brought an action for unseaworthiness. Justice Stewart speaking for a majority of the Court (himself, Chief Justice Burger and Justices White, Marshall and Blackmun) thus stated their conclusion:

> "What caused the petitioner's injuries . . . was not the condition of the ship, her appurtenances, her cargo or her crew, but the isolated personal negligent act of the petitioner's fellow longshoreman. To hold that this individual act of negligence rendered the ship unseaworthy would be to subvert the fundamental distinction between unseaworthiness and negligence that we have so painstakingly and repeatedly emphasized in our decisions." [221e]

Justice Douglas (joined by Justices Black and Brennan) entered a bitter dissent on the ground that Mahnich, Crumady and Mascuilli had established the proposition that "operational negligence" was "one sturdy type of unseaworthiness". Justice Harlan, more temperately, dissented separately, noting that he had frequently dissented from the earlier unseaworthiness cases and would welcome a "thoroughgoing reexamination" of the problem. "But [he wrote] I must in good conscience regard the particular issue in this case as having been decided by [Crumady], even if prior decisions did not inexorably point to that result. . . . Crumady cannot be distinguished from the case before us."

Apart from its possible jurisprudential implications, there is much less in Usner than meets the eye.

With respect to seamen's death and injury cases, the Usner holding is essentially meaningless. The seaman-plaintiff can recover either for negligence (under the Jones Act count) or for unseaworthiness (under the maritime law count). Since the recovery is the same under either count, the question whether he recovers for negligence or for unseaworthiness is hardly worth asking. The only effects of Usner on seamen's actions are that it perpetuates the current practice

**221d.** 400 U.S. 494, 91 S.Ct. 514, 1971 A.M.C. 277 (1971).

**221e.** 400 U.S. at p. 500, 91 S.Ct. at p. 518, 1971 A.M.C. at p. 282 (footnotes omitted). In a footnote (19) Justice Stewart suggested that the Court's per curiam reversal in Mascuilli should be taken to mean that the unseaworthiness in Mascuilli resulted from defective equipment, not from the negligent use of seaworthy equipment. The Mascuilli reversal did not refer to the facts of the case or the District Court finding (text at note 221a *supra*) but merely cited Mahnich and Crumady which Justice Stewart in his Usner footnote characterized as "defective equipment" cases. The Usner distinction between unseaworthiness and negligence is discussed at length in Earles v. Union Barge Line Corp., 486 F.2d 1097, 1973 A.M.C. 2404 (3d Cir. 1973).

of pleading the action in two counts and that trial courts will have to instruct juries on both negligence and unseaworthiness (as they have been doing all along).[221f]

At the time it was decided Usner would have had an effect on some harbor workers' unseaworthiness actions. Usner dealt with stevedore's (not shipowner's) operating negligence and the apparent meaning of Usner is that the stevedore's negligence will not be imputed to the shipowner. The longshoreman cannot sue his own employer for negligence (because of the applicable Workmen's Compensation Act) nor can he bring a maritime law negligence action against the shipowner (who, per Usner, was not negligent). Thus, in the Usner situation, the plaintiff's only hope was the unseaworthiness action (which, per Usner, did not lie).

The 1972 amendments to the Longshoremen's and Harbor Workers' Compensation Act bar the harbor worker's unseaworthiness action.[221g] Thus the only surviving effect of Usner, even in this area, is the suggestion that operating negligence for which a stevedore is solely responsible will not be imputed (as negligence) to the shipowner. Under the 1972 amendments harbor workers can bring death and injury actions against shipowners predicated on negligence chargeable to the ship or shipowner. In such actions, by a curious reverse twist, the true significance of Usner may turn out to have been its affirmation of the continuing distinction between operating negligence and unseaworthiness.

**§ 6–40.** Quite as important as the Mahnich holding was Chief Justice Stone's declaration that the shipowner's duty to furnish a seaworthy ship was absolute. Strictly speaking the declaration was dictum, or close to it, since the only way in which it could have been relevant to the case was on the debatable assumption that the defect in the rope used to rig the staging could not have been discovered by inspection. But, if the absolute-duty-regardless-of-negligence proposition was implemented in subsequent cases, the unseaworthiness doctrine would have taken another giant step forward.

The background was exceptionally obscure.[222] The second proposition of The Osceola, fountainhead of law in such matters, could be taken either way. Carlisle Packing Co. v. Sandanger,[223] on which Chief Justice Stone principally relied, was a little noticed case which had slumbered in obscurity for twenty years until its resurrection in Mahnich.

The Sandanger case affirmed a 1920 judgment of the Supreme Court of Washington in a case instituted before the passage of the

**221f.** The question might be put whether Usner overrules Waldron, discussed text following note 221c *supra*. Oddly, Justice Stewart in his Usner opinion cites Waldron as an example of unseaworthiness, see note 251k *infra* and the accompanying text.

**221g.** See § 6–46 *infra*.

**222.** The historical basis, or lack of it, for Chief Justice Stone's proposition is discussed in detail in Tetreault, *op. cit. supra* note 208.

**223.** 259 U.S. 255, 42 S.Ct. 475 (1922).

Jones Act. Sandanger was injured on a motor boat which was being used on a short trip of a few hours' duration. The allegation of the complaint was that before leaving on the trip the defendant or its agents "negligently" filled with gasoline a can labeled coal oil which was customarily used to start fires in the cooking stove. Sandanger, assuming that the can contained coal oil, poured gasoline over the fire wood, applied a lighted match and was badly burned. He claimed further that his injuries were aggravated because, before jumping into the water to put out the flames, he stopped to search for a life preserver but none had been placed aboard. The action for damages was brought in state court and tried to a jury. Both the trial court and the State Supreme Court looked on the suit as a straight common-law negligence action, without regard to maritime law, the doctrine of unseaworthiness and the four propositions of The Osceola. The case went to the jury on straight negligence instructions: if defendant was negligent; if the negligence was the proximate cause; if plaintiff was not guilty of contributory negligence. . . . There was verdict for plaintiff and the judgment was affirmed on appeal. All that, said Justice McReynolds, was as wrong as it could be. The tort was maritime, the cause of action was within the admiralty jurisdiction and the common law of negligence had nothing to do with the case even though the action was brought in state court. The error, although atrocious, was, however, harmless. If the action had been submitted to the jury on the proper theory, Justice McReynolds suggested,

> ". . . the trial court might have told the jury that without regard to negligence the vessel was unseaworthy when she left the dock if the can marked 'coal oil' contained gasoline; also that she was unseaworthy if no life preservers were then on board; and that if thus unseaworthy and one of the crew received damage as the direct result thereof, he was entitled to receive compensatory damages." [224]

On that theory the judgment for Sandanger was affirmed.

When Justice McReynolds wrote "without regard to negligence the vessel was unseaworthy" he probably meant: even if Sandanger's action was not maintainable on a theory of common law negligence (because the tort was maritime and maritime law governed even in state court), the action was maintainable on the maritime theory of unseaworthiness. He could not have meant that damages were recoverable for the unseaworthiness even though the owner was not chargeable with negligence, since, on the facts of the case, nothing could have been clearer than the owner's negligence: if putting gasoline in a can labeled "coal oil" left ready for pouring over the fire and forgetting the life preservers do not amount to negligence, what, it might be asked, would? Nevertheless, Chief Justice Stone, resurrecting the Sandanger case in Mahnich and emphasizing the words "without regard to negligence" in the passage from Justice Mc-

224. *Id.* at 259, 42 S.Ct. at 476.

Reynolds' opinion, chose to read the case as declaring that the duty to provide a seaworthy ship was absolute.[225]

**§ 6–41.** Two years after Mahnich there came to the Court a case which squarely raised the issue of the shipowner's liability without fault and in which, by an extraordinary coincidence, counsel for the shipowner, for understandable reasons of trial strategy, virtually conceded the point. The case was Seas Shipping Co. v. Sieracki,[226] which has come to replace even The Osceola as the *fons et origo* of law.

> Justice Rutledge stated the case concisely:
>
> "Sieracki was employed by an independent stevedoring company which was under contract to petitioner to load its ship, the S. S. Robin Sherwood. On December 23, 1942, he was on the vessel loading cargo. The winch he operated was controlled by a ten-ton boom at number five hatch. One part of a freight car had been lowered into the hold. The second part weighed about eight tons. While it was being put down the shackle supporting the boom broke at its crown, causing the boom and tackle to fall and injure respondent." [227]

The District Court found that the shackle had broken as the result of a defect in its forging and that visual inspection would not have disclosed the defect.[228] The ship had been built by the Bethlehem Steel Company and an affiliate, who had purchased the shackle from another company.

Sieracki brought suit on the civil side of federal court against the owner of the Robin Sherwood, which impleaded the Bethlehem companies; Sieracki then amended his complaint to state a cause of action against the third party defendants. Trial was to a jury but before testimony was completed the parties stipulated that Sieracki's damages were $9,500 and that the court should determine liability as if the jury trial had been waived. Judge Kirkpatrick gave judgment for Sieracki against the Bethlehem companies on the classical theory of McPherson v. Buick Motor Co.[229] He analyzed the case against the shipowner as follows: 1) the Jones Act did not apply because Sieracki was not suing his employer; 2) the maritime doctrine of unseaworthiness did not apply because Sieracki, a longshoreman, was not a sea-

225. A few years before Mahnich, the Second Circuit, citing the Sandanger case, had announced a doctrine of absolute liability for unseaworthiness in The H. A. Scandrett, 87 F.2d 708, 1937 A.M.C. 326 (2d Cir. 1937). The Scandrett, which was among the authorities cited by Chief Justice Stone in Mahnich, was, according to Tetreault, *op. cit. supra*, note 208 at 397 (n. 79 and accompanying text), the only pre-Mahnich case which had more than a dictum to offer in support of the absolute liability proposition.

226. 328 U.S. 85, 66 S.Ct. 872, 1946 A.M.C. 698 (1946).

227. Id. at 87, 66 S.Ct. at 874, 1946 A.M.C. at 698–699.

228. Sieracki v. Seas Shipping Co., 57 F.Supp. 724, 1944 A.M.C. 1182 (E.D. Pa.1944).

229. 217 N.Y. 382, 111 N.E. 1050 (1916).

man; 3) the action was under maritime law, since the tort was maritime, and the defendant's liability was predicated on negligence. He concluded that, under all the circumstances, the shipowner (unlike the Bethlehem companies) was not "under an affirmative duty to discover unknown and invisible defects in [the] ship's equipment," had not been negligent, and dismissed the case against it. On appeal the Third Circuit affirmed the judgment as to the Bethlehem companies but reversed as to the shipowner.[230] The Circuit agreed that the shipowner had not been negligent, but, added Judge Goodrich, citing Mahnich, that would make no difference if Sieracki was entitled to sue under the unseaworthiness doctrine. Conceding that the question was difficult and unsettled, Judge Goodrich concluded that "the logical trend of the Supreme Court authority" was in favor of extending the unseaworthiness remedy to one situated like Sieracki.

As the case came to the Supreme Court the "principal issue [was] whether the obligation of seaworthiness, traditionally owed by an owner of a ship to seamen, extends to a longshoreman injured while working aboard the ship." [231] The issue of liability without fault, while necessarily in the case, was subsidiary, allowed to go almost by default, and the main battle was fought on the other front. We are not at this point concerned with the arguments which led five justices to conclude that Sieracki was a "seaman" and therefore entitled to sue under the unseaworthiness doctrine. On the extent of the shipowner's duty, the Court was unanimous. "Due diligence of the owner", said Chief Justice Stone, dissenting from the holding that a stevedore could sue for unseaworthiness, "does not relieve him from this obligation." [232] The character of the duty, said Justice Rutledge for the majority, is "absolute", adding:

> "It is essentially a species of liability without fault, analogous to other well known instances in our law. Derived from and shaped to meet the hazards which performing the service imposes, the liability is neither limited by conceptions of negligence nor contractual in character. [Citing cases.] It is a form of absolute duty owing to all within the range of its humanitarian policy." [233]

**§ 6–42.** Mahnich and Sieracki left no doubt that the shipowner's duty to all those persons "within the range of [the] humanitarian policy" of unseaworthiness was absolute and nondelegable. Those cases left open subsidiary but not unimportant questions both as to exactly who was "within the range" and as to how far the duty extended. Mahnich had been injured while the ship was at sea as a result of defective equipment which had been on board when the ship

230. 149 F.2d 98, 1945 A.M.C. 407 (1945).

231. 328 U.S. 85, 87, 66 S.Ct. 872, 874, 1946 A.M.C. 698. For discussion of this branch of the Sieracki case, see § 6–55 *infra*.

232. *Id.* at 104, 66 S.Ct. at 881, 1946 A.M.C. at 711.

233. *Id.* at 94–95, 66 S.Ct. at 877, 1946 A.M.C. at 704.

began its voyage. Sieracki had been injured in port as a result of a defect in a piece of machinery permanently attached to the ship. Suppose that Mahnich's injury had been caused by a condition of unseaworthiness which had not existed when the ship left port for the voyage. Suppose that Sieracki's injury had been caused by defective equipment brought on board by his own employer, the master stevedore, to whom the control of the ship had been relinquished for the loading or unloading, or by negligence on the part of one of Sieracki's fellow longshoremen, like him not an employee of the shipowner. In Alaska S. S. Co., Inc. v. Petterson [234] the Supreme Court ambiguously indicated that when it said "absolute" it meant "absolute" and the shipowner was in all probability liable in all the situations mentioned.

Petterson, a longshoreman, brought suit in admiralty to recover for injuries caused by the breaking of a block which he was using on board ship in the course of a loading operation. On the evidence it was far from clear who owned the block, where it came from, and what caused it to break. The district court dismissed on the ground that it had not been proved that the block was part of the ship's regular equipment and that even Sieracki did not mean that the shipowner could be liable if the block had been part of the equipment brought on board by the stevedores.[235]

On appeal the Ninth Circuit "assumed" that the block had come from outside the ship and stated the case as presenting the question: "whether a vessel's owner is liable for injuries received by an employee of a stevedoring company (an independent contractor) on board ship while engaged in the loading of the ship where the injuries are caused by a breaking block brought on board by the stevedoring company." Judge Denman's opinion further conceded, arguendo, that control of the ship, at the time and place of Petterson's injury, had been relinquished by the shipowner to the stevedoring company and noted the absence of proof whether the block had in fact been defective (*i. e.* the ship unseaworthy). Having set up his straw men, Judge Denman bowled them over. The contention that there was no proof of anything wrong with the block was "without merit." The court applied a doctrine which it described as "similar" to that of *res ipsa loquitur* (bearing in mind that unseaworthiness is liability without fault): the district judge had found that the block was the sort of block ordinarily used in such an operation and was being used in the customary manner; therefore it would not have broken unless something had been wrong with it. As to the block's having been brought on board by the stevedoring company, Sieracki was cited to the effect that the shipowner's duty is "one he cannot delegate." That left the "relinquishment of control" argument. Beginning before and

234. 347 U.S. 396, 47 S.Ct. 601, 1954 A.M.C. 860 (1954), rehearing denied 347 U.S. 994, 74 S.Ct. 848 (1954).

235. The District Court opinion, unreported, is summarized in the Ninth Circuit's opinion, Petterson v. Alaska S. S. Co., 205 F.2d 478, 1953 A.M.C. 1405 (1953).

continuing into the Sieracki era, the Second Circuit had developed the doctrine that a shipowner was not liable for unseaworthiness arising after he had surrendered control of the ship to someone else.[236] That doctrine, as Judge Denman analyzed it in Petterson, had as its major premise the idea that the shipowner's liability for unseaworthiness is based on negligence. *Per contra,* both Mahnich and Sieracki had made clear that negligence had no part in the brave new world of unseaworthiness. "We have shown," Judge Denman concluded, "that major premise to be incorrect; thus the entire doctrine is incorrect, and it should not be applied here." Thus the Alaska Steamship Company, although it had not been in control of the ship, was liable to a stevedore injured by a block not proved to have been in any way defective assumed to have been brought on board by a stevedoring company whose general competence to do the job was not challenged.

Certiorari having been granted, the following opinion (here reprinted in full) was delivered on behalf of six members of the Supreme Court:

> "PER CURIAM. The judgment is affirmed. Seas Shipping Co. v. Sieracki, 328 U.S. 85, 100, 66 S.Ct. 872, 880; Pope & Talbot v. Hawn, 346 U.S. 406, 74 S.Ct. 202." [237] Justices Burton, Frankfurter and Jackson entered a strong dissent.

The abrupt manner in which the majority of the Court chose to handle the Petterson case made it impossible to say what the Court wanted the case to stand for and how much of Judge Denman's reasoning it approved. The only indication of what the majority could have had in mind (the Pope & Talbot citation being irrelevant to our present discussion) was the shorthand reference to the fact that the Sieracki opinion contained something relevant at page 100 of 328 U.S. The passage referred to appeared to be the discussion of the non-delegability of the shipowner's duty which had been one of the main props of the Circuit Court's decision. The inference was, therefore, that the majority of the Supreme Court agreed with Judge Denman's conclusion that the "absolute and non-delegable" duty announced in Sieracki was inconsistent with the "relinquishment of control" doctrine which the Second and Third Circuits had assumed to be still in force despite Sieracki.[238] The affirmance of the Circuit's holding

236. Grasso v. Lorentzen, 149 F.2d 127, 1945 A.M.C. 559 (2d Cir. 1945) certiorari denied 326 U.S. 743, 66 S.Ct. 57 (1945); Lynch v. United States, 163 F.2d 97, 1947 A.M.C. 1164 (2d Cir. 1947); Mollica v. Compania Sud-Americana De Vapores (Chilean Line), 202 F.2d 25, 1953 A.M.C. 299 (2d Cir. 1953) certiorari denied 345 U.S. 965, 73 S.Ct. 952 (1953). The Mollica case, while reiterating the relinquishment of control doctrine, held that, on the facts of the case, the ship's officers had temporarily resumed control in the course of a loading operation so that the shipowner, under Mahnich and Sieracki, was liable for a dangerous condition.

237. 347 U.S. 396, 47 S.Ct. 601, 1954 A.M.C. 860.

238. That the "relinquishment" cases were meant to be overruled by Petterson became clearer a month later when the Court (Justices Frankfurter,

in Petterson also seemed to indicate approval of Judge Denman's theory of inferences "similar" to res ipsa loquitur. That the Supreme Court should have been in accord on this point is not surprising, since in Jones Act cases the Court had already developed its own theory of "permissible inferences from unexplained events" which it had not scrupled to call by the name of res ipsa loquitur without qualification.[239]

Jackson and Burton still in dissent) delivered its opinion in Rogers v. United States Lines, 347 U.S. 984, 74 S.Ct. 849, 1954 A.M.C. 1088 (1954), a case in which the Third Circuit (205 F.2d 57, 1953 A.M.C. 1679 (3d Cir. 1953)) had held that a shipowner was not responsible for injuries to a longshoreman, resulting from a defective wire furnished by the master stevedore. The Supreme Court's opinion in Rogers outdid even Petterson for brevity, being in full as follows: "PER CURIAM: The petition for certiorari is granted and judgment reversed." In Tarkington v. United States Lines, 222 F.2d 358, 1955 A.M.C. 1202 (2d Cir. 1955) the Second Circuit, through Judge Frank, conceded that its earlier cases (see note 236 *supra*) were no longer good law and reversed a district court which had "correctly" applied them.

In Grillea v. United States, 229 F.2d 687, 1956 A.M.C. 553 (2d Cir. 1956) the Second Circuit gave an interesting continuation of this aspect of the Petterson case. The action, for unseaworthiness, was against the United States as owner of a ship under demise charter to the Moore-McCormack Lines. The unseaworthy condition had developed after delivery of the ship to the charterer. Considering that plaintiff had elected to proceed *in personam*, Judge Learned Hand concluded that the libel should be dismissed. Citing Petterson, he remarked that "[t]he distinction is neither thin nor unreasonable that an owner shall be liable . . . for defective gear brought on board by a stevedore, but shall not be for unseaworthiness, developing when a demisee is operating the ship." On rehearing, however (232 F.2d 919, 1956 A.M.C. 1009 (2d Cir. 1956)), the Court decided that the action had been brought *in rem*, and that, on maritime lien theory, the ship might be liable even if the owner was not. (The last-mentioned aspect of the Grillea cases is discussed Chapter IX, § 9-18(a).) The action was under the Suits in Admiralty Act which authorizes a judgment *in personam* against the United States whenever there could be a judgment *in rem* against a privately owned ship. The upshot was that the case was remanded with directions to enter a decree for the libellant. In Dimas v. Lehigh Valley R. Co., 234 F.2d 151, 1956 A.M.C. 1381 (2d Cir. 1956), an unseaworthiness action was brought against a former owner of a tug who had sold it to the present owner four years before the accident (a boiler explosion) which caused the injuries. The sale of the tug had been made "as is", "subject to complete inspection" and with an express disclaimer of any warranty of seaworthiness. Plaintiff's theory was that the boiler had been defective, and the ship unseaworthy, at the time of sale so that, under the doctrine of McPherson v. Buick, the former owner, despite the terms of sale, would be liable to the injured seaman. The trial court directed a verdict for the defendant, which was affirmed on the theory that plaintiff had not borne the burden of proving the unseaworthiness at the time of sale. Furthermore, the majority of the court (per Medina, J.) felt that, even if the unseaworthiness had been proved, plaintiff could not have recovered: " . . . we cannot find in Sieracki, even by implication, any authority for taking the step plaintiffs urge, which would impose absolute liability on a party who at the time of the accident had no relation whatever to the vessel or to the injured shipworker." Judge Frank, concurring in the disposition of the case, felt that, since "the confines of the unseaworthy doctrine still remain unsettled", the court should not have "intimated" its conclusion as to the liability of a person situated like the defendant in a case where the question was not up for decision.

239. See § 6-36 *supra*.

The lower courts wrestled with the ambiguities of Petterson for a good many years until the Supreme Court made a great effort to clarify the issues in Mitchell v. Trawler Racer, Inc.[240]

**§ 6–43.** In Dixon v. United States [241] the Second Circuit considered a case of unseaworthiness arising at a port of call during a voyage and indicated that it took a narrow view of Petterson. The case involved a ladder whose three lower rungs had been accidentally damaged by stevedores in unloading cargo at a foreign port. Repairmen were called in to make the ladder seaworthy and Dixon, the chief officer, was sent to check their work. The repairmen after finishing their job had reported to the second mate that other rungs of the ladder were in need of repair, but the testimony was in conflict as to whether that report had been passed on to Dixon. Dixon chose to go down the ladder for the purpose of inspecting the three bottom rungs, several of the upper rungs gave way, Dixon fell and was severely injured.

Dixon's libel as originally filed sought recovery both under the Jones Act for negligence and under maritime law for unseaworthiness, but at trial the Jones Act count was abandoned. Judge Harlan's opinion, after a remarkable review of the development of the unseaworthiness doctrine from The Osceola through Petterson and in particular of the shift from liability based on negligence to liability without fault, concluded that the question whether the "absolute liability doctrine [extends] to conditions arising *after* the vessel has begun her voyage" was open and unsettled. He sketched the reasons of policy which might be alleged in favor of or against such an extension and added: "We express no opinion as to which side of the line the weight of such opposing considerations falls. We simply say that the complexity of the question is such as to persuade us that it should be left open for decision in a case where there is no escape from the necessity of deciding it." The Court did not, however, feel that Dixon's case, as it then stood, required a decision on a question so "fraught with difficulty." Judge Harlan assumed that the shipowner, whose duty is non-delegable, would be liable to Dixon if the repairmen had been negligent in repairing the ladder. The abandonment of the Jones Act count did not mean an abandonment of recovery based on negligence since the shipowner, even if his liability for unseaworthiness arising during the voyage was not absolute, would be liable for a negligent failure to repair a known unseaworthy condition while the ship was at a port of call. The state of the proof on what caused the upper rungs of the ladder to give way was unsatisfactory. The case was therefore remanded to the District Court for the taking of further testimony. If it should be established that negligence in repairing the lower rungs had caused the upper rungs to give way, then Dixon would be entitled to recover for the negligence

240. 362 U.S. 539, 80 S.Ct. 926, 1960 A.M.C. 1503 (1960), discussed § 6–44(a) *infra.*

241. 219 F.2d 10, 1955 A.M.C. 498 (2d Cir. 1955).

and the thorny problem of absolute liability *vel non* would not have to be reached.

The Dixon case raised more questions than it could possibly answer. Dixon was a case of repairs in a port of call to a part of the ship's permanent structure of whose defective condition the ship owner (through the master) had notice. Beyond Dixon a host of other cases stood waiting for decision: conditions both of "permanent" and "transitory" unseaworthiness arising while the ship was on the high seas; the period during which the conditions were allowed to exist; how much notice (if any) and to whom before liability attached? [242]

**§ 6–44.** Some light was shed on these questions by the Supreme Court's opinion in Boudoin v. Lykes Bros. S. S. Co., Inc.[243] The Boudoin case was the Court's first pronouncement on a branch of the unseaworthiness doctrine which might be called unseaworthiness by defective personnel. The idea that a ship is unseaworthy if it puts to sea with an incompetent master or an untrained or fever-ridden crew is not a new one,[244] but until recent years it had not made its appearance in personal injury actions by seamen against their employers. Indeed in Keen v. Overseas Tankship Corp.,[245] Judge Learned Hand commented that the question whether "an owner is responsible for the seaworthiness of his ship in respect of personnel in the same sense that he is in respect of hull and gear" was *"res integra"*. In the Keen case the Second Circuit held that the liability for personnel was identical with that for hull and gear—*i. e.* in the light of such cases as Mahnich, absolute, non-delegable, and not conditioned on fault or notice—and reversed a district judge who had instructed a jury that the shipowner's liability for an assault with a meat cleaver by one crew member on another depended on whether the owner knew or ought to have known of the vicious character of the wielder of the cleaver. The duty, although absolute, was, however, in Judge Hand's opinion, not unlimited:

> "The warranty of seaworthiness as to hull and gear has never meant that the ship shall withstand every violence of wind and weather; all it means is that she shall be reasonably fit for the voyage in question. Applied to a seaman, such a warranty is, not that the seaman is competent to meet all contingencies; but that he is equal in disposition and seamanship to the ordinary men in the calling." [246]

242. See note 251 *infra*.

243. 348 U.S. 336, 75 S.Ct. 382, 1955 A.M.C. 488 (1955).

244. In cases involving the warranty of seaworthiness in the context of marine insurance and cargo damage, Judge Learned Hand, in Keen v. Overseas Tankship Corp., note 245 *infra*, traced the idea back as far as Tait v. Levi, 14 East 481 (K.B.1811), McLanahan v. Universal Ins. Co., 26 U.S. (1 Pet.) 170 (1828), The Gentleman, 10 Fed.Cas. 188, Case No. 5,323 (C.C.S.D.N.Y.1846).

245. 194 F.2d 515, 1952 A.M.C. 241 (2d Cir. 1952), certiorari denied 343 U.S. 966, 72 S.Ct. 1061 (1952).

246. *Id.* at 518, 1952 A.M.C. at 245.

In Jones v. Lykes Bros. S. S. Co., Inc.[247] Judge Hand had the opportunity to indicate more precisely the limits which he placed on the Keen holding. Jones had been beaten up by a fellow crew member following a dispute between them in which Jones had complained of the condition in which the other sailor had left the engine room. No weapon was used except fists and there was no evidence that Jones' assailant had a reputation for brutality or truculence. Nevertheless the beating was so severe that Jones suffered serious injury to his hip. The District Judge, sitting without a jury, thought that Keen justified the recovery. Reversing, Judge Hand suggested that in all cases in which recovery had been allowed there had been either an attack with a dangerous weapon or proof that the assailant was a man with a past history for unprovoked brutality. "All men are to some degree irascible. . . . Sailors lead a rough life and are more apt to use their fists than office employees." There was nothing to show that the assailant in Jones' case was not "equal in disposition and seamanship to the ordinary men in the calling."

In the Boudoin case, the plaintiff had been attacked with a bottle by a deckhand named Gonzales whom the District Judge found to be "a person of violent character, belligerent disposition, excessive drinking habits, disposed to fighting and making threats and assaults." [248] The Fifth Circuit reversed a judgment for plaintiff, indicating general disagreement with the Keen doctrine as well as doubt that the finding as to Gonzales' disposition was borne out by the evidence.[249] The Circuit held that there could be no recovery for unseaworthiness and none for negligence since there was no proof that the defendant or the master or any of the officers knew or ought to have known about Gonzales' violent disposition, even assuming it to have been known to his fellow crew members. The Supreme Court, in one of its few unanimous personal injury opinions since Mahnich, reinstated the District Court's judgment for plaintiff, announcing approval both of the Keen case and the Jones limitation upon it. Paraphrasing and expanding Judge Hand's formulation in Keen, Justice Douglas said:

> "We see no reason to draw a line between the ship and the gear on one hand and the ship's personnel on the other. A seaman with a proclivity for assaulting people may, indeed, be a more deadly risk than a rope with a weak strand, or a hull with a latent defect. The problem, as with many aspects of the law, is one of degree. Was the assault within the usual and customary standards of the calling? Or is it a case of a seaman with a wicked disposition, a propensity to evil conduct, a savage and vicious nature? If it is the former, it is one of the risks of the sea that every crew takes. If the

247. 204 F.2d 815, 1953 A.M.C. 1010 (2d Cir. 1953).

248. 112 F.Supp. 177, 179, 1953 A.M.C. 1089, 1092 (E.D.La.1953).

249. 211 F.2d 618, 1954 A.M.C. 666 (5th Cir. 1954).

seaman has a savage and vicious nature, then the ship becomes a perilous place. A vessel bursting at the seams might be a safer place than one with a homicidal maniac as a crew member."[250]

Holding that the recovery for unseaworthiness was justifiable, the Court found it unnecessary to reach the question of negligence.

The Boudoin case assumed that no prior notice of the condition constituting unseaworthiness had to be brought home to the owner, master or officers. The opinion also stated that there was no reason to draw a line between the personnel cases and the cases involving defects in the ship or its gear. A reasonable inference from Boudoin was that the question of liability for unseaworthiness arising after the ship had broken ground for the voyage, which the Second Circuit found both unsettled and difficult in the Dixon case, would be decided against the shipowner. Cases of "transitory unseaworthiness"—soap, oil, grease, jello or what not on floor, deck or steps—might be regarded as normal "perils of the sea," against which the owner did not insure, at least until someone had had time to clean up the mess. But the gradual disappearance from the unseaworthiness cases of any requirement of notice, which the Boudoin opinion highlighted by not even discussing the point, suggested strongly that the owner's absolute liability for anything that could be called unseaworthiness, as distinguished from a peril of the sea would not be affected by the fact that the condition arose during a voyage, whether at a port of call or on the high seas, and whether or not the condition came, or ought to have come, to the attention of the master or an officer before the accident.[251]

250. 348 U.S. 336, 339, 340, 75 S.Ct. 382, 385, 1955 A.M.C. 488, 491, 492. The Boudoin case was one of the props used to shore up the majority opinion in Waldron v. Moore-McCormack Lines, Inc., 386 U.S. 724, 87 S.Ct. 1410, 1967 A.M.C. 579 (1967), discussed text following note 221c *supra*. Held in Waldron that the District Court had erred in dismissing an unseaworthiness count where there had been evidence that a mate had ordered two men to do a job which should have been assigned to three or four men.

251. In Poignant v. United States, 225 F.2d 595, 1955 A.M.C. 1955 (2d Cir. 1955) the Second Circuit continued the discussion which it had initiated in Dixon v. United States (§ 6–43 *supra*.) In Poignant a stewardess slipped on what might have been an apple-peel in a passage-way through which garbage was carried from the galley to be dumped overboard. There was no evidence to show how the apple-peel had come to be in the passage-way, how long it had been there, or indeed that the stewardess had slipped on an apple-peel. The one incontrovertible fact was that she had slipped and had been injured. At the time of the accident the ship was at a foreign port of call. The action was brought for negligence under the Jones Act and for unseaworthiness, as well as for maintenance and cure. The District Court awarded maintenance and cure but dismissed the action for damages on both counts. The Circuit agreed as to the negligence count but reversed and remanded for the taking of further testimony on the unseaworthiness count. On the notice question, Judge Hincks read the Petterson and Boudoin cases to mean that the shipowner was liable for an unseaworthy condition without regard to notice or opportunity to remedy the condition. Going beyond the Dixon holding, Judge Hincks also concluded that the implied overruling in Petterson of the relinquishment of control cases (notes 236 and 238 *supra*) made it clear that the shipowner was liable for unseaworthy conditions, permanent or

**§ 6–44(a).** In Mitchell v. Trawler Racer, Inc.[251a] the Supreme Court attempted to answer the problems which had been puzzling the lower courts in the wake of Mahnich, Sieracki and Petterson.

Mitchell was a member of the crew of a fishing trawler which had returned to port after a voyage in the North Atlantic. Mitchell and his fellow crew-members worked on unloading the catch which was done by passing bags of fish and fish-spawn over the ship's rail. Apparently as a result of that operation, the rail, for a distance of 10 or 12 feet, became covered with slime or "fish gurry". Mitchell then prepared to go ashore. The customary method of leaving the ship was to step on the rail in order to reach a ladder attached to the pier. Mitchell did so, slipped on the slimy rail, fell and was injured. He brought the usual three-count action. The trial judge charged the jury that in order to allow recovery under either the Jones Act negligence count or the unseaworthiness count they must find that the slime or gurry had been on the rail long enough for the responsible officers to have learned about it and had it removed. Mitchell's counsel requested that the charge be amended to state that notice of the condition was not a necessary element of liability with respect to the unseaworthiness count; the request was denied. The jury awarded maintenance and cure but found for the defendant on the negligence and unseaworthiness counts. Appeal was taken solely on the ground that it was error to instruct the jury that "constructive notice was necessary to support liability for unseaworthiness." The First Circuit affirmed and the Supreme Court granted certiorari "to consider a question of maritime law upon which the Courts of Appeals have expressed differing views."

transitory, arising after the voyage had begun. That left only the question whether the hypothetical apple-peel had in fact constituted unseaworthiness. "The import of the Boudoin case," wrote Judge Hincks, "is that just as the vessel is not unseaworthy because of the misbehavior of a seamen whose disposition and skill is the equal of that of ordinary men of the calling, so it does not become unseaworthy by reason of a temporary condition caused by a transient substance if even so the vessel was as fit for service as similar vessels in similar service." (*Id.* at 598, 1955 A.M.C. at 1960.) Therefore the case was remanded for the taking of further testimony as to whether the garbage disposal methods in use on the Marine Flasher were adequate. Judge Frank concurred, making the point that liability should depend not on whether the ship had employed customary methods but on whether it would have been reasonably possible for the shipowner to have adopted or invented a method of garbage disposal which would insure that the passageways would have been free of even hypothetical apple-peels. The two opinions in Poignant generously collected the relevant cases on "transitory" unseaworthiness. The Poignant mandate, while manifestly holding that the shipowner was not entitled to notice of unseaworthiness, seemed to reintroduce the notice concept by the back door: under the reading of Boudoin offered in Poignant, the standard of seaworthiness "is not perfection but reasonable fitness", which seemed to be a way of saying that the apple-peel did not make the ship unseaworthy until someone had had time to clean up the mess.

**251a.** 362 U.S. 539, 80 S.Ct. 926, 1960 A.M.C. 1503 (1960).

Justice Stewart for a six-man majority [251b] stated that the case "presents the single issue whether with respect to so-called 'transitory' unseaworthiness the shipowner's liability is limited by concepts of common-law negligence." He further noted in the course of his opinion that the case involved "an unseaworthy condition arising after the vessel leaves her home port." Neither Justice Stewart nor Justices Frankfurter and Harlan in their separate dissents made anything of the fact that Mitchell, who had taken part in the unloading operation, presumably knew of the slippery condition of the rail before he stepped on it.

Justice Stewart reviewed at some length the history of the unseaworthiness doctrine and its modern development from The Osceola through Sandanger, Mahnich and Sieracki.[251c] He concluded:

> "From [the] day [Sieracki was decided] to this, the decisions of this Court have undeviatingly reflected an understanding that the owner's duty to furnish a seaworthy ship is absolute and completely independent of his duty under the Jones Act to exercise reasonable care. [Citing cases.]
>
> There is no suggestion in any of the decisions that the duty is less onerous with respect to an unseaworthy condition arising after the vessel leaves her home port, or that the duty is any less with respect to an unseaworthy condition which may be only temporary." [251d]

Petterson, [251e] he added, should be taken as "specific authority for the proposition that the shipowner's actual or constructive knowledge of the unseaworthy condition is not essential to his liability," and also as disposing of "the suggestion that liability for a temporary unseaworthy condition is different from the liability that attaches when the condition is permanent."

From the day it was decided Mitchell v. Trawler Racer was, so to say, the last word in the ritual string citation beginning with The Osceola which became de rigueur in all unseaworthiness cases. The proposition which the case was taken as having finally established were that liability for unseaworthiness does not depend either on negligence or on notice, that the liability is the same for conditions which arise during a voyage as for conditions which arise in port and that no distinction is to be made between "transitory" and "permanent" conditions. Indeed, with Mitchell v. Trawler Racer the Supreme Court seemed to have come to the end of the process which it had initiated fifteen years earlier with the Mahnich and Sieracki cases.

**251b.** Stewart, Warren, Black, Douglas, Clark and Brennan. Justices Frankfurter, Harlan and Whittaker dissented.

**251c.** See §§ 6–38—6–41 *supra*. Justice Stewart seems to have accepted in broad outline the reconstruction proposed in the article by Tetrault, note 208 *supra*, and in the first edition of the treatise.

**251d.** 362 U.S. at p. 549, 80 S.Ct. at p. 932, 1960 A.M.C. at pp. 1511–1512.

**251e.** On the Petterson case, see § 6–42 *supra*.

The remedy having become "absolute", there was no need to say or do anything further. Thus, during the 1960's the Supreme Court had little further to contribute to the problem.[251f]

Eleven years after the writing of the majority opinion in Mitchell v. Trawler Racer, Justice Stewart wrote the majority opinion in the Usner case (from which the surviving members of the majority in Trawler Racer bitterly dissented).[251g] Usner established (or reestablished) the proposition that the negligent operation of seaworthy equipment does not (or does not necessarily) constitute unseaworthiness. In explaining the Usner holding Justice Stewart, quoting from the Trawler Racer opinion, remarked that "what has evolved in the case law . . . is the 'complete divorcement of unseaworthiness liability from concepts of negligence'." In the Trawler Racer context the phrase had meant that there could be unseaworthiness liability without any showing of negligence. In Usner the same phrase was used to mean that, although there had been negligence, there was, on the facts before the Court, no unseaworthiness. Justice Stewart's word-play contributed to the extraordinary ambiguity of the Usner decision. On its own facts Usner may be, as we suggested earlier, essentially meaningless. On the other hand, Usner cannot be lightly dismissed if it marks the disposition of the current majority of the Supreme Court to reverse the apparent culmination in Trawler Racer of the earlier majority's reformulation of the unseaworthiness doctrine.

It is true that Justice Stewart's Usner opinion contained a notably unenthusiastic characterization of the earlier unseaworthiness cases: "from its humble origin as a dictum in an obscure case in 1922[251h] the doctrine of liability based on unseaworthiness has ex-

**251f.** In Gutierrez v. Waterman S. S. Co., 373 U.S. 206, 83 S.Ct. 1185, 1963 A.M.C. 1649 (1963) the Court, following fairly old Jones Act precedents, see note 116 *supra*, held that there could be recovery for unseaworthiness even though the injury occurred on land (or at least on the dock). Gutierrez was injured when he slipped on loose coffee beans which had been spilled from defective bags in the course of an unloading operation. Justice White, who wrote the majority opinion (Justice Harlan was the only dissenter), declined to speculate on "far-fetched hypotheticals . . . such as a suit in admiralty . . . for someone's slipping on beans that continue to leak from these bags in a warehouse at Denver." On unseaworthiness by reason of defectively packaged cargo, Gutierrez had been preceded by Atlantic & Gulf Stevedores, Inc. v. Ellerman, 369 U.S. 355, 82 S.Ct. 780, 1962 A.M.C. 565 (1962). Justice White also wrote the majority opinion in Victory Carriers, Inc. v. Law, 404 U.S. 202, 92 S.Ct. 418, 1972 A.M.C. 1 (1971) which held that there was no admiralty jurisdiction over an action by a longshoreman who had been injured on the dock in the course of a loading operation while operating a fork-lift truck owned by his employer. Justice Douglas, joined by Justice Brennan, entered a vigorous dissent. Victory Carriers, like the Usner case discussed in the following paragraph of the text, has been widely regarded as symbolizing the emergence of a new majority on the Court. Justice White, in his Victory Carriers opinion, distinguished Gutierrez but did not overrule it. The comments which follow on Justice Stewart's Usner opinion may be taken as applying equally well to Justice White's Victory Carriers opinion.

**251g.** The Usner case is discussed text following note 221d *supra*.

**251h.** The reference is to the Sandanger case, see § 6–40 *supra*, text following note 223.

perienced a most extraordinary expansion in a series of cases decided by this Court over the last 25 years. The Court's decisions in some of these cases have been severely questioned by dissenting Justices and by others, on the basis of history, reason and logic [collecting authorities].[251i] However, he had been almost as unenthusiastic in Trawler Racer: "There is ample room for argument in the light of history, as to how the law of unseaworthiness should have or could have developed. Such theories might be made to fill a volume of logic. But, in view of the decisions in this Court over the last fifteen years, we can find no room for argument as to what the law is." [251j] Perhaps Justice Stewart's attitude had not changed between 1960 and 1971: what the Court had done in the name of unseaworthiness before 1960 may not have been justified by "history, reason and logic" but, as an accomplished fact, it might as well be accepted.

Justice Stewart went to some length in Usner to indicate that the earlier cases which, like Trawler Racer, had involved "conditions" of unseaworthiness (as distinguished from an "isolated, personal, negligent act") were not meant to be affected by anything in Usner:

> "A vessel's condition of unseaworthiness might arise from any number of circumstances. Her gear might be defective, her appurtenances in disrepair, her crew unfit. The number of men assigned to perform a shipboard task might be insufficient. The method of loading her cargo or the manner of its stowage might be improper. For any of these reasons, or others, a vessel might not be reasonably fit for her intended service." [251k]

Usner may signify a new mood or even a new philosophy on the Court. However, the choice of Justice Stewart to write the majority opinion in Usner may be taken as signifying the desire of the changing Court to maintain a continuity despite the change, to accept in large measure even these past results with which the present Justices may find themselves in instinctive or reasoned disagreement.[251l]

## Rights and Disabilities of Harbor Workers: Herein of the Constitutional Requirement of National Uniformity

**§ 6–45.** The constitutionality of state workmen's compensation statutes—against the argument that the imposition on employers of liability without fault for industrial accidents violated the due process clause of the Federal Constitution—was not decided by the Supreme Court until 1917. Three cases, which involved the New York,

**251i.** 400 U.S. at p. 497, 91 S.Ct. 516, 1971 A.M.C. at pp. 279–280.

**251j.** 362 U.S. at p. 550, 80 S.Ct. 933, 1960 A.M.C. at p. 1512.

**251k.** 400 U.S. at p. 499, 91 S.Ct. at p. 517, 1971 A.M.C. at pp. 281–282 (footnotes omitted). In support of the propositions quoted Justice Stewart cited Mahnich (§ 6–39 *supra*), Sieracki (§ 6–41 *supra*), Boudoin (§ 6–44 *supra*), Waldron (§ 6–39 *supra*, text following note 221c), Gutierrez and A. & G. Stevedores (note 251f *supra*).

**251*l*.** On these matters, see our introductory discussion, § 6–1(a) *supra*.

Iowa, and Washington Acts, were on the court's docket for argument early in 1916. The Court found the question a difficult one: the three cases were restored to the docket for reargument on November 13, 1916, and were reargued on various dates during the following three months. On March 6, 1917, the Court held all three Acts constitutional, Justice Pitney writing the opinion in each case.[252] The Court was unanimous on the New York and Iowa Acts; four justices dissented without opinion from the decision on the Washington Act.

Southern Pacific Co. v. Jensen [253] was a companion case to the three already mentioned. Like them it was first argued early in 1916 and restored for reargument by the order of November 13. Presumably because both the White and Jensen cases arose under the New York Act, they were reargued together on January 31 and February 1, 1917. The White case involved an award for the death of a railroad worker; Jensen an award for the death of a longshoreman whose fatal injury had taken place on a gangway connecting the ship with the pier. The Court did not announce its decision in Jensen until May 21, more than two months after the other three cases had been decided; the holding, four justices dissenting, was that the New York Act was unconstitutional as applied to Jensen. The four justices who had dissented in the Washington case were in the Jensen majority, and one of them, Justice McReynolds, wrote the opinion; the four Jensen dissenters had been in the majority in the Washington case. The swing man on the Court was Justice Day, not known as the author of admiralty opinions, who that day made a fateful contribution to maritime law.

The reasoning which Justice McReynolds supplied for the Jensen majority was as follows: the case of a longshoreman, injured on shipboard while performing maritime work under a maritime contract, was clearly within the admiralty jurisdiction; the Constitutional grant of admiralty jurisdiction to the federal courts requires a nationally uniform system of maritime law; power to modify the maritime law is in Congress and the failure of Congress to act is equivalent to a declaration that no modification shall be made; the right conferred by the "saving to suitors" clause to litigate maritime causes outside the admiralty courts applies only to common law remedies and the remedy under a workmen's compensation act was "of a character wholly unknown to the common law"; finally, the compensation remedy was inconsistent with the Congressional policy to encourage investment in shipping evidenced by the Limitation of Liability Act (of 1851).

Justice McReynolds' reference to the Limitation Act was makeweight and the suggestion that workmen's compensation acts provided remedies "unknown to the common law" was not much better. The

252. New York Central R. Co. v. White, 243 U.S. 188, 37 S.Ct. 247 (1917); Hawkins v. Bleakly, 243 U.S. 210, 37 S.Ct. 255 (1917); Mountain Timber Co. v. State of Washington, 243 U.S. 219, 37 S.Ct. 260 (1917). The dates of argument and reargument are given in the reports.

253. 244 U.S. 205, 37 S.Ct. 524 (1917).

heart of his argument was the theory of a constitutionally required national uniformity and, in support of the theory, he offered no reasoned argument but merely a quotation from Justice Bradley's famous opinion in The Lottawanna.[254] The quotation was taken completely out of context: The Lottawanna had reaffirmed the rule of The General Smith,[255] which was that, although by maritime law no maritime liens were given for supplies and repairs furnished to a ship in her home port, such liens could be conferred by state statutes which would be enforced in the admiralty courts. The Lottawanna, then, had held that state legislatures had the power to modify the maritime law, even as to the creation of maritime liens and their enforcement by proceedings *in rem.* In the course of his discussion Justice Bradley conceded that "the Constitution must have referred to a system of law coextensive with, and operating uniformly in, the whole country," suggested that a Federal Maritime Lien Act would be a desirable and probably constitutional exercise of Congressional power, but concluded that, in the absence of a Federal Act, the states were free to legislate on maritime liens. Justice McReynolds picked up Bradley's passage about national uniformity and used it to support the conclusion that the states were powerless to modify the maritime law, where Congress had done nothing, even as to proceedings brought in their own courts or before administrative agencies. There was, of course, an impressive and uncontradicted line of Supreme Court case law, including The Lottawanna itself, which had in diverse situations acknowledged the right of state legislatures to "change, modify and affect" the general maritime law. "That this may be done to some extent," wrote Justice McReynolds, "cannot be denied . . . [But] no such legislation is valid if it contravenes the essential purpose expressed by an act of Congress or works material prejudice to the characteristic features of the general maritime law or interferes with the proper harmony and uniformity of that law in its international and interstate relations." [256] The implication was that, although it was not feasible to overrule such precedents, no further extensions along that line were to be expected.

Justice Holmes, in dissent, contributed one of his most celebrated opinions and, in a companion dissent, Justice Pitney gave substance to Holmes' epigrams in a painstaking review of the authorities. Both Holmes and Pitney took the position that there was no precedent for the Jensen proposition that the rules of maritime law applied outside the admiralty courts. There had indeed been an essential ambiguity in McReynolds' handling of that part of his argument. He had said that states could not enforce, in a maritime cause of action, a remedy "unknown to the common law"; he had not added that state courts could not enforce known common law remedies or rules merely because they might contravene the principles of "general maritime law".

254. 88 U.S.(21 Wall.) 558 (1874). See Chapter IX, § 9–28, for a discussion of The Lottawanna.

255. 17 U.S.(4 Wheat.) 438 (1819). See Chapter IX, § 9–25.

256. 244 U.S. 205, 216, 37 S.Ct. 524, 529.

Holmes and Pitney seemed to assume that McReynolds had intended the second part of the statement as well as the first and, as subsequent cases were to show, they had correctly read their colleague's mind. "The maritime law," said Holmes, "is not a *corpus juris*—it is a very limited body of customs and ordinances of the sea." Of necessity it must be supplemented and, where Congress has not acted to fill in gaps, the only available source is the law of the states, statute law as well as case law. He wrapped up his argument in language whose brilliance has caused the context in which he used it to be all but forgotten:

> "The common law is not a brooding omnipresence in the sky but the articulate voice of some sovereign or quasi-sovereign that can be identified . . . [H]itherto it has not been doubted authoritatively, so far as I know, that even when the admiralty had a rule of its own to which it adhered, as in Workman v. New York City, 179 U.S. 552, 21 S.Ct. 212, the state law, common or statute, would prevail in the courts of the State." [257]

Congressional opinion after the Jensen case was that the only sensible policy was to apply the state compensation acts to maritime workers. Therefore, Congress attempted to settle the problem by adding to the "saving to suitors" clause a phrase purporting to preserve "to claimants the rights and remedies under the workmen's compensation law of any state." [258] That solution was evidently inspired by a passage of Justice McReynolds' opinion which had stressed the inaction of Congress, treating the failure to act as tantamount to a declaration of intent that state laws should not apply. In 1920, however, the Supreme Court held the amendment to the "saving to suitors" clause unconstitutional as an invalid attempt to delegate federal power to the states.[259] The makeup of the Court had not changed between the Jensen and Stewart cases and the thin Jensen majority held its line, McReynolds again writing the opinion, with Holmes, Pitney, Brandeis and Clarke in dissent. Reading the Stewart opinion to mean that the 1917 amendment had been invalid because it had been so broadly drawn as to cover not only harbor workers but masters and crew members as well, Congress tried a second time in 1922. Under the 1922 amendment the "saving to suitors" clause preserved "to claimants for compensation for injuries to or death of persons other than the master or members of the crew of a vessel, their rights and remedies under the workmen's compensation law of any State, District, Territory, or possession of the United States." [260] The 1922 amendment came before the Supreme Court in State of Washington v. W. C. Dawson & Co.[261] Four of the members of the Jensen court had

**257.** 244 U.S. 205, 222, 37 S.Ct. 524, 531.

**258.** 40 Stat. 395 (1917).

**259.** Knickerbocker Ice Co. v. Stewart, 253 U.S. 149, 40 S.Ct. 438 (1920).

**260.** 42 Stat. 634 (1922).

**261.** 264 U.S. 219, 44 S.Ct. 302, 1924 A.M.C. 403 (1924).

now retired, two from the majority and two from the minority. All four of the new justices found the logic of the Jensen position persuasive, so that Justice McReynolds in the Dawson case spoke for a majority of seven, over the continuing dissents of Justices Holmes and Brandeis.

> "Without doubt [said the majority opinion] Congress has power to alter, amend or revise the maritime law by statutes of general application embodying its will and judgment. This power, we think, would permit enactment of a general employers' liability law or general provisions for compensating injured employees; but it may not be delegated to the several states . . . The subject is national. Local interests must yield to the common welfare. The Constitution is supreme." [262]

## The Longshoremen's and Harbor Workers' Compensation Act of 1927; Scope and Purpose of the 1972 Amendments

**§ 6–46.** After Dawson it was clear that the sensible attempts by Congress to provide industrial accident coverage for maritime employees through the existing state compensation systems had run into a Constitutional dead-end. Congress therefore went to work on Justice McReynolds' suggestion that the enactment of a federal compensation act would be within its powers.

The Longshoremen's and Harbor Workers' Compensation Act (LHCA) of 1927 [263] was modeled on the New York Compensation Act [264] and contained nothing novel in most of its substantive provisions, which will be summarized in the footnote.[265] What was novel

**262.** *Id.* at 227–228, 44 S.Ct. at 305, 1924 A.M.C. at 409.

**263.** 44 Stat. 1424 (1927), 33 U.S.C.A. §§ 901–950. The sections of the Act will be cited by their U.S.C.A. section numbers.

**264.** 3 Larson Workmen's Compensation § 89.10. The several volumes of the Larson treatise, originally published in 1952, have been reissued at various dates between 1970 and 1973 and are kept up-to-date by annual cumulative supplements.

**265.** The Act established a Compensation Commission (whose functions were subsequently transferred to the Secretary of Labor) authorized to appoint deputy commissioners to administer the Act. (Under a 1972 amendment to § 919(d), the "deputy commissioner" became a "hearing examiner." In our discussion we shall remain faithful to the "deputy commissioner.") The Act covered accidental injury or death arising out of and in the course of employment as well as employment-connected diseases and infections and injury "caused by the willful act of a third person directed against an employee because of his employment." (§ 902(2)). No compensation was payable with respect to injuries occasioned solely by the intoxication of the employee or by the willful intention of the employee to injure or kill himself or another. (§ 903(2)(b).) The employer's compensation liability under the Act was made "exclusive and in place of all other liability" to the employee, his representatives, dependents and anyone else entitled to recover damages from the employer "at law or in admiralty," except that an employer who had failed to secure payment of compensation as required by the Act could be sued for damages and in such an action the defenses of fellow servant, assumption of risk and contributory negligence were abolished. (§ 905.) The Act prescribed schedules of bene-

about the Act was a series of limitations on its coverage which will be presently explained and which left the relationship between LHCA and the otherwise applicable State Compensation Act shrouded in impenetrable confusion. Successive attempts by the Supreme Court to dispel the confusion led nowhere. Indeed, decade by decade, things seemed to get worse—from the point of view of judges and lawyers, from the point of view of the unhappy state and federal officials who had to administer overlapping compensation systems and most of all from the point of view of maritime workers who suffered injury or death in the course of their employment.

In 1972 Congress radically rewrote the provisions of LHCA relating to its coverage and consequently to its relationship to State Acts.[266] However, there is no reason to believe that Congress, in enacting the 1972 amendments, was principally motivated by the commendable desire to clarify the law in these respects. The principal motivation seems to have been the desire to overturn a series of Supreme Court decisions under which injured maritime workers covered by LHCA had been put in a position where they could recover full damages (as distinguished from the limited benefits available under a compensation system) from shipowners who in turn were entitled to be indemnified by the direct employers of the workers (master stevedores and the like). Whether the desire to overturn the Supreme Court decisions was as commendable as the desire to clarify the statutory provisions on coverage is a matter on which reasonable men may well differ. Our own bias will no doubt be revealed in the course of the following discussion.

It would be meaningless to analyze the 1972 rewrite of the coverage provisions without a preliminary consideration of the main purpose of the 1972 amendments taken as a whole. We shall therefore start with a brief outline (which will be developed in greater detail in subsequent sections) of the Supreme Court construct which the amendments were designed to do away with.

fits for various types of injuries and for death and established classes of survivors entitled to death benefits. (§§ 908–910.) Agreements under which employees purported to waive the benefits of the Act were invalidated. (§ 915.) Procedures before the deputy commissioner were set out. Compensation orders became final thirty days after filing in the deputy commissioner's office. The 1927 Act provided that injunction proceedings could be brought in federal district court to have such order suspended or set aside on the ground that they were not entered "in accordance with law." (§ 921). A 1972 amendment to the section last cited established a Benefits Review Board authorized to hear and determine appeals from compensation orders which raise "a substantial question of law or fact"; appeals from orders of the Board lie to the Circuit Courts of Appeals; payments of compensation awards are not to be stayed pending appeal unless so ordered by the Board or the Court. In any proceeding for the enforcement of a claim, it was to be presumed that the claim came within the Act, that sufficient notice of the claim had been given and that the injury had not resulted from the employee's intoxication or his willful intention to injure or kill himself or another. (§ 920.)

266. 86 Stat. 1251 *et seq.* (1972). Watson, Broadened Coverage under the LHWCA, 33 Louisiana L.Rev. 683 (1973) is an admirable review both of the pre-1972 case law and of the 1972 amendments.

When workmen's compensation systems were first conceived, the basic idea was that each side gave up something and gained something.[267] The injured employee gave up the chance of recovering a large damage award from a sympathetic jury in a tort action against his employer but gained the certainty of recovering compensation (according to established schedules) even when the employer had been in no way at fault. The employer gave up the chance of escaping scot-free (on a finding that he had not been at fault) and accepted liability for all employment-related injuries but gained in that the administratively determined awards would be set at a much lower rate than the jury verdicts. Almost as an after-thought the draftsmen of the early acts dealt with the situation in which the employee's injury was caused by tortious or wrongful acts attributable to some third party (not his employer). In that situation the typical compensation act provided that the injured worker could sue the third party in what at the time was no doubt thought of as an action in tort based on negligence. In the usual conditions of industrial employment the likelihood of employment-related injuries being caused by third-party tortfeasors is of course negligible.

When LHCA was drafted no thought, presumably, was given to the fact that maritime workers regularly work on premises (i. e., ships) owned by third parties (shipowners) which are temporarily relinquished to the employers (master stevedores) for the carrying out of, say, loading or unloading operations. Thus, the situation of employment-related injuries attributable to the acts of third parties (not employers), exceptional in the context of shore-based industrial employment, is the order of the day in maritime employment. Nevertheless, LHCA routinely followed the state compensation acts in preserving the injured employee's right to sue third parties (as distinct from his employer) outside the framework of the compensation system.

Until the 1940's an action by an injured maritime worker covered by LHCA against a shipowner (not his employer) would have been thought of as an action for a maritime tort based on negligence. Few such actions were brought. Beginning in the 1940's the Supreme Court rewrote the maritime law relating to shipowner's liability for unseaworthiness and turned it into "a species of liability without fault." [268] Seas Shipping Company v. Sieracki, which became the basic case on no-fault liability, also held that at least some harbor-workers (in addition to crew-members or Jones Act seamen) could sue under the reformulated unseaworthiness doctrine.[269] Next, the Supreme Court held that the shipowner's no-fault liability extended to conditions of unseaworthiness for which a third party (e. g., a master stevedore) to whom he had relinquished control of the ship was

267. On the matters covered in this paragraph, see generally Larson, Workmen's Compensation, note 264 *supra*.

268. See § 6–38 *et seq. supra*.

269. On the Sieracki case and "liability without fault," see § 6–41 *supra*; on the types of harbor workers who were entitled to bring actions under the unseaworthiness doctrine, see § 6–54 *infra*.

solely responsible.[270] Pressing on, the Supreme Court then held that a shipowner who was required to pay damages to a Sieracki-type plaintiff could recover in a third-party indemnity action against the plaintiff's employer (the master stevedore) if the employer had been to any degree responsible for the condition of unseaworthiness which caused the injury.[271]

The end result of the Supreme Court's labors was that many maritime workers (who were in no sense traditional seamen) could recover full damages in the unseaworthiness action and that, in many cases, their employers bore the ultimate liability. To many critics (including the minority Justices on the Court) the result seemed offensive to the basic theory of any compensation systems. To maritime workers (and their lawyers) the result seemed like pie in the sky now. The injured worker could collect his compensation benefits while he waited in line to collect the (almost) automatic jury verdict (less counsel's contingent fee) and, from his point of view, it was, of course, a matter of indifference whether shipowner or employer bore the ultimate liability. From the mid-1950's on the volume of litigation of this type (maritime worker vs. shipowner vs. employer) seemed to increase year by year almost in geometric proportion. Counsel representing shipowners and employers (who did not work on contingent fees) deplored, on grounds of conscience, the system which enriched their law firms. The already overburdened dockets of the federal courts were, unquestionably, severely strained by the Sieracki-spawned flood of litigation.

The 1972 amendments to LHCA were designed to bring this situation to an end. Under the amendments (which will be subsequently analyzed in detail) the injured maritime worker covered by LHCA may no longer sue the shipowner under the unseaworthiness doctrine although he may bring an action against the shipowner ("the vessel") for negligence. If he recovers in the negligence action, his employer "shall not be liable to the vessel for such damages directly or indirectly and any agreement or warranties to the contrary shall be void." In any political resolution of a controversy there must be a trade-off. Under the amendments the LHCA worker was to be stripped (at least in some cases) of his right to recover full damages. The trade-off was that his LHCA benefits were increased (not only over what they had previously been under LHCA but over what they would presently be under State Compensation Acts) and the coverage of LHCA, both territorially and by categories of employment, was greatly extended.

We cannot write on a fresh slate. We cannot entirely ignore the tortured history of the LHCA case law from 1927 until the effective date of the 1972 amendments—a history which makes up a not altogether uninteresting page of our maritime law and which may well determine, in considerable measure, the ultimate judicial construction which the amendments will receive. Our discussion, after a preliminary look at the problem of judicial review of compensation awards,

**270.** See § 6–42 *et seq. supra.*

**271.** See § 6–55 *infra.*

will fall into three principal categories: *first,* the case law on the coverage provision of the 1927 Act and the effect of the 1972 amendments designed to broaden the Act's coverage, *second,* the maritime worker's unseaworthiness action and the presumable effects of the 1972 amendments designed to abolish the action and to replace it with a negligence action; *third,* the shipowner's indemnity action against the injured worker's employer and the presumable effect of the 1972 amendments designed to abolish that action.

### Constitutionality of LHCA; Judicial Review of Compensation Orders

**§ 6–47.** The constitutionality of LHCA came before the Supreme Court in Crowell v. Benson,[272] a case as ill-starred in the field of administrative law as Jensen in maritime law. Crowell, the deputy commissioner, had made an award in favor of Knudsen, whom he found to have been injured while in Benson's employ and while performing service upon navigable waters. Benson challenged the award in District Court on the ground that Knudsen was not at the time of the injury Benson's employee so that the claim was not within the deputy commissioner's jurisdiction. He also raised a variety of constitutional objections to the Longshoremen's Act as a whole. The District Judge granted a hearing *de novo* on the question of employment, held that Knudsen was not Benson's employee at the relevant time and restrained enforcement of the award. On appeal the Supreme Court disposed of the constitutional objections in short order and indeed, in view of the Court's clear statement in the Dawson case that such a statute would be within Congressional power to enact,[273] it can hardly be supposed that they were seriously urged. Chief Justice Hughes devoted the greater part of his opinion to a consideration of the question of judicial review of compensation orders. The Longshoremen's Act, he pointed out, was passed under the Constitutional grant of admiralty jurisdiction. The Act would, he assumed, have been beyond the power of Congress to enact unless it had been limited to injuries occurring on navigable waters and arising out of the employment relationship. The Act provided that the deputy commissioner "shall have full power and authority to hear and determine all questions in respect of any claim brought before him" and further that the Federal court should have power to set aside an order only if not entered "in accordance with law." That appeared to mean, said the Chief Justice, that the deputy commissioner's findings of fact should not be reviewable and in most instances there could be no Constitutional objection to making administrative determinations of fact non-reviewable in the courts. A distinction, however, should be drawn between ordinary facts and "fundamental" or "jurisdictional" facts. As to the latter kind—of which the existence of the employment relationship, challenged by Benson, was one and the occurrence of the injury on navigable waters, the Chief Justice suggested, was another—Congress could not

272. 285 U.S. 22, 52 S.Ct. 285, 1932 A.M.C. 355 (1932).

273. See text at note 262 *supra.*

preclude judicial review of the administrative finding. Therefore, in order to save the Act, the deputy commissioner's authority to "hear and determine all questions" would be construed to mean all questions except the existence of the fundamental or jurisdictional facts, which must, of constitutional necessity, remain open for judicial review and on such review may be tried *de novo*.

The subsequent history of the jurisdictional fact theory is not within the scope of our discussion. As the author of a treatise on Workmen's Compensation has neatly put it:

> "This doctrine is one of those curious propositions that can be established by unanswerable logic and then demolished by an unanswerable *reductio ad absurdum*." [274]

The logic is found in Chief Justice Hughes' opinion in Crowell v. Benson. The reduction to the absurd begins when the question is asked which of the many facts necessary to support any administrative decision are, and which are not, jurisdictional. On the whole, Crowell v. Benson has had few friends, even on the Supreme Court itself. Occasionally it has been thought to be dead and buried but, although in obviously poor health, it retains a tenuous grasp on life.[275]

The Supreme Court has declined to apply the jurisdictional fact theory to new situations which on any analysis would appear to be within its scope, but it has never overruled the case itself. Thus, until the Supreme Court says No, Crowell v. Benson is still good law with respect to judicial review of orders of deputy commissioners. No new "jurisdictional facts" have been added to the two which Chief Justice Hughes suggested: the employment relationship and the question of navigable waters. Whether claimant was or was not a member of the crew,[276] whether the injury did or did not arise out of the course of employment,[277] whether or not the employer had received proper notice [278]—these are examples of "facts" held not "jurisdictional," on which under the original (1927) version of the Act there could be no review in the District Court, so long as the deputy commissioner's finding was supported by some evidence.[279] Since

**274.** Larson, note 264 *supra* § 80.41.

**275.** For an excellent discussion of the vicissitudes of Crowell v. Benson as a principle of administrative law, see Schwartz, Does the Ghost of Crowell v. Benson Still Walk?, 98 U.Pa.L. Rev. 163 (1949). For collections of cases, see Larson *loc. cit. supra* note 274.

**276.** South Chicago Coal & Dock Co. v. Bassett, 309 U.S. 251, 60 S.Ct. 544, 1940 A.M.C. 327 (1940).

**277.** Cardillo v. Liberty Mutual Ins. Co., 330 U.S. 469, 67 S.Ct. 801, 1947 A.M.C. 362 (1947); O'Leary v. Brown-Pacific-Maxon, Inc., 340 U.S. 504, 71 S. Ct. 470, 1951 A.M.C. 411 (1951), see text at note 287 *infra*.

**278.** Porter's Case (Voris v. Eikel) 346 U.S. 328, 74 S.Ct. 88, 1953 A.M.C. 1979 (1953).

**279.** The 1972 amendments to LHCA § 921 established an administrative agency to hear appeals, from whose orders appeals lie to the Circuit Courts of Appeals. See note 265 *supra* (at end).

Crowell v. Benson a handful of lower court cases has allowed review of the deputy commissioner's findings on the two jurisdictional facts and no case has denied it.[280] One lower court interpretation of Crowell v. Benson has been that the granting or denying of a trial *de novo,* even on the jurisdictional facts, lies within the discretion of the District Court.[281] That seems to be a graceful way of drawing the last remaining teeth from the case. The District Judge who considers himself obliged under Crowell v. Benson to review the deputy commissioner's findings but who declines to hold a trial *de novo* and makes his review on the record established by the commissioner may well be thought to be making a merely formal obeisance to the theory of jurisdictional fact. At all events, in the cases in which the "discretionary trial *de novo*" idea has been advanced, the trial *de novo* has been refused and the commissioner's order has been upheld.[282]

Apart from Crowell v. Benson, the deputy commissioner's findings of fact must be accepted unless, as the Supreme Court has put it, "they are unsupported by substantial evidence on the record considered as a whole." [283] Another way of putting the matter, which seems to amount to the same thing, is that the commissioner's order may be reversed or set aside only if it is "not in accordance with law" [284]—*i. e.* not supported by evidence. What these catch-phrases came to mean may be brought out by two cases which the Supreme Court decided in 1944 and 1951. In Norton v. Warner

**280.** The cases to 1949 are collected in Schwartz, *op. cit. supra* note 275 at 174 (n. 53).

**281.** See Luckenbach S. S. Co., Inc. v. Lowe, 96 F.Supp. 918, 1951 A.M.C. 1156 (E.D.Pa.1951). The doctrine of discretionary review was adopted by the Ninth Circuit in Western Boat Bldg. Co. v. O'Leary, 198 F.2d 409, 413, 1952 A.M.C. 1639, 1644 (9th Cir. 1952).

**282.** The first case to have held that the district judge had discretion to deny trial *de novo* appears to have been Moran v. Lowe, 52 F.Supp. 39 (D.N.J.1943), although the idea had been put forward in Larson, The Doctrine of "Constitutional Fact," 15 Temple L.Q. 185, 206 (1941). See discussion in Schwartz, *op. cit. supra* note 275 at 174. Another lower court reading of Crowell v. Benson, logically inconsistent with the constitutional limitations which the case imposes, is that, even as to the two jurisdictional facts, an action to set aside a deputy commissioner's award must be brought within the thirty day period specified in § 921(a); see Pillsbury v. Alaska Packers Ass'n, 85 F.2d 758, 1936 A.M.C. 1809 (9th Cir. 1936), Schwartz, *loc. cit. supra.* (In Alaska Packers Ass'n v. Pillsbury, 301 U.S. 174, 57 S.Ct. 682 (1937), the Supreme Court held that Pillsbury's appeal to the Ninth Circuit from the District Court's order setting aside the Deputy Commissioner's award had been improperly taken, but did not consider the Circuit's decision on the merits.)

**283.** O'Leary v. Brown-Pacific-Maxon, Inc., 340 U.S. 504, 508, 71 S.Ct. 470, 472, 1951 A.M.C. 411, 414 (1951). The scope of judicial review of the deputy commissioner's findings of fact, Justice Frankfurter pointed out, is governed by the Administrative Procedure Act (60 Stat. 237 (1946), 5 U.S.C. A. § 1001 *et seq.*); the "unsupported by substantial evidence" formula quoted in the text is the "standard" which the Supreme Court announced under the Administrative Procedure Act, Universal Camera Corp. v. National Labor Relations Board, 340 U.S. 474, 71 S.Ct. 456 (1951).

**284.** Porter's Case (Voris v. Eikel), 346 U.S. 328, 333, 74 S.Ct. 88, 91, 92, 1953 A.M.C. 1979, 1983 (1953).

Co.[285] claimant was employed on a barge. He lived, ate and slept on board. His duties were to take general care of the barge, and included such things as pumping it out, repairing leaks, displaying the proper navigational lights and signals, taking lines from tugs and so on. The barge had no motive power of its own and its operations were confined to waters within thirty miles of Philadelphia. At the time of the injury Rusin was the only person on the barge. The deputy commissioner found that Rusin was not "a master or member of the crew of any vessel" and awarded compensation. The Supreme Court in an opinion by Justice Douglas held that the finding on which the award was based was erroneous as a matter of law and should be set aside: "Only by a distorted definition of the word 'crew' as used in the [Longshoremen's] Act could Rusin be restricted to the remedy it affords and excluded from recovery under the Jones Act or be denied relief in admiralty."[286] In O'Leary v. Brown-Pacific-Maxon[287] the issue was whether Valak's death had arisen "out of and in the course of employment." The employer, a government contractor operating on the Island of Guam, maintained for its employees a recreation center near the shoreline, along which ran a channel so dangerous for swimmers that its use was forbidden and signs to that effect were posted. While Valak, an employee, was at the center, two men, standing on the reefs beyond the channel, called for help. Valak, with others, set out to rescue them and while attempting to swim across the channel was drowned. The deputy commissioner found that Valak's drowning arose "out of and in the course of" his employment. The District Court refused to set the award aside, but was reversed by the Ninth Circuit. On certiorari the Supreme Court directed that the award be reinstated. Justice Frankfurter wrote:

> "The Deputy Commissioner treated the question whether the particular rescue attempt described by the evidence was one of the class covered by the Act as a question of 'fact.' His doing so only serves to illustrate once more the variety of ascertainments covered by the blanket term 'fact.' Here of course it does not connote a simple, external, physical event, as to which there is conflicting testimony. The conclusion concerns a combination of happenings and the inferences drawn from them. In part at least, the inferences presuppose applicable standards for assessing the simple, external facts. Yet the standards are not so severable from the experience of industry nor of such a nature as to be peculiarly appropriate for independent judicial ascertainment as 'questions of law.' "[288]

**285.** 321 U.S. 565, 64 S.Ct. 747, 1944 A.M.C. 337 (1944).

**286.** *Id.* at 573, 74 S.Ct. at 751, 1944 A.M.C. at 343. Another bargeworker case in which plaintiff was found to be a Jones Act seaman, under the Norton case, is Bryer v. Erie R. R. Co., 1956 A.M.C. 265 (City Ct.N.Y. 1955).

**287.** 340 U.S. 504, 71 S.Ct. 470, 1951 A.M.C. 411 (1951).

**288.** *Id.* at 507–508, 71 S.Ct. at 472, 1951 A.M.C. at 413–414.

The record, the Court held, supported the finding of "fact." Three justices dissented vigorously, saying that "the finding is false and has no scintilla of evidence or inference to support it."

O'Leary v. Brown-Pacific-Maxon, which has just been reviewed, has become the leading case on the limited scope of judicial review of a Deputy Commissioner's order, which cannot be set aside if it is supported by "substantial" (which appears to mean "any") evidence. In O'Keeffe v. Smith, Hinchman & Grylls Associates, Inc.[289] the Deputy Commissioner had made an award to the dependents of a man named Ecker, who had been drowned while boating on a South Korean lake in the course of a weekend excursion which had no relationship whatever with his job. The Deputy Commissioner's theory was that employees (such as Ecker) of United States government contractors in Korea [290] were so situated that any accident they might suffer during the tenure of their employment should be considered as arising out of and in the course of their employment. The award was affirmed by the District Court but was set aside by a panel of the Fifth Circuit. A majority of the Supreme Court, in a per curiam opinion, ordered the award reinstated. According to the per curiam:

> "The Brown-Pacific-Maxon case held that the standard to be applied by the Deputy Commissioner does not require 'a causal relationship between the nature of employment of the injured person and the accident. . . . Nor is it necessary that the employee be engaged at the time of the injury in activity of benefit to his employer. All that is required is that the 'obligations or conditions' of employment create the 'zone of special danger' out of which the injury arose'." [291]

The present state of the law on the issue of judicial review of awards under LHCA may be illustrated by Plaquemines Equipment & Machine Co. v. Neuman.[292] The District Court found that:

**289.** 380 U.S. 359, 85 S.Ct. 1012, 1966 A.M.C. 1 (1965).

**290.** The Defense Bases Act, 42 U.S.C.A. § 1651, originally enacted in 1941, provided that LHCA should apply "in respect to the injury or death of any employee engaged in any employment" in various types of government activity outside the continental United States. Thus Ecker, who was not a maritime worker, was, nevertheless, covered by LHCA.

**291.** 380 U.S. at p. 362, 85 S.Ct. at p. 1014, 1966 A.M.C. at p. 4. Justice Harlan, joined by Justices Clark and White, dissented. Justice Douglas expressed himself as "dubitante." In Gondeck v. Pan American Airways, 382 U.S. 25, 86 S.Ct. 153, 1966 A.M.C. 12 (1965), another Defense Bases case, the majority of the Court, per curiam, reversed the Second Circuit and ordered a Deputy Commissioner's award reinstated with respect to a death off-duty. In earlier proceedings in Gondeck the Court had denied certiorari and denied a petition for rehearing. Gondeck was decided on the basis of O'Keeffe and Brown-Pacific-Maxon. See further Banks v. Chicago Grain Trimmers Association, Inc., 390 U.S. 459, 88 S.Ct. 1140, 1968 A.M.C. 885 (1968); O'Keeffe v. Aerojet-General Shipyards, Inc., 404 U.S. 254, 92 S.Ct. 405, 1972 A.M.C. 34 (1971), rehearing denied 404 U.S. 1053, 92 S.Ct. 702, conformed to 453 F.2d 1363 (5 Cir. 1972) (holding that a Deputy Commissioner could reopen a case under § 922 even after his original denial of the claim had become "final" under 921).

**292.** 460 F.2d 1241, 1972 A.M.C. 1612 (5th Cir. 1972).

"The Deputy Commissioner has accepted the palpably false testimony of the thoroughly impeached claimant in preference to the testimony of unimpeached disinterested witnesses.

"It is the Court's belief that claimant has demonstrated he is unworthy of belief and that his testimony is entitled to no weight. . . . The claimant was simply enmeshed in the web of his own deceit."

However, the District Court

"refused to set aside the award since, given the credibility choice which the Deputy Commissioner had made, and which was *exclusively* within his province to make, there was substantial evidence in the record as a whole to support the Deputy Commissioner's finding. . . ." [293]

A panel of the Fifth Circuit commented, per curiam:

"The District Court's holding correctly applied the law." [294]

## Coverage of LHCA—I: Its Territorial Application and Relationship with State Compensation Acts

§ 6–48. The Supreme Court's refusal, on constitutional grounds, to allow state compensation systems to cover injuries to maritime workers which occurred on navigable waters [295] drove Congress to enact LHCA in 1927. Supreme Court decisions during the 1920's had vaguely suggested the approximate location of the line beyond which state compensation systems could not constitutionally operate. The apparent intention of the Congress was to confine the operation of the Federal Act to the federal or maritime side of the Supreme Court's line; up to that line the State Acts were to continue in full force and effect. That is to say, Congress (apparently) aimed not at the broadest possible coverage (up to the full limits of its own constitutional powers) but at the narrowest possible coverage (to provide a federal compensation system only for those maritime workers who, according to the Supreme Court, could not be covered by state compensation systems). The draftsmen of the 1927 LHCA therefore wrote into the statute limitations on its territorial coverage designed to achieve that end.[296] The 1972 amendments to LHCA have greatly

293. Italics in original; footnote omitted.

294. Other examples of this state of the law are Atlantic & Gulf Stevedores, Inc. v. Neuman, 440 F.2d 908, 1971 A.M.C. 1125 (5th Cir. 1971); Continental Ins. Co. v. Byrne, 471 F.2d 257, 1972 A.M.C. 1027 (7th Cir. 1972). For a rare example of a Deputy Commissioner being reversed, see Army and Air Force Exchange Service v. Hanson, 360 F.Supp. 258 (D.Hawaii, 1970) permanently enjoining the Deputy Commissioner from enforcing an award, on the ground that the claimant was not covered by LHCA under the provisions of the Defense Bases Act, see note 290 *supra*.

295. See § 6–45 *supra*.

296. The draftsman also limited the statutory coverage with respect to the types of employment covered. The employment limitations, under the 1927 Act and the 1972 amendments, will be discussed § 6–51 *infra*.

broadened the Act's territorial coverage (perhaps up to the full limits of Congressional power). The course of decision under the 1927 Act may well influence the judicial construction of the 1972 amendments. We shall, therefore, review that sometimes astonishing course of decision before passing to the 1972 amendments.

### The 1927 Act (Herein of "Maritime but Local" and "the Twilight Zone")

**§ 6–49.** The 1927 Act provided (§ 903[a]):

> "Compensation shall be payable under this chapter in respect of disability or death of an employee, but only if the disability or death results from an injury occurring upon the navigable waters of the United States (including any dry dock) and if recovery for the disability or death through workmen's compensation proceedings may not validly be provided by State law. . . ."

The provision quoted limited the coverage of LHCA to injuries (1) which occur on navigable waters as to which (2) "recovery . . . may not validly be provided by State law." At first blush the "may not validly be provided" limitation sounds like a meaningless reiteration of the "navigable waters" limitation. For many years, however, most people thought that "may not validly be provided" meant that some injuries, even though they occurred on navigable waters, were beyond the coverage of LHCA and thus within the exclusive coverage of some State statute. To understand why most people so construed "may not validly be provided", we must go back to a couple of pre-LHCA (but post-Jensen) Supreme Court cases.

In Western Fuel Co. v. Garcia [297] Souza, a longshoreman, had been instantly killed in an accident aboard the ship which he was unloading. His administrator claimed under the California Compensation Act and an award was made in favor of his widow and children. On May 21, 1917, while the case was pending in the California courts, the United States Supreme Court decided Jensen. On the following August 6, a year and a day after Souza's death, the California Supreme Court annulled the award presumably because of Jensen.[298] The administrator promptly began an in personam suit in admiralty to recover damages for wrongful death. The California wrongful death statute had a one-year statute of limitations. When the admiralty case came to the United States Supreme Court, the holding was that the California wrongful death statute of limitations barred the action. Justice McReynolds, author of the Jensen opinion and its only true expounder, writing in Garcia for a unanimous Court, described "the subject" of the Garcia litigation (i. e.,

297. 257 U.S. 233, 42 S.Ct. 89 (1921).

298. There appears to have been no California report of the Garcia case. In a case decided somewhat later the same year the California Court annulled another compensation award in the light of Jensen, Tallac Co. v. Pillsbury, 176 Cal. 236, 168 P. 17 (1917).

a wrongful death action brought in an admiralty court under a state wrongful death statute [299]) as "maritime and local." Since "the subject", although maritime, was nevertheless local, it was not within the Jensen national uniformity principle.[300] Presumably the reason why the four Justices who had dissented from the entire line of Jensen cases concurred in Garcia was that they were willing to overlook the equities of the later case and the harshness of the decision in return for the apparent retreat of the Jensen majority from the extreme consequences of the "national uniformity" principle.

Garcia did not mean that an award for the death claim could have been made under the California Compensation Act: the decedent in Garcia had been a longshoreman killed on the ship he was unloading; thus the Garcia facts were identical with the Jensen facts. However, in Grant-Smith-Porter Ship Co. v. Rohde [301] the "maritime but local" theory of Garcia was used to support the conclusion that a maritime worker (not a longshoreman) injured on navigable waters within the State of Oregon could not bring an action against his employer in admiralty for a maritime tort but was restricted to his rights under the Oregon Compensation Act.[302] In Rohde as in Garcia Justice McReynolds wrote the opinion for a unanimous Court.[303]

The "may not validly be provided by state law" limitation in LHCA § 903(a) was generally—indeed, universally—taken to have built the Garcia-Rohde "maritime but local" category into the Act's coverage. That is, a worker like Rohde not only could not sue in admiralty; he could not claim federal compensation under LHCA either; he was restricted for all purposes to his rights under the relevant state compensation act. On the other hand, a claim for the injury or death of a worker like the decedent in Jensen (or, for that matter, Garcia) could be made only under LHCA, since the application of a state compensation act to such workers was, per Jensen, unconstitutional. And, per Garcia, a claimant who elected to pursue the wrong remedy could be time-barred from getting any relief at all. Finally, only a soothsayer with a crystal ball could tell which claimants were on the state side of the line ("maritime but local") and

299. On admiralty wrongful death actions under state statutes, see § 6–29 *et seq. supra.*

300. A little more than a year before Garcia, the Court had held in Union Fish Co. v. Erickson, 248 U.S. 308, 39 S.Ct. 112 (1919), that, under Jensen, the California Statute of Frauds could not be applied in an admiralty action on an oral contract. The Garcia opinion did not cite Erickson.

301. 257 U.S. 469, 42 S.Ct. 157 (1922).

302. Rohde, a carpenter, was injured while working on the construction of a bulkhead on a partially completed vessel lying at a dock in the Willamette River. Since a contract to build a new ship has traditionally been considered nonmaritime (see Chapter I, § 1–10) Rohde's employment was also "nonmaritime" in a technical sense.

303. There are indications that the Court, despite its unanimity, was troubled by the two cases. In 1921 the Court twice heard oral argument in Garcia before deciding the case. Rohde had been argued to the Court in December, 1920 (before either of the arguments in Garcia) but the decision was not announced until January, 1922 (after Garcia had been decided).

which were on the federal side ("maritime and national"). For a decade and a half "maritime but local" was one of the most flourishing, as it was surely one of the most depressing, branches of federal jurisprudence.

In Davis v. Department of Labor and Industries of Washington [304] the Supreme Court, having evidently come to the conclusion that the situation was intolerable, in effect abolished "maritime but local" but chose to do so in a way which guaranteed that the next stage of the debate would be marked by even more confusion. In Davis the decedent had been drowned while working on a barge moored in the Snohomish River; the job on which he had been employed was the dismantling of an abandoned drawbridge over the river and, at the time of his death, he was engaged in cutting into proper lengths pieces of steel as they were lowered from the bridge to the barge. The decedent's representative elected, not unreasonably, to claim under the Washington Compensation Act; the claim was, however, denied and the denial was affirmed by the Supreme Court of Washington on the ground that the decedent's work was "like" that of a longshoreman employed in a loading operation so that, under Jensen, the claim could be brought only under LHCA. The Supreme Court granted certiorari and reversed.

Justice Black's majority opinion reviewed the confusion that had developed in the "maritime but local" case law and the resulting injustice both to injured workers and their employers. The confusion and injustice were rooted in the Jensen doctrine but it was no longer possible to effect a cure simply by overruling Jensen. The solution adopted by the majority was to announce the existence of a "twilight zone" within which "persons such as the decedent [in Davis]" were included. Justice Black did not explain how the majority thought the twilight zone was supposed to work, beyond the obvious point that the State of Washington was being directed to consider and adjudicate the Davis claim even if the decedent had been on the Jensen side of the Supreme Court's line. Both Justice Frankfurter, concurring, and Chief Justice Stone, dissenting, thought he meant that the claim could have been brought either under the state act or under LHCA and that a deputy commissioner who had rejected the federal claim would have been reversed just as his state counterpart was reversed in the actual case. By parity of reasoning, both the deputy commissioner and his state counterpart would have been affirmed if they had made awards.[305] Such a solution, said the Chief Justice, "can

304. 317 U.S. 249, 63 S.Ct. 225, 1942 A.M.C. 1653 (1942). Justice Black's majority opinion contained a representative selection of the case law from the "maritime but local" period.

305. That reading of the "twilight zone" theory seemed to be supported by a case which the Court had decided the previous year, Parker v. Motor Boat Sales, Inc., 314 U.S. 244, 62 S.Ct. 221, 1942 A.M.C. 1 (1941). In that case the Court, reversing the Fourth Circuit, had approved an LHCA award on a set of facts which might have served as a textbook illustration of "maritime but local" (a shore-based worker, who had no maritime duties, had been drowned when he went along on a test-run of an outboard motor boat to serve as lookout for the pilot).

hardly be deemed to be within judicial competence" and was "not permissible" in the light of the fact that the Court was dealing with statutes which declared themselves to be mutually exclusive. Justice Frankfurter conceded that the solution contained a degree of "theoretic illogic" but nevertheless concurred, no doubt because the demands of justice, in this instance, outweighed the demands of reason.

Twenty years after Davis the majority of the Court announced in Calbeck v. Travelers Ins. Co.[306] a startling interpretation of the "may not validly be provided by state law" limitation. If the 1962 interpretation had been announced in 1927, all concerned would have been spared much grief and sorrow. Announcement of the new interpretation in 1962 seems to have accomplished nothing that could not have been accomplished under twilight zone theory as that theory had been explicated by the Court in a series of per curiam opinions during the 1940's and 1950's. Justice Brennan's majority opinion in Calbeck did succeed in provoking an exceptionally bitter dissent from Justice Stewart which Justice Harlan joined as well as the almost universal condemnation of the commentators. After Calbeck things were much as they had been before.

Two cases which presented almost identical facts were consolidated and heard together in Calbeck. In both cases welders had been injured on navigable waters while working on new ships under construction. That employment on new ship construction was within the "maritime but local" exception to Jensen had been undoubted since the Court's 1922 decision in Grant-Smith-Porter Ship Co. v. Rohde;[307] thus the relevant state compensation acts could "validly" have covered the injured welders. The pre-Calbeck twilight zone cases, however, seemed to leave little room for doubt that the injured welders could equally well have elected to pursue their federal remedy under LHCA. In pre-twilight zone days repair work on a completed vessel had been as firmly situated on the federal (or Jensen) side of the line as work on new construction had been, under Rohde, on the state (or maritime but local) side. Nevertheless, following Davis, the Supreme Court had held that repair work on a completed vessel was within the twilight zone, with the result that the state compensation commission was required to make an award in such a case if the injured worker elected to pursue his state remedy.[308] By parity of reasoning, it would seem that work on new ship construction would, like repair work, lie within the twilight zone, so that the injured welders in Calbeck could pursue their federal remedy if they so desired. In fact they made the federal election; the deputy commissioners made awards which were affirmed on appeal to the District

**306.** 370 U.S. 114, 82 S.Ct. 1196, 1962 A.M.C. 1413 (1962).

**307.** The Rohde case is discussed text following note 301 *supra*.

**308.** Bethlehem Steel Co. v. Moore, 335 U.S. 874, 69 S.Ct. 239 (1948) (affirming the Massachusetts Court); Baskin v. Industrial Accident Commission, 338 U.S. 854, 70 S.Ct. 99 (1949) (reversing the California Court), see further Kaiser Co., Inc. v. Baskin, 340 U.S. 886, 71 S.Ct. 208 (1950).

Court; the Fifth Circuit, which had never been enthusiastic about the twilight zone, reversed; the Supreme Court granted certiorari.

Presumably no one would have quarreled with the Calbeck majority if it had followed the Court's past practice and reversed the Fifth Circuit per curiam with a brief reference to the twilight zone cases. Instead of doing that, Justice Brennan undertook to demonstrate, through a painstaking review of the legislative history of LHCA, that Congress had never intended to incorporate the Court's "maritime but local" theory by the "may not validly be provided by state law" limitation but had instead meant that LHCA should cover all employment-related injuries which occurred on navigable waters. "Our previous decisions under the Act," wrote Justice Brennan, proceeding to review them, "are entirely consistent with our conclusion." It was no doubt that disingenuous comment which provoked the wrath of the dissenting Justices and most of the commentators. Justice Brennan's review of the legislative history had made a plausible, even a strong, case for the argument that no one in the 1927 Congress or on its relevant committees had the faintest idea what "may not validly be provided by state law" meant, so that the phrase could perfectly well be taken as merely a repetition of the "navigable waters" limitation. Most people, however, found it hard to stomach the further suggestion that the Court had, since 1927, consistently so construed the statute.[309]

Calbeck would have been a significant case if Justice Brennan's opinion could fairly have been read to mean that the twilight zone had been abolished, with the result that LHCA provided the exclusive remedy with respect to all injuries on navigable waters. There was, however, nothing in Justice Brennan's opinion to support such a reading; on the contrary he reviewed the twilight zone cases from Davis on at length and with every indication of approval. It is fair to say that the post-Calbeck consensus came to be that the twilight zone—taking that phrase to mean that there existed an area of concurrent state and federal jurisdiction over injuries on navigable waters—had not been affected by anything in Calbeck.[310]

309. Robertson, Admiralty and Federalism (1970), 214 *et seq.*, 304 *et seq.* vigorously defends Justice Brennan's position, praying in aid the techniques of symbolic logic. Professor Robertson collects, at p. 304 *et seq.*, the many attacks on the Calbeck opinion (which mostly deplored not the result but the judicial technique employed to arrive at the result).

310. See 3 Larson, note 264 *supra*, § 89.40 for an elaborate discussion and a collection of cases. Robinson, Admiralty and Federalism (1970), 212 *et seq.*, seems to accept this reading of Calbeck. In Nations v. Morris, 483 F.2d 577, 582, 1973 A.M.C. 1413, 1418 (5th Cir. 1973), Judge Brown, after reviewing the course of decision from Jensen on, commented that in Calbeck "the Supreme Court made it clear that there existed an area in which both state and federal compensation systems were competent to provide a remedy. Appellant would have us describe this as a sphere of 'concurrent jurisdiction'. [We have] referred to it as 'the doctrine of the last chance' [citing Mike Hooks, Inc. v. Pena, 313 F.2d 696, 1963 A.M.C. 355 (5th Cir. 1963)]." Held, that an accident which occurred on an oil-drilling platform in the Gulf of Mexico 40 miles from the Louisiana coast was beyond the twilight zone.

A possible reading of Calbeck was that Congress had intended the coverage of LHCA to be coextensive with the limits of admiralty jurisdiction. If that was what Calbeck meant, it should follow that LHCA awards were to be made with respect to injuries which occurred on piers and other land areas; the seaman's right to recover under the Jones Act and under maritime law had long since been extended to cover injuries which occurred on land.[311] That reading of Calbeck seemed to be supported by one of the earlier twilight zone cases, Avondale Marine Ways, Inc. v. Henderson.[312] In that case the Fifth Circuit had approved LHCA awards made with respect to deaths caused by the explosion of a barge which had been drawn up on a "marine railway" four hundred feet from the shore line. The Fifth Circuit's theory had been that a marine railway was a "dry dock" and thus within the express coverage of § 903(a).[313] The majority of the Supreme Court affirmed per curiam, citing the twilight zone cases; their citation seemed to mean that the LHCA awards were proper whether or not a marine railway is a dry dock. However, in Nacirema Operating Company, Inc. v. Johnson,[314] the newly emerging majority of the Court rejected the idea that either Calbeck or the 1948 Extension of Admiralty Jurisdiction Act[315] meant that the coverage of LHCA should be construed to "coincide with the limits of admiralty jurisdiction . . . " Justice White observed:

> "While we have no doubt that Congress had the power [to make the coverage of LHCA 'coincide' with the limits of the jurisdiction], the plain fact is that it chose instead the line in Jensen separating water from land at the edge of the pier. The invitation to move that line landward must be addressed to Congress and not to this Court."[316]

Wherefore, the Fourth Circuit, which had concluded that pier injuries to longshoremen were covered by LHCA, was reversed. The surviving members of the Calbeck majority (Justices Black, Douglas and Brennan) dissented in Nacirema.

### The 1972 Amendments

**§ 6–50.** In 1972 the Congress, accepting the suggestion which Justice White had thrown out in his Nacirema opinion,[317] rewrote the preamble to § 903(a) to read as follows:

> "Compensation shall be payable under this chapter in respect of disability or death of an employee, but only if the

311. See § 6–8 *supra* (maintenance and cure); § 6–21, note 116 *supra* (Jones Act); § 6–44, note 251f *supra* (unseaworthiness).

312. 346 U.S. 366, 74 S.Ct. 100, 1953 A.M.C. 1990 (1953).

313. The relevant provision of § 903(a) is quoted in the text at the beginning of this section.

314. 396 U.S. 212, 90 S.Ct. 347, 1969 A.M.C. 1967 (1969).

315. On the 1948 Act, see Chapter VII, § 7–17.

316. 396 U.S. at p. 223–224, 90 S.Ct. 353, 354, 1969 A.M.C. at p. 1976.

317. Text at note 316 *supra*.

disability or death results from an injury occurring upon the navigable waters of the United States (including any adjoining pier, wharf, dry dock, terminal, building way, marine railway, or other adjoining area customarily used by an employer in loading, unloading, repairing, or building a vessel.)"

LHCA has clearly crossed the Jensen line and gone ashore. How far it has gone beyond the water's edge will not be known until the Supreme Court has construed the statutory language. It seems clear enough that the piers, wharves, dry docks, terminals, building ways and marine railways which are referred to must themselves "adjoin" navigable waters. "Adjoin" presumably means something like "border on" or "have direct access to" navigable waters; all the facilities mentioned, with the possible exception of "terminals," seem to meet that linguistic test. It is less clear whether the "adjoining area[s] customarily used . . . in loading, unloading, repairing, or building a vessel" [318] must themselves "adjoin" navigable waters or whether it is sufficient that they "adjoin" piers, wharves, dry docks and so on. It may be assumed that the intent of the Congressional draftsman was to cover all employment-related injuries suffered by workers engaged in the specified activities. If that assumption is correct, "adjoin" should be broadly, not narrowly, construed; the essential test should be whether the injury occurred in the course of maritime employment and not on how close the situs of the injury was to the water's edge. Even on the level of linguistic analysis, the inclusion of "terminal[s]" in the first of the two lists may be thought to favor the broader construction of "adjoin."

A more serious problem for the Supreme Court will be whether LHCA, within its expanded territorial limits, has become the injured worker's exclusive compensation remedy or whether concurrent state and federal jurisdiction is to be recognized (1) up to the water's edge (or Jensen line) or (2) up to the limits of the pre-1972 "twilight zone" which covered injuries on navigable waters.

There is a sentence in the House Committee Report on the amendments which can be read to suggest that LHCA was to become the exclusive compensation remedy up to the new territorial limits. The Report points out that benefits for permanent total disability payable under LHCA, as amended, will be greater than benefits payable under State compensation acts. The Report then continues:

"It is apparent that if the Federal benefit structure embodied in Committee bill is enacted, there would be a substantial disparity in benefits payable to a permanently disabled longshoreman, depending on which side of the water's

318. On the extension of the LHCA coverage to include ship repair and construction, see § 6–51 *infra*.

> edge the accident occurred, *if State laws are permitted to continue to apply to injuries occurring on land.*" [319]

It may not be entirely clear that the offhand reference to state laws in the passage quoted was meant to mean that LHCA was to displace state compensation acts with respect to the land injuries to be brought within the LHCA coverage. However, even if that was the intended meaning, the statement does not appear to be entitled to much weight. The part of the Committee Report which is devoted to the shoreward extension of LHCA coverage does not so much as mention the pre-1972 case law on "maritime but local" and the "twilight zone" which we have discussed in the preceding section. (By way of contrast the part of the Report which is devoted to the abolition of the recovery for unseaworthiness by LHCA workers goes into detail about the Supreme Court cases which are to be struck down.) It may be that the writer of the Report mistakenly assumed that the LHCA had always provided the exclusive compensation remedy for injuries which occurred on navigable waters and consequently assumed that it would also be exclusive with respect to the land injuries newly covered by the amendments.

On grounds of policy it seems undesirable in the highest degree to construe the amendments as having reintroduced the idea that the federal and state compensation systems are mutually exclusive. That had of course been the construction given to the 1927 Act under the "may not validly be provided by state law" limitation. That construction led to the horrors of the "maritime but local" period, from which the Supreme Court rescued us by the invention of the twilight zone in the 1942 Davis case. The twilight zone has its own difficulties, conceptual and otherwise, but, in practice it seems to have worked reasonably well. Indeed a theory of concurrent jurisdiction (whether it is called a twilight zone or something else) seems to be the only sensible way of dealing with state and federal statutes which meet at some vaguely defined line. If LHCA is taken to be exclusive up to its new territorial limits, injured maritime workers will have to guess at where the new line (piers, wharves and so on which "adjoin" navigable waters) is located just as such workers during the 1930's and early 1940's had to guess at where the "maritime but local" line was located. Eventually the Supreme Court would no doubt find the resulting situation intolerable, and would rescue us once again by establishing a new theory of concurrent jurisdiction. But there seems to be no good reason why we should be condemned to relive the depressing episode of the 1927–1942 "maritime but local" LHCA case law.

The case for construing the amendments to provide for concurrent state and federal jurisdiction is strengthened by the fact that § 903(a), as revised, no longer contains the "may not validly be pro-

319. House Report (Education and Labor Committee) No. 92–1441, 3 U.S.C.A. Congressional and Administrative News (92nd Congress—Second Session—1972) 4698, 4707. (Emphasis supplied.)

vided by state law" limitation. It was that limitation which led to the original conclusion that the new federal system and the existing state system were to be mutually exclusive. Its deletion leaves the statute blank on the relationship of the expanded federal system to the state system. A vague idea of "federal preemption" should not lead us to the unfortunate and unnecessary conclusion that the state statutes can now operate only up to (and never beyond) the newly demarcated federal line.

If we assume a concurrent jurisdiction (or twilight zone) solution to the problem, what are its limits to be? The pre-1972 twilight zone involved the seaward extension of the coverage of state statutes, not (at least after the Nacirema case [320]) the landward extension of the coverage of LHCA. If the only purpose of twilight zone theory is to make it unnecessary for claimants to guess at the precise location of an invisible line, that purpose will be served by locating the post-1972 twilight zone at the outer limits of the landward extension of LHCA. Under that approach workers injured at or near the "adjoining navigable waters" line should be entitled to claim under either the state or the federal act. We have already suggested that "adjoining" should be broadly construed with respect to claims under LHCA; adoption of a twilight zone approach would allow both the deputy commissioner and his state counterpart to operate on both sides of the line.

A case can easily be made for a much broader area of concurrent jurisdiction, which would run at least to the water's edge and even beyond. The only theory under which a state could not provide compensation for persons injured within its territory would be one of federal preemption under LHCA. That theory, as we have suggested, seems peculiarly inappropriate under these circumstances. If the federal statute is not taken to preempt the field, the area of concurrent jurisdiction runs at least to the water's edge. If the old "maritime but local" cases are still good law, the concurrent jurisdiction area would include injuries on navigable waters which might be said to "adjoin" the land. Nothing in the 1972 amendments or in the available legislative history indicates an intention to overrule or reject the maritime but local line of cases.

The broader the area of concurrent jurisdiction, the fewer the cases will be in which claimants guess wrong as to their remedy. The argument can also plausibly be made that the injured worker should be entitled to elect whichever of the two compensation systems affords him the greater recovery.[321] Even if benefits currently payable under LHCA are greater than benefits payable under state compensation acts, cases will arise in which it will be to a claimant's advantage to pursue his state remedy. There seems to be no good reason why he should not be allowed to do so.[322]

320. On the Nacirema case, see the text following note 314 *supra*.

321. See § 6–52 *infra*.

322. Watson, Broadened Coverage Under the LHWCA, 33 Louisiana L.Rev. 683, 694 *et seq.* (1973), an excellent review of the 1972 amendments, con-

## Coverage of LHCA—II: Types of Employment

**§ 6–51.** The 1927 Act excluded from LHCA coverage (1) "a master or member of a crew of any vessel" as well as "any person engaged by the master to load or unload or repair any small vessel under eighteen tons net" [323] and (2) "an officer or employee of the United States or any agency thereof or of any State or foreign government, or of any political subdivision thereof." [324] These exclusions were carried forward without change in the Act as amended in 1972.

Seamen (or their representatives) have always resisted, so far successfully, their inclusion within any compensation system, having preferred, with good reason, to retain their rights under the Jones Act and maritime law.[325] The exclusion of longshoremen and repairmen on small vessels when they are engaged directly by the master presumably reflected the thought that such employment did not involve any national interest and could therefore be left, without constitutional objection, to the state systems. Federal employees were excluded because they were covered by the Federal Employees Compensation Act.[326] Employees of States and of foreign governments were excluded perhaps for reasons of sovereign immunity or perhaps for no reason at all except that the LHCA draftsman preferred exclusion to inclusion.

The only one of the exclusionary provisions which has accounted for much litigation has been the exclusion of Jones Act seamen. Through the 1950's maritime workers whose duties were partly on shore and partly on navigable waters frequently sought to bring Jones Act actions against their employers.[327] The Supreme Court vacillated between a broad and a narrow construction of who was a Jones Act seaman and, at least during the 1950's, seemed to think that the question of seaman's status should always (or almost always) go to the jury. The Court, however, stopped short of constructing a twilight zone between Jones Act seamen and LHCA harborworkers, except to the extent that jury verdicts are themselves a sort of twilight zone.[328] There were fewer actions of this sort during the 1960's

cludes, as we have done, that the amendments should be construed to recognize an area of concurrent jurisdiction.

323. § 902(3) (definition of "employee") and § 903(a)(1).

324. § 903(a)(2).

325. On the opposition of the maritime unions to compensation systems, see Nogueira v. New York N. H. & H. R. Co., 281 U.S. 128, 50 S.Ct. 303, 1930 A.M.C. 763 (1930) (per Hughes, C. J.); Warner v. Goltra, 293 U.S. 155, 55 S. Ct. 46, 1934 A.M.C. 1436 (1934) (per Cardozo, J.); Hust v. Moore-McCormack Lines, Inc., 328 U.S. 707, 715, 66 S.Ct. 1218, 1222 (n. 17), 1946 A.M.C. 727, 733 (n. 17) (1946).

326. See note 23 *supra*.

327. These cases are reviewed in § 6–21 *supra*.

328. Railroad workers whose duties required them to work on car ferries over navigable waters could be trapped between their remedy under FELA (if they were railroad workers) and their LHCA compensation remedy (if they were injured on navigable waters in the course of maritime employment). See Pennsylvania R. Co. v.

after the Supreme Court had established the proposition that harbor workers who were not Jones Act seamen could recover for unseaworthiness under the maritime law, at least in actions against shipowners who were not their employers and, in some circumstances, against shipowners who were their employers.[329] Now that the 1972 amendments have stripped LHCA harbor workers of their right to recover under the unseaworthiness doctrine, we may see a revival of litigation in which harbor workers of various types claim to be Jones Act seamen or, at all events, entitled to recover full damages in a tort action under the maritime law.

The problem of which classes of workers were within the coverage of LHCA (apart from the classes expressly excluded) never, before the 1972 amendments, accounted for any litigation. The 1927 Act defined both the terms "employee" (§ 902(3)) and "employer" (§ 902(4)). The "employee" definition merely excluded Jones Act seamen as well as longshoremen engaged by the master to work on small vessels. The "employer" definition provided that the term meant "an employer any of whose employees are employed in maritime employment, in whole or in part, upon the navigable waters of the United States (including any dry dock)." The odd wording "maritime employment, in whole or in part" could, and no doubt would, have led to trouble except for the fact that it was linked with the "navigable waters" limitation. As we have explained in the preceding section, LHCA, before 1972, never crossed the Jensen line to go ashore. Workers who are not seamen but who nevertheless suffer injury on navigable waters are no doubt (or so the courts have been willing to assume) engaged in "maritime employment". There was litigation, referred to in the preceding paragraph, about whether such workers could recover under the Jones Act or FELA; no one seems to have doubted that they could recover under LHCA, provided only that the proof satisfied the "navigable waters" test.

This happy state of affairs may have come to an end with the 1972 amendments. Not only has LHCA gone ashore but, or so the legislative history suggests, only some types of workers injured within the new territorial limits of LHCA are meant to be covered. If that is so, we are threatened with a spate of LHCA litigation which will be at least as depressing as the 1927–1942 "maritime but local" litigation which preceded the invention of the twilight zone. We shall attempt to demonstrate that such a result need not follow from the amendments.

The revised "employee" definition retains the exclusionary language from the original definition but adds an affirmative statement:

O'Rourke, 344 U.S. 334, 73 S.Ct. 302, 1953 A.M.C. 237 (1953) (holding that such a worker was restricted to his LHCA compensation remedy and could not sue under FELA.) See further, Weiss v. Central R.R. Co. of New Jersey, 235 F.2d 309, 1956 A.M.C. 1473 (2d Cir. 1956) in which it was held, over a dissent, that a railroad employee who had occasional duties afloat was a Jones Act seaman. See the discussion § 6–7 *supra* of who are seamen entitled to recover maintenance and cure.

329. See § 6–53 *et seq. infra.*

"The term 'employee' means any person engaged in maritime employment, including any longshoreman or other person engaged in longshoring operations, and any harbor worker including a ship repairman, ship builder, and shipbreaker . . . ." The "employer" definition reads as it did in the original Act except that the concluding parenthetical reference to "any dry dock" has been expanded to encompass the Act's new territorial limits: "(including any adjoining pier, wharf, dry dock, terminal, building way, marine railway, or other adjoining areas customarily used by an employer in loading, unloading, repairing, or building a vessel)." The language between the parentheses is repeated in the coverage section, § 903.

The new statutory language can reasonably be read to mean that all persons who suffer employment-related injuries within the Act's expanded territorial limits are covered, provided only that they are employed by an employer "any of whose employees are employed in maritime employment [of the types specified], in whole or in part . . ." If the language is so read, and if a theory of concurrent jurisdiction is accepted for the reasons advanced in the preceding section, most maritime workers injured on or near navigable waters will be able to claim benefits under either LHCA or the relevant state compensation act.

Unfortunately, the House and Senate Committee Reports prepared to accompany the bills which incorporated the amendments suggest that only some types of workers are meant to be covered, even if they suffer employment-related injuries within the specified territorial limits, are employed by an employer who is engaged in the specified activities and are themselves injured in connection with those activities. According to identical passages in the Reports:

> "The Committee does not intend to cover employees who are not engaged in loading, unloading, repairing, or building a vessel, just because they are injured in an area adjoining navigable waters used for such activity. Thus, employees whose responsibility is only to pick up stored cargo for further trans-shipment would not be covered, nor would purely clerical employees whose jobs do not require them to participate in the loading or unloading of cargo. . . . Likewise the Committee has no intention of extending coverage under the Act to individuals who are not employed by a person who is an employer [as that term is defined in the Act]. Thus, an individual employed by a person none of whose employees work, in whole or in part, on navigable waters, is not covered even if injured on a pier adjoining navigable waters."[330]

Let us, arguendo, accept the reading of the coverage amendments suggested by the Committee Reports. Presumably any worker in-

330. The passage quoted appears in the House Report, note 319 *supra*, 3 U.S.C.A.Cong. and Adm.News (1972) 4698, 4708. The same passage appears in the Senate Report (Committee on Labor and Public Welfare), S.Rep.No. 1120—92d Cong., 2d Sess. (1972).

jured on navigable waters will continue to be covered (as he has been in the past) without any inquiry into what he was doing (or supposed to be doing) at the time of his injury. However, a worker injured on an "adjoining" land area will be covered only if he was "engaged in loading, unloading, repairing, or building a vessel." As examples of workers not covered (even though they are employed by an "employer") the Reports suggest "employees" whose responsibility is only to pick up stored cargo for further trans-shipment and "purely clerical employees" whose jobs do not require them to "participate" in loading, unloading (and, presumably, repair work and construction). The line which the Committee Reports evidently sought to draw was between workers who participate directly, or physically, in the specified activities and workers whose jobs require them to be in the same area but who (like the clerical workers) do not physically "participate" or who (like the truckers) can be thought of as only indirectly involved in the strictly maritime phase of the activity.

The almost infinite range of the conditions of waterfront employment has been detailed in thousands of cases. The line between direct, physical "participation" and indirect, non-physical "participation" will be not a whit easier to draw than the line between Jensen and "maritime but local" in the years before 1942. If the Deputy Commissioners faithfully try to carry out the policy suggested by the Committee Reports, they will have their work cut out for them. And claimants who seek to avail themselves of the liberalized LHCA benefits will have to be told—by the Deputy Commissioner, or by the newly established Benefits Review Board, or by the Circuit Courts of Appeals or by the Supreme Court—that their participation in, say, a waterfront explosion was not sufficiently direct or physical to satisfy the statutory test.

If the Committee Reports are taken as holy writ, the Supreme Court will, sooner or later, have to remedy the resulting injustice by inventing a new twilight zone. The Reports do not read as if they had been divinely inspired. As essays in statutory construction, they do not commend themselves. Apart from the gloss suggested by the Reports, the 1972 coverage amendments can fairly be read to cover all employment-related injuries which occur within the Act's territorial limits. And a female secretary who works in a terminal warehouse should qualify as an LHCA harbor worker in exactly the same way that a female hair-dresser in a cruise ship's beauty salon qualifies as a Jones Act seaman. The courts wisely decided, long ago, that, for the purpose of the Jones Act and the maritime law remedies, they would not distinguish between the deck hands and the waiters, bartenders, stewards, maids and hairdressers: going to sea was a sufficient participation in the risk to entitle the injured worker to his (or her) remedy. In the same way, the fact of waterfront employment should be taken to be a sufficient participation in the risk for the purpose of entitling the injured worker to claim LHCA benefits.[331]

331. The suggestion in the Committee Reports that employment by a statutory "employer" is a pre-condition of LHCA coverage is easier to defend, on

### The Problem of Successive Awards Under LHCA and State Compensation Statutes; the Effect of the Payment of Compensation Benefits on Damage Actions

§ 6–52. An injured worker who has received payments of benefits under a state compensation act may seek a second or supplemental recovery under LHCA. Or, having received LHCA benefits, he may seek a supplemental recovery under a state act. Or, having received compensation benefits, state or federal, he may seek to recover his full damages in an action against his employer under the Jones Act or under the general maritime law. Let us assume that whatever he has received from his initial source of payments will be credited against any supplemental award or damage recovery, thus eliminating, at least theoretically, any problem of double recovery. But does his initial election of one route bar him from subsequently trying his chances at the others? [332]

We may consider first the problem of a claim under LHCA after receipt of payments under a state compensation act. Prior to the effective date of the 1972 amendments, LHCA did not cover injuries on land; thus the problem arose only with respect to injuries on navigable waters within the limits of "maritime but local" and later of twilight zone theory. With the landward extension of LHCA coverage under the 1972 amendments, the problem will obviously arise over a much broader range.

In the two preceding sections we have suggested that, under the 1972 amendments, there should be concurrent state and federal jurisdiction both as to territorial coverage and as to coverage by types of employment. If such a concurrent jurisdiction solution is finally adopted, the present problem will present no difficulty. In dry land workmen's compensation law, the problem has long been a familiar one: it arises whenever two or more states have significant contacts with the enterprise or the employment relationship. Industrial Commission v. McCartin [333] has become the leading case. Broadly stated,

grounds of statutory construction, than the suggestion that employees of such an employer be segregated according to their degrees of "participation." Assume, however, that Corporation A employs longshoremen to unload cargo on a wharf owned by Corporation B and to store it in a terminal warehouse owned by Corporation C. (Corporations A, B, and C may or may not all be wholly owned subsidiaries of a parent company.) If employees of Corporations B and C are injured in the course of the unloading operation, should they not be held to be within the LHCA coverage?

332. The matters briefly rehearsed in this section are excellently treated at length in 3 Larson, Workmen's Compensation, note 264 *supra*, § 89.50 *et seq.*, § 90.50 *et seq.* See also Larson, The Conflict of Laws Problem Between the Longshoremen's Act and State Workmen's Compensation Acts, 45 S.Cal.L.Rev. 699 (1972). We have generally followed Professor Larson's discussion; an acknowledgment of indebtedness is in order. The Larson discussion had not, at the time of writing this section, been revised to consider the possible effects of the 1972 LHCA amendments on these issues.

333. 330 U.S. 622, 67 S.Ct. 886 (1947).

the McCartin rule is that the injured worker may proceed under whichever statute seems to promise him the greater recovery and that his initial election to proceed under the State A statute does not bar him from subsequently proceeding under the State B statute: "[F]or all practical purposes," says Larson, "successive awards are now sanctioned." [334] The concurrent jurisdiction solution to the enigma of the relationship between LHCA and a state compensation act would lead to the adoption of the McCartin rule on successive awards. Employers of maritime workers would have to insure both under LHCA and the state act to protect themselves against damage suits which the typical compensation act authorizes against non-complying employers (who, in such suits, are stripped of their common law defenses).[335] According to Larson, "The assumption of the necessary insurance coverage is neither inconvenient nor unduly onerous." [335a]

If (or to the extent that) a concurrent jurisdiction solution is not adopted, the problem will be bothersome and the case law results, if the future can be judged by the past, will be erratic. During the pre-twilight zone era (1927–1942) LHCA and state compensation acts were thought to be mutually exclusive. Under that approach it would seem that receipt of state benefits would necessarily bar later LHCA proceedings; nevertheless there were cases decided during that period by respectable courts which, on one theory or another, allowed the later LHCA proceeding.[335b] It should be borne in mind that a formal award is not a pre-requisite for the payment of compensation benefits; the more informal the state compensation proceedings may have been, the weaker the argument that a subsequent LHCA proceeding should be barred on theories of election, res judicata or what have you. After the invention of the twilight zone in 1942, it would seem that the claimant's chances for success in a LHCA proceeding after having already received state benefits should have been substantially improved.[335c] After Calbeck v. Travelers' Insurance Company [335d] the

334. 3 Larson, *supra* note 332, § 85.20.

335. In Hahn v. Ross Island Sand & Gravel Co., 358 U.S. 272, 79 S.Ct. 266, 1959 A.M.C. 570 (1959), the majority of the Supreme Court held that, under twilight zone theory, a worker injured on navigable waters could bring such a suit against his employer who had elected not to insure under the Oregon compensation act (although the employer had insured under LHCA).

335a. 3 Larson, *supra* note 332, § 89.70, n. 85 and the accompanying text.

335b. *See, e. g.*, Kibaudeaux v. Standard Dredging Co., 81 F.2d 670, 1936 A.M.C. 254 (5th Cir. 1936); Great Lakes & Dredge Dock Co. v. Brown, 47 F.2d 265, 1931 A.M.C. 1159 (N.D. Ill.1930).

335c. *See, e. g.*, Newport News Shipbuilding & Dry Dock Co. v. O'Hearne, 192 F.2d 968 (4th Cir. 1951); Western Boat Building Co. v. O'Leary, 198 F.2d 409, 1952 A.M.C. 1639 (9th Cir. 1952), both upholding LHCA awards after prior receipt of state benefits.

335d. Calbeck is discussed § 6–49 *supra*, text following note 306. One of the claimants whose appeals had been consolidated in Calbeck had indeed received benefits paid under the Louisiana compensation act before he filed his LHCA claim. Justice Brennan dealt with this point at the end of his Calbeck opinion: "We hold that the acceptance of the payments does not constitute an election of the remedy under state law precluding recovery under the Longshoremen's Act. Nothing in the statute requires a contrary

claimant's chances for success in the LHCA proceeding would seem to have approached 100%. However, five years after Calbeck, the Fifth Circuit held, in Shea v. Texas Employers' Insurance Association,[335e] that an award under the Texas compensation act barred a subsequent LHCA claim. The Shea case is a sufficient illustration of the chanciness of the case law results.

To the extent that a theory of mutual exclusivity between LHCA (as amended in 1972) and state compensation acts is adopted, we shall have to relive the 1927–1942 period. The case law of that period suggests that, whatever the theoretical implication of a mutual exclusivity theory may be, courts sympathetic to a claimant's second try will find a way to allow it. The case law down through the post-Calbeck period also suggests that courts unsympathetic to the second try will find a way to bar it. Perhaps we should reflect on the proposition that: A throw of the dice will never abolish chance.

Most of what we have said about the state benefit—LHCA claim sequence applies to the reverse situation in which after receipt of LHCA benefits, a worker makes a claim under a state statute. There have never been a great many cases of this type since the LHCA benefit schedules have typically been higher than the corresponding state schedules. With the further increase in LHCA benefits under the 1972 amendments, the situation will presumably arise even less frequently than it has in the past.

Adoption of the concurrent jurisdiction solution will of course settle the problem: under the McCartin rule receipt of LHCA benefits would have no effect on the claimant's subsequent state proceeding. To the extent that a mutual exclusivity approach prevails, claimants will have to suffer the chanciness of the pre-1972 case law. It may be that in pre-twilight zone or at least in pre-Calbeck days there were conceptual difficulties in the LHCA—state act sequence which did not present themselves in the more frequently litigated state act—LHCA sequence. Initial payment of LHCA benefits would have meant that there had been a federal decision, on some level, that the federal act applied (which was also a decision that the state act could not "validly" apply). On what might be called a "federal supremacy" theory, the federal decision might have been thought entitled to greater weight than the corresponding state decision in the reverse sequence. However, the federal supremacy idea never became clearly articulated and to the extent that twilight zone theory and the Calbeck case had adopted a concurrent jurisdiction approach, became less

result. And we agree that the circumstances do not support a finding of a binding election to look solely to the state law for recovery." Justice Brennan emphasized the fact that the employer had made the payments under the Louisiana act voluntarily and apparently without an administrative hearing or a formal award. In support of his conclusion he cited the O'Hearne and O'Leary cases note 335c *supra*, as well as Massachusetts Bonding & Insurance Co. v. Lawson, 149 F.2d 853 (5th Cir. 1945).

335e. 382 F.2d 16, 1968 A.M.C. 527 (5th Cir. 1967). The case is analyzed and disapproved in 3 Larson, *supra* note 332, § 89.52.

cogent than it might have been before 1942 (twilight zone) or 1962 (Calbeck). A New Jersey case decided in the early 1950's held that receipt of LHCA benefits barred a later resort to the state act.[335f] A second New Jersey case, decided fifteen years later, held that benefits had been properly awarded under the New Jersey act even though the claimant had earlier received LHCA benefits.[335g] The sequence of New Jersey cases is of course encouraging from a claimant's point of view; it would be unwise for the claimant's counsel to assume that the 1967 New Jersey case means that his client is necessarily home free (even in New Jersey).

An injured worker who has received compensation benefits, state or federal, may subsequently bring a damage action against his employer under the Jones Act.[335h] The type of worker involved will typically be an employee who works part of the time on land and part of the time on such floating structures as dredges, barges and comparable "vessels"—that is someone whose duties put him at or near the border line between harbor worker and seaman.[335i] The Supreme Court has not constructed a twilight zone between the Jones Act (or FELA) and the compensation acts.[335j] LHCA, both as originally enacted in 1927 and as amended in 1972, expressly excludes Jones Act seamen ("a master or member of a crew of any vessel") from its coverage. So long as the Jensen case stands, a state compensation act could not constitutionally apply to a seaman. Thus there is a gulf set between the compensation remedy and the Jones Act remedy. Neither an LHCA deputy commissioner nor a state commissioner could award compensation without making a finding that the claimant was not a Jones Act seaman. Such a finding, unless reversed on appeal, would seem to bar a subsequent Jones Act action on obvious grounds of res judicata and collateral estoppel.

There are, however, a great many cases in which plaintiffs who have received compensation payments have been allowed to bring action under the Jones Act. (The statement that the Jones Act action will be "allowed" does not, of course, mean that the Jones Act plaintiff will necessarily win. Compensation is a no-fault remedy; recovery

**335f.** Dunleavy v. Tietjen & Lang Dry Docks, 17 N.J.Super. 76, 85 A.2d 343 (Hudson County Court, 1951), affirmed 20 N.J.Super. 486, 90 A.2d 84 (App. Div.1952), certiorari denied 10 N.J. 343, 91 A.2d 448 (1952).

**335g.** Hansen v. Perth Amboy Dry Dock Co., 48 N.J. 389, 226 A.2d 4 (1967).

**335h.** In the normal course of events Jones Act actions may be, or in fact have been, brought only by employees against their employers. See § 6–21(a) *supra*. On the harbor worker's pre-1972 action against a shipowner who is not his employer under the maritime law doctrine of unseaworthiness, see § 6–53 *et seq. infra*. The 1972 LHCA amendments abolished the harbor worker's unseaworthiness action but preserved his negligence action "against [the] vessel" (§ 905(b)). The harbor worker's § 905(b) action is discussed § 6–57 *infra*.

**335i.** On who are Jones Act seamen, see § 6–21 *supra*.

**335j.** See text following note 327 *supra* and note 328. Larson, note 332 *supra*, § 90.41 *et seq.* argues persuasively that a Jones Act twilight zone could, and should, be constructed.

under the Jones Act requires proof of negligence chargeable to the defendant.)[335k] The payments may have been made without the Jones Act plaintiff's ever having filed a compensation claim: in that situation, according to Larson, it is "universally accepted" that the Jones Act action is not barred.[335l] Or the payments may have been made without a formal award having been entered even though the Jones Act plaintiff had filed a compensation claim: a "substantial majority" of the cases hold that the Jones Act action is not barred.[335m] Even the payment of benefits pursuant to a formal award in a contested proceeding is not necessarily fatal to the Jones Act action. The courts have shown themselves receptive to the argument that the compensation award may have been made without a proper adjudication of the claimant's status as harbor worker or seaman.[335n] But the plaintiff who attempts to bring a Jones Act action following a compensation award in a contested proceeding may find himself barred in a court which takes res judicata and collateral estoppel seriously.[335o]

On grounds of policy the argument can be plausibly advanced that the injured worker should be entitled to try for his Jones Act recovery no matter how properly his status as a non-seaman may have been adjudicated in a contested compensation proceeding. No problem of double recovery is involved: the compensation payments will be routinely deducted from the damage recovery if the Jones Act action is successful. How is an injured worker, who is arguably a Jones Act seaman, supposed to live and support his family during the months or years which will elapse before his damage recovery, if his Jones Act action is successful, becomes collectible? The provision of compensation during this period would serve the function of the traditional maritime remedy of maintenance and cure (which has always been thought of as supplemental to the damage recovery). It is only because of a series of accidents in our legal history that the payment of medical expenses and a living allowance to an injured worker is thought to be entirely consistent with his damage recovery if the payment is called maintenance and cure but inconsistent with the damage recovery if it is called compensation. It may be that such considerations have inarticulately influenced the course of decision: the courts, while theoretically recognizing the problems of res judicata and col-

**335k.** On the standards of negligence which have evolved in the Jones Act case law, see § 6–34 *et seq. supra.*

**335*l*.** 3 Larson, note 332 *supra*, § 90.51 (collecting cases). In Tipton v. Socony Mobil Co., 375 U.S. 34, 84 S.Ct. 1, 1963 A.M.C. 2276 (1963) it was held reversible error to let a Jones Act jury know that the plaintiff had received LHCA benefits.

**335m.** 3 Larson, *loc. cit. supra* note 335*l* (collecting cases).

**335n.** Illustrative cases are Biggs v. Norfolk Dredging Co., 360 F.2d 360, 1966 A.M.C. 578 (4th Cir. 1966); Boatel, Inc. v. Delamore, 379 F.2d 850, 1968 A.M.C. 2051 (5th Cir. 1967); Toland v. Atlantic Gahagan Joint Venture Dredge, # 1, 57 N.J. 205, 271 A.2d 2 (1970). As Larson, *loc. cit. supra* note 335*l*, puts it: "[N]o one has a right to demand that the same issue between the same parties be litigated and decided twice. This certainly does not mean that a person cannot demand that the issue be genuinely litigated and decided once."

**335*o*.** *See, e. g.*, Hagens v. United Fruit Co., 135 F.2d 842, 1943 A.M.C. 741 (2d Cir. 1943).

lateral estoppel which arise from the legal inconsistency of the two remedies, have shown a great deal of judicial ingenuity in escaping from the harsh conclusion that the worker's receipt of compensation benefits bars his Jones Act action.

The sequence of a Jones Act recovery followed by a compensation claim, state or federal, is more a theoretical than a real possibility. Not only will the Jones Act recovery have been in almost all cases, greater than any available compensation but the fact that the Jones Act plaintiff has been adjudicated to be a seaman conclusively entitles him to his continuing maintenance and cure.[335p] It is hard to see why a lawyer who has won a Jones Act case for his client would attempt to recover for subsequently incurred medical expenses by the compensation route instead of the maintenance and cure route.[335q] The sequence of an unsuccessful Jones Act action followed by a compensation claim raises quite different problems. If the Jones Act action failed because the plaintiff was found not to be a "seaman", that should help his compensation claim. If the Jones Act action failed because negligence had not been proved, that should be irrelevant to his no-fault compensation claim. Other reasons for failure of the Jones Act action can easily be hypothesized relating to the employment relationship, the fact of an employment-related injury or its situs and so on which would (or could) be relevant to the later compensation claim. To the extent that factors relevant to the compensation claim have been adjudicated in the Jones Act action, the problems of res judicata or collateral estoppel which arise do not seem to be theoretically different from those which arise in the compensation claim—Jones Act sequence which has already been discussed.[335r]

## The Harbor Worker's Recovery of Damages Outside the Compensation System—I: The Sieracki-Ryan Period (1946–1972)

**§ 6–53.** The Longshoremen's and Harbor Workers' Compensation Act (LHCA) of 1927 followed the state compensation acts in providing (1) that the employer's liability for compensation was to be "exclusive and in place of all other liability" to his injured worker (or his representative) (§ 905) but (2) that, if "some person other

**335p.** See note 55c *supra* for cases in which maintenance and cure awards have been made following Jones Act recoveries.

**335q.** Indeed our mentor, Professor Larson, after exhaustive research, discovered only one case which presented the problem "in principle," Jones v. Baton Rouge Marine Contractors, 127 So.2d 58 (La.App.1961), 3 Larson, note 332 *supra*, § 90.52, text following n. 30. In that case a federal district court had dismissed a Jones Act action; while an appeal from the dismissal was pending, the parties arrived at an out-of-court settlement for $2,000. The state court held that the Jones Act plaintiffs later claim for state compensation was barred. Larson vigorously criticizes the state court's opinion.

**335r.** The Fifth Circuit has taken the position that an unsuccessful Jones Act action never bars a subsequent compensation claim. See Teichman v. Loffland Brothers, 294 F.2d 175 (5th Cir. 1961), certiorari denied 368 U.S. 948, 82 S.Ct. 388 (1961); Boatel, Inc. v. Delamore, 379 F.2d 850, 1968 A.M.C. 2051 (5th Cir. 1967). Larson, *loc. cit. supra* note 335q, text following n. 19, comments that the cases relied on by the Court do not support so sweeping a proposition.

than the employer or a person or persons in his employ is liable in damages" with respect to the injury, then the person entitled to compensation may recover damages against "such third person" and need not elect between his right to compensation and his right to recover damages (§ 933[a]).[336] In Seas Shipping Company v. Sieracki [337] the Supreme Court held that a longshoreman could recover from a shipowner, who was not his employer, under the newly reformulated doctrine of unseaworthiness. Ten years later, in Ryan Stevedoring Company, Inc. v. Pan-Atlantic Steamship Corp.[338] the Court held that a shipowner who was liable to a longshoreman under Sieracki could recover over against the longshoreman's employer in an action for indemnity. By the late 1960's further elaborations of the Sieracki-Ryan sequence had led to the result that the longshoreman's employer had become, despite the exclusive liability provision of LHCA § 905 (or the corresponding provision of a state compensation act), ultimately liable for full damages in connection with injuries to his employees. In 1972 Congress added a new subsection (b) to § 905. Under § 905(b) LHCA workers may bring third party damage actions against ships for negligence but may not sue under the unseaworthiness doctrine; LHCA employers are not to be liable, "directly or indirectly" for any damages recovered in such negligence actions.[339]

The discussion of the harbor worker's damage action which appeared in the first edition of the treatise was written at the time when the Supreme Court was considering the Ryan case; it is the writer's memory that the text had to be hastily revised just before copy went to the printer to take account of the Ryan opinions. It is clear enough from hindsight that the writer was not equipped, during the spring of 1956, with a crystal ball in good working order. If the discussion had been rewritten at any time before the enactment of § 905(b) in 1972, there would have had to be elaborate consideration of the surprising course of the post-Ryan jurisprudence in which it often seemed that the authoritative solution of any problem merely served to reveal half a dozen new problems whose existence had not been previously suspected. The evident intention of the § 905(b) draftsman was to consign the thousands of Sieracki-Ryan harbor worker cases to the scrapheap. Abolishing the past is not as simple an oper-

336. On the background, see § 6–46 *supra*. The sections of LHCA, 44 Stat. 1424 (1927), 33 U.S.C.A. §§ 901–950, will be cited by their U.S.C.A. section numbers. The provision of § 933 that the injured worker (or his representative) need not elect between compensation and damages does not mean that he can get (or keep) both. In general, a worker who has received compensation benefits and then recovers damages from a third party must repay the amount received as compensation.

337. 328 U.S. 85, 66 S.Ct. 872, 1946 A.M.C. 698 (1946).

338. 350 U.S. 124, 76 S.Ct. 232, 1956 A.M.C. 9 (1956).

339. What we have referred to (§ 6–46 *supra*) as a political trade-off for the abolition of the harbor worker's unseaworthiness action was an increase in the compensation benefits payable under LHCA and an expansion of its coverage, both territorially and by categories of employment. The coverage amendments are discussed in §§ 6–50, 6–51 *supra*.

ation as the abolishers sometimes like to believe. It is much too early to tell whether the Sieracki-Ryan construct, although abolished, will continue to rule us from the grave. It is a fair guess that the world —even the world of the harbor worker's damage action—was not created afresh on November 27, 1972, effective date of § 905(b) and the other 1972 LHCA amendments.[340] We shall therefore begin our discussion with an overview of the end state of the Sieracki-Ryan case law before proceeding to an analysis of the radically new state of things dictated by § 905(b).[341]

## Harbor Workers as Seamen

**§ 6–54.** Except for the confused sequence of events which led to the enactment of LHCA in 1927, harborworkers would in all probability have become "seamen," entitled to all the rights of seamen under the maritime law and the Jones Act. In 1914 the Supreme Court held, in Atlantic Transport Company v. Imbrovek,[342] that there was admiralty jurisdiction over an action by a longshoreman who had been injured aboard ship against his employer, a stevedoring company. Imbrovek sued his employer (no compensation statute being applicable) for violation of the duty to provide him with a safe place to work. Under the celebrated propositions of The Osceola [343] seamen had a right to recover damages for injuries caused by unseaworthiness but not for those caused by negligence. The pleading in Imbrovek should no doubt be taken as invoking the unseaworthiness doctrine.[344] The defendant argued that loading and unloading a ship were not maritime operations, so that Imbrovek's ac-

340. No court has yet suggested that the 1972 amendments are to be applied retroactively to proceedings instituted before their effective date. It is not yet clear whether they will be applied to proceedings instituted after that date with respect to injuries suffered before that date. At all events, several years will elapse before the last Sieracki-Ryan cases have been finally disposed of. It is a reasonable assumption that the final (post-1972) stage of the Sieracki-Ryan case law will be influenced by, or cross-bred with, the developing § 905(b) case law.

341. The Sieracki-Ryan case law generated an enormous law review literature. Two notable contributions written during what might be called the Sieracki-Ryan middle period were Comment, Risk Distribution and Seaworthiness, 75 Yale L.J. 1174 (1966) and Proudfoot, "The Tar Baby": Maritime Personal-Injury Indemnity Actions, 20 Stanford L.Rev. 423 (1968). George, Ship's Liability to Longshoremen Based on Unseaworthiness—Sieracki through Usner, 3 J. of Mar. Law & Commerce 45 (1971) capably reviewed the developments through 1971.

342. 234 U.S. 52, 34 S.Ct. 733 (1914).

343. See § 6–2 *supra*.

344. See the Yale Comment, note 341 *supra*, for a collection of pre-Imbrovek lower court cases which had held that longshoremen could recover for unseaworthiness against shipowners and possibly against their direct employers as well. 75 Yale L.J. at p. 1178, n. 12 and accompanying text. The action in Imbrovek had originally been brought against both the shipowner and the stevedore-employer but had been dismissed as to the shipowner on the ground (which is no longer available, see § 6–42 *supra*) that control of the ship had been relinquished to the stevedore.

tion did not lie even though he had been injured on navigable waters. Justice Hughes disposed of the argument in the following language:

> "The libelant was injured on a ship, lying in navigable waters, and while he was engaged in the performance of a maritime service. We entertain no doubt that the service in loading and stowing a ship's cargo is of this character. Upon its proper performance depend in large measure the safe carrying of the cargo and the safety of the ship itself; and it is a service absolutely necessary to enable the ship to discharge its maritime duty. Formerly the work was done by the ship's crew; but, owing to the exigencies of increasing commerce and the demand for rapidity and special skill, it has become a specialized service devolving upon a class 'as clearly identified with maritime affairs as are the mariners.' "[345]

Thirteen years after Imbrovek Justice Holmes picked up the suggestion that loading and unloading were operations "formerly . . . done by the ship's crew." International Stevedoring Co. v. Haverty[346] was, on its facts, almost identical with Imbrovek with the important exception that Imbrovek appeared to have been injured by the direct negligence of his employer while the immediate cause of Haverty's injury was the negligence of a fellow servant. The legal situation which Haverty confronted was, however, vastly changed. There was now a state compensation statute, but Haverty was deprived of that relief under the Jensen doctrine. Secondly, Congress had passed the Jones Act, which gave "seamen" the right to recover damages for "operating negligence" and abolished the fellow servant doctrine as a defense. Haverty brought suit in State court, arguing that he came under the Jones Act so that the fellow servant rule could not be used against him. The Washington Supreme Court disagreed with him as to the Jones Act but nevertheless affirmed a judgment in his favor on the "vice-principal" exception to the fellow servant rule. That complicated approach did not satisfy the Supreme Court, which affirmed but placed the ground of recovery on the Jones Act. "It is true," wrote Justice Holmes, "that for most purposes, as the word is commonly used, stevedores are not 'seamen.' But words are flexible. The work upon which the plaintiff was engaged was a maritime service formerly rendered by the ship's crew. Atlantic Transport Company v. Imbrovek, 234 U.S. 52, 62, 34 S.Ct. 733." Therefore Haverty and all other stevedores could sue under the Jones Act free of the burdensome complexities and bars of fellow servant, contributory negligence and assumption of risk. Haverty was one of the Supreme Court's very few unanimous decisions in the field of maritime injuries in the post-Jensen era. It is not unreasonable to explain the unaccustomed unanimity as a concession by the Jensen majority to the Jensen dissenters: the

345. 234 U.S. at p. 62, 34 S.Ct. at p. 735.

346. 272 U.S. 50, 47 S.Ct. 19, 1926 A.M.C. 1638 (1926).

Court had already held unconstitutional two congressional attempts to fit harbor workers into the state compensation systems; [347] longshoremen engaged in loading and unloading operations were not within the court's "maritime but local" exception to Jensen; [348] without something like Haverty this class of workers, and this class almost alone in the entire country, would have found its recovery for unavoidable industrial accidents barred by the harsh nineteenth century rules of fellow servant and the like.

Within six months after the handing down of the Haverty decision Congress enacted LHCA. The exclusive liability provision of § 905 apparently made Haverty obsolete with respect to an action by an LHCA worker against his own employer. Actions under the Jones Act, it came to be believed, could be brought only against employers; [349] if that was so, an LHCA worker could not bring a Jones Act action against a shipowner who was not his employer. At all events actions by injured harbor workers against shipowners practically disappeared from the reports between 1927 (LHCA) and 1946 when the Supreme Court decided Seas Shipping Company v. Sieracki.[350]

We have already discussed the Supreme Court's reformulation of the unseaworthiness doctrine during the 1940's and the subsequent history of the doctrine as reformulated.[351] Sieracki, which was one of the basic cases in the reformulation, also held that a longshoreman covered by a compensation act could recover full damages for unseaworthiness in a third-party action against a non-negligent shipowner. Justice Rutledge in Sieracki put the longshoreman's right to sue as a seaman under the general maritime law on the ground suggested by Justice Hughes in Imbrovek and repeated by Justice Holmes in Haverty: that loading and unloading were operations which had once been carried out by the ship's crew; the longshoreman employed by a master stevedore was entitled to bring the unseaworthiness action "because he is doing a seaman's work and incurring a seaman's hazards." [352] Justice Rutledge's acceptance of what might be called the historical rationale for Sieracki's recovery (he was doing a "seaman's work") guaranteed that there would have to be a good deal of subsequent litigation to determine how many types of harbor work-

347. See § 6–45 *supra*, text following note 257.

348. On the "maritime but local" exception to Jensen, see § 6–49 *supra*.

349. See § 6–21(a), *supra*.

350. 328 U.S. 85, 66 S.Ct. 872, 1946 A.M.C. 698 (1946).

351. See § 6–38 *et seq. supra*.

352. Tetreault, Seamen, Seaworthiness and the Rights of Harbor Workers, 39 Cornell L.Q. 381, 412 *et seq.* (1954) suggested that there was no historical basis for the Imbrovek statement. The proposition that the Court was engaging in historical fiction was accepted in most of the subsequent literature. See, however, the Yale Comment, note 341 *supra*, which concludes that "the Supreme Court [in Imbrovek] had good reason to find a close historical relationship between the two occupations [i. e. the work of longshoremen and the work of crew members]." 75 Yale L.J. at p. 1180.

ers there might be and what types of work they had to be engaged in to qualify as what came to be called Sieracki-seamen.

The Court itself during the 1950's and 1960's seems to have been almost evenly divided on whether to stand by the historical rationale ("doing a seaman's work") or scrapping that formula in favor of the broader one which Justice Rutledge's Sieracki opinion had also suggested ("incurring a seaman's hazards"). Pope & Talbot, Inc. v. Hawn,[353] majority opinion by Justice Black, seemed to mean that the broader view had won out: Hawn, a carpenter who had been brought to the ship to repair a defect which had developed in the grain loading equipment, was held to be a Sieracki-seaman. However, in United New York and New Jersey Sandy Hook Pilots Association v. Halecki [354] a different majority, in an opinion by Justice Stewart, returned to the historical rationale, holding that an electrician killed while working on a ship's generators during its annual overhaul was not a Sieracki-seaman. Halecki was followed by West v. United States [355] and Roper v. United States [356] in which the Court developed the idea that actions for unseaworthiness under the general maritime law (as well as actions under the Jones Act) do not lie to recover for injuries suffered on ships which have been "withdrawn from navigation." [357]

The Supreme Court dropped the issue at that point; the lower courts have continued to wrestle with it ever since.[358] Courts sympathetic to the harbor worker's recovery naturally stress the broad language of the majority opinion in Hawn. Courts less sympathetic to the recovery stress Halecki or the Roper-West sequence. Thus the outer limits of this aspect of the Sieracki holding have never been determined and, with the abolition of the harbor worker's unseaworthiness action, never will be determined.[359]

353. 346 U.S. 406, 74 S.Ct. 202, 1954 A.M.C. 1 (1953).

354. 358 U.S. 613, 79 S.Ct. 517, 1959 A.M.C. 588 (1959). Halecki was one of the cases in the sequence initiated by The Tungus v. Skovgaard, 358 U.S. 588, 79 S.Ct. 503, 1959 A.M.C. 813 (1959), in which the Court found itself bitterly divided on the question whether the federal maritime doctrine of unseaworthiness applied to actions brought under state wrongful death statutes. On The Tungus and its sequels, see § 6–31 *supra*, text following note 189b.

355. 361 U.S. 118, 80 S.Ct. 189, 1960 A.M.C. 15 (1959).

356. 368 U.S. 20, 82 S.Ct. 5, 1961 A.M.C. 2499 (1961).

357. Roper and West, which were unseaworthiness cases brought by harbor workers, have been discussed in the context of the Jones Act, § 6–21 *supra*, text following note 121a.

358. See, e. g., Shenker v. United States, 322 F.2d 622, 1964 A.M.C. 6 (2d Cir. 1963); Grigsby v. Coastal Marine Service of Texas, Inc., 412 F.2d 1011, 1969 A.M.C. 1513 (5th Cir. 1969), certiorari dismissed *sub nom.* Fidelity & Casualty Co. of New York v. Grigsby, 396 U.S. 1033, 90 S.Ct. 612 (1970).

359. The Supreme Court limited the scope of the harbor worker's unseaworthiness recovery in two 1971 cases. Usner v. Luckenbach Overseas Corp., 400 U.S. 494, 91 S.Ct. 514, 1971 A.M.C. 277 (1971) held that unseaworthiness does not include all types of operating negligence, see § 6–39 *supra*, text following note 221d. Victory Carriers, Inc. v. Law, 404 U.S. 202, 92 S.Ct. 418, 1972 A.M.C. 1 (1971) held that there was no admiralty jurisdiction over an injury to a longshoreman on a dock,

**The Shipowner's Indemnity Action**

§ 6–55. Before Sieracki there had been few cases in which shipowners had been held liable in damages to injured harbor workers; there were, consequently, few cases in which shipowners had sought to recover indemnity from other parties (including the harbor worker's employer) who might on some theory be chargeable with liability in connection with the accident.[360] After Sieracki counsel for shipowners naturally began to explore the possibility of passing on to others some or all of their clients' liability for unseaworthiness. They succeeded beyond their wildest hopes.

When the first of the post-Sieracki indemnity cases reached the Supreme Court, the Justices temporized. American Stevedores, Inc. v. Porello [361] was remanded for determination of the meaning of a provision in a contract between shipowner and stevedore. One of the possibilities that the provision meant that liability was to be shared when both were at fault; "a rule of comparative negligence," said Justice Reed, "is not unknown to our maritime law." The next case, Halcyon Lines v. Haenn Ship Ceiling & Refitting Corp.,[362] held that a shipowner (found to have been 25% responsible for the plaintiff's injury) could recover nothing from the stevedore-employer (75% responsible) on the ground that there is no right of contribution among joint tortfeasors. The admiralty rule of divided damages, said Justice Black, had been applied only in collision cases: "We have concluded that it would be unwise to attempt to fashion new judicial rules of contribution and that the solution of this problem should await congressional action." [363] The third case, which came to be the basis for all subsequent developments, was Ryan Stevedoring Co., Inc. v. Pan-Atlantic Steamship Corp.[364] Ryan was a case of

the injury having been caused by stevedore-owned equipment on the dock, see § 6–44(a) *supra*, note 251f.

360. In Seaboard Stevedoring Corp. v. Sogadahoc S. S. Co., 32 F.2d 886, 1929 A.M.C. 865 (9th Cir. 1929) a shipowner whose negligence was found to have been merely "passive" was allowed to recover from an "actively" negligent stevedore (who was not the injured worker's employer) the damages for which the shipowner had been held liable to the worker. The state of the law as of 1929 may be illustrated by the fact that the Court's opinion cited no authorities or precedents. Proudfoot, note 341 *supra*, cites The Tampico, 45 F.Supp. 174 (W.D.N.Y.1942), to the proposition that there were cases in which "the shipowner obtained contribution from the stevedore (usually on a 50-50 division) in a mutual fault situation." 20 Stanford L.Rev. at p. 425.

361. 330 U.S. 446, 67 S.Ct. 847, 1947 A.M.C. 349 (1947).

362. 342 U.S. 282, 72 S.Ct. 277, 1952 A.M.C. 1 (1952).

363. Twenty years later the problem was still awaiting congressional action despite which unfortunate delay the Court briefly reaffirmed the Halcyon "no contribution among joint tortfeasors" rule in Atlantic Coast Line Railroad Co. v. Erie Lackawanna Railroad Co., 406 U.S. 340, 92 S.Ct. 1550, 1972 A.M.C. 1121 (1972). The case involved an injury to a railroad worker on a freight car which was being transported across navigable waters on a car float. One railroad owned the freight car, the other owned the car float, both were found to have been negligent. No indemnity.

364. 350 U.S. 124, 76 S.Ct. 232, 1956 A.M.C. 9 (1956). Initially the Court had

concurrent negligence on the part of both shipowner and stevedore-employer.[365] The majority of the Court, in an opinion by Justice Burton,[366] held that, under the contract between shipowner and stevedore, there arose an implied "warranty of workmanlike service" running from stevedore to shipowner. Negligence chargeable to the stevedore breached the warranty; thus the shipowner, held liable to a Sieracki-seaman, was entitled to full indemnity from the stevedore-employer. Nothing in the exclusive liability provision of LHCA § 905 stood in the way of the recovery of the indemnity.[367]

The Ryan contractual indemnity theory seems to have been in hopeless contradiction with the Halcyon no contribution theory. However Justice Burton for the Ryan majority carefully distinguished Halcyon and did not overrule it. In the first edition of the treatise we commented that "it is obvious that Ryan . . . strips Halcyon

disposed of Ryan without opinion, the Justices having been equally divided, 349 U.S. 901, 75 S.Ct. 575 (1955); that judgment was vacated and the case restored to the docket for further argument, 349 U.S. 926, 75 S.Ct. 769 (1955).

365. The Second Circuit had held in Ryan that, despite Halcyon, the shipowner, whose negligence had been merely "passive," could recover indemnity from the actively negligent stevedore. The Supreme Court did not accept the "active-passive" distinction.

366. In Ryan Justice Black, joined by Chief Justice Warren and Justices Brennan and Douglas, dissented. These were, without doubt, the four members of the Court who had most enthusiastically supported the Court's expansion of remedies for harbor workers and seamen. The Ryan majority consisted of Justices Burton, Clark, Frankfurter, Harlan and Minton. Justices Frankfurter and Harlan, as long as they remained on the Court, consistently opposed the expansion championed by Justice Black and his colleagues. Thus Ryan can be described as a case in which the "conservatives" prevailed over the "liberals" on the Court. The dissenters apparently feared that under Ryan the injured harbor worker's employer would be in a position to prevent him from bringing an action against the shipowner. Under LHCA § 933(b) the employer becomes an assignee of the worker's rights against any third party when compensation is paid pursuant to a formal award. By resisting the payment of compensation until an award was made in a contested proceeding the employer could trigger the statutory assignment and thus, arguably, be able to control further proceedings. However, in a case decided shortly after Ryan, Czaplicki v. S.S. Hoegh Silvercloud, 351 U.S. 525, 76 S. Ct. 946, 1956 A.M.C. 1465 (1956), the Court decided unanimously (Justice Frankfurter concurring) that, despite such an assignment (to the employer's insurance carrier), the injured worker could maintain (and control) the third party action himself. Their fears evidently allayed by Czaplicki, the Ryan dissenters concurred (or even wrote the opinions in) the post-Ryan decisions which further extended the indemnity idea. The flood of post-Ryan indemnity litigation is sufficient proof that the situation anticipated by the Ryan dissenters did not materialize.

367. Under § 905 the employer's liability to pay compensation "shall be exclusive and in place of all other liability of such employer to the employee, [his beneficiaries] and anyone otherwise entitled to recover damages from such employer . . . on account of such injury or death . . . ." The Ryan holding on this point was that the shipowner's recovery was based on a contractual right to indemnity, hence was not "on account of" the injury and thus was not within the reach of the statutory provision. Such a right to indemnity seems to be recognized in the general law of workmen's compensation (see 3 Larson, note 264 *supra*, § 76.00) but, in the normal course of land-based industrial accidents, there will not have been a contractual relationship (like that between shipowner and stevedore) between the employer and the third-party tortfeasor.

of any surviving vitality . . . there are simply no cases left for the Halcyon rule to apply to . . ." That statement was not inaccurate but the ghostly survival of the Halcyon rule did influence the subsequent shaping of the Ryan indemnity action in ways that would have been hard to anticipate at the time we wrote our original discussion.

In the years following Ryan Justice Burton's "warranty of workmanlike service" (which most courts turned into a "warranty of workmanlike performance," abbreviated WWP, WWLP or, by one irreverent judge, WOW) had a sensational career. We need not go into detail but the Supreme Court successively held (or suggested) that the warranty was breached if the employer failed to remedy an unseaworthy condition for which the shipowner was solely responsible [368], if the employer, through the acts of his employees "brought into play" a vessel's unseaworthiness,[369] even if there was no direct contractual relationship between the shipowner and the employer [370] and even if the employer had been in no way negligent.[371]

One of the post-Ryan cases merits special treatment. In Reed v. The Yaka [372] the injured longshoreman had been employed directly by the vessel's bareboat charterer instead of by an independent stevedore. The vessel was unseaworthy by reason of acts for which the charterer was solely responsible. The action was brought in rem against the vessel; the owner appeared as claimant in the in rem proceeding and impleaded the charterer in the customary Ryan-indemnity action. The lower courts thought that the case posed the jurisprudential riddle whether a vessel could be liable in rem in a situation in which neither the owner (because he had turned over control of the vessel to the charterer who had created the unseaworthy condition) nor the charterer (because of the exclusive liability provision of LHCA § 905) was personally liable.[373] The Supreme Court sensibly declined to talk about the riddle. The majority also declined to solve the case by holding that the shipowner's absolute liability for unseaworthiness included conditions for which the charterer was solely responsible: under that approach there would have been no

**368.** Weyerhaeuser Steamship Co. v. Nacirema Operating Co., 355 U.S. 563, 78 S.Ct. 438, 1958 A.M.C. 501 (1958) (per Clark, J. for a unanimous Court).

**369.** Crumady v. The J. H. Fisser, 358 U.S. 423, 79 S.Ct. 445, 1959 A.M.C. 580 (1959) (per Douglas, J., Harlan, Frankfurter and Whitaker, JJ. dissenting).

**370.** Waterman Steamship Corp. v. Dugan & McNamara, Inc., 364 U.S. 421, 81 S.Ct. 200, 1960 A.M.C. 2260 (per Stewart, J., for a unanimous Court).

**371.** Italia Societa per Azioni di Navigazione v. Oregon Stevedoring Co., 376 U.S. 315, 84 S.Ct. 748, 1964 A.M.C. 1075 (1964) (per White, J.; Warren, C. J., Black and Douglas, JJ. dissenting). For a brilliant review of the Supreme Court's post-Ryan cases, see Proudfoot, note 341 *supra*.

**372.** 373 U.S. 410, 83 S.Ct. 1349, 1963 A.M.C. 1373 (1963) (per Black, J., Harlan and Stewart, JJ. dissenting). The Supreme Court reaffirmed Reed v. The Yaka in Jackson v. Lykes Brothers Steamship Co., 386 U.S. 731, 87 S.Ct. 1419, 1967 A.M.C. 584 (1967). A recent case following the Reed rule is Eskine v. United Barge Co., 484 F.2d 1194 (5th Cir. 1973).

**373.** This aspect of The Yaka is discussed in Chapter IX, § 9–18(a).

problem about the in rem action and the Ryan-indemnity action would have followed as a matter of course. The majority approach, which was nothing if not direct, was to say that, even if it was to be assumed that the shipowner was not personally liable for the charterer's acts (a question which was not decided), the libel in rem was supported by the bareboat charterer's status as owner pro hac vice of the vessel and the charterer, in the indemnity action, was not protected by LHCA § 905 (since he was being required to pay the damages as "charterer," not as Reed's "employer"). Or, to translate the holding from the legal gobbledegook into English: Reed could recover full damages directly from his employer, the exclusive liability provision of LHCA § 905 to the contrary notwithstanding. Justice Black's majority opinion hardly bothered to pretend that the result could be justified by a construction of the statutory language, however disingenuous. The justification was put on this ground: most longshoremen are employed by firms which do not own the ships on which they work; under Sieracki-Ryan, such longshoremen recover from the ships (or shipowners) for unseaworthiness and the shipowners are indemnified by the employers; the same result should follow when a longshoreman is employed directly by a shipowner (or owner pro hac vice).

After Reed v. The Yaka the longshoreman's action might just as well have been brought directly against his employer—which would have simplified the situation procedurally. However, in the customary employment situation, the parties, out of politeness or inertia, continued to observe the elaborate formalities of the Sieracki-Ryan ritual: longshoreman sued ship or shipowner, who impleaded employer in his third party indemnity action.[374] It is probable, however, that the very existence of Reed v. The Yaka confirmed the lower courts in their belief that the Ryan-indemnity action had become (like the Sieracki-seaworthiness action) absolute.

It is to be borne in mind that the shipowner's indemnity recovery was for 100% of the damages, even in cases where the shipowner's negligence had created the conditions of unseaworthiness and the employer had not been negligent at all.[375] We may conclude this part of our discussion with a reference to a situation which was being litigated in the lower federal courts at the end of the Sieracki-Ryan period. A ship is unseaworthy, the shipowner being solely responsible for the condition. A worker is injured as the result of the unsea-

374. In many cases the cast of characters did not stay fixed at three. In Grigsby v. Coastal Marine Service of Texas, Inc., 412 F.2d 1011, 1969 A.M.C. 1513 (5th Cir. 1969), certiorari dismissed *sub nom.* Fidelity & Casualty Co. of New York v. Grigsby, 396 U.S. 1033 (1970), Judge Brown referred to the case as "Another in that ever-growing line of multi-party 3, 4, 5, or 10 ringed amphibious Donnybrooks." The growing number of such multi-party cases no doubt reflected increasing specialization in waterfront employment. The presence of several impleaded defendants guaranteed not only protracted trials but also protracted pre-trial proceedings in the course of which the injured worker's original action was practically lost from sight.

375. See the cases described in the text at notes 368, 369, 370, 371 *supra.*

worthy condition but also as the result of his own carelessness (i. e., he is chargeable with contributory negligence, which will not bar his action but will go in mitigation of damages). May shipowner, having been held liable to the worker, recover indemnity from employer on the theory that the employee's carelessness is to be imputed to the employer, thus breaching the Ryan warranty of workmanlike performance? Yes, said the Second Circuit in McLaughlin v. Trelleborgs Angfartygs A/B.[376] In his McLaughlin opinion Judge Friendly added that, under the Halcyon case,[377] there was no possibility of the employer's shifting part of the loss back to the shipowner on the theory that the shipowner had breached his duty to provide a safe place to work. "So long as [Halcyon] remains on the books, inferior federal courts will do better to abstain from further adventures in this Wonderland and leave doctrinal development to the Supreme Court." Nor could the employer complete the circle in a McLaughlin situation by recovering from the employee for his own carelessness or contributory negligence.[378] It should be added that Judge Friendly, who wrote the McLaughlin opinion, has described the result in that and other comparable cases as "truly ludicrous." [378a] However that may be, employers of waterfront labor, contemplating the end state of the Sieracki-Ryan case law, might well have said: The buck stops here.

### The Nullification of § 905

**§ 6–56.** In effect the "liberal" majority of the Supreme Court nullified the exclusive liability provisions of LHCA and the applicable state compensation acts. It may be noted that the "liberals" initially thought that the ultimate liability under Sieracki should rest with the shipowner and not be shifted to the employer; they dissented from Ryan.[378b] At a later point, however, they embraced Ryan and turned its doctrine to their own uses, frequently over the protests of the surviving members of the Ryan majority.[378c]

The nullification of a statutory provision, whose constitutionality no one challenged, has been almost universally condemned in the professional literature. It is the received wisdom of our generation that the legislature, once it has chosen to enter a field, is supreme. If the legislature enacts an unwise statute, it is up to the legislature to confess and correct its own error. If the legislature enacts a stat-

376. 408 F.2d 1334, 1969 A.M.C. 1387 (2d Cir. 1969), certiorari denied 395 U.S. 946, 89 S.Ct. 2020 (1969). The Fifth Circuit said No. See Julian v. Mitsui O.S.K. Lines, Ltd., 479 F.2d 432, 1973 A.M.C. 1477 (5th Cir. 1973) (Thornberry, J., dissenting).

377. See text at note 362 *supra*.

378. Judge Friendly himself had thrown out this suggestion dissenting in Shenker v. United States, 322 F.2d 622, 1964 A.M.C. 6 (2d Cir. 1963). In Nicroli v. Den Norske Afrika-OG Australielinie, 332 F.2d 651, 1964 A.M.C. 1413 (2d Cir. 1964) his colleagues dismissed the suggestion as "hyperbolic," a characterization which Judge Friendly, in McLaughlin, seemed willing to accept.

378a. Friendly, Federal Jurisdiction: A General View 132 (1973).

378b. See note 366 *supra*.

378c. See the cases cited notes 368, 369, 370, 371, 372 *supra*.

ute which in the course of time becomes inadequate or obsolete or absurd, it is up to the legislature to decide that times have changed and provide whatever remedy the changed circumstances are thought to require. The limited function of the courts (theirs not to reason why) is faithfully to carry out the legislative command. Therefore, most commentators have felt, the Supreme Court's nullification of LHCA § 905 was, as Chief Justice Stone said with respect to the Court's invention of the LHCA twilight zone in 1942, met "within judicial competence" and "not permissable." [378d]

The Court's nullification of § 905 has been defended on grounds of social or economic policy. Those who work on the waterfront subject themselves to extremely high risks of injury or death; the risks are greater than in most other areas of industrial employment. (The point may be conceded for the sake of the argument, even though the available statistical evidence seems to be inconclusive.) For workers engaged in such a high risk area, the existing compensation system does not afford adequate relief. Harbor workers should therefore (like seamen under the Jones Act and railroad workers under FELA) have the right to recover full damages. The employer is the person best situated to control the risks and provide for the safety of his employees. It is appropriate that the employer of waterfront labor (like the employer of seamen under the Jones Act and the employer of railroad labor under FELA) bear the ultimate liability for employment-related accidents.[378e] Thus the Supreme Court arrived at a desirable end, however questionable its means.

The "high risk" argument, it is submitted, is unsatisfactory. A worker who is injured or killed in a low risk type of work—say, writing law books—is just as disabled or just as dead as if he had been injured or killed in high risk work. If compensation benefits are inadequate for longshoremen, they are equally inadequate for law book writers. It is hard to accept an argument which seems to say that a court would be justified in doing what the Supreme Court did to LHCA § 905 but would not be justified in doing the same thing for workers generally.

Justice Holmes once remarked that it is revolting to have no better reason for a rule of law than so it was laid down in the reign of Henry IV.[378f] Obsolete statutory rules are exactly as repulsive as obsolete judicial rules. In the second half of the twentieth century we are becoming familiar with the unhappy fact that the legislative process is much less responsive to changing circumstance than the judicial process is. An old statute, let us assume, has become inadequate or obsolete or absurd. The legislature is occupied by other matters.

**378d.** See § 6–49 *supra*, text following note 305.

**378e.** See the Yale Comment, Risk Distribution and Unseaworthiness, 75 Yale L.J. 1174 (1966). Justice Douglas seems to have associated himself with this approach in his dissent to Victory Carriers, Inc. v. Law, 404 U.S. 202, 92 S.Ct. 418, 1972 A.M.C. 1 (1971).

**378f.** The Path of the Law, in Collected Legal Papers (1920) 167, 187.

It does nothing, even though the courts have repeatedly attempted to draw its attention to the problem. For many years it goes on doing nothing. Over how long a time is society supposed to go on living by the rule laid down in the reign of Henry II?

Judicial reform of legislative inaction, however shocking the idea may be in the light of our conventional wisdom, may well have a promising future. The Supreme Court seems to have decided to carry out experiments in such reform in the field of maritime law, perhaps because the peculiar constitutional background lends itself to an unusual degree of judicial activism. The Court has been widely applauded for its revolutionary restructuring of the maritime law rule relating to actions for wrongful death even though, as we have suggested, its decision in Moragne v. States Marine Lines, Inc.[378g] had the effect of reducing the relevant statutory provisions to the level of "nonstatutory Restatements." In Sieracki, Ryan and the cases which followed the Court gave harbor workers the right to recover damages outside the compensation system and put the ultimate liability for such damages on the employers of such labor. In doing so it effectively nullified the exclusive liability provisions of the compensation acts. It is fairly arguable that the compensation system, conceived around 1910 or thereabouts, has become obsolete. No one has seriously contended for many years that the benefits payable under compensation acts (including LHCA) have been adequate. Neither the federal Congress nor the state legislatures had over many years shown the slightest interest in remedying a scandalous situation. The Supreme Court addressed itself to the problem through a series of highly technical constructions of isolated sections of LHCA. It is easy enough to say that the Court's manifest duty was to ensure that the 1910 theory of liability for industrial accidents incorporated in the compensation acts should be maintained until Congress saw fit to decree a new approach. Instead of doing that, the Court manipulated the inherent contradictions contained within the statute in such a way as to realign the statutory scheme with the theories of liability which commended themselves to the majority of the Court during the 1950's and 1960's. Judicial nullification of legislatively determined policy does not square with our current habits of thought. It may well be, however, that the canons of statutory construction which grew up during the first half of the twentieth century will seem like quaint anachronisms before the century has run its course. The Sieracki-Ryan construct may not seem, to the legal mind of the 1990's, as shocking as it did to the legal mind of the 1960's.

**378g.** 398 U.S. 375, 90 S.Ct. 1772, 1970 A.M.C. 967 (1970), discussed § 6–32 *supra*.

### The Harbor Worker's Recovery of Damages Outside the Compensation System—II: The 1972 LHCA Amendments

§ 6–57. LHCA § 905(b), added to the Act in 1972, provides:

> In the event of injury to a person covered under this chapter caused by the negligence of a vessel, then such person, or anyone otherwise entitled to recover damages by reason thereof, may bring an action against such vessel as a third party in accordance with the provisions of section 933 of this title and the employer shall not be liable to the vessel for such damages directly or indirectly and any agreements or warranties to the contrary shall be void. If such person was employed by the vessel to provide stevedoring services, no such action shall be permitted if the injury was caused by negligence of persons engaged in providing stevedoring services to the vessel. If such person was employed by the vessel to provide ship building or repair services, no such action shall be permitted if the injury was caused by the negligence of persons engaged in providing ship building or repair services to the vessel. The liability of the vessel under this subsection shall not be based upon the warranty of seaworthiness or a breach thereof at the time the injury occurred. The remedy provided in this subsection shall be exclusive of all other remedies against the vessel except remedies available under this chapter.

The two principal points are, of course, that the harbor worker may bring a third party action for negligence but not for unseaworthiness and that his employer "shall not be liable . . . directly or indirectly . . ." for any damages recovered in the negligence action. The drafting, however, suggests a few minor puzzles which we may as well attempt to deal with first.

"[*A*] *person covered under this chapter*": We have earlier discussed the new LHCA territorial limits as well as the new types of employment which are covered.[378h] It is possible that there may be "persons" so employed within the territorial limits who are not technically "covered under" LHCA. If such a person is injured, is he subject to § 905(b) or may he still, conceivably, sue as a Sieracki-seaman? Presumably the draftsman meant to abolish the entire class of Sieracki-seamen; if the section is so construed, no one could sue as a Sieracki-seaman whether or not he was technically "covered." It also seems to be consistent with the draftsman's presumable intent to conclude that harbor workers are subject to § 905(b) even if they are within the twilight zone or area of concurrent jurisdiction and entitled to claim compensation under a state act instead of under LHCA.

**378h.** §§ 6–50, 6–51, *supra*.

A more difficult problem is presented by the landward extension of the LHCA territorial limits. May a "covered person" who is injured on land (the cause of his injury being connected with the "vessel"), bring his third party negligence action? Is Gutierrez v. Waterman Steamship Co. still good law? Has Victory Carriers, Inc. v. Law been overruled in all its aspects and implications? Have the old cases which established that actions under the Jones Act could be brought for injuries suffered on land been adopted?[378i] The available legislative history suggests no answers to these questions.

*[A]n action against [the] vessel*: This terminology has customarily been used to describe what used to be called libels in rem as distinguished from libels in personam. Thus we may assume that the § 905(b) action can be brought in rem.[378j] A definition of "vessel" (§ 902[21]), added by the 1972 amendments, provides that the term means not only any vessel "upon which or in connection with which" the injury or death may have occurred but also "said vessel's owner, owner pro hac vice, agent, operator, charter [*sic*], or bareboat charterer, master, officer or crew member." Evidently the use of the phrase "against [the] vessel" was not meant to preclude actions in personam against any of the persons oddly included in the statutory definition of "vessel".

"*[E]mployed by the vessel*": The apparent purpose of the second and third sentences was to reverse Reed v. The Yaka.[378k] The language employed is somewhat confusing. Taken literally, it seems to say only that persons "employed by the vessel" cannot recover for the negligence of their fellow workers engaged in the same operation (e. g., loading). (Presumably that proposition would be equally true for persons employed by an "employer.") That leaves open the possibility that such persons could recover for negligence chargeable to the vessel, its crew, and so on, even though the "vessel" is the "employer." That is not what the Committee seemed to think it was doing but sometimes statutory language turns out to have a life of its own, independent of the wishes of whoever wrote it down. The draftsman's persistent personification of "the vessel" may have contributed to the confusion at this point.

*Contributory negligence and assumption of risk*:

According to the Committee Report:

"[T]he Committee intends that the admiralty concept of comparative negligence, rather than the common law rule

**378i.** On Gutierrez and Victory Carriers, see note 251f *supra*. On the Jones Act cases, see note 116 *supra*.

**378j.** *Cf.* the rule that actions under the Jones Act can be brought only in personam which the Supreme Court established in the course of construing the "venue" provision of the Jones Act, see § 6–22 *supra*.

**387k.** See the House Committee Report, 3 U.S.C.A. Congressional and Administrative News (92d Congress-Second Session-1972), 4698, 4705. On Reed v. The Yaka, see the text following note 372 *supra*.

as to contributory negligence, shall apply in cases where the injured employee's own negligence may have contributed to causing the injury. Also, the Committee intends that the admiralty rule which precludes the defense of 'assumption of risk' in an action by an injured employee shall also be applicable." [378l]

It would have been more satisfactory if these points had been made expressly in the statute. There is no reason, however, to anticipate that the courts will not follow such a clear expression of the legislative intent.

We may now take up the two principal points that § 905(b) was designed to make. Proceeding from the relatively simple to the relatively complex, we shall start with the language designed to abolish the Ryan-indemnity action.

"[*T*]*he employer shall not be liable to the vessel . . . directly or indirectly and any agreements or warranties to the contrary shall be void.*

The Ryan warranty of workmanlike performance (WOW) is, clearly enough, dead with respect to the shifting of liability from shipowner (or "vessel") to employer for damages recoverable in the § 905(b) negligence action. Presumably the stevedore, shipbuilder or ship repairer remains liable under normal principles of contract law for other losses caused by his default or breach.

The principal problem is whether the language is meant to adopt the rule of the Halcyon case (which is not mentioned in the Committee Reports).[378m] In Halcyon, a concurrent negligence case, the shipowner was found to have been 25% responsible for the plaintiff's injury, the employer 75% responsible. On the ground that there is no right to contribution among joint tortfeasors, the 25% responsible ship owner was denied any recovery against the 75% responsible employer. The Court, said Justice Black, would not "fashion" a comparative negligence rule, preferring to await Congressional action.

It would have been perfectly simple to adopt the Halcyon rule of no contribution in § 905(b): "The employer, even if his negligence has contributed to the injury, shall not be liable . . ." *Quaere* whether the statute as drafted "codifies" Halcyon or leaves it to the Supreme Court to decide whether the time has come when it might be appropriate for the Court to "fashion" a comparative negligence rule. It will be remembered that the Committee Report suggested that "the admiralty concept of comparative negligence" was to apply to the injured worker's § 905(b) negligence action. On grounds of policy there is much to be said for casting the employer in liability according to the degree of his fault: it gives him an incentive to take appropriate steps to protect his employees from dangerous con-

**378l.** *Loc. cit.* note 378k *supra.*

**378m.** On Halcyon, see text following note 362 *supra.*

ditions for which the shipowner is responsible. The Supreme Court in effect nullified the Halcyon no contribution rule by the Ryan indemnity rule. Indemnity (or warranty) language is no longer permissible under § 905(b). But if the Congress really meant that the 1% negligent shipowner should pay full damages to the injured worker and recover nothing from the 99% negligent employer, it might have said so more clearly.

*"The liability of the vessel . . . shall not be based upon the warranty of seaworthiness."*

What does it mean to say that "the vessel" is liable for negligence but not for unseaworthiness? The two terms overlap over most of the range of their meanings. Only at the fringes can we identify such concepts as pure operating negligence aboard a seaworthy vessel or unseaworthiness which is not caused by someone's negligence. A formula which recurs in hundreds of cases is: the defendant's negligence made the ship unseaworthy. In the seaman's action which combines a Jones Act count with an unseaworthiness count, the two counts have become, as we put in our discussion of the unseaworthiness doctrine, Siamese twins.[378n]

There are two situations in which, under the Supreme Court's doctrine, shipowners are liable for unseaworthiness without being chargeable with negligence. One is the condition of so-called transitory unseaworthiness, as to which Mitchell v. Trawler Racer, Inc.[378o] has become the leading case. Under Trawler Racer the shipowner is liable for injuries caused by conditions of unseaworthiness, however, whenever or wherever the condition may have arisen, even though no responsible officer on the ship has had time to correct the conditions or even to learn of their existence. The other is the condition of unseaworthiness caused entirely by the act of a third party (e. g., the stevedore to whom control of the ship has been relinquished for loading or unloading). On this branch of the unseaworthiness doctrine Alaska Steamship Co., Inc. v. Petterson [378p] has been regarded as the foundation case.

We may assume without further argument that the § 905(b) negligence action does not lie for injuries caused by conditions of transitory unseaworthiness under the Trawler Racer doctrine or by conditions for which no one employer by the ship is responsible under the Petterson doctrine. We may also assume that the § 905(b) action does lie for injuries caused by conditions of unseaworthiness which result from the negligence of the ship's personnel. It can hardly be seriously argued that the § 905(b) action was meant to lie only for injuries directly caused by operating negligence on the part of the crew which does not make the ship unseaworthy. The

**378n.** See § 6–38 *supra.*

**378o.** 362 U.S. 539, 80 S.Ct. 926, 1960 A.M.C. 1503 (1960), discussed § 6–44a *supra.*

**378p.** 347 U.S. 396, 74 S.Ct. 601, 1954 A.M.C. 860 (1954), discussed § 6–42 *supra*, text following note 234.

action must certainly lie for injuries caused by defective equipment and gear belonging to the ship which the crew had negligently left in a dangerous state.

The principal problem for the courts in working out the elements of the § 905(b) action will be the determination of what standards of negligence are to be applicable. It can be argued that the standards of negligence which have been developed in seamen's actions under the Jones Act should be applicable to the harbor worker's action under § 905(b). On the other hand it can be argued that negligence under the Jones Act does not (or will not) necessarily constitute negligence under § 905(b). The argument will be that a shipowner owes a higher degree of care to his own employees (crew members) than he does to longshoremen employed by a master stevedore. Thus he could be liable to a crew member suing under the Jones Act but not liable to a longshoreman suing under § 905(b), even though, let us assume, both the crew member and the longshoreman had been injured at the same time by the same cause.

It is to be hoped that the courts will reject the argument sketched at the end of the preceding paragraph and hold that Jones Act (and FELA) concepts of negligence apply to harbor workers' actions under § 905(b). In support of that position, two slightly different lines of argument may be developed.

There was a time in the development of common law theories of tort when the courts accepted the idea that landowners owed differing degrees of care to the various classes of people who might come on the land with the owner's permission or in furtherance of the owner's interest (business invitees, guests, licensees, and so on). In Kermarec v. Compagnie Générale Transatlantique [378q] it was argued that such common law distinctions should be applied to the case of a person who was injured when he was on the ship, with the permission of the executive officer, as a guest of a crew member: as a "mere licensee," the argument went, he was entitled to a lower degree of care than if he had been an "invitee". Justice Stewart, writing for a unanimous Court, first reviewed the common law history, coming to the conclusion that the earlier distinctions had largely been abandoned in favor of a unitary standard of liability. He went on:

> "For the admiralty law at this late date to import such conceptual distinctions would be foreign to its traditions of simplicity and practicality. . . . We hold that the owner of a ship in navigable waters owes to all who are on board for purposes not inimical to his legitimate interests the duty of exercising reasonable care under the circumstances of each case." [378r]

Kermarec may reasonably be cited to the proposition that the same standard of care is owed to all persons who are legitimately

**378q.** 358 U.S. 625, 79 S.Ct. 406, 1959 A.M.C. 597 (1959).

**378r.** 358 U.S. at pp. 631–632, 79 S.Ct. at p. 410, 1959 A.M.C. at p. 602.

on the ship—crew members, passengers, longshoremen, repairmen, even those who at common law would have been described as "mere licensees." For present purposes we may leave the passengers and guests to fight their own battles. The longshoremen and repairmen are on the ship in furtherance of the shipowner's commercial interests. They are, as the Supreme Court liked to put it during the Sieracki period, doing the ship's work—arguably, work that at our time was performed by the crew—they are unquestionably subject to the ship's hazards. As Justice Black, speaking of a repairman, wrote in Pope & Talbot, Inc. v. Hawn:

> "His need for protection from unseaworthiness was neither more nor less than that of the stevedores then working with him on the ship or of seamen who had been or were about to go on a voyage. All were subjected to the same danger. All were entitled to like treatment under law." [378s]

If we substitute "negligence" for "unseaworthiness" in the passage quoted, Justice Black's eloquent statement makes the case for a unitary standard of negligence in Jones Act and § 905(b) cases.

In Kernan v. American Dredging Co.[378t] the majority of the Court held that concepts of liability for violation of safety statutes which had been developed in railroad cases under FELA applied to actions under the Jones Act. Justice Brennan wrote that the FELA cases had been decided "with a view to adjusting equitably between the worker and his corporate employer the risks inherent in the railroad industry. . . . We find no difficulty in applying these principles, developed under the FELA, to the present action under the Jones Act . . ." The "risks inherent in the . . . industry" approach seems quite as applicable to harbor workers actions under § 905(b) as to seamen's actions under the Jones Act. Just as, under Kernan, the FELA standards of negligence came over to the Jones Act, so Jones Act standards of negligence should come over to actions under § 905(b).[378u]

It will be remembered that the Supreme Court once held, in International Stevedoring Co. v. Haverty,[378v] that a longshoreman could sue his employer under the Jones Act. The enactment of LHCA in 1927 seemed to make the Haverty holding obsolete: the longshoreman was restricted to his compensation remedy against his employer, the stevedore, and it came to be believed that actions under the Jones Act could be brought only against employers. The proposition that the Jones Act defendant must have been the plaintiff's employer at

**378s.** 346 U.S. 406, 413, 74 S.Ct. 202, 207, 1954 A.M.C. 1, 9 (1954).

**378t.** 355 U.S. 426, 78 S.Ct. 394, 1958 A.M.C. 251 (1958), discussed § 6–37 *supra*, text following note 202.

**378u.** On the Jones Act standards of negligence, see § 6–34 *et seq. supra*. In this connection the pre-LHCA (indeed pre-Jones Act) case of Atlantic Transport Co. v. Imbrovek, 234 U.S. 52, 34 S.Ct. 733 (1913), discussed § 6–54 *supra*, text following note 342, should also be kept in mind.

**378v.** 272 U.S. 50, 47 S.Ct. 19, 1926 A.M.C. 1638 (1926), discussed § 6–21 *supra*, text following note 107.

the time of the injury turns out, on analysis, to be less firmly based in the Jones Act case law than has often been assumed.[378w] The chances that a harbor worker's lawyer could convince a court today that his client should be allowed to bring a Jones Act action against a shipowner who was not his employer may be slim but should not be put at zero. But the harbor worker's lawyer should derive aid and comfort from the Haverty holding and the Haverty opinion even if he stops short of pleading the Jones Act. Haverty may well be cited to the proposition that the standards of negligence applicable to harbor workers should be the same as the standards applicable to seamen, since both incur the same hazards. Or it might be argued that § 905 (b) incorporates the Jones Act even though the harbor worker can no longer bring an action for unseaworthiness under the general maritime law.

Adoption of the idea that § 905(b) incorporates the Jones Act would point to a solution for a whole host of procedural problems which § 905(b) says nothing about (such as, for example, venue). The "action against [the] vessel [for negligence]" was presumably meant to be an action within the admiralty jurisdiction. No doubt the § 905(b) plaintiff may elect, under the saving to suitors clause, to bring his action on the civil side of federal court. If he does so and if there is no diversity jurisdiction, is he entitled to a jury? It would be hard to elaborate reasons of policy why Jones Act seamen are always entitled to a jury while § 905(b) harbor workers doing the same kind of work under the same conditions of danger are not. And there are, of course, many workers whose conditions of employment leave them straddling the line (wherever the line may be) which separates Jones Act seamen from LHCA harbor workers. Unless the § 905(b) action is held to incorporate the Jones Act right to a jury trial, the federal courts will have to waste their time and energies deciding a great many cases of this sort. There is another possible approach to the jury trial question through Fitzgerald v. United States Lines, Inc.[378x] in which the Supreme Court held, in effect, that it had the power to provide for jury trials in admiralty and did so with respect to a maintenance and cure count joined with a Jones Act count.

If the courts fashion the § 905(b) action in the image of the Jones Act action, they will find helpful precedents for most of the problem that will arise in litigation. If they do so, the LHCA harbor workers will be substantially in the position of the Jones Act seaman (with compensation benefits substituted for maintenance and cure) except that the harbor workers will not be entitled to recover under the no-fault fringes of the unseaworthiness doctrine. If the courts do not do that, the § 905(b) U.S.C.A. annotations will in time rival the Jones Act annotations.

**378w.** See § 6–21(a) *supra.*

**378x.** 374 U.S. 16, 83 S.Ct. 1646, 1963 A.M.C. 1093 (1963), discussed § 6–9 *supra,* text following note 45d.

### Applicability of Maritime Law in Non-admiralty Courts

**§ 6–58.** It is possible to assign a precise date to the first appearance in American admiralty law of the idea that rules of maritime law displace rules of common law in actions brought under the saving to suitors clause in non-admiralty courts. The date is May 21, 1917, decision day for Southern Pacific Company v. Jensen.

> "There is no doubt [wrote Justice Pitney, concluding an exhaustive dissent] that, throughout the entire life of the nation under the Constitution, state courts not only have exercised concurrent jurisdiction with the courts of admiralty in actions *ex contractu* arising out of maritime transactions, and in actions *ex delicto* arising upon the navigable waters, but that in exercising such jurisdiction they have without challenge until now, adopted as rules of decision their local laws and statutes, recognizing no obligation of a federal nature to apply the law maritime." [379]

That state courts were under an "obligation of a federal nature to apply the law maritime" was at most implicit in Jensen. It was a possible, but not the only possible, reading of the majority opinion. That it was the correct reading became clear the following year with Chelentis v. Luckenbach S. S. Co., Inc.[380]

Chelentis, a seaman, brought suit in New York state court (which, for diversity of citizenship, was removed to the Federal District Court on the civil side) to recover damages for an injury sustained while performing deck duties at sea. He did not question the seaworthiness of the ship but sought to recover for negligence alone. Chelentis advanced two arguments. First: that Section 20 of the Seamen's Act of 1915 (the predecessor of the Jones Act) had given seamen the right to recover damages for negligence.[381] The Court held that Section 20 had no such effect. Second: that in an action brought outside the admiralty he had, under the saving to suitors clause, "the right to recover full indemnity according to the common law," despite the maritime rule to the contrary.

In reply to the argument Justice McReynolds made explicit what had been left ambiguous in Jensen. In support of his position he found little authority to cite, and all of it (except Jensen itself) irrelevant. He started by making the point that Chelentis was suing on a maritime cause of action, and as to that there could be no dispute. He continued:

> "And unless in some way there was imposed upon the owners a liability different from that prescribed by mari-

379. 244 U.S. 205, 254, 37 S.Ct. 524, 544 (1917). Chapters X–XVI of Robertson, Admiralty and Federalism (1970) contain an elaborate and interesting discussion of the matters taken up in this section and the following sections.

380. 247 U.S. 372, 38 S.Ct. 501 (1918).

381. See § 6–20 *supra* for Section 20 of the Act of 1915 and a discussion of this aspect of the Chelentis case.

time law, petitioner could properly demand only wages, maintenance and cure. Under the doctrine approved in Southern Pacific Co. v. Jensen, no State has power to abolish the well recognized maritime rule concerning measure of recovery and substitute therefore the full indemnity rule of the common law.

. . .

"The distinction between rights and remedies is fundamental. A right is a well founded or acknowledged claim; a remedy is the means employed to enforce a right or redress an injury. Bouvier's Law Dictionary. Plainly, we think, under the saving clause a right sanctioned by the maritime law may be enforced through any appropriate remedy recognized at common law; but we find nothing therein which reveals an intention to give the complaining party an election to determine whether the defendant's liability shall be measured by common-law standards rather than those of the maritime law. Under the circumstances here presented, without regard to the court where he might ask relief, petitioner's rights were those recognized by the law of the sea." [382]

It is one of the curious facts of our legal history that after Jensen and Chelentis had established it, the doctrine of maritime law supremacy lay almost unused for a quarter of a century.[383] It is not hard to find a reason for the long delay in exploding the Chelentis time-bomb. It is in the context of personal injury cases that the maritime law vs. common law question takes on its greatest importance. The personal injury plaintiff wants a jury and to get it he must go outside the admiralty. Before Chelentis it seems to have been assumed that by going into a common law court, plaintiff subjected himself to the common law rules, including the defenses of contributory negligence, assumption of risk and fellow servant, but also freed himself from the peculiar rules of maritime law. Chelentis suggested that he carried with him his maritime rights (recovery for unseaworthiness, at that time a little used remedy) and made clear that he carried with him the limitations on his rights (no recovery for negligence). Chelentis did not decide whether plaintiff, assuming that his maritime rights followed him, would still be subject to the common law defenses: Justice McReynolds' insistence on the difference between rights and remedies could be read as meaning that the common law defenses would still be good. Plaintiff's lawyer, reading Chelentis, might well have concluded that his client would be better off in the admiralty, without a jury, where both his rights and remedies would be decided under maritime law where the common law defenses had never got a foothold. The passage of the Jones Act in 1920

382. 247 U.S. 372, 382, 384, 38 S.Ct. 501, 503–504.

383. One of its rare appearances during that period was in Carlisle Packing Co. v. Sandanger, 259 U.S. 255, 42 S.Ct. 475 (1922), opinion again by Justice McReynolds, discussed § 6–40 *supra* text following note 223.

radically simplified the problem and avoided the welter of confusion to which Chelentis might have led. Since in suits under the Jones Act the common law courts, state or federal, were dealing with a federal statute which stated its own rules, few questions could arise as to the choice between maritime and common law. Between 1920 and the early 1940's the Jones Act was the vehicle for almost all seaman's personal injury actions. During the same period almost all harbor workers' personal injury claims were settled with their employers under compensation acts. Thus, for a generation, Chelentis lay dormant.

Since the 1940's the Chelentis doctrine has become one of the leading features of maritime personal injury law. The reasons for its resurrection are of the same order which explained its earlier non-use. Since 1944 (Mahnich v. Southern S. S. Co.) [384] the action for unseaworthiness under maritime law has gradually replaced (or been fused with) the action for negligence under the Jones Act. Between 1946 (Seas Shipping Co. v. Sieracki) and 1972 (enactment of § 905 (b) of the Longshoremen's and Harbor Workers Compensation Act) harbor workers were allowed to recover against shipowners under the unseaworthiness doctrine and did so in great numbers.[385] Typically the Sieracki unseaworthiness cases were brought outside the admiralty, since the plaintiffs preferred a jury. In such cases the courts were no longer dealing with a federal statute (as they were in cases brought under the Jones Act, even when an unseaworthiness count was joined with a Jones Act count), so that the problem of maritime law vs. common law became of importance and was much discussed in the cases.[385a] Meanwhile the maritime law, as it was understood when Chelentis was decided, had been rewritten in favor of both Jones Act seamen and Sieracki-seamen. The Supreme Court, in resurrecting Chelentis and giving it an extension which even Justice McReynolds can hardly have contemplated, has thus applied it in a context which is at the opposite pole from that in which it originated.

The Supreme Court's development of a "federal supremacy" theory in maritime law during the 1940's and 1950's was not an isolated phenomenon. During the same period the Court was, in effect, federalizing large areas of the substantive law under various theories. One theory was that federal law applied to any contract or transaction to which the United States, in any of its capacities, was a party. An-

**384.** 321 U.S. 96, 64 S.Ct. 455, 1944 A.M.C. 1 (1944) discussed § 6–39 *supra*.

**385.** On harbor workers as Sieracki-seamen, see § 6–54 *supra*; on LHCA § 905(b), see § 6–57 *supra*.

**385a.** Under LHCA § 905(b), harbor workers, who can no longer sue under the unseaworthiness doctrine, are entitled to bring actions for negligence against shipowners (or "vessels") who are not their employers. Presumably the § 905(b) negligence action is quite as much an action under a federal statute as an action under the Jones Act is. We have given our reasons (§ 6–57 *supra*) for concluding that § 905(b) should be construed as having, in effect, incorporated the Jones Act. If that is correct, the problem of maritime law vs. common law will be less bothersome with respect to § 905(b) cases than it was with respect to Sieracki-unseaworthiness cases.

other was that gaps in federal statutes were to be filled by extrapolation from whatever the underlying policy of the federal statute was conceived to be and not by reference to the rules of the common law.[385b] By the mid-1960's the Court's celebrated decision in Erie Railroad Co. v. Tompkins [385c] had come to be seen as having provided the base for a new federal common law and not as having, in any meaningful sense, established the supremacy of state law.[385d] In the light of the constitutional background and the entire history of the development of admiralty jurisdiction in this country it is not (in retrospect) surprising that the Court should have hit on the maritime law as the vehicle for some of its first post-Erie federalizing decisions.[386] It should be added, however, that, as will be indicated in the following discussion, the Court has used the federal supremacy principle selectively in the maritime cases which the Justices have taken as presenting the issue of conflict (or choice) between federal and state rules.

**§ 6–59.** The Supreme Court laid the foundation for the rehabilitation of the maritime law supremacy doctrine in Garrett v. Moore-McCormack Co., Inc.[387] Garrett, a crew member, brought suit in a Pennsylvania state court to recover damages under the Jones Act and maintenance and cure under maritime law. Before commencing his action Garrett had signed a release of all claims arising from his injury, for which he had been paid $100. He had a jury verdict for $3000 on the Jones Act count and $1000 for maintenance and cure. The verdict was set aside and judgment entered for defendant on the ground that, by Pennsylvania law, the burden of proof to show that a release is invalid was on the party asserting its invalidity and that Garrett had not borne the burden. The long-established rule in admiralty, as Justice Black restated it in the Garrett case, was that "the burden is upon one who sets up a seaman's release to show that it was executed freely, without deception or coercion, and that it was made by the seaman with full understanding of his rights." [388] The Penn-

**385b.** See Chapter IX, § 9–57 *et seq.* for a discussion of these aspects of the new federalism in the context of the Ship Mortgage Act of 1920.

**385c.** 304 U.S. 64, 58 S.Ct. 817 (1938).

**385d.** See, e. g., Friendly, In Praise of Erie and the New Federal Common Law, 39 N.Y.U.L.Rev. 383 (1964).

**386.** One of the first and most perceptive studies of this phenomenon was Stevens, Erie R. Co. v. Tompkins and the Uniform General Marintime Law, 64 Harv.L.Rev. 246 (1950). See also Baxter, Choice of Law and the Federal System, 16 Stanford L.Rev. 1 (1963); Robertson, note 379 *supra.*

**387.** 317 U.S. 239, 63 S.Ct. 246, 1942 A.M.C. 1645 (1942).

**388.** The question of seamen's releases accounts for a continuing stream of litigation, with the courts in general adhering to the rule as stated in the Garrett case and casting a heavy burden on the party who sets up the release. An illustrative case is Kelcey v. Tankers Co., Inc., 217 F.2d 541, 1955 A.M.C. 31 (2d Cir. 1954). "That the release constituted a defense," wrote Judge Frank, "might be a necessary conclusion if plaintiff, on this issue, had the burden of proof. But the crucial factor here is that a release by a seaman to his employer differs markedly from a release by an ordinary worker to his employer." Judge Learned Hand, dissenting on the release issue, said: "[I]t seems to me that to allow this release to be repudiated is not only unwarranted in law, but unsanctioned in morals."

sylvania courts felt that the question of burden of proof did not go to Garrett's substantive rights but was a matter of procedure controlled by state law. The Supreme Court reversed, without dissent: "The right of the petitioner to be free from the burden of proof imposed by the Pennsylvania local rule inhered in his cause of action. Deeply rooted in admiralty as that right is, it was a part of the very substance of his claim and cannot be considered a mere incident of a form of procedure."

The Garrett case, standing by itself, was far from conclusive on how strict a rule of maritime supremacy the Supreme Court intended to establish. Justice Black's opinion did not deny that questions of "mere" procedure should be controlled by state law if the action was in a state court; the holding was that the admiralty release rule was substantive rather than procedural. And while the Pennsylvania courts were directed to apply the admiralty rule both to the Jones Act count and to the maintenance and cure count, the fact that the case was brought under a federal statute gave a lever for imposing the federal rule which might not have been present in an action brought exclusively under maritime law.

Seas Shipping Co. v. Sieracki [389] has come to be cited as a reaffirmation and broadening of the principle announced or resurrected in the Garrett case, but actually Sieracki was principally fought on other issues [390] and advanced the maritime supremacy argument only by implication. Sieracki, a stevedore, sued a non-negligent shipowner in federal district court on the civil side, alleging unseaworthiness. The defendant shipowner suggested, as one of several defenses, that an action for unseaworthiness, a doctrine peculiar to maritime law, could be maintained only in an admiralty court. Justice Rutledge cited Garrett, among other cases, to the "well settled" proposition that "a right peculiar to the admiralty may be enforced either by a suit in admiralty or by one on the law side of the court" and the balance of the opinion assumed that maritime law applied to Sieracki's civil action. The case raised no issue, however, of conflict between a common law rule and a maritime rule (such as, for example, contributory negligence on plaintiff's part) and cannot be regarded as even relevant to the supremacy issue, despite its frequent citation as a controlling authority. Sieracki did serve to set at rest any lingering doubts there may have been as to whether common law courts, state or federal, could entertain "peculiarly" maritime causes of action, such as unseaworthiness and maintenance and cure. By implication Garrett had approved submission of a maintenance and cure count to a state court jury (although the jury verdict was not made an issue in the Supreme Court). Sieracki was tried without a jury, but Garrett and Sieracki together made clear that the Court was not disposed

Releases executed by seamen as to their rights to wages and salvage must comply with statutory formalities to be valid, 46 U.S.C. § 600 (derived from Rev.Stat. § 4535).

389. 328 U.S. 85, 66 S.Ct. 872, 1946 A.M.C. 698 (1946).

390. See §§ 6–41, 6–54 *supra*.

to look with favor on any technical limitations on the rights of its favorite wards. The saving to suitors clause was to be broadly construed to allow seamen whatever strategic advantages the common law forum might afford, whether the cause of action was grounded on the Jones Act or maritime law. Subsequent cases have merely reiterated the proposition.

**§ 6–60.** After Sieracki the maritime vs. common law issue became obscurely entangled in an odd sequence of cases which involved, basically, a question of construction of the wartime agency contract under which private shipping lines operated government owned or chartered ships as "general agents" of the United States. In the first of the cases, Hust v. Moore-McCormack Lines, Inc.,[391] an injured crew member brought a Jones Act suit in state court against the general agent. The defense was that the United States, and not the general agent, was the employer, that only employers could be sued under the Jones Act, and that the suit against the United States should have been brought under the Suits in Admiralty Act. The Supreme Court of Oregon, agreeing that Moore-McCormack could be sued under the Jones Act only if it was Hust's employer, felt that the question whether an employment relationship existed was controlled by state law, decided that under Oregon law the agency contract did not make the general agent an employer and dismissed the action.[392] It was, however, according to a majority of the Supreme Court a "fallacy" to think that "the case would be controlled by the common-law rules of private agency." There was no reason to believe that the wartime shipping operation had been designed to deprive merchant seamen (even though technically employed by the United States) of their preexisting rights and to restrict them to a suit in admiralty against the United States. Consequently, the general agent could be sued under the Jones Act. Next, in Caldarola v. Eckert [393] an injured stevedore brought action in New York state court against a general agent alleging that his injury was caused by defective shipboard equipment. Like the Oregon court, the New York Court of Appeals looked to state law, held that the agent did not under the contract have possession and control of the ship to a degree sufficient to make him liable, and affirmed a judgment dismissing the action. The Hust case was distinguished on the unconvincing ground that it represented a "liberal" construction of the Jones Act not applicable in a non-statutory action.[394] Nevertheless, the Court of Appeals was upheld in its subtle distinction by the Supreme Court in an opinion by Justice Frankfurter (who had been one of the three dissenters in the Hust case), with Justices Douglas, Black, Murphy and Rutledge (all of whom had voted with the Hust majority) in dissent. The Caldarola case was widely regarded as a retreat from the Garrett principle of maritime law su-

391. 328 U.S. 707, 66 S.Ct. 1218, 1946 A.M.C. 727 (1946).

392. 176 Or. 662, 158 P.2d 275, 1945 A.M.C. 517 (1945).

393. 332 U.S. 155, 67 S.Ct. 1569, 1947 A.M.C. 847 (1947).

394. 295 N.Y. 463, 68 N.E.2d 444, 1946 A.M.C. 1319 (1946).

premacy,[395] but Justice Frankfurter's opinion was a masterpiece of contrived ambiguity: "Whether Congress [by the saving to suitors clause] recognized that there were common law rights in the states as to matters also cognizable in admiralty or whether it was concerned only with "saving" to the States the power to use their courts to vindicate rights deriving from the maritime law to the extent that their common law rights may be available, is a question on which the authorities do not speak with clarity." However, it was clear to the precariously constituted Caldarola majority that "whether New York is the source of the right or merely affords the means for enforcing it, her determination is decisive that there is no remedy in its courts for such a business invitee against one who has no control and possession of premises." Two years after Caldarola the Supreme Court finally closed the books on the question whether "general agents" were liable in personal injury actions. Cosmopolitan Shipping Co. v. McAllister [396] reproduced the Hust case: an injured crew-member sued the general agent under the Jones Act. Justice Reed, speaking for five members of the Court, commented that Caldarola had "undermined the foundations of Hust" and that from the date of the Caldarola decision "the danger of relying on Hust was apparent to the world." Hust was flatly overruled. Since the McAllister case was not decided until June of 1949, when most of the personal injury litigation arising from the period of wartime operation under agency contracts had been disposed of, it made little difference which way the case was decided (except of course to the parties litigant).

After the three agency cases the authorities still spoke with as little clarity as they had before. It now appeared that state courts could look to their own law for guidance in the interpretation of such words as "employer" in a maritime contract or for the determination of when agents were liable to business invitees. But both Caldarola and McAllister had raised issues as to which there was no well established maritime rule differing from a common law rule. Hust had been decided on humanitarian grounds rather than on a theory of maritime law supremacy. When a bare majority of the Court decided against humanitarianism as a ground of decision, the only source of law left for a court to turn to was the law of some state. If, after McAllister, a damage action had been brought against a general agent even in an admiralty court, the court would have had to look to the common law of agency in deciding whether to entertain the action, since there was no maritime rule, no general federal law of agency, and, according to the opinions in both Caldarola and McAllister, no requirement that the federal courts improvise a federal rule merely because the United States was a party to the agency contract.[397]

395. See, *e. g.*, Dickinsen and Andrew, A Decade of Admiralty Jurisdiction in the Supreme Court of the United States, 36 Calif.L.Rev. 169, 195 (1948).

396. 337 U.S. 783, 69 S.Ct. 1317, 1949 A.M.C. 1031 (1949). See § 6–21(a) *supra*, text following note 1210, for a discussion of the McAllister case and the assumed requirement that the Jones Act defendant must be the plaintiff's employer.

397. Oddly enough, in a then recent series of cases, which were not referred to in either Caldarola or McAllister,

Thus there was no reason to construe the agency cases as a retreat from the holding in Garrett that in the case of a clear conflict between a substantive maritime law rule and a common law rule, the maritime rule must be applied even in a state court. The only thing which the agency cases did make clear was the ease with which last term's dissent could become this term's majority opinion.

**§ 6–61.** It has turned out that the Caldarola-McAllister sequence did not mean that the Court had abandoned the maritime law supremacy idea any more than the 1940 Garrett case had meant that the Court was prepared to apply the idea in all possible situations with a Jensen-like rigidity. We might say that Caldarola and Garrett have continued to coexist in much the same way that Jensen itself coexisted with the "maritime but local" category in which both the Jensen majority and the Jensen dissenters had concurred in the 1920's.[398] In the context of harbor workers' compensation litigation, the Court eventually blurred the sharp line between Jensen and the maritime but local cases by inventing a twilight zone, whose meaning seemed to be that an injured worker could, within vaguely defined limits, elect either his state remedy or his federal remedy. The Court has not, in so many words, generalized its twilight zone theory into an overriding principle of plaintiff's choice, even in personal injury cases. It will be suggested, however, that most of the Supreme Court federal-state cases since 1950 are consistent with the idea of a sort of twilight zone approach.

The suggestion has been made, and has indeed acquired a certain vogue, that what the Court ought to do (arguably, what the Court has been doing) in solving federal-state conflicts is to adopt a "balancing" approach.[399] That is, when the Court is faced with a situation in which there are conflicting state (or common law) and federal (or maritime) rules (or a state rule but no federal rule) it should weigh the competing state and federal interests in the balance. If the federal interest outweighs the state interest, it should apply the federal rule (or "fashion" one if none exists). If the state interest outweighs the federal interest it should apply the state rule. The balancing idea has the merit of recognizing that cases of this sort have been sorted out into two heaps and have not, for the sake of "logical" consistency, all been forced into a single pattern of decision according to some preconceived theory. On the other hand, "balancing" ultimately explains nothing (beyond the fact that there are, and perhaps

the Court had been developing a theory that in the decision of all questions arising under contracts to which the United States was a party, state law was not applicable and a "federal rule" should be, if necessary, improvised. See D'Oench, Duhme & Co. v. Federal Deposit Ins. Corp., 315 U.S. 447, 62 S.Ct. 676 (1942); Clearfield Trust Co. v. U. S., 318 U.S. 363, 63 S. Ct. 573 (1943).

398. On "maritime but local" and the "twilight zone", see § 6–49 *supra*.

399. Robertson, Admiralty and Federalism (1970) adopts the "balancing" idea and seeks to demonstrate that most (although not all) of the Supreme Court cases can be so analyzed. The "balancing" idea had been put forward in D. Currie, Federalism and the Admiralty: "The Devil's Own Mess," 1960 Supreme Court Rev. 158.

should be, two heaps of cases). Past cases can be arranged in a sort of formal unity (with cases the writer disapproves of dismissed as failures on the Court's part to have arrived at a proper balance). Future cases cannot be predicted at all since no two lawyers (or judges) would ever agree on which of the intangible "interests" outweighs the other.

We have no all purpose theoretical solution to propose in place of the balancing solution. After we have reviewed the Supreme Court cases, we can make at least a descriptive statement about how the Court has gone about its task of sorting the cases into two heaps.

Between 1952 and 1970 the Supreme Court decided eleven cases which the Justices analyzed as presenting problems of conflict (or choice) between state common law or statutory rules and federal maritime rules (existing or to be fashioned.)[400] Arguably, other cases should be added to the list—such as the twilight zone cases culminating in Calbeck v. Travelers Ins. Co.[401] However the eleven cases we have chosen seem to us to be the cases in which the Court has confronted the state-federal problem head on. We do not believe that any significant cases, which would throw a different light on what the Supreme Court has been doing, have been omitted.

Nine of the eleven cases involved personal injury or death claims. The two which did not were Halcyon (#1) and Wilburn Boat (#5).[402] Halcyon (or the aspect of Halcyon we are presently interested in) was an attempt by a shipowner to recover from a harbor worker's employ-

**400.** The cases are listed chronologically:

1. Halcyon Lines v. Haenn Ship Ceiling & Refitting Corp., 342 U.S. 282, 72 S.Ct. 277, 1952 A.M.C. 1 (1952), discussed § 6–55 *supra*, text following note 362.

2. Levinson v. Deupree, 345 U.S. 648, 73 S.Ct. 914, 1953 A.M.C. 972 (1953), discussed Chapter IX, § 9–82, text following note 414.

3. Pope & Talbot, Inc. v. Hawn, 346 U.S. 406, 74 S.Ct. 202, 1954 A.M.C. 1 (1953), discussed § 6–54 *supra*, text following note 353.

4. Maryland Casualty Co. v. Cushing, 347 U.S. 409, 74 S.Ct. 608, 1954 A.M.C. 837 (1954), discussed Chapter X, § 10–31.

5. Wilburn Boat Co. v. Fireman's Fund Ins. Co., 348 U.S. 310, 75 S.Ct. 368, 1955 A.M.C. 467 (1955), discussed Chapter I, § 1–17.

6. The Tungus v. Skovgaard, 358 U.S. 588, 79 S.Ct. 503, 1959 A.M.C. 813 (1959), discussed § 6–30 *supra* text following note 189b.

7. Kermarec v. Compagnie Générale Transatlantique, 358 U.S. 625, 79 S.Ct. 406, 1959 A.M.C. 597 (1959), discussed § 6–57 *supra*, text following note 378q.

8. Hess v. United States, 361 U.S. 314, 80 S.Ct. 341, 1960 A.M.C. 527 (1960), discussed § 6–30 *supra*, text following note 189d.

9. Goett v. Union Carbide Corp., 361 U.S. 340, 80 S.Ct. 357, 1960 A.M.C. 550 (1960), discussed § 6–30 *supra*, text following note 189e.

10. Kossick v. United Fruit Co., 365 U.S. 731, 81 S.Ct. 886, 1961 A.M.C. 833 (1961), discussed § 6–11 *supra*, text following note 58a.

11. Moragne v. States Marine Lines, Inc., 398 U.S. 375, 90 S.Ct. 1772, 1970 A.M.C. 967 (1970), discussed § 6–32 *supra*.

**401.** See § 6–49 *supra*.

**402.** The references are to the chronological list of cases in note 400 *supra*.

er damages for which the shipowner might be held liable in the harbor worker's action for unseaworthiness as a Sieracki-seaman. The Court held for the defendant under the common law rule of no contribution among tortfeasors, declining to extend the maritime law comparative negligence rule to cover the case.[403] In Wilburn Boat the Court held that there could be a recovery under a Texas statute in a marine insurance case on the ground (disputed by most commentators) that there was no applicable rule of maritime law.

In all nine personal injury or death cases the Court held for the plaintiffs (either by affirming judgments for plaintiffs or by reversing judgments for defendants and remanding the cases for further proceedings). In four of the nine cases (Levinson [#2], Hawn [#3], Kermarec [#7], and Moragne [#11]), the Court applied (or fashioned) a federal maritime rule. In four other cases (Cushing [#4], Tungus [#6], Hess [#8], and Goett [#9]) the Court applied (or purported to apply) a state common law or statutory rule. In the ninth (and perhaps most interesting) case (Kossick [#10]) the Court seems to have given the plaintiff the benefit of one maritime rule (against a state law rule which would have been fatal to his case) and of one state law rule (against a maritime rule which would also have been fatal to his case). To avoid misunderstanding we should add that what we have said about the nine cases relates to the holdings and not to the rationales, rules, or doctrines set out in the majority opinions. It should also be added that the cases did not represent a series of victories for the "liberal" or "humanitarian" wing of the Court over the "conservative" wing. Even if it is to be assumed that the Court (rara avis) had two such wings, they did not beat in such simple-minded opposition. Indeed in what may be the two most interesting cases in the series (Kossick and Moragne) Justice Harlan, who has usually been associated with the conservatives on the Court, wrote the majority opinions, for a six man majority in Kossick, for a unanimous Court in Moragne. A third general comment relates to our arbitrary division of time periods. In most (but not all) of the pre-1950 cases (the 1940 Garrett case was a notable exception) the federal-state choice of law decisions in personal injury and death cases led to decisions against plaintiffs (Jensen, Chelentis, Garcia, Rohde, Caldarola, McAllister).[403a] It is only in the post-1950 cases of this sort that the opposite trend becomes evident.

Hawn-Tungus-Hess-Goett-Moragne may be taken as a related sequence. Hawn was a harbor worker's unseaworthiness action under Sieracki, brought on the civil side of federal court. The Hawn majority held that the maritime law rule of comparative negligence, not the common law rule of contributory negligence, applied (despite the fact that a year earlier in Halcyon the Court had held that the

403. On the Court's reaffirmance of Halcyon in 1972, see note 363 *supra*. On the Court's de facto overruling of Halcyon in the Ryan case (1956), see § 6–55 *supra*, text following note 364.

403a. On Jensen and Chelentis, see § 6–58, *supra*; on Garcia and Rohde, § 6–49 *supra*; on Caldarola and McAllister, § 6–60 *supra*.

comparative negligence rule applied only to collision cases and would not be extended to a concurrent negligence case involving a shipowner and a stevedore). Justice Black in his Hawn opinion characterized Hawn's right of recovery as "rooted in federal maritime law" and added the dictum: "Even if Hawn were seeking to enforce a State-created remedy for this right, federal maritime law would be controlling." The situation which Justice Black was presumably referring to in his Hawn dictum came up in Tungus: a wrongful death action under a state statute, the cause of the death having been non-negligent unseaworthiness. The Tungus majority (Black, Brennan, Douglas and Warren dissented) rejected the Hawn dictum and announced that the action was maintainable only if the state statute recognized non-negligent unseaworthiness as a ground of recovery. On a finding that the state statute did "encompass" unseaworthiness, a judgment for plaintiff was affirmed (all the Justices concurred in the affirmance, although Justice Frankfurter felt that the case should have been remanded for further proceedings). In the subsequent Hess and Goett cases, the Tungus majority fell apart and, with the concurrence of the Tungus dissenters, the doctrine announced in Tungus was used to support recoveries in cases in which the relevant state statute or rule arguably imposed higher standards of liability on defendants than the federal maritime law did. Finally, in Moragne, the Court was faced with the situation hypothesized in Tungus: an action for wrongful death caused by non-negligent unseaworthiness which the relevant state statute did not recognize as a ground of recovery. The response of a unanimous Court, announced in a remarkable opinion by Justice Harlan, was to solve the Tungus problem by abolishing it. Moragne, overruling precedents which went back for a hundred years, declared that a remedy for wrongful death was provided by the federal maritime law, so that any limitations on recovery contained in state wrongful death statutes had become irrelevant.[403b]

Along with Moragne, Kossick is the most interesting of the post-1950 cases. Kossick, a seaman, alleged an oral agreement with his employer under which the employer was to be responsible for the consequences of any negligent or incompetent treatment which Kossick might receive if he went to a United States Public Health Hospital. Kossick, who was entitled to maintenance and cure, went to the Hospital, allegedly received incompetent treatment which aggravated his condition, and sought to recover under the oral agreement. Kossick's action would have been time-barred under the federal maritime law. His counsel therefore pleaded the action as being for breach of contract in order to take advantage of the New York contract statute of limitation. The difficulty with that approach was that the oral agreement, even if proved, was unenforceable under the New York Statute

**403b.** Theoretically the Tungus (or Hawn) problem ("a State created remedy" for a right "rooted in federal maritime law") could arise with respect to claims of maritime liens based on state lien statutes. However, the state lien acts are, and long have been, for all practical purposes, dead. See Chapter IX, § 9–35.

of Frauds. Kossick's counsel managed to persuade six members of the Court (for whom Justice Harlan wrote the opinion) to ignore the maritime law time bar and to hold that the oral agreement (if proved) was a valid maritime contract not subject to a state statute of frauds. It is true that Justice Harlan devoted his opinion almost entirely to establishing that the oral agreement constituted a maritime contract and that it is necessary to trace the case back through the lower court opinion to discover why counsel had framed his pleadings as he had.[403c]

The remaining entries in our list of post-1950 personal injury cases [403d] may be more briefly disposed of. Levinson (#2) was a wrongful death action brought under a state statute in a federal court sitting in admiralty. The Court held, in an opinion by Justice Frankfurter, that the admiralty court was not bound by such "procedural niceties" as a state statute of limitations which was claimed to bar the action. In Cushing (#4) it was held that actions against a shipowner's insurance carrier under the Louisiana Direct Action statute were not to be dismissed because of the initiation of proceedings under the Limitation of Liability Act but would be stayed until the Limitation proceedings had been completed (four members of the Court felt that the actions against the insurance carrier should have been allowed to proceed immediately; four others felt that the actions should have been dismissed; the solution which became the mandate of the Court was supported only by Justice Clark). In Kermarec (#7), which was an action brought by a crew member's guest who had been injured on the ship while it was in port, the Court unanimously agreed, in an opinion by Justice Stewart, that state law rules on differing degrees of liability owed to invitees, licensees and so on (plaintiff, it had been argued, was a "gratuitous licensee" entitled only to the lowest standard of care) had no place in the maritime law.

In the first edition of the treatise we commented with respect to the Hawn case (which was then the Supreme Court's most recent decision on these issues): "[I]t seems arguable that the Hawn rule is not so much a rule of federal supremacy as a rule that seamen are to have the advantage in any court of whatever rules of law, substantive or procedural, may be most favorable to them." That seems on the whole to have been an accurate guess at the shape of things to come. Instead of "seamen" we should have written "personal injury plaintiffs [Kermarec] and perhaps others [Wilburn Boat]" but it remains true that harbor workers and Jones Act seamen have continued to monopolize the action. At first glance a rule (or non-rule) that op-

**403c.** See our discussion of the maintenance and cure aspect of Kossick, § 6–11 *supra*, text following note 58a. Robertson, note 399 *supra*, who does not refer to the maritime law time bar, describes Kossick (at p. 257) as "a classic application of the reverse-Erie interest-balancing process" which Professor Robertson advocates. There was ample authority for the Kossick proposition that state statutes of frauds do not apply to maritime contracts, see Union Fish Co. v. Erickson, 248 U.S. 308, 39 S.Ct. 112 (1919).

**403d.** Note 400 *supra*.

erates consistently in favor of plaintiffs may seem unprincipled.[403e] It is not, however, true that a principled devotion to the rule of law requires that victories in litigated cases be divided evenly between plaintiffs and defendants.

Between 1950 and 1970 the Supreme Court revolutionized the law relating to maritime personal injury litigation. In the Introductory Note to this long Chapter we suggested that what the Court did in this field "was not in any sense an isolated phenomenon or an aberration attributable to half a dozen Justices; it was part and parcel of the judicial revolution which has reshaped our law of civil obligations during the post-World War II period." [403f] Not infrequently the personal injury cases seemed to present a problem of choice between a federal or maritime law rule and a state common law or statutory rule. The Court never allowed itself to become doctrinaire or inflexible on this issue. State law rules which were not inconsistent with the Court's reformulation of the substantive law were allowed to continue to influence the results in litigation. The federal solution was reserved for cases in which results consistent with the reformulated substantive law required the application of an old—or the fashioning of a new—rule of maritime law. The Court's business is deciding cases, not spinning out symmetrical webs of jurisprudential theory. The opinions delivered in the sequence of cases we have been discussing may occasionally offend logicians but should not offend lawyers. In that respect the post-Moragne era is not likely to be greatly different from the pre-Moragne era.

### Federal Jurisdiction in Death and Injury Cases Brought Outside the Admiralty Under the Saving to Suitors Clause

**§ 6–62.** The privilege of prosecuting maritime causes of action in nonadmiralty courts, conferred by the "saving to suitors" clause,[404] has always been of particular importance in personal injury and death actions in which the plaintiffs prefer to have the damages assessed by a jury. The plaintiffs in such cases have long since abandoned the state courts and seek to have their jury trials on what used to be called the "civil side" of federal courts. No jurisdictional problem is presented when such an action is brought under the Jones Act, since it is established that an action brought under a federal statute is an action which "arises under the Constitution, laws or treaties of the United States" (28 U.S.C.A. § 1331). Nor is any jurisdictional problem presented when the requisite diversity of citizenship exists between the parties under 28 U.S.C.A. § 1332. However, beginning in the late 1940s, metaphysically minded lower court judges

**403e.** Thus Robertson, note 399 *supra*, who agrees that the cases had consistently gone in favor of plaintiffs, comments (at p. 200) that "the structuring of a doctrine that consistently favors one side of the case seems somehow inimical to 'neutral principles' ", citing Wechsler, Toward Neutral Principles of Constitutional Law, 73 Harv. L.Rev. 1 (1959).

**403f.** See § 6–1(a) *supra*, text following note 1g.

**404.** See Chapter I, § 1–13.

began to worry about the jurisdictional problem which was conceivably presented by actions (or counts) based not on the Jones Act but on the general maritime law in cases where there was no § 1332 diversity jurisdiction.

These worries were no doubt stimulated by the practice which developed during the 1940s of pleading all such actions (whenever it was possible to do so) in three counts—Jones Act, unseaworthiness, maintenance and cure. In time there came to be universal agreement that the Jones Act and unseaworthiness counts, which arose out of the same injury and looked toward the recovery of the same damages, could not be split apart; thus, even in a non-diversity case the unseaworthiness count went to the jury with the Jones Act count.[405] There remained the maintenance and cure count which was based on a different theory of liability and looked toward a different recovery. A controversy promptly developed as to the proper method of handling the maintenance and cure count in non-diversity cases. The First Circuit put forward the idea that, even absent diversity, there was "federal question" jurisdiction under § 1331 over general maritime law claims (so that, even in such cases, the maintenance and cure count should go to the jury with the other two counts); the Second and Third Circuits denied the jurisdiction (so that the maintenance and cure count, being cognizable only in admiralty, had to be decided by the judge and only the other two counts went to the jury).[406]

In Romero v. International Terminal Operating Company[407] the Supreme Court agreed to solve the jurisdictional puzzle. The Court divided five to four. For the majority Justice Frankfurter wrote an elaborate opinion which denied § 1331 jurisdiction over the general maritime law claims. For the dissenters Justice Brennan wrote an equally elaborate opinion which affirmed the jurisdiction. The elaborate opinions were then elaborately discussed in the law reviews.[407a] Romero, it appeared, was one of the Supreme Court's major pronouncements, destined to rank, for good or ill, at least in the field of maritime death and injury litigation, with The Osceola, with Jensen, with Sieracki. In fact, Romero has proved to be about as consequential as the medieval scholastic disputes on how many angels could dance on the head of a pin.

It is no doubt wise counsel to watch what the Supreme Court does, not what it says. What the Romero majority did, in the context of the customary three-count action, was to hold that, since the trial court had jurisdiction to decide the Jones Act claim, it also had

405. See § 6–23 *supra*.

406. See Doucette v. Vincent, 194 F.2d 834, 1952 A.M.C. 458 (1st Cir. 1952); Jordine v. Walling, 185 F.2d 662, 1951 A.M.C. 43 (3d Cir. 1950); Paduano v. Yamashita Kisen Kabushiki Kaisha, 221 F.2d 615, 1955 A.M.C. 1483 (2d Cir. 1955).

407. 358 U.S. 354, 79 S.Ct. 468, 1959 A.M.C. 832 (1959).

407a. See B. Currie, The Silver Oar and All That: A Study of the Romero Case, 27 U. of Chi.L.Rev. 1 (1959); Kurland, The Romero Case and Some Problems of Federal Jurisdiction, 73 Harv.L.Rev. 817 (1960).

jurisdiction ("pendent jurisdiction") to decide the general maritime law claims. The majority (joined by two of the dissenters) then held that American law (both the Jones Act and the general maritime law) was not applicable to the case which was an action by a Spanish seaman against his Spanish employer, and that the case against the employer had been appropriately dismissed by the trial court.[407b] Since the case was to be dismissed, the Court was not, as Justice Frankfurter put it, "called upon to decide whether the District Court may submit to the jury the 'pendent' claims under the general maritime law in the event that a cause of action be found to exist."

Thus Romero threw absolutely no light whatever on the one problem which had been bothering the lower courts—how to handle a maintenance and cure count joined to a Jones Act count in nondiversity cases. Four years after Romero the Court finally settled the matter in Fitzgerald v. United States Lines,[407c] holding that the maintenance and cure count should go to the jury along with the Jones Act count even if, under Romero, there was no § 1331 jurisdiction and even in the absence of diversity jurisdiction. With the Fitzgerald decision, the controversy which led to Romero vanished like the morning fog. In the 1966 procedural unification the revisers neither "codified" nor rejected the Romero-Fitzgerald sequence; it has been assumed without question that Romero is still the law on the metaphysics of federal jurisdiction and Fitzgerald still the law on the realities of jury trial.[407d]

Romero means that, absent diversity, there is no federal civil jurisdiction (and hence no right to a jury trial) over claims for maintenance and cure or for unseaworthiness when the general maritime law counts are not (or cannot be) joined to a Jones Act count.[407e] The Romero rule is of course applicable to death and injury actions based on maritime tort theory. The applicability of the Romero rule to two novel situations has not as yet come up in any reported case. One is the action for wrongful death under the maritime law which

**407b.** This aspect of the Romero case is discussed § 6–63 *infra*.

**407c.** 374 U.S. 16, 83 S.Ct. 1646, 1963 A.M.C. 1093 (1963), discussed § 6–9 *supra*, text following note 45d.

**407d.** See § 6–9 *supra*, note 45.

**407e.** See Dassigienis v. Cosmos Carriers & Trading Corp., 442 F.2d 1016, 1971 A.M.C. 1104 (2d Cir. 1971): "There is no basis for invoking the general maritime law of the United States as the basis for a maintenance and cure claim. Since both defendant and plaintiff are aliens there is no diversity and hence no jurisdiction. [Citing Romero]" The Court added in a footnote: "Since there is no jurisdiction under the Jones Act in this case, there is no pendent jurisdiction with respect to a general maritime law claim." See also Mahramas v. American Export Isbrandtsen Lines, 475 F.2d 165, 1973 A.M.C. 587 (2d Cir. 1973), discussed § 6–7 *supra*, text following Note 26: "In this case there was no real Jones Act claim to go to the jury, and the trial court could, as it did, properly take for itself the determination of the remaining admiralty issues. If the rule were otherwise, any plaintiff could receive a jury trial on his admiralty claims simply by alleging a Jones Act count, whether or not he had any evidence to support it, and, of course, the time has still not come when one is entitled to a jury in every admiralty suit. [Citing Romero]" (475 F.2d at 172–173, 1973 A.M.C. at p. 596).

the Supreme Court created in Moragne v. States Marine Lines, Inc.[407f] The other is the harbor worker's action for negligence under § 905(b) of the Longshoremen's and Harbor Worker's Compensation Act (added in 1972).[407g] The Moragne death action emerged from, and to some extent coexists with, an enormously complicated statutory complex: arguments for and against application of the Romero rule to the new death action might seem to be in almost even balance. Application of the Romero rule to the § 905(b) action would seem to depend on whether the action is conceived of as an action arising under a federal statute or as an action arising under the general maritime law. In our earlier discussion of § 905(b) we suggested the statutory approach.

It was predictable that the attempt would be made to reverse the Romero "pendent jurisdiction" theory—to argue, that is, that a court which had admiralty jurisdiction of general maritime law claims for maintenance and cure and unseaworthiness had "pendent jurisdiction" over a Jones Act claim: The argument surfaced in Crookham v. Muick [407h]—the usual three count pleading where the difficulty was improper venue with respect to the Jones Act count.[407i] Judge Dumbauld gave the argument short shrift, citing an earlier Third Circuit case which had presented the same situation (improper venue as to the Jones Act count) in which Judge Hastie, after citing Romero and Fitzgerald, had remarked: "If the court finds itself without power to adjudicate the principal claims, incidental power to hear the admiralty claim on the civil side must also be lacking." [407j] Thus "pendent jurisdiction" under Romero is a one-way, not a two-way street.[407k]

## Choice of Law in Actions Brought in the United States by Seamen Injured on Foreign-Flag Ships

**§ 6–63.** When a seaman brings an action to recover for personal injuries, the court must initially decide whether it has jurisdiction and, if it has, whether United States law or the law of a foreign nation is applicable. In the context of ocean shipping, there may be half a dozen or more sovereignties, each of which has contacts with the transaction which might be considered relevant on both the jurisdic-

**407f.** 398 U.S. 375, 90 S.Ct. 1772, 1970 A.M.C. 967 (1970), discussed § 6–32 *supra*.

**407g.** See § 6–57 *supra*.

**407h.** 246 F.Supp. 288, 1966 A.M.C. 1522 (W.D.Pa.1965).

**407i.** On the complicated venue provisions of the Jones Act, see § 6–22 *supra*.

**407j.** Leith v. Oil Transport Co., 321 F.2d 591, 593, 1964 A.M.C. 2152, 2154–2155 (3d Cir. 1963).

**407k.** In McCord v. Moore-McCormack Lines, Inc., 242 F.Supp. 493, 1965 A.M.C. 1873 (S.D.N.Y.1965) the Romero pendent jurisdiction theory was used to support a holding that the court's power to deny costs when the plaintiff's recovery was for less than $10,000 included the general maritime law counts as well as the Jones Act count.

See, for an unusually expansive reading of the Romero theory, as supplemented by Fitzgerald, Haskins v. Point Towing Co., 395 F.2d 737, 1968 A.M.C. 1193 (3d Cir. 1968), discussed § 6–9 *supra*, text following note 45f.

tional and choice of law issues. In Lauritzen v. Larsen [408] Justice Jackson discussed the weight to be accorded to:

1. The place of the wrongful act.
2. The law of the ship's flag.
3. The allegiance or domicile of the injured seaman.
4. The allegiance of the shipowner.
5. The place of contract (*i. e.* where the shipping articles were signed).
6. The inaccessability of a foreign forum.
7. The law of the forum.

Justice Jackson's elaborate opinion in the Lauritzen case was an attempt to formulate general propositions whose application might bring a degree of order and predictability to the disposition of actions initiated in our state and federal courts which involve one or more foreign contacts. Lauritzen was of course authoritative only on the narrow issue actually decided: which was that a seaman of Danish citizenship, who had signed articles (which provided that the rights of crew members should be governed by Danish law) in New York City, where he was temporarily resident, on a ship of Danish registry and ownership, and who was injured in Cuban territorial waters, could not sue in our courts under the Jones Act. While it would be hard to improve on Justice Jackson's discussion of the issues, the utility of the case as governing precedent was diminished by the consideration that the only conceivable point of contact which would have dictated the choice of United States law was the signing of articles in New York City. Evidently, however, the Lauritzen opinion was broadly conceived and was meant to be used as a *vade mecum* by all trial judges in travail of decision, but no one can do anything about the nature of decisional law and the difference between holding and dictum. Despite the Court's best effort, Lauritzen necessarily left unresolved all the possible combinations of "contacts" which were not exactly the Lauritzen combination (which was almost the weakest possible case for the application of domestic law). Nevertheless, with all its weaknesses, Lauritzen has continued to be the essential text.

In Lauritzen the plaintiff had pleaded only the Jones Act and had not joined counts for unseaworthiness and maintenance and cure to the Jones Act count. Thus Lauritzen could have been taken as being merely an essay in statutory construction with the result that different criteria might have been applicable to plaintiffs who invoked the general maritime law (which Justice Jackson had referred to in the course of his Lauritzen opinion as "a non-national or international law of impressive maturity and universality"). Naturally, the holding that American courts would apply the American version of the general maritime law in seamen's personal injury actions which

408. Lauritzen v. Larsen, 345 U.S. 571, 73 S.Ct. 921, 1953 A.M.C. 1210 (1953).

included counts for unseaworthiness and maintenance and cure would effectively have disposed of the Lauritzen holding. In Romero v. International Terminal Operating Co.[408a] the majority of the Supreme Court chose to remain faithful to Lauritzen and generalized the holding to include cases in which the general maritime law counts as well as the Jones Act count had been pleaded. As Justice Frankfurter put it:

> ". . . [T]he similarity in purpose and function of the Jones Act and the general maritime principles of compensation for personal injury, admit of no rational differentiation of treatment for choice of law purposes." [408b]

The plaintiff in Romero was a Spanish national who had signed articles (in Spain) to serve on a ship of Spanish registry, flag and ownership. He was injured while the ship lay in a United States port and was hospitalized and received treatment for his injuries in this country. The majority of the Court concluded that neither the situs of the injury nor Romero's treatment in this country made a case, under the Lauritzen criteria, for application of American law in Romero's action against his employer, the Spanish Line. Justice Frankfurter's opinion emphasized that the issue was one of choice of law and not of subject matter jurisdiction. That is, the District Court, having decided that Romero's action against his employer was not governed by American law, could have retained jurisdiction of the action and decided it under Spanish law. In fact the District Court had, as a matter of discretion, dismissed the action against the Spanish Line. The dismissal on forum non conveniens grounds was approved by the Supreme Court.

Romero had sought to recover damages not only from his employer but also from the Spanish Line's "husbanding agent" in New York, from a stevedoring company and from a company which was doing carpentry work on the ship preparatory to the loading of a cargo. It was held that the actions against the other three defendants should be heard and adjudicated as actions for a maritime tort. Thus Romero, assuming that he could prove some sort of negligence chargeable to one of the remaining defendants, was not deprived of a recovery in an American court of damages to be assessed by an American jury (there having been diversity of citizenship between Romero and the three tort defendants). It is to be noted, however, that the Supreme Court, although ordering that the tort actions against the "American" defendants should proceed, did not disturb the trial court's forum non conveniens dismissal of the action against the Spanish Line. It might have been argued that a court which was to determine the liability of three of four possible defendants was also a convenient forum for determining the liability of the fourth defendant, however the choice of law question was to be decided. However, that aspect of Romero seems not to have been seriously con-

**408a.** 358 U.S. 354, 79 S.Ct. 468, 1959 A.M.C. 832 (1959).

**408b.** 358 U.S. at p. 382, 79 S.Ct. at p. 485, 1959 A.M.C. at p. 854.

sidered, no doubt because everyone involved in the case was preoccupied with the essentially metaphysical question of whether there was federal jurisdiction over Romero's action against his Spanish employer.[408c]

The Supreme Court's only other contribution in recent years to the choice of law problem in personal injury litigation was in Hellenic Lines Limited v. Rhoditis.[408d] In Rhoditis the plaintiff was a Greek national who signed articles in Greece (which provided for the application of Greek law) for service on a ship of Greek flag and registry owned by a Greek corporation. The ship was regularly engaged in voyages to and from ports of the United States and Rhoditis was injured while the ship was in the port of New Orleans. It was conceded that Rhoditis could have obtained relief under Greek law in the courts of Greece. Rhoditis brought an action under the Jones Act in federal district court in Louisiana. Further facts were that 95% of the stock of the Greek corporation which owned the ship was owned by Pericles Callimanopoulos, a Greek citizen who had been a resident of the United States since 1945 and who managed the corporation out of offices in New York and New Orleans. It was also found that the entire income of the ship on which Rhoditis served was derived from voyages which either originated or terminated in the United States.

Five members of the Court held, in an opinion by Justice Douglas, that the Jones Act was applicable:

> "The Lauritzen test . . . . is not a mechanical one . . . . The significance of one or more factors must be considered in light of the national interest served by the assertion of Jones Act jurisdiction.[408e] Moreover the list of seven factors in Lauritzen was not intended as exhaustive. . . . [T]he shipowner's *base of operations* is another factor of importance in determining whether the Jones Act is applicable; and there may well be others. . . .
>
> " . . . We see no reason whatsoever to give the Jones Act a strained construction so that this alien owner, engaged in an extensive business operation in this country, may have an advantage over citizens engaged in the same business by allowing him to escape the obligations of a Jones Act 'employer.' "[408f]

**408c.** The federal jurisdiction aspect of Romero is discussed § 6–62 *supra*. On the retention of jurisdiction over a foreign defendant because of the presence of an American defendant, see § 6–64 *infra*, text following note 423.

**408d.** 398 U.S. 306, 90 S.Ct. 1731, 1970 A.M.C. 994 (1970).

**408e.** Justice Douglas at this point cited approvingly and quoted from Judge Medina's opinion in Bartholomew v. Universe Tankships, Inc., 263 F.2d 437, 1959 A.M.C. 273 (2d Cir. 1959) in which the applicability of American law had been upheld in a case which involved a plaintiff who was a resident of the United States and a defendant incorporated in Liberia, beneficial ownership being ultimately in a United States citizen.

**408f.** 398 U.S. at pp. 308–310, 90 S.Ct. at p. 1734, 1970 A.M.C. at pp. 996–997. Footnotes and citations omitted. Emphasis in original.

Justice Harlan, joined by Chief Justice Burger and Justice Stewart, dissented, principally on the ground that the "extra-territorial" effect of the Jones Act should be limited to plaintiffs who, although serving on foreign-flag ships, were either citizens or residents of the United States and thus persons whose "well-being" the United States had a legitimate interest in protecting.

Justice Douglas, who wrote the majority opinion in Rhoditis, had dissented not only from Lauritzen but from the choice of law decision in Romero. He has, thus, consistently advocated not only opening our courts to personal injury actions by foreign seamen serving on foreign-flag ships but also giving such plaintiffs the benefit of American law (both the Jones Act and the general maritime law). In Rhoditis he enlisted the support of a majority of his colleagues for a broadening of what Justice Harlan called the extra-territorial application of the Jones Act (and presumably of the domestic general maritime law as well). Rhoditis (like Lauritzen) suffers from the customary weakness of any judicial decision. Just as Lauritzen, on its facts, had been almost the weakest possible case for the application of American law on any theory, so Rhoditis was the strongest possible case for its application on what may be called the "base of operations" theory (assuming that the "base of operations" is in any way relevant, which the dissenting Justices denied). Not only had the beneficial owner been a resident of the United States for twenty years, conducting the affairs of his corporation from offices in this country, but the ship involved seems to have been employed exclusively in, and to have derived all its income from, trade with the United States. While a flat overruling of Rhoditis appears to be unlikely, extension of the base of operations doctrine to enterprises less clearly linked to the United States appears to be equally unlikely.

**§ 6–64.** In summing up the current state of the choice of law problem as the lower courts have worked it out in the light of the Supreme Court cases discussed in the preceding section, we shall start with the situations in which it is clear that American courts will not only take jurisdiction and proceed to adjudication but will apply American law. We shall then review the situations in which the courts dismiss on forum non conveniens grounds or, while refusing to dismiss, hold that the case is governed by the law of some foreign country. Our discussion assumes that no distinction is to be drawn between the question of the applicability (or non-applicability) of the Jones Act and that of the applicability (or non-applicability) of our general maritime law (unseaworthiness and maintenance and cure).[409]

American law will be applied in any personal injury or death case in which the action is brought by (or on behalf of) a citizen (or, in all probability, a long-term or permanent resident) of the United

409. See the passage quoted from Justice Frankfurter's opinion in the Romero case, text at note 408b *supra*.

States. No one has ever doubted that such seamen serving on American owned or registered ships are entitled to the benefits (and disabilities) of American law. However, when they had signed articles for service on foreign-flag ships, some of the older case law had adopted the rule that the law of the ship's flag was, for jurisdictional purposes, attributed to her crew. In Lauritzen Justice Jackson referred to In re Ross [410] in which the Supreme Court had applied such a rule and added:

> "Surely during service under a foreign flag some duty of allegiance is due. But, also, each nation has a legitimate interest that its nationals and permanent inhabitants be not maimed or disabled from self-support. In some later American cases, courts have been prompted to apply the Jones Act by the fact that the wrongful act or omission alleged caused injury to an American citizen or domiciliary [citing cases]." [411]

The fair implication of the passage quoted is that American law applies to American citizens as well as to American "domiciliaries" whether they serve on American-flag or foreign-flag ships and no matter where they may be injured.[412] There is no reason to believe that American courts would pay any attention to stipulations for foreign law in shipping articles signed by American citizens or residents; little attention is paid to such stipulations even in cases involving foreign, non-resident seamen.[413] Naturally the choice of law

410. 140 U.S. 453, 11 S.Ct. 897 (1891).

411. 345 U.S. at p. 586, 73 S.Ct. at p. 930, 1953 A.M.C. at p. 1222.

412. See the Bartholomew case, digested note 408e *supra*. For a current instance, see Nye v. A/S D/S Svendborg, 358 F.Supp. 145, 1973 A.M.C. 1708 (S.D.N.Y.1973). Nye, a ship repairman, was a citizen and resident of the United States. He was flown from New York to the Canary Islands to supervise the installation of a new pump on a Danish-flag ship lying in the port of Las Palmas. He was killed while attempting to board the ship. Holding that Nye's widow was entitled to recover, Judge Gurfein said: "The citizenship of Nye and the factors surrounding his coming from the United States to board the ship in Spanish waters are sufficient to justify applying the law of the United States" [citing Symonette Shipyards, Ltd. v. Clark, 365 F.2d 464, 1966 A.M.C. 2383 (5th Cir. 1966), certiorari denied 387 U.S. 908, 87 S.Ct. 1690 (1966), and the first edition of the treatise]. Judge Gurfein added in a footnote: "I do not mean to imply that just because a plaintiff is an American national United States law must apply. Cf. Tjonaman v. A/S Glittre, 340 F.2d 290, 1965 A.M.C. 57 (2d Cir. 1965), certiorari denied 381 U.S. 925 (1965)." In an earlier opinion in the Nye case Judge Gurfein had left the choice of law question open, 358 F.Supp. 142, 1973 A.M.C. 1705 (S.D.N.Y.1973). In the Tjonaman case cited by Judge Gurfein the Second Circuit had affirmed a holding that Norwegian law applied to the case of a Dutch national who had become a legal resident alien in the United States twenty-nine days before signing articles (in New York) for service on a Norwegian-flag ship. Tjonaman was injured in Ghanian waters. He had been a member of the Norwegian Seamen's union for two years and the articles stipulated for Norwegian law.

413. Thus the Rhoditis case, text following note 408d *supra*, Justice Douglas pointed out that the "contract of employment", signed in Greece by a Greek citizen, "provides that Greek law and a Greek collective bargaining agreement apply between the employer and the seaman and that all claims arising out of the employment con-

cases usually involve traditional, blue-water or Jones Act seamen, but there is no doubt that American harbor workers, repairmen and the like are also entitled to the application of American law.[414]

American law will also be applied in actions brought on account of injuries suffered on American-flag ships, whether the plaintiffs are American or foreign, resident or non-resident, seamen, harbor-workers, passengers, guests or, for that matter, pirates. By taking out registry in this country, the shipowner consents in effect to the application of the law of the United States. This proposition has seemed so self-evident that it appears never to have been questioned.

The application of American law with respect to injuries suffered on ships registered under foreign flags but beneficially owned by American citizens may have seemed at one time to raise greater problems than it does now. Liberian flags of convenience and Panamanian corporations will not insulate American owners from suit under American law.[415] Indeed the Rhoditis case extended the applicability of American law to the case of a foreign seaman injured on a foreign-flag ship beneficially owned by an alien on the ground that the alien, a resident of the United States, had established his "base of operations" in this country.

The doubtful cases are those which involve injuries suffered by foreign, non-resident seamen on foreign-flag ships which are not beneficially owned or controlled by citizens (or, under Rhoditis, residents) of the United States. Justice Jackson's Lauritzen opinion suggested that not much weight was to be given either to the fact that shipping articles had been signed in this country or to the fact that the injury occurred in a United States port or territorial waters. Lauritzen itself held that signing articles in this country was not enough to justify the application of American law. Romero, following Lauritzen, held that injury in a United States port followed by hospitalization and medical treatment in this country was not enough either. There is no reason to believe that a combination of the Lauritzen and Romero contacts (signing articles in the United States; injury in United States territorial waters; treatment in the United States) [416] would lead to the application of American law, although there had been some pre-Lauritzen cases which had so held.[417]

tract are to be adjudicated by a Greek court." Neither the majority opinion nor the dissent in Rhoditis paid any attention to the stipulation for Greek law and litigation in Greece.

414. Uravic v. F. Jarka Co., 282 U.S. 234, 51 S.Ct. 111, 1931 A.M.C. 239 (1931). See the Nye case, digested note 412 *supra*.

415. See the Bartholomew case, digested note 408e *supra*. Earlier cases include Zielinski v. Empresa Hondurena de Vapores, 113 F.Supp. 93, 1953 A.M.C. 1854 (S.D.N.Y.1953) (Jones Act applied in action by Polish seaman, resident in the United States, injured on Panamanian-flag ship owned by a Honduran corporation, the shipping articles having stipulated for Honduran law, the stock in the Honduran corporation having been owned by an American corporation). See also Gerradin v. United Fruit Co., 60 F.2d 927, 1933 A.M.C. 81 (2d Cir. 1932), certiorari denied 287 U.S. 642, 53 S.Ct. 92 (1932).

416. On Lauritzen and Romero, see § 6–63 *supra*.

417. See Kyriakos v. Goulandris, 151 F.2d 132, 1945 A.M.C. 1041 (2d Cir.

Once the trial court has concluded that the application of American law is not justified under the Lauritzen-Romero-Rhoditis triad, it will either dismiss the case or retain it for decision under the law of whatever foreign country may be found to be applicable. The reported cases suggest that our courts, at least in this context, are willing to assume that the maritime law of most foreign countries is the same as the maritime law of the United States. Thus, unless counsel for the defendant is in a position to prove the contrary, the court's decision to apply the law of Greece or Norway or Hong Kong may be tantamount to a decision that the plaintiff is entitled to relief under the maritime law of the United States.[417a]

Justice Jackson in his Lauritzen opinion suggested one reason why American courts should not dismiss cases out of hand even if they conclude that American law is not applicable. Under the heading "Inaccessibility of Foreign Forum" he wrote:

> "It is argued, and particularly stressed by an *amicus* brief, that justice requires adjudication under American law to save seamen expense and loss of time in returning to a foreign forum. This might be a persuasive argument for exercising a discretionary jurisdiction to adjudge a controversy; but it is not persuasive as to the law by which it shall be judged." [418]

In the light of Justice Jackson's insistence that a case should not be dismissed unless the plaintiff has some other available forum, the practice has grown up of staying the proceedings (instead of dismissing them) to allow plaintiff time to pursue his remedy in the foreign forum and of requiring defendants to agree in the American proceeding that they will not raise jurisdictional objections or plead statutes of limitation in whatever action the plaintiff elects to bring abroad.[419]

1945). Indeed, shortly before Lauritzen, the Second Circuit had held that signing articles in the United States, without more, was enough to make the Jones Act applicable. See Taylor v. Atlantic Maritime Co., 179 F.2d 597, 1950 A.M.C. 352 (2d Cir. 1950). Following Lauritzen courts in the Second Circuit concluded that the Jones Act was not applicable even though articles had been signed and the injury occurred in the United States, Nakken v. Fearnley & Eger, 1955 A.M.C. 2021 (S.D.N.Y.1955).

417a. See further text *infra* following note 429.

418. 345 U.S. 571, 589–590, 73 S.Ct. 921, 931–932, 1953 A.M.C. 1210, 1224 (1953).

419. See, e. g., Rodriguez v. Orion Schiffahrts-Gesellschaft Reith & Co., 348 F.Supp. 777, 1973 A.M.C. 364 (S.D.N.Y.1972). Judge Weinfeld wrote: "In all the facts, and in the exercise of discretion, the Court declines to retain jurisdiction. However, in view of the agreement by defendant to appear in a foreign forum, to waive any limitation statute, and to cooperate in obtaining depositions and records for use in a foreign forum, the order to be entered shall contain an appropriate provision that the dismissal shall become effective only upon proof of compliance by defendant with its undertakings." See also Ngo To Po v. Cambridge Navigation Co., Inc., 1972 A.M.C. 1810 (E.D.La.1971). Judge Christenberry concluded that he should decline jurisdiction and dismiss the suit. "However, to afford plaintiff an opportunity to file suit in a Court of the Republic of Panama or of the Province of Hong Kong, the order of dismissal will not be entered until 60 days hence." See also Fran-

There is one factor, not mentioned in Lauritzen, which has induced American courts to retain jurisdiction in actions brought by foreign, nonresident seamen against foreign registered and owned ships. 46 U.S.C.A. § 597, relating to the right of seamen to receive payment of wages while in port, provides that "this section shall apply to seamen on foreign vessels while in harbors of the United States, and the courts of the United States shall be open to such seamen for its enforcement." The preceding section, § 596, under which wages must be paid within twenty-four hours of the discharge of cargo or within four days after the seaman has been discharged, whichever first happens, with a penalty of double wages for each day's delay without sufficient cause, has also been held applicable to foreign seamen on foreign-flag ships even without the express language of § 597.[420] It appears that if a claim is well pleaded under § 596 or § 597 then, assuming that the defendant was properly served, the court must decide the claim; the exercise of jurisdiction is mandatory, not discretionary. It has also been held that the fact that the court must decide the wage claims "is a circumstance which [the court] may properly consider in deciding whether it will assume jurisdiction of the claim for damages so that the libellant may be awarded complete relief against the vessel in one suit." [421] Counsel for foreign plaintiffs have naturally picked up the implication that the inclusion of counts for wages under § 596 or § 597 is a helpful device for persuading courts to retain and decide the entire case even when American contacts (except for the fact that the plaintiff succeeded in making service on a defendant) are totally lacking. In the light of that practice, the courts have developed the idea that the exercise of jurisdiction over § 596 and § 597 claims is mandatory only when the claims are put forward "in good faith"; "good faith" is of course as elusive a concept in this context as it is in any other context.[422] Even if counsel

giskatos v. Konkar Maritime Enterprises, S. A., 471 F.2d 714, 1973 A.M.C. 333 (2d Cir. 1972). In Orgettas v. S/T Crinis, 488 F.2d 89 (4th Cir. 1973) it appeared that in earlier proceedings the plaintiff's action had been stayed on condition that the defendant would enter a general appearance in a Greek court. That was done and in the action in Greece it was held that the plaintiff had no right to recover under Greek law. The Fourth Circuit, affirming the District Court, refused to allow a further action in the United States, even though, on the alleged facts, plaintiff's right to recover maintenance and cure under United States law was crystal clear (tuberculosis contracted during the period of employment).

420. See The Fletero v. Arias, 206 F.2d 267, 1953 A.M.C. 1390 (4th Cir. 1953), certiorari denied 346 U.S. 897, 74 S.Ct. 220 (1953), citing Strathearn S. S. Co. v. Dillon, 252 U.S. 348, 40 S.Ct. 350, (1920). There are a great many cases, old and new, to the same effect.

421. The Fletero v. Arias, note 420 *supra*, 206 F.2d at p. 271, 1953 A.M.C. at p. 1394.

422. Judge Turrentine reviewed the cases in Mihalinos v. Liberian S. S. Trikala, 342 F.Supp. 1237, 1972 A.M.C. 726 (S.D.Cal.1972). He concluded that a "bare conclusory statement that wages are owing" in a complaint verified only by plaintiff's attorney on his "information and belief" did not meet the good faith test and dismissed the entire action (including the claims pleaded under §§ 596, 597). For some reason the greatest amount of litigation of this type has been in the Fourth Circuit, see The Fletero v. Arias, note 420 *supra*. Among the Fourth Circuit cases are Gkiafis v. S. S. Yiosonas, 387 F.2d 460, 1967 A.M.C.

persuades the court that the statutory wage claims have been put forward in good faith, it does not necessarily follow that the court will (or must) retain the entire case for adjudication in the absence of any other American contact. It is clear, however, that, if the count for wages survives, plaintiff's chances of persuading the court not to dismiss the rest of the case are materially improved.

A foreign seaman serving on a foreign-flag ship who is injured in an American port may bring an action against the ship (or his employer) and join as a defendant an American enterprise (stevedore, repairman or what not) allegedly chargeable with negligence in connection with his injury. This was the situation in the Romero case [423] in which the Supreme Court approved the dismissal of Romero's action against his employer, the Spanish Line, while ordering the actions against three American defendants to continue. The Court does not seem to have given much, if any, consideration to the argument that, since the liability of the American defendants was to be adjudicated, it would be a wise exercise of judicial discretion to retain jurisdiction and adjudicate the liability of the foreign defendant as well. Romero certainly cannot be taken as foreclosing that possibility.

Kearney v. Savannah Foods & Industries, Inc.[424] presented the situation discussed in the preceding paragraph. Kearney, an Irish seaman serving on a ship of Irish registry and ownership, was drowned when he fell from a "portable catwalk" used to cross over a conveyor belt that ran along the dock at the Savannah Sugar Refining plant where his ship was moored. His mother, also an Irish citizen, brought an action as his administratrix in which the Irish ship (and its owner) and the American firm (Savannah) which owned or was responsible for maintaining the catwalk were joined as defendants. The allegations were that Savannah had negligently maintained the catwalk and that the unsafe condition of the catwalk made the ship unseaworthy. Motions to dismiss were filed on behalf of the ship and its owner on the ground that a forum was available in Ireland for the

2568 (4th Cir. 1967) (holding that the District Court had abused its discretion in dismissing counts for unseaworthiness and maintenance and cure when joined with a count for wages under § 596; Boreman, J., dissented); Bekris v. M/V Aristoteles, 437 F.2d 219, 1971 A.M.C. 641 (4th Cir. 1971) (affirming dismissal of action which joined counts for unseaworthiness [semble] and maintenance and cure with a count for wages under §§ 596, 597; there were no American contacts and the plaintiff "failed to make a sufficient showing that the statutory wage claims were good faith claims"); Elefteriou v. Tanker Archontissa, 443 F.2d 185, 1971 A.M.C. 1900 (4th Cir. 1971) (reversing District Court's dismissal of action for improper service on the defendant; "If . . . the district judge finds that the [§ 596] claim was asserted in good faith, he should deny the motion to quash with respect to that cause of action, and he should also consider whether he should sustain jurisdiction with respect to the remaining causes of action"). See Grammenos v. Lemos and Nile Shipping Co., S. A., 457 F.2d 1067, 1972 A.M.C. 608 (2d Cir. 1972) (not a statutory wage claim case) for a discussion of service of process, reversing the District Court's dismissal in order to give the plaintiff another chance to obtain valid service.

423. See text following note 408a *supra*.

424. 350 F.Supp. 85, 1972 A.M.C. 2629 (S.D.Ga.1972).

adjudication of the claims against the Irish defendants. Judge Lawrence commented:

> "To decline jurisdiction in this case would leave the action between the administratrix and the American defendant to be tried in this country. Cutting a lawsuit in two and litigating the halves in different countries strikes me as an anfractuous way to handle litigation crying for single rather than piecemeal solution. I conclude that the interests of justice will be more effectively, expeditiously and inexpensively served by retaining jurisdiction over the foreign parties." [425]

Judge Lawrence, in a passage in his opinion which he characterized as "purely obiter", then discussed the relevant aspects of Irish maritime law which, he seemed to feel, were not substantially different from the comparable aspects of American maritime law. His thought apparently was that there would be no objection to adjudicating the liability of the American defendant under American law and the liability of the Irish defendants under Irish law.

There is much to be said for Judge Lawrence's solution in the Kearney case, at least where the two systems of law involved appear to be congruent or consistent. Questions of more difficulty would obviously be raised if it appeared that the two systems imposed radically different standards of liability or provided for radically different measures of recovery. Life and law being what they are, the only situations of this type which American courts will be asked to deal with are those in which American law provides a recovery while, arguably, the foreign law does not or in which American law provides for a greater recovery than would be available under the foreign law. If the lawsuit is, as Judge Lawrence put it, "cut in two," there is no reason to believe that the courts in either country would be bound by what had been done in the other country.[426]

A District Court may properly dismiss a case between a foreign, nonresident seaman and a foreign registered and owned ship (or its owner) provided only that it has been made to appear that an alternative forum is available to the plaintiff and that the defendant will consent to appear in that forum without raising jurisdictional objections or pleading the statute of limitations.[427] Dismissal may be explained in terms of lack of subject matter jurisdiction (particularly with respect to a Jones Act count) or in terms of forum non conveniens (par-

**425.** 350 F.Supp. at p. 88, 1972 A.M.C. at p. 2633.

**426.** See, by way of analogy, Mpliris v. Hellenic Lines, 323 F.Supp. 865, 1972 A.M.C. 1872 (S.D.Tex.1969–1970), affirmed per curiam 440 F.2d 1163, 1972 A.M.C. 1872 (5th Cir. 1971), a complicated case in which one of the points decided was that the American widow of a Greek seaman was not "precluded" from bringing a wrongful death action in this country by the fact that the decedent's mother had already recovered for the death in an action in Greece.

**427.** See the cases cited note 419 *supra*.

ticularly with respect to general maritime law counts) or both.[428] At least as to the general maritime law counts, given diversity jurisdiction, the court could also, as a matter of discretion, despite the absence of American contacts, retain the case for decision according to the appropriate foreign law.[429] The fact that plaintiff will not receive, in the foreign forum, the same type or quantum of relief that he could receive in an American court is not thought to be relevant to the court's decision to dismiss or retain but is, nevertheless, a factor which might be of some influence.

When an American court retains jurisdiction but determines that the case is to be decided on the merits according to the law of some foreign country, the question arises as to how rigorously the foreign law must be pleaded and proved and how strictly it will be applied. Although no clear pattern seems to emerge from the scattering of reported cases of this type, there is considerable authority to support the proposition that the courts may, without being charged with an abuse of discretion, undertake this task in what may be called a relaxed or cheerful manner on the theory that the general maritime law is not the law of any particular country but is part of the law of nations. This approach has the prestigious sanction of Justice Jackson's Lauritzen opinion, in which he wrote:

> "[C]ourts of this and other commercial nations have generally deferred to a non-national or international law of impressive maturity and universality. It has the force of law, not from extraterritorial reach of national laws, nor from abdication of its sovereign powers by any nation, but from acceptance by common consent of civilized communities of rules designed to foster amicable and workable commercial relations." [430]

In the light of Justice Jackson's characterization of the maritime law as a system of "international law of impressive maturity and universality," it is arguable that an American judge need go no further than to ascertain that the applicable foreign law bears a general resemblance to American maritime law. Having got so far, it would then not be unreasonable for him to weigh the American authorities in the balance.

428. See, e. g., the Frangiskatos case, note 419 *supra*. For discussions of forum non conveniens see Fitzgerald v. Westland Marine Corp., 369 F.2d 499, 1966 A.M.C. 2525 (2d Cir. 1966); Grammenos v. Lemos and Nile Shipping Co., 457 F.2d 1067, 1074, n. 5, 1972 A.M.C. 608, 617, n. 5 (2d Cir. 1972).

429. At least the Federal District Courts have a wide discretion in such matters. See, however, To Po Nyo v. J. Fritz Co., 1972 A.M.C. 105 (N.Y. App.Div.1971) and Lambris v. Neptune Maritime Co., 1972 A.M.C. 106 (N.Y. App.Div.1971) reversing trial courts which had refused to dismiss complaints: "It is the general policy of the courts of this State, in the absence of special circumstances, to reject actions between non-residents founded on tort, where the cause of action arises outside the State."

430. 345 U.S. at pp. 581–582, 73 S.Ct. at pp. 927–928, 1953 A.M.C. at p. 1218.

Judge Hoffman, a distinguished and experienced admiralty judge, adopted the approach which has just been outlined in Samad v. The Etivebank.[431] Having determined that English law governed an unseaworthiness action, he concluded, after investigation, that English and American theories of unseaworthiness were similar and added: "While the American law is inapplicable, the similarity of the laws of both nations would compel a consideration of our authorities on the question of liability." He held the defendant liable under English law, according to American case law interpretations of the unseaworthiness doctrine. He then went on to hold that damages were to be assessed under the law of the country where the injury was suffered—which turned out to be American law since the ship had been in an American port when the plaintiff was injured.[432] Judge Hoffman's Etivebank approach seems to reduce the pleading and proof of foreign law in such cases to little more than a formality, provided there is a showing that the foreign law affords something in the nature of a remedy available under American law.[433] The issue has never gone to the Supreme Court and has, indeed, rarely gone above the District Court level so that it cannot be said to have been authoritatively settled.[434]

In Lauritzen Justice Jackson analyzed at some length the provisions of Danish law, which was found to be applicable, concluding that "Danish law relieves [seamen's injuries] under a state-operated plan similar to our workmen's compensation system." It is entirely clear from Justice Jackson's discussion that an American court which retained jurisdiction of a Danish law case would not be justified in awarding damages for unseaworthiness, negligence, or maintenance and cure but would be restricted to the plaintiff's rights under the Danish system.[435] Conceivably an American court might make an

431. 134 F.Supp. 530, 1956 A.M.C. 1603 (E.D.Va.1955).

432. Judge Hoffman followed his Etivebank decision in Spero v. S. S. Argodon, 150 F.Supp. 1, 1957 A.M.C. 1056 (E.D.Va.1957), another English law case, commenting that English law is "substantially the same as the law of this country." However in Santorinakis v. S. S. Orpheus, 176 F.Supp. 343, 1959 A.M.C. 1883 (E.D.Va.), a Greek law case, the same judge concluded that Greek law allowed recovery for negligence but not for unseaworthiness and held that negligence had not been proved.

433. In Gkiafis v. S. S. Yiosonas, 387 F.2d 460, 1967 A.M.C. 2568 (4th Cir. 1967) Judge Craven approvingly cited Etivebank as well as the discussion in the first edition of the treatise to the proposition that a trial judge may, in appropriate cases, consider American as well as foreign materials.

434. See, as illustrations of recent judicial discussion, Kearney v. Savannah Foods & Industries, Inc., discussed text following note 424 *supra* (Irish law); Stamatakos v. Hunter Shipping Co., S. A., 1972 A.M.C. 1001 (E.D.La. 1972) (Greek law). See also The Fletero v. Arias, note 420 *supra* (Argentine law); Cruz v. Harkna, 122 F. Supp. 288, 1954 A.M.C. 1593 (S.D.N.Y. 1954) (Honduran law).

435. See Rivadeneira v. Skibs A/S Snefonn, 1973 A.M.C. 485 (S.D.N.Y.1973) (a Norwegian law case). "Plaintiff also argues that the total of the benefits and compensation afforded to an injured seaman under Norwegian law is so inadequate as compared to the damages available under the Jones Act and the unseaworthiness doctrine that a United States Court should refrain from giving Norwegian law recognition. This argument must be rejected. Norwegian law provides what is basically a workmen's compensation

award under such a system but, in all probability, plaintiff, if he had not already received what he was entitled to, would be directed to file an application for benefits through the local consulate.

type of remedy. Clearly such a remedy is not repugnant to the laws or policy of this country. [Citing Lauritzen]" (1973 A.M.C. at p. 491.) Finding that the defendants had fulfilled their obligations under Norwegian law Judge Griesa dismissed the case. Another Norwegian law case is Tjonaman v. A/S Glittre, 340 F.2d 290, 1965 A.M.C. 57 (2d Cir. 1965), digested note 412 *supra* (at end). See also the Orgettas case, digested note 419 *supra* at end of note.

# Chapter VII

# COLLISION

## The Importance of Collision

§ 7–1. We have taken up several topics, in previous chapters, which are of considerable out-of-court importance to the admiralty lawyer, but which give rise to very little litigation. The Federal reports, on the other hand, abound in collision cases.[1] Perhaps the first reaction of the lawyer without sea experience to this mass of decisions is one of wonderment at the frequency of collision itself; the ocean seems big enough that one would expect collision to be something of a rarity. But ships steam at night, and in all weather, and the combination of their huge momentum and limited braking power makes the averting of collision a matter of constant vigilance and proper and timely action; there is human failure on all these points. Crowded harbors and narrow channels remain perilous, and in some cases are growing more so. Although standardized lights and sound signals have been in use for a long time, and radar and other electronic aids have come into importance in recent decades, the marine collision is still a phenomenon of frequent incidence, and the litigation resulting from it continues to come to court in volume. While there is very rare collision litigation in state courts under the "saving clause" (see *supra* § 1–13 and *infra* § 7–6) the bulk of it comes into federal court, under the admiralty jurisdiction. The applicable law defining fault, it would seem, ought to be the maritime law [1a] (see *supra*, §§ 1–16 and 1–17), but most of it takes the form of federal statutory and regulatory material, so that the question of choice between federal and state law can rarely arise.

We shall be concerned in this chapter mainly with the problem of liabilities between colliding ships, and the less important liabilities between ship and damaged shore structure. But it is well to note that the collision case may, and often does, involve just about all the subjects taken up elsewhere in the book. Goods carried aboard one ship or both are often damaged in collision, and the adjustment of the consequent loss involves the application not only of collision law but also of the law of the carriage of goods by sea; in the discus-

1. This is true very far back; a substantial part, *e. g.*, of the nineteenth century work of the Supreme Court was in the collision field. Indispensable as a guide through this vast body of case law is Griffin, the American Law of Collision (1949, repr. 1962). The standard British treatise, often cited in our courts, is Marsden, Collisions at Sea (11th ed., 1961). Knight Modern Seamanship (14th ed. 1966) and Turpin & MacEwen, Merchant Marine Officers' Handbook (4th ed. 1965) will be found useful on practical background. See also Meadows, Preparing a Ship Collision Case for Trial (1970).

1a. Miller v. Semet-Salvay Div., Allied Chemical Corp. 406 F.2d 1037, 1969 A.M.C. 43 (4th Cir. 1969), certiorari denied 395 U.S. 921 (1969). But see *infra*, § 7–6.

sion, above, of the "Both to Blame" Clause, we have seen the very close connection of these two topics.[2] One of the results of collision may be the placing of one or both of the ships in a position of peril, where general average sacrifices or expenditures become necessary;[3] similarly, salvage charges may have to be incurred.[4] Quite often, the total of claims accruing against a vessel as a result of collision will be so great that it will be to her owner's advantage to petition for limitation of his liability, in accordance with the statute dealing with that matter.[5] Personal injuries to and deaths of people on board, whether seamen or passengers, connect the topic of collision with that of injuries to the person.[6] And, the marine underwriter is deeply concerned in all aspects of collision liability, for most of the bills will usually be his to pay at last.[7] Thus an actual case of collision may not be liquidated without laying under contribution virtually all the "topics" of maritime law.

Our focus in this chapter, however, will be on the mutual liabilities of the ships and their owners for the property damage each has sustained.

## The Elements of Collision Liability

§ 7–2. Collision liability is based on fault; the mere fact of impact has no legal consequence.[8] The rules denying liability in case of "inscrutable" fault or of "inevitable" accident should be looked on as mere obvious corollaries of this principle. Since these phrases are sometimes used, however, with a suggestion of some more artful meaning than this, it might be well to notice them briefly.

"Inscrutable fault" is said to exist when "the court can see that a fault has been committed, but is unable, from the conflict of testimony, or otherwise, to locate it." [9] The seemingly settled rule is that in such a case no one can recover anything.[10] Obviously, if liability must rest on fault, there can be no liability where proof fails as to who is at fault; in such a position, no one has made out a case on which liability can be predicated.

An accident is said to be "inevitable" not merely when caused by *vis major* or the Act of God but also when all precautions reasonably to be required have been taken, and the accident has occurred notwithstanding. That there is no liability in such a case seems only

2. *Supra* Chapter III, Part II, at note 101 *et seq.*

3. See, generally, Chapter V *supra.*

4. Chapter VIII *infra.*

5. See Chapter X *infra.*

6. See Chapter VI *supra.*

7. See Chapter II *supra.*

8. The Java, 81 U.S. (14 Wall.) 189 (1872).

9. The Worthington & Davis, 19 F. 836, 839 (E.D.Mich.1883). See also The Jumna, 149 F. 171, 173 (2d Cir. 1906).

10. The Worthington & Davis, *supra* note 9; see The Grace Girdler, 74 U. S. (7 Wall.) 196, 203 (1869); The Jumna, *supra* note 9. Cases of inscrutable fault seem rare in recent times.

one aspect of the proposition that liability must be based on fault.[11] Sometimes the use of the phrase merely conveys the judgment that nobody has been at fault; thus, where vessels taking all proper precautions and obeying all applicable rules collide in fog, as sometimes happens, courts have referred to the accident as "unavoidable" or "inevitable."[12] In such cases, all the phrase means is that neither party has been able to sustain his burden of proving the fault of the other. Sometimes, however, the "inevitable accident" notion operates practically as something superficially like an affirmative defense, after the party seeking to inculpate the vessel has made a sufficient showing of faulty maneuvering on her part to establish liability. Thus, where a vessel under a duty to reverse her engines failed to do so—a fault which would, unexplained, be sufficient to result in liability—she was exonerated on her own showing that she could not reverse the engines because of valve failure, this having occurred notwithstanding proper inspection and maintenance.[13] It will readily be seen that, as a matter of substance, this so-called "defense" is not matter of affirmative defense at all, but is in effect rebuttal of the presumption of fault created by the failure to reverse; what has happened is that the showing of a failure to maneuver properly has shifted the burden of proof, so that the vessel sought to be cast in fault may, if she can, show that her apparent fault was not really a fault at all, but that the happening was "inevitable" in the special sense of "unavoidable by the exercise of due care." It is in these terms that Judge Learned Hand treats the matter in Cranberry Creek Coal Co. v. Red Star Towing & Transp. Co.:[14]

> ". . . But there are situations in which the law does not put the duty upon the sufferer to make proof at the outset; either because the facts are especially within the owner's knowledge, or, as in the case of collisions with an anchored vessel, because usually there must be some fault, it is thought just to require the owner to explain, and if he does not, to charge him. A failure of machinery or gear is within this class of cases and the owner's duty is often spoken of as the defense of 'inevitable accident.' Strictly, it is no defense at all, but a true presumption; that is to say, a duty laid upon him to supply proof which casts him if he fails."[15]

The "inevitable accident" defense is most often invoked when a vessel has been caught in the force of a storm and driven against

11. Stainback v. Rae, 55 U.S. (14 How.) 532, 538 (1852).

12. Dunton v. Allan, S. S. Co., 119 F. 590 (3d Cir. 1903), certiorari denied 192 U.S. 606, 24 S.Ct. 850 (1904); see The Adriatic, 287 F. 257 (S.D.N.Y. 1922), affirmed per curiam 287 F. 259 (2d Cir. 1922).

13. The Rose Standish, 26 F.2d 480, 1928 A.M.C. 1322 (D.Mass.1928). A very similar recent case is Giamona v. Mineo, 125 F.Supp. 354, 1955 A.M.C. 120 (N.D.Cal.1955).

14. 33 F.2d 272 (2d Cir. 1929), certiorari denied 280 U.S. 596, 50 S.Ct. 67 (1929).

15. 33 F.2d at 274. See also Petition of Canal Barge Co., 480 F.2d 11, 1973 A.M.C. 843 (5th Cir. 1973), citing text; Ernest Const. Co. v. The Tug Commodore, 294 F.Supp. 15, 1968 A.M.C. 2541 (S.D.Ala.1968).

another vessel or vessels, or against a structure on the margin of the shore. In such a case, presumption is against the moving vessel,[16] and her efforts to rebut it take the "inevitable accident" form. In Swenson v. The Argonaut [17] (a "veritable Donnybrook Fair mélée" of libels and cross-libels, as the writing judge called it) the Argonaut had been moored to a Jersey City pier, when she was struck by a storm and broke adrift, hitting and damaging a catamaran and four barges moored nearby. The lower court had characterized the occurrence as an "inevitable accident," and exonerated the Argonaut. The appeal court, however, noted that the vessel in the position of having to overcome the "moving vessel" presumption bears a heavy burden, and, searching the record, came to the conclusion that the storm was not of unexpectably catastrophic proportions, that the master of the Argonaut had been aware that it was blowing up, and that the proper precautions, by way of strengthening the mooring, had not been taken. There was a dissent. The case, taken as a whole, illustrates well the two factors in the "inevitable accident" defense in cases of this type: (1) the reasonableness of precautions taken (2) under the circumstances as known or reasonably to be anticipated.[18]

### The Standards of Proper Action

**§ 7–3.** The concept of "fault" presupposes a standard of correct action. In collision cases, the following are the sources of such a standard:

1. The statutory Rules of Navigation. The United States has four sets of these in force, much resembling one another but applying to different waters.[19]

2. Other statutes, and regulations having the force of statutes. These include both Federal and state or local enactments, subject to the obvious requirement that the latter not contradict Federal law.[20]

16. The Louisiana, 70 U.S. (3 Wall.) 164, 173 (1866); The D. H. Miller, 76 F. 877 (1st Cir. 1896); Frost v. Saluski, 199 F.2d 460, 462, 1953 A.M.C. 579 (7th Cir. 1952); In re Barrett, 108 F. Supp. 710, 717, 1953 A.M.C. 159 (S.D. N.Y.1952), modified on other grounds 209 F.2d 487 (2d Cir. 1954); Terpe v. Yacht "Victoria", 423 F.2d 748, 1970 A.M.C. 692 (3rd Cir. 1970).

17. 204 F.2d 636 (3d Cir. 1953).

18. See also Frost v. Saluski, 199 F. 2d 460, 1953 A.M.C. 579 (7th Cir. 1952); Petition of United States v. S.S. Joseph Lykes, 425 F.2d 991, 1970 A.M.C. 2034 (5th Cir. 1970). It must be shown that the force was really irresistible, and that all precautions were taken. Boudoin v. McDermott & Co., 281 F.2d 81, 1961, A.M.C. 1457 (5th Cir. 1960).

19. See *infra* at notes 24, 26, 27, 28.

20. Of greatest importance are the so-called "Pilot Rules," issued by the Coast Guard, containing more detailed provisions than the Rules of Navigation in force in the territorial waters of the United States. See Pilot Rules for Inland Waters, 33 C.F.R. §§ 80.01–80.45 (1972); Pilot Rules for (the Great Lakes, 33 C.F.R. §§ 90.01–90.30 (1972); Pilot Rules for Western Rivers, 33 C.F.R. §§ 95.01–95.80 (1972). These Rules may not, of course, contradict the statutory Rules of Navigation. Mathieson Chemical Corp. v. The Sadie, 95 F.Supp. 221, 1951 A.M. C. 270 (D.Md.1950).

On the enforcement and investigatory functions of the Coat Guard with respect to the Rules and collision, see *infra* Chapter XI, at notes 173–174.

3. Proved local "customs" not contradicting either of the above.[21]

4. The requirements (in the interstices of the Rules and other statutory material, and in cases they do not cover) of good seamanship and due care.[22]

The Rules of the Road (1, above) are of extreme importance in the allocation of collision liability. More often than not, the finding of "fault" on the part of a ship in collision rests on her having violated one of the Rules. The general lawyer, used to the rather fast-and-loose way of a court with a statute, must accustom himself to a far different atmosphere in dealing with these Rules, for they are strictly and literally construed, and compliance is insisted upon.[23] This is as it should be, for, though they have the force of statute, they are not couched in legal terms of art, and are not lawyers' law, but are plain and simple directions addressed to ship's officers, the more competent among whom have most of them substantially committed to memory.

The United States, as we have noted, has four sets. The International Rules[24] apply to high seas navigation. The International Rules promulgated as statute by the American Congress are binding, of their own force, only on ships of the United States. But practically identical Rules have been enacted by the other maritime nations, and changes (as in the case of the new Rules mentioned in the next paragraph but one) are usually made simultaneously by some sort of international agreement. Thus, in practical effect, the International Rules constitute a code of navigation for the high seas, and American courts, where foreign law is applicable to collision cases coming before them, will take judicial notice that the other maritime nations have adopted Rules similar to ours.[25]

The remaining three sets of Rules are alike, in that all apply to the inland waters of the United States. Foreign ships, while within these waters, are of course subject to our Rules. The Great

21. See *infra* at note 108.

22. See Miller v. Semet-Solvay Div., Allied Chemical Corp., 406 F.2d 1037, 1969 A.M.C. 43 (4th Cir. 1969); certiorari denied 395 U.S. 907, 89 S.Ct. 1776 (1969). Actually, as we shall see later in the discussion of Rules 27 and 29, these requirements might be said to be inferentially a part of the Rules. See Union Oil Co. of Calif. v. M/V Issaquena, 470 F.2d 875, 1973 A.M.C. 493 (5th Cir. 1973), citing text; Wasson Barge Rental Co., Inc. v. Tug Carrie D, 296 F.Supp. 933, 1969 A.M.C. 131 (E.D.La.1969).

23. Belden v. Chase, 150 U.S. 674, 698, 14 S.Ct. 264, 271 (1893). The Emma Kate Ross, 41 F. 826, 828 (D.N.J.1890), affirmed 46 F. 872 (C.C.D.N.J.1891), modified 50 F. 845 (3d Cir. 1892).

24. See *infra* at note 30.

25. See the Scotia, 81 U.S. (14 Wall.) 170, 187–8 (1872); The Belgenland, 114 U.S. 355, 370–71, 5 S.Ct. 860, 867, 868 (1885). The Belgenland, *supra*, established that the courts of this country have jurisdiction over suits for collision even when the colliding vessels are foreign; the cause of action is a transitory one. For the forum non conveniens (*supra* Chapter I, note 166) considerations that may lead to declining jurisdiction, see Kloekner, etc., v. A/S Hakedal, 210 F.2d 754, 1954 A.M.C. 643 (2d Cir. 1954), certiorari dismissed 348 U.S. 801, 75 S.Ct. 17 (1954).

Lakes Rules[26] have a self-explanatory sphere of operation. The Western Rivers Rules[27] apply to the Mississippi and its tributaries, and to certain other streams. The Inland Rules[28] apply to all other navigable waters, including all seaports and the Intracoastal Waterway. The coverage of these Rules is precisely defined, and mariners' charts furnish exact information as to whether the line has been passed.[29] In this book, we shall deal almost entirely with the International Rules. The others are similar in scope and substance, differing from the International Rules and among themselves in ways which are, to be sure, of much importance to officers on the bridge at a time of threatening collision, but which would only clutter an elementary treatment of our subject. Where a case to which one of the other sets of Rules applied raises some interesting point of law, we will mention it. No confusion will be caused thereby, for there are no radical differences in the technique of applying the Rules, as among the different sets.

A new set of International Rules came into force on September 1, 1965, as a result of recommendations of the International Conference for the Safety of Life at Sea, London 1960.[30] The general plan of the prior Rules was not changed, and their substance was left largely the same, but the cases construing the older Rules must not be relied on without a check of the revised version.[30a] (Still another set of Rules is in the making, as a result of a 1972 conference; these will probably come into effect within a few years.)[30b]

"Fault" may be predicated on violation of some statute other than the Rules. It should be noted especially that a vessel which fails, after a collision, to remain on the scene and render aid to the other vessel, so far as she can do so without serious danger to herself, is, under the American "Stand-by Act,"[31] presumed to be at fault, though the presumption is rebuttable by proof to the contrary. (Though this provision was taken over by the United States from the law of England, this country is now virtually alone in continuing it in force, for the Brussels Collision Liability Convention of 1910,[32] to which most mari-

26. 33 U.S.C.A. §§ 241–295.

27. 33 U.S.C.A. §§ 301–356.

28. 33 U.S.C.A. §§ 151–232.

29. See 33 U.S.C.A. § 151.

30. In 1963, Congress authorized the President to promulgate the new Rules. 77 Stat. 194 (1963). In 1964, the President set Sept. 1, 1965, as the effective date. Proc. No. 3632, 29 Fed.Reg. 19167 (1964). For the text of the Rules and introductory matter see 33 U.S.C.A. §§ 1051–1094. Hereinafter, the Rules will be referred to simply by number.

30a. A canvass of the changes is in Newbould, New International Rules of the Road, 19 JAG Jour. 135 (1965).

30b. These Rules, if they come into effect, will be gazetted in the Federal Register, and carried over into the United States Code.

31. 26 Stat. 425 (1890), 33 U.S.C.A. §§ 367–8.

32. For an account of this Convention, and the text, see 6 Benedict, Admiralty 3–7 (6th ed. 1941) and pocket parts. The United States has never ratified. For an account of the forces which successfully opposed ratification by the United States, see Comment, The Difficult Quest for a Uniform Maritime Law etc., 64 Yale L.J. 878 (1955).

time nations have adhered, abolishes "legal presumptions of fault" in collision cases.[33]) A modern application of this Act was against the Douglas Victory,[34] which left the scene after damaging a barge moored in the Mobile River. Nothing appeared in that case to rebut the statutorily created presumption of fault. But it is to be noted that the presumption is a rebuttable one, and the burden of rebutting it has on occasion been successfully carried.[35]

A narrow exception to the enforcement of strict compliance with the Rules and with the standards of prudent navigation is to be found in the doctrine as to errors *in extremis.* When a vessel, through no fault of her own, is placed in a position where collision is seemingly imminent, she will not be cast in fault for action taken in violation of the Rules or, as afterthought might show, of the standards of due care in navigation, when the fault can be looked on as explained and excused by the extremity in which she was placed. Thus, in The Stifinder,[36] a steam vessel collided with a sailing ship, and was herself sunk. The steamer, which had, under the Rules, the duty of keeping out of the way of sail, had not only failed to take steps to avert the collision, but was even more grossly at fault in that she had no lookout posted. Of her attempts to show that action taken at the last moment by the sailing vessel was faulty, the court said:

> "The Stifinder's duty was to keep her course and speed in the expectation that the Selje would obey the law and keep out of the way. When it became apparent that the steamer did not intend to conform to the law, the vessels were then in extremis, and what was done or omitted to be done by the Stifinder in the agony of collision can make no difference, as it is impossible to consider a decision so made as a fault. We agree with the learned counsel who argued this case for the petitioner that to enter upon intricate calculations of what could or could not have been done in 40 seconds, illustrated by elaborate diagrams involving days of labor, and to require that the decision of a seaman, confronted with a sudden emergency and obliged to act on the instant, shall be judged by such calculations and diagrams made weeks afterwards, would be a travesty." [37]

The *in extremis* rule is not susceptible of precise formulation; it is as vague as the concept "emergency." [38] The vessel that would in-

33. Article 6.

34. Coyle Lines v. United States, 96 F. Supp. 821, 1951 A.M.C. 1598 (E.D.La. 1951), reversed on other grounds, 195 F.2d 737 (5th Cir. 1952).

35. Greaud v. The Pueblo, 77 F.Supp. 796, 1948 A.M.C. 2000 (E.D.La.1948), affirmed 174 F.2d 369 (5th Cir. 1949); see Cusumano v. The Curlew, 105 F. Supp. 428, 1952 A.M.C. 508 (D.Mass. 1952).

36. 275 F. 271 (2d Cir. 1921), overruled on other grounds in American Tobacco Co. v. The Katingo Hadjipatera, 211 F.2d 666, 1954 A.M.C. 874 (2d Cir. 1954).

37. 275 F. at 276.

38. Thus, in Pacific-Atlantic S. S. Co. v. United States, 175 F.2d 632, 640, 1949 A.M.C. 1120 (4th Cir. 1949), cer-

voke this rule must establish that the emergency she found herself in was not the result of her own fault.[38a]

## The Effect of Fault

**§ 7–4.** We will reserve to a later section a somewhat fuller discussion of the measure and allocation of damages. For now, however, the consequences of infraction of the Rules, or other fault, may be sketched.

If neither vessel is at fault each must pay its own loss, and no liability attaches to either.[39]

If a collision is attributable to the fault of one of the vessels only, that vessel must bear its own loss, and pay for the other's damages as well.[40]

Where the fault of both vessels causes the collision, the damages are divided—that is to say, such a decree is entered as shall have the effect that each bears half the total damage.[41] In effect, this involves a payment by the less injured to the more injured vessel.

It will be noted that the American law makes no provision for dividing fault—or damages—on a sliding scale of percentages. A vessel is either at fault or not at fault, and the effect of fault is never graded. Nevertheless, the operation of the so-called "major-minor fault" rule sometimes mitigates the harshness of a doctrine which would divide damages equally in the case where one vessel is grossly negligent while the other is at fault, if at all, only in some technical sense. In such cases, the courts have sometimes announced their intention to resolve all doubts in favor of the comparatively innocent vessel, shutting their eyes to what might under other circumstances have been regarded as fault, or have found that, in view of the grossness of the fault of one vessel, the minor error of the other cannot be said to be a contributory cause of the disaster.

One way of stating the major-minor fault principle may be quoted from a leading Supreme Court case:

> " . . . Where fault on the part of one vessel is established by uncontradicted testimony, and such fault is, of itself, sufficient to account for the disaster, it is not enough

tiorari denied 338 U.S. 868, 70 S.Ct. 143 (1949), the court says, "And courts are rather unwilling to judge strictly the avoiding action taken by the privileged vessel, when, as here, this action must be taken in extremis due to the fault of the burdened vessel." This is not the language of exact concept; but some reserve of vagueness is clearly necessary to prevent absurd strictness on the basis of hindsight.

38a. Bucolo, Inc. v. F/V Jaguar, 428 F.2d 394, 1970 A.M.C. 2379 (1st Cir. 1970).

39. See The Clara, 102 U.S. 200, 203 (1880); The Lepanto, 21 F. 651, 655 (S.D.N.Y.1884). And see the discussion, *supra*, of "inscrutable" fault and "inevitable" accident.

40. The Clara, 102 U.S. 200 (1880); Oaksmith v. The Mayflower, 94 F. Supp. 574, 1951 A.M.C. 296 (D.Alaska 1951), affirmed sub nom. Oaksmith v. Garner, 205 F.2d 262 (9th Cir. 1953).

41. The Catharine v. Dickinson, 58 U.S. (17 How.) *170, 177–8 (1855). See *infra* at note 158 *et seq.*

for such vessel to raise a doubt with regard to the management of the other vessel. There is some presumption at least adverse to its claim, and any reasonable doubt with regard to the propriety of the conduct of such other vessel should be resolved in its favor." [42]

The major-minor fault "rule" is vague and unreliable; in many cases a decree for evenly divided damages has been entered where the fault of one vessel was out of all proportion to that of the other. So in Tide Water Associated Oil Co. v. The Syosset,[43] one of the vessels, the Tycol, was guilty of so many and such gross faults that the appellate court said:

> "We need not burden this opinion with a recital of the litany of the Tycol's many acts and omissions from which the district court concluded that she was to blame, for she concedes her fault." [44]

Among other things, she seems to have been showing her red and green side lights alternately, in a sort of winking pattern, the consequence, apparently, of her electing to pursue a zig-zag course. Confronted with this "wildly erratic navigation," the master of the other vessel failed to signal immediately (as required by one of the Rules of Navigation) that he did not "understand the course or intention" of the Tycol. The court, holding the non-signalling Syosset for half-damages, said:

> "Nor is the major-minor fault rule of any help to the Syosset. It is true that, were we free to apportion damages according to the degree of fault as is done by those countries which have adopted the Brussels Collision Convention of 1910, we would probably agree that a 50–50 division of damages here would be unjust. But even then we certainly could not say that the Tycol should bear 100% of the damages. The discussion above shows that the Syosset's failure to sound the danger signal *immediately,* when in doubt as to the Tycol's course or intention, had more than a minor part to play in causing the collision. Therefore, under the rule administered in American admiralty, she must bear half the damages."[45]

42. The City of New York, 147 U.S. 72, 85, 13 S.Ct. 211, 216 (1893). For other formulations, see The Victory, 168 U. S. 410, 423, 18 S.Ct. 149, 155 (1897); The Great Republic, 90 U.S. (23 Wall.) 20, 35 (1874); The Oregon, 158 U.S. 186, 204, 15 S.Ct. 804, 811, 812 (1895); General Seafoods Corp. v. J. S. Packard Dredging Co., 120 F.2d 117, 1941 A.M.C. 1120 (1st Cir. 1941); Compania de Maderas, etc. v. T/S Queenston Heights, 220 F.2d 120, 1955 A.M.C. 797 (5th Cir. 1955); Pure Oil Co. v. Neilson, Inc., 135 F.Supp. 786, 1956 A.M.C. 221 (E.D.La.1955), affirmed 233 F.2d 790, 1956 A.M.C. 1256 (5th Cir. 1956).

43. 203 F.2d 264, 1953 A.M.C. 730 (3d Cir. 1953).

44. 203 F.2d at 266.

45. 203 F.2d at 268–9.

## Causation

§ 7–5. Obviously, as is presupposed by the foregoing discussion, the "fault" that is to produce liability must be not mere fault in the abstract, but fault that is a contributory cause of the collision. Where, for example, a vessel fails to maintain a proper lookout—a serious fault indeed—but where her officers actually see the approaching vessel soon enough that the defect as to lookout cannot be said to have had a causal connection with the collision, it seems settled that the vessel cannot be held liable.[46] And a prior act of negligence, merely creating a "condition" upon which the later negligence of another party acts, has been said not to give rise to liability.[46a] But it is probably accurate to say that, because recovery is not wholly defeated in admiralty, as at common law, by contributory negligence (see the statement of the "divided damages" rule just above) the maritime court has been less ready than the shore courts to find that a subsequent wrongful act by one party breaks the chain of causation connecting the accident with the prior negligence of the other party.[47] Indeed, a vessel at fault in connection with a collision usually derives little comfort from the rule that she cannot be held liable unless her fault contributed to the result; this contention is more often than not made futile by the so-called "Pennsylvania" rule (named after the case in which it was laid down by the Supreme Court [48]) which states a drastic and unusual presumption arising on its being shown that a vessel has been guilty of statutory fault before a collision. Where this appears, the vessel thus cast in fault must prove, to escape liability, not only that the fault shown probably did not but also that it *could not* have contributed to causing the collision.[49] This rule makes especially important the strictest compliance with the Rules of Navigation.

The "Pennsylvania" burden, however, is not unbeatable; vessels at fault have sometimes succeeded in satisfying the court that the

46. The Farragut, 77 U.S. (10 Wall.) 334 (1870); see The Oregon, 158 U.S. 186, 195–7, 15 S.Ct. 804, 808, 809 (1895).

46a. P. Dougherty Co. v. United States, 207 F.2d 626, 1953 A.M.C. 1541 (3d Cir. 1953), certiorari denied 347 U.S. 912, 74 S.Ct. 476 (1954).

47. See The Silvia, 2 F.2d 105, 1924 A.M.C. 1222 (E.D.N.Y.1924). The doctrine of last clear chance is thus of sparse and uncertain application in collision law. Compare the following cases: The Norman B. Ream, 252 F. 409 (7th Cir. 1918); Manhattan Lighterage Corp. v. United States, 103 F. Supp. 274, 278, 1952 A.M.C. 128 (S.D. N.Y.1951); The Sanday, 122 F.2d 325, 1941 A.M.C. 1249 (2d Cir. 1941).

48. The Pennsylvania, 86 U.S. (19 Wall.) 125 (1874).

49. 86 U.S. (19 Wall.) at 136. This rule has been followed in countless cases; see, *e. g.*, Yang-Tsze Ins. Ass'n v. Furness, Withy & Co., 215 F. 859 (2d Cir. 1914), certiorari dismissed 242 U.S. 430, 37 S.Ct. 141 (1917); Eastern S. S. Co. v. International Harvester Co. of N. J., 189 F.2d 472, 476, 1951 A.M.C. 1844 (6th Cir. 1951); Boyer v. The Merry Queen, 202 F.2d 575, 1953 A.M.C. 482 (3d Cir. 1953). It has even been applied in non-collision cases, see Director General of India Supply Mission v. S.S. Maru, 459 F.2d 1370, 1375, 1972 A.M.C. 1694 (2d Cir. 1972), but in such cases at least seems not to apply unless the catastrophe that ensues is one sought to be prevented by the statutory rule. *Ibid.*

fault could not have contributed to causing the accident.[50] It seems that this plea (that the fault was not a "contributory cause") has a much better chance of success when the other vessel has been grossly at fault; its practical operation may, therefore, not be too different from that of the "major-minor fault" rule. Both work to mitigate the rigors of the divided damages rule, insofar as it effects an equal division among vessels guilty of vastly disproportionate fault.

Thus, in National Bulk Carriers v. United States,[51] one of the vessels, the Rutgers Victory, was grossly at fault. She had no lookout; her watch officer was working at a desk in the rear of the wheelhouse. Since the crossing between the vessels was such that the other vessel, the Nashbulk, was on the starboard hand of the Rutgers Victory, the latter was the "burdened" vessel, owing a duty to keep out of the way, by stopping and reversing if necessary.[52] Of course, she did none of this, not having a lookout and so not being apprised of the presence of the Nashbulk on a crossing course, though it was broad daylight, with clear weather, calm sea, and good visibility. The Nashbulk, as privileged and required to do, held her course and speed, doubtless confident that she had been observed and that the Rutgers Victory would take appropriate measures. When the vessels were about a half-mile apart, the Nashbulk's master became apprehensive and (*without sounding his whistle*) ordered a hard right rudder, which changed his course three or four points to starboard. The Rules of Navigation require a whistle signal of such a course change. A minute later, seeing collision was imminent, the Nashbulk blew a danger signal and ordered her engines full speed astern. The vessels nevertheless collided.

On these facts, the Rutgers Victory was manifestly and grossly at fault. The Nashbulk, for not signalling her course change, was also at fault. Did her fault contribute to causing the collision? Her problem, of course, was the "Pennsylvania" rule. Could it be said that the failure to signal a course change, under these circumstances, "could not have been" one of the causes of the collision? The Rutgers Victory argued, with what grace was possible, that the required signal, if given, might have recalled her watch officer to attention, and brought about timely and perhaps effective action. The court, however, rejected this contention, and pointed to the fact that the signal required on a change of course cannot be considered as having the purpose of general warning, since no general warning, absent course change, was required, and the course change itself did not increase the peril of the situation. Of the Nashbulk, the court said:

50. See The William J. Riddle, 102 F. Supp. 884, 888, 1952 A.M.C. 398 (S.D. N.Y.1952), affirmed per curiam, 200 F.2d 608, 1953 A.M.C. 132 (2d Cir. 1952); Seaboard Tug & Barge, Inc. v. Rederi A/B Disa, 213 F.2d 772, 1954 A.M.C. 1498 (1st Cir. 1954); Compania de Maderas, etc. v. T/S Queenston Heights, *supra*, note 42.

51. 183 F.2d 405, 1950 A.M.C. 1293 (2d Cir. 1950), certiorari denied 340 U.S. 865, 71 S.Ct. 89 (1950).

52. See *infra* at note 83.

". . . She has discharged her burden under the rule of The Pennsylvania, supra, coextensive with her obligation under Article 18 [the Rule requiring the signal]. She cannot therefore be forced to pay half the damages merely because the other vessel was so grievously at fault that she needed, and might have put to good and effective use, an alerting signal which the rule did not require. Indeed, to allow that would simply put a premium upon gross negligence in navigation, for had the Rutgers Victory not been 'as blind as one who will not see' no alerting signal would have been of any use and the exoneration of the Nashbulk would have followed almost as a matter of course."[53]

Judge Learned Hand, in his dissent, strongly insists on the actual alerting function of the signal if blown, and goes on to show his awareness that the softening of the Pennsylvania rule in this case (as, one might add, in a good many modern cases) is functioning similarly to the major-minor fault rule as a means of softening the half-damage rule:

"I do not think that the Nashbulk proved beyond a reasonable doubt that, had she blown, the Rutgers Victory would not have taken the steps necessary to avoid collision; indeed, I am not sure that my brothers disagree as to that! In any event, it is eminently likely that she would have taken them, and it is clear that adequate steps were in fact open to her. I do not mean that I should divide the damages equally, if I were free to divide them proportionately to the relative fault of the vessels. An equal division in this case would be plainly unjust; they ought to be divided in some such proportion as five to one. And so they could be but for our obstinate cleaving to the ancient rule which has been abrogated by nearly all civilized nations. Indeed, the doctrine that a court should not look too jealously at the navigation of one vessel, when the faults of the other are glaring, is in the nature of a sop to Cerberus. It is no doubt better than nothing; but it is inadequate to reach the heart of the matter, and constitutes a constant temptation to courts to avoid a decision on the merits. Nevertheless, so long as our antiquated doctrine prevails, I think we should apply it unflinchingly, and in the case at bar I would divide the damages."[54]

Only "statutory" fault—*i. e.*, breach of one of the Rules of Navigation or of some other statutory norm—invokes the "Pennsylvania" rule. The ship at fault in some other regard—guilty, *e. g.*, of "negligence" by general standards—still may have the benefit of the usual rule making proof of causal connection a part of plaintiff's (or, in the pre-1966 admiralty cases, the libellant's)[54a] case. Thus, in Oriental

53. 183 F.2d at 409.

54. 183 F.2d at 410.

54a. See *supra*, Chapter I, § 1–9.

Trading & Transport Co. v. Gulf Oil Corp.[55] the Second Circuit Court of Appeals said:

> "Although it has been held—and we agree—that it is a fault not to turn on the lights of a ship in convoy when the time to take action has come, the fault is not a statutory one, and does not throw upon the delinquent ship the burden of proving that compliance with her duty would [*sic*] have prevented collision. It is a fault which the ship that asserts it, must show to have been at least one cause of the collision." [56]

But there is not entire consistency in the qualification of duties as "statutory" and "non-statutory". The principal problem is that Rule 29 (see *infra*, § 7–11) might be read to mandate generally the following of "due care", thus (since Rule 29 is statutory) making all negligence a "statutory" fault. The Circuits have not settled down to a single and consistent view on this.[56a] Realistically, this question must be evaluated against the half-and-half damage rule (see *supra*, § 7–4, and *infra* § 7–20). If "noncausation" is all that can isolate a ship guilty of minor fault from operation of the moiety rule, then any extension of the drastic Pennsylvania rule, all but conclusively presuming causation, is probably undesirable.

It has recently been held that the Pennsylvania rule does not mean that the vessel seeking to escape must show that its fault could not "by any stretch of the imagination" have contributed causally to the disaster.[56b]

On the subject of causation, it should be noted, finally, that, although the usual collision case involves immediate physical impact—indeed, that is what collision is, in the strictest sense—nevertheless liability as for collision may sometimes be incurred where the wrongdoing and victim vessels never actually touch one another. United States v. Ladd [57] presented a fairly typical situation. The libellant's sloop, the Eloise, was becalmed on the side of the channel of the Elizabeth River in Virginia. The Coast Guard cutter Mohican, heading upstream at a high rate of speed, did not hear or ignored the warning signals of the Eloise, and so failed to moderate her own speed, with the result that the swells created by the Mohican tossed the Eloise about, snapping her mast and doing damage to her sails and deck railing. The Court with counsel actually went out and took a ride on the

55. 173 F.2d 108, 1949 A.M.C. 644 (2d Cir. 1949), certiorari denied 337 U.S. 919, 69 S.Ct. 1162 (1949).

56. 173 F.2d at 110. Despite the inadvertent omission of "not" in the first sentence, the meaning is made clear by the second sentence.

56a. See, *e. g.*, Anthony v. International Paper Co., 289 F.2d 574, 1961 A.M.C. 1890 (4th Cir. 1961), and *cf.* Tempest v. United States, 404 F.2d 870, 1968 A.M.C. 2538 (4th Cir. 1968).

56b. China Union Lines v. A. O. Andersen & Co., 364 F.2d 769, 1966 A.M.C. 1653 (5th Cir. 1966), certiorari denied 386 U.S. 933, 87 S.Ct. 955 (1967).

57. 193 F.2d 929, 1952 A.M.C. 277 (4th Cir. 1952).

Mohican, observing her swells and coming to the conclusion she was at fault.[58]

## Collision Litigation

§ 7–6. Wrongful collision creates a lien in the offending vessel,[59] and, usually, a personal liability in her owner,[60] so that collision suits may be brought by action *in personam* or *in rem* or both.[61]

Practically invariably, the ship first proceeded against brings a cross-complaint. This is done because of the rule embodied in a statement by the Supreme Court in The Ella Warley—North Star:[62]

> ". . . If only one party sues, and the other merely defends the suit, and upon the proofs it appears that both parties are in fault, the court declares this fact in the decree, and decrees to the libelant one-half of the damage sustained by him,—the damage sustained by the respondent not being regarded as the subject of investigation determinable in that suit."[63]

This means that if a vessel merely "answers", denying her own fault and alleging fault in the other vessel, and if the court finds both to blame, the damages sustained by the merely answering vessel cannot be taken into account; to receive recompense, by way of set-off or otherwise, for her own damages, she must appear as plaintiff. Also, of course, it is only thus that she can hope, by casting the other vessel solely in fault, to recover her own full damages. The collision case is rare in which there is not at least some arguable reason for regarding both vessels at fault; in any case, the pleader will not want to throw away any chance he might have. Nevertheless, the cross-complaint is sometimes omitted when the vessel first proceeded against has suffered little or no damage; in such a case, merely answering, denying her own fault and setting up that of the other vessel, is enough to enable her to reduce the damages she has to pay to one-half or to nothing,

58. *Cf.* United States v. Standard Oil Co. of Kentucky, 217 F.2d 539, 1955 A.M.C. 824 (6th Cir. 1954). The libelant, owner of a tanker, sued for its destruction by fire, caused by escape of gasoline from respondent's apparatus. The court found no negligence, but it is clear from the tenor of the opinion that, if fault had been found, damages would have been recoverable just as in a physical collision case. And see American Trading & Production Corp. v. T. J. Stevenson & Co., 113 F.Supp. 332, 1953 A.M.C. 1292 (S.D.N.Y.1953), where a passing vessel was held liable when "hydraulic interaction" resulting from her excessive speed caused a collision between two other vessels.

59. The Bold Buccleugh, 7 Moo.P.C.C. 267 (1850–51); The China, 74 U.S. (7 Wall.) 53 (1869); The John G. Stevens, 170 U.S. 113, 18 S.Ct. 544 (1898); Burns Bros. v. Central R. R. of N. J., 202 F.2d 910 (2d Cir. 1953).

60. The demise charterer, as owner *pro hac vice*, may be liable. The Barnstable, 181 U.S. 464, 21 S.Ct. 684 (1901). See *supra* Chapter IV, at note 150 *et seq.*

61. See Burns Bros. v. Central R. R. of N. J., 202 F.2d 910, 1953 A.M.C. 718 (2d Cir. 1953).

62. 106 U.S. 17, 1 S.Ct. 41 (1882).

63. 106 U.S. at 22–23, 1 S.Ct. at 46.

depending upon whether her claims are supported by proof and adopted by the court.

The *in personam* liability of the owner may be enforced at common law under the saving clause.[64] This course has rarely been elected, because it is at least to be feared that the common law doctrine of contributory negligence may bar recovery entirely if the plaintiff is at fault, whereas the most the libellant in admiralty has to fear is a decree for divided damages, if mutual contributory fault is established. It seems clear that even in the common law action brought under the saving clause the admiralty divided damages rule ought to apply, for this is a matter of substance rather than of procedure, and it is absurd that a different substantive rule should govern merely because suit is brought in one court rather than in another.[65] But an early statement of the Supreme Court foreshadows this unsuitable result. In Belden v. Chase,[66] a case of collision brought originally in a New York state court, the Supreme Court said:

> "The doctrine in admiralty of an equal division of damages in the case of a collision between two vessels when both are in fault contributing to the collision, has long prevailed in England and this country. The Max Morris, 137 U.S. 1, 11 S.Ct. 29. But at common law the general rule is that if both vessels are culpable in respect of faults operating directly and immediately to produce the collision, neither can recover damages for injuries so caused. Atlee v. Packet Co., 21 Wall. 389.
>
> "In order to maintain his action, the plaintiff was obliged to establish the negligence of the defendant, and that such negligence was the sole cause of the injury, or, in other words, he could not recover, though defendant were negligent, if it appeared that his own negligence directly contributed to the result complained of." [67]

There has later appeared some reason to hope that the apparent doctrine of the Belden case is on its way out. In Intagliata v. Shipowners & Merchants Towboat Co.,[68] the Supreme Court of California squarely held the admiralty divided damages rule applicable to a collision case brought in the state court; this result seems unobjectionable even under Belden v. Chase, for the doctrine of that case, taken at its widest ought not to be regarded as *requiring* state courts to apply shoregoing rules of damage distribution to maritime torts claims, but only as permitting them to do so if their own law so dictates. And

64. See *supra* Chapter I, at note 117.

65. *Cf.* Erie R. Co. v. Tompkins, 304 U.S 64, 58 S.Ct. 817 (1938).

66. 150 U.S. 674, 14 S.Ct. 264 (1893).

67. 150 U.S. at 691, 14 S.Ct. at 269.

68. 26 Cal.2d 365, 159 P.2d 1, 1946 A.M.C. 263 (1945), noted 34 Calif.L.Rev. 599 (1946), 19 So.Calif.L.Rev. 127 (1945). See also St. Louis & Tenn. River Packet Co. v. Murray & Wathan, 144 Ky. 815, 139 S.W. 1078 (1911), noted 25 Harv.L.Rev. 387 (1912).

in Hedger Transp. Corp. v. United Fruit Co.,[69] the influential Second Circuit Court of Appeals has held that the admiralty rule is applicable to actions brought at law to enforce maritime rights. (The very case did not involve a collision, but the broad language of the court's opinion seems applicable to collision cases.) It seems probable that, if the matter gets to the Supreme Court, that tribunal will wipe the Belden v. Chase formulation off the books.[70] If this happens, we may expect a rash of state court collision cases, brought by victims who think they will stand a better chance, on facts and damages, before a jury.

Getting at the truth as to what happened in a collision case is often something of a problem for the admiralty judge. The circumstances of collision are not such as to be conducive to the exactest estimation of times, distances, and so on, or to the formation of the clearest recollection.[71] The tendency of officers and crew to "stick by the ship" on the witness stand is well-known.

### The Navigation Rules: Application and Definitions

**§ 7–7.** The International Rules begin (Rule 1) with a preliminary set of provisions prescribing their coverage and giving certain essential definitions. They are to be followed by all vessels and seaplanes upon the high seas and in all waters connected therewith navigable by sea-going vessels, except as provided in Rule 30. Rule 30 provides:

> "Nothing in these Rules shall interfere with the operation of a special rule duly made by local authority relative to the navigation of any harbour, river, lake, or inland water, including a reserved seaplane area."

From the international point of view, this Rule gives the United States the necessary permission for setting up the other three sets of Rules in force on the inland waters of this country.

Seaplanes are included under the new Rules.[72]

69. 198 F.2d 376, 1952 A.M.C. 1469 (2d Cir. 1952), certiorari denied 344 U.S. 896, 73 S.Ct. 275 (1952).

70. This result is in fact clearly foreshadowed by the decision in Pope & Talbot v. Hawn, 346 U.S. 406, 74 S.Ct. 202, 1954 A.M.C. 1 (1953). The Court affirmed a judgment, entered on the *civil side* of federal court, for 82½% of proved damages, in a longshoremen's personal injury suit, the plaintiff having been found 17½% contributorily negligent. [The admiralty rule in personal injury cases is, in effect, one of comparative negligence. The Max Morris, 137 U.S. 1, 11 S.Ct. 29 (1890); Ahlgren v. Red Star Towing Co., 214 F.2d 618, 1954 A.M.C. 1504 (2d Cir.1954)].

71. Half or more of the cases cited in this chapter, at a guess, would illustrate these points. See, *e. g.*, Cusumano v. The Curlew, 105 F.Supp. 428, 1952 A.M.C. 508 (D.Mass.1952). Logbook entries of course supplement testimony, and the gyro-compass "course recorder" is in use on some vessels. But this instrument has not always been credited; see Bushey & Sons v. Standard Oil Co. of Cal., 197 F.2d 788, 791, 1952 A.M.C. 1109 (2d Cir. 1952).

72. *Cf. supra* Chapter I, note 105.

### "Lights and Shapes"

§ 7–8. The indispensable prerequisite of intelligent action to avoid collision is knowledge as to the character and course of the craft with which collision is threatened. Rules 2–14, inclusive, embody an elaborate code of lights and "shapes," the showing of which conveys information about the vessel carrying them. The lights are for use by night, and more often than not all that the officer on the bridge can know about a vessel sighted at night is what her lights tell him. By day, most essential information can be picked up, visibility permitting, by the naked eye or with a glass, but a few of the needed facts about an encountered vessel's situation are not patent to inspection, and it is the office of the "shapes" to convey this knowledge. We cannot even summarize the elaborate code of lights and shapes, but a few examples will make their function clear.

Thus, Rule 2 provides that power-driven vessels shall carry two white lights, visible from the front, at different elevations, with the lower one forward, as well as two side lights green on starboard and red on port, visible from straight ahead to 22½ degrees abaft the beam. If the reader will draw a sketch of this and visualize the possibilities, he will see that the observer on a meeting ship can infer everything essential about the course of the vessel just from these lights. (He can also infer that she is power-driven, for a sailing vessel would carry a different set of lights.[73])

It can now be seen, for example, why, in the Syosset case, mentioned in another connection above,[74] the inference drawn from the alternation of red and green lights was that the Tycol was zigzagging. A clear visualization of these lights is a key to the understanding of much of the shorthand talk in the cases; a "green-to-green situation," *e. g.*, is one in which the vessels are in a position to pass starboard to starboard.[75]

Under Rule 3, a towing vessel carries lights in a pattern which reveals that she is towing, and which tells roughly how long the flotilla is—points of high importance if the observing vessel is considering passing astern of her, or needs to know how much dependence can be placed on her maneuverability.

The importance of towage lights is well illustrated in the case of Manhattan Lighterage Corp. v. Esso Standard Oil Co.[76] The tug National was steaming down the North River with three vessels in tow on hawsers. Astern of this flotilla, also moving south, rode Esso Barge No. 318, in tow of Esso Tug No. 3. Under the Inland Rules (applicable in these waters, and differing slightly from the International Rules) the National (as a tug with a tow on hawser astern)

73. Rule 5.

74. *Supra* at note 43 *et seq.*

75. See the district court and court of appeals opinions in The William J. Riddle, 102 F.Supp. 884, 1952 A.M.C. 398 (S.D.N.Y.1952), Id., 200 F.2d 608, 1953 A.M.C. 132 (2d Cir. 1952).

76. 97 F.Supp. 269, 1951 A.M.C. 941 (S.D.N.Y.1951).

was required to carry three white lights, not less than three feet apart, on her foremast, in such position as to be visible all around. In point of fact, the lowest of the three could not be seen from astern. The two white lights actually visible signalled, under Article 3 of the Inland Rules, that the vessel carrying them was towing a vessel *alongside*—a gross piece of misinformation, given the actual situation. Holding the National solely at fault for the resultant collision, the court characterized her fault as "obvious and egregious." [77]

In Diamond State Tel. Co. v. Atlantic Refining Co.,[78] decision went off on one of the lesser-encountered lighting Rules. A flotilla, consisting of a tug, barge, and derrick barge, had gone out to work at night on a submarine cable in the Delaware River. The three vessels were, as the Third Circuit Court of Appeals says, "lit up like a Christmas tree." [79] But they had neglected to affix the one ornament requisite in the situation—a string of three red lights in a vertical line, required, by the there applicable Rules, of all vessels engaged in cable work. An approaching tanker, narrowly missing collision with the flotilla, struck and damaged the cable. There was no question but that the tanker had been negligent; the court accepted the finding that she had disregarded the whistle-signal of danger given by the cable-repairing flotilla. The owner of the cable therefore sought to hold the tanker liable. But the appellate court, reversing the lower court, said:

> "In our view of the case, it is irrelevant that the Yeager failed to stop in the face of a danger signal, that she crossed the Adriatic's signal, and that she was also negligently navigated, because she did not collide with the Adriatic or Acco. The lights on the flotilla and the whistles by the Adriatic were successful. Because of them the Yeager was enabled to avoid collision. Maybe it was more a matter of good luck than good navigation but, in view of the final result, that should not affect the application of the classic remark, 'Proof of negligence in the air, so to speak, will not do.' The various acts and omissions charged against the Yeager were negligent toward the Acco and Adriatic and not towards libellant's cable. We are not to be understood as holding that a vessel must actually collide with another before she can be held. There are many cases holding a vessel in fault and liable even though not herself in collision. But in those cases the noncolliding vessel was negligent toward the colliding and damaged vessel. That is not our case. Here we have the unforeseeable libellant, a maritime instance of the landlubber's unforeseeable plaintiff. The scope of the Yeager's duty is not to be determined by what we know now but by what those aboard her knew or should have known as they ap-

77. 97 F.Supp. at 271.

78. 205 F.2d 402, 1953 A.M.C. 1712 (3d Cir. 1953).

79. 205 F.2d at 406.

proached the flotilla. They knew that there were one or more vessels ahead of them and that any unseamanlike navigation on their part would subject those vessels to an unreasonable risk of harm. Thus, they had a duty to navigate so as not to create such risk, and they did. They could not possibly have foreseen that poor navigation would have subjected libellant's cable to an unreasonable risk of harm because they neither knew nor should have known that the cable was there. Thus, as to the cable, there was no duty and, consequently, could be no negligence. Had the flotilla displayed the required three red lights in a vertical line, the risk of harm would have been foreseeable, thus giving birth to a duty of prudent navigation toward the cable.

"Libellant makes much of the fact that the location is marked on the chart as a cable area, contending that this is notice enough that the flotilla was engaged in cable work. We are not prepared to say that the marking on the chart to the effect that there are submarine cables there is sufficient notice that any vessels in that area have raised the cables to their decks, when those vessels are not showing the required lights. It is admitted that libellant made no effort to publish the fact of their repair work in the 'Weekly Notice to Mariners,' even though it knew three weeks beforehand that they were going to work on the cable. But, says libellant, the Contractor did display the three red lights in a vertical line, thus giving notice of cable work. The Contractor was, however, six hundred feet away from the flotilla—much too far away to help the Acco and Adriatic. Proper lights on one vessel do not satisfy the duty of every other vessel in the river. Furthermore, the rule says that the lights shall be displayed on cable-laying 'vessels,' not one vessel out of three." [80]

"The failure to carry proper lights," another court has said, "is one of the most recklessly unlawful faults a vessel can commit. . . ." [81]

As an example of the use of the "shapes," a vessel engaged in laying submarine cable or similar work must carry, by day, "in a vertical line one over the other not less than 6 feet apart, where they can best be seen, three shapes each not less than two feet in diameter, of which the highest and lowest shall be globular in shape and red in colour, and the middle one diamond in shape and white." [82]

## The Steering and Sailing Rules

**§ 7–9.** Rules 17–26 come to the heart of the matter, for they prescribe the action to be taken when the possibility of collision

80. 205 F.2d at 406–7.

81. Bradshaw v. The Virginia, 176 F.2d 526, 530, 1949 A.M.C. 1580 (4th Cir. 1949), certiorari denied 338 U.S. 892, 70 S.Ct. 244 (1949).

82. Rule 4.

enters the picture. Rule 18 deals with the case of two power-driven vessels meeting head-on, and provides that each shall alter her course to starboard, for a port-to-port passing; American automobile drivers will have no difficulty in visualizing this maneuver, and will also find readily comprehensible Rule 25, which requires every power-driven vessel in a narrow channel to keep to the starboard side of the channel. The rest of the steering and sailing rules deal with the "burdened and privileged vessel" situation. The burdened vessel is the one which, under the circumstances of the encounter, has the duty of taking action to avoid collision, while the privileged vessel maintains her prior course and speed. Thus, a steam vessel must keep out of the way of a sailing vessel, being far the more maneuverable (Rule 20), though the new Rules provide that the sailing vessel is not to hamper a powered vessel in a narrow channel. And when power-driven vessels are crossing, the one that has the other on her own starboard must maneuver to avoid collision, stopping and backing if necessary; normally, she is to slow and cross astern of the privileged vessel.[83]

The requirement (Rule 21) that the privileged vessel keep her course and speed is not permissive but mandatory, for the maneuvers of the burdened vessel cannot be intelligent unless she can assume that the situation will remain constant. Vessels have repeatedly been held at fault for changing course or speed when in the privileged position.[84] When, however, it becomes clear that evasive action by the privileged vessel is necessary, she may and must take it, as Rule 21 itself provides.[85]

With the Steering and Sailing Rules should be included Rule 28, providing for certain sound signals to be given by vessels in sight of one another. Thus, a vessel altering her course to starboard is required to indicate that fact to the vessel in sight by a single short blast on her whistle. Where a privileged vessel, required by Rule 21 to keep her course and speed, is doubtful whether the burdened vessel is actually taking sufficient action to avert collision, she may indicate her doubt by giving at least five short and rapid blasts on her whistle.[86]

### The Fog Rules

**§ 7–10.** Fog is the ancient terror of mariners. Particularly in waters bearing heavy traffic, such as areas adjacent to harbors or well-travelled ocean lanes, the presence of fog vastly increases the chances of collision. The International Rules therefore make special

83. See The Delaware, 161 U.S. 459, 465–6, 16 S.Ct. 516, 520 (1896).

84. The Britannia, 153 U.S. 130, 136–9, 14 S.Ct. 795, 797, 798 (1894); Yang-Tsze Ins. Ass'n v. Furness, Withy & Co., 215 F. 859 (2d Cir. 1914), certiorari dismissed 242 U.S. 430, 37 S.Ct. 141 (1917); see The Northfield, 154 U.S. 629, 14 S.Ct. 1184 (1878).

85. The Mauch Chunk, 154 F. 182 (2d Cir. 1907), certiorari denied 207 U.S. 586, 28 S.Ct. 255 (1907); see Postal S. S. Corp. v. El Isleo, 308 U.S. 378, 60 S.Ct. 332, 1940 A.M.C. 1 (1940); Hertz v. Consolidated Fisheries, 213 F.2d 801, 1954 A.M.C. 1164 (9th Cir. 1954).

86. See Note, 42 Geo.L.J. 95 (1953).

provision both for signalling and for navigation when fog is present. Rule 16 provides:

> "*(a)* Every vessel, or seaplane when taxi-ing on the water, shall, in fog, mist, falling snow, heavy rainstorms or any other condition similarly restricting visibility, go at a moderate speed, having careful regard to the existing circumstances and conditions.
>
> "*(b)* A power-driven vessel hearing, apparently forward of her beam, the fog-signal of a vessel the position of which is not ascertained, shall, so far as the circumstances of the case admit, stop her engines, and then navigate with caution until danger of collision is over.
>
> "*(c)* A power-driven vessel which detects the presence of another vessel forward of her beam before hearing her fog signal or sighting her visually may take early and substantial action to avoid a close quarters situation but, if this cannot be avoided, she shall, so far as the circumstances of the case admit, stop her engines in proper time to avoid collision and then navigate with caution until danger of collision is over."

The concept of "moderate speed" is of course a rather vague one. A rule of thumb, often applied, is that a speed is moderate if, given the conditions of visibility that prevail, the vessel can come to a dead stop in one-half the distance between herself and another vessel when first sighted.[87] But neither this rule nor any other can be applied mechanically; a speed is moderate which is chosen with prudent regard to the actual factors producing danger—visibility, maneuverability and backing power of the vessel, and the traffic to be anticipated. Of the many recent judicial discussions of "moderate speed," perhaps that in Gertrude Parker, Inc. v. Abrams [88] is the most helpful:

> "The 'visible distance' test of 'moderate speed' under the Rule, although useful in many situations, and frequently applicable, is not a universal one to be applied blindly. It is very generally applied in crowded waters, even though its application may require vessels, other than ferry boats to which special considerations apply, to remain moored or at anchor. But it would hardly be reasonable to apply it in such a way as to require a vessel to drift without steerageway in open waters, or to anchor in exposed or dangerous places. Furthermore, so far as we can ascertain, the test has only been applied when there was knowledge, actual or construc-

**87.** See The Umbria, 166 U.S. 404, 417, 17 S.Ct. 610, 615 (1897); The Silver Palm, 94 F.2d 754, 757, 1937 A.M.C. 1427 (9th Cir. 1937), certiorari denied 304 U.S. 576, 58 S.Ct. 1046 (1938); Standard Oil Co. v. The Wellesley Victory, 127 F.Supp. 273, 1954 A.M.C. 1835 (S.D.N.Y.1954). There is considerable confusion among the courts in the formulation of this rule; see Griffin, *op cit. supra* note 1, 292–296.

**88.** 178 F.2d 259, 1950 A.M.C. 29 (1st Cir. 1949).

tive, of the presence of other vessels in the vicinity. See The Sagamore, 1 Cir., 247 F. 743, 750. And, it has been found on adequate evidence which we are not disposed, if we are at liberty, to question, that the Gertrude Parker's whistle was not sounded until the vessels were in the jaws of collision, and the record does not indicate whether the collision occurred in much frequented waters or not.

"Of course, a vessel's speed in a fog, mist, falling snow or heavy rainstorm may be immoderate even though the 'test of sight' is inapplicable to her. Certainly a vessel would not be justified, except by the most extraordinary circumstances, in not reducing her speed at all in conditions of low visibility. The specific rule of moderate speed in a fog, to say nothing of the general rule of prudent navigation, art. 29 of the International Rules, supra, 33 U.S.C.A. § 121, requires moderate speed in conditions of low visibility regardless of whether the 'visible distance' test of moderate speed is applicable or not. But aside from that test, we are not disposed to say that the Skilligolee's speed was immoderate. We lack data on her maneuverability,—how fast she would answer her helm, or could be stopped, loaded as she was at the time of collision; whatever her loading may then have been—and data as to how frequented the waters were when and where the collision occurred. Under these circumstances we are not prepared to say that her speed of five, or even six knots through the fog was not the moderate speed required by art. 16, supra." [89]

The Supreme Court has recently held that the half-distance rule is not to be applied mechanically in a situation in which prudence did not dictate following it.[89a]

The obligation to stop engines, imposed by Rule 16(b), is independent of and in addition to the "moderate speed" requirement, and is strictly enforced by the courts. In Johnston-Warren Lines v. United States,[90] the Longview collided in fog with the Jessmore. The Longview's lookout, shortly before the collision, "thought" he heard a fog signal and reported his "thought" to the third mate. That officer, instead of taking immediate steps to comply with Rule 16(b), waited about a minute, until he heard the signal himself, when he proceeded to order "stop engines." In the interval, the Longview

89. 178 F.2d at 264. Other recent cases on moderate speed in fog: We-Four Corp. v. The Whaler, 174 F.2d 402, 1949 A.M.C. 1104 (1st Cir. 1949); Noble v. Moore-McCormack Lines, 96 F. Supp. 369, 1952 A.M.C. 69 (D.Mass. 1951); Panama Transport Co. v. United States, 102 F.Supp. 958, 1952 A.M. C. 386 (S.D.N.Y.1951); Anglo-Saxon Petroleum Co. v. United States, 222 F.2d 75, 1955 A.M.C. 985 (2d Cir. 1955).

89a. Union Oil Co. of Calif. v. Tugboat San Jacinto, 409 U.S. 140, 93 S.Ct. 368, 1972 A.M.C. 2675 (1972).

90. 196 F.2d 689, 1952 A.M.C. 1650 (2d Cir. 1952).

travelled some 600 feet further on the collision course. The Longview unsuccessfully sought to exculpate herself:

> ". . . The Longview is appealing from the decision holding it partially responsible for the collision.
>
> "She argues, we think unreasonably, as follows: Article 16 requires vessels in fog conditions to stop only when they actually 'hear'—are sure they hear—the fog signal of another vessel forward of the beam; the lookout here only 'thought' he heard a fog signal; the third mate consequently waited until he himself heard the signal, perhaps a minute later, before giving the order to stop. Thus, at a speed of six knots, over 600 feet was traveled in that interval, bringing the Longview that much nearer to the path of the Jessmore. As far as we are concerned, the only sensible interpretation of an anti-collision rule like Article 16 is that ships must stop when they hear something which they have good reason to suspect is a fog whistle ahead. This has long been held; New York & Cuba Mail S. S. Co. v. United States, 2 Cir., 16 F.2d 945; Lie v. San Francisco & Portland S. S. Co., 243 U.S. 291, 37 S.Ct. 270, 61 L.Ed. 726; Steffens v. United States, 2 Cir., 32 F.2d 206, cited by appellants, held only that where the signal did not definitely come from ahead the ship but very possibly from another direction, she was not required to stop under Article 16.
>
> "It is true that the Longview was able to stop before she ran into the Jessmore and was dead in the water when the collision occurred, and that the Jessmore, on the other hand, could not have stopped her headway in time even if she had tried on first sighting the Longview. But this fact does not excuse the Longview's failure to reverse her engines on first sighting the Jessmore, or her misleading signals proposing a port crossing when actually she was engaged in an attempt to make a starboard passing. These faults were considerable, certainly not so minor as to fall within the rule of The Umbria, 166 U.S. 404, 17 S.Ct. 610, 41 L.Ed. 1053, that 'immaterial' faults of one vessel are excused when the accident is due to the overshadowing faults of the other. We think the rule of The Pennsylvania, 19 Wall. 125, 22 L.Ed. 148, places the burden upon the Longview to show that her fault could not have contributed to the collision. We think she did not discharge that burden. For we are reasonably convinced, as was the trial judge, that, if the Longview had stopped nearly a minute sooner, when the lookout first heard the signal, and had reversed her engines at that point, no collision would have occurred; the Longview would then have been entirely outside the 170-degree course of the Jessmore." [91]

91. 196 F.2d at 691. See also Standard Oil Co. v. Pocahontas S. S. Co., 197 F.2d 422, 1952 A.M.C. 1078 (1st Cir. 1952).

(Rule 16c veiledly refers to radar; for discussion, see *infra,* § 7–12.)

Rule 15 sets out a code of sound signals for use in fog. These signals not only warn of the presence of the vessel, but also give notice of its character and situation; thus, the signals are different for powered vessels under way, vessels at anchor, vessels towing or laying cable, sailing vessels in various situations with regard to the wind, etc. The information so conveyed is of high value to other ships in the vicinity, since the degree of danger and the sort of action required vary with the factors indicated. Strict compliance with this Rule is required, and a vessel has been cast in fault for not possessing the sort of foghorn prescribed by the applicable Rule.[92]

### The "Special Circumstance" and "General Prudential" Rules—"Negligence"

**§ 7–11.** Rule 27 provides:

> "In obeying and construing these Rules due regard shall be had to all dangers of navigation and collision, and to any special circumstances, including the limitations of the craft involved, which may render a departure from the above Rules necessary in order to avoid immediate danger."

Courts, had they been so minded, could have sailed a whole armada of exceptions through the opening made by this Rule. Actually, it has been very narrowly construed, and will not excuse a violation of the plain mandate of the more specific Rules, merely because the navigator thinks it best to maneuver in some other way than in accordance with their provisions. The Supreme Court set the tone early along:

> "And while under Rule twenty-four,[93] in construing and obeying the rules, due regard must be had to all dangers of navigation and to any special circumstances which may exist in any particular case, rendering a departure from them necessary in order to avoid immediate danger, the burden of proof lies on the party alleging that he was justified in such departure. The Agra, L.R. 1 P.C. 501; The General Lee, Irish L.R. 3 Eq. 155. Indeed, in The Agra, it was ruled that not only must it be shown that the departure at the time it took place was necessary in order to avoid immediate danger, but also that the course adopted was reasonably calculated to avoid that danger. And it is the settled rule in this court that when a vessel has committed a positive breach of statute, she must show not only that probably her fault did not contribute to the disaster, but that it could not have done so. The Pennsylvania, 19 Wall. 125, 136; Richelieu &

92. The Martello, 153 U.S. 64, 74–77, 14 S.Ct. 723, 726–728 (1894).

93. A predecessor of the present Rule 27.

O. Nav. Co. v. Boston Marine Ins. Co., 136 U.S. 408, 422, 10 S.Ct. 934.

"Obedience to the rules is not a fault even if a different course would have prevented the collision, and the necessity must be clear and the emergency sudden and alarming before the act of disobedience can be excused. Masters are bound to obey the rules and entitled to rely on the assumption that they will be obeyed, and should not be encouraged to treat the exceptions as subjects of solicitude rather than the rules. The Oregon, 18 How. 570." [94]

The "special circumstances" that excuse departure must be really special. Vessels, for example, maneuvering into position alongside piers present peculiar problems to which the general steering and sailing Rules manifestly cannot apply.[95] The entry of a third vessel into a two-vessel passing or crossing situation may create complications requiring special action.[96] The presence of a breakwater, preventing normal maneuvering, is a special circumstance excusing the vessel that has not followed the Rules literally.[97] Suddenly emergent danger may require the best action possible under the circumstances, without reference to the general Rules.

Rule 29 provides:

"Nothing in these Rules shall exonerate any vessel, or the owner, master or crew thereof, from the consequences of any neglect to carry lights or signals, or of any neglect to keep a proper look-out, or of the neglect of any precaution which may be required by the ordinary practice of seamen, or by the special circumstances of the case."

This Rule, in part, may be looked on as repetitive of Rule 27, but it goes further and makes it clear that not only the steering and sailing Rules but the Rules as a whole are not a complete and comprehensive code of navigation, compliance with which is sufficient to avoid liability, but that, on the contrary, the ordinary precautions of good seamanship, as defined by custom and case law, are still required. "Negligence" in general, as well as non-compliance with the Rules, is a ground of liability.

"Negligence" at sea does not differ, in principle, from "negligence" ashore. It is an elastic and open-textured concept, defined as the correlative of the equally vague standard of "due care"; "good" or "prudent" seamanship sometimes appears as a synonym. Thus,

94. Belden v. Chase, 150 U.S. 674, 699, 14 S.Ct. 264, 272 (1893). See also Yang-Tsze Ins. Ass'n v. Furness, Withy & Co., 215 F. 859 (2d Cir. 1914), certiorari dismissed 242 U.S. 430, 37 S.Ct. 141 (1917).

95. The Servia, 149 U.S. 144, 156, 13 S. Ct. 817, 822 (1893); The Fort St. George, 27 F.2d 788 (2d Cir. 1928). *Cf.* Pure Oil Co. v. The Fred B. Zigler, 105 F.Supp. 121, 1952 A.M.C. 1518 (E.D.La.1952).

96. The C. R. Hoyt, 136 F. 671 (D.N.J. 1905).

97. Cusumano v. The Curlew, 105 F. Supp. 428, 1952 A.M.C. 508 (D.Mass. 1952).

when vessels pass in close quarters it seems that the suction generated sometimes causes the smaller vessel to move toward the larger, and collision is thus brought about; the standards of prudent navigation therefore require that speed be slackened, when necessary, to avoid this result, though the Rules say nothing about it.[98] Similarly, the Rules impose no positive requirement as to look-out, but one of the surest ways for a vessel to inculpate herself is to neglect the posting of an adequate look-out.[99]

An interesting relation between the Rules and the concept of "negligence" is found in United States v. Woodbury.[100] The submarine Sea Owl, conducting diving practice in a special area in Ipswich Bay, Mass., designated for this purpose, picked up on her periscope the fishing vessel Ariel in these waters. The Inland Rules applied, which differ from the International Rules in that the latter, but not the former, require that a vessel trawling, as the Ariel was, display a basket signal, so as to warn approaching vessels of the presence of nets. Relying, it seems, on the Inland Rules, the Ariel displayed no such signal. The Sea Owl was unaware, therefore, that the Ariel was trawling, and dove to avoid collision, fouling the nets and doing considerable damage. The court found the Ariel at fault for not displaying this signal, despite the lack of any requirement for it in the applicable rules:

> "It does not follow, however, that the Ariel was free from fault in flying no signal whatever to indicate the activity in which she was engaged at the time and place of the collision, for mere literal compliance with a specific rule of navigation is not always and under all circumstances enough to exonerate a vessel from fault. This is so for the reason that article 29 of the Inland Rules, 33 U.S.C.A. § 221, which although general in its language is just as much a statutory command as the rules couched in more specific terms, provides in pertinent part: 'Nothing in these rules shall exonerate any vessel, or the owner or master or crew thereof, from the consequences of any neglect to carry * * * signals * * * or * * * neglect of any precaution which may be required by the ordinary practice of seamen, or by the special circumstances of the case.'

98. The Fontana, 119 F. 853 (6th Cir. 1903) certiorari denied 191 U.S. 573, 24 S.Ct. 845 (1903); see The Potomac, 105 F.2d 94, 70 App.D.C. 215, 1939 A.M.C. 1296 (1939); Gulf Oil Corp. v. United States, 98 F.Supp. 988, 1951 A.M.C. 2084 (S.D.N.Y.1951).

99. Chamberlain v. Ward, 62 U.S. (21 How.) 548, 570–71 (1859); The Ariadne, 80 U.S. (13 Wall.) 475 (1872); Stevens v. United States Lines, 187 F.2d 670, 1951 A.M.C. 617 (1st Cir. 1951). Wasson Barge Rental Co., Inc. v. Tug Carrie D, 296 F.Supp. 933, 1969 A.M.C. 131 (E.D.La.1969). But even this rule is not universal, *e. g.*, where pilot justifiably relies on radar, and where posting a lookout would have been both dangerous and ineffectual because of fog, the failure to post lookout was excused. United States v. Adams 376 F.2d 459, 1968 A.M.C. 133 (3d Cir. 1967). See also § 7–5 *supra*.

100. 175 F.2d 854, 1949 A.M.C. 1471 (1st Cir. 1949).

"This rule requires, in addition to bare compliance with the literal provisions of some specific rule, the adoption either of such additional precautions as it is the ordinary practice of seamen to take in a particular situation, or of such additional precautions as the special circumstances of a particular case reasonably demand. As the Supreme Court said in The Oregon, 158 U.S. 186, 201, 15 S.Ct. 804, 810, 39 L. Ed. 943, the rules are 'supposed to make provision for all ordinary cases,' but 'Undoubtedly, where the circumstances of the case are such as to demand unusual care, such care should be exercised.'

"We have no basis for any conclusion whatever with respect to the ordinary practice of seamen when trawling in a designated submarine maneuvering area in which it is known that submarines are actually operating. But we think that trawling in such an area, knowing that submarines are actually exercising therein, constitutes a special circumstance reasonably calling for the exhibition by the fishing vessel of some appropriate signal to warn the submarine of the peril to which she is exposed by the submerged net. And an appropriate signal to fly would be the basket called for by International Rule 9(k) above, for the meaning of that signal is clear, and could not be mistaken in inland waters, since it is not specified for any other situation in those waters. Indeed in a publication of the United States Coast Guard introduced into evidence at the trial entitled 'Comparative Rules of the Road and How to Obey Them,' the basket signal of the International Rules is set out as proper, although not required, for fishing vessels with nets out making way in inland waters navigable by seagoing vessels. . . . "[101]

## Radar

**§ 7–12.** One of the most important modern aids to navigation is radar, which (by registering the reflection of a directed radio beam emitted from the ship carrying the equipment) gives as raw data the direction and distance of so-detected objects. This information can be worked (by plotting successive observations) into information about apparent course and speed.[101a] Radar does not give as much information as sighted lights or shapes, and is unreliable, especially for detecting small vessels and other objects which may ride low in the sea. Nevertheless, it is a most valuable aid to navigation under conditions of poor visibility. (There are other similar electronic aids to navigation, with slightly different names; this discussion will assimilate them all under the term "radar" used generically.)

The courts (as they must) have struggled to digest this new technique. Until 1964, the International Rules did not take any ac-

**101.** 175 F.2d at 861–2.

**101a.** See Slack, Modern Methods of Plotting, 5 Willamette L.J. 415 (1969).

count of radar. The new Rules, now in force, do treat this subject, but rather obliquely, and to a considerable extent in the form of "recommendations" rather than of binding law.[102]

An extraordinarily clear and comprehensive article by Professor Nicholas Healy [103] covers all questions that can arise under the new Rules. The discussion here following draws heavily on that article.

The new Rules are silent, first, on the obligation to have radar at all. No cases have yet held that the lack of radar makes a vessel unseaworthy, or constitutes "fault" for collision-liability purposes. The use of radar is now, however, so nearly universal that such a holding may well be imminent, with respect to large commercial ships, Judge Medina's dictum, in a case now aging, should be quoted:

> "Though the question is not before us in this case, as both ships were equipped with radar, the question arises *in limine* as to the duty of a vessel to carry radar. No statute or regulation requires this. And this is so though radar has to a considerable degree lessened the importance of other navigation aids required aboard various types of vessels. Nor have the courts as yet formulated any rule requiring radar. A District Court has found that the failure of a destroyer to carry navigational radar in 1942 did not render her unseaworthy. Anglo-Saxon Petroleum Co. v. United States, D.C.Mass.1950, 88 F.Supp. 158. However, conditions have changed since the fledgling days of radar in 1942 and the value of Anglo-Saxon Petroleum Co. as a precedent today is doubtful. Lurking in the background is T. J. Hooper, 2 Cir., 1932, 60 F.2d 737, certiorari denied, Eastern Transportation Co. v. Northern Barge Corp., 1932, 287 U.S. 662, 53 S.Ct. 220, 77 L.Ed. 571, where in 1932, despite the absence of statutes, regulations or even custom as to radio receiving sets, Judge Learned Hand found a vessel unseaworthy for lack of one. Two barges had been lost in a storm and the tugs and their tows might have sought shelter in time had they received weather reports by radio. We think this case shows which way the wind blows and have little doubt that a rule requiring radar, subject to some limitations and qualifications, will sooner or later be formulated." [104]

A general requirement for the possession of radar by all vessels is impractical, in view of the expense and other difficulties. It will

102. See Rule 1(c), Definition ix; Preliminary Note 4 to the Steering and Sailing Rules (17–24); Rule 16(c); Preliminary Note to Fog Rules (15 and 16); special new Annex to Rules.

103. Healy, Radar and the New Collision Regulations, 37 Tulane L.Rev. 621 (1963). See also Meadows, The Radar Annex and Rule 16 . . . As They Affect Navigation in Restricted Visibility, 5 Willamette L.J. 399 (1969).

104. Afran Transport Co. v. The Bergechief, 274 F.2d 469, 474, 1960 A.M.C. 1380, 1385 (2d Cir. 1960). But no holding so far, it seems, has carried this dictum into law.

be hard to draw the line; perhaps solution by an international convention is wisest here.

Secondly, the new Rules would seem to leave unimpaired the obligation to use radar if it is aboard. As Professor Healy says, the case law "is now quite abundant on this point." [105] On the closely connected question whether it is a fault under law to fail to maintain radar equipment properly, the case law still leaves the matter doubtful. Professor Healy suggests a distinction between major repairs (failure to make which he would classify as equivalent to not having radar at all, and hence not a "fault" until the possession of radar is required) and repairs performable *en route* by the crew (failure to make which he would classify with failure to use radar properly; see next paragraph). It would seem best, however, to wait for the square presentation of issues arising from particular facts, before freezing this distinction into place. Some repairs, though performable only by an expert technician in port, might be inexpensive and simple enough to justify their omission's being considered as negligence, even without going all the way and requiring the installation of radar.[106]

The "heart of the radar problem", as Professor Healy says, is touched by the first of the Recommendations respecting radar annexed to the new Rules, which cautions against the making of assumptions on the basis of "scant" radar information.[107] This Recommendation confirms existing case law; the obligation to use radar naturally comprises the obligation to use it prudently.[107a]

Other points are of less general importance: The possession and use of radar does not relieve the vessel of the obligation to maintain a visual lookout, and she may not maneuver as if another vessel were "in sight" unless that vessel is *visually* in sight; [107b] this rule recog-

105. Healy, 37 Tulane L.Rev. at 630; for recent illustration, see C.I.T. Corp. v. Oil Screw Peggy, 424 F.2d 767, 1970 A.M.C. 1550 (5th Cir. 1970). There is no duty to use radar, it has recently been held, in conditions of perfect visibility, where actual harm might have ensued from the master's interrupting his visual observations by leaving the bridge to consult radar. Maroceano Compania Naviera, S.A. v. S.S. Verdi, 438 F.2d 854, 1971 A.M.C. 584 (2d Cir. 1971), certiorari denied 404 U.S. 830, 92 S.Ct. 70 (1971).

106. Healy, 37 Tulane L.Rev. at 631–2. The Second Circuit has declared it is not negligence to have a radar on board which is out of commission. Villam & Fassio E. Compagnia v. Tank Steamer E. W. Sinclair, 313 F.2d 722, 1963 A.M.C. 610 (2d Cir. 1963). But it has been held to be negligence so to rig booms as to impair effective radar use. Hess Shipping Corp. v. S. S. Charles Lykes, 417 F.2d 346, 1969 A.M.C. 1787 (5th Cir. 1969), certiorari denied 400 U.S. 853, 91 S.Ct. 56 (1970).

107. 37 Tulane L.Rev. at 632–4.

107a. It has been held that plotting is required wherever prudence would indicate its use. Atlantic Richfield Co. v. S.S. Steel Designer, 1970 A.M.C. 1371 (C.D.Calif.1970); Orient Steam Nav. Co. v. United States, 231 F.Supp. 469, 1964 A.M.C. 2163 (S.D.Calif.1964). See also Healy, *op. cit.*, 37 Tulane L. Rev. at 632–3.

107b. See Healy, *op. cit.*, 37 Tulane L. Rev. 634–5 and cases cited. As Professor Healy says: "While the new Regulations do not specifically codify the existing case law on this point, they do provide that vessels are to be deemed in sight of one another only when they can be observed visually. From this, and from the fact that no change was made in Rule 29, the "Rule of Good Seamanship," the plain

nizes by implication that radar information, useful as it may be, is rarely as complete and reliable as visual information.

What effect does the possession and use of radar have on the definition of "moderate" speed in fog? The radar Recommendations in the new Rules speak delphically:

> (2) A vessel navigating with the aid of radar in restricted visibility must, in compliance with Rules 16(a), go at a moderate speed. Information obtained from the use of radar is one of the circumstances to be taken into account when determining moderate speed. In this regard it must be recognized that small vessels, small icebergs and similar floating objects may not be detected by radar.
>
> Radar indications of one or more vessels in the vicinity may mean that "moderate speed" should be slower than a mariner without radar might consider moderate in the circumstances.[107c]

As a practical matter, radar cuts both ways. If a reliable radar set indicates absence of any other vessels on anything like collision course, the observing ship might be justified in maintaining something near full speed. If an object appears on radar, but course and speed are not reliably shown (as is often the case) then an obligation to slow drastically or to stop may be a corollary of the general duty to navigate prudently.

One point seems definitely cleared up by the new Rules. Rules 17–24, the Steering and Sailing Rules, are to apply only if vessels are *visually* in sight of each other; the radar-sighting situation, then, is something different, and its rules will have to be worked out under a general negligence concept. This makes sense; the Steering and Sailing Rules set up a mutuality and responsiveness of obligation which can meaningfully be imposed only when there is completely reliable, instantaneous and continuous information on course and speed. That information, so far, can be derived only from mutual visual sighting.

## Custom

**§ 7–13.** Midway in definiteness between the hard-and-fast Rules and the relatively vague requirements of due care and prudence stand those customs which courts will recognize as setting a standard of

inference is that the use of radar will not dispense with the requirement of maintaining a visual lookout." 37 Tulane L.Rev. at 635.

**107c.** It has been held that reliance on radar can under certain circumstances be "reasonable", to the extent of excusing what would otherwise be the imprudence of going into New York Harbor under conditions of 75-foot visibility. Moran Towing & Transportation Co., Inc. v. United States, 263 F.Supp. 787, 1967 A.M.C. 1348 (S.D.N.Y.1967). But radar does not exempt a vessel in principle from the "moderate speed" requirement of the Fog Rules, stated in Rule 16(a). N.V. Stoomvaart Maatschappij "Nederland" v. Standard Oil of California, 398 F.2d 835, 1968 A.M.C. 1991 (9th Cir. 1968), certiorari denied 393 U.S. 980, 89 S.Ct. 448 (1968).

conduct, where they are clearly established by proof and are not in conflict with the Rules or other requirements of positive law. Since the conditions that call such customs into being are typically local in character, having reference to characteristics of particular channels and harbors, they are usually found in waters covered by the Inland or Western Rivers Rules, rather than by the International Rules.

Thus, in Union Oil Co. of California v. Tug Mary Malloy,[107d] the Fifth Circuit gave the effect of law (by faulting a flotilla that did not obey) to the long-standing custom that tugs with tow hold up to let tankers enter the Sabine-Neches Canal.

In The Luzerne,[108] the Second Circuit Court of Appeals upheld a custom giving right of way to a westbound vessel in the East River over a vessel coming out of the Harlem River. And at Hell Gate, on flood tide, a custom has been given effect by which a starboard to starboard passing is executed, rather than the port to port passing required by the Inland Rules.[109] In the latter case, the Court held that the requirements of safety justified departure from the apparently clear mandate of the Rules; the case need not be taken as overstepping the principle that custom may not contradict the Rules, for the custom itself could be regarded as an instance of the application of the Special Circumstances Rule (Rule 27) discussed in § 7–11, *supra*.[110]

## Towage in Collision Cases

**§ 7–14.** The towing situation is one presenting special problems, both practical and legal.[110a] On the practical side, the combined tug and tow constitute a far less maneuverable unit than the single powered vessel, and the presence of the tow makes close maneuvering more problematic for other vessels. For these reasons, as we have seen, tugs with a tow are required by the Rules to be marked with special lights, and to sound special signals in fog.[111] Failure to comply with any of these Rules is a serious fault.

In applying the steering and sailing Rules to tug and tow, it becomes necessary to decide just what is the "vessel" that may be "privileged" or "burdened," and that is in general charged with obeying the Rules. It is clearly settled that the flotilla as a whole, comprising tug and tow, is a unit, and must comply with the Rules as a unit.[112] Thus, an entire flotilla consisting of powered tug and her

**107d.** Union Oil Co. of California v. Tug Mary Malloy, 414 F.2d 669, 1969 A.M.C. 2254 (5th Cir. 1969).

**108.** 204 F. 981 (2d Cir. 1913).

**109.** The Transfer No. 21, 248 F. 459 (2d Cir. 1917).

**110.** On the status of custom in general, and the Mississippi River custom of "running the bends," see The John D. Rockefeller, 272 F. 67 (4th Cir. 1921), certiorari denied 256 U.S. 693, 41 S.Ct. 535 (1921).

**110a.** See Parks, Law of Tug, Tow and Pilotage (1971).

**111.** Rules 3, 15 [c] (v).

**112.** The Gladys, 144 F. 653 (2d Cir. 1906). This was an extreme case—a flotilla of tug and three barges, 4000 feet long in all.

tow must, as a powered vessel, keep out of the way of sailing ships.[113] The fact that the tug is encumbered is, however, one of the circumstances to be considered in determining whether the actions of another vessel have satisfied the requirements of prudent seamanship; clearly, the master of another vessel cannot rely on the unity of tug and tow to the point of ignoring that the encumbered tug cannot maneuver with freedom.[114]

Strangely, but as a matter of settled law, the unity of tug and tow is not carried to the point of imposing liability upon the flotilla as a whole for faults in navigation. Instead, the courts have worked out a concept of "dominant mind," the upshot of which is that only that vessel is liable whose people are actually in control of the operation, in the respect in which the flotilla is cast in fault.[115] The tug is usually the "dominant mind," since she is doing the pulling. Where, however, the collision is the result of some breach of duty on the part of the tow, such as the failure to show proper lights, she may be held liable.[116]

The refusal of the courts to impute the tug's fault to the tow has an important consequence beyond the mere immunization of the tow from liability. Where she is herself injured through the fault of her own tug and a third vessel, she can recover from them both as joint tortfeasors.[117] If she is injured by the sole fault of her tug, the latter is liable to her for the damages she sustains.[118]

## Negligence Clauses in Towage Contracts

**§ 7–15.** The operators of tugboats have for a long time sought to avoid the effects of the rules just stated by the inclusion in the contract of towage of provisions stipulating that the towage was to be at the sole risk of the tow. These provisions took many forms; their aim was to immunize the tug from liability for negligence in performing the towage service. The Supreme Court, in Bisso v. Inland Water-

113. The Civilta, 103 U.S. 699, 701–2 (1881); The Gladys, *supra* note 112.

114. The Syracuse, 76 U.S. (9 Wall.) 672, 675–676 (1870); Mitchell Transp. Co. v. Green, 120 F. 49, 57–8 (6th Cir. 1903); Western Transit Co. v. Davidson S. S. Co., 212 F. 696, 700 (6th Cir. 1914), certiorari denied 234 U.S. 764, 34 S.Ct. 998 (1914); Pure Oil Co. v. The Fred B. Zigler, 105 F.Supp. 121, 1952 A.M.C. 1518 (E.D.La.1952).

115. Sturgis v. Boyer, 65 U.S. (24 How.) 110 (1860). (Of argument in this case, the reporter says: "It was argued by *Mr. C. A. Seward* for the tug, *Mr. Williams* for the Wisconsin, and *Mr. Benedict* for the Republic. It was a triangular war."); The Fort George, 183 F. 731 (2d Cir. 1910), certiorari denied 219 U.S. 589, 31 S.Ct. 472 (1911); The John D. Rockefeller, 272 F. 67 (4th Cir. 1921), certiorari denied 256 U.S. 693, 41 S.Ct. 535 (1921).

116. The Sif, 266 F. 166 (2d Cir. 1920); see also Old Time Molasses Co. v. United States, 31 F.2d 963, 1929 A.M.C. 687 (5th Cir. 1929); The Beaverton, 273 F. 539 (S.D.N.Y.1919); In re Barrett, 108 F.Supp. 710, 1954 A.M.C. 159 (S.D.N.Y.1952), modified on other grounds 209 F.2d 487 (2d Cir. 1954). *With* the last case *compare* Dougherty Co. v. United States, 104 F.Supp. 711, 1952 A.M.C. 537 (S.D.N.Y.1951).

117. The Alabama, 92 U.S. 695 (1876).

118. The Webb, 81 U.S. (14 Wall.) 406 (1872); Great Lakes Towing Co. v. American Shipbuilding Co., 243 F. 849 (6th Cir. 1917).

ways Corp.,[119] has settled the invalidity of such clauses. The opinion, reviewing the older authorities,[120] concludes that they ". . . strongly point to the existence of a judicial rule, based on public policy, invalidating contracts releasing towers from all liability for their negligence." [121] The opinion proceeds:

> "This rule is merely a particular application to the towage business of a general rule long used by courts and legislatures to prevent enforcement of release-from-negligence contracts in many relationships such as bailors and bailees, employers and employees, public service companies and their customers. The two main reasons for the creation and application of the rule have been (1) to discourage negligence by making wrongdoers pay damages, and (2) to protect those in need of goods or services from being overreached by others who have power to drive hard bargains. These two reasons are no less applicable today than when The Steamer Syracuse and The Wash Gray were decided. And both reasons apply with equal force whether tugs operate as common carriers or contract carriers. The dangers of modern machines make it all the more necessary that negligence be discouraged. And increased maritime traffic of today makes it not less but more important that vessels in American ports be able to obtain towage free of monopolistic compulsions." [122]

In Bisso, another clause in the contract provided that the master, crews and employees of the tug should be the "servants" of the tow, in the performance of the towage service. In a suit for damage to the tow, such a clause, if held valid, would of course have had, indirectly, the same effect as the clause relieving the tug from liability for negligence. The Court makes short work of this fictitious "employment." [123]

The companion case of Boston Metals Co. v. The Winding Gulf [124] dealt with the effect of a "fictitious employment" clause in another situation. While an obsolete destroyer was in tow of a tug, a steamer collided with the destroyer. The lower courts found fault in the steamer (for negligent navigation) and in the towed destroyer (for absence of lights and crew). The latter omissions were found to be the fault of the master of the tug, which was certainly the "dominant mind" in this situation of deadship towage.[125] In the absence of contract stipulations, the tug, and not the towed destroyer, would clearly have been liable. But the contract of towage provided:

> "Tug services will be supplied upon the condition that all towing * * * of a vessel or craft of any character by a

119. 349 U.S. 85, 75 S.Ct. 629, 1955 A.M.C. 899 (1955).

120. Especially The Steamer Syracuse, 79 U.S. (12 Wall.) 167 (1871) and The Wash Gray, 277 U.S. 66, 48 S.Ct. 459, 1928 A.M.C. 923 (1928).

121. 349 U.S. at 90, 75 S.Ct. at 632.

122. 349 U.S. at 90–91, 75 S.Ct. at 632, 633.

123. 349 U.S. at 94–95, 75 S.Ct. at 635.

124. 349 U.S. 122, 75 S.Ct. 649, 1955 A.M.C. 927 (1955).

125. See *supra* at note 115.

tug or tugs owned or employed by the Tug Company is done at the sole risk of such vessel or craft and of the owners, charterers or operators thereof, *and that the Master and crew of such tug or tugs used in the said services become the servants of and identified with such vessel or craft and their owners*, and that the Tug Company only undertakes to provide motive power." [126] [Emphasis supplied]

Taken literally, this clause would mean that the faults of the master of the tug were to be imputed not to his actual employers but to the towed destroyer and her owners. This would make the latter liable to the third vessel for the tug-master's negligence in failing to light and attend his tow; the lower courts had read the contract this way and reached this result.[127] But the Supreme Court, fresh from the Bisso decision, had no trouble with this one:

> "For whatever this contract said, here as in the Bisso case, the persons who conducted these towing operations were in fact acting as employees of the towing company, not as employees of the owner of the tow. Under these circumstances it was error to hold petitioner liable for negligence of the towing company's employees." [128]

A dissent in Bisso (delivered by Mr. Justice Frankfurter and joined by Justices Reed and Burton), besides expressing a difference of opinion as to the tenor of the authorities, strikes at the policy of the decision:

> "The considerations which have governed this Court's role as arbiter of the public interest in exculpatory contracts were recently enunciated by the unanimous Court in the Sun Oil case. They bear repetition:
>
> > 'So far as concerns the service to be rendered under the agreement, respondent was not a common carrier or bailee or bound to serve or liable as such. Towage does not involve bailment * * *. There is no foundation in this case for the application of the doctrine that common carriers and others under like duty to serve the public * * * cannot by any form of agreement secure exemption from liability for loss or damage caused by their own negligence. * * * Respondent had no exclusive privilege or monopoly * * *. There is nothing to suggest that the parties were not on equal footing or that they did not deal at arm's length.' 287 U.S. at page 294, 53 S.Ct. at page 136.

126. 349 U.S. at 124, 75 S.Ct. at 650.

127. 209 F.2d 410, 1954 A.M.C. 183 (4th Cir. 1954); 72 F.Supp. 50, 1947 A.M.C. 819 (D.Md.1947). An opinion on damages, reported at 85 F.Supp. 806, 1949 A.M.C. 1149 (D.Md.1949), is discussed below in another connection. (*Infra* at note 161.)

128. 349 U.S. at 123, 75 S Ct. at 650.

These considerations of policy are equally present here and call for the result reached in Sun Oil.

> "Nothing in the record hints at any inequality of bargaining power between the parties to this contract, nor is there any basis for taking judicial notice that the tug industry as an industry is in concentrated ownership. The towing service was here undertaken by a Government corporation. Certainly we cannot assume that the Government is exploiting the maritime services it is rendering in an unreasonable or coercive manner. Nor was it suggested that no tug company available for the services involved would consent to deletion of the exculpatory clause upon payment of a reasonable consideration. Nor are we informed as to whether such clauses were uniformly found in the standard contracts offered by tug companies in the locality. Had such uniformity of practice been shown, it would not necessarily reflect more than universal satisfaction with such an arrangement; it would hardly demonstrate need for judicial wardship." [129]

With respect, it may be suggested that where a contract of towage contains the onerous conditions found in these cases it would be reasonable to regard their acceptance by the tow as economically coerced until the contrary is proven. The thesis might be sustained that owners of vessels are not likely to entrust them to the care of others who initiate the service by disclaiming responsibility for its careful performance, unless, to use common language, they have to.

The Bisso dissent makes the further (and seemingly valid) point that in the normal case both interests are insured, so that the question is really which shall carry insurance against this sort of loss.[130] But, in so far as valid, this point works both ways, for the tug with adequate P. & I. protection [131] needs no exculpatory clause. In the case where insurance is not carried, or where it for any reason fails to cover adequately or at all, the choice must be made, as between the principals, which is to bear the loss. Indeed, the insurance factor may make exculpation especially inappropriate, since it is likely best that the controlling party be under threat of premium increase.

In any case, these decisions seemed to show the Supreme Court firming up a general "set" against "negligence" clauses.[132]

The legend of "freedom of contract" is hardy. In 1963, the Court had again (in Dixilyn Drilling Corporation v. Crescent Towing and Salvage Co.[132a]) to reaffirm the Bisso rule, the Fifth Circuit Court of Appeals having upheld an exculpatory clause in a towing con-

129. 349 U.S. at 117–118, 75 S.Ct. at 646, 647.

130. 349 U.S. at 119, 75 S.Ct. at 647.

131. See *supra* Chapter II, at notes 94–95.

132. *Cf.* the Both-to-Blame decision, *supra* Chapter III, Part II, at note 101 *et seq.*

132a. 372 U.S. 697, 83 S.Ct. 967, 1963 A.M.C. 829 (5th Cir. 1963).

tract,[132b] thus placing itself as the Supreme Court saw it, "squarely in conflict" with Bisso. The per curiam reversal seemed to make it finally clear that Bisso had meant what it said.

On the other hand, an intervening development has somewhat undermined Bisso. In Southwestern Sugar & Molasses Co. v. River Terminals Corp.,[132c] the Court introduced an exception. The exculpatory clause was a part of a "tariff" filed with the Interstate Commerce Commission; the holding was that such a clause, subject as it is (and as the price of the service is) to the Commission regulatory authority, is not invalid. Just recently, Bisso has been somewhat further weakened by the Court's upholding a "choice of forum" clause in a towage contract (Houston to Italy; stipulation for British courts).[132d]

### Pilotage in Collision Cases

**§ 7–16.** A pilot may be taken on voluntarily or under the compulsion of some local statute or regulation. The voluntary pilot is in much the same position as any other crew member. Under the ordinary rules of *respondeat superior*, the shipowner is responsible for his actions, and the vessel is made liable *in rem* for collisions resulting from the faults he commits.[133]

The compulsory pilot presents a special problem. Statutes that impose a fine or imprisonment for the failure to take a pilot obviously create compulsory pilotage. Some statutes, however, allow the ship to refuse the pilot provided she pays his fee or half of it ("half-pilotage"). The Supreme Court has indicated that it does not regard the tendering of this alternative as amounting to compulsion.[134]

It makes a difference, because it is pretty well settled that if the pilotage is "compulsory" the *respondeat superior* nexus is broken, and the shipowner cannot be held personally liable for the fault of the pilot resulting in collision.[135]

132b. 303 F.2d 237, 1963 A.M.C. 831 (5th Cir. 1962).

132c. 360 U.S. 411, 79 S.Ct. 1210, 1959 A.M.C. 1631 (5th Cir. 1959).

132d. The Bremen, et al. v. Zapata Off-Shore Co., 407 U.S. 1, 92 S.Ct. 1907, 1972 A.M.C. 1407 (5th Cir. 1972). For fuller discussion of this case, see *supra* Chapter III, Part II, note 23, and *infra*, Chapter X, § 10–15.

133. See the full discussion in Homer Ramsdell Transp. Co. v. Compagnie Générale Transatlantique, 182 U.S. 406, 21 S.Ct. 831 (1901); also, The Maren Lee, 278 F. 918 (2d Cir. 1922).

134. The Merrimac, 81 U.S. (14 Wall.) 199, 203 (1872); Homer Ramsdell Transp. Co. v. Compagnie Générale Transatlantique, 182 U.S. 406, 414–15, 21 S.Ct. 831, 834, 835 (1901). But see The China, 74 U.S. (7 Wall.) 53 (1869); The Framlington Court, 69 F.2d 300, 1934 A.M.C. 272 (5th Cir. 1934), certiorari denied 292 U.S. 651, 54 S.Ct. 860 (1934); Standard Oil Co. of N. J. v. U. S., 27 F.2d 370, 1928 A.M.C. 1419 (S.D.Ala.1928).

135. Homer Ramsdell Transp. Co. v. Compagnie Générale Transatlantique, 182 U.S. 406, 21 S.Ct. 831 (1901) is usually regarded as having settled this. It held only that an action at common law did not lie against the owner personally for acts of the compulsory pilot. But the case has been generally taken to establish that no *in personam* liability, in admiralty or at common law, can be brought home to the owner in this position. See The

The ship's liability *in rem*, however, is unaffected by the fact that the pilotage is compulsory.[136] This is one of the more striking consequences of the endowment of the ship with a juristic personality independent of that of her owner.[136a]

The pilot, of course, is personally liable for his own negligence, but a judgment against him is not usually worth much. Attempts have been made to bring home liability to the pilots' association of which he is often a member, but the courts have uniformly repelled such attempts.[137]

An interesting problem involving both pilotage and towage was settled by the Supreme Court in United States v. Nielson,[138] decided along with the Bisso [139] and Boston Metals [140] cases discussed above. A towing company contracted to furnish two of its tugs to move a steamship. In performing the service, one of the tugboat captains went aboard the steamer and took charge of her as pilot. Allegedly because of his negligence, damage was done to a tug belonging to his actual employer, the tugboat company. Normally, the steamship could not, of course, have been held liable by the towing company for the negligence of one of the latter's own people. But the contract contained a "fictitious employment" clause, providing that a tugboat captain going aboard the steamer would become the "servant of the owners of the vessel assisted . . . ."

The towing company brought suit for the damage on the theory that the captain's negligence must be answered for by his "employer" under this clause. Apparently as a matter of construction of the contract, the Court held this liability could not be brought home to the steamer. Left undisturbed was the holding in Sun Oil Co. v. Dalzell Towing Co.,[141] to the effect that such a clause did serve to immunize the towing company from liability to the tow for damage caused to the latter by the pilot's negligence. The Bisso opinion [142] had already distinguished negligent *pilotage* from negligent *towage*, conceding that, while liability for the latter may not be contracted

Abangarez, 60 F.2d 543, 544, 1932 A.M.C. 1247 (E.D.La.1932); Griffin, *op. cit.*, *supra* note 1, 443–4. Certainly, the result should be the same in admiralty as at common law (*cf. supra* Chapter I, at note 163 *et seq.*) and the Ramsdell reasoning seems as applicable to one as to the other.

**136.** The China, 74 U.S. (7 Wall.) 53 (1869); Essex County Electric Co. v. Motor Ship Godafoss, 129 F.Supp. 657, 1955 A.M.C. 755 (D.Mass.1955). The latter case contains a valuable discussion of the qualifications and duties of local pilots.

**136a.** See Chapter IX, § 9–5 *et seq.*, particularly § 9–9.

**137.** Guy v. Donald, 203 U.S. 399, 27 S.Ct. 63 (1906); Dampskibsselskabet Atalanta A/S v. United States, 31 F.2d 961, 1929 A.M.C. 855 (5th Cir. 1929).

**138.** 349 U.S. 129, 75 S.Ct. 654, 1955 A.M.C. 935 (1955).

**139.** *Supra* at note 119.

**140.** *Supra* at note 124.

**141.** 287 U.S. 291, 53 S.Ct. 135, 1932 A.M.C. 149 (1932).

**142.** *Supra* at note 119.

out of, liability for the former may. The ground on which this distinction rests is thus stated in Bisso:

> "There are distinctions between a pilotage and a towage exemption clause which make it entirely reasonable to hold one valid and the other invalid. A pilotage clause exempts for the negligence of pilots only; a towage clause exempts from all negligence of all towage employees. Pilots hold a unique position in the maritime world and have been regulated extensively both by the States and Federal Government. Some state laws make them public officers, chiefly responsible to the State, not to any private employer. Under law and custom they have an independence wholly incompatible with the general obligations of obedience normally owed by an employee to his employer. Their fees are fixed by law and their charges must not be discriminatory. As a rule no employer, no person can tell them how to perform their pilotage duties. When the law does not prescribe their duties, pilots are usually free to act on their own best judgment while engaged in piloting a vessel. Because of these differences between pilots and towage employees generally, contracts stipulating against a pilot's negligence cannot be likened to contracts stipulating against towers' negligence. It is one thing to permit a company to exempt itself from liability for the negligence of a licensed pilot navigating another company's vessel on that vessel's own power. That was the Sun Oil case. It is quite a different thing, however, to permit a towing company to exempt itself by contract from all liability for its own employees' negligent towage of a vessel. Thus, holding the pilotage contract valid in the Sun Oil case in no way conflicts with the rule against permitting towers by contract wholly to escape liability for their own negligent towing." [143]

### "Ship-to-Shore" Collisions

**§ 7–17.** Ships sometimes do damage to piers, wharves, bridges, and other shore structures. In The Plymouth,[144] sparks from a burning ship set a wharf on fire. Suit was brought *in rem* against the ship, and the question was raised whether the tort lay within the admiralty jurisdiction. Holding that it did not, the Supreme Court based its decision on the localizing of the tort on shore, where the "substance and consummation" of the harm took place. Though the facts of the case were peculiar, its reasoning was broad enough to apply to all cases of damage by ships to shore structures, and the principle that such injuries were outside the purview of admiralty passed into settled law.[145] The only exception made was for the

143. 349 U.S. at 93–94, 75 S.Ct. at 634.

144. 70 U.S. (3 Wall.) 20 (1866).

145. Cleveland, T. & V. R. Co. v. Cleveland S. S. Co., 208 U.S. 316, 28 S.Ct. 414 (1908).

structure—such as a beacon—which was principally concerned with navigation.[146]

The practical result was that, as to the rather numerous injuries done by ships to bridges, docks, and the like, the aggrieved owner of the shore structure, unable to get into admiralty at all, had no maritime lien or right to proceed *in rem* against the ship, and, since the common law rule as to contributory negligence applied to his "non-maritime" injury, even his law action would be wholly defeated if he himself had been negligent.[147] Injuries to a ship by a shore structure were, on the other hand, within the admiralty jurisdiction,[148] and, while the shipowner could of course have no maritime lien on the offending shore structure, since it could not be the subject of such a lien,[149] he could, by suing in admiralty, avail himself of the divided damages rule in the both-to-blame situation.[150] Thus, in a collision, say, between a vessel and a drawbridge where both, as often happens, were at fault, the shipowner enjoyed a very considerable tactical advantage over the owner of the bridge. If the damages to the ship had been greater than those to the bridge, the shipowner could sue in admiralty and collect the balance. If the damages to the bridge had been greater than those to the ship, the owner of the ship could bide his time and wait to be sued at law, where he could defeat the bridge-owner's claim on contributory negligence grounds.

In 1948, Congress remedied this situation by providing that the admiralty jurisdiction should thenceforth extend to all injuries "caused by a vessel . . . notwithstanding that such damage or injury be done or consummated on land." [151] Under this statute, the drawbridge owner may sue in admiralty and thus invoke the benefits of the divided damages rule.

While some question existed initially as to the constitutionality of this statute, the lower courts consistently upheld it [152] and the question

146. The Blackheath, 195 U.S. 361, 25 S.Ct. 46 (1904); The Raithmoor, 241 U.S. 166, 36 S.Ct. 514 (1916). Fortunately, for a reason which appears in the text immediately following, it is no longer necessary to worry with the fine distinction suggested by these cases.

147. Under the old rule of Belden v. Chase, 150 U.S. 674, 14 S.Ct. 264 (1893), discussed *supra* at note 64 *et seq.*

148. Conklin v. City of Norwalk, 270 F. 68 (2d Cir. 1920).

149. The Rock Island Bridge, 73 U.S. (6 Wall.) 213 (1867).

150. See *supra* at note 41.

151. 62 Stat. 496 (1948), 46 U.S.C.A. § 740. Application of this statute has brought to life the situation envisaged by A. P. Herbert in his case of Rumpelheimer v. Haddock, The Uncommon Law 237 (7th ed. 1950), where a motor-car and a rowboat nearly collided on a flooded highway. In Chicago, Burlington & Quincy R. R. v. The W. C. Harms, 134 F.Supp. 636, 1955 A.M.C. 1423 (S.D.Tex.1954) collision actually occurred between a train and a vessel protruding on shore. The libellant railroad recovered; the court took occasion to find the train was "seaworthy".

152. United States v. Matson Nav. Co., 201 F.2d 610, 1953 A.M.C. 272 (9th Cir. 1953), noted 27 So.Calif.L.Rev. 312 (1954); American Bridge Co. v. The Gloria O., 98 F.Supp. 71, 1951 A.M.C. 1388 (E.D.N.Y.1951); Fematt v. City of Los Angeles, Cal., 196 F.Supp. 89, 1961 A.M.C. 2391 (S.D.Calif.1961). The Matson opinion is referred to with ev-

was seemingly resolved by the Supreme Court in 1963, in Gutierrez v. Waterman S. S. Co.[153] where, treating the issue of admiralty jurisdiction in a case concerning injuries to a longshoreman while unloading a ship, the Court squarely based its upholding of jurisdiction on the Act.[154] More recently [155] Gutierrez was limited to injury by the "appurtenances of a ship",[156] but this is clearly only a matter of interpretation of the statute, and does not touch its constitutionality, which may now be assumed.[157]

### Further on Damages

**§ 7–18.** We have already stated, in outline, the divided damages rule.[158] Somewhat fuller attention should be given to the damage problem.

Where a vessel is totally lost through collision, the damages her owner can recover are her value, measured where possible by her "market value" and pending freight.[159] As to vessels of standard type, frequent subjects of sale and purchase, market value is fairly easy to approximate. Special vessels, including private yachts, warships, and vessels having a particular business value to their owners, present a more difficult problem. In practice, in such cases, courts either guess at market value or are driven to use some other concept, such as "construction cost less depreciation"; the result often reflects a miscellany of considerations, with some rough sense of approximate justice coagulating the mass to a firm figure.[160]

In Boston Iron & Metal Co. v. The Winding Gulf,[161] an obsolete destroyer, purchased for about $6,600 and towed to the point of loss

ident approval in Diamond State Tel. Co. v. Atlantic Refining Co., 205 F.2d 402, 1953 A.M.C. 1712 (3d Cir. 1953), where jurisdiction based on the statute was accepted. In Seaboard Air Line R. Co. v. Pan Am. Petroleum Co., 199 F.2d 761, 1952 A.M.C. 1934 (5th Cir. 1952), certiorari denied 345 U.S. 909, 73 S.Ct. 649 (1953), jurisdiction was taken, without remark, of a libel by a bridge owner against a vessel.

153. 373 U.S. 206, 83 S.Ct. 1185, 1963 A.M.C. 1649 (1963).

154. 373 U.S. at 210, 83 S.Ct. at 1188, 1963 A.M.C. at 1653.

155. Victory Carriers, Inc. v. Law, 404 U.S. 202, 92 S.Ct. 418, 1972 A.M.C. 1 (1971), *rehearing denied* 404 U.S. 1064, 92 S.Ct. 731 (1972).

156. 404 U.S. at 210, 83 S.Ct. at 1188, 1972 A.M.C. at 8.

157. See 404 U.S. at 209 *et seq.*, 83 S. Ct. 1887 *et seq.*, 1972 A.M.C. at 7 *et seq.*

158. See *supra* at note 39 *et seq.* The sketch given there will not be repeated here.

159. These points are made, and the process of damage calculation thoroughly illustrated, in Ozanic v. United States, 165 F.2d 738, 1948 A.M.C. 340 (2d Cir. 1948). See also The Umbria, 166 U.S. 404, 421, 17 S.Ct. 610, 617 (1897); The I. C. White, 295 F. 593 (4th Cir. 1924). There is a discussion of the elements of collision damage law in Hewlett v. Barge Bertie, 418 F.2d 654, 1969 A.M.C. 2238 (4th Cir. 1969), certiorari denied 397 U.S. 1021, 90 S.Ct. 126 (1970).

160. Illustrative cases are: La Normandie, 58 F. 427 (2d Cir. 1893); The H. F. Dimock, 77 F. 226 (1st Cir. 1896); The Samson, 217 F. 344 (9th Cir. 1914); The President Madison, 91 F.2d 835, 1937 A.M.C. 1375 (9th Cir. 1937); The City of Alexandria, 40 F. 697 (S.D.N.Y.1889); The Lucille, 169 F. 719 (S.D.Ala.1909).

161. 85 F.Supp. 806, 1949 A.M.C. 1149 (D.Md.1949), affirmed 209 F.2d 410

at a cost of some $3,000, was sunk in collision. To her owner, who had bought her to break her up for scrap, she was almost inexpressibly dear; $46,449.32 was the amount claimed, the sum being calculated as the value of the metal. Counsel for The Winding Gulf took a more austere view, and would have limited damages to less than $10,000, a figure based on the addition of the cost of the towing expenses. The court thought, however, that this was too rigid an application of the market price concept, and concluded from all the facts that a "willing seller" could have gotten from a "willing buyer" $15,000 for the destroyer at the time and place of loss. Obviously, this is an informed and responsible guess, designed to give the victim the benefit of a good bargain.

Sometimes the "market price" concept breaks down entirely. In United States v. Eastern S. S. Lines,[162] a collision loss occurring in wartime presented the court with the problem of the total lack of a "free and open market" for vessels of the sort involved. "Reproduction cost less depreciation" was the formula selected. In Sawyer, Inc. v. Poor,[163] faced with the problem of valuing a Miami excursion vessel rammed and sunk at her pier, the Fifth Circuit Court of Appeals, noting the lack of any reliable "market value" criterion, reviewed some of the factors that go into the making of a judgment of value:

> "All agree that the usual and customary method in determining damages in cases of maritime collision is the market value of the vessel in the case of loss. See Standard Oil Co. v. Southern Pacific Co., 268 U.S. 146, 45 S.Ct. 465, 69 L.Ed. 890. But in cases where no market value has been established by recent and comparable sales other evidence is admissible touching value such as the opinion of marine surveyors, engineers, the cost of reproduction, less depreciation, the condition of repair which the vessel was in, the uses to which it can be put, the amount of insurance that the underwriters have issued, and the like. In the present case there is testimony of all of the above types and more. The opinions as to the market value ranged all the way from $10,000 to $65,000. Cost of reproduction ran from $150,000 to $200,000. It is in evidence that there was a mortgage against the vessel for $22,000 and that she was insured after a survey for insurance in the amount of $50,000. It was shown that extensive repairs had lately been made to the vessel and that she had been certificated by the Coast Guard Inspection Service and authorized to carry 283 passengers in the waters of Boston and in the waters in and around Miami and Fort Lauder-

(4th Cir. 1954), reversed on other grounds 349 U.S. 122, 75 S.Ct. 649 (1955). See *supra* at notes 124, 127.

162. 171 F.2d 589, 1949 A.M.C. 243 (1st Cir. 1948). *Cf.* Ozanic v. U. S., *supra* note 159.

163. 180 F.2d 962, 1950 A.M.C. 873 (5th Cir. 1950).

dale. There is also testimony of an offer to purchase the vessel for $60,000, and of another offer of $100,000, subject to inspection. She had recently obtained a charter on a trial basis for one month for $6,000, with the prospect of additional chartering for a longer period.

"No good purpose can be served by recounting the testimony of all of the various witnesses as to their conception of market value and the factors that each used in arriving at such value. Suffice it to say that upon controverted testimony the Commissioner fixed the value well between the limits of the highest and lowest values in evidence, and that there is substantial evidence to support even a higher value than that which the Commissioner fixed. . . ." [164]

Damage less than total loss is compensated by reference to cost of repairs,[165] and the cost of providing a substitute vessel pending repair may be allowed.[166]

§ 7–19. Damages for loss of the use of a vessel are frequently allowed. In The Gylfe v. The Trujillo,[167] the tanker Gylfe, damaged in collision, lost time to the extent of 36 days, 20 hours, and 27 minutes. Finding that there had been an active market for tonnage of her type during this period, the court allowed damages to be calculated on a *per diem* basis.[168]

The Gylfe case raises the foreign exchange question frequently important in collision damage cases. Kroner spent on repairs had depreciated between collision-day and judgment-day; the collision-day rate would therefore produce a more bounteous harvest of American dollars than the judgment-day rate. The court decided in favor of the collision-day rate, moved both by jurisprudential considerations

164. 180 F.2d at 963. Damages fixed were $30,000.

165. The Catharine v. Dickinson, 58 U.S. (17 How.) 170 (1855); Zeller Marine Corp. v. Nessa Corp., 166 F.2d 32, 1948 A.M.C. 418 (2d Cir. 1948). The repairs, which need not actually have been made at the time the decree is rendered, must be such as to restore the ship to her pre-collision state. The B. F. Guinan, 40 F.2d 277, 1930 A.M.C. 219 (E.D.N.Y.1930).

166. Petition of Sun Oil Co., 1969 A.M.C. 453 (E.D.Pa.1969). The Emma Kate Ross, 50 F. 845 (3d Cir. 1892). On the position when the libellant has used a spare boat of its own or worked its other vessels overtime, see the same cases, and Brooklyn Eastern District Terminal v. United States, 287 U.S. 170, 53 S.Ct. 103, 1932 A.M.C. 1487 (1932). On the substitution of other means of carriage for that afforded by the lost or disabled vessel, see Sinclair Refining Co. v. The America Sun, 188 F.2d 64, 1951 A.M.C. 845 (2d Cir. 1951).

167. 209 F.2d 386, 1954 A.M.C. 233 (2d Cir. 1954).

168. It is the net loss of profits that is compensated. See Agwilines, Inc. v. Eagle Oil & Shipping Co., 153 F.2d 869, 1946 A.M.C. 142 (2d Cir. 1946), certiorari denied 328 U.S. 835, 66 S.Ct. 980 (1946). Fishermen recovered damages for loss in "catch," netted and prospective, when the vessel on which they were working on "lays" was damaged in collision, in Carbone v. Ursich, 209 F.2d 178, 1954 A.M.C. 169 (9th Cir. 1953).

Damages for detention of a pleasure yacht have been awarded, on the theory that the yacht could have been chartered while she was laid up. The Lagonda, 44 F. 367 (E.D.N.Y.1890).

and by the feeling that it was "fairer to put the risk of fluctuation of foreign exchange on the tort-feasor than on the innocent injured party." Of course, no single rule can put these risks of fluctuation on any one party, as would have appeared if kroner had risen instead of fallen, in the very case. We cannot here enter into either the practical or doctrinal consideration of the foreign exchange question, which is peculiar neither to collision nor to maritime law, but simply mention it as one of the factors affecting the dollars-and-cents outcome of many collision cases.[169]

Where a vessel is damaged and repairs are not made, damages "can be measured either by estimated cost of repairs at a time immediately following the accident . . . or by the diminution in the market value of the vessel." The quotation is from United States v. Shipowners & Merchants Tugboat Co.[170] In that case, the libellant (the United States) had kept the damaged vessel unrepaired for eighteen months, and then sold it for the full statutory price at which vessels of its type could be sold as surplus by the Maritime Commission. Under these circumstances, the respondent (who had admitted sole fault in the collision) contended that damages for estimated costs of the repairs that had never been made were not allowable; the court rejected this contention, saying:

> "The respondent's argument, in effect, seeks to take advantage of the fact that the injured party was fortunate enough to find a purchaser for the damaged vessel who was willing to pay the full statutory price. It is a well-settled principle of law that a tort-feasor cannot escape the consequences of his wrongdoing merely because his victim was fortunate enough to receive reparation from a collateral source. See 1939 Edition of the Restatement of Torts, Section 920, Comment c. The law is so well settled on this point that further citation of authority appears unnecessary. Although it is not felt that the subsequent sale at the statutory sales price necessarily constitutes a reparation for the collision damages, in any way, the application of the principle of res inter alios acta, as above stated, would prevail against respondent's contention." [171]

Liabilities to third parties incurred in collision go into the final divided damages adjustment.[171a] As we have seen in the discussion of the Both-to-Blame Clause,[172] the liability which the non-carrying

169. See also Shaw, Savill, Albion & Co. v. The Fredericksburg, 189 F.2d 952, 1951 A.M.C. 1273 (2d Cir. 1951), noted 52 Colum.L.Rev. 141 (1952).

170. 103 F.Supp. 152, 153, 1952 A.M.C. 483 (N.D.Cal.1952), affirmed 205 F.2d 352 (9th Cir. 1953), certiorari denied 346 U.S. 829, 74 S.Ct. 51 (1953).

171. *Ibid.*

171a. See Weyerhaeuser S.S. Co. v. United States, 372 U.S. 597, 83 S.Ct. 926, 1963 A.M.C. 846 (1963). See also Empire Seafoods, Inc. v. Anderson, 398 F.2d 204, 1968 A.M.C. 2664 (5th Cir. 1968), certiorari denied 393 U.S. 983, 89 S.Ct. 449 (1968).

172. *Supra* Chapter III, Part II, at note 101 *et seq.*

ship incurs to cargo on the other ship is an item to be placed in the balance.

In multi-ship disasters, the American courts apportion the damages in appropriate fractions on the ships actually at fault; the record in the reports seems to be six.[173]

Where a third party is damaged, and sues two ships that are at fault, he is not prejudiced by the half-damages rule, but may collect his full damages from one if the other is unable to respond in damages, or may collect any deficiency if one cannot pay its full half.[174]

### Critique of the Divided Damages Rule

**§ 7–20.** The rule that damages are to be equally divided in both-to-blame cases is neither as widely accepted nor of as obvious justice as might be inferred from the firmness with which it is now established in the United States. As late as 1854, a federal court regarded the rule as still subject to some doubt; [175] at about the same time the Supreme Court settled the principle in our law, calling it "the most just and equitable, and as best tending to induce care and vigilance on both sides, in the navigation." [176]

It is exceedingly hard to see why the rule of equally divided damages should be thought more likely to "induce care" than any other rule that penalized negligence. As to the "equity" matter, the justice of the rule is obvious only when the respective faults are of just about the same degree of seriousness. It can produce results whose equity is highly dubious. Thus, where one vessel is grossly negligent in six ways and the other is in technical but plain fault, and where the first vessel is heavily damaged in the collision while the other vessel suffers relatively lightly, the result of the rule may be a heavy payment from the technically faulty to the grossly negligent, except where the technical fault is small enough to crawl under the fence of the major-minor fault "rule." [177] This result hardly commends itself to the sense of justice any more appealingly than does the common law doctrine of contributory negligence; actually, in the case supposed, many people might think justice better served by letting all parties walk out of court empty-handed, as the contributory negligence rule would do.[178]

173. The Norwich Victory, 77 F.Supp. 264, 1948 A.M.C. 879 (E.D.Pa.1948), affirmed on District Court opinion 175 F.2d 556 (3d Cir. 1949), certiorari denied 338 U.S. 871, 70 S.Ct. 147 (1949). As this case shows, the apportionment is by vessel and not by owner; the owner of five of the six vessels at fault paid ⅚ of the damage.

174. The Alabama, 92 U.S. 695 (1876); The Beaconsfield, 158 U.S. 303, 307, 15 S.Ct. 860, 861 (1895). See The Atlas, 93 U.S. 302 (1876).

175. Foster v. The Miranda, 9 Fed.Cas. No.4,977, at 563 (D.Ill.1854). Sprague, Divided Damages, 6 N.Y.U.L.Rev. 15 (1928), traces the history of the rule.

176. The Catharine v. Dickinson, 58 U.S. (17 How.) 170, 178 (1855).

177. See Eastern S. S. Co. v. International Harvester Co. of N. J., 189 F.2d 472, 1951 A.M.C. 1844 (6th Cir. 1951).

178. For a discussion of the proportional fault concept by land and sea, in contrast both to the admiralty rule and the contributory negligence rule, see Mole & Wilson, A Study of Comparative Negligence, 17 Cornell L.Q. 333 (1932).

The Brussels Collision Liability Convention, 1910,[179] provides, in its Article 4, for the apportionment of damages on the basis of "degree" of fault. Most of the important maritime nations have ratified or adhered to this Convention, but the United States has not done so. The consequence is that our damage rule is out of step with that of the rest of the maritime world—a fact which doubtless results in a good deal of transatlantic "shopping around" for the forum that will produce, given the probable degrees of fault and amounts of damages, the most satisfactory result from the point of view of the shopper. Thus, if we suppose that the Harriett & Bill is damaged $100,000, and (as best may be guessed) would be held 80% at fault, while the Alzada B., 20% at fault, is damaged $50,000, the final adjustment in damages payable may vary quite widely, depending on the court selected. The total damages are $150,000. In the United States, the "divided damages" rule would compel the payment of $25,000 from the Alzada B. to the Harriett & Bill, so that the net amount of damage suffered would be the same. (As a calculating convenience, this may be figured on a "cross-liability" basis—each vessel may be treated as though liable to the other for half the other's damage, and the balance struck.) On the other hand, if the Harriett & Bill is to be out 80% of the damage, as would presumably be the result in a Convention country, she must pay the Alzada B. $20,000. In many collision cases, damages run much higher than in the example; for the Harriett & Bill, getting the case into the United States court is a tactical prize of great cash value.[180]

From the point of view of the maritime world as a whole, however, the variance seems unfortunate. And the proportional negligence rule of the Convention seems in principle and in operation more just than the cruder American rule of divided damages. The only objection that really has any plausibility is the one based on the difficulty of assigning degrees of fault in exact percentages. The answer is, of course, that judges would simply approximate, as best they could, as is done every day in other cases in matters of amounts of damages, degree of disability, etc. An attempt at a division on the basis of degree of fault would at least not be foredoomed to go badly wrong in a large number of cases, as is the present rule.

Judicial dissatisfaction with the inequities of the divided damages rule has in recent decades been assuming that degree of articulateness which often presages change; courts have come full circle from the smug satisfaction with which the Supreme Court adopted

179. *Supra* note 32. For a full discussion of the Convention provisions regarding damage division, see Huger, The Proportional Damage Rule in Collisions at Sea, 13 Cornell L.Q. 531 (1928).

180. This "forum shopping" has been recognized as inevitable, given the state of the law; Petition of Bloomfield S. S. Co., 422 F.2d 728, 732 *et seq.*, 1970 A.M.C. 521, 526 *et seq.* (2d Cir. 1970). For discussion of the practical world-wide effects of the American divergence, see Sundstrom, Foreign Ships and Foreign Waters (Acta Institutae Upsaliensis Iurisprudentiae Comparativae, Uppsala 1971), esp. pp. 89–125. Isbrandtsen Co. v. Lloyd Brasiliero, 85 F.Supp. 740, 1949 A.M.C. 684 (E.D.N.Y.1949); Huger, *supra* note 179.

the rule in 1855. The pioneer case in the new trend of feeling was doubtless The Margaret,[181] where the Third Circuit Court of Appeals actually directed a division of 75%–25%, having so apportioned the fault, but modified to half-damages on rehearing, feeling itself constrained by the uniform rule applied by the Supreme Court. No court has since gone so far, but, as we have seen, dissatisfaction with the proscrustean half-damages formula has resulted in crude attempts at alleviation through the major-minor fault concept,[182] through the *in extremis* "glozing," [183] and through reluctance, despite the Pennsylvania, to find a fault "contributory" when it was a comparatively small fault committed concurrently with gross fault on the part of the other vessel.[184] And even when courts can find no way out they are complaining. Judge Learned Hand has spoken of "our obstinate cleaving to the ancient rule, which has been abrogated by nearly all civilized nations," calling the major-minor fault rule "a sop to Cerberus." [185] In Eastern S. S. Co. v. International Harvester,[186] the Sixth Circuit Court, with comparative mildness, says:

> "We are of the opinion that the District Court was in error in holding that the collision referred to in the libel was caused solely by the fault of the libelant. We are of the opinion that the fault of the Wood was far more serious than fault on the part of The International, and as pointed out in Luckenbach S. S. Co. v. United States, supra, it is a case where the Continental rule of comparative negligence would produce a more just result. . . ." [187]

And in another modern case Judge Jerome Frank, writing for the Second Circuit, said:

> "The admiralty rule of evenly-divided damages in cases of injury to property—although a highly desirable departure from the 'harsh' common-law doctrine which denies all relief to one suing for negligence if guilty of contributory negligence—has frequently received criticism as unfair. On that ground, virtually every country except ours has abandoned it. Nevertheless, we feel obligated to apply that rule until the Supreme Court or Congress instructs us otherwise. . . ." [188]

181. 30 F.2d 923, 1929 A.M.C. 1, 307 (3d Cir. 1928–9).

182. *Supra* at note 42.

183. *Supra* at note 36 *et seq.*

184. *Supra* at note 50.

185. National Bulk Carriers v. United States, 183 F.2d 405, 410, 1950 A.M.C. 1293 (2d Cir. 1950), certiorari denied 340 U.S. 865, 71 S.Ct. 89 (1950).

186. 189 F.2d 472, 1951 A.M.C. 1844 (6th Cir. 1951).

187. 189 F.2d at 476. To the same effect see Luckenbach S. S. Co. v. United States, 157 F.2d 250, 252, 1946 A.M.C. 1120 (2d Cir. 1946).

188. Ahlgren v. Red Star Towing & Transp. Co., 214 F.2d 618, 620–21, 1954 A.M.C. 1504 (2d Cir. 1954). See also, Curtis Bay Towing Co. v. The Fairwill, 110 F.Supp. 881, 1953 A.M.C. 195 (E.D.Va.1952).

In Halcyon Lines v. Haenn Ship Ceiling & Refitting Corp.,[189] the Supreme Court, though concerned with deciding another matter, used language that held out no hope to justify Judge Frank's "until." Instead, the Court spoke of the half-damage doctrine as follows:

> "Where two vessels collide due to the fault of both, it is established admiralty doctrine that mutual wrongdoers shall share equally the damages sustained by each, as well as personal injury and property damage inflicted on innocent third parties. This maritime rule is of ancient origin and has been applied in many cases, but this Court has never expressly applied it to non-collision cases. . . ." [190]

Nevertheless, it is not beyond hope that Congress or the Court may adopt someday the rule of the other civilized nations. Congress could do it either by single-shot legislation or by adhering to the Convention discussed above; the first of these methods may be preferable, for there is no use tangling the merits of this question with those of the other Convention proposals. Actually, there is no reason why the Supreme Court cannot at this late date "confess error" and adopt the proportional fault doctrine without Congressional action. The resolution to follow the divided damages rule, taken 120 years ago, rested not on overwhelming authority but on judgments of fact and of fairness which may have been tenable then [191] but are hardly so today. No "vested rights," in theory or fact, have intervened. The regard for "settled expectation" which is the heart-reason of that modified form of *stare decisis* prevailing in the United States can have no relevance in respect to such a rule; the concept of "settled expectation" would be reduced to an absurdity were it to be applied to a rule of damages for negligent collision. The abrogation of the rule would not, it seems, produce any disharmony with other branches of the maritime law, general or statutory.[192]

189. 342 U.S. 282, 72 S.Ct. 277, 1952 A.M.C. 1 (1952).

190. 342 U.S. at 284, 72 S.Ct. at 279.

191. See *supra* at note 176.

192. It now appears that the Supreme Court is ready to reconsider the half-damages rule. In Union Oil Co. of Calif. v. Tugboat San Jacinto, 409 U.S. 140, 93 S.Ct. 368, 1972 A.M.C. 2675 (1972), certiorari had been granted for the purpose of reconsidering the rule, but the Court found one of the vessels faultless, and so could not hold on the rule itself.

# Chapter VIII

# SALVAGE

## The Nature of Salvage—What Property May be Salved

§ 8–1. On land the person who rushes in to save another's property from danger is an officious intermeddler, the volunteer whom even equity will not aid. He has no right to a reward, although he may incur liability if he damages the property in the course of saving it. The person who saves life on land is similarly treated, except that he may count on a paragraph in the court's opinion paying tribute to his good character.

At sea the person who saves property receives a reward which is generously computed in the light of "the fundamental public policy at the basis of awards of salvage—the encouragement of seamen to render prompt service in future emergencies." [1] The reward, it has often been said, is not a mere recompense for work and labor done, not a *quantum meruit*. "Public policy," said Justice Clifford, "encourages the hardy and adventurous mariner to engage in these laborious and sometimes dangerous enterprises and with a view to withdraw from him every temptation to embezzlement and dishonesty allows him, in case he is successful, a liberal compensation." [2] Whether the fundamental purpose is to encourage heroism or to discourage embezzlement, the fortunate participants in a salvage operation where large values are at stake may count on a handsome reward.

Historically, the saving of life was regarded as fulfilling a moral duty but not as entitling the salvor to a reward. Thus there was a natural temptation to save property first and look around for survivors later. Life salvors now have by statute a right to a "fair share" of the award made to salvors who have saved property on the same occasion.[3] Life salvage, unaccompanied by property salvage, still goes unrewarded.[3a]

1. Clark, J., in Kimes v. United States, 207 F.2d 60, 63, 1953 A.M.C. 1335, 1338 (2d Cir. 1953).

2. The Blackwall, 77 U.S. (10 Wall.) 1, 14 (1869). "Compensation as salvage is not viewed by the admiralty courts merely as pay, on the principle of a *quantum meruit*, or as a remuneration *pro opere et labore*, but as a reward given for perilous services, voluntarily rendered . . ." (*Ibid.*) In The Clarita and The Clara, 90 U.S. (23 Wall.) 1, 17 (1874) Justice Clifford, after repeating the passage quoted in the text, went on to add: "Those liberal rules as to remuneration were adopted and are administered not only as an inducement to the daring to embark, in such enterprises, but to withdraw from the salvors as far as possible every motive to depredate upon the property of the unfortunate owner."

3. 37 Stat. 242 (1912), 46 U.S.C.A. § 729. The statute is discussed § 8–12 *infra*.

3a. In Grigsby v. Coastal Marine Service of Texas, Inc., 412 F.2d 1011, 1969 A.M.C. 1513 (5th Cir. 1969), certiorari dismissed *sub nom.* Fidelity & Casualty Co. of New York v. Grigsby, 396 U.S. 1033 (1970), a shore-based work-

The law of salvage is sometimes said to be a part of the *jus gentium*; the statement reflects a judicial awareness that the perils of the sea are not confined by national boundaries and an acceptance of the principle that international uniformity is in such a context peculiarly desirable. The other side of the *jus gentium* medal is a relaxed attitude toward foreign law and choice of law problems, on the assumption that the law of the United States and the law of other maritime countries are the same.[4] Traditionally, our courts have exercised a discretionary jurisdiction over salvage claims which had no American contact except the accidental one that the salvors had libeled the salved ship in an American port.[5]

er ventured and lost his life in an attempt to save others on board a ship which was under repair. Judge Brown concluded that the decedent's status as a "maritime life salvor" entitled him to the protection of the warranty of seaworthiness as a "vicarious seaman." On the warranty of seaworthiness, see Chapter VI, § 6–38 *et seq.*

4. The attitude also expresses itself in a willingness to be guided by foreign, particularly English, precedents. *Cf.* Frankfurter, J., in The Fisher's Hill (Lago Oil & Transport Co., Ltd. v. United States), 218 F.2d 631, 634, 1955 A.M.C. 697, 701 (2d Cir. 1955): "English admiralty decisions, with which our maritime law as a rule finds itself in accord, 'from motives of public policy' recognize salvage claims under these circumstances." The leading English treatise, Kennedy, The Law of Civil Salvage (4th ed. by McGuffie 1958) (hereafter cited as Kennedy) is regularly cited in American cases. Norris, The Law of Salvage (1958, with annual cumulative Supplement) (hereafter cited as Norris) is the American counterpart of Kennedy.

5. See, *e. g.*, Dalmas v. Stathatos, 84 F.Supp. 828, 1949 A.M.C. 770 (S.D.N.Y.1949) (libel by Greek seamen serving aboard a Greek ship for salvage services rendered to another Greek ship in the Pacific Ocean). Judge Ryan took jurisdiction despite the fact that the owners of the salving and salved ships had signed a Lloyds Salvage Agreement and arbitration proceedings under the agreement were pending in London. As to applicable law, he commented: "No problem of foreign law is here involved, for it is well settled that 'salvage is a question arising under the *jus gentium* and does not ordinarily depend upon the municipal law of particular countries'" (*id.* at 771, 829). Judge Ryan was quoting from Usatorre v. Compania Argentina Navegacion Mihanovich, Ltda. (The Victoria), 49 F.Supp. 275, 1942 A.M.C. 1170 (S.D.N.Y.1942) (libel by Argentine seamen against their own ship, of Argentine ownership and registry, for salvage following a torpedoing on the high seas). On appeal, the Usatorre case was reversed, 172 F.2d 434, 1949 A.M.C. 650 (2d Cir. 1949): Judge Frank conceded that the District Court had discretion to take jurisdiction and that ordinarily the *jus gentium* approach dispenses with proof of foreign law. The right of the crew to claim salvage, however, depended on whether the voyage for which they had signed on had been "abandoned" (see text at note 43 *infra*); the question of "abandonment" Judge Frank wrote, "must be determined, as a matter of the 'internal economy' of the ship, by the Argentine law, the 'law of the flag'." (*Id.* at 438, 655–656, citing cases). Other cases which take a *jus gentium* approach are Barkas v. Cia Naviera Coronado, S.A., 126 F.Supp. 532, 1955 A.M.C. 1787 (S.D.N.Y.1954) and Sobonis v. Steam Tanker National Defender, 298 F.Supp. 631, 1969 A.M.C. 1219 (S.D.N.Y.1969). In the Sobonis case Judge Pollack rejected the contention that the claims of Greek seamen aboard a Greek-flag ship who had rendered salvage services to an American owned ship in international waters should be determined by Greek law. See also Vernicos Shipping Co. v. United States, 349 F.2d 465, 1965 A.M.C. 1673 (2d Cir. 1965) in which Judge Friendly, after deciding a complicated jurisdictional point under the Public Vessels Act, routinely applied American precedents to the claims of Greek salvors for services to an American naval vessel in Greek waters. Choice of law questions where the American courts exercise a discre-

The judicial attitude of international orientation has more than doctrinal roots. One of the earliest of the so-called Brussels conventions was the Salvage Convention of 1910, which the United States promptly ratified.[6] The Convention was taken as codifying American salvage law with a few minor exceptions as to which American law was conformed to the Convention by the Salvage Act of 1912.[7] Except for the conforming statutory changes, the Convention has played little part in the development of American salvage law and has rarely been construed, discussed or cited.

§ 8–2. The formal requisites of an act of salvage bear a close family resemblance to those of a general average act.[8] There must be a maritime peril from which the ship or other property could not have

tionary jurisdiction over actions between foreign litigants have been much discussed in recent cases in the context of seamen's personal injury litigation, following the decision in Lauritzen v. Larsen, 345 U.S. 571, 73 S.Ct. 921, 1953 A.M.C. 1210 (1953); see discussion in Chapter VI, § 6–63 *et seq.*

6. 37 Stat. 1658 (1913).

7. 37 Stat. 242 (1912), 46 U.S.C.A. §§ 727–731. Section 727 abrogated the doctrine that common ownership of salving and salved vessels barred salvage claims by the crew of the salving vessel (see *infra* text at note 53). Section 728 imposed a duty on masters to render assistance to persons in danger at sea and provided criminal sanctions for failure to do so. In Warshauer v. Lloyd Sabaudo S. A., 71 F.2d 146, 1934 A.M.C. 864 (2d Cir. 1934), certiorari denied 293 U.S. 610, 55 S.Ct. 140 (1934) it was held that the shipowner was not liable for the master's failure to render the assistance required by § 728. Section 729 gave life salvors a right to claim salvage under certain circumstances (see § 8–12 *infra*). Section 730 provides that suits for salvage "shall not be maintainable if brought later than two years from the date when such assistance or salvage was rendered" unless during that period there has been no "reasonable opportunity" to libel the salved vessel within the jurisdiction of the court or within the territorial waters of the country where the libellant resides or has his principal place of business. In People of the Living God v. Star Towing Co., 289 F.Supp. 635, 1968 A.M.C. 2187 (E.D.La.1968), it was held that the two year period of § 730 could not be extended by reliance on a state statute which, arguably, would have tolled the limitation period. The libel included a claim for damages to the salvor's tug. Judge Heebe remarked that, even if § 730 did not apply directly to the damage claim, he would apply it analogically and hold the claim barred by laches. On his handling of the laches point, see Chapter IX, §§ 9–80, 9–81. Section 731 provides that "Nothing in sections 727–730 of this title shall be construed as applying to ships of war or to Government ships appropriated exclusively to a public service." In The Busy—The Richards (United States on behalf of the Lords Commissioners etc. v. The James L. Richards), 179 F.2d 530, 1950 A.M.C. 359 (1st Cir. 1950), it was held that, despite § 731, the two year statute of limitations of § 730 applied to bar a salvage libel brought by the United States on behalf of the British Government for services rendered by a British government-owned salvage tug in Spanish waters. In Basic Boats, Inc. v. United States, 311 F.Supp. 596, 1970 A.M.C. 1843 (E.D.Va.1970) an action was brought against the United States, for the benefit of an insurance carrier, alleging negligence on the part of a United States war vessel in carrying out a salvage operation. The United States counterclaimed for salvage after the two year period of § 730 had run. Judge Hoffman, with evident reluctance, followed The James L. Richards and held that the counter-claim, looked on as an affirmative cause of action, was time-barred. He concluded, however, that the salvage claim should be retained and treated as an "affirmative defense by way of recoupment." For subsequent proceedings in the Basic Boats case, see note 79f *infra*.

8. See Chapter V, § 5–1.

been rescued without the salvor's assistance. The salvor's act must be voluntary—that is, he must be under no official or legal duty to render the assistance.[9] The act must be successful in saving, or in helping to save, at least a part of the property at risk.[10] When property has been abandoned or become derelict, anyone may put himself forward as salvor; [10a] if the owner subsequently claims the property, he

9. On the "preexisting duty" rule, see § 8–4 *infra*. Another aspect of the requirement of "voluntariness" was illustrated in Petition of Sun Oil Co. (M/T Maumee Sun), 342 F.Supp. 976, 1972 A.M.C. 2258 (S.D.N.Y.1972), affirmed per curiam 474 F.2d 1048, 1973 A.M.C. 572 (2d Cir. 1973). After a collision caused by the fault of the Maumee Sun, the prow of the American Pilot was "embedded" in the Maumee Sun's hull. Instead of attempting to disengage, the master of the American Pilot ordered the two ships lashed together and they so remained until the Maumee Sun's cargo had been removed. Salvage claims by the officers and crew of the American Pilot were dismissed on the ground that the services had not been "voluntary." Judge Levet reached his conclusion partly on the ground that the "stand-by" act (33 U.S.C.A. § 367) required the American Pilot to act as she did but principally on the ground that any other course of action would have imperiled both ships so that the American Pilot was insuring her own safety as well as that of the Maumee Sun. On the "stand-by" act see Chapter VII, § 7–3, text at note 31 and § 8–6 *infra*, text following note 71.

See further the cases cited in note 23 *infra*.

10. In Crawford v. West India Carriers, Inc., 337 F.Supp. 262 (S.D.Fla. 1971), a many-faceted case, claims by would-be but evidently incompetent salvors were denied on the ground that their activities, although "commendable and heroic," had contributed nothing to the rescue. The statement in the text as to the formal requisites of salvage follows Kennedy *supra* note 4 at p. 5 (bearing in mind that the jurisdiction of American admiralty courts is not restricted to tidal waters and that American courts have been more lenient than English courts in passing on what types of property are subject to salvage [see § 8–3 *infra*]). See also Robinson, Admiralty 709 (1939); 1 Benedict, Admiralty § 117 (6th ed. 1940); Norris, note 4 *supra* at § 88 *et seq.*

In Complaint of Sincere Navigation Corp. (The S/S Helena), 327 F.Supp. 1024, 1971 A.M.C. 2270 (E.D.La.1971) Judge Rubin commented that "It is clear that the United States can receive no award for salvage as such because naught was saved" but went on to hold that the United States could recover some of its expenses under the Wreck Statute (33 U.S.C.A. § 409 *et seq.*). (On the Wreck Statute, see Chapter X, § 10–13, note 45 at end.)

10a. An annotation, 63 A.L.R.2d 1369, collects cases, mostly of quite ancient vintage, on: Rights in and ownership of wrecked or derelict vessels and their contents not cast upon the shore. The case annotated was State of Florida v. Massachusetts Co., 95 So.2d 902, 1962 A.M.C. 1061, 63 A.L.R.2d 1360 (Fla.1956), certiorari denied 355 U.S. 881 (1957), in which the State successfully sought to enjoin the Massachusetts Company from proceeding with the salvage of a battleship which the United States Navy had scuttled in Florida territorial waters in 1922. The United States disclaimed any interest in the sunken hull. The State prevailed on the unconvincing grounds that, under the prerevolutionary law of England, rights to derelicts and wrecks had been vested in the Crown and that the State had succeeded to those rights. In his opinion Roberts, J., indulged himself in an orgy of historical learning. Apparently the site of the wreck had become a favorite fishing spot for natives of and visitors to the sunny state of Florida—a fact which presumably explains why the action was brought in the first place.

In Rickard v. Pringle (The Acara), 293 F.Supp. 981, 1968 A.M.C. 1008 (E.D.N.Y.1968), it appeared that Rickard, after nine months labor, had succeeded in freeing the propeller from the submerged hulk of a vessel which had sunk in Long Island Sound in 1902. During Rickard's temporary absence from the site Pringle and his confederates took possession of the propeller (which was in great demand as an an-

takes it subject to the salvage claim.[11] On the other hand, so long as the owner, or his agent, remains in possession, he is entitled to refuse unwelcome offers of salvage[12]—an aspect of doctrine which, when coupled with judicial generosity in making salvage awards, gives a commercial base to the gallant behavior of masters who remain aboard otherwise abandoned ships while waiting for the owner's tugs to show up and undertake the rescue.

It would be fruitless to list the almost infinite range of acts which have been held to constitute salvage. The prototypical act is rescuing a ship in peril at sea and towing her to a place of safety. A recurrent issue is whether the service was salvage (to be compensated by a liberal award) or, as the shipowner contends, merely towage (to

tique marine artifact) and sold it. The defendants sought to justify their action on the ground that no one has any property rights in abandoned or derelict property. Judge Abruzzo held that Rickard, as "first salvor," had acquired property rights in the propeller and gave judgment against the thieves.

Brady v. S. S. African Queen, 179 F. Supp. 321, 1960 A.M.C. 69 (E.D.Va.1960) also involved claims by successive sets of salvors to an abandoned vessel. Brady and his colleagues salvaged the vessel after six months work. Warner then claimed that he was entitled to the vessel as "first salvor" because he had "posted" it before Brady had begun work. Apart from the "posting" Warner's only contribution to the salvage was to have his "proctors" send letters to Brady warning Brady of Warner's prior claim. Judgment for Brady.

In Wiggins v. 1100 Tons More or Less of Italian Marble, 186 F.Supp. 452, 1960 A.M.C. 1774 (E.D.Va.1960) the libellants were held to have acquired title to the 123 tons of marble which they had actually salvaged from the hulk of a vessel wrecked off the Virginia coast in 1894. It was also held that the Virginia Commissioner of Wrecks had acted beyond his statutory authority in granting "exclusive salvage rights" to another set of claimants (who had in fact done nothing toward salvaging the cargo).

11. However, if the owner does not claim the property he is not personally liable to the salvor. This was the situation in Lambros Seaplane Base v. The Batory, 215 F.2d 228, 1954 A.M.C. 1789 (2d Cir. 1954) in which it was held that a libel *in personam* for salvage could not be maintained against the owner of a seaplane which had been picked up at sea by a transatlantic liner outbound from New York, transported to England and deposited with the Receiver of Wrecks. Judge Hincks' opinion in the Lambros case collected and discussed the American and English authorities at 231 *et seq.*, 1798 *et seq.* The Lambros case is further discussed in the text at notes 39 and 83 *infra.* On awards to salvors where no one claims the property, see the cases digested in note 92a *infra.*

12. See Kennedy, note 4 *supra* at p. 258. "It is of course just conceivable," Kennedy adds, "that an owner or a master of a ship in distress might be guilty of such criminal negligence, so plainly reckless of his duty towards the life or property entrusted to his charge, that the Court of Admiralty would recognize and reward as salvors those who acted against his will for the preservation of the life or property in peril." In Merritt & Chapman Derrick & Wrecking Co. v. United States, 274 U.S. 611, 613, 47 S. Ct. 663, 664, 1927 A.M.C. 953, 955 (1927), in the course of an opinion in a case where salvage was denied, Justice Butler remarked: "While salvage cannot be exacted for assistance forced upon a ship . . ., her request for or express acceptance of the service is not always essential to the validity of the claim. It is enough if under the circumstances any prudent man would have accepted."

In Bonifay v. The Paraporti, 145 F. Supp. 879, 1956 A.M.C. 1898 (E.D.Va. 1956), would-be salvors who acted "without consent (express or implied) or permission of the vessel's owner, and contrary to the owner's instructions" were held to be "mere gratuitous intermeddlers" and "not entitled to compensation of any sort."

be compensated at regular towage rates).[13] In deciding the issue the courts look to the situation that existed at the time the ship was taken in tow: If she was not under command, unable to navigate or to reach port unaided, the service will be considered salvage even though the ship was not in imminent danger of destruction and even though the towage itself was calm and uneventful. Releasing a ship that has run aground or on reefs,[14] beaching a ship to keep her from running on rocks,[15] raising a sunken vessel,[16] putting out a fire,[17] are other common salvage acts. One of the classical instances where salvage was awarded was for the recapture of a ship taken by pirates; the piracy cases found a modern echo in a colorful English case which rewarded a resourceful group of British and Belgian soldiers who succeeded, on the collapse of allied intervention in the Russian revolution, in taking a ship out of Murmansk harbor under Bolshevik fire and sailing her to London, thereby saving their own lives as well as the shipowner's property.[18] The act of salvage need not be so dramatic and need not even consist in rendering physical assistance: standing by or escorting a distressed ship in a position to give aid if it becomes necessary,[19] giving information on the channel to follow to escape from an ice floe[20] or to avoid running aground,[21] carrying a message as a result of which necessary aid and equipment are forthcoming[22] have all qualified. So long as the ship is in peril, any voluntary act which contributes to her ultimate safety may rank as an act of salvage.[23]

13. Two of the older cases indicate the range of argument: McConnochie v. Kerr, 9 F. 50, (S.D.N.Y.1881) (service held salvage); The J. C. Pfluger, 109 F. 93 (N.D.Cal.1901) (service held towage). Judge Dobie's opinion in the Fra Berlanga (LaRue v. United Fruit Co.), 181 F.2d 895, 1950 A.M.C. 1312 (4th Cir. 1950) quotes from a number of the older cases. In Waterman S. S. Corp. v. Shipowners & Merchants Towboat Co., Ltd., 199 F.2d 600, 601, 1952 A.M.C. 1988, 1999 (9th Cir. 1952) certiorari denied 345 U.S. 941, 73 S.Ct. 832 (1953) the Court remarked that "the question whether the circumstances of a particular case are such as to turn towage into salvage . . . is essentially one of fact" and declined to set aside the District Court's award of salvage. In Sears v. S.S. American Producer, 1972 A.M.C. 1647 (N.D.Cal.1972), Judge Sweigert reviewed the authorities on the dividing line between salvage and towage, concluding that crew members of a tug in San Francisco harbor were entitled to a "low order" salvage award (one month's wages). See also Judge Pollack's opinion in Sobonis v. Steam Tanker National Defender, 298 F. Supp. 631, 1969 A.M.C. 1219 (S.D.N.Y. 1969).

14. The Sandringham, 10 F. 556 (E.D. Va.1882).

15. The Jason, 257 F. 438 (E.D.Va. 1919).

16. The Camanche, 75 U.S. (8 Wall.) 448 (1869).

17. The Blackwall, 77 U.S. (10 Wall.) 1 (1870).

18. The Lomonosoff [1921] P. 97.

19. The Pendragon Castle, 5 F.2d 56, 1925 A.M.C. 146 (2d Cir. 1924).

20. The Tower Bridge [1936] P. 30.

21. South American S. S. Co. v. Atlantic Towing Co., 22 F.2d 16, 1928 A.M.C. 148 (5th Cir. 1927).

22. The Cachemire, 38 F. 518 (D.S.C. 1889).

23. But see Butler, J. in Merritt & Chapman Derrick & Wrecking Co. v. United States, 274 U.S. 611, 613, 47 S. Ct. 663, 664, 1927 A.M.C. 953, 955 (1927); "All effort of plaintiff in error was put forth directly for the purpose of extinguishing fire at or about

§ 8–3. For property to become the subject of salvage, it must be on water (or at any rate on the beach) and not on land.[24] A further condition which, under the older case law, was thought requisite was that the property be maritime in nature—that is, a ship, her tackle and furnishings or her cargo. The two leading cases were The Gas-Float Whitton (No. 2)[25] in which the House of Lords held that a structure anchored in navigable waters as a beacon was not, when it came adrift, salvageable property and Cope v. Valette Dry-Dock Co.[26] in which the United States Supreme Court reached the same conclusion as to a dry-dock which had been moored in a fixed position for twenty years before it broke loose. It was agreed that cargo was salvageable, whether it was recovered from the ship, or saved along with the ship, or picked up from the water as jetsam, flotsam or ligan, or raised from the bottom or found on the beach. According to the theory, however, cargo was salvageable because, through its association with the ship, it had become maritime property and not merely because it was (or had been) afloat in navigable waters: property thrown from the shore or a wharf or, in Robinson's hypothetical example, from a railroad trestle passing over the Florida Keys,[27] would not become salvageable.

Whatever may be the present state of English law, the more recent American cases suggest that anything rescued from navigable waters, without regard to what it is or how it got there, will be considered salvageable. Indeed, despite the Supreme Court's holding in the Cope case, the American courts seem never to have matched the English courts in their strict adherence to the "maritime property" rule: in 1871 Judge Lowell allowed salvage on rafts of timber found floating in Boston Harbor, remarking it would be no defense in a salvage action "that the goods had been washed out to sea from the shore by a gale or a flood, or had been dropped from a balloon." [28]

Pier 5 and to save property not at all related to the Leviathan. The elimination of that fire contributed mediately to her safety. But, whatever the aid or benefit to her, it was incidental and indirect for which, in the absence of request for or acceptance of the service, a claim for salvage cannot be entertained." In United Boat Service Corp. v. Dailey, 1955 A.M.C. 1242 (S.D.N.Y.1955), affirmed 232 F.2d 383, 1956 A.M.C. 827 (2d Cir. 1956), the owner of a permanently moored and unmanned "station boat" claimed salvage from a barge which made fast to the station boat and sheltered behind her during a storm. The claim was denied on the ground that there was no proof that the sheltering vessel had been in real danger and also on the ground that salvage service must be voluntary and "[t]he crewless Baird was incapable of voluntary service". See also The Willis Shank—The Sailor's Splice, 1954 A.M.C. 150 (W.D.Wash.1953) (where two vessels assisted each other equally during a storm, claims for salvage by the crews of each vessel against the other were dismissed). See also Petition of Sun Oil Co. (M/T Maumee Sun), digested note 9 *supra*.

24. A vessel under repair in dry dock was held subject to salvage in The Jefferson, 215 U.S. 130, 30 S.Ct. 54 (1909).

25. [1895] P. 301.

26. 119 U.S. 625, 7 S.Ct. 336 (1887).

27. Robinson, Admiralty 712 (1939).

28. 50,000 Feet of Timber, 9 Fed.Cas. 47, Case No. 4,783 (D.Mass.1871). Norris, note 4, *supra* comments (at p. 51) that "The test should not be the place from where the property came but rather the situs of the rescue."

Two District Court cases decided during the 1940's have explored the "maritime property" limitation. In Colby v. Todd Packing Co.[29] Judge Folta allowed salvage on "fish trap frames" found adrift in navigable waters. The frames were constructed of logs lashed and bolted together into oblong structures which during the fishing season were towed to the fishing site, there anchored, and moored to the shore by cables. Between seasons they were towed to shore and moored above the low water mark, and it was from their between season mooring that they had broken loose. Judge Folta, in overruling exceptions to the salvors' libel, commented that the frames were "similar" to the log rafts which had often been held salvageable and distinguished the Cope case as being "limited to fixed structures not intended for use in trade or commerce." In Broere v. $2,133 [30] Judge Kennedy followed somewhat different analogies in awarding salvage to a boatman who had recovered from the waters of New York harbor a dead body which contained in a wallet the amount of money which was made the object of the libel *in rem.* Relying on the romantically captioned case of Hollinsworth v. Seventy Doubloons & Three Small Pieces of Gold,[31] Judge Kennedy quoted from Maltby v. Steam Derrick Boat:

> ". . . the test as to what is the subject of salvage is no longer, whether it is a vessel engaged in commerce or its cargo or furniture, but whether the thing saved is a movable thing, possessing the attributes of property, susceptible of being lost and saved in places within the local jurisdiction of the admiralty." [32]

To the "movable thing" test of the Maltby case there might be, Judge Kennedy suggested, exceptions such as the United States mails and negotiable instruments, "because neither the mails nor bills of exchange could ever be a proper subject for a proceeding *in rem, i. e.,* they could not be sold and a moiety of the avails given to the salvors for the reason that no purchaser could get a title." Money, however, whether in the form of doubloons, pieces of gold or paper currency met the test, whether it had initially been cargo, or, as in the Broere case, carried in a wallet by someone who had fallen overboard and been drowned.

The invention of the airplane raised the question whether aircraft lost at sea could be the subject of salvage and it is one of the curiosities of the legal literature that the answer has, at least in this country, been long in doubt.[33] In 1921 Judge Cardozo suggested, in

29. 77 F.Supp. 956, 1948 A.M.C. 1881 (D.Alaska 1948). In Medina v. One Nylon Purse Seine, 259 F.Supp. 769 (S.D.Calif.1966) Judge Carter made an award for the salvage of a fishing net found floating at sea.

30. 72 F.Supp. 115, 1947 A.M.C. 1523; Id., 78 F.Supp. 635, 1948 A.M.C. 1056 (E.D.N.Y.1947, 1948).

31. 12 Fed.Cas.380, Case No. 6,620 (E.D.Pa.1820).

32. 16 Fed.Cas.564, 566, Case No. 9,000 (E.D.Va.1879).

33. Knauth, Aviation and Salvage: The Application of Salvage Principles to Aircraft, 36 Colum.L.Rev. 224 (1936) reviewed the early developments.

a dictum, that a seaplane could be considered a vessel for the purposes of salvage.[34] A seaplane on land has been held not subject to a maritime lien for repairs [35] and a seaplane which crashed in flight not a "vessel" within the meaning of the Limitation of Liability Act.[36] A Scottish case which held that a seaplane and its cargo was not a subject of salvage [37] was overruled in Great Britain by the Air Navigation Act of 1936. In 1938 the United States along with other countries joined in proposing a convention covering Aviation Salvage at Sea, but the convention, not having been ratified by the required number of signatories, never came into effect. No American legislation directly covers the salvage of aircraft problem and the situation is further confused by the fact that in a variety of statutes (relating to smuggling, customs duties, navigation and shipping) the term "vessel" is sometimes defined to include, and sometimes defined to exclude, aircraft.[38]

In 1954 Judge Hincks, after a painstaking review of the material just referred to, concluded, in Lambros Seaplane Base v. The Batory,[39] that "a seaplane when on the sea is a maritime object which is subject to the maritime law of salvage." (The conclusion was, technically, dictum since the court found that, for other reasons, the salvors were not entitled to an award.[40] Nevertheless, in view of the fact that the court went out of its way to make the point, this particular dictum may be considered as only microscopically distinguishable from a holding.) The aircraft involved in the Lambros case was equipped to take off from and to land on water and had been picked up by the Batory at sea when the pilot of the hydroplane came down and asked to be rescued. Judge Hincks, properly enough, restricted his remarks in the Lambros case to "seaplanes," but if a land-based plane crashed in navigable waters and either the plane or its cargo was recovered, it can hardly be thought that the type of landing gear which the plane happened to have would be considered determinative of the salvor's right to a reward. It is clear enough that, in the absence of legislation, no one could claim salvage for recovering a plane or its cargo if the plane crashed on land, and it would make no difference whether the plane was land-based or water-based. No reason of policy suggests itself why such a distinction should be taken if the plane lands or crashes in navigable waters. It makes no great difference which way the salvage of aircraft issue is decided, but nei-

34. Reinhardt v. Newport Flying Service Corp., 232 N.Y. 115, 118, 133 N.E. 371, 372 (1921).

35. United States v. Northwest Air Service, Inc., 80 F.2d 804, 1936 A.M.C. 439 (9th Cir. 1935).

36. Noakes v. Imperial Airways, Ltd., 29 F.Supp. 412 (S.D.N.Y.1939).

37. Watson v. R. C. A. Victor Co., Inc., 50 Lloyds List Law Rep. 77, 1935 A.M.C. 1251 (Aberdeen Sheriff Ct.1934).

38. The various statutory definitions are collected in the opinion in Lambros Seaplane Base v. The Batory, 215 F.2d 228, 232–233, 1954 A.M.C. 1789, 1794–1795 (2d Cir. 1954).

39. Note 38 *supra*, at 233, 1795.

40. See note 11 *supra*.

ther is there any merit in leaving the issue unresolved and doubtful. The Lambros dictum, with respect to the salvageability of aircraft at sea, is a sensible one and will, it is hoped, be followed without regard to the type of plane that happens to be involved.

In this country there have been no further cases on the salvageability of aircraft. The well-known propensity of aircraft to crash in navigable waters has led to a good deal of litigation involving death and personal injury claim in which the trend has clearly been to uphold both the admiralty jurisdiction and the applicability of maritime law principles.[40a] If the death and personal injury claims are looked on as maritime in nature, there is no reason why, in the unusual situation in which it is possible to bring the aircraft or its cargo to safety, salvage awards (including awards for life salvage) should not be made. However, so far as direct authority on the salvage issue goes, Lambros continues to be not only the leading but the most recent case.

### Who May Become Salvors

§ 8–4. Since a salvage act must be voluntary, a person who is under a duty to render assistance cannot claim as a salvor. The duty may arise from the relationship of the salvor to the salved ship—as in the case of its own crew or passengers; or from the relationship of the salving ship to the salved ship—as in the case of tug and tow; or from the fact that the salvor was by virtue of his employment required to give aid—as in the case of pilots, municipally employed firemen and the like. The salvage-defeating duty, that is to say, must be relatively specific, and not merely the moral duty to give assistance against maritime perils or the statutory duty "to render assistance to every person who is found at sea in danger of being lost."[41] Occasionally it has been argued that a custom—say, among the vessels making up a fishing fleet—to give mutual aid should defeat salvage claims, but in most of the cases, despite proof of the custom, the argument has been rejected.[42]

The pre-existing duty problem has been most extensively litigated in cases which involved salvage claims against a ship by her own crew. As a matter of doctrine it is well settled that a crew member, no matter how heroic his acts may have been or how instrumental in saving the ship, is not entitled to salvage unless, before the acts were performed, there had been a final abandonment of the ship by the master—*sine spe recuperandi,* as the old cases put it, and *sine animo rever-*

**40a.** See, however, Executive Jet Aviation, Inc. v. City of Cleveland, 409 U.S. 249, 93 S.Ct. 493, 1973 A.M.C. 1 (1972), discussed Chapter I, § 1–10.

**41.** 37 Stat. 242 (1912), 46 U.S.C.A. § 728. See note 7 *supra.* See also discussion of the stand-by statute, 26 Stat. 425 (1890), 33 U.S.C. § 367, text at note 72 *infra.*

**42.** Stone v. The Jewell, 41 Fed. 103 (S.D.Ala.1889); The Star, 53 F.2d 890, 1931 A.M.C. 1698 (W.D.Wash.1931); Costanzo Transp. Co. v. American Barge Line Co., 35 F.Supp. 929, 1940 A.M.C. 1382 (W.D.Pa.1940); The Judith Lee Rose v. The Clipper, 169 F. Supp. 885, 1959 A.M.C. 523 (D.Mass. 1959); Nicastro v. The Peggy B., 173 F.Supp. 61, 1960 A.M.C. 914 (D.Mass. 1959).

*tendi.*[43] Recapture of ships taken by enemies or pirates were the old-fashioned illustrations of crew salvage, but the question has been restated in a contemporary context in the crop of salvage cases harvested after World War II. Thus crew salvage was denied where after a torpedoing the master had ordered the crew into lifeboats against the danger of sinking but with the intention of returning aboard if it should prove possible,[44] as well as where the master of a ship in port had ordered his men ashore to take shelter from an air raid.[45] A situation in which a final abandonment was found, and a mate rewarded for extraordinary heroism in subsequently returning to the ship, was described in The Saint Mihiel:

> "There was a hole on the top of the deck and the rough seas were going into the side of the ship and forcing the gasoline up (from No. 6 tank) and spreading it over the entire vessel and into the sea, so that soon the whole ship was afire as well as the water on the starboard side. The flames on the ship were higher than the mast. There was, of course, a fear in the minds of some of the men that the Saint Mihiel would blow up. There was ammunition on board for the use of the gun crew and it was exploding. As one may very well imagine, there was great confusion and panic. The captain was yelling 'Abandon ship, abandon ship,' about the time the burning gasoline on the water was beginning to encircle the ship.
>
> "After some difficulty the No. 2 life boat on the portside was launched, and some of the officers and men attempted to leave the vessel that way, but the flames started to come into the boat and they were compelled to jump into the sea. Most

43. The classical opinion was delivered by Dr. Lushington in The Florence [1852] 16 Jur. 572. See The Blaireau, 6 U.S. (2 Cranch) 240, 268 (1804): The Hope (Hobart v. Drogan), 35 U.S. (10 Pet.) 108, 121 (1836). The underlying idea is that by the abandonment the contractual relationship which bound the crew to the ship is dissolved. Discharge by the master is considered as having the same effect as abandonment.

In Smith v. Union Oil Co. of California (The Santa Maria), 274 F.Supp. 248, 1967 A.M.C. 1097 (W.D.Wash.1966) an award was made to the officers and crew of the Santa Maria who, after having abandoned the vessel, which was on fire and out of control following a collision, later reboarded the vessel and cooperated with other salvors in putting out the fire and ensuring the safety of the Santa Maria and its cargo. The details of the abandonment and return are given in an Editor's Note to the reprint of the case in A.M.C. and do not appear in the official report. According to the A.M.C. Editor's Note, the crew of the Santa Maria had at some point been "discharged." That a seaman still under articles is not entitled to salvage even for extraordinary services having nothing to do with the type of work for which he was taken on, see The Tashmoo, 48 F.2d 366, 1931 A.M.C. 48 (E.D.N.Y.1930). See also The Esso Copenhagen (Bertel v. Panama Transport Co.) 202 F.2d 247, 1953 A.M.C. 471 (2d Cir. 1953) certiorari denied 346 U.S. 834, 74 S.Ct. 35 (1953); The Blue Goose (Milton v. Yacht Blue Goose), 91 F.Supp. 114, 1950 A.M.C. 1162 (E.D.Va.1950).

44. The Matt W. Ransom (Drevas v. United States), 58 F.Supp. 1008, 1945 A.M.C. 254 (D.Md.1945).

45. The Lyman Abbott (Niewenhous v. United States) 66 F.Supp. 788, 1946 A.M.C. 759 (E.D.N.Y.1946).

of the men jumped into the sea from the Saint Mihiel and started to swim away. The survivors were picked up by two of the escort destroyers in the convoy, which had turned back to rescue the men. Out of the crew of 50, 27 perished including the captain and the chief mate." [46]

Passengers, like crew members, are held to be under a duty to give aid when the ship is in danger, so that, short of abandonment, their efforts are not customarily compensated. The duty, however, is not absolute as in the case of the crew and, without abandonment, exceptionally ingenious or meritorious services have occasionally been rewarded. The classical American case on passenger salvage was Towle v. The Great Eastern: [47] when that once famous and ill-fated vessel had become disabled following a gale, Towle, a passenger, devised and after twenty-four hours of labor rigged an emergency steering gear with whose aid the ship and her large complement of human cargo were brought safe to port. The ingenious Towle was rewarded by a $15,000 salvage award.[48] As the technology of shipping has increased in complexity, the occasions on which a passenger has the expertise to direct salvage operations which are beyond the competence of the officers and crew have naturally diminished to the vanishing point. Indeed no such awards appear to have been made in this century.[48a]

Municipal or other public employees, such as firemen, are not entitled to an award for saving property if they were merely performing their regular duties.[49] Licensed pilots are treated in the same way: as Judge Simonton put it in the early case of The Cachemire: "This daring and valuable body of men are allowed a monopoly of pilotage and can compel the acceptance of their service in order that experienced mariners should always be at hand to aid by their skill and knowledge vessels seeking a port. While acting in the strict line of their duty they cannot be salvors." [50] On the other hand, firemen, pilots and the like may be entitled to salvage for services which they were under no duty to render.[51] The dividing line between "duty" and "no duty" is, of course, drawn through the customary twilight zone of obscurity; the older cases suggest that presumptions run heavily against claimants so situated and there appear to be no modern cases in which such claims have been put forward.

**46.** (Baretich v. United States), 97 F. Supp. 600, 601, 1951 A.M.C. 1812, 1813 (S.D.N.Y.1951).

**47.** 24 Fed.Cas. 75, Case No. 14,110 (S. D.N.Y.1864).

**48.** One of the few other passenger cases is Candee v. Sixty-Eight Bales of Cotton, 48 F. 479 (D.Ala.1891).

**48a.** In The Donbass, 74 F.Supp. 15, 1947 A.M.C. 1559 (W.D.Wash.1947) an official of the War Shipping Administration who was a passenger on the S. S. Puente Hills aided the officers and crew in salvaging the Donbass and was given a $500 award. Norris, note 4 *supra* § 53, collects the older cases.

**49.** Fireman's Charitable Ass'n v. Ross, 60 F. 456 (5th Cir. 1893).

**50.** 38 F. 518, 522 (D.S.C.1889).

**51.** See Story, J. in The Hope (Hobart v. Drogan), 35 U.S. (10 Pet.) 108, 119 (1836).

It has long been settled that a salvage claim is not defeated under the principle of "voluntariness" by the fact that the salving vessel is specially designed for and, so to say, professionally engaged in salvage operations.[51a] Indeed it has been said that liberal awards should be made to such professional salvors in order to give them an incentive to maintain and operate their highly specialized vessels.[51b] On the other hand it has been suggested that the officers and crews of such vessels—as distinguished from the owners—would be barred from making individual salvage claims on the theory that their actions, being within the normal scope of their employment, could not be considered truly "voluntary." [51c] However, in Vernicos Shipping Co. v. United States [51d] Judge Friendly, after reviewing the "surprisingly scanty" authority on the point, concluded that there was no absolute bar to an award to the crews of Greek salvage tugs which had rendered assistance in Greek waters to United States naval vessels. In his opinion Judge Friendly noted that there was no evidence to show that the crews of the professional salvage tugs received higher wages than the crews of ordinary tugs sailing out of Greek ports and that the owner of the salvage tugs had testified that he did not pay bonuses to his crews for salvage work. Under the circumstances a "modest award" (one month's wages) for the crews was approved, in addition to an award to the owner of the tugs. Presumably evidence that the crews had been compensated by their employer, through extra wages or special bonuses, would have defeated their claims.[51e]

**51a.** Naturally the professional salvor would in any case be entitled to payment for his services. The question mooted in some of the early cases was whether the professional, like the amateur, salvor was, in the absence of a binding contract fixing his compensation, entitled to a true salvage award —that is, more than a mere *quantum meruit* (see text following note 1 *supra*). (On contract salvage, see § 8–15 *infra.*) In The Camanche, 75 U.S. (8 Wall.) 448 (1869) it was held that an incorporated professional salvor could claim salvage, despite earlier doubts that absentee owners who had not personally participated in the salvage could share in the award (see § 8–11 *infra*). Justice Clifford wrote (at p. 477): "[T]he rule is that nothing short of a contract to pay a given sum for the services to be rendered, or a binding engagement to pay at all events, whether successful or unsuccessful in the enterprise, will operate as a bar to a meritorious claim for salvage."

**51b.** See The Lamington, 86 F. 675, 684 (2d Cir. 1898) for a frequently quoted formulation of the "liberal award" idea. For awards to professional salvors in recent cases, see W. E. Rippon & Son v. United States (The Ocklawaha), 348 F.2d 627, 1966 A.M.C. 153 (2d Cir. 1965); Vernicos Shipping Co. v. United States, 349 F. 2d 465, 1965 A.M.C. 1673 (2d Cir. 1965); Devine v. S. T. Ellin (The Salvage Chief), 1969 A.M.C. 1739 (S.D. Calif.1966) (digest).

**51c.** Norris, note 4 *supra* §§ 58, 81.

**51d.** 349 F.2d 465, 1965 A.M.C. 1673 (2d Cir. 1965).

**51e.** In Sobonis v. S/T National Defender, 298 F.Supp. 631, 1969 A.M.C. 1219 (S.D.N.Y.1969) the facts were that the National Defender, carrying a cargo of wheat to Yugoslavia, became stranded in the Bahamas but was in no immediate peril. The owners, having refused offers of salvage, determined to refloat the vessel by off-loading part of the cargo. To this end they chartered The Mesologi to which the National Defender's cargo was transferred until the stranded vessel could be refloated. The Mesologi then accompanied the National

Under a contract of towage, the tug is under a duty to see to the safety of her tow. We are not here concerned with the effect of exculpatory clauses in the contract by which the tug owner seeks to insulate himself from claims for damage to the tow, but with the converse situation in which tug claims a reward, in addition to the towage hire, for rescuing her tow from danger. The doctrine which emerges from the tug-and-tow cases may be stated in two propositions. *First:* the danger from which the tow is rescued must not have been caused by the fault of the tug. *Second:* the tug and her crew will be entitled to salvage only for extraordinary efforts.[52] The mere fact that the tug has rescued her tow from a danger for which the tug is not responsible does not lead automatically to an award.

It stands to reason that an owner gets no salvage for salving his own ship, since he would merely pay the money out of one pocket into another.[52a] On this premise the nineteenth century cases erected a "common ownership" doctrine according to which when ship A was salved by ship B, both ships being in common ownership, ship B could not claim salvage against ship A. As stated, the rule is no more than a truism, but it was extended by analogy to bar salvage when the salving and salved vessels were associated in some way even though not actually owned outright by the same person.[53] It is sometimes

Defender to Yugoslavia where the cargo was delivered. Both the transfer of cargo and the subsequent voyage were uneventful. Seamen aboard the Mesologi claimed and were granted a "low order" salvage award (twice one month's wages). The owners of the Mesologi made no claim for salvage.

52. Waterman S. S. Corp. v. Shipowners & Merchants Towboat Co., 199 F. 2d 600, 1952 A.M.C. 1988 (9th Cir. 1952), certiorari denied 345 U.S. 941, 73 S.Ct. 832 (1953); The City of Portland, 298 F. 27 (5th Cir. 1924). On the effect of fault on the part of the owners of the tug, see Hendry Corp. v. Aircraft Rescue Vessels, 113 F. Supp. 198, 1953 A.M.C. 2115 (E.D.La. 1953); Fort Myers Shell and Dredging Co., Inc. v. Barge NBC 512 (Tug Nellie and Barges) 404 F.2d 137, 1969 A. M.C. 186 (5th Cir. 1968). In Valentine Waterways Corp. v. Tug Choptank, 260 F.Supp. 210, 1967 A.M.C. 1683 (E. D.Va.1966), aff'd per curiam 380 F.2d 381 (4th Cir. 1967), Judge Hoffman cited the proposition stated in the text in denying a salvage claim by tug against tow.

52a. In Continental Ins. Co. v. Clayton Hardtop Skiff, 367 F.2d 230 (3d Cir. 1966) it appeared that a former owner who had abandoned the skiff as a constructive total loss and had received payment from the insurance company later came upon the wrecked skiff and repaired her. In remanding the case for further proceedings, Judge Biggs commented (at p. 235): "Since, by operation of the doctrine of 'constructive total loss', Piperata no longer had any legal interest in the 'Skipton,' his prior ownership did not prevent him from acting as a salvor."

53. Thus no salvage could be claimed where Ship A was owned and Ship B was on a demise charter to the same person. Kennedy *supra* note 4 at p. 27. Another consequence of the rule (although the case law was confused) was that where the peril from which the salved ship had been rescued had been caused by one ship owned by X, no other ship in common ownership could claim salvage for the rescue. In Fleming v. Lay, 109 F. 952 (6th Cir. 1901) the rule was applied to deny salvage where a group of tug owners had formed a voluntary association and a tug of one owner had caused a peril from which the tug of another owner had rescued the ship in distress. The Relief, 51 F. 252 (D. Md.1892) reached a comparable result with respect to an association among the owners of pilot boats. See Kennedy at p. 26; Robinson Admiralty 756 *et seq.* The Kafiristan, [1937] p. 63, [1938] A.C. 136, seems finally to have rejected so extreme an application of the rule in England.

said that the rule did not defeat salvage claims by the crew of the salving vessel,[54] but there are suggestions in the cases that in a common ownership situation crew salvage would be denied unless the services had been out of the ordinary.[55] The Salvage Act of 1912 provided that "[t]he right to remuneration for assistance or salvage shall not be affected by common ownership of the vessels rendering and receiving such assistance or salvage services." [56] The statutory abolition of the rule does not of course mean that the owner may now claim salvage from himself. Its only effect seems to be to make clear that common ownership is to be disregarded with respect to crew salvage claims [57] and to overrule the cases where some form of association short of ownership was held to defeat the claim by the owner of the salving ship.[58] Customarily salvage is divided between owner and crew of the salving ship. In a common ownership case, where the owner gets nothing, the award to the crew is not increased: they receive only what they would have received if the salved ship had been independently owned.

Doubt whether a ship's general agent was too closely allied with the owner to receive an award was set at rest by The Fisher's Hill [59] in which Justice Frankfurter wrote the opinion for the Second Circuit. Finding "no direct precedent in American law," Justice Frankfurter referred to "the somewhat analogous case of salvage work by a tug already engaged under contract, [where] the preexisting contractual relationship has not been an obstacle to an award where the services were extraordinary in that they were beyond anything reasonably called for by the contract." Furthermore, there were English precedents in favor of the award and "our maritime law as a rule finds itself in accord" with English law on questions of salvage.[59a]

**§ 8–5.** The "preexisting duty" limitation is frequently raised when salvage services have been performed by ships owned by the United States (or a foreign government) and by merchant seamen or Navy personnel aboard such ships.

It is settled doctrine that nothing prevents a government from claiming salvage, whether the service was performed by a Navy vessel or a government-owned merchant ship. The United States usually

54. See Norris, note 4 *supra* § 298.

55. Kennedy note 4 *supra* at p. 33 et seq.

56. 37 Stat. 242 (1912), 46 U.S.C. § 727.

57. Kovell v. Portland Tug & Barge Co., 171 F.2d 749, 1949 A.M.C. 380 (9th Cir. 1948) is illustrative (salvage awarded to crew of tug for rescuing barge owned by owner of tug; no reference to the statute). See also Kimes v. United States, 207 F.2d 60, 1953 A.M.C. 1335 (2d Cir. 1953).

58. Note 53 *supra.*

59. (Lago Oil & Transport Co., Ltd. v. United States), 218 F.2d 631, 1955 A.M.C. 697 (2d Cir. 1955). For further proceedings in the case, see note 84a *infra.* In Conolly v. S. S. Karina II, 302 F.Supp. 675, 1969 A.M.C. 319 (E.D.N.Y.1969) an award was made to a claimant who was described as the "general agent" of the salving vessel. The claimant's status was not discussed in the opinion.

59a. See § 8–11 *infra* for a discussion of the interests which are entitled to share in a salvage award.

does not claim an award but that is a matter of policy and has nothing to do with legal right. In The Impoco, Judge Ward wrote:

> ". . . the United States relies upon its inherent right as an owner to recover compensation for salvage services in accordance with the ancient doctrine of the maritime law. Such services are voluntary and they are just as voluntary in the case of men of war and public vessels generally as they are in the case of private vessels; i. e. it is no part of their duty to render such services. While I can see that a sovereign would and perhaps should consider it beneath his dignity to ask for compensation for saving property at sea, I can imagine no legal reason to prevent him from doing so." [60]

The World War II cases show the United States occasionally departing from its no-salvage policy. In The Odenwald [61] the United States claimed, on its own behalf as well as for the officers and crew of a Navy cruiser, for saving a German merchant ship which its own master and crew had attempted to scuttle. In The Donbass [62] the same procedure was followed with respect to salvage services performed by a government owned tanker in the rescue of a disabled Russian ship in the Pacific. In both cases the United States ships had incurred large expenses, which may explain why the government abandoned its usual policy and sought (and received) reimbursement.[62a] The British Government has also prosecuted an occasional

60. 287 F. 400, 402, 1923 A.M.C. 82, 84 (S.D.N.Y.1922). In Petition of American Oil Co. (The Amoco Virginia), 417 F.2d 164, 1969 A.M.C. 1761 (5th Cir. 1969), certiorari denied 397 U.S. 1036, 90 S.Ct. 1353 (1970), Judge Comiskey, quoting the treatise, restated the doctrine of The Impoco. The American Oil Co. case is discussed *infra* text at note 68b. After World War II the Navy's right to make salvage claims received statutory recognition. Under 10 U.S.C.A. § 7364 (62 Stat. 209, 1948) the Secretary of the Navy was authorized to "consider, ascertain, adjust, determine, compromise, or settle and receive payment of any claim by the United States for salvage services rendered by the Department of the Navy to any vessel." A few years later (70A Stat. 592 (1951), 10 U.S.C.A. § 9804) the same authority was conferred on the Secretary of the Air Force, acting under the direction of the Secretary of Defense, with respect to claims "for salvage services performed by the Department of the Air Force for any vessel."

61. (Hamburg-American Line v. United States), 168 F.2d 47, 1948 A.M.C. 888 (1st Cir. 1948). According to Norris, supra note 4, § 79, the salvage claim was made "to obtain the arrest of the German ship by means of process under a salvage libel" since the United States and Germany were not at that time officially at war.

62. (Campbell v. The Donbass), 74 F. Supp. 15, 1947 A.M.C. 1559 (W.D. Wash.1947).

62a. In Basic Boats, Inc. v. United States, 311 F.Supp. 596, 1970 A.M.C. 1843 (E.D.Va.1970) the United States counterclaimed for salvage in an action brought for the benefit of an insurance company which alleged negligence on the part of a United States Navy vessel in carrying out a salvage operation. The main action had not been filed until three days before the expiration of the statutory period for making salvage claims, so that the counterclaim was not filed until after the period had run. For subsequent proceedings in the Basic Boats case, see note 79f *infra*. For Judge Hoffman's handling of the limitation issue, see note 7 *supra* at end. In Tampa Tugs and Towing, Inc. v. M/V Sandanger, 242 F.Supp. 576, 1965 A.M.C.

salvage claim in United States courts. In The Black Swan—The Flying Arrow,[63] the action was brought directly by "His Majesty's Government" for salvage services rendered to a privately owned American cargo vessel in Chinese waters. In The Busy—The Richards [64] the claim was for towing a stranded ship from a mud bank in Spanish waters, the salving ship having been a government-owned rescue tug and the salved ship a privately owned American cargo ship under time charter to the United States. In this instance the action was brought by "the United States of America on behalf of the Lords Commissioners for executing the office of the Lord High Admiral . . ."

Seamen employed by the United States aboard government owned or operated ships are not barred from a salvage award by the mere fact of their employment. The test becomes, as in the case of municipal and other public employees, whether the services were performed in the line of their assigned duties.[65] In Spivak v. United States [66] a civilian employee of the War Department stationed in Pusan as "Advisor" to the Korean Merchant Marine was denied salvage on the ground that his services had not been "voluntary". In Thornton v. The Livingston Roe [67] the libellant was a Naval officer assigned to port duty in Recife, Brazil, who had directed a successful and highly important salvage operation with great energy, skill and bravery, for which he received both a promotion and decorations. Although Thornton had not been charged with duty as a salvage officer, Judge Medina denied his claim on the ground that "the devotion to duty of a public official and the exercise by him of the judgment and discretion necessary to the performance of the functions of his office should not be tainted or in any way affected by the hope of private reward." [67a]

1771 (S.D.Calif.1965) United States Navy vessels cooperated with other salvors in putting out a fire on the Sandanger. The Navy claimed, and was awarded, its expenses. Judge Kunzel discussed the question whether the Navy's claim was "for a salvage award or for reasonable value of services rendered" and seems to have treated it as a claim for salvage. Salvage claims on behalf of the crews of the Navy vessels had been "waived."

63. (His Majesty's Government, etc. v. The Flying Arrow), 97 F.Supp. 182, 1951 A.M.C. 931 (S.D.N.Y.1951).

64. (United States on behalf of Lords Com'rs v. The James L. Richards), 179 F.2d 530, 1950 A.M.C. 359 (1st Cir. 1950). In this case the salvage claim was denied on the ground that the suit was brought after the two year statute of limitation of 46 U.S.C.A. § 730 had run, see note 7 supra.

65. On the perhaps special case of the Coast Guard and its personnel, see text following note 68a *infra*.

66. 203 F.2d 881, 1953 A.M.C. 866 (3d Cir. 1953).

67. 90 F.Supp. 342, 1950 A.M.C. 801 (S.D.N.Y.1950).

67a. In W. E. Rippon & Son v. United States (The Ocklawaha), 348 F.2d 627, 1966 A.M.C. 153 (2d Cir. 1965) a Captain Williams, described as being "employed by the Air Force to advise as to marine matters in and about the Port of Tripoli and to act as a pilot in Libyan waters," rendered extraordinary services in the course of a difficult salvage operation while on "administrative leave" from his regular job. The District Court felt that he would have been entitled to claim as a voluntary salvor but dismissed his claim on the ground that he had temporarily entered the employment of

Both Spivak and Thornton, who were denied awards, were officials of relatively high rank who had pursued their claims individually. Claims for crew salvage have been more warmly received. Government policy apparently discourages claims by military personnel.[67b] Civilian crews of government owned or operated ships are not, however, disqualified if their salvage efforts were not performed in the line of their regular duties. Thus in Kimes v. United States [68] the crew of a government merchant vessel received an award for salvage of cargo from another government owned vessel. The salvage in the Kimes case had been performed during the war in an active theatre of operations and the District Court had found that the crew of the salving ship, although entitled to an award in theory, had already been compensated by wartime bonus pay. On appeal the Second Circuit, in view of the public policy in favor of salvors, held them entitled to an award in addition to the extra compensation which they had received.

The United States Coast Guard, under statutory authorizations which date from the nineteenth century, has long provided a rescue service whose scope under the current formulation (14 U.S.C. § 88) is "to render aid to distressed persons, vessels and aircraft on the high seas and on waters over which the United States has jurisdiction" as well as to "persons and property imperiled by flood." The traditional policy of the Coast Guard has been not to claim salvage for property saved in the course of its rescue efforts. Both case law and commentary have not infrequently assumed that, because of the statutory base for its rescue service, the Coast Guard (unlike the Navy) was precluded as a matter of law from claiming salvage.[68a]

Rippon & Son (professional salvors) 1964 A.M.C. 2695 (S.D.N.Y.1964). However, the salvage award to Rippon & Son included an amount for Captain Williams' services. This disposition of Williams' individual claim was upheld by the Second Circuit.

**67b.** In Nolan v. A. H. Basse Rederiaktieselskab, 267 F.2d 584, 1959 A.M.C. 1362 (3d Cir. 1959) awards were made to the crews of both an Army vessel and a Navy vessel which had cooperated in the salvage of a Danish vessel on the high seas. The United States made no claim on its own behalf. Judge Biggs noted that the crew on the Army vessel "was granted specific authority by the United States Army to bring the suit at bar" but made no comparable reference to the Navy crew. (According to Norris, note 4 *supra*, § 79, the Navy's policy is "not to permit its officers and sailors to claim salvage unless consent has first been obtained from the Secretary of the Navy.") In the Nolan case the salvage action was against the owner of the cargo, since the salved Danish ship was not amenable to process in the United States. On cargo's liability for salvage, see § 8–13 *infra*.

**68.** 207 F.2d 60, 1953 A.M.C. 1335 (2d Cir. 1953). See also The Abraham Baldwin (Kittelsaa v. United States) 75 F.Supp. 845, 1948 A.M.C. 500 (E.D. N.Y.1948).

**68a.** In The Lyman M. Law, 122 F. 816 (D.Me.1903) salvage was performed jointly by private persons and a Coast Guard life-saving crew. In making an award to the private salvors, the Court said: "In fixing the amount of salvage we exclude, of course, the crew of the life-saving station from any reward." In Beach Salvage Corp. of Florida v. The Cap't Tom, 201 F. Supp. 479, 1961 A.M.C. 2244 (S.D.Fla. 1961) the Court found that "the Beach Salvage Corporation . . . was not the only salvor but the United States Coast Guard was also a salvor of the vessels even though, by reason of law, it could not actually receive a portion of any salvage award" [citing the predecessor of 14 U.S.C.A. § 88 and

In petition of American Oil Co. (United States v. American Oil Co.—The Amoco Virginia) [68b] the Coast Guard departed from its traditional policy and put forward a salvage claim. The Amoco Virginia was moored to a dock in the Houston Ship Canal in the course of loading a cargo of gasoline and heating oil when fire broke out, threatening a major disaster in the port. The Coast Guard took charge of the fire-fighting operation in which it was aided by municipal fire departments. On the following day, the fire being still not under control, all the locally available supplies of the chemical foam needed to extinguish the fire had been exhausted. Under the direction of the Coast Guard the Navy and Air Force organized an air lift and flew more than half a million pounds of foam to Houston, which made it possible for the fire to be put out by the end of the day. The United States claimed $89,676.60 as salvage—that figure representing the cost of the foam and the expenses of the Navy and Air Force in operating the air lift. The amount claimed by the United States did not include anything for the Coast Guard's own expense.

The Fifth Circuit, reversing the District Court, awarded the United States the full amount claimed. The case could perhaps have been taken as involving claims by the Navy and Air Force whose right to salvage, established under the maritime law, has received statutory recognition.[68c] Judge Comiskey, however, chose to take it otherwise: "[T]he National Government has apparently concluded as a matter of policy to make a salvage claim for services rendered by the U. S. Coast Guard to the extent, and only to the extent, that the Coast Guard used the services and supplies of the Air Force and Navy. That does not mean that the Coast Guard has no right to salvage for its own services and supplies. The pre-existing duty bar to salvage by the United States Coast Guard has not been sustained by the Courts." Judge Comiskey then reviewed the statutory authorization (14 U.S.C.A. § 88) under which the Coast Guard provides its rescue service, emphasizing that its function is "permissive," not mandatory.[68d] The post World War II legislation which recognized the right of the Navy and Air Force to claim salvage was taken as

The Kanawha, 254 F. 762 (2d Cir. 1918)]. Norris, note 4 *supra* at § 78: "The ineligibility to receive a salvage award by one who is not a volunteer is best exemplified by the United States Coast Guard."

**68b.** 417 F.2d 164, 1969 A.M.C. 1761 (5th Cir. 1969), certiorari denied 397 U.S. 1036, 90 S.Ct. 1353 (1970).

**68c.** See note 60 *supra* at end.

**68d.** Judge Comiskey also discussed the effect of the National Search and Rescue Plan (SAR) adopted in 1956 under which the Coast Guard is named the "regional SAR coordinatory" for "the maritime region" (as distinguished from "the inland region" and "the overseas region"). His conclusion was that the Coast Guard's SAR responsibilities were no bar to its salvage claim: "The SAR plan imposes no extra statutory pre-existing legal duty on the Coast Guard. The SAR plan recognizes the "statutory responsibilities" of the Coast Guard which, as we have found, are permissive." This analysis followed two earlier Fifth Circuit cases, which had not directly involved the salvage question: United States v. Gavagan, 280 F.2d 319, 1961 A.M.C. 1439 (5th Cir. 1960), certiorari denied 364 U.S. 933, 81 S.Ct. 379 (1961); United States v. DeVane, 306 F.2d 182, 1963 A.M.C. 1400 (5th Cir. 1962).

declaratory of the existing law rather than as creating the right. The facts of the Fifth Circuit case are somewhat ambiguous [68e] but the Court, for reasons best known to itself, went out of its way to construct a rationale which permits the Coast Guard to claim salvage whenever it chooses. The result appears eminently sound when the property saved belongs to a large corporation whose own corporate activities created the peril in the first instance. There is no reason to believe that the Coast Guard, under the Fifth Circuit dispensation, will make salvage claims for the rescue of small fishing boats or privately owned yachts.

Coast Guard personnel, like the Coast Guard itself, have not traditionally made salvage claims and it has usually been assumed that such claims would be barred.[68f] It is not known whether the Coast Guard will follow the lead of the Navy and authorize salvage claims on behalf of officers and crews in exceptional situations.[68g] If such claims are brought in a court which follows the lead of the Fifth Circuit in the American Oil Co. case they will presumably be treated like the comparable Navy claims and, for that matter, like the claims of municipal firemen, pilots and others who are, to some degree, already under a duty to furnish aid to a stricken vessel.[68h]

**§ 8–6.** Persons who otherwise qualify as salvors may forfeit their rights by misconduct or fault, in a maritime application of the equity clean hands rule.

The fault may be in the fact that the salving ship is herself responsible for the danger from which the salved ship is rescued, as in the case of a collision where a ship at fault renders assistance to the ship she has run down. It was in this type of case, although the facts were unusual, that Justice Clifford, in The Clarita and The Clara,[69] held that collision fault bars recovery. The Clarita was a privately owned salvage tug which had aided the municipal fire department in an unsuccessful effort to put out a fire on a ferry-boat lying at the Hoboken docks. Finally, at the request of the fire department, the Clarita undertook to tow the burning ship away from the docks, using a hempen hawser for the purpose although she either had or could easily have procured chains. The hawser quickly burnt through; indeed three successive hawsers suffered the same fate. After the third hawser had parted and before another could be made fast, the ferry-boat drifted broadside against the Clara, and set her

**68e.** Thus Norris, note 4 *supra* at § 78 (1972 Cum.Supp.) comments: "The determination and disposition of this case by the Fifth Circuit does not mean, in the opinion of this writer, that the Coast Guard would have entitlement to a salvage award for rescue activities to distressed marine property and of persons on the high seas."

**68f.** See the authorities cited *supra* note 68a. In Dominguez v. Schooner Brindicate, 204 F.Supp. 817, 1962 A.M.C. 1659 (D. Puerto Rico, 1962) Judge Magruder held that membership in the Coast Guard Auxiliary did not preclude a salvage award to a group of salvors who rendered their services voluntarily.

**68g.** On the Navy's practice, see *supra* notes 61, 62.

**68h.** See § 8–4 *supra*.

**69.** 90 U.S. (23 Wall.) 1 (1874).

on fire. The tug, having succeeded in pulling the ferry-boat away from the Clara to midstream, where it was allowed to sink, returned and labored diligently and successfully to put out the fire on the Clara. After all this activity the owners of the Clara libeled the tug to recover for the damage done by the fire and the owners of the Clarita filed a cross-libel for salvage in putting out the fire. The Clara was awarded full damages and the salvage cross-libel was dismissed. Affirming, Justice Clifford wrote that "the insuperable objection to their [cross-libellants] right of recovery is that the peril to which the schooner was exposed was caused by those who rendered the alleged salvage service, and to the rule that such libellants are not entitled to recover there are no exceptions when it appears that the suit is prosecuted in behalf of the wrongdoers."

The cross-libel for salvage in The Clarita and The Clara had been filed by the owners of the tug in an obvious attempt to secure an offset to the schooner's libel for damages. Nor does it appear from anything in the opinion that the cross-libel was brought for the crew of the tug as well as the owners. Justice Clifford's statement that "no exceptions" would be made "when . . . the suit is prosecuted in behalf of the wrong-doers" may have meant that an exception might have been made, and an award granted, if the salvage claim had been brought on behalf of the crew of the Clarita, at least if their services had been exceptionally meritorious. This interpretation becomes the more likely when it is considered that the passage in question follows a review of the situations in which salvage is ordinarily denied but may be granted in exceptional cases.

There appear to be no American cases, ancient or modern, on whether the fault of the salving ship in a collision case will be attributed to the personally innocent members of the crew to bar their salvage claims. Despite the absence of authority it has sometimes been suggested that American salvage law does bar such claims.[70] The Clarita and the Clara remains the leading case on the effect of collision fault in this seldom litigated area and Justice Clifford's remarks in that case can, as has been suggested, be read to support the crew claims at least as easily as they can be read to deny them. Nineteenth century ideas of collective fault, such as the fellow servant rule, have lost their power to persuade the legal mind. If the question is approached as an open one, as in this country it must be, no reason is apparent why the members of the crew who were not responsible for the ship's fault should be barred from salvage awards for their post-collision services.[71]

70. Norris, note 4 *supra* § 118, conceding the absence of American authority, argues that "to reward any member of the wrongdoing ship would be contrary to the spirit, if not the letter, of the law of salvage." In an earlier discussion of the point Norris had stated that "Admiralty imputes negligence of the ship at fault to her crew and identifies with the ship all those who are connected with it". (The Law of Seamen (1952) § 238, citing as principal authority The Clarita and The Clara.)

71. Robinson, Admiralty (1939) 754 *et seq.* took the position which is put forward in the text.

Earlier editions of the leading English treatise on salvage stated categorically that crew members on a ship at fault in a collision were barred from claiming salvage.[71a] Reliance was placed on a few cases of fairly ancient vintage. The editor of the current edition argues that it would be more equitable to "discriminate" between the innocent and guilty members of the crew instead of denying salvage to all alike and goes on to suggest that some of Lord Wright's remarks in The Kafiristan [71b] may be taken as undermining the authority the older cases on which the English rule is said to rest.[71c]

There is a statutory duty, in case of collision, on the master of each vessel "to stay by the other vessel until he has ascertained that she has no need of further assistance, and to render, . . . such assistance as may be practicable and as may be necessary in order to save [those aboard the other vessel] from any danger caused by the collision . . ." [72] A master who fails to stand by and render assistance is subject to criminal sanctions [73] and a presumption of fault in the collision is cast on the noncomplying vessel. In view of these provisions the argument can be made that no salvage award can be made for any post-collision assistance by any ship which had been involved, since the assistance would have been compelled by the statutory duty and not given voluntarily. The point has not been decided in any American case, although, under a substantially identical English statute, the House of Lords has decided that a salvage claim is not barred by the statute alone—although of course it will be barred if the salving ship was at fault.[74]

The Clarita and The Clara denied an award to the owners of the ship solely at fault. Assuming that the stand-by statute is irrelevant, the innocent ship would be entitled to an award for services rendered to the guilty ship. Where both ships are to some degree at fault, the English law is that neither vessel may claim a salvage award from the other; [75] there are no direct American holdings.

71a. Kennedy, The Law of Civil Salvage (3d ed. 1936) at p. 91.

71b. The Beaverbrook v. The Kafiristan, [1938] A.C. 136. The holding was that salvage claims on behalf of the Beaverbrook were not barred because the Beaverbrook and the ship which was at fault in the collision were held in common ownership. On the common ownership doctrine see note 53 *supra* and the accompanying text.

71c. Kennedy (4th ed. by McGuffie, 1958) 126 *et seq.*

72. 26 Stat. 425 (1890), 33 U.S.C.A. § 367.

73. 26 Stat. 425 (1890), 33 U.S.C.A. § 368.

74. Owners of S.S. Melanie v. Owners of S.S. San Onofre, [1925] A.C. 246. The rule of the Melanie was accepted and restated by Lord Wright in The Kafiristan, *supra* note 71b. In Petition of Sun Oil Co. (M/T Maumee Sun), 342 F.Supp. 976, 1972 A.M.C. 2258 (S.D.N.Y.1972), affirmed per curiam 474 F.2d 1048, 1973 A.M.C. 572 (2d Cir. 1973) (digested note 9 *supra*) Judge Levet, in denying salvage claims, considered the effect of the stand-by statute but seems to have grounded his decision on the conclusion that, without regard to the statute, the services were not "voluntary."

75. Robinson, Admiralty (1939) 754, citing to Kennedy. The only mutual fault case which Kennedy cites is The Duc d'Aumale [1904] P. 60 (collision between tug and tow).

**§ 8–7.** A salvor may forfeit his right to an award by carrying out the salvage so negligently or so unskillfully that the salved property is further damaged. Forfeiture is not, however, the automatic result of a finding of negligence, as it appears to be in the collision fault cases; the court may merely reduce the award. Allegations of negligence or misconduct on the part of the salvors run like a refrain through the salvage cases. Such allegations, in the context of a maritime catastrophe, are easy to make, hard to disprove, and obvious counters for the shipowner to throw into the game in his natural desire to pay as little salvage money as possible. The courts seem inclined to discount them, and at most to reduce the award instead of forfeiting it unless the negligence shown can appropriately be described as "gross".[76]

The question of negligent salvage was much discussed in Dougherty Co. v. United States (The Mohawk) [77] although the case itself touched salvage only peripherally. The action was brought by the owner of a barge which had been rescued at sea by the Coast Guard, but damaged on the way into the harbor by pounding against a breakwater. The majority of the Court found that the Coast Guard cutter had not been negligent in towing the barge into harbor, but went on to say that even if "ordinary negligence" had been found the government would still not be liable. In support of the second branch of the holding, Judge Kalodner turned for analogy to the salvage cases, concluding: "The overwhelming weight of opinion is that absent "gross negligence" or "wilful misconduct" a salvor is not liable. It was early held "the evidence must be conclusive before they (salvors) are found guilty", and the law accords the presumption of innocence in favor of salvors." Chief Judge Biggs, in an impressive dissent, undertook to demolish the position of the majority. As to the salvage cases, he wrote:

> "[I]f the salvor has not been guilty of *wilful misconduct* or of *bad faith* a salvage award to him is considered by the court. If the attempted salvage has been merely ineffectual and damage thereafter comes to the vessel attempted to be salved, no fault is found with the would-be salvor. If, on the other hand, an *independent* (viz., a distinguishable) *injury* has resulted to the salved vessel from the negligence of one undertaking a salvage service, the salvage award may be refused or diminished or an affirmative money award may be given against the salvor as Lord Justice Kennedy has pointed out. There is no magic to be found in characterizing the salvor as having been *grossly* negligent or *ordinarily* negligent. If independent (viz., distinguishable) injury has resulted from the negligence of the salvor the award is affected in almost every instance. . . . The only possible excep-

76. A typical case is The Esso Greensboro (Petition of Esso Shipping Co.), 122 F.Supp. 133, 1954 A.M.C. 734 (S.D.Tex.1954).

77. 207 F.2d 626, 1953 A.M.C. 1541 (3d Cir. 1953) certiorari denied 347 U.S. 912, 74 S.Ct. 476 (1954).

> tion is where the negligence of the salvor has been very slight." [78]

Judge Biggs' dissent seems to be an accurate rendering of the cases. Indeed in a subsequent Coast Guard case where a motor boat was rescued in a harbor his brethren seem to have nearly conceded the point, since there the United States was held liable for "ordinary negligence" on the part of the Coast Guard, the Dougherty case being distinguished on the unconvincing ground that it involved a rescue at sea.[79]

The position taken by Judge Biggs in the Dougherty case was adopted by the Fifth Circuit in The Noah's Ark v. Bentley and Felton Corporation.[79a] The Cudjoe came to the aid of the Noah's Ark, whose engine had broken down about 80 miles west of Key West, and towed her into Key West Harbor. When the two vessels arrived in port, the weather conditions were severe with winds from 60 to 72 mph and intermittent downpours of rain. The two masters had apparently agreed that the Noah's Ark should be made fast to a cable vessel which was regularly anchored in the harbor and the Cudjoe manoeuvred so that the Noah's Ark, still on the tow line, was brought parallel to and close by the cable vessel. At that point, before the Noah's Ark had been able to make fast to the cable vessel, the Cudjoe, without any plausible excuse and without any warning, cast off the tow line. The Noah's Ark, a powerless derelict, was driven against a seawall where she eventually capsized and sank. On those facts the District Court concluded that the Cudjoe was entitled to a salvage award which was diminished because of the Cudjoe's negligence in prematurely casting off the tow line but that the Noah's Ark's claim for damages against the Cudjoe should be dismissed partly because the crew of the Noah's Ark had not done all that could have been done to extricate the vessel from disaster after it had been driven against the seawall but also on the legal ground that the "negligence of the [Cudjoe] did not amount to gross negligence or wilful misconduct producing a distinguishable and separate injury to the [Noah's Ark]." The Fifth Circuit reversed on the authority of Judge Biggs' dissent in Dougherty.[79b] Judge Brown wrote:

> ". . . The key to the correct legal principle is the character of the injury inflicted—i. e., distinguishable or, as

78. *Id.* at 650, 1953 A.M.C. at 1577–1578.

79. Geertson v. United States, 223 F.2d 68, 1955 A.M.C. 1209 (3d Cir. 1955). Other cases involving allegations of negligence by Coast Guard personnel in effecting rescues are United States v. Lawter, 219 F.2d 559, 1955 A.M.C. 637 (5th Cir. 1955); Page v. United States, 105 F.Supp. 99, 1952 A.M.C. 893 (D.La.1952).

79a. 292 F.2d 437, 1961 A.M.C. 1641 (5th Cir. 1961).

79b. The Fifth Circuit had adopted the rationale of the Dougherty dissent in United States v. Gavagan, 280 F.2d 319, 1961 A.M.C. 1439 (5th Cir. 1960), certiorari denied 364 U.S. 933 (1961), a non-salvage case which involved the liability of the Coast Guard for negligently carrying out a rescue operation. Gavagan was followed in United States v. DeVane, 306 F.2d 182, 1963 A.M.C. 1400 (5th Cir. 1962).

sometimes called, independent. The requirement for wilful or gross negligence as an element of salvor liability relates to injuries of a non-distinguishable, non-independent kind. In a very broad sense the latter covers errors that made the salvage ineffectual. A distinguishable injury, on the other hand, is some type of damage sustained by the salved vessel other than that which she would have suffered had not salvage efforts been undertaken to extricate her from the perils to which she was exposed. [Citation omitted.] In other words it is a harm distinct from that from which the vessel is being saved." [79c]

The theory put forward by Judge Biggs and elaborated by Judge Brown bears a close family resemblance to the long-standing tort distinction between non-feasance and misfeasance: there may be no duty to act in the first place but, once the action has been undertaken, the actor will be held to the usual standards of liability.[79d] The position rejected in the Noah's Ark and in the Dougherty dissent has sometimes been argued in terms of a "Good Samaritan rule": since the voluntary salvor is a Good Samaritan, he should not be held to the same standard of duty or competence as other people. The answer, in the judicial discussions under review, has been that the Good Samaritan, once he has entered upon his office, will be treated like anyone else.[79e] That view seems to have been generally followed in recent litigation.[79f]

**79c.** 292 F.2d 437, 441.

**79d.** The tort distinction is conventionally traced back to the "great case" of Coggs v. Bernard, 2 Ld.Raym. 909, 92 Eng.Rep. 107 (Q.B.1703) in which it was held that: If a man undertakes to carry goods safely and securely, he is responsible for any damage they may sustain in the carriage thro' his neglect tho' he was not a common carrier and was to have nothing for the carriage.

**79e.** In Grigsby v. Coastal Marine Service of Texas, Inc., 412 F.2d 1011, 1021, 1969 A.M.C. 1513, 1524–1525 (5th Cir. 1969), Judge Brown offered this formulation: "[T]he Good Samaritan doctrine . . . has two faces —duties owed to one who, without legal obligation, voluntarily undertakes to rescue another, on the one hand, and, on the other, duties owed by such volunteer either to the one being saved or to others . . . [T]o eliminate a deterrent to voluntary, impulsive response to need as the forces of nature or man, or both, imperil ship or seamen, the law accords a considerable latitude in the standard of performance of the salvage service. The salvor is seldom held liable for just a failure to save and liability for negligent salvage is limited to situations in which the salvor, through want of due care, has worsened the position of the victim." For the facts of the Grigsby case, see note 3a *supra*.

**79f.** See United States v. Sandra & Dennis Fishing Corp., 372 F.2d 189 (1st Cir. 1967), certiorari denied 389 U.S. 836, 88 S.Ct. 52 (1967): "[T]he government makes much of the principle that a salvor who is a 'Good Samaritan' is not held to ordinary standards of care. . . . Whatever may be the limits of this principle with respect to volunteered salvage, we believe that if the Coast Guard accepts a mission it should conduct its share of the proceeding with acceptable seamanship. [Citing the Gavagan case, note 79b *supra*, and the Dougherty dissent.]" (372 F.2d at 197.) See also American Independent Oil Co. v. M/S Alkaid, 289 F.Supp. 329, 1968 A.M.C. 748 (S.D.N.Y.1967): "A salvor is liable for distinguishable independent damages caused by his ordinary negligence, that is, a failure to use reasonable care. [Citing Noah's Ark and the

A second appeal in the Noah's Ark [79g] threw further light on the Fifth Circuit doctrine. On the second trial the District Court had assessed damages in favor of the Noah's Ark against the Cudjoe only for loss which could not have been prevented even if the officers and crew of the Noah's Ark had done all that could have been done after the Cudjoe had cast off the tow line. The result was a $7500 salvage award to the Cudjoe, less damages of approximately $2000. The value of the Noah's Ark was found to have been $20,000 at the time when the Cudjoe had cast her loose and $3,000 after she capsized and sank. At that point the hapless owners of the Noah's Ark were worse off than they had been after the first trial in which a different District Judge, while refusing to consider their claim for damages against the Cudjoe, had, because of the Cudjoe's negligence, reduced the salvage award to $2,000. The Fifth Circuit reversed a second time. Judge Brown quoted a pungent formulation by Judge Learned Hand: "[The] tortfeasor cannot be allowed to escape through the meshes of a logical net. He is the wrongdoer; let him unravel the casuistries resulting from his wrong." [79h] Rather than remand the case for a third trial, the Court, with the consent of counsel, proceeded to the extraordinary step of calculating the damages itself. The $7,500 salvage award was allowed to stand; the damage award in favor of the Noah's Ark was set at $8,738.21. Thus the negligent salvor ended up paying a net balance to the victim of his negligence. Presumably if the Cudjoe's fault had been found to be "gross" or "wilfull" the salvage award would have been forfeited entirely. The possibility of large damage awards against negligent salvors raises the question whether a salvor so situated could successfully petition for limitation of liability. If the salvor's negligence was of the type for which liability can be limited under the Limitation Act—e. g. faulty navigation—there seems to be no reason why his petition should not be successful.[79i]

Dougherty dissent.] It may be added that the principle is recognized by counsel for the salvor." (289 F.Supp. at 346.) The Noah's Ark was followed in Dow Chemical Co. v. Barge UM-23B, 424 F.2d 307, 1970 A.M.C. 1622 (5th Cir. 1970) in which a salvage tug was held liable for having improperly moored a barge which broke away from the insecure mooring and damaged a third person's property. In Basic Boats, Inc. v. United States, 352 F.Supp. 44, 1973 A.M.C. 522 (E.D.Va.1972), Judge Hoffman accepted the principle of The Noah's Ark but concluded that the salving vessel (a United States naval vessel) had not been negligent. For earlier proceedings in the Basic Boats case, see note 7 *supra*.

**79g.** 322 F.2d 3, 1964 A.M.C. 59 (5th Cir. 1963).

**79h.** Navigazione Libera, TSA v. Newton Creek Towing Co., 98 F.2d 694, 697, 1938 A.M.C. 1419 (2d Cir. 1938).

**79i.** In United States v. Sandra & Dennis Fishing Corp., 372 F.2d 189 (1st Cir. 1967) Judge Aldrich concluded that the United States could limit its liability with respect to death and injury claims arising out of a negligently conducted rescue operation by the Coast Guard. The death and injury claims were subsequently adjudicated in Petition of United States, 418 F.2d 264 (1st Cir. 1969). Norris, note 4 *supra* (1972 Cum.Supp.) § 123 raises the limitation of liability point and concludes that there is no reason why the negligent salvor should be precluded from petitioning for limitation. No salvage case seems to have discussed the point. On the conditions of limitation, see Chapter X.

Another allegation of misconduct frequently brought against salvage claimants is that of pilfering, looting and theft of the salved property. Such allegations are treated like those of negligent salvage. If there is proof and if the misconduct was "gross" the award may be forfeited; for less serious misconduct there will be a reduction.[80] Salvors regularly exaggerate the value of their services, just as the owners of the salved property regularly charge the salvors with negligence and misconduct. This is understood to be part of the game; even an absurdly overstated claim will not, of itself, lead to a forfeiture.[80a]

Still another type of misconduct is that of the salvor who refuses to give aid until the master of the ship in distress has agreed to pay what the court regards as an exorbitant amount. Such agreements, if found to have been signed under duress, will be set aside.[81] As in the other misconduct cases, the gravity of the offense will determine whether the award is to be reduced or forfeited.[82]

The same principles apply where several sets of greedy salvors squabble among themselves for the privilege of playing Good Samaritan, as well as to cases where a salvor, intent on running up the largest possible bill, refuses to desist from his labors when the danger is past and the owner or master has requested him to go about his business.[82a] Normally a salvor is under a duty to return the property to the owner as quickly as possible and not to carry it with him to the ends of the earth. As might be expected a rule of reason applies: a transatlantic liner which on its outward voyage picked up a seaplane in distress a few miles out of New York harbor neither forfeited its right to salvage nor became liable in conversion by carrying the seaplane to England and there depositing it with the Receiver of Wrecks.[83]

**80.** See The Royal Oak (Danner v. United States), 99 F.Supp. 880, 1951 A.M.C. 1495 (S.D.N.Y.1951) (award forfeited; Judge Bondy's opinion collects a number of the cases). See also The Lloyd Cuarto (Breving v. The Lloyd Cuarto), 84 F.Supp. 33, 1949 A.M.C. 1016 (N.D.Cal.1949) where Judge Goodman resolved the issues in favor of the salvors. In Padilla v. The Norseman, 1967 A.M.C. 1531 (D. Puerto Rico 1967) it appeared that the salvors, in addition to stranding the Norseman, which they had in tow, engaged in looting and, in making their salvage claims, systematically exaggerated what they had done. They had also given false information to the Coast Guard in an attempt to keep the entire salvage operation to themselves. The award was held forfeited.

**80a.** Thus in Conolly v. S.S. Karina II, 302 F.Supp. 675, 1969 A.M.C. 319 (E.D.N.Y.1969) Judge Judd commented that "the demand in the libel, for awards totaling $850,000, is so excessive as to shock even a court that has observed many cases where plaintiff's attorneys put the *ad damnum* at more than ten times what they really expect to establish." However, on the theory that the fault lay more with counsel who had verified the libel than with the plaintiffs, he concluded that "the exaggeration should not affect the basic award," which was set at $6,300.

**81.** See § 8–15 *infra*.

**82.** See Higgins, Inc. v. M/V Tri-State, 99 F.Supp. 694, 1951 A.M.C. 862 (S.D. Fla.1951) (collecting cases).

**82a.** See Norris, note 4 *supra*, § 113 *et seq.*, collecting cases.

**83.** Lambros, Seaplane Base v. The Batory, 215 F.2d 228, 1954 A.M.C. 1789 (2d Cir. 1954) (the owner, who had not

### The Salvage Award: How Computed—How Distributed

§ 8–8. When an American judge reaches that part of his opinion which deals with the amount of a salvage award, he will quote from Justice Clifford's opinion in The Blackwall:

> "Courts of admiralty usually consider the following circumstances as the main ingredients in determining the amount of the award to be decreed for a salvage service:
>
> "(1) The labor expended by the salvors in rendering the salvage service.
>
> "(2) The promptitude, skill and energy displayed in rendering the service and saving the property.
>
> "(3) The value of the property employed by the salvors in rendering the service, and the danger to which such property was exposed.
>
> "(4) The risk incurred by the salvors in securing the property from the impending peril.
>
> "(5) The value of the property saved.
>
> "(6) The degree of danger from which the property was rescued." [84]

The recitation of Justice Clifford's six "ingredients" serves the useful purpose of indicating that the variables are so many and so incapable of exact measurement that it will probably be fruitless for either party to take an appeal merely on the ground that the award was incorrectly computed. If property values alone weighed in the scales, there could be the usual disputes about valuation. But who can argue successfully about such imponderables as "skill", "energy", "risk" and "danger" ? Although cases can be found in which appellate courts have increased (or, less frequently, decreased) awards, the district court's discretion will control in the great bulk of cases.[84a]

In addition to the imponderables, the Blackwall formula calls upon the judge to make a valuation of the property at risk. From the salvor's point of view this means usually the value of the salving ship plus her pending freight. Current American treatises take the po-

claimed the seaplane, was, however, held not liable *in personam* for the salvage, see note 11 *supra*).

84. 77 U.S. (10 Wall.) 1, 14 (1869).

84a. In The Fisher's Hill (Lago Oil & Transport Co., Ltd. v. United States), 232 F.2d 238, 1956 A.M.C. 544 (2d Cir. 1956) the Second Circuit ordered an award doubled, on the ground that "[a] stingy award to a salvor contravenes good public policy." A further increase in the award was subsequently ordered, 232 F.2d 283, 1956 A.M.C. 841 (2d Cir. 1956). Perhaps the judges of the Second Circuit found themselves in a stingier mood in the 1960s than in the 1950s. At all events awards were decreased in W. E. Rippon & Son v. United States (The Ocklawaha), 348 F.2d 627, 1966 A.M.C. 153 (2d Cir. 1965) and in Vernicos Shipping Co. v. United States, 349 F.2d 465, 1965 A.M.C. 1673 (2d Cir. 1965). In Nolan v. A. H. Basse Rederiaktieselskab, 267 F.2d 584, 1959 A.M.C. 1362 (3rd Cir. 1959) an award to the crew of a U.S. Army vessel was increased.

sition that the cargo on board the salving ship is not taken into account, apparently on the ground that such cargo is not entitled to share in the award.[85] The leading English treatise, on the other hand, assumes as a matter of course that cargo as well as freight are items in the valuation of the salvor's property but without discussing the allied question of cargo's right to share in the award.[86]

There is a certain illogic both in the inclusion of freight (on which all the sources agree) and in the exclusion of cargo (on which the English and American sources disagree). The property engaged in the salvage operation is valued to determine how much the salvor put at risk. A fact which should be relevant to the discussion, but which seems never to have been called to judicial attention, is that under both the Harter Act and the Carriage of Goods by Sea Act the shipowner is absolved of liability from loss or damage to cargo resulting from saving or attempting to save life or property at sea.[87] As to goods moving under Harter Act or Cogsa bills of lading, therefore, the owner of the salving ship incurs no liability to cargo by engaging in a salvage operation and may preserve his right to freight by a "lost or not lost" clause in the bill of lading. As to goods moving under a charter party where no bills of lading are issued, the same result can be achieved by a term in the charter party. If the freight is not at risk there is no reason to include it in the valuation. Different considerations apply to cargo. If, as the American writers suggest, cargo is never entitled to share in the award,[88] then (if from the salvor's point of view there is no risk) there is no reason to include it. If a court should decide that cargo on the salving ship was entitled to share in the award it should follow that, at least in such a case, cargo should also come into the valuation. While it is part of the ritual for the district court to assign a value to the property engaged in the salvage, that figure does not appear to play any great part in determining the size of the award. That fact no doubt explains why there has been so little case discussion of the freight and cargo question.

Valuation of the property salved is of the greatest importance in deciding on the award to be made and here counsel abandon the gentlemanly indifference with which they regard the attempts to value the salving property. In The Shreveport Judge Cochran wrote:

> "The great contest has been, as is usual in such cases, over the sound value of the Shreveport [the salved ship], and the necessary repairs. Experts have testified on both sides . . .

85. Robinson, Admiralty 741 (1939); Norris, note 4, *supra*, § 272. Robinson cites no authority. Of the cases cited by Norris the most recent in date is The Ereza, 124 F. 659 (D.Pa. 1903). On whether cargo is entitled to a share in the award, see text following note 107 *infra*.

86. Kennedy, note 4 *supra* p. 204 et seq. The current edition goes on to discuss the points made in the following paragraph in the text under applicable English legislation.

87. Section 3 of the Harter Act (27 Stat. 445 (1893), 46 U.S.C.A. § 191)); Section 4(4) of Cogsa (49 Stat. 1210 (1936), 46 U.S.C.A. § 1304(4).

88. See text following note 107 *infra*.

"The opinions of the experts in this case are in hopeless conflict. There is an old saying that when doctors differ, laymen may do as they please. The latitude allowed by this saying would be far too great for a court to adopt it in deciding upon conflicting expert testimony, but it has a modicum of wisdom in it. In cases of such conflict, the lay mind, being without technical knowledge upon the subject, naturally adopts the opinions of those experts which are more in accordance with the laymen's own observations and experience . . . "[89]

Judge Cochran's remarks indicate not only how hard-fought the valuation issue may be when a large ship has been salved, but the untechnical manner in which the expert testimony is handled. Valuation of the salved property is only one of the items, even though it is unquestionably the most important one, in the account. The process of valuation in salvage litigation is much more on the amateur side than the professional techniques followed by, for example, general average adjusters.

The items taken into account in valuing the salved property are typically ship, freight and cargo. When the property has been partially damaged, its value is taken as of the time when the salvage service was completed. For cargo, this means usually whatever it can be sold for in the port where it is unloaded.[89a] For the ship a customary method is to estimate the sound value of the ship—that is, its value before the collision or other cause of damage—and deduct from that figure the cost of necessary repairs.[90] The owner of the salved ship is not entitled to include repairs which were not directly occasioned by the danger from which the ship was rescued or any portion of the repair cost which puts the ship in better condition than it was in before the salvage. Intangibles, in addition to the freight, may occasionally be found to have benefited from the salvage service and

89. (Strachan Shipping Co. v. Cities Service Transport Co.), 42 F.2d 524, 1930 A.M.C. 1310 (E.D.S.C.1930).

89a. Nolan v. A.H. Basse Rederiaktieselskab, 267 F.2d 584, 1959 A.M.C. 1362 (3d Cir. 1959) raised the problem of cargo valuation on an unusual set of facts. The owner of the cargo was the sole importer of cryolite into the United States. Oresund, in Greenland, supplied the cryolite under a long-term contract which provided that the importer should take a minimum of 8,000 tons a year to be invoiced at $55 per ton. For orders above the minimum the price per ton was to be increased. The cryolite on the salved ship, invoiced at $95,324.37, happened to be the last shipment for the year at the $55 per ton rate. The invoice price for the same amount of cryolite at the increased price would have been $200,000 or more. The salvors naturally argued that the cargo should be valued at its "replacement" cost. Judge Biggs, noting that the normal rule of market value at the port of arrival was, because of the absence of a market, inapplicable, concluded, affirming the District Court, that the invoice price would control. He also commented that the burden of proof to establish value was on the libellants and that they had not shown that the importer would in fact have replaced the cargo had it been lost. The action was against the cargo owner alone since the salved vessel, a Danish-flag ship, was not subject to process in the United States.

90. The Shreveport, note 89 *supra*, contains an excellent discussion of the valuation process.

to be liable for part of the award; in such a case their value should be included.[91]

§ 8–9. From a valuation of property the trial judge passes on to an evaluation of what might be called the moral aspects of the salvage service. It is basic that more than a *quantum meruit* is involved; salvors are to be paid a bonus according to the merit of their services. It is for this reason that the value of the salving ship is calculated, so as to determine how much the salvor might have lost if his ship had perished in the danger which threatened the other ship. Other aspects of the service which the court may find worthy of mention are the promptness with which the service was rendered, the time consumed in completing the salvage, the degree of skill or ingenuity required or manifested, the extent of the danger from which the salved property was rescued, the peril which attended the work of the salvors and, in particular, instances, often extraordinary, of courage and heroism on the part of members of the salving crew and their officers. However inexact the art of property valuation may be and however loosely it may be practiced in salvage proceedings, it goes without saying that in passing on the moral worth of a salvage service the trial judge is operating on plastic material which he can shape to suit his own fancy. Having satisfactorily stirred up his ingredients, the judge will announce as his conclusion that the salvage service was of "high order", "medium order" or "low order" and will increase or decrease the award accordingly.

The salvor may suffer loss or damage in effecting the salvage. The salving ship may run aground or on rocks; her engines may be damaged in towing another ship away from danger; a fishing vessel on her way back to port may, by reason of the time spent in the rescue work, find her market gone or the fish spoiled; a vessel on her way to pick up cargo may lose a valuable contract. Both types of loss—the cost of repairing damage suffered by the salving vessel and loss of prospective profits—may be included in the award or, as is more frequently done, stated as an item of recovery in addition to the award.[92] (The reason for stating "expenses" separately is that they

91. See United States v. Cornell Steamboat Co., 202 U.S. 184, 26 S.Ct. 648 (1906) discussed *infra* text at note 122.

92. Some recent damage cases are: Perez v. Barge LBT # 4, 416 F.2d 407, 1969 A.M.C. 1804 (5th Cir. 1969); Seaman v. Tank Barge OC 601, 325 F. Supp. 1206 (opinion), 1972 A.M.C. 2408 (digest only) (S.D.Ala.1971); Tampa Tugs & Towing, Inc. v. M/V Sandanger, 242 F.Supp. 576, 1965 A.M.C. 1771 (S.D. Calif.1965). In Petition of American Oil Co. (United States v. American Oil Co.—The Amoco Virginia), 417 F.2d 164, 1969 A.M.C. 1761 (5th Cir. 1969), certiorari denied 397 U.S. 1036, 90 S. Ct. 1353 (1970) the United States recovered expenses incurred in a fire-fighting operation coordinated by the Coast Guard. The case is discussed in the text following note 68b *supra*. Among the other cases, see The Fisher's Hill (Lago Oil & Transport Co., Ltd. v. United States), 218 F.2d 631, 1955 A.M.C. 697 (2d Cir. 1955) (salvage tug driven aground and lost); The Newcomer (Kell v. Zermatten), 101 F. Supp. 898, 1952 A.M.C. 820 (S.D.Cal. 1952) (hull damage to salvage vessels); The Lloyd Cuarto (Breving v. The Lloyd Cuarto), 84 F.Supp. 33, 1949 A.M.C. 1016 (N.D.Cal.1949) ("expenses and lost earnings"); The Fearless, 76 F.Supp. 956, 1948 A.M.C. 631 (S.D.Cal.1948) (loss of catch of fish by salvor); The Melody (Rustad v. Wuori), 157 F.2d 448, 1946 A.M.C. 1637

are recovered for the benefit of the owner and are not divided between owner and crew.) The recovery of profits is subject to the customary limitations of remoteness and speculativeness. Damage to the salving ship will not be allowed if it was caused by the negligence or the unskillfulness of the salvors, although the courts, in passing on the type of salvage that has to be performed under emergency conditions and without the luxury of leisurely study of the one best way to do the job, will be slow to find against the salvors.

**§ 8–10.** Eventually the trial judge will pull an arbitrary figure out of the air. Since one of the requisites of a salvage claim is success in saving property for the benefit of the owner, the award can never be greater than the value of the salved property and in fact will never be as much (except possibly in the case of derelict and abandoned property for which no claimant appears).[92a] The older case law suggested rules of thumb, but these rules are rarely mentioned today except to state that they are no longer followed. One was the "moiety rule": half the value of the salved property to the salvors. It does not appear that awards ever regularly ran that high. If it ever was the rule, it no longer is; its abandonment is usually explained by the fact that, as steam replaced sail, the value of ships became so great that awards of a moiety would have been absurdly inflated. The reverse of the moiety rule might be said to be in effect today: the award will never be for more than half the value of the property, so that the moiety has become a ceiling instead of a floor. In fact, except where the property saved is of trifling value, the award of anywhere near 50% would be exceptional. Where large values are involved, no recent case awards more than about 20%; there is however no indication that a percentage rule is emerging to replace the moiety rule and each award continues to be a law unto itself.[93] Another of the old rules had to do with derelicts: if the property was derelict when salved the award should be larger. Like the moiety rule the derelict rule is of little surviving force except indirectly:

(9th Cir. 1946); The Odenwald, note 61 *supra*; The Donbass, note 62 *supra*. A still older damage case which is often cited is The Miskianza (Huasteca Petroleum Co. v. United States), 27 F.2d 734, 1928 A.M.C. 1332 (2d Cir. 1928). Norris, note 4 *supra* §§ 210–220 collects cases.

**92a.** In Brady v. S.S. African Queen, 179 F.Supp. 321, 1960 A.M.C. 69 (E.D. Va.1960) the owners and insurers of the African Queen publicly announced that the vessel had been abandoned after a stranding and a failure by professional salvors to refloat her. Brady and his colleagues succeeded, after several months labor, in bringing the stern section of the vessel to safety. They were awarded the entire proceeds of sale ($134,000) less court costs and some outstanding claims. In Medina v. One Nylon Purse Seine, 259 F.Supp. 769 (S.D.Calif.1966) no one appeared to claim a fishing net which had been salvaged at sea and was valued at $15,000. Judge Carter ordered the net sold and made a provisional award of $7,500 to the salvors from the proceeds of sale. If, "upon the expiration of one year and one day" the net was still unclaimed the salvors were to get the balance which would be temporarily deposited in the Registry of the Court.

**93.** Norris, note 4 *supra*, Appendix E, has a tabulation of all American salvage cases which is kept up to date in Cumulative Supplements. The Five Year Digests of American Maritime Cases contain comparable tabulations for each five year period.

there may well be more danger, and consequently more merit in the rescue, when the salved ship is derelict than when it is still manned by its crew.

The problem of inflation comes up in discussion of salvage awards as it does in other types of damage computations. In The Fairisle [94] Judge Coleman, in the course of an excellent opinion, remarked that in reaching an award of $45,000 "we are influenced to a considerable extent by the present depreciated value of the dollar, and by the fact that in considering and applying as precedent, the early decisions it would be appropriate, if given precisely the same circumstances today as are disclosed in those cases, to make a considerable increase in the awards there made." On appeal the owners of the Fairisle argued that since the amount of an award is essentially a fraction of the value of the salved ship, and since changes in the price level affect numerator and denominator alike, the awards in the older cases truly reflect the proper percentage to be awarded today. The Circuit, on the ground that awards were not made on a percentage basis anyhow, held that the trial judge could take account of inflation in fixing the award.[95] It is hard to see what the owners of the Fairisle hoped to gain by their argument. As values increase, the awards, in terms of percentages, usually decrease. Since the older cases dealt with smaller values, the percentage of the awards was higher than in recent cases.[96] The Fourth Circuit seems to have done the owners of salved property a service in rejecting the argument.[96a]

No formula precise enough to be useful can be worked out to indicate how large salvage awards will be in particular cases. The multitudinous precedents, as Judge Cochran commented in The Shreveport, are "useful as indicating the opinion of learned and experienced judges in similar matters and assisting the court in refraining from going to too great an extreme either of generosity or of parsimony." [97] The Shreveport was a tanker which exploded and burned off the Carolina coast. The master and crew abandoned the vessel and were picked up by the Aldecoa which took them to a nearby port. The Mariners Harbor, coming upon the derelict Shreveport

94. (Dean v. Waterman S.S. Corp.), 76 F.Supp. 27, 1948 A.M.C. 794 (D.Md. 1947).

95. Waterman S.S. Corp. v. Dean, 171 F.2d 408, 1949 A.M.C. 1 (4th Cir. 1948) *certiorari denied* 337 U.S. 924, 69 S.Ct. 1168 (1949). In The Lloyd Cuarto (Breving v. The Lloyd Cuarto), 84 F. Supp. 33, 1949 A.M.C. 1016 (N.D.Cal. 1949), Judge Goodman commented that Judge Coleman's holding in The Fairisle seemed to him to be erroneous.

96. The Lamington (Duff v. Merritt), 86 F. 674 (2d Cir. 1898) contains a list of awards made in salvage cases during the 19th century.

96a. The inflation problem does not seem to have been expressly discussed in any salvage case since The Fairisle. After a generation of living with inflation it has, of course, become a truism that damage awards increase as the value of the dollar decreases. See, e. g., Virginian Railway Co. v. Rose, 267 F.2d 312 (4th Cir. 1959) (personal injury) and Locklin v. Day-Glo Color Corp., 429 F.2d 873 (7th Cir. 1970) (anti-trust), both citing, among other authorities, The Fairisle.

97. (Strachan Shipping Co. v. Cities Service Transport Co.), 42 F.2d 524, 534, 1930 A.M.C. 1310, 1322 (E.D.S.C. 1930).

a few hours later, took her in tow, put out the fire and towed and escorted her to Charleston. The value of the Shreveport before the explosion was found to be just under half a million; her value as salved about $150,000. The danger from which the Shreveport had been rescued was very great; the danger to the Mariners Harbor and her crew in boarding the Shreveport, taking her in tow and putting out the fire moderately great; the salvors had acted with skill and energy. Judge Cochran made an award of one third of the salved value of the Shreveport (about $50,000) (which included expenses of about $2000 and an award of $5000 to the Aldecoa and her crew for life salvage). An illustration of a high order salvage award is The Esso Greensboro [98] where the value of the salved ship was stipulated to be $1,000,000. The salvors boarded a burning derelict in mid-ocean, searched for survivors, extinguished the fires, made changes and repairs necessary in order to take her to port and towed her to port, the entire operation consuming about eight days. No claim was made by the owner of the salving ship. In addition to an award of $4,000 for life salvage, Judge Kennedy made awards to the nine officers and thirty-one men on the salving ship which totaled $215,000; the highest individual awards, which went to the master and the chief mate, were for $25,000 each. In recent litigation the only awards which have exceeded the awards in The Esso Greensboro were made in St. Paul Marine Transportation Corp. v. Cerro Sales Corp.[98a] in which one set of salvors received $114,600 (including expenses of $35,374.-51) and another set received $200,000 (including expenses of $15,-000). The two sets of claims were adjudicated in different proceedings and apparently by different judges; at one point the set of salvors who eventually received $200,000 had put forward life salvage claims, which were dismissed.[98b] The salvage was carried out under dangerous conditions (a fire at sea) but the circumstances do not appear to have been unusually dramatic. The salved ship, which was sold for scrap, was valued at $14,000; the salved cargo, however, was stipulated to be worth $1,850,000. Judge Tavares, in making the $200,000 award, briefly explained that it was made "partly to discourage unwarranted speculation." [98c] Apart from such exceptionally profitable ventures and at the other end of the spectrum are cases of low order salvage—not much more than an uneventful tow over placid seas—

**98.** (Petition of Esso Shipping Co.), 122 F.Supp. 133, 1954 A.M.C. 734 (S.D. Tex.1954).

**98a.** (The North America) 332 F.Supp. 233 (D.Hawaii, 1971).

**98b.** For the dismissal of the life salvage claims and an explanation of the peculiar procedural posture which the case assumed, see the discussion in the text at note 111c *infra.*

**98c.** Other high awards in recent litigation are: Brady v. S.S. African Queen, 179 F.Supp. 321, 1960 A.M.C. 69 (E.D.Va.1960) ($134,000, which was the entire proceeds of the salved property, see note 92a supra); Devine v. S/T Ellen (The Salvage Chief), 1969 A.M.C. 1739 (S.D.Calif., 1966) (digest) ($135,000 to professional salvors); Tampa Tugs & Towing, Inc. v. M/V Sandanger, 242 F.Supp. 576, 1965 A.M.C. 1771 (S.D.Calif.1965) ($125,000, expenses incurred by United States Navy, crew salvage claims having been "waived," see note 62a *supra.*

where an award in the amount of double the usual towage rates has been found adequate.[99]

**§ 8–11.** The persons who share in an award are, typically, the owners of the salving ship, her officers and crew. Primitive salvage law allowed nothing to the owner as such, on the ground that the award was made as an inducement to individuals to risk their lives at sea. Owners who had not personally participated in the salvage began to be allowed to share during the nineteenth century, as ship values increased.[100] Since the owner whose valuable ship was employed in a dangerous salvage operation had a great deal to lose, he was admitted to a share of the reward. At first the lion's share was reserved to the crew, with the owner getting a third or a fourth.[101] As values continued to increase the proportion was reversed; today when a salvage service is performed by anything larger than a fishing smack the owner receives more than the crew.

The division of the award will vary according to the circumstances of the case. In high order salvage, where the individual salvors, under dangerous conditions, show skill, resourcefulness and courage, the crew's share will be upped. In low order salvage, which is just enough more than simple towage to qualify at all and where the crew has done little, the owner will get a larger than usual share. Between the two extremes, recent American cases suggest that the ordinary division is two-thirds to the owner, one-third to the crew.[102]

99. Higgins, Inc. v. M/V Tri-State, 99 F.Supp. 694, 1951 A.M.C. 862 (S.D. Fla.1951). However in Mississippi Valley Barge Line v. Indian Towing Co., Inc., 232 F.2d 750, 1956 A.M.C. 757 (5th Cir. 1956) Judge Brown concluded that there was no mandatory rule that a low order salvage award be limited to double towage; a larger award was affirmed.

100. Awards to owners appear early in the American cases: The Mary Ford (McDonough v. Dannery), 3 U.S. (3 Dall.) 149 (1796); The Blaireau (Mason v. The Blaireau), 6 U.S. (2 Cranch) 240 (1804).

101. In The Blaireau, note 100 *supra*, Chief Justice Marshall ordered one-third of the award to be divided between the owners of the salving ship and her cargo. In the Mary Ford, note 100 *supra*, District Judge Lowell gave two-thirds of the award to the owners of the salving ship (and the order was not disturbed on appeal) but the case seems exceptional for its time.

102. See, citing treatise, Nolan v. A. H. Basse Rederiaktieselskab, 267 F.2d 584, 1959 A.M.C. 1362 (3d Cir. 1959); Conolly v. S.S. Karina II, 302 F.Supp. 675, 1969 A.M.C. 319 (E.D.N.Y.1969). In St. Paul Marine Transportation Corp. v. Cerro Sales Corp., 332 F. Supp. 233 (D.Hawaii 1971) an award of $200,000 was split 65% (owners) and 35% (officers and crew). To the same effect are Rauch v. Gulf Refining Co., 129 F.Supp. 843, 1955 A.M.C. 1112 (E.D.La. 1955); Hendry Corp. v. Aircraft Rescue Vessels, 113 F.Supp. 198, 1953 A.M.C. 2115 (E.D.La.1953); Greene v. United States, 106 F.Supp. 682, 1952 A.M.C. 1542 (S.D.N.Y.1952) reversed on other grounds (sub nom. Kimes v. United States), 207 F.2d 60, 1953 A.M.C. 1335 (2d Cir. 1953). If a few salvage arbitrations reported in American Maritime Cases are representative, the arbitrators appear to give a larger proportion of the awards to the owners than do the courts. See The Aristocrates, 1952 A.M.C. 788 (arbitration at San Francisco, 1951) (four-fifths to owner); The Cape Horn, 1949 A.M.C. 2033 (arbitration at New York, 1949) (three-fourths to owner); The Ferdinand R. Hassler, 1949 A.M.C. 1911 (arbitration at Los Angeles, 1949, arbitrator's award filed with the District Court, S.D.Cal.) (three-fourths to owner); The Frej, 1948 A.M.C. 1576 (arbitration at San

According to Kennedy the "ordinary apportionment" in England, since late in the 19th century, has been three-fourths to the owner and one-fourth to the officers and crew.[103]

"Basic" awards to the crew are usually made according to rank or monthly pay; the master and senior officers receive substantially more than ordinary seamen. These awards are made to all crew members of the salving ship, whether or not they personally took part in the rescue work. Additional awards are then frequently made to individuals who played conspicuous roles: to those who boarded a derelict ship, helped to extinguish fires, or navigated her to port. Ingenuity as well as personal bravery may justify an additional award, as in the case of an officer who by noticing that, contrary to the charts, tides were higher at night than during the day, contributed the idea that made it possible to refloat a stranded ship after several daytime attempts had failed.[104]

The crew's right to awards cannot be defeated by settlements between the owners of the salving and salved ships or by arbitrations to which the crew-members have not consented. Under 46 U.S.C.A. § 600 "every stipulation by which any seaman consents . . . to abandon any right which he may have or obtain in the nature of salvage, shall be wholly inoperative." [105] Aided by the statute as well as by the judicial attitude toward releases signed by seamen, the crew members are in a position to insist that the award be made by a court and in view of the generosity with which judicial salvage awards are computed, will usually be well advised to do so.[106]

Francisco, 1948) (three-fourths to owner. No recent salvage arbitrations seem to have been reported. The members of the crew are not bound by arbitration proceedings to which they have not consented, see text at note 105 *infra*. Norris, note 4 *supra* § 282 suggests that in low order salvage an award of three-fourths to the owner is customary with the crew's share increasing as the difficulty of the salvage increases. He cites more cases of a two-thirds—one-third split than of any other apportionment.

103. Kennedy, note 4 *supra* p. 235.

104. The Fairisle (Dean v. Waterman S.S. Corp.), 76 F.Supp. 27, 1948 A.M.C. 794 (D.Md.1948), affirmed 171 F.2d 408, 1949 A.M.C. 1 (4th Cir. 1948) certiorari denied 337 U.S. 924, 69 S.Ct. 1168 (1949) (although it is not entirely clear whether the extra reward was for the contribution of the idea or additional hardship which the officer underwent).

105. 17 Stat. 268 (1872).

106. In Sobonis v. S/T National Defender, 298 F.Supp. 631, 637, 1969 A.M.C. 1219, 1227 (S.D.N.Y.1969), Judge Pollack wrote: "The general rule in this regard is clear: an agreement between the owners of the salved and salving vessels, binding though it may be between them, cannot by itself affect the independent right of the salving crew to claim an award from the vessel they have rescued." Judge Pollack found it unnecessary to decide whether the statute (46 U.S.C.A. § 600) applied to an oral agreement by Greek seamen on a Greek ship in either British or international waters. See also the discussion by Judge Sweigert in Sears v. S.S. American Producer, 1972 A.M.C. 1647 (N.D.Calif.1972). Some of the cases which have held arbitration agreements between the owners of salving and salved vessels not binding on crew members are Barkas v. Cia. Naviera Coronado, S.A., 126 F.Supp. 532, 1955 A.M.C. 1787 (S.D.N.Y.1954) (both salving and salved vessels were Panama-flag ships; arbitration pending in London; Judge McGohey took jurisdiction of crew salvage claims); Dalmas v. Stathatos, 84 F.Supp. 828, 1949 A.M.C. 770 (S.D.N.Y.1949) (salving and salved vessels were Greek-flag ships; the salvage took place in the Pacific Ocean; arbi-

When the salving ship is being operated under charter, the charter-party will usually provide for the division of the owner's share of salvage awards between owner and charterer—a customary provision in time charters is for a fifty-fifty split. In the absence of such a provision, it has been said that salvage is for the owner's account except in the case of bareboat or demise charters,[107] but the issue has been so seldom litigated that it would be overly dogmatic to say that time and voyage charterers can never share.[107a]

The owners of cargo on the salving ship are said to have no right to share in the award, even where the cargo has been damaged as a result of the salvage operation.[108] The exclusion of cargo dates from cases decided at a time when cargo could recover from the carrier any damage caused by deviation to save life or property, so that, to the extent of the carrier's solvency, the cargo was not placed at risk when the carrying ship turned aside from its voyage. As Robinson pointed out in an excellent discussion,[109] the doctrinal base was cut from under such cases by provisions in the Harter Act (later repeated in the Carriage of Goods by Sea Act) [110] under which the carrier is not liable

tration in London; Judge Ryan took jurisdiction of crew salvage claims). In Rauch v. Gulf Refining Co., 129 F. Supp. 843, 1955 A.M.C. 1112 (E.D.La. 1955) crew members were held not bound by an agreement between the owners of salved and salving ships.

107. See The Kaiser Wilhelm der Grosse, 106 F. 963 (S.D.N.Y.1901) (a demise charter case).

107a. In Chemical Carriers, Inc. v. L. Smit & Co.'s Internationale Sleepdienst, 154 F.Supp. 886, 1957 A.M.C. 2462 (S.D.N.Y.1957) a towage agreement provided for litigation of disputes in Rotterdam under Dutch law. An opinion of counsel stated that Dutch law "rewards persons entitled to the exclusive services of a vessel under a demise or time charter for salvage service performed by the chartered vessel [but] does not reward persons entitled to the services of a vessel under voyage charters, towage contracts and other contractual arrangements." Judge Bryan commented that the alleged state of Dutch law was "in contrast to the law in the United States to the effect that a party entitled to the exclusive services of a tug may be entitled to a share in salvage earned by the tug," citing The Arizonan, 144 F. 81 (2d Cir. 1906) and The Johnson Lighterage Co. No. 24, 248 F. 74 (3d Cir. 1918). In Chemical Carriers tugs had interrupted a transatlantic towing operation to go on a contract salvage mission. The owner of the tow sued in the alternative for damages for breach of the towage contract or for a share in the salvage earned by the tugs. Judge Bryan denied a motion to decline jurisdiction. No further proceedings in the case were reported.

In Conolly v. S.S. Karina II, 302 F.Supp. 675, 1969 A.M.C. 319 (E.D.N.Y.1969) a salvage award was made to Captain Conolly who was described as "general agent" of the salving ship which had been chartered. It did not appear that either the owner or the charterer had made a claim. Judge Judd commented that Captain Conolly "may well be accountable to the absentee charterer for part of what he realizes from the salvage operation, since there is authority for the charterer to share in a salvage award [citing Norris, *supra* note 4, § 54]. His award should be sufficient to make allowance for all these factors."

108. Robinson, Admiralty 749 (1939); 1 Norris, The Law of Seamen § 229 (1951); Norris, note 4, *supra* § 55. The Menominee, 300 F. 461 (S.D.N.Y. 1924), affirmed 300 F. 464, 1924 A.M. C. 828 (2d Cir. 1924). It may be noted that in some of the early cases, *e. g.* The Blaireau (Mason v. The Blaireau), 6 U.S. (2 Cranch) 240 (1804), awards were made to cargo on the salving ship.

109. *Loc. cit. supra* note 108.

110. See note 87 *supra*.

for damage to cargo resulting from salvage deviations. Since cargo, if damaged, now has no remedy under the contract of affreightment, it is placed at risk to exactly the same extent as the salving ship. Conceptually, therefore, it has as much right as the owner to share in the award.

The risk of such damage to cargo in ocean carriage is almost always covered by insurance, so that, it may be argued, the risk is not a real one. That argument, however, proves too much, or at least has a double edge. The ship owner carries hull insurance, despite which fact the owner's share has steadily increased over the past seventy-five years. The insurance question may well be relevant, although no case has ever raised it. Perhaps both insured shipowner and insured cargo-owner should be excluded from awards, which would then resume their primitive function as a reward to individuals to encourage rescues at sea. Or perhaps they should both be allowed to share on the ground that both are placed at risk.

There may be more to say in favor of the exclusion of cargo on a practical than on a doctrinal level. In the case of a general ship carrying cargo belonging to hundreds of owners, the business of figuring out the proper share of each owner would introduce into salvage proceedings the complexity of a general average adjustment. In such a case also, the resulting award to each owner would almost always be so small that the allocation would have cost a great deal and benefited no one. To allow cargo, when damaged, to recover in the same way that salving shipowners are given their "expenses" would benefit the insurance carriers at the cost of the other salvage claimants. Finally, the inclusion of cargo should not be allowed to work to the detriment of the individual salvors—the officers and crew members—who have already seen a good share of their reward diverted to the owner. The owner of the salved property is made to pay a reward which, in all conscience, seems high enough and should not be increased to benefit another absentee ownership interest. Cargo awards, if made, should come out of the two-thirds or three-fourths share which presently goes to the owner.

It seems on the whole wiser to ignore the doctrinal inconsistency in excluding cargo and to adhere to the traditional rule. That state of things is apparently acceptable to all parties concerned; at any rate no reported case has dealt with a salvage claim by cargo since Robinson's ingenious discussion made the Harter Act and Cogsa argument for reversing the rule available to anyone who can read.

It occasionally happens that some of those entitled to share in an award forebear to press their claims. The owners of the salving ship, for example, may have rendered the services under contract or may have subsequently come to an agreement with the owners of the salved property or, as in the case of the United States Navy, may simply elect not to make a claim.[110a] The owners cannot, of course, by agreements

**110a.** See Sobonis v. S/T National Defender, 298 F.Supp. 631, 1969 A.M.C. 1219 (S.D.N.Y.1969) (digested note 51e *supra*) where salvage awards were

between themselves, preclude the prosecution of salvage claims by officers and crew.[110b] It appears to be settled law that the forebearance of some of the salvors to press their claims, whatever the reason for their forebearance, does not result in a windfall recovery for those who do claim. In computing the award the District Judge will give the claimants what they would have received if all claims had been made. As Judge Butzner put it in the Dize case: "Failure or inability of salvors to prosecute a claim inures to the benefit of the salvaged vessel and not to the claiming salvors." [110c]

**§ 8–12.** By statute "Salvors of human life, who have taken part in the services rendered on the occasion of the accident giving rise to salvage, are entitled to a fair share of the remuneration awarded to the salvors of the vessel, her cargo, and accessories." [111] Although the life salvage statute has been in force since 1912, it has occasioned little litigation and few awards have been made under it.

The neglect in which the statute has mouldered is largely explained by its own limitations. In the first place, it does not provide for awards in the case of "pure" life salvage—unaccompanied, that is to say, by property salvage. Secondly, in cases where the same set of salvors has saved both life and property the statute is unnecessary. The trial court considers moral as well as economic matters in deciding on the award; therefore, the statute is not needed to justify an extra award for meritorious work in saving life any more than it is needed to justify a decrease in the award, or a forfeiture, on the ground of misconduct if salvors should pay no heed to survivors in their quest for salvageable property. The proposition that the statute is unnecessary where salvors save both life and property is neatly illustrated by two cases, which appear to be the only attempts in recent litigation to press life salvage claims. In both cases the life salvage

made to the crew of a vessel which had been chartered by the owners of a stranded vessel for the express purpose of performing the services which led to the salvage claims. Other cases of the same type are Sears v. S.S. American Producer, 1972 A.M.C. 1647 (N.D.Calif.1972); Dize v. Steel Barge Beverly, 247 F.Supp. 968, 1965 A.M.C. 1886 (E.D.Va.1965). Nolan v. A. H. Basse Rederiaktieselskab, 267 F.2d 584, 1959 A.M.C. 1362 (3d Cir. 1959) illustrates the situation in which Army and Navy crews were allowed to make salvage claims while the United States made none. In Tampa Tugs and Towing, Inc. v. M/V Sandanger, 242 F.Supp. 576, 1965 A.M.C. 1771 (S.D.Calif.1965) the situation was reversed: the Navy claimed salvage (at least for its expenses) but the claims of the crews had been "waived." The theory and practice of salvage recoveries by the United States and its personnel is discussed in § 8–5 *supra*.

**110b.** See text at note 105 *supra* and the cases cited in note 106.

**110c.** Dize v. Steel Barge Beverly, 247 F.Supp. 968, 1965 A.M.C. 1886 (E.D. Va.1965). Judge Butzner proceeded to work out what the award would have been if all the salvors had claimed. In the Nolan case, note 110a *supra*, Judge Biggs commented: "The fact that the owner of the two salving vessels, the United States, has waived its right to claim salvage, cannot and should not benefit the crew" (267 F.2d at p. 591, citing authorities).

**111.** 37 Stat. 242 (1912), 46 U.S.C.A. § 729. Jarett, The Life Salvor Problem in Admiralty, 63 Yale L.J. 779 (1954) discusses the life salvage statute and makes interesting suggestions for a system under which life salvors would be more adequately rewarded.

claims were denied but the salvors were rewarded for their contribution to property salvage. A statement of facts may suggest why the salvors were motivated to put the life salvage claims forward.

In In re Yamashita-Shinnihon Kisen [111a] the Suwaharu Maru and the Mandoil were both disabled, following a collision. The Transoneida, responding to a distress signal, interrupted its voyage and proceeded to the scene where it remained for approximately eight hours. During this period the principal service which the Transoneida performed was to give temporary asylum to the crew of the Suwaharu Maru, who were later transferred to a Coast Guard cutter. The Transoneida then resumed its voyage but, five hours later, on instructions from its owners, reversed course and returned to the collision scene where it sent a boarding party to the Mandoil and attempted unsuccessfully to take the Mandoil in tow. A salvage tug, which had been commissioned by the owners of the Mandoil, presently arrived and towed the Mandoil to port. In the salvage action it was alleged that the Transoneida, or its owners, had acted in bad faith in that the only reason for the Transoneida's return to the scene was to make an improper attempt to cut itself in on a salvage operation which it knew, or ought to have known, was already well in hand. Judge Beeks observed that there were indeed "circumstances from which a suspicion of improper motivation on the part of [the owners] might be inferred" but concluded that the charge had not been established by a fair preponderance of the evidence and declined to make a finding of bad faith or misconduct. Finding that the Transoneida had contributed to the salvage of both vessels and their cargos, he made awards to the owners and crew of $25,000. Nothing was awarded for the life salvage claims, on the authority of the Eastland.[111b] Presumably the life salvage claims were put forward as a counter to the allegations of misconduct on the Transoneida's return to the scene or in an attempt to increase the Transoneida's total award.

In St. Paul Marine Transportation Corp. v. Cerro Sales Corp.[111c] the crew of the North America was forced to abandon the vessel because of fire. The St. Paul, in response to a Coast Guard S.O.S., proceeded to the scene, rescued the crew and put a boarding party on the North America where they made efforts to control the fire. Attempts to take the North America in tow were unsuccessful. The St. Paul then took the crew of the North America to Honolulu. Eight days later the tug Malie found the North America, abandoned and derelict, and brought her to port. The owners and crew of the Malie immediately filed salvage claims but, for some reason, the owners and crew of the St. Paul did not seek to intervene until eight months later when the Malie action was ready to go to trial. The court refused to permit the belated intervention but agreed to hear the St.

**111a.** (The Suwaharu Maru and The Mandoil II), 305 F.Supp. 796, 1969 A.M.C. 2102 (D.Oregon 1969).

**111b.** Discussed in the text *infra* at note 112.

**111c.** (The North America), 313 F.Supp. 377, 1970 A.M.C. 1742 (D.Hawaii, 1970).

Paul claims separately in a later proceeding. After awards to the Malie and her crew, counsel for the St. Paul filed an action asking for a property salvage award or "in the alternative" for a life salvage award out of the awards to the Malie. The court took the case in two bites. In the first bite Judge Pence ruled against the life salvage claim, relying on the Eastland [111d] and on the Shreveport [111e] as well as on the Yamashita-Shinnihon Kisen case which has just been discussed. In the second bite [111f] Judge Tavares concluded that the St. Paul had contributed, through the efforts of its boarding party to control the fire, to the eventual salvage of the North America and its cargo and made astonishingly large awards.[111g] Here, as in the Yamashita case, the life salvage claims seem to have been put forward as a tactical counter in a confused procedural situation. In both cases the courts, refusing to be distracted, proceeded to the business of evaluating the property salvaged. It is of course possible that the "property salvage" award to the St. Paul and its crew reflected their meritorious work in saving life.

The only case in which the statute would justify an otherwise unavailable award is the unusual one where one set of salvors saves the property and an independent set saves life without participating in the property salvage. Even in this situation the statute limits its applicability to cases where the life salvors have performed their rescue work "on the occasion of the accident giving rise to salvage." This provision came into discussion in The Eastland.[112] A river excursion boat, with many passengers aboard, capsized and sank. Persons who later claimed as life salvors aided in rescuing the passengers but did nothing in connection with the sunken excursion boat, which was subsequently raised by a wrecking company working under contract. The life salvors were denied an award on the ground that the "occasion of the accident" language meant that the life salvage and the property salvage had to be performed, not only in connection with the same accident, but at about the same time. As a matter of statutory construction, the decision is entirely sound: the statute did not authorize an award for pure life salvage and, despite the subsequent refloating of the excursion boat, that was the only type of salvage which the rescue workers thought they were performing.[113] The same statutory provision was tested on a quite different set of facts in The Shreveport.[114] In that case the Aldecoa came upon the Shreveport off the Carolina coast just as the crew, after an explosion and on the

111d. Discussed in the text *infra* at note 112.

111e. Discussed in the text *infra* at note 114.

111f. 332 F.Supp. 233 (D.Hawaii 1971).

111g. On the awards to the two sets of salvors, see text at note 98a *supra*.

112. (In re St. Joseph-Chicago S. S. Co.), 262 F. 535 (N.D.Ill.1919).

113. See also The Admiral Evans, 286 F. 442, 1923 A.M.C. 327 (W.D.Wash. 1923); The Annie Lord, 251 F. 157 (D.Mass.1917).

114. (Strachan Shipping Co. v. Cities Service Refining Transport Co.), 42 F.2d 524, 1930 A.M.C. 1310 (E.D.S.C. 1930).

master's orders, had abandoned the ship. The Aldecoa picked up the survivors from the lifeboats and spent some time cruising around looking for a missing crewmember. Some of the survivors were in need of immediate medical attention and the Aldecoa carried the injured men to the nearest port. After discharging them it continued on its voyage and did not return to see if anything could be done to salvage the now derelict Shreveport. It was argued that the Aldecoa was too small a ship to have been of any assistance in salvaging the Shreveport and there was of course no way of proving whether she would have made the attempt if she had not taken the injured men to port. There was apparently no danger, either to the Aldecoa or her crew, in picking up the survivors and in all she lost only a few hours of time. Later in the same day the Mariners Harbor came upon the Shreveport, took her in tow, put out the fires and towed her to port. Judge Cochran held that the Aldecoa and the Mariners Harbor had both rendered services "on the occasion of the accident giving rise to the salvage" and made a small award to the life salvors. He based that part of his holding on the thought that the Aldecoa had "foregone an opportunity" to engage in the profitable work of property salvage. Presumably if there had been a clear showing that the Aldecoa would not under any circumstances have attempted the salvage of the Shreveport he would have denied the life salvage award. Judge Cochran's "foregone opportunity" gloss of the statute is, like the Eastland holding, a reasonable construction. The life salvors who are to be rewarded are those who, if they had not saved life, could have become property salvors.

Life salvors are entitled "to a fair share of the remuneration awarded to the [property] salvors." This means that their share must come out of the award made against the property, and that they have no statutory (or other) cause of action against the persons they have saved from death and injury. It might be argued by the owner of the salved property, who may have received no economic benefit from the saving of lives, that he should not be made to pay a premium and that the award should be calculated as if no life salvage had occurred, with the life salvors being entitled to their "fair share." That result would, in a sense, make the property salvors bear the cost of the life salvage, which may be thought to be quite as illogical as making the owner of the property bear it. If it is reasonable for a court to make a larger award to salvors who have saved both life and property than to salvors who have saved property alone, it seems equally reasonable to make the larger award when there are independent sets of life and property salvors.

If the few life salvage awards which have been made are enough to support a generalization, it can be said that it is still far more profitable to save property than to save lives. In The Shreveport,[115] out of a total award (including expenses) of just under $50,000, the life salvors received $5,000, which was divided between owner and

115. Note 114 *supra*.

crew with the owners getting four-fifths. In The Esso Greensboro [116] the disproportion was even more startling: $215,000 to the property salvors (officers and crew only, no claim by owner) against $4,000 equally divided between two sets of life salvors (also officers and crews only, no claim by owner). It should be emphasized that in both The Shreveport and The Greensboro the life salvage was accomplished without danger or difficulty while the property salvage was both dangerous and difficult. Life salvors who shared the perils and labors of the adventure would undoubtedly receive a larger "fair share" than the slightly less than 2% (Greensboro) or the slightly more than 10% (Shreveport) awarded in the cases cited.

## Liability for Salvage Award

**§ 8–13.** Any interest benefited by the salvage is liable for the fraction of an award which the value of that interest bears to the total value of the property salved. The usual contributory values are ship, freight and cargo: thus if ship and freight (taken as a unity) are worth $1,000,000 and cargo another $1,000,000, each will be liable for 50% of the award.

Usually the owner of the salved ship settles with the salvors in full and then requires cargo-owners to reimburse him for their proportionate share. As between the shipowner and the cargo-owner salvage is a general average expense; the shipowner, who has a lien against cargo for such expenses, is in a position to protect himself by holding the cargo, or requiring that a bond be posted for its release. The ratable contributions of ship, freight and cargo will be worked out in a general average adjustment.[116a]

According to Kennedy, the shipowner, despite the usual practice under which he pays and then seeks reimbursement, is liable only for his share of the award unless the salvage has been performed under a contract by which the shipowner is bound to pay the salvors in full.[117] In support of the proposition that the owner acts as a volunteer in initially paying cargo's share Kennedy cites three cases, the most

116. (Petition of Esso Shipping Co.), 122 F.Supp. 133, 1954 A.M.C. 734 (S.D.Tex.1954).

116a. In re Pacific Far East Line, Inc. (The Guam Bear—The Esso Seattle), 314 F.Supp. 1339, 1970 A.M.C. 1592 (N.D.Calif.1970). The Guam Bear was wrecked in a both-to-blame collision. The owners notified cargo that the ship was a total loss but that they had directed a salvage expert to proceed with cargo salvage "the cost of which would be initially advanced by [the owners] but would ultimately be payable in general average by Cargo interests in proportion to the value saved." Judge Beeks concluded that, under the amended Jason clause in the bills of lading under which privately owned cargo was being carried, the owners were "entitled to recover from such . . . cargo as was saved its properly adjusted proportionate share of all salvage and special charges properly incurred in getting the vessel from point of collision to the shore and in discharging cargos therefrom . . ." (314 F.Supp. at p. 1348). Since the bills of lading contained the customary "Freight-Earned" clause, the cargo owners also had to pay the full freight. (The Guam Bear had also carried cargo belonging to the United States which moved under a Government contract form which did not contain the "freight-earned" clause.)

117. Kennedy, note 4 *supra* p. 273.

recent in date having been decided in 1885. There is little discussion of the point in the American treatises and no modern case law authority.[118] A practice, voluntary in its origins, may become so well established that it is transformed into a legal duty. In view of the ease with which the shipowner may protect himself under his general average lien and the obvious convenience to all parties in his doing so, it would not be unreasonable to hold him liable to the salvors for the full award, a liability which he is usually willing to assume. If the salvors do not recover the full award from the shipowners, they may proceed directly against cargo for its ratable share of the award.[118a]

Former Admiralty Rule 18 provided that "[i]n all suits for salvage, the suit may be in rem against the property saved, or the proceeds thereof, and/or in personam against any party liable for the

118. Robinson, Admiralty 736–737 (1939) is in general agreement with Kennedy. One of the early leading cases, The Emblem, 8 Fed.Cas. 613, Case No. 4,434 (D.Me.1840), is the principal authority. The salvors, however, have a lien on the salved property and a qualified right to retain possession of it (at least if it is derelict or abandoned) until arrangements for payment have been made. Norris, note 4 *supra* § 207, comments that "The few American cases on this subject . . . are indecisive" and goes on to suggest that "the better rule would be one permitting the salvor to look to the vessel for his reward where the services have been simultaneously rendered to the vessel and cargo."

118a. In Nolan v. A.H. Basse Rederiaktieselskab, 267 F.2d 584, 1959 A.M.C. 1362 (3d Cir. 1959) the action was against cargo alone since the salved vessel was not subject to process in the United States. No attempt was made to determine what proportion of the award the vessel would have been liable for, but Judge Biggs commented that: "the awards, in all probability, would have been substantially higher if service of process could have been obtained against the ship. Where the salvage is entire, the owner of the cargo is not jointly liable for the entire salvage effort." (267 F.2d at p. 591.)

In In re Yamashita-Shinnihon Kisen (The Suwaharu Maru and the Mandoil II), 305 F.Supp. 796, 1969 A.M.C. 2102 (D.Oregon 1969) Judge Beeks stated the awards against ship and cargo separately but did not discuss the question of joint or several liability.

In St. Paul Marine Transportation Corp. v. Cerro Sales Corp., 332 F.Supp. 233 (D.Hawaii 1971) awards of over $300,000 were evidently assessed almost entirely against cargo (which had a stipulated value of $1,850,000); the salved ship, which had been sold for scrap, was valued at $14,000. The awards in The St. Paul case are discussed in the text at note 98a *supra*.

In Complaint and Petition of International Marine Development Corp., 451 F.2d 763, 1973 A.M.C. 1071 (5th Cir. 1971) it appeared that The Hulda became a constructive total loss after having been driven on the beach and stranded when Hurricane Camille hit the Gulf Coast in August, 1969. The owners of The Hulda were held entitled to exoneration from liability in proceedings under the Limitation of Liability Act. (See 328 F.Supp. 1316, 1972 A.M.C. 514 (S.D.Miss.1971)). Following the loss of The Hulda the owners of cargo incurred expenses under a contract salvage agreement for off-loading the cargo from the wreck and for transshipment. Held, that cargo could not recover the cost of salvage from the shipowner. Judge Dyer commented: "While it may be argued that the cargo was in peril and that the action the cargo owners took was necessary and was not contractually required, it does not follow that [the shipowner] is obligated for salvaging expense. The liabilities of ship and cargo to the salvor are several. 'If the service is rendered to cargo alone . . . then cargo solely must make good the award' [citing Norris, note 4 *supra* p. 331]. (451 F.2d at p. 766.)

salvage service." The currently applicable provision is Supplemental Rule C of the Federal Rules of Civil Procedure which provides:

> "An action in rem may be brought:
>
> (a) To enforce any maritime lien;
>
> (b) Whenever a statute of the United States provides for a maritime action in rem or a proceeding analogous thereto.
>
> "Except as otherwise provided by law a party who may proceed in rem may also, or in the alternative, proceed in personam against any person who may be liable. . . ."

No one has ever doubted that salvors are entitled to a maritime lien against the salved property—indeed a lien entitled to a high priority—[118b] so that the switch from Rule 18 to Supplemental Rule C leaves the salvor's alternative remedies unaffected: he may proceed *in rem* and/or *in personam* against both ships and cargo.[119] Rule 18 provided that the salvor's action lay "against any person liable for the salvage service," a phrase which has no analogue in Supplemental Rule C. The deletion seems to be of no significance: perhaps the draftsmen of the new Rule deleted it as a superfluous truism, since it is obvious that a salvage action would never lie against people who were not liable for the salvage. It should be noted, however, that an owner who abandons his property instead of claiming it has been held not liable to the salvor and thus not subject to an *in personam* suit.[120] In such a case the salvor will in all probability get the entire proceeds of the salved property [120a] and there is no need or reason to give him the right to pursue a former owner who has disclaimed any interest in the property. The verbal discrepancies between former Rule 18 and Supplemental Rule C should not be read to cast any doubt on the sensible decision in The Batory.

**§ 8–14.** "It is well settled," Judge Augustus Hand wrote in The G.L. 40 "that a salvor's remedy *in personam* is not confined to the legal ownership of the property, but extends to one who has a

118b. On the relative priority of the salvage lien, see Chapter IX, § 9–61.

119. At one time the Admiralty Rule (then Rule 19) provided that "the suit may be *in rem* . . . or *in personam*" and under that wording it was held that the ship could not be libeled *in rem* and the cargo owners *in personam* in the same action, The Sabine, 101 U.S. 384 (1879). The joinder was held permissible under the wording of Rule 18. The G.L. 40 (Cowles Towing Co., Inc. v. Grain Transit Corp.) 66 F.2d 764, 1933 A.M.C. 1439 (2d Cir. 1933). In the Suwaharu Maru, note 118a *supra*, the action was brought against the owners of the salved ships as well as against their cargos, the cargo libels being *in personam*. For no discernible reason the cargo owners moved to dismiss the libels against them on the ground that the salvor's only remedy against cargo is *in rem*. Judge Beeks naturally denied the motion, citing as his principal authority the Cornell case which is discussed in the text at note 122 *infra*.

120. Lambros Seaplane Base v. The Batory, 215 F.2d 228, 1954 A.M.C. 1789 (2d Cir. 1954).

120a. See the cases cited in note 92a *supra*.

direct pecuniary interest in its preservation." [121] The holding in The G.L. 40 was that an insurance carrier, at whose request salvage services had been performed, could be brought in by the owner as a third-party defendant in the salvage litigation and that the decree fixing the award should run both against the ship (which had been libeled *in rem*), and, secondarily, against the insurer. Judge Hand's statement that anyone "who has a direct pecuniary interest" in the property salved may be held liable to the salvors *in personam* ran far beyond the facts of his case or those in the other cases which he cited in support. If the statement is taken literally, it would have been irrelevant that the salvage to the G.L. 40 had been performed at the insurer's request; any insurer has a "direct pecuniary interest" in preserving property which it has insured and thereby decreasing its liability. The balance of the G.L. 40 opinion, however, treats the fact that the insurers had dealt directly with the salvors as decidedly relevant, so that the general statement retreats to the rank of unsupported and perhaps unjustified dictum.

The leading American case on the *in personam* liability for salvage awards of persons other than the owners of the property is United States v. Cornell Steamboat Co.[122] The salvors saved 1883 bags of sugar from destruction by fire. Customs duties had been paid on the sugar at the time it was salved, but (it was assumed) the payment would have been refunded if the sugar had been destroyed. Counsel, with remarkable ingenuity, successfully brought suit against the United States on the theory that by saving the sugar the salvors had benefited the government in the amount of the duties that would, but for the salvage, have been refunded.

The facts of the Cornell case are not likely to be duplicated and it may be that the case stands merely for the proposition that courts occasionally reward counsel who are able to fashion arguments so fresh and so novel as to tickle the judicial palate. Insurers, both of hull and of cargo, seem to be in the position of the United States in the Cornell case; by the salvage they are saved from having to pay out money to the owners of the salved property. Salvors have almost never sought to proceed against an insurer, and if the holding (as distinguished from the dictum) in The G.L. 40 is sound they would not succeed in such an action unless the insurers had, by dealings with the salvors, rendered themselves directly liable.[123] An action against

121. (Cowles Towing Co., Inc. v. Grain Transit Corp.) 66 F.2d 764, 766, 1933 A.M.C. 1439, 1441 (2d Cir. 1933).

122. 202 U.S. 184, 26 S.Ct. 648 (1906).

123. A dictum of Justice Clifford in The Sabine, 101 U.S. 384, 389–390 (1879) suggests that insurers would be liable *in personam* only if they had requested the salvage services. Star Seafood Co. v. Gulf & Atlantic Shrimp Co., 1956 A.M.C. 1694 (S.D.Fla.1956) may have been the first reported case in which salvors proceeded directly against an insurer. The libel was dismissed on the ground that the action did not lie against a Canadian insurer under a Florida statute which provided for local service of process on foreign insurance companies in proceedings brought by "the Assured or any beneficiary" of a policy. The salvors, said Judge Barker, were not "beneficiaries". In Devine v. F/V Hornet, 1969 A.M.C. 640 (D.Alaska,

a mortgagee (on the ground that the salvage had preserved his security) is even more fanciful than an action against an insurer. Rooted in unreality would be actions against a seller who had shipped goods under a contract containing a "No arrival, no sale" term (and thus except for the salvage would have lost his profits) [123a] or against a buyer who, except for the salvage, would have lost a profitable resale. None of these cases has been litigated and none is likely to be unless counsel, inspired by the lesson of the Cornell case, decide to try their hand at making some new law.[123b]

The one type of non-ownership interest which might occasionally be pursued *in personam* is that of the charterer—for example, a time charterer whose enjoyment of a valuable charter was preserved by the salvage.[124]

## Salvage Under Contract

**§ 8–15.** Two quite different types of contract salvage agreements must be distinguished. There is first the agreement entered into by the master of a ship in danger, under the stress of circumstance. Secondly, there is the agreement between the owners and a professional salvage outfit after the immediate danger has passed, to raise or refloat a sunken or stranded ship or to salvage its cargo. Both types of agreements are recognized and enforceable, but they receive notably different judicial treatment.

1967) it was held that Devine was entitled to a salvage award of $7,500 against the Hornet and its owner, Horn, and that Horn could recover over from his hull insurer, the Home Insurance Co. The opinion is unsatisfactory in that it neither cites authority nor sets out the relevant clauses of the insurance policy. Finding of Fact XXVIII was: "That the respondent Home Insurance Company was not justified in refusing to pay the salvage claim of libellant, or defend this action, and its unjustified refusal caused Horn to incur additional expense."

123a. On the meaning of the "No arrival—no sale" term, see Chapter III, § 3–7 note 56.

123b. In Brown v. Margrande Compania Naviera (The Neapolis), 281 F.Supp. 1004, 1968 A.M.C. 1565 (E.D.Va.1968) it appeared that the salved ship was under time charter to Texas Panama Co. and that the salved cargo was owned by Texas Export Co. Texaco, Inc. owned the stock of both the Panama Co. and the Export Co. and there were interlocking directorates between parent and subsidiaries. The salvors sought to join Texaco, Inc. as a defendant. The court declined to pierce the corporate veil and granted Texaco's motion to dismiss the libel. In his opinion Judge Kellam relied on the "corporate entity" cases and did not discuss the maritime law precedents.

124. In a leading English case, The Cargo ex Port Victor, [1901] P. 43, time charterers were held liable for salvage of cargo for whose loss they would have been responsible to its owners. Another English case which is often cited is Five Steel Barges, [1890] 15 P.D. 142: the barges were under construction at the time of the salvage; the shipbuilder was held liable for salvage on the theory that, except for the salvage, he would have been unable to deliver the barges under his contract and would have been liable to refund payments already made to him. In The Cardy (Lauro v. Pennsylvania R. Co.), 64 F.Supp. 902, 1946 A.M.C. 125 (E.D.N.Y.1945), in dismissing a libel, Judge Kennedy assumed that a charterer could not be held personally liable for salvage "except upon the basis of special circumstances: for instance, because he requested the salvage services".

The *in extremis* agreement will be enforced according to its terms only if the judge finds it to have been fairly negotiated. If the salvor refused assistance unless the master of the distressed ship consented to an extortionate bargain, not only will the agreement be set aside but the judge will reduce the award, or forfeit it entirely, according to the degree of the salvor's misconduct.[125] The unfairness of the agreement is usually found in the salvor's greedy overreaching but may run in the other direction. A canny master in requesting assistance may conceal aspects of the danger or of the time, labor and expense which the salvor will have to put out. Where salvors have been so entrapped, they will not be bound by the parsimonious agreement.[126]

Even if the *in extremis* agreement, being a fair one, is held to be binding on the parties to it, others who may be entitled to a share of the award, or liable for a part, will not necessarily be concluded by it. If the masters of the ships involved have acted within the scope of their authority, the agreement will bind the owners. The officers and crew of the salving ship (except for the master himself) remain free to urge their claims to a more liberal reward.[126a] Whether cargo is bound by a salvage agreement entered into by the master or owner of the salved ship is an issue which has seldom been litigated either in England or in this country. The English rule is said to be that "Neither the owners of the ship nor their master have the authority to bind the goods, or the owners of the goods, by

125. A good case of this type, where the agreement was set aside and a small award made, is Higgins, Inc. v. M/V Tri-State, 99 F.Supp. 694, 1951 A.M.C. 862 (S.D.Fla.1951). Judge Whitehurst's opinion collects the older cases. Magnolia Petroleum Co. v. National Oil Transport Co., 281 F. 336 (D.Tex.1922) is often cited as a leading case.

126. Kennedy, note 4 *supra* at p. 305 *et seq.*, collects the English cases, which are all of fairly ancient vintage. The only American case of this type cited by Norris, note 4 *supra* § 166, is The Clandeboye, 70 F. 631 (4th Cir. 1895) in which a Captain Lomm offered the services of his tug to the Clandeboye without disclosing the fact (which he knew) that the Clandeboye's owners had already made other arrangements for the salvage. The court set aside the agreement which Captain Lomm had tricked the master of the Clandeboye into accepting. As in other areas of the admiralty a certain amount of mutual deception between salvor and salvee is accepted as normal, and indeed praiseworthy, behavior. In The Henry (1851, 15 Jur. 183) the master of the ship in peril had not only failed to disclose that he was carrying a valuable cargo but had affirmatively misrepresented it as being of trifling value. The celebrated Dr. Lushington refused to set the salvage agreement aside. Kennedy, *loc cit.*, suggests that in Dr. Lushington's time the value of the salved property was given much less weight in determining the amount of salvage awards than later came to be the case.

The disappearance of the salvor entrapment cases from both the English and the American reports may reflect the worldwide practice of leaving salvage awards to be determined by arbitration in London under the Lloyds Form of Salvage Agreement, discussed in the text at note 130a *infra*. A considerable number of salvage awards continue to be judicially determined in this country. It may be that twentieth century salvors, both amateur and professional, who are in a position to press their claims in American courts, have learned that they are better advised to trust to judicial generosity after the event than to make their own bargains.

126a. See text at note 105 *supra* and cases cited in note 106.

any contract." [126b] In American Metal Co., Ltd. v. M/V Belleville [126c] the master of the Belleville, which had been stranded off the coast of Rhode Island, notified his Norwegian owners and their New York agents of the stranding. Thirty-six hours later, pursuant to their instructions, he signed a Lloyd's Form Salvage Agreement which provided for arbitration in London. Some of the cargo owners, who did not take part in the London arbitration, claimed that they were not bound by the agreement. Judge Metzner agreed:

> "In case of emergencies the master has authority to bind cargo under the concept of agent by necessity. *Alert*, 56 F. 721 (S.D.N.Y.1893). However, the agency does not arise if the master acted pursuant to superior authority, see Gillespie vs. Burns (1946), 79 Lloyds List Rep. 393 (N.S.W.) or if he had the opportunity to communicate with the cargo owner before taking action. [Citing Carver, Carriage of Goods by Lee (10th ed. 1957) § 580.]"

(Judge Metzner's citations sufficiently illustrate the dearth of authority.) Since there had been ample time to get in touch with the cargo-owners, they were not bound by the agreement.[126d]

It is usually assumed that, in the absence of a contract fixing the amount of the salvage claim, the contributory interests—typically the ship (including freight) and cargo—are liable only for their pro rata shares of the award.[126e] Presumably if the salved vessel, through her master or owners, enters into a binding contract for salvage for a fixed amount, the vessel and her owners become liable to the salvors for the entire contract amount, whether or not cargo is also bound by the agreement. That is confidently stated to be the English rule; [126f] American authority is scanty or nonexistent.[127]

**126b.** Kennedy, note 4 *supra* at p. 329, citing Lord Blackburn in Anderson v. Ocean Steamship Co., (1884) 10 App. Cas. 107, 117. Kennedy also cites The Leon Blum [1915] P. 290, 296.

**126c.** 284 F.Supp. 1002, 1970 A.M.C. 633 (S.D.N.Y.1968).

**126d.** The cargo owners in The Belleville, however, succeeded in snatching defeat out of the jaws of victory. Although they had not participated in the London arbitration, they unwisely paid their share of the award, which they were trying to recover in the New York litigation. Judge Metzner concluded that the payments, although made "under protest," had been voluntary payments which, under standard contract doctrine, could not be recovered back. Counsel for the cargo owner tried to dress the case up with allegations of negligence against the salvors, which Judge Metzner found barely worth discussion. A far-fetched claim of deviation against the Belleville also met short shrift.

**126e.** See discussion § 8–13 *supra*.

**126f.** Kennedy, note 4 *supra* at p. 325 *et seq.*, relying on The Prinz Heinrich, (1888) 13 P.D. 31.

**127.** In The Alert, 56 F. 721 (S.D.N.Y. 1893) Judge Addison Brown discussed the authority of agents of the shipowners to bind the ship to a salvage contract. He held that, on the facts of his case, both cargo and the ship were bound. Norris, *supra* note 4, who favors a rule which would permit the salvor to recover his entire claim from the ship or its owners in the first instance (see note 118 *supra*) does not, in that connection, distinguish between voluntary salvage and contract salvage.

Salvage agreements entered into with professional salvors, after the emergency has passed, with leisure to assess the situation and to communicate with all parties concerned, are naturally much less subject to judicial reformation than *in extremis* agreements. Furthermore, the officers and crew of a professional salvage tug or wrecking ship, who are doing the work they were hired to do, are not in the same position as their counterparts on ships which fortuitously engage in salvage. They receive their agreed wages and may not after each refloating or raising run to a court to ask for more.[128]

A basic principle of salvage law is, and always has been, that the salvor is rewarded only if, and to the extent that, he has been successful in saving property.[129] That aspect of doctrine may explain why most professional contract salvage is, and long has been, carried out under so-called "no cure—no pay" arrangements. It is entirely possible for a shipowner to agree to pay for salvage services to ship or cargo whether or not they are successful, although the metaphysical argument might be made that payment for unsuccessful services would not be for salvage and that a contract calling for such payments would not be within the jurisdiction of the admiralty.[129a] Most commercial enterprises like to be paid for their time, trouble and expenses. Professional maritime salvors apparently do not, possibly because they like to think of themselves as maritime salvors first and commercial enterprisers second.[129b] At all events the "no cure—no pay" principle appears to be universally accepted.

**128.** No doubt the proposition stated in the text is still the general rule. However, in Vernicos Shipping Co. v. United States, 349 F.2d 465, 1965 A.M.C. 1673 (2d Cir. 1965), Judge Friendly concluded that there was no absolute bar to such claims and made modest awards to the crews (as well as an award to the owner) of salvage tugs which had rendered assistance to United States naval vessels in Greek waters. The salvage in the Vernicos case was voluntary, not contract, salvage. The case is discussed in the text following note 51d *supra*. See also Sobonis v. S/T National Defender, 298 F.Supp. 631, 1969 A.M.C. 1219 (S.D.N.Y.1969), digested in note 51e *supra*.

**129.** See § 8–2 *supra*.

**129a.** The point was raised in Admiralty Commissioners v. Valverda (owners), [1938] A.C. 173 (House of Lords), discussed in Kennedy, note 4 *supra* at p. 101 *et seq.* It was held that a provision in the Admiralty Standard Form of Towage Agreement then in use under which the Admiralty was to be reimbursed for its expenses even though "the services [were] not successful or beneficial" did not prevent the Admiralty's claim from being considered as a salvage claim.

**129b.** Rainbow Line, Inc. v. M/V Tequila, 341 F.Supp. 459, 1972 A.M.C. 1540 (S.D.N.Y.1972), affirmed without discussion of this point, 480 F.2d 1024, 1973 A.M.C. 1431 (2d Cir. 1973), introduced a professional salvor who was indeed concerned about payment. The Tequila (then named the Linglee) ran aground off the coast of Honduras. Her owners negotiated with Murphy for the services of his salvage tug Curb in refloating her. It appeared that the vessel was uninsured and that the owners may have been in some financial difficulty. The salvage contract with Murphy provided that he was to be paid $3,600 a day from the time the Curb was dispatched on the salvage mission plus $5,000 a day for the time the Curb spent at the site of the stranding. To secure Murphy's claim the owners of the Tequila agreed to pledge 15,000 shares of their corporate stock with him. (The salvage operation was successful; Judge Metzner's opinion in the District Court does not mention whether some or all of the agreed compensation was to have become payable in the event of non-success.)

Under "no cure—no pay" the salvor gambles on his ability to complete the job successfully, short of which he gets nothing. Because of his special knowledge of local conditions or simply because of luck, the salvor may complete the job much more quickly, cheaply and easily than was contemplated. This was the situation in The Elfrida [130] when, after consultation with his owners and their insurers, the master of a steamer which had gone aground in the Mississippi agreed with a salvor on a price of $22,000 to refloat the ship, on a no cure no pay basis, the job to be done within 21 days with the master reserving the right to abandon the ship to the salvor and pay nothing if she was badly damaged in the refloating. The salvor performed the job with ease in two days and at a small fraction of the agreed price. The owners then tried to repudiate, but the Supreme Court found nothing unfair in an agreement entered into under circumstances where all parties were in a position to satisfy themselves as to the true facts. Whether the gamble turns well or badly for the salvor, the "no cure no pay" contract is everywhere recognized as enforceable, absent such invalidating causes as fraud and duress.

The most widely used form of contract salvage agreement is the Lloyd's Standard Form of Salvage Agreement/No Cure—No Pay.[130a] The use of the form appears to be worldwide, not only by professional salvage outfits but by fortuitous or amateur salvors as well.[130b] The

Eventually the Tequila was libeled and sold. Whether Murphy was entitled to be paid from the proceeds of sale depended on whether by taking security for his claim (which amounted to $61,632.08) he had waived his salvor's lien and thus forfeited the priority he would normally have enjoyed over competing lien claimants. (On the relative priority of the salvage lien, see Chapter IX, § 9–61; on waiver of liens by taking security, see § 9–38, § 9–77 *et seq.*) Judge Metzner ordered the question of waiver to stand for trial.

130. 172 U.S. 186, 19 S.Ct. 146 (1898). Unsuccessful salvors working under a "no cure no pay" agreement got nothing in The Paraporte (Bonifay & Levan v. The Paraporti), 145 F.Supp. 879, 1956 A.M.C. 1898 (E.D.Va.1956). In Fredelos v. Merritt-Chapman & Scott Corp. (The Padre Island), 447 F.2d 435, 1971 A.M.C. 1347 (5th Cir. 1971), Merritt-Chapman & Scott had entered into a no cure—no pay salvage agreement for the fixed fee of $85,000. The salved vessel, which had been valued at $620,000, was eventually sold for a price which left a fund of only $103,000 for distribution among various claimants. Nevertheless the Court approved summary judgment for the full amount of the salvage fee. However, the salvors were not yet home free. In a subsequent opinion on rehearing, 447 F.2d 435, 438, 1971 A.M.C. 2192 (5th Cir. 1971) the Court concluded that the salvage claim should be subordinated to personal injury and maintenance and cure claims which had at least the "potential" to exhaust the fund. On the relative priority of the salvage lien, see Chapter IX, § 9–61 *infra.*

130a. The Lloyd's Form is reproduced in Kennedy, note 4 *supra* at p. 292 *et seq.* and in Norris, note 4 *supra* Appendix B. Norris, Cum.Supp.1972, Appendix B, also reproduces an "American No Cure—No Pay Salvage Agreement," apparently used by the Merritt-Chapman & Scott Corporation. However in American Metal Co., Ltd. v. M/V Belleville, 284 F.Supp. 1002, 1970 A.M.C. 633 (S.D.N.Y.1968), Merritt-Chapman & Scott used Lloyd's Form in connection with salvage services performed for a Norwegian vessel which had been stranded off the Rhode Island coast. Lloyd's Form came into use during the 1890s and has been susbsequently amended several times, most recently in 1953 (Kennedy, *loc. cit. supra*).

130b. In addition to the Belleville case, note 130a *supra*, see In re Yamashita-

Form is signed by the master of the salved ship on behalf of her owners, cargo and freight.[130c] The Form provides that: "The services shall be rendered and accepted as salvage services upon the principle of 'no cure—no pay.'" A blank is provided for inserting the sum which is to be the salvor's "remuneration in the event of success" but, according to Kennedy,[130d] "in practice, a fixed sum is seldom filled in." The Form then provides in elaborate detail for arbitration in London to determine the amount of the award if no fixed sum has been written into the agreement or if such a fixed sum has been objected to by any party. The Form also provides that the salvor may use the salved vessel's equipment in the course of the salvage operation, gives a formula for remuneration for partial success and also provides for the posting of security under which the salved property may be released from the salvor's lien.

The widespread use of Lloyd's Form, with disputes to be settled in the London arbitration, has naturally resulted in a considerable decrease in the volume of salvage litigation. To judge by the latest edition of Kennedy, salvage cases have virtually disappeared from the English reports in this century. At least between owners, arbitration seems to have become the preferred method of resolving salvage disputes in this country.[130e] It is, however, well settled in this country that crews on salving ships are not bound by arbitration agreements entered into by masters or owners. A substantial amount of American salvage litigation since World War II has indeed involved claims by crew members in cases where it appeared that the owners had bound themselves to extrajudicial settlements, either by London arbitration under Lloyd's Form or otherwise.[130f] There are of course

Shinnihon Kisen (The Suwaharu Maru and The Mandoil II), 305 F. Supp. 796, 1969 A.M.C. 2102 (D.Oregon, 1969) in which Lloyd's Form was used for salvage of a Liberian-flag vessel by a Canadian salvor following a collision off the Oregon coast. A Japanese vessel involved in the same collision was brought into an American port by an American salvor, apparently for a fixed sum under contract but the form of salvage agreement used is not referred to in Judge Beeks' opinion.

**130c.** On the extent to which the master has authority to bind the cargo, see the discussion of the Belleville case, text following note 126c *supra*.

**130d.** At p. 302.

**130e.** The "American No Cure—No Pay Salvage Agreement," reproduced in Norris, *supra* note 4 (Cum.Supp.1972), Appendix B, provides for arbitration of "any dispute arising under this contract." American Maritime Cases occasionally reprints the opinions delivered in salvage arbitrations.

**130f.** See, *e. g.*, the cases cited in note 5 *supra* (where the claims were put forward by crew members on foreign-flag ships) and in note 106 *supra*.

In Devine v. S/S Irini Stefanou, 1966 A.M.C. 920 (S.D.Cal.1966) it appeared that Devine had entered into a Lloyd's Form Salvage Agreement with the ship's master. Devine then filed his libel both in personam and in rem in an attempt to obtain the security required to be posted as a prerequisite for the arbitration in London. He also moved for an order declaring that the Court would be bound by whatever salvage award might be made in the arbitration. Judge Hill concluded that "there is nothing inconsistent about [Devine's] filing the within libel and simultaneously attempting to proceed with the arbitration." He denied the motion that the arbitration award should be accepted as binding, commenting that "there is authority [citing Feltre, 1939

cases involving emergency salvage operations, particularly of derelict property, in which there was no possibility of executing a salvage agreement ahead of time or, if there was, no one involved thought about doing so. It is a reasonable hypothesis that salvage litigation will continue to decline in this country even though, because of the American rule as to rights of crew members, there is no reason to anticipate that it will disappear as it seems to have done in England. The courts and counsel will no doubt be confronted more and more frequently with situations in which the most recent judicial precedent will turn out to be one delivered in the 1930s or 1940s. As case law precedents age, judicial decision tends to become progressively more arbitrary, erratic and unpredictable. The American Maritime Law Association and its affiliated publication, American Maritime Cases, might well give thought to arranging for the regular reprinting of opinions delivered in salvage arbitration, both English and American.

Owners of salved property will not infrequently claim that a pre-existing contractual relationship between salvor and salvee—as that between a tug and her tow or between a general agent and a ship of a line which he represents—or the terms under which the salvor's assistance was requested should be a bar to an award in excess of the compensation due under the contract or under the terms of the request. As to this sort of allegation, it may be said that the presumptions run heavily in favor of the salvor and the party asserting the bar will be held strictly to his burden of proof. In The Fisher's Hill (a general agent case) Justice Frankfurter, writing for the Second Circuit, reviewed the present state of the law on this point as follows:

> "No doubt Lago would have been entitled to the compensation which it received regardless of whether or not its efforts contributed to the safety of the S. S. Fisher's Hill. Yet it is not every contract for payment irrespective of success which will preclude an award. According to The Camanche, 8 Wall. 448, 19 L.Ed. 397, "the rule is that nothing short of a contract to pay a given sum for the services to be rendered, or a binding engagement to pay at all events, whether successful or unsuccessful in the enterprise, will operate as a bar to a meritorious claim for salvage." Id., 8 Wall. at page 477, 19 L.Ed. 397. This suggests that only where the contract entered into is shown to enclose the entire undertaking, will it be a bar to recovery. The circumstances here surrounding the request for assistance do not lead to the spontaneous inference that the parties meant to

A.M.C. 1173 (D.Ore.1939)] that the Court is not bound by the London arbitration award for the purpose of distributing the fund generated by the sale of the vessel and its cargo where that award would exhaust the proceeds, leaving nothing for competing lien holders, some of whom here have claims equal in priority to Devine's."

Judge Hill did not specify what the other liens were which were "equal in priority" to Devine's salvage claims. Under the normal rules of lien priority (see Chapter IX, § 9-61) they could only have been other salvage claims, wage claims or custodial costs incurred before the sale of ship and cargo.

strike a comprehensive arrangement. The fact that Lago would have received some compensation in any event may well bear on the amount of an award. But to make this conclusive against award would unduly subordinate those "moral considerations and the considerations of policy, which enter largely into the law of salvage." Under such a doctrine the ship's agent faced with a request for assistance, instead of being encouraged to quick response, would be forced either to forego a just reward or to engage in what might be protracted negotiations when immediacy is demanded." [131]

131. 218 F.2d 631, 634, 1955 A.M.C. 697, 701–702 (2d Cir. 1955). See Fort Myers Shell & Dredging Co., Inc. v. Barge NBC 512 (Tug Nellie), 404 F.2d 137, 1969 A.M.C. 186 (5th Cir. 1968), in which the Court refused to find an "implied contract" to defeat a salvage claim in a tug and tow situation.

# Chapter IX

## MARITIME LIENS AND SHIP MORTGAGES

### Introduction: Land Liens and Maritime Liens

**§ 9–1.** The law of maritime liens has been plagued by an inept terminology, an overdose of theory and a failure to abide by Justice Holmes' admonition that general propositions do not decide concrete cases.

A maritime lien, so-called, is not a lien at all in the common-law sense of the term. A consensual dry land lien has the following characteristics:

1. It is an interest in a debtor's property held by a creditor to secure repayment of a debt contractual in its origin.

2. The lienholder may foreclose his lien only after the debtor has defaulted on the principal loan.

3. Foreclosure may be had either by legal process or through extralegal action taken by the creditor himself, who is usually empowered to repossess the collateral and sell it to satisfy his debt.

4. Priority among competing liens is in general determined by the time when they attach or become perfected: first in time is first in right. (An exception to the proposition just stated is the special priority for purchase money security interests under Article 9 of the Uniform Commercial Code as well as under much pre-Code law.)

5. The validity of most liens against third parties (creditors of the borrower or purchasers of the collateral from him) depends on the lienholder's taking possession of the collateral or on his filing public notice of his lien: absent filing or possession, good faith purchasers without notice take free of the lien, and unsecured creditors or their representatives in insolvency proceedings may avoid it.

6. The property interest in the collateral is divided between the creditor-lienor and the borrower-lienee. As co-owners, each has the right to prevent improper use of the collateral by the other—the creditor to protect his security, the borrower to defend his equity.

7. The interest of the lienholder in the property can be terminated only through payment of the debt or through foreclosure. The interest will not be lost by laches in enforcement and will most certainly not be terminated by judicial proceedings to which the lienholder is not a party.

Land liens may be voluntary—that is, consented to by the borrower in advance as a condition of the loan—or involuntary—that is, attaching to his property without his consent, by action of creditor or court. In the category of voluntary liens fall security interests under Article 9 of the Uniform Commercial Code (whose coverage includes such familiar pre-Code security devices as pledge, mortgage, conditional sale and trust receipt). The two main classes of involuntary liens are what may be called status liens (those arising in favor of mechanics, materialmen and the like) and judicial liens.

Status liens, like voluntary liens, arise out of contract: work done or services performed. By definition such a lien is intended to secure a payment that is already overdue; therefore there is no loan period. The lien may depend on the lienor's retaining possession of the object on which the work was done (like the garagemen's lien on a car for repairs) or of property of the debtor entrusted to him (like the hotelman's lien on a guest's baggage) or on his complying with filing requirements (as with most types of mechanics' liens). Status liens, like voluntary liens, rank in the order of their perfection; in some circumstances a mechanic's lien or the like may take priority over a prior voluntary lien on the theory that the work done has increased the value of the property. The status lienor is not in any sense except a fictional one a co-owner of the property; if he has it in his possession he can keep it until paid; in or out of possession, he can force its sale to satisfy his claim. There is nothing, however, that resembles the division of interest between mortgagor and mortgagee. As with the holder of a voluntary lien, the status lienor's interest will be terminated only by payment, foreclosure or judicial proceedings to which he is a party.

The judicial lien need not, in the first instance, arise from contract. It is a means of compelling payment of a debt judicially determined to be owing—or, where the lien arises by foreign attachment in advance of judgment, a means of compelling a non-resident defendant to provide security for a debt which he may be found to owe. Judicial liens are subordinate to all prior liens; among themselves they rank in order of perfection. Such liens do not relate back to the date of the happening that gave rise to the claim. Judicially created, they are judicially executed; the sheriff levies and sells at judicial sale. What the sheriff sells is the debtor's right, title and interest; the judicial sale does not cut off prior interests. Like the status lienor, the judicial lienor is not in any real sense a co-owner of the property.

§ 9–2. Not one of the propositions just stated holds true for the maritime lien:[1]

1. The maritime lien arises out of contract or tort. Only certain types of maritime claims give rise to liens. And the parties cannot by agreement confer lien status on a claim which is not by nature a lien claim or waive the conditions for attachment.

2. In the case of tort liens, there is of course no credit period and no concept of default. Except for preferred ship mortgages, the contract liens customarily arise out of extremely short-term credit extensions—30 or 60 days.

1. The general statements which follow will be documented as the several issues are discussed in the balance of the chapter.

3. The maritime lien can be "executed" (which is the admiralty terminology for "foreclosed") only by an admiralty court acting *in rem*.

4. Priority among competing maritime liens of the same type is determined by the time of their attachment, but in inverse order: last in time is first in right. The inverse order rule has become riddled with exceptions, but it is still basic to maritime lien theory. There is also an involved system of priorities among different types of liens, some being of higher rank than others.

5. The validity of a maritime lien depends neither on possession nor (except for the preferred ship mortgage, which is statutory) on notice through filing. It is therefore often referred to as a "secret" lien. It is also said to be "indelible": that is, since the maritime lien can be executed only by the admiralty court acting *in rem*, it is, until that court has so acted, good "against the world", including the good faith purchaser of the ship without notice of the lien's existence. On the same principle the maritime lien is not affected by bankruptcy or reorganization. The "indelibility" of the lien is, however, seriously affected by the doctrine of laches, to be shortly referred to.

6. The maritime lienor is not a co-owner of the ship. He has no right to control the ship's use or movements in any way. It remains the owner's ship for all purposes—subject to the lienor's right to have it arrested, wherever he can find it, on process issuing from the admiralty court. The fiction of co-ownership has nevertheless occasionally been resorted to by courts in efforts to explain the theoretical basis of the inverse order rule of priority.

7. A maritime lien is of course extinguished by payment of the underlying claim.[1a] It can also be lost by laches in its prosecution and the doctrine of laches largely destroys the lien's theoretical "indelibility". The *in rem* decree of an admiralty court following a judicial sale executes all liens—scrapes the ship free of claims—whether or not the lien claimants have intervened in, or even had notice of, the proceeding. Such a decree is given international recognition. An American claimant may find that his lien against a ship has been "executed" by an admiralty court sitting in Hong Kong or Marseille

1a. Harmon, Discharge and Waiver of Maritime Liens, 47 Tulane L.Rev. 786, 791 (1973) comments, with respect to the statement in the text: "This statement is not altogether accurate. Certainly payment of the claim that gives rise to the lien discharges the lien as between the shipowner and the claimant, but does it have this effect as to other lien claimants? And what effect does such payment have when the owner has been provided with funds to make the payment of the lien claims by some third party?" The point of Mr. Harmon's second query is that the third party who advances the funds may be entitled to assert the liens which have been paid off under theories of assignment or subrogation, see § 9–21 *infra*. Mr. Harmon does not further elucidate the point of his first query about the effect of payment on "other lien claimants". Apart from the theories of assignment and subrogation which have been referred to, it would seem that payment would discharge the lien not only as to the shipowner but as to other lien claimants as well. That an owner cannot claim a lien against his own vessel, see § 9–20 infra.

or Lisbon in a proceeding he never heard of, in which case American courts will consider themselves bound by the foreign decree. Equally, foreign claimants may find that their liens have vanished in proceedings taken in this country. What is lost, it may avoid confusion to point out, is the lien, the claim against the ship, the right to proceed *in rem:* the personal liability of any person subject to the claim is not affected by the execution of the lien. In the enforcement of this personal liability, the ship may be seized, attached, levied upon by ordinary process like any of the debtor's assets: however, once the lien has been executed, the claim is no longer entitled to its lien priority and the claimant will be subordinated to any lien claims which have accrued subsequent to the "executing" decree and are therefore not affected by it.

The maritime lien may seem to resemble the involuntary land lien more closely than it resembles the voluntary lien. Like the judicial lien, the maritime lien can be foreclosed or executed only by judicial process. And the theory of benefit to the security by which mechanics and other status liens are sometimes given priority over prior voluntary liens is a theory much repeated in discussions of maritime lien law. On the whole, however, the resemblances are deceptive. Status and judicial liens are much closer to the voluntary lien than they are to the maritime lien.

Clarity of thought is not promoted when, by an accident of linguistic history, two unlike things are called by the same name. Growth by analogy has been one of the law's great strengths but when the analogy hit upon is false the result is confusion and stalemate. The law of maritime liens might well have been worked out more satisfactorily than it has been if the unfortunate term "lien" had not come into use during the nineteenth century. The possibilities of confusion may be greater today than in the past because of the gradual disappearance of a specialized admiralty bar and even more because the federal judge sitting "in admiralty" is almost never, at the outset of his judicial service, a maritime lawyer. The beginning of wisdom in the law of maritime liens is that maritime liens and land liens have little in common. A lien is a lien is a lien, but a maritime lien is not.

### Theories About Maritime Liens: The "Personification" of the Ship

§ 9–3. Much wit and learning have been expended in analyzing the "true nature" of the maritime lien. Under what is said to be the predominant American theory the ship, personified, is itself—or herself—the defendant in a proceeding *in rem* to enforce a lien. The ship is "the offending thing"; the lien itself is, in an obscure Latin jingle which has been so often repeated that it is no longer polite to inquire what it means, *jus in re* rather than *jus ad rem.*[1b] The English theory of liens, on the other hand, is said to be merely procedural: the process *in rem* against the ship is in the nature of foreign at-

1b. No *jus ad rem*
Will comfort them
Whose *jus in re*
Has gone away.

tachment to compel the owner's appearance by subjecting to the court's control property within its territorial jurisdiction.[2]

Judges and commentators have sought to trace the origins of lien theory in the remote past. Holmes in a famous passage of The Common Law [3] suggested that the liability of the ship for her torts derived from the medieval idea of deodand, whereby inanimate objects which had been the instruments of physical harm were forfeit to the crown. The ship's liability in contract Holmes traced to the Roman *hypotheca,* which appears to have been the equivalent of our modern non-possessory security interest. The union of such unlike sources is enough to demonstrate the flimsiness of Holmes' reconstruction which, like much 19th century historical work, was ingenious rather than solid. Holmes as judge does not appear to have been impressed with the speculations of Holmes as scholar: Justice Holmes ignored the "logical" deductions which some of his fellow justices drew from the personification of the ship and did more than anyone else on the Court to rescue maritime lien law from the dead-end of historical fiction.[4]

Attempts to relate maritime lien law to medieval and Roman sources are, as Justice Holmes clearly saw, little more than fiction. Anglo-American lien law is a 19th century creation. The English admiralty courts in the 17th and 18th centuries had seen their jurisdiction shrivel away under the writs of prohibition issued by the courts of common law.[5] The vice-admiralty courts instituted in the American colonies retained, it is true, a much wider jurisdiction in the eighteenth century than did their English counterparts. Nevertheless, both in England and the colonies there was an irreparable break in the tradition. When American admiralty courts, as part of the federal court system established under the Constitution, successfully asserted a progressively wider jurisdiction, and when English admiralty courts had much of their lost jurisdiction restored to them by statute, a fresh start was made, of necessity. The evocations of the Rhodian law, the Digest of Justinian, the Code of Oleron, the Consulate of the Sea—and all that—which are frequent in 19th century opinions merely illustrate that century's addiction to the agreeable pastime of antiquarianism. A gardener may amuse himself by composing an old-fashioned garden, but he puts living plants in freshly spaded soil.[5a]

2. For a general discussion see Hebert, The Origin and Nature of Maritime Liens, 4 Tulane L.Rev. 381 (1930). Chapter I of Price, The Law of Maritime Liens (1940) is excellent. Price appears to have relied on Underhay, American and English Theories of Maritime Liens (unpublished paper in Yale Law School Library).

3. The Common Law (1881) (Howe ed. 1967) 25 *et seq.*

4. See in particular his opinion in The Western Maid, quoted *infra* § 9–14.

5. See Chapter I, § 1–4.

5a. Ryan, Admiralty Jurisdiction and the Maritime Lien: An Historical Perspective, 7 Western Ontario L.Rev. 173 (1968) is a brilliant reconstruction of the development of the action in rem and the eventual recognition (or discovery) of the maritime lien. Ac-

**§ 9–4.** Whatever the sources may be, the personification of the ship has had a notable career in American judicial opinions and has had, as literary conceptions sometimes do, an influence in shaping the law.[5b]

Three cases of forefeiture of vessels for engaging in illegal activity seem to have introduced the personification idea into American law. The first was The Little Charles [6] in which Chief Justice Marshall, sitting on circuit, dealt with a vessel forfeited for violation of the Embargo Acts of 1807 and 1808. In reply to the argument that the vessel was so used without the knowledge or consent of the owner, Marshall wrote, in an uncharacteristic flight of fancy but with a characteristic absence of authority:

> "But this is not a proceeding against the owner, it is a proceeding against the vessel, for an offence committed by the vessel, which is not less an offence, and does not the less subject her to forfeiture, because it was committed without the authority, and against the will of the owner. It is true, that inanimate matter can commit no offence. The mere wood, iron, and sails of the ship, cannot, of themselves, violate the law. But this body is animated and put in action by the crew, who are guided by the master. The vessel acts and speaks by the master. She reports herself by the master. It is, therefore, not unreasonable, that the vessel should be affected by this report." [7]

The next case was The Palmyra,[8] which was decided by the Supreme Court in 1827. The Palmyra, operating as a privateer under a Spanish royal commission, was seized by a United States war vessel as guilty of "piratical aggression" and sent with a prize crew to Charleston for condemnation under the piracy statute. The Circuit Court not only held the Palmyra not subject to condemnation for piracy but awarded damages to the Spanish owners for her wrongful detention. On appeal to the Supreme Court by the United States,

cording to Professor Ryan, the term "maritime lien" made its first appearance in Anglo-American law in Justice Story's 1831 opinion in The Nestor (see text at note 14 *infra*); the first English case to use the term, with an acknowledgment of indebtedness to Story, was The Bold Buccleugh (1851) (see text at note 18 *infra*). See further the quotation from Scrutton, L.J. in The Tervaete (1922) P. 259, note 66 *infra*. For other general reviews of maritime lien theory see Note, Personification of Vessels, 77 Harv.L.Rev. 1122 (1964); Longenecker, Developments in the Law of Maritime Liens, 45 Tulane L.Rev. 574 (1971); Toy, Introduction to the Law of Maritime Liens, 47 Tulane L.Rev. 559 (1973) (part of a valuable symposium on Maritime Liens and Securities, which will be frequently cited hereafter). English law was reviewed in Stewart-Richardson, Liens on Ships and Their Priorities, 1960 J.Bus.Law 44.

5b. In this section and the sections which follow through § 9–18 we shall discuss the career of the personification idea in the American case law. In § 9–18(a) we shall take up the present state of the still confused debate on whether there can be in rem liability without in personam liability.

6. 26 Fed.Cas. 979, Case No. 15,612 (C.C.D.Va.1819).

7. *Id.* at 982.

8. 25 U.S. (12 Wheat.) 1 (1827).

it was argued, on behalf of the Spanish owners, that the libel *in rem* alleging piracy had not been maintainable in the first place because there had been no prior conviction of the offenders *in personam*. Justice Story felt the point to be both "important and difficult". His answer, without citation of authority except for a general reference to "seizures and forfeitures, created by statute, *in rem,* cognizable on the revenue side of the Exchequer" was in the following language:

> "The thing is here [*i. e.* under such statutes] primarily considered as the offender, or rather the offence is attached primarily to the thing; and this, whether the offence be *malum prohibitum* or *malum in se.* The same principle applies to proceedings *in rem,* on seizures in the Admiralty." [9]

It will be noted that Justice Story, in replying, to the "important and difficult" point raised by counsel was not talking of admiralty law at all (except by an analogical reference) but of seizures under revenue statutes. The Palmyra was not condemned: the Supreme Court was evenly divided on the piracy issue so the judgment of the Circuit Court survived.

The third of the cases was the Brig Malek Adhel,[10] decided by the Supreme Court in 1844, the opinion again by Justice Story. The Malek Adhel, like the Palmyra, was seized under the piracy statute following a series of "piratical aggressions" whose like cannot be found outside the tuneful pages of the Pirates of Penzance.[11] There

9. *Id.* at 14.

10. 43 U.S. (2 How.) 210 (1844).

11. The details of the Malek Adhel's piratical career may amuse the reader. The brig was commanded by Captain Nunez, a terrible tempered man, whose habit it was, on the slightest provocation, to order the gunner to load the cannon and send a shot over the bows of any vessel in sight: one such shot went through the flying jib of an English brig, but no other damage was ever reported. Captain Nunez was much obsessed with time. He occasionally, being short on sailing experience, forgot to wind the "chronometer" and was always eager to "rate" his chronometer against those on other vessels he crossed. Wherefore the gunner would be ordered to load up and cause the crossing vessel to heave to in the customary manner. Nunez, although passionately attached to his chronometer, did not understand the process of rating it, so it fell to the lot of the unhappy mate, Mr. Myers, to take the Malek Adhel's chronometer on board the hove-to vessel for rating. On one such occasion, according to Myers: "Strange captain asked me why Nunez had fired at him; I said I did not know; the captain had ordered it. He asked me where we were bound. I said: 'God only knows.' When I returned to the Malek Adhel, I told Nunez what had happened, and he laughed." The only time when Nunez ordered his men to "plunder" one of his victims was when the idea occurred to him to charge the captain of one vessel twenty dollars, representing the cost of the shot which the gunner had fired, as well as ten dollars for a keg of oil which had been knocked over by the recoil of the gun; while they were about it, Nunez instructed his emissaries, they might see if there were any sweetmeats on board the other vessel. The emissaries returned with "a jar of sweetmeats, one dog and twenty dollars for the shot." They had been ashamed, one of them told Myers, to ask for the other ten for the oil.

The apparent absence of acquisitive intent of Nunez' part gave Justice Story occasion to enter into a learned discussion whether the acts alleged to be piracy must be entered into *animo furandi,* or *lucri causa.* On the

being no royal commission to justify the acts of the Malek Adhel, she was condemned and sold. It was stipulated by the proctors for the United States that the owners "never contemplated or authorized" the acts of "piracy". Under the statute, however, wrote Justice Story, the owner's innocence made no difference:

> "The vessel which commits the aggression is treated as the offender, as the guilty instrument or thing to which the forfeiture attaches, without any reference whatsoever to the character or conduct of the owner. . . . Nor is there anything new in a provision of this sort. It is not an uncommon course in the admiralty, acting under the law of nations, to treat the vessel in which or by which, or by the master or crew thereof, a wrong or offence has been done as the offender, without any regard whatsoever to the personal misconduct or responsibility of the owner thereof. And this is done from the necessity of the case, as the only adequate means of suppressing the offence or wrong, or insuring an indemnity to the injured party." [12]

As authority Justice Story then quoted Marshall's language in The Little Charles and his own remarks in The Palmyra, adding: "the same doctrine has been fully recognized in the High Court of Admiralty in England . . . and indeed in many other cases, where the owner of the ship has been held bound by the acts of the master, whether he was ignorant thereof or not".[13]

These forfeiture cases had nothing to do with maritime lien law or even with admiralty law. They brought up what we would call today "due process of law" questions. If the quoted passages from the opinions of the two great judges are read with care, it becomes apparent that neither Marshall nor Story was thinking of admiralty

whole, he concluded, they need not, or, if they did, the twenty dollars (as well as, presumably, the dog and jar of sweetmeats) sufficed. Nevertheless the learned Justice was evidently concerned to find some explanation for Nunez' behavior and, on that branch of the case, he wrote: "What Captain Nunez designed under his false and hollow pretences and excuses it may not be easy to say, with exact confidence or certainty. It may have been to train his crew to acts of wanton and piratical mischief, or to seduce them into piratical enterprises. It may have been from a reckless and wanton abuse of power, to gratify his own lawless passions. It could scarcely have been from mental hallucinations; for there was too much method in his mad projects to leave any doubt that there was cunning and craft and worldly wisdom in his course, and that he meditated more than he chose to explain to his crew." (2 How. 210, 233.) The details of the Malek Adhel's voyage are taken from the statement of the case at 210–220 of 2 How.

12. 43 U.S. (2 How.) 210, 233 (1844).

13. Justice Story cited to a note in the appendix of 2 Wheaton's Reports, which turns out to be a collection of cases respecting "blockade, contraband, . . . and the circumstances of unneutral conduct, which are visited with the forfeiture of the ship or cargo, or both." The three English cases which Story cited, The Vrouw Judith, 1 Rob.Adm. 150 (1799), The Adonis, 5 *id.* 256 (1804), The Mars, 6 *id.* 79 (1805), are also forfeiture cases.

law except in terms of the loosest possible analogy and that no "principle" of admiralty law was being laid down.

If we turn to the early lien cases which came to be considered "leading cases", we find much parade of erudition, with copious citations from the Digest and Continental sources, but no insistence on the ship as "the offender, . . . the guilty instrument or thing." One of these, The Nestor,[14] was handed down by Justice Story on circuit, in 1831—thus midway between The Palmyra and The Malek Adhel. The maritime lien, said Story in The Nestor, was not like the Roman *pignus* (pawn) which depended on possession, but more like the Roman *hypotheca* (hypothecation), although not exactly like that either. "Some obscurity too," he wrote wisely, "is thrown over the subject by the use of language borrowed from the civil and foreign law, and applied in a sense not exactly correspondent with the sense, in which it is found in that law." [15] In The Rebecca,[16] like The Nestor a Maine case decided in 1831, Judge Ware outdid even Justice Story in the stupendousness of his erudition and equally found no need to resort to the fiction of the ship's personality. Somewhat later, in 1855, Justice Curtis went over the same well-ploughed ground a third time in The Young Mechanic,[17] adding a few new citations and contributing the *jus in re* (not *jus ad rem*) tag, but was still content to look on the ship as merely a ship.

## Enforceability of Liens When Owner is not Personally Liable. (1) Good Faith Purchasers without Notice

§ 9–5. The course of litigation through the nineteenth century brought before the courts a variety of situations in which the issue for decision was whether the ship could be arrested and sold to satisfy claims for which the owner of the ship was not personally liable. In some, but not all, of these situations the decision was that the liability could be enforced against the ship. These decisions, as we shall see, were entirely reasonable on grounds of economic or public policy as a fair resolution of the multiple and conflicting interests which center around the shipping industry. It was perhaps less common in the nineteenth century than it is in our own for judges to explain their decisions in nonconceptual terms. Thus the fiction of the ship's personality, introduced as a literary flourish in the forfeiture cases, served as a convenient "reason" to explain why ships should occasionally be liable to arrest even though the underlying claims could not be enforced against the owner.

14. 18 Fed.Cas. 9, Case No. 10,126 (C.C.D.Me.1831). The question presented was whether a proceeding *in rem* could be maintained by a material man for a cable furnished to the brig.

15. *Id.* at 12.

16. 20 Fed.Cas. 373, Case No. 11,619 (D.Me.1831). The libel against the vessel alleged that the captain refused to deliver ten hogsheads of liquor, they having been lost in consequence of careless and improper stowage by the captain.

17. 30 Fed.Cas. 873, Case No. 18,180 (C.C.D.Me.1855). The *jus in re* phrase was introduced in the course of a learned discussion of whether a lien conferred by local law could be enforced against the ship after the shipowner had died insolvent.

**§ 9–6.** Chronologically, the first type of case which brought up the issue of ship's liability despite owner's non-liability was that of the good faith purchaser of a ship which was subject to unexecuted liens at the time of sale although the purchaser had no notice of the existence of the liens. In The Bold Buccleugh,[18] an English case which has ever since been recognized as a leading authority on both sides of the Atlantic, it was held that a lien for collision damage could be enforced against the offending ship in the hands of an owner who had bought her after the collision and whose good faith and lack of notice the court was willing to assume. The Bold Buccleugh was decided by the Privy Council in 1852, and the amorphous state of maritime lien law at that date is illustrated by the fact that the judges found no English precedents to rely on and had to content themselves with repeating Justice Story's general language about maritime liens in The Nestor,[19] which did not involve a good faith purchase question and, for that matter, was not a collision case. The court said:

> "A maritime lien does not include or require possession. The word is used in maritime law not in the strict legal sense in which we understand it in Courts of Common Law, in which case there could be no lien where there was no possession, actual or constructive; but to express, as if by analogy, the nature of claims which neither presuppose nor originate in possession. This was well understood in the Civil Law, by which there might be a pledge with possession, and a hypothecation without possession, and by which in either case the right traveled with the thing into whosesoever possession it came. . . . This claim or privilege [*i. e.* a maritime lien] travels with the thing into whosesoever possession it may come. It is inchoate from the moment the claim or privilege attaches, and when carried into effect by legal process, by a proceeding in rem, relates back to the period when it first attached. . . .
>
> This rule, which is simple and intelligible, is in our opinion applicable to all cases. It is not necessary to say that the lien is indelible and may not be lost by negligence or delay where the rights of third parties may be compromised; but where reasonable diligence is used, and the proceedings are had in good faith, the lien may be enforced, into whosesoever possession the thing may come." [20]

The only thing about the court's discussion of the validity of maritime liens against third parties that may seem peculiar to a modern reader, particularly to an American lawyer, is the fact that the court found the survival of the lien in any way a peculiarity of maritime law. Whatever the state of English law may have been in 1850, we are entirely familiar with the idea of property interests

18. 7 Moore, P.C. 267 (1852).

19. See note 14 *supra*.

20. 7 Moore, P.C. 267, 284–5 (1852).

"which neither presuppose nor originate in possession." Our law recognizes, and has recognized for more than a hundred years, a variety of "nonpossessory" interests in property, to which even the good faith purchaser without notice takes subject. The concept is so well recognized that no lawyer, surely, would be tempted to look on it as a novel and peculiar importation from the civil law.

**§ 9–7.** The working out in maritime law of the idea of the lien's "indelibility" has been notably different from the working out of the comparable concept in land law.

In land law most types of security holders whose liens are valid or "perfected" have an interest in the property subject to lien which can accurately be described as "indelible". The holder of a security interest in personal or real property whose interest is perfected can truly follow the collateral "into whosesoever possession the thing may come" after an unauthorized disposition by the debtor or mortgagor. The property, no matter how many times it may change hands, remains subject to the security interest—not perhaps forever, but surely through the period of the applicable statute of limitations. Whoever may have dealt with the property, whatever the state of his subjective good faith or innocence, may be held liable to the holder of the security interest as for a conversion.

The maritime lienor, as the opinion in The Bold Buccleugh indicates, does not receive nearly so tasty a serving of "indelibility". His lien may be "lost by negligence or delay where the rights of third parties may be compromised." In The Bold Buccleugh the collision had occurred on December 14, 1848. Five days later the owners of the vessel that had been damaged instituted proceedings and caused process to issue against the offending vessel. The process could not immediately be served because the Bold Buccleugh had left English for Scottish waters. Locating her in Scotland, the plaintiffs began an action in the Scottish courts on January 30, 1849, and in that proceeding the Bold Buccleugh was arrested in Leith harbor but later released on bail. She was then sold on June 26, 1849, to the present owner, said to be without notice of any of these events, and again arrested at Hull the following August on what was apparently her first return to English waters and the jurisdiction of English courts (the Scottish action being then dropped). Certainly no claimants could have been more active and diligent in asserting their claims. As our discussion of the doctrine of laches will show, the protection against third parties accorded to the maritime lienor is narrowly circumscribed by the requirement that he act promptly to assert his rights.[21]

**§ 9–8.** The law usually achieves a rough common sense, no matter how esoteric the supporting doctrine may be. The difference between the true indelibility of the perfected land lien and the limited indelibility of the maritime lien lends itself to a simple ex-

21. See infra §§ 9–77, 9–78.

planation which can be pointed up by a modern analogy. The law of land liens was shaped at a time when the principal type of chattel property which could become subject to divided ownership or a security interest was property which had a fixed situs, which stayed more or less where it was, whose movement from one point on the earth's surface to another was an out-of-ordinary-course affair. It is not unreasonable to cast on creditors and purchasers the burden of ascertaining the facts with reference to such stable property; with the exercise of reasonable diligence, they ought to be able to discover —and nine times out of ten will discover—the true state of facts; the relevant information is geographically localized, and in modern times an elaborate network of public files has been set up to aid the search. When the chattel becomes mobile, all that ceases to be true. The point has been dramatized in land law by a type of fraud prevalent since 1920 or so, which consists of buying an automobile subject to a security interest in favor of the seller in, say, New York, driving it to Arizona and there selling it. Under classical land lien theory the New York secured party, whose interest if perfected under New York law is indelible, should prevail over the good faith Arizona purchaser without notice, and indeed many cases so hold. The interesting thing about this sort of litigation, of which there has been a great deal, is that the classical theory is breaking down; a great many courts have felt that it is unreasonable to cast on the purchaser a burden of inquiry which he is, in the usual case, factually not able to undertake or which at best would be time-consuming and costly. Such courts protect the purchaser against the security holder who has not taken prompt steps to file his interest or to repossess the property in the jurisdiction to which the property has been removed.[22]

What has been looked on as a peculiarity of maritime lien law is a peculiarity of the ship rather than of the law. In the early nineteenth century, the ship was the only mobile chattel of commercial importance. As the court in The Bold Buccleugh perceived, the rules which might fit stationary chattels would not work in the case of ships which roamed the earth. Thus the special admiralty doctrine of laches developed, special in the sense that it was only the admiralty that had to evolve workable rules to fit the case. As mobile chattels have made their appearance on land, the original admiralty solution has been approximated in land law.

### Same: (2) Liens Arising from Acts of Compulsory Pilots

**§ 9–9.** The local authorities in major ports require ships proceeding into or out of the harbor to make use of the services of local pilots. These pilots, who are employed by the port authority, are assigned in rotation as ships have need of them. When the pilot takes

22. See Leary, Horse and Buggy Lien Law and Migratory Automobiles, 96 U.Pa.L.Rev. 455 (1948). For a general discussion of the problems under Article 9 of the Uniform Commercial Code and under pre-Code law, see 1 Gilmore, Security Interests in Personal Property, Ch. 22 (Interstate Movements of Collateral) (1965).

over the ship, his authority supersedes even that of the master although the regulations customarily provide that the master may resume command in case of the pilot's obvious and gross incompetence. Neither owner nor master has any choice about taking a pilot or about which of the regular pilots may be assigned. The validity of such local regulation of the shipping industry was upheld by the Supreme Court in one of the notable early cases involving the interplay between the need for national uniformity in a peculiarly national industry and the equally obvious need for local regulation of peculiarly local conditions.[23]

What now of the liability pattern when a ship under the control of a regularly assigned pilot comes into collision under conditions of fault by reason of the pilot's negligence or incompetence? During the nineteenth century it never seems to have occurred to anyone that the municipal authority which administered the pilotage regulations should itself be held liable for the torts of its employees. The idea of sovereign immunity, even for municipalities, was too deeply rooted at the time when the early cases were decided for the suggestion to have been put forward.[24] It was equally true, and in most cases irrelevant, that the pilot was himself personally liable.[24a] It would be difficult, although not impossible, to invent a plausible structure of doctrine under which a shipowner could be held personally liable for the conduct of a "servant" whom he had never chosen and over whose acts he had no control. Liability without fault has until recently

23. Cooley v. Board of Wardens of Port of Philadelphia, 53 U.S. (12 How.) 299 (1851).

24. As the idea of sovereign immunity fades away, it would be reasonable to expect that municipalities and other governmental agencies would begin to be held liable for the torts of such pilots, at least where the pilotage is compulsory, and recent cases so hold. See Gulf Oil Corp. v. Panama Canal Co., 311 F.Supp. 1307, 1970 A.M.C. 2410 (D.C.Canal Zone 1970); Waterman Steamship Corp. v. United States, 304 F.Supp. 401, 1969 A.M.C. 2100 (W.D.Wash.1969); City of Long Beach v. National Development Co. (Dona Aurora), 289 F.2d 586, 1961 A.M.C. 1105 (9th Cir. 1961), certiorari denied 368 U.S. 901 (1961); Victorias Milling Co., Inc. v. Panama Canal Co., 272 F.2d 716, 1959 A.M.C. 251 (5th Cir. 1959) (but pilot found not negligent); Pacific Transport Lines v. Territory of Hawaii, 43 Hawaii 28, 1963 A.M.C. 1321 (Sup.Ct. Hawaii, 1958); The President Van Buren (City of Long Beach v. American President Lines), 223 F.2d 853, 1955 A.M.C. 1548 (9th Cir. 1955); The Hakonesan Maru (General Petroleum Corp. v. Los Angeles), 22 Cal.App.2d 332, 70 P.2d 998, 1937 A.M.C. 1272 (1937); *Id.*, 42 Cal. App.2d 591, 109 P.2d 754, 1941 A.M.C. 510 (1941). With respect to a municipal pilot whose employment was not compulsory the Ninth Circuit held the municipality not liable for his negligence in The Lebec—The Seekonk (City of Los Angeles v. Standard Transp. Co.), 32 F.2d 988, 1929 A.M.C. 1287 (9th Cir. 1929).

24a. For examples of actions brought against pilots personally, see Tampa Ship Repair & Dry Dock Co. v. A. P. St. Philip, Inc., 440 F.2d 1193, 1971 A.M.C. 1547 (5th Cir. 1971); Bethlehem Steel Corp. v. Yates, 438 F.2d 798, 1971 A.M.C. 577 (5th Cir. 1971). Pilots' associations are typically held not liable for the torts of their members. See General v. Pilots' Ass'n for the Bay and River Delaware, 254 F. Supp. 447, 1966 A.M.C. 1734 (D.Del. 1966) (Judge Layton's opinion collects earlier cases).

seemed an abhorrent concept to most courts. It was held therefore that the owner was not personally liable.[25]

Nevertheless damage had been done, loss had been suffered and the risk had to be allocated. If the problem is looked on as a risk of the industry, it makes no difference whether the law decrees that the risk is to be borne by the class of shipowners whose ships are run down by licensed pilots or by the class whose ships do the running down, since the two classes are the same: if my ship under Pilot X runs down your ship today, your ship under Pilot Y may run mine down tomorrow. Insurance is available and always carried. The simplest and best solution would have been to let the loss rest where it fell. The law, however, prefers to find a victim, a wrongdoer, to whom the risk can be shifted and who, as a matter of morals, "ought" to pay. The municipality was thought to be immune; the pilot was judgment-proof; the owner was not liable on general theories of law. That left only the ship. To say that the owner is not liable but that his ship is may seem merely an indirect way of saying that the owner is liable to the amount of his investment in the ship—a species of limited liability. A more elegant way of putting it, however, is to say, as Justice Story had remarked, to be sure in another connection, that "the vessel . . . is treated as the offender, as the guilty instrument or thing . . ." [26]

The issue came to the Supreme Court in The China,[27] decided in 1868, which is another example of how recent a creation the law of maritime liens is. The question was not, however, an unfamiliar one, having frequently arisen on both sides of the Atlantic. Reviewing the precedents, Justice Swayne pointed out that the English cases had followed a wavering, confused and inconsistent line. At the time of The China the English rule denied the liability of the offending ship, but Justice Swayne found "little inducements . . . to establish the principle in our jurisprudence". The American cases on the other hand had consistently allowed recovery against the ship at fault, and that recovery, the Court decided, was in accord with the

25. Homer Ramsdell Transp. Co. v. La Compagnie Generale Transatlantique, 182 U.S. 406, 21 S.Ct. 831 (1901); (a common law action where a vessel collided with a pier; Justice Gray's opinion emphasized the fact that the action was at law but suggested no reason why a different result would follow in admiralty). In Ralli v. Troop, 157 U.S. 386, 402, 15 S.Ct. 657, 663 (1895) Justice Gray had suggested the same line of reasoning. That the holding in the Ramsdell case applied to actions in admiralty was accepted in Harrison v. Hughes, 125 Fed. 860 (3d Cir. 1903) certiorari denied 191 U.S. 575, 24 S.Ct. 846 (1903) and Crisp v. U. S. & Australasia S. S. Co., 124 F. 748 (S.D.N.Y.1903). In The Abengarez—The O.5 (U. S. v. United Fruit Co.), 60 F.2d 543, 1932 A.M.C. 1247 (E.D. La.1932) libellant's proctor conceded the personal nonliability of an owner for negligence of a compulsory pilot. See also City of Los Angeles v. Grace Steamship Co., 116 Cal.App. 237, 2 P. 2d 401, 1931 A.M.C. 1548 (1931) and cases cited. In Logue Stevedoring Corp. v. Tugs Dalzellance, etc., 198 F. 2d 369, 1952 A.M.C. 1297 (2d Cir. 1952) the Second Circuit left open the question whether an owner would be personally liable even for the fault of a noncompulsory pilot.

26. The Malek Adhel, 43 U.S. (2 How.) 210, 233 (1844) discussed text following note 10 *supra*.

27. 74 U.S. (7 Wall.) 53 (1868).

principles of natural justice and the maritime law, not to mention the venerable maxim: *sic utere tuo ut non laedas alienum.* According to the "commercial usages and jurisprudence of the middle ages", source of maritime law, "the primary responsibility was upon the vessel, and that of the owner was not personal, but merely incidental to his ownership . . . ." It was held, therefore, that the China, a foreign vessel, was liable for the running down of an American vessel, the collision having occurred solely by reason of the compulsory pilot's negligence. The principle, as applied to both American and foreign vessels, has never since been challenged—nor is there any reason why it should be, since it is inherently as reasonable a solution of the problem as the opposite holding would have been.[28]

## Same: (3) Liens Arising When Ship is in Control of Charterers and the Like

**§ 9–10.** Ships are frequently under the control of persons who are neither the owners nor the owners' agents. The best example of this situation is the demise charter; [29] another example is the common arrangement whereby loading and unloading are carried out by a stevedoring company, which exercises a degree of control over the vessel and whose relationship to the owner is said to be that of an independent contractor. More in the realm of fantasy than of commercial operations one may imagine ships manned by mutineers or pirates—or at any rate persons whose connection with the vessel is so irregular that an imaginative judge might find them to be like those romantic characters. In all these cases, both real and fanciful, the question arises whether the ship can be held for liabilities created while it was under the control of charterer, stevedore, mutineer or pirate.

The Barnstable [30] is cited as authority for the proposition that the ship is liable *in rem* for damage done by it while in the control of charterers. Justice Brown stated the law in words often quoted:

> " . . . the law in this country is entirely well settled, that the ship itself is to be treated in some sense as a principal, and as personally liable for the negligence of anyone who is lawfully in possession of her, whether as owner or charterer." [31]

28. See Logue Stevedoring Corp. v. Tugs Dalzellance, etc., 198 F.2d 369, 1952 A.M.C. 1297 (2d Cir. 1952) (the rule applies *a fortiori* when the pilotage is not compulsory but voluntary). See also Canadian Aviator, Ltd. v. U. S., 324 U.S. 215, 65 S.Ct. 639, 1945 A.M.C. 265 (1945). The rule of The China appears to be so firmly established that the issue has disappeared from litigation. For relatively recent restatements of the rule, see United States v. The Tug Parris Island, 215 F.Supp. 144, 1963 A.M.C. 643 (E.D.N.C.1963); United States v. S/S President Lincoln, 1964 A.M.C. 1841 (N.D. Cal.1964).

The matters taken up in this section are also discussed in Chapter VII, § 7–16.

29. For the demise charterer's liability as owner see Chapter IV, § 4–23.

30. 181 U.S. 464, 21 S.Ct. 684 (1901).

31. *Id.* at 467, 21 S.Ct. at 685–686.

For authority Justice Brown cited the usual trio of old forfeiture cases [32]—The Little Charles, The Palmyra, and The Malek Adhel —plus The China [33] on compulsory pilotage. As precedents the cases cited were remote, but Justice Brown, as this and other opinions show, was a firm believer in the doctrine of the ship's personality. In fact the issue of the ship's liability was not before the Court in The Barnstable, so that Justice Brown's statement was dictum; dictum, however, of the most authoritative kind.

The Barnstable, owned by an English corporation and chartered to the Boston Fruit Company, had run down and sunk a schooner off the coast of Massachusetts. A proceeding *in rem* was instituted, in which the English owner appeared as claimant and the Fruit Company was vouched in as a third-party defendant on the owner's allegation that by the terms of the charter the Fruit Company was liable over to the owner. After testimony had been taken, counsel for both owner and charterer admitted the fault of the Barnstable in the collision and assented to a judgment against her; the question reserved for judicial decision was whether the owner or the charterer was ultimately liable. Thus neither party raised the issue of ship's liability, and the case, as it came to the Supreme Court, presented the narrow issue of ascertaining the true meaning of the charter terms. On that issue the Court held that the "primary liability" was on the charterers, so the owners were reimbursed.

Even if the dictum in The Barnstable is accepted as settled law, the case must still be narrowly construed. In the first place the rule applies presumably only to tort claims or statutory violations: the power of a charterer to create contract liens against a vessel depends on the terms of the charter, as to which supply and repair men were, prior to a 1971 amendment to the Maritime Lien Act, put on inquiry.[34] Secondly, in Justice Brown's own phraseology, the rule applies only to those "lawfully in possession": thus the mutineers, pirates and people "like" them would not bind the ship even, as Justice Story had held long ago, for such beneficent and useful labor as pilotage.[35] The case of the stevedore-independent contractor is about as far as the rule has been or seems likely to be carried: in United States v. The Helen [36] the Second Circuit held a scow liable to a statutory penalty for discharging lumber into the tidal waters of New York harbor where the scow, on demise to a charterer, was being unloaded by an independent stevedore. The owner in The Helen was granted recovery over against both the charterer and the stevedore, who was found to be ultimately liable.[37]

32. See *supra* § 9–4 for these cases.

33. *Supra* § 9–9.

34. See *infra* § 9–39 *et seq.*

35. The Anne, 1 Fed.Cas. 955, Case No. 412 (C.C.D.Mass.1818).

36. 164 F.2d 111, 1948 A.M.C. 30 (2d Cir. 1947).

37. Recent cases holding the ship liable in rem for damage done while a charterer was in possession and control are British West Indies Produce, Inc. v. S/S Atlantic Clipper, 353 F.

### Same: (4) Liens Arising While Ship is in Custodia Legis

**§ 9–11.** It is often said to be a general rule that maritime liens do not arise against a ship which has been seized under legal process—which is, as the phrase goes, *in custodia legis.* It stands to reason that if a ship is sold under an admiralty decree in an *in rem* proceeding, no liens of any kind attach to the ship in the hands of the purchaser; the purpose of the proceeding and the effect of the decree are to execute the liens. So the rule can apply only to the proceeds of sale in such a case or to liens asserted against the ship when the legal custody was that of a non-admiralty court. If the *custodia legis* rule exists at all, it has been mostly eaten away by exceptions.

This question came before the Supreme Court in The Resolute,[38] but the case came up in such a way that the Court had no occasion to resolve the issue on the merits. A libel for wages had been filed against a ship which, at the time the services were rendered, had been in the custody of a receiver appointed by a state court. The receiver sold the vessel, and following the sale the libel was filed. The District Court assumed jurisdiction of the case, over argument that it had no jurisdiction because no lien could have arisen during the receivership. The owners thereupon took a direct appeal to the Supreme Court on the jurisdictional issue. That Court held that "the issue of lien or no lien is not one of jurisdiction but of merits" and that the appellants had mistaken their remedy, which should have been an appeal to the Circuit Court. Justice Brown's opinion was at pains to point out that the Court was not deciding the merits of the question. In a passage labeled dictum he indicated that the Court was not impressed by the contention that there could be no lien: "*Prima facie,* the rendition of mariner's services imports a lien, and the mere fact that the vessel is navigated by a receiver does not necessarily negative such lien, although there may be facts in the particular case to show [that the lien did not arise]." [39]

Since The Resolute the Supreme Court has not reconsidered the question of non-admiralty custodial claims. Justice Brown's language in The Resolute has, however, been taken to mean that liens

Supp. 548, 1973 A.M.C. 163 (S.D.N.Y. 1973); Demsey & Associates v. S/S Sea Star, 461 F.2d 1009, 1972 A.M.C. 1440 (2d Cir. 1972); United Nations Children's Fund v. S/S Nordstern, 251 F. Supp. 833 (S.D.N.Y.1965) (unreasonable deviation; Judge Levet's opinion collects older cases of this type). Some older cases in which the rule of The Barnstable was recognized and restated are: Burns Bros. v. The Carfloat Central R. R. of N. J. # 42, 202 F.2d 910, 1953 A.M.C. 718 (2d Cir. 1953); Logue Stevedoring Corp. v. Tugs Dalzellance etc., 198 F.2d 369, 1952 A.M.C. 1297 (2d Cir. 1952); Santiago v. U. S., 102 F.Supp. 425 (S.D.N.Y.1952); Davis v. M/V Esso Delivery No. 13, 100 F.Supp. 285, 1951 A.M.C. 1405 (D.Md.1951). See also Schnell v. United States, 166 F.2d 479, 1948 A.M.C. 769 (2d Cir. 1948) certiorari denied 334 U.S. 833, 68 S.Ct. 1346 (1948).

38. 168 U.S. 437, 18 S.Ct. 112 (1897).

39. *Id.* at 440, 18 S.Ct. at 113.

can arise, presumably with respect to any type of legal custody outside the admiralty.[40]

The other branch of the *custodia legis* rule relates to claims asserted against the proceeds of sale in the registry of the admiralty court for services performed after the ship has been taken into the custody of the marshal on process *in rem*. Since the ship during the period of custody is usually tied up at a wharf, most of the cases have involved claims for wages by seamen who have remained on board and claims for wharfage. Since the ship has been libeled and arrested by someone, there are necessarily prior claims outstanding. If the proceeds of sale are insufficient to pay all claims, the claimants for services rendered during custody naturally claim payment in full in priority to precustodial claims.

The law of the matter, which has reached a high point of confusion, may be stated as follows: since, as a general rule, no liens may arise against a vessel while it is *in custodia legis*, the custodial claimants have no lien for their services. Nevertheless, if equity and good conscience require that they be paid in priority to pre-custodial claimants who do have liens, the admiralty court may properly decree the prior payment. Result: sometimes the custodial claims are paid first, sometimes last and sometimes not at all, depending on what the court which decides the case thinks the dictates of "equity and good conscience" require. Thus the seamen who remain on board after the ship has been libeled, the wharf-owner who allows it to remain tied up at his wharf, as well as those who may furnish supplies or repairs are gambling on a wholly unpredictable result unless they take the precaution of having their services authorized in advance by an order of the custodial court.

The confusion stems from a 1927 decision of the Supreme Court, New York Dock Co. v. Steamship Poznan,[41] which involved a custodial claim for wharfage, where there had been no authorizing court order. Without discussion the Court agreed to the "general rule that there can be no maritime lien for services furnished a vessel while *in custodia legis*". Nevertheless the Court directed prior payment to the Dock Company as an "expense of justice" incurred for "the common benefit." For analogy Justice Stone cited Fosdick v. Schall [42] and other railroad receivership cases which had established the so-called "six months" rule for services necessary to the railroad's operation prior to the receivership period.[43] "In equity and good conscience", the Court concluded, the Dock Company's claim "should be satisfied before the libellants may enjoy the fruits of their liens."

40. Robinson, Admiralty (1939) 366. See City of Erie v. S/S North American, 267 F.Supp. 875, 1968 A.M.C. 500 (W.D.Pa.1967); The Pacific Hemlock, 3 F.Supp. 305, 307, 1933 A.M.C. 298, 301 (W.D.Wash.1932); The Washington, 296 F. 158 (E.D.N.Y.1924). But see United States v. Oil Screws Ken Jr., Linda Sue etc., 275 F.Supp. 792 (E.D.La.1967) (state receivership costs "non-maritime", subordinated to mortgage and other liens).

41. 274 U.S. 117, 47 S.Ct. 482, 1927 A.M.C. 723 (1927).

42. 99 U.S. 235 (1878).

43. See 5 Collier on Bankruptcy (14th ed. by Moore 1943, revised 1973) 573.

It would have been simpler to say in Poznan, as Justice Brown had said in The Resolute with reference to state court receiverships, that liens could accrue during the custodial period. Indeed an incidental reference by Justice Stone in a 1930 case, Collie v. Fergusson,[44] to the Poznan opinion (which he had written) suggests that Stone himself was inclined to look on Poznan as a weakening rather than an affirmation of the *custodia legis* rule. The Supreme Court, however, has had nothing further to say on the matter, and the lower courts have obediently continued to perform the two way stretch which Poznan apparently requires: deny the lien in the first instance, but pay the claim anyhow if "equity and good conscience" require it.[45]

44. 281 U.S. 52, 55, 50 S.Ct. 189, 191, 1930 A.M.C. 408, 410 (1930).

45. See, *e. g.* Murray v. The Meteor, 83 F.Supp. 212, 1949 A.M.C. 563 (E.D.N.Y. 1949), reversed 175 F.2d 72, 1949 A.M.C. 1081 (2d Cir. 1949); *Id.*, 93 F. Supp. 274, 1950 A.M.C. 2030 (E.D.N.Y. 1950). In The Meteor a wharfage claim was finally allowed against a release bond even though the vessel was held by the Second Circuit to have been a "dead ship". In recent litigation custodial claims have been paid before pre-custodial liens in Rainbow Line v. M/V Tequila, 341 F.Supp. 459, 1972 A.M.C. 1540 (S.D.N.Y.1972), affirmed without discussion of this point, 480 F.2d 1024, 1973 A.M.C. 1431 (2d Cir. 1973) (Marshal's expenses over mortgage and salvage claim); United Virginia Bank/Citizens and Marine v. O/S Sea Queen, 343 F.Supp. 1020, 1971 A.M.C. 1880 (E.D.Va.1971 (per A. M.C.) or 1972 (per official report)) (port risk insurance premium advanced by mortgagee; recoverable losses to be paid into court registry; *cf.* Moon Engineering Co., *infra* this note); Payne v. S/S Tropic Breeze, 293 F.Supp. 425, 1969 A.M.C. 930 (D. Puerto Rico 1968), affirmed 423 F.2d 236, 1970 A.M.C. 1850 (1st Cir. 1970) certiorari denied *sub nom.* Samadjopoulos v. National Western Life Ins. Co., 400 U.S. 964 (1970) (master's advances and expenses to or on behalf of crew over mortgage); Empresa Nacional "Elcano" v. M/V Tropicana, 252 F.Supp. 399, 1965 A.M.C. 2730 (E. D.La.1965), affirmed 366 F.2d 729 (5th Cir. 1966) (service and repair claims over foreign mortgage); Tampa Tugs and Towing, Inc. v. M/V Sandanger, 242 F.Supp. 576, 1965 A.M.C. 1771 (S. D.Cal.1965) (services over salvage lien); Turner & Blanchard, Inc. v. A. H. Bull S.S. Co. (S/S Emilia), 1963 A.M.C. 1448 (E.D.N.Y.1963), affirmed 322 F.2d 249, 1963 A.M.C. 1447 (2d Cir. 1963), certiorari denied, 375 U.S. 880, 84 S.Ct. 150 (1963) (Marshal's expenses for discharge of cargo over unspecified liens). The custodial court may authorize the operation of the vessel during custody and before sale; expenses incurred in such an operation were ordered paid before the pre-custodial liens in Roy v. M/V Kateri Tek, 238 F.Supp. 813, 1966 A.M.C. 1830 (E. D.La.1965) (supplies furnished to fishing vessel operated under charter); see also United States v. Audrey II, 185 F.Supp. 777, 1960 A.M.C. 1977 (N.D. Cal.1960) (advances by Maritime Administration to pay crew wages), reversed on other grounds *sub nom.* Northwest Marine Works v. United States (The Audrey II), 307 F.2d 537, 1963 A.M.C. 142 (9th Cir. 1962) (discussed note 494 *infra*). The custodial claim, instead of being paid in full, may be reduced in the discretion of the court. See Pyne v. Oil Screw F/V Chrisway, 298 F.Supp. 1160 (S.D. Ga.1969) (50% of advances by mortgagee to pay watchman on board vessel paid before tort claim which outranked the mortgage); Moon Engineering Co., Inc. v. S/S Valiant Power, 193 F.Supp. 460, 1961 A.M.C. 226 (E.D.Va.1960) (wharfage fees allowed in a reasonable amount). In the following cases, custodial claims have been subordinated to pre-custodial liens: National Bank of North America v. S/S Oceanic Ondine, 315 F.Supp. 386, 1971 A.M.C. 1816 (S.D.Tex.1970) (wharfage); Moon Engineering Co., Inc. v. S/S Valiant Power, *supra* this note (Port risk insurance premium advanced by mortgagee; *cf.* United Virginia Bank case, *supra* this note). See further the cases cited in notes 47 and 49 *infra* disallowing wage claims by crew members who remained on

In Larsen v. New York Dock Co.[46] Judge Frank explained to the successful litigant in Poznan some unsuspected traps in the "equity and good conscience" doctrine. In the Larsen case a ship which had been libeled remained at the wharf from March 19 until November 22, when it was sold. It was found that the Dock Company had looked "solely to the credit of [the owner]" until September 6 (at which time the owner had filed a petition under Chapter XI of the Bankruptcy Act). Poznan, in Judge Frank's analysis, rests on the doctrine of unjust enrichment and one aspect of that doctrine, according to Section 110 of the Restatement of Restitution, is that "A person who has conferred a benefit upon another as the performance of a contract with a third person is not entitled to restitution from the other merely because of the failure of performance by the third person." Consequently the Dock Company's claim for prior payment for the March 19–September 6 period was denied, the balance of its claim being granted. The Dock Company's success in Poznan may have caused it to rest on its laurels; it is to be hoped that the modified debacle which it suffered in Larsen has led it to take the precaution of securing a court order before allowing libeled ships to remain at its wharf.

Seamen's claims for wages earned during the custodial period might be expected to fare at least as well as wharfage claims. They have indeed recovered wages in some cases, but have been denied priority in enough cases to make it clear that they are proceeding at their own risk in staying on board.[47] Collie v. Fergusson,[48] in which Justice Stone seemed willing to concede that Poznan had shaken the foundations of the *custodia legis* rule, denied a statutory recovery of double wages for neglect or delay in paying a seaman's wages "without sufficient cause." The arrest of the ship under admiralty process, the Court held, was "sufficient cause" for the delay. And a 1948 opinion denying priority for wage claims indicates the hurdles which the custodial crew may have to clear before coming to rest in the safe embrace of Poznan:

> ". . . the crew remained on board with the acquiescence of the marshal; but their testimony as to the services performed by them after July 2 is quite vague, and it is clear

board during custody. Cunard Steamship Co. Ltd. v. S/S Caribia, 1972 A.M.C. 2310 (E.D.N.Y.1972) discusses a proposal for reconditioning a vessel held in custody submitted to and rejected by the court.

46. 166 F.2d 687, 1948 A.M.C. 756 (2d Cir. 1948). Larsen was followed in Bassis v. Universal Line, S.A., 484 F. 2d 1065, 1973 A.M.C. 1449 (2d Cir. 1973).

47. Bromfield Mfg. Co. v. The Yacht Brown, Jones & Smith, 117 F.Supp. 630, 633, 1954 A.M.C. 350, 354 (D.Mass.1954): "No maritime lien can be allowed for wages to seamen accruing after the libeling of the ship". The claim of a yacht captain was disallowed. Accord: Vlavianos v. The Cypress, 171 F.2d 435, 1949 A.M.C. 9 (4th Cir. 1948), certiorari denied 337 U.S. 924, 69 S.Ct. 1171 (1949); Old Point Fish Co. v. Haywood, 109 F.2d 703, 940 A.M.C. 145 (4th Cir. 1940).

48. See note 44 *supra*.

that the marshal did not ask them to maintain the vessel, and that the Maryland Drydock Company, with the marshal's knowledge, performed all the necessary service. The evidence spports the conclusion of the District Judge that the master and seamen remained aboard because they had no other place to sleep, were still hoping against hope that the ship might sail, and were desirous of avoiding possible complications with the immigration authorities." [49]

**Same: (5) Liens Arising While Ship is in Control of Sovereign**

**§ 9–12.** A ship which is at fault in a collision may be owned or operated by the United States or a foreign sovereign or by a State of the United States or by a municipal corporation. On grounds of sovereign immunity the victim of the collision may find himself denied recovery for the injury he has suffered, or limited in the remedies available to him. We are here concerned with the problem which arises when the offending vessel passes into or is restored to private hands. If the idea of the ship's personality is carried to a logical extreme and the ship is looked on as "the guilty instrument or thing", then the lien or claim, unenforceable during the period of government control, should obviously—or so it might be argued—be enforceable now that the impediment has been removed.

So far as ships owned by or on charter to the United States at the time of the tort are concerned, Justice Holmes in The Western Maid [50] answered the question whether recovery could be had against such ships in the hands of new owners (or the original owner after redelivery of a chartered ship) with a decisive No. Holmes, who had done as much as any one to popularize the idea that American admiralty law accepted the personification of the ship as basic theory,[51] had already expressed his disenchantment with the idea. Conceding, in a case decided in 1909, that "the fiction that a vessel may be a wrongdoer" had been carried further in the United States than in England, he went on to comment that "a fiction is not a satisfactory

49. Vlavianos v. The Cypress, 171 F.2d 435, 438, 1949 A.M.C. 9, 13 (4th Cir. 1948) certiorari denied 337 U.S. 924, 69 S.Ct. 1171 (1949).

In Putnam and Overman v. Lower, Kadlec et al., 236 F.2d 561, 1956 A.M.C. 2059 (9th Cir. 1956), Judge Stephens cited the Vlavianos case and Collie v. Fergusson, note 44 *supra*, to the propositions that: "It is well settled that no maritime lien can be allowed to seamen for wages accruing subsequent to the time the ship is taken into *custodia legis*, and particularly is this true where as here, the libel is filed by the crew of the vessel." (*Id.* at 570, 2071) The Putnam case is stated and discussed in note 351a *infra*. Wage claims by crew members who remained on board the vessel during custody were disallowed in Empresa Nacional Elcano v. M/V Tropicana, 1971 A.M.C. 1583 (E.D.La.1970) (see reference in note 45 *supra* to earlier proceedings in the case); Peterson v. S.S. Wahcondah, 216 F.Supp. 642, 1964 A.M.C. 2425 (E.D.La.1963), reversed on other grounds 331 F.2d 44, 1964 A.M.C. 2418 (5th Cir. 1964) (a claim for attorney's fees for services performed by the crew was also disallowed even though the court had at one point apparently authorized the services); Irving Trust Co. v. S/S Golden Sail, 197 F.Supp. 777, 1962 A.M.C. 2676 (D.Or.1961).

50. 257 U.S. 419, 42 S.Ct. 159 (1922).

51. See § 9–3 *supra*.

ground for taking one man's property to satisfy another man's wrong, and it should not be extended." [52] With reference to the question for decision in The Western Maid, however, it was not a case of "extending" a disreputable doctrine: the precedents, which apparently a majority of the court was not willing to overrule, indicated that the liens were enforceable once the period of sovereign control had come to an end. Holmes' opinion in The Western Maid contains some magnificent rhetoric but it cannot be said that his handling of the authorities was completely honest. Nor did his disingenuity go unremarked. Three justices joined in an angry dissent and Judge Hough, a great admiralty judge, commented in the Harvard Law Review that "when it comes to hurdling a legal difficulty Holmes, J., is *hors concours*, but in this effort he has surpassed himself," adding, in the words of "an old song":

> "It ain't so much as wot 'e said As the narsty w'y 'e said it." [53]

The question has become unimportant as to vessels owned by the United States; since the United States has consented to suit under the Public Vessels Act or under the Suits in Admiralty Act, the injured claimant will ordinarily have his relief against the sovereign and will not be tempted to pursue his claim against the ship when it reverts to private hands. But The Western Maid did not decide, or did not necessarily decide, the comparable questions which arise in connection with state and municipally owned vessels, and Holmes' curious handling of precedent has left those questions shrouded in doubt. It becomes appropriate therefore to examine what the precedents were and what surviving value, if any, they still have.

**§ 9–13.** In The Siren [54] a ship, attempting to violate the Civil War blockade of the port of Charleston, had been seized by the United States Navy and sent to Boston where she was condemned and sold as prize. In New York harbor, en route to Boston, she had under

52. The Eugene F. Moran, 212 U.S. 466, 474, 29 S.Ct. 339, 340 (1909).

53. Hough, Admiralty Jurisdiction—of Late Years, 37 Harv.L.Rev. 529, 543 (1924). Holmes was far from confessing error. See 2 Holmes-Pollock Letters 135 (1944): "In that case (The Western Maid) we held that a vessel, a military transport I believe, that had wrongly collided with another while belonging to U.S. and that couldn't be sued while belonging to the U.S. couldn't be sued after it was sold—much to the wrath of some admiralty men—*inter alios* Hough a good old admiralty judge—who wrote an amusing article . . . to me unconvincing—in which he seemed to think I had forgotten The China about [which] I discoursed in the Common Law and quoted:

"It aint so much as wot 'e said
As the narsty w'y 'e said it."

I quote as he quoted though the *as* seems wrong in the first line. Your courts decided the same way a little later (The Sylvan Arrow, (1923) P. 220). The good Hough says that I refine on the meaning of a word unknown to the admiralty law—*tort*—that the admiralty only knows *collision*, that as I conclude that there was no tort I conclude that there was no collision! This suggests several reflections too obvious to write out." The citation to The Sylvan Arrow is by the editors of the Letters. But it is entirely possible that Holmes was refering to The Tervaete, see note 66 *infra*.

54. 74 U.S. (7 Wall.) 152 (1869).

conditions of fault run down and sunk another vessel. The owner of that vessel intervened in the prize proceedings with a petition that his claim for damages be first paid out of the proceeds of sale. The petition was allowed. Justice Field commented:

> "For the damages occasioned by collision of vessels at sea a claim is created against the vessel in fault, in favor of the injured party. This claim may be enforced in the admiralty by a proceeding in rem, except where the vessel is the property of the United States. In such case the claim exists equally as if the vessel belonged to a private citizen, but for reasons of public policy, already stated, cannot be enforced by direct proceedings against the vessel. It stands, in that respect, like a claim against the government, incapable of enforcement without its consent, and unavailable for any purpose. . . .
>
> "Now, it is a settled principle of admiralty law, that all maritime claims upon the vessel extend equally to the proceeds arising from its sale, and are to be satisfied out of them. Assuming therefore, that the Siren was in fault, and that by the tort she committed a claim was created against her, we do not perceive any just ground for refusing its satisfaction out of the proceeds of her sale." [55]

The Siren did not directly involve the possible liability of the ship if, for example, it had been found to be not lawful prize and restored to its owners. Justice Field mentioned the point in passing but without discussion; the balance of his opinion suggested that there would be an enforceable liability.

The question came up again somewhat peripherally in Workman v. City of New York,[56] which involved a municipally owned fire boat, which had negligently collided with another vessel while attempting to put out a fire. Conceding that the fire boat was not subject to be libeled *in rem* because of its use in performance of a governmental function of the municipality, the Court held that the city could be sued *in personam*, under principles of maritime law which prevailed over local law by which the city was immune from suit. In a lengthy opinion Justice White had this to say:

> "Of course, as has been repeatedly declared by this court, by the general admiralty law of this country, subject to the exemption from process possessed by the national government, a ship, by whomsoever owned or navigated, is liable for an actionable injury resulting from the negligence of the master and crew of such vessel. The John G. Stevens, (1898) 170 U.S. 113, 120, 18 S.Ct. 544 and cases cited, 122 S.Ct. 548. A liability of the owners in personam, however, is not dependent upon ability to maintain a proceeding in rem because of the maritime tort. A maritime lien may not

55. *Id.* at 155, 159.

56. 179 U.S. 552, 21 S.Ct. 212 (1900).

exist in a cause of collision, for instance, when the thing occasioning the tort was not the subject of a maritime lien, The Rock Island Bridge (1867) 6 Wall. 213; or such a lien, if it exist, may not be enforceable, and so may be said to render the offending thing not the subject of a maritime lien, because of the ownership and possession of such thing being in the government of the nation. The Siren, (1869) 7 Wall. 152. Or the remedy in rem may not be available owing to the offending thing being actually in another country, or because of its loss intermediate the collision and the institution of legal proceedings." [57]

§ 9–14. In The Western Maid, several suits had been consolidated for argument, and, as it happened, the case involved a ship owned by as well as ships on charter to the United States at the time of the collisions. After the ships had been sold or in the case of the chartered ships restored to their owners, the victims of the collisions instituted libels *in rem,* relying on the propositions thought to have been established in The Siren and reiterated in the Workman case. Holmes approached the problem from on high:

> "In deciding this question we must realize that however ancient may be the traditions of maritime law, however diverse the sources from which it has been drawn, it derives its whole and only power in this country from its having been accepted and adopted by the United States." [58]

"There is," he continued, rephrasing one of his most celebrated epigrams, "no mystic overlaw to which even the United States must bow." Furthermore, "the United States has not consented to be sued for torts, and therefore it cannot be said that in a legal sense the United States has been guilty of a tort. For a tort is a tort only because the law has made it so." That left however the contention that, even if the United States had not committed a tort, the ships had, and was not a ship a person? Had not so eminent authority as Mr. Justice Holmes said in The Common Law, which counsel were careful to cite in argument, that by American law the ship *was* a person? The reply, which did *not* cite The Common Law, was brief and almost curt:

> "It may be said that the persons who actually did the act complained of may or might be sued and the ship for this purpose is regarded as a person. But that is a fiction not a fact and as a fiction is the creation of the law. It would be a strange thing if the law created a fiction to accomplish the result supposed. It is totally immaterial that in dealing with private wrongs the fiction, however originated, is in force." [59]

That left the precedents. Remarking that "Legal obligations that exist but cannot be enforced are ghosts that are seen in the law but

57. *Id.* at 572–573, 21 S.Ct. at 219–220.

58. 257 U.S. 419, 432, 42 S.Ct. 159, 160 (1922).

59. *Id.* at 433, 42 S.Ct. at 161.

that are elusive to the grasp," he distinguished The Siren by saying that "the ground of that decision was that when the United States came into court to enforce a claim [*i. e.* the United States had instituted the prize proceedings] it would be assumed to submit to just claims of third persons in respect of the same subject matter." As to Workman, he went on airily, "there was nothing decided [in that case] that is contrary to our conclusion", which is true enough if the emphasis is carefully placed on the word "decided". The dissenting justices could not see it that way. Holmes' explanation, or "gloss", of The Siren seemed to them "unjustified and inaccurate" and they flatly disagreed with his dismissal of Workman as having nothing to do with the case.[60]

**§ 9–15.** The only modern authority which Holmes cited as "favoring" his decision in The Western Maid were two cases—Ex parte New York No. 1 [61] and Ex parte New York No. 2 [62]—which the Court had decided in the immediately preceding October term. The two citations are amazing. Neither case, as the dissenting justices said politely, has "militating force". Ex parte New York No. 2 involved a collision in which a tugboat owned by the State of New York had been at fault. The tug was still owned by the State at the time of suit. It was held, on a straight sovereign immunity rationale, that property of a State used solely for its governmental purposes could not be seized under process *in rem* and that the idea of a nationally uniform maritime law depending on exclusive federal sovereignty had nothing to do with the case. Ex parte New York No. 1 is more interesting. There tugboats chartered and operated by the State had been at fault in collisions and were libeled *in rem* after redelivery to their owners. The owners, by petition under Admiralty Rule 59,[62a] sought to bring in the State's Superintendent of Public Works who had entered into the charters on behalf of the State. Monitions issued against the Superintendent, and the State, appearing in the District Court, objected to the court's jurisdiction and urged that the monitions be dismissed. On the District Court's refusal to dismiss, the State moved in the Supreme Court for writs of prohibition and mandamus. Thus the only issue which came before the Supreme Court was whether the State could, without its consent, be impleaded by admiralty process in an action between private parties. The liability of the tugs (and thus indirectly of the owners) for torts committed while the tugs had been under State control was in no way involved in the motion for writs of prohibition. The Court held that the attempt to implead the State was quite as much an action against the State as an attempt to seize its property would have been and granted the writs. It distinguished the Workman case (which had held that a city could be sued *in personam* in admiralty, despite its immunity from suit un-

60. *Id.* at 437, 439, 42 S.Ct. at 163.

61. 256 U.S. 490, 41 S.Ct. 588 (1921).

62. 256 U.S. 503, 41 S.Ct. 592 (1921).

62a. The substance of Admiralty Rule 59 (later renumbered 56) is now covered in Rule 14(c), Fed.Rules Civ.Proc.

der local law and even though its property could not be libeled *in rem*) in the following terms:

> "[Workman] dealt with a question of the substantive law of admiralty, not the power to exercise jurisdiction over the person of defendant; and in the opinion the court was careful to distinguish between the immunity from jurisdiction attributable to a sovereign upon grounds of policy, and immunity from liability in a particular case. . . . We repeat, the immunity of a State from suit *in personam* in the admiralty brought by a private person without its consent, is clear." [63]

Which seems to mean that a State and a municipal corporation are two different things.[64]

On the facts of Ex parte New York No. 1 the unfortunate owners of the tugs were presumably liable (in the sense that their tugs were liable) for the torts committed by the charterers. At least that would follow if the rule of The Barnstable [65] applied despite the charterer's sovereign immunity from suit. But the question whether The Barnstable did apply was not one of the questions raised or discussed in the phase of the litigation that came before the Supreme Court.

**§ 9–16.** Having reviewed the authorities we may return to The Western Maid. The decision in that case was entirely reasonable —*i. e.* that owners or purchasers received their ships from the sovereign free of claims which had accrued during the period of sovereign control. Indeed the English Privy Council in The Tervaete reached the same conclusion at about the same time, on a quite different conceptual or argumentative approach.[66] The only unfortunate thing

63. 256 U.S. 490, 499, 500, 41 S.Ct. 588, 590, 591 (1921).

64. See The Ferryboat West Point, 71 F.Supp. 206, 1946 A.M.C. 1532 (E.D. Va.1946) holding that under the Workman case a ferryboat jointly owned by a city and a county could be libeled *in rem*. The Workman case was also followed in The West Keats (United States v. Port of Portland) 300 F. 724, 1924 A.M.C. 1154 (9th Cir. 1924) although in The West Keats recovery was denied on other grounds.

65. See *supra* § 9–10.

66. (1922) P. 259. The action was brought in respect of a collision which occurred between a private vessel and the Belgian government-owned Tervaete. After the collision The Tervaete was sold by Belgium to a private owner. Scrutton, L. J. said: "In my view it is now established that procedure in rem is not based upon wrongdoing of the ship personified as an offender, but is a means of bringing the owner of the ship to meet his personal liability by seizing his property. The so-called maritime lien has nothing to do with possession, but is a priority in claim over the proceeds of sale of the ship in preference to other claimants. It does not appear *eo nomine* in cases of collision in the reports till The Bold Buccleugh was heard in 1851, where it is defined as a claim or privilege upon a thing to be carried into effect by legal process; and it is stated, erroneously as is now admitted, that wherever an action in rem lies there a maritime lien exists.

". . . But for a lien to arise . . . some person having by permission of the owner temporary ownership or possession of the vessel must be liable for the collision.

". . . Neither the Belgian Government could have been sued in personam, nor could their ship have been arrested in rem. If this is so, I do not understand how there could then be any maritime lien on the ship. To

about the case is that Justice Holmes, who recognized that "judges do and must legislate", felt himself unable to declare the grounds of decision more frankly, or at least more clearly. His involved and disingenuous handling of precedent, his distinctions without a difference, left the law in a state of unnecessary confusion.

What that state is may be summarized as follows: claims against ships owned or chartered by the United States do not follow the ships into private hands—although the point is no longer of much importance since the United States has, in most cases, consented to be sued. The same rule certainly applies to vessels owned or chartered by a foreign government and that may still be of considerable importance. The fog sets in when we come to State and municipal vessels. The implications from The Siren (despite Holmes' attempted distinction) and from the Workman case are that the claims run with the vessels. The underlying logic of The Western Maid is that they would not run (and that the tug owners in Ex parte New York No. 1 would have been better advised to have denied liability on the merits than to have sought to implead the State of New York).[67]

A distinction may be taken between State owned and municipally owned vessels. Ex parte New York No. 1 makes it clear that the State can neither be proceeded against directly nor impleaded in an action brought against the private owners. In that situation The Western Maid should operate to make the claims unenforceable against the owners. As to municipally owned vessels, Workman, if it is still good law,[68] says that the city may be sued *in personam* even though its property may not be libeled *in rem*. Therefore there would be nothing to prevent the private owner, if the ship were libeled *in rem*, from impleading the city. All that being true (if it is), there seems to be nothing in The Western Maid to suggest that the libel against the ship should be dismissed.

The principle established by The Western Maid has, with the decline of the sovereign immunity idea on all levels, become of purely

hold that a lien would come into existence, if the Government sold the ship to a private purchaser, would be to deprive the Belgian Government of part of their property, for such a lien about to arise must reduce the price paid to the Government and so affect the property of the government." (*id.* at 270).

Accord: The Sylvan Arrow, (1923) P. 220. While under requisition by the United States, The Sylvan Arrow was in collision with The W. I. Radcliffe. After the vessel had been released from requisition the plaintiffs commenced an action *in rem.* The court held that the defendants had surrendered the ship to the United States under compulsion, that in no sense could it be said that the master and crew derived their authority from the defendants, and that on the facts no maritime lien attached to the ship and her owners were not liable either through the vessel or otherwise.

67. In subsequent litigation arising out of the same collision the tug owners successfully resorted to this defense. The Charlotte, 299 F. 595, 1924 A.M.C. 1070 (2d Cir. 1924) certiorari denied 266 U.S. 604, 45 S.Ct. 91 (1924). The Court said, *per curiam*: ". . . The State of New York can neither be sued *in personam* for the tort complained of, nor can its property, whether absolute or owned *pro hac vice*, be made to respond for the same tort. In other words the doctrine of The Western Maid *supra* applies to and governs this case."

68. See cases cited note 64 *supra.*

theoretical interest. As a matter of jurisprudential elegance it is to be regretted that Justice Holmes so confused the issues. In the real world it is half a century or more since anyone has tried to pursue a vessel after its transfer from government to private ownership with respect to claims which accrued during the period when the vessel was owned or operated by the government. Conceivably such a case could still arise, most probably with respect to vessels at one time owned by foreign governments who may still cherish their immunity. If ever the case does arise, the result, if not the argumentation, in The Western Maid will furnish an entirely sound point of departure.

### The Libel in Rem, the Libel in Personam and the Problem of Res Judicata

**§ 9–17.** Libels in admiralty may be *in rem* or *in personam.* It is customary to say that the action *in rem* is brought against the vessel while the action *in personam* is against the owner. It might be thought to follow that, since the actions are theoretically against different parties, a decree in an *in personam* proceeding would not bar a subsequent proceeding *in rem* on grounds of *res judicata.*

An odd factual sequence suggested this interesting speculation to metaphysically minded counsel in Burns Bros. v. Central R. R. of New Jersey.[69] A carfloat owned by the Central Railroad had, while in the control of the Long Island Railroad, negligently injured libellant's barge. At the time the Central Railroad was going through a § 77 reorganization and there was doubt whether it would have been possible to arrest the carfloat by process *in rem.* The barge owner therefore brought an *in personam* action in admiralty against both the Long Island and Central Railroads. In that action judgment was entered against the Long Island, but the libel was dismissed against the Central since there was no evidence that any of its employees had been negligent. At that point the Long Island went into reorganization (which made the judgment against it of little value) and the Central's reorganization was terminated. Since the Central's property was now free from judicial control, the persistent barge owner libeled the carfloat *in rem,* which gave counsel the opportunity to make the intriguing argument that the dismissal of the *in personam* libel could not be *res judicata* as to the *in rem* libel because the two actions were against different "parties". The basis for arguing that the carfloat was liable even though the owner was not was of course the rule derived from The Barnstable (vessel redelivered to owner liable *in rem* for torts committed while under control of charterer).[70]

Judge Learned Hand, who wrote the opinion, had never been an ardent supporter of the "personification" theory, which he once described as "archaic . . . an animistic survival from remote times . . . based on . . . irrational fictions . . . atavistic . . ."[71] Conceding in his opinion in the Burns Brothers

69. 202 F.2d 910, 1953 A.M.C. 718 (2d Cir. 1953).

70. See § 9–10 *supra.*

71. The Carlotta, 48 F.2d 110, 112, 1931 A.M.C. 742, 745 (2d Cir. 1931).

case that "it has from the beginning been true that in suits *in rem* the vessel has been regarded as the tort-feasor", he nevertheless made short shrift of counsel's speculations:

> "This court has, however, twice decided that a decree *in rem* is a bar to a suit *in personam*, and we cannot see why the rule should not work both ways. Moreover, we should have so held, had there been no precedents. The reason behind the doctrine of *res judicata* is that when a party to a controversy has had one fair chance to be heard, there is no reason to suppose that the result of a second trial will be more just than the first; and it is always true that *interest reipublicae ut finis litium.* Disputes arise between human beings, not inanimate things; and it would be absurd to give the beaten party another chance because on second trial he appears as the claimant to a vessel that is, and can be, nothing but the measure of his stake in the controversy." [72]

The Burns Brothers case thus decisively rejected the theory that *in rem* and *in personam* suits can be succcessively maintained, on the "atavistic" notion of the ship's personality.[73] Sympathising, however,

72. 202 F.2d 910, 912, 913, 1953 A.M.C. 718, 721, 722 (2d Cir. 1953). The two cases that Hand referred to are: Bailey v. Sundberg, 49 F. 583 (2d Cir. 1892); Sullivan v. Nitrate Producers' S. S. Co., 262 F. 371 (2d Cir. 1919). In the Bailey case it was held that where, on a libel *in rem* for collision, the master of the libeled vessel, though not a formal party, took an active part in the defense, a dismissal on the merits rendered the question *res judicata,* as against a subsequent libel *in personam* against him. In the Sullivan case a suit *in rem* by a seaman to recover indemnity for injury on board, ending in dismissal because he was on an English ship on the high seas when injured, and under English law indemnity was not recoverable, was held a bar to a second suit *in personam* for maintenance and cure, which, although given by British statute, might have been recovered in the prior suit. The Sullivan case is no longer good law as to the proposition that a prior judgment in an indemnity action bars a subsequent action for maintenance and cure: see discussion in Chapter VI, § 6–24. In Continental Grain Co. v. Barge FBL-585, 364 U.S. 19, 25, 1961 A.M.C. 1, 6 (1960) (a transfer of venue case) Justice Black cited the Burns Brothers case as well as the Bailey and Sullivan cases with approval. In Simon v. M/V Hialeah, 431 F.2d 867, 1971 A.M.C. 95 (5th Cir. 1970) a judgment in a state court action *in personam* was held *res judicata* to bar a subsequent libel *in rem.* See also Pierce v. National Bulk Carriers, Inc., 261 F.Supp. 619, 1967 A.M.C. 1398 (synopsis only) (D.Del.1966); Anastasiadis v. Mecom, 265 F.Supp. 959, 1966 A.M.C. 2747 (S.D.Tex.1966).

73. A plaintiff who has recovered a judgment in an *in rem* action which remains in part unsatisfied may proceed against the owner *in personam* to recover the deficiency. See discussion *infra* § 9–90. A quite different situation is presented when a plaintiff who has recovered an *in personam* judgment against the owner subsequently seeks to satisfy the judgment by proceeding *in rem* against the ship and persons other than the owner (e. g., a mortgagee) claim an interest in the ship. In such a case, Baun v. The Ethel G., 15 Alaska 283, 125 F.Supp. 835, 1955 A.M.C. 374 (D.Alaska, 1954) Judge Folta held that the first action was not *res judicata* to bar the second and that neither the judgment nor the evidence in the *in personam* action was admissible in the *in rem* action since the mortgagee could not be bound by a proceeding to which he had not been a party. Judge Folta's opinion indicates the dearth of authority on this point. See also The Eastern Shore, 24 F.2d 443, 1928 A.M.C. 327 (D.Md.1928) holding that the recovery of a state court judgment in a contract action did not bar an action *in rem* by a supplier to enforce

with the curious predicament in which the successive reorganizations had placed the barge-owner, the court allowed the *in rem* action to proceed on the ground that because of the Central's reorganization the remedy had probably not been available to the libellant at the time he brought the *in personam* action.

### The "Personification" of the Ship: Conclusion

§ 9–18. The fiction of ship's personality has played a negligible role in the development of maritime lien law. The question has presented itself in each of the recurrent situations where the attempt has been to enforce against a ship a claim for which the ship's owner at the time of suit is not liable (except through his possession of the ship). If the personification theory were at the root of our law, the conclusion would follow in each case that "the ship" was liable and the claim enforceable. That is far from having been the result. With respect to the enforceability of maritime liens against good faith purchasers without notice, the maritime lien is notably less "indelible" than land liens, which might suggest that the ship is less "personified" than ordinary industrial equipment. With respect to the enforceability of liens arising when the owner was not in control of the vessel, the answers have been *ad hoc:* the "ship" liable for the negligent acts of compulsory pilots (but the risk is insured); liable for the acts of persons "lawfully in possession"—charterers, stevedores and the like —but, since the owner may have his recovery over, the risk can be covered by contract; not liable for acts committed by the sovereign, when the sovereign would be immune from direct suit. The enforceability of *custodia legis* claims against the ship or the proceeds of sale was decided on other grounds entirely. And the fanciful idea that an action *in rem* was not barred by a prior proceeding *in personam* was happily strangled at birth. It is interesting to note that English law, which is said to have rejected the "personification" theory en-

his lien against the ship. The situation involved in the Baun case *supra* came up again in Pratt v. United States, 340 F.2d 174, 1967 A.M.C. 1302 (1st Cir. 1964) where Pratt, whose *in personam* judgment against the owner had remained unsatisfied, intervened in a mortgage foreclosure action. *Held:* that he was entitled to intervene; that the judgment in his favor was not *res judicata* against the mortgagee and other lienors; but that the amount of his recovery in the *in personam* action would operate as a ceiling or "maximum limitation" in the foreclosure action. Judge Aldrich, who accepted Judge Hand's analysis in the Burns Brothers case, suggested that if judgment had gone against Pratt in the *in personam* action, that would have barred him from intervening in the foreclosure action. In McLaughlin v. Dredge Gloucester, 230 F. Supp. 623, 1964 A.M.C. 2123 (D.N.J. 1964), a judgment for wrongful death in a Jones Act action (which can be brought only *in personam*, see text at note 86 *infra*) had proved uncollectible. The judgment creditor subsequently sought to proceed *in rem* against the vessel which had been sold by the original owner to a purchaser allegedly without knowledge of the judgment. Judge Cohen concluded that the reduction of the wrongful death claim to judgment did not convert it into a martime lien and held that in any case such an action *in rem* against a good faith purchaser was barred by laches (see §§ 9–78, 9–79 *infra*).

tirely, has achieved results on most of the issues mentioned which are substantially similar to our own.[74]

It may be concluded that the fiction of ship's personality has never been much more than a literary theme. As such it reached a height of popularity toward the turn of the century. Since then even as literature it has fallen into disrepute, thanks in part to the influence of Holmes and Learned Hand. Fictions serve many useful purposes in the law. Initially their introduction is apt to be a sign of disturbance and growth. But when a fiction has served out its time and purpose, its disappearance, even when it is as agreeable and harmless as the fiction of ship's personality, is always to be welcomed.[75]

**§ 9–18(a).** Since World War II the courts and commentators have been in comfortable agreement that the personification of the ship is and always has been merely a legal fiction, is not and never has been a principle of decision.[75a] Abandonment of the fiction would seem to have been a clear gain for legal thought. In some quarters, however, the idea has found favor that, apart from the fiction, there is no rational or logical way of explaining or justifying such cases as The Barnstable [75b] or The China,[75c] and that, the fiction having been abandoned, it should (or must) follow that "*in rem* liability does not exist apart from concomitant *in personam* liability." [75d]

In recent litigation the view just expressed has been most notably illustrated by cases in the First [75e] and Third [75f] Circuits, both of which were reversed in the Supreme Court on grounds which avoided the underlying issue.[75g] The Second [75h] and Fifth [75i] Circuits, on the

74. See generally Price *op. cit. supra* note 2.

75. The ghost still walks occasionally. Thus, Justice Reed in Canadian Aviator, Ltd. v. United States, 324 U.S. 215, 224, 65 S.Ct. 639, 644, 1945 A.M.C. 265, 272 (1945): "The use of the phrase "caused by a public vessel" [in the Public Vessels Act] constitutes an adoption by Congress of the customary legal terminology of the admiralty law which refers to the vessel as causing the harm although the actual cause is the negligence of the personnel in the operation of the ship. Such personification of the vessel, treating it as a juristic person whose acts and omissions, although brought about by her personnel, are personal acts of the ship for which, as a juristic person, she is legally responsible, has long been recognized by the Court."

75a. For the acceptance of this idea at the highest level, see Justice Black's opinion in Continental Grain Co. v. Barge FBL–585, 364 U.S. 19, 1961 A.M.C. 1 (1960), holding that an action which had been brought *in rem* and *in personam* could be transferred for convenience under 28 U.S.C.A. § 1404(a) to a district where the action *in rem* could not initially have been brought.

75b. See text following note 30 *supra*.

75c. See text following note 27 *supra*.

75d. Toy note 5a *supra*, 47 Tulane L. Rev. 559, 563 (1973).

75e. Pichirilo v. Guzman, 290 F.2d 812, 1961 A.M.C. 1588 (1st Cir. 1961); Ramos v. Beauregard, Inc., 423 F.2d 916, 1970 A.M.C. 1847 (1st Cir. 1970), certiorari denied 400 U.S. 865 (1970). See also Petition of Shaver Transp. Co. (The Barge ST–15), 287 F.Supp. 339, 1968 A.M.C. 162 (D.Or.1967), following the First Circuit approach.

75f. Reed v. S/S Yaka, 307 F.2d 203, 1962 A.M.C. 1226 (3d Cir. 1962), reversed 373 U.S. 410, 83 S.Ct. 1349, 1963 A.M.C. 1373 (1963), rehearing denied 375 U.S. 872, 84 S.Ct. 27 (1963).

75g. Guzman v. Pichirilo, 369 U.S. 698, 1962 A.M.C. 1142 (1962); Reed v. S/S Yaka, 373 U.S. 410, 83 S.Ct. 1349, 1963

75h, 75i. See notes 75h, 75i on p. 617.

other hand, have taken the position that there can perfectly well be *in rem* liability even though the owner of the ship is not liable *in personam* (which of course has been the traditional view of the matter since The Barnstable and The China were decided). Neither the Circuits which have denied the *in rem* liability nor the Circuits which have affirmed it have as yet come to grips with The Barnstable or The China since the litigation has arisen in novel contexts of liability created by the Supreme Court's vast expansion of the unseaworthiness concept during the 1940's and 1950's. Only the Supreme Court can impose order on the developing chaos but, since its two more than Delphic oracles delivered in the early 1960's, that Court has refused to speak further.

Under the Supreme Court's liability construct the shipowner had an absolute duty to furnish a seaworthy ship which extended to longshoremen and harbor-workers (who were typically employed by an independent contractor) as well as to his own seagoing employees; the duty included conditions of unseaworthiness for which a longshoreman's own employer to whom control of the ship had been relinquished for, say, loading or unloading operations, was solely responsible; a longshoreman so situated could recover for death or injury from the shipowner although his recovery against his own employer was limited to the compensation provided by the relevant Workmen's Compensation Act; the shipowner having been held liable to the longshoreman could recover indemnity from the longshoreman's employer even though the Workmen's Compensation Act provided that the employer's liability under the Act was to be exclusive.[75j] It is no part of our present discussion either to applaud or deplore the Supreme Court's theories and reasons; during the 1950's and 1960's that was the pattern which had been established for the lower federal courts to work with.

Both the Guzman case in the First Circuit and the Reed case in the Third Circuit were actions to recover for personal injuries suffered by longshoremen in loading or unloading operations. In both cases the injuries were found to have been caused by unseaworthiness of the ships. In both cases the ships were being operated under charter and the charterers were found to have been responsible for the conditions of unseaworthiness. In both cases the injured longshoremen were employed directly by the charterers and not (under the more customary pattern) by independent stevedoring enterprises. In both

A.M.C. 1373 (1963), rehearing denied 375 U.S. 872, 84 S.Ct. 27 (1963).

**75h.** Grillea v. United States, 232 F.2d 919, 1956 A.M.C. 1009 (2d Cir. 1956); *cf.* Latus v. United States, 277 F.2d 264, 1961 A.M.C. 850 (2d Cir. 1960), certiorari denied 364 U.S. 827, 81 S.Ct. 65 (1960).

**75i.** Grigsby v. Coastal Marine Service, 412 F.2d 1011, 1969 A.M.C. 1513 (5th Cir. 1969), certiorari dismissed 396 U.S. 1033, 90 S.Ct. 612 (1970), on remand 317 F.Supp. 1113 (1970).

**75j.** On the elaboration of this "construct" by the Supreme Court, see Chapter VI, § 6–53 *et seq.* The statement in the text has been put in the past tense to reflect the fact that, under a 1972 statutory reform (see § 6–57), harbor-workers are no longer entitled to recover for unseaworthiness.

cases libels *in rem* were filed against the ships and in the Guzman case there was also a libel *in personam* against the owner. Both the First Circuit, in an opinion by Judge Aldrich, and the Third Circuit, in an opinion by Judge Hastie, agreed that the libels *in rem* (as well as the libel *in personam* in Guzman) should be dismissed. They reasoned: (1) the charter involved (in each case) was a demise or bareboat charter; (2) an owner-demisor is not personally liable for conditions of unseaworthiness which arise after delivery of a seaworthy ship under the demise and for which the charterer-demisee is solely responsible; the charterer-demisee, who was responsible for the unseaworthiness, was not personally liable (i. e., liable without limitation) because his liability was limited by the relevant Workmen's Compensation Act; in the absence of personal (i. e., unlimited) liability on the part of either charterer or owner, there could be no liability *in rem* on the part of the vessel. As Judge Hastie, citing the First Circuit's Guzman opinion, put it in Reed: "[T]hat court reasoned as we do that the absence of any lien-creating personal obligation of the demisor or the demisee precluded any recovery against the ship *in rem.*"

In both cases the Supreme Court granted certiorari and reversed. Both Justice Clark who wrote the majority opinion in Guzman and Justice Black who wrote the majority opinion in Reed were at pains to point out that the Court was not deciding in either case (1) whether an owner is absolved of personal liability with respect to conditions of unseaworthiness for which a demise charterer is wholly responsible, or (2) whether there can be *in rem* liability in the absence of *in personam* liability. Justice Harlan dissented in both cases (being joined by Justice Stewart in Reed), indicating in his dissents that he agreed with the reasoning of the courts below. The reversal in Guzman (which was first decided) was put on the ground that the charter had not truly been a demise, that the owner had remained in control and was therefore liable *in personam* for the unseaworthiness, whence it followed that the vessel was also liable *in rem.* The Reed reversal was more complicated since the Court agreed with the Circuit that the charter was a demise. Justice Black put the decision essentially on policy grounds: since longshoremen employed by independent contractors could, under the Court's unseaworthiness doctrine, recover in full for their injuries, it would be unjust for longshoremen to be denied that recovery because of the happenstance that they may be employed directly by the persons in control of the ship. Therefore a longshoreman so employed could recover in full from his employer, the "exclusive liability" provision of the Longshoreman's and Harbor Worker's Compensation Act to the contrary notwithstanding. The *in personam* liability of the demise charterer (or shipowner) having been thus established, the *in rem* liability of the ship followed as a matter of course.

Because of the narrow grounds on which the Court chose to decide the cases, it is impossible to say what Guzman and Reed stand for, beyond the obvious fact that a majority of the Justices voted to reverse. It is worth noting, however, that one of the questions reserved was the liability of an owner-demisor for conditions of unseaworthiness for which a charterer-demisee is wholly responsible. The Court had earlier held owners liable for such conditions when independent contractors such as stevedores were wholly responsible for them. It would not have been much of an extension to hold owners liable when demise charterers were responsible. Evidently at the time Guzman and Reed were decided a majority of the Court was not ready either to make the extension or to deny it.

The Guzman and Reed situation—injured longshoremen directly employed by demise charterers—had come up a few years earlier in the Second Circuit in Grillea v. United States.[75k] When the Court first considered the case the judges assumed that the libel against the shipowner (the United States) had been brought only *in personam*. On that assumption recovery was denied; Judge Learned Hand in his opinion accepted, like his colleagues on the First and Third Circuits, the proposition that an owner is not liable *in personam* for conditions of unseaworthiness for which the charterer is wholly responsible.[75l] On rehearing, counsel for the libellant persuaded the judges that, contrary to their initial assumption, the libel had indeed been *in rem* (or, technically, since the action was against the United States under the Suits in Admiralty Act, on *in rem* principles). So instructed, the judges reversed their original decision and granted the recovery.[75m] Judge Hand addressed himself to the question "whether a maritime lien can be imposed upon a ship for a claim on which no jural person is liable 'in personam'." He noted that the charterer, responsible for the unseaworthiness, was, under the Compensation Act, liable "only for compensation [75n]—a claim different from that in suit, both in kind and amount." He added:

> "So far as we have found, this is a question that has never come up in the books, although, as *res integra*, we see no reason why a person's property should never be liable unless he or someone else is liable 'in personam'."

Thus the libellant could recover *in rem* and the owner, under the established Supreme Court pattern, could have indemnity from the charterer.

The result in Grillea depended on the facts that there was a duty (to furnish a seaworthy ship) owed by the charterers to the libellant and that the duty had been breached; given the existence of those facts, the additional fact that the charterer's personal liability for his breach of duty was limited under the Compensation Act made no dif-

**75k.** Note 75h *supra*.

**75l.** 229 F.2d 687, 1956 A.M.C. 553 (2d Cir. 1956).

**75m.** The distinction between the two Grillea opinions has occasionally led to some confusion. See, e. g., Petition of Shaver Transp. Co. (The Barge ST–15), 287 F.Supp. 339, 1968 A.M.C. 162 (D.Or.1967).

**75n.** Judge Hand may be forgiven for not having anticipated the Supreme Court's Reed decision.

ference as to the imposition of *in rem* liability. In the absence of any duty there would of course be no liability of any kind—*in personam* or *in rem*. Judge Hand clarified this point in Latus v. United States.[75o] The Supreme Court had held in West v. United States [75p] that there was no duty to furnish a seaworthy ship with respect to a ship which had been withdrawn from navigation (a "dead ship"). Latus was injured on such a ship while it was under the control of his employer, Todd Shipyards, which was reconditioning the ship. The cause of the injury was unseaworthiness for which Todd was responsible. The holding was that, in the absence of any duty (West), there was of course no liability *in rem* which could be asserted against the United States as owner.[75q]

In Grigsby v. Coastal Marine Service [75r] the Fifth Circuit entered the debate. Grigsby was a many-sided case—an "amphibious Donnybrook", as Judge Brown described it—and only a brief passage in his remarkable opinion was devoted to the question of *in rem* liability. Grigsby was a shore-based worker who met his death as a result of unseaworthy conditions on a ship which had been temporarily put under the control of ship-repairers who were responsible for the unseaworthiness. Judge Brown concluded that the temporary withdrawal from navigation did not bring the case within the West rule and that the ship-repairers (like charterers and stevedores) owed their employees the duty to furnish a seaworthy ship (a point as to which Judge Hand had expressed doubt in Latus). Judge Brown wrote:

> "Obviously . . . the absence of possession and control may well insulate the shipowner from a liability *in personam* in the absence of conduct which somehow implicates the remote owner in the deficiency. But on principles of *in rem* liability, or concepts akin to it, there seems to be no more reason to insulate the vessel from accountability for personal injuries occasioned by unseaworthiness than there is to absolve the vessel from *in rem* liability for, say, other types of maritime torts including collision, even though the vessel, on this hypothesis, is wholly in the control of a demise charterer and, worse, being conned by a compulsory pilot." [75s]

**75o.** 277 F.2d 264, 1961 A.M.C. 850 (2d Cir. 1960), certiorari denied 364 U.S. 827, 81 S.Ct. 65 (1961).

**75p.** 361 U.S. 118, 80 S.Ct. 189, 1960 A.M.C. 15 (1959).

**75q.** Noel v. Isbrandtsen Co., 287 F.2d 783, 1961 A.M.C. 611 (4th Cir. 1961), certiorari denied 366 U.S. 975, 81 S.Ct. 1944 (1961), was, on its facts, identical with Latus and came to the same result. Both Latus and Noel are sometimes cited as being inconsistent with Grillea. It is submitted that, on a correct analysis, the three cases are entirely consistent.

**75r.** 412 F.2d 1011, 1969 A.M.C. 1513 (5th Cir. 1969), certiorari dismissed 396 U.S. 1033, 90 S.Ct. 612 (1970).

**75s.** 412 F.2d at pp. 1030–1031, 1969 A.M.C. at p. 1539. Grigsby was followed in Solet v. M/V Dufrene, 303 F.Supp. 980, 1970 A.M.C. 571 (E.D.La. 1969) in which *in rem* liability for maintenance and cure was imposed al-

We may conclude this overlong discussion by returning to our starting-point: the continuing vitality of the rule of The Barnstable and allied cases now that the fiction of ship's personality has been generally discarded. We suggest that the rule in The Barnstable (to call it that) may be generalized as follows: an owner who entrusts his ship to the control of a third party—charterer, stevedore, repairman or what not—should be charged with at least limited (i. e., *in rem*) liability for the torts and breaches of duty which occur while the third party is in control and for which the third party is (looking at the matter subjectively) wholly responsible. The Barnstable was, of course, decided at a time when it was generally assumed that civil liability, in contract or in tort, was based on subjective fault or negligence. To a nineteenth century court it would have seemed strange to hold the subjectively innocent shipowner liable without limitation (i. e., *in personam*) for torts committed while the charterer was in control of the ship. The conclusion that the shipowner should be held to a liability limited to his interest in the ship through *in rem* process may be looked on as an instinctive adjustment of theory to reality. In our century we have become accustomed to the idea of liability, indeed unlimited liability, without fault—a development which has been dramatically illustrated in maritime law by the Supreme Court's expansion of the unseaworthiness concept. In the light of our current theories of liability the rule of The Barnstable might well be expanded to one of unlimited (i. e., *in personam*) liability for the third party's torts and breaches, subject to the shipowner's right to recover indemnity from the party subjectively at fault. That is, of course, exactly what the Supreme Court has done in the case of ships turned over to third party control in the stevedoring situation. Expansion of the stevedoring rule to cover third parties who are charterers, repairmen and so on is perhaps the business of the Supreme Court (which expressly reserved the question in Guzman and Reed) and not of the lower federal courts. But, even if the rule of The Barnstable is not to be expanded (until the Supreme Court so decides), it would be most unfortunate if the rule was cut back on the flimsy pretext that we no longer personify ships. The approach taken by the First and Third Circuits in Guzman and Reed may be thus stated: in the absence of unlimited (*in personam*) liability on the part of the third party in control of the ship (and hypothetically "wholly responsible" for whatever goes wrong), not even limited (*in rem*) liability can be imposed on the shipowner. If that approach prevails, we will do well to start personifying ships again. The approach taken by the Second and Fifth Circuits in Grillea and Grigsby may be thus stated: given

though the owner was not, technically, the injured seaman's employer. Moye v. Sioux City & New Orleans Barge Lines, Inc., 402 F.2d 238, 1968 A.M.C. 2287 (5th Cir. 1968) may (although the question of *in rem* liability was not discussed) be taken as the Fifth Circuit's equivalent of the Latus and Noel cases discussed above. See further Johnson v. Oil Transport Corp., 440 F.2d 109, 1971 A.M.C. 1038 (5th Cir. 1971), rehearing denied 445 F.2d 1402 (5th Cir. 1971), certiorari denied 404 U.S. 868, 92 S.Ct. 109 (1972).

a breach of duty by the third party in control, the shipowner's limited (*in rem*) liability follows as a matter of course, whether or not the third party (e. g., an employer subject to a Workmen's Compensation Act) is entitled to a limitation of his own liability vis-à-vis his victims. That approach, it is submitted, is (as far as it goes) entirely sound and does not, for its justification, depend (any more than the rule in The Barnstable did) on the personification of the "offending vessel". Abandonment of the agreeable fiction of ship's personality will have been bought at far too high a price if twentieth century shipowners are to be absolved of liability for the tortious uses to which their ships are put by third parties to whom they have entrusted control. But an attentive study of Judge Hand's Grillea opinion and Judge Brown's Grigsby opinion should make clear that there is no reason why such a price need be paid.

## Claims Which Give Rise to Liens

**§ 9–19.** In American jurisprudence the existence of a maritime lien is synonymous with the availability of a libel *in rem*. As Justice Field wrote in The Rock Island Bridge: "The lien and the proceeding *in rem* are, therefore, correlative—where one exists, the other can be taken, and not otherwise." [76] A ship may be libeled *in rem* only in aid of a lien claim; non-lien claimants are limited to an action *in personam*, although once a lien claimant has instituted an *in rem* action certain claimants who do not have maritime liens may share in the distribution of the fund.[77] While a vessel may be levied upon and sold in satisfaction of an *in personam* judgment, that sale does not divest existing liens. Only in an *in rem* proceeding can the ship be sold free of liens, with a consequently greater fund for distribution among claimants.[78] Furthermore, in distribution of the fund lien claims (with the exception of some claims arising while the ship is *in custodia legis*) [79] are paid in full before non-lien claims are entitled to anything. What is essentially important to a claimant in having his claim ranked as a lien is in the first place the priority he receives over non-lien claimants, and secondly the availability to him of the *in rem* process by which alone liens can be executed.[80]

76. 73 U.S. (6 Wall.) 213, 215 (1867). The rule was questioned in The Lottawanna, 88 U.S. (21 Wall.) 558 (1874), but confirmed in The Resolute, 168 U.S. 437, 440, 18 S.Ct. 112, 113 (1897). Under Supplemental Rule C, F.R.C.P., "An action *in rem* may be brought (a) To enforce any maritime lien; (b) Whenever a statute of the United States provides for a maritime action *in rem* or a proceeding analogous thereto." In England the rule was announced by the Privy Council in The Bold Buccleugh, 7 Moore P.C. 267 (1852), but when Parliament restored part of the jurisdiction of the Admiralty later in the century, and granted an action *in rem* for matters formerly within the domain of the common law, it was decided that in some cases the extended jurisdiction did not include a maritime lien. See Price *op. cit. supra* note 2, at 12.

77. See §§ 9–87, 9–88, *infra*.

78. See § 9–85 *et seq.*, *infra*.

79. See § 9–11 *supra*.

80. The maritime lien attaches to the ship and her appurtenances, cargo, the wreck of these, the proceeds of sale and the freight. It may exist on the cargo for freight and salvage, and on the freight for seamen's wages and perhaps master's disbursements.

A "ship" includes those dependent on towage, The Robert W. Parsons, 191 U.S. 17, 23 S.Ct. 8 (1903), such as a barge, The New York, 93 F. 495 (E.D. N.Y.1899), affirmed 113 F. 810 (2d Cir. 1902), or a dismantled vessel which is movable, The City of Pittsburg, 45 F. 699 (W.D.Pa.1891). "Appurtenances" include the tackle, apparel, furniture, machinery and sails. ". . . though there be separate ownership of the refrigerating plant, as between the parties to the charter, it is a part of the vessel," Turner v. United States, 27 F.2d 134, 136 (2d Cir. 1928). But rented radio equipment has been held not subject to a lien on the ship, The Hirondelle, 21 F.Supp. 223, 1937 A.M.C. 1597 (S.D.Ala.1937).

The lien does not attach to an object which is permanently in place, The Rock Island Bridge, 73 U.S. (6 Wall.) 213 (1867), nor to a seaplane for repairs, The Crawford Bros. No. 2, 215 F. 269 (W.D.Wash.1914); United States v. Northwest Air Service, 80 F.2d 804 (9th Cir. 1935). The customary rule is that the lien does not attach to the proceeds of insurance, A. M. Bright Grocery Co. v. Lindsey, 225 F. 257 (S.D.Ala.1915), but see The Conveyor, 147 F. 586 (D.Ind.1906), Re Ripley, 9 Daly 252 (N.Y.1880). An unliquidated "debt may be treated as a *res* as easily as a ship. It is true that it is not tangible, but it is a right of the creditor's, capable of being attached and appropriated by the law to the creditor's duties. The ship is a *res*, not because it is tangible, but because it is a focus of rights that in like manner may be dealt with by the law. It is no more a *res* than a copyright." United States v. Freights, etc., of The Mount Shasta, 274 U.S. 466, 470, 47 S.Ct. 666, 1927 A.M.C. 943, 944 (1927).

Recent cases on "vessels" to which liens can attach include: Miami River Boat Yard, Inc. v. Houseboat, 390 F.2d 596, 1968 A.M.C. 336 (5th Cir. 1968) (houseboat without power of her own subject to lien for repairs, etc.); M/V Marifax v. McCrory, 391 F.2d 909, 1968 A.M.C. 965 (5th Cir. 1968) (vessel being reconditioned after fifteen years in moth-ball fleet subject to lien for repairs); City of Erie v. S/S North American, 267 F.Supp. 875, 1968 A.M.C. 500 (W.D.Pa.1967) (vessel in winter lay up at Great Lakes port subject to lien for wharfage); Johnson & Towers Baltimore, Inc. v. The Dredge etc., 241 F.Supp. 598, 1965 A.M.C. 1169 (D. Md.1965) (pipeline dredge engaged in sand and gravel operation on navigable waters not subject to lien); *cf.* Dann v. Dredge Sandpiper, 222 F. Supp. 838, 1964 A.M.C. 472 (D.Del. 1963) (dredge subject to lien for towage even though at time libel brought it had been removed to an inland pool); Arques Shipyards v. S/S Charles Van Damme, 175 F.Supp. 871, 1959 A.M.C. 1570 (N.D.Cal.1959) (vessel subject to lien for repairs even though after repairs made it was permanently affixed to the shore and used as a restaurant). The opinions in the cases cited collect a good many other cases, old and new. The two cases cited *supra* on dredges, which are not necessarily inconsistent, are of particular interest on the relevant criteria.

It has frequently been said that liens do not attach to "dead" vessels, permanently withdrawn from navigation. The "dead ship" cases were elaborately reviewed in Matter of The Queen, Ltd., 1973 A.M.C. 646 (E.D.Pa.1973, per Referee in Bankruptcy Goldhaber). The case involved claims for "necessaries" furnished to the former Queen Elizabeth during a period while the ship was moored in Port Everglades, Florida, and used as a tourist attraction. Referee Goldhaber commented that the denial of liens in the older "dead ship" cases seemed to be put on the ground that the admiralty court lacked jurisdiction since a "dead ship" was not a vessel (citing Hercules Co., Inc. v. Brigadier General Absalom Baird, 214 F.2d 66, 1954 A.M.C. 1201 (3d Cir. 1954)). Such cases, he felt, were not binding on him since no one would argue that the bankruptcy court lacked jurisdiction over any sort of property. Taking another tack, the Referee went on to say that the crucial factor was not whether the vessel was being used in navigation at the time the asserted liens arose but whether it was capable of being so used. That the Elizabeth was capable of being navigated was proved by the fact that, following her sale in the Bankruptcy proceedings, she was reconditioned and ultimately made a voyage to Hong Kong, where she was destroyed in a fire. Thus the claims for necessaries furnished during the period when the Elizabeth was being used as a sort of hot dog stand were entitled to maritime lien status in the distribution of the fund.

In Johnson v. Oil Transport Co., 440 F. 2d 109, 1971 A.M.C. 1038 (5th Cir. 1971), rehearing denied 445 F.2d 1402 (5th Cir. 1971), certiorari denied 404 U.S. 868, 92 S.Ct. 109 (1972), it was held,

The traditional rule in American admiralty practice has been that judgment in an action *in rem* cannot be for more than the value of the ship and freight, or her proceeds if sold. The owner must be joined in an action *in personam* before there can be a judgment in a greater amount.[81] This rule, which does not obtain in English practice,[82] has been said to reflect the American theory of personification: since the action *in rem* is against the ship, no judgment could, conceptually, be entered against the owner unless he is brought before the court by separate process. Under the currently applicable Rule, as under the former Admiralty Rules, almost all actions that can be brought *in rem* can also be brought *in personam*, so that no problem is presented by the joinder.[83] Except as a trap for counsel unfamiliar with admiralty pleading, the rule can become vexatious only when the defendant ship owner is not amenable to *in personam* process of an American court. In that situation, as Judge (later Justice) Brown held in The Monte A, the foreign owner can appear to defend the *in rem* action without rendering himself liable to a deficiency judgment *in personam*.[84]

**§ 9–20.** To give rise to a lien a claim must be in the first instance maritime. Thus we recur to the question of what is within the jurisdiction of the admiralty: what types of structures qualify as "vessels"; which contracts are maritime contracts; when a tort is a maritime tort.[85] There can be no maritime lien which does not involve a vessel, its cargo or freight and arise out of a maritime contract or a maritime tort or some peculiarly maritime operation such as salvage.

over a vigorous dissent by Judge Brown, that the warranty of seaworthiness did not extend to a shore-based workman who had been injured while working on a ship in dry-dock. Judge Ainsworth for the majority commented that "*in rem* jurisdiction was not perfected in this case by appellant. There, of course, can be no *in rem* liability without compliance with the requisites for *in rem* jurisdiction." Judge Ainsworth presumably meant that *in rem* jurisdiction could not have been perfected because there was no *in rem* liability under West v. United States, note 75, *supra* and the accompanying text.

An annotation in 3 A.L.R.Fed. 882 (1970) collects cases on: What is a "Vessel" subject to a maritime lien under 46 U.S.C.A. § 971. The case annotated is The Marifox (5th Cir. 1968), *supra* this note.

81. There are, however, indications that the traditional rule as stated in the text is beginning to break down. See § 9–90 *infra*.

82. See Price *op. cit. supra* note 2 at 13, 14.

83. Supplemental Rule C provides: "Except as otherwise provided by law a party who may proceed *in rem* may also, or in the alternative, proceed *in personam* against any person who may be liable." Rule C eliminates the provision of Admiralty Rule 15 that actions for assault and beating could be brought only *in personam* (see note 95 *infra* for cases under Rule 15) as well as the provision of Admiralty Rule 17 that suits on bottomry bonds could be brought only *in rem* (with the comment that, as a matter of hornbook law, there is no personal liability on such bonds).

84. 12 F. 331 (S.D.N.Y.1882); The Nora, 181 F. 845 (S.D.Fla.1910). But see discussion in § 9–90 *infra*. For a modern instance, see The Bournemouth, discussed in the text following note 95a, particularly note 95b.

85. See Chapter I, §§ 1–10, 1–11. On the "vessels" to which liens attach see also note 80 *supra*.

Most, but not all, maritime claims give rise to liens. It would be hard to assign persuasive reasons to explain why the occasional maritime claim which is denied lien status was relegated to inferior rank. The best that can be said usually is that some court at some point so held and, ever since, that has been "the law" of the matter. Thus the Supreme Court held, as a construction of the venue provision of the Jones Act, that a seaman's action for personal injury under that statute may not be brought *in rem* (*i. e.* that there is no lien).[86] Although an insurance contract is maritime, there is no lien in favor of the insurer for unpaid premiums.[87] Under the general maritime law a master had no lien for unpaid wages (although he could have a lien against the vessel and her freights for disbursements). The rule denying the lien for wages, which was felt to be anomalous, accounted for a fair amount of litigation [88] until it was abrogated by statute.[88a]

86. Plamals v. The Pinar Del Rio, 277 U.S. 151, 48 S.Ct. 457, 1928 A.M.C. 932 (1928). The Plamals case is discussed in Chapter VI, § 6–22. In McLaughlin v. Dredge Gloucester, 230 F.Supp. 623, 1964 A.M.C. 2123 (D.N.J. 1964) Judge Cohen rejected the "sophistic" contention that an *in personam* judgment recovered in a Jones Act action could be made the basis for a subsequent action *in rem*.

87. The Prilla, 21 F.Supp. 383, 1938 A.M.C. 97 (D.Mass.1937); The Hall, 48 F.2d 646, 1931 A.M.C. 549 (D.Mass. 1931); The American, 1931 A.M.C. 197 (D.Mass.1930); The Minnie V., 24 F. 2d 604, 1928 A.M.C. 238 (D.Mass.1927); the Man of War, 1923 A.M.C. 187 (D. Mass.1923); The Mame, 184 F. 968 (D.Conn. 1911); Learned v. Brown, 94 F. 876 (5th Cir. 1899); In re Insurance Co. of Pennsylvania, 22 F. 109 (N.D.N.Y.1884), affirmed 24 F. 559 (C. C.N.D.N.Y.1885): "But what method of investigation would enable a proposed purchaser or charterer to discover, for instance, that a lien existed in favor of a foreign insurance company for a policy issued to a former part owner?"

There are a few old cases to the contrary: The Guiding Star, 18 F. 263 (C.C.Ohio 1883) (decided under an Ohio statute which expressly gave such a lien); Provost v. The Selkirk, 20 Fed.Cas. 23, 24, Case No. 11,455 (N.D.Ohio 1878): "In the absence of loss, the enforcement of the payment of the premium note by action in rem against the ship works no wrong to any one, if there be no conflicting interest. But in case of insolvency of the ship and insufficiency of the fund in registry, it is difficult to understand that such a claim upon the fund has any foundation of principle to stand upon. It might well be regarded as of the same nature as a personal loan of money to the owner, in no sense operating as a hypothecation of or privilege upon the ship. Yet a respectful deference to the decisions of very learned judges, adverse to these views, has induced an incorporation of claims of this class in the list of maritime liens. . . ." As to state statutes creating such liens, see § 9–29 *infra*.

88. No lien for wages: Walker v. Woolsey, 186 F.2d 920, 1951 A.M.C. 471 (5th Cir. 1951); The Aguia, 72 F. Supp. 201, 1947 A.M.C. 1386 (E.D.S.C. 1947); Burdine v. Walden, 91 F.2d 321, 1937 A.M.C. 1149 (5th Cir. 1937); The Mariner, 298 F. 108, 1924 A.M. C. 882 (D.Mass. 1924): "As applied to modern conditions the rule is too strict and is often, as here, unjust; but a court of first instance must take the established law as it finds it". The "no lien for master's wages" rule appears as early as The Grand Turk, 1 Paine, 73 (C.C.N.Y. 1817) and was applied consistently through the 19th century.

In Crain v. American Waterways Corp., 143 F.Supp. 256, 258, 1956 A.M.C. 1806, 1809 (E.D.Pa.1956), Judge Kraft remarked: "Regardless of the origin of the rule, by reason of frequent repetition and application, it has now acquired the dignity and force of *stare decisis*."

Lien for disbursements: United States v. The Pomare, 92 F.Supp. 185 (D.Hawaii 1950); Ex parte Clark, 5 Fed. Cas. 832, Case No. 2,796 (D.Mass. 1843); The Packet, 18 Fed.Cas. 965, Case No. 10,654 (D.Mass.1823).

88a. See note 88a on page 626.

Owners (including part-owners and stockholders) are not entitled to a lien for advances, nor is the mysterious sort of agent who qualifies as a "general agent".[89] Nor was the ship's engineer who advanced

Contra: The Raleigh, 20 Fed.Cas. 195, 200, Case No. 11,539 (E.D.Va.1876): "I am equally bound to rule against the masters as to their claims for disbursements. These, however good against the owners or employers, do not give a lien upon the ship to the master, although they do upon the freight. The law is too well settled to be now called in question, and is founded upon the same considerations which have been stated as to wages." Bartlette v. The Viola, 2 Fed.Cas. 983, Case No. 1,083 (D.Minn.1871); The Larch, 14 Fed.Cas. 1139, Case No. 8,085 (C.C.D.Me.1855).

88a. "The master of a vessel registered, enrolled or licensed under the laws of the United States shall have the same lien for his wages against such vessel and the same priority as any other seaman serving the same vessel." 82 Stat. 107 (1968), 46 U.S.C.A. § 606.

89. Part-owners: The Frank Brainerd, 3 F.2d 664 (D.Me.1925); The Morning Star, 1 F.2d 410 (W.D.Wash.1924); The Lena Mowbray, 71 F. 720 (S.D. Ala.1895).

Stockholders: The Kongo, 155 F.2d 492, 1946 A.M.C. 1200 (6th Cir. 1946), certiorari denied 329 U.S. 735, 67 S.Ct. 99 (1946); The King Philip, 1929 A.M.C. 296 (D.Mass.1928). But see The Gloucester, 285 F. 579, 1923 A.M.C. 173 (D.Mass.1923); The Cimbria, 214 F. 131 (D.N.J.1914); The City of Camden, 147 F. 847 (D.Ala.1906).

General agents: The Maret, 145 F.2d 431, 1944 A.M.C. 1203 (3d Cir. 1944); The M. Vivian Pierce, 48 F.2d 644, 1931 A.M.C. 967 (D.Mass.1931); The American Star, 11 F.2d 479, 1926 A.M.C. 516 (3d Cir. 1926); The Owego, 292 F. 403, 1923 A.M.C. 1060 (E.D.La. 1923); The Centaurus, 291 F. 751, 1923 A.M.C. 811 (4th Cir. 1923); The Raleigh, 20 Fed.Cas. 195, 200, Case No. 11,539 (E.D.Va.1876): "It is doubtful whether the agent for a particular ship has a lien for disbursements upon that ship; but, however that may be, the agent for a line of steamers, disbursing for them generally, has no lien upon any particular vessel for a balance against the owners on general account." Many of the cases suggest, however, that the "general agent" may have a lien for disbursements made with knowledge of the owner's insolvency.

On the difference between a general agent and a special agent see Todd Shipyards Corp. v. The City of Athens, 83 F.Supp. 67, 1949 A.M.C. 572 (D.Md.1949), which also suggested that the Federal Maritime Lien Act has abrogated the rule that general agents can claim no lien.

In Compagnia Maritima La Empresa v. Pickard (M/V Eda), 320 F.2d 829, 1964 A.M.C. 109 (5th Cir. 1963) Judge Brown reviewed the case law denying liens to owners and general agents for advances before concluding that Pickard was neither and could have a lien.

A marine surveyor was denied a lien for services performed as owner's representative in Savas v. Maria Trading Corp., 285 F.2d 336, 1961 A.M.C. 260 (4th Cir. 1960).

S/S Pacific Ranger v. Bugg, 322 F.2d 250, 1964 A.M.C. 115 (5th Cir. 1963) affirmed *per curiam* a District Court order giving a ship's "servicing agent" a lien for advances to pay crew's wages. The District Court's opinion (1964 A.M.C. 117) which was evidently delivered orally cited no authorities.

Brock v. S/S Southampton, 231 F.Supp. 280, 1964 A.M.C. 800A (D.Or.1964); 231 F.Supp. 283, 1964 A.M.C. 1905 (D.Ore. 1964) is *sui generis.* At the request of the ship's general agent and her owners banks issued irrevocable letters of credit to labor unions for the payment of crew wages. Apparently without the letters of credit a crew could not have been recruited. The banks were given lien status, despite the fact that they were acting on behalf of the agent and owners.

In Freedom Line Inc. v. Vessel Glenrock, 268 F.Supp. 7, 1968 A.M.C. 507 (S.D. Fla.1967) it was held that a stockholder in and an agent of a prospective purchaser of a vessel were not entitled to liens for advances.

Roberts v. Echternach, 302 F.2d 370, 1963 A.M.C. 137 (5th Cir. 1962) is an odd case in which an owner engaged a prospective demise charterer to put the ship in seaworthy condition under an agreement that the charterer's expenses were to be deducted from the charter-hire. After the charterer had

$300 to get the captain released from jail entitled to a lien on the theory that the captain was necessary to the ship.[90]

The wide variety of claims which are given lien status (not including claims which have that status only by virtue of a state statute) will be indicated by a summary listing. The listing will be roughly in the order of priority, although it should be recognized that the only indubitable propositions about priorities are that wage and salvage claims have the highest rank and that tort claims in general outrank contract claims.[91] It must be borne in mind, with respect to many types of contract claims, that claims which are normally or by nature lien claims may, under particular circumstances, fail to qualify as such. The circumstances which may prevent a lien from attaching will be brought out in subsequent discussion.

*Seamen's claims for wages.* These are, as Justice Gray wrote in The John G. Stevens,[92] "sacred liens, and, so long as a plank of the ship remains, the sailor is entitled, against all other persons, to the proceeds as a security for his wages." [93]

done the work but before delivery under the charter, the owner sold the ship to Roberts and Sawyer, who took possession of it with knowledge of the charterer's claim. The charterer was given a lien against the ship for his expenses.

In United States v. Jane B. Corp. (The Jane B.), 167 F.Supp. 352, 1966 A.M.C. 427 (D.Mass.1958) a purchaser of a vessel who had paid off existing liens was characterized as an "equitable assignee or subrogee" of the liens he had paid. The case is probably not entitled to much weight for the reason that the issue came up in the context of a claim of the United States for taxes, which was regarded as nonmaritime, see § 9–76 *infra*.

90. Vlavianos v. The Cypress, 171 F.2d 435, 1949 A.M.C. 9 (4th Cir. 1948), certiorari denied 337 U.S. 924, 69 S.Ct. 1168 (1949).

91. Lien priorities are discussed § 9–58 *et seq. infra*.

92. 170 U.S. 113, 18 S.Ct. 544 (1898).

93. *Id.* at 119. Accord: The Chester, 25 F.2d 908, 1928 A.M.C. 638 (D.Md. 1928). Additional wages for extra-hazardous service, The Herbert L. Rawding, 55 F.Supp. 156, 1944 A.M.C. 222 (E.D.S.C.1944); statutory penalty for delayed payment, The Chester, *supra*; The President Arthur (Feldman v. American Palestine Line), 25 F.2d 1002, 1928 A.M.C. 536 (S.D.N.Y.1926); Gerber v. Spencer, 278 F. 886 (9th Cir. 1922); statutory extra pay for improper discharge, The Fort Gaines, 18 F.2d 413, 1927 A.M.C. 655 (D.Md. 1927); The Great Canton, 299 F. 953, 1924 A.M.C. 1071 (E.D.N.Y.1924); contractual discharge benefits, Gayner v. The New Orleans, 54 F.Supp. 25, 1944 A.M.C. 462 (N.D.Cal.1944); idleness of the vessel due to no fault of the seaman, Slavin v. Port Service Corp., 138 F.2d 386, 1944 A.M.C. 687 (3d Cir. 1943); The William Leishear, 21 F.2d 862, 1927 A.M.C. 1770 (D.Md. 1927). But see further the text at note 47 *supra*.

Under collective bargaining agreements shipowners are required to make payments to vacation, pension and welfare trusts of which the members of maritime unions are the beneficiaries. It has been held that the trustees are not entitled to liens for defaulted payments (claimed on the theory that the payments are, in effect, "wages of the crew"). See Long Island Tankers Corp. v. S/S Kaimana, 265 F.Supp. 723, 1967 A.M.C. 2467 (N.D.Cal.1967), affirmed *per curiam* 401 F.2d 182 (9th Cir. 1968), certiorari denied *sub nom.* Cross v. The Kaimana, 393 U.S. 1095, 89 S.Ct. 879 (1969). Judge Sweigert's opinion reviewed the case law on wages and collected other recent cases denying liens with respect to defaulted payments to trusts under collective bargaining agreements.

New England Fish Co. v. Sonya, 332 F. Supp. 463, 1972 A.M.C. 130 (D.Alaska 1971) held that claims for wages due workers on a vessel which had been

*Salvage.* A lien accrues for salvage whether performed under contract or as a voluntary service. The reason for its high rank is said to be the benefit conferred in preserving the value of ship and cargo.[94]

*Tort.* This category includes both collision claims and personal injury claims (the only exception is the seaman's action for personal injury under the Jones Act which may be brought only *in personam*).[95] While the collision claims and the personal injury claims

withdrawn from navigation and was being used for storage and generating electricity were not entitled to lien status.

National Bank of North America v. S/S Oceanic Ondine, 335 F.Supp. 71 (S.D. Tex.1971), affirmed 452 F.2d 1014, 1972 A.M.C. 744 (5th Cir. 1972) held that the United States did not have a lien, as assignee of unpaid claims, for withholding and FICA taxes. See, however, Marine Midland Trust Co. v. United States, 299 F.2d 724 (4th Cir. 1962), affirming 183 F.Supp. 932 (E. D.Va.1960), in which, at the request of seamen entitled to a wage lien, FICA and income taxes were paid, out of their wage recovery, to the United States over the objection of maritime lienors.

See Schon v. M/V Alexandra B, 1973 A. M.C. 702 (E.D.N.Y.1972) for a discussion of wage claims of various types in a highly irregular operation in which no ship's articles were signed and no shipping articles setting out the voyage, terms and so on were offered in evidence. The Special Master commented: "If the operation of this ship was less of a disaster, it would be tragic-comedy."

In Nadle v. M/V Tequila, 1973 A.M.C. 909 (S.D.N.Y.1973) Judge Gurfein assumed that claims for penalties under 46 U.S.C.A. § 596 for delayed payment of wages were entitled to lien status but referred the claims to a special master for decision on whether the statutory penalty had been incurred (which it would not have been if the owner had been insolvent at the time of his failure to pay the wages). Judge Gurfein refused to give lien status to a claim by attorneys for crew members in helping them to recover their wages: "It is not for the Court to create new species of maritime liens where precedent gives no such command."

Department of antiquarianism: those employed on board or in the navigation of a canal boat "without masts or steam power" may not libel the boat for their unpaid wages, 46 U.S.C.A. § 611, derived from 9 Stat. 38 (1846).

94. The Sabine, 101 U.S. 384 (1880). But a subcontractor of the salvor must look to his contractor, The Pelotas, 43 F.2d 571, 1930 A.M.C. 1795 (E. D.La.1930). On the priority of the salvage lien, see § 9–61 *infra*.

95. As to tow against tug for negligent towage, see § 9–61(5) *infra*. As to collision claims see cases discussed in §§ 9–6, 9–9, 9–10, *supra*.

As to the seaman's action under the Jones Act, see text at note 86 *supra*. No doubt the action for wrongful death under the general maritime law created by Moragne v. States Marine Lines, 398 U.S. 375, 90 S.Ct. 1772, 1970 A.M.C. 967 (1970) carries lien status. The Moragne case is discussed in Chapter VI, § 6–33.

Under former Admiralty Rule 15 (now eliminated, see note 83 *supra*) actions for assault and beating could be brought only *in personam*. Liens were denied under Rule 15 in The Robinson, 3 F.2d 507, 1925 A.M.C. 684 (E.D.Pa.1925); The Vueltabajo, 163 F. 594 (S.D.Ala.1908); The Fred E. Sander, 95 F. 829 (D.Wash.1899): Rule 15 was held inapplicable, although the tort resembled an assault, in The Rolph, 299 F. 52, 1924 A.M.C. 942 (9th Cir. 1924) certiorari denied 266 U.S. 614 (1924); The Western States, 159 F. 354 (2d Cir. 1908), certiorari denied 210 U.S. 433, 28 S.Ct. 762 (1908); The Lord Derby, 17 F. 265 (C.C.E.D.La.1883).

Personal injuries resulting from defective appliances, improper construction or negligence of ship's personnel, give a lien. North American Dredging Co. v. Pacific Mail S.S. Co., 185 F. 698 (9th Cir. 1911); The Anaces, 93 F. 240 (4th Cir. 1899); The Elton, 83 F. 519 (4th Cir. 1897); The Carolina, 32 F. 112 (C.C.E.D.N.Y.1887). A passenger was allowed to sue *in rem* for loss of

which have just been mentioned account for the great bulk of maritime lien tort litigation, it seems on principle that any kind of maritime tort connected with the ship or its use for which those in control of the ship are responsible should create a lien. In State of California v. S/S Bournemouth,[95a] which involved the allegedly negligent discharge of oil into navigable waters, the contention was made that only collision and personal injury claims lead to tort liens. Judge Ferguson reviewed the authorities in an able opinion and concluded that, as a general principle, any conduct which is tortious under the general law and which is connected with the ship or its use creates a maritime lien.[95b] Among the other torts which have been held to give liens are conversion and the fraudulent concealment of insolvency.[95c]

property facilitated by the negligence of the ship's officers. The Minnetonka, 146 F. 509 (2d Cir. 1906), certiorari denied 203 U.S. 589, 27 S.Ct. 777 (1906). But admiralty does not have jurisdiction of a libel *in rem* by the administratrix of a guest to whom the master had served intoxicating liquor and who fell down a stairway sustaining fatal injuries. The Westmoor, 27 F.2d 886 (D.Or.1928). A lien, however, has been allowed for failure to give a passenger proper accommodations, The Willamette Valley, 71 F. 712 (N.D.Cal.1896); for failure to give a seaman adequate instruction, causing him injury, The State of Maryland, 85 F.2d 944, 1936 A.M.C. 1515 (4th Cir. 1936); for an unauthorized act on the part of the crew, The Bulley, 138 F. 170 (S.D.N.Y.1905); for injuries to those, such as stevedores, rendering service to the ship, The General De Sonis, 179 F. 123 (W.D.Wash.1910); The Anaces, 93 F. 240 (4th Cir. 1899); The Christobal Colon, 44 F. 803 (E.D. La.1890).

A lien exists against a ship for tortious damage arising out of unauthorized use of a lighter by the ship's crew, The Atlanta, 82 F.Supp. 218, 1948 A. M.C. 1769 (S.D.Ga.1948).

**95a.** 307 F.Supp. 922, 1970 A.M.C. 642 (C.D.Cal.1969).

**95b.** Actions under the Jones Act and under former Admiralty Rule 15 would be exceptions to the general principle. See note 95 *supra*.

In further proceedings in The Bournemouth, 318 F.Supp. 839, 1971 A.M.C. 485 (C.D.Cal.1970) it was held that, under *res ipsa loquitur* theory, negligence was established and judgment for damages was entered in the *in rem* action. Unlike most lien litigation The Bournemouth did not involve priorities. The foreign owners were not amenable to process *in personam* so that the *in rem* action against the ship was, except for litigation abroad, the only possibility of recovery. The owners entered a "restricted appearance" under Supplemental Rule E(8), F.R.C.P., which provides that such an appearance when process *in rem* has issued "shall not constitute an appearance for the purposes of any other claim with respect to which such process is not available or has not been served." Rule E(8) is discussed § 9–90 *infra*, text following note 474b.

The Federal Water Quality Improvement Act of 1970, discussed Chapter X, § 10–14(b), gives maritime lien status to actions by the United States to recover its costs for cleaning up pollution of navigable waters resulting from the discharge of oil and other substances. The statute does not characterize the lien which should no doubt be categorized as a tort lien.

**95c.** On conversion see Port Welcome Cruises, Inc. v. S/S Bay Belle, 215 F. Supp. 72, 86, 1964 A.M.C. 2674, 2693 (D.Md.1963), affirmed *sub nom.* Humble Oil & Refining Co. v. S/S Bay Belle, 324 F.2d 954 (4th Cir. 1963). Richards, Maritime Liens in Tort, General Average and Salvage, 47 Tulane L.Rev. 569, 582, No. 107 (1973) collects a number of older conversion cases.

On fraudulent concealment of insolvency, see Morrisey v. S/S A. & J. Faith, 272 F.Supp. 54, 1966 A.M.C. 71 (N.D. Ohio 1965). The Henry W. Breyer, 17 F.2d 423, 1927 A.M.C. 290 (D.Md.1927) is usually cited as the leading case on this point. In Atlantic Steamer Supply Co., Inc. v. S/S Tradewind, 153 F. Supp. 354, 1957 A.M.C. 2196 (D.Md. 1957) and in Diaz v. S/S Seathunder, 191 F.Supp. 807, 1961 A.M.C. 561 (D.

*General Average.* A lien arises for general average sacrifices or contributions. The lien may be in favor of the vessel against cargo, or in favor of cargo against the vessel and her freights.[96]

*The preferred ship mortgage.* The Federal Ship Mortgage Act gives lien status and a relatively high order of priority to mortgages which comply with the Act. The statutory mortgage made available to lenders a more satisfactory financing device than the bottomry bond.[97]

*Supplies and repairs.* These liens are of great importance and account for most lien litigation. They are now, to a large extent, covered by the Federal Maritime Lien Act.[98]

*Towage, wharfage, pilotage, stevedoring etc.* These essential services create liens of equal rank with supply and repair liens.[99]

*Cargo damage caused by improper loading, stowage, custody, etc.* These hybrid claims may be looked on as arising out of contract (under the bill of lading or charter-party) or out of tort. The owner and the vessel are immune under the Harter Act and the Carriage of Goods by Sea Act for many types of damage suffered by cargo.[100] But where liability exists, such claims have lien status.[101]

Md.1961) Judge Watkins denied liens for such fraudulent concealment on the unconvincing ground that such a tort is "personal" to those responsible for it and therefore does not lead to *in rem* liability.

96. See Cia Atlantica Pacifica, S. A. v. Humble Oil & Refining Co., 274 F. Supp. 884, 1967 A.M.C. 1474 (D.Md. 1967). The lien for general average in favor of ships against cargo is also discussed in Argyll Shipping Co., Ltd. v. The Hanover Insurance Co., 297 F. Supp. 125, 1968 A.M.C. 2195 (S.D.N.Y. 1968) (the case did not involve ranking or priorities). Since litigation about a general average settlement is rare, most of the cases are fairly old. See Dupont de Nemours & Co. v. Vance, 60 U.S. (19 How.) 162 (1856); 4,885 Bags of Linseed, 66 U.S. (1 Black) 108 (1861); Ralli v. Troop, 157 U.S. 386, 400, 15 S.Ct. 657, 662 (1894). As in the case of liens for freight, the lien on cargo is dependent on possession, Det Forenede Dampskibs Selskab v. Insurance Co. of North America, 31 F.2d 658, 1929 A.M.C. 581 (2d Cir. 1929) certiorari denied 280 U.S. 571 (1929); Frederick H. Leggett & Co. v. 500 Cases of Tomatoes, 15 F.2d 270, 1926 A.M.C. 1670 (2d Cir. 1926), certiorari denied 273 U.S. 761, 47 S.Ct. 475 (1927). The Leggett case also held that if the cargo owners' contributive share of general average is neither paid nor secured, the shipowers' lien allows retention of possession; but where reasonable security is tendered, the shipowners cannot demand cash payment of the estimated amount due in general average. The Andree, 47 F.2d 874 (2d Cir. 1931), appeal dismissed 296 U.S. 668, 57 S.Ct. 756 (1936), held that where cargo is sacrificed to save the venture from fire, cargo has a lien, and that a sum recovered by the shipowner as damages for collision is a *res* to which cargo's general average lien attaches.

97. See § 9–47 *et seq. infra* for discussion of the Ship Mortgage Act.

98. For discussion of the Maritime Lien Act see § 9–30 *et seq. infra.* There is no lien under a contract to build a ship, since that is held not to be a maritime contract. Thames Towboat Co. v. The Francis McDonald, 254 U. S. 242, 41 S.Ct. 65 (1920); People's Ferry Co. v. Beers, 61 U.S. (20 How.) 393, 402 (1857).

99. Like the supply and repair liens, these liens for services are now covered by the Maritime Lien Act, see § 9–30 *et seq. infra.*

100. See Chapter III, Part II.

101. See §§ 9–22, 9–23 *infra.*

*Ship's claims against cargo for unpaid freight etc.* Where freight is unpaid (or where cargo has damaged the ship), there is a lien—*i. e.* the cargo can be libeled *in rem* and sold. The lien against cargo also includes demurrage—sometimes said to be "an extended freight"—at both the loading and the discharging port. The peculiarity of the lien against cargo is that, unlike liens against the vessel or her freight, the cargo lien is possessory, and is lost by unconditional delivery to the consignee.[101a] The universally repeated phrase in this context is a tag attributed to Cleirac:

> "Le batel est obligé à la marchandise et la marchandise au batel",

although it is hard to see exactly what this adds to the discussion.[102]

*Charter-parties.* As in the case of liens between vessel and cargo, liens arise for breach of charter-party in either direction. The charterer has a lien on the vessel for owner's breach; the owner may have a lien on cargo and sub-freights for charterer's breach (which is usually non-payment of the charter-hire).[103]

101a. This proposition, which has never been doubted, was restated in Beverly Hills National Bank & Trust Co. v. Compania de Navegacione Almirante S. A. Panama, 437 F.2d 301, 1971 A.M.C. 890 (9th Cir. 1971).

102. Cleirac, Us et Coutumes de la Mer 597 (1647). Judge Clark in Ryan Stevedoring Co. v. United States, 175 F.2d 490, 493, 1949 A.M.C. 1363, 1366 (2d Cir. 1949) suggests that cargo as such is liable *in rem* for damage caused by it: ". . . while the usual cases of liability of cargo are for freight or general average, and while clearly the fault of the ship is not imputed to the cargo also . . . it seems not beyond the realm of possibility that cargo might be considered an active cause of harm. Thus in The Lord Derby (C.C. E.D.La.1883), 17 F. 265, the libel for the bite of a dog was actually against the ship; as Robinson points out, (p. 405), the court carefully refrained from any discussion as to a libel against the dog. But why not?" Cargo has often been regarded as itself the contracting thing in the same way as a vessel. Two Hundred Seventy-Five Tons of Mineral Phosphates, 9 F. 209 (E.D.N.Y.1881); Donaldson v. McDowell, 7 Fed.Cas. 887, Case No. 3,985 (C.C.D.Mass.1873), affirming The Hyperion's Cargo, 12 Fed.Cas. 1138, Case No. 6,987 (D.Mass.1871).

Freight: The Maggie Hammond, 76 U.S. (9 Wall.) 435 (1869); The Eddy, 72 U.S. (5 Wall.) 481 (1866); 4,885 Bags of Linseed, 66 U.S. (1 Black) 108 (1861). *Cf.* California & Eastern S. S. Co. v. 138,000 Feet of Lumber, 23 F.2d 95, 1928 A.M.C. 73 (D.Md.1927).

Demurrage: The Hyperion's Cargo, *supra*, affirmed Donaldson v. McDowell, *supra;* Solberg v. Cargo of Steel Rails, 25 F.2d 125, 1928 A.M.C. 312 (D.Mass.1927); Pioneer Fuel Co. v. McBrier, 84 F. 495 (8th Cir. 1897); Hawgood v. 1,310 Tons of Coal, 21 F. 681 (E.D.Wis.1884). *Cf.* California & Eastern S. S. Co. v. 138,000 Feet of Lumber, *supra*, holding that a ship has no lien for demurrage charges paid to a railroad for the use of cars into which cargo is unloaded.

The demurrage lien is lost by unconditional delivery to the consignee, Egan v. A Cargo of Spruce Lath, 41 F. 830 (S.D.N.Y.1890), affirmed 43 F. 480 (C.C.S.D.N.Y.1890). The freight lien is lost by unconditional delivery, Eastern Transp. Co. v. United States, 159 F.2d 349, 1947 A.M.C. 194 (2d Cir. 1947); In re 9,889 Bags of Malt, 262 F. 946 (1st Cir. 1919); 4,885 Bags of Linseed, 66 U.S. (1 Black) 108 (1861). But the deposit of goods in a warehouse is not necessarily inconsistent with retention of possession. Davidson S. S. Co. v. 119,254 Bushels of Flaxseed, 117 F. 283 (W.D.N.Y.1902); The Giulio, 34 F. 909 (S.D.N.Y.1888).

103. As to the charterer's lien against the ship, see The Oceano, 148 F. 131, 133 (S.D.N.Y.1906), where Judge Hough wrote: "As soon as the performance of a charter party is com-

*Bottomry and respondentia bonds.* These once important maritime financing devices have passed out of use; most probably no living admiralty lawyer has ever seen an example of either. They are mentioned here out of a sense of history and deference for the past. A bottomry bond was a loan on the security of the vessel, and its importance lay in the fact that it did create a maritime lien, while a mortgage did not.[104] A respondentia bond was a loan on the security of cargo. Both bottomry and respondentia bonds were conditioned on the successful completion of the voyage (*i. e.* if the ship foundered, the loan was discharged). That feature, obviously unattractive to lenders, no doubt explains their disappearance.[105]

menced a lien exists on the vessel in favor of the shipper or charterer, and a suit *in rem* may be maintained for any liability of the master or owner arising therefrom . . . . Damages sustained by a charterer through breach of a charter contract constitute a lien on the vessel" (citing The Director 26 F. 708 (D.Or.1886); The Panama, 18 Fed.Cas. 1073, Case No. 10,703 (S.D.N.Y.1846). No lien arises against the ship for breach of the charter party while it is still executory, see note 114 *infra* and accompanying text.

Where cargo shipped under a charter is owned by the charterer, the Supreme Court held in an early case that the owner had a lien on the cargo by general maritime law "unless there is some stipulation in the charter-party or bill of lading inconsistent with such right of retention, and which displaces the lien." The Bird of Paradise, 72 U.S. (5 Wall.) 545, 554 (1866).

Where cargo shipped under a charter is owned by a third party, general maritime law apparently does not give the shipowner a lien against either the cargo or the freight money. Charter parties, however, customarily provide that the owner shall have a lien against cargo and freight and require the charterer to insert appropriate clauses in bills of lading subjecting the bills to the lien provision of the charter. If the owner of the cargo has notice of the lien provision, the shipowner may enforce his lien against the cargo and, after delivery, against any freight remaining unpaid. See American Steel Barge Co. v. Chesapeake & Ohio Coal Agency Co., 115 F. 669 (1st Cir. 1902); Larsen v. 150 Bales of Sisal Grass, 147 F. 783 (S.D. Ala.1906); Freights of The Kate, 63 F. 707 (S.D.N.Y.1894). In United States v. Freights, etc., of S. S. Mount Shasta, 274 U.S. 466, 47 S.Ct. 666, 1927 A.M.C. 943 (1927) it was held that a shipowner, whose charter contained the customary lien provision, could maintain a libel in rem against freight alleged to be due from a subcharterer even though the amount due was unliquidated and in dispute. The shipowner's liens against cargo belonging to and freight due from persons other than the charterer is discussed at some length in Robinson, Admiralty (1939) p. 401 *et seq.*, p. 635 *et seq.*

Recent cases affirming the propositions just stated include Rainbow Line, Inc. v. M/V Tequila, 341 F. Supp. 459, 1972 A.M.C. 1540 (S.D.N.Y. 1972), affirmed 480 F.2d 1024, 1973 A. M.C. 1431 (2d Cir. 1973); Diana Compania Maritima, S. A. v. Subfreights of the S/S Admiralty Flyer, 280 F. Supp. 607, 1968 A.M.C. 2093 (S.D.N.Y. 1968); Schilling v. A/S D/S Dannebrog, 320 F.2d 628, 1964 A.M.C. 678 (2d Cir. 1963). The owner's lien against sub-freights does not arise (or become enforceable) until there has been a default under the charter; a sub-charterer who pays freight to a charterer without notice of default will be protected. See Union Industrielle et Maritime v. Nimpex International, Inc., 459 F.2d 926, 1972 A.M.C. 1494 (7th Cir. 1972); Marine Traders, Inc. v. Seasons Navigation Corp., 422 F.2d 804, 1970 A.M.C. 346 (2d Cir. 1970); Toro Shipping Corp. v. Bacon-McMillan Veneer Mfg. Co., (The Nadine) 364 F.2d 928, 1966 A.M.C. 2290 (5th Cir. 1966).

104. For a discussion of the cases holding ship mortgages nonmaritime, see § 9–47 *infra*. Examples of a bottomry bond and a respondentia bond are set out in 1 Benedict, Admiralty (6th ed. 1940) 316, 320.

105. Bottomry bonds are within the admiralty jurisdiction even if they are

The foregoing list is not exhaustive and could not be made so, since the law of liens is, at least theoretically, open-ended. As new situations arise, it is for the courts to decide whether particular claims fall in the lien or non-lien category.[105a] It is fair to say that in recent years the courts have been disinclined to add to the list of lien claims: the prevailing attitude, which is far from being exclusively a modern one, has been that liens are disfavored. A court which denies a lien is apt to quote the language of Justice Grier in The Yankee Blade:

> "But this privilege or lien, though adhering to the vessel, is a secret one; it may operate to the prejudice of general creditors and purchasers without notice; it is therefore 'stricti juris', and cannot be extended by construction, analogy, or inference." [106]

## Advances

§ 9–21. Opinions in the older cases occasionally suggested that maritime liens could not be effectively assigned, although it was

given in part to secure nonmaritime disbursements. The Draco, 7 Fed.Cas. 1032, Case No. 4,057 (C.C.Mass.1835). In Detroit Trust Co. v. The Thomas Barlum, 293 U.S. 21, 55 S.Ct. 31, 1934 A.M.C. 1417, 1427 (1934), the same rule was applied to preferred ship mortgages, The Draco being expressly followed. *Cf.* The Wyandotte, 145 F. 321 (4th Cir. 1906). In one other fairly recent case (as cases on bottomry bonds go), Godchaux Sugars, Inc. v. The Katherine, 15 F.2d 387, 1926 A.M.C. 878 (E.D.La.1926), it was held that wireless apparatus installed in a ship is covered by a maritime lien arising from a bottomry bond, which lien is prior to that of a chattel mortgage on the apparatus. Admiralty Rule 17 (now eliminated, see note 83 *supra*) provided that suits on bottomry bonds should be *in rem* only, unless the master acted without authority or the owner had acted wrongfully.

Respondentia loans seem to have gone out when steam navigation and oceanic telegraphy came in. But in 1934 Chief Justice Hughes was still drawing parallels to preferred ship mortgages: "So, in the case of a respondentia loan, it is not necessary that it should be made before the departure of the ship on the voyage or that the money lent should be employed in the outfit of the vessel or invested in the goods on which the risk is run. It matters not, this Court has said, at what time the loan is made, or upon what goods the risk is taken." Detroit Trust Co. v. The Thomas Barlum, *supra*. For the origin of these propositions see The Draco, *supra;* Conard v. Nicoll, 4 Pet. (29 U.S.) 291, 310 (1830); Conard v. Atlantic Ins. Co., 26 U.S. (1 Pet.) 386, 437 (1828); 3 Kent's Com. (14th ed. 1896) 361, note (e).

**105a.** See, e. g., Kane v. M/V Leda, 1972 A.M.C. 2094 (E.D.La.1972) in which Judge Rubin held that, although a quasi-contractual claim for unjust enrichment is within the admiralty jurisdiction, such a claim "is purely *in personam*" and "does not . . . give rise to a lien." In a second opinion, 355 F.Supp. 796, 1973. A.M.C. 2296 (E.D.La.1972), Judge Rubin further discussed the unjust enrichment point. Judge Rubin had made the same point about no liens for quasi-contractual claims in In re Admiralty Lines, Ltd., 280 F.Supp. 601 (E. D.La.1968), affirmed per curiam 410 F.2d 398 (5th Cir. 1969), citing as authority The Eurana, 1 F.2d 684 (3d Cir. 1924). In the Admiralty Lines case Judge Rubin commented: "[A]dmiralty law has long ago ceased to create new liens. The only liens recognized today are those created by statute and those historically recognized in maritime law." (280 F.Supp. at p. 604–605.) The "no new liens" proposition is also stated in Nadle v. M/V Tequila, 1973 A.M.C. 909 (S.D.N. Y.1973), see note 93 *supra* at end.

**106.** 60 U.S. (19 How.) 82, 89 (1857).

never made clear why they could not be assigned.[107] There also grew up a considerable body of case law on the subject of "advances" and the rule came to be that persons (except owners, general agents and the like who cannot hold liens in any case) who advanced money to a ship for the purpose of discharging lien claims inherited the rank of the liens discharged.[108] The money had to be specifically advanced for the purpose and also had to be put to the designed use: thus, although the advance rule allowed a sort of assignment of lien, it did not go so far as to validate the buying up of liens without limitation. Modern cases without exception assume that liens can be assigned; the former rule to the contrary, to the extent that it ever existed, was not so much rejected as forgotten.[109]

If therefore it is possible to make effective assignments of maritime liens (on which there is general agreement), the limitations in

107. Thus in the course of his opinion in The Resolute, 168 U.S. 437, 441, 18 S.Ct. 112, 113 (1897), Justice Brown remarked without citation of authorities: ". . . a portion of libellant's claim arises by assignment from Tellefson, and the authorities are almost equally divided upon the question whether such assignment carries the lien of the assignor to his assignee." No doubt the resistance to assignments of maritime liens was part and parcel of the 19th century debate on the assignability of choses in action. On that debate see 1 Gilmore, Security Interests in Personal Property, Ch. 7 (1965).

108. See The City of Camden, 147 F. 847 (D.Ala.1906); Robinson, Admiralty (1939) 379 (n. 62). The rule appears to be so firmly established that it rarely surfaces in litigation. Caribbean Maritime Finance Co., Ltd. v. Marina Mercante Nicaraguense, S.A., 470 F.2d 277, 1973 A.M.C. 20 (5th Cir. 1972) held that a subcharterer had a lien for advances for ship's expenses despite a prohibition of lien clause in the charter. In re S/S Norberto Capay, 330 F.Supp. 825, 1971 A.M.C. 987 (N.D.Cal.1970) held that an issuer of traveler's checks used to pay crew's wages inherited the wage lien. Crustacean Transportation Corp. v. Atalanta Trading Corp. (The Crustacean), 369 F.2d 656, 1967 A.M.C. 362 (5th Cir. 1966) held that enabling advances were entitled to lien status although the repairs and supplies required by the ship had not been made or furnished when the advances were made.

109. In The Rupert City, 213 F. 263 (W.D.Wash.1914) Judge Neterer dealt with assignments of liens as if there were no question of their validity. See also The Penobscot, 1940 A.M.C. 1217 (D.Mass.1940). In modern cases there is usually no discussion at all of the assignability problem; see, *e. g.*, Handelfinanz A. G. v. S/T Evanthia, 1955 A.M.C. 340 (D.N.J.1954). In Ververica v. Drill Barge Buccaneer No. 7, 488 F.2d 880 (5th Cir. 1974) it appeared that the District Court had held that assignment of a salvage lien had "extinguished" the lien. The Circuit reversed in an opinion by Judge Bell who affirmed the assignability of liens under the modern case law. The lienor, however, was found to have "waived" his lien (see note 202e *infra*) but to be entitled to share in "surplus" (see note 458a *infra*). Of course the general consensus on the assignability of liens does not mean that all claimed assignments will be recognized, see San Rafael Compania Naviera S. A. v. American Smelting & Refining Co., 327 F.2d 581, 1964 A.M.C. 2437 (9th Cir. 1964) (denying the validity of an assignment of freights made by an insolvent charterer, with suggestions that the assignment, if made, might have been a fraudulent conveyance) and Luckenback Overseas Corp. v. Subfreights of the S/S Audrey S. Luckenback, 232 F.Supp. 572, (S.D.N.Y.1963) (holding that a charterer's order to a shipper to pay freights to a stevedore did not constitute an assignment and suggesting that such an assignment, if made, would in any case have been subordinate to the owner's lien on such freights under the charter party). See further Florida Bahamas Lines, Ltd. v. Barge Star 800, 433 F.2d 1243, 1970 A.M.C. 2189 (5th Cir. 1970) where the Court evidently regarded a claimed assignment as part and parcel of a fraudulent scheme to defraud a mortgagee.

the older case law as to when liens passed to makers of advances become irrelevant. The law of advances seems to survive principally as a trap: a claimant, whose status no one would question if he described himself as assignee, at least complicates his case and might even lose it if he claims a lien by reason of advances. Of course there is no magic in the word "assignment": an owner will fare no better as assignee than he would have under the advance rule.[110] Nor will an unrestricted advance of money to an owner to use as he sees fit entitle the person who makes the advance to a lien position with respect to claims which his money is in fact used to pay off; [111] in such a case it would make no difference whether the court talked in terms of "advances" or "assignments". Where, however, the underlying transaction amounts to an assignment of a lien to a person capable of taking one, the assignee's rights as lienor should be recognized without regard to the requirements of the older law that the "advance" be made to the ship and in fact used in specie to pay off the lien.[112]

It could well be argued that both assignments of maritime liens and advances to pay them off constitute assignments of accounts, contract rights or general intangibles under Article 9 of the Uniform Commercial Code. If that were so, the transactions could be subject to the Article 9 filing requirements even if they did not constitute transfers for security and, in the absence of filing, would be void against certain types of third party creditors or purchasers. Since the admiralty bar and the personal property security bar have little or no contact with each other, it may well be that the argument will never be made. If made, it would present some nice questions of law.[112a]

### The Executory Contract Doctrine

**§ 9–22.** No lien attaches for breach of an executory contract, even though the contract is of a type which normally gives rise to a lien. While this issue has been mostly litigated with respect to contracts of affreightment (under bills of lading and charter parties) the proposition can be stated generally. Liability arises in the admiralty as elsewhere from breach of any valid contract, but until the parties have entered on performance remedy for the breach is *in personam* only; the added advantages of lien status are reserved to claimants under executed contracts.[112b]

110. The Kongo, 155 F.2d 492, 1946 A.M.C. 1200 (6th Cir. 1946), certiorari denied 329 U.S. 735, 67 S.Ct. 99 (1946). See also The Odysseus III, 77 F.Supp. 297, 1948 A.M.C. 608 (S.D.Fla.1948).

111. See The San Francisco (International Refugee Organization v. The Maryland Drydock Co., etc.), 179 F.2d 284, 1950 A.M.C. 436 (4th Cir. 1950).

112. See The J. R. Hardee, 107 F.Supp. 379, 1952 A.M.C. 1124 (S.D.Tex.1952), holding persons who made payments to a mortgagee subrogated to the rights of the mortgagee under the Ship Mortgage Act. *Cf.* however Reconstruction Finance Corp. v. The William D. Mangold, 99 F.Supp. 651, 1951 A.M.C. 1589 (E.D.N.Y.1951).

112a. See § 6–57 *infra*, particularly note 296h and the text at that point.

112b. In Blair v. M/V Blue Spruce, 315 F.Supp. 555, 1970 A.M.C. 1298 (D.

The rule is often stated as one peculiar to the admiralty and explained on the recurrent "secret lien—stricti juris" rationalization. In fact, like most admiralty rules it has its close analogues in general law. In the pre-Code law of sales, for example, breach of a contract while it was executory (*i. e.* before property in the goods had passed from seller to buyer) was penalized by less severe sanctions than were imposed for breach after the contract had been "executed" by the passage of property.[112c] And it is not unreasonable that sanctions should be greater or less depending on the point in performance which has been reached when the breach occurs: after the contract has gone beyond the paper stage, the damage suffered by the innocent party is apt to be greater than in the case of an anticipatory repudiation or refusal to perform. The admiralty rule, like the sales rule, erects this presumption of greater damage into a rule of law.

The word "executory" is not self-defining; for clarification the stages of performance at which various types of contracts are deemed to have been "executed" will be indicated. In contracts for supplies or repairs, the crucial stage is the delivery of the supplies or the furnishing of the repairs to the ship.[113] The same point would be taken with respect to other contracts for services—wharfage, towage, salvage, pilotage and the like: the services must be furnished before a lien arises. Under charter-parties the point of "execution" would be the delivery of the vessel under the charter: mere refusal to deliver, however wrongful, would give rise only to liability *in personam* and it would make no difference if charter hire had been paid in advance.[114] Passengers who have paid in advance for a voyage sub-

Mass.1970); 329 F.Supp. 178, 1972 A.M.C. 1252 (D.Mass.1971) Judge Julian held that a pilot whose offered services had been rejected had a lien and could proceed against the vessel. In Wells Fargo Bank v. Barge Marguerita, 1970 A.M.C. 1828 (N.D.Cal.1969) Judge Tuttle held that a naval architect who had performed services (the preparation of drawings and specifications) in connection with a proposed reconditioning of a vessel which was never carried out because of the owner's insolvency was likewise entitled to a lien and could proceed *in rem.* If the two cases are taken at face value they cast doubt on the generality of the proposition stated in the text. However, neither Judge Julian nor Judge Tuttle discussed, or even mentioned, the executory contract doctrine. Thus it is impossible to say whether they intended to reject, or narrow the scope of, the doctrine or whether counsel had simply failed to draw their attention to its existence.

112c. Article 2 of the Uniform Commercial Code makes major terminological but only minor substantive changes in this branch of sales law. See Chapter III, § 3–6 *et seq.*

113. Liens for supplies, repairs and necessary services fall under the Federal Maritime Lien Act. For the lien to arise under the Act the supplies, repairs or services must have been "furnished . . . to [a] vessel". See § 9–30 *infra.* Under the construction which the Supreme Court has given to the "furnished . . . to [a] vessel" language (see § 9–36 *infra*), the Lien Act may be taken as a codification of the executory contract rule.

114. The antiquity of the doctrine is indicated by Justice Grier's opinion in The Yankee Blade, 60 U.S. (19 How.) 82 (1857): ". . . if the master or owner refused to perform his contract, or for any other reason the ship does not receive cargo and depart on her voyage according to contract, the charterer has no privilege or maritime lien on the ship for such breach of the contract by the owners, but must resort to his personal action for damages . . ." Modern cases are

sequently canceled have occasionally sought to libel the ship *in rem*, but have regularly been denied lien status: in a fairly recent case of this type, The City of Athens,[115] the result was that passenger claims in the amount of nearly $500,000 were frozen out entirely, since the proceeds of sale of the ship were exhausted by lien claims.[116] On conceptual grounds, the passenger would have a lien if the voyage were abandoned after he had gone on board the ship (thus "executing" the contract).

With respect to contracts of affreightment (evidenced by bills of lading or charter parties) the usual point of execution which will determine the existence of a lien is the delivery of the cargo to the ship. The physical placing on board, however, is not an absolute prerequisite: goods placed on board lighters for subsequent loading and even goods on wharf or dock may be sufficiently "delivered" for the lien to attach. In the wharf and lighterage cases the crucial issue becomes whether, although not actually on board, the goods are in fact subject to the control of the carrier through the master: it is more accurate, as these cases indicate, to describe the rule in terms of "control" than of "delivery".[117] If the goods on wharf or in light-

Belvedere v. Compania Plomari De Vapores, S.A., 189 F.2d 148, 1951 A.M.C. 1217 (5th Cir. 1951); The Valmar, 38 F.Supp. 618, 1941 A.M.C. 872 (E.D. Pa.1941). Judge Kalodner's opinion in The Valmar collects the authorities.

115. Acker v. The City of Athens, 177 F.2d 961, 1950 A.M.C. 282 (4th Cir. 1949). See also The Bella, 91 F. 540 (W.D.Wash.1899). The Priscilla, 114 F. 836 (2d Cir. 1902) held that a passenger had no lien for loss of baggage where the baggage had been lost on the pier without having been loaded on the ship.

116. Even though they were thus required to give up the ship, the passengers continued their pursuit of Hanioti, the owner of the City of Athens through a maze of interposed corporations, with grim determination. In Acker v. Hanioti, 276 App.Div. 78, 92 N.Y.S.2d 914, 1950 A.M.C. 283 (1949) they learned that claims by passengers for refund of prepaid passage money are equitable in nature and cannot be entertained by the New York Municipal Court. In The City of Athens (Archawski v. Hanioti) 129 F. Supp. 410, 1955 A.M.C. (S.D.N.Y.1955) Judge Walsh held that the passengers' claims against Hanioti (the corporate veils having been pierced) were cognizable *in personam* in admiralty and directed that body execution issue against the defendant who was described as "an unbelievable scoundrel, indifferent to money judgments against him because he believes himself judgment proof under the ordinary methods of execution." Judge Walsh's holding on the point of admiralty jurisdiction, after being reversed by the Circuit, 223 F.2d 406, 1955 A.M.C. 1443 (2d Cir. 1955), was reinstated by the Supreme Court, 350 U.S. 532, 76 S.Ct. 617, 1956 A.M.C. 742 (1956).

117. "There can be no delivery to the ship, in the maritime sense, whether of supplies or cargo, so as to bind the ship *in rem*, until the goods are either actually put on board the ship, or else are brought within the immediate presence or control of the officers of the ship." The Vigilancia, 58 F. 698 (S.D.N.Y.1893). See also The Gracie D. Chambers, 253 F. 182 (2d Cir. 1918), affirmed International Paper Co. v. The Schooner Gracie D. Chambers, 248 U.S. 387, 39 S.Ct. 149 (1919); The Rancagua, 256 F. 843 (5th Cir. 1919). Cargo placed on lighters furnished by the ship: Bulkley v. Naumkeag Steam Cotton Co., 65 U.S. (24 How.) 386 (1860). The only current case which has been found is Continental Grain Co. v. Toko Lines (M/S Pacific Soga), 333 F.Supp. 1349 (E.D. La.1971): lien denied where vessel had never even reached the loading port before breaching the contract. Judge Comiskey's opinion cited no other recent cases.

ers are still in the control of the shipper, or of an independent contractor or even of a charterer of the type who does not himself man the vessel, the lien has not yet arisen.

An "on board" bill of lading signed by the master is the customary evidence that goods have been delivered to the ship. But the bill is not conclusive proof of delivery, nor is its absence fatal to the shipper-libellant's case. If such a bill is issued, by fraud or mistake, without the goods having been received on board, the ship will not be bound; the fact that the bill was improperly issued will not, however, prevent the lien from attaching if the goods are subsequently delivered.[118] The fact that a bill is not signed by the master or the fact that no bill of any kind is issued will not defeat the lien: delivery can always be proved as a fact.[119] Thus a "received for shipment" bill is not inconsistent with the existence of the lien, although the bill itself proves nothing one way or the other. Even though the goods were never loaded on the ship, the lien could attach if the goods were subject to ship's control; if they were loaded, the failure of the shipper to procure an "on board" indorsement of his bill from the master would be irrelevant.

Since the lien attaches from the moment of delivery (or subjection to ship's control) it is not necessary that the ship actually break ground for the voyage, although dicta can be found in some of the older opinions suggesting the contrary.[120] The Supreme Court has not directly passed on this point, although two cases decided shortly after the First World War came close and were apparently so regarded by Justice Stone in a later case.[121] Lower court authority, however, is conclusive.[122]

118. See The Capitaine Faure, 10 F.2d 950, 1926 A.M.C. 382 (2d Cir. 1926).

119. The Esrom, 272 F. 266 (2d Cir. 1921), certiorari denied *sub nom.* J. K. Armsby Co. v. The Esrom, 257 U.S. 634, 42 S.Ct. 47 (1921). Contrariwise, where a bill has been issued, parol evidence is admissible to show that the bill did not correctly state the agreement of the parties, see The Tokyo Maru, 53 F.2d 740, 1932 A.M.C. 34 (9th Cir. 1931).

120. See, *e. g.*, Curtis, J. in The Schooner Freeman v. Buckingham, 59 U.S. (18 How.) 182, 188 (1855); "Under the Maritime law of the United States the vessel is bound to the cargo, and the cargo to the vessel, for the performance of a contract of affreightment; but the law creates no lien on a vessel as a security for the performance of a contract to transport cargo, until some lawful contract of affreightment is made, and a cargo shipped under it."

121. See Krauss Bros. Lumber Co. v. Dimon S. S. Corp. (The Pacific Cedar), 290 U.S. 117, 123 n. 1, 54 S.Ct. 105, 106 n. 1, 1933 A.M.C. 1578, 1581 (1933), citing Allanwilde Transp. Corp. v. Vacuum Oil Co., 248 U.S. 377, 39 S. Ct. 147 (1918), and International Paper Co. v. The Schooner Gracie D. Chambers, 248 U.S. 387, 39 S.Ct. 149 (1918).

122. The Capitaine Faure, 10 F.2d 950, 1926 A.M.C. 382, 401 (2d Cir. 1926): "After the goods are delivered into the custody of the master and are received on board, the failure of the ship to break ground may defeat the ship's lien for freight but it does not defeat the shipper's lien for the safe transportation of his goods". See also The Esrom, 262 F. 953 (2d Cir. 1920); The Esrom, 272 F. 266 (2d Cir. 1921) certiorari denied *sub nom.* J. K. Armsby Co. v. The Esrom, 257 U.S. 634, 42 S.Ct. 47 (1921).

§ 9–23. When the affreightment contract has been only partially performed—in the sense that only part of the cargo contracted for has been delivered to the ship or placed under its control—the lien attaches only in respect of the cargo actually delivered. Language in some of the earlier opinions had suggested the contrary result; but when the issue was squarely presented in Osaka Shosen Kaisha v. Pacific Export Lumber Co.,[123] the Supreme Court declined to give the cargo owner whose contract had been partially executed a lien against the ship for damages for the unexecuted portion. In that case, the master, after having taken on a full underdeck cargo of lumber as well as 241,559 feet on deck, refused, over the shipper's protests, to load an additional 508,441 feet. Among other things, the shipper claimed a lien for nonperformance of the affreightment contract under an Oregon statute; Justice McReynolds dismissed that contention with the brief remark that the rights of the parties depended "upon general rules of maritime law not subject to material alterations by state enactment". As to the general maritime law, the opinion, after an elaborate review of the case law, concluded that no case had actually held a lien in favor of cargo to arise for damages for the nonperformance of the unexecuted portion of a partially executed contract. Wherefore, since maritime liens are *stricti juris* and not to be extended by "construction, analogy or inference", the lien was denied.

The no-lien-for-partial-execution-of-affreightment-contracts rule of the Pacific Export case does have the merit of running both ways, as the so-called "dead freight" cases show. "Dead freight" arises when the shipper fails to deliver the amount of cargo contracted for and as a result the ship is forced to sail loaded to less than capacity. In that situation the shipowner may seek to assert a lien against the cargo shipped in aid of his claim for "dead freight" for the cargo not shipped, much as the libellant in Pacific Export was seeking to hold the ship for damages in respect of the cargo it had refused to load. The dead freight cases, which are approved in the Pacific Export case, deny the lien.[124]

Justice McReynolds' Pacific Export opinion seemed to announce a general rule that henceforward the boundaries of maritime lien law were not to be extended and that all lien claims should be denied unless the claim in suit was on all fours with a prior case, preferably decided by the Supreme Court, in which the lien had actually been granted (and dicta that the lien should be granted were not enough). A few years later, however, lower courts which took those implications seriously found themselves reversed for their pains in Krauss Bros. Lumber Co. v. Dimon Steamship Corp.[125]

The Krauss case, which did not involve an executory contract, fits into our present discussion only because of its close relationship

123. 260 U.S. 490, 43 S.Ct. 172, 1923 A.M.C. 55 (1923).

124. See 260 U.S. 490, 500, 43 S.Ct. 172, 174, 1923 A.M.C. 55, 60.

125. (The Pacific Cedar), 290 U.S. 117, 54 S.Ct. 105, 1933 A.M.C. 1578 (1933). For a discussion of this case in another connection, see Chapter I, note 94.

with the Pacific Export case. In Krauss the contract of affreightment provided for the shipment of lumber from the Pacific Coast to East Coast ports at the rate of $10 per thousand feet but with a provision that in the event "a regular intercoastal carrier moves similar cargo at a lower rate" the lower rate should apply. Payment was made at the $10 rate, both parties acting in good faith. Subsequently it was discovered that a regular intercoastal carrier had moved lumber at a lower rate and the shipper, in an action to recover the overpayment, libeled the ship *in rem*, joining an *in personam* libel against the owner. The handling of the problem in the lower courts is interesting. The District Court dismissed both libels on the ground that the suit was merely a common law action for money had and received and therefore not within the admiralty jurisdiction.[126] The Circuit Court of Appeals reversed the dismissal of the *in personam* libel, holding that since a contract of affreightment was maritime any claim for breach was within the jurisdiction; it affirmed the dismissal of the *in rem* libel, thus relegating the claim to the category of maritime claims which do not have lien status.[127] The Supreme Court ordered the *in rem* as well as the *in personam* libel reinstated.

It is difficult to say how broad a generalization the Krauss case supports. Earlier cases had held that a lien arose where the carrier had demanded and received overpayments of freight, knowing them to be overpayments.[128] If Krauss is taken narrowly, it may mean no more than that the lien exists whether or not the carrier knows that it is receiving an overpayment. Taken broadly, it might mean that whenever a maritime contract has passed the point of "execution", any claim for breach will have lien status. Counsel for the shipowner had argued that the lien in favor of cargo arose only from failure to perform the transportation contract by refusal to deliver the cargo at destination (which would have explained the cases where the carrier knowingly exacted excess freight as a condition of delivery). Justice Stone rejected the argument, citing "the numerous cases in which a lien had been imposed for some breach of the freight term." [129] Nevertheless the opinion also approved cases denying liens

126. Krauss Bros. Lumber Co. v. Dimon S. S. Corp. (The Pacific Cedar), 53 F.2d 492, 1931 A.M.C. 1476, 1775 (W.D.Wash.1931).

127. Krauss Bros. Lumber Co. v. Dimon S. S. Corp. (The Pacific Cedar), 61 F.2d 187, 1932 A.M.C. 1347 (9th Cir. 1932).

128. The John Francis, 184 F. 746 (S.D.Ala.1911); The Ada, 233 F. 325 (D. Md.1916); The Muskegon, 10 F.2d 817, 1924 A.M.C. 1512 (S.D.N.Y.1924); Tatsuuma Kisen Kabushiki Kaisha v. Robert Dollar Co., 31 F.2d 401, 1929 A.M.C. 535 (9th Cir. 1929); cf. The Oregon, 55 F. 666, 677 (6th Cir. 1893).

129. Krauss Bros. Lumber Co. v. Dimon S. S. Corp. (The Pacific Cedar), 290 U.S. 117, 123, 54 S.Ct. 105, 106, 1933 A.M.C. 1578, 1581 (1933). Justice Stone cited in illustration cases which had allowed a lien for freight paid in advance but not earned under the terms of the contract; for charges or purchase price of the cargo, collected by the master from the consignee for account of the shipper as provided in the contract of affreightment; in favor of the charterer for freight earned in violation of the charter party by the ship manned and officered by the owner; for freight overpaid, as dead freight, for shortage of cargo wrongfully exacted by threat of at-

for breaches of contract terms "which, though embodied in the contract of carriage for hire, are no necessary part of it." [130] The Supreme Court has not returned to the issue, so that the dividing line between Justice Stone's two lines of cases has not been traced by the only court which has power to trace it. At least the Krauss opinion (from which, however, four justices dissented) dispelled the possible implication of "no lien without a four-square precedent" which the Pacific Export opinion had suggested.[130a]

It is often said that the liens of cargo against ship and ship against cargo are "mutual and reciprocal", in that they depend on the "union of ship and cargo." This statement is metaphorical rather than true. Cargo's lien against the ship, as we have seen, does not arise until delivery; and the ship's lien against cargo, which is regarded as depending on possession, is lost by an unconditional delivery of the cargo to the consignee.[131] Thus far the "mutual and reciprocal" tag seems to stand up. Cargo's lien against the ship, however, survives the delivery of the cargo. Furthermore the ship's lien against cargo may extend to demurrage, both at the port of loading and the port of discharge. Demurrage at the port of discharge fits comfortably into the general theory, since the affreightment contract is no longer executory at that point. Demurrage at the loading port is harder to explain and the rule that the carrier has a lien for such charges against cargo subsequently loaded seemed to Judge Hough, whose opinion in The Saturnus gave a comprehensive survey of the executory contract doctrine, an unfortunate and unnecessary anomaly.[132]

tachment of the cargo actually shipped and delivered according to the contract; for salvage, payment of which by the cargo was fraudulently procured by the master, who had wilfully stranded the vessel; for the excess of a deposit by the cargo owner in a general average fund, the right of recovery being founded on the master's duty, and hence the ship's, to make the general average adjustment.

130. Justice Stone cited as examples an agreement to pay a commission to the broker procuring the charter party; a provision for storing cargo in the vessel at the end of the voyage.

130a. In United States v. S/S Lucie Schulte, 343 F.2d 897, 1965 A.M.C. 1516 (2d Cir. 1965) Judge Friendly concluded that, under Krauss, there would be a lien for overpayments even though the payments were not made until weeks or months after delivery of the goods and the libel asserting the lien was not filed until three and a half years later. The lien was, however, denied and the libel *in rem* ordered dismissed on other grounds (failure to inquire about the prohibition of lien clause in a charter party, see § 9–42 *et seq. infra*).

131. See cases cited in note 102 *supra*, last paragraph.

132. 250 F. 407 (2d Cir. 1918). See cases cited in note 102 *supra*. In American Anthracite and Bituminous Coal Corp. v. Arrivabene S. A., 280 F.2d 119, 1962 A.M.C. 2666 (2d Cir. 1960) it was held that a claim for demurrage at the loading port was not entitled to priority in a reorganization under Chapter XI of the Bankruptcy Act. Judge Lumbard's opinion dealt principally with the power of a trustee in bankruptcy (or a debtor in possession in a Chapter XI proceeding) to reject executory contracts. His only reference to maritime law came at the end of his opinion in response to the contention that the demurrage claim was entitled to priority under § 64a(5) of the Bankruptcy Act as "rent owing to a landlord who is entitled to priority under applicable State law . . ." Without citation of authority, Judge Lumbard wrote: "Even

### Liens Under the "General Maritime Law", State Statutes and the Federal Maritime Lien Act

**§ 9–24.** The General Smith,[133] which held that no lien is given by the general maritime law for supplies and repairs furnished to a ship in her home port, runs neck and neck with Southern Pacific Co. v. Jensen [134] (state workmen's compensation statute unconstitutional as applied to maritime workers) for the distinction of being the most ill-advised admiralty decision ever handed down by the Supreme Court. The Jensen case represented the most striking application of the Court's occasionally held theory that the Constitutional grant of admiralty jurisdiction requires a nationally uniform system of law, within which local variance must be held to an absolute minimum. The unhappy *sequelae* of Jensen are traced in another chapter.[135] From a dictum in The General Smith (that the home port lien although denied by the general maritime law may be given by state statute) has sprung the theory (which disputes with the Jensen idea of national uniformity for the Court's affections) that in many instances the general maritime law may be supplemented, filled in, perhaps modified by state legislation. It is not entirely unsound to look on the development of admiralty law as a continuing struggle between the polar principles of The General Smith and Jensen. Despite the general disapprobation of both cases, not only by commentators but by the Court itself, it is hard to see how either could have been dispensed with.

The dictum in The General Smith, implemented in subsequent decisions, led to the passage by all the states concerned with shipping of statutes creating liens for a variety of shipping services. The construction of these statutes, with a view to determining just how they fitted into the general maritime law, became the principal admiralty business of the Supreme Court over a long period. Insistent demands for a federal act led to the Maritime Lien Act of 1910 (which was amended and reenacted as part of the Ship Mortgage Act of 1920).[136] The Lien Act was not a comprehensive maritime lien statute: it did not entirely repeal the state statutes, it applied to no tort liens and to only some kinds of contract liens. Thus, despite the passage of the Lien Act, a role was reserved for state statutes and the general maritime law.

On historical grounds, an appropriate organization would be to treat first the liens by general maritime law, then the liens by state law and finally the liens subject to the Federal Lien Act. However, since 1910 most of what light there has been on maritime liens has

assuming, *arguendo*, that demurrage is "rent" . . . neither the law of New York . . . nor maritime law makes provision for such priority . . ." (280 F.2d at p. 127, 1962 A.M.C. at p. 2675.)

133. 17 U.S. (4 Wheat.) 438 (1819).

134. 244 U.S. 205, 37 S.Ct. 524 (1917). The Jensen case is discussed in Chapter VI, § 6–45.

135. See Chapter VI, § 6–46 *et seq.*

136. See § 9–30 *infra.*

been filtered through the prism of the Federal Lien Act which now supports over a hundred pages of fine print annotations in the United States Code Annotated (the Act itself taking up hardly a page).[136a] The historical background is indispensable to an understanding of the Act; the Act is indispensable to an understanding of lien law since its passage. We shall therefore describe first the history and then the Act. In analyzing the issues that have bulked largest in modern litigation, we shall indicate, so far as may be possible, the surviving distinctions between liens statutory and non-statutory, State and Federal.[136b]

### The "Home Port" Doctrine and the State-Created Lien

§ 9–25. In the General Smith libels *in rem* alleged that ship's stores had been furnished to and repairs made upon a vessel in the port of Baltimore, the vessel being the property of one Stevenson, "a merchant of Baltimore and a citizen of the United States." The District Court recognized the liens and ordered the ship sold, the Circuit Court affirmed, and the case came on appeal to the Supreme Court, which seems to have looked on it as of little interest and no importance. In an opinion just over a page long, blank of citations of any authority, the learned and prolix Justice Story reversed, saying:

> "Where repairs have been made, or necessaries furnished to a foreign ship, or to a ship in a port of the State to which she does not belong, the general maritime law, following the civil law, gives the party a lien on the ship itself for his security; and he may well maintain a suit *in rem* in the Admiralty to enforce his right. But in respect to repairs and necessaries in the port or State to which the ship belongs, the case is governed altogether by the municipal law of that State; and no lien is implied, unless it is recognized by that law." [137]

Finding that by the law of Maryland there was no lien, Story had no more to say.

Two aspects of Justice Story's remarks gave a great deal of work to later generation of jurists.

The first was: what was the "port or State to which the ship belongs"? That might have been simple had it not been for The St. Jago de Cuba,[138] decided five years after The General Smith. A ship

136a. The pace may have slackened somewhat in recent years. The 1973 U.S.C.A. Supplement, covering the period from 1958 to 1973, contributes less than twenty additional pages of annotations.

136b. The 19th century development is well traced in Robertson, Admiralty and Federalism: History and Analysis of Problems of Federal-State Relations in the Maritime Law of the United States, Chapters VI through IX (1970). Professor Robertson's conclusions appear to be, on the whole, consistent with our own. See Review of Robertson by Gilmore, 38 U. of Chicago L.Rev. 431 (1971).

137. 17 U.S. (4 Wheat.) 438, 442 (1819).

138. 22 U.S. (9 Wheat.) 409 (1824). The opinion was written by Justice Johnson, Story concurring.

whose owners lived in Baltimore, was sent to Cuba where, after a "colorable" sale to a Spanish subject, her name was changed and she was fitted out for the prohibited slave trade. The "sale", in the Court's opinion, did nothing to divest the interest of the Baltimore owners. Having set out for Africa, the ship "is pursued by hostile vessels, and in the chase sustains damage, which compels her to put into Baltimore to refit." Ultimately she was seized, condemned and sold for violation of the laws prohibiting the slave trade; before that in the course of the "refitting" at Baltimore, supply and repair claims accrued and those claimants intervened in the forfeiture proceedings, claiming a lien on the proceeds of sale. Justice Johnson's opinion conceded that "even in the home-port, a vessel may be subjected to the liabilities of a vessel in a strange port, by being falsely held up as foreign by her owners." The concession was unnecessary since all the claimants were found to have had notice of the true facts. Furthermore, Justice Johnson explained the basis of the home port rule to be that the master (and only the master) is empowered to subject a ship to liens in foreign ports, "to furnish wings and legs to the forfeited hull", to allow the ship to get on with her voyage. "But when the owner is present [*i. e.* when the vessel is in her home port], the reason ceases, and the contract is inferred to be with the owner himself, without a view to the vessel as the fund from which compensation is to be derived."

In a round-up article on the "Confusion in the Law" of supply and repair liens, published on the eve of passage of the Federal Lien Act,[139] Mr. Fitz-Henry Smith commented that the effect of The St. Jago de Cuba "has been no less fatal than that of The General Smith." The doctrine of "presumption of credit" to the owner, which Justice Johnson introduced as an explanation of the home port rule, had, according to Mr. Smith, no basis in prior law—or no more basis than The General Smith had. As we shall see, the idea of credit "to the vessel" as a prerequisite of lien, while credit "to the owner" negates the lien, is, despite the Federal Lien Act, with us still and accounts for a continuing stream of litigation.[140] Justice Johnson's other main point—that "home port" was a subjective state of mind rather than an objective fact—opened endless possibilities of refinement in which the courts wallowed for generations.[141] The Lien Act brought that discussion to an end and such cases are now of merely antiquarian interest.

The other, and more important, aspect of the litigation which flowed from The General Smith was the working out of the off-hand dictum: that, in the home port "no lien is implied, unless it is recognized by [state] law".

139. Smith, The Confusion in the Law Relating to Materialmen's Liens on Vessels, 21 Harv.L.Rev. 332, 334 (1908).

140. See § 9–38 *infra*.

141. See Smith note 139 *supra*, collecting cases.

**§ 9–26.** The first case to convert the dictum into a holding was The Planter.[142] There it was held that a claim for repairs could be enforced by libel *in rem* where the local law (in this instance a Louisiana statute) gave such a lien. A few years later Justice Story in The Orleans [143] affirmed the principle established in The Planter.

The doctrine of The Planter and The Orleans was subsequently incorporated in the first set of admiralty rules issued by the Supreme Court in 1844.[144] Rule 12 provided that supply and repair liens against foreign ships (and each State was considered "foreign" to each other State) could be enforced "against the ship and freight *in rem*, or against the master or the owner alone *in personam*", continuing: "And the like proceeding *in rem* shall apply to cases of domestic ships where by the local law a lien is given to materialmen for supplies, repairs, or other necessaries." So matters stood until 1858 when the Court revised the last quoted sentence to read: "And the like proceeding *in personam*, but not *in rem*, shall apply to cases of domestic ships for supplies, repairs, or other necessaries." [145] In 1872 the Court revised the Rule still a third time, combining the two sentences on foreign and domestic ships, so that the Rule read: "In all suits by materialmen for supplies or repairs or other necessaries, the libellant may proceed against the ship and freight *in rem* or against the master or owner alone *in personam*." According to Justice Bradley in The Lottawanna, the 1858 Rule, abrogating the *in rem*, action, was designed to avoid "the inconveniences arising from the often intricate and conflicting State laws creating such liens", while the reinstatement of the *in rem* action by the 1872 rule "was simply intended to remove all obstructions and embarrassments in the

142. Peyroux v. Howard, 32 U.S. (7 Pet.) 324 (1833). The opinion was by Justice Thompson for a unanimous Court.

143. 36 U.S. (11 Pet.) 175 (1837). The libel was, however, dismissed because the vessel was operating in waters beyond the reach of admiralty jurisdiction as it was then understood.

144. 44 U.S. (3 How.) ix (1844). The Admiralty Rules were issued in pursuance of the rule-making power given the Court by the Act of August 23, 1842, c. 188, § 6; 5 Stat. 518 (R.S. §§ 862, 917).

145. 62 U.S. (21 How.) iv (1858). The St. Lawrence, 66 U.S. (1 Black) 522 (1861), gave Chief Justice Taney an occasion to explain the nature of the change made in Rule 12 by the 1858 amendment in a manner which came to have considerable theoretical importance. The Rules should not, said the Chief Justice, be looked on as involving in any way the extent of the admiralty jurisdiction conferred by the Constitution. If the court had jurisdiction, it "could not, consistently with its duty, refuse to exercise a power which the Constitution and law had clothed it." The rules, and the 1858 amendment to Rule 12 applied merely to "the character of the process to be used in certain cases" and had nothing to do with jurisdiction. The trouble with the 1844 rule, Taney explained, had been that the state statutes contained detailed, often inconsistent, provisions as to the conditions under which liens attached or could be lost. The construction of such provisions, appropriate in the state courts, was "foreign" to the courts of admiralty. Wherefore, the Supreme Court had resolved the question by the amendment to Rule 12.

way of instituting proceedings *in rem* in all cases where liens exist by law".[146]

§ 9-27. The Court's 1858 denial of the *in rem* action to enforce state created liens led it—or so the available evidence suggests—to one of its most significant decisions. Until 1858 domestic materialmen had been well taken care of: the theoretical hole in the "general maritime law" announced in The General Smith had everywhere been plugged by state statutes which conferred liens with a generous hand and those liens were enforceable *in rem* in admiralty. By the amendment to Rule 12 they found themselves relegated to the status of non-lien creditors, whose claims would be paid off only after all liens had been satisfied. Since the admiralty action *in personam* was unsatisfactory it was natural for the materialmen to explore the possibility of relief in non-admiralty courts. At December term of 1866, the Court found on its docket two cases, The Moses Taylor [147] and The Hine v. Trevor,[148] which raised the question of how far state courts could go in adjudicating maritime liens. "It is a little singular," as Justice Miller wrote in The Hine "that, at this term of the court, we should, for the first time, have the question of the right of the State courts to exercise this jurisdiction, raised by two writs of error to State courts . . ." [149]

The Moses Taylor, the first of the two cases presented to and decided by the court, appeared to be of negligible importance; the amount in controversy was so small that the case was not even appealable to the highest state court. Counsel for the shipowners before the Supreme Court, however, included Mr. Edwards Pierrepont and Mr. William M. Evarts, who did not ordinarily appear in cases where less than two hundred dollars was at stake. The pre-eminence of counsel suggests that, beneath the surface, large interests were concerned. The facts were as follows: in 1863 one Hammons had taken passage from New York to San Francisco, by ship to Panama, by rail across the Isthmus, and by ship to San Francisco. Alleging delays as well as poor accommodations, Hammons sued the Moses Taylor, the ship employed on the Pacific leg of the journey; the suit was brought before a justice of the peace under the California lien statute which covered not only supplies, repairs and other services furnished to vessels but torts and the "nonperformance or malperformance" of any contract of affreightment or passage. The statute provided for an action "directly against the vessel," her sale and the application of proceeds to the satisfaction of any judgment. The Supreme Court decided, in an opinion by Justice Field, that the action authorized by the California statute was "a proceeding in the nature and with the incidents of a suit in admiralty"—*i. e.* an action *in rem*. Such an action, the Court for the first time decided, did not

146. 88 U.S. (21 Wall.) 558, 579 (1874). On the currently applicable provisions of Supplemental Rule C, F.R.C.P., see notes 76 and 83 *supra*.

147. 71 U.S. (4 Wall.) 411 (1866).

148. 71 U.S. (4 Wall.) 555 (1866).

149. *Id.* at 568.

fall within the "saving to suitors" clause, but lay, by the Constitutional grant, within the exclusive jurisdiction of federal courts sitting in admiralty.

The Hine v. Trevor presented the same issue: a steamboat collision on the Mississippi River near St. Louis followed by a proceeding "against the vessel" in Iowa courts under a statute like the California statute involved in The Moses Taylor. According to Justice Miller's opinion in The Hine, The Moses Taylor had been decided before The Hine was presented to the court. On the validity of the State court proceeding, the first decision controlled the second.

The Moses Taylor and The Hine made the situation of the domestic materialmen hopeless; because of Rule 12 they could not proceed *in rem* in the admiralty and comparable relief in state courts was denied them on Constitutional grounds. That the solution was not acceptable to powerful interests is a reasonable inference from the fact that within a few years the Court was persuaded to reverse its field a second time and reinstate the *in rem* action in favor of the domestic materialmen. The nonavailability of the *in rem* action, or something like the *in rem* action, in state courts became once again of purely theoretical interest.

**§ 9–28.** Following the 1872 revision of Rule 12 the Court was presented, in The Lottawanna,[150] with the opportunity to escape from the pit it had been digging for itself ever since The General Smith. The Lottawanna involved priority between mortgagees (concededly not entitled to lien status since the mortgage was not a maritime claim) and supply and repair claimants. A Louisiana statute gave a lien for supplies and repairs, but the claimants had not perfected their liens in conformity with the statute. All their claims had accrued before the rule change in 1872, but when the case came before the Court the change had been made. The materialmen argued in the first instance for a flat overruling of The General Smith. In this they were encouraged by remarks of Justice Clifford in an opinion on an earlier appeal [151] which seemed to suggest that the Court, if the issue were directly presented, was ready to overrule The General Smith. Secondly, taking advantage of the rule change, the materialmen argued that the 1872 version of Rule 12, which made no distinction between foreign and domestic liens but spoke of "all suits by materialmen", amounted to an overruling of The General Smith. Since the rules were merely procedural,[152] there could be no objection to applying the rule as amended even though the Lottawanna claims had accrued before the change.

**150.** 88 U.S. (21 Wall.) 558 (1874).

**151.** The Lottawanna, 87 U.S. (20 Wall.) 201 (1873). After reviewing the "embarrassment" and "inconveniences" inherent in the home port doctrine, Justice Clifford had concluded: "These and many other considerations have had the effect to create serious doubts as to the correctness of the decision made more than fifty years ago (The General Smith), that a maritime lien does not arise in such a case." (20 Wall. at 219).

**152.** As Taney, C. J., had said in The St. Lawrence, see note 145 *supra*.

The Court declined to take the attractive bait. Evidently there had been a change of feeling on the Court. On the first appeal Justice Clifford, writing for a unanimous court, had indicated that The General Smith would in all probability be overruled if only the issue were directly urged. On the second appeal the issue was urged but the Court decided, seven to two, to stand by The General Smith, Bradley writing for the majority with Clifford and Field in dissent.

Bradley's opinion is one of the classical statements of the basic theories of American admiralty jurisprudence. The affirmation of The General Smith was put not on the ground that the case had been correctly decided in the first place but on the ground that substantial changes in the law should not be made out of "mere expediency or love of scientific completeness". He then developed the thought that the "general maritime law" obtains in this country only so far as American courts, under the direction of the Supreme Court, choose to make it part of our domestic law. The Constitution, he went on, "must have referred to a system of law coextensive with, and operating uniformly in, the whole country"—a foreshadowing of the Jensen theory.[153] Nevertheless, until Congress had acted to establish such uniformity, the States, so long as they did not offend against the basic principles of the maritime law, were empowered to give lien status to maritime claims, and such liens would be recognized and enforced in the admiralty. "It would undoubtedly be far more satisfactory," he concluded, "to have a uniform law regulating such liens, but until such a law be adopted (supposing Congress to have the power) the authority of the States to legislate on the subject seems to be conceded by the uniform course of decisions."

Following the Court's refusal in The Lottawanna to make a fresh start, it was clear that the doctrine of State created liens enforceable only in admiralty, made necessary by the denial of home port liens, was to be a permanent feature of admiralty law. Since the Court would not, only Congress could abolish the doctrine.

**§ 9–29.** The state statutes were not limited to home port repairs and supplies. They gave lien status to both contract and tort claims which already had that status by maritime law, to claims which although maritime were not liens by that law (the New York statute gave a lien for unpaid insurance premiums) and to claims which were not (or were later held not to be) maritime claims at all (almost all the statutes gave a lien for shipbuilding contracts).[154] Why the states

153. This passage from The Lottawanna was indeed the principal authority cited by Justice McReynolds in support of the Jensen holding. See Chapter VI, § 6–45.

154. Insurance premiums: New York Lien Law, § 80(5). Ship building: § 80(1); Annotated Laws of Massachusetts, c. 255, § 14; Deering's California H. & N. C. A., § 491(c).

Among the contract claims given lien status by the New York statute of 1862, which as revised is still in force (or at least still in the statute books) were debts arising: from work done or materials furnished in the "building, repairing, fitting, furnishing, or equipping" of a vessel; from provisions and stores furnished to a vessel; from wharfage, loading, unloading, towage and pilotage. Such statutes

passed such comprehensive statutes has become obscure. There are suggestions in the arguments in The Moses Taylor and The Hine [155] that the state courts, under such statutes, had been administering a complete system of admiralty law and it may be that when the early statutes were drafted no objection to that course was perceived.

The perpetuation of the State lien system by The Lottawanna forced the Court to come to grips with the problem created by the comprehensiveness of the state statutes in the light of the decisions in The Moses Taylor and The Hine that only the admiralty courts could administer a "nationally uniform" system of admiralty law. What came out was a patchwork of many pieces.

1. State legislation has no effect on claims which are liens by maritime law. Thus, supply and repair liens against "foreign" ships continued until passage of the Federal Lien Act to be governed by general law, and state law provisions on filing, discharge and the like were disregarded.

2. State legislation can confer lien status only on maritime claims. The home port supply and repair claims were, until the passage of the Federal Lien Act, the most important claims of this type. Actions for wrongful death occurring on waters within the admiralty jurisdiction were another example. It was early held by the Supreme Court that, in admiralty as at common law, there could be no recovery for wrongful death apart from statute.[156] There was no federal statute until the Death on the High Seas Act of 1920,[157] but there were state statutes. In The Corsair [158] Justice Brown indicated that a lien given by the state statute would support an action *in rem* on the analogy of the home port supply lien. The libel in The Corsair was dismissed because nothing in the state statute gave a lien

contained provisions for regulating priorities among liens, for filing notice of lien, for duration and assignment of liens and for their enforcement. Most of the statutes were written to apply to "all vessels within this State." The New York statute adds a provision that "if a lien, created by virtue of this article, is founded upon a maritime contract, it can be enforced only by proceedings in the courts of the United States and, in any other case, in the courts of this state . . ."

155. The Moses Taylor, 71 U.S. (4 Wall.) 411, 415, 419 (1866); The Hine v. Trevor, 71 U.S. (4 Wall.) 555, 558 (1866). For other contemporary evidence of such a practice, see 2 Parsons, Shipping & Admiralty 142–155 (1869).

156. The Harrisburg, 119 U.S. 199, 213, 7 S.Ct. 140, 146 (1886): " . . . it is now established that in the courts of the United States no action at law can be maintained for such a wrong in the absence of a statute giving the right, and it has not been shown that the maritime law, as accepted and received by maritime nations generally, has established a different rule for the government of the courts of admiralty from those which govern courts of law in matters of this kind, we are forced to the conclusion that no such action will lie in the courts of the United States under the general maritime law." Accord: Butler v. Boston & Savannah S. S. Co., 130 U.S. 527, 9 S.Ct. 612 (1889). For the overruling of The Harrisburg in Moragne v. States Marine Lines, Inc., 398 U.S. 375, 90 S.Ct. 1772, 1970 A.M.C. 967 (1970), see Chapter VI, § 6–33.

157. Act of March 30, 1920, c. 111, 41 Stat. 537, 46 U.S.C. § 761.

158. 145 U.S. 335, 12 S.Ct. 949 (1892).

and the Supreme Court did not rule on the point until 1933 when in Vancouver S.S. Co., Ltd. v. Rice,[159] where the state statute did give a lien, a libel *in rem* was upheld, as it had been in several lower court cases [160] following the dictum in The Corsair. Other examples of non-lien maritime claims on which the state statutes can operate are the unpaid insurance premium covered by the New York statute and a master's claim for wages covered by many of the statutes.

3. State created liens can be enforced *in rem* only by the federal admiralty court. The Moses Taylor and The Hine block the state courts from enforcing these liens by anything resembling an action *in rem.*[161]

4. State legislation can not confer a maritime lien on a non-maritime claim. On the other hand, admiralty jurisdiction not being involved, there is nothing to prevent a state from creating any sort of lien it wants, enforceable by any sort of process, in its own courts. This was brought out most clearly in the shipbuilding contract cases: non-maritime contracts to which the state statutes almost universally gave a lien. The two sides of the rule were brought out in Edwards v. Elliott,[162] which was decided at the same term of court as The Lottawanna and directly precedes it in the reports; in the Edwards case the Court affirmed a state court judgment awarding a lien for a shipbuilding contract. Of course if the ship, after having been completed, goes into navigation and incurs true maritime liens, the state-created building lien will be subordinate to the maritime liens.

5. Insofar as state legislation creates maritime liens enforceable *in rem* the detailed provisions of the statutes (relating, for example, to filing, duration and discharge) will be applied by the admiralty court so long as they do "not contravene any acts of congress, nor work any prejudice to the characteristic features of the maritime law, nor interfere with its proper harmony and uniformity in its international and interstate relations." [163] To put it more simply: sometimes the statutory provisions will be enforced and sometimes

159. 288 U.S. 445, 53 S.Ct. 420, 1933 A.M.C. 487 (1933).

160. The Ogontz (U. S. Shipping Bd. Emergency Fund Corp. v. Greenwald), 16 F.2d 948, 1927 A.M.C. 308 (2d Cir. 1927); The Samnanger, 298 F. 620, 1924 A.M.C. 517 (D.Ga.1924); The Anglo-Patagonia, 235 F. 92 (4th Cir. 1916) certiorari denied *sub nom.* Lord v. Ledwitch, 242 U.S. 636, 37 S.Ct. 19 (1916); The Chiswick, 231 F. 452 (5th Cir. 1916) certiorari denied *sub nom.* British S. S. Co. v. Clarke, 241 U.S. 673, 36 S.Ct. 723 (1916); Aurora Shipping Co. v. Boyce, 191 F. 960 (9th Cir. 1911).

161. See § 9–27 *supra.* See Lih v. Wagner, 65 M.2d 38, 316 N.Y.S.2d 497, 1971 A.M.C. 768 (Sup.Ct.1970) dismissing for lack of jurisdiction a proceeding in state court which sought the sale of a 36-foot cabin cruiser under the New York Lien Law. *Cf.,* however, Sun Harbor Marina, Inc. v. Sellick, 250 Cal.App.2d 281, 58 Cal. Rptr. 459, 1967 A.M.C. 2783 (1967), holding that a vessel could be sold in a state court proceeding to satisfy storage charges under the California statute relating to the foreclosure of possessory liens by warehousemen, apparently with the effect of cutting off prior interests.

162. 88 U.S. (21 Wall.) 532 (1874).

163. McReynolds, J., in Southern Pacific Co. v. Jensen, 244 U.S. 205, 216, 37 S.Ct. 524, 529 (1917).

they will not. The range of possibilities is indicated by two Supreme Court cases, Union Fish Co. v. Erickson [164] and Western Fuel Co. v. Garcia.[165] Erickson involved a master's claim for wages. The contract of employment was oral and hence unenforceable by the California Statute of Frauds. *Held*: the state statute of frauds did not apply and the contract was enforceable in admiralty. Garcia involved a wrongful death claim, the action having been instituted after the state statute of limitation had run. *Held*: the state limitation statute applied and the libel in admiralty should be dismissed. Both Garcia and Erickson were libels *in personam*, not *in rem*, but the "principle" behind the two cases would seem to apply to the *in rem* action as well. As to the distinction between state statutes of frauds and state statutes of limitation, the layman who lacks the special insight of justices of the Supreme Court can only say: *Credo quia absurdum est.*[165a] More recently in Just v. Chambers,[166] the Supreme Court found that a Florida statute under which a cause of action in tort did not abate on the tortfeasor's death and could be maintained against his estate worked no prejudice to the characteristic features of the maritime law so that an *in personam* action against the owner-decedent's estate was allowed.

6. It is sometimes said that state statutes can not create liens against foreign ships, but the statement made in such general form, is not supported by the authorities usually cited. It is true that one of the pieces in the Supreme Court's jig-saw puzzle is the doctrine that state statutes do not apply where a lien is given in any case by the general maritime law: since that law gave a lien for supplies and repairs furnished to foreign or out-of-state ships, the state statutes were irrelevant in that important area. The Supreme Court case that came closest to stating the doctrine referred to was The Roanoke [167] which involved a lien claim against a foreign ship in favor of a subcontractor who had furnished materials to a contractor who had performed repairs on the ship. The subcontractor's lien, recognized by the state statute, was certainly not a lien by general law, nor was the contract between contractor and subcontractor a maritime contract. Since a nonmaritime contract was involved, the state-created lien could not have been good in admiralty. Justice Brown's opinion did discuss at some length the proposition that state statutes do not apply to foreign ships, but, as he recognized, the question was not directly raised. Another case cited in support of the doctrine is Osaka Shosen Kaisha v. Pacific Export Lumber Co.,[168]

164. 248 U.S. 308, 39 S.Ct. 112 (1919).

165. 257 U.S. 233, 42 S.Ct. 89 (1921). The Garcia case is further discussed in Chapter VI, § 6–49.

165a. See further on this mystical distinction Kossick v. United Fruit Co., 365 U.S. 731, 81 S.Ct. 886, 1961 A.M.C. 833 (1961), rehearing denied 366 U.S. 941, 81 S.Ct. 1657 (1961), discussed in Chapter VI, § 6–11.

166. 312 U.S. 383, 61 S.Ct. 687, 1941 A.M.C. 430 (1941).

167. 189 U.S. 185, 23 S.Ct. 491 (1903).

168. 260 U.S. 490, 43 S.Ct. 172, 1923 A.M.C. 55 (1923). The case is discussed § 9–23 *supra*.

in which a lien was asserted against a foreign ship for breach of a partially executed affreightment contract. One of the arguments made by the libellant was that it had a lien under the state statute. Justice McReynolds dismissed the argument with the brief remark: "Little need be written of the claim under the state statute. The rights and liabilities of the parties depend upon general rules of maritime law not subject to material alterations by state enactments." He then cited The Roanoke, Southern Pacific Co. v. Jensen and Union Fish Co. v. Erickson. The citations suggest that the point was that a state statute could not give a lien where that result would be inconsistent with general maritime law and not that there could never be a state created lien against a foreign ship. In the wrongful death actions under state statutes, the argument that liens could not arise against foreign ships seems never to have been made. Although the authorities are in a doubtful state, it is believed that the following formulation is accurate: a state statute can confer a lien against a foreign vessel provided 1) that a lien does not already exist by the general maritime law; 2) that the claim for which the lien is given is a maritime claim; and 3) that the lien does not seriously conflict with the nationally uniform system of maritime law.

### The Federal Maritime Lien Act

**§ 9–30.** In 1910 Congress enacted the "uniform law" regulating liens which Justice Bradley had called for in The Lottawanna thirty-six years earlier. The Lien Act was a useful piece of legislation; it is unfortunate that Congress delayed in passing it until the horribly complex theory of state created liens just discussed had become so deeply rooted in the law that it was nearly impossible to dig it up, and even more unfortunate that the draftsman did not take as a model one of the well-drafted, comprehensive state lien statutes such as that of New York.

The Act consists of five short sections, which are printed as Sections 971–975 of Title 46 of the United States Code and will be referred to by section number.[169] Section 971 (as amended in 1920) provides that:

> "Any person furnishing repairs, supplies, towage, use of dry dock or marine railway, or other necessaries, to any vessel, whether foreign or domestic, upon the order of the owner of such vessel, or of a person authorized by the owner, shall have a maritime lien on the vessel, which may be enforced by suit in rem, and it shall not be necessary to allege or prove that credit was given to the vessel."

Section 972, enlarging on the "person authorized by the owner" language of § 971 gives a list of persons presumed to have such authority: the managing owner, ship's husband, master or any person to whom

169. Act of June 23, 1910, c. 373, 36 Stat. 604; Merchant Marine Act of June 5, 1920, c. 250, § 30, subsections P–T, 41 Stat. 1005, 46 U.S.C.A. §§ 971–975.

the management of the vessel at the port of supply is entrusted. The section then points out that a person "tortiously or unlawfully in possession" does not have authority to bind the vessel. Section 973 continues with the authority question: the persons mentioned in § 972 still qualify when appointed by "a charterer, an owner pro hac vice, or by an agreed purchaser in possession of a vessel." Then followed a provision which sparked much litigation until it was deleted in 1971:[169a]

> " . . . nothing in this chapter shall be construed to confer a lien when the furnisher knew, or by exercise of reasonable diligence could have ascertained, that because of the terms of a charter party, agreement for sale of the vessel, or for any other reason, the person ordering the repairs, supplies, or other necessaries was without authority to bind the vessel therefor."

Section 974 goes off in a different direction. First, the section provides that liens may be waived "by agreement or otherwise" and then adds that "this chapter" [170] shall not be construed to affect existing rules with respect to (1) advances; (2) laches; (3) actions *in personam;* (4) lien priorities; (5) priorities between maritime liens and mortgages other than preferred mortgages under the Ship Mortgage Act. The final Section, § 975, deals with the state lien statutes in the following oddly chosen language:

> "This chapter shall supersede the provisions of all State statutes conferring liens on vessels, insofar as such statutes purport to create rights of action to be enforced by suits in rem in admiralty against vessels for repairs, supplies, towage, use of dry dock or marine railway, and other necessaries."

The Act bears every sign of the draftsman's earnest effort to strike a balance between conflicting interests: the materialmen, who want the lien to be easy, automatic and far reaching, and the shipowners, who would as soon take their chances with the obscurities of general maritime law and who feel that the only good lien is a dead lien. The materialmen got most, being freed from the horrors of The General Smith, the home port doctrine and the complicated business of just how far the admiralty courts might be willing to enforce local statutes. The authority provisions in §§ 972 and 973, particularly the duty to inquire as to the authority of charterers and the like, seem to have been a sop to the shipowners which, until the deletion of the "duty to inquire" provision in 1971, proved to be of great importance.

169a. 85 Stat. 285 (1971). With the deletion of this provision, § 973 consists of the provision which has just been summarized in the text.

170. As originally passed the language was "this Act" which was changed to "this chapter" when the Lien Act was reenacted in 1920 as part of the Ship Mortgage Act.

## Scope of the Lien Act: Its Relationship with State Statutes and the General Maritime Law

**§ 9–31.** Judicial theories about the scope of the Lien Act, the extent to which it repealed the state lien statutes and the extent to which a class of nonstatutory contract liens conferred by general maritime law survived the passage of the Lien Act have gone through two distinct periods. During the first period the Lien Act was generally held to have a narrow scope, so that a role remained for both the state created liens and for nonstatutory liens under general maritime law. A 1920 amendment to the language of § 971 led to the second period, in which the Lien Act has been held to have a much broader scope and, as a result, both the state created liens and the nonstatutory general maritime liens have gradually faded from sight. Nevertheless, the cases of the first period remain on the books and have never been formally overruled. Most of the critical commentary on this phase of the Lien Act was written during the 1920's and 1930's and, with good reason as of that time, assigned to the first period cases an importance which, it is believed, they have subsequently lost, more from the erosion of time and judicial forgetfulness than from conscious, deliberate action. The Supreme Court has never been called upon to consider the problem.

As a result of the complex development sketched in the preceding paragraph, it is impossible to define the present state of the law with a sharp and clear precision. At one time it seemed that we were moving toward a rigidly defined three part division of contract liens: federal statutory liens, state statutory liens and nonstatutory general maritime liens, with each class having different rules for validity and the dividing lines between classes leading to an endless spate of litigation. That nightmare pattern would have been worse than any of the disturbances which had followed in the long wake of The General Smith. Fortunately the trend of decision was reversed and we have now reached a point where it is fair to say that for most types of contract liens a uniform pattern has been established, with the Lien Act being looked to as the source of law and the state liens and nonstatutory general maritime liens all but forgotten.[170a] Only "all but" forgotten, however: as with any legal doctrine which has never died but is merely in the process of fading away, it can be brought unexpectedly to life in any given case. Only a pronouncement by the Supreme Court, in the absence of new legislation by Congress of which there is no prospect, could finally resolve the lingering shreds of doubt.

**§ 9–32.** Section 971 of the Lien Act, as passed in 1910, gave a lien to "any person furnishing repairs, supplies, or other necessaries,

**170a.** In Rainbow Line, Inc. v. M/V Tequila, 341 F.Supp. 459, 1972 A.M.C. 1540 (S.D.N.Y.1972) affirmed 480 F.2d 1024, 1973 A.M.C. 1431 (2d Cir. 1973) it was argued that there could be no lien for breach of a charter party on the ground that the only contract liens now recognized are those provided for in § 971. Judge Metzner rejected the argument in the light of "the long and volatile history of maritime jurisprudence concerning the scope and coverage of the Lien Act and the effect of claims not mentioned in the Act."

including the use of dry dock or marine railway, to a vessel, whether foreign or domestic . . ." Section 975 provided that state lien statutes were "superseded" ". . . insofar as such statutes purport to create rights of action to be enforced by proceedings in rem against vessels for repairs, supplies, and other necessaries."

The two quoted provisions shortly brought into litigation the question of what types of claims, in addition to those for supplies, repairs and the use of dry dock or marine railway, were covered. The case literature of this period was dominated by opinions delivered by the Second Circuit and the District Courts subject to its supervision. With occasional dissent from the other circuits,[171] the Second Circuit decided upon an extremely narrow construction of the Lien Act. The case for the narrow construction was first put by Judge Veeder, sitting in the Southern District of New York, in The J. Doherty;[172] Judge Veeder's reasoning was subsequently adopted by the Second Circuit in The Hatteras [173] as the officially approved rationale.

In The J. Doherty a libel *in rem* had been filed to enforce a lien for towage (which was not one of the services specifically mentioned in the 1910 Lien Act). Towage could be under the Lien Act only if it came within the meaning of the phrase "other necessaries". After an able review of the background and legislative history of the Lien Act, Judge Veeder concluded that the only services which Congress had meant to cover were those services as to which it had been held, under the doctrine of The General Smith, that, although the services were maritime and would normally import a lien, no lien would arise when the services were rendered in the vessel's home port. There had long been considerable doubt as to which home port claims were and which were not denied lien status under The General Smith but fortunately that subject had, shortly before the passage of the Lien Act, been comprehensively reviewed by the Third Circuit in The Alligator [174] and Judge Gray's Alligator opinion now became a sort of ready reference tool for courts in applying the Second Circuit theory of the Lien Act. Towage, according to Judge Gray (like pilotage, seamen's wage claims and salvage) was clearly within the class of claims which had lien status even though furnished in the home port. Accepting that analysis, therefore, and in the light of his review of the background of the Lien Act, Judge Veeder held that home port towage was not within the Lien Act but depended for lien status on general

171. Stevedoring; wireless equipment: The Rupert City, 213 F. 263 (W.D. Wash.1914); towage: Coyle & Co. v. North America S. S. Corp., 262 F. 250, (5th Cir. 1920); supplies furnished to a vessel's "slop chest": The Fortuna, 213 F. 284 (W.D.Wash.1914); but even the Western District of Washington was willing to agree that liquor was not a "necessary" for the equipment of a fishing vessel. The Sterling, 230 F. 543 (W.D.Wash.1916). "Repairs" too was narrowly construed, but not items incidental to "repairs", such as wharfage, The Geisha, 200 F. 865 (D.Mass.1912), and the services of a builder's engineer employed to see that an engine is in proper working order, and to instruct the purchaser in its operation, Ely v. Murray & Tregurtha Co., 200 F. 368 (1st Cir. 1912).

172. 207 F. 997 (S.D.N.Y.1913).

173. 255 F. 518 (2d Cir. 1918).

174. 161 F. 37 (3d Cir. 1908).

maritime law. A few years later, in The Muskegon,[175] Judge Learned Hand, with his usual felicity in generalization, drew the line between Lien Act claims and general maritime claims somewhat more clearly by pointing out that Lien Act claims were only those connected with the "outfitting" of the ship as opposed to claims connected with her "carriage of freight". Wherefore, in The Muskegon, Judge Hand held that stevedoring services did not fall within the 1910 Act, and was ritually upheld on appeal by the Second Circuit.[176]

§ 9–33. There would have been no great importance (except as a trap in pleading) in the distinction taken in the Second Circuit cases between Lien Act claims and general maritime claims, if the conditions for validity of the lien had been the same in both classes of cases. There were, however, two issues where it might make a great difference whether Lien Act or general maritime law applied. These were, first: whether credit had been extended to the ship or to the owner (in the latter case no lien would arise) and second: the effect of charter party provisions purporting to restrict or deny the charterer's power to subject the ship to liens. On the first of these issues the last clause of § 971 provided that "it shall not be necessary to allege or prove that credit was given to the vessel", a decided relaxation of requirements of proof under general maritime law. On the second, § 973 provided that "nothing in this chapter shall be construed to confer a lien when the furnisher knew, or by exercise of reasonable diligence could have ascertained" that a charter party or contract of sale denied the power to bind the ship: on the face of it that provision was ambiguous and the extent to which it changed prior maritime law could only be determined by litigation. Since both issues will be subsequently discussed in detail[177] nothing more will be said about them at this point: their importance in this connection is to show that the distinction between Lien Act liens and general maritime liens, had it survived, could have led to two substantially different bodies of case law.

The distinction also left a potentially significant area within which the state lien statutes might continue to operate. Under Learned Hand's gloss of the theory in The Muskegon the Lien Act applied only to claims connected with the "outfitting" of the ship. Claims for wharfage and stevedoring were the principal ones which were held to fall outside the Lien Act but to be liens by general maritime law even though furnished in the home port. However, there might be many types of claims which were not "outfitting" claims nor yet general maritime lien claims which, being maritime in nature, could still be given lien status by the state statutes. Nobody knew how many of these there might be, and before there was time for a case law exploration of the matter, the Second Circuit's "narrow" construction of the Lien Act received a mortal wound.

175. 275 F. 117 (S.D.N.Y.1921).

176. 275 F. 348 (2d Cir. 1921).

177. On "credit to the vessel", see §§ 9–37 to 9–38 *infra*. On "no-lien" provisions in charter parties, see §§ 9–42 to 9–46 *infra*.

§ 9–34. The Lien Act as passed in 1910 had covered "repairs, supplies, or other necessaries, including the use of dry dock or marine railway". In 1920 Congress changed the passage to read: "repairs, supplies, towage, use of dry dock or marine railway, or other necessaries . . .". At the same time, comparable language was added to § 975 on the extent to which state statutes were "superseded".

The 1920 amendment clearly reflected the dissatisfaction on the part of materialmen with the restrictive judicial construction of the 1910 Act. "Towage" was added and the reference to "dry dock or marine railway" was made to precede rather than follow "other necessaries". The amendment may seem to have been a devious way of going about the business in hand, but in its favor it must be said that it worked.

On the level of statutory construction the narrow reading of the 1910 Act had represented an application of the "*eiusdem generis*" rule: "other necessaries" included only things of the same kind as "repairs and supplies", not including even things "like" "dry dock or marine railway" since those were referred to in a phrase which followed and therefore could not qualify or add to "other necessaries". Applying the same *eiusdem generis* rule of construction, the addition of "towage" and the shift of the position of the "dry dock or marine railway" reference necessarily broadened the scope of "other necessaries" to include things "like" the three new antecedents.

One of the first courts to get the chance to comment judicially on the meaning of the Lien Act as amended was the District Court for the Western District of Washington, in a circuit which had always refused to follow the narrow approach of the Second Circuit.[178] In The Henry S. Grove,[179] Judge Cushman, with obvious pleasure, picked up Learned Hand's distinction between "outfitting" claims (covered by the Act) and "carriage" claims (not covered). Pointing out that "towage", added by the amendment, "must be held to relate to 'carriage alone' as contradistinguished from 'outfitting' ", he concluded that the whole range of claims related to carriage by the ship should now be read into the Act, and held that a claim for stevedoring services was covered. In 1924 this holding was approved and followed as to stevedoring in the Massachusetts District Court by Judge Lowell,[180] who, the following year, had occasion to extend the new doctrine even further. In re Burton S.S. Co.[181] held that charges for use of the Cape Cod Canal were for "other necessaries" within the 1920 Act (even though, as Lowell, J., meticulously pointed out, the ship could have gone around the Cape instead of using the Canal so that perhaps the canal charges were not of "strict necessity"). The Massachusetts District was highly receptive to the new approach: Judge Morton indicated in

178. See the cases cited in note 171 *supra*.

179. 285 F. 60, 61 (W.D.Wash.1922).

180. The Neponset, 300 F. 981, 1924 A.M.C. 726 (D.Mass.1924), reversed on other grounds 13 F.2d 808, 1926 A.M.C. 964 (1st Cir. 1926). Accord: The Little Charley, 31 F.2d 120, 1929 A.M.C. 398 (D.Md.1929).

181. 3 F.2d 1015, 1925 A.M.C. 335 (D. Mass.1925).

The Susquehanna [182] that a claim for fumigating passenger's baggage on orders of the Public Health Service, even though the fumigation was done on shore, would come within the Lien Act as amended (the lien, however, was denied on other grounds). By 1931 the last bastion of the narrow approach had capitulated: in The Artemis [183] Judge Woolsey held claims for winter storage of a yacht, for uniforms for the crew, and even for taxi fare run up in delivering provisions to the yacht all entitled to liens under the Lien Act.

In 1921 Judge Hough, affirming Learned Hand's decision in The Muskegon, had written that "to the full enjoyment and profitable occupation of a ship there are many services which are convenient, useful, and at times necessary," which did not necessarily bring them within the scope of the Lien Act.[184] The present state of the law is not far from the point where any service which is "convenient, useful and at times necessary" may qualify as a lien under the Lien Act.[185]

182. 3 F.2d 1014, 1923 A.M.C. 643 (D. Mass.1923).

183. 53 F.2d 672, 1932 A.M.C. 195 (S.D. N.Y.1931).

184. 275 F. 348, 350 (2d Cir. 1921).

185. In most current litigation of this type the "convenient, useful and at times necessary" slogan is ritually recited as a preliminary to holding that a contract lien of some kind exists. See, e. g., Matter of The Queen, Ltd. 1973 A.M.C. 646 (E.D.Pa.1973, per Referee in Bankruptcy Goldhaber) (claims for, inter alia, clerical services and maintenance furnished the former Queen Elizabeth which was being used as a tourist attraction in Port Everglades, Florida; for more on the case, see note 80 *supra* at end.) In re S/S Norberto Capay, 330 F.Supp. 825, 1971 A.M.C. 987 (N.D.Cal.1970) (issuer of traveler's checks used to pay crew's wages entitled to lien); Ajubita v. S/S Peik, 428 F.2d 1345, 1970 A.M.C. 1463 (5th Cir. 1970) (pilotage constitutes "other necessaries" under § 971, but no lien because of prohibition of lien clause in charter); Payne v. S/S Tropic Breeze, 423 F.2d 236, 1970 A.M.C. 1850 (1st Cir. 1970) certiorari denied *sub nom.* Samadjopoulos v. National Western Life Ins. Co., 400 U.S. 964, 91 S.Ct. 363 (1970) (Master's travel expenses on trip to secure money to keep ship from arrest are "other necessaries" under § 971); Stern, Hays & Lang, Inc. v. M/V Nili, 407 F.2d 549, 1969 A.M.C. 13 (5th Cir. 1969) (advertising for Israeli cruise ship could qualify as § 971 "other necessaries"); Wells Fargo Bank v. Barge Marguerita, 1970 A.M.C. 1828 (N.D.Cal.1969) (services of naval architect in preparing drawings and specifications for proposed reconditioning of vessel which was never carried out; see note 112a *supra*). The opinions in the cases cited collect other authorities on "convenient, useful and at times necessary." One of the few recent cases in which a contract claim (for the purchase price of a generator furnished to a vessel) has been denied lien status in Westerbeke Corp. v. Golden Fleece, 1970 A.M.C. 1740 (D.Mass.1970) (Judge Ford noted that the vessel already had two functioning generators; even if the third generator had been considered necessary, there were other grounds on which the lien would have been denied).

A good many older cases show an equally broad construction of § 971. Liquors may constitute necessaries for a pleasure yacht at a fashionable resort, Walker-Skageth Food Stores v. The Bavois, 43 F.Supp. 109, 1942 A.M.C. 211 (S.D.N.Y.1942); a repairman's claim for a proper amount, even though there were overcharges and delay in the work, The Amiga Mia, 80 F.Supp. 42, 1948 A.M.C. 647 (S.D.N.Y.1948); fumigation of a vessel, The American, 1931 A.M.C. 197 (D.Mass.1930); travel and other minor expenses incurred in securing the release of a vessel, The Egeria, 294 F. 791, 1924 A.M.C. 126 (9th Cir. 1923); *cf.* The Fannie F. Hickey, 1931 A.M.C. 794 (D.Mass.1931); repairs, even though the vessel is out of service, The V–14813 (Self v. Central Station Equipment Co.), 65 F.2d 789 (5th Cir. 1933); see The Harvard, 270 F. 668 (E.D.N.Y.1920).

§ 9–35. The broadened coverage of the Lien Act under the 1920 amendment put an end to the development of specialized learning as to the differences between statutory liens and general maritime liens. The ancient distinction between claims maritime and nonmaritime of course survives: to be a lien on any theory a claim must be in the first instance maritime. Assuming its maritime nature, almost any type of service claim will today be held within the Lien Act, so that the law has happily escaped the tripartite division with which it was threatened. In two classes of cases, however, the Lien Act is rarely, if ever, mentioned in the opinions: claims for seamen's wages and claims by cargo for breach of affreightment contracts. Seamen's wage claims are highly favored: these wards of the admiralty are not required to run the gauntlet of conditions which the materialmen must face. In the cargo lien cases, the principal Lien Act problems do not arise because the relationship of cargo to ship is different from that of materialman to ship: where cargo is concerned there is no question whether credit was extended to the ship or whether the service was furnished to the ship.

The Lien Act does not in terms repeal the State lien statutes: it merely "supersedes" them "to the extent that" they purport to create rights enforceable *in rem* as to the types of claims which are covered by the Lien Act. Nevertheless the broad coverage given to the Lien Act since 1920 has correspondingly decreased the area in which the state acts could operate. In fact for a generation or more almost no claims have been asserted, at least in reported litigation, under state statutes. In 1937 the Fifth Circuit, in Burdine v. Walden, granted a lien for master's wages under the Louisiana statute, without mention of the Lien Act in its opinion.[186] In 1949 the Second Circuit was presented with a claim for wharfage under the New York statute in Murray v. Schwartz.[187] The District Judge evidently felt the claim of lien under the state statute to be a curious one, and dealt with it at length in an able opinion, concluding that the claim could be maintained.[188] The Second Circuit, in an opinion by Judge Frank, evaded the issue with great skill by finding that the ship in question was a "dead ship"; therefore not a vessel; therefore the services were not maritime; therefore no lien could arise on any theory; therefore "we need not pass on appellant's contention" that the Lien Act had repealed the New York statute. In theory the State statutes are still in force as to whatever service liens are not covered by the Lien Act or the general maritime law.[189] In fact they are either moribund or dead.[190] One area in which the State stat-

186. 91 F.2d 321, 1937 A.M.C. 1149 (5th Cir. 1937).

187. 175 F.2d 72, 1949 A.M.C. 1081 (2d Cir. 1949).

188. Murray v. Schwartz (The Meteor), 78 F.Supp. 637 (E.D.N.Y.1948); *id.*, 83 F.Supp. 212, 1948 A.M.C. 1401, 1949 A.M.C. 563 (E.D.N.Y.1949).

189. Robinson, Admiralty (1939) 375; 1 Benedict, Admiralty (6th ed.1940) 271; Hughes, Admiralty (2d ed.1920) 117.

190. In Osaka Shosen Kaisha Line v. Pacific Export Lumber Co., 260 U.S. 490, 1923 A.M.C. 55 (1923) there was a claim of lien under the Oregon statute (see text at note 168 *supra*). The Massachusetts statute, note 154 *supra*,

utes continued to play a role until 1970 was that of wrongful death claims not covered by the Federal Death on the High Seas Act.[191]

The Lien Act had been in its origins a materialman's statute. The initial narrow construction of the Lien Act was a temporary victory for the shipowners, since it threatened to plunge the whole matter of service liens into a deeper confusion than had ever before been known. The broad construction of the Act after 1920 was a major triumph for the materialman. But, as is well known, it is possible to win every battle and lose the war. The materialman was far from being home free when he succeeded in having his various types of claim held within the Act; he still had to reckon with the fact that the Act set up certain conditions for the validity of liens, and these conditions in turn could be broadly or narrowly construed. And on this branch of the question the shipowners, a resourceful and persistent group, have fared not at all badly.

was applied in Marshall Vessels, Inc. v. Wright, 331 Mass. 487, 120 N.E.2d 286 (1954). According to a California court, a claim for unpaid repairs on a vessel taken out of service does not arise from a maritime contract enforceable in admiralty; the claimant has a possessory lien on the vessel under the California statute, see note 154 *supra*, entitling him to institute in a state court an action for conversion against persons unlawfully removing the vessel, and this is true irrespective of the Federal Maritime Lien Act, Arques v. National Superior Co., 67 Cal.App.2d 763, 155 P.2d 643 (1945). See also the Sun Harbor Marina case, note 161 *supra*. But compare The V–14813, note 185 *supra*. A watchman or caretaker of a vessel out of commission has been held by a Federal District Court not to be entitled to claim a lien under the California statute for wages or moneys advanced, on the ground that the Lien Act supersedes all provisions of state statutes covering liens on vessels enforceable by suits *in rem* in admiralty. The F. S. Loop, 63 F.Supp. 105, 1946 A.M.C. 467 (S.D.Cal.1946). Under the New York statute, note 154 *supra*, a lienor, who held a boat at his boat yard to satisfy claims for repairs and storage, had a common law lien as well as his rights under § 80 of the New York Act, and he could institute foreclosure proceedings in the same manner as any other mechanic. Davies v. Rijneers, 137 N.Y.S.2d 333 (1955). *Cf.* the Lih case, note 161 *supra*. The only relatively recent case in which a state-created contract lien has been enforced appears to be Grow v. G/S Loraine K., 310 F.2d 547, 1963 A.M.C. 2044 (6th Cir. 1962) (claim for unpaid insurance premiums given lien status by the Michigan lien statute). In Ajubita v. S/S Peik, 428 F.2d 1345, 1970 A.M.C. 1463 (5th Cir. 1970) pilots claimed a lien under the Louisiana statute; the state-lien claim was denied on the ground that pilotage came within "other necessaries" under § 971, so that, the federal statute having pre-empted the field, the state statute was inapplicable; the lien was then denied because of a prohibition of lien clause (which might not have been effective if the state-lien claim had prevailed). United States v. F/V Zarco, 187 F.Supp. 371, 1961 A.M.C. 78 (S.D.Cal.1960) also held that a claim (for repairs to an armature which was in the possession of the repairman) could not be maintained under a California statute since the claim fell under the Federal Act. In Allen v. M/V Contessa, 196 F.Supp. 649, 1961 A.M.C. 2190 (S.D.Tex.1961), Judge Garza remarked that a claim for attorney's fees under the Texas Lien Statute "does not apply to *in rem* proceedings under . . . § 971" but gave rise only to an *in personam* claim against the owner.

191. In 1970 the Supreme Court, overruling The Harrisburg (see note 156 *supra*), decided that an action for wrongful death lies under the general maritime law, Moragne v. States Marine Lines, Inc., 398 U.S. 375, 90 S.Ct. 1772, 1970 A.M.C. 967 (1970). The Moragne case is discussed in Chapter VI, § 6–33.

For another minor function which the State statutes may still have, see § 9–79 *infra*.

### "Any Person Furnishing . . . to Any Vessel"

**§ 9-36.** In the first important case decided by the Supreme Court under the Lien Act, Piedmont & George's Creek Coal Co. v. Seaboard Fisheries Co., the facts were stated as follows:

> "An oil company, owner of a fleet of fishing steamers and also of oil factories where the catch was delivered and the vessels coaled, having mortgaged this property and being without money or credit, made an agreement with a coal dealer to furnish the coal necessary for the season's operations, both parties understanding that the coal would be used by the factories as well as by the vessels, that the greater part would be used by the vessels, that the law would afford a lien on the vessels for the purchase price and that the coal dealer would thus have security. The coal was billed and delivered directly to the oil company, title passing with delivery; it was then stored by that company in its factories, and afterwards appropriated by it mainly to the vessels but partly to the factories, as occasion arose; and there was no understanding when the contract was made or at times of delivery that any part of it was for any particular vessel or for the vessels then composing the fleet." [192]

On those facts Justice Brandeis for a unanimous Court held that no lien arose. As was his habit, Justice Brandeis in the course of a moderately long opinion multiplied the facts that might be considered significant: the Coal Company did not itself "directly" deliver coal to any vessel; the coal was billed to the Oil Corporation and not to particular vessels; there was no understanding that the coal was for particular vessels; the coal was sold f. o. b. the Coal Company's piers, so that title to the coal passed at that point; the coal after delivery sometimes remained in the Oil Corporation's bins for weeks or months before being allocated to a particular vessel; some of the coal, under the agreement, was used for the factories and not for any vessel. By the time he had finished, not even the purest legal genius could have declared which of these multiple facts, or which combination of them, had resulted in the denial of lien. Consequently the case, in its specific context of supplies furnished to a fleet of ships, has ever since proved a slippery precedent to the counsel and lower court judges who have wrestled with it. The Piedmont case is all things to all men and is regularly cited on both sides of every case in which it is relevant: since some of Justice Brandeis' facts are always present, it is an authority for shipowner's counsel for denial of the lien; since all of them are never present, it is equally an authority for supplier's counsel in favor of the lien.[193]

192. 254 U.S. 1, 41 S.Ct. 1 (1920).

193. Jeffrey v. Henderson Bros., 193 F.2d 589, 593, 1952 A.M.C. 359, 366 (4th Cir. 1951): "The record is devoid of any indication that the claimants waived or intended to waive their right to liens therefor on the boat as

permitted by the statute . . . and hence it is immaterial, in considering their right to a lien for necessaries under the statute . . . that the supplies were ordered by the owner and that the sellers relied upon the credit of both the owner and the ship. Piedmont, etc. Coal Co. . . . Nor were the liens lost because the supplies were not delivered directly to the vessel but were furnished in the first instance to the owner at the seller's place or at the owner's place of business . . . or at places in the general vicinity of the vessel . . . It is established that the statutory lien for supplies ordered by an owner for use on a vessel and actually used thereon is not lost by delivering them to the owner or to some convenient place to be thence taken to the ship. . . . Piedmont, etc., Coal Co. . . .

"A situation may arise, as in Piedmont, etc., Coal Co. . . . in which supplies are furnished to an owner of a fleet of vessels, with or without other associated enterprises, in such a fashion that delivery is made to the owner rather than to the vessels themselves, and in such instances the connection may be broken and the lien is lost. But the lien is not lost when supplies are purchased and furnished to several vessels in common ownership under a single contract, since each vessel will be liable for that portion of the merchandise furnished to and used by it. Piedmont, etc., Coal Co. . . ."

American Stevedores, Inc. v. The Trajan, 118 F.Supp. 608, 610, 1954 A.M.C. 586, 588 (E.D.N.Y.1954): "The following cases make clear that a lien cannot attach to a vessel unless services or materials relied upon to support it, were ordered by the master or the owner, the ship being under charter which forbids the creation of such a lien by the charterer: . . . Cf. Piedmont & George's Creek Coal Co. . . ."

The distinguishing of the Piedmont case in Jeffrey v. Henderson Bros., *supra*, was followed in Davis v. U. S. Gas Screw Nolla Dare, 125 F.Supp. 677, 678, 1955 A.M.C. 348, 349 (E.D.N.C. 1954): "Piedmont & George's Creek Coal Company . . . relied upon by respondent does not support his position. . . . In this case the allegation is that supplies were delivered 'for use on said vessel.'

"Differing with views of counsel for respondent, I think Jeffrey v. Henderson Bros. . . . is in point for libelant. . . . While generally deliveries must be made to the vessel or alongside the wharf where she lies as observed in the Jeffrey case . . . : 'a supplyman may in effect make the owner his agent to complete the furnishing of supplies by putting the goods aboard'." For the latter proposition the Jeffrey case had relied on Bankers Trust v. Hudson River Day Line, 93 F.2d 457, 1938 A.M.C. 38 (2d Cir. 1937), which had denied the lien: "Although the supplyman may, in effect, make the owner his agent to complete the 'furnishing' by putting the goods on board, when the quantity and vessel are expressly designated, no case appears to have held that the supplyman may obtain a lien when he authorizes the owner to distribute the supplies among such of his fleet as he sees fit."

Bankers Trust relied on the Piedmont case for the denial of the lien: "The decisive words, as applied to the present case, are 'furnishing supplies to any vessel.' The meaning of these words in the substantially identical provisions of the Act of June 23, 1910, was much discussed in Piedmont Coal Co. . . . We agree with the District Court that the principle of that decision controls the case at bar. Here the buyer received on its barges fuel undesignated as to destination except that it was for vessels of the buyer's fleet. The buyer distributed it in its discretion. It was neither delivered nor billed by the seller to the vessels against which liens are sought; nor was it ordered by the buyer for any specified vessel.

"The appellant relies upon cases holding that when the supplies are ordered for a designated vessel and actually reach her, it is not fatal to a lien that they were delivered to the owner and forwarded by him to the ship. . . . The distinction between these cases and the Piedmont decision is well stated by Judge Morris in The American Eagle, *supra*, 30 F.2d 293, at page 295, 1929 A.M.C. 470, at page 474 (D.Del.1929), where he points out that the requirements for a maritime lien are met, 'if the supplies, though delivered in mass to the owner of the fleet under a single contract, are expressly ordered by the owner and delivered to him by the supplyman for the use of *named vessels in specified portions*, and are

The enduring importance of the Piedmont case has been in the attitude toward the Lien Act formulated in Justice Brandeis' opinion, which the Court has never disavowed in any Lien Act case and to which it has often turned for support. Counsel for the Coal Company had argued that by the Lien Act Congress had intended to broaden the scope of the maritime lien and that the denial of lien in their case rendered the statute inoperative in an important class of cases which it was intended to reach. "The language of the statute," wrote Justice Brandeis, "affords no basis for the latter assertion" and the Congressional Committee Reports "show that it is unfounded". According to the Committee Reports, which are cited with approval, the Act had three limited purposes: 1) to do away with the home port doctrine; 2) to do away with the related doctrine that home port contracts are presumed to be made on the credit of the owner and not of the ship; 3) to substitute a single federal statute for the state statutes. But there was to be no general relaxation of the general maritime law relating to liens, and the opinion recites the "secret lien—*stricti juris*—no extension by construction, analogy or inference" quote from The Yankee Blade.[194] At another point in the opinion Justice Brandeis developed at length a comparison between mechanics' liens and maritime liens: the former, he said, rest on the principle of unjust enrichment and are designed for the benefit of an especially deserving class of workmen; the latter are for the benefit of the ship—to enable her to prosecute her voyage by obtaining necessary credit in remote ports—and only incidentally for the advantage of the favored creditors. Thus, it follows, the fewer liens the better. The statute speaks of "any person furnishing . . . to a vessel." That simple statement, according to Justice Brandeis, has two sides. The difficulty with the Coal Company's case, he pointed out, "is not in failure to show that the coal was furnished to the vessels but in failure to prove that it was furnished by the libelant." [194a]

promptly delivered to the named vessels by their owner.' . . . Under the statute as construed by the Supreme Court the supplies must be furnished *by* the supplyman *to* the vessel. . . . 'Furnishing supplies to any vessel' must, we think, include that factor of choice; otherwise they are furnished to the owner."

194. See text at note 106 *supra*.

194a. Lien Act § 971, as construed in the Piedmont case, may be taken as a codification of the executory contract doctrine (§ 9–22 *supra*, particularly note 113). Cases like Piedmont, as well as cases under the executory contract doctrine, seem almost to have disappeared. Remote echos of Piedmont may be found in International Terminal Operating Co., Inc. v. S/S Valmas, 375 F.2d 586, 1967 A.M.C. 1727 (4th Cir. 1967) (general contract to provide stevedoring services to owner's vessels would not prevent lien from arising as services were rendered to each vessel; lien denied on other grounds); Brock v. S/S Southampton 231 F.Supp. 280, 1964 A.M.C. 800A (D.Or.1964), 231 F.Supp. 283, 1964 A.M.C. 1905 (D.Or.1964) (bank which issued letter of credit to maritime union to be used for payment of crew's wages (and which was so used) entitled to lien for wages paid although letter covered a fleet of vessels and not a single vessel). In both the cases cited, the possible implications from Piedmont were, of course, disregarded.

### "It Shall Not be Necessary to Allege or Prove That Credit was Given to the Vessel"

§ 9–37. Justice Johnson in The St. Jago de Cuba [195] introduced the idea of credit to the ship as an explanation of the home port doctrine announced in The General Smith. According to Justice Johnson, when the ship is in foreign ports, the owner not being present, it is reasonable to presume, and the law does presume, that credit for services furnished the ship was extended on the credit of the ship itself. But in the home port where the owner is usually present, or at least available, the reason for the presumption vanishes and so does the presumption.

So far as the home port doctrine was concerned, Justice Johnson's explanation was clearly fallacious. If all that happened in the home port was that the presumption of credit to the vessel vanished, then the libellant ought, by taking up the burden of proof, to have been able to establish his lien by showing that the owner was not in fact present or available or that, finding the owner's credit standing unsatisfactory, the libellant had refused to extend credit except on the security of the ship. But the home port doctrine went much further than presumptions and burden of proof; it denied the lien no matter what the state of facts might be, unless a state statute came in to aid the materialman.

As to services furnished to a ship in a foreign port and those home port services which were held not to be within the doctrine of The General Smith, the idea advanced in the St. Jago de Cuba either was or shortly became the unquestioned rule. The rule had two facets: *first* that credit to the ship, as distinguished from credit to the owner, was essential to the existence of the lien; *second* that, outside the area covered by The General Smith, credit to the ship was presumed in favor of the materialman. Thus the burden of proof was cast on the owner; if he could show that credit was extended to him personally, the claim of lien would fail.

What the shipowner was called upon to prove was, ultimately, the subjective intent of the materialman at the time he furnished services to the ship. Naturally, direct testimony on the subjective intent of the adverse party would be either unavailable or fatal to the shipowner's case: if invited to testify, the materialman could be expected to say that he had at all times wholeheartedly and exclusively relied on the ship, that the idea of extending credit to the owner, had it ever crossed his mind, would have been dismissed as fantasy. So the proof had to be indirect: what circumstances in the handling of the transaction would raise an inference of credit to the owner? Without going into the detail of the pre-Lien Act cases, we may summarize the sorts of facts that came to be generally accepted as helpful to the owner: that the contract under which services were fur-

195. 22 U.S. (9 Wheat.) 409 (1824). See text at note 138 *supra*.

nished was executed by the owner or his agent and not by the master; that the services were billed to the owner or his agent and not to the ship; that the materialman took the owner's personal obligation, in the form of a promissory note or trade acceptance, or took collateral security (other than the ship) for payment of the debt.[196]

The question of credit to the ship and the allocation of burden of proof became peculiarly involved with respect to liens asserted under state statutes. In the home port cases, according to The St. Jago de Cuba, there was no presumption of credit to the ship because of the owner's presence or availability. Indeed, apart from local statute, there was a conclusive presumption of no credit to the ship and hence no lien. Now the statute came in, so that at least the presumption of no credit was not conclusive. But, apart from specific language in the statute, was there any presumption either way, and was the issue of credit to the ship still a factor in the proceedings? By the time of the passage of the Lien Act, there had come to be three distinct theories, on which the Circuits were split, since the issue had never been resolved by the Supreme Court. One theory held that credit to the ship was still a prerequisite of lien and that the presumption ran against the materialman. A second theory, which seems to have been held in the Second Circuit, was even harder on the materialman: no lien unless he could show an agreement, or common understanding, between him and the owner that credit was extended to the ship; under this rule the materialman's own intention was not enough. A third rule, developed in the First Circuit, went the other way: under this rule, the state statute (unless it clearly provided otherwise) was deemed to have done away with the issue entirely, so that the lien arose automatically on the furnishing of services.[197] As Judge Putnam put the last mentioned rule in The Iris: [198] ". . . there is no necessity, under the local statute, of either alleging or proving that credit was given to the vessel by mutual agreement", and the balance of his opinion suggested that the qualification "by mutual agreement" could well have been deleted.

**§ 9–38.** The Lien Act contained two relevant provisions. The first (§ 971) reproduced Judge Putnam's language in The Iris: "it shall not be necessary to allege or prove that credit was given to the vessel." The second (§ 974) was that nothing in the Act should be construed to prevent the materialman from waiving his lien "by agreement or otherwise."

If the materialmen had hoped that the statutory echo from The Iris would get rid of the credit issue once and for all, they were doomed to disappointment. None of the early lower court cases even went so far as to discuss the possibility that Congress had in-

196. See generally Smith, The New Federal Statute relating to Liens on Vessels, 24 Harv.L.Rev. 182, 185 (1911).

197. On the several rules see Smith, The Confusion in the Law Relating to Materialmen's Liens on Vessels, 21 Harv.L.Rev. 332, 341 (1908).

198. 100 F. 104, 110 (1st Cir. 1900).

tended by the "not . . . necessary to allege or prove" language to dispense with credit to the ship as a prerequisite of lien. The "by agreement or otherwise" phrase in the waiver provision might have been urged in support of the position taken by the courts, since "or otherwise" had to mean something and might have been construed to mean "or by extending credit to the owner." But the question was never even seriously debated, and no changes were made in either of the two provisions when Congress amended the Lien Act in 1920. Thus all that the "not . . . necessary to allege or prove" language amounted to was that under the Lien Act the materialman got in all cases the advantage of the presumption which he had always had in foreign ship cases, and no longer had to carry the burden of proof or show a "common understanding" in home port cases.[199]

The Supreme Court put the matter beyond dispute in 1929 with The President Arthur.[200] Coal had been furnished to a ship at the owner's request. The owner had sought a longer than usual term of credit, but the coal company, doubting the owner's financial responsibility, insisted that the owner execute trade acceptances in its favor which were indorsed by three "responsible and acceptable" persons. The coal was furnished under written contracts between the coal company and the owners which did not expressly claim a lien on the ship and which provided that "the entire contract between the parties is stated above and there is no outside condition, warranty, agreement, or understanding." When one of the trade acceptances was not paid, the coal company libeled the ship, as well as instituting a state court action on the acceptances against the indorsers.

The Court unanimously denied the lien. It referred to Justice Brandeis' opinion in the Piedmont case for a statement of the limited purpose of the Lien Act and the proposition that, except for getting rid of the home port doctrine and the presumption against the materialman when he dealt directly with the owner, and substituting a single federal statute for the state statutes, "it was not intended to make any other change in the general principles of the existing law of maritime liens." Therefore, the Court felt, the pre-Lien Act credit cases were still good law (except for the shift in burden of proof). It reviewed them from 1826 on down and concluded:

> "Applying the principles stated in the foregoing cases, we think that the libellant, having made specific contracts for an express security, instead of resting on the lien which the law would otherwise give, must rely on the contracts it made for itself, and cannot now, in a change of circumstances, resort to the lien it would have had in the absence of the special agreements; and that by taking other and

199. Piedmont & George's Creek Coal Co. v. Seaboard Fisheries Co., 254 U.S. 1, 41 S.Ct. 1 (1920). A number of lower court cases came to the same conclusion.

200. 279 U.S. 564, 49 S.Ct. 420, 1929 A.M.C. 831 (1929).

different security, upon which it relied, and which it still retains, without stipulating for the retention of the lien, it has waived the lien which it otherwise would have had." [201]

The holding and opinion in The President Arthur made things difficult for the materialman who deals with the owner or his agent, particularly when he wishes to protect himself by additional security or some form of collateral agreement. Difficult but, as the subsequent cases show,[202] not impossible, provided he pays great attention to the formal aspects of the transaction. All agreements, notes, trade acceptances and what-not must expressly "stipulate for the retention of the lien." It is a useful precaution to bill all services "to the ship" or "to ship and owners," never "to owners" alone. On all possible occasions the materialman should proclaim, preferably in writing, that he has extended credit to the ship and that he has not waived his lien by agreement "or otherwise." If he does all that, his chances are on the whole good. In consequence of the law's insistence on form, it is the small outfit which most needs the lien protection which is most apt to lose it, but there is little prospect of any change.

In recent years, however, the materialmen have fared well against charges of waiver of lien by extension of credit to the owner even when they have not meticulously observed the desirable formalities outlined in the preceding paragraph. At least in the Fifth Circuit the taking of additional security for a claim otherwise entitled to lien status is realistically looked on as an indication that the lienor had no intention of trusting the owner's credit.[202a] Billing the owner instead of the vessel may not be fatal [202b] nor taking the owner's note

**201.** *Id.* at 572, 49 S.Ct. at 422–423, 1929 A.M.C. at 837.

**202.** The materialman does not waive his lien by relying on the personal credit of the owner or charterer. The Mylark, 90 F.Supp. 466, 1950 A.M.C. 826 (D.Or.1950). A lien for fuel oil furnished a ship was not waived by taking a pledge or entering into a creditor's agreement: Dampskibsselskabet Dannebrog v. Signal Oil & Gas Co., 106 F.2d 896, 1940 A.M.C. 123 (9th Cir. 1939), affirmed 310 U.S. 268, 60 S.Ct. 937, 1940 A.M.C. 647 (1940).

**202a.** Lee Point Landing, Inc. v. Alabama Dry Dock & Shipbuilding Co., 261 F.2d 861, 1959 A.M.C. 148 (5th Cir. 1958) (lien for unpaid balance of purchase price of diesel engine not waived by seller's taking a chattel (i. e., non-maritime) mortgage on the vessel plus a mortage on real estate); see also Crustacean Transportation Co. v. Atlanta Trading Corp. (The Crustacea), 369 F.2d 656, 1967 A.M.C. 362 (5th Cir. 1966). The question of waiver of lien by taking security was discussed but not decided in Rainbow Line, Inc. v. M/V Tequila, 341 F.Supp. 459, 1972 A.M.C. 1540 (S.D.N.Y.1972), affirmed without discussion of this point, 480 F.2d 1024, 1973 A.M.C. 1431 (2d Cir. 1973), which involved a salvage lien. After referring to The President Arthur, Judge Metzner commented: "Subsequent cases make clear that waiver will be found only where there is a strong showing that the party attempting to assert the lien intended to look elsewhere than the vessel for payment of its claims."

**202b.** See Layton Industries v. Gladiator, 263 F.Supp. 356, 1970 A.M.C. 2423 (D.Mass.1967), so holding. *Cf.* Esso International v. S/S Captain John, 322 F.Supp. 314, 1970 A.M.C. 2086 (S. D.Tex.1970), affirmed 443 F.2d 1144, 1971 A.M.C. 2285 (5th Cir. 1971) (no waiver of lien where fuel ordered through agent was billed to ship and owner, care of agent; no waiver from filing proof of claim in agent's bankruptcy).

and discounting it (with recourse) at a bank.[202c] And a lien in favor of a bank whose traveler's checks were used to pay crew's wages was not defeated by a showing that the bank had a "continuing commercial relationship" with the owner to whom it had provided an unsecured line of credit as well as several term loans and who maintained his checking account at the bank.[202d] The President Arthur seems to have become a sort of ghostly echo from the past and the presumption that the lienor relied on his lien has become all but conclusive.[202e]

### Authority to Subject Chartered Vessels to Contract Liens: Introductory Note

**§ 9–39.** In his opinion in The Barnstable, Justice Brown assumed that the ship could be bound—that is, subjected to lien—by the acts of anyone "lawfully" in possession.[203] In The Barnstable a ship in the possession and control of demise charterers had been at fault in a collision; the "rule of The Barnstable" was that the ship was subject to the tort lien resulting from the collision and could be libeled *in rem* (thus reaching the interest of the owners) despite the fact that the owners had not been, subjectively, chargeable with fault or responsibility in connection with the collision. No one has ever doubted the proposition that the owner who entrusts control of his ship to a third party such as a charterer thereby subjects the ship to all tort liens which may arise during the period of charterer's control; no clause in the charter party purporting to prohibit the charterer from creating liens against the ship would be effective against tort claims.

The rule of The Barnstable was never thought to be applicable to the problem of the creation of contract liens by charterers and other third parties.[203a] On the contrary, the doctrine early appeared that

**202c.** United Virginia Bank/Citizens and Marine v. O/S Sea Queen, 343 F. Supp. 1020, 1971 A.M.C. 1880 (E.D.Va. 1971 (per A.M.C.) or 1972 (per official report)).

**202d.** In re S/S Norberto Capay, 330 F.Supp. 825, 1971 A.M.C. 987 (N.D. Cal.1970).

**202e.** In Ververica v. Drill Barge Buccaneer No. 7, 488 F.2d 880 (5th Cir. 1974) a salvor agreed not to demand payment for his services until the owner had collected his insurance. In violation of his agreement he instituted an in rem action against the ship. It was held that the filing of his "premature libel" effected a "waiver" of lien although the salvor was held entitled to share in surplus after other maritime lienors (who had intervened in the action) had been paid off (see note 458a *infra*). Treakle v. Pocahontas Steamship Co., 273 F.Supp. 608, 1967 A.M.C. 2120 (E.D.Va.1967, affirmed per curiam 406 F.2d 412, 1969 A.M.C. 33 (4th Cir. 1969) may be the only other recent case denying a lien on something like waiver theory. Docking pilots asserted liens for pilotage against the ships which they docked and undocked. They were covered by a collective bargaining agreement which did not provide for pilotage charges to be made against the ships or their owners. *Held* that, by virtue of the collective bargaining agreement, the pilots were "estopped" from asserting liens. In Northwest Marine Ironworks, Inc., v. S/S Omnium Freighter, 228 F.Supp. 943, 1964 A.M.C. 1557 (D.Minn.1964) receipt of part payment was held not to constitute a waiver of lien.

**203.** See § 9–10, *supra*.

**203a.** Third parties, other than charterers, who might be in possession and control of a vessel include prospective

the creation of contract liens by charterers could be prohibited by an apt clause in the charter-party; that the prohibition of lien clause was effective against all persons dealing with the ship who either knew of the clause or could, by diligent inquiry, have found out about it; that all such persons were under a duty to inquire whether the ship was under charter and what the charter provided with respect to liens.[204]

The Maritime Lien Act of 1910 was evidently designed to codify the state of law which has just been rehearsed, including both the effectiveness of prohibition of lien clauses and the duty of would-be lienors subject to the Act to make diligent inquiry as to the charterer's actual authority. As the Lien Act case law developed, the duty to inquire became all but absolute (even if the lienor neither knew nor had reason to know that the ship was being operated under charter) and the practice of inserting a prohibition of lien clause (in language sanctified by the Supreme Court) in charter parties became universal. The end result was that the furnishers of supplies, repairs and "other necessaries", who were evidently the intended beneficiaries of the Lien Act, were no better off under the Act than they had been under the pre-statutory general maritime law; arguably they were worse off.

So matters stood until August 10, 1971—the effective date of an amendment which deleted from § 973 of the Lien Act the provision which had imposed on lienors subject to the Act the duty of inquiry as to a charterer's actual authority. Apparently the proponents of the amendment assumed that deletion of the "duty to inquire" provision was tantamount to an affirmative statement that prohibition of lien clauses were no longer effective. According to the House Committee Report which accompanied the bill:

> "The practical effect of the bill is to negate the operation of a "no lien provision" in a charter to which the American materialism [*sic*; for "materialism" read "materialman"] was not a party and of which he has no knowledge so that he will not be precluded from acquiring a lien for his services to which he would be otherwise entitled.[205]

purchasers, repairmen and so on. To avoid unnecessary repetition, we will use the term "charterers" to include all types of third parties to whom possession and control has been "lawfully" entrusted by the owner.

**204.** The Kate, 164 U.S. 458, 17 S.Ct. 135 (1896) and The Valencia, 165 U.S. 264, 17 S.Ct. 323 (1897) review the 19th century cases.

**205.** House Report (Merchant Marine and Fisheries Committee) to accompany H.R. 6239, U.S.C. Congressional and Administrative News, 1971, p. 1363 *et seq.* The reference to "American materialism" in the passage quoted reflects the fact that the bill was promoted as dealing with a problem "primarily encountered with foreign-flag vessels chartered to foreign operators." However the amendment was not restricted to foreign-flag vessels or foreign operators.

A letter to the House Committee from the General Counsel of the Department of Commerce put the matter even more forthrightly:

> "The bills are evidently intended to grant liens on vessels to suppliers of necessaries to the vessels even if the supplier knows that the persons ordering the necessaries are not authorized by the owners to bind the vessels." [206]

Evidently the 1971 amendment was looked on as a major victory for American materialmen (or materialists); whether it was as complete a victory as they may have assumed remains to be seen. It is obvious, however, that the law relating to the imposition of contract liens on chartered vessels entered a new phase on August 10, 1971. At the moment of writing, the 1971 amendment has not been construed in any reported case. In the following discussion we shall take up *first*: the state of the general maritime law prior to the enactment of the Lien Act in 1910 (which, arguably, may, by virtue of the 1971 amendment, have been restored to full force and vitality); *second* the state of the law as it developed during the Lien Act period preceding the 1971 amendment; *third* the present state of the law under the 1971 amendment so far as that can be guessed at.[207]

### Authority to Subject Chartered Vessels to Contract Liens: The General Maritime Law

**§ 9–40.** The state of the general maritime law on the imposition of contract liens on chartered vessels was conveniently summed up in two cases which were decided by the Supreme Court at its 1896 "October term" and which were, therefore, still in the area of "recent case material" when the Lien Act was passed. The Kate [208] and The Valencia,[209] which involved almost identical fact situations, have ever since been regarded as the principal "general maritime law" authorities.

In The Kate coal had been furnished in New York to a British owned vessel on charter to a New York corporation. The charterer of the British vessel had for some time operated a fleet of vessels. Until 1891 it had owned all the vessels which made up the fleet, but thereafter it also employed vessels under charter, among them the Kate. Libellant had begun supplying coal to the fleet at a time when all the vessels were owned by the New York operator, and continued during the period when the fleet was partly owned and partly chartered. To protect itself, it had filed specifications of lien under the New York lien statute. It is not absolutely clear from the report whether the coal company knew that the Kate was on charter. The

**206.** *Id.* at p. 1366. Both the Committee Report and the General Counsel's letter seem to overstate the case. On the effect of the amendment, see § 9–46a *infra.*

**207.** The order in which material will be presented and discussed from this point through § 9–46 does not correspond to the order in which the material was covered in §§ 9–39 through 9–46 of the first edition.

**208.** 164 U.S. 458, 17 S.Ct. 135 (1896).

**209.** 165 U.S. 254, 17 S.Ct. 323 (1897).

headnote, in stating the facts, said that the coal company knew the Kate and other ships "were not owned by the New York Company," but the opinion said only that "the libellant knew or could easily have known what vessels belonged to the steamship company and what vessels were operated by the latter under time charters." In any event, the coal company did not examine the charter parties or make any inquiry as to their provisions. The opinion quoted at length from the charter party under which the Kate was operated, emphasizing two provisions: "That the charterers shall provide and pay for all the coals" and "that the captain (although appointed by the owners) shall be under the orders and direction of the charterers as regards employment, agency or other arrangements." The coal furnished to the Kate was ordered by the charterer and not by the master. Bills (which apparently read "to the New York steamship company and to the vessel") were sent only to the charterer. The owners had a New York agent, a fact known to the libellant, and the agent could have supplied funds to pay for the coal. The agent did not know that the libellant was supplying coal on the credit of the vessel or that specifications of lien had been filed under the New York statute.

On those facts the Court denied the lien. Justice Harlan's reasoning is of interest. Even where supplies are ordered by the master, he said, the lien arises only where two conditions are met: *first,* that the supplies are necessary to enable the ship to get on with the voyage; and *second,* that the master has no available funds with which to pay for the supplies. Presumptions run in favor of the materialman, but if, on the facts, he knows, or ought to know, either that the supplies are not necessary or that funds are available to pay him, then he gets no lien. For the master to attempt to create liens under such circumstances is a species of bad faith towards the owner; if the materialman who knows or ought to know the facts should still claim a lien "he woud be affected with bad faith, as colluding with the master, and aiding him in violating his duty to his owner." The case of supplies ordered not by a master but by a charterer was, in Justice Harlan's opinion, *a fortiori*:

> "If no lien exists under the maritime law, when supplies are furnished to a vessel upon the order of the master, under circumstances charging the party furnishing them with knowledge that the master cannot rightfully, as against the owner, pledge the credit of the vessel for such supplies, much less is one recognized under that law where the supplies are furnished, not upon the order of the master, but upon that of the charterer who did not represent the owner in the business of the vessel, but who, as the claimant knew, or by reasonable diligence could have ascertained, had agreed himself to provide and pay for such supplies, and could not, therefore, rightfully pledge the credit of the vessel for them." [210]

210. 164 U.S. 458 at 470, 17 S.Ct. 135 at 140.

The claim of lien under the New York statute was dismissed briefly on the ground that the Court would not construe the statute to give a lien, in opposition to the "general principles of maritime law" laid down in the opinion.

The facts in The Valencia, in which Justice Harlan again wrote the opinion, were so similiar to those in The Kate that they need not be stated in detail. It does appear that the suppliers of coal in The Valencia were not aware of the existence of the charter at the time they furnished the coal, "nor did they know where the ship hailed from, whether she was foreign or domestic, nor what was her credit." As the opinion puts it: "they chose to shut their eyes and make no inquiry touching these matters." As in The Kate the charter provided that charter was "to provide and pay for all the coals", and the coal was delivered on the charterer's order. No specification of lien had been filed under the New York statute. On the doctrinal level The Valencia merely reiterated The Kate, although Justice Harlan's opinion in The Valencia went to great pains to explain and reconcile a line of old cases.

Taken together, The Kate and The Valencia established the following propositions: 1) when a materialman either knows or could easily find out that a ship is under charter (The Kate) or, preferring ignorance to knowledge, "shuts his eyes" to obvious facts (The Valencia), he is put on inquiry as to what the charter contains; 2) a charter party term requiring the charterer to "provide and pay for" certain services is enough to defeat a lien for such services in favor of a materialman who was on inquiry as to what the charter party contained.

### Authority to Subject Chartered Vessels to Contract Liens: The Lien Act (1910–1971)

**§ 9–41.** In § 971 the Act provides for a lien in favor of any person who furnishes "supplies, repairs . . . or other necessaries to any vessel, whether foreign or domestic, upon the order of the owner of such vessel, or of a person authorized by the owner . . ."

In pre-Lien Act days under the general maritime law the materialman who dealt directly with the owner was presumed (although, except in the vessel's home port, the presumption was rebuttable) not to have a lien, on the theory that in such a case he was extending credit to the owner and not to the vessel.[211] Evidently the Lien Act was intended to abolish that presumption not only in authorizing the lien for supplies or services furnished on the owner's order but also in providing in § 971 that it shall not be necessary to allege or prove that credit was given to the vessel.

The provision quoted above also gives the lien when supplies or services are furnished "upon the order of . . . a person authorized by the owner." This formula, of course, brings in all persons,

211. See § 9–37 *supra*.

whoever they may be, who are in fact authorized—who have, in agency terminology, real as distinguished from apparent authority. The "real authority" point was hardly worth making although the explicit statutory statement has simplified life for judges in cases in which it has been argued that contracts or advances which were in fact authorized by an owner should be denied lien status because of a prohibition of lien clause in a charter party.[212]

**§ 9–42.** The real problem, here as in any agency situation, arises when a principal (the shipowner) clothes his agent with all the outward trappings of authority but seeks to limit the agent's actual authority by provisions in the agreement creating the agency. The Lien Act dealt with the apparent authority problem in §§ 972 and 973 which (as originally enacted) seemed to provide *first* that materialmen are always entitled, in the absence of knowledge to the contrary, to rely on the presumption that masters, charterers and the like are authorized to incur contract liens and *second* that materialmen are never entitled to rely on the presumption that masters, charterers and the like are authorized to incur contract liens. What the draftsmen meant to accomplish by this spirit of even-handed contradiction is impossible to say. We shall first set out the statutory provisions and then see what the courts made of them.

Section 972 (unamended since the original enactment in 1910) [213] provides:

> "The following persons shall be presumed to have authority from the owner to procure repairs, supplies . . . and other necessaries for the vessel: the managing owner, ship's husband, master or any person to whom the management of the vessel at the port of supply is intrusted. No person tortiously or unlawfully in possession or charge of a vessel shall have authority to bind the vessel."

Section 973 remained as originally enacted (except for a conforming reference to § 972 added in 1920) until 1971 when the language (here printed between brackets) from the semi-colon to the end of the section was deleted.

> "The officers and agents of a vessel specified in section 972 of this title shall be taken to include such officers and agents when appointed by a charterer, by an owner pro hac vice or by an agreed purchaser in possession of the vessel; [but nothing in this chapter shall be construed to confer a lien when the furnisher knew, or by exercise of reasonable

212. See Caribbean Maritime Finance Co., Ltd. v. Marina Mercante Nicaraguense S. A., 470 F.2d 277, 1973 A.M.C. 20 (5th Cir. 1972); Schilling v. A/S D/S Dannebrog, 320 F.2d 628, 1964 A.M.C. 678 (2d Cir. 1963) (dictum); Roberts v. Echternach, 302 F.2d 370, 1963 A.M.C. 137 (5th Cir. 1962).

213. Except that when § 971 was amended in 1920 to broaden the Act's coverage (see § 9–34 *supra*), the preamble to § 972 was conformed to § 971 as amended.

diligence could have ascertained, that because of the terms of a charter party, agreement for sale of the vessel or for any other reason, the person ordering the repairs, supplies, or other necessaries was without authority to bind the vessel]."

The obvious conflict between the "presumption of authority" provisions of § 972 and the first part of original § 973 and the "duty to inquire" provision of the second part of original § 973 is the stuff of which judicial nightmares are made. Perhaps, by prodigies of judicial statesmanship, it would have been possible to harmonize the presumption of authority provisions with the duty to inquire provision in such a way that there would have been some situations in which materialmen were entitled to rely on the presumption of authority of the people with whom they dealt and other situations in which they were put under a duty of inquiry as to actual authority. The prodigies were not forthcoming; what happened was that the duty to inquire provision was, in effect, allowed to swallow up the presumption of authority provisions. This unhappy result was accomplished in three Supreme Court decisions. The first two—The South Coast [214] and United States v. Carver,[215] both opinions by Justice Holmes—have been widely regarded as irreconcilable. The third —Dampskibsselskabet Dannebrog v. Signal Oil & Gas Company,[216] opinion by Chief Justice Hughes—reaffirmed both the earlier cases. Since the Signal Oil case the Supreme Court has made no further contributions.

**§ 9–43.** In The South Coast, a ship was under a bareboat or demise charter to one Levick, who was required by the charter to pay for all supplies. The charter further provided that the owner could retake the ship "upon failure on the part of the charterer, within 30 days after incurring the same, to discharge any debts or liabilities which are liens on the vessel" and that the charterer should redeliver the ship "free from all liens" and "save [the owner] harmless . . . from all liens . . . against the said vessel". The master, although appointed by the owner, was under the orders of the charterer. Libellant furnished supplies on the order of the master. He not only knew the ship was under charter when he furnished the supplies but had received notice from the owners that he must not furnish them on the credit of the ship.

The Court, in a six to three decision, held in favor of the lien. Justice Holmes wrote a brief opinion which cited no authority and discussed no precedents. He put the decision on the ground that the charter party either gave the charterer authority to create liens or at least did not prohibit him from creating them. "The authority of the owner to prohibit or speak was displaced, so far as the charter went, by that conferred upon the charterers, who became owners

214. 251 U.S. 519, 40 S.Ct. 233 (1920).

215. 260 U.S. 482, 43 S.Ct. 181, 1923 A.M.C. 47 (1923).

216. 310 U.S. 268, 60 S.Ct. 937, 1940 A.M.C. 647 (1940).

*pro hac vice*, and therefore, unless the charter excluded the master's power, the owner could not forbid its use." The conclusion that the charter party did not prohibit liens rests on what might be called a reverse reading of the provision that the owner could retake the ship if the charterer failed to discharge liens within thirty days: that meant, said Justice Holmes, that for thirty days there could be liens.

In United States v. Carver, two ships, owned by the United States, were being operated under charters which required the charterer to pay all costs and expenses incident to their operation and further provided that the charterer "will not suffer nor permit to be continued any lien, encumbrance, or charge which has or might have priority over the title and interest of the owner in said vessel." Supplies for both ships were ordered by the charterer's "port captain" (not by the master of either of the ships). In one case the supplier "did not know of any facts tending to show that the [charterer] did not own the vessel and so far as appears made no inquiry or effort to ascertain what the facts might be." In the other the supplier's agent "knew facts putting the libellants upon inquiry but preferred to avoid making it."

A unanimous Court denied the lien both in the case where the supplier did not know of the charter's existence (and made no inquiry) and *a fortiori* in the case where the supplier did know facts sufficient to put it "upon inquiry". Once again Justice Holmes cited no authorities, except to remark that "it is unnecessary to consider whether the libellants' argument is supported" by two lower court decisions as to which certiorari had been refused, since, "as the bar has been told many times," "the denial of a writ of certiorari imports no expression of opinion on the merits of a case." The Carver opinion made two points. The first was the meaning of the "by the exercise of reasonable diligence could have ascertained" phrase in § 973:

> "We regard these words as too plain for argument. They do not allow the material-man to rest upon presumptions until he is put upon inquiry, they call upon him to inquire. To ascertain is to find out by investigation. If by investigation with reasonable diligence the material-man could have found out that the vessel was under charter, he was chargeable with notice that there was a charter; if in the same way he could have found out its terms he was chargeable with notice of its terms." [217]

The second point was the relationship of the Carver case with The South Coast, decided three years earlier. Justice Holmes explained the relationship in the following language:

> "But it is said that the charter-party if known would have shown that the master at least, if not the agent who ordered the supplies, had authority to impose a lien, since

217. 260 U.S. 482, 489, 43 S.Ct. 181, 182, 1923 A.M.C. 47, 49 (1923).

> the charter-party contemplated the possibility of one being created and provided for its removal. The South Coast, 251 U.S. 519, 40 S.Ct. 233 is cited as establishing the position. But there is a sufficient difference in the language employed there and here to bring about a different result. In The South Coast the contract went no farther than to agree to discharge liens within a month. Here the primary undertaking was that 'the charterers will not suffer nor permit to be continued any lien,' etc. We read this as meaning will not suffer any lien nor permit the same to be continued. Naturally there are provisions for the removal of the lien if in spite of the primary undertaking one is imposed or claimed. But the primary undertaking is that a lien shall not be imposed."

Like baseball players and law book writers, judges have their off days, and the day when Justice Holmes wrote his Carver opinion was one of his worst. Without the slightest warrant in the Lien Act or prior case law, he assumed that the materialman is always under a duty of inquiry as to the actual authority of the person with whom he deals and thus introduced an unnecessary confusion which has never since been dissipated. In doing this he overlooked or ignored an able discussion of the point in The Oceana,[218] one of the certiorari denied cases unavailingly cited by counsel. In the second place he put the distinction between Carver and The South Coast on narrow and formalistic grounds when more substantial ones were available. The Carver opinion nearly obliterated the distinction between supplies ordered by the master (The South Coast) who by § 972 was presumed to have authority and supplies ordered by a charterer (Carver) as to whose authority the supplier was by § 973 always under a duty of inquiry (if he had reason to know that the ship was under charter). The distinction suggested by Carver demanded an impossibly refined reading of the language used in the charter party. Both the South Coast charter and the Carver charter required the charterer to "provide and pay for" supplies, and thus were of the same general type as the charters which the Court had analyzed fifteen years before the enactment of the Lien Act in The Kate and The Valencia.[218a] But, under the Carver opinion, one charter prohibited liens and the other authorized them. Thus the lower courts were invited to engage in word-chopping games.

For nearly twenty years the District and Circuit courts continued to debate the distinction between The South Coast and Carver, with Carver on the whole in the ascendant. Several cases involved the form of sale contract used by the government in disposing of the World War I merchant marine, which required the purchaser to carry the contract among the ship's papers so as to proclaim "to the world" that he lacked authority to create liens: that was held sufficient to

218. 244 F. 80 (2d Cir. 1917).

218a. See § 9-40 *supra*.

prevent the lien.[219] The Ninth Circuit, which seems to have been traditionally favorable to materialmen, did exploit the possibilities of The South Coast line of reasoning in a series of cases,[220] but elsewhere the lien was hard to come by.

**§ 9–44.** The Supreme Court made a third effort to clarify the issue in the Signal Oil case.[221] The Oil Company had contracted to supply fuel oil to any vessel which Comyn might own, charter or operate. Comyn chartered two ships under charters which required the charterer to "provide and pay for" (among other things) fuel oil. The captain, although appointed by the owners, was "under the orders and direction of the charterers as regards employment or agency." It was further provided that nothing in the charter should be construed as a "demise" and that the owners were to remain responsible for the navigation of the vessel. "The charters contained," said the Court, disposing of the principal issue in the case in the guise of a statement of facts, "no prohibition against the creation of liens for necessary supplies ordered by the charterers." Nothing in the opinion indicated whether the Oil Company knew the ships were under charter; the opinion apparently accepted the Carver doctrine that the materialman is charged with what the charter contains in any case.

Both The Kate and The Valencia had held in effect that a "provide and pay" clause in a charter was sufficient to prevent a lien in favor of a materialman who was for some reason on notice of the charter's existence. The South Coast had allowed a lien under such a charter and Carver, although denying the lien, had found the reason for the denial in other terms of the charter. Neither The South Coast nor Carver had discussed the effect of the "provide and pay" clause or so much as mentioned The Kate or The Valencia in the opinions.

Chief Justice Hughes held in the Signal Oil case that The Kate and The Valencia, being pre-Lien Act cases, were no longer authoritative and that, under The South Coast and Carver, a "provide and pay" clause was not by itself sufficient to prevent liens from arising: there must in addition be a specific "prohibition of lien" clause like the one present in Carver. The Chief Justice also discussed possible

219. Standard Oil Co. v. United States, 1 F.2d 961, 1924 A.M.C. 1276 (4th Cir. 1924), certiorari denied 267 U.S. 591, 45 S.Ct. 228 (1924); Frey & Son v. United States, 1 F.2d 963, 1924 A.M.C. 1281 (4th Cir. 1924); The Moosabee (P. H. Gill & Sons Forge & Machine Works v. United States) 1 F.2d 964, 1924 A.M.C. 1283 (4th Cir. 1924); The Liberator, 5 F.2d 585, 1925 A.M.C. 741 (4th Cir. 1925); The Neponset, 13 F. 2d 808, 1926 A.M.C. 964 (1st Cir. 1926); The Henry S. Grove (North Coast Stevedoring Co. v. United States), 17 F.2d 874, 1927 A.M.C. 591 (9th Cir. 1927); but see Virginia Shipbuilding Corp. v. U. S. Shipping Board Emergency Fleet Corp., 11 F.2d 156, 1925 A.M.C. 668 (E.D.Va.1925).

220. The Luddco 41, 66 F.2d 997, 1933 A.M.C. 1446 (9th Cir. 1933); The Astorian, 57 F.2d 85, 1932 A.M.C. 660 (9th Cir. 1932); The Golden Gate, 52 F.2d 397, 1931 A.M.C. 1632 (9th Cir. 1931), certiorari denied 284 U.S. 682, 52 S.Ct. 199 (1932).

221. Note 216 *supra*.

distinctions based on the nature of various types of charter parties. "There is a plain distinction," he wrote, "between a case of a bareboat charter, where the charterer mans the vessel, and a case where the charter party is a mere contract for the carriage of goods." The opinion did not further explain what the "plain distinction" was but the implication seemed to be that in the demise case the charterer would have implied authority to create liens, while in the "contract of carriage" case (presumably the "voyage" charter) he would not. The Chief Justice's remarks on the necessity of a "prohibition of lien" clause may thus be understood as referring only to the sort of time charter involved in the Signal Oil case. In conclusion the Chief Justice wrote:

> "We are of the opinion that it would thwart the purpose of the statute to compel the material-man furnishing supplies to the vessel to resolve the ambiguities which may be found in such charters as those here involved. The statute was intended to afford the materialman a reasonably certain criterion. The owner has a simple and ready means of protection. All that it is necessary for him to do, as the materialman in dealing with the charterer is charged with notice of the charter, is to provide therein that the creation of maritime liens is prohibited. When the owner does not do so, he should not be heard to complain when it appears that it is the charterer's business to obtain supplies to keep the vessel on her way and the charter has not prohibited reliance upon the credit of the vessel." [222]

The Signal Oil case upheld the liens, and, since it overruled The Kate and The Valencia on the effect of the "provide and pay" clause, it might be regarded as a victory for the materialman. As our discussion of case law under the Lien Act has already shown, however, the materialman has (at least until 1971) had to be content with the shadow, while the substance went to the shipowner. Without discussion, the Signal Oil case approved Justice Holmes' unwarranted suggestion in Carver that the materialman is always charged with notice of the contents of a charter (unless, hypothetically, he can show that even by inquiry he could not have found out about it) even though there is nothing to call his attention to the fact of the charter's existence and he may reasonably suppose that he is dealing with the owner. Furthermore, the Signal Oil case clearly assumed the effectiveness of a "prohibition of lien" clause (at least with respect to time charters). Any owner who wants to keep his ship free of contract liens while under charter can do so, and it is hard to understand why any charter drawn by competent counsel should omit the "will not suffer nor permit to be continued any lien" clause which both Carver and Signal Oil cite as a sufficient "prohibition of lien". The explanation of the absence of the clause in the Signal Oil case

222. 310 U.S. 268, 280, 60 S.Ct. 937, 943, 1940 A.M.C. 647, 656 (1940).

may be that the vessels there chartered were of Norwegian ownership, and counsel for the owners may not have been familiar with the intricacies of American lien law.[222a] In its insistence on the formal nature of the transaction the Signal Oil case is reminiscent of The President Arthur, in which a lien was denied because the materialman took the owner's trade acceptances.[223]

During the pre-1971 Lien Act period the "duty to inquire" provision of § 973 effectively swallowed up the "presumption of authority" provisions of § 972 and § 973.[224] During that period it really made no difference how broadly or how narrowly the presumption of authority provisions were construed since, under the Supreme Court's Carver and Signal Oil cases, the materialman was always under a duty of inquiry as to the actual authority of the person he dealt with and the actual authority to subject the vessel to contract liens was always negated by the universal presence of the "will not suffer nor permit to be continued" prohibition of lien clause. Thus one of the necessary consequences of the 1971 amendment will be a reexamination of the presumption of authority provisions. It is to be emphasized that the pre-1971 case law on these provisions is not entitled to much, if any, weight since, after Carver and Signal Oil, it was clear that the provisions were in effect meaningless.

Four classes of people are specified in the "presumed to have authority" list of § 972: managing owner, ship's husband, master, and "any person to whom the management of the vessel at the port of supply is intrusted". These classes are generically referred to in § 973 as "officers and agents of a vessel". The generic description in § 973 suggests that the people listed in § 972 are those whose relationship to the vessel is so close that traditionally they have been presumed to have authority to bind her and whose authority as "agents" normally derives from the owner (the purpose of the first part of § 973 as originally enacted being to continue the presumption of agency in certain cases where the "officers and agents" were not in fact appointed by the owner). The "agency" reference in § 973 suggests further that a person whose status is independent of the owner (such as a charterer) would not be within the § 972 list; this suggestion which, it is believed, would have made it possible to give meaning both to the statutory presumption of authority and the duty to inquire as to lack of authority was unfortunately obscured in the case law and critical commentary.

Three of the four descriptive terms used in § 972 are not without difficulty. "Master" is clear. "Ship's husband" appears to be meaningless; no case has ever tried to assign a meaning to it and we

222a. The Norwegians appear to be slow learners. McNamara Corp. v. M/T Tabriz, 209 F.Supp. 212 (D.Minn. 1962), which involved a Norwegian-flag vessel, may well be the only case decided since 1940 in which the charter did not contain the Carver-type prohibition of lien clause.

223. See § 9–38 *supra*.

224. For the statutory text of these provisions, see § 9–42 *supra*.

may conclude that it is merely a synonym for "master". "Managing owner" is ambiguous. Since an "owner" of some sort is involved the term would not include agents or employees. Presumably it includes a part owner who undertakes management functions on behalf of the ownership group (when a ship is operated under what used to be called the "shares" system) as well as the chief executive officers of a corporate owner.[225] Finally there is "any person to whom management . . . is intrusted". The word "intrusted" is consistent with the agency language used in § 973 and, on the analysis suggested, should be taken to mean "intrusted by the owner as his agent". So construed the term would include the owner's general agent and similar people at the port where services are furnished to the ship; it would *not* include charterers, owners pro hac vice and purchasers (the people mentioned in § 973, as to whose authority the latter section as originally drafted clearly put the materialman on inquiry). If the narrow construction of "person . . . intrusted" here suggested had been followed, the statute would have made perfect sense. So long as the materialman dealt with a person whose status by long tradition was that of "owner's man" (principally the master and the ship's general agent), he could rely on that person's apparent authority, being under no duty of inquiry. If he dealt with anyone else, he would (by § 973) have been under a duty to ascertain "by reasonable diligence" the limits of his authority in fact. Thus both the statutory presumption of authority (§ 972) and the duty to inquire (§ 973) would have had a reasonably well defined area within which to operate.

By the pre-1971 Lien Act case law, however, the "person . . . intrusted" under § 972 was held to include almost anyone exercising control over the ship at the port of supply, no matter whether his traditional status had been that of owner's man or of independent actor: charterers and purchasers were alike held "persons . . . intrusted."[226] This broad construction was confirmed by Chief Justice Hughes in his opinion in the Signal Oil case:

225. In Crustacean Transportation Co. v. Atalanta Trading Corp. (The Crustacea), 369 F.2d 656, 1967 A.M.C. 362 (5th Cir. 1966) a former "sole owner" of a vessel who had transferred title to a corporation which he controlled was described as "a managing owner or an authorized person similarly situated with a ship's master under the United States Maritime Lien statutes."

226. As to charterers, see the quotation from the Signal Oil case, immediately following in the text. A prospective purchaser was held a "person . . . intrusted" in Hercules Co., Inc. v. The Brigadier General Absolom Baird, 214 F.2d 66, 1954 A.M.C. 1201 (3d Cir. 1954). See also National Bank of Fayette County v. Enterprise Marine Dock Co., 43 F.2d 547, 1931 A.M.C. 97 (4th Cir. 1930). In Harbor Service Corp. v. United States, 9 F.2d 613, 1925 A.M.C. 1036 (2d Cir. 1925), however, a receiver's power to bind the ship for repairs was put on authority from the owner; the opinion does not discuss the possibility that the receiver might have been a "person . . . intrusted" under § 972, even in the absence of owner's authorization. In the F.S. Loop, 63 F.Supp. 105, 1946 A.M.C. 467 (S.D.Cal. 1945) it was held, properly enough, that watchmen on board a vessel were not persons "to whom management . . . is intrusted."

> "In speaking of those who shall be presumed to have authority to procure supplies, the statute expressly includes not only the 'ship's husband' and 'master' but 'any person to whom the management of the vessel at the port of supply is intrusted'. . . . We think that the purpose of the statute is not properly served by construing the term 'management of the vessel' as referring to her 'navigation'. Management is a broader term connoting direction and control for the purposes for which the vessel is used. Where, as in this case, apart from mere navigation, the vessel is placed under the direction and control of the charterer as the hirer of the vessel, who as such may determine to what port she shall go and what she shall carry, subject only to specified exceptions, we think the charterer must be deemed to be intrusted with the vessel's management for the purpose of applying the statutory test of authority to obtain necessary supplies on the credit of the vessel, in the absence of a provision to the contrary." [226a]

The broad construction of "person . . . intrusted" led to the result that the persons who were "presumed to have authority" under § 972 were at the same time persons as to whose authority in fact the materialman was under a duty to inquire under § 973. That this was true is indicated by Chief Justice Hughes' offhand reference in the last phrase of the passage quoted from the Signal Oil opinion to the "absence of a provision to the contrary"—which evidently meant that the statutory presumption of authority vanished when a provision in the agreement creating the intrusted person's relationship to the ship —in the Signal Oil case, the charter party—limited or denied the actual authority. As to charterers, purchasers and the like, who, on the analysis of the statute which has been suggested, were never meant to be included within the statutory presumption, that was a perfectly correct result. The danger lay in a generalization of the broad approach suggested in the Signal Oil opinion—*i. e.*, that the statutory presumption of authority was controlled by "a provision to the contrary" in the agreement creating the relationship with respect to all the persons mentioned in the § 972 list. At that point the statutory presumption lost all force, since the materialman would be under a § 973 duty to inquire, no matter whom he dealt with, and could never rely on the presumed or apparent authority of anyone. Such a construction did the statute less than justice, and offended the basic rules of statutory construction in that § 973 was allowed to swallow § 972 whole.

Despite the possibilities of confusion in the Signal Oil opinion, the pre-1971 Lien Act case law did continue to give the hard-pressed materialman a degree of protection in cases where he dealt directly with the master without being on notice that the ship was being oper-

**226a.** 310 U.S. 268, 279, 60 S.Ct. 937, 943, 1940 A.M.C. 647, 655 (1940).

ated under charter. In such cases little was heard in the opinions of any duty on the materialman's part to inquire into possible limitations on the master's traditional authority to pledge the ship.[226b] On the other hand, if the materialman knew that the master, for whatever reason, lacked authority, he was naturally not entitled to a lien against the vessel or, for that matter, an *in personam* claim against the owner.[226c] And the materialman won a minor victory when it was held that prohibition of lien clauses in preferred ship mortgages were not effective to prevent contract liens from attaching.[226d]

**226b.** Thus in Walker-Skageth Food Stores, Inc. v. The Bavois, 43 F.Supp. 109, 1942 A.M.C. 211 (S.D.N.Y.1942) Judge Rifkind indicated that he doubted whether the § 973 duty to inquire applied to masters appointed by the owner: "If the [§ 973] limitations do not apply, then it is immaterial whether by reasonable diligence the libellant could have ascertained the master's lack of authority." On the facts before him, Judge Rifkind found that even inquiry would not have disclosed lack of authority so that the lien was good on any theory. There is a suggestion in The Kongo, 155 F.2d 492, 1946 A.M.C. 1200 (6th Cir. 1946), certiorari denied 329 U.S. 735, 67 S.Ct. 99 (1946), of a duty to investigate a master's authority, but the facts were exceptional; not only was McBride, who served as master, himself the charterer (through a dummy corporation which he controlled), but the supply man was found to be on notice of the existence of the charter. The Maret, 145 F.2d 431, 1944 A.M.C. 1203 (3d Cir. 1944), is another exceptional case. Judge Biggs commented that the § 972 presumption of master's authority was "destroyed" by the § 973 duty to inquire. The case involved a ship of Estonian registry, nationalized after Soviet occupation of Estonia in 1940, a lien being claimed by Amtorg, the Soviet Trading agency in New York. The court's attention was naturally drawn to complex problems of international law; the passing reference to the Lien Act is not entitled to great weight. In Findley v. Red Top Super Markets, 188 F.2d 834, 1951 A.M.C. 1113 (5th Cir. 1951), certiorari denied 342 U.S. 870, 72 S.Ct. 112 (1951), liens were denied for supplies and services furnished on the order of a person who "purported" to act as master. The majority of the court felt that he had never had any authority so to act from the owner; a dissenting judge commented that, "[i]f master, which position the owner had permitted him to assume, he presumptively had authority [under § 972] to bind the vessel for necessary supplies." See further on the master's presumed authority, McMillan Welding & Machine Works v. General Towing Co. (Barge TJ–248), 247 F.Supp. 402 (E.D.La.1965); McNamara Corp. v. M/T Tabriz, 209 F.Supp. 212 (D. Minn.1962). In the cases just cited the charters did not contain the customary prohibition of lien clause.

**226c.** The Majestic II, 285 F. 91 (S.D. Fla.1922); The Dawn, 1937 A.M.C. 483 (D.Mass.1936). In The Dawn the opinion, written by Fitz-Henry Smith, Jr. as Commissioner, remarks: "It has long been the law in this district that local supply men are chargeable with knowledge that fishing vessels such as the Dawn are customarily operated on lays, and that if the necessaries are of the sort that under the lay are to be paid for out of the share of the crew, the master is not authorized to bind the vessel therefor, and the furnisher cannot acquire a lien by ignoring the lay and charging the necessaries to the vessel." In Bank of New Bedford v. Dirigo First, 60 F. Supp. 675, 1945 A.M.C. 504 (D.Mass. 1945) Judge Wyzanski concluded that operation of a fishing vessel on the lay system did not preclude supply liens when the owner of the vessel served as his own master. In Epstein v. Corporacion Peruana de Vapores, 325 F.Supp. 535, 1971 A.M.C. 1259 (S. D.N.Y.1971) the fact that a master ordered quantities of cigarettes and liquors known to be in excess of his own ship's requirements was held to give the supplier notice of the master's lack of authority.

**226d.** In The Tradewind (Atlantic Steamer Supply Co. v. The Tradewind), 144 F.Supp. 408, 1956 A.M.C. 1731 (D. Md.1956), Judge Watkins, after reviewing the authorities, concluded that the notice provisions of § 973 do not apply to ship mortgages and that an antilien provision in a mortgage is conse-

§ 9–46. The Lien Act case law as it had developed at the time of the 1971 deletion of the duty of inquiry provision from § 973 may be summarized in the following propositions: [226e]

1. By the Carver and Signal Oil cases the materialman was always charged with notice of a charter's existence. This proposition seems to have been most clearly true where the services were furnished on the order of one who was in fact a charterer or purchaser (even though the materialman may have assumed him to be the owner).[226f] Where the services were furnished on the master's order, the cases, on the whole, assumed, at least where the master was appointed by the owner, that the materialman was entitled to rely on that officer's presumed authority.[226g]

2. The materialman had a theoretical escape by showing that he did in fact use "reasonable diligence to ascertain" the true facts but found out nothing. The cases did not work out any satisfactory explanation of just how thorough an inquiry "reasonable diligence" demanded. Merely to ask the person who appeared to be in possession

quently of no effect. The Tradewind is discussed in the text at and following note 356a *infra*. Subsequent cases which came to the same conclusion are Rockport Yacht & Supply Co. v. M/V Contessa, 209 F.Supp. 396 (S.D. Tex.1962) and State of Israel v. M/V Nili, 435 F.2d 242, 1971 A.M.C. 428 (5th Cir. 1970), certiorari denied 401 U.S. 994, 91 S.Ct. 1232 (1971); Esso International v. S/S Captain John, 443 F.2d 1144, 1971 A.M.C. 2285 (5th Cir. 1971). This problem arose only in the context of foreign ship mortgages under the 1954 amendment to the Ship Mortgage Act (§ 9–51 *infra*) for the reasons explained in § 9–70 *infra*.

**226e.** The 1971 deletion has presumably made most of the case law on prohibition of lien clauses of little more than theoretical importance. There continued to be a substantial number of such cases during the 1950's, 1960's and early 1970's but little new was added to the doctrinal structure which had been established by the end of the 1940's. The following footnotes, which trace the origins of the development, have been left substantially as they appeared in the first edition of the treatise. For the detail of the recent case law the reader is referred to the excellent 5-year Digests in American Maritime Cases. The opinions in the following cases are of particular interest: Schilling v. A/S D/S Dannebrog, 320 F.2d 628, 1964 A.M.C. 678 (2d Cir. 1963); United States v. S/S Lucie Schulte, 343 F.2d 897, 1965 A.M.C. 1516 (2d Cir. 1965); In re Admiralty Lines, Ltd., 280 F.Supp. 601 (E.D.La.1968), affirmed 410 F.2d 398 (5th Cir. 1969); Kane v. M/V Leda, 1972 A.M.C. 2094 (E.D.La.1972); Caribbean Maritime Finance Co., Ltd. v. Marina Mercante Nicaraguense S. A., 470 F.2d 277, 1973 A.M.C. 20 (5th Cir. 1972).

**226f.** The Maret, 145 F.2d 431, 1944 A.M.C. 1203 (3d Cir. 1944); The Kongo, 155 F.2d 492, 1946 A.M.C. 1200 (6th Cir. 1946), certiorari denied 329 U.S. 735, 67 S.Ct. 99 (1946); Morse Dry Dock & Repair Co. v. United States, 1 F.2d 233, 1924 A.M.C. 1033 (2d Cir. 1924), certiorari denied 266 U.S. 620, 4 S.Ct. 99 (1924). But supplymen could have a lien for supplies and materials furnished for the repair of a ship by the seller who had contracted to repair the ship for the buyer, where neither buyer nor seller disclosed to the supplymen that title was in the buyer or that the supplymen would not be entitled to a lien. L. W. Gunby Co. v. Steamship Willy, 1942 A.M.C. 932 (D.Md.1942). And the provision of a conditional sales contract that the buyer should keep the ship in good condition and repair "free and clear of all liens and encumbrances" did not establish that the buyer was without authority to bind the ship for supplies and necessaries. The Mylark, 90 F.Supp. 466, 1950 A.M.C. 826 (D.Or.1950).

**226g.** See the cases cited in note 226b *supra*.

or control was not enough. It was not clear whether an examination of the ship's papers was enough (since it was not clear whether the owner was under a duty to see that the charter traveled with the ship) nor was it clear what the situation was when the materialman asked to see the ship's papers but was refused permission to see them. Inquiry of the Collector of Customs at the ship's home port was sometimes suggested as a good thing for the materialman to do, but that assumed that he could somehow find out what the home port was and skirted the question whether the owner was in any case under a duty to file charters or purchase agreements with the Collector. The best thing was of course for the materialman to inquire of the owner (there was a case where a Mississippi River barge had "Property of Defense Plants Corporation" lettered on its stern, but things aren't always as easy as that). The discussion of what the materialman "ought" to have done came up almost invariably in a context where he had not done it: cases holding in his favor on the inquiry point were notably scarce.[226h]

3. The materialman could take some comfort in the thought that he would not lose his lien because of failure to make inquiry if inquiry would have revealed nothing. All that amounted to was that if the materialman dealt with a person who was in fact authorized (or if a charter, had he discovered it, contained no "prohibition of lien" clause), he got his lien, inquiry or no inquiry.

4. To prevent the lien from arising, the charter or purchase agreement had to contain a "prohibition of lien" clause and a "provide and pay" clause was not enough. With reference to charters, this was true at least as to time charters and may have been true as to other types. No court ever made anything of the "plain distinction" ambiguously hinted at in the Signal Oil case.[226i]

**226h.** The Defense Plants Corporation case was The Kongo, 155 F.2d 492, 1946 A.M.C. 1200 (6th Cir. 1946) certiorari denied 329 U.S. 735, 67 S.Ct. 99 (1946). F. E. Grauwiller Transp. Co. v. The Scow Jeanne, 131 F.Supp. 630, 1955 A.M.C. 1236 (E.D.N.Y.1955) affirmed per curiam 229 F.2d 153, 1956 A.M.C. 319 (2d Cir. 1956): The Jeanne having been cast away by a storm, Grauwiller arranged with the waterfront owner to leave her there. E. had been working on a nearby wrecked ship and also patched up The Jeanne. E. raised and towed her to R.'s yard where R. repaired her on D. Co.'s order. When repaired K. Co. towed her away, changing her name to The K-18. The court held that E. took the ship without Grauwiller's permission and he and K. Co. took unlawful possession; The Jeanne must be restored to Grauwiller in her repaired condition. Repairman R. failed to inquire about the ownership and therefore did not have a repairman's lien. As to what the repairman ought to have done, see United States v. Daniels Towing & Dry Dock, Inc., 214 F.2d 501, 1954 A.M.C. 1530 (5th Cir. 1954); The Western Wave, 77 F.2d 695, 1935 A.M.C. 985 (5th Cir. 1935), certiorari denied 296 U.S. 633, 56 S.Ct. 156 (1935); The Roseway, 34 F.2d 130, 1929 A.M.C. 957 (2d Cir. 1929), certiorari denied 280 U.S. 592, 50 S.Ct. 39 (1929); United States v. Robins Dry Dock & Repair Co., 13 F.2d 808, 1926 A.M.C. 964 (1st Cir. 1926). Cases finding that a proper inquiry had been made, without disclosing lack of authority, included The Hurricane, 2 F.2d 70, 1925 A.M.C. 42 (E.D. Pa.1924), affirmed 9 F.2d 396 (3d Cir. 1925); Esso Export Corp. v. The Cortes, 136 F.Supp. 506, 1956 A.M.C. 217 (D.Ala.1955).

**226i.** On the "plain distinction", see the discussion of the Signal Oil case § 9–44 *supra*.

### Authority to Subject Chartered Vessels to Contract Liens: Effect of the 1971 Deletion of the Duty of Inquiry Provision of § 973:

**§ 9–46a.** Congress, having been persuaded to do something for the American materialman, could perfectly well have provided that henceforth [226j] prohibition of lien clauses in charter parties, sale agreements and the like were to be ineffective, just as such clauses in preferred ship mortgages have been held ineffective.[226k] Congress did not do that. It left intact the structure of the Lien Act which, as our preceding discussion has shown, adopted from the pre-statutory general maritime law the proposition that owners can effectively deny the authority to create contract liens to charterers and other persons to whom the possession and control of the vessel may be entrusted. The Act, as we now have it, provides that contract liens may arise when services are furnished to a vessel "upon the order of the owner . . . or of a person authorized by the owner": (§ 971), and that the "managing owner, ship's husband, master or any person to whom the management of the vessel at the port of supply is intrusted" are presumed to have authority to create liens (§ 972) even though they may have been appointed by "a charterer . . . an owner pro hac vice or . . . an agreed purchaser in possession of the vessel" (§ 973).[226l] If the person who orders the services is not authorized by the owner to create liens and if the furnisher of the services has notice of the lack of authority, it is entirely clear that no lien will arise. It must be equally clear that the statutory presumption of au-

**226j.** One of the minor questions about the 1971 amendment which will presently have to be decided is what transactions the amendment (whose effective date was August 10, 1971) applies to. The cases which have so far been reported have assumed without discussion that the amendment does not apply to transactions (the furnishing of supplies, repairs and other necessaries) which took place before August 10, 1971. It is clear enough that the amendment does apply to transactions which took place after August 10 in cases where the charter to which the vessel was subject was also entered into after August 10. Quaere: whether the amendment applies to post-August 10 transactions involving vessels subject to pre-August 10 charters. There seems to be no reason, in law, logic or morals, why the amendment should not be held applicable to such transactions. By way of analogy the Uniform Commercial Code, as enacted in most states, provided that transactions which took place subsequent to the effective date of the Code under, e. g., pre-Code trust receipt or accounts receivable financing agreements were to be governed by the Code. If the 1971 amendment is held not to apply to such post-August 10 transactions, the old prohibition of lien case law will be with us for a good many years and indeed, until all the pre-August 10 charters have expired, the materialman will still, *de facto*, bear the burden of inquiry to find out whether the vessel is subject to a pre-August 10 charter. If he makes such an inquiry and discovers a post-August 10 charter, he can hardly shut his eyes to the prohibition of lien clause which the charter will undoubtedly contain. No doubt the best advice to give the materialism is that he should not make the inquiry in the first place. Life will be somewhat simpler if the courts decide that the 1971 amendment applies to all post-August 10 transactions without regard to when the relevant charter was entered into.

**226k.** See the cases cited note 226d *supra*.

**226l.** See §§ 9–41, 9–42 *supra*.

thority will be defeated by notice that the presumed or apparent authority does not exist.

It will no doubt be argued by counsel for materialmen that only "actual knowledge" (as distinguished from "notice") of lack of authority will defeat the lien. History suggests that the argument will not be persuasive. In any field of law in which the acquisition of rights is conditioned on the absence of knowledge of certain facts, the judicial criterion for determining when the fatal knowledge exists is, as the matter is usually put, objective and not subjective. That is, A will not be heard to plead personal or subjective ignorance of whatever the crucial fact may be if it appears that he knows other facts from which any reasonable man would deduce the existence of the crucial fact. During the nineteenth century the courts spent a long time working this proposition out in the context of transactions which involved the purchase of chattels, negotiable instruments and other property. The end result, particularly in commercial transactions between professionals, was that the purchaser who was allowed to take free of defenses and equities subject to which his seller held the property was the purchaser in good faith and without notice and that "good faith" and lack of "notice" were both to be objectively determined.[226m] It would be absurd for the admiralty courts to spend the rest of the twentieth century retracing the trail which the common law courts blazed in the nineteenth century. We may assume that the professional materialman will lose his lien whenever he knows (or ought to know) facts sufficient to put him on notice of the fact that the person he dealt with lacked authority to create liens.

An obvious hypothetical case suggests itself for discussion. The good ship Helen is being operated under a charter which contains an apt clause prohibiting the creation of contract liens by charterer or master. At an appropriate place (or places) on the ship is posted, under glass, the following notice:

THIS VESSEL IS SUBJECT TO A CHARTER UNDER WHICH THE CREATION OF LIENS FOR SUPPLIES, REPAIRS OR OTHER NECESSARIES UNDER UNITED STATES CODE TITLE 46 SECTIONS 971–975 BY EITHER CHARTERER OR MASTER IS PROHIBITED.

/S/ OWNER.[226n]

If the materialman (or his agent) goes on board, sees the notice and makes no further inquiry, can he claim a lien for his services? If he (or his agent) goes on board, will he be heard to say that he failed to see or didn't bother to read the notice? If he knows that owners of chartered ships customarily post such notices but refrains from go-

**226m.** See Gilmore, The Commercial Doctrine of Good Faith Purchase, 63 Yale L.J. 1057 (1954). The article cited reviews the evidence for the proposition, which is still sometimes heard, that "good faith" in the law of negotiable instruments means subjective, not objective good faith.

**226n.** See, by way of example, Kane v. M/V Leda, 1972 A.M.C. 2094 (E.D.La. 1972).

ing on board to see whether there is one, can he claim a lien? We may further hypothesize that the owner, in addition to having notices posted on the ship, causes comparable notices to be published in appropriate trade publications in the ports which his ship is scheduled to visit. Will the materialman be heard to plead that he has canceled his subscriptions to all such publications?

Enough has been said to make the point that the deletion from § 973 of the statutory duty of inquiry does not automatically solve all the materialman's problems. There is no reason to believe that the post-1971 materialman who "chooses to shut his eyes and make no inquiry" concerning the authority of the person he deals with [226o] will (or should) fare any better than his nineteenth century predecessor fared under the general maritime law. The suggestion will be ventured (subject to revision in a subsequent edition) that the principal (and desirable) effect of the 1971 amendment will prove to have been the abrogation of the absolute duty to make inquiry established in Carver and affirmed in Signal Oil [226p] and a return toward the general maritime law theory announced in The Kate and The Valencia.[226q] That is, a materialman who neither knows nor has reason to know that he is dealing with a chartered ship will be entitled to rely on the presumption of authority established by § 972. If, under all the circumstances, he has reason to know that the ship is chartered, and makes no further inquiry, a prohibition of lien clause in the charter should be effective against him.

Most contract liens are subject to the Lien Act but a few are not. One example of a contract lien not subject to the Lien Act is a shipper's (or subcharterer's) lien for breach of the contract of affreightment.[226r] In such a case, United States v. S/S Lucie Schulte,[226s] Judge Friendly, expressly following The Kate and The Valencia, concluded that the United States (as subcharterer) could not claim a lien (to which it was otherwise entitled) because of a prohibition of lien clause in the charter. If the post-1971 Lien Act case law develops along the lines suggested in the preceding paragraph, both the claimants of contract liens under the Lien Act and the claimants of contract liens under the general maritime law will be subject to the rule of The Kate and The Valencia. On the other hand, if the Lien Act case law holds that statutory contract lienors are not subject to any duty of inquiry even though they know they are dealing with chartered vessels, then the courts will have to reexamine the basis on which such cases

**226o.** See The Valencia, 165 U.S. 264, 17 S.Ct. 323 (1897) discussed § 9–40 *supra*.

**226p.** On Carver, see § 9–43 *supra*; on Signal Oil see § 9–44 *supra*.

**226q.** On The Kate and The Valencia, see § 9–40 *supra*.

**226r.** Another example is the lien for contract salvage. See Rainbow Line, Inc. v. M/V Tequila, 341 F.Supp. 459, 1972 A.M.C. 1540 (S.D.N.Y.1972); note 170a *supra*.

**226s.** 343 F.2d 897, 1965 A.M.C. 1516 (2d Cir. 1965). Another case of this type is International Terminal Operating Co., Inc. v. S/S Valmas, 375 F. 2d 586, 1967 A.M.C. 1727 (4th Cir. 1967).

as The Lucie Schulte have been decided. Materialmen do not appear to be more meritorious claimants than subcharterers and contract salvors. It is submitted that The Lucie Schulte states a sensible rule for both classes of cases.

It will be remembered that the presumption of authority provision of § 972 runs to "any person to whom the management of the vessel at the port of supply is intrusted" [226t] and that Chief Justice Hughes commented in his opinion in the Signal Oil case that "any person . . . intrusted" included a charterer.[226u] If that construction of "any person . . . intrusted" is still good, then a materialman who knows he is dealing with a charterer would be entitled to rely on the presumption of authority and make no further inquiry—contrary to the position we have taken in the preceding discussion. As we have pointed out, the broad construction of "any person . . intrusted" suggested, essentially by way of dictum, in the Signal Oil case went hand in hand with the holding that, despite the presumption of authority, the materialman was still put to his § 973 duty of inquiry as to the charterer's actual authority. With the holding undercut or abrogated by the 1971 amendment, it seems to follow that the dictum must also be reexamined. The argument for a narrow construction of "any person . . . intrusted", which would not include charterers, owners pro hac vice and purchasers, has already been made and need not be repeated.[226v]

It is to be hoped that the next time the materialmen mount a legislative campaign, they will have the foresight to retain a competent statutory draftsman. The shipping industry could no doubt live with the situation in which the materialman's lien against chartered vessels was automatic quite as easily as it has lived with the situation in which the lien has been effectively precluded by the prohibition of lien clause. Only the lawyers will profit from the unsettled state into which the 1971 amendment has plunged this aspect of maritime lien law. Unless the Supreme Court elects to clarify the issues, a generation of unnecessary litigation will be required before it becomes clear whether the materialmen won a decisive victory, or merely an insignificant skirmish, in their apparently successful 1971 campaign.

### The Ship Mortgage Act of 1920: Background and Constitutionality

**§ 9–47.** In Bogart v. The John Jay [227] the Supreme Court held that a mortgage on a ship was not a maritime contract and was therefore not within the admiralty jurisdiction. Thus the mortgagee could not bring suit in the admiralty either *in personam* on the debt or *in rem* to foreclose his security interest in the ship. Justice Swayne, noting that jurisdiction over ship mortgages had been conferred on English admiralty courts by statute, commented that until Congress should enact a similar statute the rule of no jurisdiction "must continue in the admiralty courts of the United States."

**226t.** See § 9–42 *supra*.

**226u.** See text at note 226a *supra*.

**226v.** See § 9–45 *supra*.

**227.** 58 U.S. (17 How.) 399 (1854).

At the time The John Jay was decided there was a statute on the books which the Court might have construed as giving maritime status to mortgages. The Vessel Sales and Mortgage Recording Act of 1850 provided that:

> "No bill of sale, mortgage, hypothecation, or conveyance of any vessel, or part of any vessel of the United States, shall be valid against any person other than the grantor or mortgagor, his heirs and devisees, and persons having actual notice thereof, unless such bill of sale, mortgage, hypothecation, or conveyance, be recorded in the office of the collector of customs, where such vessel is registered or enrolled." [228]

The Recording Act was not even cited in The John Jay, and bills of sale and ship mortgages continued, after its passage as before, to be considered nonmaritime. Mortgages and bills of sale covering "vessels of the United States" now depended for their validity except between immediate parties on a proper recordation under the federal statute, but actions based on such contracts could be brought only outside the admiralty—in a sense the reverse of the home port lien situation.

The relegation of the ship mortgagee to his common law remedy meant that in any foreclosure proceeding the ship would be sold subject to all maritime liens (since the liens could be executed only by the admiralty court), thus reducing the value of the mortgagee's security. Nor was the existence of the mortgage a bar to the creation of subsequent liens, even, in the case of contract liens, when the lienor had actual as well as constructive knowledge of the mortgage.[229] The owner, by appropriate provisions in a charter party, could prohibit a charterer from creating contract liens against his vessel, at least under circumstances where the materialman was on notice that he was dealing with a chartered ship. Since the mortgagee's interest was nonmaritime, no effect was given to comparable mortgage provisions designed to prevent the owner from further encumbering the ship. The materialman, knowing of the mortgage, could nevertheless furnish services to the ship and take priority over the mortgagee. The one crumb of comfort which the mortgagee received was that, when a proceeding *in rem* had been instituted by a lien claimant, the mortgagee was allowed to intervene and to receive any surplus funds which might remain after distribution had been made to all maritime claim-

**228.** Act of July 29, 1850, c. 27, § 1, 9 Stat. 440, R.S. § 4192; repealed by the Merchant Marine Act of 1920, § 30(x), 41 Stat. 988, 1006 and reenacted as part of the Ship Mortgage Act. In White's Bank v. Smith, 74 U.S. (7 Wall.) 646 (1868) the Supreme Court held that the federal recordation system established by the 1850 Act superseded all state mortgage recording statutes. See, to the same effect, Jackson v. Inland Oil and Transport Co. (The Three Jacks), 318 F.2d 802, 1963 A.M.C. 1355 (5th Cir. 1963).

**229.** Schuchardt v. The Ship Angelique, 60 U.S. (19 How.) 239 (1856); The Lottawanna, 88 U.S. (21 Wall.) 558 (1874); The J. E. Rumbell, 148 U.S. 1, 13 S.Ct. 498 (1893).

ants (with or perhaps even without liens).[230] Indeed in The Lottawanna [231] this rule was construed to allow the mortgagee to take the entire fund when it was held that the materialman who had initiated the proceeding was not entitled to a lien and had not taken the proper procedural steps to qualify him to share in the distribution as a nonlien claimant. But that was an exceptional result; in most cases the mortgagee sat at the end of the table and received little or nothing.

The only form of security interest in a ship recognized as maritime by admiralty law was the bottomry bond, which ranked as a lien with the lowest order of priority. Furthermore, the essential feature of the bottomry bond was that repayment of the bond was conditioned on the continued existence of the ship: if the ship was lost, the bondholder lost not only his security but his debt. Any attempt to keep the debt alive despite the loss of the ship turned the bond into a nonmaritime mortgage.[232]

In the course of the 19th century the bottomry bond disappeared. Occasional ship mortgages continued to be recorded but it may be assumed that these represented either friendly arrangements and not hard-fisted business deals or situations where the mortgage covered both maritime and nonmaritime property, the shore assets being the real security and the ships merely frosting on the cake.[233] In any case the booming economy of 19th century America offered many opportunities for investment more attractive than the shipping industry, nostalgically clinging to sail long after the great clipper fleet had been outdistanced by steam vessels under foreign flags. It is in the highest degree unlikely that the absence of a satisfactory security device had anything to do with the flight of private capital from investment in shipping. As an initial question, there was no satisfactory device for financing railroads either, but, the need arising, the devices were invented by imaginative lawyers and validated by commercially minded courts. The shipping industry was a victim of technology coupled with an inbred nostalgia, not of The John Jay and the peculiar incidents of bottomry.

**§ 9–48.** At the beginning of the First World War the American merchant marine had all but vanished from the seas: in 1914 there were only fifteen American ships of 1000 tons or over engaged in overseas trade. Total gross tonnage under the American flag, including the coastwise and Great Lakes fleets, amounted to not much more

230. The Hendrick Hudson, 11 Fed.Cas. 1087, Case No. 6,358 (D.C.N.Y.1855); The Lottawanna, 88 U.S. (21 Wall.) 558 (1874); The J. E. Rumbell, 148 U. S. 1, 13 S.Ct. 498 (1893).

A recent case in which common-law, non-maritime mortgagees received unusually favorable treatment with respect to surplus funds is United States v. Maryland Cas. Co., 235 F.2d 50, 1956 A.M.C. 1822 (5th Cir. 1956). See also The Three Jacks, note 228 *supra*. See further § 9–87 *infra*.

231. 88 U.S. (21 Wall.) 558 (1874).

232. The Grapeshot, 76 U.S. (9 Wall.) 129 (1869); The William D. Rice, 29 Fed.Cas. 1296, Case No. 17,691 (D. Mass.1857); Maitland v. The Atlantic, 16 Fed.Cas. 522, Case No. 8,980 (E.D. La.1855); 1 Parsons, Shipping & Admiralty 134 (1869).

233. See generally Morrison, The Constitutionality of The Ship Mortgage Act of 1920, 44 Yale L.J. 1 (1934).

than four million tons. New ship construction had become a world-wide British monopoly.

At the end of the war there were 1280 ocean-going American flag ships, of which 1107 had been built by or for the United States Shipping Board at a cost of three and one half billion dollars, and nearly half the world's new ship construction was being carried on in United States shipyards. In 1919 Congress, after some months consideration in committee but with almost no debate on the floor, approved a bill for the dismantling of the Government-owned wartime fleet and its sale to privately owned shipping lines.[234]

In considering the mechanics of getting rid of the wartime fleet, the Congressional committees soon realized that large infusions of new capital would have to be pumped into the long moribund private shipping industry. That meant credit and the credit would have to come from the Government or the banks or both. In either case the lender would demand satisfactory security. Recognizing that much of the financing would have to be done by the Government, but hoping that private capital could be induced to take its share, Congress incorporated in the Shipping Act of 1920 a statute to be known as the Ship Mortgage Act, whose purpose was to make private investment in shipping attractive as well as to protect the United States which would obviously be the principal source of credit.[235]

The Ship Mortgage Act did not immediately accomplish one of its primary purposes—that of inducing private capital to invest in shipping—and the United States had to shoulder the financing burden unaided. The principal reason for the banks' refusal to participate was most probably that in 1920 shipping did not look like a particularly profitable investment. It was also true, and may have been a contributing factor, that grave doubts were expressed as to the constitutionality of the Ship Mortgage Act and these doubts were not resolved by a Supreme Court decision until 1934.[235a]

**234.** H.R.Rep.No.443, 66th Congress, 1st Sess., 4, 9 (1919). 59 Cong.Rec. 7224 (May 18, 1920). 58 Cong.Rec. 8173 (November 8, 1919). See further Chapter XI, §§ 11–4, 11–5.

**235.** Act of June 5, 1920, c. 250, § 30, 41 Stat. 1000; 46 U.S.C.A. §§ 911–984. The sections of the Ship Mortgage Act will hereafter be referred to by their U.S.C.A. number alone. As to the purposes of the Act, with citation to the Congressional Reports, see Detroit Trust Co. v. The Thomas Barlum, 293 U.S. 21, 55 S.Ct. 31, 1934 A.M.C. 1417 (1934); The Northern No. 41, 297 F. 343, 1924 A.M.C. 583 (S.D.Fla.1924).

**235a.** Among the recent contributions to the literature on ship mortgages and ship financing patterns particular mention should be made of Gyory, Security at Sea: A Review of the Preferred Ship Mortgage, 31 Fordham L. Rev. 231 (1962)—an extraordinary piece of work which both historians and practitioners will find to be of the greatest interest. Mr. Gyory analyses the considerable amount of Ship Mortgage Act litigation which marked the early 1960's. Kriz, Ship Mortgages, Maritime Liens and their Enforcement: The Brussels Conventions of 1926 and 1952, [1963] Duke L.J. 671, [1964] Duke L.J. 70 is a most helpful review of the provisions of the Conventions on Mortgage and Liens (1926) and the Arrest of Sea-going Vessels (1952). The Conventions are in force in a considerable number of countries (see Kriz, [1963] Duke L.J. at pp. 674–675) but not in the United States or England. Note, International Uniformity of Maritime Liens and

**§ 9–49.** The constitutional issue thought to be presented by the Ship Mortgage Act was this:[236] by the Constitution the judicial power extends "to all civil causes of admiralty and maritime jurisdiction". The determination of what "causes" are within the jurisdiction is exclusively for the judiciary. Congress does not have power to confer on the admiralty courts jurisdiction over cases judicially determined not to be maritime or to prohibit the admiralty courts from exercising jurisdiction over cases that are maritime. Since the ship mortgage was nonmaritime, only a Constitutional amendment could give the admiralty courts jurisdiction over it or confer maritime lien status upon it. The argument overlooked, or did not stress, the fact that it was the Court which had determined the mortgage to be nonmaritime and that the Court had, several times in its history, reversed itself on such issues, usually in order to extend the admiralty jurisdiction.[237]

It is easy to understand why the economic interests adversely affected by the Act—the materialmen whose liens were subordinated to a properly recorded prior mortgage—should have been opposed to it. They had been given some comfort, at the time the Mortgage Act was passed, by an amendment which broadened the scope of the Lien Act,[238] but that gain was more than offset by the loss they suffered in being subordinated to long-term mortgages which would in most cases eat up the entire value of the ship. Any stick will do to beat a dog or a statute with, but it is hard to believe that the proponents of the unconstitutionality of the Mortgage Act, however sincerely they disliked the statute, really thought that they had much of a case.

Certainly the courts never gave them any reason to believe so. In several cases decided during the 1920's, the lower courts uniformly

Mortgages: The 1965 New York Conference of the Comité Maritime International, 41 N.Y.U.L.Rev. 939 (1966) reviews the progress of the so far unsuccessful effort to achieve international uniformity and reproduces an interesting draft of a Convention designed to supersede the 1926 Brussels Convention. A new Convention on Liens, designed to supersede the 1926 Convention, was adopted in Brussels in 1967 but has not, as yet, been ratified by anyone. On the 1967 Convention, see Sandström, The Changing International Concept of the Maritime Lien as a Security Right, 47 Tulane L.Rev. 681 (1973). The author comments, with respect to the 1967 Convention: "With the risk of making the understatement of the year, it may be concluded that the outcome was not a success." The Tulane Symposium on Maritime Liens and Securities (1973) contains several excellent articles: Smith, Ship Mortgages, 47 Tulane L.Rev. 608 (1973); Mahla, Some Problems in Vessel Financing—A Lender's Lawyer's View, *id.* at p. 629; Cook, Government Assistance in Financing—Title XI Federal Guarantees, *id.* at p. 653; Kominers, Federal Government Aids to Merchant Shipping, *id.* at p. 691; Angermueller, Miscellaneous Ship Financing, *id.* at p. 725; Rogers, Enforcement of Maritime Liens and Mortgages, *id.* at p. 767; Harmon, Discharge and Waiver of Maritime Liens, *id.* at p. 786.

236. See Miller, The Foreclosure of Vessel Mortgages in Admiralty, 70 U. Pa.L.Rev. 22 (1921); Jurisdiction of Mortgages, Constitutionality of the Ship Mortgage Act of 1920, 11 Calif. L.Rev. 268 (1923); Canfield, The Ship Mortgage Act of 1920, 22 Mich.L.Rev. 10 (1923); Constitutionality of the Ship Mortgage Act, 33 Yale L.J. 646 (1924).

237. See, for an example, Chapter I at note 99.

238. See § 9–34 *supra.*

ruled in favor of the Act's constitutionality.[239] In 1926 one of these cases reached the Supreme Court, Morse Drydock & Repair Co. v. The Northern Star,[240] but the Court, holding that the mortgagee had not complied with the formal requirements of the Act and therefore had no lien, did not have to pass, and chose not to pass, on the constitutional issue. Nothing in Justice Holmes' short opinion suggested, however, that the Court had any doubts about the Act's constitutionality.

The Court finally dispelled whatever remaining doubt there may have been in Detroit Trust Co. v. The Thomas Barlum,[241] with Chief Justice Hughes writing an admirable opinion for a unanimous Court. The case involved mortgages on two ships; there had been a "definite understanding" between mortgagor and mortgagee that the money advanced should be used for purposes partly maritime and partly nonmaritime, and the money had been in fact so used. On default the mortgagee brought suit in admiralty under the Mortgage Act to foreclose; the mortgagor, appearing as claimant, objected to the jurisdiction.

Before the Court reached its foregone conclusion on the constitutional issue, it had to pass on a point of construction of the Act which was quite as vital as the Act's constitutionality; whether the Act covered mortgages where the proceeds were "diverted" to nonmaritime uses. The case was a good one, since the nonmaritime use of proceeds had been an integral part of the original arrangement between mortgagor and mortgagee. Thus the Court's decision (if it upheld the mortgage) would cover not only the case where the mortgagee agreed to the nonmaritime use but, *a fortiori*, the case where the mortgagor diverted the funds without the mortgagee's knowledge or consent. A holding that the Act protected only mortgages where the funds advanced were in fact used for maritime purposes would have been almost as welcome to those who opposed the Act as a holding of unconstitutionality. In view of the difficulties of tracing the actual use to which any funds are put, not to mention the legal obscurity which shrouds the question of what uses are "maritime", no mortgage, Governmental or private, would have had much chance of prevailing over competing claims if the Barlum case had held that a maritime use was required. Fortunately, from the point of view of prospective mortgagees, the Court held that there was no such requirement. The statute contained no provision which even hinted at a solution, one way or the other; the Chief Justice dredged up some remarks of Justice Story to the effect that money advanced under bottomry bonds could be validly put to nonmaritime uses and,

239. The Oconee, 280 F. 927 (E.D.Va. 1921); The Nanking, 292 F. 642, 1923 A.M.C. 1191 (N.D.Cal.1923); The Lincoln Land, 295 F. 358, 1924 A.M.C. 194 (D.Mass.1924); The Northern No. 41, 297 F. 343, 1924 A.M.C. 583 (S.D.Fla. 1924); The Acropolis, 1924 A.M.C. 1510 (E.D.N.Y.1924); The Fort Orange, 5 F.Supp. 833, 1934 A.M.C. 240 (S.D.N.Y.1933).

240. 271 U.S. 552, 46 S.Ct. 589, 1926 A.M.C. 977 (1926).

241. 293 U.S. 21, 55 S.Ct. 31, 1934 A.M.C. 1417 (1934).

suggesting that the ship mortgage under the Act was merely a modern analogy to bottomry, held that the nonmaritime use was permissable.

In holding the Mortgage Act constitutional Chief Justice Hughes wrote a classical exposition of the roles of Court and Congress in the admiralty field. He accepted as a basic premise Chief Justice Taney's statement, with reference to the power to determine the scope of admiralty jurisdiction, that "No state law can enlarge it, nor can an act of Congress or rule of court make it broader than the judicial power may determine to be its true limits".[242] He continued:

> "The framers of the Constitution did not contemplate that the maritime law should remain unalterable. The purpose was to place the entire subject, including its substantive as well as its procedural features, under national control. From the beginning the grant was regarded as implicitly investing legislative power for that purpose in the United States. When the Constitution was adopted, the existing maritime law became the law of the United States 'subject to power in Congress to modify or supplement it as experience or changing conditions might require.'
>
> ". . . The Congress thus has paramount power to determine the maritime law which shall prevail throughout the country. . . . But in amending and revising the maritime law, the Congress necessarily acts within a sphere restricted by the concept of the admiralty and maritime jurisdiction." [243]

The opinion then traced in detail the history of Congressional action in the admiralty field, from the enactment of the Judiciary Act of 1789 to the Maritime Lien Act of 1910. With reference to the effect on Congress of the Court's holding in The John Jay that ship mortgages were non-maritime, he wrote:

> "The authority of the Congress to enact legislation of this nature was not limited by previous decisions as to the extent of the admiralty jurisdiction. We have had abundant reason to realize that our experience and new conditions give rise to new conceptions of maritime concerns. These may require that former criteria of jurisdiction be abandoned, as, for example, they were abandoned in discarding the doctrine that the admiralty jurisdiction was limited to tidewaters." [244]

The implication was that Congress, in setting the limits of admiralty jurisdiction, need not consider itself bound by the Court's prior holdings to any greater degree than the Court itself would be, subject to

**242.** The St. Lawrence, 66 U.S. (1 Black) 522, 527 (1861).

**243.** 293 U.S. 21, 43, 55 S.Ct. 31, 38, 1934 A.M.C. 1417, 1428 (1934).

**244.** *Id.* at 52, 55 S.Ct. at 41, 1934 A.M.C. at 1435.

the overriding qualification that Congress "necessarily acts within a sphere restricted by the concept of the admiralty and maritime jurisdiction" and that that concept is in the last analysis judicially determined.

### Scope of the Mortgage Act

**§ 9–50.** The Mortgage Act does not cover all mortgages on all ships. It contains limitations with respect to the nationality of the ship, the citizenship of the mortgagee and the type of ship. A mortgage not covered by the Act cannot become a "preferred mortgage" entitled to a "preferred status", but remains a common-law nonmaritime contract.[244a]

As passed in 1920, the Mortgage Act covered only a mortgage on a "vessel of the United States over 200 gross tons and upwards." [245] The term "vessel of the United States" is a word of art which is defined in § 911 to mean "any vessel documented under the laws of the United States" and "documented" is in turn defined to mean "registered or enrolled or licensed under the laws of the United States." The mysteries of registry as opposed to enrollment and licensing are briefly explored in the footnote.[246] It should be remem-

**244a.** See McCorkle v. First Pennsylvania Banking & Trust Co., 459 F.2d 243, 1972 A.M.C. 1596 (4th Cir. 1972), dismissing for lack of federal jurisdiction an action in which McCorkle sought a declaratory judgment that he held title to a yacht free of a security interest in favor of the Bank. One Murphy had bought the yacht, which was not at that time enrolled as a "vessel of the United States" (see text following note 245 *infra*), on conditional sale. The conditional sale contract was assigned to the Bank, which perfected its interest by filing a proper financing statement under the Maryland Uniform Commercial Code. Subsequently and without the Bank's knowledge Murphy succeeded in having the yacht enrolled as a "vessel of the United States" without disclosure to the Collector of Customs of the Bank's security interest. McCorkle bought the yacht from Murphy after having determined, from a search of the federal Abstract of Title kept in the appropriate Collector's office, that the yacht was apparently free of liens. *Held* that, in the absence of diversity jurisdiction, the federal court could not adjudicate McCorkle's title to the yacht against the Bank's state-created security interest. Judge Sobeloff reluctantly declined to follow the argument put forward in 7A Moore, Federal Practice ¶ 285[1] (2d ed. 1953) that, following the enactment of the Ship Mortgage Act, all mortgages and other security interests in vessels should be considered "maritime", and thus within the admiralty jurisdiction, whether or not they are "preferred mortgages" under the Federal Act. Referring to Chief Justice Hughes' opinion in the Detroit Trust Co. case (see § 9–49 *supra*) Judge Sobeloff commented: "It is the function of the Supreme Court to correct our errors; it is not our function to rectify what we may consider mistakes of the Supreme Court. If the rule embracing preferred ship mortgages within admiralty jurisdiction while excluding non-preferred ship mortgages is to be abandoned, it is for the Supreme Court or Congress to do so, not the lower federal courts." (459 F.2d at p. 249; 1973 A.M.C. at p. 1604).

**245.** § 922.

**246.** Statutes regulating the documentation of vessels go back to the earliest days of the Republic, see 1 Stat. 55 (1789); 1 Stat. 287 (1792); 1 Stat. 395 (1793). The current provisions are found in 46 U.S.C.A. Ch. 2, Registry and Recording (§§ 11–63) and Ch. 12, Regulation of Domestic Vessels (§§ 251–336). To engage in foreign trade a vessel must be registered pursuant to 46 U.S.C.A. § 11; foreign-built vessels may be registered if owned by

bered that certain small craft not subject to the documentation laws, as well as ships which for any reason are not in fact documented are not "vessels of the United States" and cannot become subjects of "preferred mortgages".

In 1935 the coverage of the Act was expanded by a relaxation of the 200 gross ton requirement. That provision had excluded from the Act practically the entire commercial fishing fleet. During the depression days of the 1930's the commercial fishermen found themselves in great need of financial aid. The Reconstruction Finance Corporation was willing to lend them money, even if the banks were not, but the RFC insisted on security for its loans and under the 200 gross ton requirement of the Mortgage Act, no security was available (unless the RFC had been willing to take a flier in bottomry bonds). A proposal was made to dispense with the tonnage requirement entirely and make the Act applicable to any "vessel of the United States". At hearings before the House Committee on Merchant Marine and Fisheries the usual conflict of interest developed between lenders who wanted safe security and materialmen who wanted prior liens. In particular, the New York Towboat Association complained that towage liens against harborcraft, largely outside the Act because of the tonnage requirement, would be subordinated to the mortgage interest. Impressed, the Committee rewrote the bill.[247] As amended, the Act was made to apply to "any vessel of the United States (other than a towboat, barge, scow, lighter, carfloat, canal boat, or tank vessel, of less than two hundred gross tons)." [248] Thus the types of vessels listed (which were by no means restricted to harborcraft) were within the Act only if they were "vessels of the United States" and of 200 gross tons or over. So the Act read until 1961 when the tonnage requirement for the types of vessels listed was reduced to 25 gross tons.[248a] All other domestic vessels are within the Act without regard to tonnage if they meet the "vessels of the United States" requirement. The strictness with which the tonnage requirement has been construed is indicated by The Angler [249] which held a vessel of $199\frac{57}{100}$ tons outside the Act on what, as Robinson happily suggests, could be considered a makeweight argument.[250]

The Mortgage Act as passed in 1920 further limited the availability of "preferred status" for mortgages by a requirement that the

citizens of the United States, but are not allowed to engage in the coastwise trade (*ibid.*) Vessels engaged in coastwise trade or the fisheries or the Great Lakes must be enrolled or licensed or both (46 U.S.C.A. §§ 251, 259, 263). The Commissioner of Customs is directed to consolidate into one document separate forms of enrollment and license which were prescribed by earlier statutes (46 U.S.C.A. § 260).

**247.** See 79 Cong.Rec. 5369 (April 10, 1935). As to the RFC, see Sen.Rep.No. 596, 74th Cong. 1st Sess. (1935).

**248.** Act of June 27, 1935, c. 319, 49 Stat. 424; 46 U.S.C.A. § 922.

**248a.** 75 Stat. 661, 46 U.S.C.A. § 922.

**249.** 23 F.Supp. 341, 1938 A.M.C. 835 (E.D.N.Y.1938).

**250.** Robinson, Admiralty (1939) 444, n. 252.

mortgagee be a "citizen of the United States" (the Reconstruction Finance Corporation, it was provided by the 1935 amendment, was to be "deemed a citizen").[251] The Act did not go on to specify how citizenship should be determined in the case of a corporate mortgagee, although it did add a helpful provision that where bonds were issued under a deed of trust the relevant citizenship was that of the trustee under the indenture rather than that of the individual bond holders. In Collier Advertising Service, Inc. v. Hudson River Day Line [252] the District Judge sensibly held that the Bankers Trust Company of New York was a citizen within the meaning of the Mortgage Act on a showing that it was organized under New York law, that its president and directors were all citizens and that more than 96% of its capital stock was held by persons with addresses within the United States. The case indicates the elaborate nature of the proof that may be required of the mortgagee in such cases. It was also argued to one court that the United States itself could not qualify as mortgagee because it was not a citizen of itself. Nonsense, said the court.[253]

Under the "citizenship" provisions of the Ship Mortgage Act it appeared that the bonds could be held by aliens so long as the trustee qualified as a citizen of the United States. However, under the Shipping Act of 1916 [253a] the sale, mortgage, lease or charter of any interest in a vessel of the United States to a non-citizen without the approval of the Secretary of Commerce was prohibited. In Chemical Bank New York Trust Company v. S/S Westhampton [253b] it appeared that the Chemical Bank was trustee under a mortgage, the entire beneficial interest being held by a German bank which had financed the reconversion of a tanker. The approval of the Secretary of Commerce for the issuance of the bond to the German bank had not been obtained. Judge Sobeloff, falling into the error of taking the statutes to mean what they said, concluded that the issuance of the bond had transferred an interest in the tanker to the German bank, that the transfer was void under the Shipping Act and that the mortgage, "infected" by the illegal transfer, was not entitled to preferred status and could not be foreclosed under the Ship Mortgage Act.[253c] The Westhampton evidently sent a thrill of horror through the financial community. Congress was speedily prevailed upon to enact "clarifying legislation", since "the Westhampton decision, if

**251.** § 922(a)(5).

**252.** 14 F.Supp. 335, 1936 A.M.C. 206 (S.D.N.Y.1936).

**253.** The Northern No. 41, 297 F. 343, 1924 A.M.C. 583 (S.D.Fla.1924).

**253a.** 39 Stat. 728, 46 U.S.C.A. §§ 801–842.

**253b.** 358 F.2d 574, 1966 A.M.C. 1136 (4th Cir. 1965), certiorari denied 385 U.S. 921, 87 S.Ct. 228 (1966).

**253c.** The same argument had been made in Moon Engineering Co., Inc. v. S/S Valiant Power, 214 F.Supp. 555, 1964 A.M.C. 1335 (E.D.Va.1963). Rejecting the argument, Judge Hoffman wrote: "Congress has seen fit to make the citizenship of the trustee the primary consideration in determining whether the mortgage is held by a citizen of this country . . . and in ascertaining the validity of any preferred mortgage . . . . We cannot rewrite the statutes."

not clarified immediately, could cast a cloud over all outstanding and future bond issues."[253d] The clarifying legislation was put in the form of an amendment to the Shipping Act[253e] and provided in effect that bonds, notes and other evidences of indebtedness secured by ship mortgages could be transferred to non-citizens if the mortgage trustee was a citizen of the United States and had been approved by the Secretary of Commerce.[253f] The legislation was given retroactive effect by a provision under which trustees under existing mortgages could apply for the Secretary's approval within a year from the effective date of the legislation. Thus the fiction that American-flag shipping will not be allowed to come under foreign control was elegantly maintained without being allowed to interfere with the realities of the marketplace.

**§ 9–51.** In 1954 the "preferred status" of mortgages under the Act was conferred on certain mortgages on foreign flag ships. The motivating force, which led to this important amendment was the same as that which had inspired the Act in 1920: the dismantling by the United States of its wartime merchant marine. Experience after the war showed that the fleet could not be successfully disposed of, on satisfactory security, so long as preferred status was limited to "vessels of the United States", particularly in the light of the post-World War II practice under which many American shipowners elected to operate their fleets under Liberian, Honduran and Panamanian flags of convenience. Thus the Act was expanded to cover foreign ship mortgages. As in the 1920's the United States was expected to be the principal beneficiary of the legislation, as the holder of most of the mortgages.[254]

Before the 1954 amendment the status of foreign ship mortgages in United States courts was, to say the least, uncertain.[255] Mortgagees of such ships had not put the issue to a test, wisely preferring to arrest the ships in foreign ports where someone might have some idea what the law was and refraining from intervening in proceedings initiated in the United States. Thus there were no American decisions and what the courts might do was a matter of pure conjecture. The question had arisen in England, whose Mortgage Act, like ours, applied only to domestic ships. In The Colorado[256] the Court of Appeal had held that, in view of the statutory recognition of the mortgage as a maritime security device, mortgages

**253d.** House Committee Report No. 1116, 89th Cong., 1st Sess., 2 U.S. Congressional and Administrative News (1965), 4231, 4233.

**253e.** 79 Stat. 1305 (1965), 46 U.S.C.A. § 808.

**253f.** The Secretary "shall grant his approval" if the trustee is a bank or trust company incorporated and doing business in the United States (or any State), subject to Federal or State regulation, and having a combined capital and surplus of at least $3,000,000.

**254.** H.R.Rep.No.1662, 83d Cong., 2d Sess. (1954); S.Rep.No.1213, 83d Cong., 2d Sess. (1954).

**255.** See generally Lord & Glenn, The Foreign Ship Mortgage, 56 Yale L.J. 923 (1947).

**256.** (1923) P. 102 (C.A.).

valid in the country of execution would be enforced in admiralty in England, although the English system of priorities and not that of the country of execution would govern distribution. American courts might follow The Colorado. On the other hand American courts had construed the American Mortgage Act with a nearly intolerable strictness. That attitude might, in a foreign ship mortgage case, be translated into a holding that the foreign mortgage was no more entitled to the benefits of the Act than were American mortgages which failed to meet the Act's requirements. Since there was nothing to stop American materialmen or any other claimants, American or foreign, whose liens were recognized under American law from arresting the ship in any United States port, the uncertain state of American law impaired vessel security throughout the world.

The 1954 amendment provided (omitting a proviso which subordinated the foreign ship mortgage to American materialmen's liens)[257] that, as used in the part of the Act relating to foreclosure of preferred mortgages:

> "the term 'preferred mortgage' shall include, in addition to a preferred mortgage made pursuant to the provisions of this chapter, any mortgage, hypothecation, or similar charge created as security upon any documented foreign vessel (other than a towboat, barge, scow, lighter, car float, canal boat, or tank vessel, of less than two hundred gross tons) if such mortgage, hypothecation, or similar charge has been duly and validly executed in accordance with the laws of the foreign nation under the laws of which the vessel is documented and has been duly registered in accordance with such laws in a public register either at the port of registry of the vessel or at a central office; and the term 'preferred mortgage lien' shall also include the lien of such mortgage, hypothecation, or similar charge." [258]

Except for the proviso, and the list of types of vessels excluded [259] the amendment copied Article I of the Brussels Convention of 1926 for the Unification of Certain Rules of Law Relating to Maritime Liens and Mortgages.[260]

The drafting of the 1954 amendment was up to the usual standard in maritime legislation. Did the amendment apply to mortgages on foreign flag ships held by aliens or only to such mortgages held by American citizens? Did the amendment apply to pre-1954 mortgages or only to mortgages executed after the effective date of the amendment? Although the statutory language did not even hint

**257.** The proviso is discussed § 9–70 *infra*.

**258.** As amended June 29, 1954, 68 Stat. 323; 46 U.S.C.A. § 951.

**259.** See text at notes 247 and 248 *supra*.

**260.** The English text of the Convention is reprinted in 6 Benedict, Admiralty 78 (6th ed. 1940). On the Convention see the articles by Kriz cited note 235a *supra*.

at an answer, the legislative history suggested that the Congressional intent had been to restrict the amendment to post-1954 mortgages held by United States citizens (or by the United States itself).[261]

The courts chose to disregard the legislative history and have construed the amendment expansively. In The Aruba, which was the first case decided under the amendment, it was held applicable to a 1949 mortgage on a Panama-flag vessel held by a Swiss bank.[262] Without dissent The Aruba has been followed in all subsequent cases, with the result that since the 1950's our courts have taken jurisdiction in mortgage foreclosure actions where the only American contact has been the accidental one that the mortgaged vessel was arrested or libeled in an American port.[262a]

The 1954 amendment was clear enough on the points that the validity of the mortgage and its proper recordation are to be governed by the law of the country in which the ship is documented.[262b] The foreign law on such matters must, of course, be pleaded and proved but the cases suggest that the courts have been taking a fairly relaxed view of the foreign law question. No cases have been found in which counsel seem to have argued such questions as whether the document (or transaction) described as a mortgage really is a mortgage ("hypothecation or similar charge") or whether the recordation was accomplished at one of the places specified in the amendment (or whether it would make any difference if the laws of the relevant country provided for recordation or registration at some other place or provided for an entirely different system of record or for no such system at all). Nothing in the 1954 amendment requires that the mortgage

**261.** See the Committee Reports cited note 254 *supra*. The legislative history of the amendment is reviewed in Comment, 9 Stanford L.Rev. 780 (1957).

**262.** Rederiaktierbolaget v. Compania de Navegacion Anne S.A., 139 F.Supp. 327, 1955 A.M.C. 1143 (The Aruba) (D. Canal Zone 1955). The decision was criticized as both unnecessary and wrong in the Stanford Comment cited note 261 *supra*.

**262a.** See, e. g., Tropicana Shipping, S. A. v. Empresa Nacional "Elcano" de la Marina Mercante (The Tropicana), 366 F.2d 729 (5th Cir. 1966) (foreclosing a mortgage in favor of a Spanish shipbuilder on a vessel owned by a Panamanian corporation documented in Greece where the mortgage had been recorded); State of Israel v. M/V Nili, 435 F.2d 242, 1971 A.M.C. 428 (5th Cir. 1970), certiorari denied 401 U.S. 994, 91 S.Ct. 1232 (1971) (foreclosing mortgage held by State of Israel on vessel owned by Israeli corporation documented in Israel where mortgage was recorded). See also Payne v. S/S Tropic Breeze, 423 F.2d 236, 1970 A.M.C. 1850 (1st Cir. 1970), certiorari denied *sub nom.* Samadjopoulos v. National Western Life Ins. Co., 400 U.S. 964, 91 S.Ct. 363 (1970); Rainbow Line, Inc. v. M/V Tequila, 341 F.Supp. 459, 1972 A.M.C. 1540 (S. D.N.Y.1972), affirmed 480 F.2d 1024, 1973 A.M.C. 1431 (2d Cir. 1973). Typically the foreign mortgagee finds himself in competition with American lien claimants but there is no suggestion in the cases that jurisdiction would be lacking, or should be declined, in the unlikely event that there were no competing claims, American or foreign.

**262b.** Typically the law of only one foreign country will be involved. It can happen that a mortgage will be executed in one country and recorded in another. See The Tropicana, note 262a *supra*, where the court considered Spanish law and practice with respect to the validity of the mortgage and Greek law with respect to its recordation.

have "preferred status" or even maritime lien status in its own country to be entitled to "preferred status" in an American court. If the amendment is taken literally, a mortgage which is non-maritime in the country of documentation might be promoted to a maritime lien if foreclosed this country. In The Nili [262c] it appeared that the mortgage had been executed to finance a ship construction contract (non-maritime under American law). Judge Watkins, in the District Court, suggested that the literal interpretation of the amendment was "preferable" but, to be on the safe side, went on to find that the mortgage was "clearly of maritime lien status under Israeli law;" on appeal the Fifth Circuit adopted this part of his opinion.[262d] With respect to the use to which the loan secured by the mortgage is put, cases like The Nili are entirely consistent with The Thomas Barlum [262e] in which the Supreme Court had held that the Ship Mortgage Act, as originally enacted, did not require that the money be put to a "maritime use".

The 1954 amendment evidently contemplated that, while foreign law was to govern the validity and the proper recordation of the mortgage, American law was to govern priorities in distribution. There was no novelty in this approach; it had long been the American, as it appears to have been the English, rule that priorities are governed by the law of the forum.[262f] In the foreign mortgage cases the American courts routinely shift from foreign to American law when they come to the adjudication of priorities.[262g] The only special

**262c.** Note 262a *supra.*

**262d.** 318 F.Supp. 1196 (S.D.Fla.1968); extracts from Judge Watkins' opinion are reprinted as an Appendix to the Fifth Circuit's opinion (note 262a *supra*). The Tropicana, note 262a *supra*, also involved a mortgage originally given to secure a ship construction contract.

**262e.** See text following note 241 *supra.*

**262f.** See Brandon v. S/S Denton, 302 F.2d 404, 1962 A.M.C. 1730 (5th Cir. 1962) in which Judge Rives reviewed the history of the American rule, citing Scotia, 35 F. 907 (S.D.N.Y.1888) (per Brown, J.) and Oconee, 280 F. 927 (E.D.Va.1922). The Denton was not a foreign mortgage case; it involved priorities between an Italian supplier and an American mortgagee as to an American-flag vessel. On the English rule, see The Colorado, text at note 256 *supra.* In Todd Shipyards Corp. v. Altema Compania Maritima, S.A., 1973 A.M.C. 176 (Sup.Ct.Canada, 1972) the Court applied Canadian law to determine priorities between an American repairman and the Panamanian holder of a mortgage on a Panamanian-owned ship which was documented in Greece where the mortgage had been recorded. Justice Ritchie's opinion reviews both the English and the Canadian cases.

**262g.** In Rainbow Line, Inc. v. M/V Tequila, 480 F.2d 1024, 1973 A.M.C. 1431 (2d Cir. 1973) Judge Anderson concluded that the choice of law question in cases involving foreign ship mortgages should be decided in the light of the guidelines laid down by the Supreme Court in Lauritzen v. Larsen, 345 U.S. 571, 73 S.Ct. 921, 1953 A.M.C. 1210 (1953). On the Lauritzen guidelines see Chapter VI, § 6–63 *et seq.* *Held* that the maritime law of the United States applied to determine both the existence of liens and their priority with respect to a Liberian-flag ship (subject to a mortgage recorded in Liberia and held by an American mortgagee) owned by a Bahamian corporation. At an earlier point the ship had been of English ownership and registry; the English owners had wrongfully withdrawn her from service under a charter party. Such a breach gives rise to a lien under American maritime law (see note 103 *supra* and accompanying text) but not

feature in the foreign mortgage cases, with respect to priorities, is the effect of the proviso in the 1954 amendment which subordinates foreign mortgages to American materialmen's liens.[262h]

### A Note on Patterns of Ship Financing

§ 9–51(a) In 1920 the Congress had evidently assumed that the provision of a satisfactory security device with maritime lien status under the Ship Mortgage Act would attract private capital to finance the construction and operation of a mercantile fleet under the American flag.[262i] That assumption proved to be mistaken even after whatever lingering doubts there may have been about the Act's constitutionality had been cleared up by the Supreme Court's 1934 decision in Detroit Trust Company v. The Thomas Barlum.[262j] The continuing reluctance, after 1934, of the normal sources of capital to make the hoped-for investment in shipping had nothing to do with investor dissatisfaction about the nature of the security device which the Ship Mortgage Act had provided. The truth was and is and will continue to be that shipping is a perhaps uniquely risky enterprise, as vulnerable to the perils of the market-place as the ships themselves are to the perils of the sea. It is also true that private sources of capital will not tolerate an unacceptable degree of risk in any investment and that, to a competently managed bank, life insurance company or pension fund, what might seem to most people a very low degree of risk is already unacceptable. The long and short of the matter was that private capital would never be attracted to ship financing until the risk factor had been removed.

Congress accepted this fact of life in the 1930's and began in 1938, under Title XI of the Merchant Marine Act of 1936, to elaborate a system of federally guaranteed or insured ship financing.[262k] Almost year by year the original Title XI was amended to make the

under English maritime law (for whose application the mortgagee unsuccessfully argued). The case also involved a salvage claim by an American salvor which had arisen after the ship's transfer to Liberian registry (see Chapter VIII, § 8–15, note 129b) and claims by the crew for unpaid wages and penalties (see § 9–20, note 93 at end *supra*). Conceivably Judge Anderson's adoption of the Lauritzen guidelines might lead to the determination of lien priorities according to the law of some foreign country in a case which did not involve any American contacts or claims. It has usually been assumed that even in such a case priorities are to be determined by the law of the forum; see the Canadian case digested note 262f *supra*.

See further the opinions in the cases cited note 262a *supra*. In addition to the opinion in The Tropic Breeze cited in note 262a, two other opinions delivered in the course of the same litigation are relevant: Payne v. S/S Tropic Breeze, 412 F.2d 707 (1st Cir. 1969); National Western Life Ins. Co. v. Tropical Commerce Corp. (S/S Tropic Breeze), 456 F.2d 137, 1972 A.M.C. 1622 (1st Cir. 1972).

**262h.** See § 9–70 *infra*.

**262i.** See §§ 9–47, 9–48 *supra*.

**262j.** See § 9–49 *supra*.

**262k.** Title XI (Federal Ship Mortgage Insurance) was added to the Merchant Marine Act by 52 Stat. 969; 46 U.S.C.A. § 1271 *et seq.* See Chapter XI, §§ 11–6, 11–7, 11–8 for a general discussion of the Merchant Marine Acts of 1936 and 1970.

proposed arrangement more attractive to lenders.[262l] By the early 1960's, according to a knowledgable commentator, the Title XI program had "virtually removed any risk factor" from ship financing eligible for federal insurance.[262m] In the Ship Financing Act of 1972 [262n] Congress consolidated, expanded and further liberalized the Title XI program in such a way as to "make ship financing virtually risk-free to the investor and hence attractive in traditional money markets." [262o]

The detail of the Title XI program, as amended, will be left to the specialized literature. Eligible for the guarantee are loans or obligations which aid in the financing (or refinancing) of the construction, reconstruction or reconditioning of vessels owned by citizens of the United States which are designed principally for research or for commercial use in domestic or foreign trade or in the fishing industry.[262p] The guarantee pledges "the full faith and credit of the United States" to the payment of principal and interest on guaranteed obligations; the guarantee of principal is restricted to 75% (or in some cases 87½%) of the cost of "construction, reconstruction or reconditioning" as determined by the Secretary of Commerce.[262q] The guarantee is to be secured by a mortgage entitled to preferred status under the Ship Mortgage Act and existing vessels may be mortgaged to secure future construction.[262r] Under the 1972 Act the mortgage is to run to the Secretary of Commerce; [262s] before 1972 the mortgage ran to the lender and was assigned to the Secretary on default.[262t] On default in the payment of principal or interest which continues uncured for thirty days, the Secretary must, on demand by the obligee, pay off the principal and interest due on the obligation; the Secretary may waive other types of default.[262u] After making payment under the guarantee the Secretary may operate, charter or

**262*l*.** The successive amendments to Title XI are traced in Cook, Government Assistance in Financing—Title XI Federal Guarantees, 47 Tulane L. Rev. 653 (1973).

**262m.** Gyory, Security at Sea: A Review of the Preferred Ship Mortgage, 31 Fordham L.Rev. 231, 269 (1962). Mr. Gyory collected the available statistics on the volume of ship financing which the Title XI program had stimulated.

**262n.** 86 Stat. 909; 46 U.S.C.A. § 1271 *et seq.*

**262*o*.** Cook, *supra* note 262*l*. The author was General Counsel, Maritime Administration, United States Department of Commerce. In his review of the 1972 Act, Mr. Cook explained various regulations under which the Department proposed to implement the legislation.

**262p.** § 1274. "Floating drydocks" may also be financed under federal guarantee. A definition of the term "vessel" (§ 1271(b)) goes into more detail on the types of vessels (and dry docks) which are included and adds the requirement that the vessels must be "documented under the laws of the United States". Under § 1274(d) the Secretary of Commerce, before making a guarantee commitment, must find that the project being financed is "economically sound" (a different formula is used with respect to fishing vessels).

**262q.** § 1273.

**262r.** § 1271(a); § 1273(b); § 1274(c)(1).

**262s.** § 1273(b).

**262t.** See Cook, *supra* note 262*l*.

**262u.** §§ 1275(a), (b).

sell any of the mortgaged vessels or, in a curious provision, place them "in the national defence reserve." [262v]

After World War II private capital, responding to the progressive assumption of all risks by the United States, did for the first time invest in ship financing. As a matter of form the financing was done on the security of the mortgaged vessel but the real security was of course the federal guarantee; the provision of the 1972 Act under which the mortgage runs directly to the Secretary of Commerce merely recognizes this fact.

If we lived in a rational world the owner of the vessel would appear in the financing arrangement as obligor-mortgagor and the lending institution as obligee-mortgagee (or, under the 1972 Act, the lending institution would be obligee and the Secretary of Commerce mortgagee, with the Secretary becoming the obligee on making payment under the guarantee). We have, however, long lived in an irrational world in which owners of property held subject to financing arrangements have found it to their advantage to describe themselves as lessees with the legal title to the property being held either by the lending institution or by some third party. In the field of personal property security law the owner's attempts to become a lessee of his own property have sometimes succeeded and sometimes failed; [262w] the courts have long distinguished between "true leases" and disguised security arrangements. The original motivation for the use of leases instead of such security arrangements as chattel mortgages and conditional sales seems to have been the lender's desire to escape from the filing requirements and the cumbersome foreclosure procedures of the chattel mortgage acts and the somewhat later conditional sales legislation. In time it was discovered that, under "approved accounting methods", a long-term lease produced a prettier balance sheet for the owner-lessee than a chattel mortgage or conditional sale did, although it is hard to believe that any one except the accountants themselves and an occasional widow or orphan was ever taken in by the balance-sheet nonsense. However the reason why industrial equipment leasing has flourished in this century, and particularly since World War II, has had little or nothing to do with either the lender's desire to escape filing and foreclosure requirements or the owner-lessee's desire to beautify his balance sheet. The reason for the growth of such leasing in our generation is that the Internal Revenue Code makes leasing more advantageous than buying or owning; if the Internal Revenue Code were to be rewritten in the light of reason, the lease advantages would presumably disappear but such a development is not to be anticipated.[262x] In the patterns of ship

262v. § 1275(c).

262w. For the long and complicated history of the matter, see 1 Gilmore, Security Interests in Personal Property, Ch. 3 (1965).

262x. We shall leave the detail of the tax advantages for leases to the specialized literature, which is, of course, enormous. For a review in the context of ship financing, see Angermueller, Miscellaneous Ship Financing, 47 Tulane L.Rev. 725 (1973). Mr. Angermueller's article deals with financing patterns both under Title XI and outside it.

financing which developed after World War II it was therefore desirable for the true or beneficial owner of the vessel being financed to appear not as owner but as lessee (or, in maritime terminology, charterer). For obvious reasons, however, the charter could not run directly to the financing institution; for the security arrangement to have maritime lien status there had to be a preferred mortgage under the Ship Mortgage Act and, whatever else a charter-party may be, it is not a preferred mortgage.[262y] For there to be a mortgage there had to be a mortgagor; since, for tax purposes, the beneficial owner must appear as charterer, some third party had to be found or invented who would hold title to the vessel for the twin purposes of chartering it to the owner and mortgaging it to the bank. This tripartite arrangement seems to have become the standard pattern of current ship financing.[262z] The title-holder will typically be a corporation created expressly for the purpose whose only asset will be the charter and whose only liability will be the mortgage.

The same sort of tripartite arrangement has, since World War II, appeared in other financing contexts. For example, a bank finances a manufacturing seller, taking as security for its loan an assignment of the moneys to be earned under a long-term contract entered into between the seller and a buyer who has agreed to take the seller's entire output. (As in the ship-financing context, the long-term contract may well be the seller's only asset and the bank loan his only liability.) Such financing on the security of long-term contract rights is relatively novel. The truth is that neither the existing case law nor the codifying statute (Article 9 of the Uniform Commercial Code) provides any clear answer to a great many problems which are implicit in this complex tripartite relationship. For present purposes it will be enough to say that the bank may get under its assignment much less security than bank counsel like to think it gets.[262aa]

The maritime adaptation of this tripartite arrangement poses a great many questions, none of which has yet been answered. Is the charterer/lessee truly a lessee or is he an owner? Is the "owner"/lessor truly a lessor or is he the holder of a disguised security interest in the vessel? Members of the admiralty bar who engage in such transactions will neglect at their peril the distinction, long elaborated in personal property security law, between "true leases" and false or security leases. What sort of interest does the mortgagee (bank or Secretary of Commerce) have in the long-term charter which,

**262y.** Thus the so-called "Philadelphia plan" equipment trust which had developed in railroad equipment financing, where the financing bank holds title to the equipment which it leases to the railroad, could not be adapted to ship financing.

**262z.** See the articles by Cook and Angermueller cited notes 262*l* and 262x *supra.*

**262aa.** See 2 Gilmore, Security Interests in Personal Property, Ch. 41 (Assignment of Contract Rights) (1965). The chapter cited appeared in somewhat different form under the title The Assignee of Contract Rights and His Precarious Security in 74 Yale L. J. 217 (1964).

much more than the vessel itself, is the real security? The bank which has a Title XI guarantee is not, of course, concerned about its security but not all ship financing transactions are eligible for the guarantee. In any event the question remains as to what rights the Secretary gets, in addition to his rights as mortgagee against the vessel, when he is required to pay under the guarantee. The "owner's" default under the mortgage obligation will of course have resulted from the "charterer's" failure to pay the charter hire. The charterer's default may have been the result of inevitable necessity (he is insolvent) or of a deliberate choice (the ship's operation is unprofitable). "Charterer" and "owner" may, before the default on the mortgage obligation, have agreed to rescind the charter or to reduce the charter rate. Is the rescission or modification good against the Secretary? There are no doubt many lawyers whose instinctive response to the question just put will be that the question is absurd because the Secretary, who is not a party to the charter, could clearly have no rights under it. Anyone who feels that the question is absurd might be well advised to look into the rapidly developing contract doctrines relating to so-called third party beneficiaries.

Another problem may be mentioned with respect to the use of the charter arrangement in ship financing. In the proceedings for limitation of liability with respect to the Torrey Canyon it appeared that that unfortunate vessel was being operated under a charter of this sort. Claimants in the limitation proceeding argued that the beneficial owner of the Torrey Canyon (the "charterer") was not the sort of person entitled to the benefits of the Limitation of Liability Act but should be held to unlimited liability. The proceedings were discontinued following an out-of-court settlement so the issue was not finally decided but, on an interlocutory appeal, the Second Circuit indicated that it looked with favor on the claimants' argument.[262bb] The dilemma in which the beneficial owner (or his counsel) finds himself is that the more he is made to look like a mere charterer or lessee, for tax purposes, the more doubtful his right to invoke the Limitation Act becomes; contrariwise, the more he is made to look like an owner, for purposes of invoking the Limitation Act, the more doubtful his right to the tax advantages becomes.

The Ship Financing Act of 1972 (like the earlier versions of Title XI) clearly contemplates the use of the tripartite arrangement we have described in transactions eligible for Title XI guarantees. We should add, by way of conclusion, that it contains no provisions relevant to any of the questions we have raised.

### "Preferred Mortgages": Formal Requisites

**§ 9–52.** The Mortgage Act outdoes the worst of the old-fashioned state chattel mortgage acts in its insistence on formalities of ex-

262bb. The Torrey Canyon limitation proceedings are discussed in Chapter X, § 10–4(a).

ecution and in the detail of its recording mechanics. An exact compliance with the host of procedural niceties which the Act sets forth is required of the mortgagee. The penalty for noncompliance is that the mortgage does not attain the status of "preferred mortgage" but is merely a common-law, nonmaritime mortgage. Thus the noncomplying mortgagee will see his libel dismissed for lack of jurisdiction and will find himself subordinated to all maritime claims even though the claimants may have known of the mortgage's existence at the time when their claims accrued.

Section 926 states three conditions which must be met before a mortgage, bill of sale or conveyance can be admitted to record:

1. the mortgage or other document must "state the interest of the grantor or mortgagor in the vessel, and the interest so sold, conveyed, or mortgaged";

2. the mortgage or other document must have been acknowledged before a notary or other qualified public official;

3. when the vessel's port of documentation is changed, the collector of customs [263] at the new port must be furnished with a certified copy of the record of the vessel at the former port. Although no litigation has arisen under the foregoing provisions, there can be no doubt that they are jurisdictional. The phraseology of the section is that "no mortgage shall be recorded unless" the conditions are complied with. If the collector of customs inadvertently accepts a defective document for record, it is believed that the mistaken recording is ineffective and the mortgage is still not a "preferred mortgage".

Section 922 establishes other requirements for the mortgage (in addition to those previously discussed relating to the type of vessel and the citizenship of the mortgagee).

Section 922(e) reads:

> "A mortgage which includes property other than a vessel shall not be held a preferred mortgage unless the mortgage provides for the separate discharge of such property by the payment of a specified portion of the mortgage indebtedness. If a preferred mortgage so provides for the separate discharge, the amount of the portion of such payment shall be indorsed upon the documents of the vessel."

By negative inference the subsection suggests that a preferred mortgage may include "property other than a vessel", which is taken to mean nonmaritime property. The subsection does not apply to a mortgage on a "vessel and her freight" (the freight being held to be

263. The functions of the "collector of customs" with respect to the recordation and indorsement of mortgages have been transferred to the United States Coast Guard. For the Coast Guard's regulations, see 46 C.F.R. § 67, .49–1 to .49–21 (1970). The Ship Mortgage Act, however, continues to refer to the "collector of customs". For convenience we shall stick with the collector.

a part of the vessel, for this purpose)[263a] nor to a mortgage on two or more vessels (the fleet mortgage being separately dealt with in the following subsection (f) of § 922). Where a mortgage does cover both a vessel and nonmaritime property, the mortgage is not a preferred mortgage unless it "provides for the separate discharge of such property by the payment of a specified portion of the mortgage indebtedness." Note that the property whose "separate discharge" must be provided for is not the vessel but the nonmaritime property.

Subsection (e) was discussed in an illuminating opinion by Judge Chesnut in The Emma Giles.[264] There the mortgage, which contained a "separate discharge" provision designed to comply with subsection (e), attached to the "separate discharge" conditions, not uncommon in trust indentures, for the protection of bondholders. It was held that the "discharge" provision relating to the nonmaritime property must be absolute and not conditional. Judge Chesnut was also bothered by the proper construction of the phrase "a specified portion of the mortgage indebtedness". In The Emma Giles the mortgage, which was for the principal amount of $175,000 and covered three ships as well as shore property, allocated specific amounts of money to the several pieces of collateral: $75,000, $10,000 and $10,000 for the three ships and $135,000 for the nonmaritime property. Judge Chesnut doubted whether such a provision would "gratify the Act". In his opinion what the Act was aiming at was a "severance" of the maritime and nonmaritime components of the mortgage collateral for purposes of foreclosure and what was required was a clause in the mortgage under which it could be determined at any particular time what "proportion" of the unpaid debt would have to be paid to secure the release, or "separate discharge", of the nonmaritime property. What Judge Chesnut evidently had in mind was a statement in terms of fractions or percentages allocated to the nonmaritime property. In Collier Advertising Service, Inc. v. Hudson River Day Line,[265] which Judge Chesnut cites in The Emma Giles with a "compare, however" reference, Judge Patterson had approved mortgages which apparently stated a "separate discharge" as to nonmaritime property in specific dollar amounts. Since Judge Chesnut had found the mortgage in The Emma Giles defective in any case because of the conditional nature of the discharge, he did not squarely rule on how the "specified portion" should be stated.

Judge Chesnut's doubts as to what subsection (e) requires (in addition to an absolute discharge) may have been stimulated by the reflection that if the subsection requires no more than the statement incorporated in the mortgage before him, it insists on a pure formality which accomplishes nothing. Assume that a mortgage covers a ship and a factory and "provides for the separate discharge" of the factory

263a. The R. Lenahan, 10 F.Supp. 497, 1935 A.M.C. 513 (E.D.Pa.1935).

264. 15 F.Supp. 502, 1936 A.M.C. 1146 (D.Md.1936).

265. 14 F.Supp. 335, 1936 A.M.C. 206 (S.D.N.Y.1936).

by the payment of $50,000. When the mortgagor has paid $50,000, other lien claimants libel the ship *in rem.* On ordinary principles of law, a creditor can allocate payments by a debtor in any way he desires, and there is nothing in the Mortgage Act to suggest that the mortgagee may not do so in this case. Thus the mortgagee in the case assumed can allocate the $50,000 paid all to the factory, or half to factory and half to ship or in any other way. If the liens are subordinate to the mortgage, there would be no way for the lienors to know, in advance of litigation, how much would have to be paid down to satisfy the ship mortgage and thus sever the maritime and nonmaritime components. If Judge Chesnut's theory were followed and the mortgage allocated 50% of the unpaid debt to the factory, the other claimants could much more easily determine the true state of facts and whether or not it would be to their advantage to litigate. That theory at least makes the subsection more than an empty gesture. The point remains as unsettled as it is obscure. Whichever way the mortgagee of a mixed mortgage chooses to jump, some court may find that he took the wrong direction. Under the circumstances a mortgagee who takes such a mortgage is inviting unnecessary trouble. The simple solution is to take separate mortgages on the maritime and nonmaritime property and avoid the whole problem.[265a] There is no discernible advantage in the composite mortgage, since there must be separate recordation of the ship and shore property and separate foreclosure actions on default.[266] If it is desired to issue bonds on the joint security, there is no reason why the bonds could not recite that they were secured by two separate mortgages on the property of the obligor.

**§ 9–53.** Section 922(f) authorizes fleet mortgages in the same offhand way that § 922(e) authorizes mixed mortgages on maritime and nonmaritime property.[267] The idea of "separate discharge" which had haunted the draftsman's mind in connection with the

**265a.** The suggested procedure was successfully followed in Port Welcome Cruises, Inc. v. S/S Bay Belle, 215 F. Supp. 72, 1964 A.M.C. 2674 (D.Md. 1963), affirmed *sub nom.* Humble Oil & Refining Co. v. S/S Bay Belle, 324 F.2d 954 (4th Cir. 1963). Judge Winter rejected the contention that the absence of a "separate discharge" provision from the ship mortgage was fatal; the theory of the argument was that § 922(e) requires the provision even though separate mortgages are used whenever the financing transaction as a whole covers both maritime and nonmaritime property. Judge Winter also refused to order a marshaling of the maritime and nonmaritime security so as to require that the security holder look first to the nonmaritime security. He based his refusal partly on jurisdictional grounds but also, more practically, on the conclusion that, on the facts of the case, the marshaling would not do the competing maritime lien claimants any good. Separate mortgages covering maritime and nonmaritime property were also held outside the scope of § 922(e) in Harrison Overseas Corp. v. American Barge Sun Coaster, 475 F. 2d 504, 1973 A.M.C. 1174 (5th Cir. 1973). Judge Brown, citing the first edition of the treatise, commented: "In the case at hand the collateral is dealt with in separate instruments and there is no need for severance."

**266.** §§ 921, 954(b).

**267.** § 922(f): "If a preferred mortgage includes more than one vessel . . . ."

mixed mortgage still rattles its chains here, but with less eerie results. The fleet mortgage may provide for the "separate discharge" of individual vessels, but if it does not it is nonetheless a preferred mortgage. When a ship covered by the mortgage comes up for sale under *in rem* process, the district judge is empowered to fix a release price upon payment of which the ship shall be discharged from the mortgage. The statutory formula for arriving at the release price is the portion of the mortgage debt which the value of the ship to be sold bears to the value of all the ships covered by the mortgage. *Quaere* what would happen if the fleet mortgage did contain a "separate discharge" provision which set a release price arrived at by some other formula? Presumably the District Judge would have the power, and might be under a duty, to substitute the statutory formula. If the duty is assumed, the statutory formula then becomes a sort of clause paramount which the statute incorporates in all fleet mortgages. Judge Chesnut's speculations on the kind of "separate discharge" provision required by § 922(e) were based in part on the apparent purpose of the § 922(f) formula: to make it possible for other claimants to determine how much must be paid down at any time to procure the ship's release from the prior lien of the mortgage. But the absence of the clause from a mixed mortgage under § 922(e) forfeits the preferred status of the mortgage, while its absence from a fleet mortgage under § 922(f) merely requires the judge to proceed as if it were in the mortgage anyhow.[267a] Whatever the draftsman may have intended to accomplish by the two subsections, the result is a horribly botched job.

To be entitled to preferred status a mortgage must include "the whole" vessel.[268] Under § 921 a mortgage may include a vessel "or any portion thereof" and still be valid against third parties if properly recorded, although if it is on less than the whole vessel it will be a common law nonmaritime mortgage. That means clearly that a mortgage on a vessel's equipment alone could not become preferred. Whether it means anything else is doubtful. A mortgage on a vessel and her freight was held not to be a mortgage on a vessel and "other property" under § 922(e) on the ground that the freight was part of the vessel.[269] But it would be absurd to hold that a mortgage which did not include freight was a mortgage of less than "the whole". The mortgagee can apparently insist on the freight if he wants it, but in most long-term financing arrangements he will have no use for it and certainly should not be required to take it. The statutory statement is that the mortgage must "at the time it is made" include the whole vessel. The implication seems to be that the right of the mortgage to preferred status will not be affected if equipment is

267a. In Pascagoula Dock Station v. Merchants and Marine Bank, 271 F.2d 53, 1959 A.M.C. 2207 (5th Cir. 1959), Judge Brown, citing the text, so construed § 922(f). For further proceedings in the case, see text at note 296j *infra*.

268. § 922.

269. The R. Lenahan, note 263 *supra*.

subsequently installed on a vessel which for some reason does not come under the mortgage lien.

Finally, under the head of formal requisites, the mortgage must not "stipulate that the mortgagee waives the preferred status thereof." [270] On the face of it, this seems to be an idiotic statement; indeed it is an idiotic statement. It is beyond belief that a mortgagee would go through all the sweat and toil necessary to create a preferred mortgage only to "stipulate" that he waives his rights. He might indeed at a later time be willing to subordinate his rights against materialmen whose services were necessary to keep the ship afloat. But no policy can be suggested which would make it reasonable to deprive a mortgagee of his preferred status because he was willing to subordinate his interest to make it possible for the ship to continue in operation. Still the provision, however idiotic, is part of the statute; mortgagees will be well advised to walk warily before agreeing to subordinate.[270a]

In The Favorite,[271] counsel for materialmen suggested an even more horrifying reading of the "must not stipulate for waiver" provision. Counsel pointed out that the Maritime Lien Act (which was incorporated as part of the Ship Mortgage Act in 1920) also contains interesting language about waiver and preferred mortgages, namely: "Nothing in this chapter shall be construed to prevent . . . the mortgagee, from waiving his right to a lien, or in the case of a preferred mortgage lien, to the preferred status of such lien, at any time by agreement or otherwise . . ." [272] Furthermore, the Lien Act section continues, nothing in the chapter shall affect the rules of law existing on the date of the Act's passage relating to (*inter alia*) "laches in the enforcement of liens upon vessels." In The Favorite a mortgagee with preferred status had not instituted foreclosure proceedings until some years after the maturity date of the mortgage. Counsel argued, with an ingenuity which must command the admira-

**270.** § 922(a)(4).

**270a.** The waiver provision has cropped up occasionally in the cases but no one has yet succeeded in making any sense of it. In Crofton Diesel Engine Co., Inc., v. Puget Sound Nat. Bank of Tacoma, 205 F.2d 950, 1953 A.M.C. 1359 (9th Cir. 1953), the Court refused to find a stipulation for waiver in a provision which made it a default under the mortgage for the mortgagor to "suffer and permit said vessel to be run in debt to an amount exceeding . . . a reasonable sum for strictly current operation and repairs to be kept currently paid within 30 days of the date incurred". In the Henry W. Breyer, 17 F.2d 423, 1927 A.M.C. 290 (D.Md.1927), Judge Soper, without referring to the waiver provisions of § 922(a)(4), held that a mortgage provision which permitted the creation of liens for supplies "is pro tanto a waiver on the part of the mortgagee of the preferred status of the preferred mortgage lien". A supply claimant was given priority over the mortgage, but the mortgage was not stripped of its preferred status. The result in the case is sensible but a mortgagee who incorporates such a clause in his mortgage is obviously asking for trouble. The § 922(a)(4) waiver provision is also discussed briefly in Judge Watkins' opinion in The Tradewind (Atlantic Steamer Supply Co. v. The Tradewind), 144 F. Supp. 408, 418, 1956 A.M.C. 1731, 1744 (D.Md.1956).

**271.** 34 F.Supp. 324, 1940 A.M.C. 958 (S.D.N.Y.1940), affirmed 120 F.2d 899, 1941 A.M.C. 1073 (2d Cir. 1941).

**272.** § 974.

tion of any lawyer, that: (1) the rule as to bottomry bonds (which Chief Justice Hughes had cited as a close analogy to preferred mortgages in The Thomas Barlum)[273] was that delay in enforcing the bond after maturity was laches which forfeited the bond; (2) delay in foreclosing a mortgage should, by analogy, have the same result, since the rules on laches are preserved by the statute; (3) if delay does not amount to a forfeiture it must at least amount to a waiver, which, under the statute, may be "by agreement or otherwise"; (4) if there is a waiver of lien, the mortgage in any case loses its preferred status and becomes nonmaritime. So brilliant an argument deserved a better fate than it received, which was to be denied out of hand by the District Judge who was affirmed by the Second Circuit on appeal. Apparently the waiver language of § 974 will not be read back into the formal requisites language of § 922.[273a]

### "Preferred Mortgages": Recordation and Indorsement on Ship's Papers

**§ 9–54.** A mortgagee who has cleared the hurdles already discussed must also comply with the public notice provisions of the Mortgage Act. These require both that the mortgage be properly recorded with the collector of customs and that certain information about the mortgage be indorsed on the ship's papers.[274]

Two documents must be placed on record. The first is the "mortgage", by which is presumably meant the original, executed by both parties. The second is an affidavit "to the effect that the mortgage is made in good faith and without any design to hinder, delay or defraud any existing or future creditor of the mortgagor or any lienor of the mortgaged vessel." The requirement is jurisdictional. If no affidavit is filed, or if an affidavit is filed but not in proper form, the mortgage does not receive preferred status. Any departure in the affidavit from the statutory language is an invitation to litigation, although minor verbal discrepancies have been held not to be fatal.[275]

273. 293 U.S. 21, 55 S.Ct. 31, 1934 A.M.C. 1417 (1934). See text following note 241 *supra*.

273a. The Favorite was followed in United States v. American Gas Screw Franz Joseph, 210 F.Supp. 581, 1963 A.M.C. 1596 (D.Alaska 1962) where it appeared that the mortgagee had failed to require payments of either principal or interest for approximately ten years prior to the forfeiture of the vessel to the United States for violation of the licensing laws. The United States in support of its forfeiture libel argued that the ten year delay or forbearance constituted laches which "destroyed" the mortgage. Judge Kilkenny, in an excellent opinion, rejected the argument.

The problem of subordinating a mortgage to later contract liens because of delay in foreclosure after default will be further discussed in § 9–83 *infra*.

274. §§ 921, 922.

275. The Nan B, 78 F.Supp. 748 (D. Alaska 1948). Gulf Coast Marine Ways v. The J. R. Hardee, 107 F.Supp. 379, 387, 1952 A.M.C. 1124, 1135 (S.D.Tex. 1952): "It is undisputed that the mortgage was in good faith and for the benefit of the vessel, to keep it going in the shrimp trade. In the absence of fraud, I think the statute should be liberally construed. In any event, so far as Coastal, the only complaining party, is concerned, the affidavit was in substantial compliance with the statute." Lake Jackson State Bank v. O/S Kingfish Too, 240 F.Supp. 450 (S.D.Tex.1965) is to the same effect. In Mastan Co., Inc. v.

The mortgage and affidavit must be recorded in the office of the collector of customs at the ship's port of documentation. Section 921, the recording section, uses the term "port of documentation", which is defined in § 911 to mean "the port at which the vessel is documented, in accordance with law"; § 911 also adds a definition of "documented", which means "registered or enrolled or licensed under the laws of the United States, whether permanently or temporarily." But the fun is just beginning. The definition of "port of documentation" carries a warning preamble: "Except as provided in section 1011". That section, which is part of the Home Port of Vessels Act of 1925,[276] provides that "wherever in the Ship Mortgage Act, 1920, the words 'port of documentation' are used they shall be deemed to mean the 'home port' of the vessel, except that the words 'port of documentation' shall not include a port in which a temporary document is issued." [277] The next section (§ 1012) provides that bills of sale, conveyances, mortgages, assignments of mortgages and hypothecations shall all be recorded in a vessel's "home port". But where is the "home port"? The earnest reader will finally run down § 18 of Title 46 U.S.C.A. (also a part of the Home Port of Vessels Act of 1925) which provides that for the purposes of both the navigation laws and the Ship Mortgage Act every "vessel of the United States" shall have a home port "which port the owner of such vessel subject to the approval of the Commissioner of Customs, shall specifically fix and determine, and subject to such approval may from time to time change." Thus the provisions as to place of recording under § 921 are superseded by the provisions of § 1012; the "port of documentation" definition in § 911 is superseded by § 1011; the part of the § 911 definition of "document" which implies that the port where a temporary document is issued is within the "port of documentation" term is also negated by § 1011; and the key phrase in §§ 1011 and 1012 is explained in § 18.

There is an explanation for this statutory merry-go-round. In 1924 the Fourth Circuit Court of Appeals held in The Susana [278] that a vessel could be validly documented only in its home port, that it home port was the port nearest to its owner's residence, and that, in the case of a corporate owner, the owner's residence was in the state under whose laws the corporation was organized. It had, however, long been the practice of corporate shipowners to document

Steinberg (S/S Sapphire Sandy), 418 F.2d 177 (3d Cir. 1969), certiorari denied *sub nom.* Mastan Co., Inc. v. Todd Shipyards, 397 U.S. 1009, 90 S. Ct. 1238 (1970) the Court rejected the contention that the affidavit had not been filed in good faith.

**276.** 43 Stat. 947–948 (1925); 46 U.S.C.A. § 18; 46 U.S.C.A. §§ 1011–1014.

**277.** If at the time of sale a vessel is in some port of the United States other than her home port according to the usual residence of her new owner, documents may be issued by the collector of the port where the vessel is. R.S. § 4159 (1878), 46 U.S.C.A. § 29. The temporary documents are required to be surrendered on arriving at the vessel's home port. R.S. § 4160 (1878), 46 U.S.C.A. § 30.

**278.** 2 F.2d 410, 1924 A.M.C. 1389 (4th Cir. 1924).

their ships in ports where they were doing business, without regard to the state of incorporation. It was estimated that under the holding in The Susana over 800 ships held in corporate ownership were improperly documented.[279] This meant that these ships were no longer "vessels of the United States". Consequently, mortgages on such ships (many of which were held by the United States) were no longer preferred mortgages under the Mortgage Act. Rather than wait and gamble on a reversal of The Susana in the Supreme Court, Congress hastily whipped up the Home Port of Vessels Act, which contains provisions, in addition to those cited, validating all documentations and recordations made prior to February 16, 1925.

The upshot is that the port of recordation is the ship's home port, and that is any port which the owner may fix, subject to the approval of the Commissioner of Customs. Two cases have involved recordation in ports fixed by the owner as the "home port", the approval of the Commissioner not having been obtained until after the recordation. In The Fort Orange,[280] Judge Knox held the recordation good; in that case the Commissioner had given oral approval at the time of recordation and written approval was filed three days later. Judge Dickinson declined to follow this holding in The R. Lenahan; [281] in that case there is no indication of a prior informal approval nor is it stated how long a time elapsed before the Commissioner's written approval was obtained. Judge Dickinson evidently felt that a port geographically remote from either the owner's place of business or the ship's area of operations had been selected as "home port" in an attempt to throw other creditors off the track. Thus the two cases are distinguishable on the facts. It is obvious that the only sound practice is to delay recordation until all the formalities of vessel documentation and home port designation have been cleared up.

Under § 911(4) a vessel once properly documented "shall be held to continue to be so documented until its documents are surrendered, with the approval of the Secretary of Transportation." Section 39 of 46 U.S.C.A. requires a registered vessel to be reregistered whenever she is sold or whenever the vessel is "altered in form or burden . . . or from one denomination to another." If she is not reregistered "she shall cease to be deemed a vessel of the United States." The provision continuing a vessel's documentation until surrender of the documents with administrative approval protects the mortgagee from loss of his preferred status by the vessel's having become no longer a "vessel of the United States." [281a] In addition § 961 provides

**279.** 66 Cong.Rec. 3559 (Feb. 12, 1925).

**280.** 5 F.Supp. 833, 1934 A.M.C. 240 (S.D.N.Y.1933).

**281.** 10 F.Supp. 497, 1935 A.M.C. 513 (E.D.Pa.1935).

**281a.** See Jackson v. Inland Oil & Transport Co. (Three Jacks), 318 F.2d 802, 1963 A.M.C. 1355 (5th Cir. 1963) (nonmaritime mortgage); Heller & Co. v. M/V Mr. Ed, 270 F.Supp. 830, 1968 A.M.C. 1089 (E.D.La.1967). In Mr. Ed a mortgagee was protected under § 911(4) against the argument that the vessel had ceased to be "a vessel of the United States" under 46 U.S.C. § 39 and regulations promulgated thereunder. In Marine Mart, Inc. v. O/S

that the Secretary of Transportation shall refuse his approval to the surrender of documents unless the mortgagee has consented, except where a vessel has been forfeited for violation of law or sold under admiralty process. In the two excepted cases the mortgagee is still protected. His interest is not terminated by forfeiture unless he "authorized, consented or conspired to effect" the act leading to the forfeiture.[282] On sale of a vessel the court is required, on appropriate motion and under the circumstances which will be explained in the footnote, to construct a new mortgage, whose terms shall be "so far as practicable" the same as those of the original mortgage.[283] If the new mortgage is given, the mortgagee shall not be paid from the proceeds of sale and the amount payable as the purchase price shall be diminished in the amount of the new mortgage. The implication is that if for some reason the new mortgage is not executed, the mortgagee would then be entitled to share in the proceeds of sale.

The mortgagee is not protected "until . . . [the] mortgage is recorded" as provided in § 921(b), which directs the collector of customs to record mortgages in "books to be kept for that purpose" and to maintain appropriate indexes. The "until . . . recorded" wording seems to throw on the mortgagee the risk of the collector's delay in recording or failure to record a mortgage properly filed with him. That the mortgagee does bear the risk of the collector's improper conduct is further suggested by the fact that under many similarly worded state chattel mortgage statutes, the risk of the filing officer's failure to do what he should was cast on the mortgagee.

**§ 9–55.** The second public notice requirement of the Mortgage Act is that there be indorsed on the ship's documents certain information about the mortgage, including the names of the parties, the amount and maturity date of the mortgage and the "time and date" when the indorsement is made on the documents.[284] The "time and

Miss Darla Down, 273 F.Supp. 353 (S.D.Tex.1967) the holding was that the failure of a mortgagee to comply with the provision of § 961 next referred to in the text had no effect on the validity of the mortgage.

**282.** § 961(b). See The Franz Joseph, digested note 273a *supra*.

**283.** Under § 961(c) when a vessel covered by a preferred mortgage is sold under in rem process for the enforcement of a maritime lien other than a preferred maritime lien [i. e., a lien with priority over the mortgage under § 953, see § 9–68 *infra*], the vessel "shall be sold free from all preexisting claims thereon" but, at the request of the mortgagee, the libellant or any intervenor, the court "shall . . . require the purchaser" to give the new mortgage referred to in the text. The only case which has been found in which this strange provision has been discussed is Moore v. United States (Tomalina), 302 F.2d 918, 1966 A.M.C. 768 (D.C. Cir. 1962). The United States libeled the Tomalina in rem in an attempt to collect various statutory penalties; the mortgagee intervened in that action. The Tomalina was arrested and custodial costs were incurred which were largely in excess of the proceeds realized when she was sold. The mortgagee's request that the purchaser be required to execute a new mortgage under § 961(c) was denied on the sensible ground that the custodial costs, entitled to first priority (see § 9–61 *infra*), exhausted the fund.

**284.** § 922(c). In Port Welcome Cruises, Inc. v. S/S Bay Belle, 215 F.Supp. 72, 1964 A.M.C. 2674 (D.Md.1963), affirmed *sub nom.* Humble Oil & Refining Co. v. S/S Bay Belle, 324 F.2d 954

date" of the indorsement are also a necessary part of the recordation of the mortgage. There is no requirement that indorsement precede recordation, but evidently the recordation is not complete until the collector has made a notation of the indorsement on his books. With its customary genius for complication, the Act does not allow the mortgagee to make the indorsement and then present appropriate proof to the collector that he has done so. The indorsement must be made by the collector—either the collector at the home port, or the collector of any port where the vessel may be, on the order of the home port collector. When, because of sale or alteration, new documents are issued to a ship, the collector must indorse the new documents. Thus the mortgagee is doubly at the collector's mercy: both for the proper recordation of the mortgage and for the making of the necessary indorsement.

That both recordation and indorsement are essential to the preferred status of a mortgage was decided by the Supreme Court in Morse Dry Dock & Repair Co. v. Northern Star.[285] A mortgage for over a million dollars had been recorded on August 11, 1920. A certified copy of the mortgage was left and kept with the ship's papers (as required by the Act) from September 23, 1920. The collector, however, did not make the required indorsement on the ship's papers until June 27, 1921. Between November 14 and 17, 1920, repairs were made to the ship at the owner's request. The mortgage contained the anti-lien provision customary in charter-parties—"not to suffer nor permit to be continued any lien." The Court held, with a single justice dissenting, that the mortgagee took no profit from the recordation or from the fact that a copy of the mortgage was kept with the ship's papers or from the anti-lien provision held effective in protecting owners against materialmen dealing with charterers. "The words of the statute", wrote Justice Holmes, "seem to us too clear to be escaped. The mortgage is made preferred only upon compliance with all the conditions specified, one of which is indorsement, and the maritime lien is preferred if it arises before the recording and indorsement of the mortgage. We see no room for construction, and there is nothing for the courts to do but bow their heads and obey." [285a]

Section 941 makes the collector of customs liable to "any person . . . [who] suffers pecuniary loss" because of the collector's failure properly to perform "any duty" required of him under the Act. The section has never been construed, and does not make clear whether the collector is liable individually or in his official capacity.

(4th Cir. 1963) the mortgage showed a maturity date of April 1, 1971 while the note which the mortgage secured showed a maturity date of April 17, 1971. *Held* that the discrepancy was irrelevant under § 922(c). In Southland Financial Corp. v. O/S Mary Evelyn, 248 F.Supp. 520 (E.D.La.1965) a demand note was held to satisfy the requirement that a maturity date be stated.

285. 271 U.S. 552, 46 S.Ct. 589, 1926 A.M.C. 977 (1926).

285a. Apparently litigants have also bowed their heads and obeyed. The issue does not appear to have been relitigated.

The mortgage does not achieve preferred status until it has been both recorded and indorsed, but the Act does not require that these acts be performed within any stated period of time. A problem, whose legal complexity makes the imagination reel, could, in the event of the mortgagor's insolvency, arise under Section 60 of the Federal Bankruptcy Act, which deals with voidable preferences. Section 60 provides, in part, that where "applicable law" requires filing (or recording) for protection of the security holder against third parties but does not require the filing to be made within any stated time, the filing must be made within 21 days from the execution of the security agreement; if the filing is made beyond the 21 day period, the transfer of the collateral covered by the agreement to the security holder "is deemed to take place" at the time the filing is made, is therefore (as of that time) for an antecedent debt, and may under certain circumstances be set aside by a trustee in bankruptcy. The involved question of the interplay between bankruptcy court and admiralty court will be discussed at a later point [286] and the preference possibility will not be further explored. It is appropriate to express the hope that all mortgagees will be lucky enough to have their mortgages recorded and indorsed within 21 days of execution and that the Section 60 problem in an admiralty context will never arise to torture some unhappy judge.

**§ 9–56.** In addition to recordation and indorsement the Mortgage Act sets a third requirement which may be dealt with under the head of "public notice": the collector of customs, on recordation, is required to deliver two certified copies of the mortgage to the mortgagor who "shall place, and use due diligence to retain, one copy on board the mortgaged vessel." [287] Both the copy of the mortgage and the ship's documents are to be exhibited by the master to any person legitimately interested. The mortgagor is made liable to any person who suffers loss as a result of his failure to comply with the certified copy provision,[288] but it is hard to see how such loss could ever arise: if the indorsement on the ship's documents has not been made, the lienor or purchaser is protected by the Supreme Court's holding in the Northern Star case; if it has been made, he certainly knows of the mortgage and can hardly claim to have been misled because the certified copy was not with the ship's papers. The certified copy provision makes no kind of sense in view of the indorsement provisions. It has properly been held that the certified copy requirement is not jurisdictional, so that the mortgage does not lose its preferred status for noncompliance.[289]

286. See §§ 9–91 to 9–95 *infra*.

287. § 923.

288. § 941(c).

289. The Oconee, 280 F. 927 (E.D.Va. 1921); The Frances C. Denehy, 94 F. Supp. 807, 1951 A.M.C. 712 (D.Me. 1950). In the Bethlehem, 4 F.2d 308, 1925 A.M.C. 569 (3d Cir. 1925) a mortgage was held not to be preferred where no certified copy was kept with the ship's papers, but the court also states that a search of the ship's documents would not have revealed the mortgage; thus it is apparent that no indorsement had been made, so that

**The Ship Mortgage Act: Applicability of State or Federal Law**

**§ 9–57.** The Mortgage Act is not a comprehensive statute. It contains the detailed provisions previously discussed on the formal requisites of a preferred mortgage and on the giving of public notice through recordation and indorsement. It has also a highly important provision regulating priorities between preferred mortgages and other maritime liens, whose discussion will be deferred until the general subject of lien priorities has been reviewed.[290] It contains sketchy provisions on foreclosure: the lien of the mortgage may be enforced by suit *in rem* in admiralty and the mortgagee may also proceed *in personam* for the recovery of any deficiency.[291] That is, however, about as far as the Act goes.

At the time the first edition of the treatise was prepared the problem of how the courts were to go about filling the gaps in the Ship Mortgage Act lurked vaguely in the background but had rarely moved to front and center stage in actual litigation. In the absence of case material we reviewed, on a high level of generality, the arguments which pointed, on the one hand, to a "federal law" solution and, on the other hand, to a "state law" solution to the gap-filling problem. During the intervening period of nearly twenty years there has been a good deal of judicial discussion of the federal law vs. state law problem in ship mortgage foreclosures. During the same period there has been a notable expansion, in a good many nonmaritime fields, of the idea that gaps in federal statutes are to be filled in by improvising a corpus of federal law which is to be extrapolated from whatever is conceived to be the basic policy of the incomplete federal statute. Another significant jurisprudential event of the intervening period is that the chaotic diversity which was a notable feature of state personal property security law during the 1940's and 1950's has been reduced to something like order by the enactment of Article 9 of the Uniform Commercial Code on Secured Transactions (which is now in force in all states except Louisiana). The only constant in the equation is that the Ship Mortgage Act is exactly as gap-ridden in the 1970's as it was in the 1920's—indeed more so since the 1954 extension of the Act to cover mortgages on foreign-flag ships, an extension which will presently entangle the courts in high-level conflict of law problems.[292] For present purposes, however, we shall eschew the additional complexities presented by the 1954 amendment and see what

the mortgage would fail under the Northern Star case, note 285 *supra.* In Brandon v. S/S Denton, 302 F.2d 404, 1962 A.M.C. 1730 (5th Cir. 1962) Judge Rives, quoting the text, concluded that failure to prove that the certified copy provision had been complied with did not affect the preferred status of a mortgage.

**290.** See § 9–68 *et seq. infra.*

**291.** §§ 951–954. See § 9–94 *infra* for discussion of whether the admiralty court has exclusive jurisdiction of foreclosure actions.

**292.** On the 1954 amendment, see § 9–51 *supra.* On the type of conflicts problems that may be expected to arise, see The Tropicana, cited in notes 262a, 262b *supra.*

we can make of the problem in the context of good old American mortgages on good old American-flag ships.

The interplay between federal and state law has long been one of the principal themes of our maritime jurisprudence.[293] The federal courts, "sitting in admiralty" have recurrently proclaimed the need for national uniformity in the maritime law—a theory which, if carried to its logical extreme, would require the federalization of all aspects of that law—while at the same time they have borrowed freely from state law to supplement what Justice Holmes once described as the "very limited body of customs and ordinances of the sea" [294] and have allowed states and municipalities to exercise considerable leeway in regulating matters of local concern. We have earlier reviewed the curious history of the state-created lien enforceable only in the federal admiralty courts [295] which we may take as symbolizing the willingness of the admiralty to resort to state law to remedy a mistaken course of decision on the admiralty side. Southern Pacific Company v. Jensen [296] is usually taken as the Supreme Court's most extreme expression of the national uniformity principle. Although the Jensen case itself has long been discredited, the Supreme Court, building on the Jensen principle, has, since 1940, erected a doctrinal structure of federal law supremacy—which, however, seems to have been restricted, de facto if not de jure, to death and personal injury cases brought by or on behalf of seamen and harbor-workers. We may conclude that the eddying cross-currents of the maritime law itself are of little help in solving our problem.

Under the doctrine of Swift v. Tyson [296a] the federal courts, for nearly a century exercised an independent judgment on matters of general commercial law. What the Swift v. Tyson doctrine meant in practice was that the federal judges, in situations where competing and conflicting rules had developed on the state law level, chose what seemed to them the better rule. The announcement of a federal rule, particularly when the announcement was made in a well-reasoned opinion by the Supreme Court, frequently served to bring the conflict and controversy to an end. Over a long period of time the sort of federal synthesis of conflicting state rules which Swift v. Tyson led to did a great deal to ensure national uniformity over a broad area of the substantive law. The Swift v. Tyson idea went into decline in this century as the Supreme Court, after 1900, gradually went out of the business of deciding commercial law cases; with the Supreme Court

293. Robertson, Admiralty and Federalism—History and Analysis of Problems of Federal-State Relations in the Maritime Law of the United States (1970) is an excellent review of the problem. Professor Robertson focuses principally on the personal injury and death cases and deals only incidentally with the lien and mortgage cases.

294. Dissenting in Southern Pacific Co. v. Jensen, 244 U.S. 205, 220, 37 S.Ct. 524, 530 (1917).

295. See § 9–24 *et seq. supra.*

296. 244 U.S. 205, 37 S.Ct. 524 (1917). This aspect of the Jensen case is discussed in Chapter VI, § 6–58 *et seq.*

296a. 41 U.S. (16 Pet.) 1 (1842).

no longer available to propose the necessary syntheses the machine broke down and had to be scrapped.

When Justice Brandeis announced in Erie Railroad Co. v. Tompkins [296b] that, for a hundred years, we had been living in constitutional sin with Swift v. Tyson, the era of the federalization of the common law seemed to be at an end. However, as things turned out, the announcement of the death of the federal principle had been greatly exaggerated. Almost simultaneously with Erie the Supreme Court began to develop a new structure of what might be called federal common law. Under this developing line of cases it appeared that federal, and not state, law applied to the resolution of disputes arising under contracts to which the United States, in any of its manifold capacities, was a party. Somewhat later the idea that federal statutes carry with them a sort of floating penumbra of potential common law—an idea that earlier generations of jurists would have dismissed without a second thought—began to gain ever increasing acceptance. The process of federalization seems also to have been obscurely at work in other areas. The Bankruptcy Act of 1898, for example, as originally drafted, provided not much more than a procedural framework for the liquidation of insolvent estates; substantive questions of property rights were implicitly left to be decided under state law. The history of our life with the Bankruptcy Act has been that decade by decade, partly as the result of successive amendments to the Act but even more as the result of the accumulating case law, the federal law component has strengthened as the state law component has weakened. And, as we know, since 1940 the federal supremacy idea has had a notable career within the confines of the maritime law itself. By the mid-1960's the revitalization of the federal law principle was so far advanced that one of our most distinguished federal judges chose, as the title for a major address: In Praise of *Erie*—and of the New Federal Common Law.[296c]

There is no question but that, under the post-Erie developments summarized in the preceding paragraph, a powerful case can be made for a root and branch federal law solution to the problem of filling the many gaps in the Ship Mortgage Act. We are concerned not only with a federal statute but with a system of ship financing which is in considerable part guaranteed by the United States under Title XI of the Merchant Marine Act [296d] and also with an area of law which is, constitutionally, committed to the "judicial power of the United States". However, before we go whole-hog for the federal law solution, we will do well to ask ourselves what goal we are aiming at and how that goal can best be achieved.

**296b.** 304 U.S. 64, 58 S.Ct. 817 (1938).

**296c.** Judge Henry Friendly in his Cardozo Lecture delivered to the Association of the Bar of the City of New York in 1964, reprinted 39 N.Y.U.L. Rev. 383 (1964). See further, Friendly, Federal Jurisdiction: A General View (1973). For a review of the post-Erie federalization process in various fields, see 1 Gilmore, Security Interests in Personal Property, Chapter 13 (1965).

**296d.** See § 9–51(a) *supra.*

Our thesis will be that the federalization of the substantive law in any area, both under the Swift v. Tyson formula and under the several post-Erie formulae, aims at the achievement of a desirable degree of national uniformity in a relatively decentralized federal system. Today as in the past the case for a federal solution becomes strongest when the state law rules, decisional or statutory, have become fragmented and diverse. There is no need for a federal solution when national uniformity has been achieved, by codification or otherwise, on a state level. Indeed the pursuit of a federal solution under such circumstances may well contribute to the destruction of the uniformity of the substantive law which the federal principle is designed to ensure.

Until the 1960's state personal property security law relating to chattel mortgages, conditional sales, trust receipts and all the other so-called security devices was, and for a hundred years had been, bewilderingly diverse. If that situation had continued, the case for a federalization of all the law relating to ship mortgages would have been overwhelming. Today (except in Louisiana) all security interests in personal property are governed by Article 9 of the Uniform Commercial Code. It is true that the versions of Article 9 enacted in some states—notably New York and California—contained a good many departures from the "official" statutory text, so that complete national uniformity has not been achieved. It is also true that a fairly comprehensive revision of Article 9 which was promulgated in 1972 may lead to a certain amount of disunity if it is enacted by some states and rejected by others.[296e] Even so, it is clear that the Article 9 codification has, for the first time, provided a uniform base for personal property security transactions which may be expected to remain relatively stable for the next generation or two. All that being true, Article 9 would seem to be the appropriate source for the federal courts to look to in working out the developing law of ship mortgages. It makes not the slightest difference whether Article 9 is applied directly as state law or indirectly or analogically as a statement of what the federal law of ship mortgages would be if there was a federal law of ship mortgages.

The point should be made that no thought was given in the drafting of either the original Article 9 or of the 1972 revision to the special problems of ship mortgages or ship financing.[296f] If Article 9 is taken as a source of law in ship mortgage foreclosure cases, the job should be done mutatis mutandis. The case will undoubtedly be that some Article 9 provisions, translated into a maritime context, will make no sense. In such a case the federal courts should feel free to improvise a federal law solution that does make sense. In many other cases the Article 9 provisions will make quite as much sense

**296e.** At the present time the 1972 revision of Article 9 has been enacted in six states. So far as is known no state legislature has rejected the proposed revision.

**296f.** The writer served as a draftsman of the original Article 9 and as a consultant to the Committee which prepared the 1972 revision.

with respect to seagoing industrial equipment as they do with respect to land-based equipment. In such cases they should be applied, directly or analogically. What is called for is a sensitive adaptation of a current state law codification to the special problems presented by the use of wandering ships as security.

So far as Article 9 itself goes, § 9–104 (captioned: Transactions Excluded from Article) provides in part:

> "This Article does not apply (a) to a security interest subject to any statute of the United States such as the Ship Mortgage Act, 1920, to the extent that such statute governs the rights of parties to and third parties affected by transactions in particular types of property . . . ." [296g]

As we have already pointed out, the Ship Mortgage Act has almost nothing to say either about the rights of the parties inter sese or about the rights of third parties affected by their transactions. Thus, in effect, § 9–104(a) proposes a state law solution to the many questions left unanswered by the Ship Mortgage Act and the other federal security statutes which cover security interests in aircraft, railroad equipment, patents, copyrights and so on. The Code provision quoted was drafted in the 1940's and has not since been changed in substance; thus it represents an approach to the problem of filling gaps in federal statutes which antedates the current theory that federal statutes are somehow to generate their own solutions to such problems. Nevertheless, for whatever it may be worth, § 9–104(a) does suggest that the facilities of Article 9 are being offered to courts which are called on to construe the incomplete and fragmentary federal security statutes.[296h]

The role which Article 9 is to play in the resolution of our problem has not as yet been determined. All the cases which have so far been reported involving a choice between federal and state law have dealt with pre-Code transactions in what are now Code states or have come up in Louisiana. On the whole—with the exception of a notable

**296g.** The specific reference to the Ship Mortgage Act was deleted from the 1972 revision.

**296h.** The only other "maritime" reference in Article 9 is an amendment promulgated in 1966 which provides that ship charters are not "chattel paper" (§ 9–105(b)) and that "All rights earned or unearned under a charter or other contract involving the use or hire of a vessel and all rights incident to the charter or contract are contract rights and neither accounts nor general intangibles" (§ 9–106). (In the 1972 version, the term "contract rights" is no longer used; what were "contract rights" under the original § 9–106 are "accounts" under revised § 9–106). It is the writer's recollection that the "charter" amendments were put forward by a group of New York counsel interested in maritime financing; their reasons for insisting on the amendments seemed to be impenetrably obscure. The only result of calling assignments of charter-hire "contract rights" (or "accounts") is that the assignments can be "perfected" only by filing a financing statement. If the charters had been treated as "chattel paper" then either filing or taking possession of the charter would have been available as methods of perfection. Evidently the proponents of the amendment assumed that state law (Article 9) applies to assignments of charter-hire.

1972 decision in the Fifth Circuit[296i]—the cases have leaned, explicitly or implicitly, toward a state law solution. Not infrequently the opinions in the state law cases have cited a comment in our discussion of the problem in the first edition of the treatise: "On a practical level . . . state law is the only [mortgage] law there is."

The Fifth Circuit seemed implicitly to adopt a state law approach in Merchants & Marine Bank v. F/V T. E. Welles.[296j] The Bank had taken a mortgage which was entitled to preferred status on March 9, 1956; for some reason the Bank, on March 29, 1957, took another mortgage, also entitled to preferred status, described as a "renewal" of the 1956 mortgage which was marked satisfied as of record. Various liens for supplies and repairs had attached to the vessel between the dates of the two mortgages. If the lien of the renewal mortgage attached on March 29, 1957, the supply and repair liens had priority. On the other hand if the mortgage lien related back to the date of the original mortgage, the mortgage had priority over the subsequent liens. Judge Brown commented that the question should be decided in the light of "generally well-accepted legal principles concerning mortgages . . . the approach ought to be one of harmony with usual security principles." The "accepted rule", he went on, quoting the Am.Jur. article on Mortgages and two A.L.R. annotations, is that a renewal mortgage is entitled to the same priority as the original mortgage. Therefore the intermediate liens were subordinated.[296k]

The implicit bias of The T. E. Welles was made explicit in several District Court cases decided during the 1960's. In Southland Financial Corporation v. O/S Mary Evelyn[296l] the mortgagors sought to have an admiralty foreclosure action dismissed on several grounds, the principal one being that the mortgage provided for future advances and that nothing in the Ship Mortgage Act authorized a future advance arrangement.[296m] Judge West, citing our discussion of the problem, commented:

> "There is no Federal law of mortgages except such as is contained in specific statutes such as the Ship's Mortgage Act.

**296i.** McDermott & Co., Inc. v. The Morning Star, 457 F.2d 815, 1972 A.M.C. 907 (5th Cir. 1972), discussed in the text following note 296s *infra*.

**296j.** 289 F.2d 188, 1961 A.M.C. 1042 (5th Cir. 1961).

**296k.** The T. E. Welles was followed in Barnouw v. S/S Ozark, 304 F.2d 717, 1962 A.M.C. 1675 (5th Cir. 1962), certiorari denied *sub nom.* Socony Mobil Oil Co. v. Wall Street Traders, Inc., 371 U.S. 923, 83 S.Ct. 291 (1962). To the authorities he had cited in The T. E. Welles, Judge Brown added, in The Ozark, a reference to Tiffany on Real Property. He also made the point that the renewal mortgage inherits the priority of the original mortgage only to the amount of the unpaid balance under the original mortgage at the time the renewal mortgage is executed. The Court's attention in The Ozark was not directed to the problem of priority for future advances.

**296l.** 248 F.Supp. 520, 1966 A.M.C. 336 (E.D.La.1965).

**296m.** Since no competing liens were involved the Court did not have to deal with the complicated problem whether later advances under the mortgage would take priority over intervening liens. For the common law

> Where voids appear, it is necessary for the Court to look to other sources for its answers. While the Federal Court may not be bound by State law in such an instance, nevertheless, the State law is the logical place to look for guidance."

Having found that future advance arrangements were recognized under the law of Louisiana and of most other states, he ruled in favor of the mortgage and its foreclosure. Judge West's decision in the Mary Evelyn was expressly followed in Bergren v. Davis.[296n] Competing lienors argued that a mortgage given by a shipowner to his mother was essentially a sham or fraud in that no money had been advanced by the "mortgagee". Judge Timbers, after paraphrasing the passage from Judge West's opinion quoted above, characterized the issue presented as being whether failure of consideration was an available defense in the light of the fact that the mortgage had been executed under seal. That issue, he said, should be decided under Maine law, Maine being the state where the mortgage had been executed and recorded (the vessel's home port being in Maine). After a careful examination of the Maine cases (nonmaritime), he concluded that the defense of failure of consideration was, if proved, available despite the seal and set the case down for trial.[296o]

The cases so far cited have suggested or held that state law is the obvious or logical or only source to look to in deciding issues raised in ship mortgage foreclosures where the Ship Mortgage Act contains nothing relevant. There have been, however, several other cases in which the opinions (as distinguished from the holdings) contain what might be described as "federalist language". In Mastan Company, Inc. v. Steinberg (S/S Sapphire Sandy) [296p] a mortgage was attacked

background and the treatment of the priority problem under Article 9 of the Code see 2 Gilmore, Security Interests in Personal Property, Chapter 35 (1965).

**296n.** 287 F.Supp. 52 (D.Conn.1968).

**296*o*.** The Mary Evelyn was also expressly followed in First Federal Savings and Loan Ass'n of Puerto Rico v. Zequiera, 288 F.Supp. 384 (D.Puerto Rico 1968). The Court commented that "the validity, effect and construction of mortgage liens is determined by the law of the state in which the mortgaged property is located." The issue presented was the confirmation of a public sale of a vessel pursuant to a default judgment in a preferred mortgage foreclosure. The Court concluded that the sale had been properly carried out under Puerto Rico law and that there was in any case no conflict between Puerto Rico law and the provisions of 28 U.S.C.A. §§ 2001, 2004 on judicial sales.

Ridings v. M/V Effort, 387 F.2d 888, 1968 A.M.C. 308 (2d Cir. 1968) may also be listed as a case leaning toward a state law solution although Judge Feinberg noted that on the point at issue (whether under negotiable instruments law the party accommodated can ever recover against the accommodating party) "we need not decide whether New York or federal law is applicable in a case under the Ship Mortgage Act [citing the first edition of the treatise], since we see no indication that New York law and general law differ." After that disclaimer, Judge Feinberg set out the relevant provisions of the Uniform Commercial Code which he followed with a string citation of cases decided under the Negotiable Instruments Law. Further proceedings in the case are reported under the same caption in 434 F.2d 183, 1971 A.M.C. 662 (2d Cir. 1970).

**296p.** 418 F.2d 177 (3d Cir. 1969), certiorari denied *sub nom.* Todd Shipyards v. Mastan Co., Inc., 397 U.S. 1009, 90 S.Ct. 1238 (1970).

by competing lienors as a fraudulent conveyance under New York law. The Court, after accepting a finding by a Special Master that the mortgage was "patently supported by full and fair consideration" (so that it was not, under any theory, a fraudulent conveyance), went on to develop the argument that federal, not state, law should provide the answers to such questions.[296q] The point need hardly be made that neither the Third Circuit nor any other court would ever hold that the Ship Mortgage Act had somehow immunized ship mortgages from attack under fraudulent conveyance theory; if the Court in Mastan had not been satisfied on the "full and fair consideration" point it would either have applied New York fraudulent conveyance law or gone on to discover that there is after all a federal law of fraudulent conveyances under § 67(d) of the Bankruptcy Act and a great deal of Bankruptcy Act case law.[296r]

The strongest statement of the case for a federal law solution to gaps in the Ship Mortgage Act is to be found in McDermott & Co., Inc. v. Morning Star.[296s] McDermott agreed to build, for a contract price of something over $2,500,000, several vessels suitable for menhaden fishing; the buyers were corporations controlled by the Smith family ("giants of the menhaden fishing world"). The Smith interests gave their note for the contract price to McDermott, secured by mortgages on the vessels, and the mortgages were properly recorded and endorsed. The vessels turned out not to be suitable for menhaden fishing. The Smith interests brought an action for breach of contract against McDermott; McDermott brought an action to foreclose its mortgages. The United States Marshal disposed of the vessels at a public sale; McDermott, who was the only bidder, bought them for $689,000. The two actions were then consolidated for trial. In the breach of contract action there was a judgment entered on a jury verdict for McDermott; in the foreclosure action, the court ordered a deficiency judgment in favor of McDermott in the amount of the difference between the proceeds of the sale and the mortgage debt represented by the note. On appeal a panel of the Fifth Circuit reversed the judgment in the breach of contract action on the ground of improper instructions to the jury. The panel also reversed the deci-

**296q.** Judge Aldisert wrote that "to engraft the various nuances of state law onto federal legislation would introduce an undesirable lack of uniformity in the interpretation of congressional enactments . . . it would condition the validity of ship mortgages on the idiosyncracies of local law rather than their conformity to national interests." (418 F.2d at p. 179.)

**296r.** Other cases in which the opinion contain "federalist language" are United States v. American Gas Screw Franz Joseph, 210 F.Supp. 581, 1963 A.M.C. 1596 (D.Alaska 1962) (holding, however, that "Under California law, the waiver in writing of the statute of limitations is valid and enforceable") and United States v. Oil Screws Ken, Jr., Linda, Sue etc., 275 F.Supp. 792 (E.D.La.1967) (in which the principal issue was not a gap in the Ship Mortgage Act but the construction of one of its express provisions).

**296s.** 431 F.2d 714, 1970 A.M.C. 2228 (5th Cir. 1970), on rehearing en banc original opinion vacated and withdrawn, 457 F.2d 815, 1972 A.M.C. 907 (5th Cir. 1972), certiorari denied 409 U.S. 948, 93 S.Ct. 271 (1972).

sion on the deficiency judgment on the ground that a Louisiana statute forbade the entry of a deficiency judgment following a public sale unless there had been a pre-sale appraisal of the property (which had not been had). As authorities for the applicability of the Louisiana statute Judge Coleman cited the first edition of the treatise, Bergren v. Davis [296t] and the Mary Evelyn.[296u] Before the breach of contract action had been retried, the Court granted a rehearing en banc on the issue of the deficiency judgment. Over the dissents of the members of the original panel, the majority of the Court held that the Louisiana statute could not be applied to bar a deficiency judgment in a foreclosure action under the Ship Mortgage Act. Judge Dyer, for the majority, pointed out that sales of property ordered by federal courts are governed by the provisions of 28 U.S.C.A. §§ 2001 and 2004, which (unlike the Louisiana deficiency statute) do not require an appraisal before a public sale. "We perceive no void in the statutory scheme here. Therefore, it is not necessary to turn to state law to implement the act with respect to deficiency judgments." [296v] In reaching his conclusion that there was "no void in the statutory scheme" Judge Dyer sketched a comprehensive argument for the federal law solution: "Congress intended that the ready availability of credit to support interstate commerce should not be impeded by parochial limitations and that the [Ship Mortgage] Act would wholly and completely supersede state law and practice in every respect."

With deference, it will be suggested that Judge Dyer's proposition that the Ship Mortgage Act "wholly and completely supersede[s] state law and practice in every respect" was unnecessary to the decision. The en banc majority felt that a federal policy with respect to deficiency judgments following court-ordered sales had been established by a federal statute other than the Ship Mortgage Act; therefore there was "no void in the statutory scheme" and no reason to turn to state law to fill a nonexistent "void". The idea that federal law, decisional or statutory, other than the Ship Mortgage Act can be used to cure the Act's deficiencies is entirely reasonable. In the same way, as we suggested in our discussion of the Mastan case, the Third Circuit, if it had thought it was dealing with a fraudulent conveyance, might well have gone on to discover a federal law of fraudulent conveyances applicable to preferred ship mortgages. There is no need to take the rhetorical exuberance of the majority opinion in McDermott as casting doubt on the earlier cases, including the Fifth Circuit cases on the priority of renewal mortgages, which had looked to state law sources in the absence of any relevant federal materials.[296w]

**296t.** Text at note 296n *supra*.

**296u.** Text at note 296*l* *supra*.

**296v.** 457 F.2d at p. 818; 1972 A.M.C. at p. 910. Judge Dyer went on to quote the passage from the Third Circuit Mastan opinion reproduced in note 296q *supra*.

**296w.** In Harrison Overseas Corp. v. American Barge Sun Coaster, 475 F.2d 504, 1973 A.M.C. 1174 (5th Cir. 1973) Judge Brown reaffirmed the "federalist" position of the McDermott case. The Sun Coaster did not, however, involve a "gap" or "void" in the Ship Mortgage Act. Under § 926(d) "A preferred mortgage

The case law results, to date, make up a reasonably harmonious pattern. In handling ship mortgage foreclosures the courts, in situations where no provision of the Ship Mortgage Act appears to be relevant, have looked to expressions of federal policy in other federal statutes or in federal decisional law; in the absence of any help from federal sources they have gone on to consult the available state law sources. On the other hand, in cases where an appropriate federal source other than the Ship Mortgage Act has been found, the opinions have occasionally seemed to say that state law can never be looked to to supplement the practically nonexistent federal law of mortgages. What the courts have been doing has made a great deal of sense; it is to be hoped that the judges who have announced an extreme "federalist" position will be astute enough to avoid tripping over their own rhetoric in later cases where there is no solution to be found on the federal level.

We suggested at an earlier point of our discussion that a federal law solution mostly involves choosing between conflicting state law rules. Since personal property security law is now represented by Article 9 of the Code in forty-nine states, the only choice that is available would seem to be between Article 9 and Louisiana law—which might conceivably be destined for an unlikely eminence as the source of a federal law of mortgages. On the other hand if Louisiana, abandoning her civil law tradition, should enact the Uniform Commercial Code, then Article 9, by default, would become the only available source for the federal law of mortgages.

### Equipment and the Title Retention Problem

**§ 9–57a.** Equipment is frequently furnished to or installed on vessels under arrangements such as leases or conditional sales whereby the furnisher seeks to retain title to the equipment. The effectiveness of the title retention device against maritime liens on the vessel is a problem that has been with us for a long time—indeed the issue first surfaced in litigation during the nineteenth century before anyone had ever heard of a ship mortgage with maritime lien status. The creation of the preferred ship mortgage led to a new variant of the old problem: the effectiveness of a title retention agreement against the mortgage. If the draftsmen of the Ship Mortgage Act had been reasonably competent, they would no doubt have provided a solution; they were not and did not. The courts were left to work

may bear such rate of interest as is agreed by the parties thereto." *Held* that the Georgia usury statute could not be pleaded in a foreclosure action. Judge Wisdom had discussed the relationship between § 926(d) and state usury laws in C.I.T. Corp. v. M/V Miss Eileen, 447 F.2d 761 (5th Cir. 1971) but had remanded the case for further proceedings without deciding the issue. On another issue in The Sun Coaster (the proper allocation of payments between principal and interest) Judge Brown rejected the application of a "federal rule" claimed to be based on an 1837 Supreme Court case. The dealings between the parties, according to Judge Brown, showed that they had chosen not to follow the federal rule. In this part of his opinion he cited, "by way of illustration", a provision of the Uniform Commercial Code.

out the not uncomplicated problem of whether the pre-1920 case law relating to the effectiveness of the title retention against real maritime liens carried over to the case of the artificial maritime lien created by the Act.

We may take The Hope [296x] as illustrative of the pre-1920 situation. The owner of the Hope, a fishing vessel, had bought two pieces of equipment on what were, in effect, conditional sale contracts: an engine (to replace an engine that had worn out) and an apparently somewhat novel piece of equipment called a net-lifter. An engine was of course essential to the vessel's operation; the net-lifter was convenient and useful but not essential. Before the purchase price of either the engine or the net-lifter had been paid in full the Hope was sunk in Gloucester Harbor; her owner was drowned. Before the sinking and death, liens for supplies and repairs had attached to the vessel; liens for wages and salvage were also proved. The conclusion that the liens prevailed over the conditional sales was foregone: even if the conditional sale contracts had created maritime liens (which of course they did not) they would, under the normal rules of priority, have been subordinated at least to the wage and salvage liens and in all probability to the supply and repair liens as well. The interesting aspect of Judge Dodge's opinion is that he carefully distinguished between the engine contract and the net-lifter contract. The supply and repair lienors, he suggested, would have priority over the seller of the engine whether the supplies and repairs were "furnished before or after the engine was put in" on the ground that the engine was "part of [the Hope's] general equipment as a vessel". On the other hand the net-lifter contract would have been good against existing contract liens at the time the net-lifter was installed since people dealing with vessels like the Hope would not assume that they would be so equipped. Contract liens arising subsequent to installation of either the engine or the net-lifter might have been subordinated to the sellers' interests if the lienors had known of the reservation of title. Finding that the lienors were not chargeable with knowledge, he ordered distribution of the fund to the maritime liens according to the usual order of priority.

Cases like The Hope are by no means free of ambiguity when the opinions are read with care. However, if the ambiguities are disregarded, the cases can be generalized and said to stand for the proposition that title retention agreements, at least those relating to essential equipment, are ineffective against all maritime liens. And if the maritime lien of a preferred mortgage is equated with the traditional maritime liens, then the title retention agreement will lose to the mortgage even when the equipment was furnished subsequent to the mortgage's execution, recordation and indorsement. That was indeed the result which was reached in First Suffolk Nat. Bank of Huntington v. The Air Brant.[296y] Subsequent to the recordation of a mortgage, fish pumps were installed on the vessel subject to a conditional sale con-

296x. 191 F. 243 (D.Mass.1911).

296y. 125 F.Supp. 709 (E.D.N.Y.1954).

tract; furthermore, certain blocks and davits were installed under what was described as a loan arrangement. Both the conditionally sold pumps and the loaned blocks and davits were found to be essential to the vessel's navigation and operation. Hence, Judge Inch concluded, citing The Hope and other cases, the Marshal was to sell the ship, including the pumps, blocks and davits, with the proceeds of the sale going to satisfy the mortgage. On the other hand it was "agreed by all parties" that other equipment on the vessel, evidently regarded as not essential to its navigation and operation, "should be removed . . . prior to the sale or excepted from the sale."

The result in cases like The Air Brant [296z] is indefensible. The mortgagee received as a windfall the value of subsequent improvements in the vessel for which he had paid nothing. If the law is that equipment installed on a vessel always and under all circumstances feeds the lien of a pre-existing mortgage, then the law is an ass. The intellectual vice in cases like The Air Brant lies in the uncritical assumption that the pre-1920 cases like The Hope carried over to the quite different situation presented by the conflict between the holder of an old mortgage and the furnishers of new equipment. In cases like The Hope the furnishers of the equipment were in conflict with lienors who had themselves furnished new value to the vessel (as by making repairs or providing supplies) or who had been injured by maritime torts for which the vessel was liable. The distinction vaguely suggested in The Hope between essential and non essential equipment really went to a question of notice: with respect to such things as engines, the lienors were entitled to rely on the assumption that the engines went with the vessel; with respect to net-lifters and the like, at least the contract lienors might be subordinated if they had reason to know that the net-lifter had not been paid for. The typical situation in the pre-1920 cases was that the liens arose, chronologically, after the installation of the equipment. Giving priority to the liens was entirely consistent with the basic principle of maritime lien law: the lien latest in time rides over earlier liens. Giving priority to the mortgage in cases like The Air Brant reverses the normal order and prefers old value to new value.

That new value (typically purchase money) equipment financing should have priority over a lien claimed under the after-acquired property clause of a general mortgage was a proposition which the courts seem to have accepted as almost self-evident when the issue first arose in litigation shortly after the Civil War in the context of railroad equipment financing. In other contexts the judicial response was the same. With the codification of security law under Article 9 of the Code the priority for purchase money interests over others was of course maintained.[296aa] It would be both unfortunate and unneces-

**296z.** For collections of other cases of the same type, see Gyory, Security at Sea: A Review of the Preferred Ship Mortgage, 31 Fordham L.Rev. 231, 263 *et seq.* (1962); Smith, Ship Mortgages, 47 Tulane L.Rev. 608, 617–618 (1973).

**296aa.** On the common law development of the purchase money priority, see 1 Gilmore, Security Interests in Personal Property, Chapter 28 (1965); on the Article 9 codification of the priority, *id.* Chapters 29, 30.

sary if the underlying and sound principle that new money should have priority over old money were to be ignored in this area of ship financing. Fortunately there are indications in some of the recent cases that a long-overdue reexamination of cases like The Air Brant is beginning to make progress.

In United States v. F/V Golden Dawn [296bb] it appeared that "certain Echo-depth Sounding Equipment" known as a "Fishfinder" had been installed on the Golden Dawn. The Fishfinder had been leased to the owners by Raytheon and bore a nameplate and property tag which described it as "Property of Raytheon Company". Subsequently the United States took a preferred mortgage on the Golden Dawn. On default under the mortgage the United States instituted foreclosure proceedings; Raytheon intervened seeking to reclaim the Fishfinder. Judge Dooling reviewed the authorities in an impressive opinion which is particularly notable for its clear differentiation between the statutory lien of a preferred mortgage and the traditional maritime lien. He assumed that the Fishfinder had been installed on the Golden Dawn in such a way that the lien of the mortgage would attach to it as between the owner and the mortgagee:

> "But that does not mean [he went on] that such a mortgage as the present one reaches leased equipment that is aboard the ship when it is mortgaged or is added after the mortgage is given. [He then noted that such equipment although not "reached" by the mortgage might nevertheless become subject to "preferred maritime liens".] The present mortgage has the preferred status defined in 46 U.S. Code, sec. 953 and the access to admiralty for enforcement granted to it by 46 U.S. Code, sec. 951; it has not the nature of a preferred maritime lien nor does it operate as they do; it remains a security instrument pledging, essentially, the mortgagor's interests of ownership for the payment of his—not the ship's—debts. Nothing in the nature of the ship mortgage, nor in the terms of its statutory implementation, suggests that its lien should extend to what the mortgagor did not own and had no right to acquire. . . . [T]he principle is plain and, if it be the case that a lessor's title fails as against the true maritime "liens" of tort claimants, seamen seeking their wages and those who furnish necessaries to the vessel when she is at a strange port . . . there is no reason to extend it beyond that to the unanalogous case of the preferred ship mortgage." [296cc]

Judge Dooling noted (citing The Air Brant and other cases, including The Hope) that "unrecorded conditional sales contracts have not presented much resistance either to maritime liens or ship mortgages." However, he concluded, in giving judgment for Raytheon, the Raytheon arrangement was a true lease, not a disguised security trans-

**296bb.** 222 F.Supp. 186, 1964 A.M.C. 691 (E.D.N.Y.1963).

**296cc.** 222 F.Supp. at pp. 188, 189; 1964 A.M.C. at pp. 695, 696–697.

action, and the United States, because of the "Property of Raytheon Company" nameplate, was on notice of Raytheon's interest when it took its mortgage.[296dd]

Judge Dooling's helpful clarification of the essential difference between the "true" maritime lien and the mortgage lien has received further support in the much-litigated First Circuit case of The Tropic Breeze.[296ee] Tropical Commerce Corporation was the time charterer of the Tropic Breeze. Under the charter Tropical was to instal cement loading, bagging and discharging equipment "reserving title thereto but with the obligation to remove at the termination of the charter" and to restore the vessel to its original state. National Western Life Insurance Company took a preferred mortgage on the vessel; the mortgage was executed before installation of the equipment but after the charter had been entered into; the Life Insurance Company knew of the terms of the charter. The equipment was installed but the operation of the vessel was unprofitable; eventually it was libeled by the crew for unpaid wages and the mortgagee along with other lien claimants intervened. Following The Golden Dawn the Court held that the charterer's retention of title to the equipment was effective against the mortgage but that the equipment, considered to be "essential to [the vessel's] navigation and operation", was nevertheless subject to the liens (the mortgagee was held to be subrogated to liens which he had paid off).

The current state of the law has been summarized, not inaccurately, as follows:

> "If title [to equipment installed on a mortgaged vessel] has been retained by a third party, the courts generally but not uniformly make a distinction between title retention based on actual ownership (*i. e.*, where the property is supplied by a lessor or charterer), and the retention of mere security title (*i. e.*, conditional sale). In the latter case, the courts have held that the owner-mortgagor is the owner and that the [mortgage] lien reaches the property. . . . When title retention is simply a security device, the courts feel that they are dealing merely with a question of priorities upon which the Act is clear. When title is retained on the basis of actual ownership and not simply a disguised conditional sale, however, the courts generally hold that the lien does not reach the property in question." [296ff]

**296dd.** The Golden Dawn was followed in C.I.T. Corp. v. O/S Peggy, 424 F.2d 767, 1970 A.M.C. 1550 (5th Cir. 1970) another "true lease" case in which radar equipment had been installed on the Peggy subsequent to the mortgage.

**296ee.** Payne v. S/S Tropic Breeze, 412 F.2d 707 (1st Cir. 1969); National Western Life Ins. Co. v. Tropical Commerce Corp. (S/S Tropic Breeze); 456 F.2d 137, 1972 A.M.C. 1622 (1st Cir. 1972). In an intervening opinion, 423 F.2d 236, 1970 A.M.C. 1850, certiorari denied, *sub. nom.* Samadjopoulos v. National Western Life Insurance Co., 400 U.S. 964, 91 S.Ct. 363 (1970), the court had disposed of various questions relating to liens and priorities.

**296ff.** Smith, Ship Mortgages, 47 Tulane L.Rev. 608, 618 (1973). Footnotes have been omitted.

If that is the current state of the law, it is submitted that change is in order. The reasons which justify giving the lessor priority over the mortgagee in The Golden Dawn and the charterer priority over the mortgagee in The Tropic Breeze apply with equal force to the case of equipment furnished under a conditional sale or an Article 9 purchase money security interest. (As The Golden Dawn and The Tropic Breeze have made clear, priority over the mortgage does not mean priority over the true or preferred maritime liens.) There is no need or reason or even excuse for the admiralty courts to engage in word-chopping games about whether the arrangement under which the equipment is furnished is a "true lease" or a "security lease" or an outright "security interest". An Article 9 secured party holding a purchase money security interest is quite as respectable and quite as meritorious as any "true lessor".

The case for priority of the security interest, lease or what-not over the mortgage seems entirely clear when (as in The Air Brant) the mortgage antedates the installation of the equipment and the mortgagee makes no further advances: in such a case the mortgagee has not relied on the equipment and receives an outrageous windfall if he is allowed to claim it with priority over the secured party or lessor. When the installation of the equipment antedates the mortgage (as in The Golden Dawn) there is a real problem of notice.[296gg] Whether admiralty courts would hold mortgagees bound by financing statements filed under Article 9 is problematical and, indeed, it is by no means clear, under the Article 9 filing provisions, where such a financing statement should be filed. (Nevertheless equipment financers might just as well make a filing for whatever it may be worth.) There is no indication in the reported cases that equipment financers have attempted filing with the Collector of Customs in the vessel's home port under 46 U.S.C.A. § 921 (the Vessel Recording Act), even though § 921, carefully read, would seem to authorize such a filing (or recording).[296hh] There remains the device of the nameplate or property tag which Judge Dooling found to be effective against a subsequent mortgagee in The Golden Dawn. Once the notice problem is solved, the case for giving priority to the purchase money equipment interest over the later mortgage seems quite as cogent in the maritime context as it has always seemed to the courts to be in the context of industrial equipment financing on land.[296ii]

**296gg.** In Merrill-Stevens Dry Dock Co. v. M/V Laissez-Faire, 421 F.2d 430, 1970 A.M.C. 38 (5th Cir. 1970) a conditional seller of radio equipment was given priority over a subsequent mortgagee who had actual knowledge of the title retention.

**296hh.** In his Golden Dawn opinion Judge Dooling commented that: "It is somewhat difficult to understand that the conditional sales cases have usually been disposed of without reference to 46 U.S.C.A. § 921 . . . presumably because of the modest language problem." (222 F.Supp. at p. 189; 1964 A.M.C. at p. 697). In The Laissez-Faire, note 296gg *supra*, the argument was made that a conditional seller ought to have filed his interest in the vessel's home port in Honduras.

**296ii.** United States v. F/V Voyager, 1973 A.M.C. 1742 (E.D.Va.1973) seems like a nightmarish switch on the cases which have been discussed. Smola (a corporation) installed a "fishscope" on the Voyager under what was de-

### Priorities Among Maritime Liens: Introduction

**§ 9–58.** "The subject of marshalling liens in admiralty is one which, unfortunately, is left in great obscurity by the authorities." Brown, J. in The City of Tawas, 1880.[297]

". . . the question in this case [is] whether a claim of a prior class is to be postponed to a claim of a subsequent class when the latter claim has been earned on a later voyage, season, or 40-day period. That question seems involved in much obscurity and is one difficult to answer." Rogers, J., in The Samuel Little, 1915.[298]

". . . much uncertainty still exists in the decisions and the textbooks as to the underlying principle controlling priorities among maritime liens." Beach, J. in the Yale Law Journal, 1924.[299]

scribed as a conditional sales contract (which was not filed or recorded). Subsequently the United States, which did not know of Smola's claim to the fishscope, took a preferred mortgage on the Voyager. The owners of the Voyager defaulted on both the fishscope contract and the mortgage (and were subsequently adjudicated bankrupts). The United States initiated a foreclosure proceeding in which Smola intervened to claim priority as to the fishscope (which was found to be "an integral part" of the ship's equipment —that is, essential to her use). Judge Hoffman, electing to follow The Air Brant (text following note 296y *supra*), concluded that the fishscope was subject to the preferred ship mortgage. Suddenly reversing his field, he then held that Smola's claim had priority over the mortgage as a pre-mortgage lien for "repairs, supplies . . . or other necessaries" (under § 971 of the Maritime Lien Act), entitled to priority under § 953(a) of the Ship Mortgage Act (see §§ 9–71 *et seq. infra*). Thus although Smola lost as a "conditional seller" he won as the holder of a "pre-mortgage maritime lien". The suggestion that furnishers of equipment, like Smola, should be treated as "maritime lienors" in priority contests with prior or subsequent mortgagees leads to outlandish results. Under the ill-advised priority provisions of the Ship Mortgage Act such a furnisher would, under Judge Hoffman's approach, always win over a subsequent mortgage (even though the mortgagee did not know and had no way of finding out about the furnisher's claim) and would always lose to a mortgage which had been recorded and indorsed before the equipment was furnished. In the foregoing discussion we have indicated our reasons for believing that the opposite results from those just suggested should be arrived at. In dry land security law there are situations in which a lender would be subordinated to competing claims as a mortgagee but would have priority over them as an ordinary unsecured creditor of the mortgagor. In such situations the courts have consistently held that a lender, if he took a mortgage, cannot divest himself of that status in order to claim as a creditor. See, e. g., McGann v. Capital Sav. Bank and Trust Co., 117 Vt. 179, 89 A.2d 123 (1952). By parity of reasoning, furnishers of maritime equipment on lease, conditional sale or purchase money security interest should stand or fall as such and should not be given a second chance as "maritime lienors". Of course, under Judge Hoffman's approach, the premortgage furnishers of the equipment will be better off as simple "lienors" without taking any security interest (or lease) in the equipment. If such a practice develops, it is to be hoped that the courts will be able to distinguish between purchase money equipment financing on the one hand and the traditional maritime liens for "repairs, supplies . . . or other necessaries" on the other.

297. 3 F. 170 (E.D.Mich.1880).

298. 221 F. 308 (2d Cir. 1915).

299. Beach, Relative Priority of Maritime Liens, 33 Yale L.J. 841 (1924).

> "The question of priority of maritime liens is filled with confusion. . . . There is the general rule that maritime liens rank in an order inverse to the order of their creation. . . . Generally speaking the law of maritime liens may be said to be made up of exceptions to the above doctrine . . ." Coleman, J. in The William Leishear, 1927.[300]

> "It is submitted that the present system of priorities among maritime liens is in need of revision. . . ." E. L. Willard Esq. in the Cornell Law Quarterly, 1931.[301]

> "Predictability is at a low level. Nonetheless, the existing rules and policies can be pinpointed, and when this is done some of the alleged uncertainty disappears, at least in the more typical cases." Connor in the Michigan Law Review, 1956.[301a]

> "There is a clear approach to the resolution of issues of rank and priorities of liens, despite text writers and commentators who irresistibly cite ancient decisions to reflect alleged current confusion that no longer exists." Varian in the Tulane Law Review, 1973.[301b]

A problem of priorities arises whenever the proceeds of sale of a ship are insufficient to satisfy all claims. The court must then proceed to a ranking of claims to determine which shall be paid in full, which shall receive partial payment and which shall be frozen out entirely. The two simplest propositions are that maritime claims outrank non-maritime claims (with the possible exception of federal and state tax claims)[302] and that maritime lien claims outrank claims which are maritime but not liens (with the exception of the costs of operating and caring for the ship while it is *in custodia legis.*)[303] The real difficulty arises in determining the priorities of liens among themselves, and that difficulty is largely attributable to the fact that there are two quite different criteria which must be applied: liens are ranked both according to class (such as wage liens, salvage liens, collision liens, and service liens: the general rule is that, except for wage and salvage liens, tort liens outrank contract liens) and according to the time of accrual (the general rule is that all liens within

300. 21 F.2d 862, 1927 A.M.C. 1770 (D. Md.1927).

301. Willard, Priorities Among Maritime Liens, 16 Cornell L.Q. 522 (1931).

301a. Connor, Maritime Lien Priorities: Cross-Currents of Theory, 54 Mich.L. Rev. 777 (1956). Mr. Connors' article had not appeared when the first edition of the treatise went to press but did appear before the treatise was published. On reading the article in preparation for this revision the writer was struck by the degree to which Mr. Connors' research had paralleled his own as well as by the general coincidence of our views.

301b. Varian, Rank and Priority of Maritime Liens, 47 Tulane L.Rev. 751 (1973). Mr. Varian expresses agreement with the proposition, § 9–59 *infra*, that, in deciding lien priorities, each court is "a law unto itself." (47 Tulane L.Rev. at p. 752.)

302. See § 9–73 *et seq. infra.*

303. On the treatment of custodial claims see § 9–11 *supra.*

a class rank in the inverse order of accrual—last in time is first in right). When all the liens asserted belong to the same class (a frequent case is a group of competing repair and supply claims), there is only the time of accrual to worry about. But let salvage and collision liens be added to the repair and supply liens, some of the services having been furnished before and some after the collision and salvage, and the question arises which Judge Rogers described in The Samuel Little as "involved in much obscurity and . . . difficult to answer." Nor is the line between tort and contract always clear: when a tug negligently causes damage to her tow, or when cargo is damaged by improper handling, is the resulting claim one for breach of contract or for a tort? Even when only liens of the same class are involved, the straight inverse order rule has become subject to so many exceptions or special rules that, as Judge Coleman said in The William Leishear, "Generally speaking, the law of maritime liens may be said to be made up of exceptions to the above doctrine." A final complication is added by the priority provisions of the Ship Mortgage Act.[303a]

**§ 9–59.** The Supreme Court has had less to say about lien priorities than about any other subject within the entire range of admiralty law: its most recent decision on lien priorities was The John G. Stevens, decided in 1898.[304] Indeed few priority cases are even carried to the Circuit Courts of Appeal: a recent Admiralty casebook[305] reprints, in a long section devoted to lien priority, one Supreme Court case (The John G. Stevens), one Second Circuit case and eight cases from various District Courts. Judge Brown remarked in 1880 that "it is scarcely too much to say that each court is a law unto itself."[306] So long as priority litigation continues to be localized at the trial court level, the confusion or, perhaps, diversity of doctrine and result will necessarily continue.

Since many priority cases involve large sums of money, it is surprising that the disappointed litigants so rarely test the trial judge's ruling on appeal. Whatever the reasons may be, appeals are rare and the trial courts enjoy an almost unfettered discretion to work out sensible solutions to the cases that come before them. While there may not be much predictability in "the law", from the point of view of appellate judges and treatise writers, there is very probably,

**303a.** In the recent literature, in addition to the articles by Connor (note 301a *supra*) and Varian (note 301b *supra*), mention should be made of the Note, Priorities of Maritime Liens, 69 Harv.L.Rev. 525 (1956). The Comment, Developments in the Law of Maritime Liens, 45 Tulane L.Rev. 574 (1971), focuses more on the claims which have lien status than on priorities in distribution but, nevertheless, contains much helpful information.

**304.** 170 U.S. 113, 18 S.Ct. 544 (1898). See text at note 316 *infra*.

**305.** Morrison and Stumberg, Cases and Materials on Admiralty 249–288 (1954). Lucas, Cases and Materials on Admiralty (1969) uses the same Supreme Court case and six District Court cases.

**306.** The City of Tawas, 3 F. 170, 172 (E.D.Mich.1880). There appears to be general agreement on this proposition. See Connor, note 301a *supra*, Varian, note 301b *supra*.

from District to District, a high degree of predictability in fact. Any branch of law that is administered at the trial level, with infrequent appellate review, is apt to become highly flexible and the law of lien priorities is no exception. General statements of doctrine, including those which follow, should be on the whole lightly regarded. Nine times out of ten, what seems fair to the trial judge will be the law of the case for all time.[306a]

**§ 9–60.** There has been little priority litigation even at the trial court level since, roughly, the 1920's. There are, obviously, as many disputes involving priorities as ever, but for a generation they have been settled at the conference table. One reason for the virtual disappearance of priority litigation may be the priority provisions of the Ship Mortgage Act: supply and repair claims arising subsequent to a "preferred mortgage" on a "vessel of the United States" are subordinated to the mortgage.[307] The mortgage is both a long-term arrangement and one that is apt to swallow up the proceeds, leaving little or nothing over for junior claims. The materialman, who has always accounted for most of the litigation in the field, is not tempted to litigate unless he can find a reason for arguing that the mortgage is not entitled to preferred status because of a failure to comply with the involved formal requisites and recordation provisions of the Mortgage Act. The United States merchant fleet which operated during the 1920's and 1930's consisted largely of vessels which had been part of the government's wartime fleet and had been sold to private owners subject to preferred mortgages. The disposal of the World War II fleet recreated the same situation during the 1950's and 1960's.[307a] Even when a foreign vessel is involved, or a domestic vessel not subject to a preferred mortgage, the materialman will in all probability not be able to claim a lien if the vessel is chartered and the charter-party contains appropriate anti-lien provisions.[307b] Thus the only case which offers the materialman a sporting chance is one involving a ship which is subject neither to a preferred mortgage nor to any of the usual forms of charter-party. A second reason for the absence of much litigation is the never to be forgotten fact of the universality of marine insurance. All cargo claims and all tort claims arising from collision (as well as many other types of claims) are insured and the insurance carriers, who sit on one side of the conference table as often as they sit on the other, are not disposed to litigate. The principal uninsured claims are those asserted by materialmen, personal injury claimants, and seamen for

**306a.** The text was quoted with approval in Fredelos v. Merritt-Chapman & Scott Corp. (The Padre Island), 447 F.2d 438, 1971 A.M.C. 2192 (5th Cir. 1971), which turned out to be the one case in ten in which the trial judge's distribution order was reversed, see note 308a *infra*.

**307.** See § 9–71 *infra*.

**307a.** See § 9–51a *supra* for a Note on Current Patterns of Ship Financing.

**307b.** See § 9–46(a) *supra* for a discussion of the 1971 amendment to the Maritime Lien Act which may have somewhat improved the materialman's position.

wages. The materialmen are discouraged from litigation for the reasons already stated. The wage claims, which outrank all others, are recognized and paid off, and the same is true in most cases for the personal injury claims.

The fact that there has been almost no priority litigation for more than a generation makes "the law" of the subject even more obscure than it may have been when the several judges quoted at the head of the section were considering it. In a priority case today, the most recent authority on any point will probably be a case decided by a District Judge thirty or forty or fifty years ago. Technological, organizational and financial changes in the method of carrying on the shipping business have been many and important. Precedents dredged from the dusty pages of the Federal Reporter (First Series) no longer have the weight they once had and lose a little more each year. Nor is there any reason to believe that there will be a substantial volume of priority litigation in the future.

Any analysis of maritime lien priorities must therefore be taken with a double *caveat*. Since priority litigation has been localized at the trial level, the discretion of the District Judge bulks much larger than doctrinal statement. Since there has been almost no priority litigation for a long time, the doctrinal statements, based as they must be on case law, are in any event out-of-date.

### Priority as Determined by Class of Lien

**§ 9–61.** There appears to be general agreement on the ranking of liens by class.[307c] It should be noted, however, that this comforting unanimity exists at a fairly high level of generality; as we descend to the level of detail, the fog rolls in.

1. Claims arising from the care and operation of the ship while it is in the custody of the court through the United States marshal are not, doctrinally, regarded as lien claims. Nevertheless, the Supreme Court held in New York Dock Co. v. The Poznan [308] that such claims should be paid as an "expense of justice" in priority to all lien claims when the dictates of "equity and good conscience" so require.

**307c.** The list which follows is essentially the same as the comparable lists which are to be found in the articles by Connor (note 301a *supra*) and Varian (note 301b *supra*) and indeed in all modern discussions of the subject. In this section we deal with custodial expenses and what may be called the true maritime liens. For the place of the statutory lien of the preferred ship mortgage in the hierarchy, see § 9–68 *et seq. infra*. For recent cases in which the ranking of various classes of liens has been discussed, see Rainbow Line, Inc. v. M/V Tequila, 341 F.Supp. 459, 1972 A.M.C. 1540 (S.D.N.Y.1972) affirmed without discussion of priorities 480 F.2d 1024, 1973 A.M.C. 1431 (2d Cir. 1973); Schon v. M/V Alexandra B., 1973 A.M.C. 702 (E.D.N.Y.1972).

**308.** 274 U.S. 117, 47 S.Ct. 482, 1927 A.M.C. 723 (1927). The Poznan and the other custodia legis cases are discussed § 9–11 *supra*.

2. Claims by seamen for wages have the highest priority among maritime liens.[308a] In general they outrank all other liens, without regard to the relative time of accrual. Some of the older cases suggest that when a ship has been at fault in a collision, claims for wages earned before the collision will be subordinated to the collision claim on the ground that the ship's fault is imputed to the crew.[309] Neither the fellow servant doctrine nor the idea of the ship's personality is in high repute today and it may be doubted that these cases have any surviving force, except possibly with respect to a crew member whose personal negligence was a cause of the collision. Some cases have suggested that wage claims will be subordinated to later salvage claims, on the theory that, except for the salvage, there would be no *res* to provide a wage fund.[310] In such cases there have often been funds available to pay both wage and salvage claims in full, so that the ranking has been unnecessary and the statements dictum. In a case where the court had to choose between salvage and wages, the wage claims would probably be preferred unless some or all of them were old enough to be called stale and unless the salvage service had been in fact vital to the preservation of the property. Or the District Judge, in the exercise of his wide discretion, might rank them equally and prorate the claims.

3. Salvage, both contract and voluntary, ranks second in the order of priority on the theory that the salvor has preserved the property for the benefit of all claimants.[311] In the case of contract salvage, if the trial judge feels that the rate of compensation is excessive, he may cut down the amount to a reasonable award.[312] Somewhat illogically, so far as the benefit or preservation of property theory goes, salvage claims outrank repair and supply claims even though the latter are subsequent to the salvage and may indeed have been

**308a.** On what are "wages", see note 93 *supra*. Under the general maritime law a master had no lien for wages but was given one by statute in 1968, see note 88a *supra*. A seaman's claim for maintenance and cure is usually thought to have the same priority as his claim for ordinary wages, a position adopted by the Fifth Circuit in Fredelos v. Merritt-Chapman & Scott Corp. (The Padre Island), 447 F.2d 438, 1971 A.M.C. 2192 (5th Cir. 1971).

**309.** The F. H. Stanwood, 49 F. 577 (7th Cir. 1892); The Nettie Woodward, 50 F. 224 (E.D.Mich.1892).

**310.** Salvage is preferred to wages previously earned: The Nika, 287 F. 717, 1923 A.M.C. 409 (W.D.Wash.1923); The Conveyor, 147 F. 586 (D.Ind. 1906); The Nettie Woodward, 50 F. 224 (E.D.Mich.1982); The Athenian, 3 F. 248 (D.Mich.1877); Collins v. The Ft. Wayne, 6 Fed.Cas. 119, Case No. 3,012 (S.D.Ohio 1861).

**311.** The City of Athens (Todd Shipyards Corp. v. Soc. Naviera Transatlantica S.A.) 83 F.Supp. 67, 1949 A.M.C. 572 (D.Md.1949); The William Leishear, 21 F.2d 862, 1927 A.M.C. 1770 (D.Md.1927). See Rainbow Line, Inc. v. M/V Tequila, 341 F.Supp. 459, 1972 A.M.C. 1540 (S.D.N.Y.1972) affirmed without discussion of this point 480 F.2d 1024, 1973 A.M.C. 1431 (2d Cir. 1973). But where salvors worked for a fixed compensation which was "not to be dependent upon the success of the services," their liens should not be given priority over liens in favor of other claimants which arose out of a single trip on the Great Lakes. The Schuyler (Munson Inland Water Lines v. Seidl), 71 F.2d 791, 1934 A.M.C. 1374 (7th Cir. 1934) certiorari denied 293 U.S. 606, 55 S.Ct. 123 (1934).

**312.** See Chapter VIII, § 8–14.

incurred to outfit the ship following the accident or disaster which occasioned the salvage.[313] Undoubtedly salvage claims among themselves rank in inverse order, the most recent having priority. Whether a salvage claim would be subordinated to a later collision claim (short of being held lost for laches or outlawed by the applicable two-year statute of limitations) is unknown.

4. Tort claims for collision and personal injury have third priority. They are as definitely subordinated to wage and salvage claims (with the possible exception that later tort claims may outrank prior salvage and wage claims) as they are superior to all the contract claims, prior or subsequent.[314] Collision and personal injury claims are usually thought of as being in the same class and ranking equally. If a choice had to be made between them, a District Judge would probably be within his discretion either in putting the personal injury claims first or in prorating the two types of claims. Priority questions often arise in the framework of a proceeding for limitation of liability and it may be noted in this connection that claims for death and personal injury, where limitation of liability is claimed with respect to a seagoing vessel, benefit from a $60 per ton fund which is set up for the payment of such claims alone.[315]

The dividing line between contract and tort, in cases which involve the negligent performance of a contractual duty, has never been precisely located and never will be. It is therefore to the advantage of lienors so situated to attempt to plead themselves into the higher priority for tort liens (just as common law plaintiffs in the same situation attempt to plead in tort instead of in contract in order to take advantage of the more liberal rules of damages thought to be available on the tort side). The desirability of such pleading has been enhanced by the provisions of the Ship Mortgage Act which give the mortgage priority over contract liens which arise subsequent to the recording and endorsement of the mortgage but subordinate

313. The William Leishear, 21 F.2d 862, 1927 A.M.C. 1770 (D.Md.1927):
"The claims are as follows:
"(1) For salvage under a written contract dated July 22, 1926, $850.
"(2) For labor and materials furnished between September 1 and November 20, 1926, $4,132.90.
"Summarizing the situation with respect to the allowed claims, it is as follows: First, wage claims, $640; second, salvage claims, $350; third, materials, supplies, and wharfage, aggregating $4,193.90. Since the first two allowances will consume all but $21.17 of the total fund in the registry of the court, there is nothing left for the claims of the third group . . ."

314. Subordinated to wages and salvage: cases cited note 311 *supra* and Great Lakes Towing Co. v. St. Joseph-Chicago S. S. Co., 253 F. 635 (7th Cir. 1918), certiorari denied *sub nom.* Bishop v. Great Lakes Towing Co., 248 U.S. 578, 39 S.Ct. 20 (1918). Possible exception as to prior wages: The James W. Follette, 1934 A.M.C. 1525 (W.D.N.Y.1934); The John G. Stevens, 170 U.S. 113, 18 S.Ct. 544 (1898); and cases cited note 309 *supra*. Superior to contract claims: cases cited note 311 *supra* and In re New England Transp. Co., 220 F. 203 (D.Conn.1914). But see Provost v. The Selkirk, 20 Fed.Cas. 23, Case No. 11,455 (N.D.Ohio 1878), which, without citation of authority, sets out a comprehensive ranking entirely at odds with modern law, and which ranks tort claims superior only to subsequent contract claims.

315. See Chapter X, § 10–7.

the mortgage to subsequent tort liens.[315a] By characterizing a lien as sounding in tort or in contract, the District Judge manipulates the priorities in whatever way may seem just and reasonable to him. The Supreme Court case next discussed in the text is, of course, the basic authority for turning what are essentially breach of contract claims into torts *pro hac vice.*

5. In The John G. Stevens, the Supreme Court's one relatively modern decision on lien priorities, it was held that a claim of tow against tug for negligent towage outranked claims for supplies furnished to the tug during the three months preceding the damage to the tow.[316] Justice Gray's opinion took the position that the negligent towage claim was like any collision claim, arose out of tort and thus outranked contract claims. Since the case has never been overruled it is unquestionably good law, at least on the specific issue decided. Whether claims for negligent towage would outrank subsequent contract claims (say, for repairs made after the collision) was not decided and was indeed an issue on which Justice Gray expressly reserved his opinion. Despite the authority of The John G. Stevens, negligent towage claims do not seem to be as firmly anchored on the tort side as ordinary collision and personal injury claims.[317]

6. Below the tort liens comes the whole host of liens for repairs, supplies and, as the Lien Act puts it, "other necessaries." Liens for wharfage, stevedoring, towage charges (as distinguished from claims for negligent towage), lighterage and so on would be included in this class. To put it generally, the class includes all claims based on contract that have lien status under the general maritime law or the Maritime Lien Act, as well as service liens arising under State lien statutes (if there is still more than a theoretical possibility of such liens). All service liens rank equally, so far as priority by class of claim is concerned; it is with reference to these claims that the rules determining priority by time of accrual become most important.

315a. See §§ 9–68, 9–69 *infra.* On current developments in maritime tort theory, and the claims which give rise to liens, see § 9–20 *supra* and the cases there cited.

316. 170 U.S. 113, 18 S.Ct. 544 (1898).

317. See The Interstate No. 1, 290 F. 926, 1923 A.M.C. 1118 (2d Cir. 1923) certiorari denied 262 U.S. 753, 43 S.Ct. 701 (1923), saying supply liens outrank both cargo damage claims and negligent towage claims on the same voyage; The Anna J. Brooks, 1927 A.M.C. 1307 (S.D.N.Y.1927), holding that repair liens outrank both claims for collision damage and negligent towage prior to the repairs. But see Stevens v. The White City, 285 U.S. 195, 202, 52 S.Ct. 347, 350, 1932 A.M.C. 468, 472 (1932) in which Justice Butler in a dictum reaffirmed the holding in The John G. Stevens: ". . . the rule that the lien for damages occasioned by negligent towage takes precedence of liens for supplies previously furnished the offending vessel rests upon the ground that the claim, like those in case of collision, is one in tort arising out of duty imposed by law and independently of any contract or consideration for the towage."

The characterization of actions for negligent towage as arising *ex delicto,* not *ex contractu,* has been frequently repeated in cases which, like The White City, did not involve lien priorities. See, e. g., National Transport Corp. v. Tug Abqaiq, 294 F.Supp. 1080, 1970 A.M.C. 203 (S.D.N.Y.1968), affirmed 418 F.2d 1241, 1970 A.M.C. 213 (2d Cir. 1969); South, Inc. v. Moran Towing & Transportation, Inc., 252 F.Supp. 500, 1965 A.M.C. 2559 (S.D.N.Y.1965).

7. Liens of cargo against ship are hard to rank with precision. By analogy to The John G. Stevens, which held negligent towage a tort, negligent custody of goods by the carrier might also be considered a tort, in which case the cargo lien would outrank the contract liens just referred to. Indeed the opinion in The John G. Stevens contains the remark that "an action . . . by an owner of goods, against a carrier, for neglect to carry and deliver in safety, is an action for the breach of a duty imposed by the law, independently of contract or of consideration, and is therefore founded in tort."[318] It is of course equally possible to look on liens of cargo against ship as based on breach of the contract of affreightment in which case they would rank below the tort liens.[318a] In The St. Paul[319] which involved the relative priority of service liens and cargo liens (which were both for damage to the goods and for recovery of prepaid freight) the cargo damage liens were even subordinated to the service liens, although the lien for prepaid freight was ranked equally with the service liens. The judge felt that the repairs and supplies furnished to the ship, like the prepaid freight, enabled the ship to set out on its voyage and were, on a "benefit" theory, entitled to a higher rank than claims on behalf of cargo which had not made any monetary contribution to the venture. He pointed out also that the cargo liens, if allowed priority over or even equality with the service liens, would often be so large as to wipe out or seriously impair the service liens (in The St. Paul the cargo liens amounted to $143,210 and the service liens to $25,489) and that the cargo owners were always insured, while the service claimants were not. The decision makes good sense and, as Judge Mayer remarked in his opinion, "In determining priorities, principles must be applied in the light of facts".

8. There are a few liens which come so rarely into priority litigation that their rank is unclear. The most important of these is cargo's lien against the ship for general average sacrifices.[320] It is

318. 170 U.S. 113, 124, 18 S.Ct. 544, 548 (1898).

318a. Judge Friendly's opinion in United States v. S/S Lucie Schulte, 343 F.2d 897, 1965 A.M.C. 1516 (2d Cir. 1965) seems to suggest a contract approach. The case did not involve lien priorities.

319. 277 F. 99 (S.D.N.Y.1921). The factual situation in the case made it unusually easy for the court to consider the cargo claims as arising from breach of contract rather than tort. The fire which damaged the cargo occurred while the ship was in custodia legis, after having been libeled by one of the service claimants; the shipowner's fault lay in breach of his Harter Act obligation to use due diligence to make the ship seaworthy and in delay in commencing the voyage which the court felt amounted to a deviation. All but two of the libels filed in behalf of cargo stated a cause of action *ex contractu* and motions to amend the libels to sound in tort had been denied.

320. See Du Pont De Nemours & Co. v. Vance, 60 U.S. (19 How.) 162 (1856); The Odysseus III, 77 F.Supp. 297, 300, 1948 A.M.C. 608, 614 (S.D.Fla.1948): ". . . general average contribution is in the nature of salvage and outranks materialmen's liens," citing Provost v. The Selkirk, note 314 *supra*, and The Pine Forest, 129 F. 700 (1st Cir. 1904). But general average ranks below salvage, Provost v. The Selkirk; The Spaulding, 22 Fed.Cas. 888, Case No. 13,215 (E.D.Mich.1871). On the general average lien see § 9–20 *supra*, cases cited in note 96.

reasonable to assume that this lien would outrank both the breach of affreightment contract liens and the service liens, not only because of the aura of maritime disaster which shrouds the general average lien but because the sacrifice of the cargo contributed to the preservation of the venture in much the same way that salvage services do. The rank of the general average lien almost never comes into litigation since general average adjustments are worked out among professionals,[321] and insurance carriers, who almost never litigate, are the only real parties in interest. The lien for pilotage is another whose rank is unsettled: although it is a service lien, it is sometimes said to rank higher than repair and supply liens.[322]

9. Liens against cargo rarely, if ever, present a priority question. In most cases the only lien claim that arises against cargo is on behalf of the shipowner for unpaid freight or for general average contributions. Inherently dangerous cargo may by explosion or otherwise cause both property and personal injury damage to a variety of claimants. If liens were held to arise against whatever might be left of the offending cargo, a court would find itself faced with a novel question of priorities.[323]

10. It is generally agreed that bottomry and respondentia liens rank at the bottom of the list.[324] Since both bottomry and respondentia have entirely passed out of use, these tranquil waters of doctrine will not be muddied or disturbed.

### Priority as Determined by Time of Accrual

**§ 9–62.** In 1824 Justice Johnson wrote in The St. Jago de Cuba:

> ". . . in every case, the last lien given will supersede the preceding. The last bottomry bond will ride over all that precede it; and an abandonment to a salvor will

321. See Chapter V, § 5–3.

322. Willard, Priorities Among Maritime Liens, 16 Cornell L.Q. 522, 532 (1931). Robinson, Admiralty 432 (1939), but what cases there are seem to go the other way. The Estrada Palma, 8 F.2d 103, 1923 A.M.C. 1040 (E.D.La.1923), "Pilotage, wharfage and watchmen are mere contract claims and there is nothing in the case that would require preferential treatment over the claims of materialmen"; Porter v. The Sea Witch, 19 Fed.Cas. 1072, Case No. 11,289 (C.C.D.La.1877): "There can be no serious question that pilotage and towage into port, etc., stand in the same rank with necessary supplies and repairs when furnished for the same voyage", citing The Emily B. Souder, 84 U.S. (17 Wall.) 666 (1873).

323. See Ryan Stevedoring Co. v. U. S., 175 F.2d 490, 1949 A.M.C. 1363 (2d Cir. 1949) certiorari denied 338 U.S. 899, 70 S.Ct. 249 (1949), where fire broke out in government-owned cargo stored on a pier and spread to nearby vessels. Although the case did not involve the priority problem referred to in the text, Judge Clark suggested that any remaining cargo might well be liable *in rem*.

324. Robinson, Admiralty (1939) 433 n. 212. The William Leishear, 21 F.2d 862, 863, 1927 A.M.C. 1770, 1772 (D. Md.1927), but see Provost v. The Selkirk, note 314 *supra*. For an explanation of bottomry and respondentia, see § 9–20 *supra*.

> supersede every prior claim. The vessel must get on; this is the consideration that controls every other . . ." [325]

Justice Johnson's statement that "in every case" the inverse order rule gives priority to the most recent lien is an overstatement, at least as to present law, and was no doubt meant to be taken metaphorically. Furthermore, the basis suggested for the rule—"the vessel must get on"—is that the most recent claim is preferred because only by the beneficial service rendered to the ship was it possible to prosecute the voyage for the benefit of all. The theory of benefit to the ship explains why contract and salvage claims should be paid off in inverse order but is hardly helpful when tort claims, to which the rule also applies, are involved. In a tort context therefore the rule is explained by saying that "in a sense" all prior lien claimants are "co-owners" of the ship, so that their equity is necessarily subjected to later claims.[326]

Outside the service lien field the inverse order rule is simple, easy to apply and causes no great difficulty or discussion. With respect to wage claims, the issue never arises: these claims have an overriding priority and are paid in full, without regard to when they were earned, before any other liens share in the distribution. If the proceeds were not enough even to pay all wages, the decision whether all wage claimants should prorate or whether the claims for more recent wages should have priority would undoubtedly lie within the discretion of the trial judge. In the salvage field, it is rare that more than one set of salvage liens is in issue: if two or more salvage operations had been performed on distinct occasions, the more recent liens would have priority as a matter of course. The same is true for collision tort liens: successive collisions are rare but they do happen; when they happen, the inverse order rule applies, even as to collisions that take place on the same voyage.[327] The problem of successive personal injury liens is seldom raised. If several such liens arise on a single occasion—collision or fire, and the ship lost—they share equally, both in the value of the ship and in the $60 per ton set up for their benefit by the Limitation of Liability Act. If the liens arise on "distinct occasions" the Limitation Act requires the setting up of separate $60 per ton funds for each occasion, so that the question of priorities between the groups of liens arising on each "occasion" could arise only if the $60 per ton funds were insufficient.[328]

Within the service lien field, the inverse order rule could not possibly be applied as a simple rule of thumb without causing chaos in the shipping industry. Lien claims for repairs, supplies, wharfage, towage, stevedoring, lighterage and the like all have the same rank. These services are furnished day by day to all ships while they are in

325. 22 U.S. (9 Wheat.) 409, 416 (1824).

326. The John G. Stevens, 170 U.S. 113, 18 S.Ct. 544 (1898); The America, 168 F. 424 (D.N.J.1909). Before The John G. Stevens there had been conflict in the cases; see The Frank G. Fowler, 17 F. 653 (C.C.S.D.N.Y.1883).

327. The America, note 326 *supra*.

328. See Chapter X, § 9–33 *et seq.*

port. The intervals between port calls may be relatively long in the case of ocean-going vessels; they are shorter for coast-wise and Great Lakes traffic; nonexistent for the swarms of harbor craft. The result of a strict application of the inverse order rule would be that each service lien claimant would have to libel the ship simultaneously with the furnishing of the services, or lose his priority to those who performed some service to the ship the next day or the next hour. Either all commercial shipping would be perpetually under arrest or the service liens would become valueless and the extension of credit by materialmen would be discouraged.

In this situation the law achieved one of its characteristic compromises: the inverse order rule was preserved in theory, but in practice was subjected to a series of special rules which in effect have largely displaced it. Under these special rules, priority periods are set up and all lien claims which accrue during the period share equally.

**§ 9–63.** The oldest of the special rules is the voyage rule which, as applied to ocean-going vessels, was well established early in the 19th century.[329] Under the voyage rule, all service liens which accrue in connection with a voyage have equal priority, and are displaced by the service liens which accrue in connection with the next voyage. At the time when the rule was formulated, a transoceanic voyage was a matter of several months. Thus the materialmen who outfitted a ship for her voyage could extend credit and be relatively secure in their liens for a fairly long period. The rule developed a certain amount of obscurity, since the key term "voyage" could be taken in a variety of ways: the voyage for which the crew was signed on, or from home port back to home port, or round trip, or one way or, when a vessel made several ports of call, the leg between each pair of ports. On various factual situations, case law authority can be found to support any one of the suggested meanings for "voyage".[330] With respect to

329. The Paragon, 18 Fed.Cas. 1084, 1088, Case No. 10,708 (D.Me.1836): "It is upon this principle that the last bottomry bond is preferred to those of older date, and that repairs and supplies furnished a vessel in her last voyage take precedence of those furnished in a prior voyage . . ." Liens connected with every new voyage start with a priority over all former ones after the ship has sailed if there has previously been opportunity to enforce them. The Fanny, 8 Fed.Cas. 993, Case No. 4,638 (D.Mass. 1876). But see The Omer, 18 Fed. Cas. 690, Case No. 10,510 (D.Va.1877); " . . . among materialmen, the one contributing 'most immediately', that is to say, at the latest stage of the voyage, to enable the vessel to complete it, has preference over those who contributed at an earlier stage of the voyage."

330. The Omer, note 329, *supra*. After return from a foreign voyage, a coasting trip for repairs and to earn freight on the way to the loading port for abroad is to be considered a voyage, when the contemplated foreign voyage is broken up by seizure; creditors on the coasting trip will be paid in full, although no funds will remain to satisfy claims on the foreign voyage, The Augustine Kobbe, 39 F. 559 (C.C.Ala.1889). In The Nissequogue, 280 F. 174 (E.D.N.C.1922), the ship's home port was New York. She was built in Brunswick, Georgia, and sailed from there. The ship called at nine ports and carried four different cargoes, not including the one she left with, before being libeled in Wilmington where she had been towed for repairs. The ship's articles called for a voyage and return to Brunswick. The court held that the voyage was as de-

ocean-going vessels, the voyage rule at the time it was formulated protected both shipowner and materialman by allowing long credit extensions before the materialman was put to the choice of libeling the ship or losing his priority to the liens of the next voyage. The voyage which took a month in the 1870's takes a few days in the 1970's, so that the rule, as a protective device for materialmen, has been a victim of technology. Under the old maxim, when the reason for a rule of law ceases, so does the rule. The voyage rule has been indeed a matter of some recent controversy, but we shall defer that discussion until the other "special rules" have been reviewed.

In 1880 in The City of Tawas [331] Judge (later Justice) Henry Brown invented, apparently out of whole cloth, the "season rule", which has ever since been accepted as the rule applicable to Great Lakes shipping. On the Lakes shipping is carried on for approximately eight months of the year; during the four months when ice makes navigation impracticable, the fleet is tied up.[331a] Lien priorities for services, Judge Brown held, would run season by season, which afforded a comfortably long credit period. It appears from The City of Tawas opinion that the novelty of the season rule did not lie in lengthening the priority period but in shortening it, and that prior practice on the Lakes had ignored the inverse order rule entirely so that all service liens (until barred by laches) shared equally without regard to the time of accrual. Judge Brown, therefore, was not departing from the principles of maritime law but returning to them. The voyage rule, he said, "certainly seems a reasonable one as applied to long voyages upon the ocean, but wholly inapplicable to the daily or weekly trips made by vessels upon the lakes." The season rule with "each year . . . considered as a voyage" seemed to him to be "a reasonable modification of the general practice" on the Lakes and the new rule would "encourage diligence in the prosecution of claims and prevent the proceeds of sale from being absorbed by dilatory creditors".

**§ 9–64.** The next of the special rules was announced by Judge Addison Brown in The Proceeds of The Gratitude.[332] The Gratitude involved a variety of libels brought against a tug whose operations were apparently confined to New York harbor. Among the libels were several for repairs, supplies and labor furnished to the tug, more than two thirds of the amounts claimed being more than a year over-

fined by the articles and was a continuing one until the ship's return to her "home port".

331. 3 F. 170 (E.D.Mich.1880). Accord: The Nebraska, 69 F. 1009 (7th Cir. 1895); The Brimstone, 69 F.2d 106, 1934 A.M.C. 283 (2d Cir. 1934); The Schuyler (Munson Inland Water Lines v. Seidl), 71 F.2d 791, 1934 A.M.C. 1374 (7th Cir. 1934) certiorari denied 293 U.S. 606, 55 S.Ct. 123 (1934); The Oswego No. 2, 23 F.Supp. 311, 1938 A.M.C. 980 (W.D.N.Y.1938). *Cf.* The John J. Freitus, 252 F. 876 (W.D.N.Y. 1918), for the extension of the season rule into the calendar year rule, where a tug was engaged the year around.

331a. In recent years attempts have been made to extend the navigation season through the use of ice-breakers.

332. 42 F. 299 (S.D.N.Y.1890).

due. New York harbor practice at the time seems to have been like Great Lakes practice before The City of Tawas: all service liens ranked equally without regard to the time of accrual. Like his namesake in Michigan, Judge Addison Brown determined to reintroduce the inverse order rule of the maritime law, modified to suit local conditions. "The long extension of time heretofore given," he commented, "has led to evils and abuses here, which observation satisfies ought to be corrected by a nearer approach to the general maritime rule." The period he decided on was 40 days, which "will give the short credit incident to the usual rendering of monthly bills, and 10 days more for settlement, or libeling the boat in case of non-payment." Furthermore, as Judge Brown pointed out, the 40 day period was roughly equivalent to the period arrived at under the voyage rule, since "it accords in some degree with the period of modern Atlantic voyages."

The 40-day rule of The Gratitude did not meet as immediate an acceptance as the season rule of The City of Tawas, even as restricted to New York harbor. In 1914 the District Court for the Eastern District of New York commented in The Towanda that "the [40 day] rule seems to have been disregarded and considered a dead letter for a long time." [333] In 1915, however, the Second Circuit reaffirmed the rule in The Samuel Little [334] and its application to New York harbor cases was not thereafter doubted.[335]

Perhaps the 40 day period selected by Judge Addison Brown was too short to serve commercial need. It has never spread beyond New York harbor, and has been held inapplicable even to craft making short trips beyond the harbor to points on Long Island Sound; [336] the District Court for the Western District of New York refused to adopt the 40-day rule for Buffalo harbor, holding the season rule applicable to both local and long-distance shipping on the Great Lakes.[337] The only approach to anything like the New York harbor

333. 216 F. 270, 271 (E.D.N.Y.1914). A similar decision was reached in an earlier opinion in The Towanda, 215 F. 232 (E.D.N.Y.1914).

334. 221 F. 308 (2d Cir. 1915). But the 40-day rule does not apply to seamen's wages. The Towanda, 215 F. 232 (E.D.N.Y.1914). The holding in The Samuel Little was that seamen's wage liens, not within the 40-day period, will be preferred to repair liens within the period, unless the wage liens are affected by laches.

335. The Baker Bros., 28 F.2d 920, 1928 A.M.C. 1600 (E.D.N.Y.1928); The Oregon, 6 F.2d 968, 1925 A.M.C. 1271 (2d Cir. 1925); The Interstate No. 1, 290 F. 926, 1923 A.M.C. 1118 (2d Cir. 1923) certiorari denied 262 U.S. 753, 43 S.Ct. 701 (1923); The Interstate No. 2, 290 F. 1015, 1923 A.M.C. 1128 (D.N.J. 1922); The Leonard F. Richards, 231 F. 1002 (E.D.N.Y.1916). No recent cases have applied the rule. Varian, note 301b *supra*, comments with reason that the rule "has for all practical purposes disappeared" (47 Tulane L.Rev. at p. 761).

336. In re New England Transp. Co., 220 F. 203 (D.Conn.1914). But see The Interstate No. 2, note 335 *supra*, holding that occasional trips by a tug to points outside New York harbor are not ground for regarding it as other than a harbor tug for purposes of the 40-day rule.

337. The John J. Freitus, 252 F. 876 (W.D.N.Y.1918). As the tug operated beyond the usual Great Lakes season, the court actually applied the calendar year rule, which it deemed "analogous to the season rule".

rule is a 90-day period which applies in Seattle harbor and the Puget Sound area. The 90-day rule was announced in 1914 by Judge Neterer in The Edith.[338] The background to the decision was the same as in The City of Tawas and The Gratitude: by local practice service liens ranked equally, subject only to a three-year statute of limitation. Judge Neterer paraphrased Judge Brown's opinion in The Gratitude on the "evils and abuses" which the local practice had led to, and came up with a 90-day period, without any explanation why he had picked 90 days rather than 40 or 180. Just as the New York 40-day rule was not allowed to spread even so far as Long Island Sound, so the Puget Sound rule was subsequently held not applicable to small craft running between Seattle and Vancouver.[339]

The season rule, on the other hand, has spread widely, usually becoming a "year rule" or a "calendar year" rule as it moves into areas where navigation is carried on throughout the year without the seasonal interruption found in the Great Lakes.[340] In one of its variants,—season, year or calendar year—it is generally assumed to be applicable to all coastwise shipping, to local shipping except possibly in New York harbor and Puget Sound, to canal boats, river shipping and so on.

Under any of the special rules, the question arises whether the rule establishes successive priority periods, fading back into the past, or merely establishes one current period, all prior claims to share alike until barred by limitation or laches. The longer the priority period, the less important the question becomes: thus in a case governed by a year rule, claims accruing during the calendar year or within twelve months of the initiating libel have first priority, claims accruing within the twelve months before that have second priority, and claims more than two years old will very likely be cut off for laches.[341] Where the priority period is short, the question can be-

338. 217 F. 300 (W.D.Wash.1914). Accord: The Sea Foam, 243 F. 929 (W.D.Wash.1917), as to liens between wage claimants.

339. The Morning Star, 1 F.2d 410, 1924 A.M.C. 1571 (W.D.Wash.1924). The Puget Sound rule, like the New York Harbor rule, see note 335 *supra* at end, has not been applied in any recent cases and may be said to have disappeared.

340. The Philomena, 200 F. 873 (D.Mass.1912); The Bethulia, 200 F. 876 (D.Mass.1912); In re New England Transp. Co., 220 F. 203 (D.Conn.1914); The John J. Freitus, 252 F. 876 (W.D.N.Y.1918); The Jack-O-Lantern, 282 F. 899 (D.Mass.1922); The Fort Gaines, 24 F.2d 438, 1928 A.M.C. 459 (D.Md.1928); The Annette Rolph, 30 F.2d 191, 1929 A.M.C. 212 (N.D.Cal.1929); The Little Charley, 31 F.2d 120, 1929 A.M.C. 398 (D.Md.1929); The Home, 65 F.Supp. 94, 1946 A.M.C. 585 (W.D.Wash.1946); Norton v. The Evan N., 109 F.Supp. 505, 1953 A.M.C. 576 (D.R.I.1952); The Odysseus III, 77 F.Supp. 297, 1948 A.M.C. 608 (S.D.Fla.1948); The City of Athens (Todd Shipyards Corp. v. Soc. Naviera Trans-Atlantica, S. A.), 83 F.Supp. 67, 1949 A.M.C. 572 (D.Md.1949): the "year rule", which ordinarily applies when the voyage rule is inapplicable, contemplates the award of priority on the basis of the calendar year and not on the basis of a 12-month period preceding the date of the libel. In Patterson Shrimp Co., Inc. v. O/S Freedom, 211 F.Supp. 852, 1963 A.M.C. 1604 (S.D.Tex.1962) the calendar year rule was applied. *Cf.*, however, The J. R. Hardee, note 341 *infra*.

341. As was done in Gulf Coast Marine Ways, Inc. v. The J. R. Hardee, 107

come significant, although it has seldom been litigated. Under the voyage rule, it is believed that successive voyages retain their identities for priority purposes: if, for example, a ship has made six voyages within a six month period and service liens have arisen on each of the voyages, the priorities will be adjusted voyage by voyage. In The Interstate No. 1,[342] a New York harbor case, the Second Circuit held that the local rule contemplated only one preferential 40-day period (measured from the date the initiating libel was filed) and that all claims from 41 days back to the cut-off by laches shared equally. The result in The Interstate No. 1 was that no claims had priority since none had accrued within the single 40-day period allowed by the court. No Puget Sound case has raised the issue under the 90-day rule.

**§ 9–65.** The season, year and harbor rules, which are stated with reference to fixed periods of time, have not been affected by technological changes in ship construction. No matter at how breathtaking a speed a tug may dash around New York harbor, the 40-day priority period is not disturbed. The voyage rule, on the other hand, has led to the safe period of credit extension to ocean-going vessels becoming shorter with each decade. The suppliers of transatlantic liners now find themselves in the unhappy position of having to choose between libeling the ship almost simultaneously with the furnishing of supplies or giving up their lien priority.

It has consequently been urged that the voyage rule should be superseded by the year rule, which would become applicable to ocean going as well as to coastwise shipping. The argument was made strongly by Mr. E. L. Willard of the New York admiralty bar in an article [343] which Professor Robinson used as a base for his discussion of lien priorities. Robinson, following Willard, wrote:

> "Even where the longer voyages of ocean steamers are concerned, the courts have ceased to apply a technical interpretation of the term 'voyage' and talk in terms of years. The year is considered representative of the voyage. [Citing several cases, none of which involved an ocean-going ship.] This shows a tendency, even in the case of larger vessels, to apply a time measured by a reasonable period of credit rather than voyage." [344]

F.Supp. 379, 1952 A.M.C. 1124 (S.D. Tex.1952). The J. R. Hardee was a shrimp boat operating out of Brownsville, Texas. Several preferred liens were allowed by the court, which then made a pro rata distribution of the remainder on liens, including material and repair, accruing within twelve months of the libel. The J. R. Hardee appears to be the only case which holds that the "year rule" contemplates a period of 12 months preceding the date of the libel rather than the calendar year. See In re England Transp. Co., 220 F. 203 (D. Conn.1914), and the quotation from The City of Athens, note 340 *supra*.

342. 290 F. 926, 1923 A.M.C. 1118 (2d Cir. 1923), certiorari denied 262 U.S. 753, 43 S.Ct. 701 (1923).

343. Willard, Priorities Among Maritime Liens, 16 Cornell L.Q. 522, 526 (1931).

344. Robinson, Admiralty 427 (1939).

The Willard-Robinson approach, however reasonable, was not supported by any authority in 1931 or 1939, and the scanty case harvest of recent years has done little to reinforce the tendency which the authors perceived.

**§ 9–66.** The City of Athens,[345] has been widely recognized as a leading case. The ship was registered under the flag of Honduras and owned by a corporation all of whose stock was held by a United States citizen. It had been used as a troop transport during the war and was converted in 1946 and 1947 for use in passenger and cargo transportation between New York and Mediterranean ports. Todd Shipyards made extensive repairs to the ship and at the time of the libel was owed $491,077, of which sum $104,972 represented work done in 1947 and $386,105 work done in 1946. The ship made four round trip voyages between New York and Europe, the first in November and December of 1946, the other three in 1947. The last voyage terminated in Baltimore in July, 1947, at which point Todd libeled her. On each of the voyages debts for supplies or other necessaries were incurred, which amounted to about $40,000 for the 1946 voyage and a little less than $200,000 for the three 1947 voyages together. After sale of the ship and payment of prior liens (wage and tort claims) there remained for distribution to Todd and the supply claimants about $320,000 to satisfy claims of over $700,000. Counsel for Todd argued for the application of a full year or twelve months rule of priority, which would have allowed Todd's claim for work done in 1946 to share equally with the 1947 claims (under that approach Todd would have received approximately $220,000, and the supply claimants $100,000). The court held, however, that the 1946 claims would be subordinated to the 1947 claims, all of which could be paid in full (so that Todd received $104,972 for the work done in 1947, and $200,000 went to the supply claimants on the three 1947 voyages). The balance left after paying the 1947 claims, the court estimated, would be in the neighborhood of $30,000, or enough to give both Todd and the 1946 voyage supply claimants a 10% dividend.

Judge Chesnut stated as a "conclusion of law" that the voyage rule still prevailed as to ocean-going vessels, despite greater rapidity of transportation and communication. If it were true that changed conditions warranted a changed rule of priorities, the framing of a new rule for ocean-going vessels, the judge suggested, was a vastly more complicated affair than the working out of local rules. A legislative committee with the ability to make a factual survey before drafting legislation would be a more satisfactory instrument for the accomplishment of such far-reaching changes than a District Judge blinkered to the facts of the case before him. Finally, Judge Chesnut was not impressed with the equities of Todd's position. While he found no evidence sufficient to charge Todd with fraud, it was nevertheless true that Todd, having run up charges in excess of the ship's

345. Todd Shipyards Corp. v. Soc. Naviera Trans-Atlantica, S. A., 83 F. Supp. 67, 1949 A.M.C. 572 (D.Md.1949).

value and apparently knowing that the owner had no other substantial assets, had allowed the ship to go out on a series of voyages in the course of which it was certain to incur large obligations to furnishers of supplies. (As a condition of letting the ship go, Todd had insisted on an assignment of freights to be earned, and before it libeled the ship had been paid more than $250,000 under the assignment.) Under the circumstances Judge Chesnut was not inclined to extend the priority period in Todd's favor.

The City of Athens was a many-sided case which lends itself to diverse interpretations. Judge Chesnut's conclusion of law that the voyage rule still applies to ocean-going shipping is diluted by his recognition that changed conditions may well have made a change in the law desirable. While it is hard to quarrel with his feeling that the change could be better accomplished by statute than by case-law, there is no indication that Congress is prepared to interest itself in the subject: if there is to be any reform, it will have to come from the courts. The holding in The City of Athens, which admitted all the 1947 claims to share equally, is not inconsistent with a "calendar year" rule (although the opinion carefully disavows any intention to adopt such a rule). And the lack of equity which Judge Chesnut found in Todd's case suggests that he might have been persuaded to a different holding in favor of a more meritorious claimant.

The present state of the voyage rule is obscure and, in view of the lack of cases in the recent past and the probability that cases will continue to be few, is likely to remain obscure. Apart from The City of Athens, the cases since 1940 have dealt with coastwise or Gulf of Mexico shipping: without discussion, the courts have assumed a full year or a calendar year rule to be in force.[346] The City of Athens itself is far from being a square holding in favor of the voyage rule. The question must be regarded as open.

**§ 9–67.** There is one setting in which the materialman may unexpectedly find himself in a priority position different from the one he counted on. A shipowner, faced with multiple claims, may petition to limit his liability to the value of his investment in the ship (which, if the ship has been lost in the course of a voyage, may be zero). The usual limitation proceeding arises out of a maritime disaster which has given rise to large tort claims, but both tort and contract claims are brought into concourse. Unless a service lien arises

346. Schon v. M/V Alexandra B., 1973 A.M.C. 702 (E.D.N.Y.1972) (semble); Patterson Shrimp Co., Inc. v. O/S Freedom, 211 F.Supp. 852, 1963 A.M.C. 1604 (S.D.Tex.1962); Norton v. The Evan N., 109 F.Supp. 505, 1953 A.M.C. 576 (D.R.I.1952); Gulf Coast Marine Ways, Inc. v. The J. R. Hardee, 107 F.Supp. 379, 1952 A.M.C. 1124 (S.D. Tex.1952); Bard v. The Silver Wave, 98 F.Supp. 271, 1951 A.M.C. 1079 (D. Md.1951); The Odysseus III, 77 F. Supp. 297, 1948 A.M.C. 608 (S.D.Fla. 1948); The Home, 65 F.Supp. 94, 1946 A.M.C. 585 (W.D.Wash.1946); The Penobscot, 1940 A.M.C. 1217 (D.Mass. 1940). A local rule of court in the Eastern District of Virginia establishes a 12-month rule and also provides that liens filed before the sale of a vessel shall be paid before liens filed after the sale. See United Virginia Bank Citizens and Marine v. O/S Sea Queen, 343 F.Supp. 1020, 1971 A.M.C. 1880 (E.D.Va.1971 (per A.M.C.) or 1972 (per official report)).

out of what is called a "personal contract", the ship owner may limit his liability in contract as well as in tort, and even when limitation is denied the fund arising from sale of the ship may be the only available asset which his creditors can reach. Furthermore, once the shipowner has petitioned for limitation, the court will adjudicate all claims on the merits even if limitation is denied.[347]

The currently applicable provisions of the Federal Rules of Civil Procedure, derived from the former Admiralty Rules of the Supreme Court, clearly contemplate that in proceedings for limitation of liability the voyage is the limitation unit: only claims arising on the last voyage are entitled to intervene in the proceeding and to share in the distribution. The historical foundations of the limitation voyage rule are almost non-existent, but there can be no doubt that the Supreme Court, in its 1948 revision of the Rules, adopted it.[348] Nor is there the least suggestion in the Rules that any distinction is to be made between ocean-going vessels, Great Lakes vessels, coastal shipping or harbor craft. Thus materialmen who have dealt with a ship subject to the season or the year rule of priorities might, in a limitation proceeding, find their priorities adjusted by the voyage with only the claims accruing on the last voyage entitled to share in the distribution.

There is no reason to believe that the Supreme Court, in drafting the Limitation Rules, had in mind the several rules other than the voyage rule which determine priorities in ordinary lien litigation. It is suggested that the "voyage" language in the Limitation Rules should not be taken to alter the priorities among service liens that would exist in the absence of a limitation proceeding. Where repairs and supplies have been furnished on the faith of a season or year rule, that rule should also determine participation in the limitation fund. And if the tendency toward the displacement of the voyage rule by the year rule, which Willard and Robinson perceived in the 1930's, is borne out by the case law, the limitation period should be comparably extended.

### Lien Priority as Affected by the Ship Mortgage Act

**§ 9–68.** In 1920 the Maritime Lien Act was amended and reenacted as part of the Ship Mortgage Act.[349] As amended, § 974 provides in part that:

> ". . . this chapter shall not be construed to affect the rules of law existing on June 5, 1920, in regard to . . (4) the rank of preferred maritime liens among themselves, or (5) priorities between maritime liens and mortgages, other than preferred mortgages, upon vessels of the United States."

Thus the traditional lien priorities were intended to survive the passage of the Mortgage Act except as they were affected by the new status given preferred mortgages.

347. See Chapter X, §§ 10–17, 10–26.

348. See Chapter X, § 10–46 *et seq.*

349. See note 235 *supra*.

Under § 952(b), on the sale of a vessel for the enforcement of a preferred mortgage lien, all claims to the vessel attach to the proceeds of sale "in accordance with their respective priorities". The subsection then provides that

> "the preferred mortgage lien shall have priority over all claims against the vessel, except (1) preferred maritime liens, and (2) expenses and fees allowed and costs taxed, by the court."

The key phrase "preferred maritime lien" is defined in § 953(a) to mean

> ". . . (1) a lien arising prior in time to the recording and indorsement of a preferred mortgage in accordance with the provisions of this chapter or (2) a lien for damages arising out of tort, for wages of a stevedore when employed directly by the owner, operator, master, ship's husband, or agent of the vessel, for wages of the crew of the vessel, for general average, and for salvage, including contract salvage."

The liens listed in § 953(a)(2) take priority over the mortgage whether they arise before or after the mortgage has achieved its preferred status.

Since tort liens against a ship at fault in a collision can easily exceed the value of the ship, the mortgagee's security interest seems at first glance to be hazardous indeed. A second glance, however, suggests that the mortgagee's position is not nearly as bad as it appears to be offhand. Except for claims for loss of life and personal injury, a shipowner may in most situations limit his liability to the value of his interest in the ship, that value being measured after the collision has taken place: if the ship has been lost without freight pending the owner's personal liability is zero. The proceeds of hull insurance, however, do not go into the limitation fund but inure to the owner's benefit.[350] Thus the insurance feeds the mortgage lien and not the tort liens which are by the Mortgage Act given priority.[351]

**§ 9–69.** The list of liens given priority by § 953(a)(2) is clear enough with the exception of exactly what is meant by the phrase "a lien for damages arising out of tort". Collision and personal injury torts are of course included. The doubt arises as to hybrid claims, which can be looked on as arising either out of contract or out of tort, such as the claim of tow against tug for negligent towage or the claim of cargo against ship for negligent custody. While The John G. Stevens[352] held that a claim for negligent towage sounded in tort,

350. The City of Norwich, 118 U.S. 468, 6 S.Ct. 1150 (1886), and see Chapter X, § 10–30.

351. See Lord & Glenn, The Foreign Ship Mortgage, 56 Yale L.J. 923, 928 (1947).

352. 170 U.S. 113, 18 S.Ct. 544 (1898).

the lower courts have tended to rank such claims as contractual and they have even been subordinated to repair and supply claims.[353] Since § 974 continues lien priorities as they existed on the effective date of the Act, the natural construction appears to be that cargo damage claims would not be within § 953(a)(2) nor would negligent towage claims unless they fell within the narrowly limited holding of The John G. Stevens.[354] It is, of course, to the advantage of any lienor whose claim arises out of the negligent performance of a contractual duty by those in control of the vessel to plead his claim as sounding not in contract but in tort. The recent case material suggests that the attempt to plead such claims in tort is being made frequently, not without success.[354a]

**§ 9–70.** Section 953(a)(2) applies to preferred mortgages on "vessels of the United States". Section 951, as amended in 1954, expanded the term "preferred mortgage" to include any "mortgage, hypothecation or similar charge" on a documented foreign vessel where certain requirements of execution and recordation in the country of the vessel's flag have been met.[355] When such foreign ship mortgages are foreclosed in the United States, they are to have the same priority as domestic mortgages subject to the following proviso:

> "That such 'preferred mortgage lien' in the case of a foreign vessel shall also be subordinate to maritime liens for repairs, supplies, towage, use of dry dock or marine railway, or other necessaries, performed or supplied in the United States."

The list of services to which the foreign ship mortgage is subordinated is copied from § 971 of the Lien Act: the case law on what claims create liens under the Lien Act applies to determine what claims are given priority over the foreign ship mortgage.[356]

353. See text at note 319 *supra*.

354. In The Henry W. Breyer, 17 F.2d 423, 1927 A.M.C. 290 (D.Md.1927), the one case which has dealt with this point under the Mortgage Act, it was held that cargo claims both for recovery of prepaid freight and for damage to the goods sounded in tort and created preferred liens with a § 953(a)(2) priority over a mortgage. The opinion drew heavily on cases involving rail carriers where the contract-tort distinction has procedural importance but has nothing to do with priorities among different classes of claims. The case cannot therefore be considered as distinguished authority.

354a. See the discussion in § 9–61 *supra*, text following note 315. See also § 9–20 *supra* and the cases there cited.

355. The amendment is discussed § 9–51 *supra*.

356. See § 9–34 *supra*. Among the cases which have applied the § 951 proviso to give liens asserted by American materialmen priority over foreign ship mortgages are Fredelos v. Merritt-Chapman & Scott Corp. (The Padre Island), 447 F.2d 438, 1971 A.M.C. 2192 (5th Cir. 1971); Payne v. S/S Tropic Breeze, 423 F.2d 236, 1970 A.M.C. 1850 (1st Cir. 1970), certiorari denied *sub nom.* Samadjopoulos v. National Western Life Ins. Co., 400 U.S. 964, 91 S.Ct. 363 (1970); Rainbow Line, Inc. v. M/V Tequila, 341 F.Supp. 459, 1972 A.M.C. 1540 (S.D.N.Y.1972), affirmed without discussion of this point 480 F.2d 1024, 1973 A.M.C. 1431 (2d Cir. 1973). In Fidelity Nat. Bank of Baton Rouge v. M/T Richlube, 302 F.Supp. 98 (D.Canal Zone 1969) Judge Crowe gave the § 951 priority to a lien for the purchase price of a generator sold by a Louisiana company and delivered to the purchaser's agent in the United States even

The priority which the § 951 proviso gave to domestic materialmen's liens over foreign ship mortgages raised a novel problem with respect to anti-lien provisions in a mortgage of the type customarily found in charter-parties.[356a] Prior to the Ship Mortgage Act, a common law mortgagee could not prevent the creation of maritime liens against the ship by any provision in the mortgage.[356b] After the passage of the Act (and before the 1954 amendment) he had no need to rely on an anti-lien clause, since § 953(a) automatically gave the preferred mortgage lien priority over all subsequently accruing materialmen's liens. (The anti-lien charter-party provisions had never been effective against the types of liens given priority over the mortgage under § 953(a)(2).) The § 951 proviso thus created for the first time the possibility of a mortgage with maritime lien status which could, without subordination by the mortgagee, become subject to subsequently accruing liens of the type against which anti-lien provisions in charter-parties are effective. In The Tradewind [356c] a preferred mortgage on a Liberian flag vessel contained a provision that: "Neither the Shipowner nor the Master has or shall have any right, power or authority to create, incur or permit to be placed or imposed upon the vessel, any liens whatsoever, other than for crew's wages or salvage." After sale of the vessel by the admiralty court, the proceeds were claimed by the mortgagee and by materialmen who had furnished supplies and services, both in United States and in foreign ports, subsequent to the date when the mortgage became preferred.[356d] In an elaborate opinion Judge Watkins concluded that a mortgagee, unlike a charterer or seller, cannot prevent subsequent service liens from arising against the ship by any provision in the mortgage, even as to materialmen who may have actual notice of the mortgage and the anti-lien provisions. Therefore the mortgage, although prior to the liens of the foreign port materialmen, would be subordinated to the Americans liens. On the level of statutory construction the Tradewind holding goes on the theory that the persons as to whose lack of authority to bind the ship materialmen are put on notice by § 973 of the Lien Act are persons whose authority (or lack of it) derives from the owner (as charterer, seller or the like); that a mortgagee is not an owner; that the notice provisions of § 973 therefore do not inure to the benefit of mortgagees.[356e] The

though the generator was installed in a vessel which lay in Panamanian waters. The same judge had refused to give the § 951 priority to liens for supplies furnished by a Panamanian corporation at ports in the Canal Zone, see Ares v. S/S Colon, 269 F. Supp. 763 (D.Canal Zone 1967). See further The Tradewind, discussed in the text following note 356c *infra* and cases cited note 226d *supra*.

**356a.** See § 9–42 *et seq. supra*.

**356b.** See text at note 229 *supra*.

**356c.** (Atlantic Steamer Supply Co., Inc. v. The Tradewind), 144 F.Supp. 408, 1956 A.M.C. 1731 (D.Md.1956).

**356d.** The case was heard on exceptions to the libel; the preferred status of the mortgage was assumed but not decided.

**356e.** In addition to the holding based on the statute, Judge Watkins suggested that the prohibitory clause in the mortgage, when read together with other provisions of the mortgage, might not in any case have been

Tradewind has been followed in several subsequent cases.[356f] Thus, **under the case law construction of the § 951 proviso, there is no** way in which a foreign ship mortgagee can preserve his security against the subsequently accruing claims of American materialmen; as to foreign service liens, the mortgage presumably has priority without regard to the presence of an anti-lien provision in the mortgage.

**§ 9–71.** Section 953(a)(1) subordinates the preferred mortgage to any lien "arising prior in time to the recording and indorsement" of the mortgage. Other provisions of the Act require the mortgagor to disclose to the mortgagee prior to the execution of the mortgage all existing liens known to the mortgagor and not to incur further liens (except for wages, general average or salvage) without the mortgagee's consent until the mortgagee has had a reasonable time to have the mortgage recorded and indorsed.[357] Failure of the mortgagor to comply with the disclosure and no-lien provision is punishable by criminal penalties and, in addition, the mortgagor is made civilly liable to any person who has entered into a contract on the credit of the ship and suffered loss by reason of the mortgagor's failure to comply.[358] The civil suit provision is obscure: it does not seem to cover the mortgagee, who may well have been prejudiced by the mortgagor's failure to disclose existing liens or to refrain from creating new ones, while the lien claimants, who are covered, do not seem to have suffered any loss since their liens have priority over the mortgage. Neither the disclosure provisions nor the penalties for noncompliance have yet come into litigation.[358a]

The only requirement under § 953(a)(1) is that the lien "arise" before the mortgage has been both recorded and indorsed. Since the mortgage itself does not achieve preferred status until both recording and indorsement have taken place, it would make no difference if the lienor knew of the mortgage before he furnished services.[359] Where repairs, being performed under contract, were begun before, but not completed until after recording and indorsement, it has reasonably been held that the entire repair claim was entitled to priority.[360] The basis of such holdings seems to be that the repair man was under a contractual duty to go forward with the work; a supply man who

found effective to prevent the creation of subsequent liens. (144 F.Supp. 408, 418, 1956 A.M.C. 1731, 1745.) For case-law precedent, Judge Watkins relied most heavily on Morse Dry Dock & Repair Co. v. Northern Star, 271 U.S. 552, 46 S.Ct. 589, 1926 A.M.C. 977 (1926), discussed in the text following note 285 *supra*.

**356f.** See the cases cited note 226d *supra*.

**357.** § 924.

**358.** § 941(b), (c).

**358a.** The § 924 disclosure provision is briefly discussed in Judge Brown's opinion in Pascagoula Dock Station v. Merchants and Marine Bank, 271 F.2d 53, 1959 A.M.C. 2207 (5th Cir. 1959).

**359.** Morse Drydock & Repair Co. v. The Northern Star, 271 U.S. 552, 46 S.Ct. 589, 1926 A.M.C. 977 (1926), and see discussion § 9–55 *supra* at note 285.

**360.** The Eastern Shore, 31 F.Supp. 964, 1940 A.M.C. 388 (D.Md.1940); The Transford, 1929 A.M.C. 727 (E.D. N.Y.1929).

continued to furnish supplies after the mortgage had been recorded and indorsed would not be entitled to priority.

Section 953 subordinates the mortgage to all preexisting liens but gives the mortgage priority over most subsequent contract liens. Section 974 says that nothing in the Chapter shall be construed to affect the rules of law relating to the "rank of preferred maritime liens among themselves". It was shortly pointed out that the two sections, read together, might be taken to create a logically insoluble puzzle.[361] Assume that one set of service liens arises before recording and indorsement, that another set arises subsequently and that the second set has priority over the first set under the applicable priority rule (voyage, season, year). Now, the first set of liens has priority over the mortgage, the mortgage has priority over the second set, but the second set (by general maritime law) has priority over the first set; thus a circular system of priorities has been set up. The argument for circularity overlooked the fact that § 974 did not refer to "maritime liens" generally but carefully used the term "preferred maritime liens". In the case assumed, the second set of liens are not "preferred maritime liens" under the definition in § 953, thus the priority over the first set of liens which they would have had by general maritime law is not preserved by § 974, and the circular system of priorities does not arise. When the hypothetical case arose it was sensibly held that the order of distribution would be *first*, the lien for supplies furnished before the mortgage was recorded and indorsed; *second*, the mortgage; and *third*, the subsequent repair and supply claims.[362]

Priorities among service liens are seriously affected by the Ship Mortgage Act. Service liens subsequent to the mortgage rank among themselves according to the usual rules but are subordinated not only to the mortgage but to all liens which antedate the mortgage. The Mortgage Act thus protects not only the mortgagee but all prior lienors. Any materialman whose claim is large enough to justify the trouble can freeze himself into a priority position by taking a mortgage on the ship.[363]

361. Kellogg, Priorities Puzzle under Ship Mortgage Act, 2 Wash.L.Rev. 117 (1927); Robinson, Admiralty 452 (1939); 3 Benedict, Admiralty 300 (6th ed. 1940).

362. The Zizania, 1934 A.M.C. 770 (D. Mass.1934); The Home, 65 F.Supp. 94, 1946 A.M.C. 585 (W.D.Wash.1946). That resolution appears to have been satisfactory to everyone; at all events the issue does not seem to have been discussed in any subsequent cases. In United Virginia Bank/Citizens and Marine v. O/S Sea Queen, 343 F. Supp. 1020, 1971 A.M.C. 1880 (E.D.Va. 1971 (per A.M.C.) or 1972 (per official report)) both pre-mortgage liens and post-mortgage liens had intervened in a foreclosure. Without discussion of the circularity point Judge MacKenzie gave first priority (after the payment of custodial costs) to a pre-mortgage lien which exhausted the available fund. See, however, The J. R. Hardee, 107 F.Supp. 379, 1952 A.M.C. 1124 (S.D.Tex.1952) and National Shawmut Bank v. Winthrop, 129 F.Supp. 661, 1955 A.M.C. 1288 (D.Mass.1955), 134 F.Supp. 370, 1955 A.M.C. 2089 (D. Mass.1955), discussed § 9–83 *infra*, in which, on theories of laches, pre-mortgage liens were subordinanted both to mortgages and to post-mortgage liens. For a general discussion of circular priority systems, see 2 Gilmore, Security Interests in Personal Property, Chapter 39 (1965).

363. See however, the discussion in § 9–83 *infra*.

§ 9–72. Notices of liens against any vessel covered by a preferred mortgage may be filed with the collector of customs at the port of documentation (where the mortgage is also filed).[364] The filing is permissive, not mandatory: the lien's status and rank are in no way affected by failure to file. A foreclosing mortgagee must give notice to any lienor who has taken advantage of the filing system; if he does not, he is liable to the filing lienor for damages "in the amount of his interest in the vessel terminated by the suit".[365] Apparently only a mortgagee who initiates a foreclosure suit is required to give notice, although the statutory language could be read to require notice when a mortgagee intervenes in an action initiated by some other libellant; libellants other than mortgagees are clearly not required to give notice or search the custom-house records.

### Priority of Government Claims

§ 9–73. At the time when the first edition of the treatise was prepared, the problem of the relative priority of maritime liens vis-à-vis claims of the United States (and of other governmental units) for taxes and other debts was distinctly unsettled. The issue had not been much litigated; such cases as there were, mostly on the District Court level, were themselves in conflict. Outside the field of maritime law the Supreme Court, in a series of cases which had begun in the late 1920's and which continued through the 1950's into the early 1960's, had been erecting a structure of doctrine under which it appeared that the United States was entitled to an absolute priority over competing claims both under the Tax Lien Statute (§§ 3670–3672 of the Internal Revenue Code) and under the so-called Priority Statute (always referred to as § 3466 of the Revised Statutes) which applies to all debts owed to the United States by an insolvent.[366] As of the 1950's the possibility that the Supreme Court might grant certiorari in a maritime lien case and extend its tax lien and § 3466 holdings to that field was far from negligible. The legal establishment, headed by the American Bar Association, had begun to agitate for remedial legislation to curb the federal monster but the prospect of a legislative solution seemed to be—and indeed was—remote. In the course of our discussion of the problem in the first edition we therefore remarked, reasonably enough, that "the relationship of government claims to maritime liens, including the

364. § 925.

365. § 951. The damage provision is obscure and could cause difficulty: "his interest" presumably means the mortgagee's interest, which would be the unpaid balance of the mortgage. Obviously the mortgagee is not automatically liable in that amount, so that the statement must mean that the mortgagee cannot be held liable in excess of that amount. The lienor will have to prove actual damages resulting from his failure to receive notice and can recover those up to the ceiling of the mortgage indebtedness. None of these provisions has yet come into litigation.

366. The best early discussion of this development was Kennedy, The Relative Priority of the Federal Government: The Pernicious Career of the Inchoate and General Lien, 63 Yale L.J. 905 (1954). The story is carried through 1965 in 2 Gilmore, Security Interests in Personal Property, Chapter 40 (1965).

lien of the preferred ship mortgage, may well give rise to more controversy in the future than it has in the past."

Our apprehensions of future controversy turn out to have been unfounded. The Supreme Court never granted certiorari in a maritime lien case. Since the early 1950's the lower federal courts have, without exception, held, in the relatively few cases that have arisen, that federal, state and local claims, being nonmaritime, are subordinate to all maritime liens (including the lien of a preferred ship mortgage) whether the maritime liens arise before or after the governmental claim becomes entitled to lien status or priority under the relevant state or federal law. The agitation for remedial legislation finally led to the Federal Tax Lien Act of 1966 [367] which was designed to give the holders of security interests and other liens more protection against federal tax claims than they had had under the Supreme Court doctrine.[368] Congress, in drafting the 1966 Act, could perfectly well have conferred maritime lien status on tax claims against ships and shipowners.[368a] Since the Act says nothing about such tax claims, the Congress may reasonably be presumed to have accepted the case law consensus which had arisen under which the tax claims, being nonmaritime, were subordinated to all maritime liens. It appears therefore that proctors in admiralty can happily go on ignoring the horrid complexities of the Federal Tax Lien Act of 1966 and the Rev.Stat. § 3466 case law. Of course we were wrong on this point in the first edition and may well be so again.

In the light of the foregoing discussion, much of the material in the following three sections has become of not much more than antiquarian interest. We have, nevertheless, preserved it for whatever it may be worth.

**§ 9–74.** The problem of how maritime liens should be treated in forfeiture cases came up in litigation a hundred years before the courts began to consider their treatment in cases where the government claim was for unpaid taxes or other debts.

Since the establishment of the Republic, ships have been liable to forfeiture to the United States for piracy, for slaving, for rum-

**367.** 80 Stat. 1125 (1966), 26 U.S.C.A. § 6323 *et seq.*

**368.** Plumb, Federal Tax Liens (3d ed. 1972) is the bible on this intricate subject. See also Mr. Plumb's remarkable series of articles, Federal Liens and Priorities—Agenda for the Next Decade, 77 Yale L.J. 228, 605, 1104 (1967–1968). Coogan, Effect of the Federal Tax Lien Act of 1966 upon Security Interests Created under the Uniform Commercial Code, 81 Harv.L.Rev. 1369 (1968) analyzes the Act and points out its unfortunate drafting deficiencies. Rev.Stat. § 3466 ought logically to have been amended to conform to the 1966 Act but was not, has not been and may never be. Thus, there is at least a theoretical possibility that a doctrine of absolute federal priority could be maintained or fashioned under § 3466. However, in the light of the obvious policy of the 1966 Tax Lien Act, such a development seems unlikely and has not in fact occurred.

**368a.** *Cf.* the Water Quality Improvement Act of 1970 (discussed in Chapter X, § 10–4(b)) which provides that claims of the United States for cleanup costs under the Act have maritime lien status.

running during prohibition, and so on. Starting with The St. Jago de Cuba,[369] it has been held in a long line of cases that maritime liens are not terminated or displaced by the forfeiture; the lienor, unless he has himself connived in the ship's illegal activity, may intervene in the forfeiture proceeding and enforce his lien against the proceeds of sale.[370] The case-law rule was given statutory force by § 961(b) of the Ship Mortgage Act which provides that the interest of a mortgagee "shall not be terminated by the forfeiture of the vessel for a violation of any law of the United States, unless the mortgagee authorized, consented or conspired to effect" the illegal act.[370a] Thus in this context the United States has consented to subordinate its claim to those of maritime lienholders.

**§ 9–75.** The Melissa Trask [371] seems to have been the first case to deal with the relative priority of government claims and maritime liens outside the forfeiture situation. The Melissa Trask was a schooner which ran between New Bedford and the Azores. Liens for supplies and equipment arose against her in 1919 and 1920. Subsequently in October, 1920 the schooner was mortgaged: the mortgage appears to have been entitled to preferred status under the Mortgage Act. In June, 1921 the schooner brought a number of aliens into the United States. The Immigration Act levied a tax of eight dollars for every alien entering the United States; the tax was required to be paid to the collector of customs by the master and the statute provided that "the tax . . . shall be a lien against the vessel . . . and shall be a debt in favor of the United States against the owner." The Melissa Trask was libeled either by the mortgagee or the materialmen and the United States intervened, claiming priority over the mortgage both for unpaid head taxes and for penalties assessed against the schooner because she did not have the space required for the number of passengers carried. Apparently the proceeds of sale were sufficient to satisfy both the supply liens and the claims of the United States. Perhaps for that reason the United States conceded that the supply liens were entitled to be paid first; since the liens had antedated the mortgage, they clearly had priority over the mortgage. The only question before the court, therefore, was the relative priority of the preferred

**369.** 9 Wheat (22 U.S.) 409 (1824).

**370.** Violation of licensing laws: United States v. American Gas Screw Franz Joseph, 210 F.Supp. 581, 1963 A.M.C. 1596 (D.Alaska 1962) (digested note 273a *supra*); rum running: The Antigostine, 44 F.2d 170, 1930 A.M.C. 2035 (E.D.N.Y.1930); tariff violations: The Ermis, 33 F.2d 763, 1929 A.M.C. 1588 (S.D.Fla.1929); rum-running; The Thomaston, 26 F.2d 279, 1928 A.M.C. 845 (D.Md.1928); sale to foreigner: The Winona, 1928 A.M.C. 108 (E.D.S.C.1927); cocaine and rum-running: The Eugenia Emilia, 298 F. 340, 1924 A.M.C. 538 (D.Mass.1924); killing seals: North American Commercial Co. v. United States, 81 F. 748 (C.C.A.Or.1897).

**370a.** In United States v. Vessel FL 4127 SE, 311 F.Supp. 1353, 1970 A.M.C. 1861 (S.D.Fla.1970) it was held that a mortgagee was not protected under § 961(b), the vessel mortgaged not having been a "vessel of the United States" (see § 9–52 *supra*, text following note 245).

**371.** 285 F. 781, 1923 A.M.C. 193 (D.Mass.1923).

mortgage and the subsequently arising claims of the United States for the head taxes (which were a statutory lien on the vessel) and penalties (which were not a lien). Judge Morton held that the tax claim came in ahead of the mortgage but that the penalty claim did not. The penalty claim seemed to him analogous to forfeitures. Such penalties, he pointed out, were not mentioned in the § 953(a)(2) list of preferred claims which are given an overriding priority over a preferred mortgage lien and the omission seemed to him "significant". Taxes, however, seemed to him to stand on an entirely different footing. They were not mentioned in the § 953(a)(2) list any more than penalties were. But that section, he went on,

> ". . . must be construed . . . with due regard to other provisions of the statutes, especially Rev.Stat. § 3466 . . . which in the strongest terms gives priority to debts or taxes due to the United States. . . . Indeed, the policy of the government to insist on priority for taxes is so fundamental, and so widely established in our law, that I should hesitate to say it had been relinquished without express language to that effect. I therefore reach the conclusion that the head tax takes precedence of the mortgage." [372]

Judge Morton's reference to the § 3466 priority was merely by analogy, since there was no showing that the owner of the schooner was insolvent, a prerequisite to a § 3466 claim. Nor was the United States claiming a tax lien under § 3670. It did, however, have a "lien against the vessel" (therefore, presumably, a maritime lien) under the Immigration Act, and that fact, although Judge Morton did not stress it, may be significant in assessing the value of The Melissa Trask as precedent.

The next case to come up was The River Queen.[373] The United States claimed a § 3670 lien for unpaid income taxes for 1918, 1919 and 1920 in the amount of $237,000. After the tax lien had attached, materialmen, whom the judge assumed to have been without notice of the lien, furnished supplies and repairs to several "gas boats" belonging to the taxpayer. Several years later the government levied on the gas boats under its tax lien and, subsequently to the levy, the materialmen filed their libels. Judge Grover considered the case to be one of first impression, pointing out that The Melissa, Trask was not in point because in that case counsel for the United States had conceded priority to the supply liens. The most nearly analogous cases, in his opinion, were the forfeiture cases, which he reviewed at length. Without the services furnished by the libellants, he continued,

> ". . . the probability is that, in the interval between the time the tax accrued and the time the levy was

372. 285 F. 781, 782, 783; 1923 A.M.C. 193, 195, 196.

373. 8 F.2d 426, 1926 A.M.C. 79 (E.D. Va.1925).

> made, nearly four years, the vessels would have become worthless; and it would seem to be a particularly hard law which would impose upon these claimants the forfeiture of their claims in behalf of the United States which, but for their services, would probably have had a bootless claim." [374]

Consequently a motion by the United States to dismiss the libels was denied as to claims covering supplies or work furnished prior to the levy under the tax lien. The right of the United States to intervene in the admiralty proceeding on the strength of its § 3670 tax lien appears not to have been questioned.

A third case, Colonna's Shipyard v. Rowe,[375] may be briefly mentioned. State and county taxes in the amount of $420 were assessed against the owner of a vessel. The vessel had been libeled on October 11, 1924, and was sold under admiralty process on December 22. Apparently the libel was in aid of claims which antedated the tax claims; at the time the libel was filed the taxes were due, although a lien for the taxes did not attach under state law until December 8. On those facts the Fourth Circuit awarded priority to the tax claims. The opinion is unsatisfactory in the last degree: it does not cite The Melissa Trask or The River Queen or any other admiralty case. In view of the court's failure to discuss, or apparently even to recognize, the difficult problems of law involved, the Colonna's Shipyard case cannot be given much weight.

The three cases just discussed were decided between 1923 and 1926. There was then a 25 year lull [376] before the question of governmental priorities came up again.

**§ 9–76.** In The J. R. Hardee [377] the United States claimed a § 3670 lien against the vessel for 1943 income taxes, the lien having attached in 1949. On August 9, 1950, a mortgage on the vessel was executed in favor of the Pan American State Bank, which on August 22 was properly filed with the collector of customs in Brownsville, Texas. On September 29, 1951, the United States filed notice of its § 3670 tax lien with the proper county official in Texas. On September 5, 1951, and October 10, 1951, other claimants had paid $2400 to the mortgagee bank under an agreement which, they claimed, entitled

374. 8 F.2d 426, 428, 1926 A.M.C. 79, 82.

375. 14 F.2d 267, 1926 A.M.C. 941 (4th Cir. 1926).

376. In North River Coal & Wharf Co. v. McWilliams Bros., Inc., 1929 A.M.C. 716 (S.D.N.Y.1929), affirmed 37 F.2d 22, 1930 A.M.C. 204 (2d Cir. 1930), it was held that the lien of a chattel mortgage prevailed over both a tax claim of the United States under § 3466 and over a claim of the State of New York for franchise taxes. The mortgage was apparently not entitled to preferred status under the Mortgage Act and neither the United States nor New York claimed maritime lien status. The action (which was not in admiralty) involved distribution of remnants and surplus proceeds in an equity receivership after maritime claims had been paid. The case does not, therefore, come into our present discussion, except as an illustration of the failure of the government claimants to have insisted on maritime lien status.

377. Gulf Coast Marine Ways, Inc. v. The J. R. Hardee, 107 F.Supp. 379, 1952 A.M.C. 1124 (S.D.Tex.1952).

them to be *pro tanto* subrogated to the Bank's mortgage lien. In addition to the government's tax claim, the mortgage claim and the subrogation claim there were various claims for repairs and supplies: some of these were furnished before August 22, 1950, (when the mortgage became preferred); others between that date and September 29, 1951 (when the tax lien became perfected); still others after September 29, 1951. Finally there was a small claim for salvage (date not specified) and another for dockage while the vessel was in the custody of the marshal after arrest under the libel which was filed November 5, 1951, by one of the materialmen. The proceeds of sale for distribution among the claimants amounted to about $5300. The government's tax claim was for about $17,000; the unpaid balance of the mortgage was $3,236; the subrogation claim was for $2,400; the service liens alone totaled more than the available fund.

The United States claimed priority not only over the mortgage, but over all the other maritime liens involved in the case (including the salvage lien and, apparently, the custodial costs). Judge Allred held that the mortgage lien (including the subrogation claim) and all the other maritime liens came in before the government.

Judge Allred's holding was based in the first instance on the finding that the United States had not perfected its lien until after the mortgage had become preferred. Since the unpaid balance of the mortgage plus the subrogation claim (which was held entitled to rank equally with the mortgage) exhausted the available fund, the opinion could, except for tidying up a few loose ends, have stopped there. Part of the subrogation claim was for $700 paid to the bank on October 10, 1951 (*i. e.* after the perfection of the tax lien). Judge Allred felt that the $700 was entitled to priority over the tax lien because the subrogees made the payment under a prior contract; thus, on a sort of relation back theory, he preferred the entire subrogation claim to the tax lien without regard to the dates of payment. Recognizing that he might be mistaken on so doubtful a point, Judge Allred then broadened his holding to include the proposition that the § 3670 tax lien is inferior to all maritime liens, even though the maritime liens accrue after the tax lien has been perfected. Having held that the service liens which antedated the mortgage were barred by laches, the judge ordered the following distribution: (1) court costs; (2) the custodial claim for dockage; (3) the salvage claim; (4) the mortgage and subrogation claims *pro rata;* (5) all other claims by materialmen whose liens arose within 12 months of the filing of the initiating libel, *pro rata.* Apparently the mortgage and subrogation claims would exhaust the fund, but, to make the holding crystal clear, it was added that, if anything was left over for the service liens given fifth priority, the government's tax lien was excluded even from that distribution.

Judge Allred put his sweeping holding on the ground that the § 3670 tax lien is nonmaritime. After pointing out that the only type of lien to which the Ship Mortgage Act gives priority over a preferred mortgage is "unquestionably . . . a *maritime* lien", he continued:

> "Since the Government's tax lien is nonmaritime, I do not believe that it has priority, even though notice is filed pursuant to a state statute, over maritime liens in general, certainly not over the preferred maritime liens created under the Ship Mortgage Act. Congress has evidenced no clear intent to give it such status. Maritime liens and proceedings are as much 'of such a specialized nature' as the Bankruptcy laws and Congress evidently intended that field of law (Maritime) to govern exclusively." [378]

In a footnote Judge Allred added that he doubted that Congress intended the § 3670 tax lien and filing provisions to cover vessels and noted that none of the state statutes made provision for recording notice of tax liens against vessels.

The narrow holding in The J. R. Hardee was that the § 3670 tax lien was subordinate to a mortgage which became preferred before the tax lien was perfected. The broad holding was that the § 3670 lien was subordinate (because it was nonmaritime) to all maritime liens without regard to dates of accrual and perfection. Judge Allred's opinion did not suggest that Congress lacked power to make the tax lien maritime; it concluded merely that Congress had not done so.

Judge Allred's broad holding in The J. R. Hardee was espoused by the First Circuit in United States v. Flood.[379] The case involved federal tax liens in competition with a preferred mortgage which antedated the tax liens and with supply liens some of which antedated the tax liens and some of which followed them. The government conceded the priority of the mortgage and of the supply liens which antedated the mortgage and argued only that the tax liens outranked subsequently arising maritime liens. Judge Magruder concluded, however, that "in our view the government's tax lien is always subordinate to a maritime lien for supplies even if the tax lien arises first." In support of his conclusion he cited The J. R. Hardee and The River Queen,[380] adding that the Colonna's Shipyard case [380a] was "entirely unpersuasive" for the reasons indicated in our discussion

378. 107 F.Supp. 379, 385, 1952 A.M.C. 1124, 1133. The "of such a specialized nature" phrase quoted by Judge Allred is from the opinion in United States v. Sampsell, 153 F.2d 731, 735 (9th Cir. 1946), which held that § 64 of the Bankruptcy Act displaced the priority for claims of the United States under R.S. § 3466 in bankruptcy proceedings.

379. 247 F.2d 209, 1957 A.M.C. 1718 (1st Cir. 1957), noted 38 B.U.L.Rev. 160 (1958). In related proceedings, Ruth v. O/S/V Marie and Winifred, 150 F. Supp. 630, 155 F.Supp. 37, 1958 A.M.C. 861 (D.Mass.1957), it was held that federal tax liens assessed against the estates of maritime lienors had priority over a subsequent assignee of the maritime liens. Apparently no appeal was taken.

380. See text following note 373 *supra*.

380a. See text following note 375 *supra*.

in the first edition of the treatise and that The Melissa Trask [380b] was distinguishable.

In subsequent cases The J. R. Hardee and United States v. Flood have been ritually cited in double harness for the proposition that tax and other governmental claims, being nonmaritime, are subordinate to maritime liens of all kinds.[380c] The issue has, indeed, almost disappeared from litigation and, unless some new factor is unexpectedly introduced into the equation, there is no reason to anticipate that it will continue to be raised.

### Loss of Lien: Laches, Limitation and Waiver

§ 9–77. The lienor who delays enforcement of his claim until after the relevant priority period has run risks having his lien subordinated to liens of a later period, but without loss of lien status. The lienor who delays until his claim has become "stale" faces the penalty of losing his lien altogether. How quickly a lien becomes stale depends largely on whether the ship is in the possession of the owner who incurred the claim or has passed into the hands of a purchaser who has bought it without notice of the lien's existence. The lapse of a short period will bar the lien against a purchaser without notice, although the underlying claim continues enforceable against the original owner. When the ship is still owned by the person who is liable on the claim, there will in most circumstances be no loss of lien status until the claim has itself become time-barred.[380d]

§ 9–78. The maritime lien which follows the ship into the hands of whomsoever it may come has never been more than theoretically indelible. The Bold Buccleugh, the leading English case which first announced the doctrine of "indelibility", did in fact enforce a collision lien against a ship which had passed into the hands of a purchaser assumed to be in good faith and without notice, but in favor of a lienor who had acted with extraordinary diligence.[381] By 1871 when the Supreme Court made its only serious contribution to the subject in The Key City,[382] Justice Miller found the law to be settled on the following propositions:

> "1. That while the courts of admiralty are not governed in such cases by any statute of limitation, they adopt the principle that laches or delay in the judicial enforcement

**380b.** See text following note 371 *supra*.

**380c.** See United States v. Jane B. Corp (The Jane B), 167 F.Supp. 352, 1966 A.M.C. 427 (D.Mass.1958), noted 73 Harv.L.Rev. 423 (1959); Pfeffer Co., Inc. v. S/S Pacific Star, 183 F. Supp. 932 (E.D.Va.1960), affirmed *sub nom.* Marine Midland Trust Co. v. United States, 299 F.2d 724 (4th Cir. 1962) (dictum); United States v. Barge Cape Flattery I, 1972 A.M.C. 345 (W.D.Wash.1972) (county tax liens nonmaritime and subordinate to maritime liens).

**380d.** See 37 Tulane L.Rev. 811 (1963), Admiralty: The Doctrine of Laches.

**381.** See § 9–6 *supra*.

**382.** 81 U.S. (14 Wall.) 653 (1871).

of maritime liens will, under proper circumstances, constitute a valid defence.

"2. That no arbitrary or fixed period of time has been, or will be, established as an inflexible rule, but that the delay which will defeat such a suit must in every case depend on the peculiar equitable circumstances of that case.

"3. That where the lien is to be enforced to the detriment of a purchaser for value, without notice of the lien, the defence will be held valid under shorter time, and a more rigid scrutiny of the circumstances of the delay, than when the claimant is the owner at the time the lien accrued." [383]

In The Key City, which involved a cargo claim, the libel was filed three and a half years after the cause of action had accrued and after the ship had been transferred from one corporation to another in the course of a corporate merger. The Court assumed that the lien would have become unenforceable if the ship had come into the possession of a good faith purchaser without notice, but on the ground that an intercorporate transfer of assets did not rise to the dignity of good faith purchase held that the lien, despite the delay, was still good.

Attempts to assert liens over the defense of good faith purchase without notice have been few and usually unsuccessful. Presumably counsel turn to such litigation as a last resort and only when the claim against the original owner is no longer worth pursuing. That was the situation in The Everosa cases [384] which offer the best modern illustration of the extent to which the good faith purchase defense has eroded the lien's indelibility.

In 1933 and 1934 the Everosa, then known as the Munorway, was owned by a Norwegian subsidiary of the Munson Lines and chartered to Munson. Between November of 1933 and May of 1934 the ship called at various Gulf ports and at Norfolk, from where it sailed for Europe on May 17. On June 11, 1934, the Munson Lines went into a § 77B reorganization. In August, 1934, the ship was sold, in Europe, to Latvian owners who renamed her and transferred her to Latvian registry. Under her new name and flag she returned to American waters and made port at Providence in November and New York in December of 1934. Her next American visit was in 1937 when she was in New York and Boston in January and again in New York in April. Since the Munson Lines were in reorganization various supply claimants attempted to assert liens against the ship on her return to American waters. The most diligent of the creditors was the Southern Coal and Coke Company which had supplied coal in Mobile, Alabama, on November 22, 1933, and again on May 8, 1934, nine days before the ship cleared for Europe from Norfolk. The Coke Company

383. *Id.* at 660.

384. The Everosa (Southern Coal & Coke Co. v. Kugniecibas), 93 F.2d 732, 1938 A.M.C. 82 (1st Cir. 1937); The Everosa (Swan & Sons, Inc. v. Kugniecibas), 20 F.Supp. 8, 1937 A.M.C. 993 (E.D.N.Y.1937).

libeled the ship in Providence on her next return to an American port, in November of 1934. On those facts the First Circuit held that the November, 1933 lien was barred for laches but that the May, 1934 lien was good.[385] Between November and May the Coke Company had had several opportunities to libel the ship, including of course the second visit to Mobile in May when the claim was already six months old. However, instead of asserting its claim at that time, the Coke Company had furnished more coal on further credit to Munson even though drafts on Munson for the November bunkering were overdue and unpaid. After the May bunkering, on the other hand, the Coke Company had had only one opportunity to arrest the ship, in Norfolk, where it stayed only one day before clearing for Europe, the May claim being then only nine days old. The Court disapproved suggestions in the older case law that a lienor who permitted a ship to go abroad was presumed to have waived his lien and held that, at least with reference to the six month period from May to November of 1934, there had been no duty on the Coke Company to pursue the ship in foreign ports and libel her there.

The Everosa, having been released from the First Circuit litigation on a stipulation for value, continued in the possession of her Latvian owners and, on her next return to the United States (in 1937), was libeled in New York by two more supply claimants whose liens had accrued in 1934, during the period of Munson's ownership. Swan and Sons, ship chandlers, had furnished supplies in Norfolk in January, 1934. Swan could have libeled the ship on her return to Norfolk in May, 1934, when his claim was four months old. His failure to have done so, joined with the fact that he had again failed to libel her on her next return to this country in November and December of 1934 (thereby showing himself to have been less diligent than the Coke Company had been in the First Circuit litigation) was enough to bar him for laches. The other New York libellant was a paint company which had sold paint to the ship in New Orleans on April 26, 1934.[386] Judge Byers felt that the paint company had been under no duty to libel the ship before her departure for Europe on May 17, particularly since there had been no return visit to New Orleans comparable to the second call at Norfolk in the case of the Swan libel. Libellant could have shown a higher degree of diligence in locating the ship, under her new name and flag in November and December, 1934, but, the judge concluded, "the equities are so nearly in balance that the libel should not be dismissed."

The two liens which were held good against the Everosa represent, so far as the American case law goes, the high water mark in enforcement of liens against good faith purchasers. In both cases less than a month had gone by after the furnishing of the supplies when the ship left for Europe (the companion liens which were held barred being at that time four and six months old). The sale to the new owners took place in Europe when the two liens which were ulti-

385. Note 384 *supra*.

386. Note 384 *supra*.

mately held enforceable were approximately three months old. Both the First Circuit and the New York District Court held that under such circumstances there was no duty on the part of the lienors to seek out and arrest the ship in Europe; they could wait until a return to an American port. The Coke Company served its libel at the first possible opportunity, despite change of name and registry, thereby demonstrating a high degree of diligence. The paint company let the first opportunity go by, but was nevertheless allowed to enforce its lien nearly two and a half years later (there having been no intervening opportunities to libel the ship in American ports). There was no evidence to suggest that the new owners had been in any way prejudiced by the mere lapse of time between 1934 and 1937 nor was there any state statute in Louisiana (where the paint company's lien arose) setting a limitation period for the enforcement of maritime liens. Furthermore it appeared that the Munson Line reorganization trustees had joined in the bill of sale to the Latvian purchasers, warranting that the ship was free from liens and that the purchaser would be held harmless from any liens that might have to be paid. Finally, the paint company's claim was only in the amount of $354. Even so Judge Byers felt that the equities were "nearly in balance" and presumably a featherweight would have tipped the scales in favor of the purchasers. It is a fair conclusion that good faith purchase without notice will bar all preexisting liens more than a few months old and that even such liens will be barred unless the lienors proceed with the utmost diligence (not, however, being required to pursue the ship in foreign ports).[387]

387. Few attempts have been made in the past generation to enforce liens against vessels which have passed into the hands of good faith purchasers.

Judge Cohen reviewed the case material, old and new, in McLaughlin v. Dredge Gloucester, 230 F.Supp. 623, 1964 A.M.C. 2123 (D.N.J.1964) and commented: "Where a maritime lien is to be enforced to the detriment of a *bona fide* purchaser without notice, the libellant must act with extraordinary diligence. As against such a purchaser such lien will be lost in equity after the lapse of a much shorter period of time under the doctrine of laches, than under analogous limitation statutes." (230 F.Supp. at p. 630; 1964 A.M.C. at p. 2133.) He concluded that a libellant who had recovered an in personam judgment in a Jones Act action could not, the judgment having proved uncollectible, bring an in rem action against the vessel six years after the accident and four years after the vessel's sale to a good faith purchaser without notice. On the attempt to bring the in rem action after judgment had been recovered in the in personam action, see note 73 *supra*, where the case is further discussed.

In Waterways Marine, Inc. v. Brooks Liquid Transport, Inc. (M/V Eddie B. ex Linda Brooks), 291 F.Supp. 703, 1968 A.M.C. 2718 (N.D.Ill.1968) supply liens were held barred by laches. Judge Robson commented: "In cases involving maritime liens on a vessel sold to a purchaser for value, a high degree of diligence is required in enforcing these liens."

Layton Industries, Inc. v. Gladiator, 263 F.Supp. 356, 1970 A.M.C. 2423 (D. Mass.1967) is the only recent case in which a lien has been enforced in rem following the vessel's sale to a good faith purchaser without notice. The lien was for the unpaid balance of the purchase price of radar equipment installed on a fishing vessel during July, 1964; the vessel was sold on August 7, 1964, to a buyer who had no notice of the lien; we are not told when the in rem libel was filed. Judge Ford's opinion was devoted almost entirely to a discussion of whether the seller of the radar had acquired a lien. He neither cited nor

§ 9–79. The great bulk of lien litigation involves ships which have continued in the same ownership from the time the lien arose until the date of the libel. There are a few types of lien claims which must be brought within statutory limitation periods: damage claims brought by cargo which moves under Cogsa bills of lading must be commenced within a year from the date when the goods were, or ought to have been, delivered; [388] the Salvage Act of 1912 requires salvage claims to be brought within two years of the act of salvage; [389] actions for wrongful death under the Death on the High Seas Act or under state death statutes must be brought within the statutory period (which is two years in the case of the Federal Act); [390] suits against the United States under the Suits in Admiralty Act must be brought within two years after the accrual of the cause of action.[391] The several limitation periods referred to bar not only the enforcement of lien but the underlying claim itself.

Other maritime claims are not directly subject to any statute of limitation but only to the bar of laches. In determining when lien

discussed any of the earlier good faith purchaser cases. The fact that the vessel was sold within a month after the installation of the equipment may justify the result.

In Todd Shipyards Corp. v. F/V Maigus Luck, 243 F.Supp. 8, 1966 A.M.C. 1608 (D.Canal Zone, 1965) repair liens nearly four years old were asserted against a vessel which a mortgagee had bought when it was sold by a Panamanian court in his foreclosure action. Judge Crowe concluded that the sale by the Panamanian court had not executed existing liens (see § 9–85 *infra*). He apparently did not look on the mortgagee as a good faith purchaser but put off until after trial decision on whether the liens had been barred by laches under the ordinary rules. Technically, Savas v. Maria Trading Corp., 285 F.2d 336, 1961 A.M.C. 260 (4th Cir. 1960) should be listed. A vessel was sold July 17, 1956. On August 10, 1956, the vessel was libeled in rem for services performed for the former owner in August and September, 1955. A decree in rem was issued against the vessel but the former owner, who appeared in the case, was held liable in personam to the purchaser on his warranty that the vessel, when sold, was free of liens. No doubt because of the presence of the former owner, the good faith purchase question seems not to have been raised and was not discussed in Judge Soper's opinion. The case is further discussed in § 9–90 *infra*, text following note 474a.

See among the older cases Phelps v. The Cecilia Ann, 199 F.2d 627, 1952 A.M.C. 1968 (4th Cir. 1952) (repair lien barred against motor boat; libels filed more than two years after furnishing of repairs; sale to good faith purchaser seven months before libels filed); The Arlene-The Bacardi (Fey v. Jewell), 1951 A.M.C. 1205 (W.D.Wash.1951) (collision tort lien: collision Sept., 1949; sale to good faith purchasers May, 1950, and July, 1950; libel filed August, 1950: *held*: lien barred); The Grace Darling, 18 F.2d 587 (D. Mass.1927) (supply lien; libel filed 15 months after supplies furnished; sale to good faith purchaser 8 months before libel filed: *held*: lien barred). In The J. W. Scott, 289 F. 495 (S.D. Fla.1923) a supply-lien was enforced against a tug sold to a good faith purchaser, the libel having been filed eight months after the supplies were furnished and five months after the sale. It appeared, however, that the tug had not been in local waters during the eight months period and that libelant had not known of the intervening sale.

388. 49 Stat. 1208 (1936); 46 U.S.C.A. § 1303(6).

389. 37 Stat. 242 (1912); 46 U.S.C.A. § 730.

390. 41 Stat. 537 (1920); 46 U.S.C.A. § 763.

391. 41 Stat. 526 (1920); 46 U.S.C.A. § 745.

status has been lost or a claim become barred, the admiralty court will look for analogy to whatever it may consider to be the applicable state or foreign statute of limitation.

Many of the state lien statutes which were in force when the Federal Maritime Lien Act was passed set short limitation periods for the enforcement of liens (as distinct from the enforcement of the underlying claims). The Lien Act provided that "nothing in this chapter shall be construed to affect the rules of law existing on June 5, 1920, in regard to . . . (2) laches in the enforcement of liens upon vessels . . . ." [392]

In the light of that provision the Second Circuit shortly held that the New York Lien Act period (12 months) still applied to a lien for supplies furnished to a vessel whose home port was New York and dismissed a libel *in rem* against the ship although allowing a libel *in personam* against the owner to proceed.[393] The decision was criticized as destructive of the uniformity which the Lien Act had been designed to create and as perpetuating the pre-Lien Act distinction between home port and foreign liens (since it was assumed that the state statutes applied only to home port liens and that foreign ship liens were under general maritime law).[394] A few years later in The Owyhee [395] the Second Circuit, acknowledging the criticism, conceded that the language in the earlier opinion "appears to have been somewhat too broad". Lien Act liens, said Judge Chase, are subject to the "general rules relating to laches in admiralty" as set out in the Supreme Court's 1871 decision in The Key City [396] and not to state lien statutes, even as to home port liens. But, he continued, "[t]he New York statute furnishes a comparative test for giving effect to time elapsed beyond it and marks the boundary between the period when liens may be enforced regardless of the time when the action is brought and the period when some explanation of the delay is required." In The Owyhee a repairman libeled a yacht *in rem* and her owner *in personam* more than a year after the completion of a rebuilding job; the holder of a duly recorded (but apparently non-maritime) mortgage on the yacht intervened in opposition to the lien claim. There had been an arbitration proceeding between repairman and owner, with an award in favor of the repairman (handed down about three months before the expiration of the statutory limitation period) which he had made "repeated attempts" to collect but without success. The Circuit, affirming the District Court, held that no sufficient excuse had been shown for delay beyond the 12 months al-

392. 41 Stat. 1005 (1920); 46 U.S.C.A. § 974.

393. The Fort Orange (Nolte v. Hudson Navigation Co.) 297 F. 758, 1924 A.M.C. 276 (2d Cir. 1924), certiorari denied *sub nom.* Conron Bros. & Co. v. Farmers' Loan & Trust Co., 264 U.S. 590, 44 S.Ct. 403 (1924).

394. 3 Benedict, Admiralty 300, n. 37 (6th ed. 1940). The criticism first appeared in the Fifth edition of Benedict, 1924.

395. (Greenport Basin & Construction Co., Inc. v. Silkworth) 66 F.2d 399, 1933 A.M.C. 1185 (2d Cir. 1933).

396. Note 382 *supra.*

lowed by the statute and dismissed the libel *in rem,* judgment going against the owner on the libel *in personam.*

The Owyhee apparently involved repairs to a domestic or home port vessel so that the rule suggested by Judge Chase of looking to the state lien act limitation provisions for a "comparative test" and requiring libellant to show an "excuse" for any delay does not necessarily have to be taken as applying to all liens, both domestic and foreign. Nevertheless, the background of the case suggests that the Court had a general rule in mind: the decision was put expressly under "general maritime law" as preserved by the Lien Act and the Court's acknowledgement of criticism of its decision in The Fort Orange, suggests that a uniform rule was contemplated. Thus The Owyhee may be taken to stand for the proposition that the State lien statutes ("superseded" but not repealed by the Federal Lien Act) [397] still have, as one of their few surviving functions, that of setting time periods for the enforcement of liens. In general the lien and the underlying claim (except where the ship has been sold to a purchaser without notice) become barred at the same point in time. Under The Owyhee, however, where the state statute has a "loss of lien" provision like that of the New York Lien Act, the lien status will be lost —*i. e.* both lien priority and the right to proceed *in rem*—before the claim itself has been barred.

The Owyhee has not been followed in any recent case and the indications are that it will not be followed if the issue is squarely presented for decision. In Merchants & Marine Bank v. T. E. Welles [397a] Judge Brown concluded that the Court need not decide the issue and thus need not undertake "the none too easy task of determining whether to approve the doctrine of Owyhee", to which he then devoted a long and disapproving footnote in the course of which he observed that "the *Owyhee* and its progenitors . . . have been severely criticized because the decision seemed to be a curious transfusion of life into state statutes in the face of comprehensive legislation designed to overcome the bewildering complexities of the old half-Federal half-State structure." [397b] The contract liens covered by the State lien statutes enjoy a low order of priority against competing liens and will be subordinated to later contract liens of the same type if the lienholders allow the relevant priority period to run without filing their libels.[397c] Since the "state" liens will be in any case subordinated there seems to be no reason why, under The Owyhee,

**397.** See §§ 9–30, 9–35, *supra.*

**397a.** 289 F.2d 188, 1961 A.M.C. 1042 (5th Cir. 1961).

**397b.** The reason why the issue did not have to be decided was that supply and repair liens which in earlier proceedings had been assumed to antedate a preferred mortgage were discovered to be post-mortgage liens and subordinate to the mortgage for that reason. In United States v. American Gas Screw Franz Joseph, 210 F.Supp. 581, 1963 A.M.C. 1596 (D.Alaska, 1962) Judge Kilkenny echoed Judge Brown's criticism of The Owyhee. The Franz Joseph was a forfeiture case in which the United States argued unsuccessfully that delay by a mortgage in foreclosing a defaulted mortgage constituted laches (see note 273a *supra.*)

**397c.** See §§ 9–61 to 9–66 *supra.*

they should be deprived of lien status in the unlikely case where there is money left in the distribution fund after all prior liens have been paid off. No doubt the shift in judicial attitudes toward laches during the 1960's, which will be discussed in the following section, makes it in the highest degree unlikely that The Owyhee will ever be heard from again. The problem of laches with respect to contract liens which antedate or postdate a preferred mortgage will be discussed in a subsequent section.[397d]

**§ 9–80.** When a claim is asserted by libel *in rem* or by libel *in personam* or both, after it has become unenforceable under the statute of limitations which would apply if the action were not in admiralty, the admiralty court will not automatically dismiss the proceeding but will consider both the extent of the delay and the degree of prejudice to the defendant resulting from the delay. In its first discussion of the admiralty doctrine of laches since 1871, the Supreme Court said in a brief *per curiam* opinion in 1951:

> "Though the existence of laches is a question primarily addressed to the discretion of the trial court, the matter should not be determined merely by a reference to and a mechanical application of the statute of limitation. The equities of the parties must be considered as well. Where there has been no inexcusable delay in seeking a remedy and where no prejudice to the defendant has ensued from the mere passage of time, there should be no bar to relief." [398]

The Gardner case was an action by a passenger to recover for personal injuries sustained on a ship owned by the Panama Railroad Company. Her first suit against the Company had been dismissed on the ground that her remedy was against the United States under the Tort

**397d.** See § 9–83 *infra.*

**398.** Gardner v. Panama R. Co., 342 U.S. 29, 30, 72 S.Ct. 12, 13, 1951 A.M.C. 2048, 2049 (1951).

In Czaplicki v. S. S. Hoegh Silvercloud, 351 U.S. 525, 76 S.Ct. 946, 1956 A.M.C. 1465 (1956), the Court reiterated the liberal attitude toward the laches problem which it had expressed in the Gardner case. After quoting the last sentence of the passage from the Gardner opinion set out in the text, Justice Harlan added: "This does not mean, of course, that the State statutes of limitation are immaterial in determining whether laches is a bar, but it does mean that they are not conclusive, and that the determination should not be made without first considering all the circumstances bearing on the issue." For the facts of the Czaplicki case, see Chapter VI, note 377.5.

In Gutierrez v. Waterman Steamship Corp., 373 U.S. 206, 83 S.Ct. 1185, 1963 A.M.C. 1649 (1963), rehearing denied 374 U.S. 858, 83 S.Ct. 1863 (1963) (a longshoreman's personal injury action for unseaworthiness) Justice White observed: "The test of laches is prejudice to the other party." The trial court had found that a libel filed two years and four months after the "analogous statute of limitations" had run was not barred by laches because there had been no prejudice to the other party. The First Circuit reversed on the ground that inexcusable delay, without more, constituted laches. Reinstating the disposition of the case by the trial court, Justice White wrote: "The Court of Appeals had no reason to reverse this finding [of no laches] as plainly erroneous merely because in some way it might have been more advantageous to respondent to question the witnesses sooner than it did."

Claims Act. She then sued the United States only to see that suit fail when Congress amended the Tort Claims Act to exclude from its coverage "any claim arising from the activities of the Panama Railroad Company". Five days after the dismissal of the second suit she instituted another action against the Railroad Company. The applicable Panama statute of limitations was one year and the third suit was begun ten months after the statute had run. On those facts, the Court held, the trial court had abused its discretion in dismissing her action for laches.

The Gardner case obviously involved an exceptionally diligent plaintiff caught in a series of procedural traps not of her own making. For some years the lower federal courts continued to assume that the discretion of a trial court in dismissing a libel for laches was not lightly to be interfered with. Thus the Fifth Circuit read Gardner as justifying a District Court's dismissal of libels by longshoremen to recover for personal injuries alleged to have been caused by poisonous fumigants in a cargo of grain, the libels being filed two and a half years after the accident, the applicable Texas statute of limitations being two years.[399] The Court held that prejudice to the defendant from delay would be presumed, unless rebutted by the plaintiffs, and that the mere fact that plaintiffs were "ignorant and unlettered persons" was no excuse. Delay occasioned by attempts to settle or compromise disputes was looked on as a good excuse[400] and the Third Circuit allowed an *in personam* action for personal injuries by a seaman to be brought five years and three months after the accident (the Pennsylvania statute being two years) where it appeared that the master, on behalf of the defendant, had promised plaintiff that he would be taken care of if he did not sue but that he would be "through on the river" if he did sue.[401] But through the 1950's the dilatory plaintiff ran a severe risk of seeing his action dismissed unless he could both excuse his own delay and prove that no prejudice to the other party had resulted.[402]

Beginning about 1960 there was a flurry of laches litigation—most of the cases involved seamen's claims for death, personal injuries, maintenance and cure or unpaid wages—in which District Courts which had dismissed actions for laches on the ground of un-

399. Morales v. Moore-McCormack Lines, Inc., 208 F.2d 218, 1954 A.M.C. 87 (5th Cir. 1953).

400. Virginia Shipbuilding Corp. v. U. S. Shipping Bd. Emergency Fleet Corp., 11 F.2d 156, 1925 A.M.C. 668 (E.D.Va.1925); see The Adour, 21 F. 2d 858, 1927 A.M.C. 1746 (D.Md.1927).

401. Taylor v. Crain, 195 F.2d 163, 1952 A.M.C. 589 (3d Cir. 1952). See also The McElroy-The Walker (Simpson Oil Co., Inc. v. The Pure Oil Co.) 127 F.Supp. 867, 1955 A.M.C. 413 (E.D.La. 1955); U. N. R. R. A. v. The Mormacmail, 99 F.Supp. 552, 1951 A.M.C. 1152 (S.D.N.Y.1951).

402. In the following cases libels were dismissed for laches: United Fruit Co. v. The M. D. Whiteman, 125 F. Supp. 898, 1955 A.M.C. 111 (E.D.La. 1954); Wilson v. Northwest Marine Iron Works, 212 F.2d 510, 1954 A.M.C. 1170 (9th Cir. 1954); Kane v. U. S. S. R., 189 F.2d 303, 1951 A.M.C. 1100 (3d Cir. 1951); Redman v. United Fruit Co., 185 F.2d 553, 1951 A.M.C. 63 (2d Cir. 1950); Redman v. United States, 176 F.2d 713, 1949 A.M.C. 1518 (2d Cir. 1949).

excused delay found themselves reversed and the cases remanded for further proceedings on the question whether the delay, although unexcused, had indeed been prejudicial to the defendant.[402a] In the course of this reevaluation of the laches problem the various Circuit Courts began to question some of their own cases decided during the previous period.[402b] Judge Brown summed up the changing attitude in Mr. Kim:[402c]

> "The inquiry on laches partakes of two parts—(1) the excuse for the delay and (2) prejudice to the pursued. As Judge Friendly's opinion in [the Larios case[402d]] carefully develops, the emphasis is more and more on (2)—prejudice—than on (1). "A weak excuse may suffice if there has been no prejudice; an exceedingly good one may still do even where there has been some." . . . The delay aspect is extremely relative."[402e]

The laches cases seem to have drawn no distinction between actions *in rem* to enforce maritime liens and actions *in personam* either on the admiralty side or the civil side. No doubt the distinct shift in the handling of the laches problem during the 1960's was connected with, or was part of, the vast expansion of seamen's remedies which the Supreme Court had initiated during the 1940's and, as we have pointed out, most of the 1960's cases did involve seamen's actions for death, personal injury, and the like. Nevertheless, the opinions were in no way restricted to the problem as it appeared in such cases. There is no reason to believe that libellants who are holders of liens for sup-

**402a.** See, *e. g.*, Claussen v. Mene Grande Oil Co., 275 F.2d 108, 1961 A.M.C. 475 (3d Cir. 1960) (action for maintenance and cure and personal injuries; nine year delay); Cities Service Oil Co. v. Puerto Rico Lighterage Co. (Royal Oak), 305 F.2d 170, 1962 A.M.C. 1941 (1st Cir. 1962) (collision libel); Larios v. Victory Carriers, Inc., 316 F.2d 63, 1963 A.M.C. 1704 (2d Cir. 1963) (seaman's action for personal injuries; delay of two months beyond running of analogous limitation statute). There was a great deal of litigation of this type in the Fifth Circuit; Judge Brown collected the Fifth Circuit cases in Molnar v. Gulfcoast Transit Co., 371 F.2d 639, 1967 A.M.C. 1925 (5th Cir. 1967) (seamen's personal injury claims; delays of from two months to over a year beyond the applicable three year statute of limitations). See also, in the Fifth Circuit sequence, Fidelity & Casualty Co. v. C/B Mr. Kim, 345 F.2d 45, 1965 A.M.C. 1944 (5th Cir. 1965); Akers v. State Marine Lines, Inc., 344 F.2d 217, 1965 A.M.C. 1395 (5th Cir. 1965); Watz v. Zapata Off-Shore Co., 431 F.2d 100, 1970 A.M.C. 2307 (5th Cir. 1970).

**402b.** Such as the Morales case, note 399 *supra* which is regularly cited as a horrible example in the later Fifth Circuit cases, note 402a *supra*.

**402c.** See note 402a *supra*.

**402d.** See note 402a *supra*.

**402e.** 345 F.2d at p. 50, 1965 A.M.C. at p. 1949. Judge Brown went on to quote further from Judge Friendly's Larios opinion: "saying that a plaintiff who has cleared each of two hurdles will win is not the same as saying that a plaintiff must fully clear each of two hurdles to win" as well as from Judge Hutcheson's opinion in the Akers case (see note 402a *supra*): "A suit in admiralty is barred by laches only when there has been both [1] unreasonable delay in the filing of the libels and [2] consequent prejudice to the party against whom suit is brought." For more on the Larios case, see text following note 409c *infra*.

plies, repairs and other necessaries will not benefit from the new approach to laches in exactly the same way that the death and personal injury libellants have.

The flurry of laches litigation, after having gone on for the better part of ten years, began to subside after the mid-1960's. Presumably, the District Courts, who until 1965 or so had been routinely following the older precedents, had learned their lesson and no longer dismissed for laches on delay alone.[402f]

**§ 9–81.** The older case law suggested that when laches was apparent on the face of the libel, the issue of laches could be raised by exception to the libel and need not be pleaded at an affirmative defense.[403] "Laches apparent on the face of the libel" seemed to mean that an inspection of the pleadings alone would reveal that the applicable limitation period had run; in such a case the libel was to be automatically dismissed on exception unless the libellant justified the delay in his original pleading or in an amended libel.[404]

The rule just stated assumed that there was no doubt as to what the applicable statute of limitations was. That was a reasonable assumption in many types of cases: supply and repair claims fell under the contract statute; collision and other tort claims fell under the tort statute. The developing case law revealed, however, a good many situations in which it was by no means clear what statute applied. Cargo damage claims presented a problem: was the action in tort for injury to property or in contract for breach of the contract of carriage? There was case authority that such cargo claims were founded in contract and thus ranked below tort claims in the hierarchy of lien priorities.[405] The Second Circuit, however, held that a three year tort statute covering "injury to property" and not a six

**402f.** On the prejudice which, combined with delay, will justify dismissal for laches Vega v. S/S Malula, 291 F.2d 415, 1961 A.M.C. 1698 (5th Cir. 1961) and its companion case Delgado v. S/S Malula, 291 F.2d 420, 1961 A.M.C. 1706 (5th Cir. 1961) are instructive. Both libellants were longshoremen; both actions were to recover for personal injuries. In Vega's case the libel was filed five years after his injury, in Delgado's case four years after his injury—well beyond the applicable limitation period in both cases. In Vega's case it was held that the action was not barred by laches since no prejudice was found to have resulted from the delay. In Delgado's case prejudice was found and the District Court's order dismissing the libel was affirmed. See also Goodwyn v. Dredge Ginger Ann, 342 F.2d 197, 1965 A.M.C. 1836 (5th Cir. 1965) affirming per curiam the District Court's dismissal for laches of a maintenance and cure action filed four and a half years after the libellant had contracted poliomyelitis.

**403.** See United States v. Alex Dussel Iron Works, 31 F.2d 535, 1929 A.M.C. 573 (5th Cir. 1929).

**404.** However, in United States v. Baltimore Towing Co., 144 F.Supp. 854, 1956 A.M.C. 2045 (D.Md.1956), Judge Thomsen, principally on the authority of the Dussel case, note 403 *supra*, concluded that "[i]t is clear that the government is not concluded by the mere passage of time and that it need not set out in its libel any reason for its delay." Judge Thomsen therefore refused to dismiss on exceptions an *in personam* libel filed in 1956 with respect to a 1947 collision, saying that respondents could set up in their answer or at trial any facts showing that they had been prejudiced by the delay or that the government should be "estopped".

**405.** See text at note 319 *supra*.

year statute covering "an action upon a contract obligation" applied to the case of a barge load of scrap iron which ended up at the bottom of a canal following a collision.[406] Actions to recover for personal injuries, whether based upon negligence or unseaworthiness, were usually assumed to come under the tort statute covering personal injury actions.[407] In 1930 the Second Circuit suggested that, while the three year tort statute applied to an unseaworthiness action, the six year contract statute applied to a suit by a seaman to recover maintenance and cure.[408] In 1955, the same court reconsidered the unseaworthiness question in Le Gate v. The Panamolga,[409] an action by a stevedore based both on negligence and unseaworthiness. The applicable New York statute prescribed a three year limitation for personal injury actions based on negligence and a six year limitation for other types of personal injury actions. On the theory that "a claim for recovery based on breach of warranty of seaworthiness is not the same as one based on negligence", the six year period was held applicable to the unseaworthiness count. However, Judge Burke continued, citing the Supreme Court's Gardner opinion, "[w]e are not disposed . . . to mechanically apply the State statutes of limitation without regard to the equities," and reached what might be considered a hybrid result. Le Gate had filed his libel three years and five months after the accident, too late for the negligence count but comfortably within what the Court found the unseaworthiness period to be. "[I]t would be a harsh result to permit the case to continue and at the same time limit its scope." Therefore the six year statute would apply to both counts but the defendants would be allowed to show that the libellant's delay in bringing suit had prejudiced them. If they should successfully bear the burden of proof on prejudice, the District Court would be within its discretion in dismissing the libel for laches even though the libel had been filed within the statutory period.

Whether the libellant was required to plead facts justifying his own delay and negativing prejudice to the other party or whether the libellee was required to plead laches as an affirmative defense, there was general agreement in the case law until the 1960's that the libellant or plaintiff bore the burden of proof both on excuse for the delay and on the lack of resulting prejudice.[409a] The reason why the burden

406. Schiavone-Bonomo Corp. v. Buffalo Barge Towing Corp., 132 F.2d 766, 1943 A.M.C. 48 (2d Cir. 1942).

407. See the Wilson, Kane and Redman cases cited in note 402 *supra*, The Adour note 400 *supra* and the Morales case note 399 *supra*.

408. Marshall v. International Mercantile Marine Co., 39 F.2d 551, 1930 A.M.C. 720 (2d Cir. 1930); followed in Benjamin v. U. S., 85 F.Supp. 948, 1949 A.M.C. 1165 (S.D.N.Y.1949).

409. 221 F.2d 689, 1955 A.M.C. 1187 (2d Cir. 1955).

The Le Gate case was reaffirmed in Tesoriero v. M. S. Molda, 232 F.2d 311, 1956 A.M.C. 836 (2d Cir. 1956). In Cummings v. Redeeriaktieb Transatlantic, 144 F.Supp. 422, 1956 A.M.C. 1336 (E.D.Pa.1956), the action was for personal injuries, with counts for negligence and for unseaworthiness. The District Judge, citing Le Gate, held that the tort statute (two years) applied to the negligence count but that the contract statute (six years) applied to the unseaworthiness count.

409a. See the Kane case and the two Redman cases cited note 402 *supra*. See also, to the same effect, Oroz v.

of proof was cast on libellant not only to excuse his own delay but also to prove that the delay had not prejudiced the other party was usually explained in terms of a "presumption of prejudice": the statutory limitation period having run, injury to the other party was presumed until the contrary was proved.[409b]

The traditional allocation of the burden of proof did not survive the reexamination of the laches problem during the 1960's which was discussed in the preceding section. Judge Friendly addressed himself to the question in Larios v. Victory Carriers, Inc.[409c] After reviewing the earlier Second Circuit cases which had adopted the traditional approach, he went on:

> "We cannot regard it as consistent with [the decisions of the Supreme Court in Gardner [409d] and Czaplicki [409e]] to hold that expiration of the analogous state statute creates a 'presumption of prejudice', save in the sense that if the plaintiff proffers no pleading or presents no proof on the issue of laches, the defendant wins. Nor can we agree that when such a plaintiff has presented evidence excusing his own delay, he should nevertheless be automatically barred unless he also presents anticipatory evidence to negate prejudice on the part of the defendant, an issue as to which the defendant, with his greater knowledge, ought to be required to come forward. Rather, when a plaintiff who asserts a maritime claim after the state statute has run, presents evidence tending to excuse his delay, the court must weigh the legitimacy of his excuse, the inference to be drawn from the expiration of the state statute, and the length of the delay, along with evidence as to prejudice if the defendant comes forward with any. Moreover, although a plaintiff who has delayed bringing suit beyond the analogous state period has the ultimate burden of persuasion both as to the excuse for his own delay and as to lack of prejudice to the defendant, see Gilmore & Black, Admiralty (1957), 631, these two factors are not to be viewed independently." [409f]

Judge Friendly's analysis of the problem was shortly adopted in the Fifth Circuit [409g] and, given its inherent reasonableness, there is every reason to believe that it will be generally followed.[409h]

American President Lines, 259 F.2d 636, 1958 A.M.C. 2343 (2d Cir. 1958); McMahon v. Pan American World Airways, Inc., 297 F.2d 268, 1962 A.M.C. 655 (5th Cir. 1962).

**409b.** For an early expression of this attitude, see McGrath v. Panama R. Co., 298 F. 303 (5th Cir. 1924).

**409c.** 316 F.2d 63, 1963 A.M.C. 1704 (2d Cir. 1963).

**409d.** See text at note 398 *supra*.

**409e.** See note 398 *supra*.

**409f.** 316 F.2d at pp. 66–67, 1963 A.M.C. at p. 1708.

**409g.** See Judge Brown's opinion in Mr. Kim, note 402e *supra* and the accompanying text quoting further from Judge Friendly's Larios opinion.

**409h.** The Third Circuit, however, declined to follow Larios and reaffirmed the "presumption of prejudice" cases in Burke v. Gateway Clipper, Inc., 441

§ 9–82. A consequence of the mobility of ships is that a libel will often be filed in the admiralty court sitting in State A in respect of an accident or transaction which occurred in another State or in a foreign country. We are not here concerned with the general issue of when such libels will be dismissed for lack of jurisdiction or on the ground of *forum non conveniens* or with the choice of law problem when the court decides to exercise jurisdiction.[410] Assuming that the court has taken jurisdiction and decided that the substantive law of another state or of a foreign country is applicable, we consider whether the court, in determining whether the action (or the lien) has become time-barred, will look to the local or to the foreign statute of limitations.

The general conflict of laws rule is that a court, in enforcing the substantive law of another jurisdiction, will apply the procedural rules of the forum.[411] Statutes of limitation are usually considered procedural, so that the local time period for bringing suit governs, although so-called "borrowing" statutes [412] are not uncommon which bar actions when they would no longer be maintainable either under the law of the forum or under the law of the jurisdiction whose substantive law applies, whichever is shorter. The rule that statutes of limitation are procedural and not substantive has often been the butt of scholastic criticism and has been described as nothing more than an accident of history.[413] Perhaps because of inarticulate judicial dissatisfaction with the rule or perhaps because to so complex a problem there is no satisfactory solution, there has grown up a counter-rule which is as well established as the rule itself. By the counter-rule the foreign statute of limitations may be considered as substantive and thus applied in preference to the local limitation rule provided the foreign statute, in an oft repeated slogan, attaches to the right and not merely to the remedy. It is not everyone who is so endowed by nature that he can unerringly distinguish between rights and remedies, so that even when both rule and counter-rule have been stated there is still room for argument and dispute.

With respect to libels in admiralty the situation becomes further complicated because of the theory that the court in most cases applies a statute of limitations only by analogy and will entertain suits

F.2d 946, 1971 A.M.C. 1623 (3d Cir. 1971).

410. Those issues are discussed in the context of seaman's suits for personal injury in Chapter VI, § 6–63 *et seq.* See also the discussion of the law applicable to foreign ship mortgages, § 9–51 *supra*, text following note 262b.

411. See generally Restatement of the Conflict of Laws (Second), Chapter 6 (1971). The doctrine was reviewed, in an admiralty setting, by Judge Harlan in Bournias v. Atlantic Maritime Co., Ltd., 220 F.2d 152, 1955 A.M.C. 523 (2d Cir. 1955). The Bournias case is discussed *infra*, text at note 416.

412. Janes v. Sackman Bros. Co., 177 F.2d 928, 1950 A.M.C. 72 (2d Cir. 1949) (not an admiralty case) contains an interesting discussion of such statutes by Clark, J. See Restatement, note 411 *supra*, § 142.

413. Harlan J. in the Bournias case, note 411 *supra*, quoting Lorenzen, Statutes of Limitation and the Conflict of Laws, 28 Yale L.J. 492 (1919).

commenced beyond the limitation period if the delay is excusable and if there has been no resulting prejudice to defendant. In Levinson v. Deupree [414] the Supreme Court made clear that federal courts sitting in admiralty are not subject to Erie-Tompkins theory and, specifically, not to the rule of Guaranty Trust Co. v. York [415] which requires federal courts sitting in equity to apply state conflict of laws rules. The question in the Levinson case, said Justice Frankfurter, was whether an admiralty court enforcing a state-created right for wrongful death "must also be bound by the dubious and perhaps conflicting intimations on *elegantia juris* to be found in local decisions [and be] imprisoned by procedural niceties . . .". The answer was No. The admiralty court, in deciding whether an action is to be barred for laches on the analogy of a foreign or of a local statute, is in a position to manipulate the concepts with a degree of flexibility not allowed to other courts.

In Bournias v. Atlantic Maritime Co., Ltd.,[416] the Second Circuit reviewed the subject and announced a rule which cannot be criticized for being unduly rigid. Bournias, a seaman, employed on a ship of Panamanian registry, brought suit in the Southern District of New York for wages, alleging as one cause of action rights based on the Panama Labor Code and as a second cause of action a right to penalties under Section 596 of Title 46 of the United States Code for his employer's failure to have paid him the amounts alleged to be due under Panama law. Thus the second cause of action, based on American law, depended on the first, based on Panama law. The Panama Labor Code provided that claims such as those advanced by Bournias were barred unless brought within a year from their accrual and Bournias did not file his libel until two years had elapsed. The New York statute of limitations for actions based on contract is six years, but New York also has the customary "borrowing" statute which provides that when a cause of action accrues outside New York in favor of a non-resident, it shall be barred in New York if either the New York or the foreign statute of limitations has run. The defense of laches having been raised in the District Court, Judge Conger concluded that, in view of the "borrowing" statute, it made no difference whether the Panama limitation statute was thought to be substantive or procedural, as going to the right or merely to the remedy, since in either case it would apply.[417] Going a step further, Judge Conger felt that, by analogy to the enforcement in admiralty of state-created wrongful death claims, this was a case where the admiralty court was required to apply the foreign statute directly, including its limitation provisions, and not to proceed on grounds of laches.

The Circuit reversed in an opinion which is not a model of lucidity. Judge Harlan apparently did not agree with the analogy

414. 345 U.S. 648, 73 S.Ct. 914, 1953 A.M.C. 972 (1953).

415. 326 U.S. 99, 65 S.Ct. 1464 (1945).

416. 220 F.2d 152, 1955 A.M.C. 523 (2d Cir. 1955).

417. 117 F.Supp. 864, 1954 A.M.C. 602 (S.D.N.Y.1954).

drawn from the state-created death claim cases, which are perhaps to be treated as *sui generis*; even though Bournias' claim was based on Panama (and not on maritime) law, the admiralty rule of laches would govern. With respect to the choice between the New York and Panama limitation periods, Judge Harlan developed a test of "specificity", drawn from an old Supreme Court case, Davis v. Mills,[418] in which Justice Holmes had discussed the subject. That is, if the foreign limitation was "directed to the newly created liability so *specifically* as to warrant saying that it qualified the right", then it is to prevail over the local limitation. If not, not. The test, Judge Harlan conceded, "leaves much to be desired":

> "It permits the existence of a substantial gray area between the black and the white. But it at least furnishes a practical means of mitigating what is at best an artificial rule in the conflict of laws without exposing us to the pitfalls inherent in prolonged excursions into foreign law. . . . We conclude, therefore, that the 'specificity' test is the proper one to be applied in a case of this type, without deciding, of course, whether the same test would also be controlling in cases involving domestic or other kinds of foreign statutes of limitation." [419]

Coming down to the facts of Bournias' case and the provisions of the Panama Labor Code, Judge Harlan concluded that the section imposing the one year limitation on Bournias' claim was not "specific" enough to prevail. Unaccountably, Judge Harlan's opinion did not mention the New York "borrowing" statute which, according to Judge Conger, made the whole discussion irrelevant. It is hard to believe that the Circuit could have meant to instruct the District Judge to apply New York law (the Panama statute having failed in "specificity") but to disregard the New York borrowing statute: however free from Erie-Tompkins the admiralty court may be, it cannot be that free.[419a] So it may be that, on the facts of the case, the reversal meant merely that the District Court should have treated the case as one of laches rather than limitation, Judge Harlan's essay on "specificity" being merely *belles-lettres*.

Looked on as a rule of law, the "specificity test" has nothing in its favor if it is really meant to be a rational device for measuring foreign statutes of limitation against some theoretical yardstick. The point need hardly be labored that one man's specificity is another man's generality. On the other hand, the several rules of thumb which the courts have worked out for determining when statutes go to the right and when to the remedy have all been found wanting. "Specificity" is as good a word as any if what is meant is that the

418. 194 U.S. 451, 24 S.Ct. 692 (1904).

419. 220 F.2d 152, 156, 157, 1955 A.M.C. 523, 529. The Restatement of Conflicts (Second), note 411 *supra*, "codifies" the right-remedy distinction in § 143. In the Reporter's Note to § 143 the Bournias opinion is referred to as "particularly notable".

419a. See The Percy Jordan, digested note 419b *infra*.

trial court should (in the absence of a "borrowing" statute) decide on the equities of the case which statute it wants to apply.[419b]

§ 9–83. Under the Ship Mortgage Act liens arising prior in time to a mortgage have priority over it while most subsequent contract liens are subordinate to it. The Act also provides that nothing in it shall be construed to affect the rules of maritime law as to priorities among liens or as to loss of lien through laches. The two provisions taken together create more than one logical puzzle. One, which involves priorities, has already been mentioned: the pre-mortgage lien, which prevails over the mortgage, may under maritime law be subordinate to the post-mortgage lien, which, in its turn, is subordinate to the mortgage. When the problem has been posed as one involving a system of circular priorities, the courts have broken out of the circle by relegating the post-mortgage lien to third place, after the pre-mortgage lien and the mortgage.[420]

Comparable questions arise when the pre-mortgage lienholder can be described as having been guilty of laches. On the lowest level of complexity is the situation of a lienholder who, knowing that a mortgage loan is about to be made, takes no steps to disclose his claim to the prospective mortgagee or affirmatively misleads the mortgagee into thinking that he has no claim.[421] The situation becomes more complex when the lienholder has no notice of the mortgage (except constructive notice from its recordation). Judge Allred dealt with this situation in The J. R. Hardee.[422] A mortgage had become preferred under the Ship Mortgage Act on August 22, 1950. Two supply liens were claimed, one for supplies furnished between February and May, 1950, the other for supplies furnished between January and July, 1950. Both lienors continued to furnish supplies for some months after recordation of the mortgage; one of them never received any payments on his account, the last payment to the other was in October, 1950. The ship was libeled by a salvage lienor in November, 1951. Judge Allred held that the pre-mortgage supply liens had lost their priority over the mortgage, being "guilty of laches by virtue of the long delay in asserting their claims, if, indeed, they did not waive them." It will be noted that the supply liens

**419b.** See Argyll Shipping Co., Ltd. v. The Hanover Ins. Co. (S/S Percy Jordan), 297 F.Supp. 125, 1968 A.M.C. 2195 (S.D.N.Y.1968) in which Judge Metzner, taking the Bournias case as governing authority, concluded that, under the New York borrowing statute, a Japanese statute of limitations should be looked to as the standard for determining laches. See further Judge Brown's discussion of these points in Vega v. S/S Malula, 291 F.2d 415, 1961 A.M.C. 1698 (5th Cir. 1961).

**420.** See § 9–71 *supra*.

**421.** See The Eastern Shore (R.F.C. v. New Castle Terminal Co.), 31 F.Supp. 964, 966, 1940 A.M.C. 388, 391 (D.Md. 1940): "[W]hile there were valid maritime liens [for certain repairs] prior to the mortgage they were at least impliedly waived and subordinated to the mortgage by the conduct of the claimant" in having failed to bring them to the mortgagee's attention.

**422.** 107 F.Supp. 379, 1952 A.M.C. 1124 (S.D.Tex.1952). The J. R. Hardee is discussed in another context § 9–76 *supra*.

thus summarily disposed of in The J. R. Hardee were by no means old or stale when the mortgage loan was made. Both liens were asserted within two years of the oldest item in the accounts, thus comfortably within the contract statute of limitations, and there is no mention of any state lien statute with "loss of lien" provisions comparable to those in the New York statute previously discussed.[423] Yet the liens were held barred against the mortgage (which swallowed up the entire fund available for distribution) on the ground of a delay in enforcement of somewhat more than a year after the execution of the mortgage, the ship having apparently been at all times in local waters and available to process.

Further complexities were suggested by Judge Aldrich in National Shawmut Bank v. The Winthrop[424] which, like The J. R. Hardee, involved a mortgage flanked by prior and subsequent contract liens. Judge Allred in The J. R. Hardee had not bothered much about the post-mortgage liens, since he found the pre-mortgage liens guilty of laches against the mortgage and the mortgage exhausted the distribution fund. In The Winthrop it occurred to Judge Aldrich to speculate on the situation which would arise if the pre-mortgage liens were not guilty of laches against the mortgagee but were guilty of laches against post-mortgage lienors. "If," he wrote, "laches occurred after the mortgage but before the post-mortgage liens, either the post-mortgage lienors may not get the due benefit of this because the ante-mortgage liens will be preferred over the mortgage which in turn is paramount to them, or, if the post-mortgage liens are given preference over the guilty liens because of their laches, this benefit will in turn accrue to the mortgage since it is paramount to the post-mortgage liens." Whereupon the case was referred back to the commissioner for the taking of further testimony. Judge Aldrich seems to have constructed his dilemma principally out of the assumption that the post-mortgage lienors were to be ranked as good faith purchasers.

In a second opinion,[425] after the taking of further testimony, Judge Aldrich, although adhering to his earlier position that subsequent lienors could be ranked as good faith purchasers for purposes of application of the laches doctrine, nevertheless chose to ignore his own speculations in the first opinion. He concluded that the proper order of distribution should be: (1) the ante-mortgage liens, except any barred by laches at the date of the mortgage; (2) the mortgage; (3) the post-mortgage liens, on the calendar year rule; (4) 1951 [*i. e.* ante-mortgage] liens guilty of laches at the date of the mortgage. Thus any post-mortgage laches on the part of the ante-mortgage lienors was disregarded, and the suggestion that the post-mortgage lienors would rank as good faith purchasers with respect to prior liens receded into dictum. On the

423. See § 9–79 *supra.*

424. 129 F.Supp. 661, 1955 A.M.C. 1288 (D.Mass.1955).

425. 134 F.Supp. 370, 1955 A.M.C. 2089 (D.Mass.1955).

other hand, the existence of the post-mortgage liens may have induced Judge Aldrich to apply a more than usually strict rule in determining which of the pre-mortgage liens had lost their statutory priority by reason of laches at the date of the mortgage, being relegated as a result to fourth and last priority. Indeed the rule which he adopted was that all pre-mortgage liens more than ten months old at the time the mortgage lien arose were guilty of laches vis-a-vis the mortgage. He remarked, without further explanation, that ten months, as the commissioner who had heard the case had found, was "the normal period . . . for laches" and cited The Everosa [426] in support of the ten month rule.

If The J. R. Hardee and The Winthrop are to be taken, on their own terms, as laches cases, it might seem that both cases would require reexamination in the light of the judicial consensus which developed during the 1960's that laches mean not so much delay as prejudice.[426a] It would surely be difficult to the point of impossibility to rationalize Judge Allred's holding in The J. R. Hardee in terms of prejudice to the mortgagee: on the assumption that the mortgage was initially subordinate to the pre-mortgage liens, no delay by the lienors, however protracted, in asserting their claims could possibly prejudice the mortgage in the sense of making his position worse than it had been to start with. It is submitted, however, that there is a great deal more to be said for both cases than would be revealed by an examination in terms of laches.

The point should be made that, apart from the Ship Mortgage Act, there has never been a problem of laches with respect to contract liens among themselves. The earlier liens were subordinated to the later liens under the relevant priority rules.[426b] Thus there was no need to inquire whether a lien, already subordinated, should be further stigmatized as guilty of laches.[426c] The Ship Mortgage Act, unwisely, gave the pre-mortgage liens a priority to which they had never been entitled under the general maritime law and stripped the post-mortgage liens of the priority to which they were entitled under that law. Short of holding the Act unconstitutional, there is no escape from the conclusion that a preferred ship mortgage must be subordinate to some pre-mortgage contract liens, just as it must have priority over some post-mortgage contract liens. It does not, however, follow, either as a matter of sound policy or as a matter of sensible statutory construction, that, without limitation of time, the mortgage must forever remain subordinate to all pre-mortgage liens or, for that matter, must forever retain its priority over all post-

426. On the Everosa cases (which involved the effectiveness of supply liens against a good faith purchaser), see text following note 384 *supra*.

426a. See § 9–80 *supra*, text following note 402.

426b. See § 9–62 *et seq. supra*.

426c. See, however, the discussion of the "loss of lien" provision of the old state lien statutes and the rule of The Owyhee, § 9–79 *supra*. For the reasons stated in our earlier discussion it seems "in the highest degree unlikely that The Owyhee will ever be heard from again."

mortgage liens. There is place for a rule of reason here as there is in the solution of most legal problems.

The Ship Mortgage Act itself invited the courts to discuss the problem of the relative priority of mortgages and liens in terms of laches. Section 974 of the Lien Act (reenacted in 1920 as part of the Ship Mortgage Act) provided in part:

> "[T]his chapter [i. e., the Ship Mortgage Act] shall not be construed to affect the rules of law existing on June 5, 1920, in regard to . . . (2) laches in the enforcement of liens upon vessels . . ."

The principal or core meaning of the word "laches" in 1920 was of course "delay". That the word suffered a sea-change of meaning during the 1960's and has come to mean "prejudice resulting from delay" should not lead on to the conclusion that the 1970 meaning of "laches" is automatically to be read back into the 1920 statute. Furthermore, the idea of laches, whether it means prejudice or merely delay, has its principal use in litigation between a libellant and a ship owner, where the most obvious type of prejudice to the shipowner is that as the result of the lapse of time he is no longer able to make an effective defense because memories have eroded, witnesses have become unavailable and so on. Where priority disputes arise between or among lienors, mortgagees and purchasers—that is, third parties who have dealt with the shipowner or the ship—laches, whatever the word means, is not a helpful concept. It is not unreasonable to take the "laches" reference in § 974(a) as inviting the courts to apply equitable principles in determining relative priorities between mortgages and liens. As Judge Brown has colorfully reminded us:

> "The Chancellor is no longer fixed to the woolsack. He may stride the quarter-deck of maritime jurisprudence and, in the role of admiralty judge, dispense, as would his land-locked brother, that which equity and good conscience impels." [426d]

And in the life history of any statute the need to resort to equitable principles for its construction increases as the statute withers away into old age.

Judge Aldrich's holding in The Winthrop can easily be rephrased in terms of equitable subordination. He held in effect that liens which were stale at the time the mortgage loan was made would be relegated to last priority. The "ten month rule" which he used to determine staleness was close to either the calendar year rule or the twelve month rule used in determining lien priorities.[426e] He held, that is, that a contract lienor who had let his lien become stale would be subordinated not only to the later pre-mortgage contract liens but

**426d.** Compania Anonima Venezolana de Navegacion v. A. J. Perez Export Co., 303 F.2d 692, 699, 1962 A.M.C. 1710, 1720 (5th Cir. 1962). The case involved laches, but not the specific problem here under discussion.

**426e.** See § 9–66 *supra.*

to the mortgage and post-mortgage liens as well. Judge Allred's holding in The J. R. Hardee that pre-mortgage liens which were not stale when the mortgage was taken out would nevertheless be subordinated because of post-mortgage delay in enforcement is more complicated. On the facts of The J. R. Hardee, the actual beneficiary of the holding was the mortgagee whose claim exhausted the distribution fund. However, if the mortgage claim had been smaller or the fund larger, the post-mortgage liens would also have shared as beneficiaries of the subordination. We cannot entirely escape from the albatross of the ill-advised priority provisions of the Ship Mortgage Act. But The Winthrop and The J. R. Hardee make life with the albatross a good deal easier than it might otherwise have been.[426f]

In Merchants and Marine Bank v. The T. E. Welles [426g] Judge Brown indicated in a thoughtful footnote that he did not think that either The Winthrop or The J. R. Hardee had been rendered obsolete by changing attitudes toward the idea of laches. The footnote was dictum since the issue did not have to be decided in The T. E. Welles [426h] but is well worth pondering. Judge Brown returned to the problem in Florida Bahamas Lines, Ltd. v. Steel Barge "Star 800" of Nassau [426i] in which he once again cited both The Winthrop and The J. R. Hardee as authoritative in such "lien-priority" contests. The case involved a lien for wharfage claimed to have priority over a preferred mortgage.[426j] The "mortgagor" and the "wharfinger", both of whom had been controlled by a man named Brown, had been in collusion to defraud the mortgagee by running up charges entitled to priority over the mortgage which would swallow up the value of the

**426f.** In Heller v. M/V Mr. Ed., 270 F. Supp. 830, 1968 A.M.C. 1089 (E.D.La. 1967), 273 F.Supp. 926, 1968 A.M.C. 716 (E.D.La.1967) a mortgagee, whose mortgage had become preferred on July 13, 1965, initiated foreclosure proceedings on June 30, 1966. Judge Rubin, without citing or discussing The J. R. Hardee, held that pre-mortgage supply liens, which had accrued immediately before the mortgage became preferred, were not barred by laches against the mortgage. It will be noted that the foreclosure proceedings were initiated within a year of the time when the liens accrued.

In United States v. F/V Voyager, 1973 A.M.C. 1742 (E.D.Va.1973) Judge Hoffman concluded that the conditional seller of a "fishscope" which was installed on the Voyager was entitled to the status of a maritime lienor (as a furnisher of "supplies, repairs . . . or other necessaries" under the Maritime Lien Act). (This aspect of the case is discussed note 296ii *supra.*) The fishscope was installed in April, 1954; the United States, which did not know of the conditional sale of the fishscope, took a preferred mortgage on the Voyager in August, 1957. The mortgagors defaulted on their mortgage payments in 1962; the United States initiated foreclosure proceedings in August, 1962. Payments under the fishscope contract had apparently been in default since 1954 but the seller made no attempt to enforce his rights until he intervened in the foreclosure. Judge Hoffman held that the seller's "lien" was not barred by laches when the mortgage was taken out and that his post-mortgage delay was irrelevant.

**426g.** 289 F.2d 188, 1961 A.M.C. 1042 (5th Cir. 1961).

**426h.** See note 397b *supra*.

**426i.** 433 F.2d 1243, 1970 A.M.C. 2189 (5th Cir. 1970).

**426j.** Since a foreign mortgage was involved, the lien would have had priority over the mortgage for post-mortgage as well as pre-mortgage services under § 951 of the Ship Mortgage Act, see § 9–70 *supra*.

vessel. Judge Brown commented that: "In the long history of the application of laches in admiralty, including lien-priority contests as our own, none is more compelling in terms of equities than this case." The upshot was that the wharfage claim "whatever its status as a maritime lien against the vessel in view of the relationship of the parties, is barred by laches as against the mortgage claim of the mortgagee." Judge Brown continued to use the traditional term "laches" but might equally well have said that the lien was being subordinated to the mortgage on equitable principles.

There remains the problem, which has so far not been much discussed in the cases, whether the mortgagee's priority over post-mortgage contract liens can ever be lost on theories of laches, equitable subordination or what not. Such an argument was made by post-mortgage lienors in The Favorite but was successively rejected by Judge Conger in the District Court and by Judge Augustus Hand in the Second Circuit [426k] and does not seem to have been advanced in any subsequent case.[426l] In The Favorite a mortgage which had become preferred on December 26, 1929, was not paid at maturity (April 1, 1930) and from then on was apparently in default although the mortgagor continued to make and the mortgagee to receive payments on account of both principal and interest. Liens for supplies and repairs accrued in 1938 and the lienors libeled the vessel in 1939 when it became apparent that the owner-mortgagor was hopelessly insolvent.[426m]

In The Favorite the mortgagee got the benefit of the repairs (which presumably increased the value of the vessel) and the supplies (presumably the payments which the mortgagor continued to make were derived from his commercial operation of the vessel). On the other hand the mortgage had been recorded with the Collector of Customs and indorsed on the ship's papers, so that the materialmen knew, or ought to have known, of it. Thus they could have protected themselves by refusing to make the repairs or furnish the supplies except for cash or other adequate security. And, from all that appears, the mortgagee had no reason to know that the mortgagor was insolvent or that the situation was hopeless, particularly in view of the fact that, although the mortgage was technically in default, the mortgagor went on making payments up to 1939 when the libels were filed.

**426k.** 34 F.Supp. 324, 1940 A.M.C. 958 (S.D.N.Y.1940), affirmed 120 F.2d 899, 1941 A.M.C. 1073 (2d Cir. 1941). See § 9–53 *supra*, text following note 271. Judge Conger cited The Red Lion, 22 F.2d 329 (E.D.N.Y.1927) as "some precedent for my holding." The opinion in The Red Lion is notably obscure but the case does not seem to have involved the problem of mortgagee's laches vis-a-vis post-mortgage liens.

**426*l*.** The Franz Joseph, digested note 273a *supra*, followed The Favorite on the laches point but the case did not involve priorities between a mortgage and post-mortgage liens.

**426m.** The District Court opinion does not give the date when the liens accrued. Judge Hand's opinion refers to repairs having been made eight years after the maturity date of the mortgage—thus in 1938.

It is not difficult, however, to construct a case in which the equities would be weighted on the side of the post-mortgage liens. Assume that a mortgagee knows that his mortgagor is insolvent and also knows that the mortgagor, if he continues to operate the vessel, will necessarily run up large bills for supplies and repairs which he will be unable to pay in the ordinary course of business. If, under such circumstances, after default, the mortgagee allows the mortgagor to continue his operations, there would be good reason to hold that the mortgage had lost its priority over the post-mortgage liens. It would make no difference whether the result was rationalized in terms of laches (the prejudice to the lienors is sufficiently obvious) or in terms of subordination on equitable principles.

The conclusion is that there is no more reason to take the mortgage's priority over post-mortgage liens as absolute than there is to take the mortgage's subordination to all pre-mortgage liens as absolute. On an appropriate set of facts the holdings in The Winthrop and The J. R. Hardee with respect to pre-mortgage liens could be duplicated in a case which involved post-mortgage liens.

**§ 9–84.** "Waiver" is a word that occasionally appears in the opinions in the older cases as a synonym for laches in cases which hold that a claimant has lost his lien by delay. The term has some meaning when it is used with reference to the failure of a lien to attach in the first place, because the materialman has extended credit to the owner and not to the ship, taken collateral security, or otherwise evidenced his intention not to insist on his lien.[427] When, however, it is conceded that a lien has attached at the time the services were furnished, "waiver", unless it refers to an express agreement by which the lienor releases his claim against the ship, seems to be merely a word which some judges like to use for stylistic effect, by itself or in double harness with its more industrious companion "laches". It is clear that the subsequent taking by the lienor of collateral security for his claim —for example, an assignment of freights [428]—or of acceptances or notes from the owner [429] or the working out with the owner of schedules of payment or the like [430] will not be stigmatized as acts of waiver. On the contrary such attempts to secure or satisfy the debt will in all probability be looked on as satisfactory evidence of the lienor's diligence and will thus serve to protect him against the charge of laches.

### Same: Execution of Liens by In Rem Decree. (Herein of Distribution of Proceeds and Effect of Stipulation for Value)

**§ 9–85.** Only the admiralty court acting *in rem* has the power to divest liens by a judicial sale. Here we touch the central point of

427. See § 9–38 *supra* and the cases there cited.

428. The City of Athens (Todd Shipyards Corp. v. Soc. Naviera Trans-Atlantica, S. A.) 83 F.Supp. 67, 1949 A.M.C. 572 (D.Md.1949).

429. The Everosa (Southern Coal & Coke Co. v. Kugniecibas), 93 F.2d 732, 1938 A.M.C. 82 (1st Cir. 1937).

430. Virginia Shipbuilding Corp. v. U. S. Shipping Bd. Emergency Fleet Corp., 11 F.2d 156, 1925 A.M.C. 668 (E.D.Va.1925).

our system of admiralty law. Here we should expect to find the winds of litigation at their most turbulent. But, just as at the eye of the hurricane the air is undisturbed, so here the law exists as in a vacuum, its purity undefiled by controversy and dispute. There are no cases —or almost none. There have never been any cases. Presumably there never will be any cases. There is only doctrine.

Any maritime lienor may have the ship arrested by filing a libel *in rem* in any district in which the ship is found.[430a] The marshal will then take the ship into custody. Notice of the libel is required to be given by publication and other claimants may intervene. If the ship is not released on a stipulation for value [431] and if a judgment in favor of the original or any intervening libellant becomes final, the ship will be sold on order of the court. The effect of such a sale is to execute or divest all liens against the ship in the hands of the purchaser— not only all liens held by claimants who intervened in or had notice of the proceeding, but all liens everywhere. The execution of liens by

**430a.** Rogers, Enforcement of Maritime Liens and Mortgages, 47 Tulane L. Rev. 767 (1973) gives a detailed account of the procedures which are followed in the seizure, custody and sale of vessels.

The Manual for United States Marshals —Procedures in Admiralty, issued by the U.S. Department of Justice, December 15, 1971, is reprinted at 1972 A.M.C. 569.

Thyssen Steel Corp. v. Federal Commerce & Navigation Co., Ltd., (World Mermaid), 274 F.Supp. 18, 1968 A.M.C. 1582 (S.D.N.Y.1967) is an odd case in which Thyssen, the owner of cargo which had been damaged in a collision with the World Mermaid, sought an order requiring the Mermaid's owners to have her make port in Halifax, Nova Scotia, so that Thyssen could obtain a "security interest" in the vessel. Judge Mansfield, commenting that Thyssen "has not advised the Court how it would obtain this security interest once the ship proceeded to Halifax," refused to issue such an order on the ground that a vessel's physical presence within the court's territorial jurisdiction is essential to *in rem* process. (Thyssen had alleged that the Mermaid was about to sink and thus destroy his lien; the owners claimed that the Mermaid, although damaged in the collision, was entirely seaworthy for her current voyage to Europe.)

In Booth Steamship Co., Ltd. v. Tug Dalzell No. 2, 1966 A.M.C. 2615 (S.D. N.Y.1966) it was held that the vessel's physical presence within the court's territorial jurisdiction was not a prerequisite to the maintenance of an *in rem* action when the shipowner entered a general appearance and claimed the vessel. Judge Cannella reviewed the "sparse" decisional authority, quoting Benedict on Admiralty: "The fictitious allegation that the *res* is within the district, the waiver of the irregularity by the claimant, enables parties to conduct suits *in rem* in any district satisfactory to them."

Everett Steamship Corp., S/A v. Liberty Navigation and Trading Co., Inc., 486 F.2d 462 (9th Cir. 1973) was a complicated case which, for our purposes, need not be digested in full. The majority of the court felt that a libel in rem filed while the ship was on the high seas would not be "cured" by the ship's subsequent arrival within the district in which the libel was filed. That approach seems inconsistent with the approach taken in the Booth Steamship case, *supra* this note, and the authorities there reviewed. The decision in the Everett case was not based on the court's feeling about the insufficiency of the in rem libel.

In Associated Metals and Minerals Corp. v. S.S. Portoria, 484 F.2d 460 (5th Cir. 1973) Judge Dyer made what would seem to be the elementary point that the District Court had erred in entering an in rem judgment where "no process in rem was issued, the Portoria was not arrested and the owner did not waive attachment of the vessel."

**431.** On stipulations for value see § 9–89 *et seq.*, *infra*.

judicial sale is given international recognition. Courts in the United States will give full effect to the sale of a ship by an admiralty court in any other country and so, it is thought, will foreign courts to sales by admiralty courts in the United States. This is so even though no two maritime countries have the same structure of lien law and it is far from clear to what extent the courts of any country will give lien status to claims which are not liens by the law of the forum but were liens in the country where they arose. On sale, all liens attach to the proceeds of sale. The court will distribute the fund to all maritime lien claimants in accordance with their respective priorities.[431a] If there remain surplus proceeds after all maritime liens have been satisfied, the court will distribute such "remnants" to nonmaritime claims which are liens by common law. It is an open question whether maritime but nonlien claims are also entitled to share in surplus. The admiralty court will not recognize claims of general common-law creditors of the shipowner but will turn over any remaining surplus to the owner (or to his trustee in bankruptcy).

The doctrine summarized above rests on the most fragile of case-law foundations. It may of course be argued that the absence of case or controversy means that the rules are so well settled and so perfectly understood that they are almost never drawn in question. Or that purported rules which have not for generations been tested in litigation or reexamined by any court are not rules in any but the most metaphysical sense of the word.

The classical case on the proposition that sale by an admiralty court acting *in rem* executes all liens everywhere is The Trenton.[432] Supplies had been furnished to the Trenton in Cleveland, her home port, and a lien was claimed under the Ohio Lien Act. The materialmen caused the ship to be arrested in Toronto under process issuing from the Maritime Court of Ontario. In the Ontario action a watchman and a seaman filed intervening petitions for wages. A demurrer was interposed to the materialmen's petition on the ground that the Ontario court had no jurisdiction to enforce a claim for necessaries supplied to an American vessel in the United States. The court sustained the demurrer and dismissed the petition. The ship was sold by the court for $1000. to satisfy the wage claims which amounted to two or three hundred dollars. Following the sale the materialmen

431a. In American Bank of Wage Claims v. District Court of Guam (M/S Galveston Navigator), 431 F.2d 1215, 1971 A.M.C. 1298 (9th Cir. 1970) it was held that distribution of the fund created by a sale under *in rem* process exhausts the court's jurisdiction. Appeals following distribution were dismissed "for lack of *in rem* jurisdiction". The appellants, it was assumed, could have prevented the distribution pending appeal by moving for a stay of execution but had not done so. The case appears to have been one of first impression. In support of the holding Judge Pence cited several cases to the proposition that "the release or removal of the vessel from the jurisdiction of the court destroys *in rem* jurisdiction, and renders moot any appeal. . . ." On the theory that the fund is substituted for the vessel, distribution of the fund was given the same effect as the physical disappearance of the vessel.

432. 4 F. 657 (E.D.Mich.1880) per Judge (later Justice) Brown.

(who had received nothing in the Canadian action) again arrested the Trenton, this time in an American port. Judge Brown held that the sale by the Ontario court had freed the ship of all pre-existing liens and, specifically, of libellants' liens. According to Judge Brown's analysis, the sale of a ship by a court possessed of admiralty power executes all liens unless the court "had no jurisdiction of the subject matter by actual seizure and custody of the thing sold" or the sale "was made by a fraudulent collusion, to which the purchaser at such sale was a party" or was "contrary to natural justice." None of those defects appearing in the Canadian proceeding, the American libellants were bound by it. The fact that the Ontario court had declined to enforce the American lien [433] had not deprived the libellant of any "right of property": "It was merely adjudged that his claim was not of that character which entitled him to set the machinery of the court in motion." Judge Brown indicated his belief that on proper motion the court would, after payment of the lien claims, have distributed the surplus to the American claimants on the theory that they did have liens under the Ohio Lien Act even if those liens were not recognized as such under Canadian law. "But," he added, "even if the foreign court should misjudge this question, and hold that, by the law of Ohio, the libellant had no lien at all upon the vessel, or should deny his petition for payment from the remnants in court, the sale would not thereby be invalidated, or the vessel remain subject to arrest in this country."

None of the case books or treatises cites any American authority subsequent to The Trenton on the central proposition that a judicial sale of a ship by a court of competent jurisdiction executes all liens, even if the sale is made by a foreign court which will not recognize or enforce American lien claims or even distribute remnants to such claimants after satisfying the local liens.[433a] The only modern case which search has revealed is The Totila ex Harald (Zimmern Coal Co. v. Coal Trading Association of Rotterdam).[434] Libellant claimed

433. In All America Cables & Radio, Inc. v. The Dieppe, 93 F.Supp. 923, 1950 A.M.C. 1863 (S.D.N.Y.1950), Judge Coxe wrote, without citation of authority: "[I]f, under the Curacao law, there was a maritime lien, . . . this court had jurisdiction to enforce that lien."

433a. Courts will examine the question whether foreign courts under whose process vessels have been sold had what we would call *in rem* jurisdiction. If the foreign court is found to have lacked such jurisdiction, the sale will not be treated as executing all liens. See Todd Shipyards Corp. v. F/V Maigus Luck, 243 F.Supp. 8, 1966 A.M.C. 1608 (D.Canal Zone 1965) (sale by Panamanian court in mortgage foreclosure proceeding, the vessel not having been within the territorial jurisdiction of the court). For an analogous English example, see The Goulandris, text following note 497 *infra*.

434. 30 F.2d 933, 1929 A.M.C. 334 (5th Cir. 1929). Loud v. United States, 286 F. 56 (6th Cir. 1923), while not directly in point, is also of interest: the United States sued Loud to recover the amount spent in straightening a vessel which had sunk in a navigable channel (for which amount the United States had a statutory lien against the vessel but no personal claim against the owners). The vessel had however been sold in a proceeding brought in a Canadian court in which the United States had not made an appearance. In the Canadian proceeding, surplus proceeds had been handed over to Loud, one of the owners, who had made advances to the wrecking company which had raised the sunken

a lien for coal furnished the Totila in New Orleans. Between the furnishing of the coal and the filing of the libel, the ship had been seized and sold by a Dutch court of general admiralty jurisdiction to enforce the lien of a mortgage. The Totila goes a step farther than The Trenton since it does not appear that the Totila libellant had had notice of the Dutch proceedings, while the Trenton libellants had at least had their day in court. "Where the proceeding is *in rem*," wrote Judge Bryan, "notice is served upon the thing itself" adding in a quotation from The Mary, 13 U.S. 126: "This is necessarily notice to all those who have any interest in the thing, and is reasonable, because it is necessary . . . " Curiously The Totila cites as governing authority not The Trenton but Hilton v. Guyot,[435] a leading but often criticized decision of the United States Supreme Court which, while restating the general doctrine that foreign judgments will be recognized in American courts, held that a French judgment would not be given conclusive effect since French courts did not give like effect to American judgments.

**§ 9–86.** Two cases have considered the effect of admiralty sales on governmental claims, state and federal. In The Forest King[436] a state court held that an admiralty sale cut off a county claim for taxes which was a lien under a state statute which provided that no sale or transfer of the property should affect the lien. In The City of Athens[437] the United States had served notice on the master of a ship (then in the custody of the admiralty court) that fines for violation of the Immigration Act might be imposed. Three days after the notice had been served, the court ordered the vessel sold and the sale was concluded about three weeks later, the Marshal's bill of sale reciting that the ship was sold free of liens. The Immigration Act provided that the Collector of Customs should refuse clearance papers to any vessel pending the determination of liability for violation of the Act, or while any fine for violation remained unpaid, unless a deposit

vessel. In holding that the United States could not recover the proceeds of sale from Loud, Judge Donahue wrote: "The question of whether this [i. e. the decree in the Canadian proceeding] was or was not a proper award is no longer open to inquiry. . . . The order distributing the proceeds of sale of a libel [*sic*] vessel to the different claimants of the fund discharges the fund so distributed from all liens against the vessel that attached to its proceeds after its sale" (*id.* at 61).

In Point Landing, Inc. v. Alabama Drydock and Shipbuilding Co., 261 F.2d 861, 1959 A.M.C. 148 (5th Cir. 1958) Judge Brown restated the proposition that the sale of a vessel under *in rem* process "cuts off the rights of all non-parties" and gives the purchaser a title "good against the world." *Held*, that a lienor who had not sought to intervene in the action until two days after the sale of the vessel (the proceeds being still in the registry of the court) was entitled to his distributive share and was not barred by laches.

Harmon, Discharge and Waiver of Maritime Liens, 47 Tulane L.Rev. 786 (1973) reviews the authorities.

435. 150 U.S. 113, 16 S.Ct. 139 (1895).

436. (Todd Drydocks, Inc. v. King County), 1931 A.M.C. 7 (Superior Ct. Wash.1930).

437. (Todd Shipyards Corp. v. Soc. Naviera Trans-Atlantica, S. A.), 73 F. Supp. 362, 1947 A.M.C. 1413 (D.Md. 1947).

or bond to secure payment should be made. The Collector therefore refused clearance and the purchaser, alleging that it was an innocent party without notice of the occasion for the fines, petitioned the admiralty court to require the Collector to furnish the necessary papers. Commenting that the case presented "a difficult question apparently of first impression", Judge Chesnut concluded that "the very explicit and clearly worded provisions of the statute authorizing the withholding of clearance papers . . . must be given effect in this case." The statute, he pointed out, did not purport to create a lien against the offending vessel, the administrative withholding of clearance papers having been substituted as a more effective remedy for the provisions of an earlier statute which did give a lien. At the time the petition was decided adversely to the purchaser, the fund arising from the sale of the ship was still in the court's registry and hearings on the many libels filed against the City of Athens had not been concluded. Judge Chesnut suggested that the purchaser post a bond or make a deposit with the Collector to secure the clearance, with leave to file a claim in the admiralty proceeding to be reimbursed from the proceeds of sale if the fines were in fact imposed. The purchaser deposited the $11,000 which the Collector required and filed its claim. Eventually the Commissioner of Immigration decided not to impose the fines, apparently on the curious ground that the violations of the Act had occurred after the ship had come into the custody of the Marshal. Since the purchaser then had a right to a return of its deposit, its claim in the admiralty proceeding failed.[438] The case is inconclusive, although Judge Chesnut's first opinion indicates that he believed the purchaser would have a valid claim to reimbursement if he were forced to pay the fines. Whether the claim would have been paid in priority to lien claims—on the analogy perhaps to claims accruing while a ship is *in custodia legis*—never had to be determined.

**§ 9–87.** The rule that the admiralty court will not distribute funds in its registry to general creditors of the owner although it will distribute surplus funds or "remnants" to common law (i. e., non-maritime) lien claimants rests on distinguished authority. The point was thoroughly discussed by Justices Clifford and Bradley on successive appeals in The Lottawanna,[439] which involved a contest between home port materialmen (who had not perfected their lien under the state lien statute) and a common law mortgagee.

On the first appeal Justice Clifford took the position that only maritime lien claimants were entitled to share in distribution, with the possible exception of the disposition of "mere remnants, if *unclaimed by the owner.*" "[T]he admiralty courts," he wrote, "are not courts of bankruptcy or of insolvency, nor are they invested with any jurisdiction to distribute such property of the owner, any more than any other property belonging to him, among his creditors. Such pro-

438. The City of Athens (Todd Shipyards Corp. v. Soc. Naviera Trans-Atlantica, S. A.), 83 F.Supp. 67, 86, 1949 A.M.C. 572, 598 (D.Md.1949).

439. 87 U.S. (20 Wall.) 201 (1873); 88 U.S. (21 Wall.) 558 (1874). The Lottawanna is discussed further § 9–28 *supra*.

ceeds, if unaffected by any lien, when all legal claims upon the fund have been discharged, become by operation of law the absolute property of the owner."[440] That Justice Clifford meant "unaffected by any *maritime* lien" is made clear by a later observation in his opinion to the effect that only those claimants who could have proceeded against the ship *in rem* (*i. e.*, who hold maritime liens) are entitled to share in proceeds.

On the second appeal, however, Justice Bradley (with Clifford in dissent) took a different tack. It had been held that the materialmen had no maritime lien either by state law or by general maritime law, and, of course, the mortgagee had no maritime lien. The mortgagee had, however, petitioned for, and received, the surplus proceeds. That, said Justice Bradley, was entirely correct and the materialmen (at least if they could show themselves entitled to a common law lien) could have done as much:

> "The court has power to distribute surplus proceeds to all those who can show a vested interest therein, in the order of their several priorities, no matter how their claims originated. The propriety of such a distribution in the admiralty has been questioned on the ground that the court would thereby draw to itself equity jurisdiction. But it is a wholesome jurisdiction very commonly exercised by nearly all superior courts, to distribute a fund rightfully in its possession to those who are legally entitled to it; and there is no sound reason why admiralty courts should not do the same. If a case should be so complicated as to require the interposition of a court of equity, the District Court could refuse to act, and refer the parties to a more competent tribunal."[441]

Justice Bradley did not refer to Justice Clifford's discussion of the distribution rule on the first appeal, but the later opinion must evidently be taken as overruling the earlier one to the extent that the two are inconsistent. Judge Brown restated the matter a few years later in The Trenton (without, curiously, any reference to The Lottawanna):

> "It is a constant practice in our courts of admiralty to decree the payment of surplus proceeds to mortgagees and other having liens which are not enforceable by original proceedings . . . It is believed to be the rule of the English as well as the American courts of admiralty, after the payment of maritime liens, to direct the surplus proceeds to be paid over to anyone who may have a lien upon such proceeds by the law of the place where the contract from which the lien arose is made."[442]

440. 87 U.S. (20 Wall.) at 223 (italics in original), 221.

441. 88 U.S. (21 Wall.) at 582, 583.

442. 4 F. 657, 664, 665 (E.D.Mich.1880). On The Trenton see text at note 432 *supra*.

The common-law lienors whom Justice Bradley and Judge Brown admitted to share in the proceeds were such claimants as mortgagees, shipbuilders and the like who had liens under the state lien statutes even though their claims were not recognized as maritime (as distinguished from the home port materialmen who were denied liens unless conferred by a state lien act but whose claims were recognized as maritime).[442a] Unpaid sellers have occasionally been awarded surplus proceeds after the ship has been libeled in the hands of the vendee and sold.[443] It is hard to see how the unpaid seller cases can be explained on a straight lien theory since the unpaid seller loses his lien by delivery of the thing sold to the buyer and becomes merely a creditor for the price. The cases may perhaps be taken to mean that, while creditors whose claims are in no way connected with the ship or its operation will not be allowed to share, creditors whose claims do derive from the ship may come in even though they are not technically lienors. Or it may be that the cases rested on a misconception of the possessory nature of the vendor's lien and were wrongly decided. It is at least true that, except for the unpaid sellers, nonmaritime nonlien claimants have been consistently denied the right to share. It is not clear whether the holder of such a claim can, by reducing his claim to judgment and acquiring a judicial lien by execution, promote himself to a sharing position. If the underlying theory of surplus distribution to nonmaritime claimants is that the claims entitled to share are those which were in their origin connected with the ship (even though technically nonmaritime—such as the claims of builders, sellers and mortgagees) then the acquisition of a judicial lien would not seem to help.[444] In The American-Imperator [445] a person (apparently a passenger) who had been injured aboard ship had brought a suit at law to recover for his injuries and in aid of that suit had attached both the American, on which he had been injured, and the Imperator,

**442a.** One of the few recent cases which have discussed the right of common law lienors to share surplus is Jackson v. Inland Oil & Transport Co. (The Three Jacks), 318 F.2d 802, 1963 A.M.C. 1355 (5th Cir. 1963). The holder of a nonmaritime mortgage was held entitled to surplus funds remaining after all maritime liens had been paid; the mortgagee was given priority over a maritime (but non-lien) claim which had been reduced to judgment in an *in personam* action. In Stern, Hays & Lang, Inc. v. M/V Nili, 407 F.2d 549, 1969 A.M.C. 13 (5th Cir. 1969), Judge Brown referred to the "usual principles of non-maritime creditors participating in surplus proceeds generated by maritime liens". The case involved a claim by an advertising agency for services rendered to a cruise ship. Judge Brown indicated that the advertising agency might well have a lien for "other necessaries" under the Lien Act (see note 185 *supra*) but that even if it did not, it could still be entitled to share in proceeds either as a lienholder under the State lien statute or under the "usual principles." See also United States v. Maryland Cas. Co., 235 F.2d 50, 1956 A.M.C. 1822 (5th Cir. 1956).

**443.** The Duchess, 201 F. 783 (E.D.N.Y. 1912); *cf.* United States v. Certain Subfreights of The Neponset, 300 F. 981, 1924 A.M.C. 726 (D.Mass.1924). But see The Ada, 250 F. 194 (2d Cir. 1918).

**444.** In The Williamette Valley, 76 F. 838 (N.D.Cal.1896) it was held that a creditor who had recovered a state court judgment "has no lien which this [the admiralty] court can recognize" [*id.* at 844] and was not entitled to surplus proceeds.

**445.** 40 F.2d 942, 1930 A.M.C. 416 (D. Mass.1930).

another ship belonging to the same owner. Both the attached ships were then libeled *in rem* by other claimants and sold by order of the court. The personal injury plaintiff was allowed to intervene in the admiralty suit, not only for the purpose of receiving surplus proceeds, if there should be any, but also for that of contesting the lien status of the libellants in the *in rem* action. The case is a curious one in that the intervening plaintiff, if he was the victim of a maritime tort, had a maritime lien himself, but had chosen to pursue his recovery outside the admiralty in order to have the advantage of a jury. Under the circumstances the decision allowing the intervention is reasonable, but the case would not support the proposition that every plaintiff in a common law action who attaches defendant's ship is thereby entitled to intervene in subsequent suits *in rem* against the ship and to share in the distribution of the proceeds of sale.

**§ 9–88.** There remains for discussion the status of maritime but non-lien claims in distribution. Such claims may for convenience be divided into several categories. *First,* maritime claims, which depend on a state statute for lien status and through failure to comply with the statutory requirements have failed to achieve such status or have lost it for failure to enforce the lien within the statutory period.[446] *Second,* maritime claims which are not given lien status either by maritime law or state statute.[447] *Third,* maritime claims which fail to qualify as liens because they arise from breach of an executory contract—such as claims for breach of a charter party by failure to deliver the ship or for breach of a contract of affreightment by failure to receive the cargo.[448] *Fourth,* claims of seamen under the Jones Act, which gives only a right *in personam* and not *in rem.*[449]

Only on the first two categories above mentioned is there modern, or relatively modern, authority. In The Edith[450] a lien was claimed under the New York statute for repairs and supplies furnished to a ship in her home port. The lien was asserted against the proceeds of sale after the ship had been libeled and sold to satisfy another lien. Justice Strong decided that under the terms of the New York statute the lien had been lost before the libellant's petition was filed. Almost as an afterthought and with no citation of authority he added that, having lost his lien, libellant had also lost his right to share in proceeds: "The court can marshal the fund only between lien-holders and owners." In The Balize[451] the district court had directed payment of surplus proceeds to satisfy the non-lien claim of the master for wages. The Circuit Court reversed on the authority of The Lottawanna,[452] citing both appeals in the case but quoting only from Justice Clifford's opinion on the first appeal, which had said

446. See, for example, The Fort Orange and The Owyhee discussed in § 9–79 *supra.*

447. For maritime claims which do not have lien status see § 9–20, *supra.*

448. See § 9–22 *et seq. supra.*

449. See text at note 86 *supra.*

450. 94 U.S. 518 (1876).

451. 52 F. 414 (6th Cir. 1887).

452. Note 439 *supra.*

(with respect to common law mortgagees) that distribution could not be made to claimants who could not have libeled the ship *in rem*. Bradley's opinion on the second appeal had not discussed the case of the maritime but non-lien claimant other than to say that materialmen who had not acquired a lien because of failure to comply with a state statute might have shared in proceeds if they had petitioned to do so and "if they had a valid lien". It is difficult to say what Justice Bradley meant by the last phrase since he had just held that the materialmen had no lien on any theory. In The Edith, however, it had been made clear that a lienor who had lost his lien was not entitled to proceeds. Conceivably that holding might govern the case of a maritime claimant who had never had a lien, but conceivably also the two cases were distinguishable: the materialman in The Edith had failed to do something which the statute required as a condition of lien; the master in The Balize had not in any way fallen short in pursuing his available remedies.

Except for The Edith and The Balize, the post-Lottawanna cases which have refused to allow non-lien claimants to share in surplus proceeds have involved non-maritime claims.[453] The language in the opinions is frequently generalized to the effect that only lien claims may share and the most recent case perpetuates the error initially made in The Balize of quoting as the last word on the subject Justice Clifford's opinion on the first appeal in The Lottawanna instead of Justice Bradley's quite different opinion on the second appeal.[454] The 1940 edition of Benedict repeats Justice Strong's concluding statement in The Edith that "In paying over a surplus, a court of admiralty marshals the fund only between owner and lien holders." [455]

The direct authority for the proposition that maritime but non-lien claims may not share in distribution after lien claims have been satisfied thus comes down to one Supreme Court case (The Edith), one Circuit Court case (The Balize) and the curious error of relying on Justice Clifford's subsequently overruled opinion on the first appeal in The Lottawanna. There was a good deal of pre-Lottawanna case authority that non-lien maritime claims could be paid from surplus [456] but these cases, never overruled, have gradually faded from

453. Bouker Contracting Co. v. Proceeds of Sale of Dredging Machine, 168 F. 428 (D.N.J.1909) (non-maritime contract for use of dredging machine); The Atlantic City, 220 F. 281 (3d Cir. 1915) (shipbuilding contract); The Paipoonge, 1925 A.M.C. 381 (E.D. Pa.1925) (nonmaritime claim of unspecified nature); The Ethel V. Stowman, 16 F.Supp. 540, 1936 A.M.C. 1802 (D.N.J.1936) (municipal tax claim).

In The Wabash, 296 F. 559, 1923 A.M.C. 923 (D.Conn.1923) Judge Thomas held the receiver of the French-American Line not entitled to proceeds of sale on the ground, *inter alia*, that he was not a lien creditor. The receiver was apparently asking that all the proceeds of sale (and not merely remnants) be paid to him in priority to maritime lien claimants. The case, thus, has nothing to do with distribution of surplus.

454. The Ethel V. Stowman, note 453 *supra*.

455. 3 Benedict, Admiralty 274 (6th ed. 1940).

456. See *e. g.* The Stephen Allen, 22 Fed.Cas.1250, Case No. 13,361 (S.D.N.Y.1830); The Boston, 3 Fed.Cas. 918, Case No. 1,669 (S.D.N.Y.1832); Zane

sight. It should also be remembered that Justice Bradley's prevailing opinion in The Lottawanna suggested, although in confusing and contradictory language, that a home port materialman who had no lien would have been entitled to share in surplus. There is some post-Lottawanna authority in favor of allowing non-lien claimants to come into distribution if their claims are maritime. The Fifth Circuit so held in The Astoria in favor of a claimant who had advanced funds for repairs to a ship under circumstances not entitling him to a lien.[457] And in The Paipoonge[458] (which involved a non-maritime claim) Judge Dickenson's opinion suggests that he regarded as open the question whether non-lien maritime claims could share.

Since the case authorities are inconclusive, the question may profitably be re-examined. The *in rem* proceeding often serves the function of bringing multiple claims into concourse and admiralty procedure has been traditionally liberal in allowing third party claimants to intervene. With respect to claims which are maritime and arise directly from transactions connected with the ship, there seems to be no good reason why the claimholders should not be allowed to intervene, both for the purpose of contesting the lien status of other claimants and for that of receiving distribution of surplus.[458a] In particular, Jones Act claims (which fail of lien status because of a judicial construction of a confusingly drafted provision of the statute) and claims which fail to qualify as liens because of the executory contract doctrine seem to have equities in their favor.

**§ 9–89.** An owner whose ship is libeled *in rem* need not allow her to remain in arrest and be sold if judgment goes against him. He may procure her release on the posting of a bond with approved surety; presumably this procedure will be followed whenever the owner has any use for the ship and her value exceeds the amount of the claims brought against her.

The release of ships from arrest has been governed both by a statutory provision (which is now 28 U.S.C.A. § 2464[459]) and by the former Admiralty Rules. The statute provided for the posting of

v. The President, 30 Fed.Cas. 909, Case No. 18,201 (C.C.E.D.Pa.1824). The cases involved mostly claims which had originally had lien status but had lost the status by reason of waiver, laches or the like.

**457.** 281 F. 618 (5th Cir. 1922).

**458.** Note 453 *supra.*

**458a.** In Ververica v. Drill Barge Buccaneer No. 7, 488 F.2d 880 (5th Cir. 1974) a salvor who was held to have lost his lien by waiver (see note 202e *supra*) was allowed to share in surplus as a maritime but non-lien claimant. Judge Bell discussed The Lottawanna and The Edith at length. In The Three Jacks, note 442 *supra*, Judge Brown had also seemed to assume that a maritime but non-lien claim (by an owner against a charterer for unpaid charter hire) was entitled to share in surplus (a tug owned by the delinquent charterer had been libeled in rem and sold to satisfy other claims which had maritime lien status) although it would be subordinated to a non-maritime mortgage. The two Fifth Circuit cases appear to represent the only recent judicial discussions of the issue.

**459.** 62 Stat. 974 (1948). The section was derived from Rev.Stat. § 941 (30 Stat. 1354, 1899).

bonds with the United States Marshal in specified amounts. The Rules provided for release on a stipulation for value entered into by the parties with the amount of the stipulation and the security therefor to be determined by the district judge if the parties could not agree. The stipulation for value was the procedure usually followed for the excellent reason (from the shipowner's point of view) that the release value under a stipulation was less than the bonds required under § 2464. The theory under which the statute could be thus overridden by court rules was explained in The Lotosland: [459a]

> "It [i. e., § 2464] would make necessary, for instance, in a libel involving a personal injury case, by setting forth damage in any ridiculous figure whatsoever, the filing of a stipulation or bond in double the amount, no matter how slight the actual injury or damage might have been. Such, certainly, could not have been the intention of the framers of the section, and, accordingly, it is not surprising to find . . . that this section does not abridge the power of a court of admiralty in a suit in rem to accept bail for less than double the amount of the libellant's demand."

Modern courts might feel that, when Congress enacts a silly statute, it is up to Congress to remedy the situation. However, no one seems ever to have questioned the power of the courts to read § 2464 out of the statute books on the ground that the draftsmen could not have meant what they said.

The matter is currently covered by Supplemental Rule E(5) (F.R. C.P.) which, according to the Advisory Committee's Note, restates the substance of the former Admiralty Rules and also incorporates 28 U.S.C.A. § 2464 "with changes of terminology, and with a substantial change as to the amount of the bond." The Committee's light-hearted approach to § 2464 is sought to be justified by citation of The Lotosland and a reference to Benedict on Admiralty. Presumably the Committee's rewriting of § 2464 is in no more danger of challenge than were the former Admiralty Rules. We shall therefore restrict ourself to Supplemental Rule E(5).

Subsections (a) and (b) of Rule E(5), which were patterned on § 2464, provide for release on the giving of a "special bond" (sub. (a)) or of a "general bond" (sub. (b)). A special bond is given with respect to libels which have already issued. If the parties cannot agree on the "amount and nature" of the security, the court is to make the determination. The amount of the bond under Rule E(5)(a) is to be set at "an amount sufficient to cover the amount of the plaintiff's claim fairly stated with accrued interest and costs; but the principal sum shall in no event exceed (i) twice the amount of the plaintiff's claim or (ii) the value of the property on due appraisement, whichever is smaller." (Under § 2464 the special bond is to be given "in

**459a.** (Haakonsen v. Lotosland Corp.), 2 F.Supp. 42, 1933 A.M.C. 263 (E.D.N.Y. 1933).

double the amount claimed by the libellant".) A general bond, under Rule E(5)(b), is given with respect to actions which may subsequently be brought in which the vessel may be attached or arrested. The amount of the bond must at all times be "at least double the aggregate amount claimed by plaintiffs in all actions begun and pending in which such vessel has been attached or arrested." When a special bond is given with respect to any particular action, liability on a previously issued general bond ceases as to that action. When a special bond is given the execution of process with respect to the action covered by the special bond is stayed. When a general bond is issued, the execution of process with respect to all future actions is stayed (so long as the bond is maintained at the required amount).

Subsection (c) of Rule E(5) reproduces the procedure which was originally authorized by the Admiralty Rules. The Marshal is authorized to release any vessel, cargo or other property in his custody, after payment of court costs and charges, on "acceptance and approval of a stipulation, bond or other security, signed by the party on whose behalf the property is detained or his attorney and expressly authorizing such release." Customarily the stipulation will be for the amount claimed in the libel, but in case of disagreement between the parties as to the award that could be made in the case, the judge will set the stipulation at what seems to him a fair figure.[460] (At least that was the practice under the former Admiralty Rules which does not seem to have been affected in any way by Rule E(5)(c).)

Bonds under § 2464 and stipulations for value under the former Admiralty Rules seem always to have been treated as identical in their legal effect.[461] Presumably, bonds under subsection (a) and (b) of Rule E(5) will continue to be treated as having the same legal effect as stipulations under subsection (c). No doubt the subsection (c) stipulation will continue to be the procedure usually followed. In our subsequent discussion we shall use the terms "bond" and "stipulation" as interchangeable parts.

The release of a ship under a special bond or stipulation has no effect on any liens except those represented by the libel (or libels) under which process had issued at the time when the release was effected.[461a] The decree in an *in rem* proceeding in which the ship has been

**460.** As was done in The Lotosland, note 459a *supra*. See also The Fairisle (Dean v. Waterman S. S. Co.) 76 F.Supp. 27, 1948 A.M.C. 794 (D.Md. 1947), affirmed 171 F.2d 408, 1949 A.M.C. 1 (4th Cir. 1948).

**461.** See the discussion in 2 Benedict, Admiralty Ch. 35 (6th ed. 1940). Forms of bond to the marshal are reproduced *id.* at 583 *et seq.*; forms of stipulation for value *id.* at 591 *et seq.*

**461a.** There is a dearth of authority on the effect of a release under a general bond, no doubt because the general bond procedure has rarely been used. The procedure itself was introduced by an Act of Congress in 1899 (see note 459 *supra*); apparently it had no roots in the earlier admiralty practice. The nature of the general bond was much discussed in a series of related cases reported as Lamprecht v. Cleveland—Erieau S. S. Co., 291 F. 876 (N.D.Ohio 1922), The Theodore Roosevelt, 291 F. 453 (N.D.Ohio 1923), reversed Kahn v. Niagara Laundry & Linen Supply Co., 10 F.2d 15 (6th Cir. 1926), certiorari denied 271 U.S. 674, 46 S.Ct. 488 (1926). Both District Judge Wes-

released executes only those liens which were made the basis of the release bond.[462] Following release, therefore, the ship may still be libeled *in rem* by lienors whose liens arose simultaneously with or before the liens from whose libels the ship was released.[463]

With respect to a lien in suit the effect of release is to transfer the lien from the ship to the fund represented by the bond or stipulation. The lien against the ship is discharged for all purposes and the ship cannot again be libeled *in rem* for the same claim.[464] In the course of a noteworthy discussion of the subject in The New England,[465] Judge Woolsey analysed the effect of a release in the following terms:

> "The stipulation for value here given has taken the place of the New England for all the purposes of this libel. She cannot be rearrested for the cause of action therein stated. . . .
>
> "The stipulation for value is a complete substitute for the *res*, and the stipulation for value alone is sufficient to give jurisdiction to a court because its legal effect is the same as the presence of the *res* in the court's custody. . . .
>
> "A stipulation for value is like any other contract. It is based on a consideration, the release of an arrested vessel or the undertaking not to arrest a vessel against which a claim *in rem* is pending. It means to the shipowner the freedom of his ship and to the libellant a new security of unfluctuating value in the place of the vessel.
>
> "A stipulation for value cannot, therefore, be lightly set aside. Fraud, which is not here involved, is, of course, a

tenhaver and Judge Denison for the Sixth Circuit commented that no precedents which discussed the general bond had been found. Judge Westenhaver seemed to feel that all liens in existence at the time the bond was issued were transferred from the vessel to the bond, so that such lienors could no longer libel the vessel *in rem*. Judge Denison and his colleagues evidently felt that Judge Westenhaver had gone too far and reversed his second decision, but Judge Denison's opinion is far from clear on what the effect of a general bond should be. Rule E(5)(b) has carefully preserved the availability of the general bond procedure, although it is hard to see why any lawyer in his senses would ever resort to this curious example of late nineteenth century Congressional whimsy. In the following discussion it is assumed that the vessel was released either under a special bond or under a stipulation for value. The nature of the mysterious general bond will not be further explored.

462. See the opinion of Sanborn, J. in Hawgood & Avery Transit Co. v. Dingman, 94 F. 1011 (8th Cir. 1899).

463. The Everosa litigation, discussed *supra*, text following note 384, is a good illustration. See also The New England (J. K. Welding Co., Inc. v. Gotham Marine Corp.) 47 F.2d 332, 1931 A.M.C. 407 (S.D.N.Y.1931).

464. The Lois (Gray v. Hopkins-Carter Hardware Co.), 32 F.2d 876, 1929 A.M.C. 875 (5th Cir. 1929). In Bushey & Sons, Inc. v. Barge B. & B. No. 5 & Hedger Transp. Corp., 70 F.Supp. 578, 585 *et seq.*, 1947 A.M.C. 621, 628 *et seq.* (E.D.N.Y.1947), affirmed 167 F.2d 9, 1948 A.M.C. 845 (2d Cir. 1948) Judge Byers suggested that the release of a ship under bond would not necessarily discharge the ship from the lien of a preferred mortgage under the Ship Mortgage Act.

465. Note 463 *supra*.

reason for so doing, but a unilateral mistake such as a statement of libellant's claim at too small a figure is not such a reason." [466]

The bonds and stipulations which we have been discussing provide for the release of vessels after their arrest under *in rem* process. However, a claimant, in lieu of having process issued under his libel, may agree to let the vessel go free in return for a promise by the ship owner, his insurer or his bank that security will be posted (or judgment paid) up to specified amounts if and when the threatened action is actually tried.[466a] Such informal or extra-legal agreements save court costs and the Marshal's fees, avoid the annoyance of having the vessel even temporarily arrested and may well be cheaper than the usual surety bond. They have not been much discussed in the literature [466b] or in judicial opinions. In Continental Grain Company v. Federal Barge Lines, Inc.,[466c] Judge Brown commented that a letter of undertaking given by a ship owner would be treated

**466.** 47 F.2d 332 at 335, 1931 A.M.C. 407 at 410, 411. In United States v. Ames, 99 U.S. 35 (1878) it was held that when property had been released under bond and a judgment rendered thereon, the insolvency of the sureties on the bond (which made the judgment uncollectible) was not sufficient reason to allow the libellant to proceed against the persons to whom the property had been released.

In the Dauntless (Hooper v. Kunkler Transp. Co.) 1 F.2d 846, 1925 A.M.C. 209 (9th Cir. 1924) a ship was released under a bond whose condition was either to pay any decree that might be entered in the action or to redeliver the ship to the marshal. On redelivery, it was held that the liens would again attach to the ship. In the Tito Campanella (United States v. Tito Campanella Societa Di Navigazione) 214 F.2d 457, 1954 A.M.C. 1519 (4th Cir. 1954) an owner who had procured the release of his ship on a cash deposit under stipulation for value was denied the right to return the ship to the marshal and withdraw the deposit.

See also The Stella R., 1 F.Supp. 998, 1932 A.M.C. 1442 (S.D.N.Y.1932).

**466a.** Such a practice seems to have been well established in the 1920's. See In re Atlantic Gulf & Western Indies S. S. Lines, Inc., 20 F.2d 975, 1927 A.M.C. 1084 (S.D.N.Y.1927), per Thacher, J.: "Proctors for the salvor . . . asked if the ship would be bonded, and were advised by the proctors for the owners that they would bond. Upon filing the libel, and pursuant to the practice which prevails among proctors representing shipping interests, the process was not issued, but assurances were obtained from the proctors representing the owners that a bond [in the sum of $30,000] would be filed in the libel proceedings . . . and that this would be accepted in lieu of a surety bond." Judge Thacher further commented: "I am not unmindful of the great importance to the owners of ships that they be not delayed in the prosecution of their business by the issuance of process, where such annoyance can be avoided without prejudice to the rights of litigants, and I think it quite important that this court should encourage and uphold the practice of its proctors in making [such] agreements . . ." His decree protected the salvage libellant under the owner's promise to give the bond.

**466b.** See, for brief discussion, Harmon, Discharge and Waiver of Maritime Liens, 47 Tulane L.Rev. 786, 796 (1973). Mr. Harmon refers to letters of undertaking from the owner's insurers ("club" letters), bank letters of credit and escrow deposits as being frequently used.

**466c.** 268 F.2d 240, 1959 A.M.C. 2158 (5th Cir. 1959), affirmed 364 U.S. 19, 80 S.Ct. 1470, 1961 A.M.C. 1 (1960). The case involved a transfer of venue question, see note 75a *supra*.

> "as though, upon the libel being filed, the vessel had actually been seized, a claim filed, a stipulation to abide decree with sureties executed and filed by Claimant, and the vessel formally released. Any other course would imperil the desirable avoidance of needless cost, time and inconvenience to litigants, counsel, ships, Clerks, Marshals, keepers and court personnel through the ready acceptance of such letter undertakings." [466d]

If, as Judge Brown suggests, the informal agreement is treated as having the same legal effect as a formal release under bond or stipulation, few questions relating to their use will ever have to be litigated. One such question did arise in In re Moore (Tug Olive L. Moore) [466e] where the owner's insurer gave a letter of undertaking in connection with an incident in which the tug had damaged a pier. In limitation proceedings which were subsequently initiated by the owner, the beneficiary of the letter argued that he was entitled to press his claim outside the limitation proceedings. Judge Freeman rejected the argument in an excellent opinion and enjoined the beneficiary's independent action until the limitation proceedings had been concluded. Counsel for the beneficiary had argued, with "unjustified emotion", that such a holding would shatter "the faith of the marine industry in letters of undertaking." Judge Freeman commented that "probability theory alone proclaims as largely groundless fears that this court's position will make these compacts obsolete." [466f]

**§ 9–90.** The libellant may be found to have a right to recover in an amount greater than that for which the ship has been released. The stipulator or the surety is of course not liable beyond the maximum amount of the bond. If an action *in personam* against the shipowner has been joined to the action *in rem* against the ship,[467] there is no difficulty in collecting the deficiency from the defendant in the *in personam* action. Although the joinder has not been made, the libellant in the *in rem* action, a part of his judgment remaining unsatisfied, may subsequently proceed against the owner personally in

**466d.** 268 F.2d at p. 243, 1959 A.M.C. at p. 2161.

**466e.** 278 F.Supp. 260, 1968 A.M.C. 818 (E.D.Mich.1968). The case is further discussed in Chapter X, §§ 10–26, 10–47.

**466f.** Narragansett Fishing Corp. v. F/V Bob 'n Barry, 425 F.2d 733, 1970 A.M.C. 1132 (1st Cir. 1970) presented a comparable question of limitation law. After a vessel had been released under bond the owner instituted limitation proceedings, in which he was required to post another bond under the provisions of the Limitation Act. The owners then moved that the first bond should be canceled, in order to avoid payment of premiums for both bonds. Judge Aldrich pointed out that, if limitation should be denied, the beneficiary of the first bond might be in a position to pursue his original action outside the limitation concourse. Therefore both bonds had to be maintained. The beneficiary of the bond in the First Circuit case seems to end up in the same position as the beneficiary of the letter of undertaking in the Moore case. Judge Aldrich commented that: "The complications, present and future, of this situation may well be thought a bucket of sea worms . . . "

**467.** See text at note 83 *supra*.

an independent action and in such action, whether it is brought in state or federal court, may have any of the defendant's property (including the ship which was the subject matter of the original libel *in rem*) attached and sold on execution.[468] Such an execution sale would not be the equivalent of a judicial sale in admiralty (even if made by the Marshal on process issuing from the admiralty court); the Marshal would not sell the ship free of liens but would sell only whatever interest the owner might have in the ship.

In the absence of a joinder *in personam* the traditional rule has been that the admiralty court in an *in rem* action will not give a personal judgment against the owner in excess of the amount of the release bond.[469] That is to say, the owner may appear to defend the *in rem* action without thereby generally submitting himself to the court's jurisdiction. The theoretical basis for the rule is said to be the American doctrine of personification of the ship according to which the ship, and not the owner, is looked on as the defendant. Under English practice, process *in rem* is looked on as merely a device for compelling the owner's personal appearance, so that there is nothing in English theory to prevent a court from handing down a personal judgment against the owner in excess of a release bond even without joinder *in personam.*

The American rule appears, however, to have been breaking down in recent years. In The Fairisle,[470] where the libel was *in rem* only, Judge Coleman entered a judgment for $45,100 after the ship had been released on stipulation for $25,000. The case is perhaps exceptional but in view of the judge's long experience in admiralty matters is not to be lightly dismissed. The Fairisle was libeled for salvage. At a preliminary hearing to determine the amount of the stipulation proctors for libellants urged that the ship be bonded at not less than $1,000,000, while for the owners it was argued that the largest award that could possibly be made would be $10,900 and that the ship should be released for that amount. Judge Coleman set a figure of $25,000 and a bond in that amount was given. On trial Judge Coleman concluded that the libellants had made out a case for a recovery of $45,100 and over the owner's strenuous objections entered a judgment for that amount. Conceding that much American case law denied a recovery in excess of the stipulation in an action only *in rem*, he distinguished the cases cited to him on the ground that they involved situations where the parties had agreed on the amount for which the vessel should be released, that amount being the estimated value of the vessel. In The Fairisle, however, the parties had been unable to come to an agreement and the amount of the stipulation merely represented the judge's guess (which on trial proved to have been an under-

468. The Susana, 2 F.2d 410, 1924 A.M.C. 1389 (4th Cir. 1924); Red Star Towing & Transp. Co. v. New York Towing & Transp. Co. (The Forrest E. Single), 5 F.Supp. 502, 1933 A.M.C. 1488 (E.D.N.Y.1933).

469. See § 9–19 *supra.*

470. (Dean v. Waterman S. S. Co.) 76 F.Supp. 27, 1948 A.M.C. 794 (D.Md. 1947), affirmed 171 F.2d 408, 1949 A.M.C. 1 (4th Cir. 1948).

estimate) as to the reasonable value of the salvage services. Judge Coleman added that "[t]he precise point . . . appears, strangely enough, to have been the subject of decision on a similar state of facts in only one reported admiralty case in this country." In The Minnetonka [471] a passenger had libeled a ship *in rem* for the value of jewelry stolen during the voyage. The value of the jewelry was stipulated at $5,000 and the ship released for that amount. Later, on expert appraisal, the jewelry was found to have been worth more and the Second Circuit approved a judgment in the *in rem* action for the full value. In addition to The Minnetonka, Judge Coleman referred to English decisions, which, as indicated above, have always proceeded on a theory quite different from the accepted American theory. After quoting Judge Coxe in The Minnetonka ("A court of admiralty has powers akin to those of a court of equity, and should not be hampered in its efforts to reach a substantial justice by the inexorable rules invoked by the claimant") Judge Coleman concluded:

> "The result of [holding the claimant-owner liable in excess of the stipulation] is not actually to engraft upon a suit *in rem* a personal liability by admiralty process, although no personal action has been brought as it might have been, but rather . . . if the owners appear to contest their liability, they may equitably be treated as if they had been brought into court by personal process." [472]

Novel as The Fairisle holding was, it shortly enlisted distinguished support. In Mosher v. Tate [473] the Ninth Circuit approved the Fairisle, pointing out that most of the cases which had held that an action *in rem* could not be converted into an action *in personam* dated back to a time when under the Admiralty Rules the two actions could not be joined. In cases where the joinder is permitted, Judge Bone commented, "there appears to be no just or logical reason for application of the former prohibition. . . ." In Logue Stevedoring Corp. v. The Dalzellance [474] the Second Circuit adhered to the traditional rule. "The ordinary practice in admiralty," wrote Judge Swan, "does not permit a personal judgment to be entered upon a mere libel *in rem.*" Judge Clark, dissenting, with a reference to Mosher v. Tate, saw "nothing erroneous, only a direct and realistic judicial act, in the action of the trial judge in entering judgment against the claimant."

In both The Fairisle and Mosher v. Tate it appeared that the libellants could initially have joined actions *in personam* to the actions

471. 146 F. 509 (2d Cir. 1906).

472. 76 F.Supp. 27, 34, 1948 A.M.C. 794, 806 (1947).

473. 182 F.2d 475, 1950 A.M.C. 1106 (9th Cir. 1950). A Note in 64 Harv.L. Rev. 164 (1950) carefully reviewed the historical background and approved the result in Mosher v. Tate.

474. 198 F.2d 369, 1952 A.M.C. 1297 (2d Cir. 1952). In the Logue Stevedoring case the judgment sought to have been entered against the owner appears to have been in excess of the ship's value. In both the Fairisle and Mosher v. Tate the judgment was in excess of the original bond or stipulation but less than the value of the ship. The cases may thus be distinguishable on this ground.

*in rem.* Thus, in allowing the *in personam* judgments to be entered in the absence of the joinder, the courts may merely have been refusing to allow themselves to become entangled in procedural red tape. The Fourth Circuit moved a step further in Savas v. Maria Trading Corporation (S/S Captain John C).[474a] Savas performed services and acquired a lien, for which he libeled the ship *in rem* on August 10, 1956. At the time the services were performed Maria Trading Corporation, a Panamanian corporation, owned the ship which, however, it sold to Associated Bulk Cargo, S. A., on July 17, 1956. The purchaser claimed the ship, secured its release under bond, filed a cross-libel against Savas and, a year later, filed an impleading petition against Maria Trading on the ground that Maria Trading had warranted the ship free of liens. Maria Trading, which had not been served with process, entered the case and filed exceptions to both the libel and the cross-libel. In its exceptions it took the position that, since it had not been served, the court lacked jurisdiction to enter an *in personam* judgment against it in favor of either Associated Bulk Cargo or of Savas. The final step in this procedural nightmare was that Savas, with the court's consent, filed an amended libel which named Maria Trading as an *in personam* respondent. After trial the District Court, in addition to giving judgment for Savas on the *in rem* libel, held Maria Trading liable *in personam* both to Savas and to Associated Bulk Cargo.

That disposition of the case was affirmed on appeal. Judge Soper, after reviewing the authorities, commented:

> "There is much to be said for the amelioration of the strict rule which permits the claimant of a vessel to resist the imposition of a lien without subjecting himself to a decree *in personam* . . . [Maria Trading's] only purpose in becoming a party to the suit was to secure an adjudication relieving it from personal liability. . . . Even if it was not validly served with process it should not be heard to say that the court had the power to decide in its favor but no power to render a decree against it. . . . Whatever be the proper rule as to the power of the court to impose personal liability upon the owner of a ship who comes into a case merely to resist a lien upon his property, there is no good reason to extend the immunity to one who no longer owns the vessel but merely seeks relief from personal liability." [474b]

Where the owner-claimant has appeared in the *in rem* action and made a defense on the merits, there seems to be no sound reason of policy why the court should not enter whatever judgment justice requires, as is done under English practice. The doctrinal basis for the American rule to the contrary—the theory of the personification of the ship—is no longer in a flourishing state of health. As the doc-

**474a.** 285 F.2d 336, 1961 A.M.C. 260 (4th Cir. 1960).

**474b.** 285 F.2d at pp. 340–341, 1961 A.M.C. at pp. 266–267.

trine loses force so should the rule which rests upon it. Legal doctrines, however, are apt to be an unconscionable time a-dying. The arguments marshaled by Judge Coleman in The Fairisle, by Judge Bone in Mosher v. Tate and by Judge Soper in the Savas case, as well as the weight to be accorded the late Judge Clark's opinions in the field of procedure, have undermined the basis of the old rule. Unless, however, the Supreme Court passes on the issue, it will undoubtedly long remain in controversy and confusion.[474c]

Supplemental Rule E(8) provides:

> "An appearance to defend against an admiralty and maritime claim with respect to which there has issued process *in rem* . . . may be expressly restricted to the defense of such claim, and in that event shall not constitute an appearance for the purposes of any other claim with respect to which such process is not available or has not been served."

According to the Advisory Committee's Note this provision, which did not appear in the former Admiralty Rules, was principally designed to insure that an appearance to defend an action initiated by *in rem* (or *quasi in rem*) process does not automatically subject the defendant to *in personam* jurisdiction with respect to nonmaritime claims which "under the liberal joinder provision of [the] unified rules" may be combined with maritime claims in the same action. The Rule does not seem to have any application to the question discussed in this section, which is whether the shipowner's appearance to defend an *in rem* action subjects him, under certain circumstances, to liability *in personam* on the same claim. It is a hundred years too late to argue that a claim *in personam* for, say, damages suffered in a collision is a different claim from the same claim pursued *in rem*. There is surely nothing in the Advisory Committee's Note to suggest that the draftsmen were thinking of this esoteric problem.[474d]

**474c.** In Stewart v. Steamer Blue Trader, 428 F.2d 361, 1970 A.M.C. 1552 (1st Cir. 1970) the plaintiff, after his action *in rem* had been dismissed, sought to amend to an action *in personam*. (The ship, which was "of foreign origin", had been allowed to sail after counsel for the shipowner had furnished a letter of undertaking (see text at and following note 466a *supra*). Presumably the foreign shipowner was not subject to process in the United States.) In a per curiam opinion the Court commented: "while the court has jurisdiction *in rem* by virtue of the stipulation, there was no service to support *in personam* recovery. The defendant's appearance to defend the *in rem* action is not enough. The Ethel, 66 F. 340, 342 (alternate holding); *see* Logue Stevedoring Corp. v. The Dalzellance, 198 F.2d 369, 372." Since the *in rem* action had been dismissed on the merits, it is hard to see what the *in personam* action could have accomplished even if it had been allowed. See § 9–17 *supra*.

**474d.** For an example of a "restricted appearance" under Rule E(8), see State of California v. S/S Bournemouth, 307 F.Supp. 922, 1970 A.M.C. 642 (C.D.Cal.1969), 318 F.Supp. 839, 1971 A.M.C. 485 (C.D.Cal.1970), discussed § 9–20 *supra*, text following note 95a. The possibility that the foreign shipowner who entered the restricted appearance to defend an *in rem* action (for oil pollution) had, or could have, thereby subjected himself to *in personam* liability was not discussed.

## Bankruptcy and Reorganization

**§ 9–91.** When bankruptcy or reorganization proceedings are instituted against a shipowner, there is much confusion as to the respective roles to be played by the bankruptcy or reorganization court and by the admiralty court in adjudicating maritime claims and in executing maritime liens asserted against the insolvent and the ships belonging to his estate.[475] The older cases held or suggested that the jurisdiction of the admiralty court was to be regarded as paramount, but such litigation was infrequent and only a few of the relevant issues and possible fact combination were ever explored or dealt with.[475a] During the late 1920's and early 1930's the depressed condition of the shipping industry stimulated a mild flurry of insolvency litigation, whose results on the whole tended to favor the bankruptcy court.[476] This depression litigation was carried on in the District and Circuit Court levels, without Supreme Court intervention. In the course of overhauling the Bankruptcy Act in 1938 Congress considered the sensible proposal of giving admiralty powers to district courts sitting in insolvency proceedings but the proposal failed.[477] There was, for obvious reasons, little or no insolvency litigation involving ships and shipowners during the 1940's. Since the 1950's a modest amount of such litigation has been reported—at the rate of one or two cases a year, mostly at the District Court level. No such case has reached the Supreme Court. The post World War II cases, like the depression cases, have been on the whole favorable to the idea that a federal district court is a federal district court and has whatever powers it has whether the proceeding before it is captioned "in bankruptcy" or "in admiralty". Needless to say, the 1966 procedural unification weighs on the same side of the balance. In the absence of word from the Supreme Court it cannot be said that the matters which will be discussed in the following sections have been authoritatively settled. Nevertheless, the admittedly meagre case law harvest of nearly half a century does testify to the good sense of the courts in

475. Landers, The Shipowner Becomes a Bankrupt, 39 U. of Chi.L.Rev. 490 (1972) is a major contribution to the literature. Professor Landers reviews the cases and issues in much greater detail than will be attempted in the following discussion.

475a. Leading cases were Moran v. Sturges, 154 U.S. 256, 14 S.Ct. 1019 (1894), Hudson v. New York & Albany Transportation Co., 180 F. 973 (2d Cir. 1910), and The Philomena, 200 F. 859 (D.Mass.1911). The traditional view was that "[t]he power to adjudicate maritime liens is vested exclusively in the admiralty courts", Fridlund, Federal Taxes and Preferred Ship Mortgages, 38 Harv.L.Rev. 1060, 1072 (1925), a position still adhered to in 1 Benedict, Admiralty 28 (6th ed. 1940). See also Fiddler, The Admiralty Practice in Montana and All That: A critique of the Proposal to Abolish the General Admiralty Rules etc., 17 Maine L.Rev. 15, 27–28 (1965). On the other hand, Robinson, Admiralty 415 *et seq.* (1939) concluded, in an excellent discussion, that even the older cases did not support so unqualified an assertion of the exclusive jurisdiction of the admiralty courts. See also Landers, note 475 *supra.*

476. See cases cited notes 478, 480, 483, 486, 487, 489, 496 *infra.*

477. See 1 Collier, Bankruptcy § 2.10 (14th ed. by Moore, 1940, revised 1971). A similar attempt failed in 1949. See Fiddler, *loc cit.* note 475a *supra.*

deciding the cases which come before them, however murky the jurisprudential and jurisdictional background may be.

Among the questions which may arise are the following:

1. On the institution of insolvency proceedings may the insolvency court enjoin the prosecution of actions in admiralty against the debtor?

2. Does the insolvency court have jurisdiction to adjudicate maritime liens? If it does, will it rank such liens among themselves according to the maritime theory of lien priorities, and will it follow the admiralty rule that maritime liens outrank all non-maritime liens?

3. Does the insolvency court have the power to sell a ship free of maritime liens?

**§ 9–92.** Whether the insolvency proceeding is in bankruptcy or reorganization the insolvency court has power to enjoin admiralty proceedings *in rem* subsequently brought against a ship which is part of the insolvent estate.[478] At least in reorganization proceedings the power to enjoin would extend to subsequently filed *in personam* actions as well as to actions *in rem*.[479] If the insolvency court finds it more convenient to allow the admiralty action to proceed for the purpose of determining the amount and rank of the maritime claim the restraining order may be modified to allow one or more such actions to proceed.[480] Even though the petitioner may be successful in the admiralty action, he will be required to return to the insolvency court which will decide for itself how the claim is to be enforced.

When a ship has been seized by the Marshal under *in rem* process before the filing of a petition in bankruptcy, the ship does not come into the control of the bankruptcy court.[481] The action cannot therefore be enjoined and will proceed to final adjudication and a sale of the ship unless the bankruptcy trustee has procured its release under bond. In general a bankruptcy court does not get control of property of the bankrupt against which an action is pending when the bankruptcy petition is filed; thus the rule is not peculiar to the admiralty.[482] The powers of a reorganization court to restrain proceed-

478. The Alabama (First Union Trust & Sav. Bank v. Consumers Co.), 53 F. 2d 972, 1932 A.M.C. 418, certiorari denied 286 U.S. 548, 52 S.Ct. 500 (1931); 63 F.2d 273, 1933 A.M.C. 976 (7th Cir. 1931, 1933); West Kentucky Coal Co. v. Dillman, 15 F.2d 25, 1926 A.M.C. 1690 (8th Cir. 1926); The Transfer No. 18 (in re New York, N.H. & H.R. Co.), 17 F.Supp. 488, 1936 A.M.C. 1580 (D.Conn.1936). In the Alabama *supra* certiorari was granted to the Circuit Court's second decision in 290 U.S. 585, 64 S.Ct. 61 (1933) and, on the ground that the cause had become moot, the Circuit Court's order was reversed and the case remanded to the District Court with mandate to dismiss the proceedings. The Alabama is discussed in the text at note 490 *infra*.

479. See 6 Collier, Bankruptcy § 3.09 (14th ed. by Moore 1940, revised 1972).

480. Pipitone v. United States, 1950 A.M.C. 1049 (E.D.N.Y.1950); In re United Marine Contracting Co., 11 F.Supp. 927 (E.D.N.Y.1935); The Artemis (Jacob v. The Irving Trust Co.) 53 F.2d 672 (S.D.N.Y.1931).

481. The Philomena, 200 F. 859 (D. Mass.1911).

482. On the matters so far discussed, see Landers, note 475 *supra*, at p. 493 *et seq.*

ings already instituted when the petition is filed are more extensive than those of the bankruptcy court. In the first edition of the treatise we commented that although the issue had not been litigated since 1938 when reorganization procedure was codified in Chapters X and XI of the Bankruptcy Act, there was no reason to doubt that a reorganization court would have power to enjoin a pending *in rem* action in admiralty. When the case came up, the predictable holding was that the reorganization court had discretionary power to stay the admiralty proceeding.[482a]

With respect to the control by the Admiralty court under pre-bankruptcy libels, it is apparently necessary to distinguish between process in rem and process quasi in rem in which the property is seized under a writ of foreign attachment. See In re Admiralty Lines, Ltd., 280 F.Supp. 601 (E.D.La. 1968), affirmed per curiam 410 F.2d 398 (5th Cir. 1969). Subfreights owed to a time-chartered vessel were so attached in New Orleans in November, 1965. Involuntary bankruptcy proceedings were instituted against the charterer in the Southern District of New York in February, 1966. The New York bankruptcy court authorized the trustee in bankruptcy to institute ancillary proceedings in Louisiana to determine the validity of certain liens asserted against the subfreights. On application by the trustee, a judge of the Louisiana court before which the admiralty proceeding was pending referred those matters to a referee in bankruptcy. The referee held that the attachment liens were void under § 67a(1) of the Bankruptcy Act (see text at note 487*l* *infra*) and that maritime liens claimed for stevedoring services had not arisen because of a prohibition of lien clause in the charter (see § 9–39 *et seq. supra*). The stevedore whose liens had been denied appealed on the grounds (inter alia) that the case should not have been referred to the referee in bankruptcy and that the trustee should have been required to intervene in the admiralty proceeding. Judge Rubin took the position that he would not review the order of reference (which had been made by another judge) but added: "However, in any event, I reach the same conclusion on the merits as did the referee and it would be pointless to belabor the issue further." The upshot was that the funds in the registry of the admiralty court were ordered paid to the trustee in bankruptcy except for $20,000 which the trustee and the owner of the vessel had stipulated was to be retained in the registry pending arbitration of the owner's claim of lien against the subfreights for unpaid charter hire. Judge Rubin's opinion seems to stop short, but not very far short, of a square holding that, under such circumstances, the jurisdiction of the bankruptcy court is paramount (which is the proposition to which Landers cites the case). The reasons for the trustee's consent to the retention of the $20,000 are not explained. The Admiralty Lines case, it might be said, casts as much darkness as it sheds light.

**482a.** In re J. S. Gissel & Co., 238 F. Supp. 130 (S.D.Tex.1965). Libels in rem and in personam were filed in the Eastern District of Louisiana to foreclose a preferred ship mortgage on November 25, 1964. The Marshal seized the vessel on November 27, 1964. A petition for reorganization of the mortgagor was filed in the Southern District of Texas on December 15, 1964. The Texas reorganization court stayed the Louisiana foreclosure action. In the reported case Judge Ingraham denied the mortgagee's motion to vacate the stay or in the alternative to require the reorganization trustee to post bond to "secure" the mortgage.

See, however, Empire Stevedoring Co., Ltd. v. Oceanic Adjusters, Ltd., 315 F.Supp. 921, 1971 A.M.C. 795 (S.D.N.Y.1970) in which a petition for reorganization was filed in the Southern District of New York a month after the petitioner's vessel had been seized under in rem process in a mortgage foreclosure action (in which other claimants intervened) in the District of Maryland. The vessel was sold in the Maryland action and the fund was distributed to maritime lien claimants by the admiralty court. There is no discussion in Judge Pollack's opinion of why the reorganization court did not stay the admiralty action or of whether it could have done so. The

The reorganization court may also enjoin the continuance of pending *in personam* actions although the power to enjoin lies in the court's discretion and may be abused. This issue reached the Supreme Court in the reorganization proceedings of the Munson Steamship Lines.[483] The administrator of a deceased seaman had commenced a Jones Act action on the civil side of federal court about four months before Munson filed its petition for reorganization under Section 77B of the Bankruptcy Act. Trustees were appointed in the § 77B proceeding and the customary order was entered which enjoined the institution or prosecution of any action at law against the debtor in reorganization. The administrator then applied to the reorganization court for leave to prosecute his Jones Act action, principally on the ground that if he recovered judgment he would have the right, under the New York Insurance Law, to proceed directly against Munson's insurance carrier. The stay of his action, he argued, was of no advantage to the debtor and benefited only the insurer. The application was denied and the denial was upheld by the Second Circuit. The Supreme Court unanimously reversed. The Court agreed that the Jones Act claim was provable and dischargeable and that the reorganization court was empowered to stay the action. However, wrote Justice Butler, "[i]n the absence of a showing of facts sufficient to require a finding that liquidation of petitioner's claim by jury trial would encumber the reorganization, the debtor and trustees were not entitled to have the injunction continued in force against petitioner." The District Judge had therefore abused his discretion in denying the administrator's application. In support of the holding, Justice Butler relied principally on Langnes v. Green which had held that a district court in a limitation of liability proceeding could not enjoin the prosecution in state court of a personal injury claim.[484] The Supreme Court did not put its "abuse of discretion" holding in Munson on the availability of the direct action against the insurer provided the administrator could prosecute his Jones Act claim to judgment but on the broader ground, suggested by the Langnes v. Green citation, that the right of a personal injury plaintiff to a jury trial is to be preserved wherever possible. The debtor or the reorganization trustees must show, therefore, that allowing the personal injury action to proceed will in some manner "encumber the reorganization proceedings."

**§ 9–93.** If the insolvency court has power to restrain admiralty actions *in rem* against a ship in the court's control, it must follow that

case is further discussed, text following note 487a *infra*.

In re Central Railroad Co. of New Jersey, 469 F.2d 857, 1973 A.M.C. 222 (3d Cir. 1972) is not directly relevant to the present discussion but does involve the intersection of maritime law and bankruptcy law. The majority of the Court held that a reorganization court lacked jurisdiction to order distribution of a fund in the registry of an admiralty court in a limitation of liability proceeding. The case is discussed and the majority holding disapproved in Chapter X, § 10–19a.

483. Foust v. Munson S. S. Lines, 299 U.S. 77, 57 S.Ct. 90, 1936 A.M.C. 1669 (1936).

484. 282 U.S. 531, 51 S.Ct. 243, 1931 A.M.C. 511 (1931). See Chapter X, § 10–19 for a discussion of Langnes v. Green.

the same court also has power to adjudicate the claims and to determine their status as liens. In the older case law it was sometimes suggested that the insolvency court could acquire no jurisdiction over maritime liens unless the lienors voluntarily submitted to the court's control [485] although, if a question of jurisdiction, resting ultimately on the constitutional grant of admiralty power, was really involved, it is hard to see how "voluntary submission" could have helped much. In the depression litigation of the thirties the courts which faced the problem assumed, without exception, that they did have the power to decide on maritime lien claims. In The Robert & Edwin [486] a shipowner became a voluntary bankrupt. The principal asset of the estate was the ship, apparently most of the bankrupt's debts had arisen from its operation and many of the claims constituted maritime liens. Some of the lienholders libeled the ship *in rem* and made the argument that under such facts the admiralty court was the better forum. Judge Morton dismissed the libel, explaining his decision in the following terms:

> "That there is weight in these reasons cannot be denied; but I think that the opposite course is, everything considered, the sounder. The bankruptcy proceeding brought all Sinagra's property including the schooner into the bankruptcy court. As has often been pointed out, bankruptcy has many of the characteristics of a proceeding *in rem.* . . .
>
> "It operates directly against the bankrupt's assets and puts them *in custodia legis.* Great confusion and difficulty might be caused by undertaking to liquidate in a separate proceeding a certain piece of property which was part of a bankrupt's estate, see The Casco, (D.C.) 230 F. 929. The trustee in bankruptcy takes the schooner in the same plight and condition as she was held by the bankrupt, i. e., subject to all valid maritime liens to be enforced with priorities according to the admiralty laws. West Kentucky Coal Co. v. Dillman, (C.C.A.) 15 F.2d 25, 1926 A.M.C. 1690. This is necessarily so because the liens attached to the vessel herself and were not merely personal claims against Sinagra. I have no doubt that the referee in bankruptcy will be able to deal correctly with the questions involved. If his conclusions should be doubted, they will be reviewed by the same judge sitting in bankruptcy who would hear the case if it were allowed to proceed on the admiralty side." [487]

485. See *e. g.*, Hudson v. New York & Albany Transp. Co., 180 F. 973 (2d Cir. 1910).

486. 32 F.2d 390, 1929 A.M.C. 686 (D. Mass.1929).

487. *Id.* at 390, 686. Other depression cases which reached the conclusion that the bankruptcy court can adjudicate maritime liens were The West Kentucky Coal Co. case and The Transfer No. 18 cited note 478 *supra*; In re Waldeck-Deal Dredging Co. (Butler v. Ellis), 45 F.2d 951, 1931 A.M.C. 77 (4th Cir. 1930); In re Southern Pacific Golden Gate Ferries, Ltd., 1942 A.M.C. 1581 (N.D.Cal.1942); De-

There were two aspects to Judge Morton's holding in the Robert & Edwin: one was that the bankruptcy court had jurisdiction to adjudicate maritime liens; the other was that the claim adjudged to have lien status would be "enforced with priorities according to the admiralty laws". In Empire Stevedoring Co., Ltd. v. Oceanic Adjusters, Ltd.,[487a] Judge Pollack commented:

> "Although there is some question whether a bankruptcy court or an admiralty court is the proper forum, it is nevertheless clear that a valid maritime lien will be enforced against a ship which is the asset of a bankrupt shipowner (or one in reorganization)." [487b]

If Judge Pollack's remarks are taken in context, there is no reason to believe that he meant to question either aspect of the holding in the Robert & Edwin.[487c] His case was an odd one in which the New York District Court before which a Chapter X reorganization proceeding was pending had made no attempt to stay a foreclosure and lien proceeding which had been commenced in the Maryland District Court.[487d] The Maryland court sold the vessel and distributed the fund to maritime lien claimants. Empire Stevedoring apparently had such a lien and would have been admitted to share in the distribution but had failed to comply with an order of the Maryland court which had directed lien claimants to file by a specified date; its claim in the Maryland admiralty proceeding was consequently dismissed. Empire then returned to the New York reorganization proceeding in which one of the assets of the debtor in reorganization was the proceeds of a general average settlement in favor of the owner of the ship which had been sold in the Maryland proceeding. On grounds which need not be stated in detail, Empire claimed a lien against the proceeds of the general average settlement (or alternatively that a constructive trust in its favor had attached to the proceeds).

Judge Pollack, sitting as judge in the reorganization proceeding, passed on Empire's claim, holding in effect that Empire had lost its maritime lien by failing to take the proper steps in the Maryland proceeding and that it had no valid claim to a lien, maritime or otherwise, on (or a trust interest in) the proceeds of the general average

fense Plant Corp. v. U. S. Barge Lines, Inc., 57 F.Supp. 14, 1944 A.M.C. 798 (S.D.N.Y.1944) affirmed 145 F.2d 766 (2d Cir. 1944) (but the point here involved was not raised on the appeal).

**487a.** 315 F.Supp. 921, 1971 A.M.C. 795 (S.D.N.Y.1970).

**487b.** 315 F.Supp. at p. 925, 1971 A.M.C. at p. 799, citing the Robert & Edwin and other cases, as well as the discussion in the first edition of the treatise.

**487c.** Landers, note 475 *supra* at p. 497, took the first part of the sentence quoted as meaning that Judge Pollack "regarded the question of the bankruptcy court's power over maritime liens as still unsettled." Professor Landers, who strongly believes that the bankruptcy (or reorganization) court does have (or should be regarded as having) the power, reviews the authorities in an illuminating discussion.

**487d.** See note 482a *supra*.

settlement. Thus Empire would rank with the other unsecured creditors in the reorganization proceeding. The case appears to be one in which the reorganization court preferred to let the admiralty court handle and dispose of the maritime lien claim. There is not the slightest suggestion that the reorganization court, if it had decided to do the job itself, would not have both adjudicated and enforced the maritime liens in accordance with the holding in the Robert & Edwin and other cases of the same type.[487e]

Even if we assume that insolvency courts both adjudicate and enforce maritime liens and that, in their enforcement, the scheme of maritime lien priorities will be followed, there remain a great many areas of doubt and obscurity which have not so far been explored in the fragmentary case law. A maritime lien claimant (subject to qualifications which will be introduced in the following paragraph) would clearly have priority over the bankrupt's general or unsecured creditors: as to them he stands in the position of the holder of a properly perfected security interest. That is true at least with respect to the bankrupt's ships and other maritime property; one case, decided by a referee in bankruptcy, may have extended the priority to cover the bankrupt's general assets.[487f] It may be hypothesized that the only assets available for distribution in a bankruptcy derive from the sale of nonmaritime property, the bankrupt's maritime property having been dissipated, lost or destroyed. In such a case a maritime lienor might plausibly claim priority in distribution over nonmaritime creditors. It is unclear whether an insolvent shipowner is entitled to petition for limitation under the Limitation of Liability Act.[487g] If he is, it is possible that the limitation fund will be distributed to one group of maritime disaster claims while other claims arising from the same disaster will be excluded from participation.[487h] That would be another situation in which the maritime lien claim excluded from the limitation proceeding could plausibly claim priority over nonmaritime creditors with respect to nonmaritime property. As a final exhibit in our chamber of hypothetical horrors we may hypothesize that the assets administered

**487e.** In addition to The Robert & Edwin and the cases cited in note 487 *supra*, the cases discussed in § 9–92 *supra* in which insolvency courts have enjoined or stayed the prosecution of admiralty proceeding necessarily rest on the theory that the insolvency court can do its own adjudication and enforcement.

**487f.** Matter of The Queen, Ltd., 1973 A.M.C. 646 (E.D.Pa.1973), digested note 80 *supra*. Referee Goldhaber's opinion does not make clear what the assets were which were available for distribution in the bankruptcy. The "vessel" against which the referee held that liens had arisen was the former Queen Elizabeth which the bankrupts had unsuccessfully attempted to operate as a tourist attraction in Florida. Following their adjudication in bankruptcy, a receiver sold the Queen Elizabeth, whose new owners sent her on a voyage to Hong Kong where she was destroyed by a fire. Evidently the bankruptcy assets included the fund created by the receiver's sale and conceivably there were no other assets. The referee held that the maritime lienors were to be paid with priority over unsecured creditors.

**487g.** See Chapter X, § 10–48 *et seq.*

**487h.** See Chapter X, § 10–40.

in a bankruptcy or reorganization include both maritime and nonmaritime property and that the claims against the estate include both maritime liens and perfected security interests in the nonmaritime property. There appears to be no case authority which is even remotely in point on the several situations we have hypothesized.

A maritime lien must, like any other claim made against an insolvent estate, run the gauntlet of the bankruptcy trustee's avoiding powers under Sections 60, 67 and 70 of the Bankruptcy Act. If a maritime lien arises out of a transaction which could have been avoided by the bankrupt's creditors as a fraudulent conveyance, it will be subject to avoidance by the trustee in bankruptcy in bankruptcy proceedings as it would be in admiralty proceedings.[487i] If a ship mortgage is taken out under circumstances constituting a voidable preference under § 60, it will be nonetheless a voidable preference for being a preferred mortgage under the Ship Mortgage Act.[487j] It is hard to see how a true maritime lien (as distinguished from the lien of a preferred mortgage) could ever be stigmatized as a voidable preference, since the true lien could never be a transfer for an antecedent debt and, under maritime law, the true lien is not subject to any filing or recording system.[487k] There is no question but that liens arising when ships are attached under writs of foreign attachment (quasi in rem process) are voidable under § 67a(1) as liens obtained by legal or equitable proceedings.[487l] The holdings just referred to led counsel, who may not have been familiar with the esoterics of maritime law, to argue that true maritime liens enforced by in rem process should also be voidable under § 67a(1) but the argument, fortunately, got nowhere.[487m]

**487i.** See, e. g., Bergren v. Davis, 287 F.Supp. 52 (D.Conn.1968), discussed text following note 296n, *supra*.

**487j.** See Liman v. Bank of Nova Scotia, 337 F.Supp. 62 (S.D.N.Y.1971). Judge Motley's opinion was devoted entirely to the question whether the trustee's action to set aside preferred mortgages as voidable preferences was time-barred. She held that it was not and certified the question for appeal under 28 U.S.C.A. § 1292b. No further proceedings in the case have been reported.

**487k.** The argument that a maritime lien was, for some unexplained reason, a voidable preference under § 60 was properly rejected by Judge Herlands in Diana Compania Maritima v. Subfreights of S/S Admiralty Flyer, 280 F.Supp. 607, 614, 1968 A.M.C. 2093, 2101 (S.D.N.Y.1968). Landers, note 475 *supra*, at p. 515 *et seq.* speculates at some length on the possibility of attacking true maritime liens as voidable preferences, including the possibility that the maritime lien could be stigmatized as an "equitable lien" voidable under § 60a(6). The chance that such attacks would be successful seems, to this writer, remote.

**487*l*.** In re North Atlantic & Gulf Steamships Co., 204 F.Supp. 899, 1963 A.M.C. 871 (S.D.N.Y.1962), affirmed *sub nom.* Schilling v. A/S D/S Dannebrog, 320 F.2d 628, 1964 A.M.C. 678 (2d Cir. 1963). The District Court's ruling on the § 67a(1) point was not contested on the appeal. See also In re Admiralty Lines, Ltd., 280 F.Supp. 601 (E.D.La.1968), affirmed per curiam 410 F.2d 398 (5th Cir. 1969), digested note 482 *supra*.

**487m.** See In re North Atlantic & Gulf Steamships Co., note 478*l* *supra*. On the appeal to the Second Circuit the trustee in bankruptcy did not "dispute" the correctness of the District Court's holding on this point. See also In re Admiralty Lines, Ltd., note 487*l* *supra*; Diana Compania Maritima v. Sub-

**§ 9–94.** A special problem may exist with respect to foreclosure of preferred mortgages under the Ship Mortgage Act.[488] According to § 951 of the Act, on default the "lien may be enforced by the mortgagee by suit in rem in admiralty. Original jurisdiction of all such suits is granted to the district courts of the United States exclusively." Under these provisions it has been held that, at least in the absence of "voluntary submission" by the mortgagee, the mortgage can be foreclosed only in admiralty.[489] In The Alabama [490] the Seventh Circuit, without disputing the proposition that exclusive jurisdiction was vested in the admiralty court, threw an interesting light on the meaning of "voluntary submission". In an equity receivership the district court, having appointed a receiver to operate a ship subject to a preferred mortgage, also enjoined the mortgagee from foreclosing his mortgage in admiralty. In affirming the action Judge Evans wrote:

> "Appellant [mortgagee] could have intervened [in the receivership], and its rights would have been fully protected in the equity court. We conclude therefore that in refusing to surrender its jurisdiction the court of equity not only did not abuse its discretion, but wisely insisted that all claimants and creditors should litigate their claims in a court which could protect them all." [491]

In Collier Advertising Service v. Hudson River Day Line,[492] the District Judge, confronted with a creditor's bill in equity as well as a libel *in rem* to foreclose a preferred mortgage in admiralty, ingeniously "consolidated" the proceedings and allowed them to proceed simultaneously, wearing now his equity hat and now his admiralty hat as required by the circumstances.[492a]

If the mortgagee can be enjoined from foreclosing his mortgage in admiralty until he chooses to submit "voluntarily" by appearing

freights of S/S Admiralty Flyer, note 487k *supra*.

**488.** 49 Stat. 2016 (1920); 46 U.S.C. §§ 911–984.

**489.** The Fort Orange (City Bank Farmers Trust Co. v. Hudson River Navigation Corp.), 5 F.Supp. 833, 1934 A.M.C. 240 (S.D.N.Y.1933); In re Munson Steamship Line, 1938 A.M.C. 837 (S.D.N.Y.1938).

**490.** (First Union Trust & Sav. Bank v. Consumers' Co.), 63 F.2d 273, 1933 A.M.C. 976 (7th Cir. 1933). For the subsequent history of this case see note 478 *supra*.

**491.** 63 F.2d at p. 274, 1933 A.M.C. at p. 979.

**492.** 14 F.Supp. 335, 1936 A.M.C. 206 (S.D.N.Y.1936).

**492a.** See the cases discussed in note 482a *supra* and the accompanying text. If a bankruptcy or reorganization court has the power to stay a foreclosure proceeding in admiralty, presumably it has the power to foreclose the mortgage itself. Since the 1966 procedural unification the metaphysical distinction between admiralty proceedings and other proceedings under the federal jurisdiction has become even more difficult to understand than it had been before 1966. There appears to have been no discussion of the issue in recent cases, perhaps because everybody is willing to admit that a federal district court can foreclose a preferred mortgage however the proceeding is captioned. Landers, note 475 *supra* at p. 507 *et seq.*, takes essentially the position outlined in the following paragraph of the text.

in the insolvency proceeding, or if the admiralty foreclosure can be "consolidated" with the insolvency proceeding, when both are instituted in the same district, there is nothing particularly bothersome about the proposition that the admiralty court's jurisdiction is exclusive. On the other hand, if, as the courts assumed in the thirties, all other maritime liens can be adjudicated by the insolvency court, then why not the lien of a preferred mortgage, without resorting to the cumbersome procedure of "consolidation" and enforced "voluntary submission"? The language of the Ship Mortgage Act, closely read, does not actually support the proposition that foreclosure jurisdiction was given exclusively to the admiralty court. Section 951 provides that the "lien may be enforced . . . in rem in admiralty" (which could not have been done before the passage of the Act because ship mortgages were not maritime). The Act also grants original jurisdiction of "all such suits to the district courts of the United States exclusively". "All such suits" means, clearly enough, all actions to foreclose a preferred mortgage. The "exclusive" jurisdiction, however, is conferred on the "district courts of the United States" and a district court sitting "in bankruptcy" or "in reorganization" is quite as much a "district court of the United States" as the district court sitting "in admiralty". The Congressional hearings on the Ship Mortgage Act indicate that it was at one time proposed to have ship mortgages foreclosed in equity but that the proposal was dropped in favor of the admiralty foreclosure provision which appears in the statute as enacted.[493] In view of the legislative history, Judge Knox felt in The Fort Orange that foreclosure in admiralty was the exclusive remedy and that an equity receivership or reorganization court lacked jurisdiction. It should be noted that the mortgage foreclosure proceeding and the equity receivership were simultaneously pending before Judge Knox—indeed he disposed of both of them in the same opinion—so that, without technically "consolidating" the proceedings, he achieved the result of a consolidation. The statute however, lends itself to the construction that the lien of the preferred mortgage, like any other maritime lien, is normally to be enforced against the ship in admiralty, but that, if insolvency proceedings are instituted and the insolvency court gets control of the property, that court (being "a district court of the United States") can foreclose the mortgage just as it can adjudicate any other maritime lien.[494]

493. The legislative history of the foreclosure provisions is reviewed in The Fort Orange, note 489 *supra*. 5 F. Supp. at 838, 1934 A.M.C. at 248.

494. Note should be made of the provisions of Chapter 14 of the Bankruptcy Act (52 Stat. 939 (1938), 11 U.S.C.A. §§ 1101–1103). Under § 1101, with respect to vessels of United States registry engaged in foreign commerce on which the United States holds preferred ship mortgages, the court in any bankruptcy or reorganization proceeding may appoint the United States Maritime Commission as sole receiver or trustee. Section 1102 provides for the operation of such vessels and the payment of operating losses by the Commission. Under § 1103 the injunction powers of courts under the Bankruptcy Act do not "affect or apply to" the United States as a creditor under a preferred ship mortgage unless the Maritime Commission files with the court a written waiver of its rights under the section.

§ 9–95. The question whether the bankruptcy court can sell a ship free of maritime liens is closely related to the question whether that court has jurisdiction to adjudicate, determine and rank the liens. Logically both questions should be answered the same way. The traditional view was that the insolvency court lacked jurisdiction on both counts, at least in the absence of "voluntary submission" by the lienors which was somehow supposed to cure the jurisdictional defect.[495] The litigation during the 1930's was predominantly in favor of recognizing the jurisdiction of the insolvency court to handle maritime lien claims and that trend has continued in the cases which have been reported since World War II.[495a] If the insolvency court has power to adjudicate liens and the power to enjoin libels *in rem*, it can hardly be doubted that it has, when the insolvent estate is liquidated, power to sell a ship free of liens and that such a sale would be recognized, at least by courts in the United States.[496] On parity of reasoning, in a reorganization proceeding the court should be able to execute pre-existing maritime liens to the same extent that it can compel other types of creditors to accept a plan of reorganization.

The United States seems never to have resorted to the Chapter 14 procedure, but its provisions were put to an odd use in Northwest Marine Works v. United States (The Audrey II), 307 F.2d 537, 1963 A.M.C. 142 (9th Cir. 1962). The United States, having filed a libel to foreclose its preferred mortgage, wanted to continue operating the Audrey II while the foreclosure action was pending. The foreclosure court, under § 952 of the Ship Mortgage Act, has discretionary authority to appoint a receiver, although the only prior reported case in which that had been done was The Southern Cross, 23 F.Supp. 613, 1938 A.M.C. 1047 (E.D.N.Y.1938) in which the United States, as mortgagee, agreed to assume operating losses incurred during the receivership. On the application of the United States and without notice to other creditors, the court appointed a receiver for the Audrey II. In the course of her operation the United States, through the Maritime Commission, advanced approximately $142,000 to pay crew wages. Subsequently, in the foreclosure proceeding after the sale of the vessel, the United States claimed that the advance should be paid as a custodial expense (§§ 9–11, 9–61 *supra*) with priority not only over the mortgage but over all pre-custodial liens. The District Court so held, United States v. Audrey II, 185 F.Supp. 777, 1960 A.M.C. 1977 (N.D.Cal.1960), see note 45 *supra*. The Ninth Circuit unanimously reversed in an opinion by Judge Duniway, who suggested that Chapter 14 (which requires the United States to bear operating losses) had, in effect, "modified" the receivership provision of the Ship Mortgage Act; thus the advance by the Maritime Commission was subordinated to the pre-custodial liens.

495. See text at note 485 *supra*.

495a. See §§ 9–91, 9–92 *supra*.

496. In In re Marine Transit Corp., 20 F.Supp. 414, 1937 A.M.C. 1515 (S.D.N.Y.1937) the bankruptcy court ordered vessels belonging to the bankrupt estate sold free of liens. No question as to the propriety of the order was raised on appeal, 94 F.2d 7, 1938 A.M.C. 743 (2d Cir. 1938).

On the power to adjudicate liens see § 9–93 *supra*; on the power to enjoin libels *in rem*, § 9–92 *supra*.

Landers, note 475 *supra* at p. 507, comments that: "The only way to obtain a precise holding on the point would be for a maritime lienor . . . to await the nonadmiralty sale [by the bankruptcy court] and then sue to enforce his lien on the ground that the sale did not execute the lien." The only case of the sort which Professor Landers cites is The Goulandris, discussed in the text at note 498 *infra*. It seems unlikely that any lienor will ever be foolish enough to waste his substance in such a pointless endeavor.

A somewhat more complicated problem is whether an execution of liens by a bankruptcy sale or a confirmation of a reorganization plan would be recognized by courts in other countries.[497] According to the classical statement of admiralty doctrine "only" the admiralty court acting *in rem* can divest or execute liens. Thus execution by an insolvency court might not be recognized, and one English case, dealing with a judicial sale of a ship by an Egyptian court which the English court analogized to a court of bankruptcy, so held.[498] On the other hand, in view of the cases discussed in the preceding sections, it could be plausibly argued that federal district courts sitting in bankruptcy or reorganization have acquired admiralty powers to an extent sufficient to entitle their execution decrees to international recognition. The problem, insoluble on a theoretical level, happily lends itself to a simple practical solution (at least in the case of sale). Just as the ecclesiastical courts were accustomed to hand over a convicted heretic to the "secular arm" for execution, so the insolvency court can easily see that, technically, the sale is carried out on the admiralty and not on the bankruptcy side.[499] It is a little harder to work out the execution of liens by confirmation of a reorganization plan, but, on the analogy of a release of a ship under a stipulation for value, it could be argued that the ship was at least freed from all liens affected by the reorganization plan.

497. 1 Benedict, Admiralty 29 (6th ed. 1940): "[F]oreign-going vessels which will come within the jurisdiction of foreign states and sovereigns should in all cases be handled by the admiralty court, inasmuch as the sale . . . by the admiralty court is likely to command much greater respect abroad than a sale by the bankruptcy court."

498. The Goulandris [1927] L.J.R. 85 (in Admiralty). *Cf.* Todd Shipyards Corp. v. F/V Maigus Luck, 243 F. Supp. 8, 1966 A.M.C. 1608 (D.Canal Zone, 1965), digested note 433a *supra*.

499. This procedure was apparently followed in The Tradewind (Atlantic Steamer Supply Co. v. The Tradewind), 144 F.Supp. 408, 1956 A.M.C. 1731 (D.Md.1956). See also the cases cited in § 9–94 *supra*.

# Chapter X

# LIMITATION OF LIABILITY

## Background and Generalities

**§ 10–1.** A recurrent feature of maritime law is the appearance of modern concepts in primitive dress. One example is the idea of risk-sharing as developed in the ancient doctrine of general average. Another is the idea of limitation of the shipowner's liability to the value of his investment—*i. e.* the ship.

Like any investor, an investor in shipping may limit his liability by incorporating his ship. Furthermore, as a carrier of cargo, the ship and shipowner are by statute freed from liability for damage to cargo in many situations in which other types of carrier are liable.[1] Finally, by the Limitation of Liability Act,[2] the shipowner, even without incorporation, may, on the occurrence of some event for which the ship is liable—to cargo, to passengers, to employees or harbor workers or to some other ship—restrict his liability to whatever value the ship may have after the event—*e. g.* a few strippings from a wreck. By reason of the almost universal use of the corporate device, limitation of liability is of much less economic importance than it once was. Nevertheless, even where a ship or a fleet of ships is owned by a corporation, the privilege of limitation will insulate the remaining corporate assets from claims to which they would otherwise be subject.

**§ 10–2.** Although limited liability had been a part of the maritime law of almost all shipowning countries,[3] it was initially rejected by American courts.[4] However, with the rise of the first great

1. The ocean carrier's liability to cargo is treated in Chapter III, Part II.

2. 9 Stat. 635 (1851), 46 U.S.C.A. §§ 181–189.

3. For judicial reviews of the history of the limitation principle, see Judge Ware's opinion in The Rebecca, 20 Fed.Cas. 373, Case No. 11,619 (D.Me. 1831); Justice Bradley in Norwich & N. Y. Transp. Co. v. Wright, 80 U.S. (13 Wall.) 104 (1871); Justice Brown in The Main v. Williams, 152 U.S. 122, 14 S.Ct. 486 (1894). Document 196 of the Maritime Law Association of the United States, The History and Present Status of Domestic and Foreign Laws concerning Limitation of Shipowner's Liability (1935) is a concise and useful summary of the general principles of American and foreign law. Eyer, Shipowners' Limitation of Liability—New Directions for an Old Doctrine, 16 Stanford L.Rev. 370 (1964) reviews the historical background.

4. The Rebecca, note 3 *supra* at 380: ". . . the commercial world seems to be satisfied with holding the owners of vessels responsible to the extent of their interest in the ship, and by abandoning the ship and freight to the creditors they are discharged. . . . It, however, has never been acknowledged in England or this country, as customary . . ." See the concurring opinion of Justice Woodbury in New Jersey Steam Navigation Co. v. Merchants' Bank (The Lexington), 47 U.S. (6 How.) 344, 434 (1848).

The first American limitation act was that of Massachusetts in 1818, c. 122, mainly based on 7 Geo. 2, c. 15 (1734). It was followed by an act in Maine, Stats. 1821, c. 14, §§ 8–10, which was nearly an exact copy of the Massachusetts statute.

American merchant marine, Congress was easily persuaded to reintroduce the limitation principle by statute. An act for the limitation of shipowner's liability was passed on March 3, 1851, with no debate in the House and only part of a day's debate in the Senate.[5] There, inexplicably, matters rested for a generation.[6] Not one of the intended beneficiaries of the Act—the shipowners—invoked its protection until the owners of the steamer City of Norwich, which had sunk following a collision in Long Island Sound on the night of the 18th of April, 1866, sought to limit their liability in a case which reached the Supreme Court in 1871 as Norwich & N. Y. Transp. Co. v. Wright.[7] The Wright case brought home to the members of the

5. 9 Stat. 635. The Act was principally taken from the English Act of 26 Geo. 3, c. 86 (1786) and from the Revised Statute of Maine, 1840, c. 47. The Maine statute had substantially adopted the provisions of the Massachusetts act.

For an extensive comparison, see 2 Parsons, Shipping & Admiralty 121 (1869).

Senator Hamlin of Maine, Chairman of the Senate Committee on Commerce, who introduced the bill, presented it as merely an adoption of English legislation: "Why not give to those who navigate the ocean as many inducements to do so as England has done? . . . That is what this bill seeks to do, and it asks no more." Of the heart of the bill, sections three and four, he said: "These two sections are substantially the English law." Sen. Rantoul of Massachusetts was willing to give even greater assurance: "They (the British) have made the alteration which we are now asked to make, and they have carried it further than this section of the bill carries it." Sen. Davis, from the same state, said: "It is simply placing our mercantile marine upon the same footing as that of Great Britain." 23 Cong.Globe 331–332, 713–720, 776–777, 31st Cong., 2d Sess. (Jan. 25, Feb. 26, March 3, 1851).

The Act was passed following a case in which American shipowners had been subjected to what was thought to be an unduly heavy burden of liability—a liability to which their competitors in other shipowning countries, notably England, were not subject. New Jersey Steam Navigation Co. v. Merchants' Bank (The Lexington), 47 U.S. (6 How.) 344 (1848). A Long Island steamer, the Lexington, en route from New York to Stonington, Connecticut, was totally destroyed by fire. Among the items lost was a simple wooden crate marked "contents unknown". It was brought out in an *in personam* libel against the owners of the Lexington that the box in fact contained $18,000 in gold and silver coin. The amount was held to be recoverable in full, in spite of a contract expressly stipulating carriage at the shipper's risk.

6. Parsons commented in 1869: "The provisions of this act are of paramount importance to the mercantile community, though the main object of the act has been frustrated by the neglect on the part of its framers to embody this intent in intelligible language." 2 Shipping & Admiralty 120 (1869).

7. 80 U.S. (13 Wall.) 104 (1871). The case arose out of a collision on Long Island Sound in which both an innocent schooner and the offending City of Norwich were sunk. The owners of the schooner sued *in personam* in the Federal District Court for Connecticut. The owners of the vessel defended on grounds of no negligence and argued, in a preliminary attempt at limitation, that the resulting loss was much higher than the value of the City of Norwich. The District Court found negligence and was in the process of decreeing full damages when defendants petitioned for limitation. Alleging that the cargo owners had begun a suit *in rem* in the Eastern District of New York, the petitioners asked the court to allow them to show the total amount of the damage sustained by all of the parties, and the value of the steamer, after which it would be proper for the court to give the Connecticut libellants their pro rata share. Libellants objected on the grounds that the Act did not apply to collisions. and that the District Court was without jurisdiction to award the relief sought.

Court the fact that the Act of 1851 was so imperfect, fragmentary and ambiguous as to be unworkable. Customarily, holes in a statute are filled in by the accumulating debris of judicial opinions, and the filling in is a time consuming process. In this instance the Court resorted to the extraordinary device of supplementing the statute by rules of court, which were issued in 1872, the year following the decision in the Wright case; the Admiralty rules on limitation, subsequently several times revised, have continued to play an important role in limitation litigation.[8]

The Wright case, together with the issuance of the rules, sufficed to bring the Limitation Act to the attention of the admiralty bar, with the result that the neglect in which the Act had mouldered for twenty years was replaced by a continuing stream of cases in which shipowners petitioned for limitation. A number of these cases reached the Supreme Court and during the '70's and '80's a series of landmark opinions authoritatively determined most of the principal issues, both of substance and procedure, arising under the Limitation Act. In addition to the Court's work in clarifying vexing problems under an abominably drawn statute, the Congress on several occasions during the same period amended the Act to extend its coverage.[9]

**§ 10–3.** The formative period for limitation law was the last quarter of the 19th century. It may be that counsel for the shipowners, in making no use of the Act between 1850 and 1870, were wise in their generation and that their clients reaped an unexpectedly rich harvest in the benign climate of the latter part of the century when the sun shone on invested capital as it has done in no other period of our history. The results were astonishingly favorable to the shipowners, and the statute, as expounded by the Supreme Court and supplemented by the industry of Congress, was expanded almost beyond belief. The purpose of the 1851 Act had been to put American shipowning interests on a competitive equality with British interests, so far as limitation of liability was concerned. English limitation law,

8. The rules prescribing the practice in limitation proceedings were issued on May 6, 1872, 80 U.S. (13 Wall.), xii–xiv. The court reasserted its power to make the rules, on the basis that the subject was "one preeminently of admiralty jurisdiction", in Providence & New York S. S. Co. v. Hill Mfg. Co., 109 U.S. 578, 593–594, 3 S.Ct. 379, 388, 389 (1883). Slightly amended, the rules were reissued on December 6, 1920 (254 U.S.Appendix, 25–29). The Mary Winkleman, 1 F.2d 774, 1924 A.M.C. 1488 (9th Cir. 1924) held that the reissue of the 1920 Rules was an indication that intervening statutes such as the Jones Act were not to be construed as evidence of an intention by Congress to depart from the principles of the Limitation Act. The Rules were considerably revised and expanded on June 21, 1948 (334 U.S. 864, 68 S.Ct. CLXII, 1948 A.M.C. 1496 (1948)). The Noronic (Petition of Canada S. S. Lines), 93 F.Supp. 549, 1950 A.M.C. 1499 (N.D.Ohio 1950), commenting extensively on the purposes and effects of the 1948 amendments held that the rules are not "jurisdictional"; that is, the trial court in its discretion may waive, overlook, or ignore noncompliance with details of the rules. Following the 1966 "unification" of admiralty and civil practice, see Chapter I, § 1–1, the rules applicable to limitation proceedings were restated in Supplemental Rule F., Fed.Rules of Civil Procedure.

9. The several amendments are discussed in § 10–5 *et seq. infra.*

it might have been supposed, was the obvious analogy to which our courts would look in developing our limitation law. However, the Supreme Court almost from the beginning cut American law loose from English influence by elaborating the theory that the 1851 Act had reincorporated in our law the theory of limitation as found in the "general maritime law";[10] thus in case of need our statute could be supplemented by general principles or particular doctrines derived from that vague corpus, from the Code of Oleron on down. By the application of its "general maritime law" theory, which reserved a wide field for judicial manoeuvre, the Supreme Court had erected by 1900 or thereabouts a structure of limitation law which gave shipowners much more protection than the British counterpart. Not only did the case by case holdings almost uniformly grant limitation, but the early opinions furnished a treasure-house of quotable passages—still regularly quoted in the briefs of counsel—on the proposition that the Limitation Act must be liberally construed so as to effectuate its beneficent purposes.

**§ 10–4.** Since approximately 1930 the early enthusiasm, both legislative and judicial, for the limitation principle has cooled. In 1935 the Congress enacted the first substantial amendments to the Limitation Act since the 1880's:[11] these amendments were adverse to the shipowning interests, the most important being a provision which required, in the case of claims for loss of life and bodily injury, a minimum limitation fund of $60. per ton. In the early '30's the Supreme Court limited the freedom with which shipowners, by filing a petition for limitation, could transfer to the juryless forum of the admiralty proceedings which plaintiffs, under the saving to suitors clause, had elected to bring on the civil side.[12] And in 1954, in a case which, without overruling, impaired the authority of one of the earliest landmark cases, Justice Black, speaking for four members of a Court divided 4–4–1, wrote:

> "Judicial expansion of the Limited Liability Act at this date seems especially inappropriate. Many of the conditions in the shipping industry which induced the 1851 Congress

10. Norwich & N. Y. Transp. Co. v. Wright, 80 U.S. (13 Wall.) 104, 127 (1871). The cutting loose from English influence was not accomplished without stirring up opposition from the shippers of goods. See Van Santvoord, Limitation of the Liability of Shipowners under the Laws of the United States (1887), sub-titled: "A review of recent decisions in the U.S. Supreme Court, on this subject, with reference to decisions in other courts, in England and in the United States, pertinent thereto, and of reproachful methods in the decisions of the Supreme Court, in subverting the specific limitations provided by Act of Congress, and displacing these limitations by substituting limitations of the Middle Ages and of foreign countries on the continent of Europe, which, as an invasion of the legislative power, Congress should not suffer to pass, without correction by legislative action, competent for it to undertake, under the political Constitution of the United States: Prepared for submission to the Judiciary Committe (sic) of the Senate and its Committee on commerce, for the consideration of Amendments to or a revision of the statutes."

11. 49 Stat. 960 (1935), 46 U.S.C.A. §§ 183, 185.

12. § 10–19 *infra.*

to pass the Act no longer prevail. And later Congresses, when they wished to aid shipping, provided subsidies paid out of the public treasury rather than subsidies paid by injured persons." [13]

Judicial attitudes are important. There is at least some reason to believe that the judicial attitude in the second half of the twentieth century will be on the whole hostile to the limitation idea, that the early cases will be whittled down if they are not flatly overruled, that the statute, even without further limiting amendments, will be narrowly and not expansively construed. Such an attitude reflects, it is suggested, not so much hostility to the shipping industry as a recognition of the fact that the Limitation Act, passed in the era before the corporation had become the standard form of business organization and before present forms of insurance protection (such as Protection and Indemnity insurance) were available, shows increasing signs of economic obsolescence.

**§ 10–4(a).** During the nearly twenty years which have elapsed since the foregoing discussion was written the limitation principle has been attacked by many and defended by almost none. Opinions in limitation cases routinely quote the passage from Justice Black's opinion in the Cushing case which has been reproduced above [13a] and not infrequently go on to add further derogatory comments.[13b] The holdings in the limitation cases which have been decided since the mid-1950's have, with a few exceptions, been adverse to the petitioning shipowner.[13c] In the low review literature the argument that the Limitation of Liability Act has served its time and should be repealed has become a commonplace.[13d]

13. Maryland Casualty Co. v. Cushing 347 U.S. 409, 437, 74 S.Ct. 608, 623, 1954 A.M.C. 837, 859 (1954).

13a. Note 13 *supra.*

13b. For a couple of current examples, *see* Complaint of Chinese Maritime Trust, Ltd., 1972 A.M.C. 1478 (S.D.N.Y.1972) ("the disfavor with which expansion of the limitation of liability statute is viewed"); Pettus v. Jones & Laughlin Steel Corp., 322 F.Supp. 1078, 1972 A.M.C. 170 (W.D.Pa.1971) ("the doctrine of limitation of liability is an anachronism in the present day and age"). See further Complaint of Barracuda Tanker Corp. (The Torrey Canyon), 409 F.2d 1013, 1969 A.M.C. 1442 (2d Cir. 1969).

13c. Thede, Statutory Limitations (other than Harter and COGSA) of Carrier's Liability to Cargo—Limitation of Liability and the Fire Statute, 45 Tulane L.Rev. 959 (1971), concludes (at p. 987): "Early cases liberally applied the 1851 legislation in favor of shipowners . . . . More recently, the trend seems to be reversing. . . . [T]he courts [have] required a higher standard of seaworthiness and demanded greater supervision by the owner than did the early cases. There is no reason to believe that this trend will not continue." In Olympic Towing Corp. v. Nebel Towing Co. Inc., 419 F.2d 230, 235, 1969 A.M.C. 1571, 1578, (5th Cir. 1969) Judge Gewin commented that "in the vast majority of cases limitation is denied for one reason or another . . ." (In the case cited, the owner was granted limitation but the claimants were allowed to prosecute actions against the insurer without limitation, see § 10–31 *infra.*)

13d. See, *e. g.*, the article by Eyer cited *supra* note 3; Note, Shipowners' Limited Liability, 3 Colum.J. of Law and Social Problems 105 (1967). For a pretty piece of invective, see Comment, 24 Nacca L.J. 223, 225 (1959): "An act which is vicious in its impact, unconscionable in its results, and out-

The Limitation Act itself has so far managed to survive unscathed but its future prospects cannot be described as bright. One more large-scale maritime disaster, following which the shipowners petition to limit their liability to a fund of $50,[13e] should suffice to bring the whole structure tumbling down. If a third edition of this book is called for, the present chapter will in all probability be of no more than historical interest.

During the early 1960's it seemed probable, or at least possible, that American limitation law would set off on a new tack with the adoption of the 1957 Brussels Convention on the Limitation of the Liability of the Owners of Seagoing Ships (or, failing adoption of the Convention itself, of legislation modeled on it).[13f] Initially, what may be called the maritime law establishment in the United States had opposed the Convention. The United States delegation to the Tenth Diplomatic Conference on Private Maritime Law held in Brussels in 1957 refused to sign the draft Convention; representatives of thirty other nations signed the draft, the only other non-signer was the Soviet Union. In 1958 the Maritime Law Association of the United States adopted a Committee Report which concluded that "the proposed Brussels Convention . . . is not acceptable to or in the best interests of American shipowners, passengers, maritime labor or shippers." [13g] However by 1961 the Maritime Law Association had reversed its first stand and supported the Convention in Congressional hearings both in 1962 and 1963.[13h] Initial American opposition to the Convention seems to have been triggered by provisions which would have established in many (although not in all) situations a larger limitation fund than the fund required under the American statute. The subsequent switch to support of the Convention seems to have reflected fears that, if something were not done to make the limitation system more palatable to its critics, Congress

moded in an age of institutionalized protective insurance, if it cannot be repealed outright, deserves only a narrow, grudging and constrictive construction."

13e. A $50 fund, representing the value of one salvaged lifeboat, was approved in American limitation proceedings which followed the stranding and sinking of the Torrey Canyon off the south-west coast of England in 1967. See In Re Barracuda Tanker Corp., 281 F.Supp. 228, 1968 A.M.C. 1711 (S.D.N.Y.1968). The English and French governments also instituted actions against the owner in Bermuda, Singapore and Rotterdam, see Haberbusch, Constitution of the Torrey Canyon Limitation Fund, 1 J. Maritime Law and Commerce, 146, 148 (1969). For the eventual settlement of the Torrey Canyon litigation, see note 13*l* *infra*. If the Torrey Canyon disaster had occurred in United States territorial waters, the public outcry in this country would no doubt have been much more strident than it was.

13f. The English text of the Convention is reproduced in 1957 A.M.C. 1971 as well as in an appendix to Comment, Limitation of Shipowners' Liability—The Brussels Convention of 1957, 68 Yale L.J. 1676, 1714 (1959). The Yale Comment analyzes the provisions of the Convention in detail.

13g. Maritime Law Association, Document 418 (1958).

13h. On the "legislative history" of the Convention in this country, see the article by Eyer, 16 Stanford L.Rev. 370 (1964) cited *supra* note 3, and the note, 3 Colum.J. of Law and Social Problems 105 (1967) cited *supra* note 13d.

might well abolish the entire structure, root and branch.[13i] However, nothing resulted from the Congressional hearings in the 1960's and it is in the highest degree unlikely that the Convention will ever be heard from again.[13j] We need shed no tears for the Convention's demise; it was a sorry job, a pathetic example of international law-making at its worst.[13k]

### The Torrey Canyon and the Pollution Problem

**§ 10–4(b).** The Torrey Canyon disaster in 1967 dramatized the long-standing problem of pollution of navigable waters by oil and other harmful substances and has led to a flurry of proposals for international conventions on liability for pollution as well as, in this country, legislation both state and federal.[13l] The present discussion is written at a time of maximum confusion. Detailed discussion of current proposals, which will in all probability be superseded by other proposals within a few years, would be out of place in a general

**13i.** "[I]f steps are not taken to liberalize our limitation of liability laws . . . there is going to be public clamor for a law which will do away with limitation in its entirety and, therefore, if we want to preserve limitation in order to encourage investment in shipping, we should try to keep up with the times and enact amendments which will make limitation more acceptable to the courts and to the public at large." Address of Chairman Nicholas J. Healy III to Ass'n of Average Adjusters of the United States, 1960 Annual Report, 313–314 (quoted, Note, 3 Colum.J. of Law and Social Problems 105, 109 (1967)).

**13j.** By its terms the Convention was to come into force six months after ratification by at least ten states of which "at least five shall be . . . States that each have a gross tonnage equal or superior to one million gross tons of tonnage" (Article 11(1)). The Convention has been ratified by most of the maritime countries of Western Europe and by England, and has been in force among the signatories since the late 1960's. Outside Western Europe, the Convention has made little headway and has not been ratified by any of the countries which provide flags of convenience for foreign-owned shipping.

**13k.** For analyses of the Convention's provisions, see the articles cited in notes 13f and 13h *supra*.

**13*l*.** The Torrey Canyon litigation, see note 13e *supra*, was eventually settled out of court for £3 million, to be equally divided between the French and English Governments (no private claims had been put forward). Following that settlement, the limitation proceedings which had been instituted in the United States (and other countries) were discontinued. See Healy and Paulsen, Marine Oil Pollution and the Water Quality Improvement Act of 1970, 1 J. of Mar. Law and Commerce 537, 552 (1970). The settlement agreement was reported in the New York Times, Nov. 12, 1969, p. 1, col. 2. In addition to the proposed international convention and the domestic legislation which will be presently discussed in the text, the Torrey Canyon episode led to private agreements under which the major world tanker owners, presumably in the hope of discouraging legislation, agreed to accept limited liability for negligent oil pollution. These agreements are known acronymically as TOVALOP (Tanker Owners Voluntary Agreement Concerning Liability for Oil Pollution) (1969) and CRISTAL (Contract Regarding an Interim Supplement to Tanker Liability for Oil Pollution) (1971). For the text of TOVALOP, see 8 International Legal Materials 497 (1969); for CRISTAL, see 2 J. of Mar. Law and Commerce 705 (1971). No legal proceedings involving either TOVALOP or CRISTAL have yet been reported. Neither TOVALOP nor CRISTAL will be examined in any detail in this discussion. To the extent that the private agreements set standards or limits of liability lower than those imposed by legislation such as the United States Water Quality Improvement Act of 1970, see text following note 13q *infra*, they are of course invalid.

treatise such as this. Therefore little more will be done in the following pages than to indicate the presently available sources. The solutions so far proposed to the pollution problem, at least on the federal level in this country, lie outside the framework of the Limitation of Liability Act (except for claims of the United States under the Water Quality Improvement Act of 1970, which will be presently discussed). The debate which has been generated by the controversy has so far focused narrowly on the problem of oil pollution and on the liability of tanker owners. That narrow focus has enveloped the proceedings in an air of unreality. A more rational approach would be to reconsider, in the light of late twentieth century conditions, the liability of shipowners (and of the enterprises—e. g., the oil companies—which use their services) for all types of property damage and personal injury—that is, to reconsider the basic principle which underlies the limitation idea. It may be that the pollution controversy will in time lead to long overdue fundamental reconsideration of the policy casually adopted more than a hundred years ago in our Limitation Act. If that happens, the present confusion will have been a small price to pay.

On the international level two draft conventions have been prepared under the auspices of the Intergovernmental Maritime Consultative Organization (IMCO) which is a specialized agency of the United Nations. These are the International Convention on Civil Liability for Oil Pollution Damage (1969) and the International Convention on the Establishment of an International Fund for Compensation for Oil Pollution Damage (1971), which will be referred to as the Liability Convention and the Fund Convention. In effect the 1971 Fund Convention was an attempt to clean up unfinished business left over from the 1969 Liability Convention. The two Conventions are closely related and it is assumed that nations which ratify the Liability Convention will also ratify the Fund Convention.[13m] In the absence of the necessary number of ratifications, neither Convention has yet come into force and, at the moment of writing, it seems probable that these Conventions will join the long list of aborted attempts to secure a degree of international uniformity in maritime and shipping law, such as the 1957 Brussels Convention of Limitation of Liability discussed in the preceding section and the 1962 Brussels Convention on the Liability of the Operators of Nuclear Ships.[13n] The United States has not ratified either the Liability Convention or the Fund Convention and is not likely to do so despite the fact that the legal establishment in this country has gone on record in support

13m. The Liability Convention is reprinted in 9 International Legal Materials 45 (1971). The Fund Convention is reprinted in 3 J. of Mar. Law and Commerce 624 (1972). Both Conventions are analyzed in Hunter, The Proposed International Compensation Fund for Oil Pollution Damage, 4 J. of Mar. Law and Commerce 117 (1972).

13n. On the Nuclear Ship Convention and related documents, see Szasz, The Convention on the Liability of Operators of Nuclear Ships, 2 J. of Mar. Law and Commerce 541 (1971), which contains, as an annex, a useful bibliography on the law of nuclear ships.

of ratification.[13o] The prospective failure of the twin conventions is not greatly to be regretted. They appear to be inadequate attempts to deal with problems of staggering complexity as to which no consensus has yet emerged.[13p]

When the efforts to find an acceptable international solution to the pollution problem had proved fruitless, the United States proceeded to what has been called a "unilateral" solution of its own in the Water Quality Improvement Act (WQIA) of 1970.[13q] WQIA is a curious example of legislation which deals with one aspect of a problem while it stubbornly ignores all the other and obviously related aspects.[13r] As drafted, the Act relates only to pollution by oil, but the President is authorized to extend its provisions to "hazardous substances, other than oil" (§ 12(a)). The only recovery for which the Act provides is on behalf of the United States for its "costs incurred . . . for the removal of [unauthorized discharges of] oil" (§ 11 [f] [1]).[13s] The Act does not provide for recovery (by the United

13o. Both the Maritime Law Association of the United States and the House of Delegates of the American Bar Association in 1972 adopted resolutions in favor of ratification of the Convention. Communication to the writer, dated February 23, 1973, from James J. Higgins, Esq., Chairman of the MLA Committee on Marine Ecology. In a message dated May 20, 1970, President Nixon urged the Senate to ratify the Liability Convention and to conform the recently enacted Water Quality Improvement Act to the Convention (New York Times, May 21, 1970, p. 1, col. 3) but no Congressional action was forthcoming.

13p. Healy, The C.M.I. and IMCO Draft Convention on Civil Liability for Oil Pollution, 1 J. of Mar. Law and Commerce 93 (1969) has some interesting material on the great range of diverse solutions which were proposed to the drafting committees. On the inadequacy of the international efforts to date, see Mendelsohn, Ocean Pollution and the 1972 United Nations Conference on the Environment, 3 J. of Mar. Law and Commerce 385 (1972).

13q. 84 Stat. 91, 33 U.S.C.A. § 1161. Mendelsohn, *supra* note 13p, suggests (at p. 393) that dissatisfaction with the 1969 Liability Convention led to the "unilateral" action by the United States. Healy and Paulsen, Marine Oil Pollution and the Water Quality Improvement Act of 1970, 1 J. of Mar. Law and Commerce, 537 (1970) analyze the Act. Canada has also proceeded "unilaterally" in the Arctic Waters Pollution Prevention Act, Bill C–203, 2d Sess. 28th Parl., 18–19 Eliz. II, 1969–1970, and related legislation. The Canadian legislation is discussed in Wilker, International Administrative Due Process and Control of Pollution—The Canadian *Arctic Waters* Example, 2 J. of Mar. Law and Commerce 499 (1971).

13r. On the legislative history of WQIA, see Healy and Paulsen, note 13q *supra*. In form WQIA is an amendment of the Federal Water Pollution Control Act, originally enacted in 1948. It also repeals the Oil Pollution Act of 1924. The territorial coverage of WQIA extends to the navigable waters of the United States, adjoining shorelines and the "contiguous zone" (12 miles) provided for by the Convention on the Territorial Sea and the Contiguous Zone, Article 24. On the Contiguous Zone, see Wulf, Contiguous Zones for Pollution Control, 3 J. of Mar. Law and Commerce, 537 (1972).

13s. No doubt the United States could authorize states, municipalities and private persons to incur costs in the removal of oil which would then become "costs of the United States" for the purpose of recovery under the Act. Section 11(d) provides in part that the United States may "coordinate and direct all public and private efforts directed at the removal of [a] threat [of a pollution hazard] . . ." One of the many obscurities of the statutory text is whether the United States could retrospectively ratify costs incurred by others without prior authorization. Section 11(c)(1) pro-

States or any one else) for property damage, loss of life or personal injuries caused by or incurred in connection with an oil discharge. The liability of "owners" or "operators" of "vessels," "onshore facilities" or "offshore facilities" is provided for in a not uncomplicated three-tier arrangement.[13t] There is no liability (exoneration) if the owner or operator "can prove that a discharge was caused solely by (*A*) an act of God, (*B*) an act of war, (*C*) negligence on the part of the United States Government, or (*D*) an act or omission of a third party without regard to whether such act or omission was or was not negligent, or any combination of the foregoing causes" (§ 11 [f] [1]). On the other hand there is unlimited liability (for "costs") "where the United States can show that [the] discharge was the result of willful negligence or willful misconduct within the privity and knowledge of the owner" (§ 11 [f] [1]). If the owner or operator cannot prove one of the excepted causes and the United States cannot show "willful negligence . . . " the owner or operator is liable for costs "in an amount not to exceed $100 per gross ton of such vessel or $14,000,000, whichever is lesser" (§ 11[f] [1]). The action may be brought in personam against the owner or operator or in rem against the vessel, the claim for costs constituting a maritime lien (of unspecified priority).[13u]

Enough has been said to indicate that the Act is as soft and spineless in its drafting as it is muddle-headed in its policy. If it is des-

vides that the owner or operator of the vessel or other "facility" responsible for the discharge may remove the oil on a finding that the removal will be "done properly". Under § 11(i)(1) the owner or operator, if he is found entitled to exoneration under the liability provisions of the Act which are next discussed in the text, is entitled to recover his "reasonable" removal costs from the United States in an action in the Court of Claims. There is no comparable provision relating to the recovery of costs by states, municipalities or private persons in the event the owner or operator is exonerated from liability.

**13t.** The term "owner or operator" is defined to mean "in the case of a vessel, any person owning, operating or chartering by demise, such vessel" (§ 11(a)(b)). Presumably the demise charterer's "willful negligencé" etc. is treated as the owner's. The reader is invited to speculate on what the apparently unnecessary word "operating" in the definition means.

**13u.** Sections 11(f)(2) and 11(f)(3) deal in comparable terms with the liability of the owners or operators of "onshore" and "offshore" facilities, whose liability, in the absence of proof of an excepted cause or a showing of "willful negligence" etc., is limited to $8,000,000. Section 11(g) takes up the liability of "third parties" whose acts or omissions have caused the discharge (excepted cause D); their liability is conditioned as under § 11(f)(1)(2) and (3) and is set, where the limitation provisions apply, at $8,000,000 in the case of owners or operators of onshore or offshore facilities and at $100 per gross ton or $14,000,000 in the case of the owners or operators of vessels.

The limitation amounts in the Act, with respect to vessel owners, seem to have been derived partly from TOVALOP, note 13*l* *supra* ($100 per gross ton, ceiling $10,000,000) and partly from the 1969 Liability Convention, text at note 13m *supra*, (approximately $134 per ton of a vessel's adjusted net tonnage, ceiling approximately $14,000,000—stated in terms of "Poincaré gold francs", thus subject to recomputation in the light of currency revaluations). For a comparison, see Healy and Paulsen, note 13q *supra*.

Other provisions of the Act require proof of "financial responsibility" and impose fines for violation of the Act's requirements.

tined to remain on the books, the courts will have their work cut out for them in making some sort of sense out of its vague, ambiguous and contradictory provisions.

*Relationship of WQIA and the Limitation of Liability Act*:

Where the limited liability provisions of WQIA apply, the United States is allowed to recover its costs against the owner and operators of a vessel, up to the ceilings stated, "notwithstanding any other provision of law" (§§ 11 [f] [i] 11 [g]). The only possible meaning of the "notwithstanding" clause is that, in actions by the United States under WQIA, the WQIA ceilings apply and the Limitation of Liability Act is, to that extent, superseded. In some cases the WQIA ceilings will be higher than the fund available under the Limitation Act but in other cases the limitation fund could easily exceed the WQIA ceilings.[13v] If the WQIA "notwithstanding" clause works both ways, the shipowner's WQIA liability would frequently be less than the liability under the Limitation Act. It could, of course, be not implausibly argued that the evident purpose of WQIA was to expand the shipowner's liability and not to cut it back, so that the "notwithstanding" clause would operate only when the WQIA ceilings provided for a recovery in excess of the limitation fund.

Under WQIA the shipowner (or operator) is exonerated from liability if he can prove that the discharge was caused by one or more of the four excepted causes. Under the Limitation Act (apart from the Fire Statute) exoneration depends on proof that the vessel was not at fault—e. g., through negligent navigation—with respect to the cause of the loss or injury. Under the Fire Statute exoneration depends on the fire's having been caused without the owner's "design or neglect." [13w] In this respect WQIA seems to set a higher standard than the Limitation Act since the shipowner (or operator) could be held liable under WQIA even though the vessel was in no way at fault unless the discharge was caused by one of the four excepted causes. In the same way the owner might be entitled to exoneration under the Fire Statute (because he was not chargeable with "design or neglect") but not entitled to exoneration under WQIA because none of the "excepted causes" was at play. These apparent distinctions may be of more theoretical than of real importance; in the absence of litigation it is impossible, or at least vain, to predict what the courts will make of the WQIA exoneration formula.

Under WQIA liability is unlimited if the United States shows "willful negligence or willful misconduct within the privity and knowledge of the owner." Under the Limitation Act liability is unlimited

13v. On the limitation fund, see § 10–29 *et seq. infra*. The basic WQIA ceiling is $100 per gross ton. The basic limitation fund is the value of the vessel and pending freight after the event giving rise to the limitation claim. In the case of recent ship construction, values are much greater than $100 per gross ton. Thus in cases where the vessel responsible for the discharge was not itself damaged or destroyed, the limitation fund would frequently be greater than the WQIA ceiling.

13w. On these provisions, see §§ 10–6, 10–7, 10–20 *et seq. infra*.

if the vessel was at fault unless the owner can show that he was not chargeable with "privity or knowledge" (or, in cases under the Fire Statute, "design or neglect") with respect to the cause of the loss. If the WQIA formula is taken literally, it seems to say that the shipowner or operator would be entitled to limit his liability to the WQIA ceilings in actions by the United States under WQIA, even though, because of "privity or knowledge" (or "design or neglect") short of "willful negligence or willful misconduct", he had lost the right to limit his liability under the Limitation Act. The idea that liability could be limited under WQIA but unlimited under the Limitation Act (or Fire Statute) makes no kind of sense. At this point the WQIA draftsmen seem to have lost sight of their objective, just as they may have done in setting the WQIA ceilings at levels which will frequently be less than the fund available under the Limitation Act. We may trust that the courts will discover that the WQIA formula means the same thing as the Limitation Act and Fire Statute formulae, except that in WQIA actions the United States bears the burden of proof which under the Limitation Act and Fire Statute is allocated to the petitioning shipowner. Indeed, if the WQIA formula is held to entitle the owner or operator to limitation in a case where he would have lost his right to limitation under the other statutes, why should the United States not disregard WQIA and sue to recover its "costs" and other losses in a tort action under the general maritime law?

There is nothing in WQIA to suggest that claims for property loss, injury or death under the general maritime law are to be in any way affected by WQIA. Indeed, § 11(o)(1) provides that: "Nothing in this section shall affect or modify in any way the obligation of any owner or operator of any vessel . . . to any person or agency under any provision of law for damages to any publicly-owned or privately-owned property resulting from a discharge of any oil or from the removal of any such oil." In this context the phrase "any provision of law" evidently includes the general maritime law, both decisional and statutory. (The failure of the clause just quoted to refer to personal injury and death claims is no doubt explained by the fact that WQIA itself deals only with the costs of removal and has nothing to do with death and injury claims.) Thus, the United States may recover its clean-up costs in a WQIA action. Claims (including claims by the United States) for property loss, injury or death may be recovered as heretofore under the general maritime law. If the shipowner is not entitled to exoneration but is entitled to limitation, he will be liable up to the WQIA ceilings in the WQIA action and liable in the amount of the limitation fund in the general maritime law action.[13x]

13x. See, to the same effect, Healy and Paulsen, note 13q *supra*, at p. 567. On the proposition that the shipowner may invoke the Limitation Act for oil pollution damage, see Petition of New Jersey Barging Corp., 144 F.Supp. 340, 1956 A.M.C. 1338 (S.D.N.Y.1956), further proceedings, 168 F.Supp. 925, 1959 A.M.C. 2532 (S.D.N.Y.1959); see further Complaint of Harbor Towing

*WQIA, The Limitation Act and State Anti-Pollution Statutes*:

WQIA provides in § 11(o)(2) that: "Nothing in this section shall be construed as preempting any State or political subdivision thereof from imposing any requirement or liability with respect to the discharge of oil into any waters within such State." That clause was apparently put in to acknowledge the fact that, at the time Congress was considering WQIA, various coastal states were considering anti-pollution legislation of their own. A number of such statutes have since been enacted. These statutes, far from being uniform, are bewilderingly diverse; their only common core of substance seems to be that they go beyond the Federal Act in setting stricter standards of liability or in decreeing higher limits of liability or in covering public or private claims for loss in addition to clean-up costs.

Such state statutes raised obvious problems of constitutionality. The Florida statute [13y] was made the vehicle for the first constitutional test in what was in effect an action for a declaratory judgment; plaintiffs included merchant shippers, world shipping associations, members of the Florida coastal barge and towing industry, the owners and operators of oil terminal facilities and heavy industry located in Florida and marine insurance companies. A three-judge District Court unanimously held the Act unconstitutional and enjoined its enforcement.[13z] Judge Tjoflat's opinion for the District Court was the most thorough-going and unqualified statement of the doctrine of the supremacy of the federal maritime law which had been delivered in any court since Southern Pacific Co. v. Jensen,[13aa]

Corp., 335 F.Supp. 1150, 1972 A.M.C. 597 (D.Md.1971), discussed in the text following note 13gg *infra*.

13y. Florida Oil Spill Prevention and Pollution Control Act (L.Fla.1970, c. 70–244). Post, Private Compensation for Injuries Sustained by the Discharge of Oil from Vessels on the Navigable Waters of the United States: A Survey, 4 J. of Mar. Law and Commerce 25 (1972) reviews (at p. 50 *et seq.*) a number of the state statutes and collects citations to the extensive law review literature on the pollution problem which has been published in recent years. The Maine statute, Maine Rev.Stat.Ann. Tit. 38 § 541–557 (Supp.1971), represents the most innovative approach: it provides for a state fund out of which claims for property loss and loss of income are to be paid and for arbitration of disputes between claimants and the persons responsible for the discharge of oil. In State of Maine v. M/V Tamano, 1973 A.M.C. 1131 (D. Maine, 1973) Judge Gignoux refused to dismiss a count in a complaint brought by the State against a vessel responsible for oil spillage in which the State claimed damages as *parens patriae* "as owner and/or trustee for the citizens of the State of Maine of all the natural resources lying in, on, over, under and adjacent to [Maine coastal waters]." Judge Gignoux did not discuss the constitutionality of the Maine statute, noting that the constitutional question had been raised in two cases pending before the Supreme Judicial Court of Maine. He also noted that the Supreme Court of the United States had upheld the constitutionality of the Florida statute in the Askew case, text following note 13bb *infra*. The Maine Court subsequently upheld the constitutionality of the Maine statute in Portland Pipe Line Corp. v. Environmental Improvement Commission, 307 A.2d 1, 1973 A.M.C. 1341 (1973).

13z. American Waterways Operators, Inc. v. Askew, 335 F.Supp. 1241, 1972 A.M.C. 91 (M.D.Fla.1971).

13aa. 244 U.S. 205, 37 S.Ct. 524 (1917). The Jensen case is discussed in Chapter VI, § 6–45 *et seq.* Judge Tjoflat

which was indeed the authority principally relied on. A unanimous Supreme Court reversed in an opinion by Justice Douglas, which gives the impression of having been written with great care so as to commit the uncharacteristically unanimous Justices to as little as possible beyond the fact that they were unwilling to strike down the Florida Act as, so to say, unconstitutional per se.[13bb] The Askew case then leaves for future decisions all the real problems raised by the State anti-pollution statutes, particularly as there is no way of knowing how much conflict and division within the Court may have been masked by the bland generalities of Justice Douglas' opinion.

Justice Douglas characterized the Florida Act as one which "imposes strict liability for any damage incurred by the State or private persons as a result of an oil spill in the State's territorial waters from any waterfront facility used for drilling oil or handling the transfer or storage of oil ("terminal facility") and from any ships destined for or leaving such facility. After a review of the WQIA provisions he pointed out that the Florida Act dealt comprehensively with damage to public and private property interests, while WQIA was restricted to clean-up costs incurred by the United States; since the two statutes, at that point, dealt with different subject matters, there was no possibility of conflict between them. Furthermore, the provisions of the Florida Act relating to "terminal facilities" could not be taken to be in conflict with the federal maritime law, which has nothing to do with such facilities. "So far as vessels are concerned," Justice Douglas noted, the Limitation of Liability Act "extends to damages caused by oil spills even where the injury is to the shore." [13cc] The Florida Act contained a section which provided for the State to recover its own clean-up costs. As to this section, Justice Douglas wrote:

> "Whether the amount of costs [Florida] could recover from a wrongdoer are limited to those specified in the Fed-

concluded: "The Florida Act here constitutes a far greater intrusion into the federal maritime domain than the New York [Workmen's Compensation] statute in the Jensen case. . . . We need not belabor the point that to permit the states severally to regulate [shipping and related] industries as Florida seeks to do would sound the death knell to the principle of uniformity." He also added that the Florida Act could not be upheld as filling a "void" or "gap" in the maritime law (see Justice Holmes' celebrated dissent in Jensen) on the altogether astonishing theory that, since Moragne v. States Marine Lines, Inc. (398 U.S. 375, 90 S.Ct. 1772, 1970 A.M.C. 967 (1970), there no longer are any "gaps". (The Moragne case is discussed in Chapter VI, § 6–33 *et seq.*) He finally suggested that the provision of WQIA § 11(o)(2) (quoted in the text following note 13x) would, if it were taken to authorize such state legislation, itself be unconstitutional as an impermissible delegation by Congress to the states of an exclusively federal power. (On Judge Tjoflat's final point, see Chapter VI, § 6–45, text following note 258.)

**13bb.** Askew v. The American Waterways Operators, Inc., 411 U.S. 325, 93 S.Ct. 1590, 1973 A.M.C. 811 (1973). On the appeal to the Supreme Court both the American Bar Association and the Maritime Law Association of the United States filed briefs amicus urging affirmance of the District Court.

**13cc.** Citing Richardson v. Harmon, 222 U.S. 96, 32 S.Ct. 27 (1911). On the Richardson case (which had nothing to do with oil spills), see text at and following note 42 *infra*.

eral Act [WQIA] and whether in turn this new Federal Act removes the pre-existing limitations of liability in the Limitation of Liability Act are questions we need not reach here. Any opinion on them is premature. It is sufficient for this day to hold that there is room for state action in cleaning up the waters of a State and recouping, at least within federal limits so far as vessels are concerned, her costs."

Thus the conclusion was that, within those ambiguously stated guidelines, the Florida Act was the sort of state regulation contemplated by WQIA § 11(o)(2).

Justice Douglas then restated his case:

"And so, in the absence of federal pre-emption and any fatal conflict between the statutory schemes, the issue comes down to whether a State constitutionally may exercise its police power respecting maritime activities concurrently with the Federal Government."

He then reviewed the history of the Jensen doctrine: "Jensen and its progeny mark isolated instances where 'state law must yield to the needs of a uniform maritime law when the Court finds inroads on a harmonious system.' "[13dd] Damage to shore property, he noted, would not have been within the admiralty jurisdiction before 1948. The Admiralty Extension Act of 1948[13ee] did not mean that "sea-to-shore injuries [had become] exclusively triable in the federal courts." Indeed, Huron Portland Cement Company v. Detroit[13ff] had reaffirmed the traditional view of the power of states and their instrumentalities to control "many areas of interstate commerce and maritime activities, concurrently with the federal government." "It follows *a fortiori* that sea-to-shore pollution—historically within the reach of the police power of the State—is not silently taken away from the States by the Admiralty Extension Act, which does not purport to supply the exclusive remedy." The grand conclusion of the discussion was:

"*Jensen* thus has vitality left. But we decline to move the *Jensen* line of cases shoreward to oust state law from any situation involving shoreside injuries by ships on naviga-

**13dd.** Quoting Justice Frankfurter in Romero v. International Terminal Co., 358 U.S. 354, 373, 79 S.Ct. 468, 480. 1959 A.M.C. 832, 847 (1959) rehearing denied 359 U.S. 962, 79 S.Ct. 795 (1959); the Romero case is discussed in Chapter VI, § 6–62. Justice Douglas also quoted at length from Chief Justice Hughes' opinion in Just v. Chambers, 312 U.S. 383, 61 S.Ct. 687, 1941 A.M.C. 430 (1941) on the extent to which the maritime law, which is "not a complete and perfect system," has traditionally been supplemented by state law. This may have been an indirect reply to the proposition in the District Court opinion, see note 13aa *supra*, that maritime law, since the Moragne case, has become a closed system. Justice Douglas carefully did not cite the Moragne case in his Askew opinion.

**13ee.** See Chapter VII, § 7–17.

**13ff.** 362 U.S. 440, 80 S.Ct. 813, 1960 A.M.C. 1549 (1960), holding vessels subject to the City's Smoke Abatement Code.

ble waters. The Admiralty Extension Act does not pre-empt state law in those situations."

Thus the state anti-pollution statutes have, like Jensen itself, some "vitality" left. How much vitality will be disclosed in due course. Justice Douglas in Askew chose, deliberately it would seem, not to refer to the only lower court case which had dealt with the relationship between such statutes and the Limitation Act. Complaint of Harbor Towing Corporation (The Barge Shamrock) [13gg] involved an oil-spillage in Baltimore Harbor. Claims for clean-up costs and for property damage aggregating over $500,000 were made both by agencies of the State of Maryland and by private parties. The Maryland anti-pollution statute provided for such recoveries, apparently without limitation of liability and without any requirement that the ship be shown to have been at fault. The owner of the barge responsible for the oil spillage petitioned for limitation of his liability to a fund of approximately $33,000. The claimants seem to have argued principally on the analogy of cases which had denied limitation for removal costs under the Wreck Statute.[13hh] Judge Northrop distinguished those cases on the ground that they involved situations necessarily within the "privity or knowledge" of the shipowner and held all the claims in his own case subject to limitation. He concluded:

> "The problem presented by this case is both novel and difficult. And it is not to be disputed that this interpretation of the Limitation Act will not encourage shipowners to proceed to engage in clean-up efforts after their own tortious acts. However, this is a question that demands a delicate balancing of policy issues. . . . The resolution of a question as complex as this demands the scrutiny of Congress, not the Judiciary." [13ii]

Justice Douglas' sybilline references to the Limitation Act in his Askew opinion do nothing whatever to resolve—nor, of course, were they meant to—the confusion which presently envelops the problem of the relationship between or among WQIA, the state anti-pollution acts and the Limitation Act. In noting that the Limitation Act "extends to damages caused by oil spills," he chose to cite an old case which had nothing to do with oil spills and to ignore more recent case authority directly in point.[13jj] His comments on whether WQIA "removes the pre-existing limitation of liability in the Limitation of Liability Act" achieve, it may well be, a new high-water mark in judi-

**13gg.** 335 F.Supp. 1150, 1972 A.M.C. 597 (D.Md.1971).

**13hh.** The Wreck Statute cases are reviewed in note 45 *infra*, at end of note.

**13ii.** Judge Northrop noted that in an action under WQIA, assuming the limited liability provision to be applicable, the owner of the barge would have been liable in the amount of $57,000.

**13jj.** See the New Jersey Barging Corp. case, note 13x *supra*, as well as, of course the Harbor Towing Corporation case.

cial ambiguity. All the Askew case tells us is that there is a great deal of litigation in store on these complex issues.[13kk]

**The Structure of the Act**

**§ 10–5.** Section 181 (R.S. § 4281) is in form an exoneration from rather than a limitation of liability. As to a specified list of commodities, whose common characteristic is high value and small bulk, the section provides that, unless the shipper gives the carrier "a written notice of the true character and value thereof" and has the information entered on the bill of lading, the carrier shall not be liable "beyond the value and according to the character thereof so notified and entered". The section was part of the original Act of 1851 and was amended in 1871 by lengthening the list of commodities to which it applied.[14] The heterogeneous list includes precious metals, jewels, watches, "trinkets", notes and securities, title deeds, "printings", pictures, glass, china, silks, furs and laces. There has been little litigation under this section and none of recent years.

**§ 10–6.** Section 182 (R.S. § 4282), often referred to as the "fire statute", is like § 181 a provision for exoneration rather than limitation. As to loss or damage to any type of cargo caused by fire on board the ship, the owner is exonerated from liability unless the fire was "caused by the design or neglect of such owner". Section 182 was part of the original Act of 1851 and has never been amended. It no longer has the importance it once had, since a provision of the Carriage of Goods by Sea Act, in slightly different wording, confers substantially the same exoneration on the carrier.[15] The principal issue which has come up in litigation under § 182 is the scope to be given the phrase "design or neglect of such owner".[16]

**§ 10–7.** Section 183 (R.S. § 4283) is the heart of the statute. It now consists of a general provision for limitation (§ 183(a)), which has been in the Act virtually unchanged since 1851, plus a series of subsections (183(b)–(f)), added in 1935 and 1936,[17] which deal with limitation against claims for "loss of life and bodily injury". Section 183(a) reads as follows (italicized words were added by the 1936 amendments):

> "The liability of the owner of any vessel, *whether American or foreign,* for any embezzlement loss or destruc-

13kk. In the Portland Pipe Line case, note 13y *supra* (at end of note), the Supreme Judicial Court of Maine, which upheld the constitutionality of the Maine anti-pollution statute in the light of the Askew case, seemed to assume that a shipowner held liable under the Maine statute would be entitled to the protection of the federal Limitation of Liability Act. (See Judge Pomeroy's opinion, 1973 A.M.C. 1341, 1382.) The Portland Pipe Line case, like the Askew case, was a suit for a declaratory judgment and did not require a decision on the issue.

14. 16 Stat. 458 (1871). The Act of 1871 also added the words "as freight or baggage", making it clear that the exoneration applies whether the goods are carried as cargo or as baggage.

15. See Chapter III, § 3–31.

16. See § 10–20 *et seq. infra.*

17. 49 Stat. 960 (1935), 49 Stat. 1479 (1936).

> tion by any person of any property, goods or merchandise shipped or put on board of such vessel, or for any loss, damage or injury by collision, or for any act, matter or thing, loss damage or forfeiture, done, occasioned or incurred, without the privity or knowledge of such owner or owners, shall not, *except in the cases provided for in subsection (b) of this section,* exceed the amount or value of the interest of such owner in such vessel, and her freight then pending."

Section 183(a) thus states, in terms of the utmost generality, the types of claims against which the privilege of limitation is conferred, conditions the privilege on the absence of "privity or knowledge" on the part of the owner, and sets, as the maximum liability of an owner entitled to limit, his interest in the vessel and her pending freight. Each of the component parts of § 183(a) has been extensively litigated, with results which will be discussed in subsequent sections of this chapter.[18]

The 1935 "loss of life" amendments (§ 183(b)–(f)) introduced a concept novel to American limitation law, although familiar in the limitation laws of other countries. In lieu of allowing the owner to limit his liability to the value of his interest in the vessel (which under § 183(a) may be zero if the vessel has sunk or been destroyed), § 183(b) requires the setting up of a fund, to be available only for the payment of loss of life or bodily injury claims, of $60 per ton, calculated with reference to a steam or motor vessel's gross tonnage.[19]

Section 183(d) provides that as to such claims the owner shall be liable "in respect of loss of life and bodily injury arising on distinct occasions to the same extent as if no other loss of life or bodily in-

18. A list of claims subject to limitation and claims not subject to limitation is set out in note 45, following the sections devoted to the structure of the Limitation Act.

19. The idea of setting up a limitation fund based on a fixed sum per ton seems to have originated in England. The Merchant Shipping Act of 1862 set limits of £15 per ton of which £7 was reserved for injury and death claims, the balance to be shared ratably with cargo claims. These limits, based on the then average value per ton of English shipping, were carried forward without change in the Merchant Shipping Act of 1894, 57 & 58 Vict., c. 60, § 503, by which time ship values had of course greatly increased. The English approach, including the 1862 limits, was copied in limitation legislation throughout the British Commonwealth.

The 1923 Brussels Convention on Limitation of Liability, which was adopted in Belgium, Brazil, Denmark, Finland, France, Italy, Netherlands, Norway, Portugal, Spain and Sweden, followed the English pattern, including the original mid-nineteenth century limits, with a proviso that the fund available for cargo claims should not exceed the value of the ship (before the disaster) and freight.

Thus the "loss of life" amendments engrafted on American limitation law one aspect of foreign limitation law.

The 1957 Brussels Convention on Limitation of Liability, see § 10–4(a) *supra,* proposed raising the limitation fund to approximately $207 per ton of the vessel's net tonnage ($140 for injury and death claims plus $67 to be divided ratably with cargo claims). (The figure of $207, which was used in most discussions of the Convention, represented a conversion into dollars, as of the 1950's, of the "Poincaré gold francs" in which the Convention's fund provisions were stated.)

jury had arisen". Although the "distinct occasions" language is in need of case law clarification,[20] it presumably means at least that, if two or more catastrophes occur on the same voyage, the owner will be liable up to the $60 per ton limit for all claims resulting from each of the "occasions".[21] Section 183(e) tightens up, to the disadvantage of the owner, the scope of the "privity or knowledge" language of § 183(a) by providing that in respect of loss of life and bodily injury the privity or knowledge of master, superintendent or managing agent at or prior to the commencement of a voyage "shall be deemed conclusively the privity or knowledge of the owner".[22] Subsections 183 (b)–(e) apply only to "seagoing vessels", a term which, as defined in § 183(f), excludes from the loss of life provisions pleasure yachts and a variety of commercial vessels whose common characteristic seems to be that they do not customarily carry passengers for hire (tugs, rowboats, tank vessels, fishing vessels, lighters, barges, scows, "nondescript vessels" whether or not self-propelled, etc.).[23] It should be noted that the types of vessels excluded from the $60 per ton requirement of § 183(b) are, by § 188, entitled to the protection of the Limitation Act as a whole.[23a] Subsections 183(b)–(f) are implemented by two further sections, confusingly numbered § 183b and § 183c.[24] Section 183b invalidates attempts by "seagoing" vessels to stipulate a shorter time than six months for giving notice of loss of life or bodily injury claims by passengers or a shorter time than one year for instituting suit on such claims.[24a] Section 183c invalidates attempts by

20. See § 10–38 *infra.*

21. Apart from § 183(d), where two or more occasions arise on the same voyage the owner is liable once only. The vessel's value, for purposes of limitation, is appraised after the final accident has occurred. See text following note 122 *infra.*

22. See § 10–37 *infra.*

23. See § 10–35 *infra.*

23a. In Pettus v. Jones and Laughlin Steel Corp., 322 F.Supp. 1078, 1972 A.M.C. 170 (W.D.Pa.1971), the argument was made that, because of the § 183(f) exclusion, barge-owners are not entitled to invoke the Limitation Act. Judge Gourley, citing the § 188 provision quoted in § 10–12 *infra,* naturally rejected the argument.

24. R.S. § 4283A, as added 49 Stat. 960 (1935); R.S. § 4283B, as added 49 Stat. 1480 (1936).

24a. In Miller v. Lykes Brothers Steamship Co., Inc., 467 F.2d 464, 1973 A.M.C. 83 (5th Cir. 1973) the claim was that Mrs. Miller had suffered "bodily injuries" in the course of a negligently supervised lifeboat drill. Mrs. Miller brought an action to recover for her injuries and her husband brought an action to recover for medical expenses and loss of consortium. The "Passenger Contract Ticket" contained a clause which adopted the § 183b time limitation but the actions were not instituted until more than a year from the date of Mrs. Miller's injury. Held (1) that the Millers were bound by the limitation clause in the ticket (Judge Godbold's opinion reviews the earlier cases on this point) and (2) that the limitation barred not only Mrs. Miller's action but also her husband's action. On the "loss of consortium" point the defendant carrier in Burstein v. United States Lines Co., 134 F.2d 89, 1943 A.M.C. 130 (2d Cir. 1943), had argued that a shorter limitation period could be applied to a husband's action for loss of consortium than was required by § 183b for the wife's own action for her injuries. In rejecting the argument, Judge Clark quoted Lord Coke's "maxim": "the Office of Judges is always to make such Construction as to suppress the Mischief and Advance the Remedy; and to suppress subtle Inventions and Evasions for Continuance of the Mis-

any vessel transporting passengers between ports of the United States and American or foreign ports to contract out of liability for negligence, or to liquidate damages in any stated amount, or to avoid the right of any claimant to a trial by a court of competent jurisdiction.[25]

The policy of the loss of life amendments was implemented by the Financial Responsibility Act of 1966 [25a] which requires American and foreign vessels having accommodations for fifty or more passengers and embarking passengers at American ports to provide proof of the owner's or charterer's financial responsibility up to $20,000. per "accommodation" for the first five hundred and in lesser amounts for "accommodations" over five hundred.

**§ 10–8.** Section 184 (R.S. § 4284) takes up the limitation story from the point of view of the claimants: its main contribution is the statement that, when the value of the vessel and her freight is not sufficient to pay all claims in full, claimants shall "receive compensation . . . in proportion to their respective losses". In contrast to the generality of the language used in § 183(a) to describe the types of claims against which limitation may be had, § 184 refers only to cargo claims and has no language referring to collision and other claims which are clearly specified in § 183(a). The Supreme Court held in an early case [26] that the verbal differences between the two sections were the result of inadvertence in drafting, and that the broader descriptive language of § 183(a) should be read into § 184: thus all claims, against which the owner may limit under § 183, share *pro rata* under § 184. The section concludes with an odd provision that the "freighters and owners of the property, and the owner or owners of the vessel, or any of them may take the appropriate proceedings in any court" for carrying out the substantive provisions of the Act. It stands to reason that there must be some kind of "appropriate proceedings" to enforce the rights and liabilities created by the Act. Section 184 is not of the least help in clarifying what the proceedings should be, except in its vague suggestions that they may be had "in any court" and that either the claimants (reading "freighters and owners of the property" to include all types of claimants) or the shipowners may "take" or initiate them. Neither of the suggestions has borne fruit in practice. The Supreme Court early announced that the admiralty court was the obvious forum for limitation proceed-

chief." In *Miller* the shoe was of course on the other foot, but Judge Godbold engagingly elected to "follow" *Burstein* down to and including the "maxim".

25. The § 183b reference to "seagoing" incorporates the definition of the term contained in § 183(f), while § 183c does not refer to "seagoing" vessels.

25a. 80 Stat. 1356, 46 U.S.C.A. § 817 (d), (e).

26. Butler v. Boston & Savannah S.S. Co., 130 U.S. 527, 9 S.Ct. 612 (1889). A passenger's administrator sued for personal injury and the shipowner petitioned for limitation. The claimant argued unsuccessfully that limitation was not available against the type of injury involved.

ings[27] and the Admiralty Rules have always so provided,[28] save that the shipowner has also been allowed to invoke the Limitation Act by way of defense in non-admiralty proceedings if he so desires.[29] It is hard to see what sense is made by the suggestion that claimants as well as the shipowner may "take" proceedings under the Act; since it will never be to their advantage to invoke the Act, "take", with reference to claimants, must mean that they are entitled to intervene in proceedings initiated by the shipowner, and the right to intervention is spelled out in the Admiralty Rules.[30]

**§ 10–9.** Section 185 (R.S. § 4285), as it read until 1936, provided that "it shall be deemed a sufficient compliance" with the Act for the owner to transfer his interest in the vessel and freight to a court-appointed trustee for benefit of claimants, "from and after which transfer all claims and proceedings against the owner shall cease". Although this was the only section in the original Act, except for the unhelpful "appropriate proceedings" language in § 184, which had any reference to the procedure to be followed under the Act, and although the transfer to a trustee was the only method stated for complying with the Act, the Admiralty Rules, from the time of their issuance in 1872, provided for the posting of a bond in the amount of the appraised value of the ship and pending freight as an alternative to the transfer to a trustee.[31] As an original question, the Court's authority to provide for the alternative procedure, for which there was

27. "Now, no court is better adapted than a court of admiralty to administer precisely such relief. It happens every day that the proceeds of a vessel, or other fund, is brought into that court to be distributed amongst those whom it may concern. Claimants are called in by monition to present and substantiate their respective claims; and the fund is divided and distributed according to the respective liens and rights of all the parties. Congress might have invested the Circuit courts . . . with the jurisdiction of such cases by bill in equity, but it did not. It is also evident that the State courts have not the requisite jurisdiction. Unless, therefore, the District Courts themselves can administer the law, we are reduced to the dilemma of inferring that the legislature has passed a law which is incapable of execution. This is never to be done if it can be avoided. We have no doubt that the District Courts, as courts of admiralty and maritime jurisdiction, have jurisdiction of the matter . . ." Norwich & N.Y. Transp. Co. v. Wright, 80 U.S. (13 Wall.) 104, 123 (1871). Prior to the procedural "unification" of 1966, see Chapter I, § 1–1 *supra*, limitation proceedings were covered in Admiralty Rules 51–55. Those Rules have been restated, apparently without change of substance, in Supplemental Rule F, FRCP (hereafter Rule F). The Admiralty Rules referred to "petitions" for limitation; the shipowner who invoked the Act was the "petitioner". Rule F refers to "complaints" for limitation; the shipowner is the "plaintiff".

28. Rule F(1) (derived from former Admiralty Rule 51).

29. See § 10–14 *infra*.

30. Rule F(3) (derived from former Rule 51) requires newspaper publication of notice of any complaint for limitation and mailing of notice to "every person known to have made any claim against the vessel or the plaintiff arising out of the voyage or trip on which the claims sought to be limited arose." The notice requires all persons having claims to file them with the Clerk of the court before a specified date (which may not be less than 30 days from issuance of the notice); the court, "for cause shown . . . may enlarge the time within which claims may be filed."

31. Rule 54, 80 U.S. (13 Wall.) xii–xiii (1872), now Rule F(1) (derived from former Admiralty Rule 51).

not the slightest statutory warrant, was far from clear; however, the provision, being a sensible one helpful to all parties, was apparently never questioned.

The final clause in the section, that "all claims and proceedings against the owner shall cease", has been of great importance when taken in connection with the Supreme Court's theory, implemented by the Admiralty Rules, that the admiralty court is the proper forum for limitation proceedings. The owner takes "appropriate proceedings" under the Act by filing a petition (or complaint) for limitation with the appropriate district court sitting in admiralty;[32] he complies with the Act by transferring his interest to a trustee or by posting bond; at that point all proceedings against him—for example, actions brought in state court under the saving to suitors clause—"shall cease", which seems to mean that the admiralty court should enjoin any other proceedings. If the suggested analysis is true, as in large part it is, we have a massive exception to the concurrent jurisdiction established by the saving to suitors clause. In recent years the Supreme Court has apparently become concerned by the breadth of the exception; the present state of the law on this point is an unhappy and shifting compromise between the diametrically opposed pulls of limitation procedure, which works to localize all litigation in the admiralty court, and the saving to suitors clause, which purports to reserve to plaintiffs a free election of the forum of litigation.[33]

Section 185 was amended in several respects in 1936. For one thing, Congress finally wrote into the statute the bond-posting procedure which had long been authorized by the Admiralty Rules; this amendment regularized the situation but made no change in long-established procedure. The most important change made in 1936 was a new preamble prefixed to the section in lieu of the "it shall be deemed a sufficient compliance" language of the original statute, which was deleted. The preamble now reads:

> "The vessel owner, within six months after a claimant shall have given to or filed with such owner written notice of claim, may petition a district court of competent jurisdiction for limitation of liability . . . "

In part the new preamble, like the bond-posting amendment, merely ratifies the procedures which the Court had originally established by rule. It adds, however, what appears to be a six month statute of limitation, running from the giving to the owner of "written notice of claim." The full implications of this change are far from having been worked out under the case law to date.[34]

A third, perhaps minor, change made by the 1936 amendments was the addition of apparently restrictive language to the "all claims and proceedings . . . shall cease" language of the original statute. The last sentence of § 185 now provides that on compliance with the requirements of the section:

32. See note 47 *infra* for a discussion of venue in proceedings for limitation of liability.

33. See §§ 10–16 to 10–19 *infra.*

34. See § 10–15 *infra.*

". . . all claims and proceedings against the owner *with respect to the matter in question* shall cease." (Italicized words added by 1936 amendment.)

**§ 10–10.** Section 186 (R.S. § 4286), unamended since 1851, provides that a charterer who shall "man, victual and navigate" the vessel "at his own expense, or by his own procurement" shall be deemed an "owner" within the meaning of the Act—*i. e.* entitled to limitation on the same footing as the owner. The importance of this section has been its negative implication that except for the owner only the type of charterer who "mans, victuals and navigates" can claim the protection of the Limitation Act. With reference to customary types of charter parties, this means that so-called bareboat or demise charterers may limit but that time charterers under the usual arrangement may not.[35] Nor may anyone other than the owner or the type of charterer described in § 186 limit his liability under the Act.[36]

35. For a discussion of the several types of charter parties, see Chapter IV. In Complaint of Caldas, 350 F.Supp. 566, 1973 A.M.C. 1243 (E.D.Pa.1972) the court concluded that a time-charterer had "not established that it [came] within the provisions of 46 U.S.C.A. § 186" and consequently was not "properly before the Court" in a limitation proceeding. See further the Torrey Canyon proceedings which are next discussed in the text.

36. But see Maryland Casualty Co. v. Cushing, 347 U.S. 409, 74 S.Ct. 608, 1954 A.M.C. 837 (1954), discussed *infra* § 10–31, in which an insurance carrier was permitted to challenge the constitutionality of a state statute as repugnant to the Limitation Act. In the Yacht Charlotte (Petition of Colonial Trust Co.), 124 F.Supp. 73, 1955 A.M.C. 1290 (D.Conn.1954) a widow who held a life interest and a trust company which was the executor of the deceased owner's estate, were both allowed to petition for limitation as "owners". After citing Flink v. Paladini, 279 U.S. 59, 49 S.Ct. 255, 1929 A.M.C. 327 (1929) to the proposition that fractional interests and the interests of shareholders of a corporation have been held within the protection of the Limitation Act, Judge Anderson continued: "If the legal relations which together comprise ownership of a vessel can be split perpendicularly so that several persons are owners, as with tenants in common, and each is able to claim the protection of the statute, there seems little reason why the statute should not also apply where those same legal relations are split horizontally as in the present case provided each holder of an interest has sufficient legal relations to constitute what has been traditionally recognized in the law as 'title' either legal or equitable with substantial rights and powers in dealing with the property; that is, something more than possession and control, for a mere bailee or lessee is not entitled to a limitation of his liability, The Severance, 4 Cir., 152 F.2d 916, 1946 A.M.C. 128; Stone v. Diamond S.S. Transp. Corp., 328 U.S. 853, 66 S.Ct. 1344, 1946 A.M.C. 967; and something more than bare legal title held for security of an obligation not in default, because such a holder cannot invoke the statute. American Car & Foundry Co. v. Brassert, 7 Cir., 61 F.2d 162, 1932 A.M.C. 1524." (*Id.* at 76, 1955 A.M.C. at 1294). See also on the question of ownership, The Milwaukee, 48 F.2d 842, 1931 A.M.C. 412 (E.D.Wis. 1931). The District Court opinion in the Torrey Canyon limitation proceedings, note 36a *infra*, collects other cases, old and new. Judge Metzner concluded: "These cases have held such diverse parties as shareholders, mortgagees, prior vendors, life tenants, trustees and government agencies operating privately-owned ships in wartime to be "owners" entitled to limit liability." (281 F.Supp. at p. 232.) On "prior vendors" see Petition of United States (The Trojan), 167 F. Supp. 576, 1959 A.M.C. 201 (N.D.Cal. 1958), affirmed per curiam *sub nom.* Todd Shipyards Corp. v. United States, 274 F.2d 402, 1960 A.M.C. 772 (9th Cir. 1960) (United States as former owner allowed to petition for limitation where it was alleged that the negligence of the United States during the

The abortive Torrey Canyon limitation proceedings cast an interesting new light on the § 186 charter provision.[36a] Barracuda Tanker Corporation was the "owner" of the Torrey Canyon, which, at the time of the stranding, was under a 20-year time charter to Union Oil Company. (The oil which the Torrey Canyon was carrying had been shipped by British Petroleum Trading, Ltd. under a voyage charter from Union, but British Petroleum and the voyage charter were not involved in the limitation proceedings.) Barracuda was a dummy corporation set up by Union for the sole purpose of holding title to the Torrey Canyon; Union at all times controlled the operation of the Torrey Canyon and, for that matter, of Barracuda.

The Torrey Canyon arrangement has, since World War II, become a common one which is by no means limited to ship financing.[36b] In the shipping context, the "true owner" (Union), instead of operating its own fleet under its own name, sets up dummies (like Barracuda) to hold title to each of its ships. The ship is subject to a long-term ship mortgage (which is the dummy corporation's only liability, except for operating expenses for which it is, of course, reimbursed by the "time charterer") and is operated under a long-term charter to the "true owner" (which is the dummy corporation's only asset). The money to be earned under the charter is assigned as further security for the mortgage but under the usual arrangement the mortgagee will not require payments of charter-hire to be made directly to it until there has been a default under the mortgage. The reasons for engaging in this complicated charade are partly to obtain fancied tax and accounting advantages for the "true owner" and partly to insulate him from the claims of the mortgagee—say, a deficiency judgment in a foreclosure action—in case the venture proves to be unprofitable. Despite the ardent belief of many eminent counsel in the effectiveness of these arrangements, neither the advantages nor the "insulation" can be guaranteed. So far, however, no arrangement of this type has run the gauntlet of litigation.

The Torrey Canyon charter from Barracuda to Union was carefully set up as a time charter. Under Article 3 the master, officers, and crew were to remain the servants of Barracuda "navigating and working the Vessel on behalf of Owner [Barracuda]" and, under Article 19, "Nothing herein contained [i. e., in the charter] shall be con-

period of its ownership had caused the subsequent explosion); Petition of Zebroid Trawling Corp. (The F/V Zebroid), 428 F.2d 226 (1st Cir. 1970) (owner of vessel at time the accident occurred allowed to petition for limitation even though, at time petition filed, the vessel had been sold in foreclosure proceedings).

36a. The proceedings are reported in Complaint of Barracuda Tanker Corp. (The Torrey Canyon), 281 F.Supp. 228, 1968 A.M.C. 1711 (S.D.N.Y.1968), reversed 409 F.2d 1013, 1969 A.M.C. 1442 (2d Cir. 1969). Following an out-of-court settlement, see note 13*l* supra, the limitation proceedings were discontinued. The opinions in the proceedings are discussed in Haberbusch, Constitution of the *Torrey Canyon* Limitation Fund, 1 J. of Mar. Law and Commerce 146 (1969).

36b. For a general discussion of this type of financing arrangement, see 2 Gilmore, Security Interests in Personal Property § 41.1 (1965). See also the Note on Patterns of Ship Financing, Chapter IX, § 9–51(a).

strued as creating a demise to the Charterer." [36c] The charter-party draftsmen were evidently concerned with making Barracuda look as much like an "Owner" as possible, for the purpose of their charade, and had momentarily forgotten about the provisions of 46 U.S.C.A. § 186.

In the Torrey Canyon litigation the claimants wasted no time in sueing Barracuda (which, with the destruction of the Torrey Canyon, was a hollow shell) but pursued Union instead. Union (and Barracuda) filed complaints for exoneration from or limitation of liability. On a motion to dismiss Union's complaint, Judge Metzner in the District Court concluded that Union, as a time charterer, was not entitled to limitation under § 186. Union's counsel, however, argued that, even if Union was not entitled to limitation as a charterer under § 186, it was, nevertheless, entitled to limitation as an "owner" under § 183(a). It is impossible not to feel a degree of sympathy for counsel driven to the desperate expedient of piercing their own corporate veil. Judge Metzner agreed that Union had made a strong enough case for its being "owner *pro hac vice*" (as the point was oddly put) to withstand the motion to dismiss and that the question of Union's liability and right to limit should be determined at trial. He therefore continued in force the customary order enjoining the prosecution of claims against Union outside the admiralty proceeding. On appeal a unanimous panel of the Second Circuit reversed. Judge Bonsal remarked that "No case has been cited to us which supports the contention of Union that, as a time charterer, it may be an 'owner' within § 183, even though it is not a 'charterer' within § 186." He also noted that the theory of the claimants' case seemed to be that "the stranding and sinking of the Torrey Canyon and the [resulting] damage . . . were caused by activities of Union unrelated to the navigation of the vessel, and that Union had something to do with the original designing and manufacturing of the Torrey Canyon in 1958 and with its enlargement in 1965." [36d] After ritually quoting the passage from Justice Black's opinion in the Cushing case on the "inappropriateness" of "[j]udicial expansion of the Limited Liability Act at this date," [36e] Judge Bonsal ordered the proceedings remanded to the District Court "with direction to modify the injunction . . . to permit Government claimants [there were no private claimants] to assert in that Court claims against Union unrelated to the navigation of the Torrey Canyon at the time of the stranding." It may be noted that neither of the Torrey Canyon opinions passed squarely on Union's contention. Judge Metzner did not hold that Union (if found to be without "privity or knowledge") was entitled to limitation as "owner *pro hac vice*"; Judge Bonsal for the Second Circuit did not hold that Union was not so entitled. With the settlement of the case, the proceedings were discontinued so that the riddle still remains unanswered.

**36c.** 281 F.Supp. at p. 231; 1968 A.M.C. at p. 1713.

**36d.** 409 F.2d at p. 1015; 1969 A.M.C. at p. 1445.

**36e.** Text at note 13 *supra*.

A great many ships are operated under the arrangement which Union employed for the Torrey Canyon and, sooner or later, one of them will repeat the Torrey Canyon's misadventure. It may be thought that the "true" or "*pro hac vice*" owners, to preserve their rights under the Limitation Act, could easily shelter under § 186 by using demise instead of time charters. The use of demise charters, however, would further undermine the already shaky structure of the financing arrangement, whose effectiveness depends on the dummy titleholder's being made to look as much like an "owner" as possible. Thus counsel who set up such arrangements are faced with a calculated gamble: if they use time charters, they may lose the protection of the Limitation Act. If they use demise charters, they may lose all the other advantages which the arrangement is designed to secure. The accidental collision of a late twentieth-century financing device with the provisions of a mid-nineteenth century statute gives an Alice in Wonderland air to the discussions.

It is difficult to disagree with the contention that Union was, in truth, the owner of the Torrey Canyon. If it is the public policy of the United States to give shipowners the benefit of limited liability, then Union should be entitled to limitation. On the other hand, the limitation idea is widely regarded as unfair, unjust, and anachronistic.[36f] Once it is accepted that the Limitation Act of 1851 is to be restrictively rather than broadly continued, the Second Circuit's opinion in the Torrey Canyon proceedings points the way to imposing unlimited liability on large corporations which, for their own corporate purposes, choose to describe themselves as "time charterers" rather than as "owners" of their fleets.

**§ 10–11.** Section 187 (R.S. § 4287), unamended except verbally since 1851, has proved to be of almost no importance. It preserves whatever remedies any "party" may have against "the master, officers, or seamen" for damage to property or for "negligence, fraud or other malversation". The remedies are preserved "notwithstanding such master or seaman may be an owner or part owner of the vessel." The last phrase is only *ex industria* in the statute, as there would presumably be privity or knowledge in such a situation, so that limitation would be denied in any case.

**§ 10–12.** Section 188 (R.S. § 4289), provides that the several sections of the Limitation Act (with the exception of the loss of life amendments) shall apply to "all seagoing vessels, and also to all vessels used on lakes or rivers or in inland navigation, including canal boats, barges, and lighters." Thus, provided that the structure seeking the benefit of the Limitation Act qualifies as a "vessel" [37] and the

36f. See § 10–4(a) *supra*.

37. On what is a "vessel" see Chapter I, § 1–11. Evansville & Bowling Green Packet Co. v. Chero Cola Bottling Co., 271 U.S. 19, 46 S.Ct. 379, 1926 A.M.C. 684 (1926), discusses the problem in the context of a limitation proceeding. A seaplane lost in flight has been held not to be a vessel within the meaning of the Act. Noakes v. Imperial Airways, 29 F.Supp. 412, 1939 A.M.C. 1048 (S.D.N.Y.1939); Dollins v. Pan-American Grace Airways, 27 F.Supp. 487, 1939 A.M.C. 691 (S.D. N.Y.1939).

event giving rise to the claims occurred on navigable waters within the Admiralty jurisdiction,[37a] the Act applies: the owner of a rowboat on a river may limit as effectively as the owner of a transatlantic liner.[38] It was not always so: Section 7 of the 1851 Act provided that the Act should *not* apply to "any canal boat, barge or lighter, or to any vessel of any description whatsoever, used in rivers or inland navigation." The exclusion of all inland shipping from the 1851 Act reflected the then legislative intent to place the American merchant marine on a level of competitive equality on the high seas; since foreign limitation laws could not operate to the disadvantage of inland shipping there was no reason to include such shipowners within the Act's coverage. The reversal of the original position and the extension of the Act to cover all shipping occurred in 1886,[39] after the Limitation Act, by reason of the Supreme Court decisions and rules, had come to the attention of shipowners. From having been in 1851 an exceptional privilege accorded ocean shipping in order to keep some sort of merchant marine afloat, it had become in 1886 a beneficent principle of the widest possible application.

**§ 10–13.** Section 189, usually considered to be a part of the Limitation Act, came in initially as Section 18 of the omnibus shipping Act of 1884.[40] The relationship of this section to the balance of

**37a.** See George v. Beavark, Inc. (The River Queen), 402 F.2d 977, 1968 A.M.C. 2759 (8th Cir. 1968), affirming the dismissal of a limitation complaint on the ground that the accident occurred on a reservoir which was not within the jurisdiction of the admiralty. In re Stephen, 341 F.Supp. 1404 (N.D.Ga. 1965) is to the same effect. In Petition of Madsen, 187 F.Supp. 411, 1963 A.M.C. 488 (N.D.N.Y.1960) a limitation petition filed by the owner of a "pleasure speed boat" was dismissed on the ground that the accident complained of had occurred on a landlocked lake in the Adirondacks which was "not a navigable water in fact of the United States". Judge Foley's opinion suggests that he was concerned about the increasing use of the Limitation Act by the owners of pleasure boats (see § 10–23 *infra*). On "navigable waters" and admiralty jurisdiction, see Chapter I, § 1–11 *supra*.

**38.** In Grays Landing Ferry Co. v. Stone, 46 F.2d 394, 1931 A.M.C. 787, (3d Cir. 1931), the Ferry Company lost six out of ten passengers from a craft 18′ x 5′ x 1½′, propelled by two sets of oars. The District Court dismissed the petition for limitation but the Circuit Court reversed, citing The Robert W. Parsons, 191 U.S. 17, 30, 24 S.Ct. 8, 12 (1903): "Neither size, form, equipment, nor means of propulsion are determinative factors upon the question of jurisdiction, which regards only the purpose for which the craft was constructed, and the business in which it is engaged." But the Supreme Court in The Robert W. Parsons, which was not a limitation case, had also said: "The modern law of England and America rules out of the admiralty jurisdiction all vessels propelled by oars simply because they are the smallest class, and beneath the dignity of the court of admiralty." (*Id.* at 32, 24 S.Ct. at 13.) The Third Circuit in the Stone case concluded that while "the ferry company used one of its smaller craft" it "was no mere skiff or rowboat."

**39.** 24 Stat. 80 (1886). The Act was a heterogeneous collection of amendments and repeals, whose only uniform characteristic seemed to be that they all related to shipping.

**40.** The act of June 26, 1884, 23 Stat. 57 was captioned "An act to remove certain burdens on the American merchant marine and encourage the American foreign carrying trade . . ." This was to be accomplished, for example, by providing that "All the officers of vessels of the United States shall be citizens . . ." Most of its 30 sections dealt with seamen and seamen's

the Act and the meaning of its cryptic language were long unsolved problems and indeed what was eventually arrived at was not so much a solution as a general agreement to ignore the section whenever possible. The section, which has not been amended since 1884, reads:

> "The individual liability of a shipowner shall be limited to the proportion of any or all debts and liabilities that his individual share of the vessel bears to the whole; and the aggregate liabilities of all the owners of a vessel on account of the same shall not exceed the value of such vessel and freight pending: *Provided,* That this provision shall not prevent any claimant from joining all the owners in one action; nor shall the same apply to wages due to persons employed by said shipowners."

No doubt when more obscure statutes are drafted, the Congress will draft them, but it is difficult to believe that any future body of law makers will ever surpass this extraordinary effort. Off hand it could have meant almost anything, including the repeal *sub silentio* of the entire Act of 1851, as amended. The Act of 1851 had provided that an owner might limit against cargo claims, collision claims, and, in fine, against "any act, matter, or thing, loss, damage, or forfeiture, done, occasioned or incurred without [his] privity or knowledge . . .", which seems comprehensive enough. The 1884 Act, improving on the generality of the original statute, says "all debts and liabilities" except (by the final proviso) wage claims, and has no reference to "privity or knowledge". As a matter of statutory construction it could have been plausibly argued that, following the 1884 Act, an owner was entitled to limit even though he had "privity and knowledge" and even as to contracts (except contracts of employment) which he had personally negotiated.[41] No such construction was given to the section, but if it did not mean that it was hard to see what it did mean. Finally in 1911 the Supreme Court in Richardson v. Harmon, an odd case involving a limitation proceeding after a collision of a ship with a bridge (the tort being therefore, as the law then stood, non-maritime), suggested that the true meaning of the Act of 1884 might be that owners could limit against non-maritime as well as against maritime claims, subject of course to the "privity or knowledge" requirements of the original statute.[42] The background to the Richardson v. Harmon holding is of interest. In Ex parte Phenix Insurance Company,[43] the Court had held that a District Court under the 1851 Act had no jurisdiction to entertain a petition for limitation of liability against a non-maritime tort (in that case a fire on shore caused by sparks escaping from a steamship's smokestack). After the fire, which occurred in 1880, state court suits were instituted against the owner of the steamer. In 1885 one of these suits ended in

rights. Section 18's inclusion is perhaps explained by the final phrase of the proviso, quoted in the text below.

41. See discussion of the "personal contract" doctrine §§ 10–26 to 10–28 *infra.*

42. 222 U.S. 96, 32 S.Ct. 27 (1911).

43. 118 U.S. 610, 7 S.Ct. 25 (1886).

judgment against the owner; four other suits were pending and still others threatened. Consequently in January of 1886 the owner petitioned for limitation; the District Court held that it had jurisdiction and ordered that the value of the steamer at the time of the fire be appraised. Plaintiffs in the tort actions (respondents in the limitation proceeding) then moved in the Supreme Court for a writ of prohibition against the District Court, which was granted on the theory that the 1851 Act did not apply to non-maritime torts. In disposing of the Phenix case in Richardson v. Harmon Justice Lurton pointed out that the tort complained of in Phenix had occurred before the 1884 Act was passed, so that the Court in its 1886 decision had no reason to consider the meaning of § 189. That point, which was perfectly correct, proved too much, so far as the Court's 1911 reading of § 189 was concerned: since the Phenix case was not decided until 1886, and since no earlier case had suggested that the 1851 Act did not apply to non-maritime torts, it becomes most unlikely that Congress in 1884 was attempting to solve a non-existent problem. However, Richardson v. Harmon gave at least a simulacrum of sense to language which was otherwise either meaningless or revolutionary. The hornbook law of the matter today is that § 189: (1) extended the Limitation Act to cover non-maritime claims; (2) excluded all wage claims, under any part of the statute, from limitation proceedings; and (3) made it clear, through the language about "individual shares", that the Limitation Act was to apply to any kind of joint ownership of a vessel as well as to sole ownership. There is no reason to believe that the courts will be inclined in the future to pump new life in § 189. Nevertheless, as in the case of any statute, there is always danger that language, judicially done to death, may be judicially restored to life. The only safe thing to do with such a statute is to repeal it,[44] but, as the foregoing discussion may have made clear, the Limitation Act is one of those statutes which Congress tinkers with every generation or two, adding a patch here and mending a leak there, but never rebuilding from the ground up.

In the first edition of the treatise the foregoing discussion was concluded with the observation: "The Limitation Act has been due for a general overhaul for the past seventy-five years; seventy-five years from now that statement will be still true, except that the overhaul will then be one hundred and fifty years overdue." The developments of the past twenty years suggest that, although the Limitation Act may never come in for a "general overhaul", its most likely fate, if it is not repealed outright, is that it will be judicially nibbled to death.[45]

44. Repeal was suggested as early as 1887 by Van Santvoord, Limitation of the Liability of Shipowners, 140, because: ". . . the first clause of this Section 18, should be entitled an Act to hinder and delay the collection of debts against shipowners . . . and to deprive them of credit . . . the second clause of Section 18 . . . is a mischievous complication, tending to confusion . . ."

45. *Claims subject to, and claims not subject to, limitation*:

In general the Limitation Act permits the owner to limit his liability against

## "The Appropriate Proceedings in Any Court"

**§ 10–14.** Until 1936 the Limitation Act (§ 185) provided, as to the procedure to be followed under it, only that either claimants or the vessel owner might "take the appropriate proceedings in any court"

all claims, whether in contract or in tort, which arise from the operation of the ship (including claims for salvage, The San Pedro, 223 U.S. 365, 32 S.Ct. 275 (1912)). The fundamental condition of the right to limit is that the owner did not have privity or knowledge of the cause of the loss, damage, injury or death (or, in the case of fire on board ship, that the fire was not caused by the owner's design or neglect); on "privity or knowledge", "design or neglect", see §§ 10–20 to 10–25 *infra.* It has been held that limitation will be denied with respect to claims arising from an accident which occurs during a deviation ordered or approved by the owner. See Companhia de Navegacao Lloyd Brasileiro v. Evans Coffee Co. (The Pelotas), 66 F.2d 75 (5th Cir. 1933). Thede, *supra* note 13c, 45 Tulane L.Rev. 959, 972 (1971) collects a few other deviation cases, all of fairly ancient vintage. See the cases cited in connection with the Harter Act and Cogsa *infra* this Note. Furthermore the right to limit is denied with respect to certain types of claims arising from so-called "personal contracts", see §§ 10–26 to 10–28 *infra.* The Limitation Act itself (§ 189, see text following note 40 *supra*) provides that seamen's wage claims are not subject to limitation.

A seaman's maintenance and cure claim was held not subject to limitation, by analogy to the "personal contract" cases (see § 10–26 *infra*) in Murray v. New York Central R. R., 171 F.Supp. 80, 1959 A.M.C. 2355 (S.D.N.Y.1959), affirmed without discussion of the maintenance and cure point, 287 F.2d 152, 1961 A.M.C. 1118 (2d Cir. 1961), certiorari denied 366 U.S. 945, 81 S.Ct. 1674 (1961). The same result was reached, on a somewhat different theory in Petition of Tiedemann (Elna II—Mission San Francisco), 236 F. Supp. 895 (D.Del.1964), reversed on procedural grounds 367 F.2d 498, 1966 A.M.C. 1934 (3d Cir. 1966). See § 10–26 *infra*, text following note 113c.

With respect to personal injury and death claims, the right to limit is available whether recovery is sought under general maritime law or under a special statute. See The Susan (Petition of Wood), 230 F.2d 197, 1956 A.M.C. 547 (2d Cir. 1956) (counts in an action for wrongful death based on unseaworthiness, the Jones Act and the Death on the High Seas Act all held subject to limitation). As to the cases where personal injury and death claimants benefit from the $60 per ton fund provided for in § 183(b), see §§ 10–33 to 10–38 *infra.* That actions brought by seamen under the Jones Act (41 Stat. 1007 (1920), 46 U.S.C. § 688) are subject to the Limitation Act was held in Re East River Towing Co. (The Edward), 266 U.S. 355, 45 S. Ct. 114, 1925 A.M.C. 33 (1925). See also Hudgins v. Gregory, 219 F.2d 255, 1955 A.M.C. 1012 (4th Cir. 1955). Recovery under the Death on the High Seas Act (41 Stat. 537 (1920), 46 U.S. C. § 761 *et seq.*) as well as recovery under a state wrongful death statute is subject to limitation. As to the Death on the High Seas Act, see *e. g.* In re Panama Transport Co. (Petition of U.S.), 98 F.Supp. 114, 1952 A.M.C. 189 (S.D.N.Y.1951), affirmed 195 F.2d 104, 1952 A.M.C. 650 (2d Cir. 1952). As to state wrongful death statutes, Butler v. Boston & Savannah S. S. Co., 130 U.S. 527, 9 S.Ct. 612 (1889); The Albert Dumois, 177 U.S. 240, 20 S.Ct. 595 (1900).

With respect to death claims against foreign shipowners, the Death on the High Seas Act provides (46 U.S.C. § 764) that actions may be maintained in American courts whenever the law of the ship's flag authorizes such a recovery "but without abatement of the amount for which recovery is authorized, any statute of the United States to the contrary notwithstanding." In The Vestris, 53 F.2d 847, 1931 A.M.C. 1553 (S.D.N.Y.1931) affirmed *sub nom.* Petition of Liverpool, Brazil & River Plate Steam Navigation Co., 57 F.2d 176, 1932 A.M.C. 608 (2d Cir. 1932) (a single-ship disaster of a British flagship on the high seas) that provision was held to mean both that the actions had to be brought within the limitation period specified in the English Fatal Accidents Act and that the English shipowner could not limit his liability. In

and that surrender of the vessel by the owner to a court-appointed trustee for claimants should "be deemed a sufficient compliance" with the requirements of the Act. In Norwich & N. Y. Transp. Co.

subsequent proceedings in The Vestris, 60 F.2d 273, 1932 A.M.C. 863 (S.D.N.Y.1932), the right to limit was denied as to cargo and all other claims. See also Petition of Donaldson Atlantic Line, 1940 A.M.C. 1408 (S.D.N.Y.1940). Cf. Bergeron v. K.L.M Royal Dutch Airlines, 188 F.Supp. 594, 1962 A.M.C. 194 (S.D.N.Y.1960) (citing The Vestris) and Petition of Chadade Steamship Co., Inc. (The Yarmouth Castle), 266 F.Supp. 517, 1967 A.M.C. 1843 (S.D. Fla.1967) (discussed text following note 188a *infra*, in which The Vestris might have been, but was not, cited). Whether English or American law would apply to claims for deaths occurring on an American flagship as a result of a collision with a British flagship was left open in The Silverpalm (Silver Line v. United States), 79 F.2d 598, 1935 A.M.C. 1506 (9th Cir. 1935); further proceedings in the case are reported at 94 F.2d 776, 1937 A.M.C. 1462 (9th Cir. 1937). British Transport Commission v. United States, 354 U.S. 129, 77 S.Ct. 1103, 1957 A.M.C. 1151 (1957) involved injury and death claims brought by and on behalf of passengers on an English ferry which had been in collision with a United States naval vessel in the North Sea. It was assumed without discussion that American limitation law applied; see the discussion of the case, § 10–42 *infra*. The Death on the High Seas Act does not apply to injuries which occur "less than a marine league from shore" (46 U.S.C. § 761); death claims resulting from such on shore accidents were held subject to the applicable state wrongful death act until Moragne v. States Marine Lines, 398 U.S. 375, 90 S.Ct. 1772, 1970 A.M.C. 967 (1970) held that the general maritime law provided a cause of action for wrongful death, see Chapter VI § 6–33.

Except in cases falling under the foreign law provision of 46 U.S.C. § 764, foreign shipowners when sued in American courts may have the benefit of the American Limitation Act; see §§ 10–43 to 10–45 *infra*.

Claims of passengers, whether for loss of property or for personal injury, are subject to the Limitation Act. 46 U.S.C. § 491 (16 Stat. 454 (1871), R.S. § 4493) provides that "Whenever damage is sustained by any passenger or his baggage, from explosion, fire, collision or other cause", the owner shall be liable to "the full amount" if the loss or injury was caused by a violation of the applicable safety laws "or through known defects in the steering apparatus or the hull". On the interrelationship of 46 U.S.C. § 491 and the Limitation Act, see Butler v. Boston & Savannah S. S. Co., 130 U.S. 527, 553, 9 S.Ct. 612, 617 (1889); The Virginia (Hines v. Butler), 278 F. 877 (4th Cir. 1921), certiorari denied 257 U.S. 659, 42 S.Ct. 185 (1922); The Princess Sophia (Petition of Canadian Pacific Ry.), 61 F.2d 339, 1932 A.M.C. 1562 (9th Cir. 1932), certiorari denied 288 U.S. 604, 53 S.Ct. 396 (1933).

The Harter Act (27 Stat. 445 (1893), § 6) and the Carriage of Goods by Sea Act, 49 Stat. 1207 (1936) § 8, 46 U.S.C. § 1308, expressly provide that the shipowner's rights under the Limitation Act are preserved as to cargo damage claims brought under those statutes. (The Harter Act, 46 U.S.C. §§ 190–195, immediately follows the Limitation Act as part of Ch. VIII of Title 46. Section 6 of the Harter Act was not carried forward to the U.S.C., but the comment to § 190 suggests that its effect was preserved by the inclusion of both statutes in the same chapter of the Code.) It has been held, however, that the right to limitation (as well as the right to exoneration under the Fire Statute) is lost when the damage was caused by an impermissible deviation. See The Pelotas, 66 F.2d 75 (5th Cir. 1933), affirming 43 F.2d 571 (E.D.La.1930); The Frederick Luckenbach, 15 F.2d 241, 1926 A.M.C. 1468 (S.D.N.Y.1926); Hoskyn & Co. v. Silver Line, 63 F.Supp. 452, 1943 A.M.C. 510 (S.D.N.Y.1943), affirmed without discussion of the point at issue 143 F.2d 462, 1944 A.M.C. 895 (2d Cir. 1944), certiorari denied 323 U.S. 767, 65 S.Ct. 116 (1944). As to the scope of permissible deviation, see Chapter III, § 3–40.

The Limitation Act covers torts both maritime and nonmaritime (see text at and following note 42 *supra*). As to the types of nonmaritime torts to which the Limitation Act has been held applicable, see The Atlas No. 7 (Petition of Wright & Cobb Lighterage Co., Inc.) 42 F.2d 480, 1930 A.M.C. 1029 (S.D.N.Y.1930) (accident on pier);

v. Wright, the first of the limitation cases to come before it, the Supreme Court concluded that it "undoubtedly has the power to make all needful rules and regulations for facilitating the course of proceed-

The Brinton (Re Pennsylvania R. Co.), 48 F.2d 559, 1931 A.M.C. 852 (2d Cir. 1931) certiorari denied 284 U.S. 640, 52 S.Ct. 21 (1931) (damage to boardwalk by barges driven on shore during a storm); The City of Bangor, 13 F.Supp. 648, 1936 A.M.C. 293 (D.Mass. 1936) (damage caused by the obstruction of a wharf); The Wichita Falls (Petition of Southern S. S. Co.), 15 F. Supp. 612, 1936 A.M.C. 1364 (S.D.Tex. 1936) (armed guards on the ship fired into a crowd of strikers gathered on the pier; limitation was denied on the ground of the owner's privity or knowledge); The Yacht Charlotte (Petition of Colonial Trust Co.), 124 F. Supp. 73, 1955 A.M.C. 1290 (D.Conn. 1954) (explosion while boat was in boathouse on land).

State laws and municipal ordinances regulating the use of canals, harbors and the like do not override the Limitation Act. See The Grand Republic —The Nassau (Petition of Highlands Navigation Corp.), 29 F.2d 37, 1929 A. M.C. 205 (2d Cir. 1929); The South Shore (City of Newark v. Mills), 35 F.2d 110, 1929 A.M.C. 1552 (3d Cir. 1929) certiorari denied 281 U.S. 722, 50 S.Ct. 237 (1930); The Central States, 9 F.Supp. 934, 1935 A.M.C. 461 (E.D.N.Y.1935).

Damage or injury caused by failure to comply with a statutory duty may deprive the owner of his right to limit unless he can bear the burden of proof required by The Pennsylvania, 86 U.S. (19 Wall.) 125 (1873), text at note 97 *infra*. See Pacific Coast Coal Co. v. Alaska S. S. Co. (The Donali), 105 F.2d 413, 1939 A.M.C. 930 (9th Cir. 1939); *Id.*, 112 F.2d 952, 1940 A.M.C. 877 (9th Cir. 1940) certiorari denied 311 U.S. 687, 61 S.Ct. 65 (1940) (failure to divide crew into proper watches as required by 46 U.S.C. § 222 *et seq.*).

Under 33 U.S.C.A. § 409 (often referred to as the Wreck Statute), which is part of the Rivers and Harbors Act of 1899, 30 Stat. 1151 *et seq.*, 33 U.S.C.A. § 401 *et seq.* the owner of a vessel which is sunk in a "navigable channel" is required to mark the sunken vessel and "diligently" attempt to remove it; his failure to do so "shall be considered as an abandonment of such craft, and subject the same to removal by the United States." In Wyandotte Transportation Co. v. United States, 389 U.S. 191, 88 S.Ct. 379, 1967 A.M.C. 2553 (1967) the United States had incurred expenses of over $3,000,000 in raising a barge loaded with liquid chlorine which had sunk in the Mississippi River. The defendant shipowner argued that, under the Wreck Statute, the United States could recover only *in rem* against the vessel and its cargo—thus, in effect, that the owner's liability was limited under the Wreck Statute even without resort to the Limitation Act. The Court held that, at least if the sinking had been negligent, the United States could recover without limitation (and, in a companion case, that it could have "declaratory or injunctive relief" to compel the owner to remove the vessel himself). Justice Fortas noted that the Court was not deciding whether claims under the Wreck Statute were subject to limitation under the Limitation Act.

In Complaint of Midland Enterprises, Inc., 296 F.Supp. 1356, 1970 A.M.C. 2437 (digest only) (S.D.Ohio, 1968) Judge Hogan discussed whether claims under the Wreck Statute were subject to limitation under the Limitation Act, noting, citing this Note as it appeared in the first edition of the treatise, that "there is considerable authority for the simple statement that a liability imposed by a failure to perform "statutory duty" is not limitable . . . ." He concluded that it was not necessary to decide the question, which he regarded as unsettled, at that stage in the proceedings before him. No further proceedings in the case have been reported.

In Complaint of Pacific Far East Line, Inc. (The Esso Seattle—The Guam Bear), 314 F.Supp. 1339, 1970 A.M.C. 1592 (N.D.Cal.1970) Judge Beeks, treating the question as "a matter of first impression", held that the shipowner could not limit with respect to wreck removal costs. (There were findings that the ship had been negligently navigated.) Judge Beeks' theory was that the costs were incurred with the "knowledge or privity" of the owner (which, of course, would always be true in such cases). In Complaint of Chinese Maritime Trust, Ltd.

ing," announced that "no court is better adapted than a court of admiralty to administer precisely such relief," [46] and promptly issued "Supplementary Rules of Practice in Admiralty" under which the "appropriate proceedings" were localized in the District Courts sitting in Admiralty. These rules, with relatively minor amendments, have ever since been in force; they now appear as Supplemental Rule F, Federal Rules of Civil Procedure (derived from former Admiralty Rules 51–55).[47]

(the S/S Sian Yung), 1972 A.M.C. 1478 (S.D.N.Y.1972) Judge Motley followed Judge Beeks' reasoning in a case which involved not the Wreck Statute but § 117.5 of the Code of Federal Regulations, applicable to sinkings in the Panama Canal. Judge Motley's disposition of the case was affirmed, 478 F.2d 1357, 1973 A.M.C. 1110 (2d Cir. 1973) on condition that the Canal Company agree to litigate its claim in the Southern District of New York before which the limitation proceeding was pending.

In Complaint of Harbor Towing Corp., 335 F.Supp. 1150, 1972 A.M.C. 597 (D. Md.1971) Judge Northrop held that claims under the Maryland Anti-Pollution Act were subject to the Limitation Act, concluding that The Guam Bear and other cases arising under the Wreck Statute were inapplicable. For a discussion of the case, see § 10–4(b) *supra*, text following note 13gg.

In Matter of Marine Leasing Services, Inc., 328 F.Supp. 589, 1971 A.M.C. 1329 (E.D.La.1971), affirmed per curiam 471 F.2d 255 (5th Cir. 1973), another barge loaded with liquid chlorine had been sunk in the Mississippi River. The cause of the sinking was the destructive force of Hurricane Betsy and it was concluded that no fault was chargeable to the barge, its owners or charterers. Judge West in the District Court, after a careful analysis of the somewhat murky language of the Wreck Statute, held that the United States could not recover removal costs where the sinking had not been the result of negligence except that the United States could recover from the charterer its costs for locating and marking the barge. This disposition of the case was approved by the Fifth Circuit in a brief per curiam opinion. The Wreck Statute is abominably drafted as to this point; it might be said that Judge West's reading is as persuasive as the opposite reading would have been. Judge West appears to have held that the charterer, who was assumed to have been a § 186 demise charterer, was liable without limitation for the costs of locating and marking the barge but, oddly, neither his opinion nor the per curiam affirmance (both the United States and the charterer had appealed) discussed the denial of limitation.

46. 80 U.S. (13 Wall.) 104, 123, 124 (1870).

47. On the 1966 procedural "unification" see note 27 *supra*.

*Venue in limitation proceedings* (Rule F(9), derived from former Admiralty Rule 54). The Rule provides for four situations:

(1) If the vessel has been attached or arrested in any district, the complaint for limitation shall be filed in that District;

(2) If the vessel has not been attached or arrested but the owner has been sued [*i. e. in personam* in state or federal court], the complaint shall be filed in any district in which the owner has been sued;

(3) If the vessel has not been attached or arrested and the owner has not been sued the "proceedings may be had in the district in which the vessel may be";

(4) If the vessel is not within any district and the owner has not been sued, "the petition may be filed in any district".

Rule F(9) further provides that "for the convenience of parties and witnesses, in the interest of justice, the court may transfer the action to any district; if venue is wrongly laid the court shall dismiss or, if it be in the interest of justice, transfer the action to any district in which it could have been brought."

The provision that the petition may be filed in any district if the vessel is "not within any district" (*i. e.* has been lost at sea or is in foreign wa-

From the outset the Rules went considerably beyond what the statute apparently authorized and provided for the payment into court of the appraised value of the ship, or the giving of a "stipulation with

ters) and the owner has not been sued was added to Rule 54 when the Admiralty Rules were revised in 1948 (see note 8 *supra*).

Subject to the provision on transfer, it appears that a claimant can localize the proceedings in a district of his choice (1) by libeling the vessel (which can of course be done only where the vessel is) or (2) by bringing suit *in personam* wherever the owner may be amenable to process, provided the libel is filed or the suit brought *before* the owner has (3) filed his petition in the district where the vessel is or (4) filed in any district if the vessel has been lost or is in foreign waters. In The Southern Districts (Petition of Southern S.S. Co.), 132 F.Supp. 316, 1955 A.M.C. 2278 (D.Del.1955) it was contended that Rule 54, the predecessor of Rule F(9), established a "priority of venue" in favor of claimants and that a shipowner could not file under (3) or (4) until some claimant had brought suit or given notice of a claim. In an excellently reasoned opinion, which carefully traced the historical development of Rule 54, Judge Rodney held that no "prority of venue" was contemplated and that a shipowner, whose ship was lost at sea, could immediately file his petition; in The Southern Districts, the petition was filed in the district of the ship's home port.

In The Southern Districts Judge Rodney had assumed that if the owner chose to wait until a claimant had filed "a libel or suit", "then the limitation proceedings must be filed in the District where such libel or suit was brought." In Petition of Tiedemann & Co., 259 F.2d 605, 1959 A.M.C. 978 (3d Cir. 1958) Judge McLaughlin distinguished the single-claim situation from the multiple-claim situation: "Where there is just one suit or libel filed, the shipowner has no choice but to bring his petition in the only court where litigation in the particular matter is pending against his vessel. But where . . . there are several causes of action pending when the limitation petition is to be filed, there is nothing in the rule [i. e. Rule 54] which in any way indicates that it must or should follow the venue of the first suit or suits." (259 F.2d at p. 605, 1959 A.M.C. at pp. 980–981). Held in Tiedemann that a petition for limitation was properly filed in Delaware where the vessel had been libeled, although in personam suits had been earlier filed in Pennsylvania and New York. In Matter of Bloomfield Steamship Co., 227 F.Supp. 615, 1964 A.M.C. 1563 (E.D.La.1964), the Court cited Tiedemann for the proposition that: "[W]here there is just one suit or libel filed . . . the shipowner has no choice but to bring his petition in the only court where litigation is pending against his vessel." (227 F. Supp. at p. 618).

The cases just cited were decided under former Rule 54 but the procedural situation under current Rule F(9) appears to be unchanged.

Until the 1948 revision, see note 8 *supra*, the Admiralty Rules said nothing about the transfer of limitation proceedings. In the 1948 revision the following transfer provision was added to Rule 54: "the District Court may, in its discretion, transfer the proceedings to any district for the convenience of the parties." Also in 1948 Congress enacted change of venue legislation (62 Stat. 937, 28 U.S.C.A. §§ 1404–1406) which provided in § 1404(a): "For the convenience of parties and witnesses, in the interest of justice, a district court may transfer any civil action to any other district or division where it might have been brought."

During the 1950's there was a depressing amount of litigation in the lower federal courts on the relationship (if any) between Rule 54 and § 1404(a) in the context of motions to transfer limitation proceedings. See Petition of Delaware River Pilots Association (The Delaware—The Corner Brook), 122 F.Supp. 896, 1954 A.M.C. 2124 (D. Del.1954) (collecting the authorities); Petition of New Jersey Barging Corp. (The Perth Amboy No. 1), 135 F.Supp., 1955 A.M.C. 2270 (S.D.N.Y.1955); Cain v. Bowater's Newfoundland Pulp & Paper Mills, Ltd., 127 F.Supp. 949, 1954 A.M.C. 2128 (E.D.Pa.1954); Petition of Diesel Tanker A/C Dodge, Inc. (The Dodge—The Michael), 117 F. Supp. 216, 1954 A.M.C. 298 (E.D.N.Y. 1954); Texas Co. v. United States (The Ruchamkin—The Washington), 116 F.Supp. 915, 1954 A.M.C. 491 (S. D.N.Y.1953), affirmed Petition of Texas Co., 213 F.2d 479, 1954 A.M.C. 1251

sureties for payment thereof" as alternatives to the transfer of the ship to a trustee. Furthermore, the Supreme Court emphasized more than once that its rules were designed to "facilitate the course of proceedings" [48] and were not meant as an exhaustive statement of all possible procedures that could be devised. As the pre-1936 practice developed, the following propositions became established:

1. The shipowner could follow the procedure set out in the Admiralty Rules and file a petition for limitation with the District Court, electing whether to transfer the ship to a trustee, pay its appraised value into court or post a stipulation for value.[49]

2. The petition could be filed in advance of any suit having been brought against the shipowner in any court.[50]

3. If suit were brought against the shipowner, he could delay filing his petition until after the entry of judgment against him.[51]

(2d Cir. 1954), certiorari denied 348 U.S. 829, 75 S.Ct. 52 (1954); Petition of Southern S.S. Co. (The Southern Districts), 132 F.Supp. 316, 1955 A.M.C. 2278 (D.Del.1955); Petition of the Baker-Whitely Towing Co. (The Nyland—The E. Kirby Smith), 145 F. Supp. 904, 1956 A.M.C. 2257 (D.Md. 1956); Petition of Clipper Fishing Corp. (The Clipper), 168 F.Supp. 130, 1959 A.M.C. 1986 (S.D.N.Y.1958); Petition of United States (The CG 95321), 221 F.Supp. 163, 1964 A.M.C. 94 (D.N. H.1963); Humble Oil & Refining Co. v. Bell Marine Service, Inc., 321 F.2d 53, 1964 A.M.C. 315 (5th Cir. 1963). After some initial hesitation, the cases seemed to be working toward the sensible conclusion that a court which felt that transfer was indicated under the circumstances could proceed either under Rule 54 or under § 1404(a), whichever seemed to fit the particular case.

The current transfer provision in Rule F(9), quoted *supra* this note, was, according to the Advisory Committee's Note, "revised to conform closely to the language of 28 U.S.Code Annotated, §§ 1404(a) and 1406(a), though it retains the existing rule's [*i. e.* Rule 54] provision for transfer to *any* district for convenience. The revision also makes clear what had been doubted: that the court may transfer if venue is wrongly laid."

Although it would still be possible to play games with the discrepancies between Rule F(9) and § 1404(a), the courts so far have shown no disposition to do so. For a relaxed (and sensible) approach, see Petition of Alamo Chemical Transportation Co. (The Tug New Work), 323 F.Supp. 789, 1972 A.M.C. 1658 (S.D.Tex.1970) and Petition of Fenwick Island, Inc. (The F/V Fenwick Island), 330 F.Supp. 1191, 1971 A.M.C. 1273 (E.D.N.C.1971) (both denying transfer).

48. Norwich & N.Y. Transp. Co. v. Wright, 80 U.S. (13 Wall.) 104, 125 (1871); The Benefactor, 103 U.S. 239, 244 (1880); The Scotland, 105 U.S. 24, 33 (1882).

49. The Scotland, 105 U.S. 24, 34 (1882); The City of Norwich, 118 U.S. 468, 493, 502, 6 S.Ct. 1150, 1156, 1161 (1886); The H. F. Dimock, 52 F. 598 (S.D.N.Y.1892).

50. In Ex parte Slayton, 105 U.S. 451, 452 (1881), Chief Justice Waite wrote: ". . . notwithstanding the admiralty rules Nos. 54, 55, 56 and 57 of this court, the owner of a vessel may institute appropriate proceedings, . . . without waiting for a suit to be begun against him or his vessel for the loss out of which the liability arises." See, however, text at note 61 *infra.*

51. The Benefactor, 103 U.S. 239, 244 (1880); The City of Norwich, 118 U.S. 468, 6 S.Ct. 1150 (1885); Larsen v. Northland Transp. Co., 292 U.S. 20, 54 S.Ct. 584, 1934 A.M.C. 501 (1934); The Ocean Spray, 117 F. 971 (N.D.Cal. 1902), penalizing laches with costs; Re Starin, 124 F. 101 (E.D.N.Y.1903); Re Moran Bros. Contracting Co., 1 F. Supp. 932, 1932 A.M.C. 910 (E.D.N.Y. 1932); The Fort Bragg, 6 F.Supp. 13, 1933 A.M.C. 1649 (N.D.Cal.1933).

4. As an alternative to proceeding by petition, the shipowner could invoke the Limitation Act as a defense in any court.[52]

The 1936 amendments to Section 185 [53] codified the pre-1936 practice in part, reversed it in part, and left still other aspects shrouded in doubt which has not yet been entirely resolved.

**§ 10–15.** Section 185, as amended, adopts the practice which the Supreme Court originally created by rule. The section provides that the vessel owner shall either pay into court the value of the vessel and her freight or post approved security therefor or transfer his interest in vessel and freight to a trustee; in any case he must also pay or give security for such sums "as the court may from time to time fix as necessary to carry out the provisions of section 183" [*i. e.* to make up the $60 per ton fund required by the loss of life amendments]. The adoption of the bond-posting procedure was a retrospective ratification of Supreme Court practice. Nevertheless, there may well be an important difference between practice which depends on rules of court and practice which depends on statute. The Admiralty Rules on limitation, it has been held, are not "jurisdictional"; [54] that is, the trial court in its discretion may waive, overlook or ignore noncompliance with details of the rules.[54a] Furthermore, the accepted pre-

52. The Scotland, 105 U.S. 24, 33–34 (1882). The rules "were not intended to prevent a defense by way of answer to a libel, or plea to an action, if the shipowners should deem such a mode of pleading adequate to their protection." California Yacht Club of Los Angeles v. Johnson (The Cyc), 65 F.2d 245, 1933 A.M.C. 943 (9th Cir. 1933).

53. See § 10–9 *supra*.

54. The Noronic (Petition of Canada S. S. Lines), 93 F.Supp. 549, 1950 A.M.C. 1499 (N.D.Ohio 1950). The case involved a petitioner who overlooked the 1948 amendments to the Rules, and followed the old procedure.

54a. The treatment of late-filed claims in limitation proceedings is instructive on the "non-jurisdictional" nature of the Rules. From their issuance in 1872 the Rules provided that the District Court with which a petition for limitation was filed should, by monition, set a date within which all claims against the owner should be filed. The practice came to be that the District Courts, as a matter of discretion, allowed claims to be filed even after the date. See, *e. g.*, Meyer v. New England Fish Co. of Oregon, 136 F.2d 315 (9th Cir. 1943), certiorari denied 320 U.S. 771, 64 S.Ct. 83 (1943) (holding a refusal to entertain a late-filed claim an abuse of the District Court's discretion). In the 1948 revision of the Admiralty Rules the Supreme Court accepted the practice by providing in Rule 51 that "the court, for cause shown, may enlarge" the date by which claims are to be filed. That provision is carried forward, without change of substance, in Rule F(4). Under the "for cause shown" formula it was held in Jappinen v. Canada Steamship Lines, Inc., 417 F. 2d 189, 1970 A.M.C. 2404 (6th Cir. 1969) that the District Court had abused its discretion in refusing to allow a claim to be filed six months late where it appeared that the claimant, who lived in a small town in Minnesota, had not heard of the order (which had been published in newspapers in Cleveland and Fort Huron). See also Texas Gulf Sulphur Co. v. Blue Stack Towing Co., 313 F.2d 359, 1963 A.M.C. 349 (5th Cir. 1963) (affirming a District Court's refusal to entertain a late-filed cargo claim but modifying the order to provide that, if limitation was ultimately denied, the cargo claim should come in but be subordinated to death and injury claims). In Petition of Vermillion Towing Corp. (The Tug Raven), 227 F.Supp. 933, 1964 A.M.C. 1733 (E.D. Va.1964) Judge Hoffman allowed a claim to be filed several years late but ruled that the claimant's "right . . . to participate in the fund will

1936 theory was that the Rules, being designed merely to "facilitate" proceedings, did not state the only possible procedure and could be varied as the ingenuity of court and counsel might suggest.[55] A statutory requirement is a different animal. Section 185 is now cast in mandatory language: "The vessel owner . . . (a) shall deposit with the court . . . or (b) at his option shall transfer . . ." and the final sentence of the section now speaks of "compliance with the requirements of this section." Before the amendments the section merely provided that "it shall be deemed a sufficient compliance on the part of such owner with the requirements of this chapter . . . if he shall transfer. . . ."

The most important change made by the 1936 amendments was the addition to Section 185 of a new preamble which provided:

> "The vessel owner, within six months after a claimant shall have given to or filed with such owner written notice of claim, may petition a district court of competent jurisdiction for limitation of liability . . ."

The Supreme Court has never authoritatively construed the 1936 preamble[56] but, after some initial confusion, the lower federal courts seem to have arrived at a stable and satisfactory reading of its somewhat obscure language.

The six months period from filing notice of claim is apparently in the nature of a statute of limitations. If the shipowner delays in filing his petition for limitation of liability beyond the six months period, it is clear that the court could not of its own motion waive the delay. It is unclear whether a stipulation entered into by the claimant to extend the six months period—for example, in the course of negotiations for a settlement—would be effective: the answer depends on whether the six months period is, or is not, taken as going to the court's jurisdiction.[56a] The pendency of suits outside the admiralty court does not affect the running of the six months period: the pre-1936 cases holding that the owner might petition for limitation at any time, even after entry of judgment, are clearly overruled to the extent that they allow the limitation petition to be filed more than six months after written notice.[57]

be subordinated to the rights of other claimants who have been diligent in filing their claims." In Petition of World Tradeways Shipping, Ltd. (The Tradeways II), 373 F.2d 860, 1968 A.M.C. 200 (2d Cir. 1965) it was held that a District Court's order allowing a late-filed claim (on behalf of a time charterer) was not subject to an interlocutory appeal.

55. 3 Benedict, Admiralty 348 (6th ed. 1940).

56. See, however, the Zapata case, discussed in the text following note 59 *infra.*

56a. "As far as the owner is concerned, the timely filing of a complaint and posting or offering to post security are jurisdictional requirements. . . ." Thede, note 13c *supra,* 45 Tulane L.Rev. 959, 975 (1971), citing the Grasselli and Goulandris cases, note 57 *infra,* as well as Standard Wholesale P. & A. Works v. Travelers Ins. Co., 107 F.2d 373 (4th Cir. 1939).

57. The Grasselli Chemical Co. No. 4, 20 F.Supp. 394, 1937 A.M.C. 1070 (S.D.N.Y.1937), which held that the purpose of the six months provision was to change the old rule and require the owner to act promptly, was approved

Pre-1936 practice permitted the Limitation Act to be raised by way of defense as an alternative to an affirmative petition.[58] There were at least three possible constructions of the 1936 preamble as it bore upon the practice of introducing the Limitation Act as a defense: 1) the six months period related only to procedure when an affirmative petition was filed; hence the pre-1936 practice was still available and the Act could be pleaded as a defense in any suit without reference to time; 2) the six months period applied both to defensive pleading and affirmative petition; hence the Act could be pleaded as a defense but only within the six months period; 3) the filing of a petition for limitation within the six months period had become the exclusive method by which a shipowner could invoke the Limitation Act; hence the possibility of pleading the Act as a defense did not exist even during the six months period, and on receiving notice of claim the vessel owner must, if he wished to avail himself on the Act's protection, promptly file his petition. In the lower federal courts the first solution (that the pre-1936 practice was not affected by the amendment) has prevailed.[59]

in Petition of Goulandris Bros., 140 F. 2d 780, 1944 A.M.C. 357 (2d Cir. 1944), certiorari denied 322 U.S. 755, 64 S.Ct. 1268 (1944). In Goulandris the owner had filed one day before the expiration of the six months period: "All we decide is that the petition as filed, with nothing further done within the six months, did not satisfy the statutory requirement. We think the appellees are correct in urging that in reality what the petitioners did amounted to no more than filing with the court a notice of their intention at some future time to initiate a proceeding for limitation . . ." (*Id.* at 782, 1944 A.M.C. at 361). In Hudgins v. Gregory, 219 F.2d 255, 1955 A.M.C. 1012 (4th Cir. 1955) there appears to be a suggestion that the six months period is not jurisdictional and could be extended. The Circuit refused to reverse the District Court's holding (that the owner was entitled to limitation) on the ground of "laches" in filing the petition for limitation. The District Court had said that the "considerable delay" in filing was "due in large measure to the understanding had between counsel and the Court that such application would be filed in event the motion for summary judgment was overruled." (*Id.* at 259, 1016).

58. See cases cited in note 52 *supra*.

59. The Third Circuit adopted that solution in The Chickie, 141 F.2d 80, 1944 A.M.C. 635 (3d Cir. 1944). In Deep Sea Tankers v. The Long Branch, 258 F.2d 757, 1959 A.M.C. 28 (2d Cir. 1958) the Second Circuit expressly followed The Chickie and reaffirmed its position a few years later in Murray v. New York Central Railroad Co., 287 F.2d 162, 1961 A.M.C. 1118 (2d Cir. 1961). No lower court seems to have doubted The Chickie since then and contrary holdings in some of the early cases, such as Cantwell v. Meade, 120 F.Supp. 406, 1954 A.M.C. 1128 (E.D.N.Y.1954) have been overruled or forgotten. For current cases adopting the rule of The Chickie, see Blunk v. Wilson Line of Washington, Inc., 341 F.Supp. 1345, 1972 A. M.C. 1501 (N.D.Ohio, 1972); Baham v. Atlantic, Gulf and Pacific Co., 333 F. Supp. 680, 1972 A.M.C. 1568 (E.D.Pa. 1971). In Odegard v. Quist, 199 F. Supp. 449 (E.D.N.Y.1961) Judge Zavatt, who was of course bound by the Second Circuit's decision in Deep Sea Tankers, held that the defendant shipowner was barred by laches from amending its answer to include a defense of limitation of liability when the motion to amend was made after a delay of two years, on the eve of trial. "To permit such an amendment," Judge Zavatt commented, "would be prejudicial to the plaintiff who had no reason to suspect that he would have to go to trial on the issue of limitation of liability. . . ." (199 F.Supp. at p. 452).

In M/S Bremen and Unterweser Reederei GMBH v. Zapata Off-Shore Company [59a] the Supreme Court declined to take advantage of an opportunity to express its views on the matters discussed in the foregoing paragraph. Unterweser (a German corporation) had contracted with Zapata (an American corporation) to tow Zapata's ocean-going oil-drilling rig Chaparral from Louisiana to the Adriatic Sea. The towage contract provided for litigation of all disputes in London; the validity of the forum-selection clause was the issue principally involved in the ensuing American litigation.[59b] The Chaparral was damaged in a storm in the Gulf of Mexico and, on Zapata's instructions, was taken to the port of Tampa, Florida, which was the nearest port of refuge. Zapata then instituted an action in the District Court for the Middle District of Florida, in rem against the Bremen and in personam against Unterweser, to recover $3,500,000. for the damages to the Chaparral, alleging negligence and breach of the towage contract. Unterweser moved to dismiss the Florida action and simultaneously instituted a breach of contract action against Zapata in London. The Florida District Court had not ruled on Unterweser's motion to dismiss at the time when the six-months period for filing a complaint for limitation under § 185 had almost run. Before the expiration of the period, Unterweser filed a complaint for limitation in the Florida District Court in which it sought to reserve all its rights under the previous motion to dismiss. The Zapata action was then refiled in the limitation proceeding.

As the litigation evolved, Zapata naturally contended that, regardless of the validity of the forum clause, Unterweser, by filing its limitation complaint in Florida, should be taken to have submitted itself for all purposes to American jurisdiction.[59c] It was in response to that contention that Chief Justice Burger, who wrote the majority opinion, turned, after having concluded that the forum clause was valid, to a consideration of the reasons which had led counsel for Unterweser to file their limitation complaint. Unterweser, he noted, had been "faced with a dilemma . . . confronted with difficult alternatives . . . " The alternative to filing the limitation complaint was, of course, to raise the defense of the Limitation Act in answer to Zapata's complaint either before or after the six-month period had run. The Chief Justice commented:

> "That course of action was not without risk, however, that Unterweser's attempt to limit its liability by answer would

59a. 407 U.S. 1, 92 S.Ct. 1907, 1972 A.M.C. 1407 (1972).

59b. By a narrow majority the Fifth Circuit, sitting en banc, had held the clause invalid, 428 F.2d 888, 1970 AM.C. 1241. The Supreme Court reversed. For a discussion of this aspect of the case, see Chapter III, § 3–25, note 23.

59c. Zapata had excellent reasons for attempting to have the case litigated in the United States under American law. An exculpatory clause in the towage contract, which was presumably invalid under American law (see Chapter VII, § 7–15), was assumed to be valid under English law. Furthermore, on the assumption that Unterweser, if found to be at fault, was entitled to limitation of liability, the American limitation fund amounted to $1,390,000 while the English limitation fund would be only slightly in excess of $80,000 (407 U.S. at p. 8, note 8, 92 S.Ct. at p. 1912).

> be held invalid. See G. Gilmore and C. Black, *Admiralty,* Sec. 10–15 (1957). We do not believe this hazardous option in any way deprived Unterweser's limitation complaint of its essentially defensive character so far as Zapata was concerned." [59d]

The conclusion was that: "There is no basis on which to conclude that this purely necessary defensive action by Unterweser should preclude it from relying on the forum clause it bargained for." [59e]

Given the context in which and the purpose for which the Chief Justice made his remarks, it is easy to understand why he emphasized the "dilemma," the "difficult alternatives", the "hazardous option" which Unterweser's counsel faced, confronted or had to decide on as well as why, for authority, he contented himself with a reference to the discussion of the point in the first edition of this treatise which had been written at a time when the resolution of the controversy over the meaning of the § 185 preamble was far from clear. There is no disposition in this quarter to quarrel with the result which the majority of the Court reached in Zapata, either on the validity of the forum clause or on the effect of Unterweser's filing of its limitation complaint. It is unfortunate that the Chief Justice did not find a formula which would have taken Unterweser off the hook without suggesting that this long-settled controversy should still have been a cause for concern in the 1970's. It is to be hoped that the Chief Justice's language will not be used by over-zealous counsel to suggest that the entirely satisfactory rule of The Chickie [59f] is in anyway open to doubt.

If we assume that the Limitation Act may be invoked either by complaint (or petition) within the six-months period of § 185 or by answer without regard to the six-months period,[59g] there remains a question of tactics which a shipowner confronted by multiple claims must decide. If he elects to file a limitation complaint, it is clear, subject to the qualifications to be discussed in the following section, that he will bring all the claims into "concourse" in the limitation proceeding and that his liability, if he is found entitled to limitation, will be the amount of the limitation fund required by § 183. If, however, several actions are brought (or could be brought) against

**59d.** 407 U.S. at pp. 19–20, 92 S.Ct. 1918, note 20.

**59e.** 407 U.S. at p. 20, 92 S.Ct. at p. 1918. Justice Douglas, dissenting, felt that: "Petitioner's petition for limitation subjects it to the full equitable powers of the Limitation Court" [which included the power to enjoin Unterweser from prosecuting its action in England]. (407 U.S. at pp. 22–23, 92 S.Ct. at p. 1919). Justice Douglas also felt that prosecution of the action in England should have been enjoined so that Zapata could get the benefit of American law on the validity of the exculpatory clause in the towage contract, see note 59c *supra.*

**59f.** See note 59 *supra.*

**59g.** Subject to the qualification suggested by Odegard v. Quist, note 59 *supra.* See also Yates v. Dann, 167 F.Supp. 882, 1961 A.M.C. 554 (digest only) (D.Del.1958), refusing to allow the defendant shipowner to amend his answer to include a Limitation Act defense eleven years and three trials after he had filed his original pleading.

him and he elects to raise the Limitation Act by answer in each action, can he be required to set up a separate § 183 limitation fund in each action? In The West Point [59h] Judge Bryan held that the shipowner in a multiple claim situation could limit to a single fund only by filing a § 185 petition and that, when he elected to proceed by answer, separate funds had to be set in each action even though, as in The West Point, the separate actions had been consolidated and were before the same court, sitting in admiralty, with which the limitation petition would have been filed.[59i] The West Point was no doubt enough to alert shipowners represented by competent counsel to the dangers of proceeding by answer in any multiple claim situation. At all events the issue did not surface in litigation again for nearly twenty-five years. In Blunk v. Wilson Line of Washington, Inc.[59j] it appeared that an excursion steamer which carried a party of Ohio school children (and, it is reassuring to learn, their "chaperones") had run aground in a fogbank at midnight and had not been refloated until the next morning. Forty actions were filed by parents of the children seeking recovery for "physical and psychic injuries" (we are not told that any actions were filed by the chaperones, who were apparently of tougher metal). The forty actions were consolidated in the District Court for the Northern District of Ohio, in which the defendant shipowner then invoked the Limitation Act by a single answer applicable to all forty complaints. Even if counsel for the shipowner had overlooked The West Point, counsel for the plaintiffs did not, so that the argument was made that forty separate limitation funds were required. Judge Green, in an elaborate opinion, concluded that "this Court must necessarily reject the holding of *West Point* as inconsistent with this Court's interpretation of the relevant portions of the Limitation of Liability Act," with the result that only one limitation fund was required. Judge Green's opinion relied principally on the older cases which had established "the proposition that the Limitation Act must be liberally construed so as to effectuate its beneficent purposes." [59k] It could well be that courts less sympathetic to the policy of the Limitation Act would find The West Point more attractive than Blunk in the occasional case in which a shipowner might seek to assert his right to limitation in a multiple claim situation by answer instead of by complaint. If the multiple claims led to action which, for procedural reasons, could not be consolidated in a single proceeding, the shipowner who elected to introduce the defense of the Limitation Act by answer in the separate actions would clearly be in danger of being required to set up a separate limitation fund in each action.[59l] To save himself the expense of filing a limi-

**59h.** 83 F.Supp. 680 (E.D.Va.1949).

**59i.** In American Tobacco Co. v. The Kantingo Hadgipatera, 211 F.2d 666, 1954 A.M.C. 874 (2d Cir. 1954), which did not involve the setting up of separate funds, Judge Chase, in a dictum, cited The West Point approvingly.

**59j.** 341 F.Supp. 1345, 1972 A.M.C. 1501 (N.D.Ohio, 1972).

**59k.** § 10–3 *supra.*

**59*l*.** Thede, note 13c *supra,* 45 Tulane L.Rev. 959, 975 (1971) cautions, citing The West Point, that "Pleading limitation complaint and posting security, a shipowner might be tempted to wait until some claimant has instituted an action and then plead the Limitation Act in his answer. However, if he is competently advised, he will always proceed by filing a § 185 complaint except in a single claim situation where he is sure the single claimant will bring his action in federal court.[59m]

Pre-1936 practice permitted a petition to be filed in advance of claims being brought against the vessel owner whenever the owner had reason to believe that two or more claims might result from an accident.[60] Only in the single claim situation did the owner have to wait for plaintiff to elect his forum.[61] The 1936 amendments to § 185 cast some doubt on both aspects of the pre-1936 rule. Read literally the 1936 language authorized the petition only after a "written notice of claim" had been "given" or "filed": merely knowing that there were outstanding claims might not be enough. However, during the period from 1936 until 1966, it seems to have been generally assumed that the pre-1936 practice had not been affected. This assumption was strengthened by the fact that Admiralty Rule 51, as revised in 1948, did not condition the filing of a petition for limitation on the petitioner's receipt of a notice of claim from some claimant.[62]

tation by answer is typically restricted to single claim cases, since the owner not proceeding under section 185 is potentially liable to *each* plaintiff up to his interest in the vessel." He adds that in any case pleading the Limitation Act by answer "is apparently restricted to federal courts, since state courts have been held to lack jurisdiction to try the owner's right to limit even where neither party challenged such jurisdiction" (citing Cooper v. Allison, 412 P.2d 356, 1966 A.M.C. 2643 (Or.1966). In the Cooper case the trial court, in a state proceeding, had ruled in favor of the shipowner on the limitation defense. The Supreme Court of Oregon reversed on the ground that a state court had no jurisdiction to try the issue of limitation and remanded the case for further proceedings. If by the time of the remand the § 185 six months period had run, as no doubt it would have, there would have been no way for the shipowner to invoke the Limitation Act. Lloyd v. Port Edgewood Inc. (The Golden Touch), 1967 A.M.C. 353 (Sup.Ct., R.I.1966), certiorari denied by the Supreme Court of Rhode Island, 101 R.I. 775, 1967 A.M.C. 356 (1967) apparently holds, *contra* Cooper v. Allison, that a state court does have jurisdiction to decide the limitation issue where the Act is pleaded in a state court proceeding.

**59m.** In Petition of Yamashita-Shinnihon Kisen (The Suwaharu Maru–Mandoil II–Transoneida), 305 F.Supp. 377, 1969 A.M.C. 2102 (D.Or.1969) the odd contention was made that the filing of a limitation proceeding under § 185 precluded any subsequent out-of-court settlement. Judge Beeks, commenting that "the argument relating to settlement restrictions is ingenious and poses a matter of first impression", rejected it on the grounds that "it is the policy of the law to encourage settlements" and that he could find nothing to the contrary in the Limitation Act. To be on the safe side in case counsel's ingenious argument met with a warmer reception on appeal, he also found that the settlements were in any case "adequate".

**60.** See note 50 *supra*.

**61.** The Alcyone (Re Putnam) 55 F.2d 73, 1932 A.M.C. 174 (2d Cir. 1932) certiorari denied 286 U.S. 558, 52 S.Ct. 641 (1932).

**62.** Rule 51 as revised in 1948 provided: "The owner or owners of any vessel who shall desire to claim the benefit of limitation of liability provided for in the third and fourth sections of the Act of March 3, 1851, may file a petition in the proper District Court of the United States, as

Since the 1966 procedural unification the matters formerly covered by Rule 51 are covered by Rule F(1) whose preamble reads:

> Not later than six months after his receipt of a claim in writing, any vessel owner may file a complaint . . . for limitation of liability pursuant to statute."

According to the Advisory Committee's Note, the 1936 amendment to § 185 "superseded to some extent the provisions of Admiralty Rule 51 . . . with respect to the time of filing the complaint . . ." The rule as revised, the Note continues, "incorporates in substance the 1936 amendment . . ." Evidently the revisers felt that the absence of a comparable provision in the 1948 revision of Rule 51 was a matter of drafting inadvertence.

Thus a limitation complaint is in technical violation of Rule F(1) if it is filed before "receipt of a claim in writing." No case has been found in which a claimant has moved to dismiss a limitation complaint on the ground that it was prematurely filed under Rule F(1). Sooner or later some court will presumably have to rule on such a motion and it is clear enough that the pre-1966 cases are no longer, of themselves, authoritative.[62a] Even so, it does not necessarily follow that the motion to dismiss, if it appeared that there had been a technically premature filing, should be automatically granted. For one thing, the statutory language (§ 185 preamble) is by no means clear on this point. For another thing, even if Rule F(1) is taken as an authoritative construction of the statute, the Admiralty Rules were never looked on as "jurisdictional"[62b] and there is no reason to believe that their incorporation in the Federal Rules of Civil Procedure has made them so. For a third thing, it is hard to see how any claimant could claim to have been prejudiced by a premature filing in the light of the traditionally liberal treatment of late-filed claims in limitation proceedings.[62c] The prudent shipowner will of course make sure that his limitation complaint is filed in technical compliance with the Rule F(1) time limits—not a minute too soon, not a minute too late. Even the prudent shipowner, however, might be, to use Chief Justice Burger's language in Zapata,[62d] faced with a dilemma in a single claim situation where the claimant had given a written notice of claim but had not, as the six months period of § 185 was about to run, instituted his action. Pre-1936 practice required

hereinafter specified. Such petition shall set forth the facts and circumstances on which limitation of liability is claimed, and pray proper relief in that behalf." That a petition for limitation could, despite the 1936 amendment, be filed in advance of notice of claim, was held in The Susan (Petition of Wood), 124 F.Supp. 540, 1954 A.M.C. 1287 (S.D.N.Y.1954) affirmed 230 F.2d 197, 1956 A.M.C. 547 (2d Cir. 1956) and The Southern Districts (Petition of Southern S.S.Co.), 132 F.Supp. 316, 1955 A.M.C. 2278 (D. Del.1955). See also The Severance (Diamond S. S. Transp. Corp. v. Peoples Sav. Bank & Trust Co., 152 F.2d 916, 1946 A.M.C. 128 (4th Cir. 1945), certiorari denied 328 U.S. 853, 66 S.Ct. 1344 (1946). No cases reached the contrary result.

**62a.** See the cases cited in note 62 *supra*.

**62b.** See text at note 54 *supra*.

**62c.** See note 54a *supra*.

**62d.** See text following note 59c *supra*.

the shipowner to wait in order to give the plaintiff his choice of forum; the statute, reinforced by Rule F(1), now requires him to move, if at all, within six months from notice. Furthermore, the Zapata case may have cast some doubt on the shipowner's right to plead the Limitation Act in his answer after the six months have run.[62e] The prudent shipowner will not be fazed by his dilemma: he will file his complaint within the six-month period and let the court wrestle with The Alcyone [63] and related problems.

The statute makes the six months period run from the "giving" or "filing" of "written notice of claim". "Written" at least excludes oral or telephonic notices; but any other type of communication which a shipowner receives relating to an outstanding claim against him might conceivably be held to be such a "notice of claim" as to set the statutory period running—or indeed, if "giving" is equivalent to "sending" the period might start to run whether or not the communication was ever received or brought to the attention of the proper officer. Nothing can be done about the latter possibility (except, of course, to argue that the combination of "giving" and "filing" in the statute as well as the use of the term "receipt" in Rule F(1), plus the equities of the case, suggest that the communication must be actually received); as to the former, prudent practice is obviously to petition for limitation within six months of receipt of anything that looks remotely like a "written notice of claim." On the other hand, several lower court decisions in the 1940's and 1950's suggest that the courts were sensibly requiring a definite statement as the type of "notice" required to start the six-months period running.[64] The issue does not appear to have been raised in recent litigation. Apparently any "notice" of any "claim" brings the six month period into play: if the statute is read literally, an owner who received notice of claim from A, which he settled or paid, and subsequently received notice of a related claim from B might learn that the six months period ran from the date of A's claim and not of B's.[65]

62e. See the discussion of Zapata, text following note 59a *supra*.

63. See note 61 *supra*.

64. See, *e. g.*, The Lavinia D. (Petition of Spearin, Preston & Burrows, Inc.), 190 F.2d 684, 1951 A.M.C. 1523 (2d Cir. 1951); The Ariel, 30 F.Supp. 110, 1939 A.M.C. 1292 (S.D.N.Y.1939) affirmed 119 F.2d 866, 1941 A.M.C. 929 (2d Cir. 1941); The Spare Time II (Petition of Hutchinson), 28 F.Supp. 519, 1939 A.M.C. 840 (E.D.N.Y.1938); Petition of Anthony O'Boyle, Inc., 51 F.Supp. 430, 1944 A.M.C. 820 (S.D.N.Y.1943); The Belleville, 35 F.Supp. 934, 1941 A.M.C. 350 (E.D.N.Y.1940). For "notices" which have been held sufficiently definite to start the period running, see Petition of Donnelly (Donnelly v. Brown), 230 F.2d 169, 1956 A.M.C. 923 (6th Cir. 1956); The Maine (Standard Wholesale Phosphate & Acid v. Travelers Ins. Co.), 107 F.2d 373, 1939 A.M.C. 1493 (4th Cir. 1939); The Irving (Petition of Conners Marine Co.), 28 F.Supp. 585, 1939 A.M.C. 825 (S.D.N.Y.1939) affirmed per curiam 107 F.2d 1011, 1940 A.M.C. 143 (2d Cir. 1939); The Graselli and Windrush, 1937 A.M.C. 847 (S.D.N.Y.1937); The Breeze, 1938 A.M.C. 327 (D.Mass. 1938).

65. This seems a most unlikely construction. But see The Grasselli Chemical Co. No. 4, 20 F.Supp. 394, 396, 1937 A.M.C. 1070, 1074–5, (S.D.N.Y.1937): ". . . a petition for limitation of liability must be filed within six months after the first writ-

**Control by the Admiralty Court of Proceedings in Other Courts**

**§ 10–16.** The last sentence of Section 185 provides that on compliance with its requirements [*i. e.* filing a petition within the six months period together with paying into court or posting a bond for the value of the ship or transferring the ship to a trustee] "all claims and proceedings against the owner with respect to the matter in question shall cease".[66] Section 1333 of the Judicial Code confers upon the District Courts exclusive original jurisdiction of any civil case of admiralty or maritime jurisdiction "saving to suitors in all cases all other remedies to which they are otherwise entitled." The two provisions are in obvious conflict. On the whole the policy of the Limitation Act has prevailed, so that in most limitation situations the "suitors" are in fact deprived of their choice of forum.

There is nothing in the Limitation Act itself which conditions the right of a shipowner to petition for limitation of liability on the existence of a multiplicity of claims or of a fund insufficient to satisfy all claims. The Act says merely that on the filing of the petition and compliance with the requirements of the Act "all claims and proceedings against the owner . . . shall cease". That language could have been construed to give the owner an absolute right, by petitioning for limitation, to transfer all proceedings against him to the admiralty. The courts, however, have not been willing to discard so easily the policy of the saving to suitors clause which reserves to plaintiff-claimant and not to defendant-shipowner the right to choose the forum. The result has been the growth of a not uncomplicated body of case law whereby the owner's right to localize proceedings in the admiralty court has been to a degree cut back in the name of the saving to suitors clause. Since the type of plaintiff who wants to sue in state court (or in federal court on the civil side) is almost always the personal injury plaintiff hoping for larger damages from a jury than he would get from the admiralty judge the cases on this point are almost without exception personal injury cases.

**§ 10–17.** The case law admits the owner's right to localize proceedings in the standard limitation situation: a multiplicity of claims, usually resulting from a maritime catastrophe, which in the aggregate clearly exceed the liability of the owner under the Limitation Act.[66a]

ten notice shall have been given of a claim arising out of the particular accident or disaster in question. If the petition is not so filed, the shipowner's privilege of limiting liability is lost entirely in respect to all claims arising out of the accident or disaster".

**66.** Institution of a limitation proceeding makes compliance with otherwise applicable state procedural statutes unnecessary. See Parham v. Pelegrin, 468 F.2d 719 (8th Cir. 1972), holding that claims filed in a limitation proceeding would not be dismissed because of the claimants' failure to comply with an Arkansas statute relating to the filing of claims against decedents' estates.

**66a.** For an authoritative statement of this proposition, see Pershing Auto Rentals, Inc. v. Gaffney, 279 F.2d 546, 1960 A.M.C. 1287 (5th Cir. 1960). Judge Brown's opinion in Gaffney was written in the light of the Supreme Court's 1957 decision in Lake

In that situation, the admiralty court, on the filing of the petition and compliance with the provisions for a limitation fund, will enjoin the continuance of any pending actions against the owner as well as the institution of any new actions.[67] Claimants are required to make proof of claim in the limitation proceeding and to litigate their rights in that proceeding.[68] Furthermore the district court, having assumed jurisdiction, will decide the entire case—that is, will pass on the merits of the individual claims as well as on the right of the shipowner to limit under the Act and will ultimately oversee the distribution of the fund among the successful claimants. Even if, on the limitation issue, the court denies the right to limit—because the owner has not succeeded in proving that he had no "privity or knowledge" of the cause of the disaster—the court may retain the case and adjudicate the claims.[69] The rule that the admiralty court may retain the case for decision in all its aspects even when it has been shown that there is either no right or no need to limit liability reflects an idea which has been given frequent expression in the opinions: that the limitation proceeding is designed to bring about a concourse of claims and to simplify the resolution of an involved, many-sided con-

Tankers Corp. v. Henn, discussed in the text following note 76b *infra*. To the same effect as Gaffney is Petition of Kahului Railroad Co. (Tug William Walsh), 214 F.Supp. 789, 1966 A.M.C. 423 (D.Hawaii, 1963).

67. The shipowner's limitation petition supersedes all other civil proceedings in every court except claims not subject to limitation, see note 45 *supra*. In Petition of Bloomfield Steamship Co. (The Ronda—The Lucille Bloomfield), 442 F.2d 728, 1970 A.M.C. 521 (2d Cir. 1970) it was held that the injunction issued in a limitation proceeding applies only to actions brought in the United States. At the time Bloomfield filed its limitation petition, Mowinckels (owner of a Norwegian-flag vessel which had been in collision with Bloomfield's vessel in international waters off the coast of France) had instituted an action against Bloomfield in England; the District Court's order refusing to stay the English action was affirmed. (Mowinckels did not file a claim in Bloomfield's American limitation proceeding.) At a later point Mowinckels also petitioned for limitation in the United States. In the Mowinckels' limitation proceeding, Bloomfield contended that Mowinckels' right to limitation in the United States should be conditioned on his withdrawing his action in England. The District Court concluded that it had power so to condition the Mowinckels petition but, as a matter of discretion, refused to do so. This order was also affirmed by the Second Circuit. On the well-settled rule that a decree granting limitation has no extraterritorial or international effect, see § 10–45 *infra*.

68. Supplemental Rule F(3), (4), derived from former Admiralty Rules 51, 52.

69. The leading case is Hartford Accident & Indemnity Co. v. Southern Pac. Co., 273 U.S. 207, 47 S.Ct. 357, 1927 A.M.C. 402 (1927); see § 10–41 *infra*.

However, if limitation is denied, plaintiffs who wish to prosecute common law actions outside the admiralty will be allowed to do so. See The Susan (Petition of Wood), 230 F.2d 197, 1956 A.M.C. 547 (2d Cir. 1956). In the Gaffney case, note 66a *supra*, Judge Brown, citing The Susan, wrote: "the claimants are the ones to determine whether such full relief from the admiralty is desired or needed. If they do not desire it, the admiralty court in its decree denying the right to limitation can make certain that they are free to pursue the petition in any other forum having requisite jurisdiction." (279 F.2d at p. 552; 1960 A.M.C. at p. 1295.) See also, to the same effect, Fecht v. Makowski, 406 F.2d 721, 1969 A.M.C. 144 (5th Cir. 1969); Narragansett Fishing Corp. v. F/V Bob n Barry, 425 F.2d 733, 1970 A.M.C. 1132 (1st Cir. 1970) also takes the position that a claimant, if limitation

troversy by bringing all parties before one judge who can then do equity in a single proceeding. The concourse of claims idea, obviously attractive to the shipowner who wishes to consolidate proceedings in which he is defendant, has proved a feeble reed when its support has been sought outside what we have called the standard limitation situation (*i. e.* multiple claims plus an insufficient fund).[70]

§ **10–18.** When either of the components in the standard situation is lacking—that is, when there is only one claim *or* when the aggregate of all claims will not exhaust the available limitation fund—the district court with which a petition for limitation of liability is filed will not enjoin the prosecution of claims in other courts, although in most situations it will retain jurisdiction of the case for the purpose of deciding the limitation issue, if, as and when such a decision becomes necessary. In this way the courts have sought, within the framework of the Limitation Act, to give effect to the policy of the saving to suitors clause. The working out of the theory has not been at all points entirely logical, but logic should not be required of courts which are obliged to implement, at one and the same time, two inconsistent and contradictory policies.

When the limitation fund exceeds the amount of all claims that could possibly be asserted against the owner, the district court must allow other actions against the owner, in state or federal court, to proceed.[71] At the outset, when its jurisdiction has been invoked by the filing of a petition, the district court must determine: 1) the amount of the limitation fund and 2) the aggregate amount of claims, including both those known to exist and those that might be asserted in the future. Only when it is satisfied that the claims exceed the fund may the court properly enjoin the prosecution of action in other courts. The mere existence of a multiplicity of claims, and the convenience (for the defendant) of bringing them into "concourse" does not justify the injunction.

The determination whether there is a "possibility" that claims, unknown as well as known, may exceed the fund is a human judgment and, as such, subject to error. On the whole the cases suggest that doubt should be resolved in favor of the shipowner, but the doubt must be a real one. In The Miss New York [72] an excursion steamer collided with a tanker in New York harbor. The steamer was appraised at $950,000; claims filed against the owner seven months later totaled only $159,000. Plaintiff, a personal injury claimant, moved to be allowed to proceed with a state court action against the owner. In denying the motion, Judge Clancy noted that there had

is denied, may return to his original action. For a somewhat different approach, see the Hanseatische case digested note 76i *infra.*

70. See § 10–41 *infra.*

71. The Aquitania, 14 F.2d 456, 1926 A.M.C. 1071 (S.D.N.Y.1926), affirmed 20 F.2d 457, 1927 A.M.C. 1320 (2d Cir. 1927); Curtis Bay Towing Co. v. Tug Kevin Moran, Inc., 159 F.2d 273, 1947 A.M.C. 51 (2d Cir. 1947).

72. (Petition of City of New York), 1941 A.M.C. 569 (S.D.N.Y.1941).

been 493 passengers on board the steamer at the time of the collision and further that the figure of $159,000 could not be taken as fixed even as to the claims already filed since there was nothing to prevent plaintiffs from increasing their demands for damages before trial. The opinion comments that "any probability," even a "highly improbable" one, that claims may exceed the fund is enough to justify the admiralty court in enjoining other actions; on the facts of the case, in view of the large number of possible claimants and the fact that the claims were unliquidated, the "possibility" or "probability" does not seem to have been too remote.[73]

Pre-1936 practice was apparently, where claims could not possibly exceed the fund, to dismiss the limitation petition out of hand.[74] The dismissal was not irrevocable, since if the assumed state of facts turned out to be wrong and it later appeared that claims did exceed the fund there was nothing to prevent the owner from filing a second petition. The 1936 amendments to the Limitation Act, which require the owner to file his petition within six months of notice of claim, have changed the situation. So that the owner may not be precluded by the six months requirement from filing a petition if the facts turn out to be other than as they are assumed, the district court should let the petition stand. In such a case, decided in 1947, Judge Learned Hand wrote:

> "It cannot prejudice claimants that the proceeding remains open, if they are free to press their suits to judgment and to collect. If meanwhile by some chance, which at the moment is too remote for practical recognition, other claims should appear which will make a concourse proper, a concourse can take over the situation as it then is; everything theretofore decided will remain decided, but the shipowner will be entitled to such part of his relief as may remain possible. Both sides will be protected in their remedies so far as it is possible to protect them without unfair invasion of the interests of either by the other." [75]

Claimants occasionally feel that the privilege of proceeding at common law is so important that they will enter into stipulations, reducing claims originally stated in larger amounts to amounts less than the limitation fund or agreeing never to enter judgments in any court for more than the amount of the limitation fund. Wheth-

73. Other cases reaching the same result as The Miss New York are The Victoria (Petition of Alaska S. S. Co.), 3 F.2d 330, 1926 A.M.C. 1096 (W.D. Wash.1924). The Tug No. 16, 237 F. 405 (S.D.N.Y.1916); The George W. Fields, 237 F. 403 (S.D.N.Y.1915); The Defender, 201 F. 189 (E.D.N.Y.1912).

74. The Aquitania, 20 F.2d 457, 1927 A.M.C. 1320 (2d Cir. 1927); Shipowners' & Merchants' Tugboat Co. v. Hammond Lumber Co. (The Dauntless), 218 F. 161 (9th Cir. 1914) certiorari denied 238 U.S. 633, 35 S.Ct. 938 (1915).

75. Curtis Bay Towing Co. v. Tug Kevin Moran, Inc., 159 F.2d 273, 276, 1947 A.M.C. 51, 55 (2d Cir. 1947). At the end of the six months' period only $32,000 in claims had been received in respect of a ship worth $209,000.

er the offer of such a stipulation, joined in by all claimants, is enough to force the district court to dissolve or modify its injunction was not, when the question first came up in litigation, entirely clear. The Second Circuit held in a series of cases decided during the 1950's that such a stipulation must be accepted and the injunction dissolved or modified.[76] Courts which thought more highly of the concourse of claims idea than did the Second Circuit, might not have been so ready to admit the ouster of jurisdiction by stipulation.[76a] However, in Lake Tankers Corporation v. Henn,[76b] the Supreme Court adopted what may be called the Second Circuit view of the matter, so that the possibility of judicial dissension was strangled at birth.

In Henn, as the result of a collision between a yacht and a tug which was push-towing a barge several passengers on the yacht were injured and one was killed. Lake Tankers (which owned both the tug and the barge) petitioned for limitation and was required to post separate bonds covering the value of the tug ($118,542.21) and the

76. Petition of Texas Co. (The Washington), 213 F.2d 479, 1954 A.M.C. 1251 (2d Cir. 1954), certiorari denied *sub nom.* Texas Co. v. United States, 348 U.S. 829, 75 S.Ct. 52 (1954). Aggregate claims of $2,225,000 having slightly exceeded the $2,109,000 limitation value of The Washington, the owner filed his petition and bond, whereupon various claimants reduced their claims until the aggregate was $350,000 less than the limitation value. The district court refused to vacate the injunction. On appeal, Judge Frank reversed, but, relying on the passage from the Curtis Bay Towing Co. case quoted in the text, at note 75 *supra*, held that "the district court will retain jurisdiction of the limitation proceeding". (This case involved appeals from two District Court orders, one by Judge Ryan which, as stated, was reversed; the other by Judge Weinfeld granting a motion to transfer the trial of a collision libel to another District which was affirmed.)

In Petition of Poling Holding Corp., 120 F.Supp. 890, 1954 A.M.C. 1733, (S.D.N.Y.1954), one argument made to sustain the right to limit was that a sufficient reduction had not been made to come under the Curtis Bay Towing Co. case. The claims amounted to within $16,000 of the $156,000 fund while in the Curtis Bay case they had been but one-seventh of the fund. The court held that the Curtis Bay case controlled since there was little likelihood of further claims.

In Petition of Trinidad Corp. (The Fort Mercer) 229 F.2d 423, 1956 A.M.C. 872 (2d Cir. 1955), the Court reaffirmed its holding in the Texas Co. case, which it had been asked to overrule. In Trinidad, however, Judge Hincks concluded that the stipulations filed with the District Court (to reduce aggregate claims below the limitation value) were for various reasons not satisfactory; the order allowing claimants to sue outside the limitation proceeding was reversed and the case remanded for further proceedings.

76a. See, for example, Judge Aldrich's opinion in Gottlieb's Claim (Petition of Boraks), 142 F.Supp. 364, 1956 A.M.C. 1342 (D.Mass.1956). Of course, in a no-fund case (where the ship has been lost with no freight pending), the right to limit must be decided in the limitation proceeding before state court actions are allowed, see The Susan (Petition of Wood), 230 F.2d 197, 1956 A.M.C. 547 (2d Cir. 1956) (where plaintiffs were, however, in order to avoid the bar of the Jones Act statute of limitations, allowed to institute their state court actions, whose prosecution would be enjoined until determination of the limitation issue).

76b. 354 U.S. 147, 77 S.Ct. 1269, 1957 A.M.C. 1165 (1957). The Henn case came up from the Second Circuit on certiorari, so that the Second Circuit's decision in Henn, 232 F.2d 573, 1956 A.M.C. 1018 (1956), affirmed on rehearing en banc, 235 F.2d 783 (1956), should be added to the list of cases digested in note 76 *supra*.

barge ($165,000.). The widow of the dead passenger, as his administratrix, had brought suit in state court in which she sought to recover $500,000. from Lake Tankers. Her state court action having been enjoined by the admiralty court, she filed a claim in the limitation proceeding for $250,000., allocating $100,000. of her alleged damage to the tug and the remaining $150,000. to the barge. (The aggregate of all the other claims filed in the limitation proceeding was less than $10,000., so that the bonds exceeded all claims.) On the widow's entering into the customary stipulation, the District Court ordered that she be allowed to proceed with her state court action. The Second Circuit affirmed, modifying the order to provide that any verdict in her favor in excess of $100,000. could be collected only if the jury allocated the amounts for which the tug and barge were found responsible. This disposition was approved by a bare majority of the Supreme Court.[76c] Justice Clark, for the majority, reviewed the history of the Limitation Act in a way that can hardly have given much comfort to shipowners. He concluded, citing Langnes v. Green:[76d]

> "The state proceeding could have no possible effect on the petitioner's claim for limited liability in the admiralty court and the provisions of the Act, therefore, do not control. . . . It follows that there can be no reason why a shipowner, under such conditions, should be treated any more favorably than an airline, bus or railway company. None of them can force a damage claimant to trial without a jury. They, too, must suffer a multiplicity of suits. Likewise, the shipowner, so long as his claim of limited liability is not jeopardized, is subject to all common-law remedies available against other parties in damage actions."[76e]

He then went on to comment on the concourse of claims idea. Referring to Justice Frankfurter's opinion in Maryland Casualty Company v. Cushing,[76f] he commented:

> "The language in [that] opinion to the effect that *concursus* is 'the heart' of the limitation system . . . refers to those cases when the claims exceed the value of the vessel and the pending freight. In that event, as we have pointed out, the *concursus* is vital to the protection of the offending owner's statutory right of limitation. But this is not to say that where *concursus* is not necessary to the protection of this statutory right it is nonetheless required."[76g]

**76c.** Justices Harlan, Frankfurter and Burton dissented. Justice Whittaker did not participate.

**76d.** 282 U.S. 531, 51 S.Ct. 243, 1931 A.M.C. 511 (1931). The case is discussed in the following section.

**76e.** 354 U.S. at p. 153, 77 S.Ct. at p. 1272.

**76f.** 347 U.S. 409, 74 S.Ct. 608, 1954 A.M.C. 837 (1954). The case is discussed in § 10–31 *infra*.

**76g.** 354 U.S. at p. 154, 77 S.Ct. at p. 1273.

Unmollified by Justice Clark's explication of his Cushing opinion, Justice Frankfurter, in Henn, joined in Justice Harlan's dissent.

In Henn only the death claimant sought (and was granted) leave to prosecute her state court action outside the limitation proceeding. However, it seems to follow from Justice Clark's opinion that the several personal injury claimants could also, on entering into the proper stipulations have pursued their common law remedies in separate civil actions. Absent the demonstrated need for a *concursus*, the shipowner, like the "airline, bus or railway company" must, as Justice Clark put it, "suffer a multiplicity of suits." In appropriate cases procedures are, of course, available for consolidating the civil actions [76h] so that the spectre of a "multiplicity of suits" is not as threatening as it sounds. It may be that if hundreds of claims were filed in the limitation proceeding, the *concursus* would be in any case maintained. However, if such a case arose in the real world, the aggregate of the claims would inevitably exceed the limitation found, so that the need for the *concursus* could be assumed.

The Henn case itself may be of no great interest, although it did serve the useful function of settling a question which otherwise might have accounted for a substantial amount of unnecessary litigation.[76i] We have quoted at some length from the majority opinions in the thought that the passages quoted, along with the oft-quoted passage from Justice Black's opinion in the Cushing case,[76j] help make the point that the majority which dominated the Court during the 1950's and 1960's was on the whole unsympathetic to the limitation idea. Henn was the last limitation case which the Court agreed to hear during that period. The Court's refusal for the better part of twenty years to pass on limitation cases of considerably more interest and importance than Henn must be counted, by the proponents of limitation, as a stroke of great good fortune. At the moment of writing the Court, as reconstituted in the 1970's, has not yet indicated whether its present membership continues to hold the attitudes

**76h.** See, by way of illustration, the Blunk case discussed in the text following note 59j *supra.*

**76i.** For an excellent analysis of the Henn case and its background in the Second Circuit cases (see note 76 *supra*), see Judge Brown's opinion in Pershing Auto Rentals, Inc. v. Gaffney, 279 F.2d 546, 1960 A.M.C. 1287 (5th Cir. 1960).

In Hanseatische Reederei Emil Offen & Co. v. Marine Terminals Corp., 1973 A.M.C. 1934 (N.D.Cal.1973), a multiple-claim inadequate-fund case, the District Court refused to allow the claimants to pursue their common law remedies outside the limitation proceeding. Judge Zirpoli observed: "Even if ordinarily . . . the claimants could be permitted to proceed in a state court, the admiralty court has the discretionary power to complete the case. [Citations omitted.] In view of the length of time that has already been spent trying the case and the small additional amount of time that would be required to complete it, the court concludes that it would be an abuse of discretion not to finally *adjudicate* this entire controversy in this court." (1973 A.M.C. at p. 1938. Emphasis in original.) The decision seems out of line with the general understanding of the meaning of the Henn case.

**76j.** See text at note 13 *supra.*

towards the purpose and policy of the Limitation Act which commended themselves to the majority of the Warren Court.

§ **10–19.** In the case of multiple claims which do not exhaust the limitation fund, it would be convenient for the defendant-shipowner to bring the claims into concourse, but there is no need for limitation: on the ground that the Limitation Act does not exist merely to provide a *forum conveniens,* the courts have refused to gather all the claims into a limitation proceeding. The case of the single claim which exceeds the limitation fund presents the opposite situation. There is no need for a concourse, but there is need for limitation. In the single claim case, as in the converse, the case law allows plaintiff to have his common law action. However, since here there is a need for limitation and since under Supreme Court theory questions of limitations are properly cognizable only in the admiralty court, plaintiff is allowed to proceed outside the admiralty only on condition that he acknowledge defendant's right to litigate the question of limitation (as distinguished from his liability on the merits) in the admiralty court.

Until 1914 there was doubt whether a shipowner had any right to petition for limitation of liability against a single claim. The doubt was based on the observation that the relevant sections of the Limitation Act referred to claims and claimants in the plural as well as on the "concourse of claims" theory of the limitation proceeding. In White v. Island Transp. Co.,[77] the Supreme Court set these doubts at rest, holding that the limitation proceeding was available in the single claim as in the multiple claim situation, thus preferring the policy of the Limitation Act over the policy of the saving to suitors clause.

In 1931 in Langnes v. Green [78] the Supreme Court reconsidered the question and this time attempted to find a solution which would preserve the policies underlying both statutes. Such a feat called for no mean powers of judicial sleight of hand; it is not surprising that the courts below found the mandate in Langnes v. Green so obscure that the case was promptly returned to the Supreme Court docket, this time captioned Ex parte Green,[79] for the Court to explain in a second opinion what it had meant by the first. The two Green cases, which in effect overruled the White case, were the Supreme Court's last contributions to the subject; they remain the essential gospel on the handling of single claim cases where plaintiff elects to sue at common law and defendant seeks to move the case into admiralty by petitioning for limitation.

77. 233 U.S. 346, 34 S.Ct. 589 (1914). A passenger, injured on board a small vessel, brought suit in a state court against the owner. The one claim, according to the petition for limitation, exceeded the value of the vessel. The Court's opinion, however, did not make the excess the basis of decision.

78. 282 U.S. 531, 51 S.Ct. 243, 1931 A.M.C. 511 (1931).

79. 286 U.S. 437, 52 S.Ct. 602, 1932 A.M.C. 802 (1932).

The facts in the Green cases were as follows: Green, an employee on board the fishing vessel Aloha, sued Langnes, owner of the vessel, in state court to recover for personal injuries. Two days before the trial date of the state court proceeding Langnes petitioned the appropriate federal district court for limitation of liability. The district court enjoined further prosecution of the state court action and issued a monition requiring all claims to be filed against Langnes within a fixed time. Green filed a claim for $25,000 and no other claim was filed. The parties stipulated the value of the Aloha to be $5,000. On this state of the proceedings Green moved to dissolve the injunction and to be allowed to proceed with his state court action. The district court denied the motion, tried the case on the merits, held that Langnes was not liable to Green in any amount and entered judgment accordingly. The Supreme Court, commenting that the problem presented to the district court was "quite simple", held that, in the exercise of its discretion, the trial court should have allowed the state court action to proceed "retaining, as a matter of precaution, the petition for a limitation of liability to be dealt with in the possible but . . . unlikely event that the right of petitioner to a limited liability might be brought into question in the state court. . . ." [80] Only in this way, said the Court, can the rights of both parties [*i. e.* under the Limitation Act and under the saving to suitors clause] be preserved, citing as governing authority the opinion of Judge Brawley, "a capable admiralty judge," in The Lotta.[81] The district judge may be sympathized with for having overlooked this "quite simple" point, since he might reasonably have imagined that the authority of The Lotta, a 1907 case, had been destroyed by the Supreme Court's 1914 holding in the White case.

The Langnes v. Green mandate remanded the case to the district court "for further proceedings in conformity with this opinion." The district court dissolved the restraining order and allowed the state court action to proceed. In that action, according to the Supreme Court's narrative in Ex parte Green, Green then "put in issue the right of the owner to limited liability, by challenging the seaworthiness of the vessel and the lack of the owner's privity or knowledge." [82] The district court, feeling that this was the "possible but . . . unlikely event" contemplated in Langnes v. Green, enjoined the state court proceedings a second time unless Green should withdraw the limitation issue from the state court proceeding. Green then moved in the Supreme Court for leave to file a petition for a writ of mandamus against the district judge requiring him "to conform to the opinion of this court in Langnes v. Green . . ." In Ex parte Green the Supreme Court denied the motion, holding that the district judge had properly interpreted the mandate and that,

80. 282 U.S. 531, 541, 51 S.Ct. 243, 247, 1931 A.M.C. 511, 518.

81. 150 F. 219 (E.D.S.C.1907).

82. 286 U.S. 437, 440, 52 S.Ct. 602, 603, 1932 A.M.C. 802, 804.

unless Green agreed to withdraw the limitation issue from the state court proceeding, the "cause became cognizable only in admiralty."

The two Green opinions established the broad outlines of the practice which has ever since been followed, although it required a substantial volume of work in the circuit courts before the details were filled in. The most important of the subsidiary details was the exact content of the stipulation that plaintiff had to agree to in the limitation proceeding as a condition of getting back into the state court, and, in particular, whether he had to concede the defendant's right to limit (as some district courts held) or merely defendant's right to have the limitation issue litigated in the admiralty court. The Second Circuit in 1947 decided that only the right to litigate had to be conceded and has since been followed by other courts.[83]

The procedure which has been worked out under the Green cases is as follows: a single claim plaintiff who wishes to prosecute a common law action after the shipowner has filed a petition for limitation must

a) file his claim in the limitation proceeding;

b) where a stipulation for value has been filed in lieu of the transfer of the ship to a trustee, concede the sufficiency in amount of the stipulation;

(c) consent to waive any claim of *res judicata* relevant to the issue of limited liability based on any judgment obtained in the state court;

d) concede petitioner shipowner's right to litigate all issues relating to limitation in the limitation proceeding.[84]

83. Petition of Red Star Barge Line, Inc., 160 F.2d 436, 1947 A.M.C. 524 (2d Cir. 1947), certiorari denied 331 U.S. 850, 67 S.Ct. 1741 (1947). The Red Star Barge case was followed in Great Lakes Dredge Co. v. Lynch (The James A. Dubbs), 173 F.2d 281, 1949 A.M.C. 986 (6th Cir. 1949): and In re Trawler Gudrun, Inc., 101 F. Supp. 586, 1952 A.M.C. 75 (D.Mass. 1951). In The Lavinia D. (Petition of Spearin), 190 F.2d 684, 1951 A.M.C. 1523 (2d Cir. 1951), the district court had erroneously required the claimant to concede the petitioner's right to limit. On appeal the error was held waived by the repeated statements of the claimant's proctor at trial that he was willing to have the admiralty court decide the issues.

84. See the Red Barge Line case, note 83 *supra*; Petition of Moran Transp. Corp., 185 F.2d 386, 1951 A.M.C. 66 (2d Cir. 1950), certiorari denied 340 U.S. 953, 71 S.Ct. 573 (1951); Walde Towing Co., Inc. v. Ricca, 227 F.2d 900, 1956 A.M.C. 73 (2d Cir. 1955). See the appendix to the opinion in the Eastern Cities—L. T. C. No. 38 (Petition of Lake Tankers Corp.), 232 F.2d 573, 1956 A.M.C. 1018 (2d Cir. 1956), for the forms of order and stipulation under which plaintiff was allowed to proceed in State court. This was the Second Circuit case affirmed *sub nom.* Lake Tankers Corp. v. Henn, 354 U.S. 147, 77 S.Ct. 1269, 1957 A.M.C. 1165 (1957). The reaffirmation of the doctrine of the Green cases in the Henn case (see text following note 76b *supra*) was so clear that the issue has almost entirely disappeared from litigation since the late 1950's. In Petition of Trawler Weymouth, Inc. (F/V. Weymouth), 223 F.Supp. 161, 1964 A.M.C. 448 (D.Mass.1963) Judge Wyzanski reviewed the history of the matter through Henn and held that an action seeking recovery both under the Jones Act and for maintenance and cure under the general maritime law should be allowed to proceed outside the limitation proceeding. Pennell v. Read, 309 F.2d 455, 1963 A.M.C. 2037 (5th

In what may be called the typical Langnes v. Green situation, the admiralty court dissolves or modifies its § 185 injunction to allow the civil action to proceed, meanwhile holding the limitation proceeding in abeyance until the result of the civil action is known. If, in that action, judgment is for the shipowner or is for the plaintiff in an amount less than the limitation fund, then the shipowner's right to limitation will never have to be decided. It is, however, possible for the admiralty court to reverse the customary sequence and decide the limitation issues first.

That procedure was followed in a case which came to the Fifth Circuit as Petition of Double D Dredging Company, Inc.[84a] Norton's administratrix brought a death action under the Jones Act. The shipowner petitioned for limitation, conceding in its petition that Norton had been a Jones Act seaman and that his death had occurred in navigable waters. The District Court decided to pass on the limitation issue first (without a jury), "consolidated" the Jones Act action and the limitation proceeding, and denied limitation. The Jones Act action then proceeded with a jury (apparently before the same District Judge) and there was a verdict for the defendant shipowner. In the jury action the shipowner was allowed to argue that Norton was not a Jones Act seaman and that his death had not occurred on navigable waters. On appeal the Fifth Circuit reversed, in an opinion by Judge Brown, on the ground that the shipowner was estopped from contesting in the jury action what he had already conceded in his limitation petition. Judge Brown suggested, somewhat obscurely, that a distinction could be drawn between the "navigable waters" concession, looked on as going to the jurisdiction of the admiralty court in the limitation proceeding, and the "Jones Act seaman" concession, not looked on as "jurisdictional" for that purpose. He added that the "navigability" issue appeared to have been "pivotal" in the jury's deliberations, so that the "concession" on that issue alone was

Cir. 1962) involved an odd switch on the usual situation: The single claimant had been injured in a Miami-Nassau yacht race. The two owners of the yacht, one a resident of Massachusetts, the other a resident of Florida, petitioned for limitation. The claimant moved to be allowed to bring separate action against each owner in Massachusetts and in Florida. The Fifth Circuit, affirming the District Court, analogized the case to the multiple claims—inadequate fund situation and held that the motion was properly denied. The claimant had offered to stipulate that, in the event of limitation being granted, each of the co-owners should be liable only in the amount of 50% of the limitation fund. The Pennell case seems inconsistent with the usual case-law interpretation of Largnes v. Green and Ex parte Green.

In Terracciano v. McAlinden Construction Co., 485 F.2d 304, 1973 A.M.C. 2111 (2d Cir. 1973) it appeared that the District Court, without objection from the defendant's counsel, had allowed the jury (in a Jones Act and unseaworthiness action) to decide whether the defendant was entitled to limitation of liability. The jury found that the defendant was liable, assessed the plaintiff's damages at $50,000 but entered a verdict for $5,000 on the theory that the defendant was entitled to limitation. The Second Circuit reversed for a variety of reasons. Judge Jameson's opinion did not say flatly that a jury can never decide the limitation issue but seemed to express surprise at the procedure.

**84a.** (Norton's case), 467 F.2d 468, 1972 A.M.C. 2377 (5th Cir. 1972).

enough to raise the estoppel. He also remarked that the District Judge, in the limitation hearing, had come "dangerously close to ruling that the shipowner was guilty of negligence and the vessel was unseaworthy, which, if intended as a finding, would have been *res judicata* or collateral estoppel in the jury case."

The Fifth Circuit's estoppel holding in Norton's case and, even more, Judge Brown's dictum about the possibility of the judge's finding in the limitation hearing being *res judicata* in the jury trial are of extraordinary interest. Both holding and dictum appear to be matters of first impression.[84b] In Norton's case the Jones Act action and the limitation proceeding had been "consolidated" and were apparently heard, successively, by the same judge. Would the same result follow if there had been no "consolidation" and if the jury trial had been held before a different judge or in a different court (state or federal)? If the District Judge, having "consolidated" the proceedings, had held the jury trial first, would the shipowner still have been "estopped" by the "concessions" in his limitation petition? Would he be estopped if the jury trial came first but in a different court? If the limitation hearing is held first, does the dictum mean that all "findings" are *res judicata* in the jury trial even if they are adverse to the plaintiff in the death action? Would not the plaintiff then be deprived of his constitutional right to a jury trial? Or does the dictum mean that findings in the limitation hearing are *res judicata* in the jury trial if they are in the plaintiff's favor but not if they are adverse to him?

The present discussion is being written so soon after the decision in Norton's case was reported that it is impossible to make even a guess as to whether the case will die unhonored and unsung or whether its apparently revolutionary implications will lead to an honorable and successful career in Shepard's Citation. Judge Brown's preeminence as an admiralty judge would seem to insure that the case will be at least pondered by the admiralty bar as well as by the membership of NACCA. It may be that shipowners' counsel, by giving thought to the matter, can prevent the Norton situation from arising again. There appears to be nothing in the relevant Rules [F (1) and F(2)] which made it necessary for the shipowner to "concede" in his limitation complaint (or petition) that Norton was a Jones Act seaman. If that is so, then that aspect of the case can be handled as a matter of proper drafting. The "navigability" point, as Judge Brown suggested, is somewhat trickier. Rule F(2) requires that the limitation complaint "state the voyage, if any, on which the demands sought to be limited arose . . ." If the vessel was indeed on a "voyage" at the time of the accident, it seems to follow that

**84b.** Judge Brown noted at the outset of his opinion that "The facts in this [Norton's] case in some respects parallel those of Davis v. Parkhill-Goodloe Co., 5th Cir., 1962, 302 F.2d 489, 1962 A.M.C. 1720." His reference was evidently to the facts and not to the legal issues involved in the 1962 case. Davis was a Jones Act case which did not in any way involve the Limitation Act.

it must also have been on "navigable waters," with the result that the "navigability concession" is inevitable.[84c] (The phrase "if any" in Rule F[2] presumably refers to cases when the vessel is in port, tied up at a wharf or, conceivably, in dry-dock.) If Judge Brown's dictum means that findings in a limitation hearing (at least if they are favorable to the plaintiff in the death or injury action) become *res judicata* in the jury trial, then counsel for petitioning shipowners may be well advised to give thought, in appropriate cases, to urging that the jury trial be held first. (Of course, if there was an unfavorable jury verdict on, say, unseaworthiness, the *res judicata* argument would run the other way, as no doubt it should.[84d])

Norton's case, to say the least, suggests possibilities of future development in an area where, it had seemed, the range of litigated issues had long since been settled.

**§ 10–19a.** In re Central Railroad of New Jersey [84e] raised, apparently for the first time, complicated questions about the interrelationship of the Limitation Act and the Bankruptcy Act in connection with the distribution of a limitation fund. In 1966 the Santa Isabel, owned by the Grace Line, had damaged a railroad drawbridge over the Raritan River in New Jersey. The New York and Long Branch Railroad (Long Branch), which owned the bridge, was itself owned in equal shares by the Central Railroad of New Jersey (Central) and the Pennsylvania Railroad Company, which later became the Penn-Central (PRR). Central and PRR operated the Long Branch under a long-term lease. Pending the determination of the Grace Line's liability, it was necessary for the railroads to advance funds for the repair of the drawbridge. Since Central's "cash position" made it impossible for it to put up its share, PRR advanced the entire amount (approximately $750,000.) under an agreement between the two railroads that PRR would be reimbursed both for its own advance and for its advance on behalf of Central out of whatever recovery might be obtained against the Grace Line. In 1966 Grace petitioned for limitation in the Southern District of New York. Central and PRR (with Long Branch joined as a nominal claimant) filed claims in the limitation proceeding. In 1967 Central petitioned for reorganization under § 77 of the Bankruptcy Act in the District of New Jersey. In 1968 the railroads and Grace, through their counsel, arrived at a settlement of the claims in the limitation proceeding which provided, inter alia, for the reimbursement to PRR of the advance for repairs which it had made both on its own behalf and on Central's. In January of 1969 Central's trustee applied to the New Jersey Reorganization Court for permission to join in the limitation

**84c.** On the extent to which plaintiffs in actions under the Jones Act and for unseaworthiness must (absent the "concession") prove that the accident occurred on navigable waters, see Chapter VI, §§ 6–21, 6–42.

**84d.** On the effect of a finding of "unseaworthiness" on the shipowner's right to limitation, see § 10–20 *et seq. infra.*

**84e.** 469 F.2d 857, 1973 A.M.C. 222 (3d Cir. 1972), certiorari denied 411 U.S. 938, 93 S.Ct. 1900 (1973).

settlement. In March of 1969 the Reorganization Court, in an "Interim Order" authorized the trustee to proceed. In September of 1969 the New York Limitation Court approved the settlement "subject to the further order of this Court regarding distribution [of the fund]." In August of 1970, no further order of the Limitation Court with respect to the distribution of the fund having been entered, the Reorganization Court, in a Memorandum opinion, ordered that the money advanced by PRR on behalf of Central should be paid (out of the limitation settlement) to Central's trustee and not to PRR (which by this time was in a § 77 reorganization itself as the Penn-Central). The New Jersey Reorganization Court thus undertook to direct distribution of the fund in the custody of the New York Limitation Court. We need not, at this point in the discussion, comment on the theory which led the Reorganization Court to its conclusion that the money advanced by PRR on Central's behalf should go to Central's trustee instead of (as things turned out) to Penn-Central's trustees.

The Penn-Central trustees naturally appealed from the order which the Reorganization Court entered in accordance with its Memorandum opinion. A panel of the Third Circuit in an opinion by Judge Kalodner held that the Reorganization Court had been without jurisdiction to order distribution of the fund which was looked on as being within the exclusive jurisdiction of the Admiralty (or Limitation) Court. Judge Adams dissented on the jurisdictional point.

Judge Kalodner's majority opinion relied principally on the traditional line of cases which have emphasized the comprehensive powers of an admiralty court with which a petition for limitation is filed.[84f] The Central case, he concluded, fell within the category of the "multiple claims—inadequate-fund" limitation cases. Consequently, "the Admiralty Court has exclusive jurisdiction . . . with respect to the distribution of [the limitation fund] now in its Registry and . . . the Reorganization Court was . . . without jurisdiction to adjudicate rights of claimants to the *res* . . . ." Judge Adams, dissenting, viewed the case as presenting the "dilemma" of "two congressional mandates [the Limitation Act and the Bankruptcy Act] in apparent conflict." However, he concluded, a "symbiosis" was possible. The "exclusive jurisdiction" of the admiralty court in limitation proceedings where there are multiple claims to an inadequate fund was designed to protect the shipowner. The Central case, he correctly pointed out, involved not multiple claims but a single claim put forward by several claimants. In any case the Admiralty Court had indeed passed on the Grace Line's liability, so that Grace had received the protection of the jurisdiction. Adjudication of the conflicting claims of the trustees of the two railroads to the proceeds of the limitation settlement had nothing whatever to do with the purpose of the limitation proceeding. In the ordinary course of events the

**84f.** In particular Providence & New York S.S. Co. v. Hill Manufacturing Co., 109 U.S. 578, 3 S.Ct. 379, 617 (1883) (see § 10–2 *supra*, note 8) and Hartford Accident & Indemnity Co. v. Southern Pacific Co., 273 U.S. 207, 47 S.Ct. 357, 1927 A.M.C. 402 (1927) (see § 10–41 *infra*).

limitation court distributes the fund among claimants.[84g] But where, as in the Central case, the proper distribution of the fund depends on the resolution of a dispute between a claimant in reorganization (or bankruptcy) proceedings and one of his creditors, the reorganization (or bankruptcy) court is in a much better position than the admiralty court to resolve the dispute.

It is in the highest degree unlikely that the peculiar facts of the Central case will ever be duplicated. On the other hand the case illustrates a situation which can come up whenever a property damage claimant in a limitation proceeding is in reorganization or bankruptcy proceedings at the time when a limitation fund is to be distributed. The Central case is, therefore, far from being a freakish occurrence.

Proper distribution of the fund between the Central and PRR depended on the resolution of some notably obscure questions of bankruptcy and personal property security law which, since they are not germane to a discussion of admiralty law, may be relegated to a footnote.[84h] The Federal judges assigned to the Southern District of New York are, of course, quite as knowledgeable about obscure questions of bankruptcy and personal property security law as are the Federal judges assigned to the District of New Jersey. However, the New Jersey District Court which had been conducting the Central reorganization was already in command of the facts relating to the Central's transactions with PRR and its other creditors, secured and unsecured. At the very least it will be an enormous waste of judicial time and effort (to say nothing about the multiplication of counsel fees) if the New York admiralty court, before distributing the limitation fund, has to learn all about the no doubt intricate ramifications of the Central reorganization. Judge Adams' dissent seems infinitely preferable to Judge Kalodner's majority opinion, both as a matter of law and as a matter of policy. If future cases of this sort come up, it is to be hoped that the limitation court will find some plausible way of getting the reorganization court to decide the questions of distribution which have nothing to do with the limitation proceeding itself.

**84g.** On distribution of the fund, see § 10–39 *et seq. infra.*

**84h.** Briefly: if Central's claim against Grace for damage to the drawbridge was an asset of Central's (as it apparently was) and if PRR's advance of Central's part of the repair costs was in effect a loan to Central (as it seems to have been) and if PRR did not take security for its loan and perfect its security interest (apparently it did neither), then the District Court before which the Central reorganization proceeding was pending was (in all probability) correct in concluding that the PRR claim was invalid against Central's trustee and that the money should be paid to the trustee. All three members of the Third Circuit panel (including Judge Adams) agreed that the District Court was (in all probability) wrong. So far as the facts can be disentangled from the narrative in the reported case, the position will be maintained here that the learned Circuit Judges were wrong and that the learned District Judge was right. Adequate discussion of the points of bankruptcy and personal property security law which were involved in the Central case would require a separate chapter. They will not be further pursued here.

### The Conditions of Limitation: "Privity or Knowledge"

**§ 10–20.** The shipowner's right to limit his liability is made, by the key phrase of Section 183, to depend on his "privity or knowledge" of the cause of the loss. Only if he is without privity or knowledge may he limit; if he is chargeable with privity or knowledge, his personal liability remains unaffected. By a similar phrase in Section 182 (the "fire statute") the owner is exonerated from liability to cargo for fire damage unless the fire is caused by the owner's "design or neglect".

"Privity or knowledge" and "design or neglect" are phrases devoid of meaning. They are empty containers into which the courts are free to pour whatever content they will. The statutes might quite as well say that the owner is entitled to exoneration from liability or to limitation of liability if, on all the equities of the case, the court feels that that result is desirable; otherwise not. Since, in the infinite range of factual situations no two cases will ever precisely duplicate each other, no judge with the slightest flair for the lawyer's craft of distinguishing cases need ever be bound by precedent: "privity like knowledge," the Supreme Court has remarked, "turns on the facts of particular cases." [85]

Judicial attitudes shape the meaning of such catch-word phrases for successive generations. In the heyday of the Limitation Act it seemed as hard to pin "privity or knowledge" on the petitioning shipowner as it is thought to be for the camel to pass through the needle's eye. To the extent that in our own or a subsequent generation the philosophy of the Limitation Act is found less appealing, that attitude will be implemented by a relaxed attitude toward what constitutes "privity or knowledge," "design or neglect." The Act, like an accordion, can be stretched out or narrowed at will.

The principle of the Limitation Act is the same as that found in the Harter Act and the Carriage of Goods by Sea Act: because of the extraordinary hazards of seaborne commerce and because the owner can exercise only a nominal control over his "servants" once the ship has broken ground for the voyage, the owner should be entitled to exoneration from liability, or at least to a limitation of liability, for whatever happens after the ship has passed beyond his effective control. Contrariwise, he should be held to liability for all loss resulting from his failure to exercise effective control when he had the chance. Although the Limitation Act uses a vocabulary different from that of Harter and Cogsa, the concept of liability is the same: the shipowner is not chargeable with "privity or knowledge" or with "design or neglect" when he has used "due diligence" to furnish a seaworthy ship; he is so chargeable when he has failed in his duty of "due dili-

85. Coryell v. Phipps (The Seminole), 317 U.S. 406, 411, 63 S.Ct. 291, 293, 1943 A.M.C. 18, 22 (1943).

gence" and has sent out a ship unseaworthy in some respect that proximately contributes to the loss.[85a] The foregoing comment is not meant to suggest that courts customarily cross-cite Limitation Act cases and Harter Act or Cogsa cases. There is indeed authority for the proposition that the Limitation Act imposes on the shipowner a lower standard of care than do the Harter Act and Cogsa; that is, failure to have exercised "due diligence" under Harter or Cogsa does not automatically deprive the shipowner of his defense under the Fire Statute or the Limitation Act.[86] No recent cases, however, have restated the doctrine of the lower Limitation Act standard, at least so far as the Fire Statute is concerned.[87] Whether the right to limitation of liability (as distinguished from exoneration from liability) is automatically lost when the right to exoneration under Harter or Cogsa is lost has been a matter of considerable discussion in recent litigation which will be presently reviewed.[87a] If the older cases are in time overruled or forgotten, in line with the discernible judicial trend to narrow the Limitation Act by construction, the situation would then be that, if the carrier is liable to cargo under Harter or Cogsa, it would also lose its privilege under the Limitation Act. As to cargo liability, then, the Limitation Act would be in effect superseded by

**85a.** See further the discussion in § 10–24 *infra* with respect to ships held in corporate ownership.

**86.** In Earle & Stoddart v. Ellerman's Wilson Line, 287 U.S. 420, 53 S.Ct. 200, 1933 A.M.C. 1 (1932), Justice Brandeis pointed out that the Harter Act's non-delegable duty of due diligence did not apply under the Fire Statute: "The courts have been careful not to thwart the purpose of the fire statute by interpreting as 'neglect' of the owners the breach of what in other connections is held to be a non-delegable duty". El Sol and The Sac City (Southern Pac. Co. v. United States), 72 F.2d 212, 215, 1934 A.M.C. 1185, 1189 (2d Cir. 1934): "Personal diligence is not a condition upon limitation, as it is upon immunity under the Harter Act".

**87.** The question of the relation between the Fire Statute's "design or neglect" and Cogsa's "actual fault or privity" was presented in Accinanto, Ltd. v. Cosmopolitan Shipping Co. (The Ocean Liberty), 99 F.Supp. 261, 1951 A.M.C. 1464 (D.Md.1951), reversed in part 199 F.2d 134, 1952 A.M.C. 1681 (4th Cir. 1952) certiorari denied 345 U.S. 992, 73 S.Ct. 1129 (1953). The District Court had said: ". . . 'actual fault or privity' contained in Cogsa is to be construed as substantially equivalent to 'design or neglect' in the fire statute". In reversing, the Fourth Circuit agreed to the identity of the two statutes: "We do not think that the carrier can be held liable on the theory that stowage of cargo was a non-delegable duty, negligence in performance of which should be imputed to the carrier in determining whether it had exercised due care to make the vessel seaworthy. Directly in point is the case of Earle & Stoddart v. Ellerman Wilson Line, *supra*, 287 U.S. 420, 53 S.Ct. 200, 1933 A.M.C. 1, in which a vessel was held to be exempted from liability by reason of the fire statute, although she was rendered unseaworthy before leaving port as the result of the negligent stowage of coal in her bunkers by her chief engineer. The exemption of the fire statute is admittedly the same as that provided by the Carriage of Goods by Sea Act . . .

"The purpose of the fire exemption in the Carriage of Goods by Sea Act is the same as the purpose of the fire statute . . ."

In Asbestos Corp. Ltd. v. Compagnie de Navigation Fraissinet, 345 F.Supp. 814, 1972 A.M.C. 2581 (S.D.N.Y.1972) affirmed 480 F.2d 669, 1973 A.M.C. 1683 (2d Cir. 1973). Judge Levit commented: "'Actual fault or privity' under COGSA and 'design or neglect' under the Fire statute have the same meaning." Exoneration was denied.

**87a.** See § 10–24 *infra*.

Harter and Cogsa, and would continue to be of importance only with respect to collision, loss of life and personal injury claims.

**§ 10–21.** The Fire Statute conditions the shipowner's exoneration on the absence of his "design or neglect"; the Limitation Act on the absence of his "privity or knowledge." Are the two phrases equivalents or does the Fire Statute set one standard and the Limitation Act a different and presumably lower one? The older case law suggested that different standards were involved, and that a shipowner who was not, because of neglect, entitled to exoneration for fire loss might nevertheless, on a holding of no privity, successfully urge his privilege of limitation.[88] The more recent cases, on the other hand, take "design or neglect" and "privity or knowledge" as synonyms, so that if the right to exoneration under the Fire Statute is lost the right to limitation automatically vanishes.[89] In the balance of our discussion the equivalence of the two sets of catchwords will be assumed and what is said of "privity or knowledge" with respect to limitation may be taken to apply equally to "design or neglect" with respect to exoneration for fire loss.

**§ 10–22.** The "privity or knowledge" must be that of the owner himself. He is not ordinarily held responsible for the negligence of his servants or employees; the theory of the Limitation Act and the doctrine of *respondeat superior* are at opposite poles. Two qualifications must immediately be attached to the proposition just stated. The first is that the principle of the shipowner's irresponsibility has been much more successfully maintained with respect to his seagoing

88. Providence & New York S.S. Co. v. Hill Mfg. Co., 109 U.S. 578, 602 3 S.Ct. 379, 395 (1883): ". . . there is no inconsistency or repugnancy in allowing a partial exemption in cases falling within the 3d section; that is, cases of loss by fire happening without the privity or knowledge of the owners. They may not be able under the 1st section, to show that it happened without any neglect on their part, or what a jury may hold to be neglect; whilst, they may be very confident of showing, under the 3d section, that it happened without their privity or knowledge. The conditions of proof, in order to avoid a total or partial liability under the respective sections, are very different." La Bourgogne, 210 U.S. 95, 103, 28 S.Ct. 664, 665 (1908); Hines v. Butler, 278 F. 877 (4th Cir. 1921); Hockley v. Eastern Transp. Co., 10 F.Supp. 908 (D.Md.1935).

89. The Doris Kellogg, 18 F.Supp. 159, 169 (S.D.N.Y.1937) affirmed per curiam 94 F.2d 1015, 1938 A.M.C. 158 (2d Cir. 1938); Great Atlantic & Pac. Tea Co. v. Lloyd Brasileiro, 159 F.2d 661, 664, 1947 A.M.C. 306, 311 (2d Cir. 1947) certiorari denied 331 U.S. 836, 67 S.Ct. 1519 (1947); The Edmund Fanning (Petition of United States), 105 F.Supp. 353, 371, 1952 A.M.C. 1147, 1168 (S.D.N.Y.1952) affirmed as to Fire Statute and the Limitation Act (but liability held limited under Cogsa), 201 F.2d 281, 1953 A.M.C. 86 (2d Cir. 1953). Thede, *supra* note 13c, 45 Tulane L.Rev. 959, 982 (1971), after referring to the proposition stated in the text, comments: "It is difficult to find a positive statement by any court to this effect, but it is certainly the 'flavor' of modern cases" (citing the cases referred to in this Note). The contention that the two catchphrases carry different meanings does not seem to have been made in any reported case since the 1950's. In Complaint of Caldas (The M/S Caldas), 350 F.Supp. 566, 1973 A.M.C. 1243 (E.D.Pa.1972), Judge Huyett, citing the treatise, remarked: "We shall treat the requirements of 'design or neglect' and 'privity or knowledge' as being essentially identical." For the holding in the case, see note 105t *infra*.

employees than with respect to his shoreside organization. Just as the Harter Act and Cogsa exempt the carrier from liability to cargo caused by faulty navigation or "management" of the ship, so has the Limitation Act been construed to protect the shipowner against claims deriving from the actual operation of the ship at sea. The "privity or knowledge" of the crew, officers or master is not imputed to the owner—with the exception that the 1935 loss of life amendments provide that the "privity or knowledge of the master . . . shall be deemed conclusively the privity or knowledge of the owner of the vessel." The second qualification lies in the difference between individual and corporate ownership; in the case of the corporate owner, which can act only through agents of the corporation, it is obvious that there must come a point in the corporate hierarchy where the knowledge of some officer becomes the knowledge of the corporation.

**§ 10–23.** Two cases decided during the 1940's which both involved private pleasure yachts indicate the traditional view of the extent of protection which the individual owner can hope to receive under the Limitation Act. In The Seminole (Coryell v. Phipps) the Supreme Court held the owner of the Seminole entitled to limitation.[90] A leak in the machinery or equipment of the Seminole allowed gasoline fumes to collect in the engine room. As a result a fire broke out which damaged or destroyed other vessels lying in the harbor. The fire occurred on June 24, 1935. It appeared that the Seminole had been examined and pronounced fit by an experienced ship surveyor in February, 1935; that in April, following a cruise, she had been left in proper condition; that "she was repeatedly examined by competent men between April 15 and June 24, 1935, who discovered nothing wrong with her." The court drew a distinction between cases involving individual owners and those involving corporate owners. In cases involving corporate owners, wrote Justice Douglas,

> ". . . liability may not be limited under the statute where the negligence is that of an executive officer, manager or superintendent whose scope of authority includes supervision over the phase of the business out of which the loss or injury occurred. . . . In the case of individual owners it has been commonly held or declared that privity as used in the statute means some personal participation of the owner in the fault or negligence which caused or contributed to the injury. . . . Some cases, however, have barred the individual owner from the benefits of the statute even though the element of personal participation in the fault or negligence was not present. Thus it has been thought that the scope of authority delegated by an individual owner to a subordinate may be so broad as to justify imputing privity

90. 317 U.S. 406, 63 S.Ct. 291, 1943 A.M.C. 18 (1943). The Seminole was in fact (or in law) owned by a corporation which had been set up by Phipps, who owned half the stock (the other half being owned by his sister). The case was decided, however, on the ground that "even if the corporation be disregarded, Phipps was without 'privity or knowledge' . . ."

> . . . as well as knowledge. . . . [E]ven were we to assume without deciding that for the purposes of sec. 4283 [*i. e.* § 183] privity as well as knowledge of an individual owner may be constructive rather than actual, it does not follow that Phipps should be barred from limiting his liability. One who selects competent men to store and inspect a vessel and who is not on notice as to the existence of any defect in it cannot be denied the benefit of the limitation as respects a loss incurred by an explosion during the period of storage, unless 'privity' or 'knowledge' are to become empty words." [91]

In The Trillora II,[92] a yacht owned by Guggenheim, which was being recommissioned after having been laid up during World War II, exploded, causing extensive property damage as well as loss of life. Guggenheim had turned over to Rothschild full authority to do whatever was right, proper, or necessary in connection with the upkeep, maintenance and operation of the yacht. The actual work of recommissioning was entrusted to a Captain Gott, who held an unlimited master's license for steam and motor vessels. The evidence strongly suggested that the cause of the explosion was negligence on the part of Gott. Guggenheim was held entitled to limit on the theory that he was not responsible for Gott's negligence and on findings that neither Guggenheim nor Rothschild was chargeable with privity or knowledge. After reviewing the cases Judge Waring, however, underscored by dictum the Supreme Court's statement in Coryell v. Phipps that "the scope of authority delegated by an individual owner to a subordinate may be so broad as to justify imputing privity . . . as well as knowledge . . .". "It is clear," wrote Judge Waring, discussing the authority delegated to Rothschild, "that if Rothschild had privity or knowledge of defects, such knowledge would be imputed to Guggenheim."

The individual owner will not, then, be chargeable with the privity or knowledge of his employees unless he has handed over to them plenary power with respect to the operation of the ship, and will not in any case be responsible for the acts of the master or crew even

91. *Id.* at 410–412, 63 S.Ct. at 293–294, 1943 A.M.C. at 21–23. Justice Douglas cited the following cases as illustrative of the proposition that "the scope of authority delegated by an individual owner may be so broad as to justify imputing privity . . . as well as knowledge." In re New York Dock Co. (Converse & Co.), 61 F.2d 777, 1932 A.M.C. 1492 (2d Cir. 1932): an individual contractor who chartered a floating pile driver and entrusted its inspection, rigging and operation to his general superintendent, had delegated such broad authority that the superintendent's privity or knowledge was in law that of the contractor. In re Great Lakes Transit Corp. (The Glenbogie), 81 F.2d 441, 1936 A.M.C. 267 (6th Cir. 1936): failure to drain a seacock in laying up a barge for the winter on the Great Lakes and failure to repair a leaking cargo port showed absence of due diligence on the part of the superintendent of the individual owner. "The statute does not require that knowledge be actual; it may be imputed if some one in charge for the owner had general authority to act for him and by the exercise of ordinary care could have discovered the fault".

92. (Petition of Guggenheim), 76 F. Supp. 50, 1948 A.M.C. 132 (E.D.S.C. 1947).

when the ship is in port and thus theoretically subject to control. Most of the recent individual ownership cases involve pleasure yachts and owners who are amateur yachtsmen.[92a] The Limitation Act, originally passed to afford a measure of relief to a hard-pressed and highly competitive industry, has become a charter of irresponsibility for a few wealthy individuals. The individual owner of, say, a small fishing vessel which explodes in port may well find himself liable to respond in damages under circumstances where the absentee yacht-owner will go free. No theory can justify the results reached in Coryell v. Phipps or The Trillora, under which the owner of yacht or speedboat, who is provident enough to hire someone else to run the boat for him, is granted a general license to kill and destroy.[93]

The Limitation Act covers any sort of "vessel" from a rowboat up and restriction of its coverage to commercial enterprises could be achieved only by amendment. Nevertheless the very vagueness of the "privity or knowledge" phrase leaves a wide area for judicial construction; a more liberal construction of the phrase in the individual ownership cases than the precedents suggest would be desirable.

92a. Maslin v. M/S Heering Lotte, 1972 A.M.C. 2203 (D.Md.1972) is one of the few recent individual ownership cases which did not involve a private pleasure boat. The owner of a Chesapeake Bay pilot launch was granted limitation with respect to the death of a pilot which, it was found, had been caused by the negligent navigation of the launch which was under the command of an experienced master.

93. See The Spare Time II (Petition of Hutchinson), 36 F.Supp. 642, 1941 A.M.C. 417 (E.D.N.Y.1941); The Trim Too (Petition of Ferguson), 39 F.Supp. 271, 1941 A.M.C. 1147 (D.Mass.1941); The Yacht Charlotte, 124 F.Supp. 73, 1955 A.M.C. 1290 (D.Conn.1954).

The owner who operates his own pleasure craft is of course not entitled to petition for limitation. Petition of Davis, 1950 A.M.C. 1028 (N.D.Cal. 1950): "The undenied exceptive allegations in support of claimants' exceptions to the petition for limitation . . . as well as the testimony under oath of the petitioner . . . that he was in control of and operating his pleasure motorboat at the time of the occurrence of the events upon which claimants' claims are based stamp the petition as sham. It should never have been filed. To derogate the historical and traditional purposes of the limitation statute to the end sought by the petitioner is shocking to the sense of justice. The restraining order heretofore ill-advisedly issued is vacated and dissolved" and the petition dismissed, affirmed *sub nom.* Davis v. United States, 185 F.2d 938, 1951 A.M.C. 93 (9th Cir. 1950), certiorari denied 340 U.S. 932, 71 S.Ct. 495 (1951). Accord: King, Adm'r v. Liotti, 190 Misc. 652, 76 N.Y.S.2d 98, 1948 A.M.C. 476 (N.Y. Sup.Ct.1947). The same rationale has been applied when the owner's wife ran the boat: Schoremeyer v. Barnes, 190 F.2d 14, 1951 A.M.C. 1527 (5th Cir. 1951). If the owner is on board when the accident occurs he will lose his right to limit even though he has taken more than usually elaborate steps to insulate himself from liability. Thus in Petition of H. & H. Wheel Service, Inc., 219 F.2d 904, 1955 A.M.C. 1017 (6th Cir. 1955), a forty-seven foot motor cruiser was owned by a corporation, whose president, manager and almost exclusive stockholder was one Hiles. The boat was used for Hiles' personal pleasure and for entertaining business customers. The cruiser, Hiles being aboard, ran down a small outboard motor boat, killing two men and severely injuring a third; it was found that the cruiser was being operated in a grossly negligent manner. The corporate owner petitioned for limitation of liability which was denied on the ground that "Hiles, its president, agent and representative was privy to and had knowledge of all happenings aboard the Fourth Marie that night." (*Id.* at 912, 1955 A.M.C. at 1027.) See further the cases cited in note 93f *infra.*

Since the foregoing discussion was written in the 1950's, the anomaly of the availability of the defense of the Limitation Act to the owners of pleasure craft has continued to gnaw at the consciences of the District Judges who are required to rule on such petitions. In Petition of Porter (The Yacht Julaine) [93a] Judge Seals collected in his opinion the considerable literature, judicial and academic, which, since the 1950's has deplored this perversion of the original purpose of the Limitation Act. After quoting from the preceding paragraph of the treatise, he added that:

> "Recent law review articles . . . have pointed out that as small boat sales and traffic increase, so will the number of accidents and potential situations in which claimants may find themselves with pitifully inadequate recompense for serious injuries or death. It is urged that the result of this situation is to allow liability insurance companies to become the true beneficiaries by limiting their liability to the value of the vessel." [93b]

However, Judge Seals concluded, he was bound by the precedents and, given "the silence of the Supreme Court and the Court of Appeals for the Fifth Circuit on this issue," could do nothing to set things right. He invited the claimant to take an interlocutory appeal from his decision, but the Fifth Circuit denied the appeal [93c] and no further proceedings were reported in the case.

So the matter stands.[93d] It seems as unlikely that the Supreme Court will ever consent to reconsider the applicability of the Limitation Act to pleasure boats as it is that Congress will act to exclude them from the Act.

The immunity for pleasure boat owners is not, of course, absolute. Much pleasure boating takes place on technically non-navigable waters, beyond the jurisdiction of the admiralty and the reach of the Limitation Act.[93e] And owners careless enough to operate (or be on board) their own boats when an accident occurs need not hope for much sympathy.[93f] Finally, as has already been suggested, "privity

**93a.** 272 F.Supp. 282, 1968 A.M.C. 2310 (S.D.Tex.1967).

**93b.** 272 F.Supp. at p. 285, 1968 A.M.C. at p. 2314. Judge Seals cited law review articles by Harolde, 37 Temple L.Q. 423 (1964), Stolz, 51 Calif.L.Rev. 661 (1963) and a Comment, 19 Villanova L.Rev. 721 (1965).

**93c.** See the report of the case in 1968 A.M.C. 2310.

**93d.** See also, holding a pleasure boat owner entitled to limitation, Petition of Klarman (The Sloop Fling), 295 F. Supp. 1021, 1969 A.M.C. 1446 (D.Conn. 1968).

**93e.** See the cases cited in note 37a *supra*, particularly Petition of Madsen, 187 F.Supp. 411, 1963 A.M.C. 488 (N.D.N.Y.1960).

**93f.** In addition to the cases cited in note 93 *supra*, see Fecht & McAllister v. Makoski, 406 F.2d 721, 1969 A.M.C. 144 (5th Cir. 1969); Nuccio v. Royal Indemnity Co., 415 F.2d 228, 1969 A.M.C. 1825 (5th Cir. 1959) (both opinions collect other citations). The owner's presence is not necessarily fatal to his right to limit if the evidence suggests that his conduct was in all respects prudent, see Petition of Reading (The Crow's Nest II A), 169 F.Supp. 165, 1959 A.M.C. 1753 (N.D.N.Y.1958), affirmed per curiam on the opinion below 271 F.2d 959, 1960 A.M.C. 214 (2d Cir. 1959).

or knowledge" is an essentially manipulable phrase. For example, in the typical situation in which a pleasure boat is owned by a parent and operated by teenage children, it would not seem far-fetched to hold that parents of adolescent children are chargeable with knowledge of the unhappy fact (testified to by automobile insurance rates) that adolescents tend to operate motor vehicles, whether on land or on water, recklessly and to the public danger.[93g]

§ **10–24.** When is a corporate shipowner chargeable with the "privity or knowledge" which will defeat his right to a limitation of liability? Most discussions of the problem, including the discussion in the first edition of the treatise, seem to have foundered in a bottomless bog of semantic confusion. During the 1950's and 1960's the hazards of litigation brought up a number of notable "corporate privity or knowledge" cases, none of which went beyond the level of the Circuit Courts of Appeal. Despite the absence of a unifying or synthesizing opinion by the Supreme Court, which has steadfastly denied certiorari in such cases, it is believed that recent judicial analysis reveals a general consensus in the light of which, it may be hoped, the confusion which has long plagued discussion will presently come to an end. Parts of our earlier discussion seem to have played a part in stimulating the ultimately clarifying judicial analysis. For that reason we cannot entirely ignore what was said in the first edition even though the approach there taken now appears to have been unduly and unnecessarily complex.

A preliminary discussion of the reasons for the prevalent semantic confusion may be in order. When Congress drafted and passed the Limitation Act of 1851, the corporation was still a relatively novel, little understood form of business organization whose explosive potentialities were far from having been understood. The phraseology of the Act suggests that the draftsmen were thinking of shipowners who were individuals, not corporations—an assumption which, at the time, may well have been justified. The Act itself, although it was based on a principle well-known to the traditional maritime law,[94] may be looked on, as of its own time, as an attempt to give individual shipowners the benefits of limited liability without requiring them to go through the ritual of incorporation. In time, of course, the shipowner, like the owners of all other large enterprises, incorporated. Indeed, since the shipowner soon learned to incorporate ship by ship, he may be said to have outstripped his railroad colleagues who never seem to have thought of the idea of incorporating each engine and freight-car separately.

As an initial matter it could perfectly well have been held that the Limitation Act applied only to individually owned ships and that shipowners who sought the benefit of limited liability through incorporation would be left to the developing law of corporations and held liable for the acts, torts and crimes of their agents, employees

**93g.** See Application of Theisen, 349 F. Supp. 737, 1973 A.M.C. 730 (E.D.N.Y. 1972).

**94.** See § 10–1 *supra*.

and servants in exactly the same way that, say, railroads were. Such an idea may well have lurked behind one of the early landmark cases in the development of limitation law, Providence & New York Steamship Company v. Hill Manufacturing Company.[95] The shipowner, a corporation, instituted limitation proceedings in the Southern District of New York, which enjoined proceedings in all other courts. Despite the injunction Hill, a cargo-owner, brought suit in Massachusetts state court. The Massachusetts court treated the injunction as a "nullity" and, in successive opinions,[96] dealt with the Steamship Company's liability as an ordinary problem of corporate responsibility which had no special maritime flavor.[97] Hill had a jury verdict and judgment, apparently for the full amount of his loss. On appeal the Supreme Court, in an opinion by Justice Bradley, over a dissent by Justice Field (in which Justice Gray joined), reversed on the ground that the Massachusetts court was bound by the Limitation Court's injunction and had been without jurisdiction to hear the case. The Hill case may be taken as having established, almost by inadvertence, the propositions that corporate, as well as individual, shipowners were entitled to the protection of the Limitation Act and that the corporate shipowner's liability, like that of the individual shipowner, depended on "his" "privity or knowledge" under the Limitation Act case law, not on developing standards of corporate responsibility under the general law of corporations.

The individualistic or subjective phraseology of the Limitation Act unquestionably had an influence on the development of the "privity or knowledge" case law, which, from the time of the Hill case on, was worked out almost exclusively in the context of ships held in corporate ownership. As a matter of usage, the petitioner was always referred to as "the shipowner," never as "the corporation." The inquiry into "privity or knowledge" was never put in terms of: What are the duties of the corporation?[98] Instead, the inquiry was: Is someone in the shipowner's organization chargeable, subjectively, with knowledge of the cause of the accident? If so, and if the "someone" was at a fairly high level in the executive hierarchy, then "the shipowner" was chargeable with "privity." It was not, indeed, until

95. 109 U.S. 578, 3 S.Ct. 379, 617 (1883).

96. 113 Mass. 495 (1873), 125 Mass. 292 (1878).

97. In the second opinion the following jury instructions (125 Mass. at p. 301) were approved: "It becomes necessary for you to inquire whether there was any negligence on the part of the defendant corporation . . . . The corporation is the owner, and the liability of the corporation is the exact liability of the owner. The corporation provides ships, docks, piers and places for the transaction of the business incident to its enterprise. Now, if there is a failure to do what is proper for the reasonably setting in motion and carrying on the business of the corporation, that is in law a neglect of the corporation. The case here rests upon the provision made by the corporation for the purpose of doing the business. It is like the case of a railroad company that is bound to furnish the railroad with a good roadbed, with a properly constructed road, with suitable equipment, with a proper depot."

98. *Cf.* the jury instructions in the Massachusetts case, note 97 supra.

the 1940's that judicial opinions in limitation cases began to distinguish the "corporate ownership" situation from the "individual ownership" situation. It may well have been Justice Douglas's 1943 opinion in Coryell v. Phipps that drew attention to the distinction.[99] Thus it is only for the past twenty or thirty years that judicial attention has been sharply focused on the problem of what "privity or knowledge" means (or ought to mean) in the case of a corporate shipowner as distinguished from the case of an individual shipowner.

The nineteenth century Limitation Act case law insisted on the "subjective" nature of the "knowledge" (if we take care of "knowledge," "privity" will take of itself) which would deprive corporate shipowners of the protection of the Act. In this century there has been a gradual shift toward what might be called an "objective" approach to the problem. The question to be asked (and answered) when a corporate shipowner invokes the Limitation Act is not: What did the chairman of the board or the president or the executive vice-president actually know? but rather: What, as responsible corporate officers, ought they to have known? It is not surprising that the shift has taken place—such a process of "objectification" is common in any field of law in situations where liability *vel non* is conditioned on concepts such as knowledge, good faith and the like. However the process of objectifying the "privity or knowledge" requirement in the Limitation Act case law has been more than usually obscure and subterranean.

In our discussion in the first edition we suggested two formulae under which corporate shipowners should be held to have "privity or knowledge" even when that conclusion might seem doubtful under the purely subjective approach. One formula, borrowed from the Harter Act and Cogsa case law, was that certain duties—particularly the duty to use due diligence to make the ship seaworthy for the voyage—were "nondelegable": if the ship's unseaworthiness was causally related to the accident and if due diligence had not been used to make her seaworthy, then the shipowner would lose his right to limitation of liability just as he would lose his right to exoneration under Harter or Cogsa. The other formula based on a 1932 Supreme Court case which will be presently discussed, was phrased in terms of a "duty to control," with the comment that: "the factual possibility of control leads to a duty to exercise the control at a 'sufficiently high' level to bind the corporation, and the failure to do so will itself be 'privity or knowledge' . . . whether president or office boy was left in charge." The vice of our discussion was that the two formulae were treated as different approaches to the problem instead of as two ways of putting the same question, that is: What duties are imposed on the corporation? That confusion in our own discussion has perpetuated itself in the case law with the result, for example, that the Ninth Circuit in a recent case denounced the idea of "nondelega-

99. See note 90 *supra*.

bility" while at the same time embracing the idea of "a duty to control (or supervise)." [100] It should be added that the case-law authority cited in support of the "nondelegability" proposition in our earlier discussion was, to say the least, inadequate.[101]

The Supreme Court's "duty to control" case was Spencer Kellogg & Sons, Inc. v. Hicks (The Linseed King).[102] Spencer Kellogg operated a factory in Edgewater, New Jersey. It was the company's practice to ferry employees across the Hudson River from New York City in a motor launch; the launch was concededly unseaworthy to run when ice had formed in the river; the executive officers of the company had instructed Stover, who was in charge of the Edgewater plant, that the launch should never be run through ice and the master of the launch had "definite and positive instructions" to that effect. Nevertheless, the launch was operated on a day when ice had formed, ran into an ice floe and sank with considerable loss of life. It did not appear that Stover, the works manager, knew that the launch would be operated that day or had been consulted by the master.

Justice Roberts assumed that Stover was "sufficiently high" in the corporate hierarchy so that his "privity or knowledge" would be chargeable to the corporation. The difficulty was that Stover, at least subjectively, did not know anything about the launch's operation on the fatal day and that proper instructions had been given the master. The case could thus be analogized, as counsel for Spencer Kellogg urged, to the many cases in which limitation had been grant-

100. Waterman Steamship Corp. v. Gay Cottons (The Chickasaw), 414 F.2d 724, 1969 A.M.C. 1682 (9th Cir. 1969), discussed in the text following note 105j *infra*.

101. The only case cited in the first edition to support the proposition that the duty to furnish a seaworthy ship is nondelegable was Grace & Co. v. Charleston Lighterage & Transfer Co., 193 F.2d 539, 1952 A.M.C. 689 (4th Cir. 1952). More than one commentator has pointed out that the case cited, despite the statement in Judge Dobie's opinion that "unseaworthiness of a ship is not a risk excepted by [the Limitation] Act," does not support the "nondelegability" proposition since the holding was based on the so-called "personal contract" doctrine (which is discussed in § 10–26 *et seq. infra*). See Wood, Limitation of Liability: Gilmore and Black's Concept of Privity Based on "Primitive Unseaworthiness", 5 Willamette L.J. 393 (1969); Thede, note 13(c) *supra*, 45 Tulane L. Rev. 959, 969 (1971). See further Judge Duniway's opinion in Waterman S. S. Corp. v. Gay Cottons (The Chickasaw), note 100 *supra*. The Charleston case was an action to recover for cargo damage caused by the unseaworthiness of a barge. The action was brought against both the charterer and the owner of the barge. It was held that the charterer had warranted seaworthiness to cargo under the contract of affreightment and that the owner had warranted seaworthiness to the charterer under the charter-party. Since all the parties were before the court, judgment was entered directly against the owner; it was at that point in his opinion that Judge Dobie made the remark quoted above. As the commentators have pointed out, if the Charleston case is all the case law authority there is to support the nondelegability proposition, then the proposition does not have (or, at least, did not have when it was put forward in the first edition) much case law support.

102. 285 U.S. 502, 52 S.Ct. 450, 1932 A.M.C. 503 (1932).

ed where the accident had resulted from a master's failure to follow proper instructions. Justice Roberts wrote:

> "But there is a vast difference between the cases relied on and the instant one. The launch was used for ferriage over a distance of about a mile and a third. She was known to be unseaworthy and unfit if there was ice on the river. There is no analogy between such a situation and that presented in the cited cases where the emergency must be met by the master alone. In these there is no opportunity of consultation or cooperation or of bringing the proposed action of the master to the owner's knowledge. The latter must rely on the master's obeying rules and using reasonable judgment. The conditions on the morning in question could have been ascertained by Stover, if he had used reasonable diligence, and we think the evidence is adequate to support the finding that the negligence which caused the disaster was with his, and therefore with the owner's privity or knowledge."[103]

Justice Roberts' Linseed King opinion was of course highly ambiguous. He emphasized the local nature of the Linseed King's operation ("ferriage over a distance of about a mile and a quarter"). On the other hand he explained that the cases granting limitation in situations which involved a "master's failure to obey rules and instructions when on the high seas" depended on the basic fact that "the emergency must be met by the master alone . . . [without the] opportunity of consultation or cooperation [with the owner] . . . " Under that explanation it should, arguably, make no difference whether the vessel was crossing the Hudson River or the Pacific Ocean. And the holding was entirely clear that the shipowner was denied limitation not because of what Stover knew but because of what Stover ought to have found out.[104]

103. 285 U.S. at p. 511–512, 52 S.Ct. at pp. 452–453.

104. "[Stover] was under obligation to assure himself by inquiries or by personal inspection that the "Linseed King" should not incur the hazard of colliding, as she did, with ice floes in the river." (285 U.S. at p. 510). The "ought to know" theme recurs frequently in limitation cases decided during the 1940's. The Cleveco, 154 F.2d 605, 1946 A.M.C. 933 (6th Cir. 1946) (tug and tow lost in a storm on Lake Erie because of the tug's unseaworthiness): "[K]nowledge means not only personal cognizance but also the means of knowledge—of which the owner or his superintendent is bound to avail himself . . . ". (154 F.2d at p. 613). Great Atlantic & Pacific Tea Co. v. Lloyd Brasileiro, 159 F.2d 661, 1947 A.M.C. 306 (2d Cir. 1947) (a Fire Statute case, involving a voyage from a Brazilian port to New York): "The measure [of knowledge] is not what the owner knows, but what he is charged with finding out." (159 F.2d at p. 665, per L. Hand, J.). In Avera v. Florida Towing Corp., 322 F.2d 155, 1963 A.M.C. 2110 (5th Cir. 1963) Judge Brown quoted both the passages just cited in denying limitation under the authority of The Linseed King. He also quoted approvingly, from the discussion of The Linseed King in the first edition of the treatise, the proposition that "the duty to control increases along with the possibility of control. . . ."

In States Steamship Company v. United States (The Pennsylvania)[105] the facts were startlingly similar to the facts in The Linseed King, with the notable exception that the case did indeed involve a trans-Pacific instead of a trans-Hudson crossing. The Pennsylvania was a welded steel vessel which was lost with all hands in the North Pacific in January, 1952, in weather which, it was found, was not unusual in those waters and at that time of year.[105a] On a previous voyage the Pennsylvania had suffered a crack in its hull. The crack had been repaired but it was known that welded steel vessels which had once suffered a crack were thereafter "crack-sensitive," particularly in cold weather and heavy seas. Vallet and Brenneke, who were "managerial employees or officers" of the corporate shipowner, were in charge of the repairs. They knew or ought to have known of the crack-sensitiveness of welded steel vessels. The Pennsylvania was about to depart on a voyage from Portland, Oregon to Japan. They knew that the customary route for such a voyage would take the Pennsylvania through the Gulf of Alaska where "violent storms, low temperatures and mountainous seas were to be expected at that time of year . . . ." They did not instruct the master to take a more southerly route through warmer waters. The Pennsylvania was lost in the Gulf of Alaska.

The District Judge found that the Pennsylvania was unseaworthy and that due diligence had not been used to make her seaworthy. (These findings were not disturbed on appeal.) He therefore denied exoneration (under Cogsa) but granted limitation of liability on the ground that the owners were not chargeable with privity or knowledge. This disposition of the case was initially affirmed but, on rehearing, the Ninth Circuit, in an opinion by Judge Pope, reversed on the question of limitation and decreed full liability. In a third *per curiam* opinion the Court attempted to "clarify the basis" for its denial of limitation. In reversing the grant of limitation Judge Pope relied principally on The Linseed King. In the "clarifying" *per curiam* opinion the holding in The Linseed King was generalized in this way:

> "[W]here the circumstances are such that the owners or managing agents have a duty to act to see that the vessel is made seaworthy, a neglect or failure to take such action will require denial of limitation. Mere instructions to subordinate employees will not suffice to give the owner the benefit of the limitation act.[105b]

105. 259 F.2d 458, 1957 A.M.C. 1181, 2277, 1958 A.M.C. 1775 (9th Cir. 1957, 1958), certiorari denied 358 U.S. 953, 79 S.Ct. 316 (1959). The three opinions which the Ninth Circuit delivered in the case are printed seriatim in the official report.

105a. The case involved only cargo claims; no death claims were put forward.

105b. 259 F.2d at p. 472. The opinion also quoted (p. 474, n. 6) the passages from The Cleveco and The Lloyd Brasileiro case reproduced in note 104 *supra*.

Following the analysis of The Linseed King the *per curiam* opinion also quoted at some length and with apparent approval from the discussion of "nondelegable duties" in the first edition of the treatise, italicizing the comment that "[the shipowner] should be held to liability for all loss resulting from his failure to exercise effective control when he had the chance." [105c] The Court made no attempt to explain what it conceived the relationship to be between the "nondelegable duty" idea and the "duty to act to see that the vessel is made seaworthy" which it found in The Linseed King.

The Second Circuit presently provided a counterpoint to whatever it was the Ninth Circuit had done in The Pennsylvania. Petition of Kinsman Transit Company (The Shiras) [105d] dealt with an almost unbelievable series of events which took place on the Buffalo River during the night of January 21, 1959. These events, which laid waste to the City of Buffalo, were precipitated when Kinsman's vessel Shiras broke loose from its winter moorings in the river during a sudden thaw. Kinsman petitioned for limitation of liability. Kinsman's head office was in Cleveland. Captain Davies, who had been master of the Shiras during the 1958 navigation season, was put in charge of seeing that the Shiras was properly moored for the winter in Buffalo. Although Davies' "competence was established," he did not see to it that the Shiras was properly and safely moored. Thus if his knowledge (or negligence) had been the knowledge (or negligence) of the corporation, limitation would have been denied.

Judge Friendly's discussion of the limitation issue reads suspiciously like an invitation to the Supreme Court to grant certiorari and reverse; if that is what he was about, he was doomed to disappointment, since certiorari was routinely denied. After having concluded that Captain Davies was not "sufficiently high" in the hierarchy to bind Kinsman, Judge Friendly commented that, under the doctrine of The Linseed King, Kinsman would be denied limitation if its home office had been in Buffalo instead of Cleveland. "[O]ne might [he added] query the good sense of [such] a distinction . . . in this age of rapid communication and transportation . . .", particularly since it appeared that Captain Davies knew more about the mooring operation than any corporate officer who might have come on from Cleveland. Warming to his work, Judge Friendly continued:

> "Indeed the whole rationale of the doctrine is of questionable application in a case like this where there was no need for the owner to rely on the skill of a master or other agents as he must when a vessel is at sea or in a distant port. All this, however, is not for us; shipowners and their insurers are entitled to rely on the statute and the decisions

105c. § 10–20 *supra*.

105d. 338 F.2d 708, 1964 A.M.C. 2503 (2d Cir. 1964), certiorari denied *sub nom.* Continental Grain Co. v. City of Buffalo, 380 U.S. 944, 85 S.Ct. 1026 (1965).

applying it, and we must take these as we find them until a higher authority intervenes." [105e]

He then cited four cases granting limitation (the most recent of which had been decided in 1918) and seven cases, including the Ninth Circuit's decision in The Pennsylvania, (all but one of which had been decided since 1944) denying limitation. "We are aware [he wrote] of the difference in the ages of the two sets of decision, but we find nothing in the later cases reflecting on the authority of the earlier ones on fact situations within their sweep . . ." Kinsman being "closer" on its facts to the old cases than to the new limitation was decreed.[105f]

A few years later the Second Circuit had another opportunity to express its views on "privity or knowledge" in Federazione Italiana dei Consorzi Agrari v. Mandask Compania de Vapores (The Perama).[105g] The Perama (like the Pennsylvania in the Ninth Circuit case) was a "crack-prone" vessel. Cracks which had appeared on an earlier voyage had been repaired but on the vessel's final voyage new cracks appeared which led to its sinking. (There was no loss of life, and as in The Pennsylvania, only cargo claims were involved). Limitation was denied. In his opinion Judge Anderson [105h] put the decision on two grounds. One: The agents of the owners who had supervised the repairs of the cracks "were sufficiently high in the managerial hierarchy of the appellant so that their general and detailed knowledge and their close privity to the repair project was imputed to the corporation." Two:

> "The trial court . . . found . . . that because of a lack of due diligence on the part of the appellant the *Perama* was sent to sea in an unseaworthy condition. This alone is a sufficient basis for denying limitation of liability. . . . the corporate owner's duty to make the vessel seaworthy, at least to the point of providing it with sufficient integrity to meet the ordinary perils of the sea, is not delegable to anyone. Under the circumstances of this case the

**105e.** 338 F.2d at p. 715.

Monsanto Co. v. Port of St. Louis Investments, Inc., 350 F.Supp. 502, (E.D.Missouri, 1972) was another "negligent mooring" case in which the Becky Thatcher (a riverboat restaurant) and the Santa Maria (a replica of the original) broke loose in a storm and damaged property of Monsanto. Judge Harper denied limitation, citing The Linseed King, Kinsman and the treatise. He wrote: "Thus, a corporation cannot, in all instances, delegate authority to one whose privity and knowledge cannot be imputed to the corporation and be held to be without privity and knowledge." (350 F.Supp. at p. 519).

**105f.** Judge Friendly also noted the suggestion in the treatise that the duty to use due diligence to make a ship seaworthy is nondelegable but concluded that the failure to see that the Shiras was properly moored was not "unseaworthiness", at least in the "primitive" or traditional sense of that term.

**105g.** 388 F.2d 434, 1968 A.M.C. 315 (2d Cir. 1968), certiorari denied 393 U.S. 828, 89 S.Ct. 92 (1968).

**105h.** Judge Friendly, who had written the opinion in the Kinsman case, was on the panel which decided The Perama and concurred.

appellant is held to have knowledge and privity as a matter of law." [105i]

The year after the Second Circuit had decided the Perama, the Ninth Circuit returned to the fray in Waterman Steamship Corporation v. Gay Cottons (The Chickasaw).[105j] The Chickasaw ran aground on Santa Rosa Island off the coast of Southern California; the vessel was a total loss and there was a substantial loss of cargo. The Chickasaw's navigational equipment appears to have been almost ludicrously defective: the radio direction finder could not be used because no current correction or compensation chart was carried; the vessel's mechanical sounding device "had been pried off the deck in Japan and sold for scrap"; the third mate had reported to the master that the fathometer was "inoperative" but the master had not had the fathometer checked when the Chickasaw next made port; the radar had been broken for over a month. Naturally the Chickasaw was found to have been unseaworthy and exoneration vis-a-vis the cargo claims was denied. Limitation of liability was also denied on the ground that the owners were chargeable with privity or knowledge with respect to the Chickasaw's failure to carry a current correction chart for the radio direction finder as required by federal statutes and regulation. Judge Duniway concluded his opinion with these observations:

> "We do not think that an owner can so completely delegate its statutory duty, even to the [Federal Communications Commission]. The regulation requires an FCC certificate, but that is stated as in addition to the duty imposed on the shipowner, not a substitute for it. . . . [Citations omitted.] And it does not excuse Waterman's failure to carry out its own duty to see that there was a current accurate deviation chart on board, or its duty to see that its responsible personnel knew how to use it.
>
> [A]n owner cannot close its eyes to what prudent inspection would disclose. [Citing the 1957 decision in The Pennsylvania.] That is just what Waterman did in this case. We conclude that a finding of lack of privity or knowledge on Waterman's part would be clearly erroneous." [105k]

So far as we have gone, The Chickasaw appears to be in line with Judge Friendly's analysis (although not with the holding) in Kinsman. It remains to be added that Judge Duniway devoted the greater part of his opinion to an elaborate demonstration of the proposition that "all cases denying limitation of liability to a corporate shipowner have emphasized that the negligence or lack of due diligence

105i. 388 F.2d at p. 439. Judge Anderson cited as authority the Ninth Circuit's decision in The Pennsylvania, Grace & Co. v. Charleston Lighterage & Transfer Co. (see note 101 *supra*) and the first edition of the treatise.

105j. 414 F.2d 724, 1969 A.M.C. 1682 (9th Cir. 1969).

105k. 414 F.2d at p. 739, 1969 A.M.C. at pp. 1702–1703.

to make seaworthy was attributable to managerial personnel." [105l] He concluded that "standards under the Limitation Act are different from those under Cogsa" (the Cogsa duty to use due diligence to make the ship seaworthy being, concededly, nondelegable). He dismissed as "dictum" any suggestions in either The Pennsylvania or The Perama that the duty to make seaworthy is nondelegable for purposes of the Limitation Act. This part of Judge Duniway's opinion was written in response to the contention (which the District Court had accepted) that limitation should be denied because of the failure of Captain Patronas (who was not only the master of the Chickasaw but the person to whom the owners had delegated their "entire managerial responsibility as respects repairs") to have the fathometer checked after having been notified by the third mate that it was "inoperative." On this part of the case the conclusion was that what Captain Patronas "knew" was irrelevant since, although he exercised managerial functions he was not a "managerial employee." [105m]

Judge Duniway's emphatic rejection of the proposition that the duty to use due diligence to make a ship seaworthy is nondelegable under the Limitation Act as it is under Cogsa will undoubtedly lead to a good deal more litigation of this sort before this tired issue is finally put on the shelf. His simultaneous acceptance of the "duty to control" proposition will of course make it possible for his opinion to be cited on both sides of all unseaworthiness cases.[105n] On the facts of The Chickasaw Judge Duniway may well have been suggesting a not unreasonable distinction between conditions of unseaworthiness which arise during the course of a voyage (the inoperative fathometer) and conditions which ought to have been corrected before the voyage was undertaken (the absence of current correction charts for the radio direction finder).

**105*l*.** In support of his proposition Judge Duniway cited forty-five cases (if our count is accurate) which he followed with a "cf." citation to the Brasileiro case (note 104 *supra*) and to Williams S. S. Co. v. Wilbur, 9 F. 2d 622, 1926 A.M.C. 32 (9th Cir. 1925), noting that both the cases were Fire Statute cases. Judge Duniway's list of square holdings included The Linseed King, The Pennsylvania and The Perama.

**105m.** Judge Duniway went on to make clear that, once the managerial level is reached, the standard of "knowledge" is objective, not subjective. "[A]n owner cannot close its eyes to what prudent inspection would reveal. An owner must avail itself of whatever means of knowledge are reasonably necessary to prevent conditions likely to cause losses. 'If lack of actual knowledge were enough, imbecility, real or assumed, on the part of owners would be at a premium' [quoting Hough, J., in Argent, 1940 A.M.C. 509 (S.D.N.Y.1915)]." (414 F.2d at p. 732.) Judge Duniway also quoted approvingly the discussion in the first edition of the treatise on the "duty to control" as the principle underlying The Linseed King.

**105n.** "If the owner can delegate performance of the task but remains responsible in a supervisory capacity to insure that the task is performed properly, there is no difference between the duty to supervise and the rule of non-delegability as enunciated by Gilmore and Black." Thede, note 13c *supra*, 45 Tulane L.Rev. 959, 971 (1971) (discussing The Chickasaw.)

"Unseaworthiness" is a term which has suffered from a strange expansion of meaning. It seems clear enough that an owner who sends a ship to sea which is unseaworthy in the sense that it has structural defects [105o] or defective navigational equipment [105p] or is improperly manned [105q] will be denied limitation. The denial of limitation will be explained, as the facts of the case may suggest and the opinion-writing judge's predilections may dictate, on the ground that a "sufficiently high" managerial employee or corporate officer had "privity or knowledge" or on the ground that the corporation failed in its duty to supervise or control or on the ground that the duty to provide a seaworthy ship is nondelegable. Conditions of unseaworthiness which arise in the course of a voyage (e. g., the inoperative fathometer in The Chickasaw) or which are caused by improper loading (or by overloading) of cargo in a distant port may be treated differently. It is certainly true that the older case law assumed that the vessel had passed beyond the owner's effective control once it had broken ground for the voyage, so that he should not be stripped of the protection of the Limitation Act with respect to events which he could not, in fact, control. Instantaneous worldwide communication and the airplane have of course largely destroyed the factual assumption on which the older case law rested.[105r] We may assume that the case law will gradually reflect the technology of the twentieth century and that corporate shipowners will be held to a duty of exercising control over their voyaging ships to the extent that it is reasonably possible for them to do so.[105s] So long as the Limitation Act is on

**105o.** The Pennsylvania, text following note 105 *supra*; The Perama, text following note 105g *supra*.

**105p.** The Chickasaw, text following note 105j *supra*; China Union Lines, Ltd. v. Anderson & Co. (The Union Reliance—The Berean), 364 F.2d 769, 1966 A.M.C. 1653 (5th Cir. 1966) (collision caused by defective steering equipment).

**105q.** Empire Seafoods, Inc. v. Anderson (The Shrimper Bera-Bora), 398 F. 2d 204, 1968 A.M.C. 2664 (5th Cir. 1968) ("[the owner] had a non-delegable duty to provide a qualified master and crew for the intended voyage of the vessel.") Judge Dyer's opinion collects other cases of this sort, of which there are a great many going back at least as far as In re Pacific Mail S.S. Co., 130 F. 76 (9th Cir. 1904), certiorari denied 195 U.S. 632, 25 S.Ct. 790 (1904).) See also State of Oregon Highway Commission v. Tug Go-Getter, 468 F.2d 1270, 1973 A.M.C. 243 (9th Cir. 1972); Chesapeake Bay Bridge & Tunnel District v. Oil Screw Prince (Barge NL–5), 298 F.Supp. 881, 1968 A.M.C. 1427 (E.D.Va.1968).

Petition of Great Lakes Towing Co. (The Tug North Carolina), 1970 A.M. C. 2169 (W.D.N.Y.1969), presented an interesting variant on the owner's duty to make sure that a ship is seaworthy. The petitioner for limitation was directed to answer interrogatories on whether his ship had been involved in other collisions during the three years preceding the collision which led to the limitation proceeding. Answers to the interrogatories, Judge Henderson pointed out, "may establish a pattern of wrongdoing on the part of the North Carolina which may be within the "privity or knowledge" of the Great Lakes Towing Company . . .".

**105r.** See Judge Friendly's opinion in the Kinsman case, text following note 105d *supra*.

**105s.** It may be that the beginning of such a case-law shift can be traced back to two notable cases on improper loading decided in 1943 and 1953. In Consumers Import Co. v. Kabushiki Kaisha Kawasaki Zosenjo (The Venice Maru), 320 U.S. 249, 64 S.Ct. 15, 1943 A.M.C. 1209 (1943) exoneration was

the books, the owner will of course be entitled to limitation for events which occur during the voyage which lie beyond the possibility of his control.[105t]

**§ 10–25.** An underlying question in the privity or knowledge cases, whatever type of ownership may be involved, is which side bears the burden of proof. Two problems are involved: first, the establishment of liability of the shipowner to the claimant, as to which the claimant (or libellant) bears the burden; second, the burden of establishing privity or knowledge or their absence. It seems reasonable that the shipowner who invokes the Limitation Act, should bear the

granted under the Fire Statute. Justice Jackson wrote: "The cause of the fire is found to be negligent stowage . . . which made the vessel unseaworthy. The negligence was that of a person employed to supervise loading [in the port of Kobe, Japan, where the demise-charterer's main office was located] to whom responsibility was properly delegated and who was qualified by experience to perform the work. No negligence or design of the owner or charterer is found." In Petition of Isbrandtsen (The Edmund Fanning), 201 F.2d 281, 1953 A.M.C. 86 (2d Cir. 1953) Isbrandtsen was the demise-charterer of an American-flag vessel. The improper loading took place at a German port. Judge Augustus Hand, affirming the District Court, wrote briefly: "Isbrandtsen's responsibility for the negligent stowage was held to be established because of the acts of its agent, Captain Praast, who was authorized to, and in fact did, supervise the loading of the cargo. Consequently the Fire Statute, 46 U.S.C.A. § 182, and the Limitation Statute, 46 U.S.C.A. § 183, were held inapplicable." The question of exoneration under the Fire Statute for improper or negligent loading was much—indeed too much—discussed in Verbeeck v. Black Diamond Steamship Corp. (The Black Gull), 250 F.2d 777, 1958 A.M.C. 277 (2d Cir. 1957), certiorari denied 356 U.S. 933, 78 S.Ct. 772 (1958); 269 F.2d 68, 1960 A.M.C. 163 (2d Cir. 1959); 273 F.2d 61, 1960 A.M.C. 175 (2d Cir. 1959), certiorari denied 361 U.S. 934, 80 S.Ct. 374 (1960); 302 F.2d 114, 1962 A.M.C. 1205 (2d Cir. 1962). The District Court twice granted exoneration and was twice reversed. In its second opinion (269 F.2d 68) the Second Circuit held that exoneration should be finally denied but that opinion was "vacated and withdrawn" (273 F.2d 61) and a third trial ordered. Instead of going through a third trial, the litigants settled (see 302 F.2d 114). So many opinions expressing so many different points of view were written by so many judges that it is impossible to determine what the case stands for beyond the obvious point that the judges were much divided in their minds. Moore-McCormack Lines, Inc. v. Armco Steel Corp. (The Mormackite), 272 F.2d 873, 1960 A.M.C. 185 (2d Cir. 1959), certiorari denied 362 U.S. 990 (1960) was another hard-fought improper loading case in which it was eventually determined that Moore-McCormack could limit its liability with respect to cargo claims but not with respect to death and injury claims under the "loss of life" amendments to § 183 (see § 10–33 *et seq. infra*). A more recent improper loading case in which exoneration and limitation were denied is Petition of Long (The Smith Voyager), 439 F.2d 109, 1971 A.M.C. 1147 (2d Cir. 1971). In the light of the sequence of cases reviewed in this note, it would be foolhardy to say that the present state of the law as to owner's responsibility for improper loading is clear.

**105t.** For an interesting current example see Complaint of Caldas (The M/S Caldas), 350 F.Supp. 566, 1973 A.M.C. 1243. (E.D.Pa.1972) (exoneration granted under the Fire Statute). The ship, found to be seaworthy and properly manned, was destroyed at sea by a fire of unexplained origin. It was alleged that the fire had been set by Meijo, a depressed and perhaps insane member of the crew, but Judge Huyett concluded that the evidence was "not sufficient to permit us to conclude that Meijo was responsible." Judge Huyett's opinion may be read to suggest that if it had been proved that Meijo had set the fire, exoneration would have been denied.

burden of proving the absence of privity or knowledge: as to that branch of the case he is the moving party and the facts are peculiarly within his knowledge. That is evidently the Supreme Court's view of the matter; in Coryell v. Phipps Justice Douglas commented, citing earlier cases: "Thus respondent [shipowner] has satisfied the burden of proof, which is on those who seek the benefit of sec. 4283 [*i. e.* § 183], of establishing the lack of privity or knowledge." [106] This allocation has been universally accepted; every limitation case decided since the 1940's has routinely recited the Coryell v. Phipps formula.[106a]

There is no reason why the allocation of the burden of proof should be different in Fire Statute cases from the universally accepted allocation in Limitation Act cases. Many cases have, however, assumed that if the owner in a Fire Statute case proves that the cargo damage or loss was caused by fire, the burden is on the claimants not only to prove negligence or fault but also to prove that the fire was, in the words of the Fire Statute, "caused by the design or neglect of such owner." [106b] It may be that the use of the term "neglect" in the Fire Statute led to judicial confusion: just as the plaintiff in a tort case bears the burden of proving the defendant's "negligence", so (it may have seemed to follow) the claimant in a Fire Statute case must bear the burden of proving the owner's "neglect."

It was suggested in the first edition of the treatise that, the cases to the contrary notwithstanding, the burden of proof rule in the Fire Statute cases should be the same as in the Limitation Act cases: burden on the claimant to show negligence or fault; burden on the owner to show that the fire was not "caused by [his] design or neglect." At one point the Second Circuit accepted that suggestion, in an opinion by Judge Clark, but subsequent proceedings in the case left the issue, so far as the Second Circuit was concerned, "somewhat uncertain." [106c] The burden of proof in Fire Statute cases has been little

**106.** (The Seminole) 317 U.S. 406, 409, 63 S.Ct. 291, 292, 1943 A.M.C. 18, 21 (1943).

**106a.** For a current example, see The Marine Sulphur Queen, 460 F.2d 89, 101, 1972 A.M.C. 1122, 1136 (2d Cir. 1972). See also Petition of Northern Fishing & Trading Co., Inc., 477 F.2d 1267, 1973 A.M.C. 1283 (9th Cir. 1973).

**106b.** Thede, *supra* note 13c, 45 Tulane L.Rev. 959, 985 (1971) traces this handling of the burden of proof question back to Keene v. The Whistler (14 Fed.Cas. 208 [D.Cal.1873]) which announced, without citing any authority, that "the burden of proof is on libellant [claimant] to show that such fire was caused by the design or neglect of the owners of the vessel." According to Thede, "*Keene* was followed in *The Strathdon* [89 F. 374 (E.D.N.Y.1898)] which, in turn, was followed in case after case, despite the establishment of a contrary rule in limitation cases . . . ". The most recent case following "the rule of The Strathdon" appears to be Hershey Chocolate Corp. v. The S.S. Robert Luckenbach, 184 F.Supp. 134, 1960 A.M.C. 1143 (D.Or. 1960), affirmed without discussion of the burden of proof point, 295 F.2d 619, 1961 A.M.C. 2215 (9th Cir. 1961). See also Hoskyn & Co. v. The Silver Line, Ltd., 143 F.2d 462, 1944 A.M.C. 895 (2d Cir. 1944), certiorari denied 323 U.S. 767, 65 S.Ct. 116 (1944); Fidelity Phoenix Fire Ins. Co. v. Flota Mercante Del Estado, 205 F.2d 886, 1953 A.M.C. 1348 (5th Cir. 1953).

**106c.** The case was Verbeeck v. Black Diamond Steamship Corp.; for the tortured history of the case, see note 105s *supra*, at end. Judge Clark's opinion was the opinion reported at 269 F.2d 68, which was "vacated and

discussed in recent years: in 1960 the Oregon District Court followed the traditional view; in 1972 the Pennsylvania District Court held that the burden of proof to show absence of "design or neglect" or "privity or knowledge" was on the owner both in Fire Statute cases and in Limitation Act cases.[106d]

The Marine Sulphur Queen [106e] dramatically illustrates the decisive importance which the burden of proof allocation can have. The Queen had been built as an oil tanker but was converted for the carriage of molten sulphur at extremely high temperatures. Little was known about the carriage of molten sulphur. The Queen's conversion was described by a Coast Guard engineer as "a calculated risk"; it was, Judge Anderson observed, "largely the owner's experiment, to which the officers and men of the ship had been committed." Over a period of two years the Queen successfully carried molten sulphur, making 63 round-trip voyages. On February 2, 1963, the Queen, laden with molten sulphur, left Beaumont, Texas. She was last heard from on February 4, after which she disappeared from sight. No unusual weather conditions were reported. The District Court found that the Queen, as converted, was unseaworthy—a finding which the Second Circuit accepted. The claimants, of course, bore the burden of proving that the unseaworthiness was causally connected with the Queen's loss—the fact being that no one knew what had caused the loss. Judge Anderson commented, citing cases, that: "It is settled that when a vessel disappears in expectable weather under otherwise unknown circumstances, proof . . . of some element of unseaworthiness will permit the trier of fact to infer that the unseaworthiness was the proximate cause of the loss." Since the inference could not be rebutted by the owner, the claimants had made out their case and the burden on the limitation issue shifted to the owner to prove that the unseaworthiness was without their privity or knowledge. Judge Anderson concluded: "In light of the fact that no one knows what caused the loss, it is impossible for [the owner] to bear its burden . . . . Because [the owner] could show nothing at all about causation for the disappearance of the Queen and her crew, the district court properly denied it limitation." [106f]

withdrawn" in 273 F.2d 61. Judge Clark (dissenting) seemed to feel that the "vacating" opinion had rejected the burden of proof proposition but Judge Moore's language, read with care, seems, at most, ambiguous. The phrase "somewhat uncertain" in the text is from the discussion by Thede, note 106b *supra*.

**106d.** For the Oregon case, see note 106b *supra*. The Pennsylvania case (per Huyett, J.) is Complaint of Caldas (The M/V Caldas), 350 F.Supp. 566, 1973 A.M.C. 1243 (E.D.Pa.1972). Judge Huyett cites Coryell v. Phipps (note 106 *supra*), Judge Clark's Verbeeck opinion (note 106c *supra*) and the treatise.

**106e.** 460 F.2d 89, 1972 A.M.C. 1122 (2d Cir. 1972).

**106f.** 460 F.2d at p. 101, 1972 A.M.C. at p. 1136. Martinson & Robertson, Ltd. v. The Steamship Barcelona, 1968 A.M.C. 331 (S.D.Fla.1967) was another unexplained disappearance case. Judge Choate, without citing authority, wrote: "It is concluded thus the respondents, . . . being the owner and the bareboat charterer . . . of the S. S. Barcelona, which vessel sank for reasons and

In cases where the vessel's unseaworthiness constitutes a statutory violation, the shipowner may find himself obliged to carry the staggering burden of proof imposed by the so-called "statutory fault" rule of The Pennsylvania [106g]—that is, that the fault or violation "could not have been" the cause of the accident. In imposing the "statutory fault" rule in The Chickasaw, Judge Duniway quoted from an earlier Ninth Circuit case: "This burden is frequently extremely difficult, if not impossible, for the violator to discharge, in the nature of things; and therein lies the true penalty imposed on him." [106h]

### The "Personal Contract" Doctrine

**§ 10–26.** Claims against which a shipowner may desire to limit may arise out of contract or out of tort. The tort claims arising from a collision may be distinguished from claims brought against a shipowner by cargo interests, charterers or suppliers with whom the shipowner had, before the loss, entered into a contractual relationship. The importance of the distinction lies in an ambiguous and enigmatic doctrine under which the shipowner loses the right to limit when his liability arises from a "personal contract." [107]

The Supreme Court first indicated its approval of the doctrine when in 1911, in Richardson v. Harmon,[108] it tackled the unpleasant task of making sense out of § 189. Justice Lurton, indicating approval of several lower court opinions, commented:

> "Thus construed, the section [*i. e.* § 189] harmonizes with the policy of limiting the owner's risk to his interest in

causes unknown, is therefore presumed to have been unseaworthy, have therefore been unable to establish their lack of privity or knowledge of the said unseaworthiness and so, are not entitled to limit their liability." (1968 A.M.C. at p. 336.) The burden of proof rule of The Marine Sulphur Queen was reaffirmed in Terracciano v. McAlinden Construction Co., 485 F.2d 304, 1973 A.M.C. 2111 (2d Cir. 1973).

**106g.** 86 U.S. (19 Wall.) 125 (1874). See Chapter VII, § 7–5 *supra.*

**106h.** The Chickasaw is discussed in the text following note 105j *supra.* The case quoted from was The Princess Sophia, 61 F.2d 339, 1932 A.M.C. 1562 (9th Cir. 1932). The Second Circuit also applied the "could not have been" rule of The Pennsylvania in Petition of Long (The Smith Voyager), 439 F.2d 109, 1971 A.M.C. 1147 (2d Cir. 1971). In The Marine Sulphur Queen, note 106e *supra,* Judge Anderson, who had written the Smith Voyager opinion, cautioned that the rule of The Pennsylvania should not be applied where the relevant statutes "do not delineate a precise and clearly defined duty, but rather call for interpretation and judgment in their application." (460 F.2d at p. 98, 1972 A.M.C. at p. 1132). There have been suggestions in some cases that the "statutory fault" rule does not apply to Fire Statute cases. See Automobile Insurance Co. v. United Fruit Co., 224 F.2d 72, 1955 A.M.C. 1429 (2d Cir. 1955); Hershey Chocolate Corp. v. The S. S. Robert Luckenbach, 184 F.Supp. 134, 1960 A.M.C. 1143 (D.Or.1960), affirmed without discussion of the point, 295 F.2d 619, 1961 A.M.C. 2215 (9th Cir. 1961). If it is accepted that the allocation of burden of proof under the Fire Statute should be the same as under the Limitation Act, as suggested in the text, there seems to be no reason to distinguish between the two statutes with respect to the applicability of the "statutory fault" rule.

**107.** See generally Castles, The Personal Contract Doctrine: An Anomaly in American Maritime Law, 62 Yale L.J. 1031 (1953).

**108.** 222 U.S. 96, 32 S.Ct. 27 (1911). See § 10–13 *supra.*

the ship in respect of all claims arising out of the conduct of the master and crew, whether the liability be strictly maritime or from a tort non-maritime, but leaves him liable for his own fault, neglect, *and contracts*" [emphasis added].[109]

The statement that the shipowner is to be liable, without benefit of limitation, for "his . . . contracts" might have been taken to mean that the Limitation Act was available to the shipowner only against pure tort claims—typically arising out of collisions—and perhaps against claims arising out of contracts entered into by the master in foreign ports. There is no reason to believe that so broad a construction was intended by the Court; in any event the subsequent case law progressively narrowed the scope of the doctrine. It is by no means clear exactly what a "personal contract" is, but it is clear that not all contracts are "personal", even though entered into personally by the shipowner.

Bills of lading are not personal contracts—with the important result that the shipowner may limit against cargo claims. This has been accepted doctrine since the Supreme Court's decision in Earle & Stoddart, Inc. v. Ellerman's Wilson Line, Ltd., in which Justice Brandeis wrote:

> "The bills of lading, which are said to contain 'personal contracts,' were not executed by the respondent or by any of its officers or managers. They were given, in large part, by agents of railroads or other steamship companies and are to be regarded merely a ship's documents." [110]

Justice Brandeis' insistence on the manner in which the bills of lading involved in the Earle & Stoddart case were executed leaves some theoretical ambiguity on the point. Bills of lading are typically issued either by some agent for the carrier or by the master or by some relatively minor clerk. All such bills would, in Justice Brandeis' terminology, be merely "ship's documents" and not personal contracts. However, even in the unlikely event that the president of a shipping line himself signed a bill of lading there is no reason to believe that such a bill would be held a personal contract any more than a bill issued in more customary fashion.

A charter party is the clearest example of what is, under current case law, held to be a "personal contract". Of the five Supreme Court cases which have involved the "personal contract" doctrine, one (the Earle & Stoddart case) refused to apply the doctrine to bills of lading; the other four all arose under charter parties, which were held "personal" and the owner denied limitation.[111] Indeed Justice

109. *Id.* at 106, 32 S.Ct. at 30.

110. 287 U.S. 420, 429, 53 S.Ct. 200, 202, 1933 A.M.C. 1, 6 (1932).

111. Capitol Transp. Co. v. Cambira Steel Co., 249 U.S. 334, 39 S.Ct. 292 (1919); Pendleton v. Benner Line, 246 U.S. 353, 38 S.Ct. 330 (1918); Luckenbach v. W. J. McCahan Sugar Refining Co., 248 U.S. 139, 39 S.Ct. 53 (1918); Cullen Fuel Co. v. W. E. Hedger, Inc., 290 U.S. 82, 54 S.Ct. 10, 1933 A.M.C. 1584 (1933). In the Tem-

Brandeis, in his opinion in Earle & Stoddart, remarked that "the rule . . . has been applied by this court only to private charter parties executed by the owner", which gives some ground for arguing that, in the Supreme Court's opinion, the doctrine covers charter parties and nothing else.

However, although the Supreme Court has never passed on the point, contracts for supplies and repairs have been held "personal" in several District and Circuit Court decisions of relatively ancient vintage.[112] Some of the cases, which go back to the days when no maritime lien was created for supplies and repairs furnished in the vessel's home port, suggest a distinction between contracts which would create a lien on the ship and those which would not—the latter being "personal contracts", hence not subject to limitation; the former not "personal" since entered into on the credit of the ship, and subject to limitation. Changes both of law and technology make such a distinction difficult to support today. In the first place, under the Federal Maritime Lien Act, suppliers and repairmen may have a lien on the ship whether their services were performed in the home port or elsewhere.[113] In the second place, modern communications by telegraph, cable and radio, make the idea, which was often true in fact a hundred years ago, of credit extended "to the ship" in foreign ports without the owner's authorization fictional indeed. It is fair to conclude that if any contracts for supplies, repairs and the like are "personal", all of them are. Although the point has never been authoritatively determined in a modern case, it is probable that all repair and supply contracts are "personal", home port or foreign port, lien or no lien.

An ingenious but unsuccessful attempt to expand the boundaries of the personal contract doctrine was made in The Susan.[113a] The action, for wrongful death, included a count for unseaworthiness (as well as counts under the Jones Act and the Death on the High Seas Act). With respect to the unseaworthiness count, counsel argued that the shipowner's liability was contractual, hence "personal", and not subject to limitation. The Court dismissed the argument with the remark that: "the owner's liability to seamen for unseaworthiness,

ple Bar (Petition of Temple S.S. Co.) 45 F.Supp. 608, 1942 A.M.C. 1125 (D. Md.1942) affirmed 137 F.2d 293, 1943 A.M.C. 835 (4th Cir. 1943), Judge Coleman held, relying on the Earle & Stoddart case, that a charter for the carriage of an entire cargo for a single shipper which was executed not by the owner but by his brokers was not a "personal contract". Thus there may be charters and charters.

112. The Havana, 92 F. 1007 (3d Cir. 1899); Great Lakes Towing Co. v. Mill Transp. Co., 155 F. 11 (6th Cir. 1907) certiorari denied 207 U.S. 596, 28 S.Ct. 262 (1907); The Mary Morgan, 28 F. 196 (E.D.Pa.1886); The Amos D. Carver, 35 F. 655 (S.D.N.Y. 1888); McPhail v. Williams, 41 F. 61 (D.Mass.1890); Gokey v. Fort, 44 F. 364 (S.D.N.Y.1890).

113. On the home port doctrine and its abrogation by the Lien Act, see Chapter IX, § 9–25 *et seq.*

113a. (Petition of Wood), 230 F.2d 197, 1956 A.M.C. 547 (2d Cir. 1956).

like the liability for negligence, is . . . neither voluntary nor 'personal', and is therefore subject to the Limitation Act."[113b]

In Murray v. New York Central Railroad Company[113c] Judge Murphy, without citing The Susan, held that a seaman's claim for maintenance and cure "being an incident of the employment relationship, is sufficiently contractual to put it in the contract category and thus place it outside the compass of limitation." He had found, he commented, no cases in point and none had been cited to him, but "reason dictates that an award for maintenance and cure does not come within the limitation proceeding." Murray involved a single maintenance and cure claim which Judge Murphy liquidated in the amount of $2,800. The plaintiff had received a $75,000 jury verdict in an action under the Jones Act (a count for unseaworthiness having been dismissed); the Jones Act recovery was held subject to limitation and the limitation fund was determined to be $16,000. The ultimate recovery was thus $18,800.

Judge Murphy's holding in Murray was followed in Petition of Tiedemann[113d] where considerably larger amounts were involved: Tiedemann was held entitled to limitation with respect to a large number of personal injury and death claims which resulted from a collision in the Delaware River. The limitation fund was set at $179,000. Judge Layton concluded that Tiedemann must pay, in addition to the $179,000, maintenance and cure claims which aggregated $166,000. In explaining his conclusion he wrote:

> "[T]he duty [to pay maintenance and cure] is a unique one and quite different from duty to make reparation for personal injuries. Congress cannot be presumed to have created the possibility that this duty can be wiped out. . . . Therefore, despite the broad language of the [Limitation Act], I hold, upon principle, that such a liability is not one which is extinguished by the granting of a petition to limit liability."[113e]

**113b.** The Susan was cited and followed, on this point in Petition of Reed (The Yacht Meridian), 224 F. Supp. 241, 1967 A.M.C. 645 (S.D.Fla. 1963).

**113c.** 171 F.Supp. 80, 1959 A.M.C. 2355 (S.D.N.Y.1959), affirmed without discussion of maintenance and cure or the personal contract doctrine, 287 F. 2d 152, 1961 A.M.C. 1118 (2d Cir. 1961) certiorari denied, 366 U.S. 945, 81 S. Ct. 1674 (1961).

**113d.** (The Elna II—The Mission San Francisco), 236 F.Supp. 895 (D.Del. 1964), reversed as to this point on procedural grounds, 367 F.2d 498, 1966 A.M.C. 1934 (3d Cir. 1966). In Hugney v. Consolidation Coal Co., 345 F. Supp. 1079 (W.D.Pa.1971) Judge Marsh, in dictum, expressed the opinion that claims for maintenance and cure (as well as actions under the Jones Act for damages resulting from the employer's failure to provide maintenance and cure) are not subject to limitation of liability. Judge Marsh did not cite the cases discussed in the text but referred to 1 Edelman, Maritime Injury and Death 578 (1960).

**113e.** 236 F.Supp. at p. 912. Judge Layton commented that "in the absence of authority to the contrary" he was following Judge Murphy's decision in Murray. It will be noted that Judge Layton's holding was not based on the personal contract doctrine.

In reversing Judge Layton's award of the additional $166,000 for the maintenance and cure claims, Judge Hastie, for the Third Circuit, did not deal with the merits of the issue; the reversal was predicated on the ground that the issue had been raised too late in the proceedings (which at the time of Judge Layton's 1964 award had been pending since 1957 and had been the subject of two previous appeals to the Third Circuit.)

Except for the District Court maintenance and cure cases which have been reviewed, the personal contract doctrine has remained in a state of suspended animation for the past generation.[113f] It is hard to understand why this should be so. Potentially, the doctrine seems to have explosive (and, from a shipowner's point of view, frightening) possibilities. The Limitation Act has long outlived its popularity. The courts have shown themselves eager to deny limitation on almost any theory. There must be many claimants—both for property damage and for death and injury—who could plausibly argue themselves within the ill-defined limits of the personal contract doctrine. It seems particularly surprising that no one has seriously challenged the doctrine of The Susan.[113g] If the shipowner's duty to provide maintenance and cure to his sea-going employees is "sufficiently contractual" to be "outside the compass of limitation", why is his duty to furnish them a seaworthy ship not equally so? And, for that matter, if a shipowner warrants seaworthiness to a charterer and thus waives his right to limitation, why is it that the same result should not follow in a seaman's action for death or injury under the unseaworthiness doctrine? It is true that acceptance of the arguments which have just been sketched would amount to a judicial repeal of the Limitation Act with respect to all seamen's death and injury claims; since such claims have been held subject to limitation for a hundred years, courts to which such arguments were addressed might well think twice before plunging forward. And yet it is, to repeat, surprising that counsel for such claimants have been so uncharacteristically meek in accepting The Susan as holy writ.

A type of contractual obligation which is not unfamiliar in other maritime contexts made what appears to have been its first appearance in a limitation proceeding in In re Moore (The Tug Olive L. Moore).[113h] In order to induce a claimant to forbear from bringing an in rem action against a vessel, the owners (or their insurers) may

113f. A fairly desperate effort to invoke the doctrine was made in Steuart Investment Co. v. Bauer Dredging Construction Co., Inc., 323 F.Supp. 907, 1971 A.M.C. 1447 (D.Md.1971). It appeared that Bauer's vessels were in the habit of buying gasoline at Stewart's dock. Following such a purchase, a tug and barge owned by Bauer were driven against the dock in a storm and damaged it. Counsel for Stewart argued that the purchase of gasoline was a "personal contract" so that Bauer's right to limitation should be denied. Judge Northrop, who may have been amused by the argument, naturally rejected it. If Stewart's claim had been for the price of the gasoline instead of for the damage to the dock, the case might have stood in a different footing.

113g. Text following note 113a *supra*.

113h. 278 F.Supp. 260, 1968 A.M.C. 818 (E.D.Mich.1968).

furnish the claimant with a "letter of undertaking" in which it is agreed that, if owner is held liable to claimant, the final judgment will be paid up to whatever amount is specified in the letter. In Moore the tug had put into the port of Muskegon for repairs. Huron Cement gave permission for the use of one of its piers in connection with trials of the tug after completion of the repairs. In the course of the trials the tug damaged Huron's pier in an amount estimated at $75,000. The tug's insurers gave Huron a letter of undertaking "in customary form" in which the insurer agreed to pay any final judgment against Moore up to $30,000 (which was slightly more than the tug's estimated value at the time of the pier incident). The tug, unlibeled, then resumed its interrupted voyage which, however, was finally abandoned when the tug's engines went dead in the Straits of Mackinac. The owners filed a petition for limitation and surrendered the tug to a trustee, who sold it for $16,000. Claims for more than $250,000 were filed in the limitation proceeding; the nature of the claims, other than Huron's claim for damage to its pier, were not specified in the opinion.

Huron moved that the "contractual commitment" in the letter of undertaking should have the effect of allowing it "to press its claim for this amount [$30,000] independently of these [limitation] proceedings." [113i] Judge Freeman denied the motion principally on the ground that if Huron had libeled the tug and the owners had procured her release by filing a surety bond, Huron would have had to come into the limitation proceeding; it should be no better off as the beneficiary of the letter of undertaking which was, in effect, a substitute for the bond. Judge Freeman declined to become "entangled" at that stage in the proceedings with speculations as to what Huron's rights would be, in the limitation proceeding or under its letter of undertaking, in the event that the owners of the tug were held entitled to limitation. In denying Huron's motion to be allowed to proceed "independently", he did not cite either the "personal contract" cases or the cases in which claimants have been allowed to proceed against insurers, outside limitation proceedings, under so-called "direct action" statutes.[113j] No further proceedings were reported in Moore; the case obviously raises a great many more questions than it answers. We shall follow Judge Freeman's sensible decision not to become entangled in such speculative matters in the absence of further judicial elucidation of the effect of an insurer's letter of undertaking in an owner's subsequent limitation proceeding.

**§ 10–27.** The discussion is not, however, at an end even if we conclude that charter parties certainly are, that supply and repair contracts probably are, that maintenance and cure (and conceivably

113i. Huron also argued, unsuccessfully, that the damage to the pier had taken place before the tug set out on the limitation voyage so that, as a pre-voyage claimant, Huron could not be compelled to come into the limitation proceeding. This aspect of the case is discussed, text following note 205a *infra*.

113j. On the cases under the "direct action" statutes, see § 10–31 *infra*, particularly text following note 131a.

seamen's personal injury and death) claims possibly are and that bills of lading certainly are not, personal contracts. To call a given type of contract "personal" does not automatically lead to the conclusion that the shipowner will under all circumstances be denied the right to limit against the claims of his promisee. The early cases, which frequently equated "personal" with "personally executed or signed by the owner", may well have assumed that to call a contract personal to the owner was equivalent to saying that the owner, being in privity with his promisee, could not limit. In 1919, however, Judge Learned Hand, sitting on the District Court, had occasion, in The Soerstad, to draw a distinction which has since enlisted a considerable following.[114]

The Soerstad was an action against the owner of a tug which had negligently collided with and sunk a vessel it had in tow. Judge Hand, assuming that the contract of towage was "personal", nevertheless allowed the tug owner to limit on the theory that the doctrine as developed by the Supreme Court denied limitation only when not merely the contract but the resulting breach was personal. A breach of warranty—such as the warranty of seaworthiness—is personal in both senses, or so Judge Hand concluded after a learned discussion of the nature of the action of warranty, which dipped back as far as the yearbooks for helpful precedent. On the other hand the owner's contractual obligation to tow in a non-negligent manner was personal only in the first sense. Having selected a competent master for the tug, the owner was not responsible for his subsequent negligence, had no "privity or knowledge" of the events leading to the sinking of the tow, and was entitled to limit.

The Supreme Court has denied limitation on the personal contract doctrine in only one case decided since The Soerstad. Cullen Fuel Co., Inc. v. W. E. Hedger, Inc.[115] denied limitation in a charter party case where it was held that the owner had breached an implied warranty of seaworthiness. The case was, therefore, of the type which, even according to Judge Hand's analysis, fell within the doctrine and afforded no occasion for accepting or rejecting the narrowing of the rule in The Soerstad. Nevertheless, Justice Roberts' opinion indicated approval of the narrower approach:

> "The petitioner urges that the denial of limitation in cases like this will sweep away much of the protection af-

114. 257 F. 130 (S.D.N.Y.1919). The Soerstad was followed in: The E. S. Atwood, 289 F. 737, 1923 A.M.C. 99 (S.D.N.Y.1923); The No. 34, 25 F.2d 602, 1928 A.M.C. 780 (2d Cir. 1928) certiorari denied *sub nom.* Hogan & Sons Inc. v. L. Boyer's Sons Co., 278 U.S. 606, 49 S.Ct. 11 (1928); The Nat. Sutton (Petition of W. E. Hedger Transp. Co., Inc.), 62 F.2d 787, 1933 A.M.C. 338, on rehearing 63 F.2d 1021, 1933 A.M.C. 507 (2d Cir. 1933). The most recent citation of the Soerstad appears to have been in Judge Friendly's opinion in Petition of Kinsman Transit Co., (The Shiras) 338 F.2d 708, 716, n. 3, 1964 A.M.C. 2503 (2d Cir. 1964). The Kinsman case is discussed text following note 105d *supra.* Judge Friendly seemed to think that The Soerstad was still as good as gold.

115. 290 U.S. 82, 54 S.Ct. 10, 1933 A.M.C. 1584 (1933).

forded to shipowners by the acts of Congress. But this view disregards the nature of the warranty. The fitness of the ship at the moment of breaking ground is the matter warranted, and not her suitability under conditions thereafter arising which are beyond the owner's control" [citing as authority The Soerstad and subsequent cases].[116]

Under The Soerstad the personal contract doctrine, with respect to charter parties, contracts for towage and the like, would deprive the owner of his right to limit only where breach of a warranty or of a promise of indemnity was involved, and it is hard to think of any warranty except that of seaworthiness which would come up. Despite the "personal" nature of the contract, the owner would still be entitled to limit against claims arising from negligent management or navigation of the ship during the voyage. With respect to contracts for supplies and repairs (assuming them to be "personal"), Soerstad would not appear to have any effect. The supplier or repairman performs his services while the ship is at port or in drydock. The owner's promise is to pay money, and his obligation is complete when the services have been performed. There is no occasion for the Soerstad distinction between warranties and contractual promises to carry out the contract in a proper manner. If, therefore, supply and repair contracts are considered "personal", the result is that such contractual claims can never be limited against, Soerstad or no Soerstad.

**§ 10–28.** Section 186 of the Limitation Act (R.S. § 4286) provides that a charterer who shall "man, victual and navigate" a vessel shall be deemed the "owner" for purposes of limitation—*i. e.* entitled to limit as if he were the owner. By negative implication, the charterer who does not "man, victual and navigate" is not to be deemed the owner and not entitled to the benefit of the Limitation Act. The time charterer or the voyage charterer, where the owner continues to man, victual and navigate the vessel, may not limit.[116a] The time or voyage charterer frequently issues bills of lading in his own name. Assume now that cargo carried under bills of lading so issued is damaged as a result of unseaworthiness of the ship existing at the beginning of the voyage. As we know, bills of lading are considered "ship's documents" and not personal contracts, so that when the owner issues the bills he may limit against cargo claims. The time or voyage charterer, however, is not the owner nor entitled to limit, so that, if liability is established under the Harter Act or Cogsa, he must pay cargo in full. But the time or voyage charter is a personal contract, so that if the warranty of seaworthiness was breached at the beginning of the voyage it seems that the charterer can recover from the owner all that he may have had to pay out to cargo.[117] But

116. *Id.* at 88–89, 54 S.Ct. at 11, 1933 A.M.C. at 1586.

116a. See § 10–10 *supra.*

117. Castles, op. cit. supra note 107 at 1033. Grace & Co. v. Charleston Lighterage Co., 193 F.2d 539, 1952 A.M.C. 689 (4th Cir. 1952); The M. J. Woods—The Skipper (petition of Reliance Marine etc., Corp.) 206 F.2d 240, 1953 A.M.C. 1615 (2d Cir. 1953). And see Judge Learned Hand's opin-

this possibility, like most other aspects of the personal contract doctrine, has remained largely unexplored in the case law.

### The Limitation Fund

§ **10–29.** Except as to claims for loss of life and bodily injury, the liability of an owner entitled to limitation "shall not exceed," in the language of § 183, "the amount or value of the interest of such owner in such vessel, and her freight then pending." The provision is echoed, without change of substance, in § 189: "the aggregate liabilities of all the owners of a vessel on account of the same shall not exceed the value of such vessel and freight pending." Section 189 further provides that the "individual liability" of an owner shall be limited to "the proportion of any or all debts and liabilities that his individual share of the vessel bears to the whole."

Nothing in the statute indicated at what point in time the owner's interest should be valued. In the case of the ship lost at sea, should it be the value at the beginning of the voyage or the value after the loss—*i. e.* zero? Although § 185 now provides for posting a bond and transfer of the owner's interest to a trustee as alternative methods of complying with the Act, the original Act provided only for the transfer to a trustee, the bond posting procedure having been authorized first by the Supreme Court's Admiralty Rules and subsequently ratified by amendment of the statute.[118] Thus the Supreme Court's initial determination of when the owner's interest should be valued—and necessarily that point would have to be determined in the first case in which the Court should hold the Limitation Act applicable—involved construction of a statute which provided as an exclusive method of compliance the transfer of the owner's interest to a trustee. The English rule was that the owner's interest in a collision case was the value of the ship just before the collision,[119] and the English rule had been followed by the Massachusetts court in a case decided under the Massachusetts limitation statute after the passage of the federal act in 1851.[120] In Norwich & N. Y. Transp. Co. v. Wright,[121] however, the Supreme Court refused to follow the English precedents and the Massachusetts court and adopted instead what it considered to

ion in Cannella v. Lykes Brothers S. S. Co., 174 F.2d 794 (2d Cir. 1949), certiorari denied 338 U.S. 859, 70 S.Ct. 102 (1949) (since an injured longshoreman could recover from a charterer without limitation and the charterer from the owner, there is no reason why the longshoreman could not proceed directly against the owner to avoid "circuity of action").

118. See § 10–9 *supra.*

119. Brown v. Wilkinson, 15 M. & W. 391 (1846); The Mary Caroline, 3 W. Rob. 101 (1848); Leycester v. Logan, 3 K. & J. 446 (1857). These cases were decided under the English Limitation Act of 1813, which had amended the Act of 1786; the 1786 Act was one of the principal sources of the American Limitation Act of 1851. (See note 5 *supra.*) The English Merchant Shipping Act of 1862 (25 & 26 Vict. c. 63) had adopted a different method of limiting shipowner's liability: £8 per ton for property damage, £15 per ton for personal injury or death.

120. Walker v. Boston Ins. Co., 80 Mass. (14 Gray) 288 (1859).

121. 80 U.S. (13 Wall.) 104 (1871). The facts of the case are stated in note 7 *supra.*

be the rule of the "general maritime law"—that the owner's interest is to be calculated according to the value of the ship after the collision or other cause of loss has taken place. Thus if the ship is lost, the value is zero; if a few strippings from the wreck and a life boat or two are saved, those may be solemnly handed over to a trustee or their value ascertained and a bond posted. Since the voyage is the limitation unit,[122] if more than one accident or collision should occur in the course of a voyage, the owner's interest is the ship's value after the last of the accidents has occurred. If the voyage is completed, the value to be used is the ship's value at the end of the voyage. All these propositions, decided in or necessarily implied from the court's holding in Norwich Company v. Wright, have ever since been fixed points of American limitation law. The 1935 loss of life amendments created a statutory exception to the rule which, otherwise, has not been judicially questioned or even discussed since its first formulation.[123]

§ **10–30.** The decision in Norwich Co. v. Wright left unsettled a point quite as important as when the shipowner's interest should be valued: assuming, as the Wright case held, that the time is after the collision and not before, does the term "interest" used in the Limitation Act include the proceeds of insurance carried by the owner on the vessel? Since hull insurance is universally carried, the owner whose vessel is lost or damaged can largely make himself whole if he is not required to turn over to court or trustee the amounts received as insurance. On the other hand, if "interest" includes insurance, the shipowner will stand to lose the entire value of his investment.

The insurance question came to the Court in 1885 in three cases, which were decided together: The City of Norwich,[124] which was a subsequent appeal in the same litigation which had brought Norwich Co. v. Wright to the Court, The Scotland,[125] and The Great Western.[126] The cases were elaborately briefed and argued to the Court: the roster of counsel and *amici curiae* is a blue book of the admiralty bar of the period. The question was clearly felt as one of great difficulty, particularly since the Court's announced policy of looking to "general maritime law" for aid in construing the American Limitation Act was here of not the slightest help. The question whether insurance proceeds had to be abandoned along with the ship to obtain limitation of liability had been a matter of violent controversy among European commentators for several hundred years and nineteenth century legislative developments in such maritime countries

122. §§ 10–46 to 10–49 *infra.*

123. However, as late as 1887, Van Santvoord, Limitation of the Liability of Shipowners 137, suggested on behalf of cargo: (1) the English rule of valuation of the ship just before the collision or other cause of loss; (2) the rule that the valuation should be taken as at the commencement of the voyage in the case of more than one accident.

124. 118 U.S. 468, 6 S.Ct. 1150 (1886).

125. 118 U.S. 507, 6 S.Ct. 1174 (1886).

126. 118 U.S. 520, 6 S.Ct. 1172 (1886).

as France, Holland and the German states reflected a continuing divergence of opinion. The difficulty which the Court felt with the cases is indicated by the sequence of argument. The Scotland was first argued on March 12 and 13, 1885; argument in The Great Western was heard on October 19 and 20, which was followed on October 20 and 21 by reargument in The Scotland; finally The City of Norwich was heard on November 16 and 17. Decision in the three cases was not announced until May 10, 1886, a year and two months after the first argument in The Scotland.

By a 5–4 majority the Court, through Justice Bradley, held that "interest" did not include insurance, so that the proceeds need not be surrendered by the shipowner. Justices Miller, Harlan, Matthews and Gray published a vigorous dissent.[127] In view of the confusion of the Continental authorities, looked to as sources of "general maritime law", the absence of any indication of what the legislative intent may have been in 1851, and the blank ambiguity of the Limitation Act itself, the holding in the three cases might be described, in current terminology, as a policy decision, vaguely shored up in the majority opinion by makeweight speculations as to the "nature" of property insurance (a "collateral contract", "personal to the insured", of "indemnity merely", which "does not attach itself to the thing insured, nor go with it when it is transferred"). In essence all that can be said of the cases is that five justices felt that allowing the shipowner to retain the proceeds of insurance was wise and statesmanlike, and that four justices did not.

The battle of the insurance proceeds, like the battle of Waterloo in the Duke of Wellington's opinion, was "a damned close-run thing". Nevertheless, once settled, it stayed settled.[128] The shipowner's right to retain the proceeds of his insurance has long been regarded as a point quite as firmly settled as his right to have his "interest" measured after the collision and not before. Not even during the Congressional consideration of the Limitation Act in 1935 and 1936 was there any disposition on anyone's part to call either of these two settled issues into question.

**§ 10–31.** In 1954 Maryland Casualty Co. v. Cushing,[129] brought novel questions of the interrelationship between insurance and limitation law before the Supreme Court, which found itself even more hopelessly divided than it had been seventy years earlier on The City of Norwich and its companion cases. The owner of a towboat, oper-

127. 118 U.S. 468, 526, 6 S.Ct. 1150, 1164. The dissent applied to all three cases.

128. An unsuccessful attempt was made to persuade Congress to amend the Limitation Act to include insurance proceeds in the limitation fund. See Van Santvoord, Limitation of the Liability of Shipowners 138 (1887). In 1957 Senator Morse introduced legislation which would have required that insurance proceeds go into the limitation fund; no action was ever taken on the proposal. See Note, Shipowners' Limited Liability, 3 Colum.J. of Law and Social Studies 105, 109 (1967).

129. 347 U.S. 409, 74 S.Ct. 608, 1954 A.M.C. 837 (1954).

ating in Louisiana waters, carried policies of liability insurance which provided that payment should be made by the insurance carrier only when the insured should have been held liable in damages. Five seamen were drowned in a collision of the towboat with a bridge; the owner and charterer petitioned for limitation of liability and the District Court enjoined suit against the petitioners outside the limitation proceeding. A Louisiana statute authorized a direct action against the insurance company by injured claimants. Representatives of the drowned seamen, who had challenged the right to limitation in the admiralty proceeding, brought actions against the insurance company as authorized by the state statute. The insurance company sought to defend on the ground that the actions were in direct conflict with the Limitation Act.

Four members of the Court agreed with the insurance company and thought that the actions should be dismissed. Their principal argument, expressed in an opinion by Justice Frankfurter, was the following: death claims already filed amounted to $600,000; the liability insurance was for $180,000; the value of the towboat had not been established in the limitation proceeding, but assume that it was $25,000. If the direct actions are allowed, claimants may recover $180,000 from the insurance companies. Thereafter, if limitation is allowed, they may recover from the owner whatever value may be placed on the ship in the limitation proceeding. The owner will not be able to recoup from the insurance companies, since their liability under the policies will have been exhausted in the direct actions. Therefore the owner will have been deprived of the benefit of his insurance which, under The City of Norwich, the Limitation Act allows him to keep.

Four other members of the Court, in an opinion by Justice Black, found nothing in the Limitation Act to prevent the actions against the insurance companies. For one thing, the insurance companies could not be looked on as beneficiaries of the Act nor even as entitled to plead it as a defense. For another, the present case had nothing to do with the makeup of the limitation fund and thus no connection with the rule of The City of Norwich which the four justices who joined in the Frankfurter opinion had thought ultimately decisive of the case.

> "There is [wrote Justice Black] a vital difference between liability insurance and hull insurance with which The City of Norwich dealt. . . . It is a far cry from the decision in The City of Norwich that a shipowner is entitled to keep the insurance collected for loss of his own ship to today's holding that States cannot assure seamen that they instead of the shipowner can get the full benefit of liability policies bought in order to pay their just claims for injuries caused by the ship." [130]

130. *Id.* at 434–435, 74 S.Ct. at 621, 1954 A.M.C. at 857.

The four justices who joined in the Black opinion would have allowed the actions against the insurance companies to proceed.

The ninth man on the Court, Justice Clark, had his own way of solving the case. The actions against the insurance companies should be stayed until completion of the limitation proceeding. If the shipowner in that proceeding should be found liable but entitled to limitation and the value of the vessel appraised at $25,000, the insurance companies could then pay that amount into the limitation proceeding for *pro rata* distribution among the claimants. Thereafter the claimants could proceed directly against the insurance companies, whose liability under their policies would of course be reduced by the amount previously paid into the limitation proceeding. Justice Clark's ingenious solution gave the claimants the possibility of recovering the full amount of the insurance without subjecting the shipowner to the hazard of paying a judgment in the amount of the ship's value which he could not then recover under his insurance policies. Although Justice Clark stood alone in his analysis of the case, his solution became the mandate of the Court since the four justices who had joined in the Frankfurter opinion agreed to remand the case in accordance with Justice Clark's views "in order to breach the deadlock . . . and to enable a majority to dispose of this litigation".

Because of the Court's extraordinary division, it is impossible to say what the Cushing case stands for, beyond the fact that it presumably established a procedure to be followed by lower courts in handling similar cases until the Supreme Court further clarified the issues. It cannot be said that the Cushing case in any way weakened the rule of The City of Norwich. The members of the Court for whom Justice Black spoke betrayed some impatience with the idea of limited liability, but felt that The City of Norwich was in no way involved. Justice Clark commented that "Though the holding in The City of Norwich does not control, . . . the reasoning of that case is pertinent". And the four justices who joined in Justice Frankfurter's opinion felt that The City of Norwich ultimately controlled the Cushing case. The manner in which the case was remanded suggested that state law would be allowed to have a regulatory effect on marine insurance policies,[131] but it must not be forgotten that only one justice thought the Cushing case was properly disposed of. In any event, the rule of The City of Norwich seems to be too firmly established a rule of federal maritime law to be displaced by state action.

The Fifth Circuit, in the absence of further guidance from the Supreme Court, naturally became the only true expounder of the meaning of the Cushing case as applied to actions brought directly against insurers under the Louisiana statute. It would be inappro-

131. See the discussion of Wilburn Boat Co. v. Fireman's Fund Ins. Co., 348 U.S. 310, 75 S.Ct. 368, 1955 A.M.C. 467 (1955) in Chapter II, § 2–7.

priate in a general treatise to pursue the horrid complexities which the Fifth Circuit has uncovered in its attempts to reconcile the language of the Louisiana Direct Action statute and related provisions of the Louisiana Civil Code with the meaning and policy of the Limitation Act revealed as through a glass darkly in the Supreme Court's 4–1–4 split in Cushing. Olympic Towing Corporation v. Nebel Towing Company, Inc.[131a] appears to be the Fifth Circuit's definitive attempt to read the riddle.[131b] The holding in the Nebel case, stated in an oversimplified form, was that, in limitation proceedings, direct, actions against insurers should be allowed to proceed but that the Limitation Court, by injunction, consolidation or whatever other device might occur to it, should "devise effective procedures" to make sure that the insurance fund will not be exhausted before the shipowner has received the benefit of his insurance. Judge Gewin concluded, citing Cushing:

> There is no question that the Limitation Act was designed to assist the maritime industry and that it was in no way intended to benefit the insurance industry. Thus it is patent that statutory limitation of liability is only available to a shipowner; the status of insurer is not covered by the public policy underlying the Limitation Act. We therefore hold that limitation of liability under the federal statute is a personal defense which cannot be availed of by an insurer under Louisiana law.[131c]

The question whether actions not subject to limitation can be brought against insurers under the Louisiana statute with respect to accidents occurring outside Louisiana territorial water has not, at the moment of writing, been clearly answered.[131d]

**131a.** 419 F.2d 230, 1969 A.M.C. 1571 (5th Cir. 1969), rehearing en banc denied 419 F.2d 238 (5th Cir. 1969), certiorari denied 397 U.S. 989, 90 S.Ct. 1120 (1970).

**131b.** Judge Brown's dissent from the order denying a rehearing en banc, 419 F.2d 238, collects the Court's earlier decisions on the point.

**131c.** 419 F.2d at p. 238. For more on the Nebel case and the Louisiana statute see Judge Brown's opinion in Alcoa S.S. Co. v. Charles Ferran & Co., Inc., 443 F.2d 250, 1971 A.M.C. 1116 (5th Cir. 1971), certiorari denied 404 U.S. 854, 92 S.Ct. 98 (1971) (the Alcoa case did not involve the Limitation Act). See further, applying the rule of the Nebel case in a limitation proceeding, Complaint of Sincere Navigation Corp. (The S/S Helena), 317 F. Supp. 1, 1971 A.M.C. 991 (E.D.La. 1970).

**131d.** Continental Oil Co. v. The London Steam-Ship Owners' Mutual Insurance Association, Ltd., 417 F.2d 1030, 1969 A.M.C. 1882 (5th Cir. 1969) held that the Louisiana Direct Action statute did not apply to litigation arising from the collision of a ship with an oil drilling platform on the Continental Shelf but the decision rested on the provisions of a federal statute (the Outer Continental Shelf Lands Act, 43 U.S.C.A. § 1331 *et seq.*). In Sassoni v. Savoie, 327 F.Supp. 474, 1971 A.M.C. 1910 (E.D.La.1971) Judge Rubin concluded that the question was "open" under the Continental Oil case and the Nebel case (text following note 131a *supra*) and held that a direct action lay against an insurer where the plaintiff was a Louisiana

The only other "direct action" statute comparable to the Louisiana statute which has so far surfaced in limitation litigation is a Puerto Rico statute.[131e] In other jurisdictions where the attempt has been made to proceed against insurers (or to hold owners liable without benefit of limitation) under the rule of the Cushing case, the answer has been that the relevant jurisdiction did not have a Louisiana-type statute and that the action was not maintainable.[131f]

**§ 10–32.** After the principal issues of when the owner's interest was to be valued and who was entitled to insurance proceeds had been decided, there remained to be worked out a number of subsidiary details regarding the makeup of the limitation fund. The draftsmen of the Limitation Act seem to have contemplated that the shipowner would transfer his interest in the vessel to a court-appointed trustee and that the limitation fund would eventually be established by a sale of the vessel. However, the Limitation Rules, from the time of their promulgation by the Supreme Court in 1872, have always provided, in lieu of a transfer to a trustee, for the deposit with the Limitation Court of money or security in the amount of his interest.[132] Since the shipowner almost invariably posts bond and keeps his ship, the first step in any limitation proceeding is to decide how his interest is to be valued and how much he must put up.[133]

The question of valuation comes up for judicial discussion in limitation cases as it does in collision, general average and salvage cases. There do not appear to be any special limitation rules applicable to the

resident who had been injured (on the "high seas") aboard a fishing vessel which operated out of a Louisiana port.

131e. See Torres v. Interstate Fire and Casualty Co., 275 F.Supp. 784, 1968 A.M.C. 367 (D.Puerto Rico 1967) holding that injury and death claimants could proceed with their actions against an insurer without waiting for conclusion of the limitation proceeding. Ema v. Compagnie Generale Transatlantique (the S.S. Antilles), 353 F.Supp. 1286 (D.Puerto Rico 1972) is to the same effect.

131f. See In re Pacific Inland Navigation Co., 263 F.Supp. 915 (D.Hawaii, 1967) (Hawaii law); Pettus v. Jones & Laughlin Steel Corp., 322 F.Supp. 1078, 1972 A.M.C. 170 (W.D.Pa.1971) (Pennsylvania law); Complaint of Harbor Towing Corp., 335 F.Supp. 1150, 1972 A.M.C. 597 (D.Md.1971) (Maryland law).

On the effect of an insurer's "letter of undertaking" in an owner's subsequent limitation proceeding, see In re Moore (The Tug Olive L. Moore), 278 F.Supp. 260, 1968 A.M.C. 818 (E.D. Mich.1968), discussed text following note 113 *supra*.

132. On the Rules, see §§ 10–2, 10–9 *supra*.

133. It has been held that demise or bareboat charterers who are entitled to limitation under § 186 (see § 10–10 *supra*) must post bond in the amount of the vessel's appraised value and not merely in the amount of the charterer's own "interest". See Petition of McAllister Bros. Inc., 96 F.Supp. 575, 1951 A.M.C. 967 (E.D.N.Y.1951). In Avera v. Florida Towing Corp., 322 F.2d 155, 162 (n. 10), 1963 A.M.C. 2110, 2116 (n. 10) (5th Cir. 1963), Judge Brown, citing McAllister, commented that: "Though precedents are scarce, the value to be surrendered or bonded by a bareboat charterer is the same as that exacted of an owner."

vessel valuation problem.[134] In The Main v. Williams [134a] Justice Brown remarked that:

> The real object of this [Limitation] act . . . was to limit the liability of vessel owners to their interest in the *adventure*; hence, in assessing the value of the ship, the custom has been to include all that belongs to the ship, and may be presumed to be the property of the owner, not merely the hull, together with the boats, tackle, apparel, and furniture, but all the appurtenances comprising whatever is on board for the object of the voyage, belonging to the owner, whether such object be warfare, the conveyance of passengers, goods, or the fisheries.

In a hyper-modern application of that principle it has been held that removable refrigerated cargo containers, not assigned to any particular vessel except by coincidence for a particular voyage, were to be valued and included in the limitation fund as "appurtenances . . . risked on the vessel for the object of the adventure." [134b] The Supreme Court held long ago that a shipowner who has recovered damages from another ship with which his own had been in collision must, if he petitions for limitation, include the damages recovered in the valuation of his "interest".[134c] Presumably the rule would require the valuation of all the owner's claims against third parties which arose out of the operation of the vessel (at least those on the relevant voyage) whether or not the claims had been reduced to judgment.[134d] In fine, the vessel is to be valued free of pre-existing liens.[134e]

The vessel is to be valued in its state at the end of the relevant voyage. "Voyage" is not, of course, a self-defining term: if a ship puts in at an intermediate port for repairs following an accident and then resumes her original voyage in the course of which she suffers

134. In petition of Bloomfield Steamship Co. (The Ronda–The Lucille Bloomfield), 422 F.2d 728, 1970 A.M.C. 521 (2d Cir. 1970), Judge Palmieri commented that: "The limitation value was the value after collision and the district court correctly followed Norwich & N.Y. Transp. Co. v. Wright, 80 U.S. 104 (1871), in determining her limitation value to be her stipulated sound value minus the cost of collision repairs." He also cited Standard Oil Co. of New Jersey v. Southern Pacific Co. (The Cushing—The Proteces), 268 U.S. 146, 45 S.Ct. 465, 1925 A.M.C. 779 (1925), a limitation case in which the valuation question was discussed not for the purpose of establishing a limitation fund but for the purpose of calculating collision damages. Olson & Co. v. American Steamship Marine Leopard, 356 F.2d 728, 1966 A.M.C. 1064 (9th Cir. 1966) also discusses valuation in a limitation proceeding for the purpose of calculating collision damages.

134a. 152 U.S. 122, 131, 14 S.Ct. 486, 488 (1894).

134b. Complaint of Pacific Far East Line (The Esso Seattle—The Guam Bear), 314 F.Supp. 1339, 1970 A.M.C. 1592 (N.D.Cal.1970). Thede, note 13(c) *supra*, 45 Tulane L.Rev. 959, 962 (1971) collects other cases.

134c. O'Brien v. Miller, 168 U.S. 287, 303 *et seq.*, 18 S.Ct. 140, 146 (1897).

134d. The rule of O'Brien v. Miller was applied in Olson & Co. v. American Steamship Marine Leopard, 356 F.2d 728, 1966 A.M.C. 1064 (9th Cir. 1966).

134e. See § 10–48 *infra*.

a second accident, has she been engaged in a single interrupted voyage or in two separate voyages? This issue can become of importance not only for the purpose of valuation but, since the voyage is the limitation unit, for the purpose of determining which creditors or claimants may share in the fund.[134f] It occasionally happens that an owner has his vessel repaired before he gets around to filing his limitation complaint. In such a case the claimants will naturally argue that, for the purposes of the limitation fund, the vessel should be valued in its repaired state. Under the "voyage" theory, the question for decision is whether the repairs were made before or after the voyage had come to an end; the prudent shipowner will make as clear as possible to all potential claimants that the voyage is at an end before the repairs are undertaken.[134g] Even better, he will file his limitation complaint first.

The Limitation Act (§ 183(a)) requires the owner to surrender his interest not only in the "vessel" but also in "her freight then pending". Norwich and New York Transp. Co. v. Wright [134h] made it clear that only money actually earned was to be considered "pending"; if the termination of the voyage short of destination discharged the duty to pay, then the freight which would have been earned if the voyage had been successfully completed did not come in. And subsequently it was held that where the event leading to the limitation proceeding occurs on the return half of a round trip voyage, only the freight on the return voyage should be considered "pending".[134i] In The Main

134f. See § 10–46 *et seq. infra.* In re Moore, (The Tug Olive L. Moore), 278 F.Supp. 260, 1968 A.M.C. 818 (E.D. Mich.1968) (discussed text following note 205a *infra*) has an interesting discussion of the "interrupted voyage" question.

134g. See Rice Growers Ass'n of California v. Rederiaktiebolaget Frode (The Frej), 176 F.2d 401, 194, 1949 A.M.C. 1761 (9th Cir. 1949), certiorari denied 338 U.S. 879, 70 S.Ct. 159 (1949) in which the shipowner was held not liable for the value of repairs made after he had notified cargo that the voyage had been abandoned (even though the ship, following the repairs, carried the cargo to its original destination). But see Petition of Cuba Distilling Co., Inc. (The Lara), 1947 A.M.C. 27 (S.D.N.Y.1946) in which the owner was required to include the value of repairs in the limitation fund. Another case in which the contention that the value of repairs should be included in the limitation fund was made, and rejected is Complaint of Pacific Inland Navigation Company, Inc. (The Diesel Tug Shinn), 263 F.Supp. 915 (D.Hawaii, 1967).

134h. 80 U.S. (13 Wall.) 104, 126 (1871).

134i. La Bourgogne, 210 U.S. 95, 28 S. Ct. 664 (1908); The Steel Inventor (Petition of the U. S. Steel Products Co.), 36 F.2d 399, 1929 A.M.C. 1610 (S. D.N.Y.1929); The Black Eagle and Concordia, 87 F.2d 891, 1937 A.M.C. 198 (2d Cir. 1937). But if a round trip voyage is found to constitute a "single adventure", the freight for the round trip must be surrendered even if the collision occurs on the return trip after delivery of the cargo at destination, The William J. Riddle (Petition of United States), 111 F.Supp. 657, 1953 A.M.C. 531 (S.D.N.Y.1953).

In Complaint of Pacific Inland Navigation Co., Inc. (The Diesel Tug Shinn), 263 F.Supp. 915 (D.Hawaii, 1967) it was contended that there should be included in the limitation fund, as "freight pending", the total earnings of the vessel (a tug) under a six-month charter which had about two months to run at the time of the accident. Judge Tavares reviewed the "freight pending" cases, elected to follow La Bourgogne and denied the contention. See further Cross Contracting Co. v. Law, discussed in the text following note 134k *infra.*

v. Williams[134j] Justice Brown commented that "There is no reason . . . for giving to the word 'freight' a narrow and technical definition" and held that passenger fares should be included as well as any money payable for the carriage of goods. Under Justice Brown's approach it would seem that the owner's total earnings from whatever "adventure" the vessel was engaged in at the time of the accident should be included in the limitation fund. Such an argument was made to the Fifth Circuit in a novel context in Cross Contracting Co. v. Law.[134k] The "adventure" was the construction of a levee in connection with a flood control project undertaken by the Army Corps of Engineers in Lake Okochobee, a "navigable waterbody" in Florida. In the contractor's limitation proceeding claimants argued that all the money earned under the contract should be considered "freight pending". Judge Ainsworth, for the majority of the court, rejected the argument, observing that: "there is little relationship between pending freight as used in the commonly accepted maritime cases, and money due for the construction of a levee . . . ". Judge Godbold, building on Justice Brown's opinion in The Main and collecting other cases illustrating a broad reading of "freight", entered a persuasive dissent.

The interest which the owner is required to transfer or post security for is described in § 183(a) as his interest in "such vessel". From their use of the singular noun, it seems a reasonable hypothesis that the draftsmen had not given any thought to what should happen when two or more vessels under common ownership—the most obvious example is a tug and her tow—are involved in the same accident. Must all the vessels be surrendered or valued and included in the limitation fund or only the vessel found to be principally or actively at fault? The confusion which would in any case have followed from the draftsmen's oversight was compounded by an unfortunate sequence of Supreme Court cases in the early 1920's. The Supreme Court has made no further contribution to the problem which, under the somewhat misleading rubric of "the flotilla doctrine", continues to account for a substantial amount of litigation.

In Liverpool, Brazil and River Plate Steam Navigation Company v. Brooklyn Eastern District Terminal[134l] it appeared that a tug owned by the Terminal had been at fault in a collision with the Navigation Company's Vauban, which was moored to a Brooklyn pier. At the time of the collision a car float was lashed to the tug's port side and a disabled tug was lashed to its starboard side. Both the car float and the disabled tug were owned by the Terminal, which successfully pleaded the Limitation Act. The issue presented to the Supreme Court was whether the Terminal's liability should be limited to the value of

134j. 152 U.S. 122, 14 S.Ct. 486 (1894). See the quotation from Justice Brown's opinion, text following note 134a *supra*.

134k. 454 F.2d 408, 1972 A.M.C. 1008 (5th Cir. 1972). *Cf.* Complaint of Pacific Inland Navigation Co., Inc., note 134i *supra*.

134*l*. 251 U.S. 48, 40 S.Ct. 66 (1919).

the tug under power or whether the value of the car float and the other tug should also be included. Justice Holmes, in a notably simplistic opinion, said in effect that "such vessel" meant "such vessel" and that the owner would not be getting the protection contemplated by the Limitation Act if the courts were to "profess a formal compliance with the words but . . . artificially [construe] 'such vessel' to include other vessels if only they are tied to it." The tug under power, he said, was "actively responsible" and the car float (which had in fact collided with the Vauban was merely a "passive instrument". In a characteristic flourish he added the not particularly helpful thought that: "[I]f you surrender the offending vessel you are free, just as it was said by a judge in the time of Edward III, 'If my dog kills your sheep and I freshly after the fact tender you the dog you are without recourse against me.' "[134m]

It might be said that the holding in the Liverpool case, however outrageous, was at least clear. Its clarity, however, did not survive a distinction suggested by Justice Sutherland (for a unanimous Court) in Sacramento Navigation Company v. Salz.[134n] The Salz case was not a limitation proceeding (although it is often cited as if it had been) but involved the construction of the phrase "any vessel transporting merchandise" in § 3 of the Harter Act. "Any vessel", said Justice Sutherland, included both a tug and a barge which she had in tow. The distinction between Salz and Liverpool, he added, was "plain":

> "There [Liverpool] the libel was for an injury to a ship in no way related to the flotilla. It was a pure tort—no contractual obligations were involved; and the simple inquiry was, What constituted the 'offending vessel'? Here we must ask, What constituted the vessel by which the contract of transportation was to be effected? a very different question."[134o]

The Salz distinction may have been as nonsensical as the Liverpool holding was outrageous. Why on earth should an owner, several of whose vessels have been used in the commission of a tort, be entitled to limit his liability to the one "actively responsible" vessel while an owner who has used several of his vessels in performing a contractual obligation must put up the value of the whole "flotilla" if anything goes wrong? However that may be, the "flotilla doctrine" limitation litigation has ever since revolved around the opposite poles of Liverpool ("pure tort") and Salz ("contractual obligation").

The current state of the Liverpool or "pure tort" horn of the dilemma is neatly illustrated by Complaint of Midland Enterprises,

**134m.** Citing Fitz. Abr., Barre, 290. In his later years Justice Holmes not infrequently lived off the fat of his youthful erudition. See The Common Law, (1881 (Howe ed. 1963)), 21.

**134n.** 273 U.S. 326, 47 S.Ct. 368, 1927 A.M.C. 397 (1927).

**134*o*.** 273 U.S. at p. 332, 47 S.Ct. at p. 370.

Inc.[134p] The tug, Orco, had been engaged in towing fourteen barges up the Ohio River. Orco, having been summoned to the aid of one of its sister ships, left its string of barges moored to the river bank. The barges broke loose; a number of the barges crashed into a dam, causing substantial damage, and eight barges sank; six barges were undamaged (and, apparently, undamaging). Midland, owner of the Orco and of thirteen of the fourteen barges, claimed that it should be entitled to limit to the value of the sunken and consequently valueless barges. The United States, as owner of the dam, claimed that the value of the tug and all fourteen barges had to be accounted for. Judge Hogan, in a remarkable opinion, delivered a judgment of Solomon: Midland must put the value of the tug as well as the six sunken barges into the limitation fund. As to the six undamaged barges, he indicated that if he were free to exercise an independent judgment he would order their value included but, being bound by Liverpool, he concluded that Midland need not pay their value into the fund.[134q]

The lower federal courts which have reluctantly followed Liverpool when they could find no way of escaping from it have enthusiastically embraced the "contractual obligation" theory and carried it light years beyond the contracts of towage which Justice Sutherland was talking about in Salz. One tour de force was contributed by Judge Learned Hand in Standard Dredging Co. v. Kristiansen.[134r] Kristiansen was a seaman employed by Standard on a dredge who was ordered to perform duties on a barge (which was not physically attached to the dredge) and was injured on the barge. Held: that Standard owed a "contractual obligation" to Kristiansen as his employer and, as a condition of limitation, must surrender both dredge and barge (or their value). Judge Hand indulged himself in the course of his opinion with a reference to the "archaic notion" which Justice Holmes had espoused in Liverpool and concluded (perhaps tongue in cheek):

134p. 296 F.Supp. 1356, 1970 A.M.C. 2437 (digest only) (S.D.Ohio, 1968).

134q. Complaint of American Commercial Lines, Inc. (M/V James L. Hamilton), 353 F.Supp. 872, 1973 A.M.C. 319 (E.D.Kentucky, 1973) was another Ohio River tug and barge case in which the Court reluctantly followed the Liverpool "pure tort" rule. Judge Swinford commented that: "it is at least doubtful whether the Liverpool doctrine is responsive to the realities of the situation" (353 F.Supp. at p. 875, note) and went on to quote from Judge Medina's opinion in Deep Sea Tanker's Ltd. v. The Long Branch, 258 F.2d 757, 773, 1959 A.M.C. 28 (2d Cir. 1958): "We are not at liberty to disregard this binding precedent [i. e. Liverpool] simply because a contrary view may seem to reach a conclusion more in keeping with the realities of this particular case." The cases were again reviewed by Judge Northrop in Steuart Investment Co. v. Bauer Dredging Construction Co. Inc., 323 F.Supp. 907, 1971 A.M.C. 1447 (D.Md. 1971), who succeeded in holding, Liverpool to the contrary notwithstanding, that a tug and her barge in tow (the barge alone having damaged a pier) "should be treated together as the 'offending vessel'." For an example of the complexities which can result when the Liverpool rule is followed, consider the separate bonds for tug and tow which the Second Circuit felt obliged to order in Lake Tankers Corp. v. Henn, discussed in the text following note 76b *supra*.

134r. 67 F.2d 548, 1933 A.M.C. 1621 (2d Cir. 1933), certiorari denied 290 U.S. 704, 54 S.Ct. 372 (1934).

> "[W]e read [Salz] as meaning that when the duty violated, though imposed by law, presupposes at least the relation of master and servant, the owner must surrender all those vessels which share in the execution of the venture; collectively they are 'such vessel' within [§ 183(a)]." [134s]

Kristiansen has become the standard authority in flotilla cases where a court can find some handhold of "contractual obligation". Thus in Brown & Root Marine Operators, Inc. v. Zapata Offshore Co.[134t] Judge Coleman applied Kristiansen to a situation in which the limiting shipowner had contracted to do construction work on off-shore oil installation in the Gulf of Mexico and in Cross Contracting Company v. Law [134u] Judge Ainsworth found Kristiansen equally persuasive with respect to a "flotilla" of vessels engaged in constructing a levee in Lake Okochobee.

The flotilla litigation is an unhappy illustration of our judicial system at its worst. There is, and long has been, universal agreement that the Liverpool decision was as ill-advised in law as it was in policy—a great judge's momentary aberration. Consequently, the absurd distinction suggested in Salz has been exploited for all it is worth. It seems in the highest degree unlikely that the Supreme Court will ever agree to hear another flotilla case.[134v] Occasionally the Erie-bound inferior federal courts, faced with some state court clinker vintage 1880, will free themselves of their burden by speculating that the state court, if it had the opportunity to reconsider the issue, would reverse its unfortunate precedent. Perhaps some daring federal judge will come forward to give the Liverpool case that cavalier treatment. The worst that could happen to him would be to be reversed.[134w]

**134s.** 67 F.2d at p. 551. A quarter of a century later Judge Hand had a second opportunity to pay his respects to the Liverpool doctrine in Petition of United States Dredging Corp. (The Motor Launch Nip), 264 F.2d 339, 1959 A.M.C. 1110 (2d Cir. 1959) certiorari denied 360 U.S. 932, 79 S.Ct. 1452 (1959). On the authority of Kristiansen (and, of course, Salz) the shipowner-employer had to put up the value of five vessels engaged in a common venture. For some reason the flotilla question in an employment relationship was passed on by a state court in Rank v. Colonial Sand & Stone Co., Inc., 69 Misc.2d 749, 331 N.Y.S.2d 290, 1972 A.M.C. 2074 (Sup.St.1972). Judge Lane, rejecting several ingenious distinctions suggested by counsel for the shipowner, elected to follow Judge Hand in the Kristiansen and Dredging cases.

**134t.** 377 F.2d 724, 1967 A.M.C. 2684, 9 ALR Fed. 759 (5th Cir. 1967). The ALR annotation contains an exhaustive collection of the cases on this dreary subject through 1971.

**134u.** 454 F.2d 408, 1972 A.M.C. 1008 (5th Cir. 1972).

**134v.** Conceivably the Court could have discussed the flotilla question in Lake Tankers Corp. v. Henn, text following note 76b *supra*, but did not.

**134w.** See the Yarmouth Castle, discussed text following note 188a *infra*, in which a District Judge may have come "perilously close" to overruling another venerable Supreme Court decision in which Justice Holmes once again wrote the opinion.

### Claims for Loss of Life and Bodily Injury

**§ 10–33.** On September 8, 1934, the steamship Morro Castle burned off the coast of New Jersey with a loss of 135 lives. The vessel was largely destroyed and the owners petitioned to limit their liability to $20,000. The Morro Castle disaster stirred wide interest which became indignation when the peculiar (from a layman's point of view) provisions of the Limitation Act came to public attention. The subsequent hue and cry led to the first major amendments to the Limitation Act since its passage in 1851.[135]

The purpose of the amendments was to insure the availability of a fund (to the extent of the owner's solvency) [135a] out of which personal injury and death claims could be compensated even though the ship itself had been totally destroyed. The main features of the new legislation were adopted from British limitation law which, since 1862, has provided, with respect to property as well as injury and death claims, for the establishment of a limitation fund calculated on the basis of a vessel's registered tonnage.[136] Congress let pass the opportunity of rewriting the Limitation Act as a whole and merely piled the personal injury and loss of life amendments on top of the old ramshackle structure. The amendments themselves present difficult problems of construction which have not as yet been resolved and in all probability never will be. Curiously, the amendments have repeated the experience under the original Act of 1851 and have now lain fallow for a generation since their enactment.[136b]

The key provision of the amendments reads as follows:

> "In the case of any seagoing vessel, if the amount of the owner's liability as limited under subsection (a) [*i. e.* old § 183] is insufficient to pay all losses in full, and the portion of such amount applicable to the payment of losses in respect

135. See Springer, Amendments to the Federal Law Limiting the Liability of Shipowners, 11 St. Johns L.Rev. 14 (1936); Purdy, Recent Amendments to the Limitation of Liability Statutes, 5 Brooklyn L.Rev. 42 (1935); Colomb, The Effect of the Recent Amendments to the Federal Limitation of Liability Act, 10 Tulane L.Rev. 119 (1935).

The Morro Castle litigation was settled before trial. The settlement is reported in detail in 1939 A.M.C. 895. The proctors for the many damage claimants organized a proctors' committee, only one proctor with three personal injury clients declining to cooperate. The committee negotiated a settlement under the terms of which the owner placed a fund of $890,000 at the disposal of the committee in full settlement of all the claims. An additional $10,000 was contributed by cargo in the guise of a proportional reduction of their claims. Aggregate damage claims amounted to $1,450,000.

135a. The Financial Responsibility Act of 1966 (text at note 25a *supra*), applicable to certain passenger-carrying vessels, is designed to make sure that a fund will be available in any event.

136. Merchant Shipping Acts, 1862, 25 & 26 Vict., c. 63, § 64; 1894, 57 & 58 Vict., c. 60, § 503. See note 119 *supra*.

136b. The statement in the text has been left as it appeared in the first edition. During the period of nearly twenty years which has elapsed since the first edition was prepared, only four cases have been found which discuss the amendments.

> of loss of life or bodily injury is less than $60 per ton of such vessel's tonnage, such portion shall be increased to an amount equal to $60 per ton, to be available only for the payment of losses in respect of loss of life or bodily injury." [137]

That provision does not, at least in the first instance, establish a separate fund for the payment of injury and death claims. By its terms it comes into operation only after the owner's liability has been determined in a limitation proceeding under what may be called the old Act (*i. e.* the value of the owner's interest in the vessel and pending freight under § 183(a)). Only if the amounts allocated to injury and death claims from the § 183(a) fund are insufficient to pay those claims in full is the $60 per ton fund to be set up. The amount of the additional § 183(b) fund is whatever is necessary to increase the recovery of the death and injury claimants, who have already received something from the § 183(a) fund (unless the vessel was a total loss with no freight pending), to the maximum figure of $60 per ton.

**§ 10–34.** The amendment does not indicate the procedure to be followed. Under § 185 the owner who petitions for limitation must surrender his interest to a trustee or post bond within six months after he has received notice of claim. The six months limitation (which was written into the Act concurrently with the amendments now under discussion) obviously does not apply to the establishment of the $60 per ton fund, since the facts on which the setting up of that fund depend could not be shown by the mere filing of claim. What is not clear, however, is when and how and under what conditions the court can order the fund to be set up. Assume that death and injury claims have been filed against a shipowner who petitions for limitation, alleging that the value of the ship (which has been lost) is zero. Could the court with which the limitation petition is filed require the owner, as a condition of limitation, to post bond in an amount sufficient (up to the statutory ceiling) to satisfy his maximum liability under the claims (which are still unliquidated); or should the court first determine the basic questions of liability and right to limitation before requiring the owner to provide funds or sureties to satisfy the judgments? The first alternative would be more satisfactory to claimants, who would be protected against supervening insolvency of the shipowner or dissipation of assets during possibly protracted judicial proceedings; the second alternative would be more to the shipowner's liking. The statute offers no sure guide to solution, although, on a purely verbal level of statutory construction, the statement that the $60 per ton fund comes into operation only "if the amount of the owner's liability as limited under subsection (a) is insufficient" might be read to suggest that the questions of liability and limitation under § 183(a) must be first settled before the additional fund is set up.[138] However, in two recent cases where the aggregate

137. 49 Stat. 960 (1935), 49 Stat. 1479 (1936), 46 U.S.C.A. § 183(b).

138. In The Park Victory (Petition of Luckenbach S.S. Co., Inc.), 1953 A.M.C.

of the death and injury claims was many times in excess of the § 183 (a) fund, the trial judges sensibly ordered that § 183(b) funds be set up at the outset of the proceedings.[138a]

Other procedural problems may come up in cases where the claimants, under the theory of Langnes v. Green, are allowed to prosecute their actions outside the admiralty court despite the filing of a limitation petition.[138b] If, in such a case, the owner's right to limit and the amount of his liability under § 183(a) have been determined by the admiralty court, would a state court, having given judgment for death or injury in excess of the § 183(a) fund, have jurisdiction to decree the setting up of an additional fund up to $60 per ton; or would the matter have to be referred back to the admiralty court? The more prudent procedure would seem to be to return to the admiralty court, since under Langnes v. Green the claimant must stipulate that all questions relating to the owner's right to limit are to be decided in that court. It could be argued that setting up a fund under § 183 (b) has nothing to do with the right to limit or questions of limitation law, being merely a matter of ascertaining the vessel's tonnage and multiplying by 60; but counsel who made such an argument would seem to be asking for unnecessary trouble.

**§ 10–35.** The § 183(b) fund is to be available, under the circumstances explained above, only "in the case of any seagoing vessel". Section 183(f) limits the term "seagoing vessel" by giving a list of types of vessels which are not to be included in the term for the purposes of the subsections relating to the § 183(b) fund.[139] The common characteristic of the vessels excluded seems to be that they do not customarily carry passengers for hire. If that is the true meaning of the exclusionary language, neither the crews of the various

808 (S.D.N.Y.1953) Judge Ryan refused to order a $90,000 bond given under § 183(a) increased to $400,000 under § 183(b) until it should be determined that the § 183(a) fund was insufficient to pay the death and personal injury claims in full.

**138a.** In Complaint of Panoceanic Tankers Corp. (S/S Panoceanic Faith), 332 F.Supp. 313, 1971 A.M.C. 1163 (S.D.N.Y.1971) it appeared that the § 183(a) fund was $100 and the death and injury claims were $28,500,000. Judge Cooper distinguished the Park Victory, note 138 *supra*, on the ground of the "grossly insufficient" § 183(a) fund in his own case and ordered that a § 183(b) fund be set up before the questions of liability and limitation were disposed of.

Petition of Alva S.S. Co. (The M/T Alva Cape), 262 F.Supp. 328, 1967 A.M.C. 2363 (S.D.N.Y.1966) is to the same effect. In Alva the § 183(a) fund was $162,400.30; the death and injury claims were in excess of $32,000,000.

Supplemental Rule F(7) provides, in part, that "any claimant may demand that the deposit or security be increased on the ground that it is insufficient to carry out the provision of the statutes relating to claims in respect of loss of life or bodily injury . . . ". There was no comparable reference to the "loss of life" amendments in Admiralty Rule 52 from which Rule F(7), according to the Advisory Committee's Note, was derived. To the extent that the Rule F(7) reference means anything, it should presumably be taken to increase the Limitation Court's discretion in granting such "demands". This provision of Rule F(7) does not appear to have been the subject of any judicial discussion.

**138b.** On Langnes v. Green, see § 10–19 *supra*.

**139.** See § 10–7 *supra*.

types of commercial vessels listed, nor the crew of or guests aboard a "pleasure yacht", nor third persons injured by such vessels could claim the benefit of the $60 per ton fund to satisfy their claims. However, the cases which have considered the point have uniformly concluded that the loss of life amendments are not limited to "passenger-carrying" vessels and that crews of commercial vessels are entitled to the $60 per ton fund.[139a] Even so, to be on the safe side, the potential victim should be careful to be injured or killed by a "seagoing" passenger-carrying vessel.

The term "seagoing", even as limited by § 183(f), carries serious ambiguities. Does the adjective refer to types of vessels or to types of voyages? The narrowest construction would be that the § 183(b) fund is available only for the benefit of claimants who were injured or killed "at sea" or "on the high seas"—excluding, for example, claims deriving from an accident on board a vessel which, after completing an ocean voyage, was proceeding up the Mississippi River to the port of New Orleans. The broadest construction would be that the term "seagoing" means any vessel capable of going to sea, as a matter of ship construction, whether the vessel, at the time of the accident leading to the claim, is at sea or in a harbor, lake, river, sound, canal or even dry dock. Various intermediate positions are possible—for example that the term includes a vessel which regularly goes to sea, even though it may be temporarily, at the time of the accident, somewhere else. Vessels used on the Great Lakes present a problem of their own. And would passenger-carrying ferryboats plying New York harbor or San Francisco Bay or Puget Sound be "seagoing" for this purpose? The exclusionary list in § 183(f), which is drawn up by types of vessels, may faintly suggest that the term as used in § 183(b) should also be taken to mean a type of vessel, and that suggestion, if adopted, leads to a broad construction.[139b] Even if,

**139a.** Petition of Panama Transport Co. (The J.H. Senior), 73 F.Supp. 716, 1947 A.M.C. 651 (S.D.N.Y.1947) ("tank vessel", collision at sea; the exclusion of "tank vessels" in § 183(f) was meant "to refer to tank vessels which are of the harbor or river type"); Petition of the Diesel Tanker A.C. Dodge, Inc., 282 F.2d 86, 1961 A.M.C. 233, (2d Cir. 1962) ("tanker", collision in Delaware River; "it is by no means clear that 'tank vessels' and 'tankers' are synonymous" (per Waterman, J.)); Olson & Co. v. American Steamship Marine Leopard, 356 F.2d 728, 1966 A.M.C. 1064 (9th Cir. 1966) (lumber-carrying vessel in coastwise trade, collision "at sea" (see 279 F.2d 662 (9th Cir. 1960)); "the restriction of section 183(b) to passenger-carrying vessels only, would be an unwarrantable limitation . . ." (356 F.2d at p. 737, n. 4)). It was assumed without discussion that the loss of life amendments applied to a cargo vessel in Moore-McCormack Lines, Inc. v. Armco Steel Corp. (The Mormackite), 272 F.2d 873, 1960 A.M.C. 185 (2d Cir. 1959), certiorari denied 362 U.S. 990, 80 S.Ct. 1079 (1960) (subsequent proceedings in The Mormackite are discussed in § 10–40 *infra*). The same assumption was made, also without discussion, with respect to a cargo vessel in The Alva Cape, note 138a *supra*.

**139b.** In The Alva Cape, note 138a *supra*, the vessel was (1) in a collision in the Kill Van Kull off Bergen Point, New Jersey and (2) destroyed in an explosion while moored in Gravesend Bay. Judge Bonsal assumed that both events were subject to the loss of life amendments. The vessel was clearly of a seagoing type, having just com-

as the cases have suggested, commercial vessels which do not carry passengers are included,[139c] the known background from which the legislation stemmed—the Morro Castle disaster—makes it reasonable to conclude that all passenger-carrying vessels, no matter where they ply their trade, should also be included.

**§ 10–36.** The amendments do not distinguish between claims of passengers, claims of crew-members and claims of third parties. All alike are entitled to claim the benefit of the $60 per ton fund, provided that the accident did not occur on a vessel excluded from the amendments under § 183(f).[140] It has long been established that claims of crew-members under the Jones Act or maritime law as well as claims brought under the federal Death on the High Seas Act and comparable state statutes are subject to the Limitation Act,[140a] and that foreign shipowners, sued in the United States, may equally with American shipowners, claim the benefit of the American limitation system.[141]

**§ 10–37.** The loss of life amendments carry forward, with one important change, the "privity or knowledge" requirements of the original Act. The change is made by § 183(e) which provides that:

> "In respect of loss of life or bodily injury the privity or knowledge of the master of a seagoing vessel or of the superintendent or managing agent of the owner thereof, at or prior to the commencement of each voyage, shall be deemed conclusively the privity or knowledge of the owner of such vessel."

Apparently the main change sought to be made from prior law was in making the master's "privity or knowledge" of the cause of the disaster "at or prior to the commencement of the voyage" equivalent to the owner's privity or knowledge. Thus if the ship is unseaworthy at the beginning of the voyage, and the master knows or ought to know of the unseaworthiness, and the unseaworthiness leads to death and injury claims, the owner will be denied the right to limit his liability against those claims. As in the past he may continue to limit, even against death and injury claims, caused by the master's negligence in navigation. The bracketing of the owner's "superintendent or managing agent" along with the master in this context is confusing, since it was clearly established by prior case law that the privity or knowledge of such officials was enough to bind the owners

pleted a voyage from Pakistan. In The Dodge, note 139a *supra*, the "tanker" (neither the type nor the destination was specified) was in collision on the Delaware River. In the other cases that have been found the accident occurred "at sea" or its location was not specified.



**139c.** Note 139a *supra* and accompanying text.

**140.** See § 10–35 *supra*.

**140a.** See note 45 *supra*.

**141.** See § 10–42 *infra*.

in any case.[142] The inclusion of superintendent and managing agent in § 183(e) which is restricted to "loss of life and bodily injury" might suggest by negative inference that where only property claims are involved the privity or knowledge of the named officials would no longer bind the owner. However there is nothing in the legislative history and background of the amendments to suggest that such an inference was intended. The intent was to extend the shipowner's liability with respect to death and injury claims; there is no suggestion that his property liability was to be narrowed. It may be concluded therefore that superintendent and managing agent were included in § 183(e) merely by way of lily-gilding.

A further interesting point about § 183(e) is that it is not limited to claims under the $60 per ton amendments but applies to all claims for "loss of life or bodily injury"—*i. e.* under § 183(a) as well as under § 183(b). It is reasonable to conclude that this result was not inadvertent, since the next following subsection (on types of vessels which are not to be considered "seagoing") is carefully limited to claims under the $60 per ton fund. Thus in any case in which the master's privity or knowledge is attributable to the owner under § 183(e), the result is that the owner is liable without limitation with respect to the death and injury claims.

The imputation of the master's "privity or knowledge . . . at or prior to the commencement of each voyage" has become, with respect to unseaworthiness (and it is hard to see what the provision could be taken to refer to except unseaworthiness), much less important now than it may have seemed to be when § 183(e) was drafted. Under the current "privity or knowledge" case law, limitation against all types of claims will be denied whenever it appears that, at the commencement of the voyage, the ship was unseaworthy in the sense of having structural defects or defective navigational equipment or of being inadequately manned.[142a] Conditions of unseaworthiness which arise while a ship is at sea are not covered by § 183(e) —although the "at or prior to the commencement of each voyage" language should not be taken to mean that an owner is conclusively entitled to limitation with respect to such conditions even under circumstances where he could (and therefore should) have taken steps to remedy the situation. The only situation in which § 183(e) could lead to a denial of limitation with respect to death and injury claims where the owner would still be entitled to limitation against other types of claims would seem to be the case of unseaworthiness caused by improper or negligent loading at a distant port—and indeed the only case in which § 183(e) has ever been applied involved the negligent loading and stowage of cargo in a Brazilian port of an American-flag ship which, because of the resulting unseaworthiness, was later lost at sea.[142b] Under the developing case law it is by no means as

142. See § 10–24 *supra*.

142a. See § 10–24 *supra*, particularly text at and following note 105o.

142b. Moore-McCormack Lines, Inc. v. Armco Steel Co. (The Mormackite), 272 F.2d 873, 1960 A.M.C. 185 (2d Cir. 1959), certiorari denied 362 U.S. 990,

clear as it may once have been that an owner is entitled, in such a case, to limitation even against cargo claims.[142c] Thus it is entirely possible that the first appearance of § 183(e) in litigation will prove to have been its last appearance since the provision is irrelevant in any case where the "owner" is chargeable with privity or knowledge under the § 183(a) case law.

**§ 10–38.** There remains to be noticed one other significant change which the amendments worked in the structure of the Limitation Act for the benefit of death and injury claimants. Subsection 183(d) reads as follows:

> "The owner of any such seagoing vessel shall be liable in respect of loss of life or bodily injury arising on distinct occasions to the same extent as if no other loss of life or bodily injury had arisen."

The obvious purpose of this amendment was to reverse, in the case of death and injury claims, the rule of The Scotland,[143] under which, when a vessel on the same voyage suffers two or more causally unrelated accidents, the vessel's value, for purposes of limitation, is appraised after the final accident has occurred. "Distinct occasions" is borrowed from the English statute and presumably English case-law would be persuasive on when an "occasion" is to be considered "distinct". The general meaning of the phrase is free from doubt, however much argument can be anticipated in detail. If the good ship Anne (a) allows a passenger or crew-member to fall overboard and drown on Monday and (b) runs down a fishing vessel on Tuesday, killing the crew, and (c) strikes an iceberg and is sunk with all hands on Wednesday, the events of that catastrophic half-week, being in no causal relationship to each other, are "distinct occasions". On the other hand the diverse results that can flow from a single cause, even though separated in time and space, would not be "distinct". "Distinctness" in this context is a matter of fact and of degree and is just the sort of thing that courts are instituted to decide.

The only case which has so far considered the "distinct occasions" provision is Petition of Alva Steamship Co., Ltd. (The M/T Alva Cape).[143a] the Alva Cape was in a collision off the New Jersey coast, after which she was towed to Gravesend Bay. The New York City Fire Commissioner directed that her cargo tanks be "inerted" through the introduction of carbon dioxide into the tanks. While that was be-

80 S.Ct. 1079 (1960) (limitation granted against cargo claims but denied, because of the master's knowledge of the improper stowage, as to death and injury claims; Judge Learned Hand's opinion did not expressly cite § 183(e) which was, of course, the only basis for the decision). Complicated problems with respect to the distribution of the limitation fund which were raised in subsequent proceedings in The Mormackite are discussed in § 10–40 *infra*.

142c. See text following note 105r *supra* and the improper loading cases reviewed in note 105s.

143. 105 U.S. 24 (1882).

143a. 262 F.Supp. 328, 1967 A.M.C. 2363 S.D.N.Y.1966).

ing done, the vessel exploded. Death and injury claims resulted both from the collision and from the explosion (which occurred twelve days later). Judge Bonsal discussed at some length whether the collision and the explosion were to be regarded as "distinct occasions", citing several English cases as well as the discussion in the first edition of the treatise. He concluded that the issue could not be resolved in advance of trial but seems to have ordered that the owner should post separate bonds setting up two § 183(b) funds.[143b]

There is more difficulty in determining how the owner's liability is affected when death or injury claims arise on two or more occasions which, we shall assume, have been judicially held to be "distinct". The statute says that on each "occasion" the owner shall be liable "to the same extent as if no other loss of life or bodily injury had arisen". That means at least that the death and injury claims arising on each occasion are entitled to the setting up for their benefit of the $60 per ton fund. If the vessel was of a thousand tons burden and there were three "distinct occasions", the owner could be held to pay out $60,000 to each of the three sets of claimants. Assume, further, that the value of the owner's interest in the vessel after all the "occasions" have occurred is $100,000, and that the claims arising on each occasion amount to $150,000. Disregarding possible property claims, there is, before the court proceeds to set up the several $60 per ton funds called for by § 183(b), the basic § 183(a) fund in the value of the ship. The obvious solution is that the several sets of claimants should first share *pro rata* in the § 183(a) fund ($100,000), after which, to the extent necessary to meet deficiencies, § 183(b) funds would be drawn on. The exact language of the statute, however, is that, for each "occasion", the shipowner is to be liable "as if" no other death and injury claims had arisen. Literally construed, that language suggests the possibility that the shipowner might be required to set up three § 183(a) funds ($300,000) as well as three § 183(b) funds ($180,000). Subsection 183(d) is not restricted to claims under the $60 per ton provision of § 183(b) but apparently applies to all claims arising from "loss of life or bodily injury" on "seagoing" vessels; thus the argument can plausibly be made that the "distinct occasions" concept applies both to § 183(a) and § 183(b). If it can be argued that the extent of the shipowner's liability in respect of death and injury claim is, under § 183(a), to be measured by the value of the ship just after each "distinct occasion", results even more uncomfortable to the shipowner than those already suggested can be readily perceived. Nothing in the legislative history of the amendments suggests which of the solutions was intended. None of these esoteric points has yet been raised in litigation.

143b. The headnote to the A.M.C. reprint of the case states: "petitioning shipowner must post two separate bonds, each in the statutory amount, to secure both sets of claims." The opinion may not be quite as clear as the headnote suggests.

### The Nature of the Limitation Proceeding

**§ 10–39.** The final decree in a limitation proceeding determines both the owner's liability *in personam* and the ship's liability *in rem.*[144] Since the voyage is the limitation unit,[145] claims arising on voyages prior or subsequent to the voyage as to which limitation is sought are not affected. But all claims arising on the relevant voyage are required to come into the limitation proceeding. When the owner's liability or non-liability to the various claimants has been determined, the available fund is to be "divided pro rata, subject to all relevant provisions of law, among the several claimants in proportion to the amounts of their respective claims, duly proved, saving, however, to all parties any priority to which they may be legally entitled." [146] Since the owner may limit against nonmaritime as well as maritime claims,[147] it is apparent that both types of claimants may share in the fund, contrary to the stricter rule said to be applicable to the ordinary preceeding *in rem.*[148]

The question whether maritime lien priorities are to be observed in the distribution of the limitation fund is one on which it would be unwise to speak with dogmatic finality. The natural meaning of the "saving . . . priority" language in Rule F(8) (whose substance has stood unchanged since the Rules were promulgated in 1872) [149] would seem to be that lien priorities are to be observed. Nevertheless a commentator observed in black-letter text in 1901: "Under the express provisions of the statute, all claims filed, whether they have an admiralty lien attached or are mere personal claims against the owner, are paid pro rata." [150] Robinson, on the other hand, assumed, without discussion of the point, that in distribution of a limitation fund, "[t]he usual priorities will be followed".[151] The 1940 edition of Benedict played it both ways, saying, *First*: "The questions of priority among claimants having been reported by the commissioner . . . such priorities are to be observed in the distribution"; and *Second*: "Every admissible claim is a statutory lien on the fund and claims that are maritime liens have no preference as such." [152]

144. Hartford Accident & Indemnity Co. v. Southern Pacific Co., 273 U.S. 207, 47 S.Ct. 357, 1927 A.M.C. 402 (1927); The Venice Maru (Consumers Import Co., Inc. v. Kabushiki Kaisha Kawasaki Zosenjo), 320 U.S. 249, 64 S.Ct. 15, 1943 A.M.C. 1209 (1943) (a fire statute case).

145. See §§ 10–46 to 10–49 *infra*.

146. Supplemental Rule F(8) (FRCP), taken without change of substance from former Admiralty Rule 52.

147. See § 10–13 *supra*.

148. See Chapter IX, §§ 9–88, 9–89.

149. 80 U.S. (13 Wall.) xii (1872), Rule 55.

150. Hughes, Admiralty § 174 (1901). The statement was carried forward without change in the second edition (1920). Neither edition identified "the express provisions of the statute". The balance of Hughes' discussion suggests that he was thinking mostly of the fact that *prior* liens do not participate in a limitation proceeding because of the rule that the voyage is the limitation unit.

151. Robinson, Admiralty 929 n. 115 (1939).

152. 3 Benedict, Admiralty § 530 (6th ed. 1940). The explanation of the con-

Limitation proceedings usually arise from a maritime disaster and the claims against which limitation is sought are for death, personal injury, damage to cargo and damage to other ships or shore property. Seamen's wage claims are not subject to limitation by § 189, nor are supply and repair claims (if it be assumed that such claims arise from "personal contracts").[153] In any event materialmen's claims do not figure in the limitation cases. Death, personal injury and property damage claims all sound in tort and, under maritime lien doctrine, are entitled to the same high order of priority. The Supreme Court has held that cargo damage claims are also in tort, but they have nevertheless been ranked below the other tort claims in distribution of funds in proceedings *in rem*.[154]

In view of the types of claims asserted in limitation proceedings, the importance of our question seems to lie in the possible priority of the property damage claims and of personal injury or death claims, which do not benefit from the 1935 loss of life amendments, over the cargo damage claims. There appears to be no modern authority on the problem, which may be an indication that the claimants to whose benefit it would be to raise the issue have acquiesced in the denial of priority suggested by Hughes and the second statement in the last two editions of Benedict. It should be noted, however, that limitation decrees do not receive international recognition; cargo may sue in one country while the collision claimants sue in another, with the possibility of still another set of proceedings being brought in a third country by death and personal injury claimants.[155]

In the absence of modern authority, we shall consider the early cases adduced by Benedict in support of his two statements on the distribution rule.[156] The Lakeland Transp. Co. case arose out of a

tradictory statements seems to be the propensity of successive editors to add to the original text in lieu of revising it. The first edition of Benedict to discuss the Limitation Act was the Third (1894) which said, after remarking that the fund is divided pro rata among claimants: "If there is, however, any right to a priority of payment on the part of one claimant as against others, that right is preserved to him by the terms of Rule 55" (§ 581). The editor of the Fourth edition (1910) revised the section to include the first, but not the second, of the two statements quoted in the text (§ 556). The editor of the Fifth edition (1925) let the prior text stand but added the second statement (§ 517). The Sixth edition carried the section forward without change, adding no new citations of authority.

153. See §§ 10–26 to 10–28 *supra*.

154. See Chapter IX, § 9–61(7).

155. See *e. g.* The Norwalk Victory and The Western Farmer, discussed in § 10–45 *infra*.

156. In favor of observing priorities: Re Lakeland Transp. Co., 103 F. 328 (E.D.Mich.1900), affirmed with modification *sub nom.* The George W. Roby, 111 F. 601 (6th Cir. 1901) certiorari denied *sub nom.* Lakeland Transp. Co. v. Miller, 183 U.S. 699, 22 S.Ct. 936 (1901), Miller v. Lakeland Transp. Co., 184 U.S. 699, 22 S.Ct. 939 (1902); Re California Navigation & Imp. Co., 110 F. 678 (N.D.Cal.1901); The Mauch Chunk, 139 F. 747 (S.D.N.Y.1905), affirmed 154 F. 182 (2d Cir. 1907), certiorari denied *sub nom.* Central R. Co. of N. J. v. Wren, 207 U.S. 586, 28 S.Ct. 255 (1907). Against maritime lien priorities: The Catskill, 95 F. 700 (S.D.N.Y.1899); Boston Marine Ins. Co. v. Metropolitan Redwood Lumber Co., 197 F. 703 (9th Cir. 1912).

mutual fault collision; with respect to priorities it was held that seamen's claims (for loss of personal effects) would be subordinated to cargo damage claims on the theory that cargo was innocent while the ship's negligence was imputed to the seamen. In the California Navigation Co. case, a salvage claim was ordered paid in full, other claimants (for personal injury and property damage) to share pro rata. The opinion assumed without discussion that maritime lien priorities govern distribution. In The Mauch Chunk, a mutual fault collision case, the damage claim of one of the ships at fault was subordinated to personal injury and cargo claims. Turning to the two cases cited for the proposition that lien priorities are not observed, The Catskill involved the same situation as The Mauch Chunk and reached the same result—indeed The Mauch Chunk (a 1905 case) was decided on the authority of The Catskill (1899). In the course of his Catskill opinion, Judge Brown wrote: [T]he statute itself [§ 185] not only makes the fund derived from the sale of the vessel a fund applicable to all claims pro rata (see, also, rule 55 in admiralty), but . . . bars all other remedy. The necessary effect of this is to make every admissible claim a statutory lien upon the fund. The fund must be distributed, therefore, according to the statute itself, i. e., pro rata among the claims arising from the collision . . . saving any special equitable rights between the parties."[157] The Boston Marine Insurance Co. case also arose out of a mutual fault collision. "Certain of the claimants" (the nature of their claims is not specified) argued that under Rule 55 lien priorities should govern the distribution. The Court disagreed, relying on The Catskill and citing La Bourgogne[158] as a case where "it appears that the court considered the rights of claimants whose claims were diverse, such as those in the case at bar, and recognized the right of all to share in the fund pro rata." La Bourgogne had in fact approved a pro rata distribution but it does not appear from Justice White's opinion that the priority question was considered by the Court.[159]

The authorities, then, stand principally for the proposition that a claimant whose ship was in fault in a collision will be subordinated to cargo and personal injury claims, which is certainly a reasonable rule. It is true that the Ninth Circuit in the Boston Marine Insurance case stated generally that distribution will be made without regard to lien priorities, but it is not clear what types of claims it was dealing with and La Bourgogne is not satisfactory authority.

157. 95 F. 700, 703. Judge Brown's language is of course the source of the second statement in Benedict, see text at note 152 *supra*.

158. 210 U.S. 95, 28 S.Ct. 664 (1908).

159. In The San Pedro, 223 U.S. 365, 376, 32 S.Ct. 275 (1912), which held that a salvage claim was subject to limitation, so that a salvor could not bring suit outside a limitation proceeding, Justice Lurton remarked: "The claim is, therefore, of a highly meritorious character. But the question of preference in payment out of the fund is one to be determined in the limited liability case. We, therefore, express no opinion as to whether such a claim may be preferred or must share *pro rata* with others."

The Catskill was delivered by a distinguished admiralty judge; it may be emphasized that Judge Brown said (and held) that "equitable rights between the parties" will be observed and qualified his general statement on pro rata distribution with a parenthetical reference to Rule 55.[159a]

On principle it is hard to see why lien priorities should not be observed (with the sensible exception suggested in the mutual fault collision cases). If the applicable rules of law establish priorities among a debtor's creditors, why should the unilateral act of the debtor (in filing a petition for limitation) destroy the priorities? One might as reasonably suggest that on the filing of a petition in bankruptcy secured and unsecured creditors should share alike in the debtor's assets. If a ship is libeled *in rem* and sold, certain types of claims will outrank others. The shipowner's act in converting the *in rem* proceeding into a limitation proceeding should not, it is suggested, alter that result. If the question is whether collision claims should (absent fault) be preferred to cargo damage claims, it is hard to become excited over the answer; both types of claims are insured and the dispute is between the insurance carriers. On the other hand the death and injury claims of merchant seamen who may not be covered by the $60 per ton provision of § 183(b)[160] are not insured. On equitable as well as legal principles they should be preferred to the insured claims with which they may compete.

The $60 per ton provision in favor of certain death and injury claims could present a puzzle in this context. The $60 per ton fund is to be set up only if the initial fund (the value of the owner's interest in ship and pending freight) is inadequate to pay all claims in full. The idea seems to be that in the first instance the death and injury claims are to share pro rata with the property claims and are then to be made whole through the fund set up for their exclusive benefit. In a case which falls within § 183(b) the argument for a pro rata distribution in the division of the § 183(a) fund is stronger than in the usual case, although even then it need not be regarded as overwhelming.

No doubt the real reason why we have been able to get on so well for so long without knowing whether lien priorities are to be observed

159a. The idea that claimants chargeable with fault will be subordinated, on equitable principles, to other claimants seems to be alive and well. See Petition of Kinsman Transit Co. (The Shiras), 338 F.2d 708, 726–727, 1964 A.M.C. 2503, 2530 (2d Cir. 1964), certiorari denied *sub nom.* Continental Grain Co. v. City of Buffalo, 380 U.S. 944, 85 S.Ct. 1026 (1965); Petition of Tugboat Dalzellea, Inc., 254 F.Supp. 298, 1966 A.M.C. 28 (S.D.N.Y.1965) (late-filed claims subordinated); Petition of Marina Mercante Nicaraguense, S.A. (The M/V El Salvador—Tug Russell No. 18) 248 F.Supp. 15, 37–38, 1966 A.M.C. 1777, 1808 (S.D.N.Y.1965) ("tortfeasor" not entitled to participate in fund as against "innocent claimants" whose claims exhausted it). See also Judge Waterman's approving reference to The Catskill in Petition of the Diesel Tanker A. C. Dodge, Inc., 282 F.2d 86, 89, 1961 A.M.C. 233, 237 (2d Cir. 1960): "[A]ppellants appear to ask us to depart from venerable precedent [i. e. The Catskill] in order that we may be free in the future to reach improper results. We refuse to do so."

160. As to the coverage of § 183(b), see § 10–35 *supra*.

in the distribution of limitation funds is the principle of equitable subordination derived from The Catskill and other early cases. Under this admirably flexible approach the Limitation Court can rank claims in order of merit without concerning itself with the ambiguities and complexities of maritime lien law.

**§ 10–40.** An owner, entitled to limitation against some claims, may be liable without limitation with respect to other types of claims which have arisen on the same voyage. Such a mixed situation, which became more than a theoretical possibility with the enactment of the loss of life and bodily injury amendments of 1935, was finally made flesh in Moore-McCormack Lines, Inc. v. Armco Steel Co. (The Mormackite),[160a] in which Moore-McCormack was held entitled to limitation against cargo claims but liable without limitation to death and injury claims.

In subsequent proceedings, captioned Moore-McCormack Lines, Inc. v. Richardson (The Mormackite),[160b] several questions, which we had discussed on a purely hypothetical level in the first edition of the treatise, came up for decision in the real world.

The Mormackite capsized and sank on the high seas with considerable loss of life as well as the loss of her cargo. In the limitation proceeding initiated by Moore-McCormack, the District Court found that the cause of the Mormackite's loss was an unseaworthy condition which resulted from the improper storage of cargo loaded at a Brazilian port.[160c] On the basis of that finding, which was not disturbed on appeal, the District Court held Moore-McCormack liable without limitation both to the cargo claimants and to the death and injury claimants. On appeal the Second Circuit affirmed as to the death and injury claimants [160d] but reversed as to the cargo claimants.[160e] Since the Mormackite was a total loss, the § 183(a) limitation fund, to which the cargo claimants were now restricted, consisted of pending freight and perhaps a lifeboat or two. Following the remand there were further proceedings in the District Court and on a second appeal the Circuit Court had to decide some novel questions of limitation law.[160f]

One question was what should be done, with respect to the nonlimitable death and injury claims, about the customary injunction staying all proceedings in other courts and compelling all claimants to come into the limitation proceeding.[160g] There was no practical problem in The Mormackite since all the death and injury claimants had elected to have their claims adjudicated by the Limitation Court instead of seeking jury trials under the saving to suitors clause. It

**160a.** 272 F.2d 873, 1960 A.M.C. 185 (2d Cir. 1959), certiorari denied 362 U.S. 990, 80 S.Ct. 1079 (1960).

**160b.** 295 F.2d 583, 1962 A.M.C. 804 (2d Cir. 1961), certiorari denied 368 U.S. 989, 82 S.Ct. 606 (1962), rehearing denied 370 U.S. 965, 82 S.Ct. 1580 (1962).

**160c.** 164 F.Supp. 198, 1958 A.M.C. 1497 (S.D.N.Y.1958).

**160d.** See § 10–37 *supra.*

**160e.** Citation at note 160a *supra.*

**160f.** Citation at note 160b *supra.*

**160g.** See §§ 10–16 to 10–19 *supra.*

was, however, at least a theoretical possibility that there were death and injury claims which had not been filed in the limitation proceeding. Judge Lumbard sensibly concluded that such claims, if they existed, should be barred only by the running of the applicable statute of limitation and that the injunction, as to them, should be dissolved. He also made clear that the injunction would have been dissolved as to the death and injury claims which had been filed in the limitation proceeding if any of the claimants had so elected.

A more complicated question was whether the non-limitable death and injury claims should share with cargo claims in the § 183(a) limitation fund (which amounted to only a small fraction of the cargo claims alone) or whether the § 183(a) fund should go entirely to cargo with the no-limitation claimants left to reach, by normal process, whatever corporate assets might be available. Judge Lumbard, emphasizing the fact that Moore-McCormack appeared to be eminently solvent, concluded, citing the first edition of the treatise, that the entire fund should go to the cargo claims.

Judge Lumbard's emphasis on the happy fact of Moore-McCormack's solvency may suggest that, had Moore-McCormack appeared to be insolvent (or, even worse, in bankruptcy or reorganization proceedings), the no-limitation claims would have been allowed to share in the fund pro rata with (or perhaps with priority over) the cargo claims. Judge Lumbard and his colleagues were, of course, deciding only the case which was before them and there is no disposition here to quarrel with the result which they reached: there is surely no reason to allow the no-limitation claims to take the already inadequate limitation fund when they can be made whole from other sources. However, it does not seem to follow that Moore-McCormack's insolvency should necessarily lead to the opposite result. It is at least arguable that only solvent shipowners—solvent, that is, apart from the claims that are forced into the limitation proceeding—are entitled to the protection of the Limitation Act and that, once overall insolvency appears, the proceeding should be dismissed—or limitation denied as to all claims—with the erstwhile limitation claimants left to compete with other creditors in whatever insolvency proceeding may be instituted. On the other hand, if insolvents are entitled to limitation against some disaster claims but not against others, there still seems to be no good reason for allowing the no-limitation claims to share in an inadequate limitation fund instead of going into the insolvency proceeding—particularly as there is no reason to believe that the insolvency court would not recognize maritime lien priorities.[160h]

**160h.** On whether insolvents are entitled to the protection of the Limitation Act, see §§ 10–48, 10–49 *infra.* On the recognition of lien priorities in insolvency proceedings, see Chapter IX, § 9–91 *et seq.* It may be noted that the death and injury claims, like those in the Mormackite, are, as tort liens, entitled to a high priority (see Chapter IX, § 9–58 *et seq.*) and, specifically, to a priority over the lien of a preferred ship mortgage under the Ship Mortgage Act (see Chapter IX, § 9–68 *et seq.*).

Our argument that the shipowner's insolvency should not reverse the result in The Mormackite is based on the assumption that there are corporate assets other than the owner's interest in the limitation vessel and that the no-limitation claims should be left to pursue those assets in the insolvency proceeding, in which they may be expected to come out with priority over most competing claims. A different situation would be presented if the only available corporate asset was indeed the owner's interest in the limitation vessel. In such a case the no-limitation claimants should not be prejudiced by the fact that the owner is liable to them in full and would have to be admitted to a share in the limitation fund (whether to a pro rata share with the limitation claims or with priority over them is a question that can best be left to the court which may some day have to wrestle with the problem). In cases where a large corporate enterprise elects to incorporate each of its vessels separately, setting up dummy corporations to hold title, it is to be hoped that the courts, with the aid of the corporate veil-piercing device or whatever other device may suggest itself, will find their way past the legal titleholder to the beneficial owner.[160i]

**§ 10–41.** In the usual case the question of the owner's right to limit will not be determined until an advanced stage of the proceedings has been reached. If he is held entitled to limitation the proceeding runs its ordinary course, ending in the distribution of the fund among claimants. Assume, however, that the owner is denied the right to limit. Should the admiralty court now dismiss the limitation proceeding or should it proceed to dispose of the case and finally

160i. See the discussion of the Torrey Canyon limitation proceedings, § 10–10 *supra*, text following note 36a.

Recent litigation has revealed another situation in which the same maritime disaster may produce both limitable and non-limitable claims. See the cases under the Wreck Statute digested note 45 *supra*, at end. In Complaint of Chinese Maritime Trust, Ltd. (The S/S. Sian Yung), 1972 A.M.C. 1478 (S.D.N.Y.1972) (a case which arose not under the Wreck Statute but under the regulations applicable to sinkings in the Panama Canal) Judge Motley assumed (1) that the claim of the Panama Canal Co. for wreck-removal costs was not subject to limitation, (2) that the Canal Co. could have participated in the limitation proceeding but that (3) the limitation injunction would, on the Canal Co's motion, be modified to allow the Canal Co. to prosecute its claim outside the limitation proceeding. Judge Motley did not, of course, have to decide whether the Canal Co. would be entitled to participate in the limitation fund. That disposition of the case was affirmed, 478 F.2d 1357, 1973 A.M.C. 1110 (2d Cir. 1973) on condition that the Canal Co. agree to litigate its claim in the Southern District of New York before which the limitation proceeding was pending.

If the cases which have held that maintenance and cure claims are not subject to limitation (see § 10–26 *supra*, text following note 113c) are followed, the same problem can arise in that context as well as under any further extensions of the personal contract doctrine.

Comparable problems seem almost certain to arise in connection with the as-yet-totally-mysterious relationship of the Limitation Act to the Federal Water Quality Improvement Act of 1970 and to state anti-pollution statutes (see § 10–4(b) *supra*).

Thus the Mormackite may have a considerable future as a precedent even if there is never another case under the 1935 loss of life amendments and the privity or knowledge provision of § 183(e) (see § 10–37 *supra*).

adjudicate the owner's liability to the claimants who have been brought before the court by the limitation petition? This problem did not receive an authoritative solution until 1927, when the Supreme Court held that the admiralty court, having once assumed jurisdiction of the case, should continue to a final adjudication, whichever way the limitation question is decided.[161] Chief Justice Taft's analysis of the nature of a limitation proceeding has been quoted ever since as a classical exposition:

> "It is quite evident from these cases that this Court has by its rules and decisions given the statute a very broad and equitable construction for the purpose of carrying out its purpose and for facilitating a settlement of the whole controversy over such losses as are comprehended within it, and that all the ease with which rights can be adjusted in equity is intended to be given to the proceeding. It is the administration of equity in an admiralty court. Dowdell v. United States District Court, C.C.A., 139 F. 444, 445. The proceeding partakes in a way of the features of a bill to enjoin a multiplicity of suits, a bill in the nature of an interpleader, and a creditor's bill. It looks to a complete and just disposition of a many cornered controversy, and is applicable to proceedings *in rem* against the ship as well as to proceedings *in personam* against the owner, the limitation extending to the owner's property as well as to his person.
>
> "The jurisdiction of the admiralty court attaches *in rem* and *in personam* by reason of the custody of the res put by the petitioner into its hands. The court of admiralty, in working out its jurisdiction, acquires the right to marshal all claims, whether of strictly admiralty origin or not, and to give effect to them by the apportionment of the *res* and by judgment *in personam* against the owners, so far as the court may decree. It would be most inequitable if parties and claimants, brought in against their will and prevented from establishing their claims in other courts, should be unable to perfect a remedy in this proceeding promptly, and should be delayed, until after the possible insolvency of the petitioner, to seek a complete remedy in another court, solely because the owner can not make his case of personal immunity. 1 Benedict's Admiralty, 5th ed., 488. If Congress has constitutional power to gather into the admiralty court all claimants against the vessel and its owner, whether their claims are strictly in admiralty or not, as this court

161. Hartford Accident & Indemnity Co. v. Southern Pacific Co., 273 U.S. 207, 47 S.Ct. 357, 1927 A.M.C. 402 (1927). The National Oil Transport Co. filed a petition for limitation and executed an *ad interim* stipulation after an explosion on one of its oil barges. Limitation was denied. The surety on the bond then argued that he should be discharged on the theory that with the denial of limitation there was no longer a res in court. It was held that he remained liable.

has clearly held, it necessarily follows as incidental to that power that it may furnish a complete remedy for the satisfaction of those claims by distribution of the *res* and by judgments *in personam* for deficiencies against the owner, if not released by virtue of the statute." [162]

Chief Justice Taft's description of the limitation proceeding as "partaking in a way of the features of a bill to enjoin a multiplicity of suits" and as looking to "a complete and just disposition of a many cornered controversy" has often been cited in favor of the proposition that one of the essential purposes of the Limitation Act is to enable the shipowner to bring multiple claims "into concourse" and to avoid the undeniable burden of having to defend individual suits in various forums. The "concourse" theory of limitation was forcefully restated by Justice Frankfurter, speaking for four members of the Court in Maryland Casualty Co. v. Cushing:

> "The heart of this system [*i. e.* limitation of liability] is a *concursus* of all claims to ensure the prompt and economical disposition of controversies in which there are often a multitude of claimants. . . . The ship's company [if direct actions against the insurance carrier were allowed to proceed] would be subject to call as witnesses in more than one proceeding, perhaps in diverse forums. Conflicting judgments might result. Ultimate recoveries might vary from the proportions contemplated by the statute." [163]

It cannot be said, however, that the concourse theory is today in a flourishing state, despite the generalities of Chief Justice Taft and the more specific language of Justice Frankfurter.[163a] The lower courts have on the whole found that the Supreme Court's Langnes v. Green theory—that plaintiffs, by virtue of the saving to suitors clause, should be allowed to choose the forum of litigation—overrides the shipowner's claim to the benefits of a "concourse". The Second Circuit emphatically stated the anti-concourse position in a series of cases decided in the 1940's and 1950's.[164] In Petition of the Texas Co.

162. *Id.* at 215–217, 47 S.Ct. at 359, 1927 A.M.C. at 406–408. The position taken in the Hartford Accident & Indemnity case was reiterated in Just v. Chambers, 312 U.S. 383, 61 S.Ct. 687, 1941 A.M.C. 430 (1941).

163. 347 U.S. 409, 415, 417, 74 S.Ct. 608, 611, 612, 1954 A.M.C. 837, 842, 843 (1954). See discussion of the Cushing case § 10–31 *supra.*

163a. Little need be added to the following discussion which has been left substantially in the form in which it appeared in the first edition. On the continuing decline of the concourse theory, see §§ 10–17, 10–18 *supra* and the authorities there cited as well as the post-Cushing "direct action" cases against insurers (§ 10–31 *supra*, text following note 131a). On a plaintiff's right to proceed outside the admiralty if limitation is denied, see the cases cited in note 69 *supra.* See also Complaint of Chinese Maritime Trust, Ltd., note 160i *supra.*

164. Petition of Trinidad Corp., 229 F. 2d 423, 1956 A.M.C. 550 (2d Cir. 1955); Petition of The Texas Co. (The Washington), 213 F.2d 479, 1954 A.M.C. 1251 (2d Cir. 1954) certiorari denied 348 U.S. 829, 75 S.Ct. 52 (1954); Petition of Moran Transp. Corp., 185 F.2d 386, 1951 A.M.C. 66 (2d Cir. 1950) cer-

Judge Frank summed up the thought of the members of that influential court:

> "We have several times announced the principles which we think must apply here: Absent an insufficient fund (1) the statutory privilege of limiting liability is not in the nature of a *forum non conveniens* doctrine, and (2) the statute gives a shipowner, sued in several suits (even if in divers places) by divers persons, no advantage over other kinds of defendants in the same position. Concourse is to be granted 'only when . . . necessary in order to distribute an inadequate fund.' The 'purpose of the limitation proceedings is not to prevent a multiplicity of suits but, in an equitable fashion, to provied a marshalling of assets—the distribution of an inadequate fund among claimants, none of whom can be paid in full.' We see nothing to the contrary in Maryland Casualty Co. v. Cushing, 347 U.S. 409, 74 S.Ct. 608, 1954 A.M.C. 837, where the claims aggregated $600,000 and the Court was advised the valuation was but $25,000." [165]

A dramatic illustration of the case for a concourse arose in the litigation which followed a catastrophic explosion in the port of South Amboy, New Jersey, on May 19, 1950.[166] Twenty suits, involving approximately 8600 plaintiffs, had been instituted in New Jersey state courts against thirteen defendants. In addition there were many civil suits brought in the federal courts against the United States and other defendants. Finally, a petition for limitation of liability had been filed by one of the defendants in the admiralty court. Another of the defendants (not the petitioner for limitation) moved under Rule 42(a) of the Federal Rules of Civil Procedure to consolidate 56 of the pending suits so that they could all be disposed of in the limitation proceeding. The motion was sought to be supported by Chief Justice Taft's theories as expressed in the Hartford Accident & Indemnity case. Judge Forman, however, after reviewing Langnes v. Green and the then recent Second Circuit cases, denied the motion, commenting that in deciding against the motion "regard is being paid to the equities of the plaintiffs in their state court actions, which seem to be greater than advantages that can be realistically expected to flow from attempted consideration in the limitation proceedings of all the complicated issues and forms of action in these numerous suits." [166a]

tiorari denied 340 U.S. 953, 71 S.Ct. 573 (1950); Curtis Bay Towing Co. v. Tug Kevin Moran, Inc., 159 F.2d 273, 1947 A.M.C. 51 (2d Cir. 1947).

165. (The Washington), 213 F.2d 479, 482, 1954 A.M.C. 1251, 1254. See Lake Tankers Corp. v. Henn, discussed text following note 76b *supra*, for the Supreme Court's post-Cushing view of the concourse idea.

166. Petition of Healing & Son, Inc., 124 F.Supp. 46, 1954 A.M.C. 1763 (D. N.J.1954).

166a. See Petition of Chadade Steamship Co. (The Yarmouth Castle), 1967 A.M.C. 1081 (S.D.Fla.1966) on the procedure adopted by a Limitation Court in a proceeding in which 460 claims aggregating more than $59,000,000 had been filed.

**§ 10–42.** According to the Limitation Rules which the Supreme Court issued in 1872 "the said owner or owners [who have petitioned for limitation of liability] shall be at liberty to contest his or their liability, or the liability of said ship or vessel . . ."[167] This provision was a deliberate departure from English limitation practice under which the owner was required to admit fault as a condition of petitioning for limitation.[168] The right of the owner to petition for exoneration from, as well as for a limitation of, liability has ever since been a characteristic feature of American limitation law; all petitions (or complaints) are and, presumably since 1872 have been, so drawn.[169] Thus the typical limitation proceeding has for a hundred years been conceived of as essentially a "defensive" proceeding in which all the claims arising from a maritime disaster are brought into concourse before the Limitation Court which will then adjudicate all aspects of the case against the owner.[170]

The characterization of a limitation proceeding as defensive seems to have led at one time to the curious conclusion that the only business before a Limitation Court was the adjudication of the owner's liability, the liquidation of claims and the distribution of the limitation funds. Under that theory the Limitation Court could not entertain cross-libels by the petitioner against claimants (for example, against a claimant who was the owner of another ship allegedly at fault in the collision out of which the limitation proceeding arose) or cross-claims among claimants or motions to implead third parties.[171] These restrictions on third-party practice in limitation proceedings seem all the more curious in the light of the fact that third-

167. 80 U.S. (13 Wall.) xiii, Rule 56.

168. Justice Bradley in the course of his opinion in The Benefactor, 103 U.S. 239, 243 (1880), commented on the reasons which led the Court to reject the "onerous requirement" of English law.

169. Rule 56 was later renumbered Rule 53. Supplemental Rule F(2), FRCP, currently provides: "The [limitation] complaint may demand exoneration from as well as limitation of liability."

170. On the present state of the "concourse" theory, see § 10–41 *supra.*

171. The theory outlined in the text seems to have been particularly in vogue in the Second Circuit. See Petition of the Texas Co. (The Latin American), 81 F.Supp. 758, 1948 A.M.C. 1933 (S.D.N.Y.1948); New Jersey Barging Corp. v. T.A.D. Jones & Co. (The Perth Amboy No. 1), 135 F.Supp. 97, 1955 A.M.C. 2270 (S.D.N.Y.1955). In Algoma Central & Hudson Bay R. Co. v. Great Lakes Transit Corp., 86 F.2d 708, 1937 A.M.C. 50 (2d Cir. 1936) Judge Learned Hand, emphasizing the defensive nature of limitation proceedings, remarked: "At no time can the owner recover a dollar by means of it [the limitation proceeding] from anybody." This remark was ritually repeated in the later cases which refused to allow cross-libels or impleaders, although in fact the Algoma case had nothing to do with such questions. However, even before the Supreme Court had rejected the theory in question in the British Transport Commission case which will be presently discussed in the text, the Second Circuit appeared to be having second thoughts; see Moore-McCormack Lines, Inc. v. McMahon, 235 F.2d 142, 1956 A.M.C. 1487 (2d Cir. 1956). Department of Highways v. Jaknke Service, Inc., 174 F.2d 894, 1949 A.M.C. 1144 (6th Cir. 1949) took the same position on impleaders as the earlier Second Circuit cases.

party practice in admiralty proceedings generally, under Admiralty Rule 56, had always been extremely liberal.[172]

The Supreme Court finally disposed of such unnecessarily restrictive theories in British Transport Commission v. United States.[173] The Haiti Victory, owned by the United States, and the Duke of York, owned by the Commission, were in collision in the North Sea. The United States filed a limitation petition in the United States and the Commission claimed in that proceeding for collision damage to the Duke of York, estimated at $1,500,000. (Death, injury and property claims were also filed by or on behalf of passengers on the Duke of York, a cross-channel ferry.) The United States and the other claimants then filed cross-claims against the Commission, alleging that the collision had been caused by the negligence of the Duke of York. The District Court held that the Duke of York had been solely at fault, but dismissed all the cross-claims under the "defensive" theory of limitation proceedings. The Fourth Circuit reversed, in an admirable opinion by Judge Dobie.[174] The Supreme Court, in an opinion by Justice Clark, affirmed the Circuit, holding in effect that the rules of third-party practice applicable to admiralty proceedings generally were also applicable to limitation proceedings, quoting Chief Justice Taft's description of a limitation proceeding as "the administration of equity in an admiralty court . . . [looking] to a complete and just disposition of a many cornered controversy." [175] Three dissenting justices (Brennan, Harlan, Frankfurter) argued that, since the Commission had filed in the American proceeding in reliance on the cases which had denied the availability of cross-claims, it could not fairly, on a sort of estoppel theory, be subjected to affirmative liability. According to the dissenters, the Commission should have been allowed to institute its own limitation proceeding, presumably in England (on the facts of the case English limitation law was apparently more favorable to the Commission than American limitation law), in which, it was assumed, the American court's decision on liability would be treated as res judicata.[176] To the argument that holding the Commission liable to cross-claims would cause

172. The substance of Admiralty Rule 56 is now incorporated in Rule 14, F.R.C.P.; 14(c) deals specifically with "admiralty and maritime claims". Rule 56 had provided for third party practice "in any suit, whether *in rem* or *in personam.*" The technical explanation for the refusal to apply the provision of Rule 56 in limitation proceedings was that a limitation petition was not a "suit", either in rem or in personam, but rather a statutory proceeding sui generis. See Learned Hand's opinion in the Algoma case, note 171 *supra* in which the issue was whether venue had been properly laid.

173. 354 U.S. 129, 77 S.Ct. 1103, 1957 A.M.C. 1151 (1957).

174. 230 F.2d 139, 1956 A.M.C. 275 (4th Cir. 1956).

175. See text at note 162 *supra*.

176. Presumably, under the Supreme Court's decision, the Commission was entitled to petition for limitation under American law (although there would have been some technical problems under the six-months provision of § 185 (see § 10–15 *supra*)). However, none of the opinions delivered in the case discussed the point and no further proceedings were reported.

foreign claimants to refrain from entering American limitation proceedings, Justice Clark, for the majority, replied in effect: So What?, adding the comforting reassurance that "self-protection would balance things out." [177]

Since the decision in the British Transport Commission case, limitation proceedings have been as "offensive" as any other type of maritime proceeding. Litigants seem to have adjusted to the situation and the problem has all but disappeared from current litigation. The British Transport Commission case itself involved cross-claims within the limitation proceeding but no one has questioned the proposition that the holding covers not only such cross-claims but impleaders of third parties.[177a]

**§ 10–43.** Foreign shipowners, when sued in American courts, may have the benefit of limitation on the American plan equally with American shipowners.[178] Furthermore, on the theory that limitation law is procedural rather than substantive, so that, on received principles of the conflict of laws, the law of the forum should govern, it has been assumed that American courts will apply American limitation law in any limitation proceedings properly before them. With respect to property claims, American law limits liability to the owner's interest in the vessel and pending freight. In those countries

177. On the proposition that decrees in limitation proceedings do not receive international recognition, see §§ 10–43 to 10–45 *infra*. Thus the hypothetical foreign claimants who shunned the American proceeding could sue the American shipowner anywhere in the world where he was subject to process (*e. g.* any port in which any of his ships docked).

177a. See, for example, the Marine Sulphur Queen, 460 F.2d 89, 1972 A.M.C. 1122 (2d Cir. 1972). The Queen, which had been built as an oil tanker, was converted for the carriage of molten sulphur. Bethlehem had carried out the conversion work for the owners. The Queen having been lost at sea, Bethlehem was impleaded in the owners' limitation proceeding. The propriety of the impleader was not even discussed in the case; apparently Bethlehem raised no objection to it. Ultimately all the claims against Bethlehem were dismissed.

Petition of Klarman (The Sloop Fling), 270 F.Supp. 1001, 1967 A.M.C. 2641 (D.Conn.1967) allowed the Town of Westport to be impleaded in a limitation proceeding on the allegation that the negligence of a town employee had caused the accident. Judge Timbers' opinion reviewed the background of the impleader question and collected cases. He commented that impleader under Rule 14(c) presented the same problems as impleader under former Admiralty Rule 56 (see note 169 *supra*).

See also Petition of Evangelistria Shipping Corp. (The Kimon), 1967 A.M.C. 974 (S.D.Tex.1966) in which the limitation petitioner brought a cross-claim against a claimant in the proceeding who in turn impleaded a third party. Both the cross-claims and the impleader were allowed.

In Petition of Sheffield Tankers Corp. (The Trojan), 168 F.Supp. 446, 1959 A.M.C. 206 (N.D.Cal.1958), the United States, as claimant in a limitation proceeding, was allowed to interplead a third party. The same third party, in a related limitation proceeding, had moved to implead the United States. Since the two proceedings were consolidated, it appears that both impleaders were allowed.

*Cf.* In re Northern Transatlantic Carrier Corp. (The Ocean Eagle), 423 F.2d 139, 1970 A.M.C. 517 (1st Cir. 1970).

178. Except with respect to certain death claims under the Death on the High Seas Act, see note 45 *supra*. The Titanic, discussed in the text following note 180 *infra*, was decided before the Death on the High Seas Act was enacted.

which adhered to the 1923 Brussels Convention on Limitation of Liability, the owner's liability was limited to the value of the vessel, her freight and accessories in an amount not to exceed £8 per ton of the vessel's tonnage. In counties which have adhered to the 1957 Brussels Convention, the limitation ceilings have been raised to approximately $207 per ton ($140 for death and injury claim plus $67 to be divided ratably with cargo claims).[179] Thus, under varying circumstances, American law or foreign law might turn out to be more favorable to one party or the other. When the vessel has been lost, American law is most favorable to the shipowner against property claims; when the vessel survives and is worth more than the limitation ceilings set by the Brussels Convention, American law is to the advantage of the claimants while foreign law is to the advantage of the shipowner.[179a] Frequently therefore in limitation proceedings in American courts between foreign litigants or arising out of a tort committed within the territorial waters of another sovereign, either the claimants or the petitioning shipowner would find it advantageous to argue for the application of foreign rather than American limitation law.

The Titanic [180], a British-flag ship, sank after collision with an iceberg. A petition for limitation of liability was filed in the United States. Claimants, both English and American, argued that English limitation law, which provided a fund for recovery even though the ship was lost, should apply. The Supreme Court, through Justice Holmes, rejected the argument. Admitting that American substantive law "does not control or profess to control the conduct of a British ship on the high seas" and that "the foundation for recovery upon a British tort is an obligation created by British law," Holmes went on to say that "the laws of the forum may decline altogether to enforce that obligation on the ground that it is contrary to the domestic policy, or may decline to enforce it except within such limits as it may impose." [181] It resulted, Holmes concluded, from prior decisions of the Court that litigants who chose to sue the owners of the Titanic in United States courts were limited in their recovery by the American law of limitation.

**§ 10–44.** The Titanic was followed as a matter of course for nearly forty years.[182] In 1949, however, Justice Frankfurter, in an

**179.** On the 1957 Brussels Convention, see § 10–4(a) and Notes 13j and 19 supra.

**179a.** For a dramatic example, see M/S Bremen and Unterweiser Reederei GMBH v. Zapata Off-Shore Company, 407 U.S. 1, 92 S.Ct. 1907, 1972 A.M.C. 1407 (1972) (discussed, text following note 59a *supra*) in which it appeared that the American limitation fund would have been $1,390,000 while the limitation fund under English law was $80,000.

**180.** (Oceanic Steam Navigation Co. v. Mellor), 233 U.S. 718, 34 S.Ct. 754 (1914).

**181.** 233 U.S. at 732, 34 S.Ct. at 755, 756.

**182.** Royal Mail Steam Packet Co. v. Companhia de Navegacao Lloyd Brasileiro, 31 F.2d 757, 758, 1929 A.M.C. 195, 196 (E.D.N.Y.1928): In an action for collision in Belgian waters, "The fact that libellant (claimant) amended, alleging the Belgian statutory rule that damages will be ordered according to the degree of fault, does not

extraordinarily obscure opinion in The Norwalk Victory,[183] cast some doubt over the continuing vitality of The Titanic. In the Norwalk Victory, an American vessel, on its way down the Schelde River and within Belgian territorial waters, first ran down and sank a British vessel and then, in extricating itself, struck and damaged the bank of the River. The owners of the cargo lost on the British vessel sued the owners of the American vessel in the United States. The value of the American vessel was admitted to be about $1,000,000. Nevertheless the owners in their petition for limitation argued that Belgian (*i. e.* Brussels Convention) law applied and that under that law their maximum liability was $325,028.79. Consequently, they tendered with their petition a bond in that amount. The District Court, inspired by The Titanic, dismissed the petition.[184] The Second Circuit, affirming the dismissal, elaborated an engaging fantasy on the inextricable "dilemma" in which the shipowners had placed themselves: if they were right in arguing that Belgian law established their maximum liability, then they were not entitled to petition for limitation since the admitted value of the vessel was several times greater than their claimed liability; if they were wrong, then the proffered bond was not in compliance with the requirements of the Limitation Act.[185] Justice Frankfurter, speaking for a bare majority of his colleagues, made short shrift of this virtuoso performance, while expressing great respect for the "wisdom of that most experienced of admiralty courts"—*i. e.* the Second Circuit. The case was reversed and remanded for further proceedings with the suggestion that the owners should be required to post a bond in the amount of the value of the ship ($1,000,000) "not because sec. 4285 [*i. e.* § 185] demands it, but as an exercise of its power to preserve the *status quo* pending appeal." On the question of law, Justice Frankfurter offered, in Sibylline language, several alternative hypotheses:

> ". . . if, indeed, the Belgian limitation attaches to the right, then nothing in The Titanic, 233 U.S. 718, 34 S.Ct. 754 stands in the way of observing that limitation . . .

change the respondent's position, because the weight of authority in our courts seems to be that while the rights and liabilities of the parties will be determined in accordance with the law of the foreign country, the right to limit liability will be controlled by the limited liability statute of our country, which will be applied to foreign ships and foreign collisions," citing The Titanic. The Mandu, 102 F.2d 459, 463, 1939 A.M.C. 287, 293 (2d Cir. 1939): "Liability for tort caused by collision in the territorial waters of a foreign country is governed by the laws of that country. . . . That law not only determines the existence of the liability but also generally determines the measure of it. . . . But on limitation of liability in maritime cases the statutes permitting limitation are regarded as relating to remedy, and the law of the forum controls."

183. (Black Diamond S.S. Corp. v. Robert Stewart & Sons, Ltd.), 336 U.S. 386, 69 S.Ct. 622, 1949 A.M.C. 393 (1949).

184. Petitions of Black Diamond S. S. Co. & United States, 1948 A.M.C. 816 (E.D.N.Y.1947).

185. United States & Black Diamond S. S. Corp. v. Robert Stewart & Sons, Ltd., 167 F.2d 308, 1948 A.M.C. 815 (2d Cir. 1948).

> "If, on the other hand, the Convention merely provides procedural machinery by which claims otherwise created are brought into concourse . . . we would respect the equally well settled principle that the forum is not governed by foreign rules of procedure. . . . Nor do we mean to imply that these apparently clear-cut alternatives are exhaustive. A limit which attaches not to an individual's right of recovery but to the aggregate claims arising from a given tort can be said to be "attached to the right" only in a special sense of that phrase, and a rule which operates to cut down the amount recoverable by a claimant cannot be fitted within any but a very broad definition of the term 'procedure'." [186]

What this apparently meant was that the District Court should look into the question whether by Belgian law the limitation convention was regarded as substantive or procedural (or something in between); if substantive ("attaching to the right"), then the owner's maximum liability would be determined by Belgian law; if "merely . . . procedural," then our own Limitation Act would determine liability. There was no subsequent elucidation of the true meaning of Justice Frankfurter's baffling hypotheses, since no further opinions in the case, following remand, were reported. It may be that the parties, appalled at the complexities which the Second Circuit and Supreme Court had successively revealed, decided that settlement was the better part of valor.

Unless the Supreme Court chooses some day to explain the matter further, it appears that we shall have to go on living with the riddle of to what extent, if at all, The Norwalk Victory unsettled the rule of The Titanic.

The Second Circuit in 1954 apparently felt that The Titanic was as good as ever. In The Western Farmer [187] German owners of cargo, which had been lost following a collision and sinking in the English Channel, sued the owners of the non-carrying ship, a Norwegian vessel. Other litigation against the Norwegian shipowner was pending in England and the shipowner moved to have the American action dismissed so that the entire matter could be decided in the English proceeding. The District Judge agreed and dismissed the libel on the ground that the most just disposition of the case could be made by the English courts of admiralty. On appeal one of the arguments made in support of the dismissal was that the English limitation statute should apply. Disagreeing, Judge Learned Hand wrote curtly:

> "it is necessary to say no more than that The Titanic, 233 U.S. 718, 34 S.Ct. 754, finally settled it for us that such statutes are part of the remedy, and that the law of the for-

186. 336 U.S. 386, 395–396, 69 S.Ct. 622, 627, 1949 A.M.C. 393, 400.

187. (Kloeckner Reederei, etc. v. A/S Hakedal), 210 F.2d 754, 1954 A.M.C. 643 (2d Cir. 1954) appeal dismissed 348 U.S. 801, 75 S.Ct. 17 (1954).

um applies. What the respondent finds in Black Diamond S. S. Co. v. Robert Stewart & Sons, 336 U.S. 386, 69 S.Ct. 622 [i. e. The Norwalk Victory], that qualifies this, we have been unable to discover." [188]

Wherefore the District Court's dismissal of the libel was reversed.

The only subsequent case in which the issue has been raised was Petition of Chadade Steamship Co., Inc. (The Yarmouth Castle).[188a] The Yarmouth Castle, a Panamanian-flag cruise ship which operated out of Miami, burned and sank on the high seas. Death, injury and property claims amounted to more than $59,000,000.[188b] The owners of the Yarmouth Castle, in their limitation petition, proposed a basic (§ 183(a)) limitation fund of $33,000, which was the estimated value of the strippings from the wreck together with passage money, plus the $60 per ton § 183(b) fund required by the 1934 loss of life and bodily injury amendments.[188c] Claimants moved that the basic § 183 (a) fund should be determined not by the American Limitation Act but by the relevant provision of the Panamanian Commercial Code which required that insurance proceeds go into the limitation fund.

Judge Mehrtens rehearsed the sequence of The Titanic and The Norwalk Victory in a scholarly opinion and concluded, as the Second Circuit had in the Western Farmer, that the later case had not overruled the earlier case. He was therefore required, under the Norwalk Victory, to determine whether the Panamanian limitation provisions were procedural or substantive. He concluded that they were substantive, so that the larger bond, including the insurance proceeds, had to be posted. Judge Mehrtens added that, if he was wrong about the substance-procedure distinction, then he thought that the decision in The Titanic should be "reexamined" on the ground that that 1914 decision is sadly out of line with modern conflict of laws theories.

Judge Mehrtens Yarmouth Castle opinion can be read to suggest that the foreign limitation law will be applied (as "substantive") if it sets higher limits of liability than does the American Limitation Act (at least in proceedings which involve death and injury claims which greatly exceed the aggregate of the § 183(a) and § 183(b) funds). He concluded his discussion with the observation that:

"Having deliberately sought and obtained the benefits given by a foreign law, there seems no basis in equity and justice upon which the foreign ship owner should be enabled

188. *Id.* at 757, 647. Judge Learned Hand's assumption that nothing in The Norwalk Victory weakened The Titanic may have been bolstered by the fact that in Lauritzen v. Larsen, 345 U.S. 571, 73 S.Ct. 921, 1953 A.M.C. 1210 (1953), Justice Jackson cited The Titanic approvingly, without referring to The Norwalk Victory, in an opinion joined by Justice Frankfurter.

188a. 266 F.Supp. 517, 1967 A.M.C. 1843 (S.D.Fla.1967).

188b. See the earlier proceedings in The Yarmouth Castle reported at 1967 A.M.C. 1081 (S.D.Fla.1966).

188c. On the $60 per ton §§ 183(b) fund, see § 10–33 *et seq. supra.*

> to receive those benefits and yet evade the burdens that may accompany them." [188d]

On the other hand foreign limitation laws which, on given sets of facts, set lower limits of liability (which was the situation in The Norwalk Victory) would be classified as "procedural". Judge Mehrtens did not suggest that playing games with the substance-procedure distinction was a sensible way of resolving such questions; his own preference, as he made clear, would have been to scrap The Titanic (and The Norwalk Victory) and to approach the problem in the light of modern choice of law doctrines which "are based essentially on the concept of justice corresponding to the moral and social values which are held by society." The Yarmouth Castle reproduced the situation in The Titanic: the foreign law set higher limits of liability. It may be thought that in The Yarmouth Castle District Judge Mehrtens came perilously close, de facto if not de jure, to overruling a unanimous decision of the Supreme Court announced by no less a jurist than Justice Holmes. But in situations in which the Supreme Court reexamines its ancient precedents on an average of once every fifty years or so, it is hard to see how else the system can be kept viable.

§ **10–45.** Under the rule in The Titanic, the limitation proceeding is procedural and not substantive; it attaches, to use Justice Frankfurter's terminology in The Norwalk Victory, not to the right but to the remedy. It follows that the law of the forum applies. A closely related proposition is that the decree in a limitation proceeding is given merely a domestic and not an international recognition. It is generally agreed that the judicial sale of a ship pursuant to a decree of a court of admiralty in any country, handed down in an action *in rem*, discharges all maritime liens against the ship and will be given that effect in the courts of all other countries.[189] A decree entered in a limitation proceeding, which in many respects resembles an action *in rem*, does not have any juridical force beyond the national boundaries.

Justice Holmes' opinion in The Titanic clearly assumed the merely domestic effect of a limitation decree:

> "The question is not [he wrote] whether the owner of the Titanic by this proceeding can require all claimants to come in and can cut down rights vested under English law, as against, for example, Englishman living in England, who do not appear. . . .
>
> "We see no absurdity in supposing that if the owner of the Titanic were sued in different countries, each having a

188d. 266 F.Supp. at p. 524, 1967 A.M.C. at p. 1852. It is odd that Judge Mehrtens, with respect to the death claims, did not cite the cases which have held that claims against foreign-flag ships are not subject to limitation under the American Limitation Act because of § 4 of the Death on the High Seas Act (see note 45 *supra*).

189. See Chapter IX, §§ 9–85, 9–86.

different rule affecting the remedy there, the local rule should be applied in each case." [190]

The facts in The Norwalk Victory dramatically illustrated what Holmes had in mind. There the owners of the vessel had been sued in England for collision damages in the amount of $1,000,000. Cargo then sued in the United States for damages of another $1,000,000. There was the possibility of other suits, wherever the owners might have assets subject to attachment, for damage to the bank of the Schelde River and for death and personal injury claims. A comparable situation was presented in The Western Farmer. The owners who were being sued in New York by cargo had already been sued in England for collision; it was held that the action of the District Court in dismissing the libel was an abuse of discretion.[190a]

The owner whose ships move in international trade receives only a limited benefit from the international acceptance of the principle of limited liability. Wherever he may have assets subject to arrest, within whatever national boundaries his ships may move to take on and discharge passengers or cargo, he may expect suit. The courts of each country will apply local law on the question of limitation; no country will give effect to a foreign limitation decree as barring further suit; and, as The Western Farmer indicates, courts will not decline jurisdiction, even in actions between foreign litigants on a tort taking place in foreign waters, on grounds of comity or *forum non conveniens*. This obviously leads to a good deal of forum shopping by litigants. American collision law, which does not impute the fault of the carrying ship to cargo, is more favorable to cargo interests than the laws of most other countries; [191] cargo is therefore most apt to prosecute its claim in the United States. The law of most countries except the United States accepts the principle of proportional fault in collision cases; [192] that will frequently make it in the interest of the collision plaintiff to proceed outside the United States.

In a recent Second Circuit case Judge Palmieri summed up the situation in this way:

> "The owners of ships moving in international trade and colliding in international waters may well expect to be involved in legal proceedings in more than one country. Forum shopping in this context is not a term of opprobrium but a way of life and each party seeks what appears to be the best legal haven. Additionally, the absence of an international

190. 233 U.S. 718, 732, 734, 34 S.Ct. 754, 755, 756 (1914).

190a. For more recent illustrations, see the Torrey Canyon litigation described in note 13e *supra* and Petition of Bloomfield Steamship Co. (The Ronda–The Lucille Bloomfield), 422 F.2d 728, 1970 A.M.C. 521 (2d Cir. 1970) (in which litigation was instituted in the United States, England and France).

191. The Chattahoochee, 173 U.S. 540, 19 S.Ct. 491 (1899).

192. See Chapter VII, § 7–20.

concursus which can be obtained only through the treaty making processes of the United States leaves the decree in a limitation proceeding clothed with domestic, not international recognition." [192a]

### The Voyage as the Limitation Period (Herein of the Treatment of Prior and Subsequent Claims)

**§ 10–46.** The claims against which a shipowner may limit his liability are in general those arising from a single accident.[193] In most situations this is the same as saying that all claims arising on a particular voyage (except claims not subject to limitation) may be required to come into the limitation proceeding and accept a distributive share of the fund and that all such claims will be concluded by the court's decree. Claims arising on prior and subsequent voyages can not be brought into the proceeding and are not affected by it.

The Limitation Act was by no means clear on how claims were to be grouped. Under § 183(a) the owner's liability was not to exceed "the amount or value of the interest of such owner in such vessel and her freight then pending". Section 184 added the thought that when loss "is suffered by several freighters or owners of goods . . . on the same voyage, and the whole value of the vessel and her freight for the voyage, is not sufficient to make compensation to each of them, they shall receive compensation . . . in proportion to their respective losses." Section 189, added to the Act in 1884, said merely that an owner's liability "shall be limited to the proportion of any or all debts and liabilities that his individual share of the vessel bears to the whole", with no voyage reference to qualify the "debts and liabilities". The § 184 reference to loss "suffered by . . . owners . . . on the same voyage" was at least consistent with the idea that the privilege of limitation was to extend only to the group of claims which might arise on a single voyage but hardly compelled such a construction. The absence of comparable language in § 189 confused an already obscure picture. Nor did the Admiralty Rules governing practice in limitation proceedings which the Supreme Court issued in 1872 [194] do anything to clarify the problem.

No case directly involving the voyage question ever came to the Supreme Court, although in La Bourgogne Justice White quoted with approval the statement that:

> "The phrase is added [in § 184] 'on the same voyage' to confine the participation in the apportionment to the freighters of a single voyage and not to permit the shipowner to

192a. Petition of Bloomfield Steamship Co., note 190a *supra*, 422 F.2d at p. 736, 1970 A.M.C. at p. 533. Under the 1957 Brussels Convention, limitation decrees are entitled to international recognition among signatory countries (see note 13j supra).

193. 3 Benedict, Admiralty 400 (6th ed. 1940); Robinson, Admiralty 930, n. 116 (1939); Hughes, Admiralty 364 (2d ed. 1920).

194. 80 U.S. (13 Wall.) xii (1872).

bring into the compensation losses sustained on the prior or other voyages." [195]

There were not a great many cases in which shipowners asserted the right to limit without restriction of time, but the few lower court opinions which dealt with the problem were consistent in holding that the Act required a voyage by voyage grouping of claims. In The Alpena, which seems to have been the first case on the point, Judge Blodgett succinctly stated the issue of policy:

> "I am clearly of opinion that the casualties or losses of different voyages cannot be aggregated or grouped together, say at the end of a season, or when a final catastrophe ensues, and all the losers be cited in to share what has been saved from shipwreck or other disaster, together with the pending freight, and have a decree entered exonerating the owners from personal liability. It seems to me that each voyage or trip, each separate journey, which the ship makes from one port to another, must be treated as a separate venture, involving its own particular hazards, losses and earnings; and that when each such voyage is ended it is for the owner to decide whether the losses have been such as to make it expedient for him to invoke the protection given by this act of congress. If he does not decide to do this, but sends his ship upon a new voyage, he thereby concedes his personal liability for the damages incurred on the past voyage." [196]

The Supreme Court finally put the voyage question beyond doubt by the 1948 revision of the Limitation Rules.[197] Under Rule 51 the petition for limitation was required to state "the voyage on which the demands sought to be limited arose, with the date and place of its termination" and the form of "Notice of Petition for Exoneration from or Limitation of Liability" which the Rule set forth read that the right is claimed "for all claims arising on the voyage of the vessel ______ from ______ to ______ terminating on ______."

That language from Rule 51 was copied into Supplemental Rule F(2) with the addition of the words "if any" after the word "voyage". The reason for the "if any" addition is not explained in the Advisory Committee's Notes; presumably the added phrase was meant to cover cases in which the vessel was not, strictly speaking,

195. 210 U.S. 95, 135, 28 S.Ct. 664 (1908). Justice White gave as the source of his quotation Norwich & N. Y. Transp. Co. v. Wright, 80 U.S. (13 Wall.) 104 (1871), citing to p. 111 of 13 Wallace. Curiously, the passage he refers to was not a part of the Court's opinion but a summary of the arguments of counsel. The point was at best remote from the issues presented in the case (see note 7 *supra*) and Justice Bradley did not bother to discuss it in his opinion.

196. 8 F. 280 (N.D.Ill.1881). Other early cases which came to the same conclusion were The Rose Culkin, 52 F. 328 (S.D.N.Y.1892) and The Puritan, 94 F. 365 (N.D.Ill.1899).

197. 334 U.S. 864, 68 S.Ct. clxll 1948 A.M.C. 1496 (1948).

engaged in a voyage at the time of the accident but was, *e. g.*, in port or even in dry dock.[197a]

§ 10–47. In Norwich & N. Y. Transp. Co. v. Wright [198] the Supreme Court had decided that the value to which a shipowner was entitled to limit was the value of the ship after the loss had taken place. In The City of Norwich, a later appeal in the same proceeding, the Court said that, in the case of a ship which had sunk following a collision, that meant "the value which she had when she had sunk, and was lying at the bottom of the sea. That was the termination of the voyage." [199] In The Great Western,[200] it was found that the value of the ship immediately after a high seas collision, was $150,000. The ship, which had not been damaged, continued on her voyage but was stranded and wrecked before making port by careless navigation; the collision and the later stranding were not causally related. After the stranding the strippings from the wreck were sold for $1794.14. On these facts the Court held that the voyage had not been completed until the ship was stranded and that the owner could limit to the value of the strippings.[201]

The ship need not be actually engaged on something that could be called a "voyage" to come within the Limitation Act. The owner will not be deprived of his right to limit because the vessel is tied up at a wharf or even in drydock on the occasion of an accident.[202] On the

197a. See note 202 *infra* and the accompanying text. The form of "Notice of Petition" which was set forth in the 1948 version of Rule 51 no longer appears in Rule F.

198. 80 U.S. (13 Wall.) 104 (1871).

199. 118 U.S. 468, 493, 6 S.Ct. 1150, 1156 (1886).

200. 118 U.S. 520, 6 S.Ct. 1172 (1886).

201. The Americana, 230 F. 853 (N.D. Cal.1915) is an example of what might be called the voyage-splitting technique. The Americana left San Francisco, stopped at another West Coast port and then cleared for Australia, but was lost at sea with all hands. A seaman who had been injured on the coastwise leg of the trip brought suit. The shipowner invoked the Limitation Act, arguing that the ship should be valued at the end of the voyage—*i. e.* as it lay at the bottom of the Pacific Ocean. The court held that there had been two voyages and that, with respect to the seaman's claim, the owner could limit only to the value of the ship at the end of the coastwise voyage.

202. See The Agwisun (Petition of Atlantic, Gulf & West Indies S. S. Lines), 49 F.2d 263, 1931 A.M.C. 957 (2d Cir. 1931); The Glenbogie (Petition of Great Lakes Transit Corp.), 53 F.2d 1022, 1931 A.M.C. 1740 (N.D.Ohio 1931), affirmed 63 F.2d 849, 1933 A.M. C. 1019 (6th Cir. 1933) but limitation was ultimately denied on other grounds, 81 F.2d 441, 1936 A.M.C. 267 (6th Cir. 1936). In the Pump Boat 600 (Lehigh Valley R. Co. v. Jones), 50 F.2d 828, 1931 A.M.C. 1182 (3d Cir. 1931), the owner of a structure which was used in putting out fires in New York Harbor petitioned for limitation. The pump boat was without motive power and was towed out to wherever it was used. An engineer was injured aboard the boat at a time when it was tied up at a pier. Judge Woolsey held both that the pump boat was a vessel within the Limitation Act and that the owner was entitled to petition for limitation even though the "vessel" had not been on a voyage. The Snug Harbor (Petition of United States), 53 F.2d 407, 1931 A.M.C. 1487 (E.D.N.Y.1931) affirmed 59 F.2d 984, 1932 A.M.C. 964 (2d Cir. 1932) raised the question whether the owner could limit against claims which arose sub-

other hand his protection, time-wise, is limited to the group of claims which arise from the particular accident. Also in the case of vessels such as harbor or other craft which are continually engaged in trips of short duration, the grouping of claims is by the accident and the seagoing voyage rule does not apply.[203]

Following an accident the owner may continue the original voyage to destination; in that case the limitation value is the value at the end of the voyage and it has been held that, if repairs have been made at an intermediate port, the value of the repairs may not be deducted from the fund.[204] On the other hand, the owner, by abandoning the voyage after the accident, may fix his liability at the time of abandonment. If he does so, subsequent repairs are for his own account and their value does not swell the limitation fund.[205]

The only modern case in which the ancient learning about what is a "voyage" for limitation purposes has been reviewed is In re Moore (The Tug Olive L. Moore).[205a] The tug set out from Chicago for a voyage through the Great Lakes and the St. Lawrence Seaway. Twenty-four hours out of Chicago the tug suffered storm damage and was forced to put into the port of Muskegon where it remained for more than five weeks while repairs were being made. On completion of the repairs the tug had to be put through certain trials and Huron Cement gave permission for the use of one of its piers. In the course of the trials the pier was damaged in an amount estimated at $75,000. The tug (which was not itself damaged in the pier incident) then set out a second time on its interrupted voyage. On this occasion she got as far as the Straits of Mackinac where her engines went dead. At this point the owner gave up, abandoned the voyage, filed a limitation petition and turned the tug over to a trustee who eventually sold her for $16,000 (her value when she left Muskegon had been estimated to be slightly less than $30,000). Claims aggregating $250,000 were filed in the limitation proceeding (the nature of the claims, other than Huron's claim for damages to its pier, is not specified in Judge Freeman's opinion). Huron claimed that the tug had in effect engaged in two voyages from Chicago to Muskegon and then from Muskegon to the Straits of Mackinac, that its pier had been damaged before the commencement of the second and final voyage, that it was therefore a pre-voyage claimant as to whom limitation was not available.[205b]

sequent to the termination of the voyage by sinking (other ships had run against the wreck). The owner was held to have lost his right to limit by failure to comply with the Wreck Statute (see note 45 *supra*) so the question did not have to be decided.

**203.** 3 Benedict, Admiralty 401 (6th ed. 1940).

**204.** The Lara (Petition of Cuba Distilling Co., Inc.), 1947 A.M.C. 27 (S.D. N.Y.1946).

**205.** See The Frej (Rice Growers Ass'n of Cal. v. Rederiaktiebolaget Frode), 176 F.2d 401, 1949 A.M.C. 1761 (9th Cir. 1949) certiorari denied 338 U.S. 878, 70 S.Ct. 159 (1949).

**205a.** 278 F.Supp. 260, 1968 A.M.C. 818 (E.D.Mich.1968).

**205b.** On the treatment of pre-voyage claim, see § 10–48 *infra*.

Judge Freeman reviewed the venerable "voyage" authorities in a careful opinion and concluded that the tug had been engaged in a single voyage, which had been temporarily interrupted at Muskegon. He placed that conclusion principally on the ground that the tug's master and owner had the right to determine whether to abandon or continue the voyage and that they had decided to continue until the tug suffered her second misadventure in the Straits of Mackinac. Thus Huron had to come into the limitation proceeding and the tug's value for limitation purposes was what she had been sold for after the termination of the voyage.

If the owner continues to operate his ship after the completion of a voyage on which claims have arisen it is clear that the claimants do not take the risk of subsequent deterioration in the ship's condition. Judge Blodgett in The Alpena went so far as to suggest that if the owner "sends his ship upon a new voyage, he thereby concedes his liability for the damages incurred on the past voyage"[206]—that is, gives up once and for all the right to limit. Judge Brown in The Rose Culkin took a more moderate position: "[A]lthough the mere subsequent navigation of the vessel cannot be treated as a personal assumption of the debt such as to exclude all right to limit liability afterwards . . . yet if the Rose Culkin had been stranded, or otherwise so damaged, or so depreciated in her subsequent voyages, as to be of substantially less market value than immediately after this collision, I should have held that the right to proceed by *surrender* [*i. e.* of the vessel in its deteriorated condition to a trustee] was gone, and that the owner must resort to some one of the other modes of proceeding [*i. e.* give a bond or other security for the vessel's value after the collision] to obtain the benefit of the act."[207] Although the point has not been much litigated, Judge Brown's moderate position seems to state the general understanding.

**§ 10–48.** Claims arising on voyages prior to the limitation voyage cannot be required to come into the limitation proceeding; indeed, it is stated to be a condition of the owner's right to limit on a subsequent voyage that prior voyage claims be first satisfied.[208] It follows from this that the fund for distribution among claimants on the limitation voyage is not to be reduced by the amount of prior claims. If the ship is surrendered to a trustee, the surrender must be made free of preexisting liens—*i. e.* such liens must have been independently paid or secured. If the ship is released on a stipulation for value, the stipulation must be in the amount of the ship's value unencumbered by prior liens.

Authority for the propositions just stated is, it must be admitted, scant.[209] It seems entirely consistent with the purpose of the Limita-

**206.** See text at note 196 *supra*.

**207.** 52 F. 328, 332–333 (S.D.N.Y.1892).

**208.** 3 Benedict, Admiralty 458 (6th ed. 1940); Robinson, Admiralty 928 *et seq.* (1939); Hughes, Admiralty § 168 (2d ed. 1920).

**209.** The case relied on by Hughes and Robinson (note 208 *supra*) was The Leonard Richards, 41 F. 818 (D.N.J.

tion Act that prior voyage claims should not be affected by a limitation proceeding, that the owner's personal liability should continue unabated as to such claims, and that the limitation fund should be made up without reference to them. The Limitation Act was designed to give shipowners a limited immunity from the consequences of large scale disaster at sea; it was never meant to serve as an informal bankruptcy proceeding for the benefit of owners who had been improvidently operating their ships at a loss and piling up large amounts of debt. The intended beneficiary of the Act is, it might be said, the prudent shipowner who is able to meet his obligations as they become due, but who is, by reason of circumstances beyond his control, confronted with catastrophic claims which he could not foresee and which, in the early days of limited insurance coverage, he could not protect himself against. The limitation proceeding, as between the shipowner and the claimants, has been described as a general average among the participants in a maritime disaster: [210] the shipowner contributes the remaining value of his investment; the claimants share that fund among them. It would surely be unreasonable to require the disaster claimants to admit prior creditors, whose claims would in most instances represent supplies and repairs furnished to the ship, to share in the distribution, or to reduce the fund available for distribution by allowing such prior claims to be deducted from the ship's value. Even without a limitation proceeding, the prior claims would usually be subordinate to the limitation claims. The limitation claims are typically tort claims, which would, on maritime lien theory, outrank contract claims; secondly, being later in time, they would in any event outrank the prior claims, whether the prior claims were in contract or in tort.[211] Prior lien claims would be executed if the ship were sold in an ordinary proceeding *in rem*; they are no worse off if the ship is sold free of liens in a limitation proceeding. If the ship is bonded and released on a stipulation for value, prior liens would not be affected whether the proceeding was *in rem* or for limitation.

Thus it is hard to see how prior claims can be adversely affected by a limitation proceeding. In fact, under the rules as usually stated, they seem to have become the unintended beneficiaries of the Act, since it has usually been assumed that they are to be paid in full while later claims of higher rank, to which they would, absent limitation, be subordinate, will receive only a partial satisfaction and must abandon any personal claim against the shipowner. At this point the rule that a shipowner will be denied limitation unless he has satisfied prior

1890). Hughes also cited Gokey v. Fort, 44 F. 364 (S.D.N.Y.1890). Benedict cited no case authority. Admiralty Rule 51 required that if the petitioner offers to surrender the vessel or her wreckage to a trustee "the petition must further show any prior paramount liens thereon . . . ". That provision was carried forward without change in Supplemental Rule F(2).

210. Knappen, J., in Monongahela River Consolidated Coal & Coke Co. v. Hurst, 200 F. 711, 713 (6th Cir. 1912).

211. See Chapter IX, § 9–58 *et seq.*

claims (or at least prior liens) becomes of peculiar interest.[212] At first blush, the rule sounds like a bit of unnecessary favoritism to the prior creditors: they are to be paid off in full before the limitation claimants get a penny. On further analysis, however, the rule seems to have quite a different effect. Almost by necessary hypothesis the shipowner who cannot take care of his prior ordinary course of business debts is insolvent. Short of bankruptcy or reorganization he will not continue in the shipping business. The idea behind the Limitation Act was to keep shipowners in the business of operating ships. If limitation of his liability to a group of disaster claimants will not accomplish that end, no purpose is served by granting a decree. Denial of the decree on such a state of facts would mean that the disaster claimants would be on an equal footing with prior creditors with regard to subjecting to their claims, with or without the aid of insolvency proceedings, any personal assets which the owner may have in addition to the ship. With regard to the ship, the disaster claims, which are typically liens of a higher rank, would in any case have priority over the prior claims.[213] The rule that limitation will be denied unless prior claims are satisfied is therefore a rule of protection for the disaster claims, not for the prior creditors, in a situation where it is no longer possible to achieve the basic purpose of the Limitation Act.

Petition of Zebroid Trawling Corporation (The F/V Zebroid)[213a] is the first case in the better part of a hundred years which has actually dealt with some of the issues considered in the foregoing discussion (which has been left substantially in the form in which it appeared in the first edition). The facts of The Zebroid, so far as they can be determined from the two brief opinions which were delivered in the case, are obscure and some aspects of the holding are, at least to this writer, equally obscure.

212. The only source for this proposition is 3 Benedict, Admiralty 458 (6th ed. 1940): "[I]t is the duty of the court, in its distribution of the res in such a proceeding, to take into account both the claims which have arisen out of the matter which gave rise to the proceeding, and also other existing liens, and to protect such other existing liens, so far as possible, as an admiralty court will always strive to do. It accomplishes this by refusing to grant the decree of limitation until such liens, if prior to the particular liens or claims of the limitation proceedings, have been paid off or secured." No cases were cited as authority but reference was made to the Admiralty Rules of the Southern and Eastern Districts of New York (S.D. N.Y. Rule 32; E.D.N.Y. Rule 32). Benedict was writing with reference to proceedings in which the ship has been surrendered to a trustee and is to be sold free of liens. To the point that a ship may be sold free of liens in a limitation proceeding, Benedict cited The Mendota, 14 F. 358 (S.D. N.Y.1882). The position taken in the text is that, for reasons rather different from those suggested by Benedict, the rule should be considered one of general application.

213. Insolvency courts in bankruptcy or reorganization proceedings will recognize and adjudicate maritime liens. See Chapter IX, § 9–92 *et seq.*

213a. 428 F.2d 226 (1st Cir. 1970), affirming 1970 A.M.C. 113 (D.Mass.1969). The statement of facts which follows in the text borrows from both opinions.

The Zebroid, a fishing trawler, was subject to a preferred ship mortgage (amount and unpaid balance unspecified) held by the First National Bank of Cape Cod. So encumbered, the Zebroid departed on a voyage on December 30, 1967; in the course of the voyage the master was washed overboard in a storm and lost. On the following April 10 the Bank instituted an action to foreclose its mortgage. On May 22 the master's widow, as administratrix of his estate, was allowed to intervene in the foreclosure action; she alleged that she intended to bring an action under the Jones Act, the general maritime law and the Death on the High Seas Act, to recover for her husband's death and asserted that her claim had priority over the mortgage lien in the foreclosure action.[213b] The Zebroid was sold by order of the court in the foreclosure action for $45,000; the court approved the sale on May 27 and the proceeds were deposited in the registry of the court. On the same day (May 27) Zebroid Corporation, the owner of the trawler, was adjudicated a bankrupt (apparently the bankruptcy proceedings were pending in the same court in which the foreclosure action had been brought). On July 3 Zebroid Corporation [or its trustee in bankruptcy?] filed a complaint for limitation (the limitation complaint seems to have been filed in the same court in which the foreclosure and bankruptcy proceedings were already pending). The court in the limitation proceeding enjoined the prosecution of the widow's death claim; this seems to have been done by way of anticipation since we are also told that the widow's action was not instituted until November 12. At an unspecified date the Bank was allowed to intervene in the limitation proceeding. Zebroid Corporation [or its trustee] moved in the limitation proceeding that the $45,000 in the registry of the court [*i. e.*, the proceeds of the foreclosure sale] be taken as security for the fund required in the limitation proceeding.

Both the District Court and the First Circuit agreed that the Corporation [or its trustee] could not use the proceeds of the foreclosure sale as security for the limitation fund. (Indeed the suggestion that the proceeds could be so used seems insane). The two courts were, however, in strenuous disagreement on their reasons for that conclusion.

The District Court, following and citing the discussion in this and the following section in the first edition of the treatise, held in effect that the Corporation, as the former owner of the Zebroid, could not invoke the Limitation Act (1) because it was a bankrupt and (2) because it had not paid off the pre-voyage liens (*i. e.*, the mortgage). Under this approach the limitation proceeding would evidently have been dismissed and the widow would have been entitled to reduce her claim in the death action to judgment, to assert her priority over the Bank to the proceeds of sale in the foreclosure action and to

213b. Her claim, if proved, did indeed have priority over the mortgage. See Chapter IX, § 9–68 *et seq.*

claim as a judgment creditor (to the extent that her claim had not been satisfied out of the proceeds of the foreclosure sale) against any other corporate assets in the custody of the bankruptcy trustee.[213c]

The First Circuit, in an opinion by Judge Aldrich, took an entirely different approach. He made several points. *One*: a person (like the Zebroid Corporation) who was the owner of a vessel at the time of an accident may subsequently petition for limitation against claims arising from the accident even though before his petition is filed he has sold (or, as in Zebroid, been compelled to transfer) his interest in the vessel. (This point, which no one would quarrel with, is comfortably supported by the prior case law.) [213d] *Second*: In a limitation proceeding, "the full value of the vessel [free of lien] must be tendered into court." Since pre-voyage obligations [*e. g.*, the Zebroid mortgage] "remain unaffected by the [limitation] proceeding . . . it must follow that [the owner] cannot throw the security interests of these [pre-voyage] lieners into the pot." Therefore, the owner cannot use the proceeds of the mortgagee's foreclosure sale as security for his limitation fund, simply because of the happenstance that the proceeds are on deposit in the court's registry. (No one would quarrel with Judge Aldrich's second point). *Third*: It is not a condition of the right to file a limitation complaint that "prior liens" (by which Judge Aldrich evidently meant pre-limitation-voyage liens) be paid off. All that is required is that "a stipulation must be filed [in the limitation proceeding] to protect the limitation claimant in the amount of the value of the vessel."

Let us try to see how the case would come out under Judge Aldrich's third point. Assume that the widow recovers $200,000 in her wrongful death action. Under the Ship Mortgage Act her claim has priority over the mortgage; therefore the proceeds of the foreclosure sale ($45,000) will be paid to her. If the Zebroid was the Corporation's only asset, that is the end of the matter. Assume further, however, that there were other corporate assets which are now being administered in the bankruptcy proceeding. Apart from the limitation proceeding, the widow could claim in the bankruptcy proceeding for the unpaid balance of her judgment and, since her claim is based on a high-order maritime lien, would in all probability be given priority over the claims of competing creditors (including the Bank). But, according to Judge Aldrich, the limitation proceeding can be maintained if the Corporation's trustee in bankruptcy posts bond in the amount of the Zebroid's value (presumably $45,000). It is not im-

213c. It is entirely possible that the Zebroid had been the Corporation's only asset—on that hypothesis, the bankruptcy proceeding would have been a no-asset case and the only fund available would have been the proceeds of the foreclosure sale. One of the many things we are not told about the case is whether the Corporation was a dummy, set up to hold title by a large enterprise which controlled a fleet of separately incorporated ships or whether the Corporation was in truth the beneficial owner of the Zebroid (and, if so, whether it had any other assets).

213d. See note 36 *supra*.

possible, or even difficult, to imagine a situation in which it would be to the benefit of the Corporation's other creditors to freeze the widow out of the bankruptcy and restrict her to the $45,000 limitation fund. The apparent meaning of Judge Aldrich's third point is that this can be done (it would make no kind of sense to say that the widow could collect $45,000 in the limitation proceeding and still claim for the unpaid balance of her judgment in the bankruptcy proceeding).

If we have correctly understood Judge Aldrich's third point and if the consequences outlined in the preceding paragraph follow from it, then we must respectfully disagree. If a bankrupt shipowner's trustee can initiate a limitation proceeding and if, on limitation being decreed, the result is to restrict the limitation claimants to the limitation fund and preclude them from claiming against other assets in the bankruptcy proceeding, then the beneficiaries of the limitation proceeding will be the bankrupt's creditors who cannot be forced into that proceeding. Furthermore the creditors so benefited would almost certainly hold claims which would, on one theory or another, be subordinated to the limitation claims in any direct confrontation. With deference we suggest that such a result cannot be justified, no matter what the underlying purpose of the Limitation Act of 1851 is conceived to be. It may be that Judge Aldrich did not distinguish clearly enough between liens which arise on the limitation voyage (which do not have to be paid or secured since they are forced to take a distributive share of the limitation fund) and pre-limitation-voyage liens (which, it had always been assumed until The Zebroid was decided, must be paid or secured as a condition of invoking the Limitation Act).

Judge Aldrich commented in his Zebroid opinion that there is "little decisional authority" of these issues—which is surely an understatement. Nevertheless, such authority as there is has, since the early days of limitation law, been to the effect that the ability to pay debts incurred in the ordinary course of business is a condition of the right to limit liability against a group of disaster claimants. It is submitted, The Zebroid to the contrary notwithstanding, that that was (and is) a sound rule.

**§ 10–49.** Claims arising on voyages subsequent to the limitation voyage are, like prior voyage claims, thought not to be entitled to intervene in the limitation or to share in distribution of the fund. It follows that the owner's personal liability towards subsequent voyage claims is not affected by a decree granting limitation on a prior voyage. There appears to be no case law authority dealing with subsequent voyage claims; there is merely a vacuum of doctrine.[214]

214. That subsequent claims do not come into, and therefore are not affected by, the limitation proceeding is clear from Supplemental Rule F(2) which was copied without change of substance from Admiralty Rule 51. Rule F(2) provides in part that if the limitation plaintiff offers to surrender the vessel or her wreckage to a trustee, "the complaint must further show . . . what voyages or trips, if any, she has made since the voyage or

Assume that claims exceeding the value of the ship arise on voyage A. The owner makes any necessary repairs and sends the ship out on subsequent voyages, on which claims also arise. Subsequently, when claims are filed or suits commenced by the victims of the voyage A disaster, the owner petitions for limitation as to that voyage. The voyage A limitation fund will be the value of the ship at the end of that voyage, and there is no more reason why the fund should be reduced by subsequent claims than by prior claims.[215] Should it also follow that the owner will be denied the right to limit on voyage A unless he has satisfied subsequent claims in the same way that he is said to be required to satisfy prior claims? It is believed that the reasons suggested for the rule requiring satisfaction of prior claims also apply to the case of subsequent claims: unless, after a limitation decree, the owner is in a position to continue operating his ships there is no reason to grant limitation in the first place. If, apart from the limitation claims, he is unable to meet all his obligations in full, then all his creditors should be allowed an equal chance at his remaining assets. Furthermore, subsequent lien creditors might, under maritime lien theory, be entitled to priority over the limitation voyage liens. If the shipowner is insolvent, it is hard to see why they should be deprived of their prior right in the ship by a sale free of liens in a case where the ship has been surrendered to a limitation trustee. Thus, at least in certain types of cases, the argument for denying limitation unless subsequent claims are satisfied may be even stronger than the argument for satisfaction of prior claims.[215a] A conceivable situation is that a ship might be so unlucky as to run into a limitation situation—claims exceeding her value—on successive voyages. Presumably, if the owner were able to set up two limitation funds he could limit separately against each group of claim-

trip on which the claims sought to be limited arose, and any existing liens arising upon any such subsequent voyage or trip, with the amounts and causes thereof, and the names and addresses of the lienors, so far as known; and whether the vessel sustained any injury upon or by reason of such subsequent voyage or trip." In The Pelotas-The Omoa (Cuyamel Fruit Co. v. The Pelotas), 21 F.2d 236, 1927 A.M.C. 1347 (E.D.La.1927), a shipowner had petitioned for limitation and surrendered the ship to a trustee. While the ship was in the custody of the United States marshal, pending sale in the limitation proceeding, it was allowed to drag its anchor, by the negligence of those aboard, and came into collision with another ship. Judge Burns said that in a limitation proceeding: "[T]he owner must surrender the vessel or have it appraised free of all prior and all subsequent liens. The law seems, plainly, to contemplate that where the surrender is made at a time subsequent to the actual termination of the voyage, the owner can be compelled to pay all liens accruing after that date and for any diminution in value." (*Id.* at 329, 1927 A.M.C. at 1352). It was held that "the ship" was responsible for the subsequent collision, which seems to mean that, since the ship was *in custodia legis* at the time, the subsequent collision lienor was to be paid in priority to the limitation claimants. On liens arising while a ship is *in custodia legis*, see Chapter IX, § 9–11.

215. See The Pelotas, note 214 *supra;* The Rose Culkin, text at note 207 *supra.*

215a. See, however, The Zebroid, discussed text following note 213a *supra.* The Zebroid involved not "subsequent" but "prior" claims (a pre-limitation-voyage mortgage).

ants. If he could not (being insolvent) there would be no reason to allow limitation for either of the voyages.

It is, perhaps, not unreasonable to conclude that if the cases just discussed have not been litigated in the past hundred and twenty-five years, they will probably not be litigated in the next hundred and twenty-five either.

## Chapter XI

# GOVERNMENTAL ACTIVITY IN SHIPPING

§ 11–1. This book has been mainly concerned with the private law of shipping, in its commercial aspects and in connection with the problem of injuries to shipping personnel and to third persons. But the practicing admiralty lawyer, as well as the student of shipping law, soon becomes aware that there is a vast network of public law governing the subject—that statutes in great number and of high complexity regulate the conduct of the business in both its physical and its commercial aspects, and that a huge amount of governmental administrative activity must be taken into daily account. The sheer volume of the public law dealing with this industry would lead to an inference that is abundantly confirmed by the nature of the legal dispensations encountered: Shipping is a matter of close and often anxious governmental concern, to an extent far greater than is normal for most industries of comparable size.

It is not hard to see why this should be so. Two main characteristics of the industry make it the inevitable concern of statecraft—and the plaything of politics.[1] First, the patterns of shipping—trade routes, volume, rates, nationality—affect in turn the whole scheme of geographic distribution of population and of economic activity. Shipping is not just another service; it is the necessary condition of access to materials and markets.[2] Second, and closely connected, is the strategic aspect of the industry. The merchant marine has always been an indispensable military asset, and its importance in this regard has increased rather than diminished in modern times, for wars have become global in potentiality, and the quantities of troops and material required for conducting them grow steadily greater.[3]

Separately considered, either of these factors—the economic-political or the strategic—might force the subject of shipping on the

1. For a general (and still generally useful) survey of the modern relations of the maritime industries and the State, see Hutchins, The American Maritime Industries and Public Policy, 1789–1914, 3–36 (1941).

2. U.N. Conference on Trade and Development, Shipping and the World Economy (1966); also U. S. Maritime Commission, Economic Survey of the American Merchant Marine 5–9 (1937); Hutchins, *op. cit. supra* note 1, at 9–12; National Industrial Conference Board, The American Merchant Marine Problem 6–14 (1929). For an emerging problem, see Rajwar and others, Shipping and Developing Countries, International Conciliation No. 582 (1971).

3. U. S. Maritime Commission, *op. cit. supra* note 2, at 9–13; Hutchins, *op. cit. supra* note 1, at 6–9.

It must be strongly noted here that the patterns of power, and of the uses and usefulness of power, may now be so changing that the fighting of the kind of war that requires heavy marine transport may be turning unprofitable and unattractive; if this happens, the strategic value of marine transport will of course vanish. There is always the danger that we may, in forming our policy toward shipping, be planning to fight World War II over again—a thing very unlikely to happen.

attention of statesmen, and impose near-imperatives on political action. Together, they make the subject a prime public concern—and, for an obvious reason, make it a matter of rare accident for a wholly consistent shipping policy to be formulated. For they pull in opposite directions; the drive for rational ordering of shipping, so as to produce a maximum of economic enjoyment, need not (and usually does not) tend to the same result as the urge toward the building of an industry optimally suited for employment in war.[4] Shipping policy, in recent times at least, is the troubled resultant of these two pulls; to criticize it on the ground of lack of rationality is to miss the main point, which is that it aims at compromising the never totally reconcilable. (Which is not to say that the compromise at any moment is the best that could be attained. The atmosphere in which policy is set is by no means as lofty or serene as the foregoing paragraphs might indicate; like anything that gets into politics, shipping policy is heavily influenced from time to time by the insistent clamors of those whose primary motivation is that they want something for themselves, and who have perhaps persuaded themselves, and would persuade others, that their getting what they want is a necessary corollary of political wisdom and patriotism).[5]

This chapter will deal with the history of the concern of the state with shipping, with the principal measures employed to implement shipping policy, and with the present legal dispensations which implement the shipping policy of the United States. We will go into a few of the problems that arise when the government enters shipping as an actual participant. Some of the principal regulatory material will be mentioned. The hope is that such a treatment of all these matters will give the student some sense of the all-pervading importance, from the lawyer's point of view, of the governmental concern with shipping. This is all that can be done here; full description and balanced evaluation would be the work of many books, rather than of a surveying chapter. The subject has fascination; in the notes will be found leads for pursuing it further.[5a]

## The Past

**§ 11–2.** The remotest history of shipping furnishes abundant evidence of governmental concern. When the Egyptian fleets sailed to trade in the "land of Punt", it was the Pharoahs that sent them there.[6] King Solomon "made a navy of ships . . . And they

**4.** Hutchins, *op. cit. supra* note 1, at 12–20.

**5.** See Zeis, American Shipping Policy, Chapter XIII, The Pressure Group Basis of American Shipping Policy, pp. 206–212 (1938). There is no reason to think there has been any significant recent change in this regard.

**5a.** John B. Kuhns, Yale Law School 1972, was extraordinarily helpful in the revision of this chapter for this edition; many of his ideas and suggestions are in the product. He is of course not responsible for any of the views on policy herein expressed.

**6.** For a summary account of several interesting Egyptian voyages, with citations, see Hourani, Arab Seafaring 7–8 (1951); see also Savile, Ancient Harbors, 15 Antiquity 209 (1941); Fayle, A Short History of the World's Shipping Industry 34 *et seq.* (1933).

came to Ophir and fetched from thence gold, four hundred and twenty talents, and brought it to King Solomon." [7] Athens was dependent for life on the Black Sea grain trade; it was a major concern of her policy to keep the sea-lanes open.[8] The Romans suffered early from lack of a fleet of their own, and took remedial action as the price of rule.[9] In the great Maurya Empire of India (around the third century B.C.) shipping was sufficiently "affected with a public interest" to be made a state monopoly.[10] Later, the Venetians closely controlled their powerful merchant marine,[11] and Ferdinand and Isabella instituted a system of ship bounty in their kingdom.[12] To the Mercantilist theory of the seventeenth century, shipping was a prime national asset, for to pay foreigners for the service of transport was needlessly to lose gold.[13] Fouquet and Colbert built up the French merchant marine by subsidy and by discriminatory taxation on foreign vessels.[14]

To us, the English experience is of the most interest. King Alfred is said actually to have sought to encourage merchant shipping by rewarding Englishmen who had made three voyages over the seas in vessels of their own,[15] and a statute of Richard II moved in the direction of fostering the growth of the Kingdom's trading fleet by forbidding English subjects' freighting their goods on any but English ships.[16] In the time of Henry VII, a statute was passed prohibiting the importation of certain commodities in a ship not owned by English subjects and manned in greater part by them [17]—a dispen-

7. 1 Kings 9, 26, 28.

8. Fayle, *op. cit. supra* note 6, at 45 *et seq.;* 1 Lindsay, History of Merchant Shipping 72 (1874).

9. 1 Lindsay, *op. cit. supra* note 8, at 162 *et seq.*

10. Mookerji, Indian Shipping 102 (1912).

11. Indeed, the city "built and owned most of the large Venetian round ships and galleys" and "in general exercised a careful supervision over all that had to do with trade." Clough & Cole, Economic History of Europe 59 (3d ed. 1952). The Venetians also employed the ship subsidy; Hutchins, *op. cit. supra* note 1, at 48.

12. Clough & Cole, *op. cit. supra* note 11, at 207. The interconnections of shipping, politics, and the structure of empire are rarely more neatly illustrated than in a later item in the Spanish experience, the Manila-Acapulco trade; see Schurz, The Manila Galleon (1939). On the Spanish and Portuguese policies in general, see Fayle, *op. cit. supra* note 6, at 127 *et seq.;* also Borah, Early Colonial Trade and Navigation Between Mexico and Peru, Ibero-Americana: 38 (1954).

13. Hutchins, *op. cit. supra* note 1, at 3, citing 2 Heckscher, Mercantilism 34 (Shapiro trans. 1935).

14. Clough & Cole, *op. cit. supra* note 11, at 319, 322, 329. *Cf.* the interest in matters maritime shown by Colbert's sponsorship of the Ordonnance de la Marine, *supra*, Chapter I, note 27. On the French experience in general, those happy in the language will be interested in Charliat, Trois Siècles D'Économie Maritime Française (1931).

15. Harper, The English Navigation Laws 19 (1939).

16. 5 Rich. II, stat. 1, c. 3 (1381), cited in Harper, *loc. cit. supra* note 15.

17. 4 Hen. VII, c. 10 (1487), cited and discussed in Harper, *op. cit. supra* note 15, at 21. On British shipping in these early times, see Burwash, English Merchant Shipping, 1460–1540 (1947).

sation which shows awareness of the need for building both a national merchant marine and the corps of men to sail it. By the time of Elizabeth I, detailed legislation was on the books, aimed at developing shipping in its material and personnel aspects; [18] it had even been ordained that large landholders must plant a certain amount of flax, for use in sails and cordage! [19]

In 1651 was passed the first of the great Navigation Acts,[20] aimed at the Dutch carrying trade but phrased in terms of general prohibition of importation into England or its colonies by other than English ships—with certain exceptions, the most important of which was that European goods might be imported in ships of the country of origin. The coasting trade was entirely closed to foreigners. This Act is said to have "consolidated the foundations of England's colonial and maritime system." [21] It stated a principle which (though the Act itself was soon and frequently amended, to meet evasion, to except favored groups or trades, and in general to fit emergent circumstances) was the cornerstone of British shipping policy until well into the nineteenth century: that of the reservation of empire trade, in the main, to British vessels. This policy, whatever its effect on other matters, was designed and operated primarily with the aim of building and maintaining a strong merchant marine; from this point of view, one of its most thorough modern students has pronounced it a success.[22] Though partially eroded by treaties in the early nineteenth century, the Navigation Acts were not entirely done away with until 1849.[23]

By this time, steam was well on its way. The natural advantages enjoyed by the British in this regard (access to coal, long experience in iron working [24]) were supplemented by mail contract subsidies and other governmental aid, with the consequence that British shipping came overwhelmingly to dominate the North Atlantic and the world. Close cooperation by the Admiralty, with subsidization where needful, have been the tools of British policy since the repeal of the Navigation Acts.[25]

18. Harper, *op. cit. supra* note 15, at 25 *et seq.*

19. 24 Hen. VIII, c. 4 (1532–33).

20. Act of Oct. 8, 1651 (F. & R. II, 559).

21. Clough & Cole, *op. cit. supra* note 11, at 345.

22. Harper, *op. cit. supra* note 15, at 365–378, esp. 377–8.

23. 12 & 13 Vict. c. 29 (1849).

24. Clough & Cole, *op. cit. supra* note 11, at 595.

25. A detailed and documented account of British aids to shipping is found in American Maritime Council (Otterson, chmn.), Foreign Trade and Shipping 10–133 (1945). The book as a whole is a plea for "all possible aids to our foreign trade and shipping under whatever name." *Id.* at 7. For a detailed discussion of the development of steam and governmental involvement in Great Britain, see Thornton, British Shipping, 2d ed., 1–64 (1959).

§ 11–3. It might be well, before moving to the American experience, to list the principal means that have been used by governments to foster and control merchant shipping:[26]

(a) First, as we have seen, a monopoly for vessels owned by nationals and registered domestically may be established in such carrying trades as can be controlled. The British Navigation Acts exemplify this method. Reservation of domestic ("coastwise") commerce to domestic vessels is a common mode; as we shall see, this is a leading feature of American policy.

(b) Subsidies or bounties may be paid to the shipping or the shipbuilding industries of the nation. These subsidies may be open or disguised; a common form of operational subsidy has been the "mail contract," carrying a far higher rate of compensation than the current free rates for transporting like matter. Subsidies may take many forms.[27] In rare cases, they have even been paid to foreign vessels, where the government concerned judged that its economy would be benefited by the establishment of a regular shipping service, but where no national industry existed capable of furnishing this.[28] Subsidies may be and commonly are used not merely to reward shipping activity generally but to form the pattern of the industry and of its routes and services, by awarding subsidies differentially to favored activities.[29]

(c) Shading off from subsidy, and resembling it in net effect, is the furnishing by government, at less than cost, of various services essential to the conduct of shipping. These may range from the commercial (*e. g.*, government insurance on ship mortgages) to the literally physical (*e. g.*, maintenance of lighthouses).

(d) Direct regulation may form the pattern of the industry; thus, discrimination of various kinds may be prohibited. Similarly, the benefits of national registration (and with it, perhaps, the monopoly in certain trades mentioned in (a) above) may be made to depend on a vessel's being built within the country, or owned or manned by nationals.

26. The listing follows, with some adaptations, that set out by Hutchins, *op. cit. supra* note 1, at 39–40. Mance, International Sea Transport 70–90 (1945) summarizes the shipping policies of the principal maritime countries at the time of writing. Saugstad, Shipping and Shipbuilding Subsidies (Dept. of Commerce, Bureau of Foreign and Domestic Commerce, Trade Promotion Series No. 129, 1932) goes into great detail on the aid given to shipping in the maritime nations in times past.

27. See Saugstad, *op. cit. supra* note 26, *passim.*

28. Brazil, for ten years beginning in 1864, paid a subsidy to an American steamship line for foreign trade operation from Brazilian ports; Saugstad, *op. cit. supra* note 26, at 444.

29. See, *e. g.*, the "essential trade routes" concept shaping the present American subsidy program, *infra* at note 68.

Such measures are aimed at strengthening the domestic shipbuilding industry, insuring a supply of trained seamen-nationals, or placing the fleet firmly under governmental control.

(e) The government may itself participate in the shipping industry, either making this a state monopoly or conducting operations of its own in a generally "private" field.[30]

These are only the salient and most direct means employed. Hundreds of kinds of laws may affect shipping in one way or another. But the realization that the above listing reflects widespread and long-continued practice among maritime nations will make American policy more comprehensible.

## The American Experience

**§ 11–4.** Before the Revolutionary War, the American colonies led the world in shipbuilding,[31] though the conduct of Empire shipping operations was largely in British hands. With independence, the United States found themselves cut out of the closed shipping system created by the Navigation Laws; the maintenance of the shipbuilding industry, and the creation of an operating merchant marine, were among the most urgent tasks facing the Congress and the nation. Economic conditions favored the accomplishment of these tasks. American ships (because, basically, of the proximity of suitable timber) were both better and cheaper than those that could be built in England,[32] and, since that country would not register under her flag ships built in America, the British shipping industry operated under higher costs, and the American carriers enjoyed an advantage over their recent foe and chief competitor. Further, the wars in which Europe was engaged gave an impetus to shipping as a whole, and a special advantage to neutral American vessels.[33]

Congress assisted shipping and shipbuilding in this early period, by a series of measures. The coastwise trade was early reserved to domestic vessels,[34] and registry under the American flag was limited to vessels built and owned here.[35] Discriminatory tonnage taxes were

30. See *supra* note 11; *infra* at notes 125–127.

31. Hutchins, *op. cit. supra* note 1, at 130–157; Bryant, The Sea and the States 44 (1947).

32. Hutchins, *op. cit. supra* note 1, at 171 *et seq.*

33. Zeis, *op. cit. supra* note 5, at 4–5.

34. In 1789, in the second law passed under the new Constitution, Congress enacted a discriminatory tax on foreign vessels in the coasting trade, making it impracticable economically for them to operate, 1 Stat. 27. In 1817, the coastwise trade was prohibited outright to foreign ships, a disposition that has lasted down to now. 3 Stat. 351.

35. R.S. § 4132 (1875); 1 Stat. 287 (1792). Despite constant agitation for its removal, this provision remained law until 1912. Panama Canal Act of 1912, c. 390, § 5, 37 Stat. 562. *Cf.* note 47, *infra*. The present law in substance provides for registry of any

imposed on foreign vessels using our ports and on the goods they carried—but these measures were of short duration, for the natural competitive advantage of American shipping in these times was such that an even break was all that was needed for success, and the discriminatory taxes became important chiefly as weapons for negotiating the removal of similar taxes on American ships in foreign ports; this "reciprocity" policy was largely successful by around 1830.[36]

These policies, and the natural advantage they exploited, ushered in the Golden Age of Sail for the United States.[37] But there were ominous signs on the horizon, even in the greatest days of the Yankee clippers. Steam navigation had become practicable,[38] and steel construction of hulls was moving to the end of its experimental stage. The shipping interests in this country were reluctant to admit the importance of developments that threatened the destruction of the competitive advantages (timber and accumulated know-how) under which our shipping operated. But the menace could no longer be ignored, as the Cunard steamers, under mail contract to the British government, chalked up an impressive record of reliable transatlantic service.[39] In 1845, Congress passed a law authorizing subsidy under the guise of mail contracts; the Ocean Steam Navigation Company, running between New York and Bremen, became the chief beneficiary.[40] In 1847 (under the same disguise) a subsidy was granted to the Collins Line, for a New York to Liverpool run in direct competition with the Cunarders.[41]

Neither of these measures worked out well. The Collins Line was in difficulty from the start; increases in its subsidy crystallized public opinion against the whole subsidy system, which was virtually abandoned in 1858.[42] Meanwhile, it was becoming apparent that steam had come to stay, and the competitive advantage in shipbuilding and shipping passed to the British. Then, during the Civil War,

suitable vessel wherever built, but bars foreign-built vessels from the coasting trade. 46 U.S.C.A. § 11.

36. Hutchins, *op. cit. supra* note 1 at 246 *et seq.*, sketches this development; see also Zeis, *op. cit. supra* note 5, at 3–4.

37. Denison, America's Maritime History 85 *et seq.* (1944); Bryant, *op. cit. supra* note 31, at 263 *et seq.* The period of highest American activity and prestige, in the 'forties and 'fifties, curiously coincides with our early fumblings and failures with steam—with all that meant. While the British were introducing electric lighting, we were developing the kerosene lamp to its peak of perfection.

38. See Fayle, *op. cit. supra* note 6, at 226 *et seq.*, for an account of the nearly simultaneous use of the "clippers" and steam, and the ultimate triumph of the latter. See also Denison, *op. cit. supra* note 37, at 110–118.

39. Clough & Cole, *op. cit. supra* note 11, at 596; McKee, The Ship Subsidy Question in U. S. Politics, 8 Smith College Studies in History 5, 15–16 (1922); see Hutchins, *op. cit. supra* note 1, at 336 *et seq.*, on the development of the world-wide British steamship network.

40. Hutchins, *op. cit. supra* note 1, at 348 *et seq.*; McKee, *supra* note 39, at 18 *et seq.*

41. Hutchins, *op. cit. supra* note 1, *at* 353 *et seq.*; McKee, *supra* note 39, at 21–22.

42. Hutchins, *op. cit. supra* note 1, at 357–358; McKee, *supra* note 39, at 22–28; see 11 Stat. 364 (1858).

American ships in great numbers were transferred to the British flag, because of the hazard to American flag vessels created by the Confederate cruisers, and the consequent high war-risk insurance rates. Retransfer was forbidden by law.[43]

Thus, when the Civil War ended, American shipping, which, within the easy memory of men in their prime, had been a chief asset of the nation and the wonder of the world, had become the chronic problem-child which it has remained ever since. Now operating at a competitive disadvantage, in a nation in which all the factors of production were pouring inland to develop the West, the industry had nowhere to go but down, and its decline was not slowed by Congressional studies [44] or by the pleas of private citizens who from time to time cried out in the wilderness.[45] By 1900, the British steamers were supreme in most important trades, and the American merchant marine was utterly insignificant.[46] Postal subsidies and other half-hearted aid could do no more than keep it from disappearing entirely. It is against this bleak background that the experience and expedients of the twentieth century must be evaluated.[47]

**§ 11–5.** World War I thrust upon the country the necessity of building up a merchant fleet. Even before we entered the war, the

43. For a full account, with background and tracing out of effects, see Dalzell, The Flight from the Flag (1940).

44. Perhaps the most celebrated was that of the "Lynch Committee"—an *ad hoc* group appointed by the House of Representatives in 1870, to study the shipping decline and to recommend measures. See House Committee Report 28, 41st Cong., 2d Session. The shipbuilding bounty bill proposed by the chairman of this committee failed to pass. Later "studies" were slightly more successful in getting legislation passed, but not in reviving the shipping industry. See Zeis, *op. cit. supra* note 5, at 29–53.

45. *E. g.*, Bates, American Marine (1893); Bates, American Navigation (1902); Kelley, The Question of Ships (1884). The most amusing volume on the theme during this epoch (at least of those examined), Hill, History of American Shipping (1883), depicts on its cover a loose-robed female figure, "American Shipping," her head bowed down by a weight labelled "Booty, Foreign Shipping Agents and Lobbyists," hands manacled to other weights marked "Bounties to Competitors" and "Burden Local National." On an inner page, "Columbia," eyeglass pointed seaward, "Looks in Vain for Our Merchant Marine," while "Foreign Lobbyist" sings of "The Ships o' Clyde." The language of the text is correspondingly strong.

46. Denison, *op. cit. supra* note 37, at 121 *et seq.*; Bryant, *op. cit. supra* note 31, at 378–9.

47. Virtually omitted, in this sketch, is the history of the unremitting pressure of the shipping and shipbuilding interests (not always at one with each other) to secure subsidy and other government aid. The works cited in note 45, *supra*, are samples of the polemic. There were occasional minor successes; the Ocean Mail Act of 1891 (26 Stat. 830–33) was the most important. This Act, like all other measures taken in these times, failed to achieve its purpose; see Zeis, *op. cit. supra* note 5, at 32–36. Also constantly pressed, during the period, was the drive to open American registry (and the coasting trade) to foreign-built vessels; in this "free ship" controversy, the shipowners and shipbuilders were at loggerheads, for obvious reasons. The great sensation of the period (and one which colored attitudes toward subsidy for a long time) was the disclosure that the Pacific Mail S. S. Co., in 1872, spent some $900,000 in mysterious ways to secure the passage of its subsidy bill. For full accounts of the whole depressing period, see Hutchins, Zeis, and McKee, *op. cit. supra*, at appropriate chapters.

withdrawal of foreign tonnage, and the departure of freight rates for the stratosphere, forced the passage of the Shipping Act of 1916,[48] creating the United States Shipping Board, and the formation of the Shipping Board Emergency Fleet Corporation. The Board was a regulatory and policy-forming body charged with the task of developing a merchant marine, and the Corporation was empowered actually to build, buy, charter, and operate merchant vessels. Our entry into the war vastly increased the importance of these agencies.

After the first World War (as after the second [49]) the problem changed from one of shortage of tonnage to one of surplus. The Merchant Marine Act of 1920 [50] continued the Shipping Board in being, empowered it to study and to fix policy with regard to the operations of the merchant marine, and enacted a number of miscellaneous provisions designed to foster shipping; a "construction loan fund" was established. The Board itself, under the Act, continued to operate vessels in a number of trades, though actual operation was in most cases conducted by private companies under commission contracts.

A new Act, in 1928,[51] liberalized the "construction loan" program, and extended and strengthened the mail subsidy program which had been half-heartedly revived.[52] During this period, the sale of ships by the Board, at prices far below cost, constituted, in effect, an additional subsidy.[53] Nevertheless, progress was far from satisfactory, and in 1933 the Black Committee of the Senate uncovered extensive abuses in the operation of the subsidy system and of the merchant marine in general.[54] Thoroughly convinced that strategic factors, if not economic ones, imperatively called for the maintenance of a healthy shipping industry, Congress, under the then persuasive stimulus of an urgent plea from President Franklin Roosevelt,[55] passed the Merchant Marine Act of 1936,[56] which, through the 1970 Act (to be discussed below), directly and recognizeably set the pattern of our present governmental policy toward shipping.

The Act created, in place of the older agencies, the United States Maritime Commission [56a], whose most important functions had to

48. 39 Stat. 728, 46 U.S.C.A. § 801 *et seq.*

49. See *infra* at note 59.

50. 41 Stat. 988, 46 U.S.C.A. § 861 *et seq.*

51. 45 Stat. 689, 46 U.S.C.A. § 891 *et seq.*

52. See *supra*, note 47.

53. See Zeis, *op. cit. supra* note 5, at 135–6.

54. Hearings Before The Special Senate Committee to Investigate Air Mail and Ocean Mail Contracts, 73d Cong., 2d Sess. (1933).

55. See Zeis, *op. cit. supra* note 5, at 187.

56. 49 Stat. 1985, 46 U.S.C.A. § 1101 *et seq.*

56a. Here we begin an exceedingly confusing set of continually changing names for governmental maritime agencies. The present position is summed up at and in n. 61b, *infra.*

do with the formation and implementing of overall shipping policy. The Act gave a general directive:

> It is necessary for the national defense and development of its foreign and domestic commerce that the United States shall have a merchant marine (a) sufficient to carry its domestic water-borne commerce and a substantial portion of the water-borne export and import foreign commerce of the United States and to provide shipping service on all routes essential for maintaining the flow of such domestic and foreign water-borne commerce at all times, (b) capable of serving as a naval and military auxiliary in time of war or national emergency, (c) owned and operated under the United States flag by citizens of the United States in so far as may be practicable, and (d) composed of the best-equipped, safest, and most suitable types of vessels, constructed in the United States and manned with a trained and efficient citizen personnel. It is hereby declared to be the policy of the United States to foster the development and encourage the maintenance of such a merchant marine.[57]

It will be noted that the formula gives weight both to the economic and to the strategic factors that have pulled at shipping policy through the ages. Before the Commission could do much more than start on its long-range program, the strategic element became wholly dominant, with the advent of World War II. To take over the unprecedentedly acute shipping problem created by that conflict, a War Shipping Administration came into being, and operated vessels on its own account in many principal trades.[58]

After the war, the country found itself with a glut of ships, mostly built during hostilities.[59] Transport made necessary by the Korean conflict somewhat eased the position, but only temporarily.

By an Executive Order, implementing one of the governmental Reorganization Plans, President Truman, in 1950, transferred the functions of the Maritime Commission to the Department of Commerce.[60] In that Department, a Maritime Board was to exercise the regulatory and quasi-judicial functions of the old Maritime Commission, in independence of the Secretary of Commerce. The rest of the

57. 49 Stat. 1985 (1936), 46 U.S.C.A. § 1101.

58. The WSA was created by Exec.Order No. 9054, 7 Fed.Reg. 837 (1942). The National Shipping Authority (established in 1951, under Exec.Order No. 10219, § 201(c), Feb. 28, 1951) differed from WSA, its World War II predecessor, in that it was planned as a built-in unit of the Maritime Administration, whereas WSA was an independent wartime agency existing side-by-side with the Maritime Commission.

59. See *infra* at notes 82, 100–101, 103–105.

60. Reorganization Plan No. 21 of 1950, transmitted 13 March 1950. This Plan, the result of a study of the Maritime Commission by the Hoover Commission, is printed, with discussion and some interesting background, in S.Rep.No.1674, 81st Cong., 2d Sess. (1950).

functions of the Commission—policy formation, ship operation and procurement, etc.—were to be performed either by the Secretary of Commerce or by a Maritime Administration, responsible to the Secretary but headed by a Maritime Administrator who was the same individual as the chairman of the Maritime Board.[61]

In 1961, by yet another Executive Order,[61a] the Board was abolished and its regulatory functions have been vested in a Maritime Commission independent of the Department of Commerce. The subsidy functions are now in the Maritime Administration. The Maritime Administrator is an Assistant Secretary of Commerce for Maritime Affairs.[61b]

This brings us almost down to now in this very broad sketch of the history of American shipping policy, for the Act of 1970, to be discussed in § 11–8 *infra,* changed important details rather than overall pattern. There are three phases: (1) The great days of sail, when a minimum of governmental activity was needed to insure the success of an industry enjoying great advantages. (2) The period between the Civil War and World War I, when our shipping declined to insignificance, but when Congress saw no imperative reason for effective resuscitative action. (3) The modern period, starting with World War I, when felt strategic necessities have forced and probably will continue to force some kind of government action to maintain the shipping and shipbuilding industries. This period continued through the Viet Nam war, when great ocean transport capacity was required.[61c]

The problems of the present period are simple in outline, though endlessly complex in their ramifications. There are two salient factors: (1) The American merchant marine as a whole seemingly cannot now or in the foreseeable future operate in free competition; our ships are too expensive and our wages too high for that. (2) The United States, it has seemed necessary to assume, cannot sustain its responsibilities as a world power without a merchant marine; the acceptance of this judgment as orthodoxy has made it unnecessary to

61. Formally, the Reorganization Plan vested all the functions other than the regulatory and quasi-judicial in the Secretary of Commerce, who might delegate them as he saw fit within the Department. He delegated a number of these functions to the Maritime Administrator. The lines of responsibility were not so clearly drawn as might perhaps be desired; thus, the Board was given "final" authority over the making, terminating, etc., of subsidy contracts (Plan, § 105(1)), but the Secretary of Commerce retained the right to guide "policy" (Plan, § 106) with respect to these matters. There was an Undersecretary of Commerce for Transportation, who exercised most of the Secretary's functions in this field. See U. S. Dept. of Commerce, Manual of Orders Part 1 (Dept. Order 117, Sept. 3, 1953), Organization and Functions of the Federal Maritime Board and the Maritime Administration.

61a. See Reorganization Plan No. 7 of 1961, 26 F.R. 7315; for the Plan as amended by later statutes, see 46 U.S.C.A. following § 1111.

61b. The award, amendment and termination of subsidy contracts is delegated by this Assistant Secretary to a Maritime Subsidy Board, of which he himself is *ex officio* chairman. Maritime Administration Annual Report 37–38 (1971).

61c. *Ib.,* 15.

debate the dubious economic advantages of maintaining our own shipping, instead of using the shipping services of other countries.[62]

There can be only two answers, given the premises: government operation or subsidy. Both clash to some extent with current folklore, but the former is probably regarded generally as a good deal more objectionable than the latter, as least in peacetime.[63] Accordingly, subsidy was the basic method employed under the 1936 Act, and remains the basic method under the 1970 Act; tax benefits, themselves a kind of subsidy, are, under the latter Act, extremely important.

We can now turn to the relatively recent working of schemes for promotion of the strength of our merchant marine.

### U. S. Shipping Policy Under the 1936 Act

**§ 11–6.** The Merchant Marine Act of 1936 ended the mail contract subsidy system, and committed the nation to a policy of outright subsidization of those activities in shipping which were determined to be essential. In this strategic regard the 1936 Act set shipping policy down to now. The old Maritime Commission had general charge of the subsidy program. Under the divided organizational scheme described in the last section, however, subsidy *policy* was set by the Secretary of Commerce, while actual award of subsidy contracts, being conceived as a quasi-judicial function, was performed by the Maritime Board.[64]

The underlying theory of the subsidy system set up by the 1936 Act was simple. American shipping, where such action was judged to implement the national interest, was to be placed on terms of competitive equality with foreign shipping.[65] Two disadvantages had to

62. For a doubt now no bigger than a man's hand, see *supra*, n. 3.

A treatment of policy problems, under the 1936 Act, with useful bibliography (including Committee hearings and reports) is House Committee on Merchant Marine and Fisheries, Survey: The American Merchant Marine, Policies and Problems (Committee Print, 1954). Also useful is the voluminous Merchant Marine Study and Investigation, Hearings Before a Subcommittee of the Senate Committee on Interstate and Foreign Commerce, 81st Cong., 1st and 2d Sess. (1949–50). For immediate background to the 1970 Act (§ 11–8 *infra*) see *infra*, n. 98.

63. On the record, it is questionable whether government operation in the full sense—that is, actual operation by the government, as opposed to assumption by government of the financial risks of operation actually performed by private operators for liberal compensation—is really as "wasteful" and "inefficient" as claimed—or, at least, whether it is any more so than "private" operation. See Zeis, *op. cit. supra* note 5, at 125 *et seq.* Obviously, the question is one of the focal points of pressure and emotionalism in the field; summary judgment on a rational basis is correspondingly difficult. What is certain is that extensive government operation in peacetime is not a real political possibility in the foreseeable future, though, if the maintenance of shipping is a strategic objective, there seems no theoretical, as opposed to possible practical, objection.

64. See *supra* note 61.

65. This objective is patent on the face of the Act (as detailed) in the text immediately following) and is the "philosophy" stated in all the surrounding literature. See, *e. g.*, U. S. Maritime

be overcome: The high cost of shipbuilding in the United States, and the high cost of United States flag operation, owing mainly to the high wages commanded by American crews. To answer the first of these, the "construction-differential subsidy" [66] paid the difference between domestic and foreign construction cost. The second disadvantage was to be equalized by the "operating-differential subsidy".[67] Under the 1936 Act, the availability of either of these subsidies was limited by the "essential routes" concept. Under a separate section of the Act,[68] the Commission was to determine what routes were "essential for the promotion, development, expansion, and maintenance of the foreign commerce of the United States . . . " The construction subsidy was to be available only to vessels destined for operation on such routes; the operational subsidy was to be granted only for essential route operations. Under an amendment to the Act, contained in the so-called Long Range Shipping Act of 1952, the construction subsidy was made theoretically available for any vessel to be used in the foreign commerce of the United States, without regard to its plying an "essential route",[69] though the Maritime Board or Administration negotiated few contracts for the building of vessels not to be used on "essential routes". The operating subsidy remained limited to "essential route" operations.

The administration of any subsidy program is likely, despite the simplicity of its philosophy, to be a matter of considerable complexity. The statute required, for the granting of a construction subsidy, that the Board find:

> (1) the plans and specifications call for a new vessel which will meet the requirements of the foreign commerce of the United States, will aid in the promotion and development of such commerce, and be suitable for use by the United States for national defense or military purposes in time of war or national emergency; (2) the applicant possesses the ability, experience, financial resources, and other qualifications necessary to enable it to operate and maintain the proposed new vessel, and (3) the granting of the aid applied for is

Commission, *op. cit. supra* note 2, at 70. The formula, as shown in the text, is not a simple one to administer. It is to be doubted whether it is even theoretically sound. The final goal perhaps ought to be envisioned in terms of *result*—a going-concern merchant marine of the kind required by strategic and other considerations—rather than of "fair competition." The instrumental question could then emerge with clarity: "What does it take to motivate the desired conduct?" As it stands, the Act not only lays down a formula excessively difficult to administer, but also confuses the issues, which are: "What is indispensably required, and what are the necessary means for getting it?" A useful and well-documented summation of the shipping industry's point of view on subsidies is found in an Analysis of Construction and Operating Subsidies (1953) prepared by the Ocean Shipping Panel.

66. 46 U.S.C.A. §§ 1151–1161.

67. 46 U.S.C.A. §§ 1171–1182. There was a third type of subsidy permitted under the Act—the so-called "countervailing subsidy," to offset subsidies granted by foreign nations. 46 U.S.C.A. § 1174.

68. 46 U.S.C.A. § 1121.

69. 66 Stat. 760.

reasonably calculated to replace worn-out or obsolete tonnage with new and modern ships, or otherwise to carry out effectively the purposes and policy of this chapter.[70]

The applicant had to be a citizen, and the Department of the Navy had to certify approval of the construction plans, on the basis of the suitability of the vessel for conversion to military use.[71] The Board was then to receive bids from American shipyards, and the shipbuilding contract was entered into directly between the Board and the successful bidder. Concurrently, the Board was to enter into a contract with the subsidy, applicant, for sale of the vessel to him at a price "corresponding to the estimated cost . . . of building such vessel in a foreign shipyard." The net effect was that the government paid the difference between domestic and foreign construction, and that the subsidy applicant was placed in the same competitive position as the purchaser of a foreign-built ship.[72]

It will be seen that a principal effect of this scheme was the subsidy of shipbuilding as well as shipping; the same result, from the ship operator's point of view, could at least theoretically be attained, without cost to the government, by permitting the American shipowner to purchase his vessels abroad without incurring any disadvantage. But from the strategic point of view the maintenance of the shipbuilding industry, at least in cadre, was thought to be as important as the maintenance of operational shipping.

The grant of operating subsidy required determinations of public interest, competence and responsibility of the applicant, etc., similar to those required for the award of the construction subsidy.[73] The result of these determinations, and of the negotiations with the applicant, was a contract for annual subsidy payments for a period not longer than twenty years. The estimated amount of the payment was fixed by taking all the items (wages, insurance, etc.) as to which the applicant stood in a disadvantageous cost position vis-a-vis foreign competition; the cost differences were estimated item by item, and the total of these cost differences was the subsidy limit. The actual amount payable was reckoned by a periodic accounting reflecting actu-

70. 46 U.S.C.A. § 1151.

71. 46 U.S.C.A. § 1151(b).

72. 46 U.S.C.A. § 1152(a). In addition to the "differential" subsidy, the Board was also to pay for "national defense features"—those added to the vessel to make it more useful in wartime.

The subsidy applicant did not have to pay cash or arrange private financing for even the entire purchase price set by the Board; he was to pay 25% of the price, with twenty years to pay the balance at 3½% interest on the unpaid balance. 46 U.S.C.A. § 1152(c).

An alternative procedure (46 U.S.C.A. § 1154) permitted the applicant to finance the construction of the vessel himself, with the Board simply joining his contract and making up the difference between his cost and "foreign" cost (plus an adjustment for "national defense features"). In view of the obvious advantage of the favorable government financing terms, it is not surprising to find that this concession to "private enterprise" has not appealed to many applicants.

73. 46 U.S.C.A. § 1171.

al experience with the same items.[74] In exceptional cases, additional subsidies might be paid to equalize those paid by foreign governments.[75]

Operating subsidy arrangements were subject to elaborate "recapture" provisions. If the operator's profits during any ten-year period were greater than 10 percent on "necessarily" invested capital, then the operator had to pay the government one-half of this excess, but only up to the amount of subsidy payments actually received.[76] "Reserve funds" were required to be set up for this purpose, and elaborate accounting provisions were set forth in the statute for administration of these.[77]

The actual working out of the 1936 Act's subsidy program was more restricted, as to the number of subsidy beneficiaries, than might have been inferred from the general language of the statutory plan as so far described. Instead of determining the "essentiality" of each proposed route *ad hoc,* the Maritime Commission conducted a study of the foreign commerce of the United States, and set out a pattern of "essential routes." These were over thirty in number; they link the Atlantic and Pacific ports of this country, respectively, with the important trade areas of Europe, Asia, Africa and South America.[78] The following are typical:

No. 9: North Atlantic ports (Baltimore to Boston range) to Atlantic French ports and the Vigo to Bilbao range in Spain.

No. 26A: Pacific Coast ports to United Kingdom.

No. 31: Gulf of Mexico ports to West Coast of South America.

The routes designated differed among themselves with respect to the sort of service considered essential, on that route, for American trade. Thus, one route might require mainly passenger service, while freight movement might be the prime consideration on some other route. (Because of the dominance of air travel, the passenger component is now pretty well moribund).

74. 46 U.S.C.A. § 1173. The actual calculations required are staggering in number and difficulty. See Maritime Subsidy Policy, (a Report prepared by the Office of the Under Secretary of Commerce for Transportation and the Maritime Administration, 1954) pp. 96–98.

75. See *supra* note 67.

76. 46 U.S.C.A. § 1176. It is to be observed that only *half* the excess profit can be recaptured; thus, an operator who averaged 25% profit could keep not only the first 10%, but ½ of the remainder, or 7½%, making a total of 17½%. Also, the 10%, allowed before recapture of a moiety begins, is a ten-year average; an operator who in five lean years made only 6% clear could make 14% in the next five years without incurring any repayment liability. These provisions seem not ungenerous. But see Analysis of Construction and Operating Subsidies, *supra* note 65, at 30, for statistics indicating that, during the period 1943–1945, the profits of subsidized lines were well below the 10% figure, and note that the 1970 Act (*infra* § 11–8) has abolished the "recapture" provisions.

77. 46 U.S.C.A. § 1177.

78. A description of these, with accompanying map, is found in McDowell & Gibbs, Ocean Transportation 83–91 (1954).

The restrictive characteristic of the administration of the program is seen principally in the fact that, for each route, (with the exception of later addition to subsidized operators in the Pacific trade), one and only one American line was chosen as recipient of subsidy benefits.[79] Some companies were subsidized for operation on more than one route. Not all "essential" routes were actually subsidized. The consequence was that scarcely more than a dozen companies became the beneficiaries of operating subsidies. The concept was one of selection of a "chosen instrument" in each essential trade. This development doubtless could have been foreseen, since it would seem to be self-defeating, in general, for the government to subsidize American operators to compete against one another. Nevertheless, grave doubts about the subsidy program as a whole were bound to arise as long as (for example) non-subsidized American companies could operate, apparently profitably, in the same trades as the "Twelve Apostles" (as the dozen lines to whom subsidies were at one time limited were called).[79a]

## Problems After World War II

§ **11–7.** The operating-differential subsidies were discontinued during World War II but were resumed in 1947.[80] The construction-subsidy program ran into a number of snags in the years following and could not be said to function at anything even approaching efficiency.[81] As to ordinary cargo vessels, those constructed and operated by the government during the war, and sold to private operators, so saturated the demand that little new construction (except that directly undertaken by the Maritime Administration) went forward.[82] An even more difficult situation arose with regard to the subsidization of passenger ship construction. The experience of the war seemed to indicate that one of the prime needs of the country in any future conflict would be for ships easily convertible to troop transports; at the same time, United States flag passenger tonnage was seriously depleted by wartime losses. Accordingly, the Maritime Commission (later the Maritime Board) entered into subsidy contracts for the

79. The Act itself stated a restrictive policy with respect to "double tracking." 46 U.S.C.A. § 1175(c). Administration followed this lead. "The government is in fact a partner in such operations and strongly inclined therefore to guard its interests by restricting the number of subsidized lines in any service . . ." Recommendations of the Dept. of Commerce and the Maritime Administration [on the So-called Long-Range Shipping Bill], Senate Committee on Interstate and Foreign Commerce, 82d Cong., 1st Sess. (1951), p. 1.

79a. Some previously subsidized lines are now relinquishing this status; see Maritime Administration, Annual Report 7 (1971).

80. Maritime Subsidy Policy, *supra* note 74, at 95.

81. "At present, not a single ship is being constructed under the subsidy provisions of the 1936 Act." Maritime Subsidy Policy, *supra* note 74, at 88.

82. See *supra* at note 59; *infra* at notes 100–101, 103–105.

construction of a number of "super-liners," with "national defense" features facilitating conversion to the transport of troops.[83]

Several of these ships were taken over by the government during the Korean war, but three (the United States, the Constitution, and the Independence), were transferred to private owners. Out of the subsidy transactions underlying the building of these ships came numerous problems. Foremost was the difficulty of determining the foreign cost of building similar vessels. Where a subsidy was to be over 33⅓%, as it was in all three cases mentioned, the 1936 Act required "convincing" evidence of foreign construction costs.[84] Clearly this meant evidence of a fairly high degree of concreteness and solidity. Yet, since the earliest days of operation under the Act, the Maritime Administration and its predecessor agency had emphasized the enormous difficulty of assembling even moderately reliable data on foreign ship cost.[85] In the first place, foreign shipyards are not eager to furnish the necessary data; a confidential character surrounds their transactions with their own customers. Secondly, the selection of a "representative" country for reference is difficult, and in the end quite largely arbitrary. Thirdly, even within any given country costs will vary widely. Finally, the fluctuating and uncertain nature of foreign exchange—with, often, both an "official" and a more realistic rate—makes conversion of foreign cost into dollar cost a matter of subtlety and even indeterminacy.

Operational subsidy experience under the Act was also exceedingly complex.[96]

### The Merchant Marine Act of 1970

**§ 11–8.** Perhaps partly as a result of problems such as those described in the preceding section, the United States merchant fleet was widely thought to be in a deplorable condition in the late 1960's.[98] (The reader attentive so far will be aware that this deplorability is chronic, having lived its century.) It ranked fifth in the world in tonnage, carrying only six percent of United States foreign trade. In 1970, the United States flag fleet mustered just under a thousand ships, only some two-thirds of which were in foreign trade. About three-fourths of American vessels were twenty years old or older;

83. See McDowell & Gibbs, *op. cit. supra* note 78, at 261–264, for a consecutive account of the transactions mentioned here. See also Statement of Ralph E. Casey, Assoc. Gen. Counsel, Gen. Accounting Office, before House Merchant Marine and Fisheries Committee, Apr. 1, 1953, reported in 1953 A.M.C. 1685; Statement of Chairman Gatov of the Federal Maritime Board, before the same Committee, reported 1953 A.M.C. 1992.

84. 46 U.S.C.A. § 1152(b).

85. U.S. Maritime Commission, *op. cit. supra* note 2, at 70–72; Maritime Subsidy Policy, *supra* note 74, at 88–89.

96. On this aspect, see Whitehurst, The Merchant Marine Act of 1936: An Operational Subsidy in Retrospect, 8 Journ. of Law and Econ. 223 (1965).

98. For the facts on the American shipping industry discussed in this section, see Senate Committee of Commerce, 91st Cong., 2d Sess., Report No. 91–1080, to accompany H.R. 15424, to amend the Merchant Marine Act, 1936.

many were ready to be scrapped. It was estimated that, given the current low rate of ship construction, the foreign trade fleet would be reduced to less than 300 ships by 1974. The majority of these, moreover, had not benefited from recent technological improvements in speed and carrying capacity. The shipping industry did not seem able to reverse this trend without further governmental action, plagued as it was by all its chronic troubles—high building and operating costs, production delays, and labor disputes.

While the American shipping industry has been declining, the worldwide industry has been expanding. The tonnage of cargo carried by sea has doubled since 1950, and is expected to double again before 2000. Though such a long-range projection is obviously fallible, it is clear enough that, whatever may be the case as to passenger traffic, surface cargo carriage continues to thrive in the face of air competition. More than three-fourths of the freighters operating under foreign flags were less than twenty years old in 1970, and more than two-thirds of the dry bulk carriers with foreign registry were less than ten years old.[99]

The Merchant Marine Act of 1970 [100] was passed for the stated purpose of revitalizing our Merchant Marine. In form, it consists in a series of amendments to the 1936 Act. The desire for new legislation was based in part on much the same statement of policy as was contained in the opening section of the 1936 Act, as quoted in § 11–5, *supra*.

A 1970 Senate Report offers elaboration on the policy behind the 1970 Act.[101] The legislation is said to provide an imperatively needed emergency sealift capacity. It is argued, moreover, that growth of the merchant marine would permit the United States to exert more influence on world freight rates, particularly since strong American flag representation in various shipping conferences would strengthen our influence in conference ratemaking. The new program, it is contended, should also contribute to the U. S. balance of payments position by direct contributions through earnings of exchange from foreign nationals and by lessening the outflow of dollars that would take place if shipping services were purchased from foreign flag companies. Finally, it is thought that unemployment should decrease as a result of new job opportunities both in shipyards and on ships. These are, it will easily be noted, pretty much the same arguments as those always made for subsidy; one must begin to wonder about them as one program after another proves disappointing.

Significant changes were made by the 1970 legislation, aimed at remedying felt shortcomings of the 1936 Act. The new Act calls for a subsidy level for construction of thirty ships a year for a ten-year

99. *Id.* at 13.

100. 84 Stat. 1018 (1970). See Bowman, The Merchant Marine Act of 1970, 2 Journal of Maritime Law and Commerce 715 (1971).

101. Senate Committee of Commerce Report, *supra* n. 98, at 21.

period,[101a] although the percentage of costs that are subsidized is to be gradually decreased. The 1970 legislation states that the maximum permissible construction subsidy would be 55% until July 1, 1970, and then be reduced to 50%. Provisions are also included for gradual reduction of the subsidy in years to come.[101b] Construction differential subsidies may be paid directly to shipbuilders.[101c]

Both construction and operational subsidies will be available for the first time to bulk carriers—operators of ships designed to carry ore, grain, or oil.[101d] The "fixed route" concept will thus not always be applicable, for bulk carriers do not operate on specific routes, but are commonly tramps (see *supra* § 4–2); it is now our policy, therefore, to subsidize tramps.[101e] (It remains to be seen how far this policy will be implemented; tramp shipping does not pack much political punch, but shipyards constructing vessels designed for bulk cargoes may.)

Because of the increased level of anticipated ship construction, the ceiling on federally insured mortgages was increased from one to three billion dollars. Further, the elaborate "recapture" provisions of the 1936 Act were eliminated, so that subsidized lines no longer have to pay back to the government a portion of their profits.[101f] The Maritime Administration was made an integral part of the Department of Commerce, instead of remaining an independent executive agency.[101g] The President appoints, with the advice and consent of the Senate, an Assistant Secretary of Commerce for Maritime Affairs.

A number of other changes were made, including more specific provisions for fixing construction and operational subsidies.[101h] Recomputations of equivalent foreign ship-construction cost are to be made yearly, if significant changes in the market have occurred. The new Act requires that an explanation of the estimated foreign cost determination be made public.

Changes were made in operational subsidies. The 1936 Act provided that these "shall not exceed the excess of" parity with foreign operating costs.[101i] To lessen uncertainty as to amount, the new legislation provides that the subsidy "shall equal" the difference between certain American and foreign operating costs.[101j] Changes of a tech-

**101a.** 46 U.S.C.A. § 1119, as amended.

**101b.** 46 U.S.C.A. § 1152, as amended.

**101c.** 46 U.S.C.A. § 1151(c).

**101d.** *Id.* See *supra*, Chapter IV, § 4–2.

**101e.** Actually, this has been the *de jure* policy since 1952, so far as construction subsidies went; 66 Stat. 760.

**101f.** 46 U.S.C.A. § 1271, as amended. Pub.L. 91–469 (1970) struck out the recapture provisions formerly found in 46 U.S.C.A. § 1155, section 505 of the 1936 Merchant Marine Act.

**101g.** 46 U.S.C.A. § 1111.

**101h.** 46 U.S.C.A., Subchapter 5.

**101i.** 46 U.S.C.A. § 1173, prior to 1970 Amendment.

**101j.** 46 U.S.C.A. § 1173, as amended.

nical nature were made in the approach for determining the subsidizable wage costs of U. S. officers and crews.[101k]

Many important policies of the 1936 Act remained virtually unaltered in the 1970 legislation. For example, materials used in subsidized vessel construction must, if practicable, be manufactured in the United States; the vessel itself must be built in an American shipyard.[101l] At least half of certain government-generated cargoes must be carried in American bottoms.[101m]

The 1970 Act widened tax-deferment privileges for shipowners. Under the 1936 Act, each shipowner in foreign trade who received an operating differential subsidy could establish both a "capital reserve fund" and a "special reserve fund".[101n] The first of these was for the purchase and replacement of vessels and for the payment of shipmortgage indebtedness, while the second was to be applied to maintenance. Although the 1936 Act provided that the earnings deposited in these funds were to be "exempt from all Federal taxes", other sections suggested that these funds were only to be tax-deferred. The issue was settled in 1947, when the subsidized operators entered into closing agreements with the Internal Revenue Service, which treated these funds as tax-deferred.[101o] No tax was to be imposed when money was deposited in the funds, but when assets were withdrawn for ship construction, the depreciation basis of the ships was lessened by the amount that tax-deferred earnings or capital gain were used to finance them. If the amount withdrawn from the fund was not used for ship construction, it was taxed as earned income in the year of withdrawal. The 1970 Merchant Marine Act made these same tax deferment privileges available to all operators in foreign trades. The Senate Committee on Commerce concluded that this section of the bill would "do more than any other provision . . . to build ships in United States shipyards to be operated under the American flag".[101p] A more specific statutory framework for administering the various funds was provided.[101q]

On the whole, the 1970 Act seems to constitute a very good deal for shipping companies. Some of its provisions—*e. g.*, the subsidy of fishing vessels—seem quite indefensible; most if not all are exceedingly favorable. It is too early to evaluate the Act—and too early, more importantly, to evaluate the probability that new patterns of power, by making long-distance land wars unwinnable, may have affected drastically the indispensable premise of all ship-construction and shipping subsidy legislation—the premise that a national carrying fleet is essential to defense and to national power.[101r]

**101k.** *Id.*

**101*l*.** 46 U.S.C.A. § 1155.

**101m.** 46 U.S.C.A. § 1241.

**101n.** 46 U.S.C.A. § 1177.

**101*o*.** See Senate Commerce Committee Report, *supra* n. 98 at 41.

**101p.** *Id.* at 42–44.

**101q.** 46 U.S.C.A. § 1177, as amended.

**101r.** See Chapter IX, § 9–51(a) for a discussion of the federal guaranty program in ship mortgage financing under Title XI of the Act of 1936 as amended through the Ship Financing Act of 1972.

### Government as Promoter

**§ 11–9.** The promotional activities of the Maritime Administration are not confined to the subsidy program set up under the 1936 and 1970 Acts. Under existing legislation, the Administration itself has authority to contract directly with shipyards for the construction of new vessels.[102]

The Administration also operates a training program, centering in the Merchant Marine Academy at Kings Point, N. Y.[104] A course leading to licensing as merchant marine officers is offered to cadets in this school. There is now provision for aid to states in establishing maritime academies.[105] Various specialist courses are offered to all personnel of the merchant marine.[106]

Beyond these specific responsibilities (and the regulatory activities to be discussed later) the Administration has the general task of keeping abreast of all matters affecting shipping policy.

Other governmental agencies also do valuable work aimed at the promotion of shipping. These activities range from the most literally physical assistance in the operation of ships to various forms of commercial and diplomatic assistance required by the industry. The Coast Guard, in cooperation with other nations, conducts the North Atlantic Ice Patrol, aimed at minimizing the danger to shipping on the great-circle lanes that swing far north.[107] Weather reports are collected and disseminated by the Environmental Sciences Services Administration,[107a] into which the Coast and Geodetic Survey is also covered, in cooperation with the Coast Guard and its ocean stations.[108] The Army Corps of Engineers (with the cooperation of the Coast Guard) oversees the preservation and protection of navigable waters —keeping channels dredged,[109] policing the building of bridges,[110] re-

102. 46 U.S.C.A. § 1192. See note 61, *supra*. For material descriptive of recent activity, see Annual Reports of the Administration.

104. 46 U.S.C.A. § 1126.

105. 46 U.S.C.A. §§ 1381 *et seq.*

106. On all these matters, up-to-date information is to be found in the Annual Reports of the Administration.

107. A vivid account of this and other functions of the Coast Guard mentioned in the text is found in Armed Forces Talk No. 482 (1955). Current problems are discussed in Proceedings of the Merchant Marine Council, published monthly at Coast Guard Headquarters. On the International Ice Patrol specifically, see the Annual Reports of the Department of Transportation.

107a. Comprising the former Weather Bureau; see Reorg. Plan No. 2 of 1965, 30 F.R. 8819, 79 Stat. 1318.

108. 14 U.S.C.A. §§ 90, 147. In a single year the "ocean stations"—vessels on extended patrol in selected areas far out to sea—transmitted over 70,000 weather reports, besides their search and rescue work, air navigation assistance, and other duties. 1953 Report of the Secretary of the Treasury 154. See also U. S. Coast Guard, Weathermen of the Sea (1950). In 1967, the four ocean stations spent 75,370 hours on patrol, providing meteorological data. 1967 Annual Report of the Department of Transportation.

109. 33 U.S.C.A. §§ 541, 603a.

110. 33 U.S.C.A. Chapter 11.

moving obstructions.[111] The successor agency to the Coast and Geodetic Survey [111a] furnishes charts indispensable to navigation.[112] The Coast Guard, again, conducts oceanographic studies of value to shipping,[113] maintains lighthouses, lightships, buoys and other aids to navigation in our waters,[114] and conducts operations of search and rescue.[115]

Besides these directly physical aids, the agencies of government assist our shipping in various intangible ways. A considerable volume of diplomatic activity, conducted by the State Department, has the promotion of shipping as its goal; conventions on important legal and technical matters have been negotiated in this way.[116] A form of diplomatic activity perhaps more important from the nationalist point of view is the constant effort made by the State Department, in cooperation with the Maritime Administration, to deal diplomatically with discriminations against U. S. shipping imposed by foreign governments.[117] Consular services of various sorts are also furnished to our vessels abroad.[118]

Governmental agencies also service shipping by furnishing information of commercial value. The Bureau of the Census reports on shipping statistics.[119] The Bureau of Foreign Commerce collects and distributes information on foreign trade and shipping.[120] The Depart-

111. 33 U.S.C.A. § 414; 14 U.S.C.A. § 86.

111a. See *supra,* n. 107a.

112. 33 U.S.C.A. §§ 883a–883e.

113. 14 U.S.C.A. § 2, as amended by Public Law 87–396 (1961).

114. 14 U.S.C.A. § 81. The Supreme Court has held that the government is suable under the Federal Tort Claims Act for negligent operation of a lighthouse. Indian Towing Co. v. United States, 350 U.S. 61, 76 S.Ct. 122, 1956 A.M.C. 27 (1955). See also Afran Transport Co. v. United States, 309 F.Supp. 650, 1969 A.M.C. 1897 (S.D.N.Y.1969), affirmed 435 F.2d 213, 1971 A.M.C. 335 (2d Cir. 1970) holding that, once the Coast Guard established a buoy, it must use due care to keep the buoy in good condition.

115. 14 U.S.C.A. § 88. Lower court cases seem to establish that, while this section creates no obligation (privately enforceable) to undertake rescue, rescue once undertaken must be well conducted, or government liability results. In re American Oil Co., 417 F.2d 164, 1969 A.M.C. 1761 (5th Cir. 1969), certiorari denied 397 U.S. 1036, 90 S.Ct. 1353 (1970); Frank v. United States, 250 F.2d 178, 1958 A.M.C. 796 (3rd Cir. 1957), certiorari denied 356 U.S. 962, 78 S.Ct. 1000 (1958); United States v. Devane, 306 F.2d 182, 1963 A.M.C. 1400 (5th Cir. 1962).

116. Such as the Conventions on: Safety of Life at Sea—T.S. 910 (1929) 50 Stat. 1121 (1937), amended T.S. 921 (1930), 51 Stat. 13 (1937); Assistance and Salvage at Sea, T.S. 576 (1910), 37 Stat. 242 (1912).

117. For material on the "discrimination" problem, see Discriminatory Acts of Foreign Governments Affecting Our Merchant Marine, Hearings Before the Subcommittee On Merchant Marine and Maritime Matters of the Senate Committee On Interstate and Foreign Commerce, 82d Cong., 2d Sess. (1952). The Maritime Board is directed by statute to investigate complaints of discrimination against American shipping, and to report its findings to the President for diplomatic action. 46 U.S.C.A. § 825.

118. 22 U.S.C.A. § 1173.

119. U. S. Govt. Organization Manual 261 (1954–55).

120. *Id.* at 266–7.

ment of Labor conducts studies on the all-pervasive problems of labor relations in this as in other fields.[121] And of course the Maritime Administration, in the discharge of its general function, constantly collects and disseminates shipping information of all sorts.[122]

The Maritime Administration has addressed itself of late to the problems of intermodal transportation, seeking new methods of facilitation, and consulting with other agencies on port development.[122a]

The maritime states of the Union have from earliest times concerned themselves with the promotion of shipping. Perhaps the most striking present-day example is the Port of New York Authority, created by interstate compact between New York and New Jersey, in 1921.[123] As a joint instrument of the public policy of the two constituent states, this body concerns itself with the development and promotion of the port, which comprises the waterfronts of Greater New York and the New Jersey communities opposite. It owns and operates, either directly or through lease or other arrangement, a number of terminal and transportation facilities. It represents the interests of the port of New York in legislative and administrative proceedings, and conducts promotional activity in the United States and abroad.[124]

### Government as Participant

**§ 11–10.** Closely connected with the promotional activities described, but formally distinguishable, is the entrance of government into the picture as an actual participant in the shipping industry.[125] Generally speaking, when some essential shipping activity cannot be performed by "private" enterprise (even when subsidized and otherwise favored), the government is likely to be found on the scene in an active capacity. So strong is the pressure against this sort of activity, however, that military necessity is usually the only reason good enough to overcome it. And the entrances of government are always partial and to some extent peripheral; the private operators are invariably present in some relation to the transaction.

Illustrative of all these points is the activity of the government, in both World Wars, as owner of merchant ships. The bulk of the hastily constructed merchant fleet of World War II was built for the United States, and the government retained title and the control that went with it, operating these vessels, and others acquired by purchase or demise charter, for its own account, through the War Shipping Administration.[126] Formally, the officers and crews were employees of

121. *Id.* at 293 *et seq.*

122. See current Annual Reports of the Federal Maritime Commission and Maritime Administration.

122a. Annual Report of the Maritime Administration 17–19 (1971).

123. Authorized by c. 154, Laws of N. Y. (1921) and c. 151, Laws of N. J. (1921); approved by Public Resolution No. 17, 67th Cong., 1st Sess., 42 Stat. 174 (1921).

124. Port of New York Authority 1970 Annual Report, *passim*, esp. 21 *et seq.*

125. *Cf. supra* at note 30.

126. See *supra* note 58.

the United States, and of course the vessels were under the control of the War Shipping Administration as to voyages, cargoes taken, charters fixed, and so on. Actually, the details of operation were taken care of by private companies, related to the government by so-called "general agency agreements," and compensated in accordance with the terms of these contracts.[127] To the lawyer, the main interest of this arrangement lies in its putting the United States in the owner's position, for purposes of all the maritime rights and liabilities connected with ownership. This arrangement, more than anything else, explains the large number of ordinary maritime cases, involving collision, cargo damage, general average, etc., in which the United States figures as a party.

At various times, the United States has appeared in each of the capacities possible under charter parties. During World War II, ships were frequently requisitioned by the government on demise charter, rather than by taking title to the vessel. The government has time-chartered vessels, too, leaving the owner in control of navigation and management.[128] On the other hand, the government, when it has had on its hands a surplus of vessels and when sale of these has proved impossible (as to some extent after World War II) has demise-chartered them to private operators.[129]

On the other side of the picture, the government is a large shipper of cargo, and may therefore often be encountered in litigation on the cargo-interest side of the fence.

During World War II, private underwriters proved unwilling to write war risk insurance [129a]; in consequence, it became necessary for the government, through the instrumentality of the War Shipping Administration, to enter directly into the marine insurance business.[130]

127. The present National Shipping Authority (see *supra* note 58) has made extensive use of the General Agency Agreement. See 1951 Annual Report of Federal Maritime Board and Maritime Administration 15–16. For the current form of the Agreement, see 32A C.F.R. p. 259 (1953). See also Hust v. Moore-McCormack Lines, 328 U.S. 707, 66 S.Ct. 1218, 1946 A.M.C. 727 (1946), esp. Mr. Justice Douglas's concurring opinion, 328 U.S. at 734 *et seq.*, 66 S.Ct. at 1231 *et seq.*

128. For a case illustrating both these practices, with references to forms, see Sinclair Refining Co. v. United States, 124 F.Supp. 628, 1954 A.M.C. 2201 (Ct.Cl.1954).

129. The Ship Sales Act of 1946, 60 Stat. 41–50, 50 U.S.C.A. §§ 1735–1746, authorized this procedure. For the charter form used, see 46 C.F.R. § 299.82 (1954). See Schnell v. U. S., 166 F.2d 479 (2d Cir. 1948), certiorari denied 334 U.S. 833, 68 S.Ct. 1346 (1948).

129a. See *supra* Chapter II.

130. Under the War Risk Insurance Act of June 29, 1940, 54 Stat. 689. (*Cf.* War Risk Insurance Act 1914, 38 Stat. 711). The 1940 Act, despite its title, authorized both war and marine risk insurance. (See *supra*, Chapter II, at note 80.) This statute was repealed in 1947, 61 Stat. 449, but at present (until Sept. 7, 1960) the Administration is authorized to insure war and marine risks (Act of Sept. 7, 1950, 64 Stat. 773, 46 U.S.C.A. § 1294, as amended 69 Stat. 440 (1955)). The main activity currently seems to consist in the writing of "interim war risk" insurance, which is to come into effect only if and when commercially underwritten war risk insurance terminates, in accordance with a now standard policy clause, 48 hours after outbreak of hostilities. See Winter, Marine Insurance 344 (1952).

During this period, the government handled the bulk of war risk insurance.[131]

The pattern of all these governmental interventions into the shipping world and its commercial ambient is a simple one: the United States merely assumes one of the roles or capacities already familiar—owner, demise charterer, shipper, underwriter, employer, etc., etc. The underlying pattern of maritime law and industrial practice is little changed; the government just takes a place within that pattern.

### Government as Litigant

**§ 11–11.** In litigation, where the United States is plaintiff, no special problem is created; but where liability is claimed against the government the sovereign immunity problem arises. There has been a comprehensive waiver by the United States, in the Suits in Admiralty Act of 1920.[132] The Act first provides that no vessel or cargo owned or possessed by or operated by or for the United States as a government corporation shall be subject to *in rem* process.[133] It then goes on to provide that in cases where, if such vessel or cargo were privately owned or possessed, a proceeding in admiralty could be maintained, and where the vessel is a merchant vessel (or a tugboat operated by a government corporation) then a libel *in personam* may be brought against the United States in admiralty.[134] Recovery *in personam* may be had against the United States where either an *in rem* or an *in personam* liability would have arisen on the same facts as against a private owner.[135] Obviously, the pattern of this statute supports the statement made in the last paragraph, to the effect that the government, in entering the shipping world as a participant, simply assumes a normal role in the antecedent pattern.

The statute does result in two peculiarities as to the enforcement of liabilities against the government. First, no *in rem* process is available; this is, of course, of complete unimportance, since the maritime lien is a security device, and the government's credit is good. Secondly, since this statute constitutes the only waiver the government has made as to cases coming within its terms, the remedy in admiralty is exclusive, and therefore a jury cannot be had, either under the "saving clause" or under the special Jones Act jurisdictional pattern. This fact is of great importance in seaman's injury cases; where the government is the "employer," the injured seaman must accept the findings of fact and the estimate of damages made by a federal judge rather than by a jury.

Employment "as a merchant vessel" is one of the concepts limiting the operation of this Act; naval ships and other vessels carrying

131. Winter, *op. cit. supra* note 130, at 345–6.

132. 41 Stat. 525–528, 46 U.S.C.A. §§ 741–752.

133. 46 U.S.C.A. § 741.

134. 46 U.S.C.A. § 742.

135. Eastern Transp. Co. v. U. S., 272 U.S. 675, 47 S.Ct. 289, 1927 A.M.C. 124 (1927).

on "public" functions are not within its scope. But in 1925 Congress enacted a waiver statute [136] providing that the United States was to be suable in admiralty "for damages caused by a public vessel of the United States, and for compensation for towage and salvage services, including contract salvage, rendered to a public vessel of the United States . . ." [137] Thus, the would-be libellant under the 1920 Act, even if the vessel involved was not employed in merchant service, may still sue the government in admiralty, if his claim is one within the categories listed in the 1925 Act.

The Supreme Court seemed to indicate its intention of so construing these statutes, where possible, as to make them meet, so that no suits which might otherwise be brought against the United States in admiralty will fall outside the coverage of both of them.[138] One of the problems encountered was the fact that, unless the concept of "employment as a merchant vessel" is given quite a liberal interpretation, it might well happen that a ship, though not susceptible of being treated as a "public" vessel, would not pass the test of employment as a "merchant" vessel, and so would fall between the Acts. In the very case which announced the principle of construction just mentioned, the vessel involved was voyage-chartered by the United States. Clearly, it was "operated for the United States"; equally clearly, it would seem, it was not a public vessel. But the cargo consisted entirely of war material, being carried to an active theatre. The pivotal question then became whether a ship so laden and thither bound could be said to be operating as a "merchant" vessel. The Court decisively rejected a test based on the nature of the cargo, and took the fact that the vessel was operated for hire for the United States as sufficient to establish her "merchant" character.[139]

The Court, realistically, took into consideration the fact that even a dismissal on the ground of non-coverage by the Suits in Admiralty (or for that matter the Public Vessels) Act would not be tantamount to a holding that the government was unsuable on the facts.[140] The more general immunity-waiver statutes would in most cases still permit suit somewhere—in the Court of Claims or on the civil side of the District Court.[141] Thus a narrow technical construc-

136. The so-called "Public Vessels Act," 43 Stat. 1112–1113 (1925), 46 U.S.C.A. §§ 781–790.

137. 46 U.S.C.A. § 781.

138. Calmar S. S. Corp. v. United States, 345 U.S. 446, 73 S.Ct. 733, 1953 A.M.C. 943 (1953); see Aliotti v. United States, 221 F.2d 598, 1955 A.M.C. 1048 (9th Cir. 1955). But see *infra*, at note 148.

139. 345 U.S. at 456, 73 S.Ct. at 738.

140. 345 U.S. at 455, 73 S.Ct. at 737.

141. See Moran v. United States, 102 F.Supp. 275 (D.Conn.1951) (discussing the meeting-point of the admiralty waiver statutes and the Federal Torts Claims Act, 28 U.S.C.A. §§ 2671–2680); Prudential S. S. Corp. v. United States, 220 F.2d 655, 1955 A.M.C. 990 (2d Cir. 1955) on relations between the Tucker Act and the admiralty statutes. With the latter case *compare* Lykes Bros. S. S. Co. v. United States, 124 F.Supp. 622, 1954 A.M.C. 2192 (Ct.Cl.1954), certiorari denied 348 U.S. 971, 75 S.Ct. 530 (1955). See also Matson Navigation Co. v. United States, 284 U.S. 352, 52 S.Ct. 162, 1932

tion of the two admiralty Acts would merely have the effect of sending many claims having a maritime flavor to a forum less apt for dealing with them.

Undoubtedly, another problem that has to be dealt with, in the attempt to make these Acts meet and jointly cover all maritime claims arising out of government shipping activity, is encountered when it is noted that the Public Vessels Act of 1925 does not purport to cover *all* such liabilities incurred by public vessels, but only those damages "caused by" such vessels, and towage and salvage services. Towage and salvage are relatively inelastic concepts. "Cause" is an utterly Protean word. Perhaps the most natural usage would take "damages caused by a public vessel" to mean physical damages arising out of her operation. But there is nothing compulsive about such an understanding, and in Thomason v. United States [142] the Ninth Circuit Court of Appeals held that wage claims of seamen employed aboard tugboats operated by the United States in the European Theatre of Operations—clearly public vessels—were within the Public Vessels Act, and hence suable only in Admiralty. "The phrase," said the court, "includes damages arising from those acts for which a private ship is held legally responsible as a juristic person under the customary legal terminology of the admiralty law." [143]

In reaching this conclusion, the court relied heavily on Canadian Aviator, Ltd. v. United States.[144] In that case, the Supreme Court held that, where a public vessel [145] ordered a steamship to follow it into port, and then so negligently led the way that the following vessel struck a wreck, the damage might be said to be "caused by" the public vessel. It is easy to see that this holding, while it expands the "causation" concept beyond the narrowest possible meaning—physical impact—nevertheless is a long way short of standing foursquare for the proposition that the Public Vessels Act authorizes suits on maritime claims in general, including those sounding in contract. In Canadian Aviator there was at least a physical connection of the ship with the ensuing occurrence. In American Stevedores v. Porello,[146]

A.M.C. 202 (1932); Andrews & Co. v. United States, 124 F.Supp. 362, 1954 A.M.C. 2221 (Ct.Cl.1954).

142. 184 F.2d 105, 1950 A.M.C. 1649 (9th Cir. 1950).

143. 184 F.2d at 107–8. Eastern S. S. Lines v. United States, 187 F.2d 956, 1951 A.M.C. 1844 (1st Cir. 1951) seems to have held (187 F.2d at 959) that a contract claim arising under a bareboat charter was not within the Public Vessels Act, but the point was not discussed, and was apparently conceded by counsel. The case antedates Calmar. In Sinclair Refining Co. v. United States, 124 F.Supp. 628, 1954 A.M.C. 2201 (Ct.Cl.1954) the court takes Calmar as clearly intimating that the Public Vessels Act covers contract claims under charters. See also Waterman S. S. Corp. v. United States, 124 F.Supp. 634, 1954 A.M.C. 2196 (Ct.Cl.1954), certiorari denied 348 U.S. 971, 75 S.Ct. 530 (1955).

144. 324 U.S. 215, 65 S.Ct. 639, 1945 A. M.C. 265 (1945).

The United States has even been held liable for damage resulting from inaccuracy of Coast and Geodetic Survey charts. De Bardeleben Marine Corp. v. United States, 451 F.2d 140, 1971 A.M.C. 2131 (5th Cir. 1971).

145. A navy patrol boat.

146. 330 U.S. 446, 67 S.Ct. 847, 1947 A. M.C. 349 (1947).

it is true, the Court held that personal injuries as well as property damage were within the Act, but this again is rather a declining to limit the meaning of the crucial phrase in an unnatural manner than a decision to expand it as far as it will stretch. In a final footnote to Calmar,[147] the Court says:

> It is not to be assumed that all claims sounding in contract can form the basis of a suit under the Public Vessels Act. The Act expressly authorizes towage and salvage claims. We intimate no opinion as to other claims, and do not suggest that all or any of the causes of action in this very suit would or would not qualify under the Public Vessels Act. There are cases in which jurisdiction over contract claims other than towage or salvage has been assumed. Thomason v. United States, 9 Cir., 184 F.2d 105; United States v. Loyola, 9 Cir., 161 F.2d 126. But cf. Eastern S. S. Lines v. United States, 1 Cir., 187 F.2d 956. All that matters for our purpose is that there is a class of cases, no matter how narrow, which, if the cargo test of jurisdiction is applied, will be heard by the District Courts in admiralty when a vessel owned by the United States is involved, and in the Court of Claims when the vessel was chartered as was the Portmar. It is not our task, of course, to torture the Suits in Admiralty and Public Vessels Acts into an all-inclusive grant of jurisdiction to the District Courts. But equivocal language should be construed so as to secure the most harmonious results.[148]

The trend, then, was to read these two Acts together as part of a grand scheme of waiver of immunity and channeling of maritime claims against the government to the admiralty side of the District Courts.

It has already been pointed out that, where neither of the admiralty immunity waiver Acts applies, the government can usually be sued under one of the other waiver statutes, in the Court of Claims or elsewhere. Disputes about subsidy payments, e. g., are clearly not within the admiralty jurisdiction, but may form the subject matter of suits in the Court of Claims.[149]

**147.** *Supra* note 138.

**148.** 345 U.S. at 456, 73 S.Ct. at 738.

**149.** This section has not discussed the problem of the foreign vessel sought to be attached or otherwise subjected to liability in our courts. Of course, foreign public vessels are exempt from *in rem* process. A vessel possessed by a foreign government, though employed by it as a merchant ship, is also exempt. Berizzi Bros. v. S. S. Pesaro, 271 U.S. 562, 1926 A.M.C. 958 (1926). On the other hand, a vessel certified by our State Department to be the property of a foreign government, but which was not in the possession of that government, has been held not immune. Republic of Mexico v. Hoffman, 324 U.S. 30 (1945). The subject is exhaustively discussed in Shephard, Sovereignty and State-Owned Commercial Entities (1951), esp. pp. 100 *et seq.* See also Riesenfeld, Sovereign Immunity of Foreign Vessels in Anglo-American Law, 25 Minn.L.Rev. 1 (1940); Raymond, Sovereign Immunity in Modern Admiralty Law, 9 Texas L.Rev. 519 (1931).

Until 1960, there remained certain very practical difficulties about this whole scheme of immunity. Counsel could not always be sure which was the correct court to sue in, and risked dismissal (after, it might be, the Statute of Limitations had run) if he chose wrong.[149a] In 1960, Congress enacted amendments providing free transfer between the Court of Claims and the District Courts.[149b]

### Regulatory Activity

**§ 11–12.** It will be noted that so far this chapter has not touched on any activities which, within our orthodox assumptions, could be considered "normal" for government. We have had to do with activity of an intensively promotional character, directed not toward enforcing the "rules of the game" but toward attempting to insure, by whatever means are available, the prosperity or at least the survival of the shipping industry. But in a field so deeply affected with a public interest, touching the national life at so many vital spots, there must be a very great deal of governmental activity which might be classed as regulatory rather than promotional—as aimed at protecting or furthering the public safety, health or welfare in ways and with emphases comparable to those found in respect to industries not enjoying the favored position of shipping.

It is not feasible to effect a clearcut separation of "regulatory" from "promotional" activity. A mere formal criterion will not do, for a provision in form regulatory (such as that reserving the coastal trade to domestic vessels) may have a purely or predominantly promotional purpose; on the other hand, a good deal of regulatory effect can be found in the device of making benefits (*e. g.*, subsidies) available only on condition that certain modes of business conduct be adhered to. But there is a huge body of law—statutory and administrative—which rather clearly has as its main purpose some objective classifiable under the police power rather than one purely or mainly promotional.

Shipping activity, in fact, picks its way through such a network of regulation that it is difficult to impart any clarity of shape to the totality. Several devices might be used to give some order to the picture, but let's choose the one of following a ship through its life-phases.

From the moment when a new vessel becomes so much as a thoughtful expression on the face of someone with the power to set things rolling toward her construction, governmental regulatory activity comes into the calculations. The plans of passenger vessels must be approved by the Commandant of the Coast Guard; [150] builders of cargo vessels proceed with innumerable regulations in mind, and in the knowledge that inspection is in the offing. If a vessel is

**149a.** There is an excellent brief sketch on this in Healy and Currie, Cases and Materials on Admiralty, 863–864 (1965).

**149b.** 28 U.S.C.A. §§ 1406, 1506.

**150.** 46 U.S.C.A. § 369.

being built under subsidy, the plans as a whole must be approved as well by the Secretary of Commerce and by the Navy.[151] During and immediately after construction, inspections will be conducted to ascertain actual conformity to plans and regulations,[152] and throughout the life of the vessel periodic and unscheduled inspections (especially by the Coast Guard) will keep her up to the mark.[153]

The financing of construction will very likely involve the use of the "preferred ship mortgage"—already discussed in another chapter.[154] The United States Customs Bureau takes care of the registry (or, for the coasting trade, of enrollment and license) which is the basic document attesting the vessel's identity and nationality.[155] At this stage, too, the vessel is assigned an "admeasurement" or tonnage, based on complicated (and, on the international scene, somewhat controversial) formulae relating to allowances for crew space, ballast, engines, and so on.[156]

Any new vessel must be measured and marked for purposes of compliance with the Loadline Statute.[157] This requires some explanation. The interest of shipowners led them, in early times, to load vessels to a point beyond safety; the greater the weight of the vessel's load, of course, the lower she rides in the water, and the more vulnerable she is to heavy seas. Many seamen consequently lost their lives. Britain led the way in establishing standards of depth in the water believed to be safe; Samuel Plimsoll, M.P., was the moving spirit, and gave his name to the Plimsoll mark, now seen on the side of all large vessels, which marks the limits of safety for different seas and seasons.[158] Since 1929, the United States has made mandatory the placing of and compliance with loadline marks,[159] and in 1931 we adhered to the International Load Line Convention of 1930, establishing worldwide standards in this matter.[160] In 1966, a new Convention, somewhat altering prior rules, was entered into.[160a] The Coast Guard polices shipping for compliance.[161]

151. 46 U.S.C.A. § 1151.

152. Documentation is conditioned on the possession of a certificate of inspection. 46 U.S.C.A. § 496.

153. 46 U.S.C.A. § 391. The marine inspection laws have justly been called a "maze of regulation." Kelly v. Washington, 302 U.S. 1, 4, 58 S.Ct. 87, 89, 1937 A.M.C. 1490 (1937). The basic statutes are collected in 46 U.S.C.A. §§ 361–436.

154. *Supra*, Chapter IX.

155. See generally 46 U.S.C.A. § 11 *et seq.*

156. 46 U.S.C.A. §§ 71–83k.

157. 46 U.S.C.A. §§ 85–85g. For coastwise and Great Lakes vessels: 46 U.S.C.A. §§ 88–88i.

158. Fayle, *op. cit. supra* note 6, at 284–5. Quite early, the Venetians had stringent "load-line" statutes; *id.*, at 77. By the shipping interests of his day, Plimsoll was considered a most unconstructive man; his statue now overlooks the Thames.

159. *Supra* note 157.

160. 47 Stat. 2228.

160a. International Convention on Load Lines, (1966), 18 U.S.T. 1857. For full discussion, see Kushner, The 1966 Load Line Convention: Compatibility of Greater Carrying Capacity with Safety of Life and Property, 3 J. of Maritime Law and Commerce 375 (1972).

161. 46 U.S.C.A. §§ 85–85b. The Commandant of the Coast Guard is autho-

**§ 11–13.** Thus the mere physical preparation of a ship for service is a matter of great complexity, supervised at every turn by governmental agencies and hedged round with statutes and regulations. The same may be said of the procurement of personnel. In the first place, "manning scales" are established and enforced by the Coast Guard, setting out minimum requirements of numbers, for officers' complement and crew.[162] Personnel must be licensed or certified by the Coast Guard;[163] health requirements of various sorts are also in force.[164] The fact that maritime labor is strongly unionized means that contact with the administrative bodies—mainly the National Labor Relations Board—dealing with union matters will be expectable. The "articles" the seamen sign,[165] and the conditions under which they work,[166] are regulated with some particularity, by statutes and Coast Guard regulations. Throughout the life of the vessel, disciplinary problems will be handled in strict accordance with governmental regulations.[167] When a pilot is taken aboard in United States waters, his qualifications, and his duties to the ship, will be regulated in detail by statute and administrative rule.[168]

The entrance of the ship on active operations—the carriage of goods—brings into play a host of additional regulations. The loadline statute, of course, must be complied with.[169] Special regulations govern the loading and carriage of explosives and other dangerous goods.[170] Special goods of various sorts (*e. g.*, cattle) are subject to statutory and regulatory dispensations peculiar to them.[171] The inbound cargo ship will of course have to deal with Customs, and even

rized to appoint "the American Bureau of Shipping [a private organization] or such other American corporation or association for the survey or registry of shipping as may be selected by him" to determine whether the load lines are correctly placed. 46 U.S.C.A. § 85b. Apparently the American Bureau of Shipping was appointed in this capacity.

162. 46 U.S.C.A. §§ 222–223. Failure to comply with these provisions creates a presumption of fault in the event of collision. The New York Marine No. 10, 109 F.2d 564 (2d Cir. 1940); The Denali, 112 F.2d 952, 1940 A.M.C. 877 (9th Cir. 1940), certiorari denied 311 U.S. 687, 61 S.Ct. 65 (1940).

163. 46 U.S.C.A. § 672 (crews); 46 U.S.C.A. § 224 (officers).

164. Under 46 U.S.C.A. § 672(a), the Coast Guard is authorized to prescribe physical standards. For some of the problems that may arise, see 12 Proceedings of the Merchant Marine Council 31 (1955).

165. 46 U.S.C.A. §§ 563–568. A schedule of the required form for the articles is set out in 46 U.S.C.A. § 713. Articles must be signed in the presence of a shipping commissioner.

166. See, *e. g.*, 46 U.S.C.A. § 669. (Every seaman on a voyage longer than 14 days is to have "one suit of woolen clothing", and the use of a "safe and warm room" in cold weather. This is a good example of the particularity of these regulations.)

167. 46 U.S.C.A. §§ 701–707.

168. 46 U.S.C.A. §§ 211–215.

169. See *supra* note 157.

170. 46 U.S.C.A. § 170. The Commandant of the Coast Guard is authorized to promulgate regulations governing dangerous cargo; see 46 C.F.R. 146 (1953).

171. See, *e. g.*, 46 U.S.C.A. §§ 466a–466b.

outbound vessels must clear with that agency and file various documents, such as outgoing manifests.[172]

The movements of the ship will be constantly subject to statute and rule, and to the policing and administrative activities of governmental agencies. The Navigation Rules, which we have taken up in another chapter, are in part enforced by the Coast Guard,[173] as well as by the private liability system we studied there. On the occurrence of a marine casualty in our waters or involving an American vessel, the Coast Guard "immediately" (by which is meant, often, within twenty-four hours) holds a hearing to determine causation and fault.[174] Where the hearing turns up evidence of negligence or incompetence on the part of any one of the officers or crew of either vessel, those responsible may be penalized by suspension or revocation of licence.[175] In cases of a gravity warranting it, the Coast Guard may turn the evidence it collects over to the United States Attorney, for prosecution of the offender.[176]

The keeping of that all-important record of events at sea—the ship's log—is regulated by law.[177]

There is now in effect a comprehensive Water Quality Improvement Act, affecting vessels in many ways, but especially with regard to oil pollution.[178] Immigration regulations govern all persons brought here on any sort of vessel,[179] and the subject of port security (obviously of high importance today) is committed primarily to the Coast Guard.[180]

This section merely mentions a few of the salient federal controls applicable to shipping. Omitted entirely are the innumerable state and local laws, ordinances, rules, etc.[181] (Aside from those obviously aimed principally at shipping, any local enactment may affect ship operation; a good example is the New York City smoke control ordinance.) Yet even this small sample may convey some notion of the complexity of the regulatory machinery governing the industry. We have left entirely out of consideration, and can only mention here, the

172. 19 U.S.C.A. §§ 1431–1467; 46 U.S.C.A. §§ 91, 93–4, 96.

173. Violation of the International Rules is apparently penalized only by the incurring of civil liability; all the Coast Guard can do is to note and report violation. But the Inland, Great Lakes, and Western Rivers Rules are sanctioned with penalties. 33 U.S.C.A. §§ 158–159, 244, 303, 354–355. The Coast Guard is given authority to supplement these Rules by regulations. 33 U.S.C.A. §§ 157, 243.

174. 46 U.S.C.A. § 239.

175. 46 U.S.C.A. § 239(g).

176. 46 U.S.C.A. § 239(h).

177. 46 U.S.C.A. §§ 201–203.

178. 33 U.S.C.A. 1151 *et seq.* See Healy and Paulsen, Marine Oil Pollution and the Water Quality Improvement Act of 1970, 1 Journal of Maritime Law and Commerce 537 (1970). The Act is discussed and its relationship to the Limitation of Liability Act is analyzed in Chapter X, § 10–4(b), text following note 13q.

179. For some of the principal duties of the master of any vessel in this regard, see 8 U.S.C.A. § 1221.

180. 50 U.S.C.A. § 191.

181. *Cf. supra* at notes 123–124; *supra* Chapter I, at note 161.

extremely complex network of private associations which so largely structure and discipline the shipping world; the underwriters' associations, the classification societies, the general average adjusters' associations, the trade organizations of shipowners, the maritime unions, and many other such groups, actually exert a decided structuring function;[182] on occasion, the responsibilities of government have been delegated to them.[183]

Mention should be made, also, of the international organizations devoted to shipping problems. The International Maritime Committee and the International Law Association have contributed to the unification of world maritime law, as have the International Chamber of Commerce and the International Union of Marine Insurance. Cogsa and the York-Antwerp Rules are the result of the labors of organizations such as these, and a respectable number of Conventions and other arrangements dealing with technical matters have come into being as a result of efforts on the international level.[184] The United Nations has brought together a number of specialized international organizations dealing with problems of interest to shipping.[185] There has been established an Intergovernmental Maritime Consultative Organization under the UN.[186]

### Regulation of Rates and Trade Practices—The "Conferences"

**§ 11–14.** We have left to the last, for emphasis, the regulatory machinery applicable to freight rates, "discrimination," and other commercial aspects of cargo carriage. Since 1940, the Interstate Commerce Commission has exercised a general regulatory function, including that of rate approval, over water carriers in domestic commerce.[187] But since our main interest, here as elsewhere throughout the book, is in shipping in foreign trade, we will focus the discussion on the regulatory activities of the Federal Maritime Commission.[187a]

182. *E. g.:* the Committee of American Steamship Lines, the Pacific American Steamship Asso., the American Asso. of Shipowners, the Lake Carriers Asso., American Waterways Operators, the American Tramp Shipowners Asso., the American Merchant Marine Institute. The American Bureau of Shipping is the insurance classification society, and the National Cargo Bureau issues "certificates of proper loading" for insurance purposes. The Asso. of Average Adjusters of the United States, and the Society of Naval Architects, have self-explanatory functions. The Maritime Law Asso. of the United States is composed mainly of lawyers interested in the field. British organizations are listed and discussed in Dover, The Shipping Industry 276 *et seq.* (1952).

183. *E. g.*, the delegation to the American Bureau of Shipping of Coast Guard functions regarding load-lines, *supra* note 161.

184. The more important of these are summarily described in McDowell & Gibbs, *op. cit. supra* note 78, at 434 *et seq.*

185. *Id.* at 440 *et seq.*

186. See: Intergovernmental Maritime Consultative Organization, Basic Documents (1962).

187. 54 Stat. 929–952 (1940), 49 U.S.C.A. §§ 901–923.

187a. On this section generally, see Gordon, Shipping Regulation and the Federal Maritime Commission, 37 U.Chic.L.Rev. 90, 256 (1969–70); also, Comment, Ocean Shipping Conferences and the Federal Maritime Commission, 53 Cornell L.Rev. 1070 (1968);

That body has no authority to fix or control rates; in that sense its regulatory power is short of that usually vested in analogous bodies supervising land transportation. Ocean freight rates are subject to international considerations, and it would be difficult for one country to regulate them. This is not to say, however, that the Board has no concern with rates; the subject must be approached by a brief description of the "conference" system, which was mentioned in Chapter I.

As the pattern of modern shipping took form in the nineteenth century, the British took the lead in organizing, for each trade area (*e. g.*, the North Atlantic) a loose association or "conference" of steamship lines, whose main purpose—not to take too seriously the various euphemisms which have been employed—was to keep freight rates up, in the face of a tendency toward keen competition. Baldly, the "conferences" set up tariff schedules which their members agree to follow.[188] Very often (if not always) the arrangements have gone further than this—into "pooling" of business, for example—but for present purposes we need consider conferences only in their rate-fixing aspect.

It is manifest that such arrangements on their face violate the anti-trust laws. Since, however, the American shipping interests considered it to their advantage to join, and since (as so often) they were able to persuade Congress that their interest and the national interest coincided, Congress, as a part of the Shipping Act of 1916, provided that such arrangements were to be exempt from the anti-trust laws, where not disapproved by the predecessors of the present Maritime Commission.[189] (The latter body has of course inherited this function.) Most large American operators now belong to the Conferences for which they are eligible, though a few have held out and operated in genuine competition.[189a]

Problems of interest center around the question of means permitted to the conferences for insuring that shippers patronize conference lines exclusively; the conference scheme works only imperfectly if shippers feel free to use cheaper transportation when it becomes available, and to use conference vessels only when a better deal

Comment, Regulating Ocean Shipping: Powers and Problems of the Federal Maritime Commission, 51 Calif.L.Rev. 986 (1963); Note, Rate Regulation in Ocean Shipping, 78 Harv.L.Rev. 635 (1965). A valuable discussion of the relation of conferences to containerization (see *supra*, § 1–5) is in Note, Containerization and Intermodal Service in Ocean Shipping, 21 Stanford L. Rev. 1077, at 1078 *et seq.* (1969).

188. McDowell & Gibbs, *op. cit. supra* note 78, at 394–399. Clough & Cole, *op. cit. supra* note 11, at 596–7. See *supra*, Chapter I at note 43, and works there cited.

189. 39 Stat. 733, 46 U.S.C.A. § 814. See Comment, Accommodation of Anti-Trust Law and Ocean Shipping, 4 Tex.Int. Law Forum 393 (1968).

189a. On international problems created by American regulation, see Drechsel, Kelly, and Lamberton, The Shipping Act of 1916 and the Dual Rate Amendment: A Problem of Enforcement, 4 Va.J. of Intl.L. 215 (1964). And see reference in note 1930 *infra*. For an economic evaluation, see Bennathan and Walters, Shipping Conferences: An Economic Analysis, 4 Journal of Maritime Law and Commerce 93 (1972).

is not at hand. Various forms of preferential treatment have been devised for rewarding the faithful and penalizing those who stray. The "rebate," at the end of a year, to those who have used only conference ships, has long been forbidden in this country.[190] But a device, similar in effect, which is now being tested, is the "dual rate" system, under which two rates are quoted: one for the shipper who agrees to use only conference tonnage, and a higher one for the shipper with a fickle nose for bargains.[190a]

It is required by statute that conference operators file with the Maritime Commission schedules of the rates they propose to charge, as part of the conference agreement. Schedules have embodied the dual rate provision, and the Commission (or its predecessor "Board") earlier gave its approval.

In 1958, after years of uncertainty as to the legality of these arrangements, the Supreme Court, in Federal Maritime Board v. Isbrandtsen Co., Inc. held that the dual-rate contract in the case at bar constituted a "resort to other discriminating or unfair methods" to stifle outside competition in violation of (the Shipping Act of 1916) Section Third." [191] Although the holding may be qualified by the fact that the system in question was thought "predatory" by the Court, it cast doubt on all dual-rate arrangements.

After the Isbrandtsen decision, Congress passed legislation suspending impact of the holding so that the matter might be further studied.[192] Extensive congressional hearings followed; witnesses for the Federal Maritime Board, the steamship industry, and other groups argued that the dual-rate system was "indispensable to the strength of a conference" and responsible for "assuring the stability of rates necessary to permit and encourage forward trading" by exporters and importers.[193] Despite substantial opposition to these arguments from Senator Kefauver, from the Antitrust Subcommittee of the House Judiciary Committee, and from the Justice Department, Congress decided against banning dual-rate arrangements through anti-trust laws,[193a] but did set restrictions on the terms of such contracts, as conditions to their approval.

190. 46 U.S.C.A. § 812.

190a. See Magnusson, Shipping Conference Dual-Rate Contract Arrangements as a Competitive Weapon, 38 St. John's L.Rev. 221 (1964); Bush, Steamship Conference Contract Rate Agreements and the Dual Rate System, 40 I.C.C.Prac.J. 14 (1972).

191. 356 U.S. 481, 493, 78 S.Ct. 851, 859 (1958).

192. Act of August 12, 1958, P.L. 85–626, 72 Stat. 574 (expired June 30, 1960). For a history of this moratorium, see Antitrust Subcomm. of the House Comm. on the Judiciary, The Ocean Freight Industry, H.R.Rep. No. 1419, 87th Cong., 2d Sess. (1962).

193. Antitrust Subcomm. of the House Comm. on the Judiciary, supra note 9, at 216; Hearings on the Ocean Freight Industry Before the Antitrust Subcomm. of the House Comm. on the Judiciary, 86th Cong., 1st & 2d Sess., ser. 14, pt. 1, vols. I–IV and pt. 2, vols. I–II (1959–60); *id.*, 87th Cong., 1st Sess., ser. 10, pt. 3, vols. I–II (1961).

193a. 107 Cong.Rec. 19334–19374, 19409–19428 (1961). The line up of different governmental agencies on different sides shows how very com-

There were other amendments in 1961. One of these has already become a source of controversy. Section 15 of the 1916 Act establishes a number of conditions for agreements between competing carriers which eliminate rate and service competition.[193b] In addition to several specific requirements, the Commission may disapprove any such agreement if it finds that it

(a) is "unjustly discriminatory or unfair as between carriers, shippers, exporters, importers, or ports, or between exporters from the United States and their foreign competition";

(b) operates "to the detriment of the commerce of the United States";

(c) is "contrary to the public interest"; or

(d) is "in violation of this chapter."

Section (c) was added to the Act in 1961, the other sections having been part of the 1916 Act. The Supreme Court has understandably interpreted section (c) as granting the Commission "considerably broader authority" than previously existed to determine the legality of these agreements.[193c] In the American Society of Travel Agents (ASTA) decision, the Court reversed a D. C. Court of Appeals judgment invalidating a Commission ruling that approval will only be given to those agreements interfering with antitrust policy when the conference can "bring forth such facts as would demonstrate that the . . . (conference arrangement) was required by a serious transportation need, necessary to secure important public benefits or in furtherance of a valid regulatory policy of the Shipping Act." [193d] The possible impact of this decision is suggested by the Court's reasoning rather than by its holding. Rejecting past application of the antitrust exemption, the Court declared "[O]nce an antitrust violation is established, this alone will normally constitute substantial evidence that the agreement is 'contrary to the public interest,' unless other evidence in the record fairly detracts from the weight of this factor." [193e] Thus, it appears the Court shifted a substantial burden of proof to the conference member by articulating for the first time the assumption that all section 15 agreements *prima facie* violate the antitrust laws.

Commission activity under other provisions of the Shipping Act has come under fire in the decade just past. Sections 16, 17, and 18 (b)(5) of the Act are concerned with direct rate regulation. The Commission has been authorized to distinguish between the merely

plicated and ambiguous the "governmental interest" in shipping is. For an interesting account, see Gordon, Shipping Regulation and the Federal Maritime Commission, 37 U.Chi.L. Rev. 90, 95–99 (1969).

**193b.** 46 U.S.C. § 814, as amended by P.L. 87–346, 75 Stat. 762 (1961).

**193c.** FMC v. Aktiebolaget Svenska Amerika Linien, 390 U.S. 238 at 243, 88 S.Ct. 1005, at 1008.

**193d.** *Id.*

**193e.** *Id.* at 245–46.

discriminatory or preferential rate and the unreasonably discriminatory or preferential rate. Section 18(b)(5) grants the Commission power "to disapprove any conference, rate, fare, or charge which after hearing it finds to be so unreasonably high or low as to be detrimental to the commerce of the United States." In recent years the Commission, yielding to Congressional pressure, has increased its activity under these sections, thereby meeting serious opposition both from the shipping industry and from foreign governments resentful of our efforts to control international shipping.[193f] This activity has resulted in extensive administrative proceedings and litigation. We may briefly refer to a couple of the more important cases, by way of illustration.

*Investigation of Rates in the Hong Kong-United States Atlantic Gulf Trade* [193g] was the first case to be brought under section 18(b)(5) of the Shipping Act. The dispute involved a rate war between member lines of the New York Freight Bureau and a group of independent carriers. One of these, the Sabre Line, after a round of particularly sharp rate-cutting, filed a protest with the Commission, alleging that the rates had become "unreasonably low and detrimental to the commerce of the United States." [193h] After an investigation lasting over four years, the hearing examiner determined that the rates in question were illegal, because they were noncompensatory of the "direct costs" incurred in serving the port of Hong Kong, and had therefore resulted in the Sabre Line's being forced to quit that trade.[193i] The Commission, neither affirming nor reversing the hearing examiner, determined that the case had become moot as a result of the five-year investigation, since the trade had "long since regained an element of stability".[193j] But the Commission did enunciate two important rules:

1. [A] rate which fails to meet out-of-pocket costs of the carrier quoting the rate is unreasonably low.
2. [A] carrier may, by proving his own out-of-pocket costs, establish a rebuttable presumption of the out-of-pocket costs prevailing generally in the trade.[193k]

**193f.** See Joint Economic Comm., Discriminatory Ocean Freight Rates and the Balance of Payments, S.Rep. 89th Cong., 1st Sess. (1965); Hearings on H.R. 4299 Before the Special Subcomm. on Steamship Conferences of the House Comm. on Merchant Marine and Fisheries, 87th Cong., 1st Sess. 140–4, 158–64 (1961); Hearings on H.R. 6775 Before the Merchant Marine and Fisheries Subcomm. of the Senate Comm. on Commerce, 87th Cong., 1st Sess., pt. I at 51–70 (1961).

**193g.** 11 FMC 168, No. 1083 (Nov. 3, 1967) (opinion of the Commission).

**193h.** 11 FMC 168, supra note 193g, at 172.

**193i.** Investigation of Rates in the Hong Kong—United States Atlantic and Gulf Trade, FMC No. 1083 at 19 (April 20, 1967) (initial decision of the hearing examiner).

**193j.** 11 FMC 168, supra note 193g, at 181.

**193k.** 11 FMC 168, supra note 1, at 172.

In effect, the Commission removed much of the effectiveness of the statute by placing reliance on out-of-pocket costs, rather than on direct costs. The former are limited to cargo handling expenses and other directly assignable costs. Direct costs, on the other hand, may include such factors as amortization of capital, interest, and voyage vessel operating costs as well as out-of-pocket costs.

The Iron and Steel Rate Disparities Investigation [193l] was instituted by the Commission (after considerable Congressional pressure was exerted) under sections 15 and 18(b)(5) of the Shipping Act "to determine (1) whether the outbound and inbound rates on iron and steel items assessed by the conferences and common carriers in the United States North Atlantic and Gulf/United Kingdom and Continent trades and in the United States Atlantic, Gulf and Pacific trades with Japan were so unreasonably high or low as to be detrimental to the commerce of the United States, and (2) whether the discrepancy between such [outbound and inbound] rates results in unjust prejudice to exporters of the United States as compared with their foreign competitiors." [193m] After extensive investigation, the Commission held that there was no factual basis for these charges, and found in favor of the respondent carriers and conferences. Perhaps to placate critics, the Commission adopted a rule requiring the carrier quoting the higher rate in such a rate disparity case to demonstrate the reasonableness of the disparate rates.

The foregoing paragraphs do no more than illustrate modern problems, but may give the student some feel for the setting in which new problems continually arise.[193n]

Various acts of unfair competition are forbidden by the 1916 Act as amended.[194] Among these are rebates, use of a "fighting ship" (for temporarily undercutting a carrier so as to drive him out of business) and "discrimination." The Commission hears complaints of violations of these provisions. It is partly to facilitate the work of policing discrimination that the filing of rate schedules is required; even though the Commission has no general rate-making power, it may order a change in an "unjustly discriminatory or prejudicial rate, fare, or charge." [195]

**193*l*.** Iron and Steel Rates, Export-Import, 9 F.M.C. 180 (1965).

**193m.** J. S. Gordon, Shipping Regulation and the Federal Maritime Commission, 37 U.Chi.L.Rev. 90, 143 (1969), quoting 9 F.M.C. 180, supra note 22, at 181.

**193n.** For an overview on regulation of conferences, see Lowenfeld, "To Have One's Cake . . . "—The Federal Maritime Commission and the Conferences, 1 Journal of Maritime Law and Commerce 21 (1969).

**194.** 46 U.S.C.A. §§ 812–817.

**195.** 46 U.S.C.A. § 817. In dealing with violations of the Shipping Act (even though the same actions might transgress the broader prohibitions of the general anti-trust laws) the jurisdiction of the Board is primary and "exclusive"; *i. e.*, the courts seemingly are excluded from enforcing the antitrust laws in the normal way in such cases, and are confined to reviewing actions of the Board. U. S. Navigation Co. v. Cunard S. S. Co., 284 U.S. 474, 52 S.Ct. 247, 1932 A.M.C. 209 (1932); Far East Conference v. United States, 342 U.S. 570, 72 S.Ct. 492, 1952 A.M.C. 433 (1952); United States v. Borax Consolidated, Ltd., 141 F.

## Conclusion

§ 11–15. Shipping, from earliest times and down to now, has been the subject of solicitous national concern. A great deal of the political sensitivity to the subject in this country is doubtless factitious, being stimulated by the well-heeled insistencies of people who know what they want for themselves, and know just what strings to pluck to get it. One may justifiably lament the dearth of disinterested continuing studies of merchant shipping policy, in the face of changing conditions of world power, and it is easy to become irritated at the solemn pretenses of "educational" drives and dead-pan "testimony", with their refurbishing of time-tested platitudes just enough to make them fit the latest headlines and appear to support, with the urgency of contemporaneity, something the "educator" or the "witness" actually finds desirable for an altogether different and much less complicated reason. But this irritation ought not to blind one to the fact that there has been plausibility in the assertion that strategic considerations require the maintenance of a merchant marine. This evaluation may change in the next decades, if the fighting of faraway wars becomes unthinkable, a thing recent events make quite likely.

In any case, this national interest, genuine and stimulated, has expressed itself in our history in ways which are not new; we have chosen among classic devices on the basis of felt need and present pressure. The coastwise monopoly, the covert and overt subsidy, and all the minor devices are part of the stock-in-trade of statecraft, in dealing with this industry. This country's aid to and regulation of shipping may continue pretty much along the present lines, or some new formula may be worked out. But the whole history of the subject, here and abroad, recently and remotely, justifies the expectation that the concerns of shipping will for some time continue to interest the state, and that, through the intermediacy of politics, law will continue to reflect this fact.

Supp. 396, 1956 A.M.C. 404 (N.D.Calif. 1955); American Union Transport Co. v. River Plate and Brazil Conferences, 126 F.Supp. 91, 1955 A.M.C. 1063 (S.D.N.Y.1954), aff'd *per curiam* 222 F.2d 369, 1955 A.M.C. 1068 (2d Cir. 1955). It may be questioned whether the cases have given sufficient weight to the language of the Shipping Act § 15—"Before approval . . . it shall be unlawful to carry out . . . any such agreement." 46 U.S.C.A. § 814. In any case, a contract unlawful under the Shipping Act cannot be *affirmatively* enforced prior to Maritime Board action. River Plate and Brazil Conferences v. Pressed Steel Car Co., 227 F.2d 60, 1955 A.M.C. 2186 (2d Cir. 1955).

## Appendix A

# THE DOCUMENTARY COUNCIL OF THE BALTIC AND WHITE SEA CONFERENCE

## UNIFORM GENERAL CHARTER

As Revised 1922

CODE NAME: GENCON.

______ 19__

**Owners—Position—Charterers.**

1. It is this Day Mutually Agreed between ______ Owners of the ______ steamer or motor-vessel ______ of ______ tons gross/net Register and carrying about ______ tons of dead-weight cargo, now ______ and expected ready to load under this Charter about ______ and Messrs. ______ of ______ as Charterers.

**Where to Load—Cargo—Destination—Rate of Freight.**

That the said vessel shall proceed to ______ or so near thereto as she may safely get and lie always afloat, and there load a full and complete cargo (if shipment of deck cargo agreed same to be at Charterers' risk) of ______ (Charterers to provide all mats and/or wood for dunnage and any separations required, the Owners allowing the use of any dunnage wood on board if required) which the Charterers bind themselves to ship, and being so loaded the vessel shall proceed to ______ as ordered on signing Bills of Lading or so near thereto as she may safely get and lie always afloat and there deliver the cargo on being paid freight—on delivered/intaken quantity—as follows ______

**Owners Responsibility-Clause.**

2. Owners are to be responsible for loss of or damage to the goods or for delay in delivery of the goods only in case the loss, damage or delay has been caused by the improper or negligent stowage of the goods (unless stowage performed by shippers or their stevedores or servants) or by personal want of due diligence on the part of the Owners or their Manager to make the vessel in all respects seaworthy and to secure that she is properly manned, equipped and supplied or by the personal act or default of the Owners or their Manager.

And the Owners are responsible for no loss or damage or delay arising from any other cause whatsoever, even from the neglect or default of the Captain or crew or some other person employed by the Owners on board or ashore for whose acts they would, but for this clause, be responsible, or from unseaworthiness of the vessel on loading or commencement of the voyage or at any time whatsoever.

Damage caused by contact with or leakage, smell or evaporation from other goods or by the inflammable or explosive nature or insufficient package of other goods not to be considered as caused by improper or negligent stowage, even if in fact so caused.

**Deviation Clause.**

3. The vessel has liberty to call at any port or ports in any order, for any purpose, to sail without pilots, to tow and/or assist vessels in all situations, and also to deviate for the purpose of saving life and/or property.

**Payment of Freight.**

4. The freight to be paid in cash without discount on delivery of the cargo at mean rate of exchange ruling on day or days of payment, the receivers of the cargo being bound to pay freight on account during delivery, if required by Captain or Owners.

Cash for vessel's ordinary disbursements at port of loading to be advanced by Charterers if required at highest current rate of exchange, subject to two per cent, to cover insurance and other expenses.

**Loading.**

5. Cargo to be brought alongside in such a manner as to enable vessel to take the goods with her own tackle and to load the full cargo in ______ running working days. Charterers to procure and pay the necessary men on shore or on board the lighters to do the work there, vessel only heaving the cargo on board.

If the loading takes place by elevator cargo to be put free in vessel's holds, Owners only paying trimming expenses.

Any pieces and/or packages of cargo over two tons weight shall be loaded, stowed and discharged by Charterers at their risk and expense.

Time to commence at 1 p. m. if notice of readiness to load is given before noon and at 6 a. m. next working day if notice given during office hours after noon.

The notice to be given to the Shippers, Messrs. ______

Time lost in waiting for berth to count as loading time.

**Discharging.**

6. Cargo to be received by Merchants at their risk and expense alongside the vessel not beyond the reach of her tackle and to be discharged in ______ running working days. Time to commence at 1 p. m. if notice of readiness to discharge is given before noon, and at 6 a. m. next working day if notice given during office hours after noon.

Time lost in waiting for berth to count as discharging time.

**Demurrage.**

7. Ten running days on demurrage at the rate of ______ per day or pro rata for any part of a day, payable day by day, to be allowed Merchants altogether at ports of loading and discharging.

**Lien Clause.**

8. Owners shall have a lien on the cargo for freight, dead-freight, demurrage and damages for detention. Charterers shall remain responsible for dead-freight and demurrage (including damages for detention), incurred at port of loading. Charterers shall also remain responsible for freight, and demurrage (including damages for detention) incurred at port of discharge, but only to such extent as the Owners have been unable to obtain payment thereof by exercising the lien on the cargo.

**Bills of Lading.**

9. The Captain to sign Bills of Lading at such rate of freight as presented without prejudice to this Charter-party, but should the freight by Bills of Lading amount to less than the total chartered freight the difference to be paid to the Captain in cash on signing Bills of Lading.

**Strike-, War- and Ice-Clauses.**

10. *Strike-Clause, War-Clause and Ice-Clause as below.*

**Cancelling-Clause.**

11. Should the vessel not be ready to load (whether in berth or not) on or before the ______ Charterers have the option of cancelling this contract, such option to be declared, if demanded, at least 48 hours before vessel's expected arrival at port of loading. Should the vessel be delayed, on account of average or otherwise, Charterers to be informed as soon as possible, and if the vessel is delayed for more than 10 days after the day she is stated to be expected ready to load, Charterers have the option of cancelling this contract, unless a cancelling date has been agreed upon.

**General Average.**

12. General average to be settled according to York-Antwerp rules, 1950, Proprietors of cargo to pay the cargo's share in the general expenses even if same have been necessitated through neglect or default of the Owners' servants (see clause 2).

**Indemnity.**

13. Indemnity for non-performance of this Charter-party, proved damages, not exceeding estimated amount of freight.

**Agency.**

14. In every case the Owner shall appoint his own Broker or Agent both at the port of loading and the port of discharge.

**Brokerage.**

15. _____% brokerage on the freight earned is due to ______

In case of non-execution at least ⅓ of the brokerage on the estimated amount of freight and dead-freight to be paid by the Owners to the Brokers as indemnity for the latter's expenses and work. In case of more voyages the amount of indemnity to be mutually agreed.

**General Strike Clause.**

Neither Charterers nor Owners shall be responsible for the consequences of any strikes or lock-outs preventing or delaying the fulfilment of any obligations under this contract.

If there is a strike or lock-out affecting the loading of the cargo, or any part of it, when vessel is ready to proceed from her last port or at any time during the voyage to the port or ports of loading or after her arrival there, Captain or Owners may ask Charterers to declare, that they agree to reckon the laydays as if there were no strike or lock-out. Unless Charterers have given such declaration in writing (by telegram, if necessary) within 24 hours, Owners shall have the option of cancelling this contract. If part cargo has already been loaded, Owners must proceed with same, (freight payable on loaded quantity only) having liberty to complete with other cargo on the way for their own account.

If there is a strike or lock-out affecting the discharge of the cargo on or after vessel's arrival at or off port of discharge and same has not been settled within 48 hours, Receivers shall have the option of keeping vessel waiting until such strike or lock-out is at an end against paying half demurrage after expiration of the time provided for discharging, or of ordering the vessel to a safe port where she can safely discharge without risk of being detained by strike or lock-out. Such orders to be given within 48 hours after Captain or Owners have given notice to Charterers of the strike or lock-out affecting the discharge. On delivery of the cargo at such port, all conditions of this Charter party and of the Bill of Lading shall apply and vessel shall receive the same freight as if she had discharged at the original port of destination, except that if the distance of the substituted port exceeds 100 nautical miles, the freight on the cargo delivered at the substituted port to be increased in proportion.

**General War Clause.**

If the nation under whose flag the vessel sails should be engaged in war and the safe navigation of the vessel should thereby be endangered either party to have the option of cancelling this contract, and if so cancelled, cargo already shipped shall be discharged either at the port of loading or, if the vessel has commenced the voyage, at the nearest safe place at the risk and expense of the Charterers or Cargo-Owners.

If owing to outbreak of hostilities the goods loaded or to be loaded under this contract or part of them become contraband of war whether absolute or conditional or liable to confiscation or detention according to international law or the proclamation of any of the belligerent powers each party to have the option of cancelling this contract as far as such goods are concerned, and contraband goods already loaded to be then discharged either at the port of loading, or if the voyage has already commenced, at the nearest safe place at the expense of the Cargo-Owners. Owners to have the right to fill up with other goods instead of the contraband.

Should any port where the vessel has to load under this Charter be blockaded the contract to be null and void with regard to the goods to be shipped at such port.

No Bills of Lading to be signed for any blockaded port, and if the port of destination be declared blockaded after Bills of Lading have been signed, Owners shall discharge the cargo either at the port of loading, against payment of the expenses of discharge, if the ship has not sailed thence, or, if sailed, at any safe port on the way as ordered by Shippers or if no order is given at the nearest safe place against payment of full freight.

## GENERAL ICE CLAUSE.

**Port of Loading.**

a) In the event of the loading port being inaccessible by reason of ice when vessel is ready to proceed from her last port or at any time during the voyage or on vessel's arrival or in case frost sets in after vessel's arrival, the Captain for fear of being frozen in is at liberty to leave without cargo, and this Charter shall be null and void.

b) If during loading the Captain, for fear of vessel being frozen in, deems it advisable to leave, he has liberty to do so with what cargo he has on board and to proceed to any other port or ports with option of completing cargo for Owner's benefit for any port or ports including port of discharge. Any part cargo thus loaded under this Charter to be forwarded to destination at vessel's expense but against payment of freight, provided that no extra expenses be thereby caused to the Receivers, freight being paid on quantity delivered (in proportion if lump sum), all other conditions as per Charter.

c) In case of more than one loading port, and if one or more of the ports are closed by ice, the Captain or Owners to be at liberty either to load the part cargo at the open port and fill up elsewhere for their own account as under section B or to declare the charter null and void unless Charterers agree to load full cargo at the open port.

d) This Ice Clause not to apply in the Spring.

**Port of Discharge.**

a) Should ice (except in the Spring) prevent vessel from reaching port of discharge Receivers shall have the option of keeping vessel waiting until the re-opening of navigation and paying demurrage, or of ordering the vessel to a safe and immediately accessible port where she can safely discharge without risk of detention by ice. Such orders to be given within 48 hours after Captain or Owners have given notice to Charterers of the impossibility of reaching port of destination.

b) If during discharging the Captain for fear of vessel being frozen in deems it advisable to leave, he has liberty to do so with what cargo he has on board and to proceed to the nearest accessible port where she can safely discharge.

c) On delivery of the cargo at such port, all conditions of the Bill of Lading shall apply and vessel shall receive the same freight as if she had discharged at the original port of destination, except that if the distance of the substituted port exceeds 100 nautical miles, the freight on the cargo delivered at the substituted port to be increased in proportion.

# Appendix B

## TIME CHARTER

### GOVERNMENT FORM

*Approved by the New York Produce Exchange*

November 6th, 1913—Amended October 20th, 1921;
August 6th, 1931; October 3rd, 1946

THIS CHARTER PARTY, made and concluded in ______ day of ______

19__. Between ______ Owners of the good ______ { Steamship / Motorship }

______ of ______ of ______ tons gross register, and ______ tons net register, having engines of ______ indicated horse power and with hull, machinery and equipment in a thoroughly efficient state, and classed ______ at ______ of about ______ cubic feet bale capacity, and about ______ tons of 2240 lbs. deadweight capacity (cargo and bunkers, including fresh water and stores not exceeding one and one-half percent of ship's deadweight capacity, allowing a minimum of fifty tons) on a draft of ______ feet ______ inches on ______ Summer freeboard, inclusive of permanent bunkers, which are of the capacity of about ______ tons of fuel, and capable of steaming, fully laden, under good weather conditions about ______ knots on a consumption of about ______ tons of best Welsh coal—best grade fuel oil—best grade Diesel oil, now ______ and ______ Charterers of the City of ______.

WITNESSETH, That the said Owners agree to let, and the said Charterers agree to hire the said vessel, from the time of delivery, for about ______ within below mentioned trading limits. Charterers to have liberty to sublet the vessel for all or any part of the time covered by this Charter, but Charterers remaining responsible for the fulfillment of this Charter Party.

Vessel to be placed at the disposal of the Charterers, at ______ in such dock or at such wharf or place (where she may safely lie, always afloat, at all times of tide, except as otherwise provided in clause No. 6), as the Charterers may direct. If such dock, wharf or place be not available time to count as provided for in clause No. 5. Vessel on her delivery to be ready to receive cargo with clean-swept holds and tight, staunch, strong and in every way fitted for the service, having water ballast, winches and donkey boiler with sufficient steam power, or if not equipped with donkey boiler, then other power sufficient to run all the winches at one and the same time (and with full complement of officers, seamen, engineers and firemen for a vessel of her tonnage), to be employed, in carrying lawful merchandise, including petroleum or its products, in proper containers, excluding

______ (vessel is not to be employed in the carriage of Live Stock, but Charterers are to have the privilege of shipping a small number on deck at their risk, all necessary fittings and other requirements to be for account of Charterers), in such lawful trades, between safe port and/or ports in British North America, and/or United States of America, and/or West Indies, and/or Central America, and/or Caribbean Sea, and/or Gulf of Mexico, and/or Mexico, and/or South America ______ and/or Europe and/or Africa, and/or Asia, and/or Australia, and/or Tasmania, and/or New Zealand, but excluding Magdalena River, River St. Lawrence between October 31st and May 15th, Hudson Bay and all unsafe ports; also excluding, when out of season, White Sea, Black Sea and the Baltic, ________________

________________________________________

as the Charterers or their Agents shall direct, on the following conditions:

1. That the Owners shall provide and pay for all provisions, wages and consular shipping and discharging fees of the Crew; shall pay for the insurance of the vessel, also for all the cabin, deck, engine-room and other necessary stores, including boiler water and maintain her class and keep the vessel in a thoroughly efficient state in hull, machinery and equipment for and during the service.

2. That the Charterers shall provide and pay for all the fuel except as otherwise agreed, Port Charges, Pilotages, Agencies, Commissions, Consular Charges (except those pertaining to the Crew), and all other usual expenses except those before stated, but when the vessel puts into a port for causes for which vessel is responsible, then all such charges incurred shall be paid by the Owners. Fumigations ordered because of illness of the crew to be for Owners account. Fumigations ordered because of cargoes carried or ports visited while vessel is employed under this charter to be for Charterers account. All other fumigations to be for Charterers account after vessel has been on charter for a continuous period of six months or more.

Charterers are to provide necessary dunnage and shifting boards, also any extra fittings requisite for a special trade or unusual cargo, but Owners to allow them the use of any dunnage and shifting boards already aboard vessel. Charterers to have the privilege of using shifting boards for dunnage, they making good any damage thereto.

3. That the Charterers, at the port of delivery, and the Owners, at the port of re-delivery, shall take over and pay for all fuel remaining on board the vessel at the current prices in the respective ports, the vessel to be delivered with not less than ______ tons and not more than ______ tons and to be re-delivered with not less than ______ tons and not more than ______ tons.

4. That the Charterers shall pay for the use and hire of the said Vessel at the rate of ______ United States Currency per ton on vessel's total deadweight carrying capacity, including bunkers and stores, on ______ summer freeboard, per Calendar Month, commenc-

ing on and from the day of her delivery, as aforesaid, and at and after the same rate for any part of a month; hire to continue until the hour of the day of her re-delivery in like good order and condition, ordinary wear and tear excepted, to the Owners (unless lost) at ______ unless otherwise mutually agreed. Charterers are to give Owners not less than ______ days notice of vessels expected date of redelivery, and probable port.

5. Payment of said hire to be made in New York in cash in United States Currency, semi-monthly in advance, and for the last half month or part of same the approximate amount of hire, and should same not cover the actual time, hire is to be paid for the balance day by day, as it becomes due, if so required by Owners, unless bank guarantee or deposit is made by the Charterers, otherwise failing the punctual and regular payment of the hire, or bank guarantee, or on any breach of this Charter Party, the Owners shall be at liberty to withdraw the vessel from the service of the Charterers, without prejudice to any claim they (the Owners) may otherwise have on the Charterers. Time to count from 7 a. m. on the working day following that on which written notice of readiness has been given to Charterers or their Agents before 4 p. m., but if required by Charterers, they to have the privilege of using vessel at once, such time used to count as hire.

Cash for vessel's ordinary disbursements at any port may be advanced as required by the Captain, by the Charterers or their Agents, subject to 2½% commission and such advances shall be deducted from the hire. The Charterers, however, shall in no way be responsible for the application of such advances.

6. That the cargo or cargoes be laden and/or discharged in any dock or at any wharf or place that Charterers or their Agents may direct, provided the vessel can safely lie always afloat at any time of tide, except at such places where it is customary for similar size vessels to safely lie aground.

7. That the whole reach of the Vessel's Hold, Decks, and usual places of loading (not more than she can reasonably stow and carry), also accommodations for Supercargo, if carried, shall be at the Charterers' disposal, reserving only proper and sufficient space for Ship's officers, crew, tackle, apparel, furniture, provisions, stores and fuel. Charterers have the privilege of passengers as far as accommodations allow, Charterers paying Owners ______ per day per passenger for accommodations and meals. However, it is agreed that in case any fines or extra expenses are incurred in the consequence of the carriage of passengers, Charterers are to bear risk and expense.

8. That the Captain shall prosecute his voyages with the utmost despatch, and shall render all customary assistance with ship's crew and boats. The Captain (although appointed by the Owners), shall be under the orders and directions of the Charterers as regards employment and agency; and Charterers are to load, stow, and trim the cargo at their expense under the supervision of the Captain, who

is to sign Bills of Lading for cargo as presented, in conformity with Mate's or Tally Clerk's receipts.

9. That if the Charterers shall have reason to be dissatisfied with the conduct of the Captain, Officers, or Engineers, the Owners shall on receiving particulars of the complaint, investigate the same, and, if necessary, make a change in the appointments.

10. That the Charterers shall have permission to appoint a Supercargo, who shall accompany the vessel and see that voyages are prosecuted with the utmost despatch. He is to be furnished with free accommodation, and same fare as provided for Captain's table, Charterers paying at the rate of $1.00 per day. Owners to victual Pilots and Customs Officers, and also, when authorized by Charterers or their Agents, to victual Tally Clerks, Stevedore's Foreman, etc., Charterers paying at the current rate per meal, for all such victualling.

11. That the Charterers shall furnish the Captain from time to time with all requisite instructions and sailing directions, in writing, and the Captain shall keep a full and correct Log of the voyage or voyages, which are to be patent to the Charterers or their Agents, and furnish the Charterers, their Agents or Supercargo, when required, with a true copy of daily Logs, showing the course of the vessel and distance run and the consumption of fuel.

12. That the Captain shall use diligence in caring for the ventilation of the cargo.

13. That the Charterers shall have the option of continuing this charter for a further period of ______ on giving written notice thereof to the Owners or their Agents ______ days previous to the expiration of the first-named term, or any declared option.

14. That if required by Charterers, time not to commence before ______ and should vessel not have given written notice of readiness on or before ______ but not later than 4 p. m. Charterers or their Agents to have the option of cancelling this Charter at any time not later than the day of vessel's readiness.

15. That in the event of the loss of time from deficiency of men or stores, fire, breakdown or damages to hull, machinery or equipment, grounding, detention by average accidents to ship or cargo, drydocking for the purpose of examination or painting bottom, or by any other cause preventing the full working of the vessel, the payment of hire shall cease for the time thereby lost; and if upon the voyage the speed be reduced by defect in or breakdown of any part of her hull, machinery or equipment, the time so lost, and the cost of any extra fuel consumed in consequence thereof, and all extra expenses shall be deducted from the hire.

16. That should the Vessel be lost, money paid in advance and not earned (reckoning from the date of loss or being last heard of) shall be returned to the Charterers at once. The act of God, enemies, fire, restraint of Princes, Rulers and People, and all dangers and

accidents of the Seas, Rivers, Machinery, Boilers and Steam Navigation, and errors of Navigation throughout this Charter Party, always mutually excepted.

The vessel shall have the liberty to sail with or without pilots, to tow and to be towed, to assist vessels in distress, and to deviate for the purpose of saving life and property.

17. That should any dispute arise between Owners and the Charterers, the matter in dispute shall be referred to three persons at New York, one to be appointed by each of the parties hereto, and the third by the two so chosen; their decision or that of any two of them, shall be final, and for the purpose of enforcing any award, this agreement may be made a rule of the Court. The Arbitrators shall be commercial men.

18. That the Owners shall have a lien upon all cargoes, and all sub-freights for any amounts due under this Charter, including General Average contributions, and the Charterers to have a lien on the Ship for all monies paid in advance and not earned, and any overpaid hire or excess deposit to be returned at once. Charterers will not suffer, nor permit to be continued, any lien or encumbrance incurred by them or their agents, which might have priority over the title and interest of the owners in the vessel.

19. That all derelicts and salvage shall be for Owners' and Charterers' equal benefit after deducting Owners' and Charterers' expenses and Crew's proportion. General Average shall be adjusted, stated and settled, according to Rules 1 to 15, inclusive, 17 to 22, inclusive, and Rule F of York-Antwerp Rules 1924, at such port or place in the United States as may be selected by the carrier, and as to matters not provided for by these Rules, according to the laws and usages at the port of New York. If such adjustment disbursements in foreign currencies shall be exchanged into United States money at the rate prevailing on the dates made and allowances for damage to cargo claimed in foreign currency shall be converted at the rate prevailing on the last day of discharge at the port or place of final discharge of such damaged cargo from the ship. Average agreement or bond and such additional security, as may be required by the carrier, must be furnished before delivery of the goods. Such cash deposit as the carrier or his agents may deem sufficient as additional security for the contribution of the goods and for any salvage and special charges thereon, shall, if required, be made by the goods, shippers, consignees or owners of the goods to the carrier before delivery. Such deposit shall, at the option of the carrier, be payable in United States money and be remitted to the adjuster. When so remitted the deposit shall be held in a special account at the place of adjustment in the name of the adjuster pending settlement of the General Average and refunds or credit balances, if any, shall be paid in United States money.

In the event of accident, danger, damage, or disaster, before or after commencement of the voyage resulting from any cause whatsoever, whether due to negligence or not, for which, or for the consequence of which, the carrier is not responsible, by statute contract, or otherwise, the goods, the shipper and the consignee, jointly and severally, shall contribute with the carrier in general average to the payment of any sacrifices, losses, or expenses of a general average nature that may be made or incurred, and shall pay salvage and special charges incurred in respect of the goods. If a salving ship is owned or operated by the carrier, salvage shall be paid for as fully and in the same manner as if such salving ship or ships belonged to strangers.

Provisions as to General Average in accordance with the above are to be included in all bills of lading issued hereunder.

20. Fuel used by the vessel while off hire, also for cooking, condensing water, or for grates and stoves to be agreed to as to quantity, and the cost of replacing same, to be allowed by Owners.

21. That as the vessel may be from time to time employed in tropical waters during the term of this Charter, Vessel is to be docked at a convenient place, bottom cleaned and painted whenever Charterers and Captain think necessary, at least once in every six months, reckoning from time of last painting, and payment of the hire to be suspended until she is again in proper state for the service. ________

________________________________________

22. Owners shall maintain the gear of the ship as fitted, providing gear (for all derricks) capable of handling lifts up to three tons, also providing ropes, falls, slings and blocks. If vessel is fitted with derricks capable of handling heavier lifts, Owners are to provide necessary gear for same, otherwise equipment and gear for heavier lifts shall be for Charterers' account. Owners also to provide on the vessel lanterns and oil for night work, and vessel to give use of electric light when so fitted, but any additional lights over those on board to be at Charterers' expense. The Charterers to have the use of any gear on board the vessel.

23. Vessel to work night and day, if required by Charterers, and all winches to be at Charterers' disposal during loading and discharging; steamer to provide one winchman per hatch to work winches day and night, as required, Charterers agreeing to pay officers, engineers, winchmen, deck hands and donkeymen for overtime work done in accordance with the working hours and rates stated in the ship's articles. If the rules of the port, or labor unions, prevent crew from driving winches, shore Winchmen to be paid by Charterers. In the event of a disabled winch or winches, or insufficient power to operate winches, Owners to pay for shore engine, or engines, in lieu thereof, if required, and pay any loss of time occasioned thereby.

24. It is also mutually agreed that this Charter is subject to all the terms and provisions of and all the exemptions from liability contained in the Act of Congress of the United States approved on the 13th day of February, 1893, and entitled "An Act relating to

Navigation of Vessels, etc.," in respect of all cargo shipped under this charter to or from the United States of America. It is further subject to the following clauses, both of which are to be included in all bills of lading issued hereunder:

U. S. A. Clause Paramount

> This bill of lading shall have effect subject to the provisions of the Carriage of Goods by Sea Act of the United States, approved April 16, 1936, which shall be deemed to be incorporated herein, and nothing herein contained shall be deemed a surrender by the carrier of any of its rights or immunities or an increase of any of its responsibilities or liabilities under said Act. If any term of this bill of lading be repugnant to said Act to any extent, such term shall be void to that extent, but no further.

Both-to-Blame Collision Clause

> If the ship comes into collision with another ship as a result of the negligence of the other ship and any act, neglect or default of the Master, mariner, pilot or the servants of the Carrier in the navigation or in the management of the ship, the owners of the goods carried hereunder will indemnify the Carrier against all loss or liability to the other or non-carrying ship or her owners in so far as such loss or liability represents loss of, or damage to, or any claim whatsoever of the owners of said goods, paid or payable by the other or non-carrying ship or her owners to the owners of said goods and set off, recouped or recovered by the other or non-carrying ship or her owners as part of their claim against the carrying ship or carrier.

25. The vessel shall not be required to enter any ice-bound port, or any port where lights or light-ships have been or are about to be withdrawn by reason of ice, or where there is risk that in the ordinary course of things the vessel will not be able on account of ice to safely enter the port or to get out after having completed loading or discharging.

26. Nothing herein stated is to be construed as a demise of the vessel to the Time Charterers. The owners to remain responsible for the navigation of the vessel, insurance, crew, and all other matters, same as when trading for their own account.

27. A commission of 2½ per cent is payable by the Vessel and Owners to

______________________________________________

on hire earned and paid under this Charter, and also upon any continuation or extension of this Charter.

28. An address commission of $2\frac{1}{2}$ per cent payable to ______ on the hire earned and paid under this Charter.

By cable authority from

As ______ For Owners

The original Charter Party in our possession.

BROKERS.

# TABLE OF CASES

References are to pages

## A


Aaby v. States Marine Corp., 229
Aakre, The 160
Abangarez, The, 520, 599
Abbe v. Erie R. Co., 97
Abraham Baldwin, The, 549
Acara, The, 535
Accinanto v. Cosmopolitan Shipping Co., 878
Ace Tractor & Equipment Co. v. Olympic S. S. Co., 207
Acker v. Hanioti, 637
Acker v. The City of Athens, 637
Acropolis, The, 693
Actieselskabet Dampsk. v. Harrison & Co., 233
Ada, The, 26, 640, 793
Adams, United States v., 510
Admiral Evans, The, 572
Admiral Peoples, The, 23
Admiralty Lines, In re, 633, 683, 808, 813
Adour, The, 772
Adriatic, The, 487
Aetna Ins. Co. v. United Fruit Co., 87, 91
Aetna Ins. Co. v. Sacramento-Stockton S. S. Co., 73
Afran Transport Co. v. The Bergechief, 512
Afran Transport Co. v. United States, 979
Aguia, The, 625
Aguilar v. Standard Oil Co., 289
Aguirre v. Citizens Cas. Co., 65
Agwilines, Inc. v. Eagle Oil & Shipping Co., 526
Agwisun, The, 948
Ahlgren v. Red Star Towing & Transp. Co., 500, 530
Ahmed v. United States, 288
Air Brant, The, 729
Ajubita v. S/S Peik, 658, 660
Akers v. State Marine Lines, Inc., 773
Aktieselskabet Fido v. Lloyd Brasileiro, 213, 254
Alabama, The, 516, 528, 807, 814
Alamo Chemical Transp. Co., Petition of, 852
Alaska Packers Ass'n v. Pillsbury, 414
Alaska S. S. Co., Petition of, 865
Alaska S. S. Co. v. Petterson, 394, 452
Albers Bros. Milling Co. v. Drumheller, 97
Albert Dumois, The, 846
Alcoa S. S. Co. v. Charles Ferran & Co., 911
Alcona, The, 255
Alcyone, The, 859, 861
Alert, The, 580
Alexandervich v. Gallagher Bros., 308
Alex Dussel Iron Works, United States v., 774
Algoma Central & Hudson Bay R. Co. v. Great Lakes Transit Corp., 937
Aliotti v. United States, 983, 985
All America Cables & Radio, Inc. v. The Dieppe, 789
Allanwilde Transp. Corp. v. Vacuum Oil Co., 228, 638
Allen v. M/V Contessa, 660
Alligator, The, 655
Alva Cape, The, 922
Alvarez v. American Export Isbrandtsen Lines, Inc., 288
Alva S. S. Co., Petition of, 921, 925
A. M. Bright Grocery Co. v. Lindsey, 623
Amell v. United States, 284
America, The, 743
Americana, The, 948
American Anthracite & Bituminous Coal Corp. v. Arrivabene S. A., 641
American Bank of Wage Claims v. District Court of Guam, 788
American Bridge Co. v. The Gloria O., 47, 523
American Car & Foundry Co. v. Brassert, 840
American Commercial Lines, Inc., Complaint of, 917
American Eagle, The, 662
American Gas Screw Franz Joseph, United States v., 712, 725, 759, 784
American-Hawaiian S. S. Co. v. Bennett & Goodall, 73
American-Imperator, The, 793

American Independent Oil Co. v. M/S Alkaid, 556
American Ins. Co. v. Bryan & Maitland, 73
American Ins. Co. v. Canter, 45
American Mail Line v. Tokyo Marine & Fire Ins. Co., 170, 267.
American Merchant Marine Ins. Co. v. Liberty Sand & Gravel Co., 76
American Merchant Marine Ins. Co. v. Margaret M. Ford Corp., 65
American Metal Co. v. M/V Belleville, 580, 582
American Oil Co., Petition of, 547, 550, 562, 979
American Oil Co. v. S. S. Ionian Challenger, 209
American Oil Co.—The Amocoa Virginia, United States v., 550, 562
American President Lines v. Federal Maritime Board, 211
American Star, The, 626
American Steel Barge Co. v. Chesapeake & Ohio Coal Agency Co., 233, 632
American Stevedores, Inc. v. Porello, 29, 442, 984
American Stevedores, Inc. v. The Trajan, 662
American, The, 625, 658
American Tobacco Co. v. Goulandris, 184
American Tobacco Co. v. The Katingo Hadjipatera, 184, 222, 491, 530, 858
American Trading & Production Corp. v. T. J. Stevenson & Co., 498
American Union Transport Co. v. River Plate and Brazil Conferences, 995
American Waterways Operators, Inc. v. Askew, 830
Ames, United States v., 800
Amiga Mia, The, 658
Amoco Virginia, The, 547
Amos D. Carver, The, 900
Anaces, The, 628, 629
Anastasiadis v. Mecom, 614
Anchawski v. Hanioti, 637
Anderson v. Ocean Steamship Co., 580
Andree, The, 630
Andrew J. Smith, The, 27
Andrews v. Essex Fire & Marine Ins. Co., 41
Andrews & Co. v. United States, 983
Angler, The, 696
Anglo-Argentine Agency v. Temperley Shipping Co., 262
Anglo-Patagonia, The, 650
Anglo-Saxon Petroleum Co. v. United States, 506
Anna J. Brooks, The, 740
Annette Rolph, The, 747
Annie Lord, The, 572
Ansaldo San Giorgio I, The v. Rheinstrom Bros. Co., 188
Artemis, The, 658
Anthony v. International Paper Co., 497
Anthony O'Boyle, Inc., Petition of, 861
Antigostine, The, 759
Aquascutum of London v. S. S. American Champion, 14
Aquitania, The, 864, 865
Arbib and Houlberg v. Second Russian Ins. Co., 73, 162
Archawski v. Hanioti, 27
Ares v. S/S Colon, 754
Argonaut Navigation Co. v. French Supply Council, 202
Argyll Shipping Co. v. Hanover Ins. Co., 245, 630, 780
Ariadne, The, 510
Ariel, The, 861
Aristocrates, The, 566
Arizona, The v. Anelich, 353, 385
Arizonan, The, 568
Arkell & Douglas, Inc. v. United States, 161
Arlene-The Bacardi, The, 768
Armco International Corp. v. Rederi A/B Disa, 158, 170
Armour & Co. v. Ft. Morgan S. S. Co., 29
Armstrong Cork Co. v. Farrell Line, 29
Army and Air Force Exchange Service v. Hanson, 417
Arques v. National Superior Co., 660
Arques Shipyards v. S/S Charles Van Damme, 623
Artemis, The, 658, 807
Aruba, The, 700
Asbestos Corp. v. Compagnie de Navigation Fraissinet, 161, 878
Askew v. American Waterways Operators, Inc., 50, 831
A/S Nye Kristianborg, State, to Use of Maines v., 35
Associated Metals and Minerals Corp. v. S. S. Portoria, 787
Astorian, The, 677
Astraea, The, 231
Atamanchuck v. Atamanchuck, 25
Athenian, The, 738
Atkins v. Disintegrating Co., 206
Atkins v. Fiber Disintegrating Co., 205, 206
Atlanta, The, 229, 629
Atlantic & Gulf Stevedores, Inc. v. Ellerman, 403
Atlantic & Gulf Stevedores, Inc. v. Neuman, 417
Atlantic City, The, 795

Atlantic Coast Line R. R. Co. v. Erie Lackawanna R. R. Co., 50, 442
Atlantic Fruit Co. v. Solari, 236
Atlantic, Gulf & Western Indies S. S. Lines, Inc., In re, 800, 948
Atlantic Ins. Co. v. Storrow, 73
Atlantic Mutual Ins. Co. v. Poseidon Schiffahrt, 181
Atlantic Mutual Ins. Co., United States v., 173, 251, 270
Atlantic Refining Co., United States v., 213
Atlantic Richfield Co. v. S. S. Steel Designer, 513
Atlantic Steamer Supply Co. v. S/S Tradewind, 629, 682, 711, 754, 817
Atlantic Transport Co. v. Imbrovek, 23, 438, 439, 454
Atlas No. 7, The, 242, 846
Atlas, The, 528
Atwater Fuels v. Pocahontas Fuel Co., 212
Audrey II, The, 816
Audrey II, United States v., 604, 816
Augustine Kobbe, The, 744
Aurora Shipping Co. v. Boyce, 650
Austin Friars S. S. Co. v. Spillers & Bakers, 262
Automobile Ins. Co. v. United Fruit Co., 161, 898
Avera v. Florida Towing Corp., 888, 912
Avondale Marine Ways, Inc. v. Henderson, 423

# B

Baham v. Atlantic, Gulf and Pacific Co., 855
Bailey v. Sundberg, 614
Baker v. Ocean Systems, Inc., 292
Baker Bros., The, 746
Baker-Whitely Towing Co., Petition of the, 852
Balado v. Lykes Bros. S. S. Co., 347
Balfour, Guthrie & Co. v. American-West African Line, 189
Balize, The, 794
Baltimore S. S. Co. v. Phillips, 344, 358
Baltimore Towing Co., United States v., 774
Banco Espanol de Credito v. State Street Bank and Trust Co., 121
Bangor, The City of, 849
Bankers Trust v. Hudson River Day Line, 662
Bank of East Asia v. Pang, 129
Bank of Italy v. Colla, 99, 113, 168
Bank of Italy v. Merchants' Nat. Bank, 122
Bank of New Bedford v. Dirigo First, 682
Bank of Nova Scotia v. San Miguel, 112
Banks v. Chicago Grain Trimmers Ass'n, Inc., 416
Barclay's Bank D.C.O. v. Mercantile Nat. Bank, 115
Bard v. The Silver Wave, 750
Baretich v. United States, 543
Barge Cape Flattery I, United States v., 764
Barge NL-5, p. 894
Barge Shamrock, The, 833
Barge ST-15, The, 619
Barge TJ-248, p. 682
Barkas v. Cia Naviera Coronado, 533, 567
Bark San Fernando v. Jackson, 265
Bark San Fernando v. Jackson and Manson, 25
Barnard v. Adams, 245, 256
Barnouw v. S/S Ozark, 723
Barnstable, The, 36, 242, 498, 600, 611, 616
Barr v. Int'l Mercantile Marine Co., 158
Barracuda Tanker Corp., In re, 822, 823, 841
Barrett, In re, 488, 516
Barrett v. Bank of the Manhattan Co., 133
Barrios v. Louisiana Constr. Materials Co., 334, 339
Bartholomew v. Universe Tankships, Inc., 474
Bartlette v. The Viola, 626
Basic Boats, Inc. v. United States, 534, 547, 556
Baskin v. Industrial Accident Commission, 421
Bassis v. Universal Line, 605
Baun v. The Ethel G., 614
Beach Salvage Corp. of Florida v. The Cap't Tom, 549
Beaconsfield, The, 528
Beadle v. Spencer, 353, 385
Beaverbrook, The v. The Kafiristan, 553
Beaverton, The, 516
Beck v. The Vizcaya, 168
Bekris v. M/V Aristoteles, 480
Belden v. Chase, 489, 499, 509, 523
Belgenland, The, 489
Bella, The, 637
Belle of Portugal, 73
Belleville, The, 861
Belvedere v. Compania Plomari De Vapores, S. A., 216, 637
Benefactor, The, 852, 937
Bergren v. Davis, 726
Benjamin v. United States, 775

Benjamin Noble, The, 151
Benson v. American Export Isbrandtsen Lines, Inc., 357
Bentaloe v. Pratt, 66
Bentley v. Albatross S. S. Co., 291
Benton v. United Towing Co., 302
Bergeria v. Marine Carriers, Inc., 288, 296
Bergeron v. K. L. M. Royal Dutch Airlines, 846
Bergren v. Davis, 724, 813
Berizzi Bros. v. S. S. Pesaro, 985
Berke v. Lehigh Marine Disposal Corp., 299
Bertel v. Panama Transp. Co., 542
Berwind-White Coal Mining Co. v. City of New York, 28
Bethlehem, 717
Bethlehem Steel Co. v. Moore, 421
Bethlehem Steel Corp. v. Yates, 598
Bethulia, The, 747
Beverly Hills Nat. Bank & Trust Co. v. Compania de Navegacione Almirante S. A. Panama, 631
B. F. Guinan, The, 526
Biays v. Chesapeake Ins. Co., 75
Biggs v. Norfolk Dredging Co., 435
Bird of Paradise, The, 187, 190, 215, 632
Bishop v. Great Lakes Towing Co., 739
Bishop & Co., v. Midland Bank, 99, 113, 168
Bisso v. Inland Waterways Corp., 147, 199, 516, 521
Bjornefjord, The, 235
Black Diamond S. S. Corp. v. Robert Stewart & Sons, 941
Black Diamond S. S. Co v. United States, Petitions of, 941
Black Eagle and Concordia, The, 914
Black Gull, The, 895
Blackheath, The, 523
Black Swan—The Flying Arrow, The, 548
Blackwell, The, 532, 537
Blair v. M/V Blue Spruce, 635
Blaireau, The, 542, 566, 568
Blake v. Delaware & Hudson R. Co., 308
Blake v. Farrell Lines, Inc., 296
Blanchard Lumber Co. v. S. S. Anthony II, 156
Blatz Brewing Co. v. Richardson and Richardson, 113
Bloomfield S. S. Co. Petition of, 529, 851, 863, 913, 945, 946
Blouin v. American Export Isbrandtsen Lines, Inc., 291
Blue Goose, The, 542
Blunk v. Wilson Line of Washington, Inc., 855, 858
B. M. Heed, Inc. v. Roberts, 128
Boatel, Inc. v. Delamare, 283, 435, 436
Bogart v. The John Jay, 27, 688
Bold Buccleugh, The, 36, 187, 498, 595
Bonifay and Levan v. The Paraporti, 536, 582
Booth S. S. Co. v. Tug Dalzell No. 2, p. 787
Boraks, Petition of, 866
Borax Consolidated, United States v., 995
Borup v. Western Operating Corp., 228
Boston Iron & Metal Co. v. The Winding Gulf, 524
Boston Marine Ins. Co. v. Metropolitan Redwood Lumber Co., 928
Boston Metals Co. v. The Winding Gulf, 147, 517, 521
Boston, The, 795
Boudoin v. Lykes Bros. S. S. Co., Inc., 348, 398, 399, 400
Boudoin v. McDermott & Co., 488
Bouker Contracting Co. v. Proceeds of Sale of Dredging Machine, 795
Bournemouth, The, 629
Bournias v. Atlantic Maritime Co., 777, 778
Boyer v. The Merry Queen, 494
Bradlie v. Maryland Ins. Co., 57, 84, 85, 226
Bradshaw v. The Virginia, 503
Brady v. S. S. African Queen, 536, 563, 565
Braen v. Pfeifer Oil Transportation Co., 328
Brahms v. Moore-McCormack Lines, Inc., 303
Brandon v. S/S Denton, 701, 718
Branic v. Wheeling Steel Corp., 347
Brazil Oiticica v. The Bill, 188
Breeze, The, 861
Bremen, The, 192
Bremen, The v. Zapata Off-Shore Co., 520
Breving v. The Lloyd Cuarto, 558, 562, 564
Brig Malek Adhel, United States v. 36, 592
Brimstone, The, 745
Brinton, The, 849
Britiannia, The, 504
British S. S. Co. v. Clarke, 650
British Trans. Commission v. United States, 846, 938
British West Indies Produce, Inc. v. S/S Atlantic Clipper, 166, 601
Brittan v. Barnaby, 22
Brock v. S/S Southampton, 115, 626, 663
Broere v. $2,133, p. 539

Bromfield Mfg. Co. v. The Yacht Brown, Jones and Smith, 605
Brooklyn Eastern District Terminal v. United States, 526
Brown v. Margrande Compania Naviera, 578
Brown v. Wilkinson, 906
Brown & Root, Inc. v. American Home Assur. Co., 91
Brown & Root Marine Operators, Inc. v. Zapata Offshore Co., 918
Brunswick, The, 165
Bryer v. Erie R. Co., 415
Btesh v. Royal Ins. Co. of Liverpool, 62
Bucolo, Inc. v. F/V Jaguar, 492
Bulkley v. Naumkeag Steam Cotton Co., 186, 216, 637
Bulkley v. Protection Ins. Co., 66
Bullard v. Roger Williams Ins. Co., 63
Bulley, The, 629
Bundy v. Meyer, 104
Burdine v. Walden, 625, 659
Burgess v. Equitable Marine Ins. Co., 66
Burke v. Gateway Clipper, Inc., 301, 350, 776.
Burn Line v. United States & A. S. S. Co., 210
Burns Bros. v. The Carfloat Central R. Co. of N. J. #42, pp. 498, 602, 613
Burstein v. United States Lines Co., 836
Burt v. Brewers' & Malsters' Ins. Co., 83, 193
Burton S. S. Co., In re, 657
Bushey & Sons, Inc. v. Barge B. & B. No. 5 & Hedger Transp. Corp., 799
Bushey & Sons, Inc. v. Standard Oil Co. of Cal., 500
Busy—The Richards, The, 534, 548
Butler v. Boston & Savannah S. S. Co., 649, 837, 846
Butler v. Ellis, 810
Butler v. Whiteman, 332

# C

Cabot Corp. v. S. S. Mormacscan, 149
Cachemire, The, 537, 543
Caddy v. Texaco, Inc., 382
Cain v. Bowater's Newfoundland Pulp & Paper Mills, Ltd., 851
Calbeck v. Travelers Ins. Co., 421, 432, 464
Caldarola v. Eckert, 51, 461
Caldas, Complaint of, 840, 879, 895, 897
Caledonia, The, 151, 208
California & Eastern S. S. Co. v. 138,000 Feet of Lumber, 216, 631
California Conserving Co. v. D'Avanzo, 96
California Navigation & Imp. Co., Re, 928
California Yacht Club of Los Angeles v. Johnson, 852, 853
Calmar S. S. Corp. v. Scott, 16, 55, 56, 72, 77, 84, 85, 195, 226
Calmar S. S. Corp. v. Taylor, 288, 293, 300
Calmar S. S. Corp. v. United States, 983, 985
Camanche, The, 537, 544
Campbell v. The Donbass, 547, 551
Canada S. S. Lines, Petition of, 820, 853, 860
Canada Sugar-Refining Co. v. Insurance Co. of North America, 85
Canadian Aviator v. United States, 600, 616, 984
Canadian Pacific Ry., Petition of, 846
Canal Barge Co., Petition of, 372, 373, 374, 487
Candee v. Sixty-Eight Bales of Cotton, 543
Cannella v. Lykes Brothers S. S. Co., 906
Cannella v. United States, 242
Cantwell v. Meade, 855
Cape Horn, The, 566
Capitaine Faure, The, 638
Capitol Transp. Co. v. Cambria Steel Co., 151, 209, 899
Carbone v. Ursich, 526
Carbon Slate Co. v. Ennis, 207
Carcich v. Rederi A/B Nordie, 196
Cardillo v. Liberty Mutual Ins. Co., 413
Cardy, The, 578
Cargo ex Port Victor, The, 578
Caribbean Maritime Finance Co. v. Marina Mercante Nicaraguense, S.A., 634, 637, 683
Carib Prince, The, 152, 208
Carle & Montanari, Inc. v. American Export Isbrandtsen Lines, Inc., 149
Carlisle Packing Co. v. Sandanger, 390, 457
Carlotta, The, 613
Carolina, The, 628
Carr v. Austin & N. W. R. Co., 219
Carr v. Security Ins. Co., 83, 193
Carver, United States v., 674, 675
Catharine, The v. Dickinson, 492, 526, 528, 531
Caterpillar Overseas, S. A. v. S. S. Expeditor, 142, 148, 160.
Carnation Co. v. Pacific Westbound Conference, 12
Catskill, The, 928
Centaurus, The, 626

Central R. Co. of New Jersey, In re, 809, 874
Central R. Co. of New Jersey v. Wren, 928
Central States, The, 849
Centrosoyus-America, Inc. v. United States, 178
Ceres, The, 231
Cerro De Pasco Copper Corp. v. Knut Knutsen, 146
Certain Subfreights of The Neponset, United States v., 793
Chadade Steamship Co., Petition of, 846, 936, 943
Chadwicke, The, 219, 222
Chamberlain v. Ward, 510
Chaparral, The, 856
Chapman v. City of Grosse Point Farms, 30
Charbonnier, United States v., 161
Charles Pfizer & Co. v. 912 Bags of Tarter and 58 Bags of Uva Ursi Leaves, 254
Charlotte, The, 612
Charter Shipping Co. v. Bowring, Jones, & Tidy, 51, 253
Chase v. Hammond Lumber Co., 59
Chattahoochee, The, 945
Chelentis v. Luchenback S. S. Co., 51, 325, 456, 457
Chellew v. Royal Commission on Sugar Supply, 264
Chemical Bank New York Trust Co. v. S/S Westhampton, 697
Chemical Carrier, Inc. v. L. Smit & Co.'s Internationale Sleepdienst, 568
Chesapeake Bay Bridge & Tunnel District v. Oil Screw Prince, 894
Chester, The, 627
Chicago, Burlington & Quincy R. R. v. The W. C. Harms, 523
Chicago, M., etc. R. Co. v. Acme Freight, 14
Chickasaw, The, 887, 892, 894, 898
Chickie, The, 855, 857
Chilean Line, 395
Chilean Nitrate Sales Corp. v. The Nortuna, 220
China, The, 36, 498, 520, 521, 601, 616
China Union Lines v. A. O. Andersen & Co., 497, 894
Chinese Maritime Trust, Ltd., Complaint of, 822, 849, 933, 935
Chiswick Products v. S. S. Stolt Avance, 162
Chiswick, The, 650
Christobal Colon, The, 629
Christophersen v. Donald S. S. Co., 230
Church Cooperage Co. v. Pinkney, 208
Cia. Atlantica Pacifica S. A. v. Humble Oil & Refining Co., 245, 251, 252, 630
Ciconett v. Home Ins. Co., 67, 75
Cimbria, The, 626
C. I. T. Corp. v. M/V Miss Eileen, 727
C. I. T. Corp. v. Oil Screw Peggy, 513, 731
Cities Service Oil Co. v. Puerto Rico Lighterage Co., 773
Cities Service Transp. Co. v. Gulf Oil Refining Co., 206
Citta Di Messina, The, 183
City Bank Farmers Trust Co. v. Hudson River Navigation Corp., 814
City of. See name of City
City of Alexandria, The, 524
City of Athens, The, 637, 738, 747, 748, 749, 786, 790, 791
City of Camden, The, 626, 634
City of New York, The, 493, 530
City of Norwich, The, 752, 852, 907, 908, 909
City of Pittsburgh, The, 623
City of Portland, The, 545
City of Tawas, The, 733, 735, 745, 746
City Stores Co. v. Sun Ins. Co., 58
Civil v. Waterman S. S. Corp., 361, 364
Civilta, The, 516
C. J. Hendry Co. v. Moore, 38
Clandeboye, The, 579
Clara, The, 492, 532, 551
Clarita, The, 532, 551
Clark, Ex parte, 625
Clark v. Barnwell, 140, 141
Clark v. Barnwell & Ravenal, 162
Clarke S. S. Co. v. Munson S. S. Line, 165
Claussen v. Mene Grande Oil Co., 773
Claveresk, The, 224, 239
Clearfield Trust Co. v. U. S., 463
Cleirac, Us et Coutumes de la Mer, 631
Clemens Horst & Co. v. Biddell Bros., 114
Cleveco, The, 888
Cleveland, T. & V. R. Co. v. Cleveland S. S. Co., 522
Clipper Fishing Corp., Petition of, 852
Clipper, The, 852
Clyde Commercial S. S. Co. v. West India S. S. Co., 234, 238
Coast Wrecking Co. v. Phoenix Ins. Co., 25, 81
Coggs v. Bernard, 556
Colby v. Todd Packing Co., 539
Coles v. Marine Ins. Co., 73
Collie v. Fergusson, 604, 605, 606
Collier Advertising Service, Inc. v. Hudson River Day Line, 697, 708, 814

Collins v. The Ft. Wayne, 738
Colonial Trust Co., Petition of, 840, 849
Colonna's Shipyard, 763
Colonna's Shipyard v. Rowe, 761
Colorado, The, 698, 701
Columbian Ins. Co. v. Ashby & Stribling, 254, 257
Columbian Ins. Co. v. Catlett, 66
Comegys v. Vasse, 91
Commercial Molasses Corp. v. New York Tank Barge Corp., 208
Commercio Transito Internationale, Ltd. v. Lykes Bros. Steamship Co., 145
Commissioners v. Valverda, 581
Commonwealth v. King, 33
Compagnia de Navegazione Rome v. Kulukundis, 215
Compagnia Maritima La Empresa v. Pickard, 626
Compagnie de Navigation Fraissinet and Cyprien Fabre, S. A. v. Mondial United Corp., 162
Compagnie Francaise de Navigation v. Bonnasse, 29
Compagnie Francaise de Navigation a Vapeur v. Bonnasse, 25, 81
Companhia de Navegacao Lloyd Brasileiro v. Evans Coffee Co., 846
Compania Anonima Venezolana de Navegacion v. A. J. Perez Export Co., 783
Compania de Maderas, etc. v. T/S Queenston Heights, 493, 495, 503
Compania de Navegacion Interior, S. A. v. Fireman's Fund Ins. Co., 65
Compania de Navigacion La Flecha v. Brauer, 141, 199
Compania De Vapores Insco, S. A. v. Missouri Pac. R. Co., 163
Compania Maritima Astra, S. A. v. Archdale, 90
Compania Transatlantica Centroamericana, S. A. v. Alliance Asur. Co., 63, 72
Compania Trasatlantica v. Charles Pfizer & Co., 254
Conard v. Atlantic Ins. Co., 633
Conard v. Nicoll, 633
Conklin v. City of Norwalk, 523
Connecticut Fire Ins. Co. v. Davison Chemical Corp., 56, 57, 226
Conners Marine Co., Petition of, 861
Connors v. Brown S. S. Co., 33
Conolly v. S. S. Karina II, 546, 558, 566, 568
Conron Bros. & Co. v. Farmers' Loan & Trust Co., 769
Consumers Import Co. v. Kabushiki Kaisha Kawasaki Zosenjo, 894, 927
Continental Grain Co. v. Armour Fertilizer Works, 215
Continental Grain Co. v. Barge FBL–585, pp. 614, 616
Continental Grain Co. v. City of Buffalo, 46, 890, 930
Continental Grain Co. v. Federal Barge Lines, Inc., 800
Continental Grain Co. v. Toko Lines, 637
Continental Ins. Co. v. Byrne, 417
Continental Ins. Co. v. Clayton Hardtop Skiff, 545
Continental Oil Co. v. The London Steam-Ship Owners' Mutual Insurance Association, Ltd., 911
Continental Sea Foods, Inc. v. New Hampshire Fire Ins. Co., 70
Continex, Inc. v. S. S. Flying Independent & Isbrandtsen Co., Inc., 123
Converse & Co., 881
Conveyor, The, 623, 738
Cook v. Belden Concrete Products, Inc., 34, 334
Cooley v. Board of Wardens of Port of Philadelphia, 598
Cooper v. Allison, 859
Cooper v. Pinedo, 216
Copco Steel & Engineering Co. v. The Prins Frederik Hendrik, 168
Cope v. Vallette Dry-Dock Co., 33, 334, 538
Copelin v. Phoenix Ins. Co., 85
Cordova, United States v., 34
Cornell Steamboat Co., United States v., 562, 577
Corrado Societa Anonima Di Navigazione v. L. Mundet & Son, 251, 268
Corsair, The, 649
Corsair v. J. D. Spreckels & Bros. Co., 158
Cortes v. Baltimore Insular Line, 311, 376
Cory Bros. & Co. v. United States, 26
Coryell v. Phipps, 877, 886, 897
Cosmopolitan Shipping Co. v. McAllister, 337, 462
Costanzo Transp. Co. v. American Barge Line Co., 541
Cowles Towing Co. v. Grain Transit Corp., 576, 577
Coyle & Co. v. North America S. S. Corp., 655
Coyle Lines v. United States, 491
Cox v. Roth, 352
Crain v. American Waterways Corp., 625
Cranberry Creek Coal Co. v. Red Star Towing & Transp. Co., 487
Crawford v. West India Carriers, Inc., 535

Crawford Bros. No. 2, The, 623
C. R. Hoyt, The, 509
Crisp v. U. S. & Australasia S. S. Co., 599
Crofton Diesel Engine Co. v. Puget Sound Nat. Bank of Tacoma, 711
Cromwell v. Slaney, 242
Crookham v. Muick, 471
Crooks v. United States, 308, 309
Cross v. The Kaimana, 627
Cross Contracting Co. v. Law, 915, 918
Crossman v. Burrill, 217
Crosson v. N. V. Stoomvaart Mij "Nederland", 70
Crosson v. Vance, 30
Crowell v. Benson, 412
Crow's Nest II A, The, 883
Crumady v. The J. H. Fisser, 387, 444
Crustacean, The, 634
Crustacean Transportation Corp. v. Atalanta Trading Corp., 634, 667, 680
Crustacea, The, 667, 680
Cruz v. Harkna, 483
Cuba Distilling Co., Petition of, 914, 949
Cullen Fuel Co. v. W. E. Hedger, Inc., 899, 904
Cummings v. Redeeriaktieb Transatlantic, 775
Cummins Diesel Michigan, Inc. v. The Falcon, 43
Cunard Steamship Co. v. S/S Caribia, 605
Curtis Bay Towing Co. v. The Fairwill, 530
Curtis Bay Towing Co. v. Tug Kevin Moran, Inc., 864, 865, 936
Cushing, The—The Proteces, 913
Cusumano v. The Curlew, 491, 500, 509
Cutler v. Rae, 24, 25, 81
Cuyamel Fruit Co. v. The Pelotas, 956
Cyc, The, 853
Cypria, The, 163
Cyrus, The, 384
Czaplicki v. S. S. Hoegh Silvercloud, 771

# D

Dabney v. New England Mutual Marine Ins. Co., 259
Dalmas v. Stathatos, 533, 567
Dampskibsselskabet Atlanta A/S v. United States, 521
Dampskibsselskabet Dannebrog v. Signal Oil & Gas Co., 36, 230, 667, 674
Daniel Ball, The, 32
Daniels Towing & Dry Dock, Inc., United States v., 684
Dann v. Dredge Sandpiper, 623
Danner v. United States, 558
D'Aprille v. Turner-Looker Co., 103
Dardar v. State of Louisiana, 308, 310
Dassigienis v. Cosmos Carriers & Trading Corp., 470
Dauntless, The, 800, 865
David Crystal, Inc. v. Cunard Steamship Co., 93, 148
Davidson S. S. Co. v. 119,254 Bushels of Flaxseed, 631
Davies v. Rijneers, 660
Davis, Petition of, 882
Davis v. City of Jacksonville Beach, 30
Davis v. Department of Labor and Industries of Washington, 420
Davis v. Mills, 779
Davis v. M/V Esso Delivery No. 13, p. 602
Davis v. Parkhill-Goodloe Co., 873
Davis v. United States, 32, 882
Davis v. United States Gas Screw Nolla Dare, 662
Davison v. Von Lingen, 200, 201
Davison Chemical Corp. v. The Henry W. Card, 240
Dawn, The, 682
Dayton v. Parke, 220
D. C. Andrews & Co. v. United States, 29
Dean v. Waterman S. S. Corp., 564, 567, 798, 802
De Bardeleben Marine Corp. v. United States, 984
Deep Sea Tankers v. The Long Branch, 855, 917
Defender, The, 865
Defense Plant Corp. v. U. S. Barge Lines, Inc., 810
Delaware River Pilots Ass'n, Petition of, 851
Delaware, The, 173, 504
Delaware, The—The Corner Brook, 851
Delgado v. S/S Malula, 774
De Lovio v. Boit, 1, 11, 20, 21, 42, 53
Delta Supply v. Liberty Mutual Ins., 84
Demko, United States v., 284
Demsey and Associates, Inc. v. S. S. Sea Star, 186, 233, 602
Denali, The, 988
Denholm Shipping Co. v. W. E. Hedger Co., 200, 201, 229
Denton, The, 701
Department of Highways v. Jaknke Service, Inc., 937
Desmond v. United States, 300, 324
Desper v. Starved Rock Ferry Co., 331
Det Forenede Dampskibs Selskab v. Insurance Co. of North America, 249, 265, 630
Detroit Trust Co. v. The Thomas Barlum, 633, 691, 693, 702

DeVane, United States v., 550, 555, 556, 979
Devine v. F/V Hornet, 577
Devine v. S/S Irini Stefanou, 583
Devine v. S. T. Ellin, 544, 565
Dexter & Carpenter Co. v. United States, 201
De Zon v. American President Lines, 311
D. H. Miller, The, 488
Diamond S. S. Transp. Corp. v. Peoples Sav. Bank & Trust Co., 860
Diamond State Tel. Co. v. Atlantic Refining Co., 502, 524
Diana Compania Maritima, S. A. v. Subfreights of the S/S Admiralty Flyer, 632, 813
Diaz v. S/S Seathunder, 629
Diesel Tanker A/C Dodge, Inc., Petition of, 851, 922, 930
Diesel Tug Shinn, The, 914
Dietrich v. United States Shipping Board, 178
Dimas v. Lehigh Valley R. Co., 395
Director General of India Supply Mission v. S. S. Maru, 494
Director, The, 632
Dixilyn Drilling Corp. v. Crescent Towing & Salvage Co., 519
Dixon v. United States, 397
Dixon, Irmaos & Cia. Ltda. v. Chase Nat. Bank, 127
Dize v. Steel Barge Beverly, 570
D'Oench, Duhme & Co. v. Federal Deposit Ins. Corp., 463
Dodge, The, 923
Dodge—The Michael, The, 851
Dollins v. Pan-American Grace Airways, 843
Dominguez v. Schooner Brindicate, 551
Donaldson v. McDowell, 631
Donaldson Atlantic Line, Petition of, 846
Donali, The, 849
Donbass, The, 543
Donnelly, Petition of, 861
Donnelly v. Brown, 861
Doris Kellogg, The, 879
Dorsid Trading Co. v. S. S. Rose, 123
Double D Dredging Co., Petition of, 872
Doucette v. Vincent, 347, 469
Dougherty Co. v. United States, 516, 554
Dow Chemical Co. v. Barge UM-23B, p. 556
Dow Chemical Co. v. Dixie Carriers, Inc., 32
Doyle v. Albatross Tanker Corp., 364
Draco, The, 633
Drevas v. United States, 542
DuBose v. Matson Navigation Co., 356
Duc d'Aumale, The, 553
Duche v. Thomas & John Brockelbank, 163
Duchess, The, 793
Dudley v. Bayou Fabricators, 29
Duff v. Merritt, 564
Dugas v. National Aircraft Corp., 365
Duke of York, 938
Dunleavy v. Tietjen & Land Dry Docks, 434
Dunn v. Wheeler Shipbuilding Corp., 23
Dunton v. Allan S. S. Co., 487
DuPont de Nemours v. S. S. Mormacvega, 182
Du Pont de Nemours & Co. v. Vance, 24, 81, 630, 741

# E

Eagle Star & British Dominions v. Tadlock, 56
Eagle Star & British Dominions Ins. Co. v. George Moore & Co., 63
Eagle, The, 32
Earle & Stoddart v. Ellerman Wilson Line, 878, 899
Earles v. Union Barge Line Corp., 389
Earnmoor S. S. Co. v. New Zealand Ins. Co., 263
Eastern Marine Corp. v. Fukaya Trading Co., 196, 229
Eastern Mass. St. Ry. Co. v. Transmarine Corp., 206
Eastern Shore, The, 614, 755, 780
Eastern S. S. Co. v. International Harvester Co. of N. J., 494, 528, 530
Eastern S. S. Lines v. United States, 984
Eastern S. S. Lines, United States v. 525
Eastern Transp. Co. v. United States, 631, 982
Eastland, The, 572
Easton, Ex parte, 20, 21, 22
East River Towing Co., In re, 846
Eclipse, The, 41, 43
Economu v. Bates, 28
Eddy, The, 216, 631
Edith, The, 747, 794
Edmond Weil, Inc. v. American West African Line, Inc., 153
Edmund Fanning, The, 130, 160, 879, 895
Edward Pierce, The, 243
Edward, The, 846
Edwards v. Elliott, 650
Egan v. A Cargo of Spruce Lath, 631
Egeria, The, 658
Elefteriou v. Tanker Archontissa, 480
Elfrida, The, 582
Eliza Lines, The, 217, 222

Ella Warley—North Star, The, 498
Elna II—The Mission San Francisco, The, 847, 901
El Sol, 878
Elton, The, 628
Ely v. Murray & Tregurtha Co., 655
Ely & Walker Dry Goods Co. v. Adams Mfg. Co., 104
Ema v. Compagnie Generale Transatlantique, 912
Emblem, The, 575
Emilia S. De Perez, The, 25, 81
Emily B. Souder, The, 742
Emma Giles, The, 708
Emma Kate Ross, The, 489, 526
Empire Seafoods, Inc. v. Anderson, 527, 894
Empire Stevedoring Co. v. Oceanic Adjusters Ltd., 252, 808, 811
Empire Transp. Co. v. Philadelphia & R. Coal & Iron Co., 213
Empresa Central Mercantil de Representacoes v. Republic of the United States of Brazil, 123
Empresa Nacional "Elcano" v. M/V Tropicana, 604, 606
Encyclopedia Britannica, Inc. v. S. S. Hong Kong Producer, 144, 145, 176, 182, 183, 185
Engel v. Davenport, 340, 350
England Transp. Co., In re, 748
Enochasson v. Freeport Sulphur Co., 309
Epstein v. Corporacion Peruana de Vapores, 682
Ereza, The, 560
Erie & St. Lawrence Corp. v. Barnes Ames Co., 151, 152
Erie, City of v. S/S North American, 603, 623
Erie R. Co. v. Tompkins, 51, 70, 318, 324, 459, 499, 720
Ermis, The, 759
Ernest Constr. Co. v. The Tug Commodore, 487
E. S. Atwood, The, 904
Eskine v. United Barge Co., 444
Esrom, The, 638
Essex County Electric Co. v. Motor Ship Godafoss, 521
Essex S. S. Co. v. Langbehn, 226
Esso Belgium, The, United States v., 173
Esso Copenhagen, The, 542
Esso Export Corp. v. The Cortes, 684
Esso Greensboro, The, 554, 565, 574
Esso International v. S/S Captain John, 667, 683
Esso Seattle—The Guam Bear, The, 849, 913
Esso Shipping Co., Petition of, 554, 565, 574
Esso Standard Oil Co. v. United States, 79
Estrada Palma, The, 165, 742
Ethel, The, 805
Ethel V. Stowman, The, 795
Eugene F. Moran, The, 607
Eugenia Emilia, The, 759
Eurana, The, 633
Evangelistria Shipping Corp., Petition of, 939
Evansville & Bowling Green Packet Co. v. Chero Cola Bottling Co., 33, 843
Everett Steamship Corp., S/A v. Liberty Navigation & Trading Co., 787
Everosa, The, 765, 766, 782, 786
Executive Jet Aviation, Inc. v. City of Cleveland, 26, 31, 541
Export S. S. Corp. v. American Ins. Co., 57, 226

# F

Fairisle, The, 564, 567, 798, 802, 803
Fair Pavillions, Inc. v. First Nat. City Bank, 115, 119
Fannie F. Hickey, The, 658
Fanny, The, 744
Far East Conference v. United States, 995
Farnarjian v. American Export Isbrandtsen Lines, Inc., 382
Farr v. Hain S. S. Co., 202, 209
Farragut, The, 494
Farrell v. United States, 287, 290, 309
Farr Sugar Corp., United States v., 173
Favorite, The, 711, 712, 785
Fearless, The, 562
Fecht v. Makowski, 863, 883
Federal Maritime Board v. Isbrandtsen Co., 992
Federal Maritime Comm. v. Aktiebolaget Svenska Am. L., 12
Federal No. 2, The, 316, 319
Federazione Italiana dei Consorzi Agrari v. Mandask Compania de Vapores, 891
F. E. Grauwiller Transp. Co. v. The Scow Jeanne, 684
Feinberg v. Insurance Co. of North America, 74
Feldman v. American Palestine Line, 627
Felicione & Sons Fish Co. v. Citizens Cas. Co. of N. Y., 74
Feltre, 583
Fematt v. City of Los Angeles, 523
Fenwick Island, Inc., Petition of, 852

Ferdinand R. Hassler, The, 566
Ferguson, Petition of, 882
Ferrante v. Detroit Fire & Marine Ins. Co., 55, 75, 195
Ferryboat West Point, The, 611
Fey v. Jewell, 768
F. H. Stanwood, The, 738
Fidelity & Cas. Co. v. C/B Mr. Kim, 773
Fidelity & Cas. Co. of New York v. Grigsby, 441, 445, 532
Fidelity Nat. Bank of Baton Rouge v. M/T Richlube, 753
Fidelity-Phenix Ins. Co. v. Chicago Title & Trust Co., 67
Fidelity Phoenix Fire Ins. Co. v. Flota Mercante Del Estado, 896
Field Line v. South Atlantic S. S. Line, 233
50,000 Feet of Timber, 538
Findley v. Red Top Super Markets, 682
Fink v. Shepard S. S. Co., 337
Fireman's Charitable Ass'n v. Ross, 543
Fireman's Fund Ins. Co. v. City of Monterey, 23
Firestone Synthetic Fibers v. M/S Black Heron, 158
First Federal Savings & Loan Ass'n of Puerto Rico v. Zequiera, 724
First Nat. Bank of McClusky v. Rogers-Amundson-Flynn Co., 111
First Suffolk Nat. Bank of Huntington v. The Air Brant, 728
First Union Trust & Sav. Bank v. Consumers Co., 807, 814
Fisher's Hill, The, 533, 559, 562
Fitzgerald v. United States Lines Co., 279, 294, 295, 312, 348, 455, 470
Fitzgerald v. Westland Marine Corp., 482
Five Steel Barges, 578
Flanagan & Sons, Inc. v. Carken, 282
Fleming v. Lay, 545
Fletcher v. Keystone Tankship Corp., 291
Fletero, The v. Arias, 348, 479
Flink v. Paladini, 840
Flood, United States v., 763, 764
Florence, The, 542
Flores, United States v., 44
Florida Bahamas Lines v. Steel Barge "Star 800" of Nassau, 634, 784
Flota Maritima v. Motor Vessel Ciudad de la Habana, 26
FMC v. Aktiebolaget Svenska Amerika Linien, 993
Folmina, The, 163
Fontana, The, 510
Forest King, The, 790
Forrest E. Single, The, 802
Forster v. Insurance Co. of North America, 58
Fort Bragg, The, 852
Fort Gaines, The, 230, 627, 747
Fort George, The, 516
Fort Mercer, The, 866
Fort Myers Shell & Dredging Co., Inc. v. Barge NBC 512, pp. 545, 585
Fort Orange, The, 693, 714, 769, 794, 814, 815
Fort St. George, The, 509
Fortuna, The, 655
Forward v. Pittard, 163
Fosdick v. Schall, 603
Foster v. The Miranda, 528
Four Sisters, The, 362, 364
4,885 Bags of Linseed, 187, 216, 631
Foust v. Munson S. S. Lines, 809
Fra Berlanga, 537
Framlington Court, The, 520
Frances C. Denehy, The, 717
Francesco v. Massey, 217
Frangiskatos v. Konkar Maritime Enterprises, S. A., 478
Frank v. United States, 979
Frank Brainerd, The, 626
Frank C. Sparks Co. v. Huber Baking Co., 320
Frankel v. Foreman & Clark, Inc., 102, 103
Frank G. Fowler, The, 743
Franklin Ins. Co. v. Lord, 25
Franz Joseph, The, 715, 785
Fredelos v. Merritt-Chapman & Scott Corp., 284, 582, 736, 738, 753
Frederick H. Cone & Co. v. The Tai Shan, 179, 181
Frederick H. Leggett & Co. v. 500 Cases of Tomatoes, 630
Frederick Luckenbach, The, 846
Fred E. Sander, The, 628
Freedman v. The Concordia Star, 123
Freedom Line Inc. v. Vessel Glenrock, 626
Freights, etc., of The Mount Shasta, United States v., 623, 632
Freights of The Kate, 632
Frej, The, 566, 914, 949
Fretz v. J. C. Bull & Co., 32
Frey & Son v. United States, 677
Frey, The, 162, 183
Frost v. Saluski, 488
F. S. Loop, The, 660, 680
F/V Fenwick Island, The, 852
F/V Golden Dawn, United States v., 730
F/V Voyager, United States v., 732, 784
F/V Weymouth, 871
F/V Zarco, United States v., 660
F/V Zebroid, The, 841, 952

## G

Gallagher, United States v., 315, 322
Gans S. S. Line v. Wilhelmsen, 163, 165
Gardner v. Panama R. Co., 771
Garrett v. Moore-McCormack Co., 293, 459
Gas-Float Whitton (No. 2), The, 538
Gaudet v. Sea-Land Services, Inc., 370
Gavagan, United States v., 550, 555, 556
Gayner v. The New Orleans, 627
Gaynor v. Agwilines, Inc., 337
Gazelle, The, 203
Geertson v. United States, 555
Geisha, The, 655
General v. Pilots' Ass'n for the Bay and River Delaware, 598
General De Sonis, The, 629
General Foods Corp. v. The Troubador, 155, 184
General Foods Corp. v. United States, 166
General Hide & Skin Corp. v. United States, 178
General Interest Ins. Co. v. Ruggles, 59, 62
General Motors Overseas Operation v. S. S. Goettingen, etc., 191
General Petroleum Corp. v. Los Angeles, 598
General Seafoods Corp. v. J. S. Packard Dredging Co., 493, 530
General Smith, The, 22, 36, 406, 642, 647
Genesee Chief v. Fitzhugh, 32
Gentleman, The, 398
George v. Beavark, Inc., 844
George v. Chesapeake and Ohio R. Co., 283, 302, 308
George F. Hinrichs, Inc. v. Standard Trust & Sav. Bank, 111
George W. Fields, The, 865
George W. Roby, The, 928
Gerber v. Spencer, 627
German v. Carnegie-Illinois Steel Corp., 347
Germanic, The, 158
Gerradin v. United Fruit Co., 477
Gertrude Parker, Inc. v. Abrams, 505
Giamona v. Mineo, 487
Gianfala v. Texas Co., 332
Gilbert Knapp, The, 21
Gilchrist Transp. Co. v. Boston Ins. Co., 148, 160
Gillespie v. United States Steel Corp., 363
Giulia, The, 162
Giulio, The, 631
Gkiafis v. S. S. Yiosonas, 479, 483
Gladys, The, 515
Glass v. The Sloop Betsey, 20, 44
Glass & Co. v. Misroch, 102
Glenbogie, The, 881, 948
Glidden v. Manufacturers' Ins. Co., 66
Glidden Co. v. Hellenic Lines, 228
Glide, The, 50
Globe & Rutgers Fire Ins. Co. v. United States, 251, 268
Gloster v. Pennsylvania R. Co., 338
Gloucester, The, 626
Glover v. Philadelphia Ins. Co., 73
Godchaux Sugars, Inc. v. The Katherine, 633
Goett v. Union Carbide Corps., 366, 464
Gokey v. Fort, 900, 951
Gold v. Groves, 378
Gold Dust Corp. v. Munson S. S. Line, 151
Golden Dawn, The, 730, 731, 732
Golden Gate, The, 677
Golden Touch, The, 859
Gomes v. Eastern Gas & Fuel Associates, 293, 299, 315, 317, 320
Gondeck v. Pan American Airways, 416
Gooden v. Sinclair Refining Co., 284, 322
Goodwyn v. Dredge Ginger Ann, 774
Gore v. Clearwater Shipping Corp., 284, 288, 314, 322
Gottlieb's Claim, 866
Goulandris Bros., Petition of, 855
Goulandris, The, 817
Goumas v. K. Karras and Son, 26
Gow v. Gans S. S. Line, 235
Grace & Co. v. Charleston Lighterage & Transfer Co., 887, 892, 905
Grace & Co. v. Toyo Kisen Kabushiki Kaisha, 178
Grace Darling, The, 768
Gracie D. Chambers, The, 637
Grammenos v. Lemos and Nile Shipping Co., S. A., 480, 482
Grand Banks Fishing Co. v. Styron, 26
Grand Republic—The Nassau, The, 849
Grand Turk, The, 625
Grant-Smith-Porter Ship Co. v. Rohde, 419, 421
Grapeshot, The, 25, 690
Graselli and Windrush, The, 861
Grasselli Chemical Co. No. 4, The, 854, 861
Grasso v. Lorentzen, 395
Gray v. Hopkins-Carter Hardware Co., 799
Grays Landing Ferry Co. v. Stone, 844
G. R. Booth, The, 168
Great Atlantic & Pac. Tea Co. v. Lloyd Brasileiro, 879, 888, 889
Great Canton, The, 627

Great Lakes & Dredge Dock Co. v. Brown, 432
Great Lakes Dredge Co. v. Lynch, 871
Great Lakes Towing Co., Petition of, 894
Great Lakes Towing Co. v. American Shipbuilding Co., 516
Great Lakes Towing Co. v. Mill Transp. Co., 900
Great Lakes Towing Co. v. St. Joseph-Chicago S. S. Co., 739
Great Lakes Transit Corp., In re, 881, 948
Great Republic, The, 493, 530
Great Western Ins. Co. v. Fogarty, 83, 193
Great Western, The, 907, 908, 948
Greaud v. The Pueblo, 491
Green, Ex parte, 869, 870
Greene v. United States, 566
Greene v. Vantage S. S. Corp., 372, 373, 374
Greenport Basin & Construction Co., v. Silkworth, 769
Green Star Shipping Co. v. London Assur., 264
Grigsby v. Coastal Marine Service of Texas, Inc., 441, 445, 532, 556, 617, 620
Grillea v. United States, 395, 617, 619
Grimes v. Raymond Concrete Pile Co., 332
Groban v. S. S. Pegu, 123
Gronvold v. Suryan, 29
Grow v. G/S Loraine K., 660
Guam Bear—The Esso Seattle, The, 574
Guaranty Trust Co. v. York, 778
Guaranty Trust Co., United States v., 131
Guggenheim, Petition of, 881
Guiding Star, The, 22, 625
Gulf Coast Marine Ways v. The J. R. Hardee, 712, 747, 750, 761
Gulf Oil Corp., Petition of, 365
Gulf Oil Corp. v. Panama Canal Co., 598
Gulf Oil Corp. v. United States, 510
Gulf Refining Co. v. Atlantic Mutual Ins. Co., 87, 90
Gulfstream Cargo v. Reliance Ins. Co., 62
Gulledge v. United States, 291
Gutierrez v. Waterman S. S. Corp., 23, 403, 524, 771
Guy v. Donald, 521
Guzman v. Pichirilo, 240, 616
Gylfe, The v. The Trujillo, 526
Gypsum Carrier, Inc. v. Handelsman, 308

## H

Haakonsen v. Lotosland Corp., 797
Hadjipateras v. Pacifica, S. A., 28, 43
Hagan v. Scottish Union & Nat Ins. Co., 62
Hagens v. United Fruit Co., 435
Hahn v. Ross Island Sand & Gravel Co., 432
Haiti Victory, The, 938
Hakonesan Maru, The, 598
Halcyon Lines v. Haenn Ship Ceiling & Refitting Corp., 315, 442, 464, 531
Hall & Co. v. Jefferson Ins. Co., 61, 62
Hall, The, 625
Hamburg-American Line v. United States, 547, 551
Hamilton, The, 48, 359, 364, 365
Handelfinanz A. G. v. S/T Evanthia, 634
H. & H. Wheel Service, Inc., Petition of, 882
Hanover Fire Ins. Co. v. Holcombe, 63
Hanseatische Reederei Emil Offen & Co. v. Marine Terminals Corp., 868
Hansen v. Perth Amboy Dry Dock Co., 434
Hanson v. Haywood Bros. & Wakefield Co., 158
Harbor Service Corp. v. United States, 680
Harbor Towing Corp., Complaint of, 829, 833, 850, 912
Harden v. Gordon, 25, 281, 289
Harmer v. Bell, 187
Haroco Co. v. The Tai Shan, 179, 181
Harriman, The, 210
Harriman v. Midland S. S. Line, 310
Harrisburg, The, 359, 649, 660
Harrison v. Hughes, 599
Harrison Overseas Corp. v. American Barge Sun Coaster, 709, 726
Hart v. Delaware Ins. Co., 59
Hartford Accident & Indemnity Co. v. Southern Pac. Co., 863, 875, 927, 934
Harvard, The, 658
H. A. Scandrett, The, 392
Haskell v. Socony Mobil Oil Co., 292
Haskins v. Point Towing Co., 286, 296, 471
Hatteras, The, 655
Haughton v. Blackships, Inc., 307
Havana, The, 900
Hawgood v. 1,310 Tons of Coal, 631
Hawgood & Avery Transit Co. v. Dingman, 799
Hawkhurst S. S. Co. v. Keyser, 165
Hawkins v. Bleakly, 405
Hawley v. Alaska S. S. Co., 378

Hazard's Adm'r v. New England Marine Ins. Co., 62, 73
Hazelton v. Luckenbach S. S. Co., 288
Healing & Son, Inc., Petition of, 936
Hearn v. Equitable Safety Ins. Co., 63, 200, 201
Hearne v. Marine Ins. Co., 66
Hearty v. Ragunda, 164
Hedger Transp. Corp. v. United Fruit Co., 500
Helen, The, United States v., 601
Helgar Corp. v. Warner's Features, Inc., 113
Hellenic Lines v. Embassy of Pakistan, 219
Hellenic Lines v. Rhoditis, 474
Heller & Co. v. M/V Mr. Ed., 714, 784
Heman v. Compagnie Generale Transatlantique, 163
Hendrick Hudson, The, 690
Hendry Corp. v. Aircraft Rescue Vessels, 545, 566
Hendy Corp. v. Clavel, 310
Henjes v. Aetna Ins. Co., 63, 67
Henjes Marine, Inc. v. White Const. Co., 238
Henry S. Grove, The, 657, 677
Henry, The, 579
Henry W. Breyer, The, 629, 711, 753
Herbert L. Rawding, The, 627
Hercules Co. v. The Brigadier General Absolom Baird, 27, 34, 623, 680
Herd & Co. v. Krawill Machinery Co., 149
Hershey Chocolate Corp. v. The S. S. Robert Luckenbach, 896, 898
Hertz v. Consolidated Fisheries, 504
Hess v. United States, 366, 464
Hess Shipping Corp. v. S. S. Charles Lykes, 513
Hewlett v. Barge Bertie, 524
Heye v. North German Lloyd, 249
H. F. Dimock, The, 524, 852
Higa v. Transocean Airlines, 40
Higgins, Inc. v. M/V Tri-State, 558, 566, 579
Highlands Navigation Corp., Petition of, 849
Hill v. Atlantic Navigation Co., 347, 378
Hills Bros. Co. v. United States, 262
Hilton v. Guyot, 790
Hinkins, S. S. Agency v. Freighters, Inc., 28
Hine, The, 649
Hine, The v. Trevor, 32, 38, 39, 646, 649
Hines v. Butler, 848, 879
Hirondelle, The, 623
Hirsch v. The San Pablo, 41
Hirsch Lumber Co. v. Weyerhaeuser S. S. Co., 166
His Majesty's Government, etc. v. The Flying Arrow, 548
Hobart v. Drogan, 542, 543
Hobson v. Lord, 262
Hockley v. Eastern Transp. Co., 879
Hogan & Sons Inc. v. L. Boyer's Sons Co., 904
Holden v. S. S. Kendal Fish, 147
Holland-Ameriklijn, 282
Holliday v. Pacific Atlantic S. S. Co., 310
Hollinsworth v. Seventy Doubloons & Three Small Pieces of Gold, 539
Home Ins. Co. of New York v. Merchants Transp. Co., 28
Homer Ramsdell Transp. Co. v. Compagnie Generale Transatlantique, 520, 599
Home, The, 747, 750, 756
Hooper v. Kunkler Transp. Co., 800
Hooper v. Robinson, 60, 62
Hope, The, 542, 543, 728, 729
Horn v. Cia de Navegacion Fruco, S. A., 152, 154, 159, 199, 200, 201, 208
Hoskyn & Co. v. Silver Line, 249, 267, 846, 896
Hostetter v. Park, 177, 190
Houseman v. Cargo of the Schooner North Carolina, 24
Howard v. Dobbins-Trinity Coal Co., 241
Huasteca Petroleum Co. v. United States, 563
Hudgins v. Gregory, 846, 855
Hudson v. New York & Albany Transp. Co., 806, 810
Hudson Valley Lightweight Aggregate Corp. v. Windsor Bldg. & Supply Co., 241
Hudspeth v. Atlantic & Gulf Stevedores, Inc., 283, 308, 314
Hugg v. Augusta Ins. & Banking Co., 58, 83
Hugg v. Baltimore & Cuba Smelting & Mining Co., 263
Hughes v. J. S. Hoskins Lumber Co., 211
Hughes v. Union Ins. Co., 66
Hugney v. Consolidation Coal Co., 301, 901
Humble Oil & Refining Co. v. Bell Marine Service, Inc., 852
Humble Oil & Refining Co. v. S/S Bay Belle, 629, 709, 715
Huron Portland Cement Co. v. Detroit, 832
Hurricane, The, 684

Hust v. Moore-McCormack Lines, Inc., 427, 461, 981
Hutchinson, Petition of, 861, 882
Hydaburg Cooperative Ass'n v. Alaska S. S. Co., 154
Hyperion's Cargo, The, 631

# I

I. C. White, The, 524
Igneri v. Cie. de Transports Oceaniques, 46
Impoco, The, 547
Indemnity Marine Assur. Co. v. Cadiente, 85
Indian Towing Co. v. United States, 979
India, The, 211
Indrani, The, 158
Indussa Corp. v. S. S. Ranborg, 146
Industrial Commission v. McCartin, 431
Industrial Y Frutera Colombiana v. The Brisk, 196
Inland Waterways Corp. v. Doyle, 284
Inman v. South Carolina R. Co., 176
Instituto Cubano De Estabilizacion Del Azucar v. The Golden West, 220
Insurance Co. v. Dunham, 20, 21, 22, 25, 55, 70, 81
Insurance Co. v. Lyman, 59
Insurance Co. v. Thwing, 67, 68
Insurance Co. of Pennsylvania, In re, 625
Insurance Co. of the Valley of Va. v. Mordecai, 58
Intagliata v. Shipowners & Merchants Towboat Co., 499
Intermondale Trading Co. v. North River Ins. Co., 73
International Convention on Load Lines, 987
International Drilling Co. v. M/V Deriefs, 182
International Marine Development Corp., In Complaint and Petition of, 575
International Nav. Co. v. Atlantic Mutual Ins. Co., 58, 89, 90, 261
International Nav. Co. v. Farr & Bailey Mfg. Co., 160
International Paper Co. v. The Schooner Gracie D. Chambers, 228, 637, 638
International Refugee Organization v. Maryland Drydock Co., etc., 635
International Stevedoring Co. v. Haverty, 278, 330, 439, 454
International Terminal Operating Co., Inc. v. S/S Valmas, 663, 687
Interocean S. S. Corp. v. Amelco Engineering Co., 28
Interstate No. 1, The, 740, 746, 748
Interstate No. 2, The, 746
Iona, The, 219
Ionian S. S. Co. of Athens v. United Distillers of America, Inc., 208
Iris, The, 665
Irmaos & Cia. Ltda. v. Chase Nat. Bank, 107
Iroquois, The, 310
Irrawaddy, The, 266, 269
Irving, The, 861
Irving Trust Co. v. S/S Golden Sail, 606
Irwin v. Eagle Star Ins. Co., 49
Irwin v. United States, 320
Isbrandtsen Co., Petition of, 130, 895
Isbrandtsen Co. v. Federal Ins. Co., 268
Isbrandtsen Co. v. Lloyd Brasiliero, 529
Isbrandtsen Co. v. United States, 22, 188
Isis, The, 152, 155
Island Yachts, Inc. v. Federal Pacific Lakes Line, 188
Isle of Mull, 237
Israel, State of v. M/V Nili, 683, 700
Isthmian S. S. Co. v. California Spray-Chemical Corp., 148, 160
Italia Societa per Azioni di Navigazione v. Oregon Stevedoring Co., 444

# J

Jack Nielson, Inc. v. Tug Peggy, 196
Jack-O-Lantern, The, 747
Jackson v. Inland Oil and Trans. Co., 38, 689, 714, 793
Jackson v. Lykes Brothers Steamship Co., 444
Jacob v. The Irving Trust Co., 807
James A. Dubbs, The, 871
James W. Follette, The, 739
Jane B. Corp., United States v., 627, 764
Jane B, The, 764
Janes v. Sackman Bros. Co., 777
Jappinen v. Canada Steamship Lines, Inc., 853, 860
Jason, The, 266, 537
Java, The, 486
J. B. Effenson Co. v. Three Bays Corp., 199, 209
J. C. Pfluger, The, 537
J. Doherty, The, 655
Jeanie, The, 156
Jeffcott v. Aetna Ins. Co., 84
Jefferson Chemical Co. v. M/T Grena, 196, 217, 219
Jefferson Myers, The, 315
Jefferson, The, 538
Jeffrey v. Henderson Bros., 661, 662
Jensen, Tallac Co. v. Pillsbury, 418
J. E. Rumbell, The, 689, 690

Jewell v. The Ohio River Co., 296, 301, 312.
J. Gerber & Co. v. S. S. Sabine Howaldt, 130
J. H. Senior, The, 922
J. K. Armsby Co. v. The Esrom, 638
J. K. Welding Co., Inc. v. Gotham Marine Corp., 799
Johansen v. United States, 284
John D. Rockefeller, The, 515, 516
John Francis, The, 640
John G. Stevens, The, 36, 46, 498, 627, 735, 739–741, 743, 752
John H. Cannon, The, 260
John J. Freitus, The, 745–747
John Perkins, The, 259
Johnson v. Oil Transp. Corp., 621, 623
Johnson v. United States, 284, 305, 306, 377
Johnson & Towers Baltimore, Inc. v. The Dredge, etc., 623
Johnson Lighterage Co., The, 568
Johnston-Warren Lines v. United States, 506
John T. Clark & Son v. Cunard Steam-Ship Co., 93
Jones v. Baton Rouge Marine Contractors, 436
Jones v. Lykes Bros. S. S. Co., Inc., 399
Jones v. The Flying Clipper, 181, 182
Jones v. Waterman S. S. Corp., 309, 316, 317
Jones Constr. Co. v. Niagara Fire Ins. Co., 82
Jordan, Inc. v. Mayronne Drilling Service, 209
Jordine v. Walling, 294, 469
Joseph J. Hock, The, 158
J. P. Donaldson, The, 259
J. R. Hardee, The, 635, 756, 761, 763, 764, 780–782, 784, 786
J. S. Gissel & Co., In re, 808, 811
Judith Lee Rose, The v. The Clipper, 541
Julia Fowler, The, 354
Julian v. Mitsui O. S. K. Lines, 446
Just v. Chambers, 651, 832, 935
J. W. Scott, The, 768

# K

Kahn v. Niagara Laundry & Linen Supply Co., 798
Kahului R. Co., Petition of, 863
Kaiser Co., Inc. v. Baskin, 421
Kaiser Wilhelm der Grosse, The, 568
Kalimian v. Liberty Mut. Fire Ins. Co., 61
Kamara v. The Atlantic Emperor, 26
Kanawha, The, 549
Kane v. M/V Leda, 633, 683, 686
Kane v. U. S. S. R., 772
Karobi Lumber Co. v. S. S. Norco, 243
Karran v. Peabody, 201
Kate, The, 669–672, 676, 678, 687
Kearney v. Savannah Foods & Industries, Inc., 480, 483
Keen v. Overseas Tankship Corp., 398
Keene v. The Whistler, 896
K–18, The, 684
Kelcey v. Tankers Co., Inc., 459
Kell v. Zermatten, 562
Keller v. Dravo Corp., 34
Kelly v. Washington, 987
Kendall Produce Co. v. Terminal Warehouse & Transfer Co., 97
Kenney v. New York Central & H. R. Co., 141
Kenny v. City of New York, 33, 241
Kermarec v. Compagnie Generale Transatlantique, 453, 464
Kernan v. American Dredging Co., 364, 375, 379, 454
Key City, The, 764, 769
Kibaudeaux v. Standard Dredging Co., 432
Kimes v. United States, 532, 546, 549, 566
Kimon, The, 939
King v. Aetna Ins. Co., 62
King v. Testerman, 30
King, Adm'r v. Liotti, 882
King Philip, The, 626
Kinsman Transit Co., Petition of, 46, 890, 904, 930
Kittelsaa v. United States, 549
Klarman, Petition of, 883, 939
Kloekner, etc. v. A/S Hakedal, 489, 942
Knapp, Stout & Co., The v. McCaffrey, 22, 37, 38
Knickerbocker Ice Co. v. Stewart, 48, 407
Knott v. Botany Worsted Mills, 146, 157
Kongo, The, 626, 635, 682–684
Koch-Ellis Marine Contractors, Inc. v. Phillips Petroleum Co., 27
Koistinen v. American Export Lines, Inc., 291
Koninklijke Nederlandsche Stoomboot Maatschappij v. Yglesias & Co., 41
Korthinos v. S. S. Niarchos, 25
Koslusky v. United States, 300, 305
Kossick v. United Fruit Co., 49, 303, 351, 464, 651
Kovell v. Portland Tug & Barge Co., 546
Krauss Bros. Lumber Co. v. Dimon S. S. Corp., 27, 638–640

Kuljis v. Union Marine & General Ins. Co., 73
Kulukundis v. Norwich Union Fire Ins. Society, 58
Kulukundis Shipping Co. v. Amtorg Trading Corp., 196, 198
Kunglig Jarnvagsstyrelsen v. Dexter & Carpenter, Inc., 110
Kupfermann v. United States, 184
Kurt Orban Co. v. S. S. Clymenia, 146
Kyriakos v. Goulandris, 478

# L

La Bourgogne, 879, 914, 929
Ladd, United States v., 497
Ladjimi v. Pacific Far East Line, Inc., 311, 312
Lafcomo, The, 181, 188
Lagonda, The, 526
Lago Oil & Trans. Co. v. United States, 533, 546, 559, 562
Lake Jackson State Bank v. O/S Kingfish Too, 712
Lakeland Transp. Co., Re, 928
Lakeland Transp. Co. v. Miller, 928
Lake Tankers Corp., Petition of, 871
Lake Tankers Corp. v. Henn, 866, 871, 917, 918, 936
Lamborn v. National Bank of Commerce, 112
Lambris v. Neptune Maritime Co., 482
Lambros Seaplane Base v. The Batory, 34, 265, 536, 540, 558, 576
Lamington, The, 544, 564
Lamp v. United States Steel Corp., 372, 373, 374
Lamprecht v. Cleveland-Erieau S. S. Co., 798
Lanasa Fruit S. S. & Importing Co. v. Universal Ins. Co., 73, 76
Landers, 807, 811, 813, 816
Lange v. Emery Co., 260, 261
Langnes v. Green, 867, 869, 921
La Normandie, 524
Lara, The, 914, 949
Larch, The, 626
Larios v. Victory Carriers, Inc., 773, 776
Larsen v. Insurance Co. of North America, 81
Larsen v. 150 Bales of Sisal Grass, 233, 632
Larsen v. New York Dock Co., 605
Larsen v. Northland Transp. Co., 852
LaRue v. United Fruit Co., 537
Latin American, The, 937
Latus v. United States, 617, 620
Laudisi v. American Exchange Nat. Bank, 122
Lauritzen v. Larsen, 52, 472, 534, 701, 943
Lauro v. Pennsylvania R. Co., 578
Lavinia D., The, 861, 871
Lawler v. Matson Nav. Co., 290
Lawrence v. Minturn, 260
Lawter, United States v., 555
Layton Industries, Inc. v. Gladiator, 667, 767
Learned v. Brown, 625
Leary v. United States, 242
Leather's Best, Inc. v. S. S. Mormaclynx, 148, 188
Lebec—The Seekonk, The, 598
Lee Point Landing, Inc. v. Alabama Dry Dock & Shipbuilding Co., 667
Le Gate v. The Panamolga, 775
Lehigh Valley R. Co. v. Jones, 948
Leith v. Oil Transport Co., 471
Lekas & Drivas, Inc. v. Goulandris, 170, 184
Lena Mowbray, The, 626
Leo v. Ins. Co. of North America, 87
Leon v. Galceran, 37
Leonard F. Richards, The, 746, 950
Leon Blum, The, 580
Lepanto, The, 492
Levatino Co. v. S. S. Hellenic Hero, 148, 160
Levine v. Aetna Ins. Co., 67, 70
Levinson v. Deupree, 464, 778
Lexington, The, 818, 819
Leycester v. Logan, 906
Libby, McNeil & Libby v. United States, 79
Liberator, The, 677
Lih v. Wagner, 650
Liman v. American Steamship Owners Mutual Protection and Indemnity Ass'n, 69
Liman v. Bank of Nova Scotia, 813
Lincoln Land, The, 693
Lindgren v. United States, 362
Linseed King, The, 887
Little Charles, The, 591, 601
Little Charley, The, 657, 747
Liverpool & Great Western Steam Co. v. Phenix Ins. Co., 91, 142, 162, 176, 266
Liverpool, Brazil & River Plate Steam Nav. Co., Petition of, 846
Liverpool, Brazil and River Plate Steam Nav. Co. v. Brooklyn Eastern District Terminal, 915
Lloyd v. Port Edgewood, Inc., 859
Lloyd Cuarto, The, 558, 562, 564
Lockett Co. v. Cunard S. S. Co., 140, 158
Locklin v. Day-Glo Color Corp., 564
Loe v. Goldstein, 242

Logue Stevedoring Corp. v. Tugs Dalzellance, etc., 599, 600, 602, 803, 805
Lois, The, 799
Lomonosoff, The, 537
London Assur. v. Companhia de Moagens do Barreiro, 82, 89
London Guarantee & Accident Co. v. Industrial Accident Commission of Cal., 23
Long, Petition of, 895
Long Beach, City of v. American President Lines, 598
Long Beach, City of v. National Development Co., 598
Long Island Sound, 746
Long Island Tankers Corp. v. S/S Kaimana, 627
Lord v. Ledwitch, 650
Lord Derby, The, 628, 631
Los Angeles, City of v. Grace Steamship Co., 599
Los Angeles, City of v. Standard Transp. Co., 598
Los Angeles Soap Co., United States v., 262, 268
Lotosland, The, 797, 798
Lotta, The, 870
Lottawanna, The, 21, 405, 622, 647, 689, 690, 791, 794
Loud v. United States, 789
Louisiana, The, 488
Lovell v. Davis, 200
Lowber v. Bangs, 201
L. T. C. No. 38, p. 871
Lucchese v. Malabe Shipping, 191
Lucille, The, 524
Luckenbach v. W. J. McCahan Sugar Co., 191, 230, 899
Luckenbach S.S. Co., Inc. v. Lowe, 414
Luckenbach S.S. Co., Petition of, 920
Luckenbach S.S. Co. v. United States, 530
Luckenback Overseas Corp. v. Subfreights of the S/S Audrey S. Luckenback, 634
Luddeo, The, 677
Luria Bros. & Co. v. Eastern Transp. Co., 158
Luth v. Palmer Shipping Corp., 302, 311
Lux, Jr., Mercantile Co. v. Jones, 97
Luzerne, The, 515
L. W. Gunby Co. v. Steamship Willy, 683
Lykes Bros. S.S. Co., Inc. v. Boudoin, 399
Lykes Bros. S.S. Co. v. United States, 983
Lyman Abbott, The, 542
Lyman M. Law, The, 549
Lynch v. United States, 395

# M

McAllister v. Magnolia Petroleum Co., 348, 349, 352
McAllister Bros. Inc., Petition of, 912
McAndrews v. Thatcher, 261
McCarthy v. American Eastern Corp., 293, 346
McConnochie v. Kerr, 537
McCord v. Moore-McCormack Lines, Inc., 471
McCorkle v. First Pennsylvania Banking & Trust Co., 695
McCorpen v. Central Gulf S.S. Corp., 288
McDermott & Co. v. The Morning Star, 723, 725
MacDonald v. United States, 26
McDonough v. Dannery, 566
McElroy—The Walker, The, 772
McGann v. Capital Sav. Bank & Trust Co., 733
McGhee v. United States, 347
McGrath v. Panama R. Co., 776
McGuire v. City of New York, 30
McLanahan v. Universal Ins. Co., 62, 398
McLaughlin v. Dredge Gloucester, 615, 625, 767
McLaughlin v. Trelleborgs Angfartygs A/B, 446
McMahon v. Pan American World Airways, Inc., 776
McMillan Welding & Machine Works v. General Towing Co., 682
McNamara Corp. v. M/T Tabriz, 679, 682
McNiel, Ex parte, 22
McPhail v. Williams, 900
McPherson v. Buick Motor Co., 392
Madole v. Johnson, 30, 33
Madruga v. Superior Court of California, 39, 40
Madsen, In Petition of, 33, 844, 883
Maggie Hammond, The, 216, 631
Magnolia Petroleum Co. v. National Oil Transport Co., 579
Magnolia, The, 32
Mahnich v. Southern S. S. Co., 384, 386, 458
Mahramas v. American Export Isbrandtsen Lines, Inc., 282, 285, 296, 305, 321, 331, 335, 470
Main, The v. Williams, 818, 913, 915
Maine Seaboard Paper Co. v. The Maurice R. Shaw, 241
Maine, The, 861
Maitland v. The Atlantic, 690
Majestic II, The, 682
Major William H. Tantum, The, 257
Malek Adhel, The, 599, 601
Maltby v. Steam Derrick Boat, 539

Mame, The, 625
Mamiye Bros. v. Barber S. S. Lines, 164, 184
Mandu, The, 941
Manhattan Fruit Exp. Corp. v. Royal Netherlands S. S. Co., 185
Manhattan Lighterage Corp. v. Esso Standard Oil Co., 501
Manhattan Lighterage Corp. v. United States, 494
Man of War, The, 625
Marcardier v. Chesapeake Ins. Co., 73, 84
Maren Lee, The, 520
Maret, The, 626, 682, 683
Margaret, The, 530
Margarethe Blanca, The, 260
Maria, The, 155, 268
Marifax, The, 624
Marina Mercante Nicaraguense, S. A., Petition of, 930
Marine Leasing Services, Inc., Matter of, 850
Marine Mart, Inc. v. O/S Miss Darla Down, 714
Marine Midland Grace Co. of N. Y. v. Banco del Pais, 120, 128
Marine Midland Trust Co. v. United States, 628, 764
Marine Space Enclosures v. Federal Maritime Commission, 12
Marine Sulphur Queen, The, 896, 897, 898, 939
Marine Traders, Inc. v. Seasons Navigation Corp., 632
Marine Transit Corp., In re, 816
Mariner, The, 625
Maroceano Compania Naviera, S. A. v. S. S. Verdi, 513
Marshall v. International Mercantile Marine Co., 775
Marshall Vessels, Inc. v. Wright, 660
Martello, The, 508
Martin v. Delaware Ins. Co., 66
Martinson & Robertson v. The Steamship Barcelona, 897
Mary Caroline, The, 906
Mary Evelyn, The, 726
Mary F. Barrett, The, 266
Mary Ford, The, 566
Mary Morgan, The, 900
Mary, The, 790
Mary Winkleman, The, 820
Maryland Cas. Co. v. Cushing, 50, 464, 822, 840, 867, 868, 908, 935
Maryland Cas. Co. v. Paton, 320
Maryland Cas. Co., United States v., 690, 793
Mascuilli v. United States, 387
Maslin v. M/S Herring Lotte, 882
Mason v. The Blaireau, 24, 566, 568
Massachusetts Bonding & Ins. Co. v. Lawson, 433
Massari v. Forest Lumber Co., 201
Mastan Co. v. Steinberg, 712, 724
Mastan Co. v. Todd Shipyards, 713
Mathieson Chemical Corp. v. The Sadie, 488
Matson Nav. Co., United States v., 523, 983
Matt W. Ransom, The, 542
Mauch Chunk, The, 504, 928
Maurice O'Meara Co. v. National Park Bank, 120
Max Morris, The, 500
Mechling Barge Lines, Inc. v. Derby Co., 199
Medina v. Erickson, 310
Medina v. One Nylon Purse Seine, 539, 563
Melissa Trask, The, 759, 760, 764
Melody, The, 562
Mencke v. A Cargo of Java Sugar, 203
Mendota, The, 952
Menominee, The, 568
Merchants & Marine Bank v. F/V T. E. Welles, 723, 770, 784
Merida, The, 158
Merrill-Stevens Dry Dock Co. v. M/V Laissez-Faire, 732
Merrimac, The, 520
Merritt & Chapman Derrick & Wrecking Co. v. United States, 536, 537
Meteor, The, 659
Meyer, In re, 183
Meyer v. Dollar S. S. Line, 291
Meyer v. New England Fish Co. of Oregon, 853, 860
Miami River Boat Yard, Inc. v. 60 Foot Houseboat, 34, 623
Middle East Agency v. The John B. Waterman, 188
Midland Bank v. Seymour, 122
Midland Enterprises, Inc., Complaint of, 849, 917
Mihalinos v. Liberian S. S. Trikala, 479
Miller v. Lakeland Transp. Co., 928
Miller v. Lykes Brothers Steamship Co., 836
Miller v. Semet-Salvay Div., Allied Chemical Corp., 485, 489
Miller v. Standard Oil Co., 33
Milton v. Yacht Blue Goose, 542
Milwaukee Bridge, The 158
Milwaukee, The, 840
Ministry of Commerce, etc., Greece v. Marine Tankers Corp., 223
Minnetonka, The, 629, 803

Minnie V., The, 625
Minturn v. Maynard, 26
Miskianza, The, 563
Mississippi Shipping Co. v. Zander & Co., 152
Mississippi Valley Barge Line v. Indian Towing Co., 566
Miss New York, The, 864, 865
Missouri S. S. Co., In re, 142
Mitchell v. Trawler Racer, Inc., 397, 401, 452
Mitchell v. Weiner, 104
Mitchell Transp. Co. v. Green, 516
Mitsubishi Goshi Kaisha v. J. Aron & Co., 112
M. J. Woods—The Skipper, The, 905
Mobile & Montgomery R. Co., v. Jurey, 91
Mobile Life Ins. Co. v. Brame, 359
Mohawk, The, 554
Mollica v. Compania Sud-Americana De Vapores, 395
Molnar v. Gulfcoast Transit Co., 773
Monarch of Nassau, The, 199
Monongahela River Consolidated Coal & Coke Co. v. Hurst, 951
Monroe v. British & Foreign Marine Ins. Co., 83
Monrosa v. Carbon Black Export Co., 146
Monsanto Co. v. Port of St. Louis Investments, Inc., 891
Monte A., The, 624
Monte Icair, The, 141
Moon Engineering Co. v. S/S Valiant Power, 604, 697
Moore, In re, 801, 902, 912, 914, 949
Moore v. United States, 715
Moore-McCormack Lines v. Boston Line & Service Co., 315
Moore-McCormack Lines v. The Esso Camden, 263
Moore-McCormack Lines, Inc. v. Armco Steel Corp., 895, 922, 924, 931
Moore-McCormack Lines, Inc. v. McMahon, 937
Moore-McCormack Lines, Inc. v. Richardson, 931
Moosabee, The, 677
Moragne v. States Marine Lines, Inc., 24, 46, 273, 311, 327, 359, 367, 379, 448, 464, 471, 628, 649, 660, 831, 848
Morales v. Moore-McCormack Lines, Inc., 772
Moran v. Lowe, 414
Moran v. Sturges, 806
Moran v. United States, 983
Moran Bros. Contracting Co., Re, 852
Moran No. 16, The, 259
Moran Towing & Transp. Co. v. United States, 514
Moran Transp. Corp., Petition of, 871, 935
Morean v. U. S. Ins. Co., 83
Morewood v. Enequist, 16, 21, 22, 193
Morgan v. Insurance Co. of North America, 8
Mormackite, The, 895, 922, 924, 931
Morning Star, The, 626, 747
Morrisey v. S. S. A. & J. Faith, 154, 629
Morrison S. S. Co. v. Greystoke Castle, 252
Morro Castle, The, 919
Morse Dry Dock & Repair Co. v. Northern Star, 693, 716, 755
Morse Dry Dock & Repair Co. v. United States, 683
Moses v. Delaware Ins. Co., 62
Moses Taylor, The, 22, 38, 39, 646, 649
Mosher v. Tate, 803, 805
Moss v. Hendy Corp., 293
Motor Launch Nip, The, 918
Mountain Timber Co. v. State of Washington, 405
Moye v. Sioux City & New Orleans Barge Lines, Inc., 621
Mpliris v. Hellenic Lines, 481
Mroz v. Dravo Corp., 333, 357
M/S Bremen and Unterweser Reederei GMBH v. Zapata Off-Shore Co., 146, 856, 861, 940
M/S Caldas, The, 879, 895
M/S Galveston Navigator, 788
M/S Pacific Soga, 637
M/T Alva Cape, The, 921, 925
M/T Maumee Sun, 535, 538, 553
Muise v. Abbott, 317
Muller v. Globe & Rutgers Fire Ins. Co., 77
Mulvaney v. Dalzell Towing Co., 26
Munorway, The, 765
Munson Inland Water Lines v. Seidl, 738, 745, 814
Murphy v. Light, 291
Murray v. New York Central R. Co., 846, 855, 901
Murray v. Schwartz, 27, 659
Murray v. The Meteor, 604
Muscelli v. Frederick Starr Contracting Co., 242
Muskegon, The, 640, 656, 658
M/V Caldas, The, 897
M/V Eda, 626
M/V Eddie B ex Linda Brooks, 767
M/V El Salvador-Tug Russell No. 18, The, 930
M. Vivian Pierce, The, 626
M/V James L. Hamilton, 917

M/V Marifax v. McCrory, 34, 623
M/V Marilena P, United States v., 224
Mylark, The, 667, 683
Myles v. Quinn Menhaden Fisheries, Inc., 321
Mystic Terminal Co. v. Thibeault, 315

# N

Nacirema Operating Co. v. Johnson, 423
Nadine, The, 632
Nadle v. M/V Tequila, 628, 633
Nakken v. Fearnley & Eger, 478
Nan B., The, 712
Nanking, The, 693
Naples Maru, The, 163
Narragansett Fishing Corp. v. F/V Bob 'n Barry, 801, 863
National Bank of Commerce v. Morgan, 113
National Bank of Fayette County v. Enterprise Marine Dock Co., 680
National Bank of North America v. S/S Oceanic Ondine, 604, 628
National Board of Marine Underwriters v. Melchers, 25, 81, 253
National Bulk Carriers v. United States, 495, 530
National Importing & Trading Co. v. E. A. Bear & Co., 112
National Shawmut Bank v. The Winthrop, 756, 781
National Trans. Corp. v. Tug Abqaiq, 740
National Union Fire Ins. Co. v. Republic of China, 73
National Western Life Ins. Co. v. Tropical Commerce Corp., 702, 731
Nations v. Morris, 422
Nat Sutton, The, 904
Navegacion Goya, S. A. v. Mutual Boiler and Machinery Ins. Co., 69
Navigazione Generale Italiana v. Spencer Kellogg & Sons, 251, 255
Navigazione Libera, TSA v. Newton Creek Towing Co., 557
Navois Corp. v. The Ulysses II, 229
Neapolis, The, 578
Nebraska, The, 745
Neff v. Dravo Corporation, 299
Neponset, The, 657, 677
Nestor, The, 35, 594, 595
Nettie Woodward, The, 738
Newark, City of v. Mills, 849
New Bedford Dry Dock Co. v. Purdy, 26
Newcomer, The, 562
New England Fish Co. v. Sonya, 627
New England S. S. Co. v. Howard, 208
New England, The, 799
New England Transp. Co., In re, 739, 746, 747
New Jersey Barging Corp., Petition of, 829, 851
New Jersey Barging Corp. v. T.A.D. Jones & Co., 937
New Jersey Steamboat Co. v. Brockett, 23
New Jersey Steam Nav. Co. v. Merchants' Bank, 21, 22, 141, 818, 819
New Orleans, T. & M. R. Co. v. Union Marine Ins. Co., 63
Newport News Shipbuilding & Dry Dock Co. v. O'Hearne, 432
Newport, The, 148, 160
Newport Rolling Mill Co. v. Mississippi Valley Barge Co., 189
New York & Cuba Mail S. S. Co. v. Guayaquil & Q. R. Co., 216
New York & Cuba Mail S. S. Co. v. Royal Exchange Assur., 87
New York & Oriental S. S. Co. v. Automobile Ins. Co. of Hartford, 58
New York Central R. Co. v. White, 405
New York, City of, Petition of, 864
New York Dock Co., In re, 881
New York Dock Co. v. Steamship Poznan, 603, 737
New York Marine No. 10, The, 988
New York, N. H. & H. R. Co., In re, 807
New York No. 1, Ex parte, 610–612
New York No. 2, Ex parte, 610
New York State Waterways Ass'n v. Diamond, 43
Ngo To Po v. Cambridge Nav. Co., Inc., 478
Nicaraguan Long Leaf Pine Lumber Co. v. Moody, 246, 260, 261
Nicastro v. The Peggy B., 541
Nichimen Co. v. M/V Farland, 144, 196
Nickerson v. American Dredging Co., 358
Nicroli v. Den Norske Afrika-OG Australielinie, 446
Nielson, United States v., 521
Niewenhous v. United States, 542
Nika, The, 738
Niles-Bement-Pond Co. v. Dampkiesaktieselskabet Balto, 177, 180
Nili, The, 701
9,889 Bags of Malt, In re, 631
Nissequogue, The, 744
Noah's Ark, The, 556
Noah's Ark, The v. Bentley and Felton Corp., 555
Noakes v. Imperial Airways, 34, 540, 843
Noble v. Moore-McCormack Lines, 506
Noel v. Isbrandtsen Co., 620
Nogueira v. New York N. H. & H. R. Co., 427

Nolan v. A. H. Basse Rederiaktieselskab, 549, 559, 561, 566, 570, 575
Nolte v. Hudson Nav. Co., 769
Nora, The, 624
Norman B. Ream, The, 494
Noronic, The, 820, 853, 860
North America, The, 565, 571
North American Commercial Co. v. United States, 759
North American Dredging Co. v. Pacific Mail S. S. Co., 628
North American Steel Products Corp. v. Andros Mentor, 219
North Atlantic & Gulf Steamships Co., In re, 813
North Coast Stevedoring Co. v. United States, 677
Northern Fishing & Trading Co., Inc., Petition of, 896
Northern No. 30, The, 259
Northern No. 41, The, 691, 693, 697
Northern S. S. Co. v. Earn Line S. S. Co., 235
Northern Star, 718
Northern Transatlantic Carrier Corp., In re, 939
Northfield, The, 504
North Pac. S. S. Co. v. Hall Bros. Marine Ry. & Shipbuilding Co., 22
North River Coal & Wharf Co. v. McWilliams Bros., Inc., 761
Northwest Air Service, Inc., United States v., 540, 623
Northwestern Mutual Life Ins. Co. v. Linard, 71
Northwest Marine Ironworks, Inc. v. S/S Omnium Freighter, 668
Northwest Marine Works v. United States, 604, 816
Norton v. The Evan N., 747, 750
Norton v. Warner Co., 414
Norton's Case, 872
Norwich & N. Y. Transp. Co. v. Wright, 25, 818, 819, 821, 838, 852, 906, 913, 914, 947, 948
Norwich Victory, The, 528
Noyes v. Munson S.S. Line, 235
Nuccio v. Royal Indemnity Co., 883
Nugent v. Smith, 163
No. 34, The, 904
Nunes v. Farrell Lines, Inc., 347, 378
N. V. Stoomvaart Maatschappij "Nederland" v. Standard Oil of California, 514
Nye v. A/S D/S Svendborg, 476
Nyland—The E. Kirby Smith, The, 852
New York, N. H. & H. R. R. Co. v. Gray, 65, 73

# O

Oaksmith v. Garner, 492
Oaksmith v. The Mayflower, 492
Obrecht v. Crawford, 103
O'Brien v. Miller, 913
Oceana, The, 676
Ocean Eagle, The, 939
Oceanic Steam Navigation Co. v. Mellor, 940
Oceanic Trading Corp. v. Vessel Diane, 233
Ocean Liberty, The, 878
Oceano, The, 631
Ocean Spray, The, 852
Ocklawaha, The, 544, 548, 559
Oconee, The, 693, 701, 717
Odegard v. Quist, 855, 857
Odenwald, The, 547
O'Donnell v. Great Lakes Dredge & Dock Co., 332
Odysseus, The, 270, 635, 741, 747, 750
Offshore Co. v. Robison, 283
Offshore Oil Co. v. Robinson, 334
Ogontz, The, 650
Oil Screws Ken Jr., Linda Sue, etc., United States v., 603, 725
Oil Transfer Corp. v. Spentonbush Fuel Transport Service, 203
O'Keefe v. Smith, Hinchman & Grylls Associates, Inc., 416
O'Keeffe v. Aerojet-General Shipyards, Inc., 416
Old Point Fish Co. v. Haywood, 287, 605
Old Time Molasses Co. v. United States, 516
O'Leary v. Brown-Pacific-Maxon, Inc., 413–415
Oliver v. Maryland Ins. Co., 66
Oliver J. Olson & Co. v. American Steamship Marine Leopard, 263, 913, 922
Olsen v. Hunter-Benn & Co., 200
Olympic Towing Corp. v. Nebel Towing Co., 822, 911
Omer, The, 744
Onco, The, 917
O'Neill v. Perini Corp., 292
Oregon, The, 493, 494, 530, 640, 746
Ore S. S. Corp. v. D/S A/S Hassel, 208
Orgettas v. S/T Crinis, 479
Oriental Trading & Transport Co. v. Gulf Oil Corp., 496
Orient Mid-East Lines v. Bowen, 29
Orient Mutual Ins. Co. v. Wright, 58
Orient Steam Navigation Co. v. United States, 513
Oritani, The, 160
Orleans, The, 645
Oroz v. American President Lines, 776

Osaka Shosen Kaisha v. Pacific Export Lumber Co., 187, 216, 639, 651, 659
Osceola, The, 23, 25, 285, 384
Oswalt v. Williamson Towing Co., 302
Owego, The, 626, 745
Owyhee, The, 769, 794
O/Y Finlayson-Forssa A/B v. Pan-Atlantic S. S. Corp., 173
Ozanic v. United States, 524, 525
Ozark, The, 723

# P

Pacific-Atlantic S. S. Co. v. United States, 491
Pacific Cedar, The, 638–640
Pacific Coast Coal Co. v. Alaska S. S. Co., 849
Pacific Far East Line, Inc., In re, 574, 849, 913
Pacific Freighters Co. v. St. Paul Fire & Marine Ins. Co., 246
Pacific Hemlock, The, 603
Pacific Inland Navigation Co., Complaint of, 912, 914, 915
Pacific Mail S. S. Co., In re, 894
Pacific S. S. Co. v. Peterson, 282, 293, 342, 358
Pacific Surety Co. v. Leatham & Smith Towing & Wrecking Co., 25, 81
Pacific Transport Lines v. Territory of Hawaii, 598
Pacific Veg. Oil Corp. v. M/S Norse Commander Corp., 193
Packet, The, 625
Padilla v. The Norseman, 558
Padre Island, The, 582, 736, 738, 753
Paduano v. Yamashita Kisen Kabushiki Kaisha, 469
Page v. United States, 555
Paipoonge, The, 795, 796
Palmyra, The, 591, 601
Palsgraf v. Long Island R. Co., 46
Panama, The, 632
Panama R. Co. v. Johnson, 47, 327, 340, 353, 375
Panama R. Co. v. Vasques, 341
Panama Transport Co., In re, 846, 922
Panama Transport Co. v. United States, 506
Pan-Am Trade & Credit Corp. v. The Campfire, 189
P & E Shipping Corp. v. Empresa Cubana Exportadora E Importadora De Alimentos, 178, 179
Panoceanic Tankers Corp., Complaint of, 921
Paragon, The, 744
Paramount Clause, The, 191
Paraporte, The, 582
Parham v. Pelegrin, 862
Parker v. Motor Boat Sales, Inc., 420
Park S. S. Co. v. Cities Service Oil Co., 206, 207, 230
Park Victory, The, 920, 921
Pascagoula Dock Station v. Merchants & Marine Bank, 710, 755
Patapsco Ins. Co. v. Coulter, 58, 73
Pate v. Standard Dredging Corp., 347, 357, 358
Paterson v. Dakin, 41
Patten v. Darling, 260
Patterson v. United States, 284
Patterson Shrimp Co. v. O/S Freedom, 747, 750
Payne v. S/S Tropic Breeze, 43, 604, 658, 700, 702, 731, 753
Payne v. Tanker Co., 310
P. D. Marchessini & Co. (N. Y.) v. Pacific Marine Corp., 28
P. Dougherty Co. v. United States, 494
Pedersen v. Eugster, 211
Pelotas, The, 628, 846, 956
Pelotas-The Omoa, The, 956
Pendergast v. Globe & Rutgers Fire Ins. Co., 59
Pendleton v. Benner Line, 899
Pendragon Castle, The, 537
Pennell v. Read, 871
Pennsylvania, Grace & Co. v. Charleston Lighterage & Transfer Co., 892
Pennsylvania, The, 494, 849, 889, 898
Pennsylvania, The, in Petition of Long, 898
Pennsylvania R. Co., Re, 849
Pennsylvania R. Co. v. Moore-McCormack Lines, Inc., 214
Pennsylvania R. Co. v. O'Rourke, 427
Penobscot, The, 165, 634, 750
People of the Living God v. Star Towing Co., 534
People's Ferry Co. v. Beers, 16, 21, 630
Perama, The, 891, 894
Perez v. Barge LBT No. 4, 562
Permanente S. S. Co. v. Hawaiian Dredging Co., 238
Pershing Auto Rentals, Inc. v. Gaffney, 862, 868
Perth Amboy No. 1, The, 23, 851, 937
Peters v. Warren Ins. Co., 73
Peterson v. S. S. Wahcondah, 231, 606
Petroleum Export Corp. v. Kerr S. S. Co., 201
Petterson v. Alaska S. S. Co., 394
Pettus v. Jones & Laughlin Steel Corp., 822, 836, 912
Peyroux v. Howard, 36, 645
Pfeffer Co. v. S/S Pacific Star, 764

Phelps v. The Cecilia Ann, 768
Phenix Ins. Co., Ex parte, 845
P. H. Gill & Sons Forge & Machine Works v. United States, 677
Philadelphia, W. & B. R. R. v. Philadelphia & Havre de Grace Steam Towboat Co., 23
Phillips v. Clark, 141
Phillips v. United States, 344
Philomena, The, 747, 806, 807
Phoenix Ins. Co. v. Erie & Western Transp. Co., 191
Pichirilo v. Buzman, 616
Piedmont & George's Creek Coal Co. v. Seaboard Fisheries Co., 661, 666
Pierce v. National Bulk Carriers, Inc., 614
Pillsbury v. Alaska Packers Ass'n, 414
Pine Forest, The, 741
Pioneer, The, 309
Pioneer Fuel Co. v. McBrier, 631
Pioneer Import Corp. v. The Lafcomo, 188
Pipitone v. United States, 807
Plamals v. The Pinar Del Rio, 36, 341, 385, 625
Planter, The, 645
Plaquemines Equipment & Machine Co. v. Neuman, 416
Pleason v. Gulfport Shipbuilding Corp., 33
Plow City, The, 163, 263
Plymouth, The, 21, 24, 522
Poignant v. United States, 400
Point Brava, The, 151
Point Landing, Inc. v. Alabama Drydock & Shipbuilding Co., 790
Polar S. S. Corp. v. Inland Overseas S. S. Corp., 239
Poling Holding Corp., Petition of, 866
Pomare, The, United States v., 625
Pontin Lighterage Co. v. American Export Lines, 28
Pope & Talbot v. Blanchard Lumber Co., 228
Pope & Talbot v. Hawn, 51, 70, 348, 355, 441, 454, 464, 500
Porter v. The Sea Witch, 742
Porter's Case, 413, 414
Portland Pipe Line Corp. v. Environmental Improvement Commission, 830, 834
Port of Portland, United States v., 611
Portsmouth, The, 266
Port Welcome Cruises, Inc. v. S/S Bay Belle, 629, 709, 715
Postal S. S. Corp. v. El Isleo, 504
Potomac, The, 510
Powers v. Bethlehem Steel Corp., 334
Pratt v. United States, 615
President Arthur, The, 627, 666
President Madison, The, 524
President Polk, The, 160
President Van Buren, The, 598
Preston v. Grant Advertising, Inc., 358
Prilla, The, 625
Princess Sophia, The, 846, 898
Priscilla, The, 637
Proceeds of The Gratitude, The, 745
Proctor & Gamble Co. v. Peters, White & Co., 104
Production Steel Co. of Illinois v. S. S. Francois L. O., 220
Progreso, The, 164, 201
Propeller Commerce, The, 35
Propeller Niagara v. Cordes, 140
Providence & New York S. S. Co. v. Hill Mfg. Co., 820, 875, 879, 885
Provost v. The Selkirk, 625, 739, 741, 742
Prudential S. S. Corp. v. United States, 983
Pullman's Palace-Car Co. v. Commonwealth of Pennsylvania, 135
Pump Boat 600, 948
Pure Oil Co. v. Geotechnical Corp., 320
Pure Oil Co. v. Neilson, Inc., 493, 530
Pure Oil Co. v. The Fred B. Zigler, 509, 516
Puritan, The, 947
Putnam, Re, 859, 861
Putnam and Overman v. Lower, Kadlec et al., 606
Pyne v. Oil Screw F/V Chrisway, 604

## Q

Queen Ins. Co. of America v. Globe & Rutgers Fire Ins. Co., 56, 64
Queen, In the Matter of The, 262, 623, 658, 812
Quinlivan v. Northwestern Fire & Marine Ins. Co., 73

## R

Rainbow Line, Inc. v. M/V Tequila, 581, 604, 632, 654, 667, 687, 700, 701, 737, 738, 753
Raithmoor, The, 523
Raleigh, The, 626
Ralli v. Troop, 259, 266, 599, 630
Ramos v. Beauregard, Inc., 616
Rancagua, The, 637
Randolph v. Waterman S. S. Corp., 193
Rank v. Colonial Sand & Stone Co., 918
Rapid Transit, The, 258
Rauch v. Gulf Refining Co., 566, 568

Ravenscroft v. United States, 254
Rayner & Co. v. Hambro's Bank, 122
Read v. Agricultural Ins. Co., 72
Reading, Petition of, 883
Rebecca, The, 594, 818
R. F. C. v. New Castle Terminal Co., 780
R. F. C. v. The William D. Mangold, 635
Red Cross Line v. Atlantic Fruit Co., 38, 196
Rederi A/B Pulp v. Republic Chemical Co., 216
Rederiaktierbolaget v. Compania de Navegacion Anne S. A., 700
Red Lion, The, 785
Redman v. United Fruit Co., 772
Redman v. United States, 772
Redna Marine Corp. v. Poland, 75
Red Star Barge Line, Petition of, 871
Red Star Towing & Transp. Co. v. New York Towing & Transp. Co., 802
Reed, Petition of, 901
Reed v. Canfield, 281
Reed v. People-to-People Health Foundation, 314
Reed v. S. S. Yaka, 242, 444, 445, 450, 616
Reed v. United States, 242
Reinhardt v. Newport Flying Service Corp., 540
Reliance Ins. Co. v. The Escapade, 67
Reliance Marine, etc., Corp., Petition of, 905
Relief, The, 545
Republic of China v. National Union F. I. Co., 62
Republic of Mexico v. Hoffman, 985
Resolute, The, 35, 602, 622, 634
Rhederel Actien Gesellschaft Oceana v. Clutha Shipping Co., 26
Rhinelander v. Insurance Co. of Pa., 84
Rice v. Charles Dreifus Co., 41
Rice Growers Ass'n of California v. Rederiaktiebolaget Frode, 914, 949
Richard Bertram & Co. v. Yacht Wanda, 26
Richardson v. Harmon, 831, 845, 898
Richardson v. St. Charles-St. John the Baptist Bridge and Ferry Authority, 283, 308, 316, 320
Richardson & Sons v. Jenkins S. S. Co., 210
Richard Winslow, The, 26
Richelieu & Ontario Navigation Co. v. Boston Marine Ins. Co., 63
Rickard v. Pringle, 535
Ridings v. M/V Effort, 724
Rio Verde, The, 181
Rita Sister, The, 159, 167
Rivadeneira v. Skibs A/S Snefonn, 483
Rivera v. Farrell Lines, Inc., 355
Rivera v. Rederi A/B Nordstjernan, 356
River Plate and Brazil Conferences v. Pressed Steel Car Co., 996
River Queen, The, 760, 763
Riverside Coal Co. v. Elman Coal Co., 103
Riverstone Meat Co. v. Lancashire Shipping Co., 152
R. Lenahan, The, 708, 714
Roach v. Hapag-Lloyd, 146
Roanoke, The, 258, 651
Robert & Edwin, The, 810–812
Roberts v. Echternach, 626, 673
Robert Stewart & Sons, Ltd., United States & Black Diamond S. S. Corp. v., 941
Robert W. Parsons, The, 32, 623, 844
Robin Gray, The, 218
Robins Dry Dock & Repair Co., United States v., 684
Robinson, The, 628
Robinson v. Baltimore & Ohio Railroad, 338
Robinson v. Pocahontas, Inc., 302, 310, 313
Rock Island Bridge, The, 35, 36, 523, 623
Rockport Yacht & Supply Co. v. M/V Contessa, 683
Rock Transport Properties Corp. v. Hartford Fire Ins. Co., 84
Roddick v. Indemnity Mutual Marine Ins. Co., 61
Rodrigue v. Aetna Cas. & Surety Co., 27, 334
Rodriquez v. National Bulk Carriers, Inc., 358
Rodriquez v. Orion Schiffahrts-Gesellschaft Reith & Co., 478
Rofer v. Head & Head, Inc., 303, 310
Rogers v. Missouri Pacific R. Co., 383
Rogers v. United States Lines, 395
Rolph, The, 628
Romano v. West India Fruit & S. S. Co., 178, 181, 200, 201, 240
Romero v. International Terminal Operating Co., 29, 38, 52, 294, 348, 469, 473, 832
Ronda—The Lucille Bloomfield, The, 863, 913, 945
Roper, The, 333
Roper v. United States, 333, 441
Rosalia, The, 183
Rose Culkin, The, 947, 950, 956
Rosenquist v. Isthmian S. S. Co., 288, 294

Rosenthal v. Poland, 87
Rose Standish, The, 487
Roseway, The, 684
Ross, In re, 476
Ross, United States v., 44
Rounds v. Cloverport Foundry & Machine Co., 37, 38
Roux v. Salvador, 83
Rowald v. Cargo Carriers, Inc., 283, 309
Roy v. M/V Kateri Tek, 604
Royal Mail Steam Packet Co. v. Companhia de Navegacao Lloyd Brasileiro, 940
Royal Oak, The, 558, 773
Royal Typewriter Co. v. Hamburg-Amerika Linie, 188
R. T. Jones Lumber Co. v. Roen S. S. Co., 151, 162, 209
Rubens v. Ludgate Hill S. S. Co., 142
Ruchamkin—The Washington, The, 851
Ruggles v. General Interest Ins. Co., 62
Rupert City, The, 634, 655
Rupp v. International Terminal Operating Co., 149
Russo v. Matson Navigation Co., 308
Rustad v. Wuori, 562
Ruth v. O/S/V Marie and Winifred, 763
Ryan, Czaplicki v. S. S. Hoegh Silvercloud, 443
Ryan Stevedoring Co. v. Pan-Atlantic Steamship Corp., 315, 437, 442
Ryan Stevedoring Co. v. United States, 631, 742
Rygja, The, 232

## S

Saar v. Sun Oil Co., 288
Sabine, The, 576, 577, 628
Sac City, The, 878
Sacramento Navigation Co. v. Salz, 147, 260, 916
S/A Industrias Reunidas F. Matarazzo v. Compania De Vapores San Antonio, S. A., 28
St. Jago de Cuba, The, 643, 664, 742, 759
St. Johns N. F. Shipping Corp. v. S. A. Companhia Geral, etc., 182, 188
St. Joseph-Chicago S. S. Co., In re, 572
St. Lawrence, The, 645, 647, 694
St. Louis & Tenn. River Packet Co. v. Murray & Watham, 499
St. Louis Iron Mountain & Southern R. Co. v. Craft, 361
St. Paul, The, 741
St. Paul Marine Transp. Corp. v. Cerro Sales Corp., 565, 566, 571, 575
Salant v. Pennsylvania R. Co., 97
Salmons Dredging Corp. v. The Herma, 240
Salvage Chief, The, 544, 565
Samad v. The Etivebank, 483
Samadjopoulos v. National Western Life Ins. Co., 604, 658, 700, 731, 753
Samland, The, 158
Sammon v. Central Gulf S. S. Corp., 288
Samnanger, The, 650
Sampsell, United States v., 763
Samson, The, 524
Samuel Little, The, 733, 746
Samuel W. Hall, The, 201
Sanday, The, 494
Sanday v. United States Shipping Board Emergency Fleet Corp., 201
Sandra & Dennis Fishing Corp., United States v., 556, 557
Sandringham, The, 537
San Francisco, The, 635
Sanib Corp. v. United Fruit Co., 189
San Pedro, The, 846, 929
San Rafael Compania Naviera S. A. v. American Smelting & Refining Co., 634
Santa Anna Maria, The, 251, 542
Sante Fe, P. & P. R. Co. v. Grant Bros. Constr. Co., 176
Santorinakis v. S. S. Orpheus, 483
Sarnia Steamships v. Continental Grain Co., 212
Saskatchewan Govt. Ins. Office v. Ciaramitaro, 67
Saskatchewan Govt. Ins. Office v. Spot Pack, Inc., 64
Sassoni v. Savoie, 911
Saturnus, The, 215, 216
Saugerties Bank v. Delaware & Hudson Co., 99
Savannah Sugar Refining Corp. v. S. S. Hudson Deep, 220
Savas v. Maria Trading Corp., 626, 768
Savoie v. Apache Towing Co., 321
Sawyer, Inc. v. Poor, 525
Scarburgh v. Compania Sud-Americana De Vapores, 144
Schackman v. Cunard White Star, 145
Schade v. National Surety Corp., 268
Schiavone-Bonomo Corp. v. Buffalo Barge Towing Corp., 775
Schiemann v. Grace Line, Inc., 336
Schilling v. A/S D/S Dannebrog, 632, 673, 683, 813
Schnell v. The Vallescura, 170
Schnell v. United States, 602, 981
Schoening v. 102 Jute Bags of Standard 3R Asbestos Spinning Fibre, 29
Schon v. M/V Alexandra B., 628, 737, 750

Schooner Freeman, The v. Buckingham, 638
Schooner Mahukona Co. v. Charles Nelson Co., 202
Schooner Tilton, The, 25
Schoremeyer v. Barnes, 882
Schroeder Bros., Inc. v. The Saturina, 130, 166
Schuchardt v. The Ship Angelique, 689
Schulz v. The Pennsylvania R. Co., 378
Schuyler, The, 738, 745
S. C. Loveland Co. v. United States, 260
Scotia, The, 489, 701
Scotland, The, 852, 853, 907, 908, 925
Seaboard Air Line R. Co. v. Pan Am Petroleum Co., 524
Seaboard Pioneer, The, 212
Seaboard Shipping v. Jocharanne Tugboat Co., 86
Seaboard Stevedoring Corp. v. Sogadachoc S. S. Co., 442
Seaboard Tug & Barge, Inc. v. Rederi A/B Disa, 495, 530
Sea Foam, The, 747
Sea Gull, The, 371, 374
Sea-Land Services, Inc. v. Gaudet, 360, 369
Seaman v. Enterprise Fire & Marine Ins. Co., 61
Seaman v. Tank Barge OC601, p. 562
Seapool, The, 262
Searoad Shipping Co. v. E. I. duPont de Nemours & Co., 182
Sears v. S. S. American Producer, 537, 567, 570
Sears Oil Co. v. Reinauer Transp. Co., 241
Seas Shipping Co. v. Sieracki, 330, 365, 392, 393, 437, 440, 458, 460
Seas Shipping Co. v. United States War Shipping Administration, 230
Seely v. City of New York, 315
Self v. Central Station Equipment Co., 658
Sellers v. Dixilyn Corp., 292
Seminole, The, 877, 886, 896
Senko v. LaCrosse Dredging Corp., 331
Servia, The, 509
Severance, The, 840, 860
Shamrock Towing Co. v. American Ins. Co., 70
Shaver Transp. Co., Petition of, 616, 619
Shaw, Savill, Albion & Co. v. The Fredericksburg, 527
Shea v. Texas Employers' Ins. Ass'n, 433
Shea, United States v., 240
Sheffield Tankers Corp., Petition of, 939
Shenker v. United States, 441, 446
Sheppard v. Taylor, 22
Shipowners' & Merchants' Tugboat Co. v. Hammond Lumber Co., 865
Shipowners' & Merchants' Tugboat Co., United States v., 527
Shiras, The, 890, 904, 930
Shoe v. George F. Craig & Co., 262, 263
Shogry v. Lewis, 33
Shreveport, The, 573
Shrimper Bera-Bora, The, 894
Siders v. The Ohio River Co., 288, 293, 303
Siegelman v. Cunard White Star, 15, 23, 195
Sieracki v. Seas Shipping Co., 392, 393
Sif, The, 516
Sillanpa v. Cornell Steamboat Co., 320
Silva v. Bankers Commercial Corp., 27
Silver Line v. United States, 846
Silver Palm, The, 505, 848
Silvia, The, 494
Simmes v. Marine Ins. Co., 58.
Simon v. M/V Hialeah, 614
Simonetti v. Foster, 200, 201
Simpson v. Knutsen, 372–374
Simpson Oil Co v. The Pure Oil Co., 772
Sims v. Marine Catering Service, 283, 285, 337
Sims v. United States War Shipping Administration, 299, 300, 311
Sincere Navigation Corp., Complaint of, 535, 911
Sinclair Refining Co. v. The American Sun, 526
Sinclair Refining Co. v. United States, 981, 984
Siren, The, 607, 608
Skolar, The, 343
Skolar v. Lehigh Valley R. Co., 343, 347
Slade, Inc. v. Scurlock Oil Co., 321
Slavenburg Corp. v. Boston Ins. Co., 58
Slavin v. Port Service Corp., 627
Slayton, Ex parte, 852, 859
Sloop Fling, The, 883, 939
Smith v. The Ferncliff, 189
Smith v. Union Oil Co. of Caifornia, 542
Smith v. United States, 290
Smith Voyager, The, 895, 898
Snug Harbor, The, 948
Sobonis v. S/T National Defender, 533, 537, 544, 567, 569, 581
Sobosle v. United States Steel Corp., 300
Sociedade Brasileira De Intercambio Comercial E. Industrial, Ltda. v. S. S. Punta Del Este, 146
Societe Purfina Maritime v. 8598.09 Long Tons of Diesel Oil, 210, 228
Socony Mobil Oil Co. v. Wall Street Traders, Inc., 723

Socony-Vacuum Oil Co. v. Smith, 354, 356, 385
Soerstad, The, 904
Solberg v. Cargo of Steel Rails, 631
Solet v. M/V Capt. H. V. Dufrene, 243, 286, 314, 337, 620
Son Shipping Co. v. De Fosse & Tanghe, 220
Sorensen v. Keyser, 211
Sorenson v. Boston Ins. Co., 63
Sound Marine & Machine Corp. v. Westchester County, 41
South American S. S. Co. v. Atlantic Towing Co., 537
South Chicago Coal & Dock Co. v. Bassett, 413
South Coast, The, 674, 676.
Southern Coal & Coke Co. v. Kugniecibas, 765, 782, 786
Southern Cross, The, 816
Southern Districts, The, 851, 852, 860
Southern Pacific Co. v. Jensen, 48, 278, 405–407, 456, 642, 650, 719, 830
Southern Pacific Co. v. United States, 878
Southern Pacific Golden Gate Ferries, In re, 810
Southern Prince, The, 253
Southern S. S. Co., Petition of, 849, 851, 852, 860
South, Inc. v. Moran Towing & Transp. Inc., 740
Southland Financial Corp. v. O/S Mary Evelyn, 716, 723
South Shore, The, 849
South Star, The, United States v., 199
Southwark, The, 151, 209
Southwestern Sugar & Molasses Co. v. River Terminals Corp., 520
Southwestern Sugar & Molasses Co. v. The Eliza Jane Nicholson, 220
Spare Time II, The, 861, 882
Spaulding, The, 741
Spearin, Preston & Burrows, Inc., Petition of, 861, 871
Spellman v. American Barge Line, 310
Spencer Kellogg & Sons v. Great Lakes Transit Corp., 184
Spencer Kellogg & Sons, Inc. v. Hicks, 887
Spero v. S. S. Argodon, 483
Spivack v. United States, 548
Spooner & Sons v. Connecticut Fire Ins. Co., 73
S. S. Antilles, The, 912
S. S. Bournemouth, State of Cal. By and Through Dept. of Fish and Game v., 23
S/S Helena, The, 535, 911
S/S Lucie Schulte v. United States, 687
S/S Lucie Schulte, United States v., 641, 683, 741
S. S. Melanie v. Owners of S. S. San Onofre, 553
S/S Norberto Capay, In re, 634, 658, 668
S/S Pacific Ranger v. Bugg, 626
S/S Panoceanic Faith, 921
S/S Percy Jordan, 780
S/S President Lincoln, United States v., 600
S/S Sapphire Sandy, 713, 724
S/S Sian Yung, 850, 933
Stacey-Vorwerk Co. v. Buck, 99, 113, 168
Stag Line v. Foscolo, Mango & Co., 181
Stainback v. Rae, 487
Stamatakos v. Hunter Shipping Co., S. A., 483
Standard Dredging Co. v. Kristiansen, 917
Standard Electrica S. A. v. Hamburg Sudamerikanische, etc., 188
Standard Marine Ins. Co. v. Nome Beach Lighterage & Transp. Co., 87
Standard Oil Co. v. Pocahontas S. S. Co., 507
Standard Oil Co. v. The Wellesley Victory, 505
Standard Oil Co. v. United States, 677
Standard Oil Co. of Cal., United States v., 23, 318
Standard Oil Co. of Kentucky, United States v., 498
Standard Oil Co. of New Jersey v. Southern Pacific Co., 913
Standard Oil Co. of New Jersey v. United States, 78, 520
Standard Varnish Works v. The Bris, 228
Standard Wholesale Phosphate & Acid v. Travelers Ins. Co., 854, 861
Stankiewicz v. United Fruit S. S. Corp., 379
Stanovich v. Jurlin, 299
Stapp v. The Steamboat Clyde, 33
Star, The, 541
Starin, Re, 852
Star of Hope, The, 248, 254
Star Seafood Co. v. Gulf & Atlantic Shrimp Co., 577
State of Cal. By and Through Dept. of Fish and Game v. S. S. Bournemouth, 23, 629, 805
State of Florida v. Massachusetts Co., 535
State of Maine v. M/V Tamano, 830
State of Maryland, The, 629
State of Oregon Highway Commission v. Tug Go-Getter, 894

State of Washington v. W. C. Dawson & Co., 48, 407
States Marine Corp. of Delaware, Application of, 196
States Steamship Co. v. United States, 889
State, to Use of Maines v. A/S Nye Kristianborg, 35
Steamer Syracuse, The, 517
Steamship Co. of 1912 v. C. H. Pearson & Son Hardwood Co., 216
Steamship Rutherglen Co. v. Howard Houlder & Partners, 213, 222
Steel Inventor, The, 914
Steel Navigator, The, 152, 160
Stella R., The, 800
Stendze v. The Neptune, 293
Stephen, In re, 844
Stephen Allen, The, 795
Sterling, The, 655
Stern, Hays & Lang, Inc. v. M/V Nili, 43, 658, 793
Stetson v. Insurance Co. of North America, 63
Steuart Investment Co. v. Bauer Dredging Constr. Co., 902, 917
Steuer v. N. V. Nederl-Amerik Stoomvaart Maatschappf, 282
Stevens v. Seacoast Co., 241
Stevens v. The White City, 740
Stevens v. United States Lines, 510
Stewart v. Steamer Blue Trader, 805
Stifinder, The, 491, 530
Stirnimann v. The San Diego, 188
Stone v. Diamond S. S. Transp. Corp., 840
Stone v. The Jewell, 541
Strachan Shipping Co. v. Cities Service Transport Co., 561, 564, 572, 573
Straits of Dover S. S. Co. v. Munson, 232
Strathearn S. S. Co. v. Dillon, 479
Sturgis v. Boyer, 516
Sullivan v. Nitrate Producers' S. S. Co., 614
Sun Coaster, The, 726
Sun Harbor Marina, 660
Sun Harbor Marina, Inc. v. Sellick, 650
Sun Mutual Ins. Co. v. Ocean Ins. Co., 62
Sun Oil Co., Petition of, 526, 535, 538, 553
Sun Oil Co. v. Dalzell Towing Co., 521
Susan, The, 846, 860, 863, 866, 900, 902
Susana, The, 713, 714, 802
Susquehanna, The, 658
Suwaharu Maru and The Mandoil II, The, 571, 575, 576, 583
Suwaharu Maru-Mandoil II—Transoneida, The, 859
Swan & Sons, Inc. v. Kugniecibas, 765, 782
Swanson v. Marra Bros., Inc., 330
Swenson v. The Argonaut, 488
Swift v. Tyson, 719
Swift & Co. Packers v. Compania Colombiana Del Caribe, S. A., 41, 42
Sword Line, Inc. v. United States, 27
Sylvan Arrow, The, 607, 612
Symonette Shipyards v. Clark, 476
Syracuse, The, 516
Sztejn v. J. Henry Schroder Banking Corp., 120

# T

Tait v. Levi, 398
Tampa Ship Repair & Dry Dock Co. v. A. P. St. Philip, Inc., 598
Tampa Tugs and Towing, Inc. v. M/V Sandanger, 259, 547, 562, 565, 570, 604
Tampico, The, 442
Tangled Seine, The, 346
Tankers Corp. v. Henn, 863
Tarkington v. United States Lines, 395
Tashmoo, The, 542
Tatsuuma Kisen Kabushiki Kaisha v. Robert Dollar Co., 640
Taylor v. Atlantic Maritime Co., 478
Taylor v. Crain, 49, 51, 772
Teichman v. Loffland Bros., 436
Tempest v. United States, 497
Temple Bar, The, 900
Temple S. S. Co., Petition of, 900
Teneria El Popo v. Home Ins. Co., 86
Terne, The, 206
Terpe v. Yacht "Victoria", 488
Terracciano v. McAlinden Constr. Co., 872, 898
Tesoriero v. M. S. Molda, 775
T. E. Welles, The, 723, 784
Texas Co., Petition of, 851, 866, 935, 937
Texas Co. v. Hogarth Shipping Co., 224
Texas Co. v. Lea River Lines, 207
Texas Co. v. United States, 851, 866
Texas Gulf Sulphur Co. v. Blue Stack Towing Co., 853, 860
Thames & Mersey Marine Ins. Co. v. Hamilton, Fraser & Co., 74
Thames Towboat Co. v. The Francis McDonald, 16, 33, 630
Theisen, Application of, 884
Themis, The, 165
Theodore Roosevelt, The, 798
Thibeault v. Boston Towboat Co., 315
Thomas v. Humble Oil & Refining Co., 308
Thomas Barlum, The, 25, 701, 712

Thomas Jefferson, The, 31
Thomason v. United States, 984
Thomaston, The, 759
Thornton v. The Livingston Roe, 548
Three Jacks, The, 689, 690, 714, 793, 796
Thyssen Steel Corp. v. Federal Commerce & Navigation Co., 787
Tide Water Associated Oil Co. v. The Syosset, 493, 501
Tiedemann & Co., Petition of, 847, 851, 901
Tipton v. Socony Mobil Co., 435
Titanic, The, 940
Tito Campanella Societa Di Navigazione, United States v., 800
Tjonaman v. A/S Glittre, 484
Todd Drydocks, Inc. v. King County, 790
Todd Shipyards Corp. v. Altema Compania Maritima, S. A., 701
Todd Shipyards Corp. v. City of Athens, 35, 626
Todd Shipyards Corp. v. F/V Maigus Luck, 768, 789, 817
Todd Shipyards Corp. v. Mastan Co., 724
Todd Shipyards Corp. v. Soc. Naviera Trans-Atlantica, S. A., 738, 747, 749, 786, 790, 791
Todd Shipyards Corp. v. United States, 840
Tokyo Maru, The, 638
Toland v. Atlantic Gahagan Joint Venture Dredge, No. 1, 435
Toledo, The, 151, 208
To Po Nyo v. J. Fritz Co., 482
Toronto, The, 165
Toro Shipping Corp. v. Bacon-McMillan Veneer Mfg. Co., 632
Torres v. Interstate Fire & Cas. Co., 912
Torrey Canyon, The, 822, 841
Totila ex Harald, The, 789
Towanda, The, 746
Tower Bridge, The, 537
Towle v. The Great Eastern, 543
Tradewind, The, 682, 711, 754, 817
Trans-Amazonica Iquitos, S. A. v. Georgia Steamship Co., 130
Transatlantic Financing Corp. v. United States, 228
Transfer No. 18, The, 807, 810
Transfer No. 21, The, 515
Transford, The, 755
Traupman v. American Dredging Co., 382
Trawler Gudrun, Inc., In re, 871
Trawler Weymouth, Inc., Petition of, 871
Treakle v. Pocahontas Steamship Co., 668
Tregenna, The, 181
Trenton, The, 37, 788, 792
Trillora II, The, 881
Trim Too, The, 882
Trinidad Corp., Petition of, 866, 935
Trojan, The, 840, 939
Tropical Marine Products Co. v. Birmingham Fire Ins. Co., 73
Tropicana Shipping, S. A. v. Empresa Nacional "Elcano" de la Marina Mercante, 700, 718
Tropic Breeze, The, 702, 731, 732
Troupe v. Chicago, Duluth & Georgian Bay Transit Co., 51
Tugboat Dalzellea, Petition of, 930
Tug Manzanillo, United States v., 315, 318
Tug Nellie, 585
Tug New Work, The, 852
Tug North Carolina, The, 894
Tug No. 16, The, 865
Tug Olive L. Moore, The, 801, 902, 912, 914, 949
Tug Parris Island, The, United States v., 600
Tug Raven, The, 853, 860
Tug William Walsh, 863
Tungus, The, 367
Tungus, The v. Skovgaard, 365, 441, 464
Turner v. United States, 623
Turner & Blanchard, Inc. v. A. H. Bull S. S. Co., 604
Tweedie Trading Co. v. Clan Line, 230
Two Hundred Seventy-Five Tons of Mineral Phosphates, 631

## U

Umbria, The, 505, 524
Union Fish Co. v. Erickson, 303, 419, 467, 651
Union Industrielle et Maritime v. Nimpex International, Inc., 632
Union Ins. Co. of Philadelphia v. Smith, 63, 64, 152
Union Marine Ins. Co. v. Charles D. Stone & Co., 74
Union Oil Co. of Cal. v. M/V Issaquena, 489
Union Oil Co. of Cal. v. Tugboat San Jancinto, 506, 531
Union Oil Co. of Cal. v. Tug Mary Malloy, 515
Union Reliance—The Berean, The, 894
United Boat Service Corp. v. Dailey, 538
United Fruit Co. v. The M. D. Whiteman, 772
United Fruit Co. v. United States Shipping Board Fleet Corp., 29
United Fruit Co., United States v., 599

United Marine Contracting Co., In re, 807
United Nations Children's Fund v. S/S Nordstern, 602
United New York and New Jersey Sandy Hook Pilots Ass'n v. Halecki, 366, 441
United States, Petition of, 557, 840, 846, 852, 879, 914, 948
United States v. Adams, 510
United States v. Alex Dussel Iron Works, 774
United States v. American Gas Screw Franz Joseph, 712, 725, 759, 770, 784
United States v. American Oil Co.—The Amoco Virginia, 550, 562
United States v. Ames, 800
United States v. Atlantic Mutual Ins. Co., 173, 251, 270
United States v. Atlantic Refining Co., 213
United States v. Audrey II, 604, 816
United States v. Baltimore Towing Co., 774
United States v. Barge Cape Flattery I, 764
United States v. Borax Consolidated, 995
United States v. Brig Malek Adhel, 36
United States v. Carver, 674, 675
United States v. Certain Subfreights of The Neponset, 793
United States v. Charbonnier, 161
United States v. Cordova, 34
United States v. Cornell Steamboat Co., 562, 577
United States v. Daniels Towing & Dry Dock, Inc., 684
United States v. Demko, 284
United States v. DeVane, 550, 555, 556, 979
United States v. Eastern S. S. Lines, 525
United States v. Farr Sugar Corp., 173
United States v. Flood, 763, 764
United States v. Flores, 44
United States v. Freights, etc., of the Mount Shasta, 623, 632
United States v. F/V Golden Dawn, 730
United States v. F/V Voyager, 732, 784
United States v. F/V Zarco, 660
United States v. Gallagher, 315, 322
United States v. Gavagan, 550, 555, 556
United States v. Guaranty Trust Co., 131
United States v. Jane B. Corp., 627, 764
United States v. Ladd, 497
United States v. Lawter, 555
United States v. Los Angeles Soap Co., 262, 268
United States v. Maryland Cas. Co., 690, 793
United States v. Matson Navigation Co., 523
United States v. M/V Marilena P, 224
United States v. Nielson, 521
United States v. Northwest Air Service, Inc., 540, 623
United States v. Oil Screws Ken Jr., Linda Sue, etc., 603, 725
United States v. Port of Portland, 611
United States v. Robins Dry Dock & Repair Co., 684
United States v. Ross, 44
United States v. Sampsell, 763
United States v. Sandra & Dennis Fishing Corp., 556, 557
United States v. Shea, 240
United States v. Shipowners & Merchants Tugboat Co., 527
United States v. S/S Lucie Schulte, 641, 683, 687, 741
United States v. S/S President Lincoln, 600
United States v. Standard Oil Co. of Cal., 23, 318
United States v. Standard Oil Co. of Kentucky, 498
United States v. The Esso Belgium, 173
United States v. The Helen, 601
United States v. The Pomare, 625
United States v. The South Star, 199
United States v. Tito Campanella Societa Di Navigazione, 800
United States v. Tug Manzanillo, 315, 318
United States v. Tug Parris Island, 600
United States v. United Fruit Co., 599
United States v. Vessel FL 4127 SE, 759
United States v. Waterman S. S. Co., 246
United States v. Webb, Inc., 45
United States v. Wessel, Duval & Co., 199, 255
United States v. Woodbury, 510
United States & Black Diamond S. S. Corp. v. Robert Stewart & Sons, 941
United States Dredging Corp., Petition of, 918
United States Navigation Co. v. Cunard S. S. Co., 995
United States on behalf of the Lords Commissioners, etc. v. The James L. Richards, 534, 548
United States, Petition of v. S. S. Joseph Lykes, 488
United States Shipping Board Emergency Fund Corp. v. Greenwald, 650
United States Steel Corp., In re, 372, 373, 374

United States Steel Products Co., Petition of the, 914
United Virginia Bank/Citizens and Marine v. O/S Sea Queen, 604, 668, 750, 756
Universal Camera Corp. v. National Labor Relations Board, 414
Universal Tramp Shipping Co. v. Irish Salt Mining Co., 206
Universo Ins. Co. of Milan v. Merchants Marine Ins. Co., 55
Uravic v. F. Jarka Co., 477
U. N. R. R. A. v. The Mormacmail, 772
Urti v. Transport Commercial Corp., 357
Usatorre v. Compania Argentina Navegacion Mihanovich, 533
Usner v. Luckenbach Overseas Corp., 273, 279, 379, 389, 403, 441

# V

Valencia, The, 669, 670, 672, 676, 678, 687
Valentine Waterways Corp. v. Tug Choptank, 545
Valmar, The, 637
Vancouver S. S. Co. v. Rice, 50, 650
Vaughan v. Atkinson, 43, 306, 307, 312, 321, 322
Vega v. S/S Malula, 774, 780
Venice Maru, The, 267, 894, 927
Venizelos, S. A. v. Chase Manhattan Bank, 119
Venore Transp. Co. v. Oswego Shipping Co., 207
Verbeeck v. Black Diamond Steamship Corp., 895, 896
Vermillion Towing Corp., Petition of, 853, 860
Vernicos Shipping Co. v. United States, 533, 544, 559, 581
Ververica v. Drill Barge Buccaneer No. 7, 634, 668, 796
Vessel FL 4127 SE, United States v., 759
Vestris, The, 846
Vickers v. Machinery Warehouse & Sales Co., 113
Victoria, The, 533, 865
Victoria v. Luckenbach S. S. Co., Inc., 291
Victorias Milling Co. v. Panama Canal Co., 598
Victory, The, 493, 530
Victory Carriers, Inc. v. Law, 273, 403, 441, 447, 524
Vigilancia, The, 637
Villam & Fassio E. Compagnia v. Tank Steamer E. W. Sinclair, 513
Vincent v. Harvey Well Service, 283, 292
Virginian R. Co. v. Rose, 564
Virginia Shipbuilding Corp. v. United States Shipping Board Emergency Fleet Corp., 677, 772, 786
Virginia, The, 848
Virgin Islands Corp. v. Merwin Lighterage Co., 163
Vitco v. Joncich, 309
Vitozi v. Balboa Shipping Co., 242
Vizcaya, The, 168
Vlavianos v. The Cypress, 605, 606, 627
Voris v. Eikel, 413, 414
Vueltabajo, The, 628

# W

Wabash, The, 795
Waldeck-Deal Dredging Co., In re, 810
Walde Towing Co. v. Ricca, 871
Waldron v. Moore-McCormack Lines, Inc., 388, 400
Walker v. Boston Ins. Co., 906
Walker v. The Western Transp. Co., 161
Walker v. Woolsey, 625
Walker-Skageth Food Stores v. The Bavois, 658, 682
Wall Street Traders v. Sociedad Esponola de Construcion N., 33, 52
Walsh v. Tadlock, 56
Waring v. Clarke, 21, 23, 32
Warner v. Goltra, 427
Warner v. The Bear, 22, 27
Warren v. United States, 290, 323
Warren v. Weber & Heidenthaler, Inc., 347
Warren Corp. v. Britain S. S. Co., 211
Warren Corp. v. Picton S. S. Co., 202
Warshauer v. Lloyd Sabaudo S. A., 534
Washburn & Moen Mfg. Co. v. Reliance Marine Ins. Co., 79
Wash Gray, The, 517
Washington, The, 603, 866, 935, 936
Wasson Barge Rental Co. v. Tug Carrie D, 489, 510
Waterman S. S. Co., United States v., 246
Waterman Steamship Corp. v. Dean, 564
Waterman Steamship Corp. v. Dugan & McNamara, Inc., 444
Waterman Steamship Corp. v. Gay Cottons, 887, 892
Waterman Steamship Corp. v. Jones, 289
Waterman Steamship Corp. v. Shipowners & Merchants Towboat Co., 537, 545
Waterman Steamship Corp. v. United States, 246, 598, 984
Waters v. Merchants' Louisville Ins. Co., 73
Waterways Marine, Inc. v. Brooks Liquid Transport, Inc., 767

Wathen v. Public Fire Ins. Co., 62
Watson v. Joshua Hendy Corp., 291
Watson v. Providence Washington Ins. Co., 74
Watson v. R. C. A. Victor Co., Inc., 540
Watts v. J. B. Camors & Co., 200
Watz v. Zapata Off-Shore Co., 46, 773
W. C. Dawson & Co., State of Washington v., 48
Webb, The, 516
Webb Inc., United States v., 45
We-Four Corp. v. The Whaler, 506
W. E. Hedger Transp. Co., Petition of, 904
Weinstein v. Eastern Airlines, 30
Weiss v. Central R. Co. of New Jersey, 282, 294, 308, 428
Welded Tube Co. v. Hartford Fire Ins. Co., 62
Wellman v. Morse, 270
Wells Fargo Bank v. Barge Marguerita, 636, 658
Welsh v. Utah Dredging Co., 286
W. E. Rippon & Son v. United States, 544, 548, 559
Wessel, Duval & Co., United States v., 199, 255
Wessels v. The Asturias, 162
West, The, 333
West v. Marine Resources Commission, 301
West v. United States, 333, 441, 620, 624
West Arrow, The, 268
West Cape, The, 344
Westerbeke Corp. v. Golden Fleece, 658
Western Assur. Co. v. Southwestern Transp. Co., 87
Western Assur. Co. of Toronto v. Shaw, 72
Western Boat Building Co. v. O'Leary, 414, 432
Western Canada S. S. Co. v. United States, 232
Western Farmer, The, 942
Western Fuel Co. v. Garcia, 365, 418, 651
Western Hat & Mfg. Co. v. Berkner Bros., Inc., 102, 104
Western Maid, The, 45, 606, 607, 609, 612
Western States, The, 628
Western Transit Co. v. Davidson S. S. Co., 516
Western Wave, The, 684
West Keats, The, 611
West Kentucky Coal Co. v. Dillman, 807, 810
West Kyska, The, 168, 188
Westmoor, The, 629
West Nosska, The, 212
West Point, The, 858
Weyerhaeuser Steamship Co. v. Nacirema Operating Co., 444
Weyerhaeuser Steamship Co. v. United States, 527
Whatley v. United States, 291
White v. Island Transp. Co., 869
White's Bank v. Smith, 689
Wichita Eagle & Beacon Publishing Co. v. Pacific Nat. Bank of San Francisco, 114, 115
Wichita Falls, The, 849
Wiggins v. 1100 Tons More or Less of Italian Marble, 536
Wilburn Boat Co. v. Fireman's Fund Ins. Co., 32, 48, 56, 67–69, 464, 910
Wildwood, The, 228
Willamette Valley, The, 629, 793
Willcox, Peck & Hughes v. American Smelting & Refining Co., 254, 258, 261
Willdomino, The, 140
Willdomino v. Citro Chemical Co., 177, 180
William D. Rice, The, 690
Wm. H. Muller & Co. v. Swedish-American Line, 145
William J. Riddle, The, 495, 530, 914
William Leishear, The, 627, 734, 738, 739, 742
Williams v. New England Ins. Co., 56
Williams v. Theobald, 213
Williams v. Tide Water Associated Oil Co., 347
Williams v. United States, 300, 302, 304
Williamson v. Western Pacific Dredging Corp., 292, 308
Williams S. S. Co. v. Wilbur, 161, 893
Wilson v. Bank of Victoria, 263
Wilson v. Northwest Marine Iron Works, 772
Winona, The, 759
Winthrop, The, 782, 786
Winthrop v. Union Ins. Co., 66
Woodbury, United States v., 510
Wood, Petition of, 846, 860, 863, 866, 900
Wordsworth, The, 254
Work v. Leathers, 208, 241
Workman v. City of New York, 608
World Mermaid, 787
World Tradeways Shipping, Petition of, 854
World Wide S. S. Co. v. India Supply Mission, 181, 270
Worthington & Davis, The, 486
Wright & Cobb Lighterage Co., Petition of, 846
Wyandotte, The, 633
Wyandotte Transp. Co. v. United States, 849

X

Xantho, The, 140, 141, 162

Y

Yacht Charlotte, 840, 849, 882
Yacht Julaine, The, 883
Yacht Meridian, The, 901
Yamashita-Shinnihon Kisen, In re, 571, 572, 575, 582, 859
Yang-Tsze Ins. Ass'n v. Furness, Withy & Co., 494, 504, 509
Yankee Blade, The, 636, 663
Yarmouth Castle, The, 846, 936, 943
Yates v. Dann, 293, 347, 857
Yone Suzuki v. Central Argentine R., 221
Young Mechanic, The, 594
Yourk-Shipley, Inc. v. Atlantic Mutual Ins. Co., 61
Yungay, The, 160

Z

Zane v. The President, 795
Zapata, 860
Zebroid, The, 956
Zebroid Trawling Corp., Petition of, 841, 952
Zeller Marine Corp. v. Nessa Corp., 526
Zielinski v. Empresa Hondurena de Vapores, 477
Zimmern Coal Co. v. Coal Trading Ass'n of Rotterdam, 789
Zizania, The, 756

# INDEX

References are to Pages

**ABANDONMENT**
See Insurance; Salvage.

**ACT OF GOD**
Carrier, when not liable for cargo damage, 139.
Cogsa provision, 163, 164, 168.
Collision, 486.

**ACTION**
See In Personam Suit; In Rem Proceeding.

**ACTUAL TOTAL LOSS**
See Insurance.

**ADJUSTER**
See, also, General Average.
General average, 248–254.

**ADMIRALTY JURISDICTION**
See Jurisdiction.

**ADMIRALTY LAW**
Definition, 1.

**ADMIRALTY RULES**
See, also, Federal Rules of Civil Procedure.
Joinder of ship and owner, 624.
Limitation proceedings,
Generally, 820, 837, 838, 859–861.
Intervention, 838.
Priorities, 927, 929.
Third party practice, 937–939.
Federal Rules of Civil Procedure, 938 (note).
Transfer, 850 (note), 851 (note), 852.
Not jurisdictional, 645 (note).
Salvage, 575, 576.
Federal Rules of Civil Procedure, 576.
State-created liens, 645.
Supreme Court's rule-making power, 645 (note).
Venue, 850.
Voyage as limitation unit, 751.

**ADVANCES**
See Maritime Lien.

**AFFREIGHTMENT**
See Cargo; Carriage of Goods; Cogsa.

**AGENCY**
See, also, Broker; Respondeat Superior.
Apparent authority,
Incurring of liens, 671 et seq.

**AGENCY**—Continued
General agency agreements, 240.
General agent,
Not entitled to lien, 626.
Right to salvage award, 546, 585.
Master,
General average acts, 264.

**AIR NAVIGATION ACT** (Eng.), 540.

**AIRPLANES,** 34 (note).
See, also, Salvage; Seaplanes.
Salvage, 539–541.

**AMALFI, TABLETS OF,** 5.

**AMERICAN BUREAU OF SHIPPING,** 987, 988 (note).

**AMERICAN SOCIETY OF TRAVEL AGENTS,** 993.

**ANTI-TRUST LAWS**
Conference agreements exempt, 12, 30, 991.

**ARBITRATION**
Bill of lading clause, 220 (note).
Charter parties, 196.
Demurrage, 212.
Contract salvage, Lloyd's Form, 583.
Federal Arbitration Act, 196 (note).
Salvage awards, 566 (note), 567.

**ARMY CORPS OF ENGINEERS,** 978.

**ARREST**
See In Rem Proceeding; Maritime Lien.

**ARTICLES AND WAGES**
See Seamen.

**ARTICLES OF CONFEDERATION,** 11 (note).

**ASSIGNMENT**
Liens, assignment of, 633–635.
Effect of Uniform Commercial Code, 635.
Mortgage, assignment of, 713.

**ASSUMPTION OF RISK**
See, also, Seamen.
FELA, 351–357.
Versus contributory negligence, 354–357.
Jones Act, 351–357.
Versus contributory negligence, 354–357.

**ASSURED AND ASSURER,** 56.

**ATTACHMENT**
Goods under order bills of lading, 94.
Lien as foreign attachment [English rule], 590, 802.
Ship,
Action at law, 802.
Where owner is personally liable, 589.

**ATTORNEY FEES**
Maintenance and cure action, 313.

**AVERAGE**
See, also, General Average.
Average warranty, 68, 74, 79–82.
Defined, 80.
Memorandum clause, 79–82.
Particular average, 81.

**AVIATION SALVAGE AT SEA CONVENTION,** 540.

**BALTIC EXCHANGE,** 198.

**BANK**
See Letter of Credit; Sale of Goods.

**BANKRUPTCY AND REORGANIZATION**
See, also, Maritime Lien; Ship Mortgage Act.
Jurisdiction, 791, 806–817.

**BAREBOAT CHARTER**
See Charter Party.

**BARRATRY,** 73.

**BERTH**
Safe berth, 202, 230 (note).

**BILL OF EXCHANGE,** 111.

**BILL OF LADING**
See, also, Cogsa; Harter Act; Negotiable Instrument; Sale of Goods; Uniform Customs and Practice for Commercial Documentary Credits.
Generally, 93–192.
Benefit of insurance clause, 191.
Both-to-blame clause, 173–176.
Carrier's liability,
Generally, 139–192.
Clause paramount, 145 (note), 146 (note), 186.
Exceptions, 140.
Negligence disclaimers, 142, 143.
"Overriding obligations", disclaimer of, 141.
Pro rata clause, 189 (note).
Requirement that bill of lading be issued, 185, 186.
Charter party, issuance under, 14, 125, 195, 217–221, 232, 233.
Charterer as holder, 218, 219.
Incorporation clause, 125, 217–221.
Notice of charter terms, 218.
Clean bill, 122, 123.
Conflict of laws, 130 et seq.
Conflict of laws problems, 130 et seq.
Custody bill, 124.
Defined, 93.
Documentary sale, 13, 110–114.
Execution of underlying contract, 637.
Federal Bills of Lading (Pomerene) Act, 95, 96.
Foreign commerce, 95, 96.
Foul bill, 122.
Functions of, 13, 93.
General average, provisions concerning, 266–270.
Interstate commerce, 95, 96.
Jason clause, 266–270.
Limitation of liability,
Notation of value and character of goods, 834.
Personal contract doctrine, 898, 899.

**BILL OF LADING**—Continued
Negotiability,
Generally, 93–100.
General average liability, effect of, 265.
Good faith purchaser, 97.
Law governing, 94–96.
Ocean bills, 94.
Quasi-negotiability, 95.
Railroad bills, 94.
Negotiable instrument compared, 96.
Non-negotiable bill, 96.
On board bill, 106, 522.
Order bill,
Discharge of carrier's duty, 96.
Indorsement, 99.
Thief, issuance to, 97.
Warranties of indorser, 99.
Parol evidence 637 (note).
Parts, issuance in, 125, 126.
Indemnity for missing part, 127.
Pledge of bill, 111.
Pomerene Act, 95, 96.
Port bill, 124.
Received for shipment bill, 106, 124, 637.
Sailing vessels, 124.
Sale, bill used to finance, 13, 96, 97, 110–114.
Sets, issuance in, 125, 126.
Shipowner's liability to holder, 232, 233.
"Subject to" bill, 125, 217–221.
Through bill, 124.
"Type-contract", 14.
Uniform Bills of Lading Act, 95.
York-Antwerp Rules, stipulation for, 253, 268, 269.

**BINDER,** 57.

**BLACK BOOK OF THE ADMIRALTY,** 9 (note).

**BONDS**
General, 797, 798.
Special, 797, 798.

**BOTH-TO-BLAME CLAUSE,** 173–176.

**BOTTOMRY BOND**
Defined, 25 (note), 632.
Low priority, 690, 742.
Obsolescence, 632, 690, 742.

**BREAKDOWN CLAUSE,** 233–236.

**BROKER**
Marine insurance, 56, 57.

**BRUSSELS CONVENTION**
Collision Liability Convention (1910),
Presumptions of fault abolished, 490, 491.
Proportional negligence rule, 529, 530.
Limitation of Liability Convention (1923), 835 (note), 940.
Maritime Liens and Mortgages Convention (1926), 699.
Salvage Convention (1910), 534.

**BUOY,** 979.

**BURDEN OF PROOF**
Cargo damage actions,
Bill of lading exceptions, 141, 184.
Cogsa provisions, 167, 183–185.
Notice of damage claim, 189.
Fire Statute cases, 896.
General average, payability of, 254.
Inevitable accident, 487, 488.
Jones Act, suit, 377, 378.
Laches, 775, 776.
Limitation of liability, 895–898.
Maritime liens,
Credit to the ship, 664–668.
Release, invalidity of, 459.
Seaworthiness, 898.
Special circumstances, rule, 508.

**BUYER**
See Sale of Goods.

**BYNKERSHOEK,** 8 (note), 46.

**CARGO**
See, also, Carriage of Goods; Cogsa; Freight; General Average; Harter Act; Salvage.
Baggage, 834 (note).
Carrier's duties, 155.
Decay, 262, 263.
Explosives and dangerous goods, 742, 988.
General average, cargo interest in, 245, 246, 574.
General cargo, 13.
Governmental regulation, 988.
Improper packing, 167.
Insurance against particular average, 79–82.
Jettison, 260, 261.
Latent defects, 167.
Lien against, 215, 232, 233, 270, 630, 742.
Lien against ship for damage to cargo, 630, 741, 753.
Limitation proceedings, damage claims, 928.
Salvage award, cargo interest in, 560, 561, 574, 579.
Ship's negligence, not imputed to, 173.

**CARRIAGE OF GOODS**
See, also, Cogsa; Harter Act.
Carrier's duty to fulfill contract, 262.
Carrier's prestatutory liability,
Generally, 139–142.
Burden of proof, importance, 141.
Exceptions, 139, 140.
Negligence, stipulations against liability for, 142, 143, 167, 172.
Overriding obligations, 141.
Shipper's prima facie case, 141.
Warranty of seaworthiness, 141, 151 (note).
Charter, carriage under, 207–209.
Containerization, 144.
Delivery of goods under bills of lading, 96.
Liability, lost or damaged goods, 139–192.
Warranty of seaworthiness, 150–155.

**CARRIAGE OF GOODS BY SEA ACT**
See Cogsa.

**CARRIER**
See Carriage of Goods; Insurance.

**CASAREGIS,** 8 (note).

**CENSUS, BUREAU OF,** 979.

**CESSER CLAUSE,** 215–217, 221–223.

**CESSER OF HIRE CLAUSE,** 234.

**CHARTER PARTY**
Generally, 193–243.
Arbitration, demurrage, 196, 212.
Bareboat charter, see this title, Demise charter.
Bill of lading issued under, 14, 125, 195, 217–221, 232, 233.
Bulk shipment, 13.
Cogsa,
Charter not governed by, 125, 207.
Stipulation for, 199, 209.
Construction of charter terms, 198, 199.
Defined, 193.
Demise charter,
Generally, 193, 239–243.
Charterer as owner, 242, 498 (note).
Condition at end of term, 241.
Control of vessel, 239–241.
Distinguishing features, 239–241.
General agency agreements, 240, 981.
Government, use by, 240, 981.
Inspection of vessel, 241.
Insurance, 241.
Jones Act, 242.
Liens incurred by charterer, 242, 243.
Limitation of liability, 242, 840.
Respondeat superior, 242.
Seamen, 242.
Seaworthiness, 241.
Voyage nature, 193, 194.
Execution, when accomplished, 636, 637.
Gencon, 199, 997–1002 (Appendix A).
Harter Act, stipulation for, 199, 209.
Insurance premium, effect of deviation on, 230.
Liens incurred by charterer, 215–217, 242, 243, 600, 615, 636, 637.
Part of ship, charter of, 193.
Personal contract doctrine, 899.
Rules of Civil Procedure, applicability, 193.
Salvage,
Award, 568.
Liability for, 578.
Standardized contract, 15, 195, 199 et seq.
Subcharter, 195.
Time charter, 229–239.
Generally, 193, 194, 229 et seq., 1003.
Basic arrangement, 229, 230.
Bill of lading issued under, 232, 233.
Breakdown clause, 233–236.
Deficiency of men, 234.
Dispatch, 231.
Exceptions clause, 233–236.
Frustration, 236.

**CHARTER PARTY**—Continued
Time charter—Continued
Fumigation, 230.
Liens on charter and subfreight, 232, 233.
N. Y. Produce Exchange Charter, (1946), 1003.
Loading and unloading, 231.
Non-demise nature, 194.
Overlap and underlap, 231, 232.
Restraint of princes, 234.
Safe ports, 230.
Seaworthiness, 229.
Trading limits, 230.
Warranties, 229.
Type-contract, 15, 195, 199 et seq.
Voyage charter,
Generally, 193, 197–229, 997–1002.
Basic terms, 200 et seq.
Bills issued by charterer, 217–221.
Cancellation date, 201, 202.
Cargo damage, 207–209.
Cesser clause, 215–217, 221–223.
Charterer's misperformance of charter duties, 207 (note).
Constructive conditions, 223.
Delay, 201.
Demurrage, 211–215.
Deviation, 209, 210.
Dispatch money, 212.
Freight, payment of, 210.
Frustration, 223–229.
Gencon, 199, 997–1002.
General average, 229.
Ice, 223.
Impossibility, 223–229.
Jason clause, 229.
Lay days, 211.
Liens, 215–217.
Loading and unloading, 210–215.
Port of loading, 202.
Running days, 211.
Safe berths clause, 202.
Safe ports clause, 202.
Scope of voyage, 209.
Strikes, 223.
War, 223.
Warranties, 200, 201.
Weather working days, 211.
Working days, 211.

**CHARTERER**
Bill of lading, rights as holder, 218.
Charterer as consignee, 223.
Demise charterer as "owner", 242, 498 (note).
Insurance, 230, 241.
Liability to owner, 215–217, 221–223.
Liens, power to create, 242, 243.
Limitation of liability, 839, 905.
Seamen, responsibility to, 242.

**CHOICE OF LAW**
See Conflict of Laws.

**C.I.F.**
Term defined, 106, 114.

**CLAIMANT,** 36.

**CLASSIFICATION SOCIETIES,** 57.

**CLEIRAC,** 8 (note), 146, 187, 631.

**COAST AND GEODETIC SURVEY,** 978, 979.

**COAST GUARD**
Activities of, 978.
Inspection of vessels, 987.
License revocation, 989.
Loadline Statute enforcement, 987.
Navigations Rules enforcement, 989.
Oil pollution, 989.
Passenger vessels, approval of plans, 986.
Personnel of ships, certification, 988.
Pilot Rules, 488 (note).
Port security, 989.
Salvage, 549–551, 554.

**COASTWISE TRADE**
Calendar year rule, 747.
Domestic vessels, 963.
Foreign vessels, 696 (note).

**CODES**
Sea-codes, Mediterranean, 5, 6.

**COGSA (CARRIAGE OF GOODS BY SEA ACT)**
See, also, Bill of Lading; Carriage of Goods; Hague Rules; Harter Act; Seaworthiness.
Generally, 93–192.
Absolute liability eliminated, 150.
Act of God, 163, 164, 168.
Benefit of insurance clause, 191.
Bill of lading controlled by, 145, 185, 186.
Bill of lading must be issued, 185.
Bills of lading giving notice of charter terms, 218.
Bills of lading subject to Act, 145 (note), 185, 186.
Bills of lading "subject to" charter, 217–221.
Burden of proof, 167, 183–185.
Cargo, care of,
Generally, 155.
Effect of voyage clause on duty of care, 182.
Navigation and management, distinguished, 156.
Peril of the sea, distinguished, 162.
Carriage liens, 186, 187.
Carrier's "responsibilities and liabilities", 149, 150.
Carrier's "rights and immunities", 149, 150.
"Catch-all", exception, 167, 168.
Charter, bill incorporating terms of, 217–221.
Charterer, bills issued by, 217–221, 232, 233.
Charters, Act incorporated in, 198, 209.
Charters not governed by Act, 125, 207.
Choice of law: see this title. Conflict of laws.
Claims, 187–189.
Clause paramount, 145 (note), 146 (note), 186.
Coastwise option, 148.

**COGSA (CARRIAGE OF GOODS BY SEA ACT)**—Continued
Concurrent negligence, 172.
Conflict of laws, 130.
    Stipulation for foreign law, 145, 146 (note).
Customary freight, unit, 187.
Damages,
    Determination of, 188.
    Minimization of, 170.
    Notice of, 189.
Demised ship, liability of, 243.
Deviation, 176–183, 269, 560.
Domestic commerce, not covered by Act, 147.
Fire, 161, 834.
Foreign commerce, covered by Act, 147.
General average, 267–270.
Harter Act, Cogsa coverage, compared, 144–149.
Incorporation of charter terms, 217–221.
Inherent vice, 169.
Jason clause, 267, 268.
Labor disputes, 164–166, 169.
Latent defects, 167, 169.
Liens, stipulations against, 186, 187.
Life salvage, 167.
Marks, inadequacy of, 167.
Maximum recovery, 187, 188.
Navigation and management, immunity,
        Generally, 155–160, 169, 170.
    Absolute immunity under, Cogsa, 155.
    Both-to-blame clause, 173–176.
    Care of cargo, distinguished, 156.
    Conditional immunity, under Harter Act, 155, 156.
    Diligence to make seaworthy, distinguished, 159, 160.
Negligence, substantive effect of, 169–173.
Overwhelming human force, 164–166.
Package, recovery limit, 187, 188.
Packing, 167.
Perils of the sea, 162, 163, 169.
Pro rata clause invalid, 189 (note).
Public enemy, act of, 164, 169.
Quarantine, 164, 169.
Restraint of princes, 163, 164, 169.
Rights acquired by negotiation, 130.
Riot and civil commotion, 164, 169.
Salvage, 560.
Seaworthiness,
        Generally, 150–155.
    Duty to use due diligence, 150 et seq.
    Latent defects, 167, 169.
    Relation to perils of the sea, 163.
    Warranty abolished, 151.
    When obligation must be met, 151.
Seizure under legal process, 164, 169.
Ship, carrier's duties in furnishing, 150–155.
Shipper, fault of, 167, 169.
Statute of limitations, 768.
Statutory construction, 171–173, 175, 176.
Stipulation for foreign law, 145, 146.
Strikes, 164–166, 169.
Valuation, 187–189.

**COGSA (CARRIAGE OF GOODS BY SEA ACT)**—Continued
War, act of, 164, 169.
York-Antwerp Rules, 268–270.

**COLLISION**
Generally, 485–531.
Act of God, 486.
Breakwater, 509.
Burden of proof, 487.
Causation, 494–498.
Contact, absence of, 497.
Contributory negligence, 492, 493, 499.
Cross-complaint, failure to bring, 498, 499.
Custom, 489, 509, 514, 515.
Damages, 492, 493, 524–531.
Demise charterer's liability, 498.
Docking, 509.
Elements of liability, 486–488.
Errors in extremis, 491, 530.
Evidence, 499, 500.
Fault,
Generally, 486–488, 492, 493.
Basis of liability, 486–488.
Both vessels at fault, 492, 528.
Breach of statutory standard, 488 et seq.
Effect of, 492, 493.
Major-minor fault rule, 492, 493, 529, 530.
Neither vessel at fault, 492.
One vessel at fault, 492.
Statutory fault, 494–498, 508, 848, 849.
Great Lakes Rules, 489, 490, 989 (note).
Inevitable accident, 487, 488.
Inland Rules, 490, 515.
Inscrutable fault, 486.
International Rules,
Generally, 489–491, 500–514.
Application of, 500.
Burdened and privileged vessel, 495, 504, 515.
Cable-laying vessels, 501–503, 508.
Definitions, 500.
Fog, 504–508.
Foghorn, 508.
General prudential Rule, 509–511.
Lights, 501–503.
Local Rules, 500.
Negligence, 509–511.
Power vessels, 503, 504.
Privileged vessel, must keep course, 504.
Seaplanes, 500.
Shapes, 501, 503.
Signals not specifically required, 510, 511.
Sound signals, 505, 508.
Special circumstances, 508.
Speed, 505, 506.
Steering and sailing Rules, 503, 504.
Stop engines, requirement, 505–507.
Towage, 501.
Violation, penalty for, 989.
Visible distance test, 505, 507.

**COLLISION**—Continued
Intervening negligence, 494.
Jury trial, 500.
Last clear chance, 494 (note).
Lien for wrongful collision, 498, 628, 739, 743, 752.
Litigation, 498–500.
Lookout, failure to maintain, 494, 510.
Machinery, failure of, 487.
Navigation Rules, 488, 500–514.
Pennsylvania Rule, 494–498, 530, 848, 849, 898.
Pilot Rules, 488 (note).
Pilotage,
Generally, 520–522.
Compulsory pilots, 520, 521.
Half-pilotage, 520.
Negligence clauses, 521, 522.
Presumption of fault, 487, 490, 494–498.
Radar, 511–514.
Rules of the Road, 489, 500–514.
Ship to shore collisions, 522–524.
Standards of proper action, 488–492.
Stand-by Act, 490, 491, 553.
Statutory fault, 494–498, 848, 849.
Third vessel, 509.
Towage, 515–520.
Negligence clauses, 516–520.
Unavoidable accident, 487, 488.
Vis major, 486.
Western Rivers Rules, 490, 515, 989 (note).

**COMMERCE, DEPARTMENT OF,** 967, 976.

**COMMON LAW**
Common law defenses, 456, 457.

**COMMON LAW REMEDY**
See Jurisdiction.

**COMPARATIVE NEGLIGENCE,** 351, 500 (note).

**COMPENSATION COMMISSION,** 408, 409.

**COMPENSATION ORDERS**
Judicial review, 412.

**COMPLAINT**
See, also, Libel.
Cross complaint,
Collision, action, 498.

**CONFERENCE SYSTEM**
Anti-trust exemption, 12, 30, 991.
Dual rate system, 992.
Purpose, 12, 991.
Rebates, 992.

**CONFLICT OF LAWS**
Generally, 47–51, 130, 463–468, 471–484, 777–780, 939–946.
Bankruptcy sale, foreign recognition of, 817.
Bills of lading, 130, 130 et seq.
Borrowing statutes, 777–780.
Collision, 489.

**CONFLICT OF LAWS**—Continued
Death claim against foreign shipowner, 847 (note).
Erie-Tompkins Rule, 318, 459, 720, 778, 779.
Federal-state, 47–52.
Federal supremacy, 47–51, 68–71, 458, 459, 463–468.
Foreign shipowner, 847, 928, 939–946.
General average adjustment, 253.
International, 51, 52.
Lien execution, international recognition of, 788.
Limitation decree, extent of international recognition of, 928.
Limitation of liability, 939–946.
Maritime law in non-admiralty court, 456 et seq.
Pollution control, 50.
Salvage, 533.
Saving clause, 50, 51.
Seamen's actions, 471–484.
Ship Mortgage Act, 718–727.
Ship mortgages, 700, 718–727.
State vs. federal, 463–468.
Statutes of limitation, 777–780.
Stipulation for foreign law, 23 (note), 145, 146 (note).
Twilight zone, 463.
United States vs. foreign law, 471–484.
Workmen's compensation system as foreign law, 483.

**CONGRESS**
Judiciary Act (1789), 18, 19, 37.
Power to alter admiralty jurisdiction, 692–695.

**CONSOLIDATION**
Admiralty and insolvency proceedings, 814, 815.

**CONSTITUTION OF THE UNITED STATES**
Admiralty jurisdiction, 11, 19, 45, 404, 692–695.
Due process of law, 404.
Longshoremen's Act, 412.
National uniformity, 404–408, 642.
State workmen's compensation acts, 404.

**CONSTRUCTIVE TOTAL LOSS**
See Insurance.

**CONSULAT DE MAR**, 5, 590.

**CONTAINERIZATION**
Generally, 144.
Carrier liability, 188, 191.
Insurance, 58.
Mode of shipping, 14.

**CONTRACT**
Anticipatory repudiation, 636.
Charter party, 14, 193, 899.
Exculpatory clauses, 142, 143, 151, 186, 187, 516–520, 836.
Executory contracts, 635–641.
Frustration, 197–203, 223–229, 236.
Impossibility, 223–229.
Insurance policy, 53, 56.
Jurisdiction, see Jurisdiction.
Mixed contracts, 28.

**CONTRACT**—Continued
Passage, contract of, 23 (note).
Personal contract, 751, 898–906.
Quasi-contract, 27, 41.
Reformation, 579, 580.
Sale of vessel, 26.
Salvage, 578–585.
Separability, 29 (note).
Shipbuilding contract, 16, 26, 650.
Substantial performance, 112 (note).
Towage, 515–520, 904.
"Type-contract", 15, 195.

**CONTRIBUTION,** 314.
Joint tortfeasors, 314, 315.

**CONTRIBUTORY NEGLIGENCE**
See, also, Collision, Jurisdiction, Seamen.
Collision actions, 499.
FELA, 354–357.
Jones Act, 354–357.

**CONVERSION,** 558.

**CORPORATION**
Government corporations, 982.
Insurers, 55.
Personal fault, 161, 884 et seq.
Shipowners, 12.

**COST, INSURANCE, FREIGHT,** 106–108.

**COST AND FREIGHT,** 107.

**COTTON,** 124.

**COURT OF CLAIMS,** 983, 985.

**COURTS**
Maritime, history of, 5–11.

**CRIMINAL OFFENSES**
Jurisdiction, 44.

**CROSS-LIBEL**
See Libel.

**CUSTOMARY FREIGHT UNIT,** 188.

**CUSTOMS, COLLECTOR OF**
Clearance papers, 790.
Notice of lien, filing, 757.
Ship mortgages, 707, 712–717.
Tax on aliens entering U. S., 759.

**CUSTOMS, COMMISSIONER OF,** 696 (note).

**CUSTOMS BUREAU,** 987, 988.

**DAMAGES**
Breakdown clause, 233.
Brussels Liability Convention (1910), 529.
Cargo damage, 187–189.
Collision, 492, 493, 524–531.

**DAMAGES**—Continued
Contribution, 314, 442.
Detention of pleasure yacht, 526 (note).
Divided damages,
Generally, 492, 493, 524–531.
Both-to-blame clause, 173.
History, 528.
Multi-ship collisions, 528.
Non-collision cases, 442.
Personal injury action, 442.
Third parties, 527.
Exceptions clause, 235.
Foreign exchange fluctuations, 526.
Harbor worker's action, 438 et seq.
Liquidated damages, 235, 836.
Lost profits, 526 (note).
Maintenance and cure, 293 et seq.
Pro rata clause, 189 (note).
Proportional negligence, 492, 495, 496, 528–531.
Salvage award, 559–574.
Stipulation of value, 188, 189.
Valuation,
Cargo, 187–189.
Vessel, 524–526.
Vessel,
Less than total loss, 526–528.
Loss of use, 526.
Total loss, 524.

**DEATH**
See, also, Damages; Seamen; Wrongful Death.
Recovery for, 272 et seq.

**DEATH ON THE HIGH SEAS ACT**
See Jurisdiction; Passengers; Seamen; Wrongful Death.

**DEFENDANT,** 35.

**DEFICIENCY JUDGMENT**
In personam action, 801–805.

**DEFINITIONS**
Foreign trade, 108.
Shipping terms, 105–109.

**DEMISE CHARTER**
Generally, 239–243.

**DEMURRAGE**
Generally, 211–215.
Consignee, liability of, 220, 221.
Contract demurrage, 211.
Damages for detention, 212.
Lien for, 631, 641.
Non-contract demurrage, 211, 212.
Vis major, 214.

**DEPOSITION,** 35.

**DERELICT**
See Salvage.

**DEVIATION**
Carriage of goods,
Generally, 176–183.
Causation, 180–182.
Definition of voyage, 177.
Liberties clause, 178 (note).
Life salvage, 178, 183, 185.
Misconduct of carrier, 182, 183.
Ouster of contract, 180, 181.
Reasonable deviation, 178, 179.
Salvage, 568, 569.
Scope of voyage clause, 179.
Fire statute, 848 (note).
General average, 269.
Insurance, 66, 67, 176, 230.
Limitation of liability, 848 (note).
Salvage operations, 568, 569.
Voyage charter, 209, 210.

**DISBURSEMENTS**
See Insurance; Maritime Lien.

**DISPATCH,** 212, 231.
Dispatch money, 212.

**DIVIDED DAMAGES**
See Damages.

**DOCK RECEIPT,** 13.

**DOCUMENTARY SALE**
See, also, Sale of Goods.
Generally, 110–114.

**DOCUMENTATION,** 712–715, 987 (note).
See Enrollment and Licensing; Registry; Ship Mortgage Act.

**DRAFT,** 110–112.

**DUE DILIGENCE**
See Cogsa; Seaworthiness.

**ELECTION OF REMEDIES**
See Seamen.

**EMERIGON,** 8 (note).

**ENROLLMENT AND LICENSING,** 696, 712, 713, 987.
See Documentation; Registry.

**EQUIPMENT**
Title retention, 727–732.

**EQUITY**
Fraudulent transfer, 42.
Jurisdiction, 38, 41–43, 792.
Limitation proceeding, 934.
Remedies, 38, 41–43.

**ERIE-TOMPKINS RULE**
See Conflict of Laws.

**ESSENTIAL ROUTES,** 970–973, 976.

**EXECUTION SALE,** 802.

**F.A.S.,** 106.
Term defined, 106.

**F.O.B.,** 106.
Term defined, 106.

**FAULT**
See Collision; General Average.

**FEDERAL ARBITRATION ACT,** 196 (note).

**FEDERAL BILLS OF LADING ACT**
Cogsa, effect of, 95.
Foreign commerce, 95, 96.
Interstate commerce, 95, 96.
Parts, bills issued in, 125, 126.

**FEDERAL COURTS,** 19.
Erie-Tompkins rule, 318, 459, 720, 778, 779.

**FEDERAL EMPLOYEES' COMPENSATION ACT,** 284.

**FEDERAL EMPLOYERS' LIABILITY ACT**
See Seamen.

**FEDERAL JURISDICTION**
See Jurisdiction.

**FEDERAL MARITIME BOARD**
See Maritime Board.

**FEDERAL MARITIME COMMISSION,** 990.

**FEDERAL MARITIME LIEN ACT**
See Maritime Lien.

**FEDERAL RULES OF CIVIL PROCEDURE**
Applicability to admiralty actions, 2, 19, 34, 37, 193, 317, 576, 610, 624, 629, 751, 797, 805, 820 (note), 838, 850, 859–861, 927, 938 (note), 947.

**FEDERAL TAX LIEN ACT,** 758.

**FINANCIAL RESPONSIBILITY ACT,** 837.

**FIRE**
Cogsa, liability under, 161, 169.
Carrier's negligence, 161, 169.
General average, 258, 259.
Insurance, 73.
Jason clause, 267.

**FIRE STATUTE**
Burden of proof, 896.
Cogsa, effect of, 161.
Design or neglect, 878.
Deviation, 848 (note).
Jason clause, 267.
Limitation of Liability Act, 834.

**FISHERMEN**
Limitation of liability, 836
Loss of catch, damages for, 526 (note).
Maintenance and cure, 287.
Mortgage on fishing vessel, 696.
Salvage award despite custom of giving aid, 541.
Trawling signals, 510.

**FIXED ROUTE,** 976.

**FLEET OR FLOTILLA**
Demurrage, 212.
Fleet mortgages, 709, 710.
Lien for supplies, 662 (note).
Lights, 502.
Limitation of liability, 918.
Unit, when considered as, 515, 516.

**FOG**
Navigation rules, 503–508.

**FOREIGN COMMERCE, BUREAU OF,** 979.

**FORFEITURE,** 715.

**FORUM**
Selection clause, 856, 857.

**FORUM NON CONVENIENS**
Generally, 51, 489 (note).
Foreign litigants, suits between, 945.
Limitation of liability proceedings, 869, 936.

**FRAUDS, STATUTE OF,** 651.

**FRAUDULENT TRANSFER,** 42.

**FREE ALONGSIDE,** 106.

**FREE ON BOARD,** 106.

**FREIGHT,** 915.
Assignment of, 786.
Charter party option, 202.
Dead freight, 207 (note), 215, 639.
Defined, 245.
Dual rate system, 992.
General average, 245–248.
Insurance, 58.
Lien on, 624.
Limitation fund, 835 (note).
Overpayment, 640.
Prepaid freight, 218 (note), 753 (note).
Rate fixing and regulation, 990–995.
Rebates, 992.
Salvage, 559–561.
Voyage charter, 209, 210.

**FREIGHT FORWARDER,** 14.
Function of, 13, 14.

**FRUSTRATION,** 236.
Doctrine of, 223–229, 236.

**FUMIGATION,** 230.

**GARNISHMENT,** 113.

**GENCON,** 997–1002.

**GENERAL AVERAGE**
See, also, Average.
Generally, 244–271.
Adjuster, 248–254.

**References are to Pages**

**GENERAL AVERAGE**—Continued
Adjustment,
Illustrated, 247.
Master's duty to procure, 248, 249 (note).
Not binding, 251.
Agency theory, 264.
Basic elements, 245.
Bill of lading provision, 267–270.
Bond required of consignee, 248 (note), 249, 254 (note), 265, 574.
Burden of proof, 254.
Cargo,
Interest of, 245, 246, 574.
Release of, to consignee, 249, 254 (note), 270, 574.
Charter provisions, 229.
Choice of law, 253.
Cogsa, 267–270.
Common venture, 259, 260.
Contributing interests, 245, 246, 250.
Decay, 262, 263.
Defined, 80, 246.
Deposit required of consignee, 248 (note), 249, 254, 265 (note), 270, 574.
Deviation, 269.
Disease control regulations, 262 (note).
Engines, extraordinary use of, 261.
Expenditures in excess of value, 264.
Fault, effect of, 266–270.
Fire, 267.
Freight, interest of, 245, 246.
General average acts, 248.
General average agreement, 249, 251.
General average expenditure, 247, 248, 262, 263.
Harter Act, effect of fault under, 266–270.
History of, 4, 244.
Insurance, 80, 86, 250.
Jason clause, 229, 266–268.
Jettison, 260, 261.
Jurisdiction, 270.
Liens, 270, 630, 742.
Litigation, rare, 250, 251.
Peril,
Generally, 245, 254–260.
Degree of danger required, 255, 256.
Fire, 258, 259.
Inevitable loss, 256–258.
Mistaken belief as to, 254, 255.
Stranding, 255–259.
Voluntariness, effect on, 256–258.
Port of refuge expenses, 247, 248, 262.
Sacrifice, 245, 248, 256–258.
Salvage, 261 (note), 574.
Salvage payments, 262.
Sea protest, 250.
Security required of consignee, 248 (note), 249, 254 (note), 270, 574.
Ship, interest of, 245, 246.
Statement of general average, 250.
Stipulated place of adjustment, 253.
Subsequent total loss, 264.
"Substituted expenses", 263.
Temporary repairs, 262.

**GENERAL AVERAGE**—Continued
Third parties, liability to, 261.
Towage, 259, 260.
Underwriter's guarantee of deposit, 249, 254.
Unjust enrichment theory, 265.
Valuation, 263–265.
Voluntary sacrifice, 245, 256–258.
York-Antwerp Rules, 252–254.

**GENERAL BOND,** 798.

**GENERAL SHIP,** 13.

**GOTLAND SEA LAWS,** 6 (note).

**GOVERNMENTAL ACTIVITY IN SHIPPING**
See History; United States.

**GREAT LAKES**
Enrollment and licensing, 696 (note).
Jurisdiction, 32, 33.
Jury trial, 33.
Navigation rules, 489, 490, 989 (note).
Personal injury limitation fund, 922.
Season rule, 745.

**GUIDON de la MER,** 54.

**HAGUE RULES,** 143, 165, 179.

**HANSA TOWNS, LAWS OF,** 6.

**HARBOR WORKERS**
See Seamen.

**HARTER ACT**
Generally, 93, 142.
Bill of lading,
Exculpatory clauses, 142, 143, 151, 186, 187.
Requirement that bill be issued, 185.
Rights acquired by negotiation, 131.
Charter party stipulation, 199, 209.
Cogsa coverage compared,
Generally, 144–149.
Coastwise trade, 147, 148.
Harter Act cases as Cogsa precedent, 148, 149.
Pre-loading custody, 147.
Diligence to make ship seaworthy, 143, 151.
Domestic commerce, 147.
Foreign commerce, 147.
General average, 266.
Navigation and management, 142, 143, 155.
Salvage, damage resulting from, 560.
Towage, 147 (note).

**HISTORY**
Generally, 3–11.
Ancient,
Customary law, 3, 4.
England,
Generally, 8–10.
Jurisdiction of admiralty, 8–10, 590.
Jury trial, 9.

**HISTORY**—Continued
England—Continued
Lord High Admiral, 9.
Modern status of court, 10.
Richard II, Statutes of, 9.
Medieval,
Amalfi, Tablets of, 5.
Civil law, 8.
Codes, 5, 6.
Hansa Towns, laws of, 6.
Law merchant, 5.
Oleron, Rules of, 7, 46, 244, 590.
Tribunals, 5.
Wisby, Laws of, 6.
Mediterranean origins, 4–7.
Rhodes and the Rhodian law, 3, 244, 590.
Rome, 3, 4, 244, 960.
Shipping policy,
Generally, 958 et seq.
Direct regulation, 962, 963.
English Navigation Act, 961–963.
Governmental participation, 963, 980.
Monopoly, 962, 963.
Subsidy, 962, 969–977.
United States,
Generally, 11 et seq., 21.
Break from English tradition, 589, 590.
Constitutional provision, 11.
Judiciary Act of 1789, 11.
Shipbuilding, 963, 964.
Shipping policy, 963 et seq.
Steam navigation, 964, 965.

**HOLDER IN DUE COURSE,** 96–98.

**HOME PORT DOCTRINE**
See Maritime Lien.

**HOME PORT OF VESSELS ACT (1925),** 713

**HONOR POLICY,** 61.

**HULL INSURANCE,** 58

**HYPOTHECATION,** 713

**ICE PATROL,** 978.

**IDENTIFICATION**
Goods, sale, 109.

**IMMUNITY**
See Sovereign Immunity.

**IMPLEADER**
Charterer, in suit against shipowner, 601, 610–613.
Insurer, in salvage suit, 576, 577.
Limitation proceedings, 937–939.
State, in action against ship for liens while in state control, 610–613.
Third party tortfeasor in seaman's actions, 316–319, 392.

**IMPUTED NEGLIGENCE**
Carrying ship's negligence not imputed to cargo, 945.
Ship's negligence, whether imputed to crew, 552, 739, 929.

**IN PERSONAM SUIT**
See, also, In Rem Proceeding; Res Judicata.
Charter party, action for breach, 193, 216.
City, admiralty suit against, 608, 610, 612.
Defense of in rem action no submission to in personam liability, 801–805.
Deficiency judgment, 801–805.
Defined, 35.
Demise charterer, 242.
Executory contract, breach of, 635, 636, 640.
Joinder with in rem action, 801–805.
Limitation decree, effect of, 927.
Non-lien claimant, 622.
Saving clause, 37.
Shipowner's personal liability,
Bill of lading, holder of, 233.
Collision, 498.
Compulsory pilot, 520 (note).
Deficency judgment, 624, 801–805.
Harbor workers, suit by, 277, 278.
Salvage, 536, 576, 577.
Seaman's maintenance and cure suit, 293.
State, admiralty suit against, 610, 612.
United States, suit against, 982.
Unseaworthiness action, 616–621.

**IN REM PROCEEDING**
See, also, Maritime Lien; Res Judicata.
Appearance not submission to in personam liability, 801–805.
Arrest, release from, 796 et seq.
Attachment and levy, 38.
Bill of lading, holder's action, 233.
Charter party, breach of, 193, 216.
Collision, 498, 521.
Compulsory pilot's negligence, 520, 521.
Decree's international effect, 786–790.
Defined, 35.
Effect of personal appearance, 805.
English theory, 589, 590, 802.
Executory contracts, 635–641.
Federal jurisdiction, exclusive, 38.
Foreign public vessels, 985 (note).
General bond, 797–800.
Harbor worker's suit, 278.
Intervention by non-lien claimant, 796.
Joinder with in personam action, 801–805.
Jones Act, 341.
Judgment, limited amount of, 624.
Lien,
Generally, 35–37, 622–624.
Cargo, 186.
Execution of, 587, 786–790.
Seamen's actions, 293, 341.
Limitation proceeding,
Effect of decree, 927.
Personification of ship, 589, 590.
Salved property, 575, 576.
Special bond, 797–800.
State-created liens, 645–647, 650.
Stipulation for value, 796 et seq.

**IN REM PROCEEDING**—Continued
Unseaworthiness action, 616–621.
United States, action against, 982.

**INCHMAREE CLAUSE**
See Insurance.

**INDEMNITY**
Shipowner's action, 442–446.

**INHERENT VICE**
Carrier not liable, 139, 169.

**INJUNCTION,** 809, 863, 867, 870, 872.

**INJURIES**
Recovery for, generally, 272 et seq.

**INLAND RULES**
See Collision.

**INSPECTION,** 987.

**INSURABLE INTEREST**
See Insurance.

**INSURANCE**
Generally, 17, 53–92.
Acceptance, 57.
All risk insurance, 75.
Application, 57.
Assured, 56.
Assurer, 56.
Barratry, 73.
Benefit of insurance clause, 189–191.
Binder, 57.
Broker, 56.
Cargo insurance,
Generally, 189–191.
F.P.A. clause, 82, 190.
Loan receipt, 191.
Seaworthiness admitted, 154, 155.
Subrogation, 189–191.
Carrier, 55.
Charter party,
Charterer's duty to insure, 241.
Trading limits, 230.
Classification societies, 57.
Club insurance, 76.
Codification, 55, 56.
Collision, 76, 87.
Commissions, insurance on, 58, 59.
Concealment, 62.
Conflict of laws, 68.
Containerization, 58.
Corporate insurers, 55.
Coverage, 57–59.
Deviation, 66, 67, 176 et seq.
Extra premium, 182, 230.
Direct action statutes, 908–912.
Disbursements, insurance on, 58, 61.
Fire, 73.

**INSURANCE**—Continued
Freight, insurance on, 58.
Frustration, 58, 223–229.
General average, 80, 86.
History, 54–56.
Hull insurance, 58, 76.
Insurable interest,
Generally, 59–62.
Defined, 60.
Disbursements, 61.
Policy proof of interest (P.P.I.), 61.
Unspecified interest, 62.
International Union of Marine Insurance, 990.
Lien,
Insurance proceeds, 623 (note), 752.
Unpaid premiums, no lien for, 625, 648, 650.
Limitation fund, proceeds excluded from, 752, 907–912.
Lloyd's, 55.
Loss,
Actual total, 83.
Constructive total, 83–85.
Partial, 79–82, 87.
Total, 83–86.
Marine Insurance Act (Eng.), 60.
Misrepresentation, 62.
Ordinary marine insurance, 71, 72.
Particular average, 79–82, 86.
Perils clause, 71 et seq.
Construction, 74.
Principal types, 86.
Pilferage, 73, 74.
Policy,
Generally, 56–58.
All risk policy, 75, 190.
Certificates under open policy, 58 (note).
Collision and running down clause, 76.
Deductible average clause, 82.
Floating policy, 58, 107 (note).
Free of Capture and Seizure (F.C. & S.) clause, 71, 72.
Free of Particular Average, American Conditions, 82.
Free of Particular Average, English Conditions, 82.
Free of Particular Average (FPA) clause, 79–82.
General average, coverage of, 250.
Held covered clause, 177, 182.
Honor policy, 61.
Hull policy, 58, 76, 82.
Inchmaree clause, 74 (note), 75 (note).
Lost or not lost, 59.
Memorandum clause, 79–82.
Mimimum franchise clause, 82.
Open policy, 58, 107.
Ordinary marine policy, 71.
Perils clause, 71–76, 190.
Protection and Indemnity (P. & I.) policy, 59, 76.
Sue and labor clause, 75, 86.
Valued policy, 86–90.
Formulae and calculations, 88–90.
War risk policy, 71, 72, 189.
Profits, insurance on, 58, 59.

**INSURANCE**—Continued
Protection and Indemnity (P. & I.) insurance, 59, 519, 822.
Proximate cause, 76–79.
Rates, 57.
Representation, 62.
Risks insured against, 71–76.
Salvage award, assurer's liability for, 576, 577.
State legislation, effect of, 48, 68–71.
Subrogation, 91, 92, 189–191.
Sue-and-labor clause, 75, 86.
Thievery, 73, 74.
Uberrimae fidei, 62.
War Risk Insurance Act, 981.
Warranty, see Seaworthiness; Warranty.
Total loss, 83–86.
Valuation, procedure, 88–90.
Valued policy, 86–90.
War risk Insurance, 71, 72, 79, 955, 981.
Warranties,
Express, 67–71.
Federal supremacy, 68–71.
Warranty of seaworthiness, 63–67.

**INSURED,** 56.

**INSURER,** 56.

**INTERGOVERNMENTAL MARITIME CONSULTATIVE ORGANIZATION,** 825.

**INTERNATIONAL CHAMBER OF COMMERCE,** 990.

**INTERNATIONAL CONVENTION ON CIVIL LIABILITY FOR OIL POLLUTION DAMAGE,** 825.

**INTERNATIONAL LAW ASSOCIATION,** 990.

**INTERNATIONAL LOAD LINE CONVENTION (1930),** 987.

**INTERNATIONAL MARITIME COMMITTEE,** 990.

**INTERNATIONAL RULES**
See Collision.

**INTERNATIONAL UNION OF MARINE INSURANCE,** 990.

**INTERPLEADER,** 98.

**INTERSTATE COMMERCE COMMISSION,** 990.

**INTERVENTION**
Admiralty proceedings, generally, 787, 793, 794.
Limitation proceedings, 838, 930, 931.
Mandatory intervention, 930, 931.
Non-lien claimants, 796.
United States, intervention to protect tax lien, 760.

**INTRACOASTAL WATERWAY,** 490.

**INVOICE,** 122.

**JASON CLAUSE,** 266–268.

**JETTISON**
See General Average.

**JOINDER**
Deficiency judgment requisite, 624, 801–805.
In rem and in personam actions, 801–805.
Maintenance-cure action with Jones Act action, 295.
Seamen's actions,
Jones Act and unseaworthiness counts, 279, 342–346.
Maintenance and cure and other counts, 293.
Shipowner and third party tort-feasor, 314, 319.
Ship and cargo owners in salvage award action, 576, 577.
Ship and shipowner, 624.

**JONES ACT**
See, also, Seamen.
Generally, 325–383.
Claim under jurisdiction, 294–296.

**JUDGMENT**
See In Rem Proceeding.

**JUDICIAL NOTICE,** 489.

**JUDICIAL REVIEW**
Compensation orders, 412.
LHCA compensation orders, 412.

**JURISDICTION**
Generally, 11, 18–50, 624–633, 692–695.
Admiralty Rules, 645 (note).
Airplane crashes, 30.
Articles of Confederation, 11 (note).
Bankruptcy, 791, 806–817.
Bottomry bond, suit on, 25.
Breach of agreement to procure insurance, 27.
Choice of law, see Conflict of Laws.
Collision between foreign vessels, 489 (note).
Colonial Vice-Admiralty courts, 10.
Complaint, allegation of, 19.
Consequences of admiralty jurisdiction, 34–37.
Constitutional provision, 11, 19.
Contracts,
Generally, 22.
Carriage of goods, 22, 187.
Carriage of passengers, 22.
Charter party, 193.
Fee for procuring charter, 26.
Insurance premiums, 22.
Marine insurance policy, recovery on, 22.
Pilotage, 22.
Sale of vessel, 26.
Ship,
Chartering of, 22.
Repairs and supplies furnished to, 22, 788.
Services rendered to, 22, 26.
Shipbuilding 16, 26.
Towage, 22.
Wharfage, 22.
Criminal causes, 44.
Diversity of citizenship, 20, 37.
English admiralty court, 8–10.
Equitable remedies, 792.
Federal courts, 2.

**JURISDICTION**—Continued
Federal Employers' Liability Acts, 351, 352.
Federal Rules of Civil Procedure, 2, 19, 34, 37, 193, 576, 805, 820.
Forum non conveniens, 51, 489 (note), 869, 936, 945.
General agency agreements, 28.
General average claims, 24, 270.
Great Lakes, 32.
Jones Act claim, 294–296.
Judiciary Act (1789), 11, 18, 19, 37.
Jurisdictional amount, 37.
Land structure damaged by vessel, 522–524.
Liens, 624–633.
Limitation, effect of denial, 683, 933–936.
Limitation of liability proceeding, 23, 838, 839, 862 et seq.
Locality test, 9, 21.
Maintenance and cure action, 24, 294–296.
Management of vessel agreements, 28.
"Mixed" contracts, 28.
Motorboat accidents, 30.
Navigable rivers, 31.
Non-admiralty court, see this title, Saving clause.
Personal jurisdiction over in rem defendant-owner, 801.
Prize proceedings, 44.
Products liability, 29.
Quasi-contractual claims, 27.
Removal of causes, 352, 357.
Reorganization, 806–817.
Respondentia bond, suit on, 25.
Sale of ship, 688, 689.
Salvage claim, 24, 533.
Saving clause,
Generally, 2, 20, 37–40, 193.
Collision action, contributory negligence defense in, 499.
Common law remedies, 456, 457.
Constitution, 20.
Equitable remedies, 38.
Harbor worker's action, 279.
Lien adjudication by state court, 646, 647.
Maritime action in non-admiralty court, 460, 461, 468.
Maritime law controlling, 279, 456 et seq.
Passenger's personal injury suit, 23 (note).
Saving to suitors clause, 468.
Seaman's action for maintenance and cure, 293, 294.
Seaman's unseaworthiness action, 277, 278, 461.
State workmen's compensation action, 404–408.
United States, jury trial in suit against, 982.
Seamen's actions,
Generally, 471 et seq., 627.
Discretionary jurisdiction, 479.
Federal non-admiralty jurisdiction, 468.
Foreign seaman's suit, 475–484.
Foreign shipowner, suit against, 477.
Harbor worker, 438.
Jones Act, 326, 340.
Longshoremen's Act, 412–417.
Ship mortgage foreclosure, 27, 40, 41, 688–695, 814, 815.
Ship wrongfully taken, recovery of, 25.
Shipbuilding contract, 16, 26.
Shore structure, collision with, 522–524.

**JURISDICTION**—Continued
State court, see this title, Saving clause.
Surfboard accidents, 30.
Test by waters, 31.
Three mile limit, 31.
Torts,
Generally, 23.
Cargo damage, 23.
Collision, 23.
Damage caused by vessel, 23.
Inducing breach of contract, 29.
Injury on artificial island drilling rigs, 27.
Personal injury, 23, 326, 340, 471.
Ship, damage to, 23.
Unseaworthiness actions, 294–296.
Vessels, 33.
Voluntary submission, 810.
Waters, 31–33.

**JURY TRIAL**
See Collision; Great Lakes; Seamen; United States.

**JUSTINIAN'S DIGEST,** 4, 244.

**LABOR DEPARTMENT,** 979, 980.

**LACHES**
See, also, Limitations, Statute of; Maritime Lien.
Burden of proof, 775, 776.
Maritime lien, 739, 747, 764 et seq.
Ship mortgage foreclosure, 712.

**LAND LIEN**
Characteristics, 586.

**LATENT DEFECTS**
See Inherent Vice.

**LAW MERCHANT,** 5.

**LAY DAYS,** 211.

**LETTER OF CREDIT**
Generally, 114–130.
Bank as pledgee of bill of lading, 129.
Bank's remedies, 128, 129.
Bills of lading in parts, 125, 126.
Clean credit, 115.
Confirming bank, 127 (note).
Documentary credit, 115.
Documentary sale, 110–114.
Elements of, 120.
History of law, 116.
Indemnity agreements, 127.
Non-conforming goods, 121.
Perfect tender rule, 121.
Reimbursement, 121, 129.
Security interest, perfection, 129, 130, 133–138.
Trust receipt, use of, 129.
UCC, Art. 9, pp. 129, 133–138.
Uniform Customs and Practice for Commercial Documentary credits (UCP), 118 et seq.

**LEVY**
On ship, 589.

**LIABILITY**
Lost or damaged goods,
Generally, 139–192.

**LIBEL**
Arrest of ship by, 787.
Cross libel,
Limitation proceeding, 937–939.
Defined, 35.
In personam, 35.
In rem, 35.
Notice, 787, 790.
Petitory and possessory libels, 25 (note).

**LIBELLANT,** 35, 36.

**LIBERTIES CLAUSE,** 178 (note).

**LICENSING**
See Enrollment and Licensing.

**LIEN**
See Maritime Lien.

**LIFE SALVAGE**
See Salvage.

**LIGHTERAGE,** 740, 743.

**LIGHTHOUSES AND LIGHTSHIPS,** 979.

**LIGHTS**
Navigation rules, 501–503.

**LIMITATION OF LIABILITY**
Generally, 818–957.
Admiralty court, proper forum, 837.
Selection clause, 856, 857.
Admiralty Rules, 849, 850, 859–861.
Not jurisdictional, 853.
Supplementation of Act, 819, 820.
"Appropriate proceedings", 847.
Bankruptcy, effect of, 953–955.
Bankruptcy Act, effect on limitation fund distribution, 874–876.
Bond posted by owner, 838, 839.
British Commonwealth, 835 (note).
Brussels Convention, 835 (note).
Burden of proof, 895–898.
Cargo, notice of value, 834.
Cargo damage claims, 928.
Charterer, petition by, 839, 905.
Charterers, 840–843.
Claim,
Generally (types of claims subject to, and not subject to, limitation), 846, 847 (note).
Cargo claim, 848 (note), 928.
Non-maritime, 844–846, 927.
Notice of, 854, 861.
Passenger's claim, 848 (note).
Premature filing, 860.

**LIMITATION OF LIABILITY**—Continued
Claim—Continued
  Prior voyage, 927, 949 et seq.
  Property damage, 928.
  Single claim, 859, 864 et seq.
  Subsequent voyage, 927, 955–957.
  Total claimed less than fund, 864–868.
Concourse of claims, 864, 867, 868.
Concourse of claims theory, 864, 867, 868, 933–936.
Conditions of limitation, 877 et seq.
Conflict of laws, principles, 939–946.
Containers, 913.
Contractual obligations, 917, 918.
Control of proceedings in other courts, 862–876.
Corporate ownership of vessel, 884 et seq.
Cross-libels, 937–939.
Decree,
  Determines in personam and in rem liability, 927.
  International recognition withheld, 928, 944, 945.
Defense, Act pleaded as, 838, 853, 855–859.
Defensive nature of proceeding, 937.
Denial of limitation, 863, 933–936.
Design or neglect, 877.
Deviation, effect of, 848 (note).
Direct action against insurer, 908–912.
"Distinct occasions", provision, 836.
Employees, acts of, 879–884.
Exculpatory clauses, 836.
Filing of claim, premature, 860.
Financial Responsibility Act (1966), 837.
Fire Statute, 834.
Flotilla, 918.
Foreign shipowner, 847 (note), 923, 939–946.
Forum selection clause, 856, 857.
Freight, term defined, 915.
History, 818–824.
Impleader, 937–939.
Injunction against pending actions, 809, 863, 870, 872.
Inland shipping, 843, 844.
Insurance proceeds, 752, 907–912.
Intervention, 838.
  Claimant not subject to limitation, 930, 931.
Joint owner, 846.
Liability insurance, 908–912.
Lien priorities, 927–931.
Limitation fund, 906 et seq.
Limitation of Liability Act, future of, 822 et seq.
Loss of life and bodily injury,
    Generally, 821, 835, 847, 848, 919–926.
  Calculation of fund, 919 et seq.
  Crew members, 929.
  Master's privity or knowledge, 923, 924.
  Non-admiralty actions, 919, 920.
  Passengers, 23, 923.
  Seagoing vessel requirement, 921, 922.
  Separate accidents, 925, 926.
  Sixty dollar per ton fund, 919–926, 930.
  Third parties, 928.
  When fund must be set up, 920, 921.

**LIMITATION OF LIABILITY**—Continued
Master and crew, remedies against, 843.
Mortgagee, status of, 752.
Nondelegable duties, 890.
Notice of claim, 854, 861.
"Owner", defined, 840–843.
Payment to court of vessel's value, 853.
Pennsylvania rule, effect of, 849 (note).
Personal contract doctrine,
Generally, 751, 846, 847 (note), 898–906.
Bill of lading, 899.
Breach of warranty, 904.
Charter party, 899.
Charterer, 905.
Letter of undertaking, 903.
Maintenance and cure, 901, 902.
Personal breach, 904.
Supply and repair contracts, 900.
Towage contract, 904.
Unseaworthiness, 900.
Personal injury claims, 928.
Petition,
After entry of judgment, 852.
Filing in advance of claim, 852 (note), 853.
Form of, 947, 948.
Notice of, 947, 948 (note).
Procedural Rule, 947, 948 (note).
When may be filed, 852 et seq.
Who may file, 839.
Pollution liability, 824–834
International conventions, 825.
State acts, 830–834.
Water Quality Improvement Act, 826–834.
Prior claimant, 950.
Prior voyage, 949 et seq.
Priorities, 341, 342, 743, 750, 751, 927–931.
Private pleasure yachts, 880–884.
Privity or knowledge,
Generally, 836, 877–895.
Burden of proof, 895–898.
Corporate owners, 884 et seq.
Design or neglect, 877.
Due diligence, 877.
Individual owners, 879–884.
Loss of life or bodily injury, 923, 924.
Negligence of employees, 879 et seq.
Procedural Rules, 849, 850, 859–861.
Pro rata distribution of fund, 837, 927–931.
Purpose of Act, 950–952.
Remedies against master and crew, 843.
Reorganization Court, effect on distribution of funds, 874–876.
Res judicata, 871, 873, 874, 938.
Retention of case where limitation denied, 863.
Rowboat, 844 (note).
Salvage claim, 929 (note).
Satisfaction of prior claims, 950–952.
Satisfaction of subsequent claims, 955–957.
Saving clause, suits under, 839, 862 et seq.
Seagoing vessel, 836.

**LIMITATION OF LIABILITY**—Continued
Seamen's claims,
  Jones Act, 341, 847 (note).
  Mutual fault collision, 928, 929.
  Unseaworthiness, action for, 341, 847 (note).
  Wage claim, 844–846, 928.
Security, 851, 934 (note).
Servants, acts of, 879–884.
Ship, sale free of liens, 952 (note).
Six-month period, 839, 854–861.
Special commodities, 834.
State laws and municipal ordinances, 849 (note).
Statute of limitations, 854–861.
Statutory fault, effect of, 849 (note).
Stipulation for value, 851, 852, 934 (note), 950.
Stipulation to avoid limitation proceedings, 865.
Structure of Act, 834–846.
Subsequent claimants, 955–957.
Subsequent voyages, 955, 957.
Surrender to trustee, 852, 950, 952 (note).
Termination of proceedings against owner, 839.
Third party practice, 937–939.
Torrey Canyon disaster, 824, 841–843.
Transfer of interest to trustee, 839.
Transfer of proceedings, 821, 850 (note), 851 (note), 852 (note).
Valuation, 905, 906, 948–950.
Venue, 850 (note).
Voyage,
  Defined, 913, 914, 949, 959.
  The limitation period, 751, 907, 927, 946 et seq.
Voyage splitting 948 (note).
Wreck Statute, compliance with, 849, 850 (note), 949 (note).

**LIMITATION OF LIABILITY ACT**
Financial Responsibility Act (1966), 837.

**LIMITATIONS, STATUTE OF**
  See, also, Laches.
Cogsa, 189, 768.
Death on the High Seas Act, 768.
Federal Employers Liability Act, 352.
Jones Act, 351, 352.
Limitation of liability, petition, 854–861.
Maritime liens, 768–786.
Salvage, 534 (note), 768.
State-created liens, 651, 768–771.
State limitations periods, 418, 768.
United States, claims against, 768.
Wrongful death claims, 418, 768.

**LINER,** 13, 194, 197.

**LLOYD'S** 55.

**LOADING AND UNLOADING**
Time charter, 231.
Voyage charter, 110–115.

**LOADLINE STATUTE,** 987, 988.

**LOG,** 249, 989.

**LONGSHOREMEN**
See Seamen.

**LONGSHOREMEN'S AND HARBOR WORKERS' COMPENSATION ACT**
See, also, Seamen.
Generally, 278.
Concurrent federal-state jurisdiction, 417 et seq.
Constitutionality of Act, 412.
Coverage of Act, 417 et seq.
Relationship with state compensation acts, 417–426.
Territorial application, 417–426, 449, 450.
Types of employment, 427–430, 450.
Employment covered under Act, 427–430, 450.
Judicial review of compensation orders, 412.
1972 Amendments, 273, 275, 280, 330, 380, 390, 408 et seq., 417–438.
Relationship with state compensation acts, 417.
State limitations on remedy, 418 et seq.
Successive state, LHCA, Jones Act awards, 431 et seq.
Territorial application, 417, 449, 450.

**LOSS**
See Insurance.

**MAINTENANCE AND CURE**
See, also, Seamen.
Remedy, nature of, 281 et seq.

**MANNING SCALES,** 988.

**MARINE HOSPITALS,** 301.

**MARINE INSURANCE**
See Insurance.

**MARINE INSURANCE ACT (Eng.),** 60.

**MARITIME ADMINISTER,** 968.

**MARITIME ADMINISTRATION**
Generally, 968, 976, 978–980.
Merchant Marine Academy, 978.
National Shipping Authority, 967 (note), 981 (note).
Shipping information, 979.
Subsidized vessels, inspection of plans, 986.

**MARITIME BOARD**
Generally, 967.
Chairman, 968.
Subsidy contracts, 970, 971.
Surrender of documents, 715.

**MARITIME COMMISSION,** 968–970.
Rate regulation, 990–995.

**MARITIME COURTS**
History of, 5–11.

**MARITIME LAW**
Generally, 1, 45–51.
Absence of maritime rule, 48, 68–71.
Carrier's liability, 139–142, 207.
Common law defenses, 458.
Conflict of laws, principles, see Conflict of Laws.
Constitutional silence, 45.
Federal-state conflicts, 47–52.

**MARITIME LAW**—Continued
History, 3–11.
Home port doctrine, 643, 644.
Indemnity action, 319.
Law of nations, 482.
Liens, 654–660.
National uniformity, 404–408, 642.
Non-admiralty courts, 456.
Pollution, state law, 50.
Saving clause, actions under, 456; See, also, under Jurisdiction.
Sovereign immunity, 608, 611.
State power to modify, 48–50, 404–408, 418, 642, 649–652.
State powers, 49, 50.
Statutory law, 45.
Substantive, 45–52.

**MARITIME LIEN**
See, also, In Rem Proceeding; Ship Mortgage.
Generally, 35–37, 586–817.
Advances, 626, 633–635, 653.
Appurtenances, 622, 623 (note).
Arrest of ship, 588, 787, 796–801.
Assignment of lien, 633–635.
Effect of UCC, 635.
Attachment and levy on ship, 589.
Authority to incur, 668 et seq.
Authority to subject chartered vessels to contract liens, 668–688.
Agents authority, 673.
Duty of inquiry, 624 et seq.
1971 abolition of duty, 669, 685–688.
General maritime law, 670–672.
Knowledge of authority, 673.
Lien Act (1910–1971), 672–685.
1971 deletion of duty of inquiry, 685–688.
Presumption of authority, 674–688.
Bankruptcy and reorganization,
Generally, 588, 613–615, 806–817.
Claim to general average settlement funds, 811, 812.
Consolidation, 814, 815.
Foreign recognition of decree, 817.
Injunction against admiralty action, 806–809, 815 (note).
Insolvency court's adjudication of liens, 806–817.
Jurisdiction of admiralty court, 791.
Limitation fund, 812.
Priorities, 811, 812.
Ship mortgage foreclosure, 814, 815.
Voidable preferences, 813.
Voluntary submission, 810.
Benefit theory, 589, 741, 743.
Bond, 796 et seq.
Bottomry bond, 25 (note), 632, 690, 742.
Cargo, lien on,
Cesser clause, 215, 221–223.
Charter hire, 216.
Dead freight, 639.
Demurrage, 631, 641.
Freight, 36, 186, 187, 215.
General average, 270.
Mutual and reciprocal liens, 187, 641.

**MARITIME LIEN**—Continued
Cargo lien against ship,
Damage, 186, 187, 630.
General average, 270.
Non-delivery, 232, 233.
Carriage lien, 186, 187.
Charter breach, lien for, 193.
Charterer's power to incur liens, 600, 615.
Collateral security, effect on lien, 786.
Collision, lien for, 498, 628, 739, 743, 752.
Compulsory pilot's acts, 597–600, 615.
Municipal non-liability, 498 (note).
Custodia legis, ships in, 602–606, 615.
Dead ships, 623 (note).
Deficiency judgment, 801–805.
Demise charterer, 243.
Disbursements, lien for, 625 (note).
Enforceability of liens when owner not personally liable, 594 et seq.
English theory of liens, 589, 598, 802.
Equipment, title retention, 727–732.
Execution of liens, 588, 774–779, 786–790.
Arrest, release from, 796–801.
Bond, 796–801.
Decree, international recognition, 788.
Deficiency judgment, 801–805.
Fraudulent sale, 789.
General bond, 797, 798.
Rule E(5), 797, 798.
Maritime non-lien claims, 794–796.
Non-maritime lienor, 692–694.
Notice, 787, 790.
Remnants, 788, 692–694.
Sale, effect of, 786–790.
Special bond, 797, 798.
Rule E(5), 797, 798.
State statute lienor, 794–796.
Stipulation for value, 796 et seq.
Unsecured creditors, 692–694.
Executory contract, breach of, 635–641, 794, 796.
When executed, 635–638.
Executory contract doctrine, 635–641.
Extinguishment of lien, 587.
Federal Maritime Lien Act,
Generally, 630, 642–688.
Advances, 653.
Anti-lien provisions, 716.
"Any person furnishing . . . to any vessel", 661–663.
Authority, inquiry concerning, 669 et seq.
1971 Amendment of Act, 669, 685–688.
"Carriage of freight", 656, 657.
Charter, knowledge of terms, 656.
Contractual limitations on liens, 716.
Credit to the ship, 656, 664–668.
Dry dock, 652, 655, 657.
Executory contracts, 636 (note).
Fleet, supplies furnished to, 662 (note).
"Furnishing", directness of, 661–663.
General maritime law, 654–660.
In personam actions, 653.

**MARITIME LIEN**—Continued
Federal Martime Lien Act—Continued
Laches, 653.
Marine railway, 652, 653, 655, 657.
Merchant Marine Act of 1920, 326.
Necessaries, 654, 657, 658.
"Outfitting" ship, 656, 657.
Priorities, 653.
Provisions of Act, 652, 653.
Purposes of Act, 663.
Sales contract, knowledge of terms, 656.
Scope of Act, 654–660.
State statutes, 654–660.
Supply and repair liens, 630.
Towage, 655, 657, 658.
Waiver, 653, 665–668.
Foreign government vessel, 612, 985 (note).
Forfeiture of vessel, 591–594, 759.
Freight, overpayment of, 640.
General agent, 626 (note).
General average claims, 270, 630.
General bond, 797, 798.
Good faith purchaser without notice, 36, 588, 594–597.
Historical development, 589 et seq.
History, 589 et seq.
Home port doctrine, 643, 644.
Credit to the ship theory, 644, 664.
Effect of Federal Lien Act, 663.
Home port, what constitutes, 643, 644.
Home port claims having lien status, 655.
Home Port of Vessels Act (1925), 713.
In rem libel, 622–624.
Indelibility, 588, 595–597, 615.
Independent contractor, acts of, 600.
Insurance premium, 625, 648, 650.
Insurance proceeds, 622, 623 (note).
Involuntary lien compared with, 586, 589.
Jones Act, 796.
Judicial lien, compared with, 586.
Laches and limitation,
Generally, 588, 653, 764–786.
Cargo damage claim, 768, 744.
Conflict of laws, 777–780.
Death claim, 768.
Excusable delay, 771 et seq.
Good faith purchaser, 764–767.
Libel, laches apparent on face, 774.
Personal injury action, 775.
Pre-mortgage lienholder, 780 et seq.
Priorities, pre and post mortgage liens, 782–786.
Salvage claim, 768.
Same owner, lien asserted against, 768–786.
State lien statutes, 768–771.
United States, claim against, 768.
Waiver, 786.
Land lien, compared with, 585–589.
Limitation proceeding,
Priorities, effect on, 341, 927–931.
Sale of ship, 952 (note).

**MARITIME LIEN**—Continued
Loss of lien, 764–805.
Execution of liens by in rem decree, 786–805.
Laches, limitation and waiver, 764–786.
Maritime claims, 624–633.
Marshal, ship in custody of, 603.
Marshalling liens, 794.
Materialman's lien, 35, 230 (note), 630.
Mechanic's lien, 660 (note), 663.
Mortgage, see under title Ship Mortgage.
Municipally-owned vessels, 606 et seq.
Mutineers, acts of, 601.
Mutual and reciprocal, 641.
Non-lien claimants, 622, 794–796.
Non-maritime lienor, 650, 791, 794.
Notice of lien, 588, 757.
Owner,
Charterer's acts, liability for, 232, 233, 242, 243.
Lack of knowledge or consent, 591–594.
Non-liability, effect of, 36, 594–513.
Not entitled to lien, 626 (note).
Part-owner, 626 (note).
Personification of ship, 589, 590, 615, 616.
Persons unlawfully in possession, acts of, 602.
Pilotage, claim for, 630.
Pirates, acts of, 601.
Possession, 36, 586, 588, 595.
Preferred ship mortgage, see under title Ship Mortgage.
Priorities, 733–764.
Generally, 588, 627, 733–764, 780.
Bottomry lien, 742.
Calendar year rule, 747, 750.
Cargo, lien against, 742.
Cargo damage lien, 741, 753.
Charges while ship in custodia legis, 734, 737.
Class, lien ranked by, 734, 737–742.
Collision claims, 739, 752.
Contract liens, 734, 739, 743.
Determined by class of lien, 737–742.
Determined by time of accrual, 742–751.
Effect of Ship Mortgage Act, 751–757.
Federal Maritime Lien Act, 653.
Federal Tax Lien Act, 758.
Forty-day rule, 745–748.
General average lien, 742.
Government claims, 757–764.
Great Lakes rule, 745.
Inverse order rule, 588, 734, 739, 742–751.
Lighterage claim, 740, 743.
Limitation, voyage rule, effect of, 750, 751.
Limitation proceeding, effect on, 739, 743, 750, 751.
New York Harbor rule, 745–748.
Ninety-day rule, 747.
Non-lien maritime claims, 734.
Non-maritime claims, 734.
Personal injury claim, 739, 743.
Pilotage lien, 742.
Post-mortgage liens, laches, 782–786.
Preferred maritime lien, 751, 752.

**MARITIME LIEN**—Continued
Priorities—Continued
Preferred mortgage, 736, 751–757.
Pre-mortgage liens, laches, 782–786.
Priority periods, 747.
Proration, 738, 740, 743.
Puget Sound rule, 747.
Repair claims, 738, 753.
Respondentia lien, 742.
Salvage lien, 734, 738, 739, 743, 752.
Season rule, 745.
Service lien, 740, 742–745, 757.
Ship Mortgage Act, effect of, 751–757.
Special rules, 744–751.
Stevedore's claim, 740, 743, 752.
Supply claims, 738, 753.
Tax claims, 734, 757–764.
Tax liens, 757 et seq.
Time of accrual, lien ranked by, 734, 742–751.
Tort liens, 734, 739, 743, 752.
Towage claim, 740, 743, 753.
Voyage rule, 743, 745, 748–750.
Wage lien, 734, 738, 743, 752.
Wharfage claims, 740, 743.
Year rule, 747, 748–750.
Procedural theory of liens, 589, 590.
Proceedings where lienholder not party, 587.
Remnants, 692–694.
Reorganization, see Bankruptcy under this title.
Repairs, 630.
Res judicata, 613–615.
Respondentia bond, 632.
Sale, proceeds of, 622, 623 (note).
Salvage, 628, 655.
Salved property, 575.
Seamen's claims,
Jones Act, 341, 796.
Maintenance and cure, 284.
Seaplane, 539, 540.
Secret lien, 588, 633, 663.
Ship Mortgage, see under that title.
Sovereign, liens on ship in control of, 606–613.
State court, adjudication of liens by, 646, 647.
State lien statutes,
Generally, 643–652.
Claims having lien status at maritime law, 648–652.
Credit to the ship, 665.
Death claims, 649, 659, 660.
Federal Maritime Lien Act, effect of, 654–660.
Foreign vessel, lien on, 651, 652.
Insurance premiums, 647, 650.
Limitation periods, 768–771.
New York statute, 648 (note).
Non-compliance with statutory requirements, 794.
Non-maritime claims, 650.
Shipbuilding contract, 648 (note), 650.
Statute of frauds, 651.
Statutes of limitation, 651.
Wage claim, 651.

**MARITIME LIEN**—Continued
State-owned vessels, 606 et seq.
Stevedore, act of, 600.
Stevedoring, 630, 656–658, 752.
Stipulation for value, 796 et seq.
Stockholder, 626 (note).
Subfreight, lien against, 125, 232, 233.
Subject-matter of liens, 622, 623 (note).
Supplies, 35, 230 (note), 630.
Tort claims, 628.
Towage, claim for, 630, 655.
United States, vessels owned by, 606 et seq.
Unsecured creditors, 692–694.
Wages, claim for, 35, 36, 627, 651, 656, 659, 660, 794.
Waiver, 786.
Wharfage, 630, 656.
When liens attach, 636 et seq.

**MARKS**
Bill of lading, 185.
Inadequacy, 167.

**MARSHAL**
Bond, 798, 799.
Custody of ship, 787.

**MASTER**
Chartered vessel, 232.
General average acts, 264.
Remedies against, 843.
Wages, no lien for, 625.

**MEMORANDUM CLAUSE**
See Insurance.

**MERCHANT MARINE ACADEMY,** 978.

**MERCHANT MARINE ACT (1920),** 326, 327, 966.

**MERCHANT MARINE ACT (1936),** 966, 967, 969–978.

**MERCHANTS' SHIPPING ACT (Eng. 1876),** 276.

**MISSISSIPPI RIVER,** 490.

**MORTGAGE**
See Ship Mortgage.

**NATIONAL LABOR RELATIONS BOARD,** 988.

**NATIONAL SHIPPING AUTHORITY,** 967 (note), 981 (note).

**NAVIGATION AND MANAGEMENT**
See Cogsa.

**NAVIGATION RULES**
See, also, Collision.
Application and definitions, 500.
Fog, 504–508.
Lights, 501–503.
Radar, 511–514.
Sailing, 504.
Special circumstances, 508.
Steering, 504.

**NAVY DEPARTMENT,** 971, 987.

**NECESSARIES,** 654, 657, 658.

**NEGLIGENCE**
See, also, Cogsa; Collision; Seamen.
Recovery for injury or death, 272 et seq.
See, also, Seamen.
Standards of, 453.

**NEGOTIABLE INSTRUMENT**
See, also, Bill of Lading.
Attachment, 94.
Conflict of laws, 131, 132.
Good faith purchaser, 94, 125.
Holder's rights, 94.
Indorser's warranties, 99.
Merger, 94.
Post-maturity purchaser, 99.
Thief, bill of lading, issued to, 97.
Underlying debt, discharge of, 94.

**NEGOTIABLE INSTRUMENTS LAW,** 95.

**NEW YORK FREIGHT BUREAU,** 994

**NEW YORK HARBOR,** 745, 746.

**OIL POLLUTION ACT,** 989.

**OLERON, RULES OF,** 7, 46, 244, 590.

**ORDONNANCE DE LA MARINE OF LOUIS XIV,** 8, 960 (note).

**OVERALL WAR-MARINE RISK SETTLEMENT AGREEMENT,** 79.

**OVERLAP AND UNDERLAP,** 231, 232.

**OWNER**
Defined, limitation of liability, 841–843.

**PARTICULAR AVERAGE**
See Average.

**PASSENGER**
Carrier-passenger relationship, 23 (note).
Death on the High Seas Act, 24.
Intervention in admiralty proceeding, 793, 794.
Lien,
Cancellation of passage contract, 636, 637.
Personal injury, 628, 629.
Limitation of liability, 837, 848 (note).
Personal injury suit, 23.
Salvage award, 543.

**PENNSYLVANIA RULE,** 849, 898.

**PERIL**
See Cogsa; General Average; Insurance; Salvage.

**PERILS OF THE SEA**
Cogsa provision, 162.

**PERSONAL INJURY**
See, also, Passenger; Seamen.
Lien, 739, 743.

**PERSONAL INJURY**—Continued
Limitation of liability, 821, 846–849, 928.
Statute of limitations, 775.

**PILFERAGE,** 73, 74.

**PILOT RULES**
See Collision.

**PILOTAGE**
See Collision; Maritime Lien.

**PIRACY,** 591–594, 601.

**PLAINTIFF,** 35.

**PLEDGE,** 111.

**PLIMSOLL MARK,** 987.

**POLICYHOLDER,** 56.

**POLLUTION**
International conventions, 825.
Liability, 824–834, 850.
State acts, 830–834.
State control, 50.
Water Quality Improvement Act, 826–834.
Relationship to Limitation of Liability Act, 828–834.

**POMERENE ACT**
See, also Federal Bills of Lading Act.
Applicability, 95, 96.

**PORT**
Safe port, 202, 230.
Security, 989.

**PORT OF NEW YORK AUTHORITY,** 980.

**POTHIER,** 8 (note).

**PRACTICE AND PROCEDURE**
See, also, Impleader; Interpleader; Joinder; Jurisdiction; Libel.
Generally, 34–37.
Criminal causes, 44.
Possessory and petitory actions, 25 (note).
Prize proceedings, 44.
Procedural unification, 2, 19, 34, 37, 820 (note), 850.

**PRIVATE ASSOCIATIONS,** 987, 988 (note), 990.

**PROCEDURE**
See Practice and Procedure.

**PROCTOR,** 35.

**PROPER VICE**
See Inherent Vice.

**PROXIMATE CAUSE,** 76–79.

**PUBLIC ENEMY, ACT OF,** 139, 164, 169.

**PUBLIC VESSELS ACT**
Contract claims under charters, 984.
Private ownership, liens upon reversion to, 607.

**PUBLIC VESSELS ACT**—Continued
Provisions of, 983.
Public vessel, 983.
Seamen in government service,
 Wage claims, 984.
Suits in Admiralty Act, relation to, 983–986.

**PUGET SOUND,** 747.

**QUARANTINE,** 164, 169, 234, 235.

**QUASI-CONTRACT**
General average, 265.
Jurisdiction, 27, 41.
Restitution, 27 (note).
Unjust enrichment, 265.

**RADAR,** 511–514.
Navigation rule, 511–514.

**RATES**
Regulation of, 990–995.

**REFORMATION OF INSTRUMENTS,** 41.

**REGISTRY**
  See, also, Documentation; Enrollment and Licensing.
 Generally, 695, 696 (note).
Domestically-built vessel, 963.
Port of documentation, 713.
Reregistration, 714.
Seamen's action, effect of U. S. registry in, 479.
United States Customs Bureau, 987.

**REGULATION OF SHIPPING**
See United States.

**REMEDIES,** 40–43.
Election of, 463.

**REMOVAL OF CAUSES,** 352, 357, 358.

**REORGANIZATION**
See Maritime Lien.

**RES IPSA LOQUITUR**
See Seamen.

**RES JUDICATA**
In personam judgment, 613–615.
In rem decree, 613–615.
Limitation proceeding, 871, 873, 874, 938.
 Jones Act, suit, 342–346.
 Maintenance and cure, 342–346, 614.
 Unseaworthiness, 342–346.

**RESPONDEAT SUPERIOR**
Cogsa, 150.
Demise charterer, 242.
Fire Statute, 161.
Harter Act, 142.
Pilot, 520.

**RESPONDENT,** 35.

**RESPONDENTIA BOND,** 25 (note), 632, 742.

**RESPONDENTIA LIENS,** 742.

**RESTITUTION**
See Quasi-contract.

**RESTRAINT OF PRINCES**
Carriage of goods, 164.
Charter party, 234.

**RHODES**
See History.

**RIOT AND CIVIL COMMOTION,** 164, 169.

**ROCCUS,** 8 (note).

**ROME**
See History.

**RUNNING DAYS,** 211.

**SAFE BERTH,** 203, 204, 230 (note).

**SAFETY CONFERENCE, LONDON (1948),** 490.

**SAFETY STATUTES,** 355, 381.

**SAILING VESSEL,** 124.

**SALE OF GOODS**
See, also, Letter of Credit.
Generally, 100–110.
Appropriation rules, 104, 109.
Defective tender, 112, 113.
Documentary sale,
Generally, 110–114.
Bank collection or discount, 111.
Buyer's remedies, 113.
Consular certificate, 110.
Draft, buyer's duty to pay or accept, 110.
Garnishment, 113.
Insurance certificates, 110 (note).
Insurance policy, 111.
Perfect tender rule, 111, 125.
Presenting bank, 111.
Tender, 110–114.
Fraud by insolvency, 96 (note).
History of law, 102.
Identification of goods, 109.
Passage of ownership, time, 102, 108.
Presumptions, 99.
Remedies,
Buyer, 102, 103, 113.
Seller, 102.
Risk shifting, 109.
Shipping terms, 105–108.
Stoppage in transit, 96 (note).
Substantial performance, 112 (note).
Title, passage of, 108.
Uniform Commercial Code, 100–109.
Uniform Sales Act, 100 et seq.
Voidable title, 98.
Warranties of seller, 99.

**SALE OF SHIP**

Action on contract, jurisdiction, 26, 689.
Admiralty sale, effect on mortgage, 715.
Bill of sale executed by marshal, 790.
Limitation proceeding, sale, 952 (note).
Recordation of bill of sale, 713.
Unpaid seller's right to admiralty sale surplus, 793.

**SALVAGE**

Generally, 532–585.
Abandonment, 535, 563, 576.
Act of salvage, 534–537.
Airplane, 539–541.
Award, how computed,
Generally, 559–574.
Expenses of salvor, 562, 563.
Inflation, 564.
Insurance, effect of, 569.
Life salvage, 570–574.
Loss or damage suffered by salvor, 562.
Moiety rule, 563.
Moral aspects, 562.
Negligent salvage, reduction for, 554.
Not quantum meruit, 532, 562.
"Order" of salvage service, 562.
Shares of owner, crew, 566.
Value after salvage, 563.
Value of property risked, 559.
Value of property salved, 559.
Brussels Salvage Convention (1910), 534.
Cargo, salvage of, 538.
Cargo interest, 560, 561, 574, 579.
Cargo of salvor, 559–560.
Coast Guard, 549–551, 554.
Collision, salvage following, 453.
Common ownership, 534 (note), 545, 546.
Conflict of laws, 533.
Contract salvage,
Agreement form, Lloyd's, 582, 583.
Agreement in extremis, 579–581.
Arbitration, 583.
"No cure, no pay" contract, 582, 583.
Officers and crew, rights of, unaffected, 580, 581.
Pre-existing contractual relationship, 584.
Professional salvors, 581, 582.
Crew of salved ship, 541, 542.
Crew of salvor, 546, 552.
Custom of giving aid, 541.
Customs duties, 577.
Derelict, 536, 563.
Disputes among salvors, 558.
Duress, 558.
Duty to salve, 535, 541–551.
Fault of salvor, 551–553.
Firemen, 543.
Forfeiture of right to award, 554–558.
General agent, 546.
General average expense, 262, 574.
Government vessels, 546–551.
In personam proceeding, 575, 576.

**SALVAGE**—Continued
In rem proceeding, 575, 576.
Jurisdiction, 533.
Liability for award,
Generally, 574–578.
Cargo owner, 574.
Charterer, 578.
General average contribution, 574.
In personam suit, 575, 576.
In rem proceeding, 575, 576.
Insurer, 576, 577.
Others than owner, 576–578.
Pecuniary interest in salved property, 576, 577.
Shipowner, 574.
Lien for, 627, 655, 752.
Life salvage,
Generally, 570–574.
Award, how computed, 570–574.
Cogsa, 167, 178, 183, 185.
Deviation, 178, 183, 185.
Property salvage necessary for award, 532.
Property salved by other salvor, 570, 571.
Statutory right to award, 532.
Limitation of liability, 847 (note), 929 (note).
Maritime property rule, 538.
Misconduct of salvor, 551–553.
"Moveable thing", test, 539.
Negligent salvage, 554–558.
Passengers, 543.
Peril, 434.
Persons entitled to award,
Generally, 566–576.
Cargo owners excluded, 568, 569.
Chartered salvor, 568.
Crew, 566, 567.
Salving shipowner, 566.
Settlement between salved and salving shipowners, 567.
Pilfering, looting, or theft, 558.
Pilots, 543.
Pre-existing duty to salve, 535, 541–551.
Professional salvors, 544.
Property subject to salvage, 538–541.
Public employees, 543, 548.
Refusal of salvage, 536.
Return of property by salvor, 558.
Rules of Civil Procedure, 576.
Salvage Act (1912), 534, 546.
Seamen on government vessels, 548.
Seaplane, 539–541.
Statute of limitations, 534 (note).
Success, 535.
Towage distinguished, 536, 545.
Tug and crew, 543.
United States, suit against, 983.
Voluntary act of salvor, 535, 541.

**SALVAGE ACT (1912)**, 534.

**SAVING CLAUSE**
See Jurisdiction.

**SEA-CODES**
Mediterranean, 5, 6.

**SEA PROTEST,** 250.

**SEAMEN**
Articles, 287, 988.
Assumption of risk, 351–357, 408 (note), 439.
Charterer, liability of, 242.
Comparative negligence, 351, 352, 410 (note).
Contributory negligence, 290, 408 (note), 439.
Death, see Wrongful Death.
Death,
Generally, 359 et seq.
Death on the High Seas Act, 359 et seq.
Foreign shipowner, claim against, 847 (note).
Jones Act recovery, 359 et seq.
State death acts, 359.
Statute of limitations, 768.
Election between unseaworthiness and Jones Act remedies, 278, 279, 342.
Harbor workers,
Assumption of risk, 408 (note), 450.
Bargeworker, 415.
Comparative negligence, 450.
Compensation commission, 408 (note).
Compensation legislation, 48.
Conflict of laws, 477.
Constitutionality of Longshoremen's Act, 412.
Contributory negligence, 408 (note), 450.
Coverage of Longshoremen's Act, 278, 330, 408 et seq.
1972 Amendments of Act, 273, 275, 280, 330, 380, 390, 408 et seq., 417–438, 449–455.
Employer's indemnity to shipowner, 442.
Fellow servant rule, 408 (note).
Intoxication and willful misconduct, 408 (note).
Joinder of negligence, unseaworthiness counts, 348.
Joint tortfeasors, 442–446.
Jurisdiction, 438, 477.
Jurisdictional facts, 412–417.
"Local" exception, 418 et seq.
Longshoremen's and Harbor Workers' Compensation Act (1927), 278, 330, 408 et seq., 417–438.
1972 Amendment, 273, 275, 280, 330, 380, 390, 408 et seq., 417–438, 449–455.
Maritime but local exception, 418 et seq.
National uniformity requirement, 404–408.
Navigable waters, injuries on, 413, 417.
Recovery of damages outside compensation system, 436–455.
1972 Amendments to LHCA, 449–455.
Relationship of federal and state acts, 279, 404–408, 418 et seq.
Review of compensation orders, 409 (note), 412–417.
"Seaman", harbor worker as, 278, 282, 328, 438–441.
Shore injuries, 438.
Standards of negligence, 453.
State limitations period, applicability of, 418.
Stevedore, 410, 411.
Third party, liability of, 278, 279, 436 et seq., 449.
Third party action, 449.
"Twilight Zone", 418 et seq.
Waiver of rights, 409 (note).
Imputed fault of ship, 929.

**SEAMEN**—Continued
Joinder of unseaworthiness and Jones Act counts, 278, 279, 342–351.
Jones Act,
Generally, 277, 278, 325–383.
Amendments to FELA, effect of, 354.
Assumption of risk, 351–357.
Assumption of risk vs. contributory negligence, 354–357.
Bargeworker, 415.
Burden of proceeding with evidence, 377.
Contributory negligence, 277, 351, 352.
Death, recovery for, 326, 359 et seq.
Defendant, 335–339.
Demise charterer, 242.
Election between Jones Act and unseaworthiness recovery, 342–351.
Election between law, admiralty actions, 342, 346.
Federal Employe Liability Act, relation to, 351–377.
Fellow servant's negligence, 277, 278, 325 et seq.
In rem proceeding, 341.
Insolvency court's power to enjoin, 809.
Jurisdiction, 326, 340–342.
Jury trial, 277, 326, 340–351.
Limitation of liability, 341, 847.
"Negligence" defined, 374–383.
Non-exclusive remedy, 375.
Non-lien status of claim, 625, 794, 796.
Off-duty injuries, 277.
Plaintiff, 328–334.
Pleading and practice, 348–351.
Provisions of, 326.
Removal to federal court, 357.
Res ipsa loquitur, 377.
Res judicata in later unseaworthiness suit, 342–346.
"Seaman", classification, 328–334.
Shore injuries, 438.
Statute of limitations, 349, 350.
Stevedore, 438, 439.
Unseaworthiness, recovery, compared, 342–346, 375, 379.
Venue, 341.
Jurisdiction,
See also Jurisdiction.
Federal non-admiralty court, 468.
Foreign seaman's actions, 471–484.
Harbor workers, 477.
United States citizens on foreign ships, 477.
Jury trial,
Jones Act, suit, 277, 278, 326, 340–351.
Maintenance and cure suit, 294.
United States, suit against, 982.
Unseaworthiness action, 277, 278, 342–351.
Limitation of liability,
Generally, 923.
Shipowner's remedies against seamen, 843.
Wage claims, 845, 846, 928.
Longshoremen, see this title, Harbor workers.
Maintenance and cure,
Generally, 279, 281 et seq.
Amount of recovery, 293 et seq.
Attorney fees, 313.
"Care" and "cure", 299.

**SEAMEN**—Continued
Maintenance and cure—Continued
- Causal relation between duties and injury, 289–292, 298.
- Commuter seamen, 292.
- Contributory negligence, 290.
- "Cure" as "improvement", 299.
- Deduction of other income, 306–308.
- Distinguished from Jones Act actions, 285.
- Duration of liability, 297–314.
- Employer liable, 284.
- Employment by one other than shipowner, 285.
- Failure to provide, Jones Act claim, 312.
- Future expenses, 299, 300.
- Harbor worker, 282.
- Hospitals, 301–304.
- Impleader of third-party tortfeasor, 316–319.
  - Federal Rule, 14, p. 317.
- Improper care, 301, 311.
- In rem action, 286, 287.
- Incurable ailments, 297–299.
- Joinder of actions, 293.
- Joinder with Jones Act claim, 294–296.
- Jurisdiction, 294–296.
- Jury trial, 294.
- Lump sum award, 297, 298.
- Maintenance distinguished from cure, 302.
- Maximum cure, point of, 298.
- Mental disease, 302, 310 (note).
- Mitigation of damages, 306–308.
- Nature of remedy, 281, 282.
- Non-exclusive remedy, 281.
- Past expenses, 300.
- Per diem allowance, 307.
- Personal contract doctrine, 901, 902.
- Physicians, 301.
- Pre-employment illness, 288.
- Pre-employment physical examination, 288.
- Pre-judgment interest, 314.
- Prior suit not a bar, 300, 301.
- Refusal to undergo treatment, 300, 301.
- Removal to federal court, 358.
- Res judicata, 342–346, 614.
- Separate action, 293.
- Shipowner's duty to procure treatment, 310.
- Shipowners' Liability Convention, 323, 324.
- Shore-leave injuries, 289–292.
- State court action, 293 (note).
- Successive employers, 284 (note).
- Third-party tortfeasor, 314–322.
- Transportation to place of treatment, 310.
- Unearned wages, 309, 310.
- Union contract clause, 307.
- Wages, recovery of, 305.
- Waiver of right, 287.
- Who entitled to, 282.
- Willful misconduct, 291.

Maritime law in non-admiralty court, 456 et seq.

**SEAMEN**—Continued
Negligence, recovery for,
Generally, 272 et seq.
Comparative negligence, 500 (note).
Death, 311, 359 et seq.
Fellow servant rule, 275–277.
Judicial trends, 272–275.
Navigation and management, 276.
Operating negligence, 279.
Unseaworthiness distinguished, 277.
See also Jones Act, this title.
Non-admiralty court, action in, 456 et seq.
Pro hac vice, 280.
Recovery for injury and death, 272 et seq.
Release of injury claim, 317, 459.
Salvage award, 567.
State legislation, 47.
Unionization, 988.
United States, suit against, 284, 982.
Unseaworthiness,
Generally, 275, 383–404.
Absolute duty, 276–278.
Condition arising after beginning of voyage, 397, 398.
Defined, 279, 842–846.
Diligence to make seaworthy, 277–279.
Election between unseaworthiness and Jones Act, 342–351, 379.
Equipment, 386, 387.
Harbor worker's actions, 277–279, 438.
Independent contractor, 393–396.
Joined with negligence count, 388.
Jones Act, effect of, 375, 379.
Jury trial, 277.
Liability without fault, 390–393.
Limitation of liability, 341, 342.
Merchant's Shipping Act (Eng.1876), 276.
Negligence distinguished, 387.
Non-admiralty court, 460, 461.
Non-delegable duty, 393–396.
Notice of unseaworthy condition, 398 et seq.
Operating negligence, 384–390.
Personnel, defects in, 398 et seq.
Relinquishment of control, 393–396.
Res ipsa loquitur, 394, 396.
Res judicata, 342–346.
Saving clause, suit under, 277.
Shore injuries, 438.
Structural defects, 386, 387.
Transitory unseaworthiness, 398, 402.
Lien for, 35, 36, 627, 655, 659, 734, 738, 743, 752.
Limitation of liability, 845, 846, 928.
Public Vessels Act, 984.
Ship in custody of marshal, 605.

**SEAPLANES**
Collision, 500.
Lien, 539, 540.
Limitation of liability, 539, 540.
Salvage, 539–541.

**SEAWORTHINESS**

See, also, Cogsa; Seamen.
Burden of proof, 898.
Carrier,
Generally, 141, 150–155, 159, 160.
Cargo, fitness to carry, 207.
Cogsa, 149–155.
Due diligence, exercise of, 143, 150–155, 167, 207, 208.
Harter Act, 142, 148, 149.
Navigation and management distinguished, 159, 160.
Charter party, 207, 208, 229, 230.
General average, 267, 268.
Insurance contract,
Generally, 63.
Breach, effect of, 63.
Time policy, 63.
Radar, 512.
Warranty of, 150–155, 452.
When ship must be seaworthy, 63, 151 (note), 151.

**SEIZURE**

Free of capture and seizure,
Cogsa, 164.
Insurance, 71, 72.
Under legal process, 163, 164.

**SELLER**

See Sale of Goods.

**SHAPES**

Navigation Rules, 501, 503.

**SHIP**

See, also, Maritime Lien; Sale of Ship; Ship Mortgage; Shipbuilding.
Admeasurement, 987.
Dead ship, 604 (note).
Foreign ship, 695, 696 (note).
Forfeiture for violation of law, 715.
General average, interest in, 245–248.
General ship, 13, 125, 195, 197.
Liner, 13, 197.
Merchant vessel, 982, 983.
Port of documentation, 712–715.
Public vessel, 983.
Seagoing vessel, 836, 921, 922.
Tonnage, 987.
Tramp, 13, 197.

**SHIP FINANCING**

See, also, Ship Mortgage.
Merchant Marine Act of 1936, Title XI, 702–706.
Patterns of, 702–706.
Ship Financing Act of 1972, pp. 703–706.

**SHIP MORTGAGE**

Affidavit of good faith, 712.
Anti-lien provision, 716.
Assignment of mortgage, 713.
Bankruptcy, status of unrecorded mortgage in, 717.
Bankruptcy or reorganization, 814, 815, 953–955.
Bond, release of ship under, 800 (note).

**SHIP MORTGAGE**—Continued
Certified copy requirement, 717.
Citizenship of mortgagee, 696, 697.
Disclosure provision, 755.
Documentation of vessel, 695, 712–715.
Federally insured mortgages, 976.
Fleet mortgage, 709, 710.
Foreclosure, 757, 814, 815.
Foreign ship mortgage, 698, 753–755.
Forfeiture of vessel, 715.
Formal requisites, 706–717.
Gross tonnage requirement, 696.
Home port, 713, 714.
Indorsement on ship's papers, 715, 716, 755–757.
Insolvency court, submission to, 814, 815.
Insurance proceeds, 752.
Jurisdiction, 40, 41, 688–695.
Laches, 712, 780–786.
Lien of preferred mortgage, 630, 751–753.
Limitation of liability, 752.
Mixed mortgages, 707–709.
Mortgagor, duties of, 755.
Notarization, 707–709.
Notice of foreclosure, 757.
Notice of lien, 757.
Port of documentation, 712–715.
Pre-existing lien, 755–757.
Preferred maritime lien, 751–753.
Preferred mortgage, 706, 953.
  Formal requisites, 706–712.
  Recordation and indorsement, 712–717.
Priority, 735, 736, 751–757.
Proceeds applied to non-maritime use, 693.
Public notice, 717.
Reconstruction Finance Corporation, 697.
Recordation and indorsement, 712–717.
Recordation with collector of customs, 707–709.
Sale of vessel by admiralty court, 715.
Services completed after recordation, 755, 756.
Ship financing, patterns of, 702–706.
Ship Mortgage Act,
    Generally, 688–732.
  Applicability of state or federal law, 718–727.
    Article 9 of UCC, 718, 722, 727.
    Erie doctrine, 720.
    History, 718–721.
  Conflict of laws, state-federal, 718–727.
  Constitutionality, 692–695.
  Enactment of, 327, 691.
  Scope of Act, 695–702.
Statement of interest, 707–709.
Surrender of documents, 715.
Vessel of the United States, 695, 714, 736, 753.
Vessel Sales and Mortgage Recording Act (1850), 689.
Waiver of preferred status, 711.
"Whole vessel" requirement, 710, 711.

**SHIP MORTGAGE ACT**
See Ship Mortgage.

**SHIPBUILDING**
Construction differential subsidy, 970 et seq., 976.
Construction loan program, 965, 976.
Contracts, jurisdiction over, 16, 26, 650.
Cost, 970.
Financing by preferred ship mortgage, 987.
History, 963–965.
Maritime Administration, 968, 976, 978–980.
Navy department approval, 971.
Passenger vessels, 973, 974, 986.
Subsidization, 962, 969–977.
Tax deferment privileges, 977.

**SHIPOWNER**
Indemnity,
  From charterer, 232, 233.
  From seaman's tortfeasor, 314–322.
Indemnity actions, 442–446.
  From harbor worker's employer, 442.
Salvage award, 566, 574–576.

**SHIPOWNERS' LIABILITY (SICK AND INJURED SEAMEN), CONVENTION,** 323, 324.

**SHIPPER**
  See, also, Carriage of Goods; Cogsa.
Bulk shipments, 12.
Fault of, 167.
Freight forwarder, 14.
Less-than-shipload shipment, 13.
Prima-facie case against carrier, 141.

**SHIPPING ACT (1916)**
  Generally, 966, 991–995.
Amendments to Act (1961), 993–995.

**SHIPPING BOARD,** 327, 966.

**SHIPPING BOARD EMERGENCY FLEET CORPORATION,** 966.

**SHIPPING INDUSTRY**
Bulk carriers, 976.
Conference agreements, 991 et seq.
Corporate form, 12.
Essential routes, 970 et seq., 976.
Fixed or essential routes, 970 et seq., 976.
Government as participant, 980–982.
Government as promoter, 978–980.
Government regulation, 986–990.
Liners, 13, 197.
Operating differential subsidy, 971 et seq.
Private associations, 990.
Statistics, 979.
Tax deferment privileges, 977.
Tramp shipping, 13, 197, 976.

**SHIPPING POLICY**
See History; Shipbuilding; Shipping Industry; United States.

**SHIPPING TERMS,** 105–108.

**SHIPS**
Dead ship, 623 (note).

**SHIP'S HUSBAND,** 672, 673.

**SHORE APPARATUS,** 167.

**SOVEREIGN IMMUNITY**
See, also, In Personam Suit; Maritime Lien; Public Vessels Act; Suits in Admiralty Act; United States.
Foreign public vessel, 985 (note).

**SPECIAL BOND,** 797, 798.

**SPECIFIC PERFORMANCE,** 41.

**STAND-BY ACT**
Presumption of fault, 490.
Salvage award, 453.

**STATE COMPENSATION ACTS**
Relationship to LHCA, 417 et seq.
Successive state, LHCA, Jones Act awards, 431 et seq.

**STATE DEPARTMENT,** 979.

**STATE LAW**
Collision action, 499.
Insurance, 48, 68–71.
Lien statutes, 647–652.
Non-admiralty courts, 456 et seq.
Shipowner's indemnity action, 317, 319.
State-created remedies, 456.

**STATUTE OF FRAUDS,** 651.

**STATUTE OF LIMITATIONS**
See, also, Limitations, Statute of.
Jones Act, 349.

**STEERING**
Navigation rules, 503.

**STEVEDORE**
See Maritime Lien; Seamen.

**STIPULATION FOR VALUE**
See In Rem Proceeding; Limitation of Liability; Maritime Lien.

**STOWAGE,** 209.

**STRANDING,** 255–258.

**STRIKES AND LOCKOUTS,** 164–166, 169.

**SUB-FREIGHTS,** 125, 233.

**SUBROGATION**
See, also, Insurance.
Doctrine of, 91, 92.

**SUBSIDY**
See, also, Shipbuilding; Shipping Industry; United States.
Merchant marine industry, 962, 969–977.

**SUCCESSIVE AWARDS**
State, LHCA, Jones Act compensation awards, 431 et seq.

**SUE AND LABOR CLAUSE**
See Insurance.

**SUITS IN ADMIRALTY ACT**
Lien against ships reverting to private ownership, 607.
Limitations, statute of, 302 (note), 768.
Merchant vessels, 982, 983.
Personal injuries, 282 (note).
Provisions of, 982.
Public Vessels Act, 983, 985.

**SUPREMACY**
Federal-state conflicts, 45–51.

**SUPREMACY CLAUSE**
Federal supremacy, 47–51, 68–71, 458, 459.

**TAXES**
See Maritime Lien; United States.

**TENDER**
See Charter Party; Sale of Goods.

**THIRD PARTY ACTION**
Generally, 436.
Harbor workers, 449.

**TIGER POLICY,** 54.

**TIME CHARTER**
See, also, Charter Party.
Generally, 229–239.
Government form, 1003.

**TORTS**
See Jurisdiction; Maritime Tort.

**TORT CLAIMS ACT,** 983 (note).

**TOWAGE**
See, also, Fleet or Flotilla.
Collision, 515–520.
General average, 259, 260.
Harter Act, 147 (note).
Lien, 630, 655.
Lights, 501.
Negligence clause in towage contract, 516–520.
Negligent towage, 740, 753.
Personal contract, 904.
Pilot's exculpation distinguished, 521, 522.
Salvage award, 545.
Salvage distinguished, 536, 545.
Tug as "dominant mind", 516, 517.
United States, suit against, 983.

**TRADING LIMITS,** 230.

**TRAMP,** 13, 197.

**TRAMP SHIPPING**
Generally, 197.

**TRIAL**
See Collision; Great Lakes; Seamen; United States.

**TRUST RECEIPT,** 129, 133–137.

**TUCKER ACT,** 983 (note).

**UNDERLAP,** 231, 232.

**UNDERWRITER,** 56.

**UNIFORM BILLS OF LADING ACT**
Acceptance, 111.
Negotiability, 95.
Parts, bills issued in, 125, 126.

**UNIFORM COMMERCIAL CODE**
Applicability, 93, 94.
Documentary sale, 110–114.
Fraud by insolvency rule, 96 (note).
Indemnity agreements, 127.
Installment contracts, 113 (note).
Letters of credit, 94, 114–130.
Negotiable Instruments Law, 95, 96.
"No arrival, no sale", term, 107.
Sale of goods, 100 et seq.
Sets, bills issued in, 125 (note).
Tender, 112, 113 (note).

**UNIFORM CUSTOMS AND PRACTICE FOR COMMERCIAL DOCUMENTARY CREDITS**
Generally, 118 et seq.
Bank's duties, 118.
Charter, bill of lading subject to, 125.
"Clean" shipping document, 122, 123.
Commercial invoice, 122.
Forwarding agent's bill of lading, 124.
Indemnity agreement, 127.
Letter of credit distinct from sales contract, 121.
New York, 118, 119.
Sailing vessel's bill of lading, 124.

**UNIFORM GENERAL CHARTER (GENCON, 1922),** 997–1002.

**UNIFORM TRUST RECEIPTS ACT,** 129.

**UNITED NATIONS INTERGOVERNMENTAL MARITIME CONSULTATIVE ORGANIZATION,** 990.

**UNITED STATES**
Admiralty sale, effect on government claim, 790, 791.
Cargo, shipment by government, 981.
Charters, use of, 194, 240, 981.
Citizen for Ship Mortgage Act purposes, 696, 697.
Consent to suit, 982.
Courts of Claims, 983, 985.
General agency agreements, 240, 461, 981.
In rem proceeding, 982.
Jury trial in suit against, 982.
Priority of government claims, 757–764.
Salvage claim by, 546.
Seamen employed by, 284, 461.
Shipping policy,
Generally, 963 et seq.
American registry, 963.
Anti-trust laws, 12, 30, 991, 993.
Coast Guard, 978.
Coastwise trade, 963.
Conference system, 12, 30, 991 et seq.

**UNITED STATES**—Continued
Shipping policy—Continued
Construction, differential subsidy, 970 et seq., 976.
Construction loan program, 966, 976.
Countervailing subsidy, 970 (note).
Department of Commerce, 967, 976.
Essential routes, 970 et seq., 976.
Factors affecting, 958, 959, 967–969.
History, 963–969.
Loadline statute, 987.
Maritime Administration, 968, 976, 978–980.
Maritime Commission, 967, 968, 991–996.
National Shipping Authority, 967 (note).
Operating differential subsidy, 971 et seq.
Passenger vessel plans approval, 986.
Postal subsidy, 965, 966, 969.
Private association, 990.
Problems after World War II, 973, 974.
Promotional activities, 978–980.
Shipowner, government as, 981.
Shipping Board, 327, 966.
Subsidies, 964, 965, 969–977, 985.
Subsidization of tramp shipping, 976.
Subsidized vessel, inspection of, 986.
Subsidy "recapture" provisions, 972, 976.
Suits in Admiralty Act (1920), 982.
Under 1936 Act, 969–973.
Under 1970 Act, 974–977.
War risk insurance, 981.
War Shipping Administration, 967, 980.
Sovereign immunity, 982–985.
Statute of limitations on claims against, 768.
Tax-liens, 757–764, 791.

**UNITED STATES PUBLIC HEALTH SERVICE,** 301, 302.

**UNJUST ENRICHMENT**
See Quasi-contract.

**UNSEAWORTHINESS ACTION**
In personam suit, 616–621.
In rem proceeding, 616–621.

**VALIN,** 8 (note).

**VALUATION**
See, also, Damages; Insurance.
Generally, 912 et seq.
Collision, ship lost in, 524–526.
Goods listed in bill, 834.
Insurance,
Constructive total loss, 83–85.
Valued policy, 86–90.
Limitation of liability proceeding, 905, 906.
Salvage,
Property at risk, 559–561.
Property salved, 560–563.

**VALUED POLICY**
See Insurance; Valuation.

**VENUE**
Generally, 850 (note).
Seaman's Jones Act suit, 341.

**VESSEL**
See Ship.

**VESSEL SALES AND MORTGAGE RECORDING ACT (1850),** 689.

**VIS MAJOR**
Collision, 486.
Demurrage, 214.

**VOYAGE,** 913, 914.

**VOYAGE CHARTER**
See Charter Party.

**WAGES**
See Maritime Lien; Seamen.

**WAR**
Cogsa provision, 164.

**WAR SHIPPING ADMINISTRATION,** 967, 980.

**WARRANTIES**
See, also, Seaworthiness.
Charter party statements, 200, 231.
Defined, 63 (note), 67.
Express warranty,
Generally, 67–71.
State legislation, 48, 68–71.
Seaworthiness, 63–67, 150–155, 452.
Special use of term, 67, 68.
State-federal conflict, 68–71.

**WATER QUALITY IMPROVEMENT ACT,** 989.
Generally, 826–834.
Relationship to Limitation of Liability Act, 828–834.

**WEATHER BUREAU,** 978.

**WEATHER WORKING DAYS,** 211.

**WESTERN RIVERS RULES**
See Collision.

**WHARFAGE**
Lien for, 656.

**WISBY, LAWS OF,** 6.

**WORKING DAYS,** 211.

**WORKMEN'S COMPENSATION**
See, also, Constitution of the United States; Seamen.
State Acts, 404.

**WRECK STATUTE,** 949 (note).

**WRONGFUL DEATH**
See, also, Seamen.
Generally, 359–374.
Compared with survival statutes, 360.
Death on the High Seas Act, 24 (note), 359 et seq., 659, 660.

**WRONGFUL DEATH**—Continued
Foreign shipowners, claims against, 847 (note).
Liens under state statutes, 649, 652, 659, 660.
Limitation of liability, 821, 847 (note).
Minimum limitation fund, 821.
No recovery at maritime law, 48.
Recovery under DOHSA, 359 et seq.
Recovery under FELA, 359 et seq.
Recovery under Jones Act, 359 et seq.
  Jones Act plaintiffs, high seas death, 363.
    On shore deaths, 362.
Recovery under maritime law, 359 et seq.
Recovery under state statutes, 359.
State legislation, 48.
Statute of limitations, 768.
Statutory recovery formulae, 360–362.

**YORK-ANTWERP RULES**
  Generally, 252–254, 990.
Bill of lading stipulation, 253, 268.
Deck cargo, jettison, 260, 261.
Fault, effect of, 268.
Fire, extinguishment of, 258, 259.
General average act, 255.
Jettison, damage caused by, 260, 261.
Substituted expenses, 263.
Value, calculation of, 263.
Voluntary stranding, 257.

END OF VOLUME